FORD MUSTANG
1994-98 REPAIR MANUAL

Deleted

President	Dean F. Morgantini, S.A.E.
Vice President–Finance	Barry L. Beck
Vice President–Sales	Glenn D. Potere
Executive Editor	Kevin M. G. Maher
Production Manager	Ben Greisler, S.A.E.
Project Managers	Michael Abraham, George B. Heinrich III, Will Kessler, A.S.E., Richard Schwartz
Editor	George B. Heinrich III

CHILTON™ Automotive Books
PUBLISHED BY W. G. NICHOLS, INC.

Manufactured in USA
© 1997 W. G. Nichols
1020 Andrew Drive
West Chester, PA 19380
ISBN 0-8019-8823-3
Library of Congress Catalog Card No. 97-77322
1234567890 6543210987

Contents

Contents

SAFETY NOTICE

Proper service and repair procedures are vital to the safe, reliable operation of all motor vehicles, as well as the personal safety of those performing repairs. This manual outlines procedures for servicing and repairing vehicles using safe, effective methods. The procedures contain many NOTES, CAUTIONS and WARNINGS which should be followed along with standard procedures to eliminate the possibility of personal injury or improper service which could damage the vehicle or compromise its safety.

It is important to note that the repair procedures and techniques, tools and parts for servicing motor vehicles, as well as the skill and experience of the individual performing the work vary widely. It is not possible to anticipate all of the conceivable ways or conditions under which vehicles may be serviced, or to provide cautions as to all of the possible hazards that may result. Standard and accepted safety precautions and equipment should be used when handling toxic or flammable fluids, and safety goggles or other protection should be used during cutting, grinding, chiseling, prying, or any other process that can sauce material removal or projectiles.

Some procedures require the use of tools specially designed for a specific purpose. Before substituting another tool or procedure, you must be completely satisfied that neither your personal safety, not the performance of the vehicle will be endangered.

Although information in this manual is based on industry sources and is complete as possible at the time of publication, the possibility exists that some vehicle manufacturers made later changes which could not be included here. While striving for total accuracy, W. G. Nichols, Inc. cannot assume responsibility for any errors, changes or omissions that may occur in the compilation of this data.

PART NUMBERS

Part numbers listed in this reference are not recommendations by Chilton for any product by brand name. They are references that can be used with interchange and aftermarket supplier catalogs to locate each brand supplier's discrete part number.

SPECIAL TOOLS

Special tools are recommended by the vehicle manufacturer to perform their specific job. use has been kept to a minimum, but where absolutely necessary, they are referred to in the text by the part number of the tool manufacturer. These tools can be purchased, under the appropriate part number, from your local dealer or regional distributor, or an equivalent tool can be purchased locally from a tool supplier or parts outlet. Before substituting any tool for the one recommended, read the SAFETY NOTICE at the top of this page.

ACKNOWLEDGMENTS

W. G. Nichols, Inc. expresses appreciation to Ford Motor Company for their generous assistance.

1

GENERAL
INFORMATION
AND
MAINTENANCE

HOW TO USE THIS BOOK

Chilton's Total Car Care manual for the 1994–98 Ford Mustang is intended to help you learn more about the inner workings of your vehicle while saving you money on its upkeep and operation.

The beginning of the book will likely be referred to the most, since that is where you will find information for maintenance and tune-up. The other sections deal with the more complex systems of your vehicle. Operating systems from engine through brakes are covered to the extent that the average do-it-yourselfer becomes mechanically involved. This book will not explain such things as rebuilding a differential for the simple reason that the expertise required and the investment in special tools make this task uneconomical. It will, however, give you detailed instructions to help you change your own brake pads and shoes, replace spark plugs, and perform many more jobs that can save you money, give you personal satisfaction and help you avoid expensive problems.

A secondary purpose of this book is a reference for owners who want to understand their vehicle and/or their mechanics better. In this case, no tools at all are required.

Where to Begin

Before removing any bolts, read through the entire procedure. This will give you the overall view of what tools and supplies will be required. There is nothing more frustrating than having to walk to the bus stop on Monday morning because you were short one bolt on Sunday afternoon. So read ahead and plan ahead. Each operation should be approached logically and all procedures thoroughly understood before attempting any work.

All sections contain adjustments, maintenance, removal and installation procedures, and in some cases, repair or overhaul procedures. When repair is not considered practical, we tell you how to remove the part and then how to install the new or rebuilt replacement. In this way, you at least save the labor costs. Backyard repair of some components is just not practical.

Avoiding Trouble

Many procedures in this book require you to "label and disconnect . . ." a group of lines, hoses or wires. Don't be lulled into thinking you can remember where everything goes—you won't. If you hook up vacuum or fuel lines incorrectly, the vehicle will run poorly, if at all. If you hook up electrical wiring incorrectly, you may instantly learn a very expensive lesson.

You don't need to know the official or engineering name for each hose or line. A piece of masking tape on the hose and a piece on its fitting will allow you to assign your own label such as the letter A or a short name. As long as you remember your own code, the lines can be reconnected by matching similar letters or names. Do remember that tape will dissolve in gasoline or other fluids; if a component is to be washed or cleaned, use another method of identification. A permanent felt-tipped marker can be very handy for marking metal parts. Remove any tape or paper labels after assembly.

Maintenance or Repair?

It's necessary to mention the difference between maintenance and repair. Maintenance includes routine inspections, adjustments, and replacement of parts which show signs of normal wear. Maintenance compensates for wear or deterioration. Repair implies that something has broken or is not working. A need for repair is often caused by lack of maintenance. Example: draining and refilling the automatic transmission fluid is maintenance recommended by the manufacturer at specific mileage intervals. Failure to do this can ruin the transmission/transaxle, requiring very expensive repairs. While no maintenance program can prevent items from breaking or wearing out, a general rule can be stated: MAINTENANCE IS CHEAPER THAN REPAIR.

Two basic mechanic's rules should be mentioned here. First, whenever the left side of the vehicle or engine is referred to, it is meant to specify the driver's side. Conversely, the right side of the vehicle means the passenger's side. Second, most screws and bolts are removed by turning counterclockwise, and tightened by turning clockwise.

Safety is always the most important rule. Constantly be aware of the dangers involved in working on an automobile and take the proper precautions. See the information in this section regarding SERVICING YOUR VEHICLE SAFELY and the SAFETY NOTICE on the acknowledgment page.

Avoiding the Most Common Mistakes

Pay attention to the instructions provided. There are 3 common mistakes in mechanical work:

1. Incorrect order of assembly, disassembly or adjustment. When taking something apart or putting it together, performing steps in the wrong order usually just costs you extra time; however, it CAN break something. Read the entire procedure before beginning disassembly. Perform everything in the order in which the instructions say you should, even if you can't immediately see a reason for it. When you're taking apart something that is very intricate, you might want to draw a picture of how it looks when assembled at one point in order to make sure you get everything back in its proper position. We will supply exploded views whenever possible. When making adjustments, perform them in the proper order; often, one adjustment affects another, and you cannot expect even satisfactory results unless each adjustment is made only when it cannot be changed by any other.

2. Overtorquing (or undertorquing). While it is more common for overtorquing to cause damage, undertorquing may allow a fastener to vibrate loose causing serious damage. Especially when dealing with aluminum parts, pay attention to torque specifications and utilize a torque wrench in assembly. If a torque figure is not available, remember that if you are using the right tool to perform the job, you will probably not have to strain yourself to get a fastener tight enough. The pitch of most threads is so slight that the tension you put on the wrench will be multiplied many times in actual force on what you are tightening. A good example of how critical torque is can be seen in the case of spark plug installation, especially where you are putting the plug into an aluminum cylinder head. Too little torque can fail to crush the gasket, causing leakage of combustion gases and consequent overheating of the plug and engine parts. Too much torque can damage the threads or distort the plug, changing the spark gap.

There are many commercial products available for ensuring that fasteners won't come loose, even if they are not torqued just right (a very common brand is Loctite®). If you're worried about getting something together tight enough to hold, but loose enough to avoid mechanical damage during assembly, one of these products might offer substantial insurance. Before choosing a threadlocking compound, read the label on the package and make sure the product is compatible with the materials, fluids, etc. involved.

3. Crossthreading. This occurs when a part such as a bolt is screwed into a nut or casting at the wrong angle and forced. Crossthreading is more likely to occur if access is difficult. It helps to clean and lubricate fasteners, then to start threading with the part to be installed positioned straight in. Then, start the bolt, spark plug, etc. with your fingers. If you encounter resistance, unscrew the part and start over again at a different angle until it can be inserted and turned several times without much effort. Keep in mind that many parts, especially spark plugs, have tapered threads, so that gentle turning will automatically bring the part you're threading to the proper angle, but only if you don't force it or resist a change in angle. Don't put a wrench on the part until it's been tightened a couple of turns by hand. If you suddenly encounter resistance, and the part has not seated fully, don't force it. Pull it back out to make sure it's clean and threading properly.

Always take your time and be patient; once you have some experience, working on your vehicle may well become an enjoyable hobby.

TOOLS AND EQUIPMENT

Naturally, without the proper tools and equipment it is impossible to properly service your vehicle. It would also be virtually impossible to catalog every tool that you would need to perform all of the operations in this book. Of course, It would be unwise for the amateur to rush out and buy an expensive set of tools on the theory that he/she may need one or more of them at some time.

The best approach is to proceed slowly, gathering a good quality set of those tools that are used most frequently. Don't be misled by the low cost of bargain tools. It is far better to spend a little more for better quality. Forged wrenches, 6 or 12-point sockets and fine tooth ratchets are by far preferable to their less expensive counterparts. As any good mechanic can tell you, there are few worse experiences than trying to work on a vehicle with bad tools. Your monetary savings will be far outweighed by frustration and mangled knuckles.

Begin accumulating those tools that are used most frequently: those associated with routine maintenance and tune-up. In addition to the normal assortment of screwdrivers and pliers, you should have the following tools:

• Wrenches/sockets and combination open end/box end wrenches in sizes from ⅛–¾ in. or 3mm–19mm (depending on whether your vehicle uses standard or metric fasteners) and a ¹³⁄₁₆ in. or ⅝ in. spark plug socket (depending on plug type).

➡ **If possible, buy various length socket drive extensions. Universal-joint and wobble extensions can be extremely useful, but be careful when using them, as they can change the amount of torque applied to the socket.**

• Jackstands for support.
• Oil filter wrench.
• Spout or funnel for pouring fluids.
• Grease gun for chassis lubrication (unless your vehicle is not equipped with any grease fittings—for details, please refer to information on Fluids and Lubricants found later in this section).
• Hydrometer for checking the battery (unless equipped with a sealed, maintenance-free battery).
• A container for draining oil and other fluids.
• Rags for wiping up the inevitable mess.

In addition to the above items there are several others that are not absolutely necessary, but handy to have around. These include Oil Dry® (or an equivalent oil absorbent gravel—such as cat litter) and the usual supply of lubricants, antifreeze and fluids, although these can be purchased as needed. This is a basic list for routine maintenance, but only your personal needs and desire can accurately determine your list of tools.

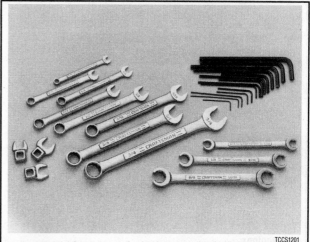

TCCS1201

In addition to ratchets, a good set of wrenches and hex keys will be necessary

TCCS1202

A hydraulic floor jack and a set of jackstands are essential for lifting and supporting the vehicle

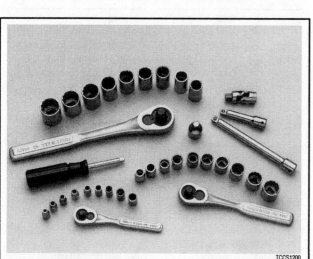

TCCS1200

All but the most basic procedures will require an assortment of ratchets and sockets

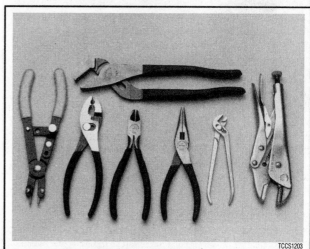

TCCS1203

An assortment of pliers, grippers and cutters will be handy for old rusted parts and stripped bolt heads

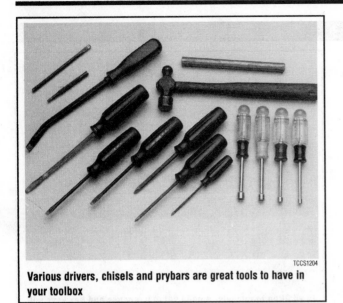

Various drivers, chisels and prybars are great tools to have in your toolbox

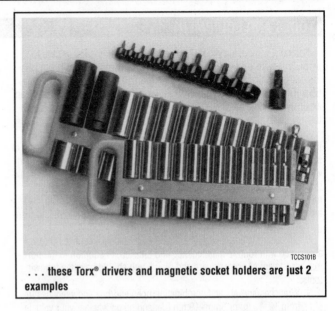

. . . these Torx® drivers and magnetic socket holders are just 2 examples

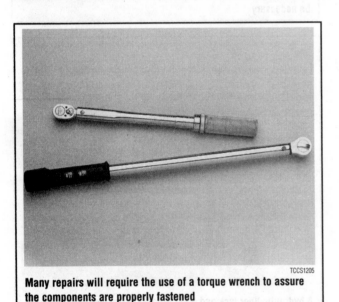

Many repairs will require the use of a torque wrench to assure the components are properly fastened

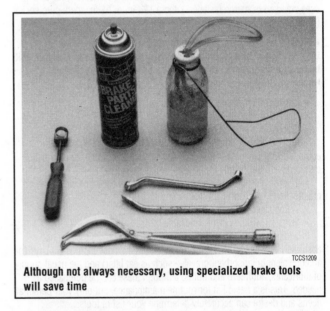

Although not always necessary, using specialized brake tools will save time

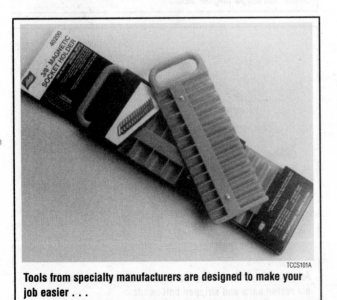

Tools from specialty manufacturers are designed to make your job easier . . .

A few inexpensive lubrication tools will make maintenance easier

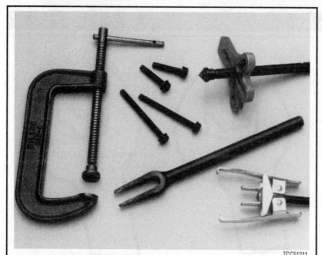

TCCS1211

Various pullers, clamps and separator tools are needed for many larger, more complicated repairs

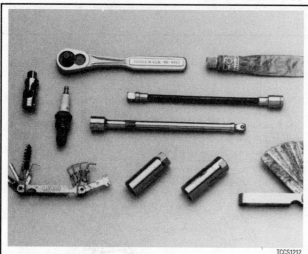

TCCS1212

A variety of tools and gauges should be used for spark plug gapping and installation

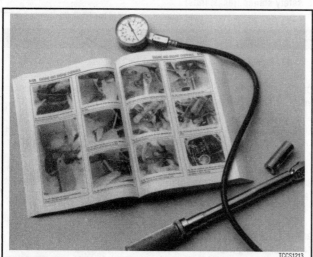

TCCS1213

Proper information is vital, so always have a Chilton Total Car Care manual handy

After performing a few projects on the vehicle, you'll be amazed at the other tools and non-tools on your workbench. Some useful household items are: a large turkey baster or siphon, empty coffee cans and ice trays (to store parts), ball of twine, electrical tape for wiring, small rolls of colored tape for tagging lines or hoses, markers and pens, a note pad, golf tees (for plugging vacuum lines), metal coat hangers or a roll of mechanics's wire (to hold things out of the way), dental pick or similar long, pointed probe, a strong magnet, and a small mirror (to see into recesses and under manifolds).

A more advanced set of tools, suitable for tune-up work, can be drawn up easily. While the tools are slightly more sophisticated, they need not be outrageously expensive. There are several inexpensive tach/dwell meters on the market that are every bit as good for the average mechanic as a professional model. Just be sure that it goes to a least 1200–1500 rpm on the tach scale and that it works on 4, 6 and 8-cylinder engines. (If you have one or more vehicles with a diesel engine, a special tachometer is required since diesels don't use spark plug ignition systems). The key to these purchases is to make them with an eye towards adaptability and wide range. A basic list of tune-up tools could include:

- Tach/dwell meter.
- Spark plug wrench and gapping tool.
- Feeler gauges for valve or point adjustment. (Even if your vehicle does not use points or require valve adjustments, a feeler gauge is helpful for many repair/overhaul procedures).

A tachometer/dwell meter will ensure accurate tune-up work on vehicles without electronic ignition. The choice of a timing light should be made carefully. A light which works on the DC current supplied by the vehicle's battery is the best choice; it should have a xenon tube for brightness. On any vehicle with an electronic ignition system, a timing light with an inductive pickup that clamps around the No. 1 spark plug cable is preferred.

In addition to these basic tools, there are several other tools and gauges you may find useful. These include:

- Compression gauge. The screw-in type is slower to use, but eliminates the possibility of a faulty reading due to escaping pressure.
- Manifold vacuum gauge.
- 12V test light.
- A combination volt/ohmmeter
- Induction Ammeter. This is used for determining whether or not there is current in a wire. These are handy for use if a wire is broken somewhere in a wiring harness.

As a final note, you will probably find a torque wrench necessary for all but the most basic work. The beam type models are perfectly adequate, although the newer click types (break-away) are easier to use. The click type torque wrenches tend to be more expensive. Also keep in mind that all types of torque wrenches should be periodically checked and/or recalibrated. You will have to decide for yourself which better fits your purpose.

Special Tools

Normally, the use of special factory tools is avoided for repair procedures, since these are not readily available for the do-it-yourself mechanic. When it is possible to perform the job with more commonly available tools, it will be pointed out, but occasionally, a special tool was designed to perform a specific function and should be used. Before substituting another tool, you should be convinced that neither your safety nor the performance of the vehicle will be compromised.

Special tools can usually be purchased from an automotive parts store or from your dealer. In some cases special tools may be available directly from the tool manufacturer.

SERVICING YOUR VEHICLE SAFELY

▶ **See Figures 1, 2, 3 and 4**

It is virtually impossible to anticipate all of the hazards involved with automotive maintenance and service, but care and common sense will prevent most accidents.

The rules of safety for mechanics range from "don't smoke around gasoline," to "use the proper tool(s) for the job." The trick to avoiding injuries is to develop safe work habits and to take every possible precaution.

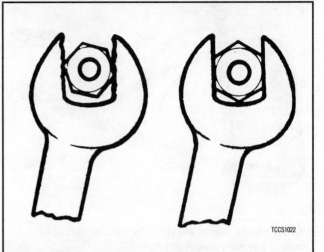

Fig. 3 Using the correct size wrench will help prevent the possibility of rounding off a nut

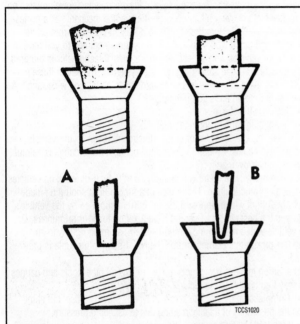

Fig. 1 Screwdrivers should be kept in good condition to prevent injury or damage which could result if the blade slips from the screw

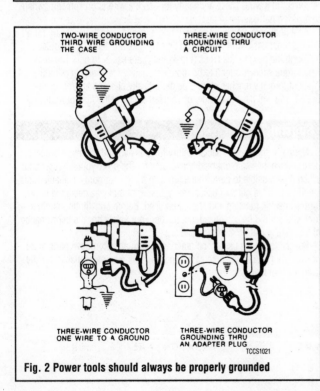

Fig. 2 Power tools should always be properly grounded

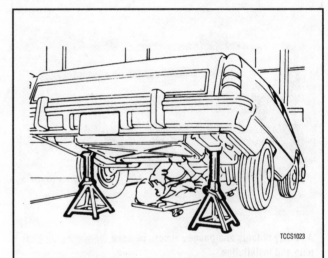

Fig. 4 NEVER work under a vehicle unless it is supported using safety stands (jackstands)

Do's

- Do keep a fire extinguisher and first aid kit handy.
- Do wear safety glasses or goggles when cutting, drilling, grinding or prying, even if you have 20–20 vision. If you wear glasses for the sake of vision, wear safety goggles over your regular glasses.
- Do shield your eyes whenever you work around the battery. Batteries contain sulfuric acid. In case of contact with the eyes or skin, flush the area with water or a mixture of water and baking soda, then seek immediate medical attention.
- Do use safety stands (jackstands) for any undervehicle service. Jacks are for raising vehicles; jackstands are for making sure the vehicle stays raised until you want it to come down. Whenever the vehicle is raised, block the wheels remaining on the ground and set the parking brake.
- Do use adequate ventilation when working with any chemicals or hazardous materials. Like carbon monoxide, the asbestos dust resulting from some brake lining wear can be hazardous in sufficient quantities.
- Do disconnect the negative battery cable when working on the electrical system. The secondary ignition system contains EXTREMELY HIGH VOLTAGE. In some cases it can even exceed 50,000 volts.

• Do follow manufacturer's directions whenever working with potentially hazardous materials. Most chemicals and fluids are poisonous if taken internally.

• Do properly maintain your tools. Loose hammerheads, mushroomed punches and chisels, frayed or poorly grounded electrical cords, excessively worn screwdrivers, spread wrenches (open end), cracked sockets, slipping ratchets, or faulty droplight sockets can cause accidents.

• Likewise, keep your tools clean; a greasy wrench can slip off a bolt head, ruining the bolt and often harming your knuckles in the process.

• Do use the proper size and type of tool for the job at hand. Do select a wrench or socket that fits the nut or bolt. The wrench or socket should sit straight, not cocked.

• Do, when possible, pull on a wrench handle rather than push on it, and adjust your stance to prevent a fall.

• Do be sure that adjustable wrenches are tightly closed on the nut or bolt and pulled so that the force is on the side of the fixed jaw.

• Do strike squarely with a hammer; avoid glancing blows.

• Do set the parking brake and block the drive wheels if the work requires a running engine.

Don'ts

• Don't run the engine in a garage or anywhere else without proper ventilation—EVER! Carbon monoxide is poisonous; it takes a long time to leave the human body and you can build up a deadly supply of it in your system by simply breathing in a little every day. You may not realize you are slowly poisoning yourself. Always use power vents, windows, fans and/or open the garage door.

• Don't work around moving parts while wearing loose clothing. Short sleeves are much safer than long, loose sleeves. Hard-toed shoes with neoprene soles protect your toes and give a better grip on slippery surfaces.

Jewelry such as watches, fancy belt buckles, beads or body adornment of any kind is not safe working around a vehicle. Long hair should be tied back under a hat or cap.

• Don't use pockets for toolboxes. A fall or bump can drive a screwdriver deep into your body. Even a rag hanging from your back pocket can wrap around a spinning shaft or fan.

• Don't smoke when working around gasoline, cleaning solvent or other flammable material.

• Don't smoke when working around the battery. When the battery is being charged, it gives off explosive hydrogen gas.

• Don't use gasoline to wash your hands; there are excellent soaps available. Gasoline contains dangerous additives which can enter the body through a cut or through your pores. Gasoline also removes all the natural oils from the skin so that bone dry hands will suck up oil and grease.

• Don't service the air conditioning system unless you are equipped with the necessary tools and training. When liquid or compressed gas refrigerant is released to atmospheric pressure it will absorb heat from whatever it contacts. This will chill or freeze anything it touches. Although refrigerant is normally non-toxic, R-12 becomes a deadly poisonous gas in the presence of an open flame. One good whiff of the vapors from burning refrigerant can be fatal.

• Don't use screwdrivers for anything other than driving screws! A screwdriver used as an prying tool can snap when you least expect it, causing injuries. At the very least, you'll ruin a good screwdriver.

• Don't use a bumper or emergency jack (that little ratchet, scissors, or pantograph jack supplied with the vehicle) for anything other than changing a flat! These jacks are only intended for emergency use out on the road; they are NOT designed as a maintenance tool. If you are serious about maintaining your vehicle yourself, invest in a hydraulic floor jack of at least a 1½ ton capacity, and at least two sturdy jackstands.

FASTENERS, MEASUREMENTS AND CONVERSIONS

Bolts, Nuts and Other Threaded Retainers

♦ See Figures 5, 6, 7 and 8

Although there are a great variety of fasteners found in the modern car or truck, the most commonly used retainer is the threaded fastener (nuts, bolts, screws, studs, etc.). Most threaded retainers may be reused, pro-

vided that they are not damaged in use or during the repair. Some retainers (such as stretch bolts or torque prevailing nuts) are designed to deform when tightened or in use and should not be reinstalled.

Whenever possible, we will note any special retainers which should be replaced during a procedure. But you should always inspect the condition of a retainer when it is removed and replace any that show signs of damage. Check all threads for rust or corrosion which can increase the torque

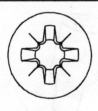

POZIDRIVE   PHILLIPS RECESS   TORX®   CLUTCH RECESS

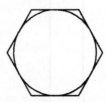
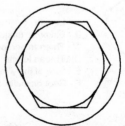

INDENTED HEXAGON   HEXAGON TRIMMED   HEXAGON WASHER HEAD

TCCS1037

Fig. 5 Here are a few of the most common screw/bolt driver styles

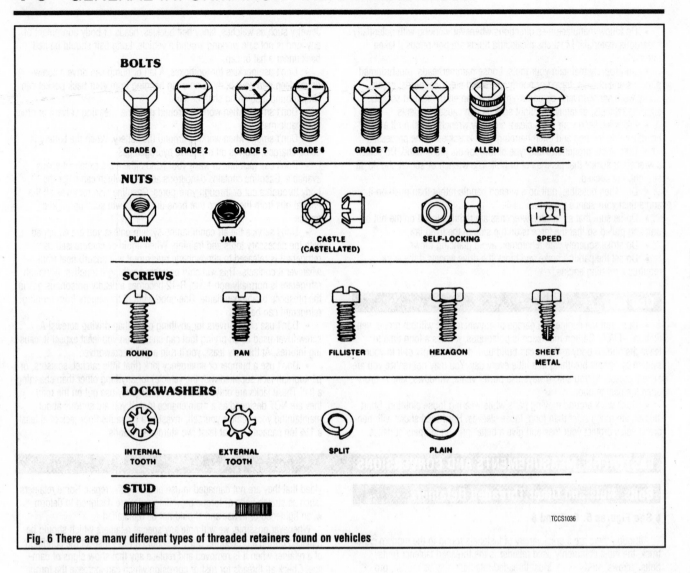

BOLTS

GRADE 0 GRADE 2 GRADE 5 GRADE 6 GRADE 7 GRADE 8 ALLEN CARRIAGE

NUTS

PLAIN JAM CASTLE (CASTELLATED) SELF-LOCKING SPEED

SCREWS

ROUND PAN FILLISTER HEXAGON SHEET METAL

LOCKWASHERS

INTERNAL TOOTH EXTERNAL TOOTH SPLIT PLAIN

STUD

TCCS1036

Fig. 6 There are many different types of threaded retainers found on vehicles

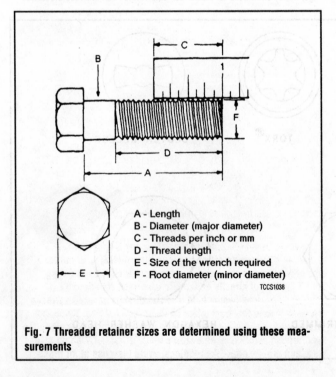

A - Length
B - Diameter (major diameter)
C - Threads per inch or mm
D - Thread length
E - Size of the wrench required
F - Root diameter (minor diameter)

TCCS1038

Fig. 7 Threaded retainer sizes are determined using these measurements

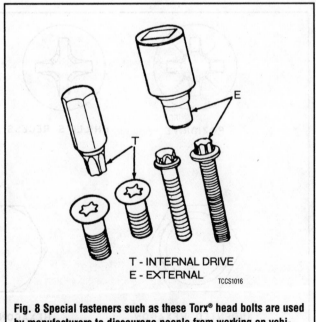

T - INTERNAL DRIVE
E - EXTERNAL

TCCS1016

Fig. 8 Special fasteners such as these Torx® head bolts are used by manufacturers to discourage people from working on vehicles without the proper tools

necessary to achieve the desired clamp load for which that fastener was originally selected. Additionally, be sure that the driver surface of the fastener has not been compromised by rounding or other damage. In some cases a driver surface may become only partially rounded, allowing the driver to catch in only one direction. In many of these occurrences, a fastener may be installed and tightened, but the driver would not be able to grip and loosen the fastener again. (This could lead to frustration down the line should that component ever need to be disassembled again).

If you must replace a fastener, whether due to design or damage, you must ALWAYS be sure to use the proper replacement. In all cases, a retainer of the same design, material and strength should be used. Markings on the heads of most bolts will help determine the proper strength of the fastener. The same material, thread and pitch must be selected to assure proper installation and safe operation of the vehicle afterwards.

Thread gauges are available to help measure a bolt or stud's thread. Most automotive and hardware stores keep gauges available to help you select the proper size. In a pinch, you can use another nut or bolt for a thread gauge. If the bolt you are replacing is not too badly damaged, you can select a match by finding another bolt which will thread in its place. If you find a nut which threads properly onto the damaged bolt, then use that nut to help select the replacement bolt. If however, the bolt you are replacing is so badly damaged (broken or drilled out) that its threads cannot be used as a gauge, you might start by looking for another bolt (from the same assembly or a similar location on your vehicle) which will thread into the damaged bolt's mounting. If so, the other bolt can be used to select a nut; the nut can then be used to select the replacement bolt.

In all cases, be absolutely sure you have selected the proper replacement. Don't be shy, you can always ask the store clerk for help.

✲✲ WARNING

Be aware that when you find a bolt with damaged threads, you may also find the nut or drilled hole it was threaded into has also been damaged. If this is the case, you may have to drill and tap the hole, replace the nut or otherwise repair the threads. NEVER try to force a replacement bolt to fit into the damaged threads.

Torque

Torque is defined as the measurement of resistance to turning or rotating. It tends to twist a body about an axis of rotation. A common example of this would be tightening a threaded retainer such as a nut, bolt or screw. Measuring torque is one of the most common ways to help assure that a threaded retainer has been properly fastened.

When tightening a threaded fastener, torque is applied in three distinct areas, the head, the bearing surface and the clamp load. About 50 percent of the measured torque is used in overcoming bearing friction. This is the friction between the bearing surface of the bolt head, screw head or nut face and the base material or washer (the surface on which the fastener is rotating). Approximately 40 percent of the applied torque is used in overcoming thread friction. This leaves only about 10 percent of the applied torque to develop a useful clamp load (the force which holds a joint together). This means that friction can account for as much as 90 percent of the applied torque on a fastener.

TORQUE WRENCHES

➧ See Figures 9 and 10

In most applications, a torque wrench can be used to assure proper installation of a fastener. Torque wrenches come in various designs and most automotive supply stores will carry a variety to suit your needs. A torque wrench should be used any time we supply a specific torque value for a fastener. A torque wrench can also be used if you are following the general guidelines in the accompanying charts. Keep in mind that because there is no worldwide standardization of fasteners, the charts are a general guideline and should be used with caution. Again, the general rule of "if you are using the right tool for the job, you should not have to strain to tighten a fastener" applies here.

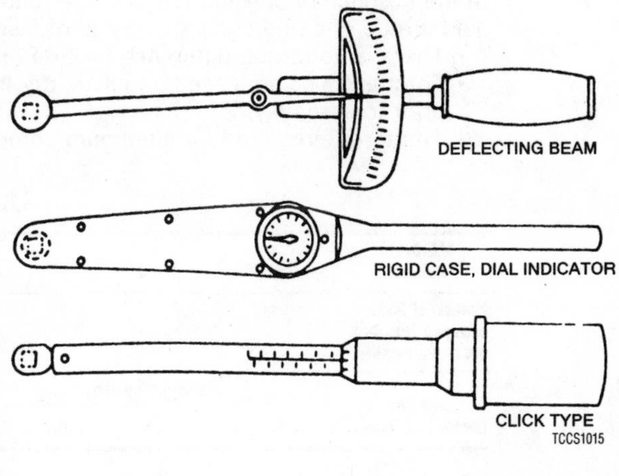

Fig. 9 Various styles of torque wrenches are usually available at your local automotive supply store

Beam Type

➧ See Figure 11

The beam type torque wrench is one of the most popular types. It consists of a pointer attached to the head that runs the length of the flexible beam (shaft) to a scale located near the handle. As the wrench is pulled, the beam bends and the pointer indicates the torque using the scale.

Click (Breakaway) Type

➧ See Figure 12

Another popular design of torque wrench is the click type. To use the click type wrench you pre-adjust it to a torque setting. Once the torque is reached, the wrench has a reflex signalling feature that causes a momentary breakaway of the torque wrench body, sending an impulse to the operator's hand.

Pivot Head Type

➧ See Figure 13

Some torque wrenches (usually of the click type) may be equipped with a pivot head which can allow it to be used in areas of limited access. BUT, it must be used properly. To hold a pivot head wrench, grasp the handle lightly, and as you pull on the handle, it should be floated on the pivot point. If the handle comes in contact with the yoke extension during the process of pulling, there is a very good chance the torque readings will be inaccurate because this could alter the wrench loading point. The design of the handle is usually such as to make it inconvenient to deliberately misuse the wrench.

➡ It should be mentioned that the use of any U-joint, wobble or extension will have an effect on the torque readings, no matter what type of wrench you are using. For the most accurate readings, install the socket directly on the wrench driver. If necessary, straight extensions (which hold a socket directly under the wrench driver) will have the least effect on the torque reading. Avoid any extension that alters the length of the wrench from the handle to the head/driving point (such as a crow's foot). U-joint or Wobble extensions can greatly affect the readings; avoid their use at all times.

Standard Torque Specifications and Fastener Markings

In the absence of specific torques, the following chart can be used as a guide to the maximum safe torque of a particular size/grade of fastener.
- There is no torque difference for fine or coarse threads.
- Torque values are based on clean, dry threads. Reduce the value by 10% if threads are oiled prior to assembly.
- The torque required for aluminum components or fasteners is considerably less.

U.S. Bolts

SAE Grade Number	1 or 2			5			6 or 7		
Number of lines always 2 less than the grade number.									
Bolt Size (Inches)—(Thread)	Maximum Torque			Maximum Torque			Maximum Torque		
	Ft./Lbs.	Kgm	Nm	Ft./Lbs.	Kgm	Nm	Ft./Lbs.	Kgm	Nm
¼ — 20	5	0.7	6.8	8	1.1	10.8	10	1.4	13.5
— 28	6	0.8	8.1	10	1.4	13.6			
⁵/₁₆ — 18	11	1.5	14.9	17	2.3	23.0	19	2.6	25.8
— 24	13	1.8	17.6	19	2.6	25.7			
⅜ — 16	18	2.5	24.4	31	4.3	42.0	34	4.7	46.0
— 24	20	2.75	27.1	35	4.8	47.5			
⁷/₁₆ — 14	28	3.8	37.0	49	6.8	66.4	55	7.6	74.5
— 20	30	4.2	40.7	55	7.6	74.5			
½ — 13	39	5.4	52.8	75	10.4	101.7	85	11.75	115.2
— 20	41	5.7	55.6	85	11.7	115.2			
⁹/₁₆ — 12	51	7.0	69.2	110	15.2	149.1	120	16.6	162.7
— 18	55	7.6	74.5	120	16.6	162.7			
⅝ — 11	83	11.5	112.5	150	20.7	203.3	167	23.0	226.5
— 18	95	13.1	128.8	170	23.5	230.5			
¾ — 10	105	14.5	142.3	270	37.3	366.0	280	38.7	379.6
— 16	115	15.9	155.9	295	40.8	400.0			
⅞ — 9	160	22.1	216.9	395	54.6	535.5	440	60.9	596.5
— 14	175	24.2	237.2	435	60.1	589.7			
1 — 8	236	32.5	318.6	590	81.6	799.9	660	91.3	894.8
— 14	250	34.6	338.9	660	91.3	849.8			

Metric Bolts

Relative Strength Marking	4.6, 4.8			8.8		
Bolt Markings						
Bolt Size Thread Size x Pitch (mm)	Maximum Torque			Maximum Torque		
	Ft./Lbs.	Kgm	Nm	Ft./Lbs.	Kgm	Nm
6 x 1.0	2–3	.2–.4	3–4	3–6	.4–.8	5–8
8 x 1.25	6–8	.8–1	8–12	9–14	1.2–1.9	13–19
10 x 1.25	12–17	1.5–2.3	16–23	20–29	2.7–4.0	27–39
12 x 1.25	21–32	2.9–4.4	29–43	35–53	4.8–7.3	47–72
14 x 1.5	35–52	4.8–7.1	48–70	57–85	7.8–11.7	77–110
16 x 1.5	51–77	7.0–10.6	67–100	90–120	12.4–16.5	130–160
18 x 1.5	74–110	10.2–15.1	100–150	130–170	17.9–23.4	180–230
20 x 1.5	110–140	15.1–19.3	150–190	190–240	26.2–46.9	160–320
22 x 1.5	150–190	22.0–26.2	200–260	250–320	34.5–44.1	340–430
24 x 1.5	190–240	26.2–46.9	260–320	310–410	42.7–56.5	420–550

TCCS1098

Fig. 10 Standard and metric bolt torque specifications based on bolt strengths—WARNING: use only as a guide

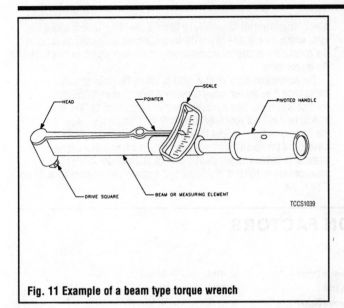

Fig. 11 Example of a beam type torque wrench

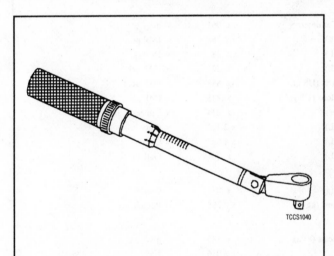

Fig. 12 A click type or breakaway torque wrench—note this one has a pivoting head

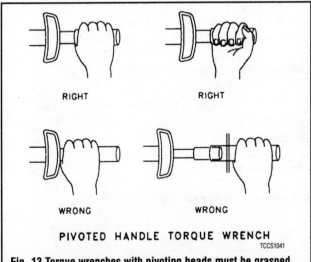

PIVOTED HANDLE TORQUE WRENCH

Fig. 13 Torque wrenches with pivoting heads must be grasped and used properly to prevent an incorrect reading

Rigid Case (Direct Reading)

♦ See Figure 14

A rigid case or direct reading torque wrench is equipped with a dial indicator to show torque values. One advantage of these wrenches is that they can be held at any position on the wrench without affecting accuracy. These wrenches are often preferred because they tend to be compact, easy to read and have a great degree of accuracy.

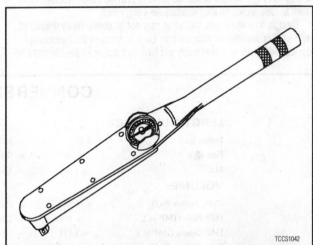

Fig. 14 The rigid case (direct reading) torque wrench uses a dial indicator to show torque

TORQUE ANGLE METERS

♦ See Figure 15

Because the frictional characteristics of each fastener or threaded hole will vary, clamp loads which are based strictly on torque will vary as well. In most applications, this variance is not significant enough to cause worry. But, in certain applications, a manufacturer's engineers may determine that more precise clamp loads are necessary (such is the case with many aluminum cylinder heads). In these cases, a torque angle method of installation would be specified. When installing fasteners which are torque angle tightened, a predetermined seating torque and standard torque wrench are usually used first to remove any compliance from the joint. The fastener is then tightened the specified additional portion of a turn measured in degrees. A torque angle gauge (mechanical protractor) is used for these applications.

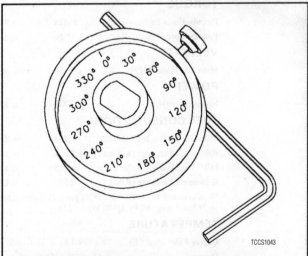

Fig. 15 Some specifications require the use of a torque angle meter (mechanical protractor)

Standard and Metric Measurements

♦ **See Figure 16**

Throughout this manual, specifications are given to help you determine the condition of various components on your vehicle, or to assist you in their installation. Some of the most common measurements include length (in. or cm/mm), torque (ft. lbs., inch lbs. or Nm) and pressure (psi, in. Hg, kPa or mm Hg). In most cases, we strive to provide the proper measurement as determined by the manufacturer's engineers.

Though, in some cases, that value may not be conveniently measured with what is available in your toolbox. Luckily, many of the measuring devices which are available today will have two scales so the Standard or Metric measurements may easily be taken. If any of the various measuring tools which are available to you do not contain the same scale as listed in the specifications, use the accompanying conversion factors to determine the proper value.

The conversion factor chart is used by taking the given specification and multiplying it by the necessary conversion factor. For instance, looking at the first line, if you have a measurement in inches such as "free-play should be 2 in." but your ruler reads only in millimeters, multiply 2 in. by the conversion factor of 25.4 to get the metric equivalent of 50.8mm. Likewise, if the specification was given only in a Metric measurement, for example in Newton Meters (Nm), then look at the center column first. If the measurement is 100 Nm, multiply it by the conversion factor of 0.738 to get 73.8 ft. lbs.

CONVERSION FACTORS

LENGTH–DISTANCE

Inches (in.)	x 25.4	= Millimeters (mm)	x .0394	= Inches
Feet (ft.)	x .305	= Meters (m)	x 3.281	= Feet
Miles	x 1.609	= Kilometers (km)	x .0621	= Miles

VOLUME

Cubic Inches (in3)	x 16.387	= Cubic Centimeters	x .061	= in3
IMP Pints (IMP pt.)	x .568	= Liters (L)	x 1.76	= IMP pt.
IMP Quarts (IMP qt.)	x 1.137	= Liters (L)	x .88	= IMP qt.
IMP Gallons (IMP gal.)	x 4.546	= Liters (L)	x .22	= IMP gal.
IMP Quarts (IMP qt.)	x 1.201	= US Quarts (US qt.)	x .833	= IMP qt.
IMP Gallons (IMP gal.)	x 1.201	= US Gallons (US gal.)	x .833	= IMP gal.
Fl. Ounces	x 29.573	= Milliliters	x .034	= Ounces
US Pints (US pt.)	x .473	= Liters (L)	x 2.113	= Pints
US Quarts (US qt.)	x .946	= Liters (L)	x 1.057	= Quarts
US Gallons (US gal.)	x 3.785	= Liters (L)	x .264	= Gallons

MASS–WEIGHT

Ounces (oz.)	x 28.35	= Grams (g)	x .035	= Ounces
Pounds (lb.)	x .454	= Kilograms (kg)	x 2.205	= Pounds

PRESSURE

Pounds Per Sq. In. (psi)	x 6.895	= Kilopascals (kPa)	x .145	= psi
Inches of Mercury (Hg)	x .4912	= psi	x 2.036	= Hg
Inches of Mercury (Hg)	x 3.377	= Kilopascals (kPa)	x .2961	= Hg
Inches of Water (H_2O)	x .07355	= Inches of Mercury	x 13.783	= H_2O
Inches of Water (H_2O)	x .03613	= psi	x 27.684	= H_2O
Inches of Water (H_2O)	x .248	= Kilopascals (kPa)	x 4.026	= H_2O

TORQUE

Pounds–Force Inches (in–lb)	x .113	= Newton Meters (N·m)	x 8.85	= in–lb
Pounds–Force Feet (ft–lb)	x 1.356	= Newton Meters (N·m)	x .738	= ft–lb

VELOCITY

Miles Per Hour (MPH)	x 1.609	= Kilometers Per Hour (KPH)	x .621	= MPH

POWER

Horsepower (Hp)	x .745	= Kilowatts	x 1.34	= Horsepower

FUEL CONSUMPTION*

Miles Per Gallon IMP (MPG)	x .354	= Kilometers Per Liter (Km/L)
Kilometers Per Liter (Km/L)	x 2.352	= IMP MPG
Miles Per Gallon US (MPG)	x .425	= Kilometers Per Liter (Km/L)
Kilometers Per Liter (Km/L)	x 2.352	= US MPG

*It is common to covert from miles per gallon (mpg) to liters/100 kilometers (1/100 km), where mpg (IMP) x 1/100 km = 282 and mpg (US) x 1/100 km = 235.

TEMPERATURE

Degree Fahrenheit (°F)	= (°C x 1.8) + 32
Degree Celsius (°C)	= (°F – 32) x .56

TCCS1044

Fig. 16 Standard and metric conversion factors chart

SERIAL NUMBER IDENTIFICATION

Vehicle

VEHICLE IDENTIFICATION NUMBER (VIN) PLATE

The Vehicle Identification Number (VIN) is stamped onto a metal tag mounted in the upper left-hand corner of the instrument panel, visible through the windshield from the outside of the vehicle. The VIN is also presented on various other labels and identifiers found throughout the vehicle.

The VIN is an identification code comprised of a seventeen-digit combination of numbers and letters. Each letter, number or combination represents different items, such as manufacturer, type of restraint system, line, series and body type, engine, model year and consecutive unit number.

Note that some VIN plates may convey additional information, such as whether a vehicle has an air bag

The last six digits of the VIN indicate the assembly plant production sequence number of each individual vehicle manufactured at the factory. The unit numbers are divided as follows by manufacturer:
- 000,001 through 599,999—Ford division vehicles
- 600,000 through 999,999—Lincoln and Mercury division vehicles

Refer to the acompanying specifications chart and illustrations for VIN breakdown.

VEHICLE CERTIFICATION LABEL

▶ See Figure 17

The vehicle certification label is affixed to the driver's side door pillar. The vehicle certification label displays various, important information regarding your particular vehicle, such as the following:
- Name of the manufacturer
- Month and year of manufacture
- Gross Vehicle Weight Rating (GVWR)
- Gross Axle Weight Rating (GAWR)
- Certification statement
- Vehicle Identification Number (VIN)
- Vehicle color
- Vehicle body type
- Brake type

- Moulding option (if applicable)
- Tape stripe or paint stripe option (if applicable)
- Interior trim option (if applicable)
- Radio type (if applicable)
- Axle ratio identification
- Transmission identification
- Spring identification
- District sales office
- Special order codes

Refer to the accompanying illustration for the location of the specific identification codes on the label.

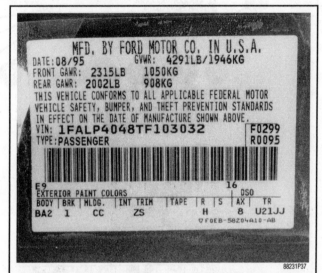

The vehicle certification label provides various important information regarding your vehicle

Engine

▶ See Figure 18

The engine, with which your specific vehicle is equipped, can be most easily identified by the Vehicle Identification Number (VIN), located on either the VIN tag, mounted in the upper left-hand corner of the instrument panel, or on the vehicle certification label, located on the driver's side door pillar. The engine identifying code is the 8th digit of the VIN. The engine VIN codes are as follows:
- 4—3.8L SFI engine
- D—5.0L SFI SHP engine
- T—5.0L SFI HO engine
- V—4.6L 4V SFI (DOHC) engine
- W—4.6L 2V SFI (SOHC) engine

All Ford Mustangs should also have an engine emission calibration number label affixed to the driver's side door or door post pillar. The calibration number should be used when ordering replacement parts or when checking calibrations. Because engine parts will often differ, even within a given Cubic Inch Displacement (CID) family, verifying the calibration number will ensure that the proper parts are obtained. Consult your local dealer's parts department to determine any pertinent information regarding dates, optional equipment or revisions concerning the code for your engine.

1FABP43F2RZ100001

VEHICLE IDENTIFICATION NUMBER

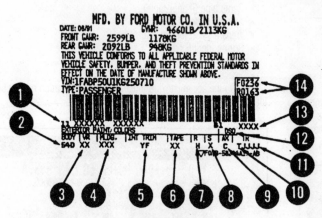

MFD. BY FORD MOTOR CO. IN U.S.A.
DATE: 06/91 GVWR: 4660LB/2113KG
FRONT GAWR: 2599LB 1178KG
REAR GAWR: 2092LB 948KG
THIS VEHICLE CONFORMS TO ALL APPLICABLE FEDERAL MOTOR VEHICLE SAFETY, BUMPER, AND THEFT PREVENTION STANDARDS IN EFFECT ON THE DATE OF MANUFACTURE SHOWN ABOVE.
VIN: 1FABP50U1KG250710
TYPE: PASSENGER

UNITED STATES

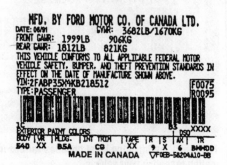

MFD. BY FORD MOTOR CO. OF CANADA LTD.
DATE: 06/91 GVWR: 3682LB/1670KG
FRONT GAWR: 1999LB 906KG
REAR GAWR: 1812LB 821KG
THIS VEHICLE CONFORMS TO ALL APPLICABLE FEDERAL MOTOR VEHICLE SAFETY, BUMPER, AND THEFT PREVENTION STANDARDS IN EFFECT ON THE DATE OF MANUFACTURE SHOWN ABOVE.
VIN: 2FABP35X9KB218512
TYPE: PASSENGER

MADE IN CANADA

CANADA

DECAL APPLIED TO CANADA BUILT UNITS

MFD. BY FORD MOTOR CO. IN U.S.A.
DATE: 06/91 GVWR: 4900LB/2222KG
FRONT GAWR: 2557LB 1159KG
REAR GAWR: 2430LB 1102KG
VIN: 1FABP50H4KA253107
TYPE: U.S.CERT VOID-EXPORT

UNITED STATES EXPORT LABEL SHOWN (CANADIAN EXPORT LABEL TYPICAL)

NOTE: X'S ON LABELS ARE SHOWN IN PLACE OF ACTUAL NUMBERS TO REPRESENT TYPICAL LABELS ONLY.

I
F } WORLD MANUFACTURER IDENTIFIER
A
B — RESTRAINT SYSTEM TYPE
P — MANUFACTURER SPECIFICATION
4
3 } LINE, SERIES, BODY TYPE
F — ENGINE TYPE
2 — CHECK DIGIT
R — VEHICLE MODEL YEAR
Z — ASSEMBLY PLANT
1
0
0
0 } PRODUCTION SEQUENCE NUMBER
0
1

1 — EXTERIOR PAINT COLOR CODES
2 — BODY TYPE CODES
3 — VINYL ROOF CODES
4 — MOULDING CODES
5 — INTERIOR TRIM CODES — (FIRST CODE LETTER = FABRIC AND SEAT TYPE, SECOND CODE = COLOR)
6 — TAPE STRIPE CODES
7 — RADIO TYPE CODES
8 — SUN ROOF/MOON ROOF CODES
9 — AXLE RATIO CODES
10 — TRANSMISSION/TRANSAXLE CODES
11 — SUSPENSION SPRING CODES
12 — DISTRICT CODES
13 — SPECIAL ORDER CODES
14 — ACCESSORY RESERVE LOAD CODES

88231G01

Fig. 17 The codes on the vehicle certification label can be deciphered as shown

VEHICLE IDENTIFICATION

Code	Liters	Cu. In. (cc)	Cyl.	Fuel Sys.	Eng. Mfg.		Code	Year
4	3.8 (3802)	232	6	SFI	Ford		R	1994
D	5.0 (4949)	302	8	SFI	Ford		S	1995
T	5.0 (4949)	302	8	SFI	Ford		T	1996
V	4.6 (4593)	281	8	SFI	Ford		V	1997
W	4.6 (4593)	281	8	SFI	Ford		W	1998

(Engine Code columns; Model Year columns: Code / Year)

SFI – Sequential Fuel Injection

88231C00

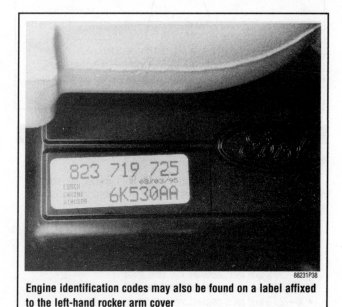

Engine identification codes may also be found on a label affixed to the left-hand rocker arm cover

CALIBRATION
ÉTALONNAGE
CALIBRACIÓN

8-25F-R00   E8AE-6E061-**AAA**

CALIBRATION
REVISION NUMBER

88231G02

Fig. 18 An engine calibration label is usually found on the driver's door or pillar

ENGINE IDENTIFICATION

Year	Model	Engine Displacement Liters (cc)		Engine Series (ID/VIN)	Fuel System	No. of Cylinders	Engine Type
1994	Mustang	3.8 (3802)		4	SFI	6	OHV
	Mustang Cobra	5.0 (4949)	①	D	SFI	8	OHV
	Mustang	5.0 (4949)	②	T	SFI	8	OHV
1995	Mustang	3.8 (3802)		4	SFI	6	OHV
	Mustang Cobra	5.0 (4949)	①	D	SFI	8	OHV
	Mustang	5.0 (4949)	②	T	SFI	8	OHV
1996	Mustang	3.8 (3802)		4	SFI	6	OHV
	Mustang Cobra	4.6 (4593)	①	V	SFI	8	DOHC
	Mustang	4.6 (4593)	②	W	SFI	8	SOHC
1997	Mustang	3.8 (3802)		4	SFI	6	OHV
	Mustang Cobra	4.6 (4593)	①	V	SFI	8	DOHC
	Mustang	4.6 (4593)	②	W	SFI	8	SOHC
1998	Mustang	3.8 (3802)		4	SFI	6	OHV
	Mustang Cobra	4.6 (4593)	①	V	SFI	8	DOHC
	Mustang	4.6 (4593)	②	W	SFI	8	SOHC

SFI - Sequential Fuel Injection
OHV - Overhead Valve
SOHC - Single Overhead Camshaft
DOHC - Double Overhead Camshaft
① - Special high performance
② - High output

88231C01

Transmission

▶ **See Figures 19, 20 and 21**

The transmission identification code is either located on a metal tag or plate attached to the transmission housing, or is stamped directly into the housing. The transmission code can also be found on the vehicle certification label, which should be affixed to the driver's side door or door post pillar. The transmission identification codes displayed on the vehicle certification label are as follows:

- 5—T50D manual
- 6—T450D manual
- P—Automatic Overdrive (AODE)
- U—Automatic Overdrive (AODE) 4R70W

Refer to the Transmission Identification chart in this section for more details.

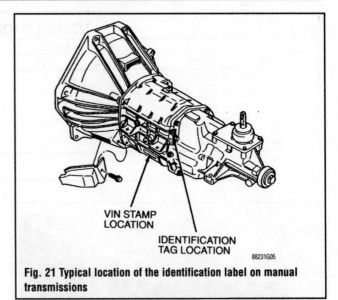

Fig. 21 Typical location of the identification label on manual transmissions

Drive Axle

▶ **See Figures 22 and 23**

The drive axle code can be found either stamped on a tag secured by one of the differential housing cover bolts, or on the vehicle certification label. The rear axle identification codes are as follows:

1994 models:
- 2—3.55 axle ratio, conventional differential
- 4—3.42 axle ratio, conventional differential
- 5—3.27 axle ratio, conventional differential
- 6—3.73 axle ratio, conventional differential
- 7—3.07 axle ratio, conventional differential
- 8—2.73 axle ratio, conventional differential
- A—3.63 axle ratio, conventional differential
- B—2.47 axle ratio, conventional differential
- D—3.42 axle ratio, Traction-Lok® limited-slip differential
- E—3.27 axle ratio, Traction-Lok® limited-slip differential

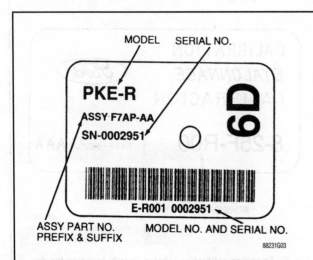

Fig. 19 A typical automatic transmission identification label displays the model and serial numbers, as well as an identifying bar code

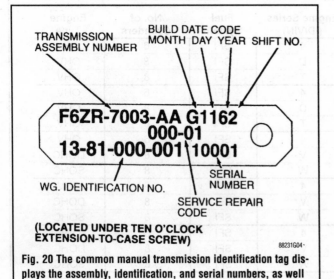

Fig. 20 The common manual transmission identification tag displays the assembly, identification, and serial numbers, as well as the build date code

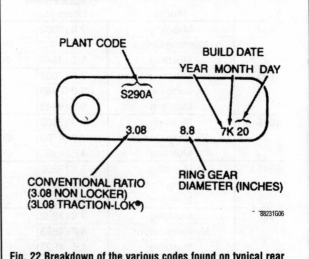

Fig. 22 Breakdown of the various codes found on typical rear axle tags

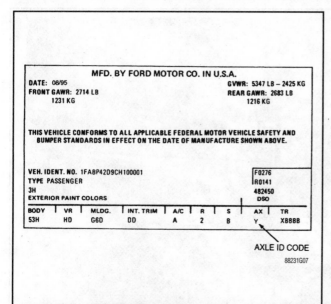

Fig. 23 The axle identifier code on the vehicle certification label is found on the lower right-hand corner

- F—3.45 axle ratio, conventional differential
- J—3.85 axle ratio, conventional differential
- K—3.55 axle ratio, Traction-Lok® limited-slip differential
- M—2.73 axle ratio, Traction-Lok® limited-slip differential
- R—3.45 axle ratio, Traction-Lok® limited-slip differential
- W—3.73 axle ratio, Traction-Lok® limited-slip differential
- Y—3.08 axle ratio, conventional differential
- Z—3.08 axle ratio, Traction-Lok® limited-slip differential

1995 models:
- 8—2.73 axle ratio, conventional differential
- E—3.27 axle ratio, Traction-Lok® limited-slip differential
- M—2.73 axle ratio, Traction-Lok® limited-slip differential
- Z—3.08 axle ratio, Traction-Lok® limited-slip differential

1996 models:
- 1—2.73 axle ratio, conventional differential
- A—2.73 or 3.08 axle ratio, Traction-Lok® limited-slip differential
- C—3.27 axle ratio, Traction-Lok® limited-slip differential

1997 models:
- 1—2.73 axle ratio, conventional differential
- A—2.73 or 3.08 axle ratio, Traction-Lok® limited-slip differential
- C—3.27 axle ratio, Traction-Lok® limited-slip differential

1998 models:
- 1—2.73 axle ratio, conventional differential
- A—2.73 or 3.08 axle ratio, Traction-Lok® limited-slip differential
- C—3.27 axle ratio, Traction-Lok® limited-slip differential

ROUTINE MAINTENANCE AND TUNE-UP

Proper maintenance and tune-up is the key to long and trouble-free vehicle life, and the work can yield its own rewards. Studies have shown that a properly tuned and maintained vehicle can achieve better gas mileage than an out-of-tune vehicle. As a conscientious owner and driver, set aside a Saturday morning, say once a month, to check or replace items which could cause major problems later. Keep your own personal log to jot down which services you performed, how much the parts cost you, the date, and the exact odometer reading at the time. Keep all receipts for such items as engine oil and filters, so that they may be referred to in case of related problems or to determine operating expenses. As a do-it-yourselfer, these receipts are the only proof you have that the required maintenance was performed. In the event of a warranty problem, these receipts will be invaluable.

The literature provided with your vehicle when it was originally delivered includes the factory recommended maintenance schedule. If you no longer have this literature, replacement copies are usually available from the dealer. A maintenance schedule is provided later in this section, in case you do not have the factory literature.

Air Cleaner (Element)

GENERAL INFORMATION

The air cleaner is a dry-type, chemically treated, pleated paper element. The paper cartridge should be replaced every 30,000 miles (48,000 km).

➡**Check the air filter more often if the vehicle is operated under severe (especially dusty) conditions and replace or clean it as necessary.**

The air inducation system functions as follows:
1. Outside air flows from an air intake into the air tray through an opening in the front fender.
2. The incoming air is filtered by the paper element in the air tray.
3. From the air tray, the filtered air flows through the Mass Air Flow (MAF) sensor and air cleaner outlet tube into the trhottle body.

➡**The Positive Crankcase Ventilation (PCV) system uses filtered air from the induction system. The air for the PCV system is taken from the air cleaner outlet tube via a fitting and hose.**

On 3.8L and 5.0L engines, air induction noise is controlled by means of a sealed cover with an integral resonator, which is a part of the MAF sensor unit.

REMOVAL & INSTALLATION

▶ **See Figures 24, 25, 26 and 27 (p. 22–25)**

1. Disconnect the negative battery cable.
2. Label and disconnect all hoses, tubes and wires connected to the air filter assembly or outlet hose.
3. Unfasten the clamps that attach the air tray to the MAF sensor housing.
4. Separate the MAF sensor housing from the air tray and position the MAF sensor aside.

➡**Before removal, be sure to note the proper positioning of the element within the housing for installation purposes.**

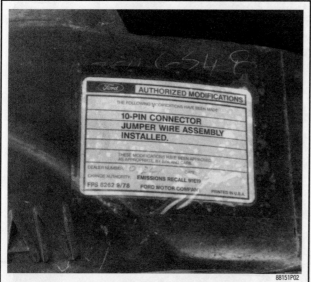

Dealers will usually install underhood labels to indicate if special recall service has been performed

GENERAL MAINTENANCE ITEMS—3.8L ENGINE

1. Brake master cylinder and reservoir
2. Engine oil fill cap
3. Engine oil dipstick
4. Battery
5. Radiator fill cap
6. Power steering reservoir
7. Accessory drive belt
8. Coolant reservoir fill cap
9. Cooling system bleed port
10. Accessory drive belt automatic tensioner
11. Warning and information labels
12. PCV valve (beneath the air intake hose)
13. Automatic transmission fluid dipstick (behind the air intake hose)
14. Air filter and housing (air tray)
15. Upper radiator hose
16. Spark plug wires
17. Windshield washer reservoir

8231P70

GENERAL MAINTENANCE ITEMS (CONTINUED)—3.8L ENGINE

1. Grease fittings (outer tie rod ends)
2. Radiator drain petcock
3. Lower radiator hose
4. Engine oil filter
5. Accessory drive belt
6. Ignition timing marks (on crankshaft damper)
7. Engine oil drain plug
8. Torque converter drain access plug (automatic transmissions)
9. Automatic transmission fluid pan

GENERAL MAINTENANCE ITEMS—4.6L ENGINES

1. Battery
2. Cooling system reservoir and fill cap
3. Power steering fluid reservoir and fill cap
4. Engine oil dipstick
5. Windshield washer reservoir and fill cap
6. Engine oil fill cap
7. Brake master cylinder fluid reservoir and fill cap
8. PCV valve
9. Accessory drive belt
10. Upper radiator hose
11. Air cleaner housing (filter element inside)
12. Accessory drive belt automatic tensioner
13. Spark plug wires

88231P72

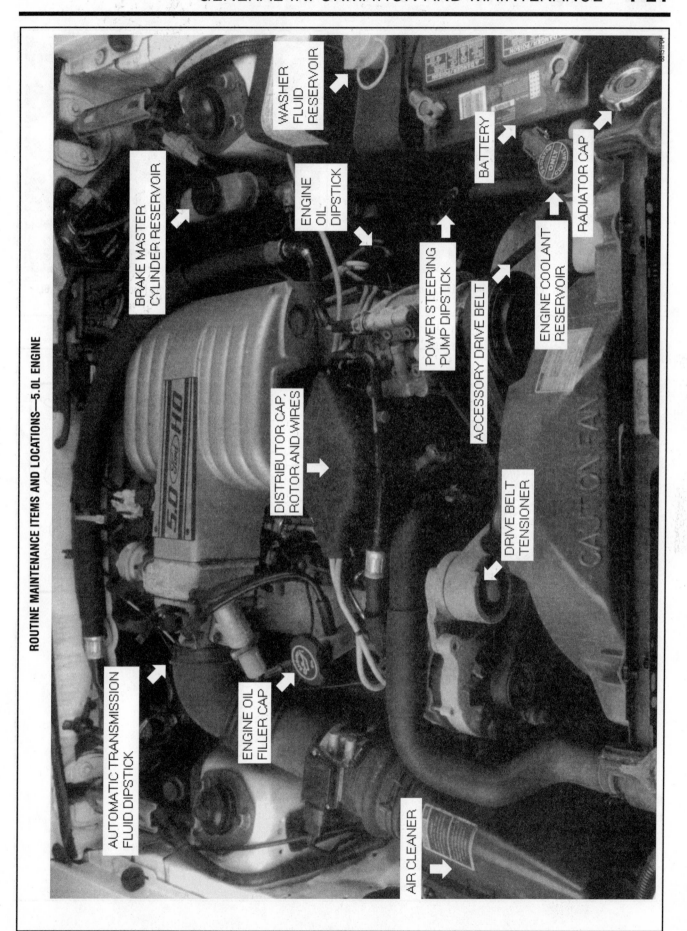

ROUTINE MAINTENANCE ITEMS AND LOCATIONS—5.0L ENGINE

To remove the air filter, separate the MAF sensor housing from the air tray . . .

. . . then slide the air filter out of the housing—3.8L and 4.6L engines

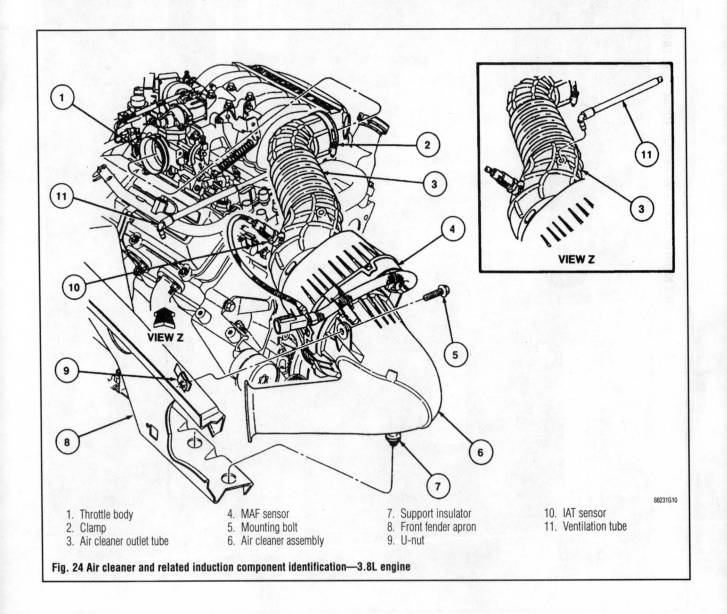

1. Throttle body
2. Clamp
3. Air cleaner outlet tube
4. MAF sensor
5. Mounting bolt
6. Air cleaner assembly
7. Support insulator
8. Front fender apron
9. U-nut
10. IAT sensor
11. Ventilation tube

Fig. 24 Air cleaner and related induction component identification—3.8L engine

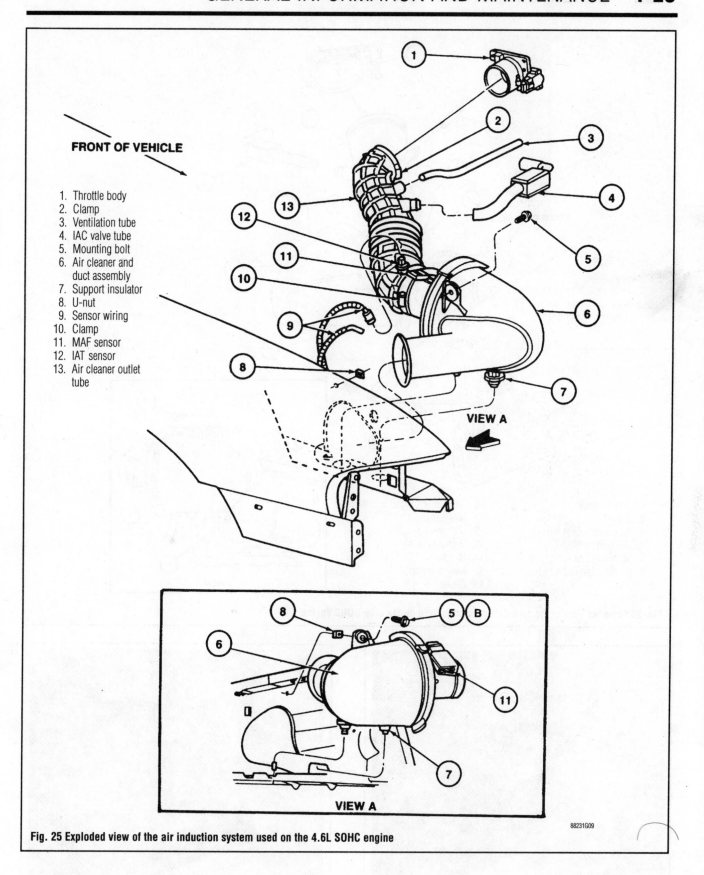

FRONT OF VEHICLE

1. Throttle body
2. Clamp
3. Ventilation tube
4. IAC valve tube
5. Mounting bolt
6. Air cleaner and duct assembly
7. Support insulator
8. U-nut
9. Sensor wiring
10. Clamp
11. MAF sensor
12. IAT sensor
13. Air cleaner outlet tube

VIEW A

VIEW A

88231G09

Fig. 25 Exploded view of the air induction system used on the 4.6L SOHC engine

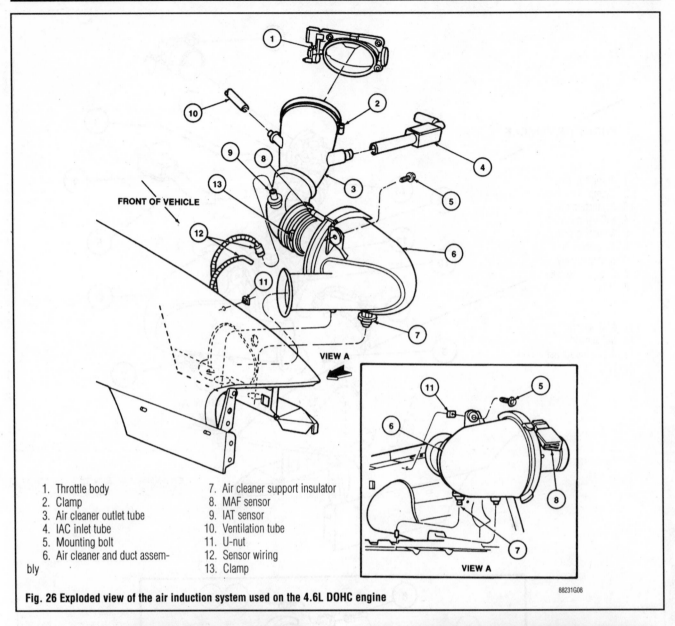

FRONT OF VEHICLE

VIEW A

1. Throttle body
2. Clamp
3. Air cleaner outlet tube
4. IAC inlet tube
5. Mounting bolt
6. Air cleaner and duct assembly
7. Air cleaner support insulator
8. MAF sensor
9. IAT sensor
10. Ventilation tube
11. U-nut
12. Sensor wiring
13. Clamp

VIEW A

88231G08

Fig. 26 Exploded view of the air induction system used on the 4.6L DOHC engine

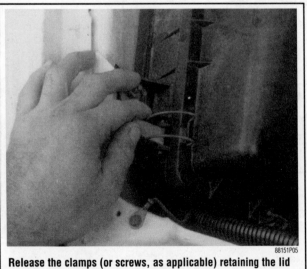

88151P05

Release the clamps (or screws, as applicable) retaining the lid to the air filter housing—5.0L engine

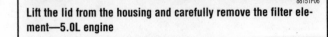

88151P06

Lift the lid from the housing and carefully remove the filter element—5.0L engine

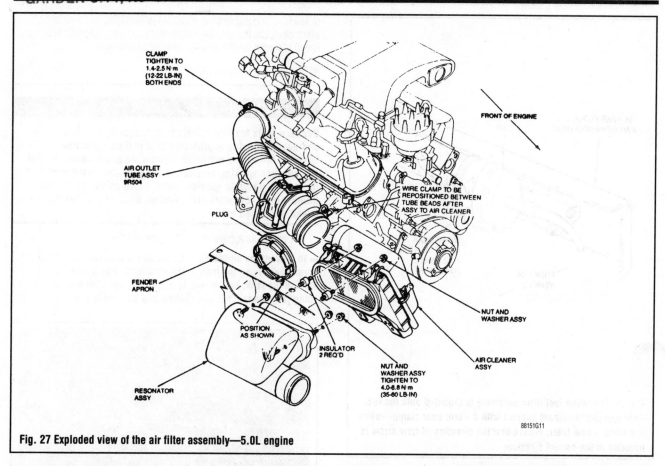

CLAMP
TIGHTEN TO
1.4-2.5 N·m
(12-22 LB-IN)
BOTH ENDS

FRONT OF ENGINE

AIR OUTLET
TUBE ASSY
9R504

WIRE CLAMP TO BE
REPOSITIONED BETWEEN
TUBE BEADS AFTER
ASSY TO AIR CLEANER

PLUG

FENDER
APRON

NUT AND
WASHER ASSY

POSITION
AS SHOWN

AIR CLEANER
ASSY

INSULATOR
2 REQ'D

NUT AND
WASHER ASSY
TIGHTEN TO
4.0-6.8 N·m
(35-60 LB-IN)

RESONATOR
ASSY

88151G11

Fig. 27 Exploded view of the air filter assembly—5.0L engine

5. Remove the filter element from the air tray.
To install:
6. Using a damp rag, clean all of the inside surfaces of the air tray.
7. Install the air filter element (as noted during removal) and position the MAF sensor against the air tray.
8. Fasten the retaining clamps, then connect all hoses, tubes and wires to the air induction components.
9. Connect the negative battery cable.

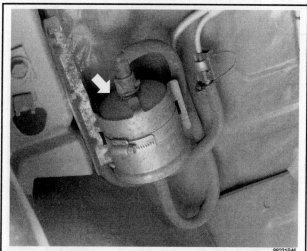

88231P46

The fuel filter (arrow) is mounted to the underside of the vehicle near the fuel tank

Fuel Filter

The inline fuel filter on the Mustang is normally found under the vehicle, near the fuel tank, mounted to the rear crossmember.

GENERAL INFORMATION

◆ **See Figures 28 and 29**

Fuel is filtered at 3 separate locations on these vehicles:
1. Fuel pump inlet filter—A nylon filter element is attached to the electric fuel pump inlet inside the fuel tank. It is used to protect the fuel pump from possible tank contamination.
2. Inline fuel filter—The inline fuel filter is designed to filter material which could damage the tiny metering orifices of the injector nozzles. The filter is located downstream of the electric fuel pump and is usually mounted to the rear crossmember. The inline filter is of one-piece construction, meaning that it cannot be cleaned and must be replaced as an assembly should it become clogged. Because flow will vary between filter elements, be sure to only use the proper replacement part which is designed for your engine's fuel system.
3. Injector filter screen—Each fuel injector contains a filter screen at the top (fuel inlet point). If the injector screen becomes clogged, the complete injector assembly must be replaced.

Of these 3 fuel filters, only the inline type has ever really been considered a maintenance item. The others are expected to serve the life of the components to which they are attached. But even the inline fuel filters have become more efficient, so no periodic replacement interval is recommended by the manufacturer. It is never a bad idea to replace the filter on a older vehicle or a used vehicle where the quality of gasoline which may have been used in the car is not known. Likewise, any vehicle that shows signs

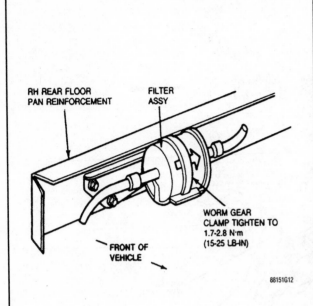

Fig. 28 The inline fuel filter assembly is mounted onto the rear floor pan reinforcement support with a worm gear clamp—when installing a new filter, ensure that the direction-of-flow arrow is pointing in the correct direction

Fig. 29 Along with the fuel pump filter and the inline filter, each fuel injector uses a small filter screen for additional protection—the fuel injector filter screens are not serviceable

of fuel filter clogging (such as hesitation or stumbling on acceleration, which cannot be traced to the ignition system or other fuel system components) is a good candidate for an inline filter replacement.

REMOVAL & INSTALLATION

✳✳ CAUTION

Because of its toxicity, refrain from breathing gasoline vapors and avoid exposing unprotected skin to liquid gasoline. Since gasoline fumes are extremely flammable and volatile, NEVER smoke when working around or near gasoline. Make sure that there is no possible ignition source (such as sparks or open flames) near your work area. Always work on the fuel system in a well-ventilated area.

This procedure applies only to the inline fuel filter.

➡To prevent the siphoning of fuel from the tank when the filter is removed, raise the front of the vehicle slightly above the level of the tank, but be sure to properly support the vehicle using jackstands. Fuel line clamps may be used to prevent

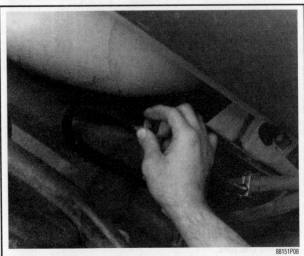

Even though fuel line clamps can be used to prevent leakage, MAKE SURE the line is not damaged

Once the hairpin clip is removed, the push-connect fitting may be disengaged from the filter

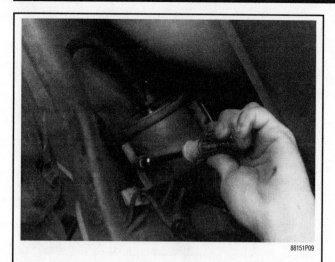

If you have trouble getting to the push-connect fittings, try loosening the worm clamp and repositioning the filter slightly.

leakage, but ONLY WITH CAUTION. Old, brittle fuel lines may be damaged by the clamps and could leak afterwards. If a clamp is used, BE SURE to thoroughly inspect the lines after installation of the fuel filter. Any damaged line should be immediately replaced.

1. Disconnect the negative battery cable.
2. Properly relieve the fuel system pressure using a test gauge at the fuel pressure relief valve. For more details, please refer to Section 5 of this manual.
3. Raise and safely support the rear of the vehicle on jackstands.
4. Detach the fuel lines from both ends of the fuel filter by disengaging both push-connect fittings (for details on push-connect fitting removal, please refer to Section 5 of this manual). Install new retainer clips in each push-connect fitting prior to reassembly.

➡Position a rag below the filter to catch any fuel which may spill as it is disconnected and removed.

5. Remove the fuel filter from the bracket by loosening the worm gear clamp. Note the orientation of the direction-of-flow arrow on the fuel filter, as installed in the bracket, to ensure proper fuel flow through the replacement filter.

To install:
6. Install the fuel filter into the bracket, ensuring the proper direction of flow. Tighten the worm gear clamp to 15–25 inch lbs. (2-3 Nm).
7. Install the push-connect fittings onto the filter ends. Connect the negative battery cable, then start the engine and check for fuel leaks.

✳✳ CAUTION

Use extreme caution when starting and running an engine which is supported by jackstands. ENSURE that no drive wheels are on the ground. Also, ensure that the wheels which are on the ground are properly blocked so the vehicle cannot move.

8. Lower the vehicle.

Positive Crankcase Ventilation (PCV) Valve

➡For more information on the Positive Crankcase Ventilation (PCV) system, please refer to Section 4 of this manual.

GENERAL INFORMATION

The PCV valve system vents crankcase gases into the engine air/fuel intake system where they are burned with the air/fuel mixture. The PCV valve system keeps pollutants from being released into the atmosphere, and also helps to keep the engine oil clean, by ridding the crankcase of moisture and corrosive fumes. The system consists of the PCV valve, its mounting grommet, the nipple in the air intake and the connecting hoses. On most applications, the system contains some form of oil separator to remove oil from the vapors.

Because of the function this system serves in keeping the crankcase ventilated, it is extremely important that the valve be checked periodically and replaced if clogged. A restricted PCV valve will allow pressure to build in the crankcase, which can decrease gas mileage, cause gasket oil leaks and, most importantly, allow the build-up of dangerous oil sludge/acids.

For details concerning PCV system component testing or replacement, please refer to Section 4 of this manual.

REMOVAL & INSTALLATION

The PCV valve should be replaced at a minimum of every 60,000 miles (96,000 km); sooner if the vehicle is driven under severe conditions, such as: stop-and-go driving, very hot or cold climates, especially dusty conditions, short and frequent trips.

3.8L and 4.6L Engines

▶ See Figures 30, 31 and 32

1. On 4.6L SOHC engines, remove the air cleaner outlet tube from the vehicle by loosening the clamps and detaching the tube from the air cleaner assembly and the throttle body.
2. Detach the ventilation hose from the PCV valve, mounted in the right-hand rocker arm cover.
3. Pull the valve out of its rubber mounting grommet.
4. Inspect the valve and grommet for deterioration or other damage; replace if necessary.

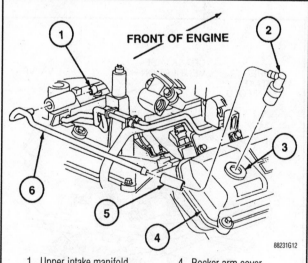

1. Upper intake manifold	4. Rocker arm cover
2. PCV valve	5. Hose
3. Grommet	6. Ventilation tube

Fig. 30 Exploded view of the Positive Crankcase Ventilation (PCV) system used on 3.8L engines

To install:

5. Insert the PCV valve into the rubber mounting grommet until it is fully seated.

6. Attach the ventilation hose to the valve.

7. If necessary, install the air cleaner outlet tube. Tighten the retaining clamps until snug.

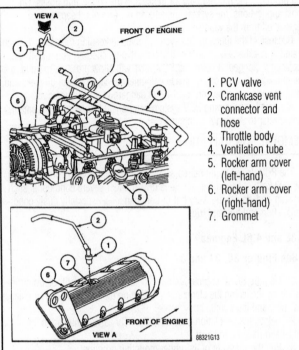

1. PCV valve
2. Crankcase vent connector and hose
3. Throttle body
4. Ventilation tube
5. Rocker arm cover (left-hand)
6. Rocker arm cover (right-hand)
7. Grommet

Fig. 31 Positive Crankcase Ventilation (PCV) system component identification—4.6L SOHC engine

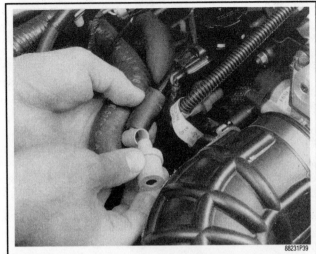

To remove the PCV valve, pull it out of the rocker arm cover grommet and separate it from the vacuum hose

5.0L Engine

▶ **See Figure 33**

➡**5.0L engines are equipped with a crankcase vent oil separator element, located in the intake manifold just beneath the PCV valve mounting grommet. This crankcase emission filter element should be replaced every 30,000 miles (48,000 km). Of course, as long as you are removing the PCV valve for access to the element, it is a good time to check and/or replace the valve as well.**

1. Pull the PCV valve out of the rubber mounting grommet, located at the rear of the lower intake manifold.

2. Detach the ventilation hose from the PCV valve, then remove the grommet from the lower intake manifold to access the crankcase vent oil separator element.

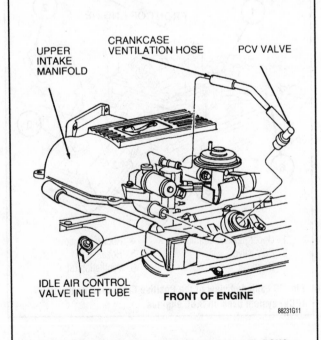

Fig. 32 PCV system component identification for 4.6L DOHC engines

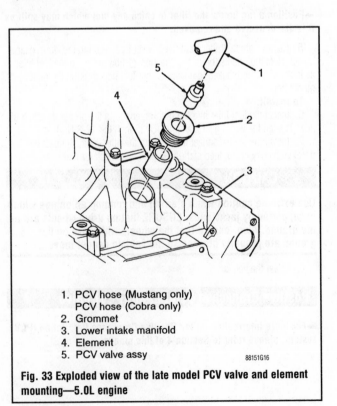

1. PCV hose (Mustang only)
   PCV hose (Cobra only)
2. Grommet
3. Lower intake manifold
4. Element
5. PCV valve assy

Fig. 33 Exploded view of the late model PCV valve and element mounting—5.0L engine

3. Remove the crankcase vent oil separator element from the intake manifold.

4. Inspect the valve and grommet for deterioration or other damage; replace if necessary.

To install:

5. Install a new crankcase vent oil separator element into the intake manifold.

6. Attach the ventilation hose to the PCV valve.

7. Install the rubber mounting grommet, then the PCV valve into the rear of the lower intake manifold.

8. Start the engine and check for leaks.

Evaporative Canister

SERVICING

▶ **See Figures 34, 35 and 36**

➡For more information on the Evaporative Emissions system, please refer to Section 4 of this manual.

The canister is located either under the right-hand front fender, mounted onto the underside of the fender apron (3.8L and 4.6L engines), or under the hood on the inside of the right-hand fender (5.0L engine).

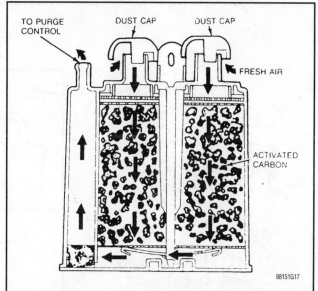

Fig. 34 Cross-sectional view of a typical activated carbon (charcoal) canister

1. Fuel and vapor return line
2. Evaporative emission hose
3. Push-pin
4. Ventilation tube
5. Bracket
6. Evaporative emission canister purge valve
7. Connector
8. Front fender apron
9. Evaporative emission return hose
10. Bolt
11. Evaporative emission canister bracket
12. Evaporative emission canister
13. Bolt

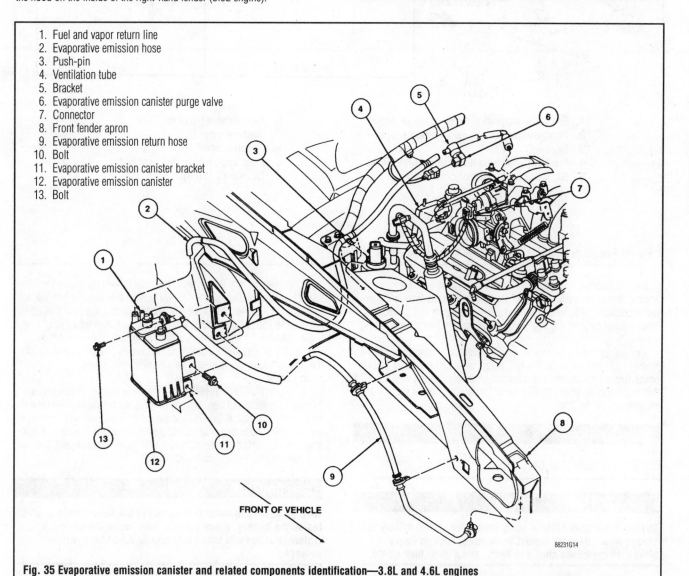

FRONT OF VEHICLE

Fig. 35 Evaporative emission canister and related components identification—3.8L and 4.6L engines

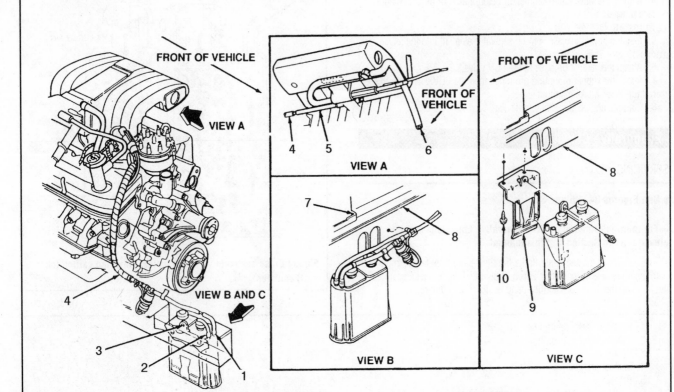

1. Engine evaporator hose to large nipple
2. Tank evaporator hose to small nipple
3. Screw
4. Fuel vapor return hose and valve assy
5. EGR vacuum control connector
6. Crankcase hose to PCV
7. Battery tray
8. Sidemember
9. Fuel vapor canister bracket
10. Screw (2 req'd)

88151G19

Fig. 36 Evaporative canister mounting and hose routing—5.0L engine

The fuel evaporative emission control system stores gasoline vapors which rise from the sealed fuel tank. The system prevents these unburned hydrocarbons from polluting the atmosphere. It consists of a charcoal vapor storage canister, check or purge valves and the interconnecting vapor lines.

The canister and vapor lines should be inspected for damage or leaks at least every 24,000 miles (38,500 km). Repair or replace any old or cracked hoses. Replace the canister if it is cracked or damaged in any way. Other than inspecting the lines and the canister for damage, there is no periodic maintenance for this item.

Battery

REMOVAL & INSTALLATION

✳✳ CAUTION

To reduce the possibility of burns caused by spilled battery acid, always wear adequate protective clothing, such as heavy gloves, long-sleeved shirt and pants, and a clear face shield.

1. Loosen the nuts which secure the cable ends to the battery terminals. Using a twisting motion, lift the negative battery cable from the terminal, followed by the positive cable. If there is a battery cable puller available, use it.
2. If so equipped, lift the battery cover up and off of the battery.
3. Remove the hold-down nuts from the battery hold-down bracket. Remove the bracket and the battery. Lift the battery straight up and out of the vehicle, being sure to keep it level to avoid spilling acid.

To install:

4. Before installing the battery in the vehicle, make sure that the battery terminals are clean and free from corrosion. Use a battery terminal cleaner on the terminals and on the inside of the battery cable ends. If a cleaner is not available, use coarse grade sandpaper to remove the corrosion. A mixture of baking soda and water poured over the terminals and cable ends will help remove and neutralize any acid buildup.

✳✳ CAUTION

Take great care to avoid getting any of the baking soda solution inside the battery. If any solution gets inside the battery a violent reaction will take place and/or the battery will be damaged.

5. Before attaching the cables to the terminals, install a pair of anti-corrosive felt washers. These washers, which are available at most auto parts stores, are impregnated with a solution that will help keep oxidation to a minimum.

6. Position the battery in the vehicle. Install the cables onto the terminals, negative terminal last.

7. Tighten the nuts on the cable ends until secure.

8. Smear a light coating of grease on the cable ends and tops of the terminals. This will further prevent the build-up of oxidation on the terminals and the cable ends.

9. Install and tighten the nuts of the battery hold-down bracket.

10. If so equipped, install the battery cover.

Belts

INSPECTION

▶ **See Figures 37, 38, 39 and 40**

Although Ford recommends that the drive belt(s) be inspected every 30,000 miles (48,000 km), it is really a good idea to check them at least once a year, or at every major fluid change. Whichever interval you choose,

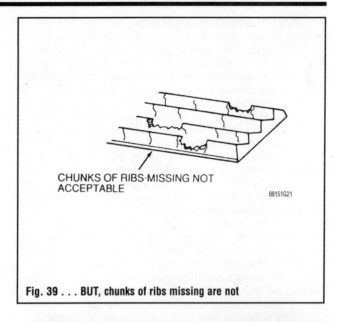

Fig. 39 . . . BUT, chunks of ribs missing are not

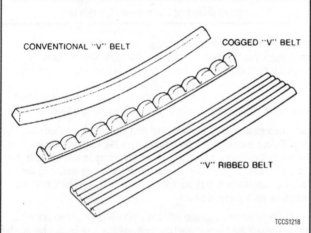

Fig. 37 There are typically 3 types of accessory drive belts found on vehicles today—the V-ribbed serpentine drive belt is found on vehicles covered by this manual

Make sure the belt tensioner arrow falls within the range markings on the tensioner's face—5.0L engine

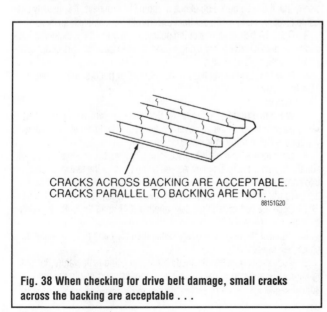

Fig. 38 When checking for drive belt damage, small cracks across the backing are acceptable . . .

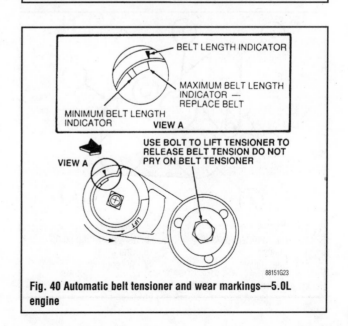

Fig. 40 Automatic belt tensioner and wear markings—5.0L engine

the belts should be checked for wear or damage. Obviously, a damaged drive belt can cause problems should it give way while the vehicle is in operation. But, improper length belts (too short or long), as well as excessively worn belts, can also cause problems. Loose accessory drive belts can lead to poor engine cooling and diminished output from the alternator, air conditioning compressor or power steering pump. A belt that is too tight places a severe strain on the driven unit and can wear out bearings quickly.

The V-ribbed serpentine drive belts used by these engines should be inspected for rib chunking (pieces of the ribs breaking off), severe glazing, frayed cords or other visible damage. Any belt which is missing sections of 2 or more adjacent ribs which are ½ in. (13mm) or longer must be replaced. You might want to note that V-ribbed belts do tend to form small cracks across the backing. If the only wear you find is in the form of one or more cracks across the backing, and NOT parallel to the ribs, the belt is still good and does not need to be replaced.

As for belt tension, an automatic spring-loaded tensioner is used on these vehicles to keep the belt properly adjusted at all times. The tensioner is also useful as a wear indicator. When the belt is properly installed, the arrow on the tensioner housing must point within the acceptable range lines on the tensioner's face. If the arrow falls outside the range, either an improper belt has been installed or the belt is worn beyond its useful lifespan. In either case, a new belt must be installed immediately to assure proper engine operation and to prevent possible accessory damage.

ADJUSTMENT

All engines covered by this manual utilize automatic drive belt tensioners; therefore, periodic drive belt tensioning is not necessary.

REMOVAL & INSTALLATION

▶ **See Figures 41 thru 46 (p. 32–34)**

The Mustang engines utilize one or more wide-ribbed V-belts to drive the engine accessories such as the water pump, alternator, air conditioner compressor, air pump, etc. Because these belts use a spring loaded tensioner for adjustment, belt replacement tends to be somewhat easier than it used to be on engines where accessories were pivoted and bolted in place for tension adjustment. Basically, belt replacement involves pivoting the tensioner to loosen the belt, then sliding the belt off of the pulleys. The two most important points are to pay CLOSE attention to the proper belt routing (since serpentine belts tend to be "snaked" all different ways through the pulleys) and to make sure the V-ribs are properly seated in all the pulleys.

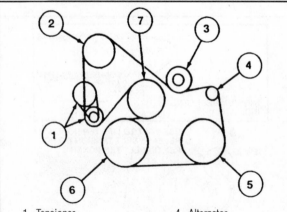

1. Tensioner
2. A/C compressor or idler pulley
3. Idler pulley
4. Alternator
5. Power steering pump
6. Crankshaft
7. Water pump

88231G17

Fig. 41 Accessory drive belt routing—3.8L engine

1. Alternator
2. Water pump
3. Power steering pump
4. Crankshaft
5. A/C compressor
6. Drive belt
7. Tensioner
8. Idler pulley

88231G18

Fig. 42 Accessory drive belt routing—4.6L engines

Although belt routing diagrams have been included in this section, the first places you should check for proper belt routing are the labels in your engine compartment. These should include a belt routing diagram which may reflect changes made during a production run.

1. Disconnect the negative battery cable for safety. This will help assure that no one mistakenly cranks the engine with your hands between the pulleys.

➡**Take a good look at the installed belt and make a note of the routing. Before removing the belt, make sure the routing matches that of the belt routing label or one of the diagrams in this book. If, for some reason, a diagram does not match (you may not have the original engine or it may have been modified), carefully note the changes on a piece of paper.**

2. For tensioners equipped with a ½ square hole (as shown in the accompanying illustration), insert the drive end of a large breaker bar into the hole. Use the breaker bar to pivot the tensioner away from the drive belt. For tensioners not equipped with this hole, use the proper-sized socket and breaker bar (or a large handled wrench) on the tensioner idler pulley center bolt to pivot the tensioner away from the belt. This will loosen the belt sufficiently that it can be pulled off of one or more of the pulleys. It is usually easiest to carefully pull the belt out from underneath the tensioner pulley itself.

3. Once the belt is off one of the pulleys, gently pivot the tensioner back into position. DO NOT allow the tensioner to snap back, as this could damage the tensioner's internal parts.

4. Now finish removing the belt from the other pulleys and remove it from the engine.

To install:

5. While referring to the proper routing diagram (which you identified earlier), begin to route the belt over the pulleys, leaving whichever pulley you first released it from for last.

6. Once the belt is mostly in place, carefully pivot the tensioner and position the belt over the final pulley. As you begin to allow the tensioner back into contact with the belt, run your hand around the pulleys and make sure the belt's ribs are properly seated. If not, release the tension and seat the belt.

7. Once the belt is installed, take another look at all the pulleys to double check your installation.

8. Connect the negative battery cable, then start and run the engine to check belt operation.

9. Once the engine has reached normal operating temperature, turn the ignition **OFF** and check that the belt tensioner arrow is within the proper adjustment range.

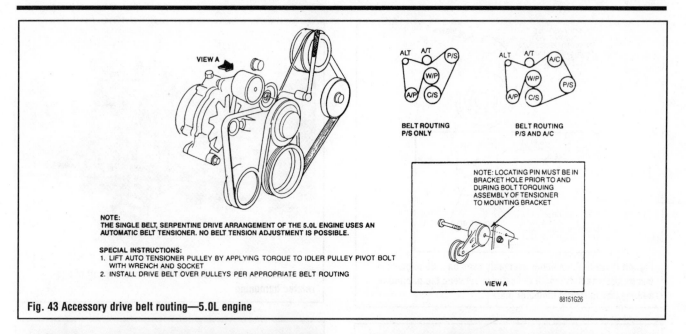

VIEW A

NOTE:
THE SINGLE BELT, SERPENTINE DRIVE ARRANGEMENT OF THE 5.0L ENGINE USES AN AUTOMATIC BELT TENSIONER. NO BELT TENSION ADJUSTMENT IS POSSIBLE.

SPECIAL INSTRUCTIONS:
1. LIFT AUTO TENSIONER PULLEY BY APPLYING TORQUE TO IDLER PULLEY PIVOT BOLT WITH WRENCH AND SOCKET
2. INSTALL DRIVE BELT OVER PULLEYS PER APPROPRIATE BELT ROUTING

ALT A/T P/S
W/P
A/P C/S

**BELT ROUTING
P/S ONLY**

ALT A/T A/C
W/P
A/P C/S P/S

**BELT ROUTING
P/S AND A/C**

NOTE: LOCATING PIN MUST BE IN BRACKET HOLE PRIOR TO AND DURING BOLT TORQUING ASSEMBLY OF TENSIONER TO MOUNTING BRACKET

VIEW A

Fig. 43 Accessory drive belt routing—5.0L engine

Often the labels in the engine compartment display the routing for the serpentine drive belt (arrow)

After installing the drive belt, ensure that it is properly routed around all the pulleys

To remove the drive belt, pivot the automatic tensioner away from the belt, then remove the belt

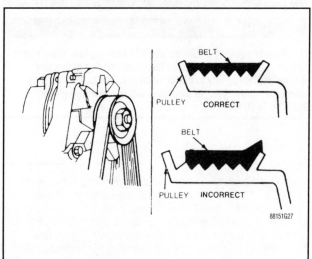

BELT
PULLEY CORRECT

BELT
PULLEY INCORRECT

Fig. 44 Also MAKE SURE the belt is properly seated on all the pulleys during installation

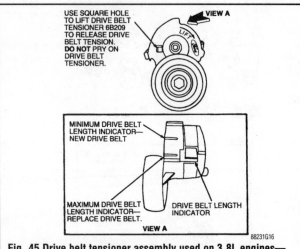

Fig. 45 Drive belt tensioner assembly used on 3.8L engines—ensure that the belt length indicator is between the minimum and maximum length indicator marks

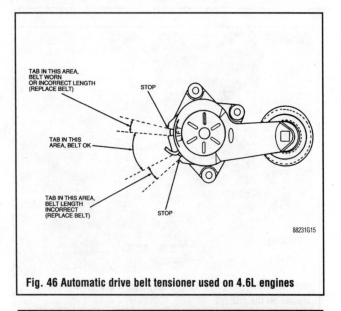

Fig. 46 Automatic drive belt tensioner used on 4.6L engines

Hoses

✳✳ CAUTION

On models equipped with an electric cooling fan, disconnect the negative battery cable or fan motor wiring connector before replacing any radiator or heater hose. The fan may come on, under certain circumstances, even though the ignition is OFF.

INSPECTION

Upper and lower radiator hoses, along with the heater hoses, should be checked for deterioration, leaks and loose hose clamps at least annually or every 12,000 miles (19,000 km), whichever comes first. It is also wise to check the hoses periodically in early spring and at the beginning of the fall or winter when you are performing other maintenance. A quick visual inspection could uncover a weakened hose which may leave you stranded if it remains unrepaired.

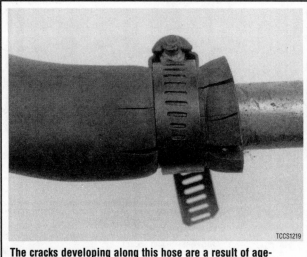

The cracks developing along this hose are a result of age-related hardening

A hose clamp that is too tight can cause older hoses to separate and tear on either side of the clamp

A soft spongy hose (identifiable by the swollen section) will eventually burst and should be replaced

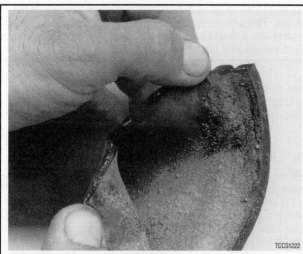

TCCS1222

Hoses are likely to deteriorate from the inside if the cooling system is not periodically flushed

Whenever you are checking the hoses, make sure the engine and cooling system are cold. Visually inspect for cracking, rotting or collapsed hoses, and replace as necessary. Run your hand along the length of the hose. If a weak or swollen spot is noted when squeezing the hose wall, the hose should be replaced.

REMOVAL & INSTALLATION

3.8L and 5.0L Engines

1. Disconnect the negative battery cable for safety purposes.

> ✷✷ **CAUTION**
>
> **Never remove the pressure cap while the engine is hot or running, or personal injury from scalding hot coolant or steam may result. If possible, wait until the engine has cooled to remove the pressure cap. If this is not possible, wrap a thick cloth around the pressure cap and turn it slowly to the first stop. Step back while the pressure is released from the cooling system. When you are sure all the pressure has been released, use the cloth to turn and remove the cap.**

2. Remove the radiator pressure cap.
3. Position a clean container under the radiator and/or engine draincock or plug, then open the drain and allow the cooling system to drain to an appropriate level. For some upper hoses, only a little coolant must be drained. To remove hoses positioned lower on the engine, such as a lower radiator hose, the entire cooling system must be emptied.

> ✷✷ **CAUTION**
>
> **When draining coolant, keep in mind that cats and dogs are attracted to ethylene glycol antifreeze, and are likely to drink any that is left in an uncovered container or in puddles on the ground. This will prove fatal in sufficient quantity. Always drain coolant into a sealable container. Coolant may be reused unless it is contaminated or several years old.**

4. Loosen the hose clamps at each end of the hose requiring replacement. Clamps are usually either of the spring tension type (which require pliers to squeeze the tabs and loosen) or of the worm gear screw type (which require screw or hex drivers to loosen). Slide the clamps down the hose away from the connection.

5. Twist, pull and slide the hose off the fitting, taking care not to damage the neck of the component from which the hose is being removed.

➡**If the hose is stuck at the connection, do not try to insert a screwdriver or other sharp tool under the hose end in an effort to free it, as the connection and/or hose may become damaged. Heater connections, especially, may be easily damaged by such a procedure. If the hose is to be replaced with a new one, use a single-edged razor blade to make a slice along the portion of the hose which is stuck on the connection, perpendicular to the end of the hose. Do not cut so deep that the connection is damaged. The hose can then be peeled from the connection and discarded.**

6. Clean both hose mounting connections. Inspect the condition of the hose clamps and replace them, if necessary.

To install:

7. Dip the ends of the new hose into clean engine coolant to ease installation.
8. Slide the clamps over the replacement hose, then slide the hose ends over the connections and into position.
9. Position and secure the clamps at least ¼ in. (6.35mm) from the ends of the hose. Make sure they are located beyond the raised bead of the connector. If you are using worm gear screw type clamps, tighten them to 20–30 inch lbs. (2–4 Nm). Do not overtighten hose clamps, as they will cut into the hose (possibly causing a leak).
10. Close the radiator or engine drains and properly refill the cooling system with the clean engine coolant drained earlier or a suitable mixture of fresh coolant and water, as follows:

   a. Fill the radiator with coolant until it reaches the radiator filler neck seat.

   b. Reconnect the negative battery cable, then start the engine and allow it to idle until the thermostat opens (the upper radiator hose will become hot).

   c. Turn the engine **OFF** and refill the radiator until the coolant level is at the filler neck seat.

   d. Fill the engine coolant overflow tank with coolant to the FULL HOT mark, then install the radiator cap.

11. If available, install a pressure tester and check for leaks. If a pressure tester is not available, run the engine until normal operating temperature is reached (allowing the system to naturally pressurize), then check for leaks.

> ✷✷ **CAUTION**
>
> **If you are checking for leaks with the system at normal operating temperature, BE EXTREMELY CAREFUL not to touch any moving or hot engine parts. Once the temperature has been reached, shut the engine OFF, and check for leaks around the hose ends and connections which were separated earlier.**

4.6L Engines

▶ **See Figures 47 and 48**

1. Disconnect the negative battery cable for safety purposes.

> ✷✷ **CAUTION**
>
> **Never remove the pressure cap while the engine is hot or running, or personal injury from scalding hot coolant or steam may result. If possible, wait until the engine has cooled to remove the pressure cap. If this is not possible, wrap a thick cloth around the pressure cap and turn it slowly to the first stop. Step back while the pressure is released from the cooling system. When you are sure all the pressure has been released, use the cloth to turn and remove the cap.**

2. Remove the pressure cap from the degas (overflow) container.

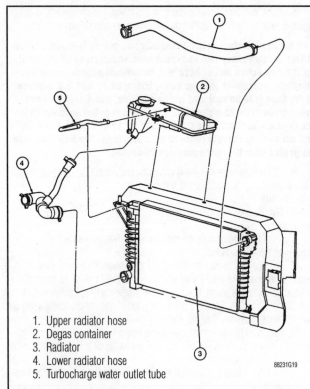

1. Upper radiator hose
2. Degas container
3. Radiator
4. Lower radiator hose
5. Turbocharge water outlet tube

88231G19

Fig. 47 Exploded view of the cooling hose routing on 4.6L engines

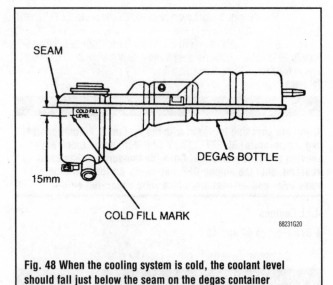

88231G20

Fig. 48 When the cooling system is cold, the coolant level should fall just below the seam on the degas container

3. Position a clean container under the radiator and/or engine draincock or plug, then open the drain and allow the cooling system to drain to an appropriate level. For some upper hoses, only a little coolant must be drained. To remove hoses positioned lower on the engine, such as a lower radiator hose, the entire cooling system must be emptied.

✲✲ CAUTION

When draining coolant, keep in mind that cats and dogs are attracted to ethylene glycol antifreeze, and are likely to drink

any that is left in an uncovered container or in puddles on the ground. This will prove fatal in sufficient quantity. Always drain coolant into a sealable container. Coolant may be reused unless it is contaminated or several years old.

4. Loosen the hose clamps at each end of the hose requiring replacement. Clamps are usually either of the spring tension type (which require pliers to squeeze the tabs and loosen) or of the worm gear screw type (which require screw or hex drivers to loosen). Slide the clamps down the hose away from the connection.
5. Twist, pull and slide the hose off the fitting, taking care not to damage the neck of the component from which the hose is being removed.

➡**If the hose is stuck at the connection, do not try to insert a screwdriver or other sharp tool under the hose end in an effort to free it, as the connection and/or hose may become damaged. Heater connections, especially, may be easily damaged by such a procedure. If the hose is to be replaced with a new one, use a single-edged razor blade to make a slice along the portion of the hose which is stuck on the connection, perpendicular to the end of the hose. Do not cut so deep that the connection is damaged. The hose can then be peeled from the connection and discarded.**

6. Clean both hose mounting connections. Inspect the condition of the hose clamps and replace them, if necessary.

To install:
7. Dip the ends of the new hose into clean engine coolant to ease installation.
8. Slide the clamps over the replacement hose, then slide the hose ends over the connections and into position.
9. Position and secure the clamps at least ¼ in. (6.35mm) from the ends of the hose. Make sure they are located beyond the raised bead of the connector. If you are using worm gear screw type clamps, tighten them to 20–30 inch lbs. (2–4 Nm). Do not overtighten hose clamps, as they will cut into the hose (possibly causing a leak).
10. Close the radiator or engine drains and properly refill the cooling system with the clean engine coolant drained earlier or a suitable mixture of fresh coolant and water, as follows:
    a. Fill the degas (overflow) container with coolant until it reaches the MAX mark. (The radiator will be filled by the degas bottle, so it may take a while until the degas container coolant level reaches the MAX mark.)
    b. Install the cap on the degas container.
11. Bleed the cooling system as follows:
    a. Connect the negative battery cable, then, from inside the vehicle, turn the heater on to the hottest setting.
    b. Start the engine and allow it to idle. While the engine idles, feel the air coming from the heater vents to check for heat. The air should become hot, the engine coolant temperature gauge should maintain a stable reading in the middle of the NORMAL range, and the upper radiator hose should feel hot.

➡**If the heater air remains cool and the temperature gauge does not move, engine coolant level is too low. Stop the engine, allow it to cool and refill the cooling system.**

12. Continue running the engine and check for leaks.

✲✲ CAUTION

If you are checking for leaks with the system at normal operating temperature, BE EXTREMELY CAREFUL not to touch any moving or hot engine parts. Once the temperature has been reached, shut the engine OFF, and check for leaks around the hose ends and connections which were separated earlier.

13. Allow the engine to cool completely, then top off the degas container with coolant, if necessary.

Spark Plugs

▶ See Figure 49

A typical spark plug consists of a metal shell surrounding a ceramic insulator. A metal electrode extends downward through the center of the insulator and protrudes a small distance. Located at the end of the plug and attached to the side of the outer metal shell is the side electrode. The side electrode bends in at a 90° angle so that its tip is just past and parallel to the tip of the center electrode. The distance between these two electrodes (measured in thousandths of an inch or hundredths of a millimeter) is called the spark plug gap.

The spark plug does not produce a spark, but instead provides a gap across which the current can arc. The coil produces anywhere from 20,000 to 50,000 volts (depending on the type and application) which travels through the wires to the spark plugs. The current passes along the center electrode and jumps the gap to the side electrode, and in doing so, ignites the air/fuel mixture in the combustion chamber.

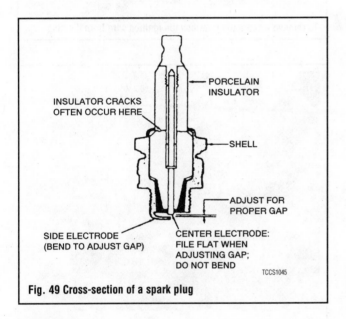

Fig. 49 Cross-section of a spark plug

SPARK PLUG HEAT RANGE

▶ See Figure 50

Spark plug heat range is the ability of the plug to dissipate heat. The longer the insulator (or the farther it extends into the engine), the hotter the plug will operate; the shorter the insulator (the closer the electrode is to the block's cooling passages), the cooler it will operate. A plug that absorbs little heat and remains too cool will quickly accumulate deposits of oil and carbon since it is not hot enough to burn them off. This leads to plug fouling and consequently to misfiring. A plug that absorbs too much heat will have no deposits but, due to the excessive heat, the electrodes will burn away quickly and might possibly lead to preignition or other ignition problems. Preignition takes place when plug tips get so hot that they glow sufficiently to ignite the air/fuel mixture before the actual spark occurs. This early ignition will usually cause a pinging during low speeds and heavy loads.

The general rule of thumb for choosing the correct heat range when selecting a spark plug is: if most of your driving is long distance, high speed travel, use a colder plug; if most of your driving is stop and go, use a hotter plug. Original equipment plugs are generally a good compromise between the 2 styles and most people never have the need to change their plugs from the factory-recommended heat range.

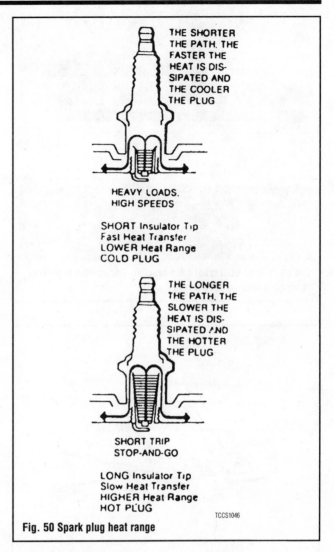

Fig. 50 Spark plug heat range

REMOVAL & INSTALLATION

▶ See Figure 51

A standard set of spark plugs usually requires replacement after about 20,000–30,000 miles (32,000–48,000 km), depending on your style of driving. In normal operation, plug gap increases about 0.001 in. (0.025mm) for every 2,500 miles (4,000 km). As the gap increases, the plug's voltage requirement also increases. It requires a greater voltage to jump the wider gap and about two to three times as much voltage to fire the plug at high speeds than at idle. The improved air/fuel ratio control of modern fuel injection, combined with the higher voltage output of modern ignition systems, will often allow an engine to run significantly longer on a set of standard spark plugs, but keep in mind that efficiency will drop as the gap widens (along with fuel economy and power).

When you're removing spark plugs, work on one at a time. Don't start by removing the plug wires all at once, because, unless you number them, they may become mixed up. Take a minute before you begin and number the wires with tape. The best location for numbering is near where the wires come out of the distributor cap or the coil pack (as applicable).

➡**Apply a small amount of silicone dielectric compound (D7AZ-19A331-A or equivalent) to the inside of the terminal boots whenever an ignition wire is disconnected from the plug, ignition coil, or a distributor cap (when applicable).**

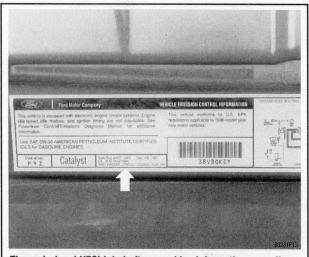

The underhood VECI label often provides information regarding spark plug type and gap (arrow)

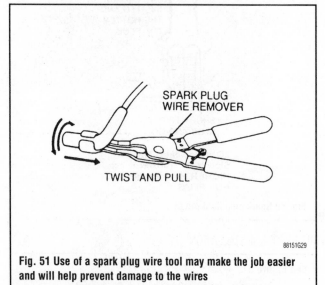

Fig. 51 Use of a spark plug wire tool may make the job easier and will help prevent damage to the wires

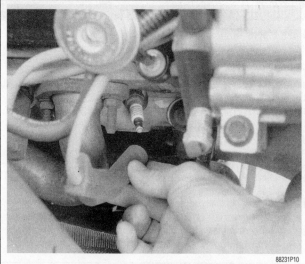

To remove a spark plug, detach the ignition wire from the plug . . .

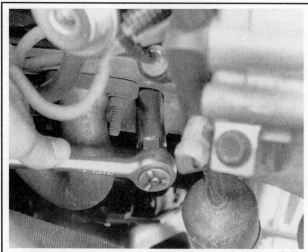

. . . and loosen the plug with a spark plug socket and ratchet wrench . . .

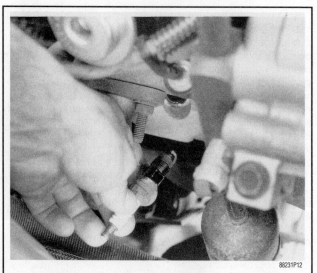

. . . then unthread the plug from the cylinder head by hand

1. Disconnect the negative battery cable and, if the vehicle has been run recently, allow the engine to thoroughly cool.

2. Carefully twist the spark plug wire boot to loosen it, then pull upward and remove the boot from the plug. Be sure to pull on the boot and not on the wire, otherwise the connector located inside the boot may become separated.

3. Using compressed air, blow any water or debris from the spark plug well to assure that no harmful contaminants are allowed to enter the combustion chamber when the spark plug is removed. If compressed air is not available, use a rag or a brush to clean the area.

➡Remove the spark plugs when the engine is cold, if possible, to prevent damage to the threads. If removal of the plugs is difficult, apply a few drops of penetrating oil or silicone spray to the area around the base of the plug, and allow it a few minutes to work.

4. Using a spark plug socket that is equipped with a rubber insert to properly hold the plug, turn the spark plug counterclockwise to loosen and remove it from the bore. Be sure to hold the socket straight on the plug; this will avoid breaking the plug or rounding off the hex flats on the plug.

✳✳ WARNING

Be sure not to use a flexible extension on the socket. Use of a flexible extension may allow a shear force to be applied to the plug. A shear force could break the plug off in the cylinder head, leading to costly and frustrating repairs.

5. Once the plug is out, inspect it for signs of wear, fouling or damage. This is crucial, since plug readings are a vital sign of internal engine condition.

To install:

6. Inspect the spark plug boot for tears or damage. If a damaged boot is found, the spark plug wire must be replaced.

7. Using a wire feeler gauge, check and adjust the spark plug gap. When using a gauge, the proper size should pass between the electrodes with a slight drag. The next larger size should not be able to pass while the next smaller size should pass freely.

8. Squirt a drop of penetrating oil on the threads of the new plug (don't oil it too heavily), then carefully thread the plug into the bore by hand. If resistance is felt before the plug is almost completely threaded, back the plug out and begin threading again. In small, hard-to-reach areas, an old spark plug wire and boot could be used as a threading tool. The boot will hold the plug while you twist the end of the wire and the wire is supple enough to twist before it would allow the plug to crossthread.

✳✳ WARNING

Do not use the spark plug socket to thread the plugs. Always thread the plug carefully by hand or by using an old plug wire to prevent the possibility of crossthreading and damaging the cylinder head bore.

9. Carefully tighten the spark plug. If the plug you are installing is equipped with a crush washer, seat the plug, then tighten about ¼ turn to crush the washer. If you are installing a tapered seat plug, tighten the plug to specifications provided by the vehicle or plug manufacturer.

10. Apply a small amount of silicone dielectric compound to the end of the spark plug lead or inside the spark plug boot to prevent sticking, then install the boot to the spark plug and push until it clicks into place. The click may be felt or heard, then gently pull back on the boot to assure proper contact.

INSPECTION & GAPPING

▶ **See Figures 52 and 53 (p. 40–41)**

Check the plugs for deposits and wear. If they are not going to be replaced, clean the plugs thoroughly. Remember that any kind of deposit will decrease the efficiency of the plug. Plugs can be cleaned on a spark plug cleaning machine, which can sometimes be found in service stations, or you can do an acceptable job of cleaning with a stiff brush. If the plugs are cleaned, the electrodes must be filed flat. Use an ignition points file, not an emery board or the like, which will leave deposits. The electrodes must be filed perfectly flat with sharp edges; rounded edges reduce the spark plug voltage by as much as 50%.

Check spark plug gap before installation. The ground electrode (the L-shaped one connected to the body of the plug) must be parallel to the center electrode and the specified size wire gauge must pass between the electrodes with a slight drag. (Refer to the Tune-Up Specifications chart for correct gap specifications.)

➡ **NEVER adjust the gap on a used platinum type spark plug.**

Always check the gap on new plugs, as they are not always set correctly at the factory. Do not use a flat feeler gauge when measuring the gap on a used plug, because the reading may be inaccurate. A round-wire type gapping tool is the best way to check the gap. The correct size gauge should pass through the electrode gap with a slight drag. If you're in doubt, try one size smaller and one larger. The smaller gauge should go through easily, while the larger one shouldn't go through at all. Wire gapping tools usually

A normally worn spark plug should have light tan or gray deposits on the firing tip

A carbon fouled plug, identified by soft, sooty, black deposits, may indicate an improperly tuned vehicle. Check the air cleaner, ignition components and engine control system

Tracking Arc
High voltage arcs between a fouling deposit on the insulator tip and spark plug shell. This ignites the fuel/air mixture at some point along the insulator tip, retarding the ignition timing which causes a power and fuel loss.

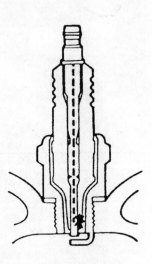

Wide Gap
Spark plug electrodes are worn so that the high voltage charge cannot arc across the electrodes. Improper gapping of electrodes on new or "cleaned" spark plugs could cause a similar condition. Fuel remains unburned and a power loss results.

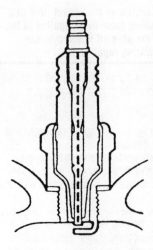

Flashover
A damaged spark plug boot, along with dirt and moisture, could permit the high voltage charge to short over the insulator to the spark plug shell or the engine. A buttress insulator design helps prevent high voltage flashover.

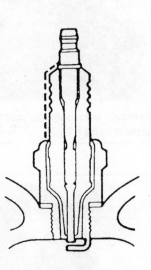

Fouled Spark Plug
Deposits that have formed on the insulator tip may become conductive and provide a "shunt" path to the shell. This prevents the high voltage from arcing between the electrodes. A power and fuel loss is the result.

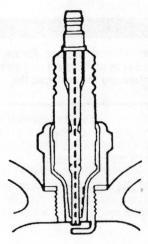

Bridged Electrodes
Fouling deposits between the electrodes "ground out" the high voltage needed to fire the spark plug. The arc between the electrodes does not occur and the fuel air mixture is not ignited. This causes a power loss and exhausting of raw fuel.

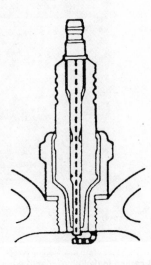

Cracked Insulator
A crack in the spark plug insulator could cause the high voltage charge to "ground out." Here, the spark does not jump the electrode gap and the fuel air mixture is not ignited. This causes a power loss and raw fuel is exhausted.

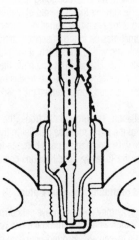

TCCS201A

Fig. 52 Used spark plugs which show damage may indicate engine problems

GAP BRIDGED

IDENTIFIED BY DEPOSIT BUILD—UP CLOSING GAP BETWEEN ELECTRODES.

CAUSED BY OIL OR CARBON FOULING. REPLACE PLUG, OR, IF DEPOSITS ARE NOT EXCESSIVE THE PLUG CAN BE CLEANED.

OIL FOULED

IDENTIFIED BY WET BLACK DEPOSITS ON THE INSULATOR SHELL BORE ELECTRODES.

CAUSED BY EXCESSIVE OIL ENTERING COMBUSTION CHAMBER THROUGH WORN RINGS AND PISTONS, EXCESSIVE CLEARANCE BETWEEN VALVE GUIDES AND STEMS, OR WORN OR LOOSE BEARINGS. CORRECT OIL PROBLEM. REPLACE THE PLUG.

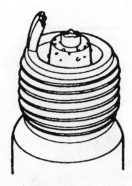

CARBON FOULED

IDENTIFIED BY BLACK, DRY FLUFFY CARBON DEPOSITS ON INSULATOR TIPS, EXPOSED SHELL SURFACES AND ELECTRODES.

CAUSED BY TOO COLD A PLUG, WEAK IGNITION, DIRTY AIR CLEANER, DEFECTIVE FUEL PUMP, TOO RICH A FUEL MIXTURE, IMPROPERLY OPERATING HEAT RISER OR EXCESSIVE IDLING. CAN BE CLEANED.

NORMAL

IDENTIFIED BY LIGHT TAN OR GRAY DEPOSITS ON THE FIRING TIP.

PRE-IGNITION

IDENTIFIED BY MELTED ELECTRODES AND POSSIBLY BLISTERED INSULATOR. METALIC DEPOSITS ON INSULATOR INDICATE ENGINE DAMAGE.

CAUSED BY WRONG TYPE OF FUEL, INCORRECT IGNITION TIMING OR ADVANCE, TOO HOT A PLUG, BURNT VALVES OR ENGINE OVERHEATING. REPLACE THE PLUG.

OVERHEATING

IDENTIFIED BY A WHITE OR LIGHT GRAY INSULATOR WITH SMALL BLACK OR GRAY BROWN SPOTS AND WITH BLUISH-BURNT APPEARANCE OF ELECTRODES.

CAUSED BY ENGINE OVER-HEATING, WRONG TYPE OF FUEL, LOOSE SPARK PLUGS, TOO HOT A PLUG, LOW FUEL PUMP PRESSURE OR INCORRECT IGNITION TIMING. REPLACE THE PLUG.

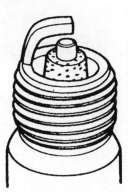

FUSED SPOT DEPOSIT

IDENTIFIED BY MELTED OR SPOTTY DEPOSITS RESEMBLING BUBBLES OR BLISTERS.

CAUSED BY SUDDEN ACCELERATION. CAN BE CLEANED IF NOT EXCESSIVE, OTHERWISE REPLACE PLUG.

TCCS2002

Fig. 53 Inspect the spark plug to determine engine running conditions

A variety of tools and gauges are needed for spark plug service

Checking the spark plug gap with a feeler gauge

A physically damaged spark plug may be evidence of severe detonation in that cylinder. Watch that cylinder carefully between services, as continued detonation will not only damage the plug, but could also damage the engine

An oil fouled spark plug indicates an engine with worn piston rings and/or bad valve seals, allowing excessive oil to enter the chamber

have a bending tool attached. Use that to adjust the side electrode until the proper distance is obtained. Absolutely NEVER attempt to bend the center electrode. Also, be careful not to bend the side electrode too far or too often, as it may weaken and break off within the engine, requiring removal of the cylinder head to retrieve it.

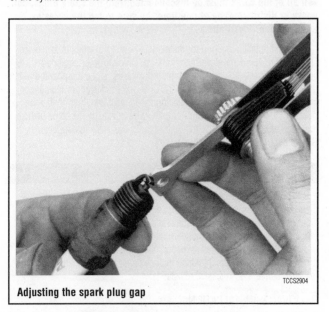

Adjusting the spark plug gap

TCCS2904

TCCS2140

A bridged or almost bridged spark plug, identified by a build-up between the electrodes caused by excessive carbon or oil build-up on the plug

TCCS2139

This spark plug has been left in the engine too long, as evidenced by the extreme gap. Plugs with such an extreme gap can cause misfiring and stumbling, accompanied by a noticeable lack of power

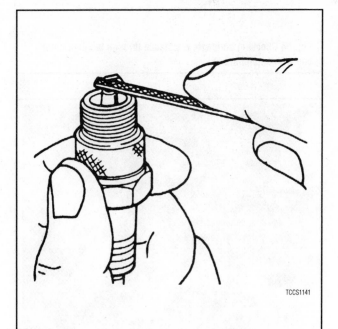

TCCS1141

If the plug is in good condition, the electrode may be filed flat and reused

Spark Plug Wires

TESTING & REPLACEMENT

♦ **See Figure 54**

At every tune-up/inspection, visually check the spark plug cables for burns, cuts, or breaks in the insulation. Start by wiping the wires with a clean, damp cloth. Then, carefully inspect the surface of the wires. Check the boots and the nipples on the distributor cap and/or ignition coil (as applicable). Replace any damaged wiring.

Every 50,000 miles (80,000 km) or 60 months, the resistance of the wires should be checked with an ohmmeter. Wires with excessive resistance will cause misfiring, and may make the engine difficult to start in damp weather. To check resistance on the 3.8L and 4.6L engines (these engines utilize a distributorless ignition system), remove a wire from both the spark plug and the ignition coil pack tower, then use an ohmmeter probe at each end. On the 5.0L engine, remove the distributor cap, then unplug only 1 wire at a time from the spark plug. Check resistance from the inside terminal of the distributor cap to the spark plug end of the cable. In both cases, resistance of any given spark plug wire should be

LESS than 7000 ohms per foot of wire. Therefore, a 2 foot long spark plug wire with 10,000 ohms of resistance would be acceptable (less than the 14,000 ohm maximum), while the same wire should be discarded if resistance is 15,000 ohms.

➡ **If all of the wires must be disconnected from the spark plugs, coil packs or distributor cap at one time, be sure to tag the wires to assure proper installation.**

The best possible method for installing a new set of wires is to replace ONE AT A TIME so there can be no mix-up. On distributor equipped engines, don't rely on wiring diagrams or sketches, since the position of the distributor can be changed (unless the distributor is keyed for installation in only one position). Start by replacing the longest wire first. Install the boot firmly over the spark plug. Route the wire in exactly the same path as the original and connect it to the distributor or coil pack (as applicable). Repeat the process for each shorter wire.

Distributor Cap and Rotor

Of the engines covered by this manual, only the 5.0L engine utilizes a distributor ignition system. The 3.8L and 4.6L engines use distributorless electronic ignition systems, in which separate ignition coils fire the spark plugs directly through the secondary ignition wires.

It is normally a good idea to inspect the distributor cap and rotor any time you perform a tune-up, which includes checking the spark plug wires for wear, damage or excessive resistance.

REMOVAL & INSTALLATION

1. Disconnect the negative battery cable for safety purposes.
2. If equipped, remove the protective rubber boot from the distributor assembly by carefully lifting at the edges.

➡ **Depending on the reason you have for removing the distributor cap, it may (in some cases) make more sense to leave the spark plug wires attached. This is the case, for example, if you are testing spark plug wires, or if removal is necessary to access other components (and wire play allows you to reposition the cap out of the way).**

3. Tag and disconnect the spark plug wires from the distributor cap towers. THIS STEP IS CRITICAL. Do not attempt to rewire the cap based only on a diagram; this often leads to confusion and miswiring.
4. Disconnect the ignition coil lead from the distributor cap.
5. Loosen the distributor cap hold-down screws and/or release the hold-down clamps. Most original equipment distributors and caps utilize the hold-down screws.

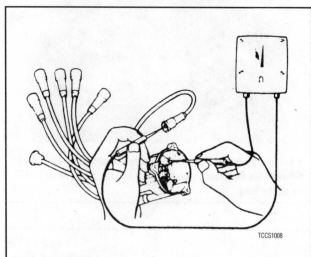

TCCS1008

Fig. 54 Checking plug wire resistance through the distributor cap with an ohmmeter

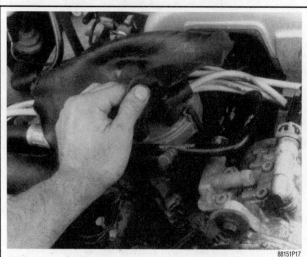

TCCS1009

Checking individual plug wire resistance with a digital ohmmeter

88151P17

If equipped, remove the protective rubber boot from the top of the distributor assembly

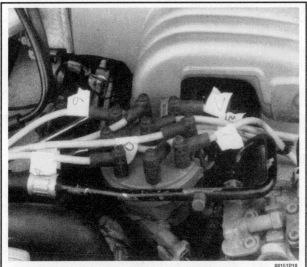

Tag ALL of the spark plug wires before disconnecting them

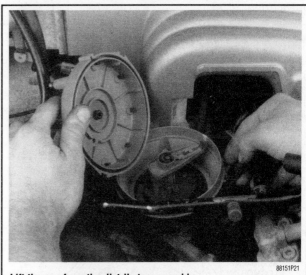

Lift the cap from the distributor assembly

Disconnect some or all of the wires (as necessary for the job) from the cap

If necessary, grasp and pull the rotor from the distributor shaft

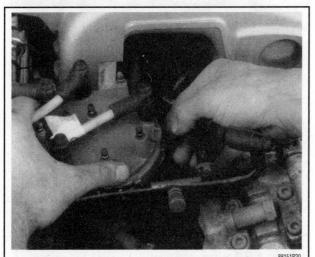

Release the cap hold-down screws and/or (in this case) the retaining clamps

6. Carefully lift the distributor cap STRAIGHT up and off the distributor, in order to prevent damage to the rotor blade and spring.

7. If necessary, grasp the rotor by hand and pull upward to remove it from the distributor shaft and armature.

8. Inspect both the distributor cap and rotor for damage; replace as necessary.

To install:

9. Align the locating boss on the rotor with the hole on the armature, then carefully seat the rotor on the distributor shaft. Make sure the rotor is fully seated, but do not force it, as the plastic components often break easily.

10. Position the distributor cap on the base, noting the square alignment locator.

11. Secure the cap using the hold-down screws and/or the release clamps. If used, tighten the cap hold-down screws to 18–23 inch lbs. (2.0–2.6 Nm).

12. Connect the ignition coil lead to the center tower of the distributor cap.

13. If removed, connect the spark plug wire leads as tagged during removal.

14. If equipped, reposition and seat the protective rubber boot over the distributor assembly.

15. Connect the negative battery cable.

INSPECTION

◆ See Figures 55 and 56

After removing the distributor cap and rotor, clean the components (both inside and outside of the cap) using soap and water. If compressed air is available, carefully dry the components (wearing safety goggles) or allow the parts to air dry. You can dry them with a clean, soft cloth, but don't leave any lint or moisture behind.

Once the cap and rotor have been thoroughly cleaned, check for cracks, carbon tracks, burns or other physical damage. Make sure the distributor cap's carbon button is free of damage. Check the cap terminals for dirt or corrosion. Always check the rotor blade and spring closely for damage. Replace any components where damage is found.

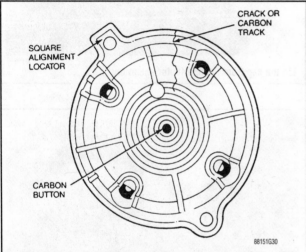

Fig. 55 Check the distributor cap for cracks, a damaged carbon button or carbon tracks

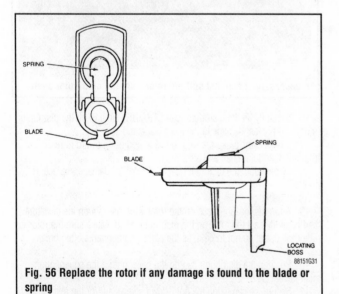

Fig. 56 Replace the rotor if any damage is found to the blade or spring

Ignition Timing

➥No periodic checking or adjustment of the ignition timing is necessary for any of the vehicles covered by this manual. However, the distributor ignition system used by the 5.0L engine does allow for both, should the distributor be removed and installed or otherwise disturbed.

GENERAL INFORMATION

Ignition timing is the measurement, in degrees of crankshaft rotation, of the point at which the spark plugs fire in each of the cylinders. It is measured in degrees before or after Top Dead Center (TDC) of the compression stroke.

Because it takes a fraction of a second for the spark plug to ignite the mixture in the cylinder, the spark plug must fire a little before the piston reaches TDC. Otherwise, the mixture will not be completely ignited as the piston passes TDC and the full power of the explosion will not be used by the engine.

The timing measurement is given in degrees of crankshaft rotation Before Top Dead Center (BTDC). If the setting for the ignition timing is 5° BTDC, the spark plug must fire 5° before each piston reaches TDC. This only holds true, however, when the engine is at idle speed.

As the engine speed increases, the pistons go faster. The spark plugs have to ignite the fuel even sooner if it is to be completely ignited when the piston reaches TDC. On all engines covered by this manual, spark timing changes are accomplished electronically by the engine and ignition control computers.

If the ignition is set too advanced (BTDC), the ignition and expansion of the fuel in the cylinder will occur too soon and tend to force the piston down while it is still traveling up. This causes engine ping. If the ignition spark is set too retarded, or After Top Dead Center (ATDC), the piston will have already passed TDC and started on its way down when the fuel is ignited. This will cause the piston to be forced down for only a portion of its travel. This will result in poor engine performance and lack of power.

Timing marks consisting of 0 marks or scales can be found on the rim of the crankshaft pulley and the timing cover. The mark(s) on the pulley correspond(s) to the position of the piston in the No. 1 cylinder. A stroboscopic (dynamic) timing light is used, which is hooked into the circuit of the No. 1 cylinder spark plug. Every time the spark plug fires, the timing light flashes. By aiming the timing light at the timing marks while the engine is running, the exact position of the piston within the cylinder can be easily read, since the stroboscopic flash makes the pulley appear to be standing still. Proper timing is indicated when the mark and scale are in proper alignment.

Because these vehicles utilize high voltage, electronic ignition systems, only a timing light with an inductive pick-up should be used. This pick-up simply clamps onto the No. 1 spark plug wire, eliminating the adapter. It is not susceptible to cross-firing or false triggering, which may occur with a conventional light, due to the greater voltages produced by electronic ignition.

The ignition timing marks (arrow) are often stamped into the crankshaft damper assembly

CHECKING & ADJUSTING

3.8L and 4.6L Engines

The 3.8L and 4.6L engines utilize the Distributorless Ignition System (DIS). On this system, ignition coil packs fire the spark plugs directly through the spark plug wires. All spark timing and advance is determined by the ignition control module and engine control computer. No ignition timing adjustments are necessary or possible.

5.0L Engine

♦ See Figure 57

SETTING INITIAL (BASE) TIMING

➡Specific instructions and specifications for setting initial timing can be found in the Vehicle Emission Control Information (VECI) label in the engine compartment. Because this label contains information regarding any specific calibration requirements for YOUR vehicle, those instructions and specifications should be followed if they differ from the following.

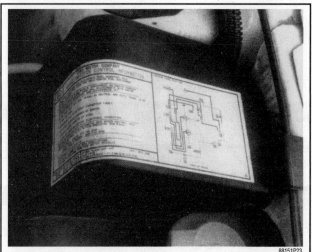

VECI information is specific to YOUR car and should always be used if it differs from another source

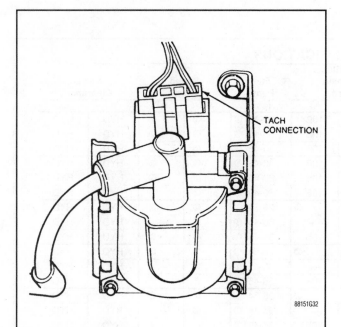

Fig. 57 Using an alligator clip, a tachometer may be hooked up to the ignition coil connector

If adjustment is necessary, loosen the distributor hold-down bolt

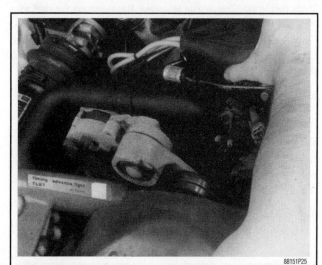

Adjust the timing by rotating the distributor while observing the timing marks

This procedure should not be used as a periodic maintenance adjustment. Timing should only be set after the distributor has been disturbed (removed and re-installed) in some way. If problems are encountered setting the initial timing with this procedure, and no mechanical causes are found, follow the spark timing advance check procedure later in this section.

➡Do not change the ignition timing by the use of a different octane rod without having the proper authority to do so. Federal emission requirements will be affected.

1. Start the engine and allow it to run until it reaches normal operating temperature.

❊❊ CAUTION

NEVER run an engine in a garage or building without proper ventilation. Carbon monoxide will quickly enter the body, excluding oxygen from the blood stream. This condition will cause dizziness, sleepiness and eventually death.

2. Once normal operating temperature has been reached, shut the engine **OFF**.
3. Firmly apply the parking brake and block the drive wheels. Place the transmission in **P** (A/T) or **NEUTRAL** (M/T), as applicable.

4. Make sure the heater and A/C, along with all other accessories, are in the OFF position.

5. Connect an inductive timing light, such as the Rotunda 059-00006 or equivalent, to the No. 1 spark plug wire, according the tool manufacturer's instructions.

6. Connect a tachometer to the ignition coil connection using an alligator clip. This can be done by inserting the alligator clip into the back of the connector, onto the dark green/yellow dotted wire.

➥DO NOT allow the alligator clip to accidentally ground to a metal surface while attached to the coil connector, as that could permanently damage the ignition coil.

7. Disconnect the single wire inline SPOUT connector which connects the control computer (usually terminal 36) to the ignition control module. This will prevent the electronic ignition from advancing the timing during the setting procedure.

8. Using a suitable socket or wrench, loosen the distributor hold-down bolt slightly at this time, BUT DO NOT ALLOW THE DISTRIBUTOR TO MOVE, or timing will have to be set regardless of the current conditions.

➥A remote starter must NOT be used to start the vehicle when setting the initial ignition timing. Disconnecting the start wire at the starter relay will cause the ignition control module to revert to Start Mode timing after the vehicle is started. Reconnecting the start wire after the vehicle is running WILL NOT correct the timing.

9. Start the engine (using the ignition key and NOT a remote starter to assure timing will be set correctly) and allow the engine to return to normal operating temperature.

10. With the engine running at the specified rpm, check the initial timing. If adjustments must be made, rotate the distributor while watching the timing marks. Once proper adjustment has been reached, make sure the distributor is not disturbed until the hold-down bolt can be secured.

11. Reconnect the single wire inline SPOUT connector and check the timing to verify that the distributor is now advancing beyond the initial setting.

12. Shut the engine OFF and tighten the distributor bolt while CAREFULLY holding the distributor from turning. If the distributor moves, you will have to start the engine and reset the timing.

13. Restart the engine and repeat the procedure to check the timing and verify that it did not change.

14. Shut the engine OFF, then disconnect the tachometer and timing light.

CHECKING SPARK TIMING ADVANCE

Spark timing advance is controlled by the Electronic Engine Control (EEC) system. This procedure checks the capability of the ignition module to receive the spark timing command from the EEC module. The use of a volt/ohmmeter is required.

1. Turn the ignition switch OFF.

2. Disconnect the pin-inline connector (SPOUT connector) near the TFI module.

3. Start the engine and measure the voltage, at idle, from the SPOUT connector to the distributor base. The reading should equal battery voltage.

4. If the result is okay, the problem lies within the EEC-IV system.

5. If the result is not satisfactory, separate the wiring harness connector from the ignition module. Check for damage, corrosion or dirt, and service as necessary.

6. Measure the resistance between terminal No. 5 and the pin-inline connector. This test is done at the ignition module connector only. The reading should be less than 5 ohms.

7. If the reading is okay, replace the TFI module.

8. If the result is not satisfactory, service the wiring between the pin-inline connector and the TFI connector.

Valve Lash

No periodic valve lash adjustments are necessary or possible on these engines. All engines utilize hydraulic valve trains to automatically maintain proper valve lash.

Idle Speed and Mixture Adjustments

The engines covered by this manual utilize sophisticated Sequential Fuel Injection (SFI) systems in which an engine control computer utilizes information from various sensors to control idle speed and air/fuel mixtures. No periodic adjustments are either necessary or possible on these systems. If a problem is suspected, please refer to Sections 4 and 5 of this manual for more information on electronic engine controls and fuel injection.

TUNE-UP SPECIFICATIONS

Year	Engine ID/VIN	Engine Displacement Liters (cc)	Spark Plugs Gap (in.)	Ignition Timing (deg.) MT	Ignition Timing (deg.) AT	Fuel Pump (psi)	Idle Speed (rpm) MT	Idle Speed (rpm) AT	Valve Clearance In.	Valve Clearance Ex.
1994	4	3.8 (3802)	0.054	10B	10B	30-45 ①	②	②	HYD	HYD
	D	5.0 (4949)	0.054	10B	10B	30-45 ①	②	②	HYD	HYD
	T	5.0 (4949)	0.054	10B	10B	30-45 ①	②	②	HYD	HYD
1995	4	3.8 (3802)	0.054	10B	10B	30-45 ①	②	②	HYD	HYD
	D	5.0 (4949)	0.054	10B	10B	30-45 ①	②	②	HYD	HYD
	T	5.0 (4949)	0.054	10B	10B	30-45 ①	②	②	HYD	HYD
1996	4	3.8 (3802)	0.054	②	②	28-54 ①	②	②	HYD	HYD
	V	4.6 (4593)	0.054	10B	—	35-45 ①	②	—	HYD	HYD
	W	4.6 (4593)	0.054	10B	10B	35-45 ①	②	②	HYD	HYD
1997	4	3.8 (3802)	0.054	②	②	28-54 ①	②	②	HYD	HYD
	V	4.6 (4593)	0.054	10B	—	35-45 ①	②	—	HYD	HYD
	W	4.6 (4593)	0.054	10B	10B	35-45 ①	②	②	HYD	HYD
1998	4	3.8 (3802)	0.054	②	②	28-54 ①	②	②	HYD	HYD
	V	4.6 (4593)	0.054	10B	—	35-45 ①	②	—	HYD	HYD
	W	4.6 (4593)	0.054	10B	10B	35-45 ①	②	②	HYD	HYD

① Fuel pressure with the engine running and the pressure regulator vacuum hose connected.
② Refer to the Vehicle Emission Control Information (VECI) label.

88231C02

Air Conditioning System

SYSTEM SERVICE & REPAIR

➡️**It is recommended that the A/C system be serviced by an EPA Section 609 certified automotive technician utilizing a refrigerant recovery/recycling machine.**

The do-it-yourselfer should not service his/her own vehicle's A/C system for many reasons, including legal concerns, personal injury, environmental damage and cost. The following are some of the reasons why you may decide not to service your own vehicle's A/C system.

According to the U.S. Clean Air Act, it is a federal crime to service or repair (involving the refrigerant) a Motor Vehicle Air Conditioning (MVAC) system for money without being EPA certified. It is also illegal to vent R-134a refrigerant into the atmosphere.

State and/or local laws may be more strict than the federal regulations, so be sure to check with your state and/or local authorities for further information. For further federal information on the legality of servicing your A/C system, call the EPA Stratospheric Ozone Hotline.

➡️**Federal law dictates that a fine of up to $25,000 may be levelled on people convicted of venting refrigerant into the atmosphere. Additionally, the EPA may pay up to $10,000 for information or services leading to a criminal conviction of the violation of these laws.**

When servicing an A/C system you run the risk of handling or coming in contact with refrigerant, which may result in skin or eye irritation or frostbite. Although low in toxicity (due to chemical stability), inhalation of concentrated refrigerant fumes is dangerous and can result in death; cases of fatal cardiac arrhythmia have been reported in people accidentally subjected to high levels of refrigerant. Some early symptoms include loss of concentration and drowsiness.

Also, refrigerants can decompose at high temperatures (near gas heaters or open flame), which may result in hydrofluoric acid, hydrochloric acid and phosgene (a fatal nerve gas).

R-134a refrigerant is a greenhouse gas which, if allowed to vent into the atmosphere, will contribute to global warming (the Greenhouse Effect).

It is usually more economically feasible to have a certified MVAC automotive technician perform A/C system service to your vehicle. While it is illegal to service an A/C system without the proper equipment, the home mechanic would have to purchase an expensive refrigerant recovery/recycling machine to service his/her own vehicle.

PREVENTIVE MAINTENANCE

▶ **See Figures 58 and 59**

Although the A/C system should not be serviced by the do-it-yourselfer, preventive maintenance can be practiced and A/C system inspections can be performed to help maintain the efficiency of the vehicle's A/C system. For preventive maintenance, perform the following:

• The easiest and most important preventive maintenance for your A/C system is to be sure that it is used on a regular basis. Running the system for five minutes each month (no matter what the season) will help ensure that the seals and all internal components remain lubricated.

➡️**Some newer vehicles automatically operate the A/C system compressor whenever the windshield defroster is activated. When running, the compressor lubricates the A/C system components; therefore, the A/C system would not need to be operated each month.**

• In order to prevent heater core freeze-up during A/C operation, it is necessary to maintain a proper antifreeze protection. Use a hand-held coolant tester (hydrometer) to periodically check the condition of the antifreeze in your engine's cooling system.

➡️**Antifreeze should not be used longer than the manufacturer specifies.**

Fig. 58 A coolant tester can be used to determine the freezing and boiling levels of the coolant in your vehicle

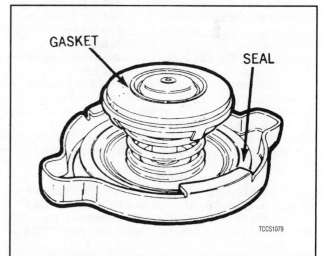

Fig. 59 To ensure efficient cooling system operation, inspect the radiator cap gasket and seal

• For efficient operation of an air conditioned vehicle's cooling system, the radiator cap should have a holding pressure which meets manufacturer's specifications. A cap which fails to hold these pressures should be replaced.

• Any obstruction of or damage to the condenser configuration will restrict air flow which is essential to its efficient operation. It is, therefore, a good rule to keep this unit clean and in proper physical shape.

➡️ **Bug screens which are mounted in front of the condenser (unless they are original equipment) are regarded as obstructions.**

• The condensation drain tube expels any water, which accumulates on the bottom of the evaporator housing, into the engine compartment. If this tube is obstructed, the air conditioning performance can be restricted and condensation buildup can spill over onto the vehicle's floor.

SYSTEM INSPECTION

▶ **See Figure 60**

Although the A/C system should not be serviced by the do-it-yourselfer, preventive maintenance can be practiced and A/C system inspections can be performed to help maintain the efficiency of the vehicle's A/C system. For A/C system inspection, perform the following:

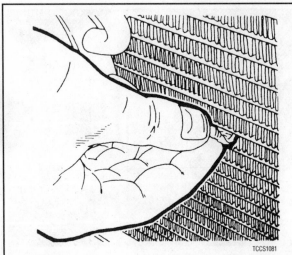

Fig. 60 Periodically remove any debris from the condenser and radiator fins

The easiest and often most important check for the air conditioning system consists of a visual inspection of the system components. Visually inspect the air conditioning system for refrigerant leaks, damaged compressor clutch, abnormal compressor drive belt tension and/or condition, plugged evaporator drain tube, blocked condenser fins, disconnected or broken wires, blown fuses, corroded connections and poor insulation.

A refrigerant leak will usually appear as an oily residue at the leakage point in the system. The oily residue soon picks up dust or dirt particles from the surrounding air and appears greasy. Through time, this will build up and appear to be a heavy dirt impregnated grease.

For a thorough visual and operational inspection, check the following:

• Check the surface of the radiator and condenser for dirt, leaves or other material which might block air flow.

• Check for kinks in hoses and lines. Check the system for leaks.

• Make sure the drive belt is properly tensioned. When the air conditioning is operating, make sure the drive belt is free of noise or slippage.

• Make sure the blower motor operates at all appropriate positions, then check for distribution of the air from all outlets with the blower on **HIGH** or **MAX**.

➡**Keep in mind that under conditions of high humidity, air discharged from the A/C vents may not feel as cold as expected, even if the system is working properly. This is because vaporized moisture in humid air retains heat more effectively than dry air, thereby making humid air more difficult to cool.**

• Make sure the air passage selection lever is operating correctly. Start the engine and warm it to normal operating temperature, then make sure the temperature selection lever is operating correctly.

Windshield Wipers

ELEMENT (REFILL) CARE & REPLACEMENT

For maximum effectiveness and longest element life, the windshield and wiper blades should be kept clean. Dirt, tree sap, road tar and so on will cause streaking, smearing and blade deterioration if left on the glass. It is advisable to wash the windshield carefully with a commercial glass cleaner at least once a month. Wipe off the rubber blades with the wet rag afterwards. Do not attempt to move wipers across the windshield by hand; damage to the motor and drive mechanism will result.

To inspect and/or replace the wiper blade elements, place the wiper switch in the **LOW** speed position and the ignition switch in the **ACC** position. When the wiper blades are approximately vertical on the windshield, turn the ignition switch to **OFF**.

Examine the wiper blade elements. If they are found to be cracked, broken or torn, they should be replaced immediately. Replacement intervals will vary with usage, although ozone deterioration usually limits element life to about one year. If the wiper pattern is smeared or streaked, or if the blade chatters across the glass, the elements should be replaced. It is easiest and most sensible to replace the elements in pairs.

If your vehicle is equipped with aftermarket blades, there are several different types of refills and your vehicle might have any kind. Aftermarket blades and arms rarely use the exact same type blade or refill as the original equipment. Here are some typical aftermarket blades; not all may be available for your vehicle:

The Anco® type uses a release button that is pushed down to allow the refill to slide out of the yoke jaws. The new refill slides back into the frame and locks in place.

Some Trico® refills are removed by locating where the metal backing strip or the refill is wider. Insert a small screwdriver blade between the frame and metal backing strip. Press down to release the refill from the retaining tab.

Other types of Trico® refills have two metal tabs which are unlocked by squeezing them together. The rubber filler can then be withdrawn from the frame jaws. A new refill is installed by inserting the refill into the front frame jaws and sliding it rearward to engage the remaining frame jaws.

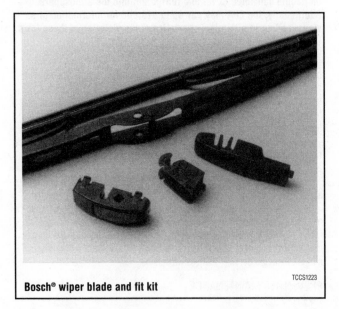

Bosch® wiper blade and fit kit

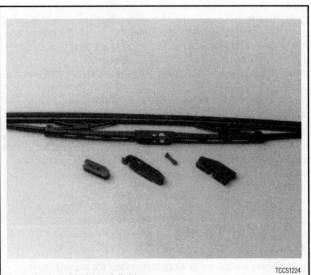

Lexor® wiper blade and fit kit

Pylon® wiper blade and adaptor

TCCS1225

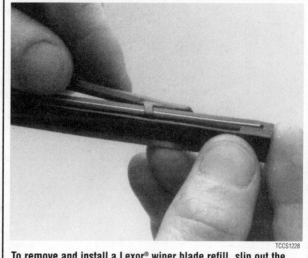

To remove and install a Lexor® wiper blade refill, slip out the old insert and slide in a new one

TCCS1228

Trico® wiper blade and fit kit

TCCS1226

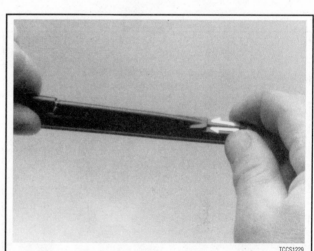

On Pylon® inserts, the clip at the end has to be removed prior to sliding the insert off. Don't forget to attach the clip after the new insert is installed

TCCS1229

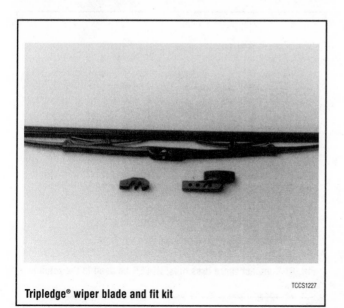

Tripledge® wiper blade and fit kit

TCCS1227

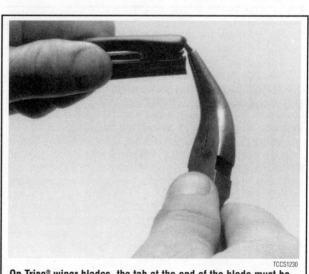

On Trico® wiper blades, the tab at the end of the blade must be turned up . . .

TCCS1230

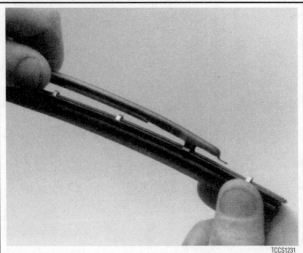

. . . then the insert can be removed. After installing the replacement insert, bend the tab back

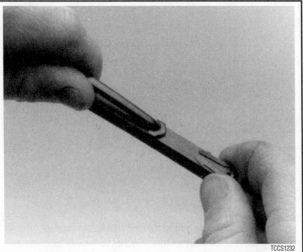

The Tripledge® wiper blade insert is removed and installed using a retaining clip

There are usually four jaws; be certain when installing that the refill is engaged in all of them. At the end of its travel, the tabs will lock into place on the front jaws of the wiper blade frame.

Another type of refill is made from polycarbonate. The refill has a simple locking device at one end which flexes downward out of the groove into which the jaws of the holder fit, allowing easy release. By sliding the new refill through all the jaws and pushing through the slight resistance when it reaches the end of its travel, the refill will lock into position.

To replace the Tridon® refill, it is necessary to remove the wiper blade. This refill has a plastic backing strip with a notch about 1 in. (25mm) from the end. Hold the blade (frame) on a hard surface so that the frame is tightly bowed. Grip the tip of the backing strip and pull up while twisting counterclockwise. The backing strip will snap out of the retaining tab. Do this for the remaining tabs until the refill is free of the blade. The length of these refills is molded into the end and they should be replaced with identical types.

Regardless of the type of refill used, be sure to follow the part manufacturer's instructions closely. Make sure that all of the frame jaws are engaged as the refill is pushed into place and locked. If the metal blade holder and frame are allowed to touch the glass during wiper operation, the glass will be scratched.

Tires and Wheels

Common sense and good driving habits will afford maximum tire life. Fast starts, sudden stops and hard cornering are hard on tires and will shorten their useful life span. Make sure that you don't overload the vehicle or run with incorrect pressure in the tires. Both of these practices will increase tread wear.

➡**For optimum tire life, keep the tires properly inflated, rotate them often and have the wheel alignment checked periodically.**

Inspect your tires frequently. Be especially careful to watch for bubbles in the tread or sidewall, deep cuts or underinflation. Replace any tires with bubbles in the sidewall. If cuts are so deep that they penetrate to the cords, discard the tire. Any cut in the sidewall of a radial tire renders it unsafe. Also look for uneven tread wear patterns that may indicate the front end is out of alignment or that the tires are out of balance.

TIRE ROTATION

▶ **See Figure 61**

Tires must be rotated periodically (about every 6,000 miles/9,500 km) to equalize wear patterns that vary with a tire's position on the vehicle. Tires will also wear in an uneven way as the front steering/suspension system wears to the point where the alignment should be reset.

Rotating the tires will ensure maximum life for the tires as a set, so you will not have to discard a tire early due to wear on only part of the tread. Regular rotation is required to equalize wear.

When rotating "unidirectional tires," make sure that they always roll in the same direction. This means that a tire used on the left side of the vehicle must not be switched to the right side and vice-versa. These tires are marked on the sidewall as to the direction of rotation; observe the mark when reinstalling the tire(s).

Some styled or "mag" wheels may have different offsets front to rear. In these cases, the rear wheels must not be used up front and vice-versa. Furthermore, if these wheels are equipped with unidirectional tires, they cannot be rotated unless the tire is remounted for the proper direction of rotation.

➡**The compact or space-saver spare is strictly for emergency use. It must never be included in the tire rotation or placed on the vehicle for everyday use.**

If your car is equipped with tires having different load ratings on the front and the rear, the tires should not be rotated front to rear. Rotating these tires could affect tire life (the tires with the lower rating will wear faster, and could become overloaded) and upset the handling of the car.

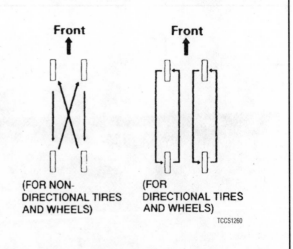

Fig. 61 Compact spare tires must NEVER be used in the rotation pattern

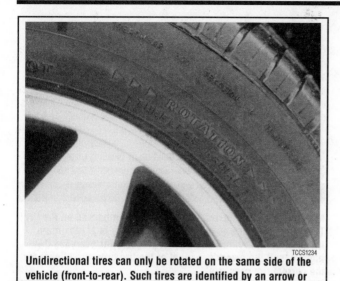

Unidirectional tires can only be rotated on the same side of the vehicle (front-to-rear). Such tires are identified by an arrow or the word "rotation"

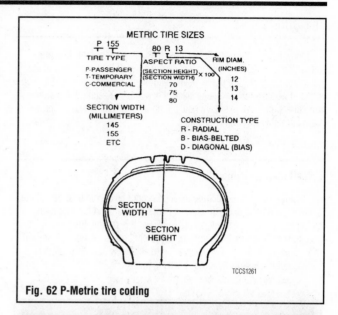

Fig. 62 P-Metric tire coding

TIRE USAGE

The tires on your car were selected to provide the best all-around performance for normal operation when inflated a specified. Oversize tires (load range D) will not increase the maximum load carrying capacity of the vehicle, although they will provide an extra margin of tread life. Be sure to check overall height before using larger size tires which may cause interference with suspension components or wheel wells. When replacing conventional tire sizes with other tire size designations, be sure to check the manufacturer's recommendations. Interchangeability is not always possible because of differences in load ratings, tire dimensions, wheel well clearances and rim size. Also, due to differences in handling characteristics, 70-series and 60-series tires should be used only in pairs on the same axle. Radial tires should be used only in sets of four.

The wheels must be the correct width for the tires. Tire dealers have charts of tire and rim compatibility. A mismatch can cause sloppy handling and rapid tread wear. The old rule of thumb is that the tread width should match the rim width (inside bead to inside bead) within an inch. For radial tires, the rim width should be 80% or less of the tire (not tread) width.

The height (mounted diameter) of the new tires can greatly change speedometer accuracy, engine speed at a given road speed, fuel mileage, acceleration and ground clearance. Tire manufacturers furnish full measurement specifications. Speedometer drive gears are available for correction.

➡ **Dimensions of tires marked the same size may vary significantly, even among tires from the same manufacturer.**

TIRE DESIGN

♦ See Figure 62

For maximum satisfaction, tires should be used in sets of five. Mixing of different types (radial, bias-belted, fiberglass belted) must be avoided. In most cases, the vehicle manufacturer has designated a type of tire on which the vehicle will perform best. Your first choice when replacing tires should be to use the same type of tire that the manufacturer recommends.

Radial tires are recommended for use on all Ford cars. If they are used, tire sizes and wheel diameters should be selected to maintain ground clearance and tire load capacity equivalent to the minimum specified tire. Radial tires should always be used in sets of five, but in an emergency, radial tires can be used—with caution—on the rear axle only. If this is done, both tires on the rear should be radial.

✻✻ CAUTION

Radial tires should never be used on only the front axle.

When selecting tires, pay attention to the original size as marked on the tire. Most tires are described using an industry size code sometimes referred to as P-Metric. This allows the exact identification of the tire specifications, regardless of the manufacturer. If selecting a different tire size or brand, remember to check the installed tire for any sign of interference with the body or suspension while the vehicle is stopping, turning sharply or heavily loaded.

Snow Tires

Good radial tires can produce a big advantage in slippery weather, but in snow, a street radial tire does not have sufficient tread to provide traction and control. The small grooves of a street tire quickly pack with snow and the tire behaves like a billiard ball on a marble floor. The more open, chunky tread of a snow tire will self-clean as the tire turns, providing much better grip on snowy surfaces.

To satisfy municipalities requiring snow tires during weather emergencies, most snow tires carry either an M + S designation after the tire size stamped on the sidewall, or the designation "all-season." In general, no change in tire size is necessary when buying snow tires.

Most manufacturers strongly recommend the use of 4 snow tires on their vehicles for reasons of stability. If snow tires are fitted only to the drive wheels, the opposite end of the vehicle may become very unstable when braking or turning on slippery surfaces. This instability can lead to unpleasant endings if the driver can't counteract the slide in time.

Note that the number of snow tires, whether 2 or 4, will affect vehicle handling in all non-snow situations. The stiffer, heavier snow tires will noticeably change the turning and braking characteristics of the vehicle. Once the snow tires are installed, you must relearn the behavior of the vehicle and drive accordingly.

➡ **Consider buying extra wheels on which to mount the snow tires. Once done, the "snow wheels" can be installed and removed as needed. This eliminates the potential damage to tires or wheels from seasonal removal and installation. Even if your vehicle has styled wheels, see if inexpensive steel wheels are available. Although the look of the vehicle will change, the expensive wheels will be protected from salt, curb hits and pothole damage.**

TIRE STORAGE

If they are mounted on wheels, store the tires at proper inflation pressure. All tires should be kept in a cool, dry place. If they are stored in the garage or basement, do not let them stand on a concrete floor; set them on strips of wood, a mat or a large stack of newspaper. Keeping them away from direct moisture is of paramount importance. Tires should not be stored upright, but in a flat position.

INSPECTION

▶ **See Figures 63 thru 68**

The importance of proper tire inflation cannot be overemphasized. A tire employs air as part of its structure. It is designed around the supporting strength of the air at a specified pressure. For this reason, improper inflation drastically reduces the tires's ability to perform as intended. A tire will lose some air in day-to-day use; having to add a few pounds of air periodically is not necessarily a sign of a leaking tire.

Two items should be a permanent fixture in every glove compartment: an accurate tire pressure gauge and a tread depth gauge. Check the tire pressure (including the spare) regularly with a pocket type gauge. Too often, the gauge on the end of the air hose at your corner garage is not accurate because it suffers too much abuse. Always check tire pressure when the tires are cold, as pressure increases with temperature. If you must move the vehicle to check the tire inflation, do not drive more than a mile before checking. A cold tire is generally one that has not been driven for more than three hours.

A plate or sticker which shows the proper tire pressures is normally provided somewhere on the vehicle (door post, hood, tailgate or trunk lid). Never counteract excessive pressure build-up by bleeding off air pressure (letting some air out). This will cause the tire to run hotter and wear quicker.

✻✻ CAUTION

Never exceed the maximum tire pressure embossed on the tire! This is the pressure to be used when the tire is at maximum loading, but it is rarely the correct pressure for everyday driving. Consult the owner's manual or the tire pressure sticker for the correct tire pressure.

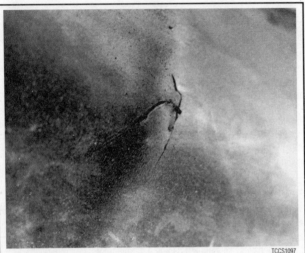

Tires should be checked frequently for any sign of puncture or damage

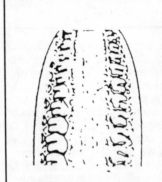
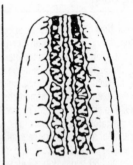

• DRIVE WHEEL HEAVY ACCELERATION
• OVERINFLATION

• HARD CORNERING
• UNDERINFLATION
• LACK OF ROTATION

TCCS1262

Fig. 63 Examples of inflation-related tire wear patterns

Tires with deep cuts, or cuts which show bulging, should be replaced immediately

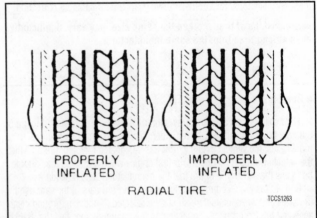

PROPERLY INFLATED

IMPROPERLY INFLATED

RADIAL TIRE

TCCS1263

Fig. 64 Radial tires have a characteristic sidewall bulge; don't try to measure pressure by looking at the tire. Use a quality air pressure gauge

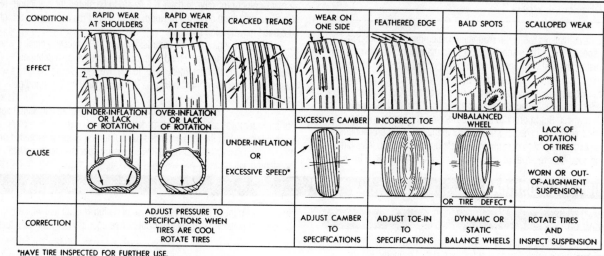

CONDITION	RAPID WEAR AT SHOULDERS	RAPID WEAR AT CENTER	CRACKED TREADS	WEAR ON ONE SIDE	FEATHERED EDGE	BALD SPOTS	SCALLOPED WEAR
EFFECT							
CAUSE	UNDER-INFLATION OR LACK OF ROTATION	OVER-INFLATION OR LACK OF ROTATION	UNDER-INFLATION OR EXCESSIVE SPEED*	EXCESSIVE CAMBER	INCORRECT TOE	UNBALANCED WHEEL OR TIRE DEFECT *	LACK OF ROTATION OF TIRES OR WORN OR OUT-OF-ALIGNMENT SUSPENSION.
CORRECTION	ADJUST PRESSURE TO SPECIFICATIONS WHEN TIRES ARE COOL ROTATE TIRES			ADJUST CAMBER TO SPECIFICATIONS	ADJUST TOE-IN TO SPECIFICATIONS	DYNAMIC OR STATIC BALANCE WHEELS	ROTATE TIRES AND INSPECT SUSPENSION

*HAVE TIRE INSPECTED FOR FURTHER USE.

TCCS1267

Fig. 65 Common tire wear patterns and causes

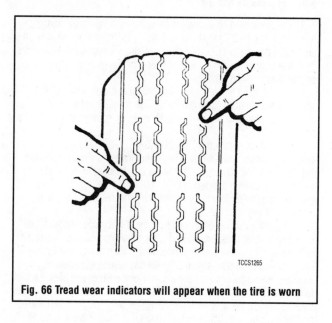

TCCS1265

Fig. 66 Tread wear indicators will appear when the tire is worn

TCCS1266

Fig. 68 A penny works well for a quick check of tread depth

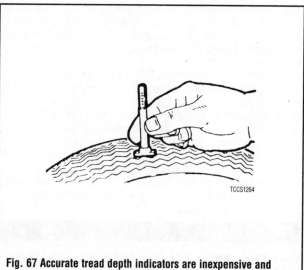

TCCS1264

Fig. 67 Accurate tread depth indicators are inexpensive and handy

Once you've maintained the correct tire pressures for several weeks, you'll be familiar with the vehicle's braking and handling personality. Slight adjustments in tire pressures can fine-tune these characteristics, but never change the cold pressure specification by more than 2 psi. A slightly softer tire pressure will give a softer ride but also yield lower fuel mileage. A slightly harder tire will give crisper dry road handling but can cause skidding on wet surfaces. Unless you're fully attuned to the vehicle, stick to the recommended inflation pressures.

All tires made since 1968 have built-in tread wear indicator bars that show up as ½ in. (13mm) wide smooth bands across the tire when $\frac{1}{16}$ in. (1.5mm) of tread remains. The appearance of tread wear indicators means that the tires should be replaced. In fact, many states have laws prohibiting the use of tires with less than this amount of tread.

You can check your own tread depth with an inexpensive gauge or by using a Lincoln head penny. Slip the Lincoln penny (with Lincoln's head upside-down) into several tread grooves. If you can see the top of Lincoln's head in 2 adjacent grooves, the tire has less than $\frac{1}{16}$ in. (1.5mm) tread left and should be replaced. You can measure snow tires in the same manner by using the "tails" side of the Lincoln penny. If you can see the top of the Lincoln memorial, it's time to replace the snow tire(s).

CARE OF SPECIAL WHEELS

If you have invested money in magnesium, aluminum alloy or sport wheels, special precautions should be taken to make sure your investment is not wasted and that your special wheels look good for the life of the vehicle.

Special wheels are easily damaged and/or scratched. Occasionally check the rims for cracking, impact damage or air leaks. If any of these are found, replace the wheel. But in order to prevent this type of damage and the costly replacement of a special wheel, observe the following precautions:

• Use extra care not to damage the wheels during removal, installation, balancing, etc. After removal of the wheels from the vehicle, place them on a mat or other protective surface. If they are to be stored for any length of time, support them on strips of wood. Never store tires and wheels upright; the tread may develop flat spots.

• When driving, watch for hazards; it doesn't take much to crack a wheel.

• When washing, use a mild soap or non-abrasive dish detergent (keeping in mind that detergent tends to remove wax). Avoid cleansers with abrasives or the use of hard brushes. There are many cleaners and polishes for special wheels.

• If possible, remove the wheels during the winter. Salt and sand used for snow removal can severely damage the finish of a wheel.

• Make certain the recommended lug nut torque is never exceeded or the wheel may crack. Never use snow chains on special wheels; severe scratching will occur.

FLUIDS AND LUBRICANTS

Fluid Disposal

Used fluids such as engine oil, transmission fluid, antifreeze and brake fluid are hazardous wastes and must be disposed of properly. Before draining any fluids, consult with your local authorities; in many areas waste oil, etc. is being accepted as a part of recycling programs. A number of service stations and auto parts stores are also accepting waste fluids for recycling.

Be sure of the recycling center's policies before draining any fluids, as many will not accept different fluids that have been mixed together.

Fuel and Engine Oil Recommendations

FUEL

➡ **Some fuel additives contain chemicals that can damage the catalytic converter and/or oxygen sensor. Read all of the labels carefully before using any additive in the engine or fuel system.**

All vehicles covered by this manual are designed to run on unleaded fuel. The use of a leaded fuel in a vehicle requiring unleaded fuel will plug the catalytic converter and render it inoperative. It will also increase exhaust backpressure to the point where engine output will be severely reduced. Obviously, use of leaded fuel should not be a problem, since most companies have stopped selling it for quite some time.

For all Mustang models, except the Cobra, the minimum octane rating of the unleaded fuel being used must be at least 87 (as listed on the pumps), which usually means regular unleaded. Some areas may have 86 or even lower octanes available, which would make 87 midgrade or even premium. In these cases, a minimum fuel octane of 87 should STILL be used. Mustang Cobra models were designed to use gasoline with a minimum octane rating of 91; however, an octane rating of 87 may be used occasionally, if absolutely necessary.

Fuel should be selected for the brand and octane which performs best with your engine. Judge a gasoline by its ability to prevent pinging, its engine starting capabilities (cold and hot) and general all-weather performance. The use of a fuel too low in octane (a measurement of anti-knock quality) will result in spark knock. Since many factors such as altitude, terrain, air temperature and humidity affect operating efficiency, knocking may result even though the recommended fuel is being used. If persistent knocking occurs, it may be necessary to switch to a different brand or grade of fuel. Continuous or heavy knocking may result in engine damage.

➡ **Your engine's fuel requirement can change with time, mainly due to carbon buildup, which will in turn change the compressio ratio. If your engine pings or knocks, switch to a higher grade of fuel. Sometimes just changing brands will cure the problem.**

The other most important aspect is that the fuel contains detergents designed to keep fuel injection systems clean. Many of the major fuel companies will display information right at the pumps telling you that their fuels contain these detergents. The use of a high-quality fuel which contains detergents will help assure trouble-free operation of your car's fuel system.

OIL

▶ **See Figures 69 and 70**

The recommended oil viscosities for sustained temperatures ranging from below 0°F (-18°C) to above 32°F (0°C) are listed in the section. They are broken down into multi-viscosities and single viscosities. Multi-viscosity oils are recommended because of their wider range of acceptable temperatures and driving conditions.

When adding oil to the crankcase or changing the oil and filter, it is important that oil of an equal quality to original equipment be used in your car. The use of inferior oils may void the warranty, damage your engine, or both.

The Society of Automotive Engineers (SAE) grade number of the oil indicates the viscosity of the oil-its ability to lubricate at a given temperature. The lower the SAE number, the lighter the oil; the lower the viscosity, the easier it is to crank the engine in cold weather, but the less the oil will lubricate and protect the engine in high temperatures. This number is marked on every oil container.

Oil viscosities should be chosen from those oils recommended for the lowest anticipated temperatures during the oil change interval. Due to the need for an oil that embodies both good lubrication at high temperature and easy cranking in cold weather, multigrade oils have been developed. Basically, a multigrade oil is thinner at low temperatures and thicker at high temperatures. For example, a 10W-40 oil (the W stands for winter) exhibits the characteristics of a 10-weight (SAE 10) oil when the car is first started and the oil is cold. Its lighter weight allows it to travel to the lubricating surfaces quicker and offer less resistance to starter motor cranking than a heavier oil. But after the engine reaches operating temperature, the 10W-40 oil begins acting like straight 40-weight (SAE 40) oil. It behaves as a heavier oil, providing greater lubrication and protection against foaming than lighter oils.

The American Petroleum Institute (API) designations, also found on oil containers, indicate the classification of engine oil used for given operating conditions. Only heavy duty detergent oils designated for Service SG (or the latest superceding designation) should be used in your car. Oils of the SG-type perform many functions inside the engine besides their basic lubrication. Through a balanced system of metallic detergents and polymeric dispersants, the oil prevents high and low temperature deposits and also keeps sludge and dirt particles in suspension. Acids, particularly sulfuric, as well as other by-products of engine combustion, are neutralized by the oil. If these acids are allowed to concentrate, they can cause corrosion and rapid wear of the internal engine parts.

❊❊ WARNING

Non-detergent motor oils or straight mineral oils should never be used in your Ford gasoline engine.

Fig. 69 Recommended oil viscosities—5.0L engine

Fig. 70 Recommended oil viscosities for 3.8L and 4.6L engines

OIL LEVEL CHECK

Check the engine oil level every time you fill the gas tank. The oil level should be between the ADD and FULL marks on the dipstick. Make sure that the dipstick is inserted into the crankcase as far as possible and that the vehicle is resting on level ground. Also, allow a few minutes after turning the engine **OFF** for the oil to drain into the pan, otherwise an inaccurate reading may result. One good way to assure enough time for the oil to run back into the pan is to fill the fuel tank first, then check the oil after paying for the gas.

1. Open the hood, then locate and remove the engine oil dipstick.
2. Wipe the dipstick with a clean, lint-free rag and reinsert it. Be sure to insert it all the way.
3. Pull out the dipstick and note the oil level. It should be between the FULL (safe or max.) and the ADD (low or min.) marks.

➡Use a high quality multigrade oil of the proper viscosity.

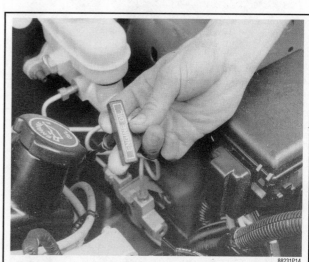

To check the engine oil, park the car on level ground, open the hood and withdraw the dipstick

Look for the API oil identification label when choosing your engine oil

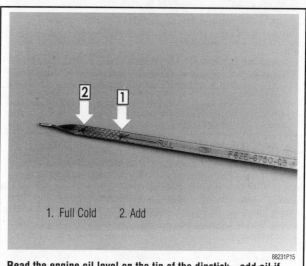

1. Full Cold   2. Add

Read the engine oil level on the tip of the dipstick—add oil if the level is below the ADD mark

4. If the level is below the lower mark, install the dipstick and add fresh oil to bring the level within the proper range by adding oil through the oil filler cap. Do not overfill the engine.

5. Recheck the oil level and add more engine oil, if necessary.

6. Close the hood.

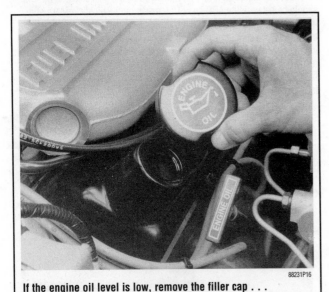

If the engine oil level is low, remove the filler cap . . .

. . . and, using a funnel to avoid messy spills, add the proper amount and type of clean engine oil

OIL & FILTER CHANGE

➡The engine oil and oil filter should be changed at the mileage recommended on the Maintenance Intervals Charts (found later in this section). Though some manufacturers may recommend changing the filter only at every other oil change, we recommend that you ALWAYS change the filter with the oil. The benefit of fresh oil is quickly lost if the old filter is clogged and unable to do its job. Also, leaving the old filter in place leaves a significant amount of dirty oil in the system.

The oil should be changed more frequently if the vehicle is being operated in a very dusty area. Before draining the oil, make sure that the engine is at operating temperature. Hot oil will hold more impurities in suspension and will flow better, allowing the removal of more oil and dirt.

➡It is a good idea to place your ignition key in the box or bag with the bottles of fresh engine oil. In this way, it will be VERY HARD to forget to refill the engine crankcase before you go to start the engine.

1. Raise and support the vehicle safely on jackstands. Make sure the oil drain plug is at the lowest point on the oil pan. If not, you may have to raise the vehicle slightly higher on one jackstand (side) than the other.

2. Before you crawl under the car, take a look at where you will be working and gather all the necessary tools, such as a few wrenches or a strip of sockets, the drain pan, a few clean rags and, if the oil filter is more accessible from underneath the vehicle, you will also want to grab a bottle of oil, the new filter and a filter wrench at this time.

3. Position the drain pan beneath the oil pan drain plug. Keep in mind that the fast flowing oil, which will spill out as you pull the plug from the pan, will flow with enough force that it could miss the pan. Position the drain pan accordingly and be ready to move the pan more directly beneath the opening as the oil flow lessens to a trickle.

➡The 5.0L engine is equipped with 2 drain plugs (one in front of the crossmember and one behind it, closer to the transmission). Both should be removed to assure proper pan draining, but if the front end is raised and supported on ramps or jackstands, the oil may not fully drain from the front plug. The best way to assure all oil has been drained is to pull the plugs, then remove the jackstands and carefully lower the vehicle (make sure your drain pans are properly positioned because the relative positioning of the drain holes will change as the vehicle is lowered). Once you are sure the front portion of the oil pan has sufficiently drained, raise the vehicle and support it again with jackstands.

4. Loosen the drain plug with a wrench (or socket and driver), then carefully unscrew the plug with your fingers. Use a rag to shield your fingers from the heat. Push in on the plug as you unscrew it so you can feel when all of the screw threads are out of the hole (and so you will keep the oil from seeping past the threads until you are ready to remove the plug). You can then remove the plug quickly to avoid having hot oil run down your arm. This will also help assure that you have the plug in your hand, not in the bottom of a pan of hot oil.

✳✳ CAUTION

Be careful of the oil; when at operating temperature, it is hot enough to cause a severe burn.

5. Allow the oil to drain until nothing but a few drops come out of the drain hole. Check the drain plug to make sure the threads and sealing surface are not damaged. Carefully thread the plug into position and tighten it with a torque wrench to 15–25 ft. lbs. (20–34 Nm). If a torque wrench is not available, snug the drain plug and give a slight additional turn. You don't want the plug to fall out (as you would quickly become stranded), but the pan threads are EASILY stripped from overtightening (and this can be time consuming and/or costly to fix).

6. The oil filter is located on the bottom left-hand side of all the engines installed in these vehicles; position the drain pan beneath it. To remove the filter, you may need an oil filter wrench, since the filter may have been fitted too tightly and/or the heat from the engine may have made it even tighter. A filter wrench can be obtained at any auto parts store and is well worth the investment. Loosen the filter with the filter wrench. With a rag wrapped around the filter, unscrew the filter from the boss on the side of the engine. Be careful of hot oil that will run down the side of the filter. Make sure that your drain pan is under the filter before you start to remove it from the engine; should some of the hot oil happen to get on you, there will be a place to dump the filter in a hurry and the filter will usually spill a good bit of dirty oil as it is removed.

7. Make sure that the old gasket was removed with the used oil filter and wipe the base of the mounting boss with a clean, dry cloth. Before you install the new filter, smear a small amount of fresh oil on the gasket with your finger, just enough to coat the entire contact surface. When you tighten the filter, rotate it about a half-turn after the gasket contacts the mounting boss (or follow any instructions which are provided on the filter or parts box).

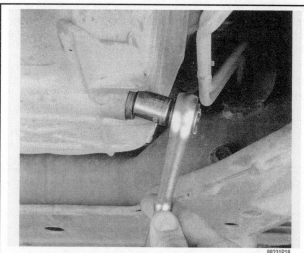

With the engine fully warmed up, raise and support the vehicle, then loosen the oil pan drain plug

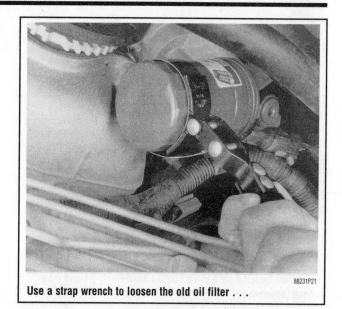

Use a strap wrench to loosen the old oil filter . . .

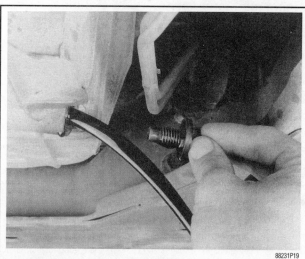

Once the plug threads are free, pull your hand away from the drain hole quickly to avoid being burned

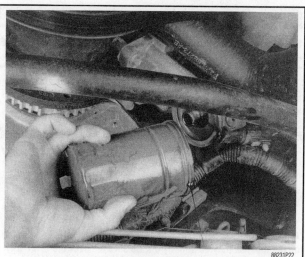

. . . then remove the filter by hand—be cautious, the filter holds about 1 pt. (0.47L) of hot, dirty engine oil

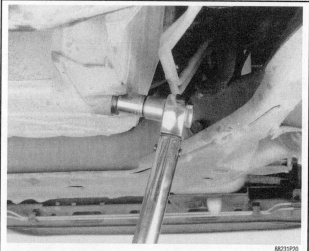

Whenever possible, use a torque wrench to tighten the drain plug to the manufacturer's specification

Before installing a new oil filter, lightly coat the rubber gasket with clean oil . . .

. . . then install it onto the mounting boss—only tighten it by hand, otherwise it will be difficult to remove

✖✖ WARNING

Never operate the engine without engine oil, otherwise SEVERE engine damge will be the result.

8. Remove the jackstands and carefully lower the vehicle, then IMME-DIATELY refill the engine crankcase with the proper amount of oil. DO NOT WAIT TO DO THIS because if you forget and someone tries to start the car, severe engine damage will occur.

9. Refill the engine crankcase slowly, checking the level often. You may notice that it usually takes less than the amount of oil listed in the capacity chart to refill the crankcase. But, that is only until the engine is run and the oil filter is filled with oil. To make sure the proper level is obtained, run the engine to normal operating temperature, shut the engine **OFF**, allow the oil to drain back into the oil pan, and recheck the level. Top off the oil at this time to the FULL mark.

➡ **If the vehicle is not resting on level ground, the oil level reading on the dipstick may be slightly off. Be sure to check the level only when the car is sitting level.**

10. Drain your used oil in a suitable container for recycling and clean up your tools, as you will be needing them again in a few thousand miles/kilometers.

Manual Transmission

FLUID RECOMMENDATIONS

The manual transmissions covered by this manual use Mercon® automatic transmission fluid for lubrication. DO NOT use improper fluids such as gear oil. Use of improper fluids could lead to leaks or transmission damage.

LEVEL CHECK

◗ **See Figure 71**

The fluid level should be checked every six months or 6,000 miles (9,600 km), whichever comes first.
1. Park the car on a level surface, turn the engine **OFF**, FIRMLY apply the parking brake and block the drive wheels.

➡ **Ground clearance may make access to the transmission filler plug impossible without raising and supporting the vehicle, BUT, if**

this is done, the car MUST be supported at four corners and level. If only the front or rear is supported, an improper fluid level will be indicated. If you are going to place the car on four jackstands, this might be the perfect opportunity to rotate the tires as well.

2. Remove the filler plug from the side of the transmission case using a ⅜ in. drive ratchet and extension. The fluid level should be even with the bottom of the filler hole.
3. If additional fluid is necessary, add it through the filler hole using a siphon pump or squeeze bottle.
4. When you are finished, carefully install the filler plug, but DO NOT overtighten it and damage the housing.

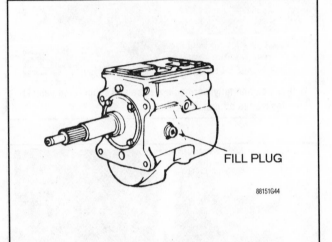

FILL PLUG

Fig. 71 The manual transmission filler/inspection plug is normally found on the middle-to-upper side of the housing

DRAIN & REFILL

◗ **See Figure 72**

Under normal conditions, the manufacturer claims that manual transmission fluid should not need to be changed. However, if the car is driven in deep water (as high as the transmission casing), it is a good idea to replace the fluid. Little harm can come from a fluid change when you have just purchased a used vehicle, especially since the condition of the transmission fluid is usually not known.

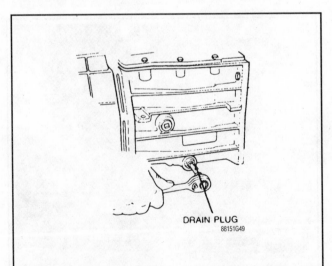

DRAIN PLUG

Fig. 72 The transmission fluid is removed through the drain plug in the lower portion of the housing

If the fluid is to be drained, it is a good idea to warm the fluid first so it will flow better. This can be accomplished by 15–20 miles (24–32 km) of highway driving. Fluid which is warmed to normal operating temperature will flow faster, drain more completely and remove more contaminants from the housing.

1. Drive the vehicle to ensure that the fluid is at normal operating temperature.

2. Raise and support the vehicle securely on jackstands. Remember that the vehicle must be supported level (usually at four points) so the proper amount of fluid can be added.

3. Place a drain pan under the transmission housing, below the drain plug. Remember that the fluid will likely flow with some force at first (arcing outward from the transmission), and will not just drip straight downward into the pan. Position the drain pan accordingly and move it more directly beneath the drain plug as the flow slows to a trickle.

➡**To ensure that the fill plug is not frozen or rusted in place, remove it from the transmission BEFORE removing the drain plug. It would be unfortunate to drain all of your transmission fluid and then realize that the fill plug is stripped or frozen in place.**

4. Remove the fill plug, then the drain plug and allow the transmission fluid to drain out.

➡**The transmission drain plug is usually a square receiver which is designed to accept a ⅜ in. driver, such as a ratchet or extension.**

5. Once the transmission has drained sufficiently, install the the drain plug until secure.

6. Fill the transmission to the proper level with the required fluid.

7. Reinstall the filler plug once you are finished.

8. Remove the jackstands and carefully lower the vehicle.

Automatic Transmission

FLUID RECOMMENDATIONS

The automatic transmissions covered by this manual use Mercon® automatic transmission fluid for lubrication. DO NOT use improper fluids such as gear oil. Use of improper fluids could lead to leaks or transmission damage.

On automatic transmissions, the fluid type is normally stamped on the dipstick. Be sure to double check the dipstick before adding any fluid.

LEVEL CHECK

It is very important to maintain the proper fluid level in an automatic transmission. If the level is either too high or too low, poor shifting operation and internal damage are likely to occur. For this reason, a regular check of the fluid level is essential.

Although it is best to check fluid at normal operating temperature, it can be checked "overnight cold" if the ambient temperatures are 50–95°F (21–35°C). If so, refer to the dots on the transmission dipstick instead of the cross-hatched area and level marking lines.

1. Drive the vehicle for 15–20 minutes, allowing the transmission to reach operating temperature.

➡**If the car is driven at extended highway speeds, is driven in city traffic in hot weather or is being used to pull a trailer, fluid temperatures will likely exceed normal operating and checking ranges. In these circumstances, give the fluid time to cool (about 30 minutes) before checking the level.**

2. Park the car on a level surface, apply the parking brake and leave the engine idling. Make sure the parking brake is FIRMLY ENGAGED. Shift the transmission and engage each gear, then place the selector in **P** (PARK).

3. Open the hood and locate the transmission dipstick. Wipe away any dirt in the area of the dipstick to prevent it from falling into the filler tube. Withdraw the dipstick, wipe it with a clean, lint-free rag and reinsert it until it fully seats.

With the engine hot and idling, remove the Automatic Transmission Fluid (ATF) dipstick . . .

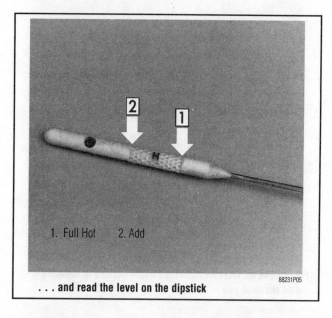

1. Full Hot   2. Add

. . . and read the level on the dipstick

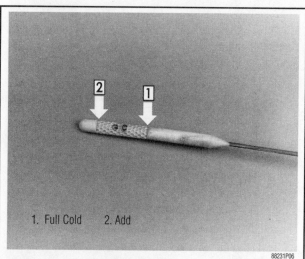

1. Full Cold   2. Add

The ATF dipstick is also equipped with a fluid level range to check the engine when it is cold

4. Withdraw the dipstick and hold it horizontally while noting the fluid level. It should be between the upper (FULL) and the lower (ADD) marks.

5. If the level is below the lower mark, use a funnel and add fluid in small quantities through the dipstick filler neck. Keep the engine running while adding fluid and check the level after each small amount. DO NOT overfill, as this could lead to foaming and transmission damage or seal leaks.

➡**Since the transmission fluid is added through the dipstick tube, if you check the fluid too soon after adding fluid, an incorrect reading may occur. After adding fluid, wait a few minutes to allow it to fully drain into the transmission.**

DRAIN & REFILL/PAN & FILTER SERVICE

Transmission Assembly

▶ **See Figures 73, 74, 75 and 76**

Under normal service (moderate highway driving excluding excessive hot or cold conditions), the manufacturer feels that automatic transmis-

sion fluid should not need periodic changing. However, if a major service is performed to the transmission, if transmission fluid becomes burnt or discolored through severe usage, or if the vehicle is subjected to constant stop-and-go driving in hot weather, trailer towing, or long periods of highway use at high speeds, the fluid should be changed to prevent transmission damage. A preventive maintenance change is therefore recommended for most vehicles at least every 90,000 miles (145,000 km).

➡**Although not a required service, transmission fluid changing can help assure a trouble-free transmission. Likewise, changing the transmission filter at this time is also added insurance.**

1. Raise the car and support it securely on jackstands.

➡**The torque converters on some transmissions are equipped with drain plugs. Because it may take some time to drain the fluid from the converter, you may wish to perform that procedure at this time, then come back to the pan and filter removal.**

2. Place a large drain pan under the transmission.

3. Loosen all of the pan attaching bolts to within a few turns of complete removal, then carefully break the gasket seal, allowing most of the fluid to drain over the edge of the pan.

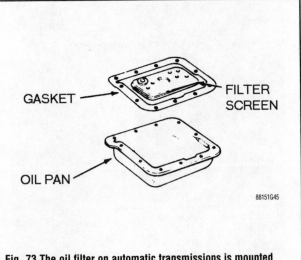

Fig. 73 The oil filter on automatic transmissions is mounted inside the fluid pan

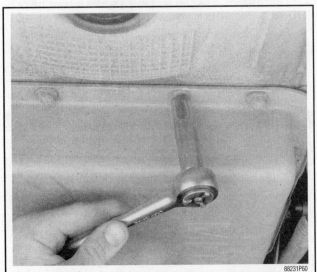

Remove all but a few of the transmission pan mounting bolts . . .

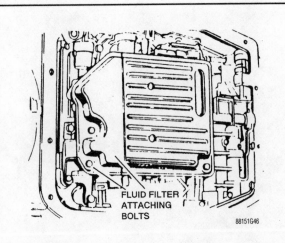

Fig. 74 Some filters are attached to the transmission with bolts around the perimeter

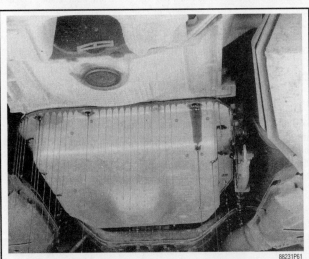

. . . then gently separate the pan from the transmission to drain the initial amount of fluid

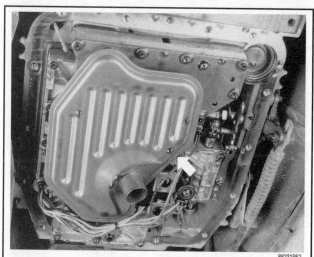

Remove the transmission pan to access the ATF fluid filter (arrow)

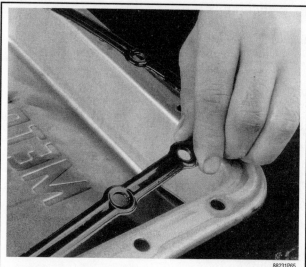

Prior to installation, position a new pan gasket on the fluid pan

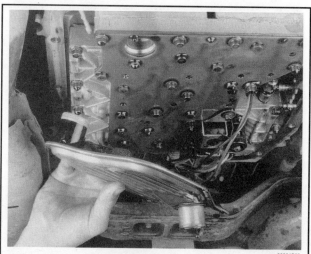

Remove any mounting bolts (if equipped) and pull the filter down and off of the transmission valve body

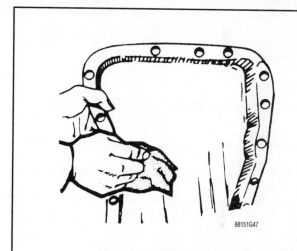

Fig. 75 If a cloth is used to clean the oil pan, MAKE SURE that no bits of lint are left behind

Clean the fluid pan of all dirt and old fluid; also clean the pan magnet (shown), if so equipped

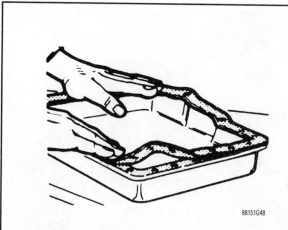

Fig. 76 Position the new gasket on the pan to assure a proper fit before installation

※※ WARNING

DO NOT force the pan while breaking the gasket seal. DO NOT allow the pan flange to become bent or otherwise damaged.

4. When fluid has drained to the level of the pan flange, remove the pan bolts and carefully lower the pan, doing your best to drain the rest of the fluid into the drain pan.

5. Clean the transmission oil pan thoroughly using a safe solvent, then allow it to air dry. DO NOT use a cloth to dry the pan, since it might leave behind bits of lint. Discard the old pan gasket.

6. If necessary, remove the Automatic Transmission Fluid (ATF) filter mounting bolts, then remove the filter by pulling it down and off of the valve body. Make sure any gaskets or seals are removed with the old filter. The transmission usually has one round seal and a rectangular gasket.

7. Install the new oil filter screen, making sure all gaskets or seals are in place, then secure using the retaining screws, if applicable.

8. Place a new gasket on the fluid pan, then install the pan to the transmission. Tighten the attaching bolts to 71–119 inch lbs. (8–13 Nm).

9. Add three quarts of appropriate fluid to the transmission through the filler tube.

10. Remove the jackstands and carefully lower the vehicle.

11. Start the engine and move the gear selector through all gears in the shift pattern. Allow the engine to reach normal operating temperature.

12. Check the transmission fluid level. Add fluid, as necessary, to obtain the correct level.

Torque Converter

Some torque converters, such as those usually used on the AOD transmission, are equipped with drain plugs. If so, you will probably want to drain the fluid in the converter also at the time of a transmission pan fluid change. Just make sure that you compensate for the additional fluid drained during the refilling process.

1. Remove the lower engine dust cover or the torque converter drain rubber access plug.

2. Rotate the torque converter until the drain plug comes into view.

3. Remove the drain plug and allow the transmission fluid to drain. This could take some time, so you may wish to perform the other transmission service (fluid pan and filter removal) while waiting.

4. Once the fluid has drained, install the drain plug.

5. Install the engine dust cover or access plug.

6. Make sure the transmission is properly refilled with appropriate fluid before attempting to drive the vehicle.

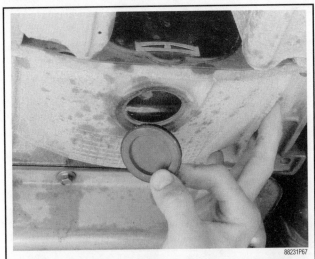

. . . then remove the small rubber access plug from the transmission

Use a socket wrench to remove the drain plug . . .

Remove the cover plate from the transmission and turn the converter until the drain plug can be seen . . .

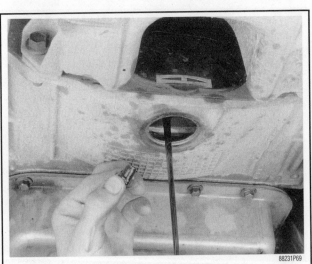

. . . and allow the torque converter fluid to drain into a catch pan

Rear Axle

FLUID LEVEL CHECK

The fluid level in the rear axle should be checked at each oil change. Like the manual transmission on the Mustang, the rear axle does not have a dipstick to check its fluid level. Instead, a filler plug is located in the side of the housing (or in the side of the cover), just barely above the level to which fluid should fill the housing.

1. Make sure the transmission is in **P** (A/T) or in gear (M/T), then FIRMLY set the parking brake and block the drive wheels.

2. Check under the vehicle to see if there is sufficient clearance for you to access the filler plug on the side of the differential housing. If not, you will have to raise and support the vehicle using jackstands at four points to make sure it is completely level. Failure to support the vehicle level will prevent you from properly checking or filling the rear axle fluid.

3. Thoroughly clean the area surrounding the fill plug. This will prevent any dirt from entering the housing and contaminating the gear oil.

4. Remove the fill plug and make sure that the gear oil is up to the bottom of the fill hole. If a slight amount of lubricant does not drip out of the hole when the plug is removed, additional lubricant should be added. Use hypoid gear lubricant SAE 80 or 90.

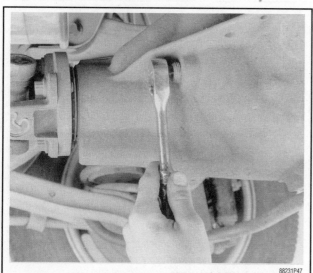

To check the rear axle fluid level, remove the fill plug

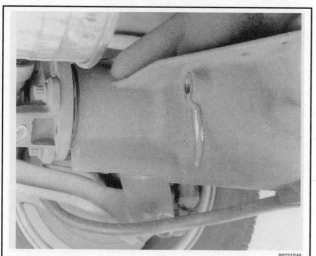

If the fluid is at the correct level, a little oil should dribble out of the fill hole (as shown) . . .

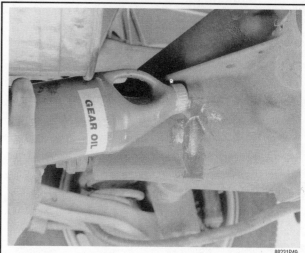

. . . otherwise, add SAE 80 or 90 weight hypoid gear oil through the fill hole

➡️**If the differential is a Traction-Lok limited-slip unit, be sure to use 4 oz. of Ford Friction Modifier C8AZ-19B546-A or equivalent special limited-slip additive with the lubricant.**

5. Once you are finished, install the fill plug, then (if raised) remove the jackstands and lower the vehicle.

DRAIN & REFILL

Drain and refill the rear axle housing every 100,000 miles (160,000 km) or any time the vehicle is driven in high water (up to the axle). Although some fluid can be removed using a suction gun, the best method is to remove the rear cover to ensure that all of any present contaminants are removed. As with any fluid change, the oil should be at normal operating temperature to ensure the best flow/removal of fluid and contaminants.

1. Drive the vehicle until the lubricant reaches normal operating temperature.

2. If necessary for access, raise and support the vehicle safely using jackstands, but be sure that the vehicle is level so you can properly refill the axle when you are finished.

3. Use a wire brush to clean the area around the differential. This will help prevent dirt from contaminating the differential housing while the cover is removed.

4. Position a drain pan under the rear axle.

5. Loosen and remove all but one or two of the rear cover upper or side retaining bolts. The remaining bolt(s) should then be loosened to within a few turns of complete removal. Use a small prytool to carefully break the gasket seal at the base of the cover and allow the lubricant to drain. Be VERY careful not to force or damage the cover and gasket mating surface.

6. Once most of the fluid has drained, remove the final retaining bolt(s) and separate the cover from the housing.

To fill the differential:

7. Carefully clean the gasket mating surfaces of the cover and axle housing of any remaining gasket or sealer. A putty knife is a good tool to use for this. You may want to cover the differential gears using a rag or piece of plastic to prevent contaminating them with dirt or pieces of the old gasket.

8. Install the rear cover using a new gasket and sealant. Tighten the retaining bolts using a crisscross pattern.

➡️**Make sure the vehicle is level before attempting to add fluid to the rear axle, otherwise an incorrect fluid level will result.**

9. Refill the rear axle housing using the proper grade and quantity of lubricant, then install the filler plug. Lower the vehicle, if applicable, then operate the vehicle and check for any leaks.

To drain the rear axle fluid, raise and safely support the vehicle on jackstands to access the cover (arrow)

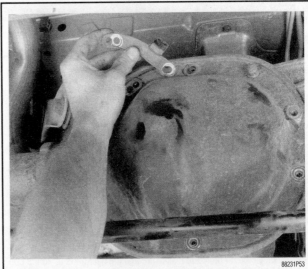

Remove any hose or wire brackets from the differential cover . . .

Clean all dirt and debris from the differential cover with a wire brush . . .

. . . then gently pry the cover away from the housing and drain the oil into a large catch pan

. . . then remove all but one differential cover mounting bolt—only loosen the last bolt

Remove the last bolt and separate the differential cover from the housing

Allow the remaining oil to drain from the housing . . .

. . . then cover the differential gears with a rag and clean all old gasket material from the housing

Cooling System

▶ See Figure 77

✳✳ CAUTION

Never remove the radiator cap under any conditions while the engine is running! Failure to follow these instructions could result in damage to the cooling system and/or personal injury. To avoid having scalding hot coolant or steam blow out of the radiator, use extreme care when removing the radiator cap from a hot radiator. Wait until the engine has cooled, then wrap a thick cloth around the radiator cap and turn it slowly to the first stop. Step back while the pressure is released from the cooling system. When you are sure the pressure has been released,

ALWAYS heed warning labels found in the engine compartment— this one includes suggestions for safe cooling system service

press down on the radiator cap (with the cloth still in position), turn and remove the cap.

FLUID RECOMMENDATIONS

The recommended coolant for all vehicles covered by this manual is a 50/50 mixture of ethylene glycol or (other suitable aluminum-compatible formula) and water for year-round use. Choose a good quality antifreeze with water pump lubricants, rust inhibitors and other corrosion inhibitors, along with acid neutralizers.

INSPECTION

▶ See Figure 78, 79 and 80 (p. 68–69)

Any time you have the hood open, glance at the coolant recovery tank (known as the degas bottle on 4.6L engines) to make sure it is properly filled. Top off the cooling system using the recovery tank and its markings as a guideline. If you top off the system, make a note of it to check again soon. A coolant level that consistently drops is usually a sign of a small, hard to detect leak, although in the worst case it could be a sign of an internal engine leak (blown head gasket or cracked block . . . check the engine oil for coolant contamination). In most cases, you will be able to trace the leak to a loose fitting or damaged hose (and you might solve a problem before it leaves you stranded). Evaporating ethylene glycol antifreeze will leave small, white (salt-like) deposits, which can be helpful in tracing a leak.

At least annually or every 12,000 miles (19,000 km), all hoses, fittings and cooling system connections should be inspected for damage, wear or leaks. Hose clamps should be checked for tightness, and soft or cracked hoses should be replaced. Damp spots, or accumulations of rust or dye near hoses or fittings indicate possible leakage. These must be corrected before filling the system withfresh coolant. The pressure cap should be examined for signs of deterioration and aging. The fan belt and/or other drive belt(s) should be inspected and adjusted to the proper tension. Refer to the information on drive belts found earlier in this section. Finally, if everything looks good, obtain an antifreeze/coolant testing hydrometer in order to check the freezing and boilover protection capabilities of the coolant currently in your engine. Old or improperly mixed coolant should be replaced.

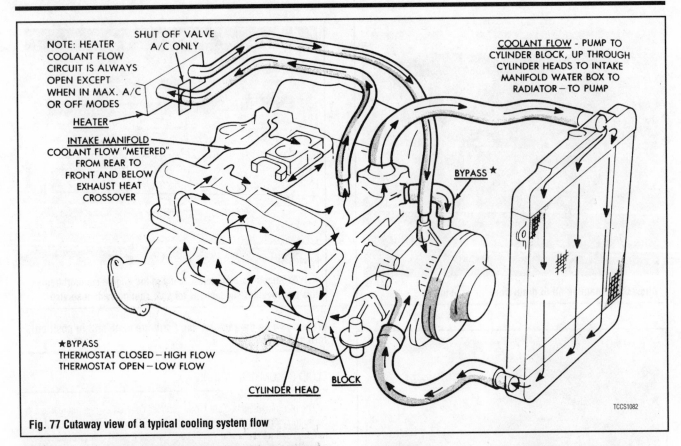

NOTE: HEATER COOLANT FLOW CIRCUIT IS ALWAYS OPEN EXCEPT WHEN IN MAX. A/C OR OFF MODES

SHUT OFF VALVE A/C ONLY

COOLANT FLOW - PUMP TO CYLINDER BLOCK, UP THROUGH CYLINDER HEADS TO INTAKE MANIFOLD WATER BOX TO RADIATOR - TO PUMP

HEATER

INTAKE MANIFOLD COOLANT FLOW "METERED" FROM REAR TO FRONT AND BELOW EXHAUST HEAT CROSSOVER

BYPASS ★

★BYPASS
THERMOSTAT CLOSED – HIGH FLOW
THERMOSTAT OPEN – LOW FLOW

CYLINDER HEAD

BLOCK

TCCS1082

Fig. 77 Cutaway view of a typical cooling system flow

❊❊ CAUTION

When draining coolant, keep in mind that cats and dogs are attracted to ethylene glycol antifreeze, and are likely to drink any that is left in an uncovered container or in puddles on the ground. This will prove fatal in sufficient quantity. Always drain coolant into a sealable container. Coolant may be reused unless it is contaminated or several years old.

At least once every 3 years or 36,000 miles (48,000 km), the engine cooling system should be inspected, flushed and refilled with fresh coolant. If the coolant is left in the system too long, it loses its ability to prevent rust and corrosion. If the coolant has too much water, it won't protect against freezing.

If you experience problems with your cooling system, such as overheating or boiling over, check for a simple explanation before expecting the complicated. Make sure the system can fully pressurize (are all the connections tight/is the radiator cap on properly, and is the cap seal intact?). Ideally, a pressure tester should be connected to the radiator opening and the system should be pressurized and inspected for leaks. If no obvious problems are found, use a hydrometer-type antifreeze/coolant tester (available at most automotive supply stores) to check the condition and concentration of the antifreeze in your cooling system. Excessively old coolant or the wrong proportions of water and coolant will adversely affect the coolant's boiling and freezing points.

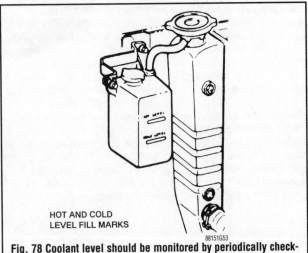

HOT AND COLD LEVEL FILL MARKS

88151G53

Fig. 78 Coolant level should be monitored by periodically checking the coolant recovery tank—overflow tank used with 5.0L engines shown

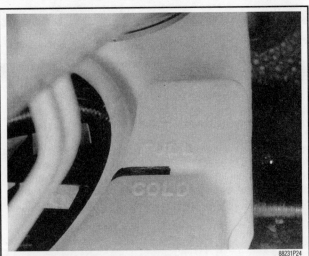

88231P24

If the coolant level in the overflow reservoir is not to the FULL COLD mark when the engine is cold . . .

... remove the reservoir cap ...

88151P51

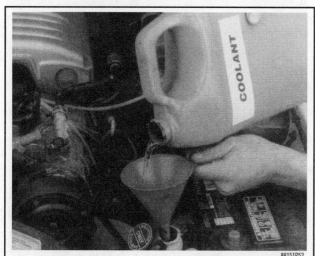

... and add small amounts of coolant until the proper level is reached

88151P52

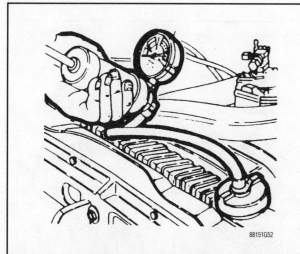

Fig. 79 If possible, pressure check the system at least once a year to help catch problems before something fails

88151G52

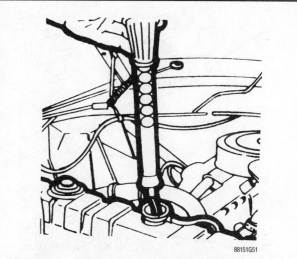

88151G51

Fig. 80 Use an antifreeze/coolant testing hydrometer to check the condition of the coolant in your engine

Check the Radiator Cap

▶ See Figure 81

While you are checking the coolant level, check the radiator cap for a worn or cracked gasket. If the top doesn't seal properly, fluid will be lost and the engine will overheat. Worn caps should be replaced with new ones.

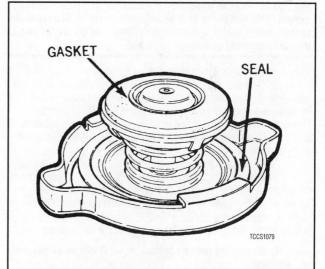

GASKET

SEAL

TCCS1079

Fig. 81 Be sure the rubber gasket on the radiator cap has a tight seal

Clean Radiator of Debris

▶ See Figure 82

Periodically, clean any debris—leaves, paper, insects, etc.—from the radiator fins. Pick the large pieces off by hand. The smaller pieces can be washed away with water pressure from a hose.

Carefully straighten any bent radiator fins with a pair of needlenosed pliers. Be careful; the fins are very soft. Don't wiggle the fins back and forth too much. Straighten them once and try not to move them again.

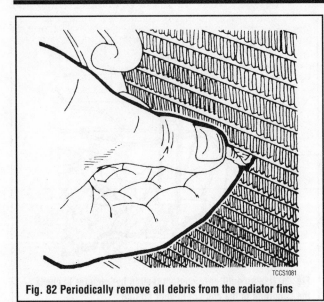

Fig. 82 Periodically remove all debris from the radiator fins

To drain and refill the coolant, remove the radiator and overflow reservoir caps

DRAIN, FLUSH & REFILL

3.8L and 5.0L Engines

> **✳✳ CAUTION**
>
> **When draining coolant, keep in mind that cats and dogs are attracted to ethylene glycol antifreeze, and are likely to drink any that is left in an uncovered container or in puddles on the ground. This will prove fatal in sufficient quantity. Always drain coolant into a sealable container. Coolant may be reused unless it is contaminated or several years old.**

A complete drain and refill of the cooling system at least every 30,000 miles (48,000 km) or 3 years will remove the accumulated rust, scale and other deposits. The recommended coolant for most late model cars is a 50/50 mixture of ethylene glycol (or other suitable aluminum-compatible formula) and water for year-round use. Choose a good quality antifreeze with water pump lubricants, rust inhibitors and other corrosion inhibitors along with acid neutralizers.

1. Position a catch pan and drain the existing coolant. Open the radiator and engine drains (petcocks) or disconnect the bottom radiator hose at the radiator outlet. The engine block drain plugs can also be temporarily removed to drain coolant, but they are often hard to get at and it is not really necessary for this procedure. On 3.8L engines, also remove the upper bleed port cap (located on the center front portion of the intake manifold).

➡ **Before opening the radiator petcock, spray it with some penetrating lubricant.**

2. Close the petcock(s) or reconnect the hose (and install any block drain plugs which may have been removed), then fill the system with water.
3. Add a can of quality radiator flush.
4. On 3.8L engines, install the upper bleed port cap.
5. Idle the engine until the upper radiator hose gets hot.
6. Drain the system again.
7. Repeat this process until the drained water is clear and free of scale.
8. Close all drains/petcocks and connect any loose hose(s). On 3.8L engines, leave the bleed port open.
9. If equipped with a coolant recovery system, flush the reservoir with water and leave it empty.
10. Determine the capacity of the cooling system, then properly refill the system with a 50/50 mixture of fresh coolant and water, as follows:
    a. Fill the radiator with coolant until it reaches the radiator filler neck seat.

On the 3.8L engine, be sure to remove the bleed port cap . . .

. . . by loosening the center mounting bolt . . .

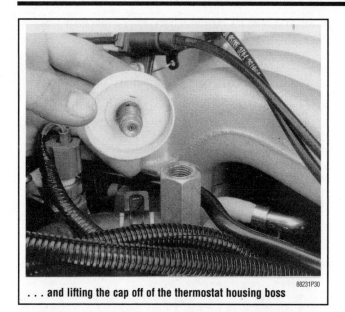

... and lifting the cap off of the thermostat housing boss

Attach any loosened hose(s) and close all drain plugs/petcocks, then fill the radiator ...

Locate the radiator petcock (arrow) ...

... until the coolant level is up to the fill neck—install the radiator cap and run the engine until hot ...

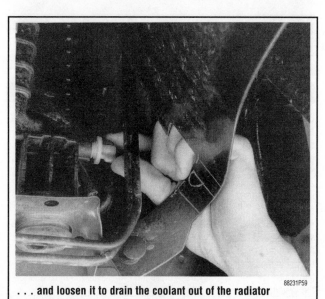

... and loosen it to drain the coolant out of the radiator

... then refill the radiator and overflow tank (shown). On 3.8L engines, be sure to close the bleed port

b. Start the engine and allow it to idle until the thermostat opens (the upper radiator hose will become hot). Coolant will flow out of the bleed port on 3.8L engines—this means that all of the trapped air has been bled from the system.

c. Turn the engine **OFF** and refill the radiator until the coolant level is at the filler neck seat. On 3.8L engines, close the bleed port.

d. Fill the engine coolant overflow tank with coolant to the FULL HOT mark, then install the radiator cap.

11. If available, install a pressure tester and check for leaks. If a pressure tester is not available, run the engine until normal operating temperature is reached (allowing the system to naturally pressurize), then check for leaks.

❄❄ CAUTION

If you are checking for leaks with the system at normal operating temperature, BE EXTREMELY CAREFUL not to touch any moving or hot engine parts. Once operating temperature has been reached, shut the engine OFF, and check for leaks around the hose fittings and connections which were removed earlier.

12. Check the level of protection with an antifreeze/coolant hydrometer.

4.6L Engines

♦ See Figure 83

❄❄ CAUTION

When draining coolant, keep in mind that cats and dogs are attracted to ethylene glycol antifreeze, and are likely to drink any that is left in an uncovered container or in puddles on the ground. This will prove fatal in sufficient quantity. Always drain coolant into a sealable container. Coolant may be reused unless it is contaminated or several years old.

A complete drain and refill of the cooling system at least every 30,000 miles (48,000 km) or 3 years will remove the accumulated rust, scale and other deposits. The recommended coolant for most late model cars is a 50/50 mixture of ethylene glycol (or other suitable aluminum-compatible formula) and water for year-round use. Choose a good quality antifreeze with water pump lubricants, rust inhibitors and other corrosion inhibitors along with acid neutralizers.

1. Position a catch pan and drain the existing coolant. Open the radiator and engine drains (petcocks) or disconnect the bottom radiator hose at the radiator outlet. The engine block drain plugs can also be temporarily removed to drain coolant, but they are often hard to get at and it is not really necessary for this procedure.

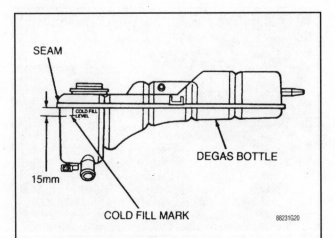

SEAM

COLD FILL LEVEL

DEGAS BOTTLE

15mm

COLD FILL MARK

88231G20

Fig. 83 When the cooling system is cold, the coolant level should fall just below the seam on the degas container

➡**Before opening the radiator petcock, spray it with some penetrating lubricant.**

2. Close the petcock or reconnect the hose (and install any block drain plugs which may have been removed), then fill the system with water.

3. Add a can of quality radiator flush.

4. Idle the engine until the upper radiator hose gets hot.

5. Drain the system again.

6. Repeat this process until the drained water is clear and free of scale.

7. Close all drains/petcocks and connect any loose hoses.

8. If equipped with a coolant recovery system, flush the reservoir with water and leave it empty.

9. Properly refill the cooling system with a 50/50 mixture of fresh coolant and water, as follows:

a. Fill the degas (overflow) container with coolant until it reaches the MAX mark. (The radiator will be filled by the degas bottle, so it may take a while until the degas container coolant level reaches the MAX mark.)

b. Install the cap on the degas container.

10. Bleed the cooling system as follows:

a. From inside the vehicle, turn the heater on to the hottest setting.

b. Start the engine and allow it to idle. While the engine idles, feel the air coming from the heater vents to check for heat. The air should become hot, the engine coolant temperature gauge should maintain a stable reading in the middle of the NORMAL range and the upper radiator hose should feel hot.

❄❄ CAUTION

If the heater air remains cool and the temperature gauge does not move, the engine coolant level is too low. Stop the engine, allow it to cool and refill the cooling system.

11. Continue running the engine and check for leaks.

❄❄ CAUTION

If you are checking for leaks with the system at normal operating temperature, BE EXTREMELY CAREFUL not to touch any moving or hot engine parts. Once the temperature has been reached, shut the engine OFF, and check for leaks around the hose fittings and connections which were removed earlier.

12. Allow the engine to cool completely, then top off the degas container with coolant, if necessary.

13. Check the level of protection with an antifreeze/coolant hydrometer.

Brake Master Cylinder

FLUID RECOMMENDATIONS

❄❄ WARNING

BRAKE FLUID EATS PAINT. Take great care not to splash or spill brake fluid on painted surfaces. Should you spill a small amount on the car's finish, don't panic, just flush the area with plenty of water.

When adding fluid to the system, ONLY use fresh DOT 3 (or superseding) brake fluid from a sealed container. DOT 3 brake fluid will absorb moisture when it is exposed to the atmosphere, which will lower its boiling point. A container that has been opened once, closed and placed on a shelf will allow enough moisture to enter over time to contaminate the fluid within. If your brake fluid is contaminated with water, you could boil the brake fluid under hard braking and lose all or some of the brake system. Don't take the risk; buy fresh brake fluid whenever you must add to the system.

LEVEL CHECK

Brake fluid level and condition is a safety related item and it should be checked ANY TIME the hood is opened. Your vehicle should not use brake fluid rapidly (unless there is a leak in the system), but the level should drop slowly in relation to brake pad wear.

The master cylinder reservoir is located under the hood, on the left side of the firewall. All vehicles covered by this manual should be equipped with a see-through plastic reservoir. This makes checking the level easy and helps reduce the risk of fluid contamination (since you don't have to expose the fluid by opening the cap to check the level). Fluid should be kept near the FULL line or between the MIN and MAX lines, depending on how the reservoir is marked.

If it becomes necessary to add fluid to the system, take a moment to clean the area around the cap and reservoir. Use a clean rag to wipe away dust and dirt which could enter the reservoir after the cover is removed. If the level of the brake fluid is less than half the volume of the reservoir (and the brake pads are not approaching a replacement point), it is advised that you check the brake system for leaks. Leaks in the hydraulic system often occur at the wheel cylinders.

The brake master cylinder fluid level should be at the MAX mark

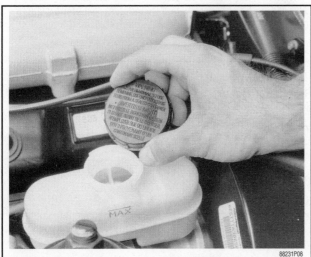

If the fluid level is low, unscrew the master cylinder reservoir cap . . .

. . . and fill the reservoir with clean DOT 3 brake fluid

Power Steering Pump Reservoir

FLUID RECOMMENDATIONS

1994–95 Models

The 1994–95 Mustangs use either Type F Automatic Transmission Fluid (ATF) or Ford Premium Power Steering Fluid meeting Ford specification ESW-M2C33-F. Ensure that the fluid added to the power steering pump reservoir is new and clean.

1996–98 Models

The 1996–98 Mustangs use Mercon® Automatic Transmission Fluid (ATF). Ensure that the fluid added to the power steering pump reservoir is new and clean.

LEVEL CHECK

The level of the power steering fluid should be checked in the reservoir periodically, at least once a year. Fluid is checked using the dipstick which is attached to the reservoir cap. Although the dipstick is equipped with range markings so that you can check the fluid hot or cold, it is recommended that you check the fluid at normal operating temperature (HOT).

✳✳ WARNING

Extensive driving with a low power steering fluid level can damage the power steering pump.

➡The power steering pump on 1994–95 vehicles requires the use of power steering fluid that meets Ford's specification ESW-M2C33-F, or an equivalent Type F ATF. 1996–98 models require Mercon® ATF.

1. Warm the fluid to normal operating temperature by driving for at least one mile, or start the engine and allow it to idle for five minutes.
2. With the engine idling, turn the steering wheel back-and-forth several times from lock-to-lock, then center the wheels and shut the engine **OFF**.
3. Locate the power steering pump reservoir. Twist and remove the cap/dipstick and note the level as indicated by the markings. To be sure of your reading, put the cap back in position, remove it again and double check the level.
4. If the level is below the indicator markings, add fluid to bring it up to the proper level (a funnel is usually very helpful). If you are checking the level after running the engine or driving, make sure you add enough fluid to bring it to the FULL HOT range, but like most automotive fluids, DO NOT overfill.
5. When you are finished, install the cap and be sure it is secure.

To check the power steering fluid, twist and remove the fill cap/dipstick from the reservoir . . .

. . . then read the fluid level on the dipstick—the dipstick has markings for when the engine is cold . . .

If the fluid level is low, add the recommended type of clean fluid to the reservoir

Chassis Greasing

Chassis greasing should be performed every 12 months or 12,000 miles (19,000 km) for most cars. Greasing can be performed with a commercial pressurized grease gun or at home by using a hand-operated grease gun. Wipe the grease fittings clean before greasing in order to prevent the possibility of forcing any dirt into the component.

There are far fewer grease points on the modern automotive chassis than there were on cars of yesteryear. The tie rod ends on these vehicles should be checked and lubricated periodically, and the front suspension should be checked for grease fittings.

A water resistant long-life grease that meets Ford's ESA-M1C75-B specification should be used for all chassis greasing applications.

Body Lubrication

Whenever you take care of chassis greasing, it is also advised that you walk around the vehicle and give attention to a number of other surfaces which require a variety of lubrication/protection.

HOOD/DOOR LATCH & HINGES

Wipe clean any exposed surfaces of the door hatches and hinges, hood latch and auxiliary catch. Then, treat the surfaces using a multi-purpose grease spray that meets Ford's ESR-M1C159-A specification.

LOCK CYLINDERS

These should be treated with Ford Lock Lubricant, Part No. D8AZ-19587-AA or equivalent. Consult your local parts supplier for equivalent lubricants.

DOOR WEATHERSTRIPPING

Spray the door weatherstripping using a silicone lubricant to help preserve the rubber.

CLUTCH, THROTTLE VALVE (TV) & KICKDOWN LINKAGE

A water resistant long life grease that meets Ford's ESA-M1C75-B specification should be used for all linkages.

. . . and hot—it is better to check the fluid when the engine is hot

TRAILER TOWING

The 1994–98 Mustang cars were not designed with trailer towing in mind. Because of the additional strain placed on your car's engine, drive train, steering, braking and other systems when towing a trailer, and because of the Mustang's frame and lower body valance design, it is a good idea to avoid towing a trailer with a Mustang.

TOWING THE VEHICLE

Preferred Method—Flatbed

▶ **See Figure 84**

For maximum safety to the components of your drive train and chassis, it is most desirable to have your vehicle towed by on a flatbed or whole car trailer. The only way to properly place the vehicle on a flatbed is to have it pulled on from the front.

✳✳ WARNING

For the Mustang Cobra model, a flatbed is a requirement, as any other method will likely damage body components.

Alternate Method—T-Hook

▶ **See Figure 85**

If a flatbed is unavailable, your car (unless it is a Cobra) can be towed using a T-hook wrecker. In this case, it is best to tow from the rear, with the rear wheels off the ground, as this will prevent wear and tear on the drive train. Make sure the transmission is in N (Neutral) and that the parking brake is released. Tow vehicle speed should not exceed 35 mph (56 km/h) when using this method.

When necessary, you can tow using the T-hook in the front, with the rear wheels on the ground, BUT all of the previous conditions for rear towing

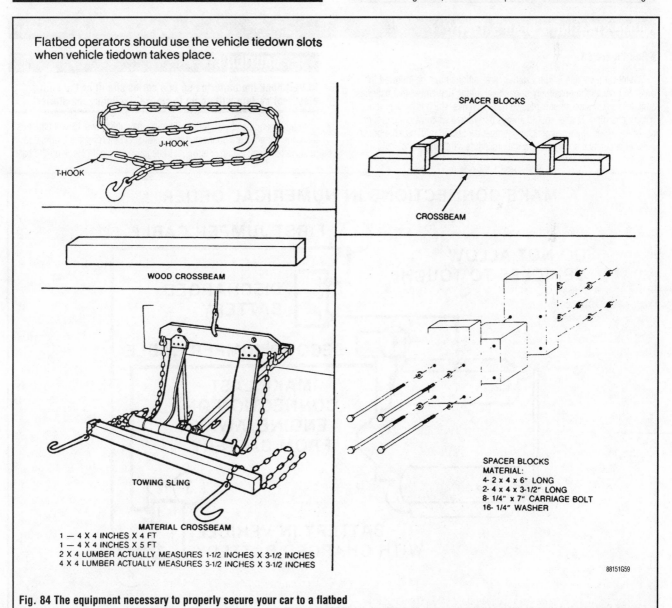

Flatbed operators should use the vehicle tiedown slots when vehicle tiedown takes place.

J-HOOK

T-HOOK

WOOD CROSSBEAM

TOWING SLING

MATERIAL CROSSBEAM
1 — 4 X 4 INCHES X 4 FT
1 — 4 X 4 INCHES X 5 FT
2 X 4 LUMBER ACTUALLY MEASURES 1-1/2 INCHES X 3-1/2 INCHES
4 X 4 LUMBER ACTUALLY MEASURES 3-1/2 INCHES X 3-1/2 INCHES

SPACER BLOCKS

CROSSBEAM

SPACER BLOCKS
MATERIAL:
4- 2 x 4 x 6" LONG
2- 4 x 4 x 3-1/2" LONG
8- 1/4" x 7" CARRIAGE BOLT
16- 1/4" WASHER

88151G59

Fig. 84 The equipment necessary to properly secure your car to a flatbed

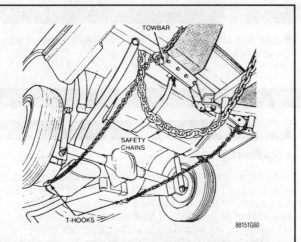

Fig. 85 When necessary, the car (unless it is a Cobra) can be towed from the rear (with the rear wheels off the ground) using a T-hook

are applicable AND the total distance towed should NOT EXCEED 50 miles (80 km). Otherwise, transmission damage may occur unless the driveshaft is removed.

Last Chance Method—Dolly

If absolutely necessary, you can tow your vehicle with either the front or rear wheels on a dolly. Again the preferred method would be to leave the front wheels on the ground and the rear on the dolly so the drive train is not turning. All conditions which apply to the T-hook method also apply to the dolly method.

JUMP STARTING A DEAD BATTERY

▶ **See Figure 86**

Whenever a vehicle is jump started, precautions must be followed in order to prevent the possibility of personal injury. Remember that batteries contain a small amount of explosive hydrogen gas which is a by-product of battery charging. Sparks should always be avoided when working around batteries, especially when attaching jumper cables. To minimize the possibility of accidental sparks, follow the procedure carefully.

❊❊ CAUTION

NEVER hook the batteries up in a series circuit or the entire electrical system will go up in smoke, including the starter!

Vehicles equipped with a diesel engine may utilize two 12 volt batteries. If so, the batteries are connected in a parallel circuit (positive terminal to positive terminal, negative terminal to negative terminal). Hooking the bat-

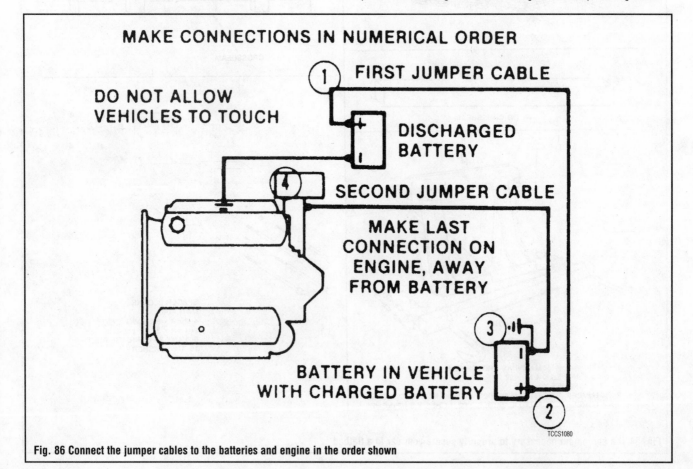

Fig. 86 Connect the jumper cables to the batteries and engine in the order shown

teries up in parallel circuit increases battery cranking power without increasing total battery voltage output. Output remains at 12 volts. On the other hand, hooking two 12 volt batteries up in a series circuit (positive terminal to negative terminal, positive terminal to negative terminal) increases total battery output to 24 volts (12 volts plus 12 volts).

Jump Starting Precautions

- Be sure that both batteries are of the same voltage. Vehicles covered by this manual and most vehicles on the road today utilize a 12 volt charging system.
- Be sure that both batteries are of the same polarity (have the same terminal, in most cases NEGATIVE grounded).
- Be sure that the vehicles are not touching or a short could occur.
- On serviceable batteries, be sure the vent cap holes are not obstructed.
- Do not smoke or allow sparks anywhere near the batteries.
- In cold weather, make sure the battery electrolyte is not frozen. This can occur more readily in a battery that has been in a state of discharge.
- Do not allow electrolyte to contact your skin or clothing.

Jump Starting Procedure

1. Make sure that the voltages of the 2 batteries are the same. Most batteries and charging systems are of the 12 volt variety.
2. Pull the jumping vehicle (with the good battery) into a position so the jumper cables can reach the dead battery and that vehicle's engine. Make sure that the vehicles do NOT touch.
3. Place the transmissions/transaxles of both vehicles in **Neutral** (MT) or **P** (AT), as applicable, then firmly set their parking brakes.

➡️**If necessary for safety reasons, the hazard lights on both vehicles may be operated throughout the entire procedure without significantly increasing the difficulty of jumping the dead battery.**

4. Turn all lights and accessories OFF on both vehicles. Make sure the ignition switches on both vehicles are turned to the **OFF** position.
5. Cover the battery cell caps with a rag, but do not cover the terminals.
6. Make sure the terminals on both batteries are clean and free of corrosion or proper electrical connection will be impeded. If necessary, clean the battery terminals before proceeding.

7. Identify the positive (+) and negative (-) terminals on both batteries.
8. Connect the first jumper cable to the positive (+) terminal of the dead battery, then connect the other end of that cable to the positive (+) terminal of the booster (good) battery.
9. Connect one end of the other jumper cable to the negative (& minus;) terminal on the booster battery and the final cable clamp to an engine bolt head, alternator bracket or other solid, metallic point on the engine with the dead battery. Try to pick a ground on the engine that is positioned away from the battery in order to minimize the possibility of the 2 clamps touching should one loosen during the procedure. DO NOT connect this clamp to the negative (-) terminal of the bad battery.

✳️✳️ CAUTION

Be very careful to keep the jumper cables away from moving parts (cooling fan, belts, etc.) on both engines.

10. Check to make sure that the cables are routed away from any moving parts, then start the donor vehicle's engine. Run the engine at moderate speed for several minutes to allow the dead battery a chance to receive some initial charge.
11. With the donor vehicle's engine still running slightly above idle, try to start the vehicle with the dead battery. Crank the engine for no more than 10 seconds at a time and let the starter cool for at least 20 seconds between tries. If the vehicle does not start in 3 tries, it is likely that something else is also wrong or that the battery needs additional time to charge.
12. Once the vehicle is started, allow it to run at idle for a few seconds to make sure that it is operating properly.
13. Turn ON the headlights, heater blower and, if equipped, the rear defroster of both vehicles in order to reduce the severity of voltage spikes and subsequent risk of damage to the vehicles' electrical systems when the cables are disconnected. This step is especially important to any vehicle equipped with computer control modules.
14. Carefully disconnect the cables in the reverse order of connection. Start with the negative cable that is attached to the engine ground, then the negative cable on the donor battery. Disconnect the positive cable from the donor battery and finally, disconnect the positive cable from the formerly dead battery. Be careful when disconnecting the cables from the positive terminals not to allow the alligator clips to touch any metal on either vehicle or a short and sparks will occur.

JACKING

▶ See Figure 87

Your vehicle was supplied with a jack for emergency road repairs. This jack is fine for changing a flat tire or other short term procedures not requiring you to go beneath the vehicle. If it is used in an emergency situation, carefully follow the instructions provided either with the jack or in your owner's manual. Do not attempt to use the jack on any portions of the vehicle other than specified by the vehicle manufacturer.

✳️✳️ CAUTION

It is very important to be careful about running the engine on vehicles equipped with limited slip differentials while on a jack. When the drive train is engaged, power is transmitted to the wheel with the best traction. If one drive wheel is in contact with the ground, the vehicle will drive off the jack, possibly resulting in severe injury or damage.

Always raise a Ford car from under the axles, suspension arms or frame rails, and be sure to block the diagonally opposite wheel. Place jackstands under the vehicle at the indicated points or directly under the frame when you are going to work under the vehicle.

With the exception of a hoist (which most of us would love to have, but where would we put it?), the most convenient way of raising the vehicle is the use of a garage or floor jack. You may use the floor jack on any of the frame and suspension points illustrated.

Never place the jack under the radiator, engine or transmission components. Severe and expensive damage will result when the jack is raised. Additionally, never jack under the floorpan or bodywork; the metal will deform.

✳️✳️ CAUTION

NEVER WORK OR EVEN REACH UNDER A VEHICLE THAT IS NOT PROPERLY SUPPORTED. We are talking about your life here and the few minutes it takes to position a set of jackstands are precious little to ask to protect it.

Whenever you plan to work under the vehicle, you must support it on jackstands or ramps. NEVER use cinder blocks or stacks of wood to support the vehicle, even if you're only going to be under it for a few minutes. Never crawl under the vehicle when it is supported only by the tire-changing jack or other floor jack.

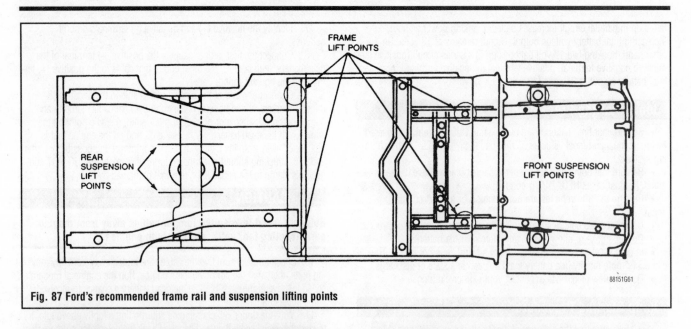

Fig. 87 Ford's recommended frame rail and suspension lifting points

Raise the front of the vehicle with a floor jack beneath the No. 2 crossmember . . .

Raise the rear of the vehicle with a floor jack beneath the rear jacking support . . .

. . . and secure the vehicle with jackstands beneath the jacking/support points, behind the front wheels

. . . and support it with jackstands positioned under the rear axle tubes

➡**Always position a block of wood or small rubber pad on top of the jack or jackstand to protect the lifting point's finish when lifting or supporting the vehicle.**

Small hydraulic, screw, or scissors jacks are satisfactory for raising the vehicle. Drive-on trestles or ramps are also a handy and safe way to both raise and support the vehicle. Be careful though, some ramps may be too steep to drive your vehicle onto without scraping the front bottom panels. The ground effects on many of the performance Mustangs will not easily clear the steep grade of the ramps (although one option might be to use the ramps like jackstands that you place under the tires once the vehicle is raised). Never support the vehicle on any suspension member (unless specifically instructed to do so by a repair manual) or by an underbody panel.

Jacking Precautions

The following safety points cannot be overemphasized:
- Always block the opposite wheel (or wheels) to keep the vehicle from rolling off the jack.
- When raising the front of the vehicle, firmly apply the parking brake.
- DON'T run the engine while the vehicle is on jackstands, ESPECIALLY if one or more drive wheels are remaining on the ground.
- When the drive wheels are to remain on the ground, leave the vehicle in gear to help prevent it from rolling.
- Always use jackstands to support the vehicle when you are working underneath. Place the stands beneath the vehicle's jacking brackets. Before climbing underneath, rock the vehicle a bit to make sure it is firmly supported.

CAPACITIES

Year	Model	Engine ID/VIN	Engine Displacement Liters (cc)	Engine Oil with Filter	Transmission (pts.) T-45 ①	Transmission (pts.) T-50 ①	Transmission (pts.) Auto. ②	Rear Drive Axle (pts.)	Fuel Tank (gal.)	Cooling System (qts.)
1994	Mustang	4	3.8 (3802)	5.0	—	5.6	25.0	③	15.4	11.8
	Mustang Cobra	D	5.0 (4949)	5.0	—	5.6	25.0	③	15.4	14.1
	Mustang	T	5.0 (4949)	5.0	—	5.6	25.0	③	15.4	14.1
1995	Mustang	4	3.8 (3802)	5.0	—	5.6	27.2	③	15.4	11.8
	Mustang Cobra	D	5.0 (4949)	5.0	—	5.6	27.2	③	15.4	14.1
	Mustang	T	5.0 (4949)	5.0	—	5.6	27.2	③	15.4	14.1
1996	Mustang	4	3.8 (3802)	5.0	—	5.6	27.2	③	15.4	11.8
	Mustang Cobra	V	4.6 (4593)	6.0	6.4-6.7	—	—	③	15.4	14.1
	Mustang	W	4.6 (4593)	④	6.4-6.7	—	27.2	③	15.4	14.1
1997	Mustang	4	3.8 (3802)	5.0	—	5.6	27.2	③	15.4	11.8
	Mustang Cobra	V	4.6 (4593)	6.0	6.4-6.7	—	—	③	15.4	14.1
	Mustang	W	4.6 (4593)	④	6.4-6.7	—	27.2	③	15.4	14.1
1998	Mustang	4	3.8 (3802)	5.0	—	5.6	27.2	③	15.4	11.8
	Mustang Cobra	V	4.6 (4593)	6.0	6.4-6.7	—	—	③	15.4	14.1
	Mustang	W	4.6 (4593)	④	6.4-6.7	—	27.2	③	15.4	14.1

Note: All capacities are approximate. Add fluid gradually and check to be sure a proper fluid level is obtained.
① 5-speed manual transmission
② 5-speed manual transmission
③ 7.50" axle: 3.5 pts.
   8.80" axle: 3.75 pts.
④ Automatic transmission: 6.7 qts.
   Manual transmission: 6.4 qts.

88231C05

MANUFACTURER RECOMMENDED MAINTENANCE INTERVALS

VEHICLE MILEAGE INTERVAL (x1000)

TO BE SERVICED	5 / 95	10 / 100	15 / 105	20 / 110	25 / 115	30 / 120	35 / 125	40 / 130	45 / 135	50 / 140	55 / 145	60 / 150	65 / 155	70 / 160	75 / 165	80 / 170	85 / 175	90 / 180
Adjust clutch	✓	✓	✓	✓	✓	✓	✓	✓	✓	✓	✓	✓	✓	✓	✓	✓	✓	✓
Change ATF and filter						✓						✓						✓
Change engine coolant and flush the cooling system						✓						✓						✓
Change engine oil and filter ①	✓	✓	✓	✓	✓	✓	✓	✓	✓	✓	✓	✓	✓	✓	✓	✓	✓	✓
Change rear axle lubricant ②		✓																
Inspect accessory drive belt						✓						✓						✓
Inspect brake pads and rotors						✓						✓						✓
Inspect engine cooling system ③			✓			✓			✓			✓			✓			✓
Inspect exhaust heat shields						✓						✓						✓
Replace air cleaner element						✓						✓						✓
Replace PCV valve ④												✓						
Replace spark plugs												✓						
Rotate tires and check air pressure	✓		✓		✓		✓		✓		✓		✓		✓		✓	

① The engine oil and filter should be changed every 5,000 miles (8,000 km) or 6 months, whichever occurs first.
② Change the rear axle lubricant every 100,000 miles (160,000 km) or whenever the rear axle is submerged in water.
③ Perform this service every 15,000 miles (24,000 km) or 12 months, whichever occurs first.
④ On the 5.0L engine, this includes replacing the crankcase emission air filter.

88231C03

MANUFACTURER RECOMMENDED SEVERE MAINTENANCE INTERVALS①

VEHICLE MILEAGE INTERVAL (x1000)

TO BE SERVICED	3 / 63 / 123	6 / 66 / 126	9 / 69 / 129	12 / 72 / 132	15 / 75 / 135	18 / 78 / 138	21 / 81 / 141	24 / 84 / 144	27 / 87 / 147	30 / 90 / 150	33 / 93 / 153	36 / 96 / 156	39 / 99 / 159	42 / 102 / 162	45 / 105 / 165	48 / 108 / 168	51 / 111 / 171	54 / 114 / 174	57 / 117 / 177	60 / 120 / 180
Adjust clutch	✓	✓		✓		✓		✓		✓		✓		✓		✓		✓		✓
Change ATF and filter														✓						
Change engine coolant and flush the system ②																✓				
Change engine oil and filter ③	✓	✓	✓	✓	✓	✓	✓	✓	✓	✓	✓	✓	✓	✓	✓	✓	✓	✓	✓	✓
Change rear axle lubricant ④										✓										
Inspect accessory drive belt															✓					✓
Inspect brake pads and rotors					✓					✓					✓					✓
Inspect engine cooling system										✓										✓
Inspect exhaust heat shields										✓										✓
Replace air cleaner element ⑤										✓										✓
Replace PCV valve										✓										✓
Replace spark plugs–5.0L engine										✓										✓
Replace spark plugs–except 5.0L engine																				✓
Rotate tires and check air pressure		✓			✓			✓			✓			✓			✓			✓

① If a vehicle is operated under any of the following conditions it is considered severe service:
- Extremely dusty areas.
- 50% or more of the vehicle operation is in 90°F (32°C) or higher temperatures, or constant operation in temperatures below 32°F (0°C).
- Prolonged idling (vehicle operation in stop-and-go traffic).
- Frequent short running periods (engine does not warm to normal operating temperature).
- Police, taxi, delivery usage or trailer towing usage.

② Initially change the coolant at the 48,000 mile (76,800 km) mark. Thereafter, replace it every 30,000 miles (48,000 km).

③ Change the engine oil every 3,000 miles or 3 months, whichever occurs first.

④ Change the rear axle lubricant every 100,000 miles (160,000 km) or whenever the rear axle is submerged in water.

⑤ On 5.0L engines, replace the crankcase emission air filter as well.

88231C04

ENGLISH TO METRIC CONVERSION: MASS (WEIGHT)

Current **mass** measurement is expressed in pounds and ounces (lbs. & ozs.). The metric unit of mass (or weight) is the kilogram (kg). Even although this table does not show conversion of masses (weights) larger than 15 lbs, it is easy to calculate larger units by following the data immediately below.

To convert ounces (oz.) to grams (g): multiply th number of ozs. by 28
To convert grams (g) to ounces (oz.): multiply the number of grams by .035

To convert pounds (lbs.) to kilograms (kg): multiply the number of lbs. by .45
To convert kilograms (kg) to pounds (lbs.): multiply the number of kilograms by 2.2

lbs	kg	lbs	kg	oz	kg	oz	kg
0.1	0.04	0.9	0.41	0.1	0.003	0.9	0.024
0.2	0.09	1	0.4	0.2	0.005	1	0.03
0.3	0.14	2	0.9	0.3	0.008	2	0.06
0.4	0.18	3	1.4	0.4	0.011	3	0.08
0.5	0.23	4	1.8	0.5	0.014	4	0.11
0.6	0.27	5	2.3	0.6	0.017	5	0.14
0.7	0.32	10	4.5	0.7	0.020	10	0.28
0.8	0.36	15	6.8	0.8	0.023	15	0.42

ENGLISH TO METRIC CONVERSION: TEMPERATURE

To convert Fahrenheit (°F) to Celsius (°C): take number of °F and subtract 32; multiply result by 5; divide result by 9

To convert Celsius (°C) to Fahrenheit (°F): take number of °C and multiply by 9; divide result by 5; add 32 to total

Fahrenheit (F)		Celsius (C)		Fahrenheit (F)		Celsius (C)		Fahrenheit (F)		Celsius (C)	
°F	°C	°C	°F	°F	°C	°C	°F	°F	°C	°C	°F
−40	−40	−38	−36.4	80	26.7	18	64.4	215	101.7	80	176
−35	−37.2	−36	−32.8	85	29.4	20	68	220	104.4	85	185
−30	−34.4	−34	−29.2	90	32.2	22	71.6	225	107.2	90	194
−25	−31.7	−32	−25.6	95	35.0	24	75.2	230	110.0	95	202
−20	−28.9	−30	−22	100	37.8	26	78.8	235	112.8	100	212
−15	−26.1	−28	−18.4	105	40.6	28	82.4	240	115.6	105	221
−10	−23.3	−26	−14.8	110	43.3	30	86	245	118.3	110	230
−5	−20.6	−24	−11.2	115	46.1	32	89.6	250	121.1	115	239
0	−17.8	−22	−7.6	120	48.9	34	93.2	255	123.9	120	248
1	−17.2	−20	−4	125	51.7	36	96.8	260	126.6	125	257
2	−16.7	−18	−0.4	130	54.4	38	100.4	265	129.4	130	266
3	−16.1	−16	3.2	135	57.2	40	104	270	132.2	135	275
4	−15.6	−14	6.8	140	60.0	42	107.6	275	135.0	140	284
5	−15.0	−12	10.4	145	62.8	44	112.2	280	137.8	145	293
10	−12.2	−10	14	150	65.6	46	114.8	285	140.6	150	302
15	−9.4	−8	17.6	155	68.3	48	118.4	290	143.3	155	311
20	−6.7	−6	21.2	160	71.1	50	122	295	146.1	160	320
25	−3.9	−4	24.8	165	73.9	52	125.6	300	148.9	165	329
30	−1.1	−2	28.4	170	76.7	54	129.2	305	151.7	170	338
35	1.7	0	32	175	79.4	56	132.8	310	154.4	175	347
40	4.4	2	35.6	180	82.2	58	136.4	315	157.2	180	356
45	7.2	4	39.2	185	85.0	60	140	320	160.0	185	365
50	10.0	6	42.8	190	87.8	62	143.6	325	162.8	190	374
55	12.8	8	46.4	195	90.6	64	147.2	330	165.6	195	383
60	15.6	10	50	200	93.3	66	150.8	335	168.3	200	392
65	18.3	12	53.6	205	96.1	68	154.4	340	171.1	205	401
70	21.1	14	57.2	210	98.9	70	158	345	173.9	210	410
75	23.9	16	60.8	212	100.0	75	167	350	176.7	215	414

ENGLISH TO METRIC CONVERSION: LENGTH

To convert inches (ins.) to millimeters (mm): multiply number of inches by 25.4

To convert millimeters (mm) to inches (ins.): multiply number of millimeters by .04

Inches		Decimals	Milli-meters	Inches to millimeters		Inches		Decimals	Milli-meters	Inches to millimeters	
				inches	mm					inches	mm
	1/64	0.051625	0.3969	0.0001	0.00254		33/64	0.515625	13.0969	0.6	15.24
1/32		0.03125	0.7937	0.0002	0.00508	17/32		0.53125	13.4937	0.7	17.78
	3/64	0.046875	1.1906	0.0003	0.00762		35/64	0.546875	13.8906	0.8	20.32
1/16		0.0625	1.5875	0.0004	0.01016	9/16		0.5625	14.2875	0.9	22.86
	5/64	0.078125	1.9844	0.0005	0.01270		37/64	0.578125	14.6844	1	25.4
3/32		0.09375	2.3812	0.0006	0.01524	19/32		0.59375	15.0812	2	50.8
	7/64	0.109375	2.7781	0.0007	0.01778		39/64	0.609375	15.4781	3	76.2
1/8		0.125	3.1750	0.0008	0.02032	5/8		0.625	15.8750	4	101.6
	9/64	0.140625	3.5719	0.0009	0.02286		41/64	0.640625	16.2719	5	127.0
5/32		0.15625	3.9687	0.001	0.0254	21/32		0.65625	16.6687	6	152.4
	11/64	0.171875	4.3656	0.002	0.0508		43/64	0.671875	17.0656	7	177.8
3/16		0.1875	4.7625	0.003	0.0762	11/16		0.6875	17.4625	8	203.2
	13/64	0.203125	5.1594	0.004	0.1016		45/64	0.703125	17.8594	9	228.6
7/32		0.21875	5.5562	0.005	0.1270	23/32		0.71875	18.2562	10	254.0
	15/64	0.234375	5.9531	0.006	0.1524		47/64	0.734375	18.6531	11	279.4
1/4		0.25	6.3500	0.007	0.1778	3/4		0.75	19.0500	12	304.8
	17/64	0.265625	6.7469	0.008	0.2032		49/64	0.765625	19.4469	13	330.2
9/32		0.28125	7.1437	0.009	0.2286	25/32		0.78125	19.8437	14	355.6
	19/64	0.296875	7.5406	0.01	0.254		51/64	0.796875	20.2406	15	381.0
5/16		0.3125	7.9375	0.02	0.508	13/16		0.8125	20.6375	16	406.4
	21/64	0.328125	8.3344	0.03	0.762		53/64	0.828125	21.0344	17	431.8
11/32		0.34375	8.7312	0.04	1.016	27/32		0.84375	21.4312	18	457.2
	23/64	0.359375	9.1281	0.05	1.270		55/64	0.859375	21.8281	19	482.6
3/8		0.375	9.5250	0.06	1.524	7/8		0.875	22.2250	20	508.0
	25/64	0.390625	9.9219	0.07	1.778		57/64	0.890625	22.6219	21	533.4
13/32		0.40625	10.3187	0.08	2.032	29/32		0.90625	23.0187	22	558.8
	27/64	0.421875	10.7156	0.09	2.286		59/64	0.921875	23.4156	23	584.2
7/16		0.4375	11.1125	0.1	2.54	15/16		0.9375	23.8125	24	609.6
	29/64	0.453125	11.5094	0.2	5.08		61/64	0.953125	24.2094	25	635.0
15/32		0.46875	11.9062	0.3	7.62	31/32		0.96875	24.6062	26	660.4
	31/64	0.484375	12.3031	0.4	10.16		63/64	0.984375	25.0031	27	690.6
1/2		0.5	12.7000	0.5	12.70						

ENGLISH TO METRIC CONVERSION: TORQUE

To convert foot-pounds (ft. lbs.) to Newton-meters: multiply the number of ft. lbs. by 1.3

To convert inch-pounds (in. lbs.) to Newton-meters: multiply the number of in. lbs. by .11

in lbs	N-m	in lbs	N-m	in lbs	N-m	in lbs	N-m	in lbs	N-m
0.1	0.01	1	0.11	10	1.13	19	2.15	28	3.16
0.2	0.02	2	0.23	11	1.24	20	2.26	29	3.28
0.3	0.03	3	0.34	12	1.36	21	2.37	30	3.39
0.4	0.04	4	0.45	13	1.47	22	2.49	31	3.50
0.5	0.06	5	0.56	14	1.58	23	2.60	32	3.62
0.6	0.07	6	0.68	15	1.70	24	2.71	33	3.73
0.7	0.08	7	0.78	16	1.81	25	2.82	34	3.84
0.8	0.09	8	0.90	17	1.92	26	2.94	35	3.95
0.9	0.10	9	1.02	18	2.03	27	3.05	36	4.0

TCCS1C02

ENGLISH TO METRIC CONVERSION: TORQUE

Torque is now expressed as either foot-pounds (ft./lbs.) or inch-pounds (in./lbs.). The metric measurement unit for torque is the Newton-meter (Nm). This unit—the Nm—will be used for all SI metric torque references, both the present ft./lbs. and in./lbs.

ft lbs	N-m	ft lbs	N-m	ft lbs	N-m	ft lbs	N-m
0.1	0.1	33	44.7	74	100.3	115	155.9
0.2	0.3	34	46.1	75	101.7	116	157.3
0.3	0.4	35	47.4	76	103.0	117	158.6
0.4	0.5	36	48.8	77	104.4	118	160.0
0.5	0.7	37	50.7	78	105.8	119	161.3
0.6	0.8	38	51.5	79	107.1	120	162.7
0.7	1.0	39	52.9	80	108.5	121	164.0
0.8	1.1	40	54.2	81	109.8	122	165.4
0.9	1.2	41	55.6	82	111.2	123	166.8
1	1.3	42	56.9	83	112.5	124	168.1
2	2.7	43	58.3	84	113.9	125	169.5
3	4.1	44	59.7	85	115.2	126	170.8
4	5.4	45	61.0	86	116.6	127	172.2
5	6.8	46	62.4	87	118.0	128	173.5
6	8.1	47	63.7	88	119.3	129	174.9
7	9.5	48	65.1	89	120.7	130	176.2
8	10.8	49	66.4	90	122.0	131	177.6
9	12.2	50	67.8	91	123.4	132	179.0
10	13.6	51	69.2	92	124.7	133	180.3
11	14.9	52	70.5	93	126.1	134	181.7
12	16.3	53	71.9	94	127.4	135	183.0
13	17.6	54	73.2	95	128.8	136	184.4
14	18.9	55	74.6	96	130.2	137	185.7
15	20.3	56	75.9	97	131.5	138	187.1
16	21.7	57	77.3	98	132.9	139	188.5
17	23.0	58	78.6	99	134.2	140	189.8
18	24.4	59	80.0	100	135.6	141	191.2
19	25.8	60	81.4	101	136.9	142	192.5
20	27.1	61	82.7	102	138.3	143	193.9
21	28.5	62	84.1	103	139.6	144	195.2
22	29.8	63	85.4	104	141.0	145	196.6
23	31.2	64	86.8	105	142.4	146	198.0
24	32.5	65	88.1	106	143.7	147	199.3
25	33.9	66	89.5	107	145.1	148	200.7
26	35.2	67	90.8	108	146.4	149	202.0
27	36.6	68	92.2	109	147.8	150	203.4
28	38.0	69	93.6	110	149.1	151	204.7
29	39.3	70	94.9	111	150.5	152	206.1
30	40.7	71	96.3	112	151.8	153	207.4
31	42.0	72	97.6	113	153.2	154	208.8
32	43.4	73	99.0	114	154.6	155	210.2

TCCS1C03

ENGLISH TO METRIC CONVERSION: FORCE

Force is presently measured in pounds (lbs.). This type of measurement is used to measure spring pressure, specifically how many pounds it takes to compress a spring. Our present force unit (the pound) will be replaced in SI metric measurements by the Newton (N). This term will eventually see use in specifications for electric motor brush spring pressures, valve spring pressures, etc.

To convert pounds (lbs.) to Newton (N): multiply the number of lbs. by 4.45

lbs	N	lbs	N	lbs	N	oz	N
0.01	0.04	21	93.4	59	262.4	1	0.3
0.02	0.09	22	97.9	60	266.9	2	0.6
0.03	0.13	23	102.3	61	271.3	3	0.8
0.04	0.18	24	106.8	62	275.8	4	1.1
0.05	0.22	25	111.2	63	280.2	5	1.4
0.06	0.27	26	115.6	64	284.6	6	1.7
0.07	0.31	27	120.1	65	289.1	7	2.0
0.08	0.36	28	124.6	66	293.6	8	2.2
0.09	0.40	29	129.0	67	298.0	9	2.5
0.1	0.4	30	133.4	68	302.5	10	2.8
0.2	0.9	31	137.9	69	306.9	11	3.1
0.3	1.3	32	142.3	70	311.4	12	3.3
0.4	1.8	33	146.8	71	315.8	13	3.6
0.5	2.2	34	151.2	72	320.3	14	3.9
0.6	2.7	35	155.7	73	324.7	15	4.2
0.7	3.1	36	160.1	74	329.2	16	4.4
0.8	3.6	37	164.6	75	333.6	17	4.7
0.9	4.0	38	169.0	76	338.1	18	5.0
1	4.4	39	173.5	77	342.5	19	5.3
2	8.9	40	177.9	78	347.0	20	5.6
3	13.4	41	182.4	79	351.4	21	5.8
4	17.8	42	186.8	80	355.9	22	6.1
5	22.2	43	191.3	81	360.3	23	6.4
6	26.7	44	195.7	82	364.8	24	6.7
7	31.1	45	200.2	83	369.2	25	7.0
8	35.6	46	204.6	84	373.6	26	7.2
9	40.0	47	209.1	85	378.1	27	7.5
10	44.5	48	213.5	86	382.6	28	7.8
11	48.9	49	218.0	87	387.0	29	8.1
12	53.4	50	224.4	88	391.4	30	8.3
13	57.8	51	226.9	89	395.9	31	8.6
14	62.3	52	231.3	90	400.3	32	8.9
15	66.7	53	235.8	91	404.8	33	9.2
16	71.2	54	240.2	92	409.2	34	9.4
17	75.6	55	244.6	93	413.7	35	9.7
18	80.1	56	249.1	94	418.1	36	10.0
19	84.5	57	253.6	95	422.6	37	10.3
20	89.0	58	258.0	96	427.0	38	10.6

TCCS1C04

ENGLISH TO METRIC CONVERSION: LIQUID CAPACITY

Liquid or fluid capacity is presently expressed as pints, quarts or gallons, or a combination of all of these. In the metric system the liter (l) will become the basic unit. Fractions of a liter would be expressed as deciliters, centiliters, or most frequently (and commonly) as milliliters.

To convert pints (pts.) to liters (l): multiply the number of pints by .47
To convert liters (l) to pints (pts.): multiply the number of liters by 2.1
To convert quarts (qts.) to liters (l): multiply the number of quarts by .95

To convert liters (l) to quarts (qts.): multiply the number of liters by 1.06
To convert gallons (gals.) to liters (l): multiply the number of gallons by 3.8
To convert liters (l) to gallons (gals.): multiply the number of liters by .26

gals	liters	qts	liters	pts	liters
0.1	0.38	0.1	0.10	0.1	0.05
0.2	0.76	0.2	0.19	0.2	0.10
0.3	1.1	0.3	0.28	0.3	0.14
0.4	1.5	0.4	0.38	0.4	0.19
0.5	1.9	0.5	0.47	0.5	0.24
0.6	2.3	0.6	0.57	0.6	0.28
0.7	2.6	0.7	0.66	0.7	0.33
0.8	3.0	0.8	0.76	0.8	0.38
0.9	3.4	0.9	0.85	0.9	0.43
1	3.8	1	1.0	1	0.5
2	7.6	2	1.9	2	1.0
3	11.4	3	2.8	3	1.4
4	15.1	4	3.8	4	1.9
5	18.9	5	4.7	5	2.4
6	22.7	6	5.7	6	2.8
7	26.5	7	6.6	7	3.3
8	30.3	8	7.6	8	3.8
9	34.1	9	8.5	9	4.3
10	37.8	10	9.5	10	4.7
11	41.6	11	10.4	11	5.2
12	45.4	12	11.4	12	5.7
13	49.2	13	12.3	13	6.2
14	53.0	14	13.2	14	6.6
15	56.8	15	14.2	15	7.1
16	60.6	16	15.1	16	7.6
17	64.3	17	16.1	17	8.0
18	68.1	18	17.0	18	8.5
19	71.9	19	18.0	19	9.0
20	75.7	20	18.9	20	9.5
21	79.5	21	19.9	21	9.9
22	83.2	22	20.8	22	10.4
23	87.0	23	21.8	23	10.9
24	90.8	24	22.7	24	11.4
25	94.6	25	23.6	25	11.8
26	98.4	26	24.6	26	12.3
27	102.2	27	25.5	27	12.8
28	106.0	28	26.5	28	13.2
29	110.0	29	27.4	29	13.7
30	113.5	30	28.4	30	14.2

TCCS1C05

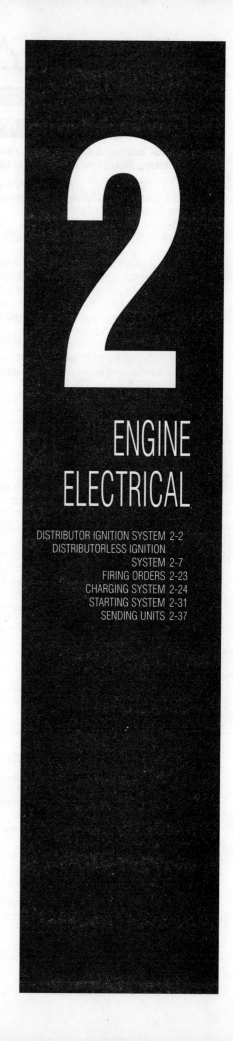

2

ENGINE ELECTRICAL

DISTRIBUTOR IGNITION SYSTEM

General Information

➡**For additional information on understanding and troubleshooting electrical systems, please refer to Section 6 of this manual.**

Only the 5.0L engine is equipped with the distributor ignition system. The distributor ignition system consists of the following components:
- Ignition Control Module (ICM)
- Distributor
- Camshaft Position (CMP) sensor (a Hall-effect PIP sensor)
- Ignition coil

The distributor ignition system designed by Ford has two distinct configurations. The first configuration is known as the distributor mounted system, because the ICM is mounted directly on the distributor housing. The second configuration is known as a remote mount system, since the ICM is mounted on the front fender apron. The 5.0L Mustang engine is only equipped with the remote mount configuration.

The distributor used by this system is sealed and houses the CMP sensor. The distributor does not utilize vacuum or centrifugal advance mechanisms; the ignition timing is automatically controlled by the Powertrain Control Module (PCM) and the ICM.

SYSTEM OPERATION

▶ **See Figures 1, 2, 3, 4 and 5**

The CMP sensor, housed inside the distributor, responds to a rotating metallic shutter mounted on the distributor shaft. This rotating shutter produces a digital Profile Ignition Pick-up (PIP) signal, which is used by the PCM and ICM to provide base timing information and to determine engine speed (rpm) and crankshaft position. The distributor shaft rotates at one-half crankshaft speed; therefore, the shutter rotates once for every two crankshaft revolutions.

The ICM functions in either one of two modes: push start or Computer Controlled Dwell (CCD). The push start mode allows for increased dwell, or coil ON time, when starting the engine. During this mode, the ICM determines when to turn the ignition coil ON based on engine speed information. The coil is turned OFF, thereby firing, whenever a rising edge of a

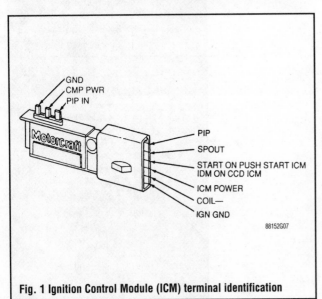

Fig. 1 Ignition Control Module (ICM) terminal identification

SPark OUTput (SPOUT) signal is received. The SPOUT signal is generated by the PCM, and provides spark timing information to the ICM. During the push start mode, the SPOUT signal only indicates the timing for coil firing; the falling edge of the SPOUT signal is ignored. Despite the name, the push start mode is also enabled during engine starting with the ignition key.

➡**Do not attempt to push start a vehicle equipped with an automatic transmission.**

During the CCD mode, both edges of the SPOUT signal are utilized and, with this one exception, the SPOUT signal is used by the ICM in the same manner as during the push start mode. The falling edge of the SPOUT signal is generated to control the timing for turning the ignition coil ON (the ICM no longer controls this function as during the push start mode). During the CCD mode, the coil ON time, or dwell, is entirely controlled by the PCM through the SPOUT signal.

In the event that the SPOUT signal from the PCM is disrupted, the ICM will use the PIP signal from the CMP to fire the ignition coil, which results in a fixed spark angle and dwell.

Diagnosis and Testing

SERVICE PRECAUTIONS

- Always turn the key **OFF** and isolate both ends of a circuit whenever testing for shorts or continuity.
- Never measure voltage or resistance directly at the processor connector.
- Always disconnect solenoids and switches from the harness before measuring for continuity, resistance or energizing by way of a 12-volt source.
- When detaching connectors, inspect for damaged or pushed-out pins, corrosion, loose wires, etc. Service if required.

PRELIMINARY CHECKS

1. Visually inspect the engine compartment to ensure that all vacuum lines and spark plug wires are properly routed and securely connected.
2. Examine all wiring harness and connectors for insulation damage, burned, overheated, loose or broken conditions. Ensure that the ICM is securely fastened to the front fender apron.
3. Be certain that the battery is fully charged and that all accessories are OFF during the diagnosis.

TEST PROCEDURES

➡**Perform the test procedures in the order in which they are presented here.**

Ignition Coil Secondary Voltage Test

CRANK MODE

1. Connect a spark tester between the ignition coil wire and a good engine ground.
2. Crank the engine and check for spark at the tester.
3. Turn the ignition switch **OFF**.
4. If no spark occurs, check the following:

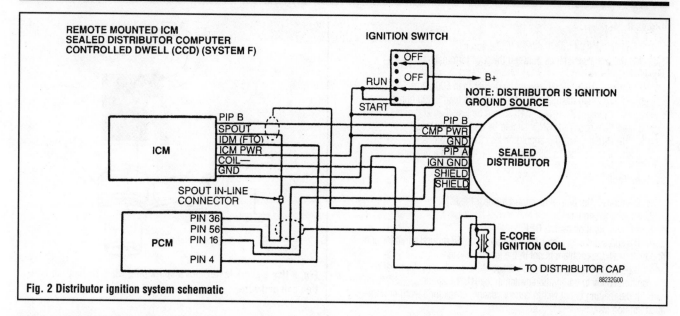

REMOTE MOUNTED ICM
SEALED DISTRIBUTOR COMPUTER
CONTROLLED DWELL (CCD) (SYSTEM F)

Fig. 2 Distributor ignition system schematic

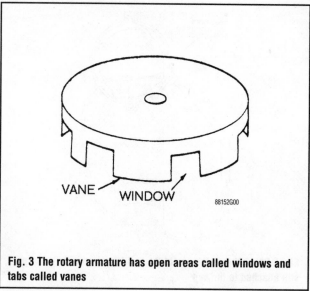

Fig. 3 The rotary armature has open areas called windows and tabs called vanes

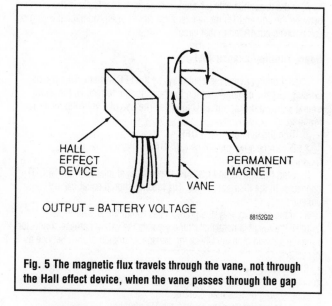

OUTPUT = BATTERY VOLTAGE

Fig. 5 The magnetic flux travels through the vane, not through the Hall effect device, when the vane passes through the gap

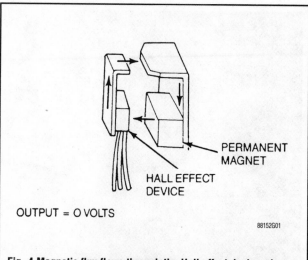

OUTPUT = O VOLTS

Fig. 4 Magnetic flux flows through the Hall effect device when a window in the armature passes through the gap

   a. Inspect the ignition coil for damage or carbon tracking.
   b. Check that the distributor shaft is rotating when the engine is being cranked.
   c. If the results in Steps a and b are okay, go to Module Test.
   5. If a spark did occur, check the distributor cap and rotor for damage or carbon tracking. Go to the Ignition Coil Secondary Voltage (Run Mode) Test.

RUN MODE

   1. Fully apply the parking brake. Place the gear shift lever in Neutral (manual transmission) or Park (automatic transmission).
   2. Disconnect the **S** terminal wire at the starter relay. Attach a remote starter switch.
   3. Turn the ignition switch to the **RUN** position.
   4. Using the remote starter switch, crank the engine and check for spark.
   5. Turn the ignition switch **OFF**.
   6. If no spark occurred, the problem lies with the wiring harness. Inspect the wiring harness for short circuits, open circuits and other defects.
   7. If a spark did occur, the problem is not in the ignition system.

ICM Test

1. Remove the ICM from the front fender apron.
2. Measure the resistance between the ICM terminals as shown below:
    a. GID(em dash)PIP IN: should be greater than 500 ohms.
    b. PIP PWR(em dash)PIP IN: should be less than 2,000 ohms.
    c. PIP PWR(em dash)TFI PWR: should be less than 200 ohms.
    d. GND(em dash)IGN GND: should be less than 2 ohms.
    e. PIP IN(em dash)PIP: should be less than 200 ohms.
3. If any of these checks failed, replace the ICM with a new one.

System Test

1. Disconnect the pin-inline connector near the ICM.
2. Crank the engine.
3. Turn the ignition switch **OFF**.
4. If a spark did occur, check the PIP and ignition ground wires for continuity. If okay, the problem is not in the ignition system.
5. If no spark occurs, check the voltage at the positive (+) terminal of the ignition coil with the ignition switch in the **RUN** position.
6. If the reading is not within battery voltage, check for a worn or damaged ignition switch.
7. If the reading is within battery voltage, check for faults in the wiring between the coil and TFI module terminal No. 2, or any additional wiring or components connected to that circuit.

Spark Timing Advance Test

Spark timing advance is controlled by the EEC system. This procedure checks the capability of the ignition module to receive the spark timing command from the EEC module. The use of a volt/ohmmeter is required.
1. Turn the ignition switch **OFF**.
2. Disconnect the pin-inline (SPOUT) connector near the TFI module.
3. Start the engine and measure the voltage, at idle, from the SPOUT connector to the distributor base. The reading should equal battery voltage.
4. If the result is okay, the problem lies within the EEC-IV system.
5. If the result is not satisfactory, separate the wiring harness connector from the ignition module. Check for damage, corrosion or dirt. Service as necessary.
6. Measure the resistance between terminal No. 5 and the pin-inline connector. This test is done at the ignition module connector only. The reading should be less than 5 ohms.
7. If the reading is okay, replace the TFI module.
8. If the result was not satisfactory, service the wiring between the pin-inline connector and the TFI connector.

Ignition Coil

TESTING

▸ **See Figures 6 thru 11**

1. Disconnect the ignition coil connector and check for dirt, corrosion or damage.
2. Substitute a known good coil and check for spark using the spark tester.

➡**Dangerous high voltage may be present when performing this test. Do not hold the coil while performing this test.**

3. Crank the engine and check for spark.
4. Turn the ignition switch **OFF**.
5. If a spark did occur, measure the resistance of the ignition coil wire, replace it if the resistance is greater than 7000 ohms per foot. If the readings are within specification, replace the ignition coil.
6. If no spark occurs, the problem is not the coil.

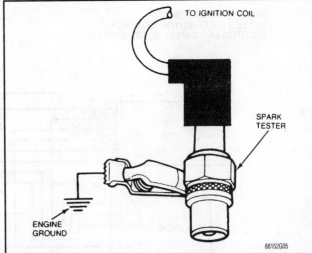

Fig. 6 Use a spark tester, not a spark plug when testing the ignition coil and wire

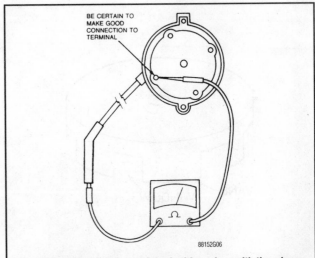

Fig. 7 Check the resistance of the ignition wires with the wires still attached to the cap

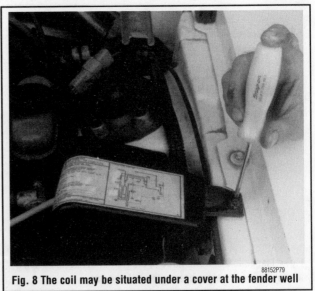

Fig. 8 The coil may be situated under a cover at the fender well

Fig. 9 Remove the cover to access the coil for the tests

Fig. 10 Pull the connector off after releasing the clip at the front

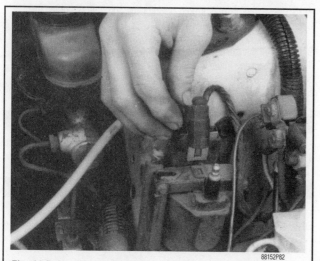

Fig. 11 Pull on the boot, not the wire, when removing the coil wire from the terminal

REMOVAL & INSTALLATION

▶ **See Figure 12**

1. Disconnect the negative battery cable.
2. Label and detach all wiring from the ignition coil.
3. Remove the ignition coil-to-bracket bolts, then remove the ignition coil.
4. If necessary, the radio ignition interference capacitor can now be removed from the ignition coil.

To install:

5. If applicable, install the radio interference capacitor onto the ignition coil. Tighten the mounting bolt to 25–35 inch lbs. (2.8–4.0 Nm).
6. Position the ignition coil onto the mounting bracket, then install and tighten the mounting bolts to 25–35 inch lbs. (2.8–4.0 Nm).
7. Attach all wiring to the ignition coil, then connect the negative battery cable.

Ignition Control Module (ICM)

REMOVAL & INSTALLATION

▶ **See Figure 13**

1. Disconnect the negative battery cable.
2. Label and detach all wiring from the ICM.
3. Remove the ICM/heatsink-to-fender apron bolts, then remove the ICM/heat sink.
4. If necessary, the ICM can now be removed from the heat sink.

To install:

5. Apply an approximately 1/32 in. (0.80mm) thick layer of silicone dielectric compound (D7AZ-19A331-A or equivalent) to the base plate of the ICM.
6. Install the ICM onto the heat sink. Tighten the mounting bolts to 15–35 inch lbs. (1.7–4.0 Nm).
7. Position the ICM onto the right-hand, front fender apron, then install and tighten the mounting bolts to 90–120 inch lbs. (10–14 Nm).
8. Attach all wiring to the ICM, then connect the negative battery cable.

Distributor

REMOVAL & INSTALLATION

1. Rotate the engine until the No. 1 piston is at Top Dead Center (TDC) of its compression stroke.
2. Disconnect the negative battery cable. Disconnect the vehicle wiring harness connector from the distributor. Before removing the distributor cap, mark the position of the No. 1 wire tower on the cap for reference.
3. Loosen the distributor cap hold-down screws and remove the cap. Matchmark the position of the rotor to the distributor housing. Position the cap and wires out of the way.
4. Scribe a mark in the distributor body and the engine block to indicate the position of the distributor in the engine.
5. Remove the distributor hold-down bolt and clamp.

➡ **Some engines may be equipped with a security-type distributor hold-down bolt. If this is the case, use distributor wrench T82L-12270-A or equivalent, to remove the retaining bolt and clamp.**

6. Remove the distributor assembly from the engine. Be sure not to rotate the engine while the distributor is removed.

To install:

7. Make sure that the engine still has the No. 1 piston at TDC of its compression stroke.

➡ **If the engine was disturbed while the distributor was removed, it will be necessary to remove the No. 1 spark plug and rotate the crankshaft clockwise until the No. 1 piston is on its compression stroke. Align the timing pointer with TDC on the crankshaft damper or flywheel, as required.**

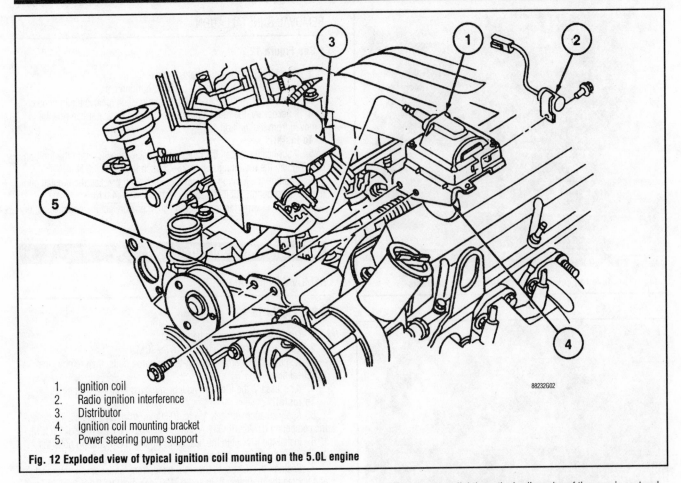

1. Ignition coil
2. Radio ignition interference
3. Distributor
4. Ignition coil mounting bracket
5. Power steering pump support

Fig. 12 Exploded view of typical ignition coil mounting on the 5.0L engine

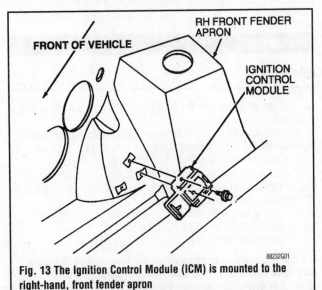

Fig. 13 The Ignition Control Module (ICM) is mounted to the right-hand, front fender apron

8. Check that the O-ring is installed and in good condition on the distributor body.
9. On all vehicles:
   a. Rotate the distributor shaft so the rotor points toward the mark on the distributor housing made previously.

b. Turn the rotor slightly so the leading edge of the vane is centered in the vane switch state assembly.
   c. Rotate the distributor in the block to align the leading edge of the vane with the vane switch stator assembly. Make certain the rotor is pointing to the No. 1 mark on the distributor base.

➡**If the vane and vane switch stator cannot be aligned by rotating the distributor in the cylinder block, remove the distributor enough to just disengage the distributor gear from the camshaft gear. Rotate the rotor enough to engage the distributor gear on another tooth of the camshaft gear. Repeat Step 9 if necessary.**

10. Install the distributor hold-down clamp and bolt(s); tighten them slightly.
11. Attach the vehicle wiring harness connector to the distributor.
12. Install the cap and wires. Install the No. 1 spark plug, if removed.
13. Recheck the initial timing.
14. Tighten the hold-down clamp and recheck the timing. Adjust if necessary.

Camshaft Position (CMP) Sensor

For Camshaft Position (CMP) sensor procedures, please refer to Section 4 in this manual.

Crankshaft Position (CKP) Sensor

For Crankshaft Position (CKP) sensor procedures, please refer to Section 4 in this manual.

DISTRIBUTORLESS IGNITION SYSTEM

General Information

▶ **See Figures 14, 15 and 16**

The distributorless ignition system used on 3.8L and 4.6L engines is referred to as the Electronic Ignition (EI) system, and eliminates the conventional distributor by utilizing multiple ignition coils instead. The EI system consists of the following components:

- Crankshaft Position (CKP) sensor
- Ignition Control Module (ICM) (1994–95 models only)
- Ignition coil(s)
- The spark angle portion of the Powertrain Control Module (PCM)
- Related wiring

➡**The function of the ICM was incorporated into the PCM beginning with the 1996 model year; otherwise the newer system operates in the same manner.**

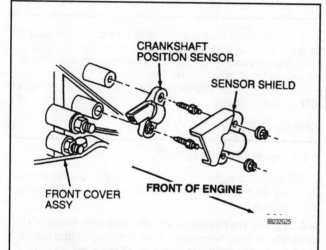

Fig. 14 The CKP sensor is mounted onto the front of the engine block, near the crankshaft damper/pulley unit—3.8L engine

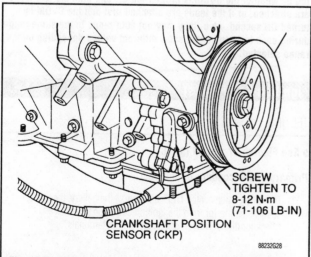

Fig. 15 The CKP sensor for the 4.6L engines is mounted onto the side of the front engine cover, near the crankshaft damper

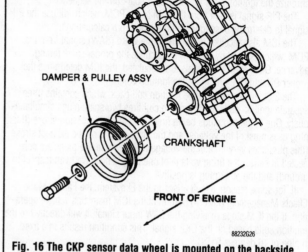

Fig. 16 The CKP sensor data wheel is mounted on the backside of the crankshaft damper

SYSTEM OPERATION

The CKP sensor is a variable reluctance sensor, mounted near the crankshaft damper and pulley.

The crankshaft damper has a "36-minus-1-tooth wheel" (data wheel) mounted on it. When this wheel rotates, the magnetic field (reluctance) of the CKP sensor changes in relationship with the passing of the teeth on the data wheel. This change in the magnetic field is called the CKP signal.

➡**The base ignition timing is set at 10 (plus or minus 2 degrees) degrees Before Top Dead Center (BTDC) and is not adjustable.**

1994–95 Models

▶ **See Figure 17**

The CKP signal is sent to the ICM, where it is used to create the Profile Ignition Pick-up (PIP) signal.

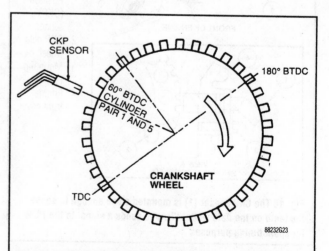

Fig. 17 The CKP sensor notes the changes in its magnetic field, which corresponds to the passing of the data wheel teeth, and sends this as a digital signal to the ICM

The one missing tooth on the data wheel creates one large space between two of the teeth. The ICM utilizes this large space as a reference to help determine base ignition timing and engine speed (rpm), and to synchronize the ignition coils for the proper spark timing sequence.

The PIP signal is sent from the ICM to the PCM, which will use the PIP signal to determine base ignition timing and rpm calculations.

The ICM also receives the Spark Angle Word (SAW) signal from the PCM, which is used by the ICM to calculate the proper spark timing advance. Once all of the signals are calculated, the ICM determines the proper ON and OFF timing for the ignition coils.

The 3.8L engine utilizes one ignition coil pack, which contains three separate ignition coils. Each ignition coil fires two spark plugs simultaneously. One of the two plugs being fired is on the compression stroke (this plug uses most of the voltage) and the other plug is on the exhaust stroke (this plug uses very little of the voltage). Since these two plugs are connected in series, the firing voltage of one plug is negative (with respect to ground) and the other plug is positive.

If, for some reason, a fault arises in the EI system, the Failure Mode Effects Management (FMEM) portion of the ICM maintains vehicle operation. If the ICM stops receiving the SAW input signal, it will directly fire the ignition coils based on the CKP signal. This condition results in a fixed timing of 10 degrees BTDC.

1996–98 Models

♦ See Figure 18

The CKP signal is sent to the PCM, which uses the signal to determine base ignition timing and rpm calculations.

The one missing tooth on the data wheel creates one large space between two of the teeth. The PCM utilizes this large space as a reference to help determine base ignition timing and engine speed (rpm), and to synchronize the ignition coils for the proper spark timing sequence.

The 3.8L engine utilizes one ignition coil pack, which contains three separate ignition coils, whereas the 4.6L engines use two separate ignition coil packs, each of which contains two ignition coils. Each ignition coil

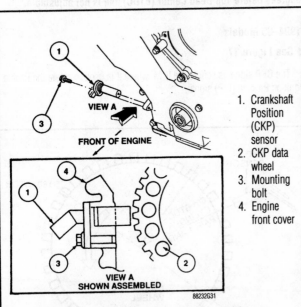

1. Crankshaft Position (CKP) sensor
2. CKP data wheel
3. Mounting bolt
4. Engine front cover

88232G31

Fig. 18 The CKP sensor (1) is mounted close enough to sense the teeth on the data wheel (2), and sends a signal to the PCM for spark timing purposes

fires two spark plugs simultaneously. One of the two plugs being fired is on the compression stroke (this plug uses most of the voltage) and the other plug is on the exhaust stroke (this plug uses very little of the voltage). Since these two plugs are connected in series, the firing voltage of one plug is negative (with respect to ground) and the other plug is positive.

Diagnosis and Testing

SERVICE PRECAUTIONS

- Always turn the ignition key **OFF** and isolate both ends of a circuit whenever testing for shorts or continuity.
- Never measure voltage or resistance directly at the processor connector.
- Always disconnect solenoids and switches from the harness before measuring for continuity, resistance or energizing by way of a 12-volt source.
- When detaching connectors, inspect for damaged or pushed-out pins, corrosion, loose wires, etc. Service if required.

PRELIMINARY CHECKS

1. Visually inspect the engine compartment to ensure that all vacuum lines and spark plug wires are properly routed and securely connected.
2. Examine all wiring harnesses and connectors for insulation damage, burned, overheated, loose or broken connections.
3. Be certain that the battery is fully charged and that all accessories are **OFF** during the diagnosis.

GENERAL SYSTEM TEST

♦ See Figures 19 thru 36 (p. 9–17)

This is a general system test for a no-start condition. Use the accompanying flow charts for this test. For ignition coil testing, refer to the ignition coil procedures.

➡Most Digital Volt Ohmmeters (DVOMs) used today belong to a class referred to as "averaging." Some averaging DVOMs include the Rotunda® 007-00001, the Fluke® 70, 20 series and the Fluke® 88. Recently, a new class of DVOMs, referred to as True RMS DVOMs (such as the Fluke® 87, 8060A, 8062A, etc.), are being used. True RMS DVOMs should not be used for the tests presented here, because they may display different voltage readings, depending on whether the DVOM is first turned ON and then the test leads are attached, or if the leads are attached first and the DVOM is turned ON second. Also, they may not auto range to the same range during each test, and some show different values depending on the range selected.

Ignition Coil Pack(s)

TESTING

♦ See Figures 37 and 38 (p. 18)

Primary and Secondary Circuit Test

1. Turn the ignition switch **OFF**, disconnect the battery, then detach the wiring harness connector from the ignition coil to be tested.
2. Check for dirt, corrosion or damage on the terminals.

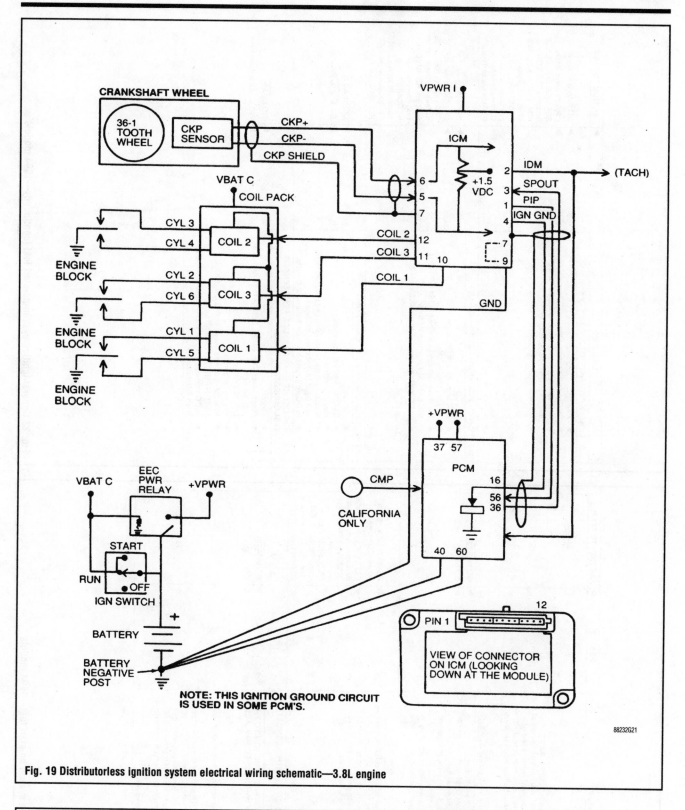

Fig. 19 Distributorless ignition system electrical wiring schematic—3.8L engine

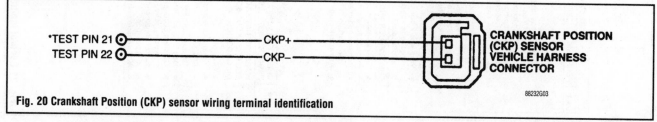

Fig. 20 Crankshaft Position (CKP) sensor wiring terminal identification

	TEST STEP	RESULT	ACTION TO TAKE
A5	CHECK PWR GND TO ICM—KEY OFF		
	• Key off. • DVOM on 200 ohm scale. • Measure resistance between J27 (PWR GND) and J7 (B-) at breakout box. • **Is resistance less than 5.0 ohms?**	Yes No	▲ GO to A6. ▲ CHECK connectors, SERVICE or REPLACE harness. PWR GND to ICM is open. REMOVE all test equipment. RECONNECT all components. CLEAR Continuous Memory. RERUN Quick Test.
A6	CHECK FOR VPWR TO ICM—KEY OFF		
	• Key off. • DVOM on 40 volt DC scale. • Key on, engine off. • Measure voltage between (+)J51 (VPWR I) and (-)J7 (B-) at breakout box. • **Is DC voltage greater than 10.5 volts?**	Yes No	▲ GO to A7. ▲ CHECK connectors, SERVICE or REPLACE harness. VPWR to ICM is open. REMOVE all test equipment. RECONNECT all components. CLEAR Continuous Memory. RERUN Quick Test.
A7	CHECK CKP+ BIAS AT ICM—KOEO		
	• Key off. • DVOM on 40 volt DC scale. • Key on, engine off. • Measure voltage between (+)J35 (CKP+ I) and (-)J7 (B-) at breakout box. • **Is DC voltage between 1.0 and 2.0 volts?**	Yes No	▲ GO to A21. ▲ GO to A8. Bias fault.
A8	CHECK CKP+ —BIAS FAULT—CKP SENSOR DISCONNECTED—KOEO		
	• Key off. • Disconnect CKP sensor from vehicle harness connector. • DVOM on 40 volt DC scale. • Key on, engine off. • Measure voltage between (+)J35 (CKP+ I) and (-)J7 (B-) at breakout box. • **Is DC voltage greater than 1.0 volt but less than 2.0 volts?**	Yes No	▲ GO to A9. ▲ GO to A29. Bias fault.

Fig. 22 General ignition system no-start test (continued)—1994 models

	TEST STEP	RESULT	ACTION TO TAKE
A1	PERFORM EEC QUICK TEST		
	NOTE: These diagnostic procedures are designed to correct one ignition failure at a time. When a component is replaced or a service is completed, remove all test equipment, reconnect all components and rerun Quick Test.		
A2	CHECK FOR SPARK DURING CRANK—KOEC		
	• Using a Neon Bulb Spark Tester (Special Service Tool D89P-6666-A) or Air Gap Spark Tester (Special Service Tool D81P-6666-A), check for spark at all spark plug wires while cranking. • **Was spark consistent on all spark plug wires (one spark per crankshaft revolution)?**	Yes No	▲ GO to A13. ▲ GO to A3.
A3	CHECK PLUGS AND WIRES—KEY OFF		
	• Check spark plug wires for insulation damage, looseness, shorting or other damage. • Remove and check spark plugs for damage, wear, carbon deposits and proper plug gap. • **Are spark plugs and wires OK?**	Yes No	▲ REINSTALL plugs and wires. GO to A4. ▲ SERVICE or REPLACE damaged component. REMOVE all test equipment. RECONNECT all components. CLEAR Continuous Memory. RERUN Quick Test.
A4	CHECK FOR VEHICLE START WITH DIAGNOSTIC HARNESS INSTALLED		
	WARNING: NEVER CONNECT THE PCM TO THE EEC BREAKOUT BOX WHEN PERFORMING EI DIAGNOSTICS. • Key off. • Install EI diagnostic harness to breakout box and ICM. • **Do not connect CKP sensor tee or coil tee.** • Use EI (High Data Rate) 6 overlay. • Connect EI diagnostic harness negative lead to battery, leave positive lead disconnected. • Set EI diagnostic harness box type switch to 4/6 position. • **Will vehicle start and run?**	Yes No	▲ GO to A32. ▲ GO to A5.

Fig. 21 General ignition system no-start test—1994 models

TEST STEP	RESULT	ACTION TO TAKE
A12 CHECK CKP. — FOR SHORT HIGH — BIAS HIGH FAULT — CKP SENSOR AND ICM DISCONNECTED — KOEO • Key off. • Disconnect ICM from ICM tee; leave EI diagnostic harness connected to vehicle harness connector. • DVOM 40 volt DC scale. • Key on, engine off. • Measure voltage between (+)J48 (CKP-I) and (-)J7 (B-) at breakout box. • **Is DC voltage less than 0.5 volts?**	Yes No	REPLACE ICM. CKP- shorted high. REMOVE all test equipment. RECONNECT all components. CLEAR Continuous Memory. RERUN Quick Test. CHECK connectors, SERVICE or REPLACE harness. CKP- is shorted high. REMOVE all test equipment. RECONNECT all components. CLEAR Continuous Memory. RERUN Quick Test.
A13 CHECK PIP AT ICM — KOEC **WARNING: NEVER CONNECT THE PCM TO THE EEC BREAKOUT BOX WHEN PERFORMING EI DIAGNOSTICS.** • Key off. • Install EI diagnostic harness to breakout box and ICM. • **Do not connect CKP sensor tee or coil tee.** • Use EI 6 overlay. • Connect EI diagnostic harness negative lead to battery, leave positive lead disconnected. • Set EI diagnostic harness type switch to 4 / 6 position. • DVOM on 40 volt AC scale. • Crank engine and measure voltage between J43 (PIP I) and J7 (B-) at breakout box. • **Is settled AC voltage reading greater than 3.5 volts?**	Yes No	GO to A14. GO to A18. PIP fault.
A14 CHECK FOR PIP OPEN TO PCM — PCM DISCONNECTED — KEY OFF • Key off. • DVOM on 200 ohm scale. • Install a second EEC breakout box to PCM vehicle harness connector. • Measure resistance between J43 (PIP I) at breakout box and Pin 56 (PIP) at second EEC breakout box. • **Is resistance less than 5.0 ohms?**	Yes No	GO to A15. CHECK connectors, SERVICE or REPLACE harness. PIP is open. REMOVE all test equipment. RECONNECT all components. CLEAR Continuous Memory. RERUN Quick Test.

Fig. 24 General ignition system no-start test (continued)—1994 models

TEST STEP	RESULT	ACTION TO TAKE
A9 CHECK CKPS — BIAS — CKP SENSOR DISCONNECTED — KOEO • Key off. • DVOM on 40 volt DC scale. • Key on, engine off. • Measure voltage between (+)J48 (CKP-I) and (-)J7 (B-) at breakout box. • **Is DC voltage between 1.0 and 2.0 volts?**	Yes No	REPLACE CKP sensor. Short to ground. REMOVE all test equipment. RECONNECT all components. CLEAR Continuous Memory. RERUN Quick Test. GO to A10.
A10 CHECK FOR BIAS HIGH OR BIAS LOW FAULT — BIAS FAULT • **Was bias voltage reading in Step A9 less than 1.0 volt?**	Yes No	GO to A11. Bias fault. GO to A12. Bias fault.
A11 CHECK CKP- CIRCUIT — FOR SHORT TO GROUND — BIAS LOW FAULT — CKP SENSOR AND ICM DISCONNECTED • Key off. • Disconnect ICM from ICM tee, leave EI diagnostic harness connected to vehicle harness connector. • DVOM on 20K ohm scale. • Measure resistance between J48 (CKP-I) and J7 (B-) at breakout box. • **Is resistance greater than 10K ohms?**	Yes No	REPLACE ICM. CKP- shorted low. REMOVE all test equipment. RECONNECT all components. CLEAR Continuous Memory. RERUN Quick Test. CHECK connectors, SERVICE or REPLACE harness. CKP- is shorted low. REMOVE all test equipment. RECONNECT all components. CLEAR Continuous Memory. RERUN Quick Test.

Fig. 23 General ignition system no-start test (continued)—1994 models

	TEST STEP	RESULT	ACTION TO TAKE
A15	CHECK IGN GND AT ICM—PCM DISCONNECTED—KEY OFF • Key off. • DVOM on 2K ohm scale. • Measure resistance between J47 (IGN GND I) and J7 (B-) at breakout box. • **Is resistance less than 1050 ohms?**	Yes No	GO to A16. GO to A17. Ground fault.
A16	CHECK FOR IGN GND OPEN TO PCM—PCM DISCONNECTED • Key off. • DVOM on 2K ohm scale. • Measure resistance between J47 (IGN GND I) at breakout box and Pin 16 (IGN GND) at second EEC breakout box. • **Is resistance less than 1050 ohms?**	Yes No	Ignition system is OK. REMOVE all test equipment. RECONNECT all components. CLEAR Continuous Memory. RERUN Quick Test. GO to Section 2A for no start problems. CHECK connectors, SERVICE or REPLACE harness. IGN GND is open. REMOVE all test equipment. RECONNECT all components. CLEAR Continuous Memory. RERUN Quick Test.
A17	CHECK PWR GND TO ICM—PWR GND FAULT • Key off. • DVOM on 200 ohm scale. • Measure resistance between J27 (PWR GND) and J7 (B-) at breakout box. • **Is resistance less than 5.0 ohms?**	Yes No	REPLACE ICM. IGN GND open. REMOVE all test equipment. RECONNECT all components. CLEAR Continuous Memory. RERUN Quick Test. CHECK connectors, SERVICE or REPLACE harness. Power ground to ICM is open. REMOVE all test equipment. RECONNECT all components. CLEAR Continuous Memory. RERUN Quick Test.

Fig. 25 General ignition system no-start test (continued)—1994 models

	TEST STEP	RESULT	ACTION TO TAKE
A18	CHECK PIP AT ICM—PIP FAULT—PIP CIRCUIT OPEN—KOEC • Key off. • DVOM 40 volt AC scale. • Push and hold EI diagnostic harness PIP push button down (opens PIP circuit to PCM). • Crank engine and measure voltage between J43 (PIP I) and J7 (B-) at breakout box. • **Is settled AC voltage reading greater than 3.5 volts?**	Yes No	GO to A19. REPLACE ICM. No PIP output. REMOVE all test equipment. RECONNECT all components. CLEAR Continuous Memory. RERUN Quick Test.
A19	CHECK FOR PIP SHORT HIGH—ICM AND PCM DISCONNECTED—KOEO • Key off. • DVOM on 40 volt DC scale. • Key on, engine off. • Measure voltage between J43 (PIP I) and J7 (B-) at breakout box. • **Is DC voltage less than 0.5 volts?**	Yes No	GO to A20. CHECK connectors, SERVICE or REPLACE harness. PIP is shorted high. REMOVE all test equipment. RECONNECT all components. CLEAR Continuous Memory. RERUN Quick Test.
A20	CHECK FOR PIP SHORT TO GROUND—ICM AND PCM DISCONNECTED—KEY OFF • Disconnect PCM. • Disconnect ICM from ICM tee. Leave EI diagnostic harness cable connected to vehicle harness connector. • DVOM on 20K ohm scale. • Measure resistance between J43 (PIP I) and J7 (B-) at breakout box. • **Is resistance greater than 10K ohms?**	Yes No	REPLACE PCM. PIP shorted. REMOVE all test equipment. RECONNECT all components. CLEAR Continuous Memory. RERUN Quick Test. CHECK connectors, SERVICE or REPLACE harness. PIP is shorted low. REMOVE all test equipment. RECONNECT all components. CLEAR Continuous Memory. RERUN Quick Test.
A21	CHECK CKP AMPLITUDE AT ICM • Key off. • DVOM on 40 volt AC scale. • Crank engine and measure voltage between J35 (CKP+ I) and J48 (CKP- I) at breakout box. • **Is settled AC voltage reading greater than 0.4 volts?**	Yes No	The problem lies with the ignition coil. GO to A22. Amplitude fault.

Fig. 26 General ignition system no-start test (continued)—1994 models

	TEST STEP	RESULT	ACTION TO TAKE
A26	CHECK CKP CIRCUIT FOR OPEN—RESISTANCE HIGH FAULT—KEY OFF		
	• Key off. • DVOM on 20K ohm scale. • Measure resistance between J32 (CKP- S) and J48 (CKP- I) at breakout box. • **Is resistance less than 2050 ohms?**	Yes	REPLACE CKP sensor. High resistance. REMOVE all test equipment. RECONNECT all components. CLEAR Continuous Memory. RERUN Quick Test.
		No	CHECK connectors, SERVICE or REPLACE harness. CKP- open. REMOVE all test equipment. RECONNECT all components. CLEAR Continuous Memory. RERUN Quick Test.
A27	CHECK CKPS AIR GAP AND TRIGGER WHEEL		
	• Key off. • Check trigger wheel and CKP sensor for damage. • **Is CKP sensor and trigger data wheel OK?**	Yes	REPLACE CKP sensor. No output from sensor. REMOVE all test equipment. RECONNECT all components. CLEAR Continuous Memory. RERUN Quick Test.
		No	SERVICE or REPLACE bad parts. REMOVE all test equipment. RECONNECT all components. CLEAR Continuous Memory. RERUN Quick Test.

88232G11

Fig. 28 General ignition system no-start test (continued)—1994 models

	TEST STEP	RESULT	ACTION TO TAKE
A22	CHECK CKP AMPLITUDE AT ICM—AMPLITUDE FAULT—ICM DISCONNECTED—KOEC		
	• Key off. • Disconnect ICM from ICM tee, leave EI diagnostic harness connected to vehicle harness connector. • DVOM 40 volt AC scale. • Crank engine and measure voltage between J35 (CKP+ I) and J48 (CKP- I) at breakout box. • **Is settled AC voltage reading greater than 0.4 volts?**	Yes	REPLACE ICM. CKP is shorted in ICM. REMOVE all test equipment. RECONNECT all components. CLEAR Continuous Memory. RERUN Quick Test.
		No	GO to A23.
A23	CHECK CKP CIRCUIT RESISTANCE—ICM DISCONNECTED—AMPLITUDE FAULT—KEY OFF		
	• Key off. • DVOM on 20K ohm scale. • Measure resistance between J48 (CKP- I) and J35 (CKP+ I) at breakout box. • **Is resistance between 2580 and 2700 ohms?**	Yes	GO to A27.
		No	GO to A24. Resistance fault.
A24	CHECK FOR RESISTANCE HIGH OR RESISTANCE LOW FAULT		
	• **Was the resistance from Step A23 or A32 less than 2580 ohms?**	Yes	GO to A28. Resistance low fault.
		No	GO to A25. Resistance high fault.
A25	CHECK CKP+ OPEN—RESISTANCE HIGH FAULT—KEY OFF		
	• Key off. • Connect CKP sensor tee to CKP sensor and vehicle harness connector. • DVOM on 20K ohm scale. • Measure resistance between J31 (CKP+ S) and J35 (CKP+ I) at breakout box. • **Is resistance less than 2050 ohms?**	Yes	GO to A26.
		No	CHECK connectors, SERVICE or REPLACE harness. CKP + open. REMOVE all test equipment. RECONNECT all components. CLEAR Continuous Memory. RERUN Quick Test.

88232G10

Fig. 27 General ignition system no-start test (continued)—1994 models

	TEST STEP	RESULT	ACTION TO TAKE
A31	CHECK CKPS+ CIRCUIT FOR SHORT HIGH—BIAS HIGH FAULT—CKP SENSOR AND ICM DISCONNECTED—KOEO • Key off. • Disconnect ICM from ICM tee, leave EI diagnostic harness connected to vehicle harness connector. • DVOM on 40 volt DC scale. • Key on, engine off. • Measure voltage between + J35 (CKP+ I) and -J7 (B-) at breakout box. • Is DC voltage less than 0.5 volts?	Yes No	▲ REPLACE ICM. REMOVE all test equipment. RECONNECT all components. CLEAR Continuous Memory. RERUN Quick Test. ▲ CHECK connectors, SERVICE or REPLACE harness. CKP+ is shorted high. REMOVE all test equipment. RECONNECT all components. CLEAR Continuous Memory. RERUN Quick Test.
A32	CHECK CKP CIRCUIT RESISTANCE—ICM DISCONNECTED—KEY OFF • Key off. • Disconnect ICM from ICM tee, leave EI diagnostic harness connected to vehicle harness connector. • DVOM on 20K ohm scale. • Measure resistance between J48 (CKP- I) and J35 (CKP+ I) at breakout box. • Is resistance between 2300 and 2500 ohms?	Yes No	▲ REPLACE ICM. REMOVE all test equipment. RECONNECT all components. CLEAR Continuous Memory. RERUN Quick Test. ▲ GO to [A24]. Resistance fault.

88232G13

Fig. 30 General ignition system no-start test (continued)—1994 models

	TEST STEP	RESULT	ACTION TO TAKE
A28	CHECK FOR CKP+ SHORTED TO CKP.—RESISTANCE LOW FAULT—CKP SENSOR AND ICM DISCONNECTED—KEY OFF • Key off. • Disconnect CKP sensor from vehicle harness connector. • DVOM on 20K ohm scale. • Measure resistance between J35 (CKP+ I) and J48 (CKP- I) at breakout box. • Is resistance greater than 3K ohms?	Yes No	▲ REPLACE CKP sensor. Shorted sensor windings. REMOVE all test equipment. RECONNECT all components. CLEAR Continuous Memory. RERUN Quick Test. ▲ CHECK connectors, SERVICE or REPLACE harness. CKP+ shorted to CKP- in harness. REMOVE all test equipment. RECONNECT all components. CLEAR Continuous Memory. RERUN Quick Test.
A29	CHECK FOR BIAS VOLTAGE HIGH OR BIAS VOLTAGE LOW FAULT • Was bias voltage reading in Step [A8] less than 1.0 volts?	Yes No	▲ GO to [A30]. Bias voltage low fault. ▲ GO to [A31]. Bias voltage high fault.
A30	CHECK CKPS+ CIRCUIT FOR SHORT TO GROUND—CKP SENSOR AND ICM DISCONNECTED—BIAS LOW FAULT—KEY OFF • Key off. • Disconnect ICM from ICM tee, leave EI diagnostic harness connected to vehicle harness connector. • DVOM on 20K ohm scale. • Measure resistance between J35 (CKP+ I) and J7 (B-) at breakout box. • Is resistance greater than 10K ohms?	Yes No	▲ REPLACE ICM. REMOVE all test equipment. RECONNECT all components. CLEAR Continuous Memory. RERUN Quick Test. ▲ CHECK connectors, SERVICE or REPLACE harness. CKP+ is shorted low. REMOVE all test equipment. RECONNECT all components. CLEAR Continuous Memory. RERUN Quick Test.

88232G12

Fig. 29 General ignition system no-start test (continued)—1994 models

Test Step		Result		Action to Take
JD6	CHECK CKP- BIAS FAULT			
	• Key off. • Disconnect CKP sensor from vehicle harness connector. • Key on, engine off. • Measure voltage between Test Pin 22 (CKP-) at the breakout box and (B-). • **Is dc voltage between 1.0 and 2.0 volts?**	Yes	▲	Short to ground. REPLACE CKP sensor. REMOVE all test equipment. RECONNECT all components. COMPLETE PCM Reset to clear DTCs. RERUN Quick Test.
		No	▲	Bias fault. GO to JD7.
JD7	DETERMINE IF BIAS HIGH OR BIAS LOW FAULT			
	• Key off. • **Was bias voltage reading in JD6 less than 1.0 volt?**	Yes	▲	Bias low fault. GO to JD8.
		No	▲	Bias high fault. GO to JD9.
JD8	CHECK CKP- FOR SHORT TO GROUND FOR BIAS LOW FAULT			
	• Key off. • Disconnect CKP sensor from vehicle harness connector. • Disconnect PCM from breakout box. • When making measurements on a wiring harness, both a visual inspection and continuity test must be performed. • Measure resistance between Test Pin 22 (CKP-) at the breakout box and (B-). • **Is the resistance greater than 10K ohms?**	Yes	▲	CKP- is shorted low. REPLACE PCM. REMOVE all test equipment. RECONNECT all components. RERUN Quick Test.
		No	▲	CKP- is shorted low. CHECK connectors, SERVICE or REPLACE harness. REMOVE all test equipment. RECONNECT all components. RERUN Quick Test.
JD9	CHECK CKP- SHORTED HIGH FOR BIAS HIGH FAULT			
	• Key off. • Disconnect CKP sensor from vehicle harness connector. • Disconnect PCM from breakout box. • Key on, engine off. • Measure voltage between Test Pin 22 (CKP-) at the breakout box and (B-). • **Is dc voltage less than 0.5 volt?**	Yes	▲	CKP- shorted high. REPLACE PCM. REMOVE all test equipment. RECONNECT all components. RERUN Quick Test.
		No	▲	CKP- is shorted high. CHECK connectors, SERVICE or REPLACE harness. REMOVE all test equipment. RECONNECT all components. RERUN Quick Test.

Fig. 32 General ignition system no-start test (continued)—1995–98 models

88232G15

Test Step		Result		Action to Take
JD1	CHECK PLUGS AND WIRES			
	NOTE: Electronic Ignition engine timing is entirely controlled by the PCM. Electronic Ignition engine timing is NOT adjustable. Do not attempt to check base timing. You will receive false readings. • Check spark plug wires for insulation damage, looseness, shorting or other damage. • Remove and check spark plugs for damage, wear, carbon deposits and proper plug gap. • Examine all wiring harnesses and connectors for damaged, burned or overheated insulation, damaged pins and loose or broken conditions. • Check sensor shield connector. • **Are spark plugs and wires OK?**	Yes	▲	REINSTALL plugs and wires. GO to JD4.
		No	▲	SERVICE or REPLACE damaged component. REMOVE all test equipment. RECONNECT all components. COMPLETE PCM Reset to clear DTCs. RERUN Quick Test.
JD4	CHECK CKP+ BIAS AT PCM			
	• Key off. • Disconnect Scan Tool from DLC. • Disconnect PCM. Inspect for damaged or pushed out pins, corrosion and loose wires. Service as necessary. • Install breakout box and connect PCM. NOTE: Do not use an incandescent lamp to check CKP+ or CKP-. The lamp will prevent the circuit from operating. • Key on, engine off. • When making a voltage check, a ground reading means any value within a range of zero to 1 volt. Also, VPWR readings mean any value within a range of B+ to 2 volts less than B+. When making a voltage check and a reference to ground is made, use the negative battery lead. B+ means the battery positive cable at the battery. • Measure voltage between test Pin 21 (CKP+) at the breakout box and (B-). • **Is dc voltage between 1.0 and 2.0 volts?**	Yes	▲	GO to JD10.
		No	▲	Bias fault. GO to JD5.
JD5	CHECK CKP+ BIAS FAULT			
	• Key off. • Disconnect CKP sensor from vehicle harness connector. • Key on, engine off. • Measure voltage between Test Pin 21 (CKP+) at the breakout box and (B-). • **Is dc voltage greater than 1.0 volt but less than 2.0 volts?**	Yes	▲	GO to JD6.
		No	▲	Bias fault. GO to JD18.

Fig. 31 General ignition system no-start test—1995–98 models

88232G14

Test Step	Result	Action to Take
JD10 CHECK CKP SENSOR AMPLITUDE AT PCM • Key off. • Crank engine and measure voltage between Test Pin 21 (CKP+) and Test Pin 22 (CKP-) at breakout box. • **Is settled ac voltage reading greater than 0.4 volt?**	Yes No	The problem most liekly lies within the ignition coil(s). Amplitude fault. GO to JD11.
JD11 CHECK CKP AMPLITUDE AT PCM FOR AMPLITUDE FAULT • Disconnect PCM from breakout box. • Crank engine and measure voltage between Test Pin 21 (CKP+) and Test Pin 22 (CKP-) at breakout box. • **Is settled ac voltage reading greater than 0.4 volt?**	Yes No	CKP is shorted in PCM. REPLACE PCM. REMOVE all test equipment. RECONNECT all components. RERUN Quick Test. GO to JD12.
JD12 CHECK CIRCUIT RESISTANCE FOR AMPLITUDE FAULT • Key off. • When making measurements on a wiring harness, both a visual inspection and continuity test must be peformed. • Measure resistance between Test Pin 22 (CKP-) and Test Pin 21 (CKP+) at breakout box. • **Is resistance between 300 and 800 ohms?**	Yes No	GO to JD16. CKP circuit resistance fault. GO to JD13.
JD13 DETERMINE IF RESISTANCE HIGH OR RESISTANCE LOW FAULT • **Was the resistance from JD12 less than 300 ohms?**	Yes No	Low resistance fault. GO to JD17. High resistance fault. GO to JD14.

Fig. 33 General ignition system no-start test (continued)—1995–98 models

Test Step	Result	Action to Take
JD14 CHECK FOR CKP+ HARNESS OPEN FOR RESISTANCE HIGH FAULT • Key off. • Install Electronic Ignition (EI) System Adapter (EDIS Systems Adapter) to 60-Pin breakout box and the CKP sensor and vehicle harness. • Connect EI diagnostic harness negative lead to battery, leave positive lead disconnected. • **For 8 Cylinder Applications:** • Use Integrated Electronic Ignition 8 Overlay (Rotunda T97L-50-A3 or equivalent). • Set EI diagnostic harness box type switch to 8 cylinder position. • **For 6 Cylinder Applications:** • Use appropriate Integrated Electronic Ignition 6 Overlay (Rotunda T97L-50-A5/6 or equivalent). • Set EI diagnostic harness box type switch to 4/6 cylinder position. • **For 2.3L Ranger:** • Use Integrated Electronic Ignition 4 Dual Plug Overlay (Rotunda T97L-50-A4 or equivalent). • Set EI diagnostic harness box type switch to 4/6 cylinder position. • **All other 4 Cylinder Applications:** • Use Integrated Electronic Ignition 4 Overlay (Rotunda T97L-50-A1 or equivalent). • Set EI diagnostic harness box type switch to 4/6 cylinder position. • Measure resistance between J31 (CKP+ S) at the EI breakout box and Test Pin 21 (CKP+) at the PCM breakout box. • **Is resistance less than 1050 ohms?**	Yes No	GO to JD15. CKP+ open. CHECK connectors, SERVICE or REPLACE harness. REMOVE all test equipment. RECONNECT all components. COMPLETE PCM Reset to clear DTCs. RERUN Quick Test.
JD15 CHECK FOR CKP HARNESS OPEN FOR RESISTANCE HIGH FAULT • Key off. • Measure resistance between J32 (CKP- S) at the EI breakout box and Test Pin 22 (CKP-) at PCM breakout box. • **Is resistance less than 1050 ohms?**	Yes No	High resistance. REPLACE CKP sensor. REMOVE all test equipment. RECONNECT all components. COMPLETE PCM Reset to clear DTCs. RERUN Quick Test. CKP- open. CHECK connectors. SERVICE or REPLACE harness. REMOVE all test equipment. RECONNECT all components. COMPLETE PCM Reset to clear DTCs. RERUN Quick Test.

Fig. 34 General ignition system no-start test (continued)—1995–98 models

Test Step	Result	Action to Take
JD19 CHECK CKP+ HARNESS FOR SHORT TO GROUND FOR LOW BIAS FAULT • Key off. • Disconnect CKP sensor from vehicle harness connector. • Disconnect PCM from breakout box. • When making measurements on a wiring harness, both a visual inspection and resistance test must be performed. • Measure resistance between Test Pin 21 (CKP+) at the PCM breakout box and (B-). • **Is resistance greater than 10K ohms?**	Yes ▲	▲ CKP+ is shorted low. REPLACE PCM. REMOVE all test equipment. RECONNECT all components. RERUN Quick Test.
	No ▲	▲ CKP+ is shorted low. CHECK connectors, SERVICE or REPLACE harness. REMOVE all test equipment. RECONNECT all components. RERUN Quick Test.
JD20 CHECK CKP+ HARNESS FOR SHORTED HIGH FOR BIAS VOLTAGE HIGH FAULT • Key off. • Disconnect CKP sensor from vehicle harness connector. • Disconnect PCM from breakout box. • Key on, engine off. • Measure voltage between Test Pin 21 (CKP+) at the PCM breakout box and (B-). • **Is dc voltage less than 0.5 volt?**	Yes ▲	▲ CKP+ shorted high. REPLACE PCM. REMOVE all test equipment. RECONNECT all components. RERUN Quick Test.
	No ▲	▲ CKP+ is shorted high. CHECK connectors, SERVICE or REPLACE harness. REMOVE all test equipment. RECONNECT all components. RERUN Quick Test.

88232619

Fig. 36 General ignition system no-start test (continued)—1995–98 models

Test Step	Result	Action to Take
JD16 CHECK CKP SENSOR AND TRIGGER WHEEL • Key off. • Check trigger wheel and CKP sensor for damage. • **Is CKP sensor and trigger data wheel OK?**	Yes ▲	▲ No output from sensor. REPLACE CKP sensor. REMOVE all test equipment. RECONNECT all components. COMPLETE PCM Reset to clear DTCs. RERUN Quick Test.
	No ▲	▲ SERVICE or REPLACE damaged parts. REMOVE all test equipment. RECONNECT all components. COMPLETE PCM Reset to clear DTCs. RERUN Quick Test.
JD17 CHECK FOR CKP+ SHORTED TO CKP- FOR RESISTANCE LOW FAULT • Key off. • Disconnect CKP sensor from vehicle harness connector. • Measure resistance between test Pin 21 (CKP+) and Test Pin 22 (CKP-) at breakout box. • **Is resistance greater than 1000 ohms?**	Yes ▲	▲ Shorted sensor windings. REPLACE CKP sensor. REMOVE all test equipment. RECONNECT all components. COMPLETE PCM Reset to clear DTCs. RERUN Quick Test.
	No ▲	▲ CKP+ shorted to CKP- in harness. CHECK connectors. SERVICE or REPLACE harness. REMOVE all test equipment. RECONNECT all components. COMPLETE PCM Reset to clear DTCs. RERUN Quick Test.
JD18 DETERMINE IF BIAS VOLTAGE HIGH OR BIAS VOLTAGE LOW FAULT • **Was bias voltage reading in JD5 less than 1.0 volt?**	Yes ▲	▲ Low bias voltage fault. GO to JD19.
	No ▲	▲ High bias voltage fault. GO to JD20.

88232618

Fig. 35 General ignition system no-start test (continued)—1995–98 models

PRIMARY RESISTANCE

1. Use an ohmmeter to measure the resistance between the following terminals on the ignition coil, and note the readings:

3.8L engine
- B+ to Coil 1
- B+ to Coil 2
- B+ to Coil 3

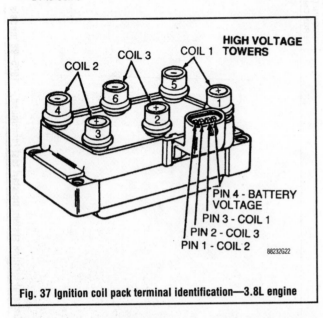

Fig. 37 Ignition coil pack terminal identification—3.8L engine

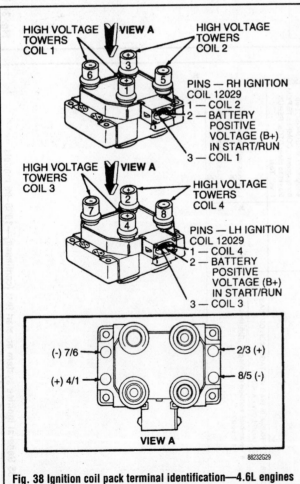

Fig. 38 Ignition coil pack terminal identification—4.6L engines

4.6L engines
- B+ to Coil 1
- B+ to Coil 2

or,
- B+ to Coil 3
- B+ to Coil 4

The resistance between all of these terminals should have been 0.3–1.0 ohms. If the resistance was more or less than this value, the coil should be replaced with a new one.

SECONDARY RESISTANCE

1. Measure, using the ohmmeter, and note the resistance between each corresponding coil terminal and the two spark plug wire towers on the ignition coil. The coil terminals and plug wires towers are grouped as follows:

3.8L engine
- Terminal 3 (coil 1)—spark plugs 1 and 5
- Terminal 2 (coil 3)—spark plugs 2 and 6
- Terminal 1 (coil 2)—spark plugs 3 and 4

4.6L engines—right-hand coil pack
- Terminal 1 (coil 2)—spark plugs 3 and 5
- Terminal 3 (coil 1)—spark plugs 1 and 6

4.6L engines—left-hand coil pack
- Terminal 1 (coil 4)—spark plugs 2 and 8
- Terminal 3 (coil 3)—spark plugs 4 and 7

If the resistance for all of the readings was between 6,500–11,500 ohms, the ignition coils are OK. If any of the readings was less than 6,500 ohms or more than 11,500 ohms, replace the corresponding coil pack.

➡️**On 4.6L engines, if one coil pack is found to be defective, the other pack does not need to be replaced.**

REMOVAL & INSTALLATION

◗ **See Figures 39 thru 44 (p. 18–22)**

➡️**The 3.8L engine utilizes one coil pack containing three separate coils, and the 4.6L engines use two coil packs containing two separate coils each.**

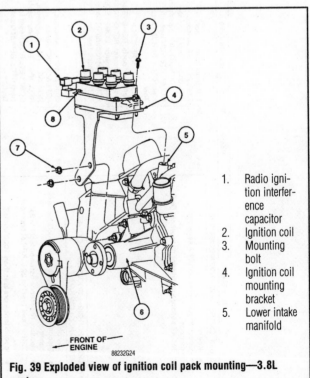

1. Radio ignition interference capacitor
2. Ignition coil
3. Mounting bolt
4. Ignition coil mounting bracket
5. Lower intake manifold

Fig. 39 Exploded view of ignition coil pack mounting—3.8L engine

1. Disconnect the negative battery cable.
2. Unplug the electrical harness connector from the ignition coil pack.
3. Label and remove the spark plug wires from the ignition coil terminal towers by squeezing the locking tabs to release the coil boot retainers.
4. Remove the coil pack mounting screws and remove the coil pack.

To install:

5. Install the coil pack and the retaining screws. Tighten the retaining screws to 40–62 inch lbs. (4.5–7 Nm).

➡**Be sure to place some dielectric compound into each spark plug boot prior to installation of the spark plug wire.**

6. Attach the spark plug wires and electrical harness connector to the coil pack.
7. Connect the negative battery cable.

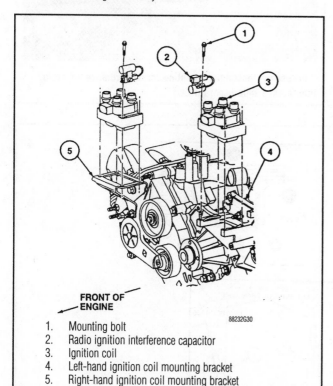

FRONT OF
ENGINE

1. Mounting bolt
2. Radio ignition interference capacitor
3. Ignition coil
4. Left-hand ignition coil mounting bracket
5. Right-hand ignition coil mounting bracket

88232G30

Fig. 40 Exploded view of coil pack mountings—4.6L engines

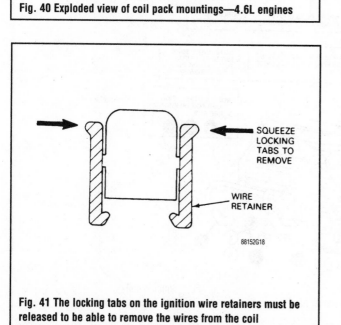

SQUEEZE
LOCKING
TABS TO
REMOVE

WIRE
RETAINER

88152G18

Fig. 41 The locking tabs on the ignition wire retainers must be released to be able to remove the wires from the coil

88232P07

To remove the ignition coil, depress the plug wire retaining tabs (arrows) and pull off the wires

88232P08

Note that the plug wires may already be marked (arrow) with their respective cylinder numbers

88232P09

Disengage the engine control wiring connector . . .

... and the radio interference suppressor connector

88232P10

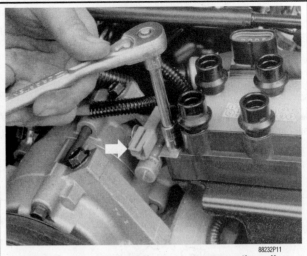

If necessary, loosen the mounting screw to remove the radio interference suppressor (arrow)

88232P11

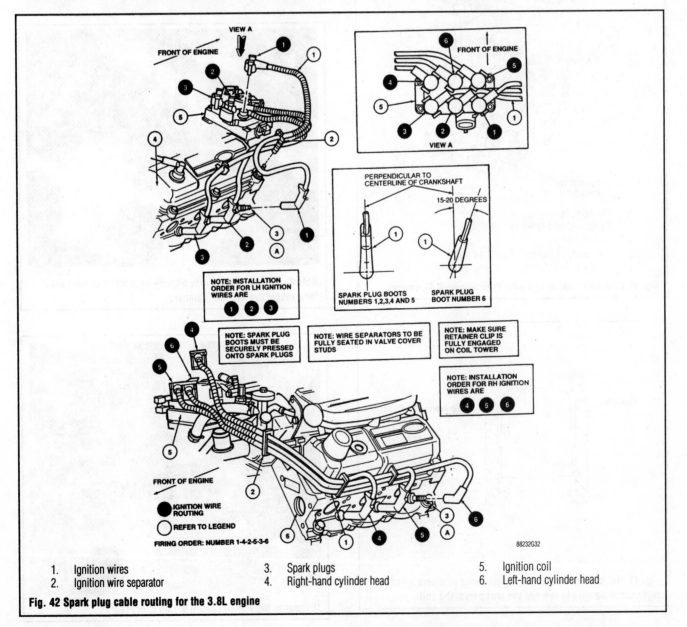

1. Ignition wires
2. Ignition wire separator
3. Spark plugs
4. Right-hand cylinder head
5. Ignition coil
6. Left-hand cylinder head

Fig. 42 Spark plug cable routing for the 3.8L engine

Remove the four mounting screws and lift the ignition coil off of the support bracket . . .

. . . or loosen the bracket attaching bolts and remove the coil, along with the bracket, from the engine

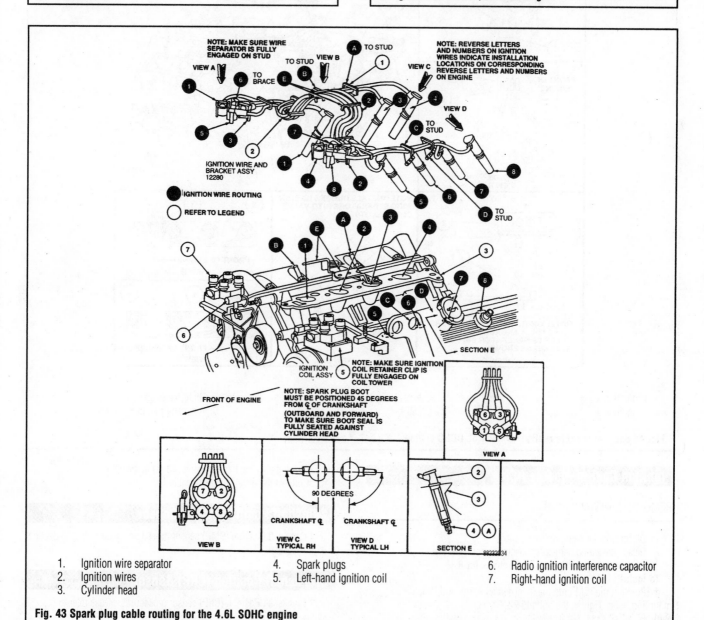

Fig. 43 Spark plug cable routing for the 4.6L SOHC engine

1. Ignition wire separator
2. Ignition wires
3. Cylinder head
4. Spark plugs
5. Left-hand ignition coil
6. Radio ignition interference capacitor
7. Right-hand ignition coil

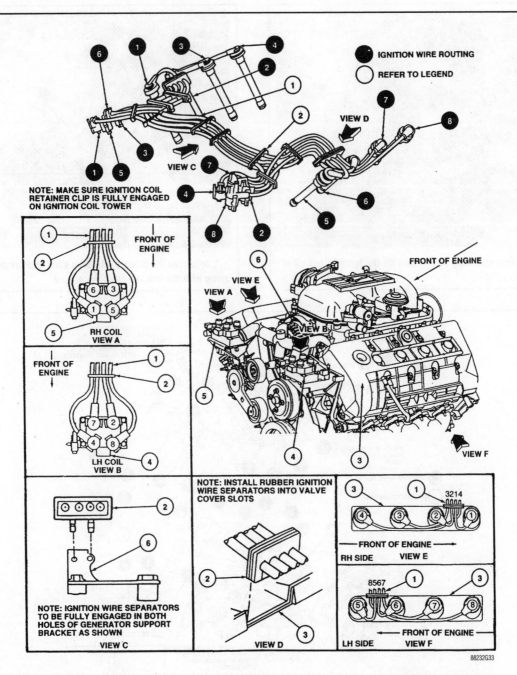

1. Ignition wires
2. Ignition wire separator
3. Rocker arm cover
4. Left-hand ignition coil
5. Right-hand ignition coil
6. Alternator mounting bracket

Fig. 44 Spark plug cable routing for the 4.6L DOHC engine

Ignition Control Module (ICM)

REMOVAL & INSTALLATION

1. Disconnect the negative battery cable.
2. Detach the wiring harness connector(s) from the ICM.
3. Remove the mounting bolts, then remove the ICM.
   To install:
4. Position the ICM onto the inner fender apron and install the mounting bolts. Tighten the bolts to 22–31 inch lbs. (2.5–3.5 Nm).

5. Attach the wiring harness connector(s) to the ICM.
6. Connect the negative battery cable.

Camshaft Position (CMP) Sensor

For Camshaft Position (CMP) sensor procedures, please refer to Section 4 in this manual.

Crankshaft Position (CKP) Sensor

For Crankshaft Position (CKP) sensor procedures, please refer to Section 4 in this manual.

FIRING ORDERS

♦ See Figures 45, 46 and 47

➡To avoid confusion, remove and tag the wires one at a time, for replacement.

If a distributor is not keyed for installation with only one orientation, it could have been removed previously and rewired. The resultant wiring would hold the correct firing order, but could change the relative placement of the plug towers in relation to the engine.

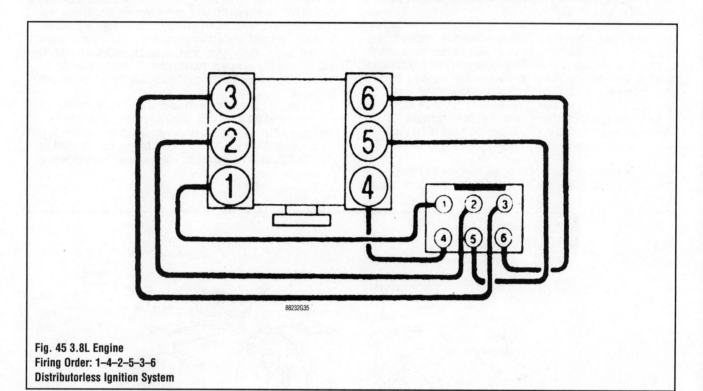

88232G35

Fig. 45 3.8L Engine
Firing Order: 1–4–2–5–3–6
Distributorless Ignition System

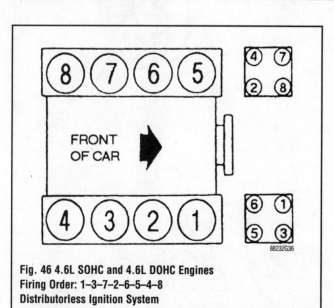

88232G36

Fig. 46 4.6L SOHC and 4.6L DOHC Engines
Firing Order: 1–3–7–2–6–5–4–8
Distributorless Ignition System

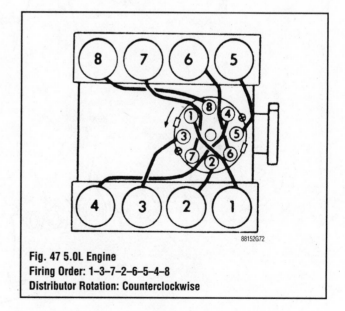

88152G72

Fig. 47 5.0L Engine
Firing Order: 1–3–7–2–6–5–4–8
Distributor Rotation: Counterclockwise

CHARGING SYSTEM

General Information

▶ **See Figure 48**

The charging system is a negative (−) ground system which consists of an alternator, a regulator, a charge indicator, a storage battery, wiring connecting the components, and fuse link wire.

The alternator is belt-driven from the engine. Energy is supplied from the alternator/regulator system to the rotating field through two brushes to two slip-rings. The slip-rings are mounted on the rotor shaft and are connected to the field coil. This energy supplied to the rotating field from the battery is called excitation current and is used to initially energize the field to begin the generation of electricity. Once the alternator starts to generate electricity, the excitation current comes from its own output rather than the battery.

The alternator produces power in the form of alternating current. The alternating current is rectified by 6 diodes into direct current. The direct current is used to charge the battery and power the rest of the electrical system.

When the ignition key is turned **ON**, current flows from the battery, through the charging system indicator light on the instrument panel, to the voltage regulator, and to the alternator. Since the alternator is not producing any current, the alternator warning light comes on. When the engine is started, the alternator begins to produce current and turns the alternator light off. As the alternator turns and produces current, the current is divided in two ways: one part to the battery to charge the battery and power the electrical components of the vehicle, and one part is returned to the alternator to enable it to increase its output. In this situation, the alternator is receiving current from the battery and from itself. A voltage regulator is wired into the current supply to the alternator to prevent it from receiving too much current, which, in turn, would cause it to produce too much current. Conversely, if the voltage regulator does not allow the alternator to receive enough current, the battery will not be fully charged and will eventually drain.

The battery is connected to the alternator at all times, whether the ignition key is turned **ON** or not. If the battery were shorted to ground, the alternator would also be shorted. This would damage the alternator. To prevent this, a fuse link is installed in the wiring between the battery and the alternator. If the battery is shorted, the fuse link melts, thereby protecting the alternator.

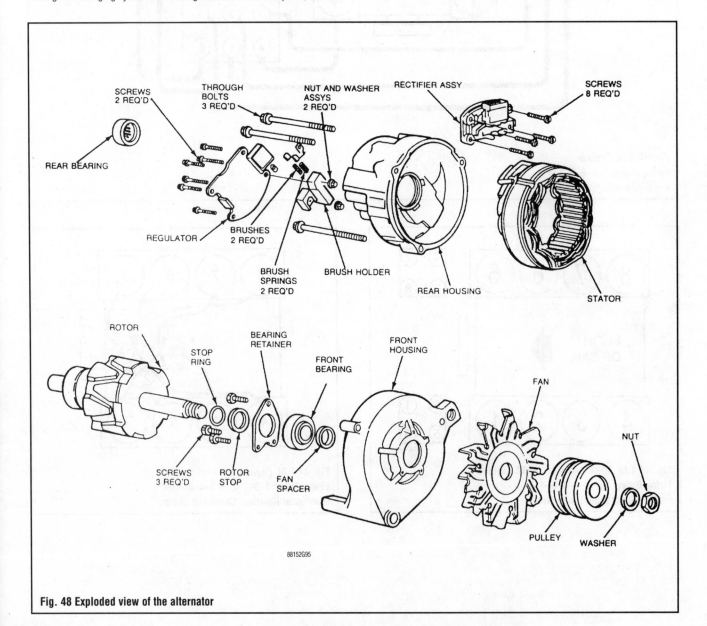

88152G95

Fig. 48 Exploded view of the alternator

Alternator Precautions

To prevent damage to the alternator and regulator, the following precautions should be taken when working with the electrical system:

- Never reverse the battery connections.
- Booster batteries for starting must be connected properly: positive-to-positive and negative-to-ground.
- Disconnect the battery cables before using a fast charger; the charger has a tendency to force current through the diodes in the opposite direction for which they were designed. This burns out the diodes.
- Never use a fast charger as a booster for starting the vehicle.
- Never disconnect the voltage regulator while the engine is running.
- Avoid long soldering times when replacing diodes or transistors. Prolonged heat is damaging to AC generators.
- Do not use test lamps of more than 12 volts for checking diode continuity.
- Do not short across or ground any of the terminals on the AC generator.
- The polarity of the battery, generator, and regulator must be matched and considered before making any electrical connections within the system.
- Never operate the alternator on an open circuit. Make sure that all connections within the circuit are clean and tight.
- Disconnect the battery terminals when performing any service on the electrical system. This will eliminate the possibility of accidental reversal of polarity.
- Disconnect the battery ground cable if arc welding is to be done on any part of the vehicle.

Alternator

TESTING

▶ See Figures 49 and 50

General Information

There are many possible ways in which the charging system can malfunction. Often the source of a problem is difficult to diagnose, requiring special equipment and a good deal of experience. This is usually not the case, however, where the charging system fails completely and causes the dashboard warning light to come on or the battery to discharge. To troubleshoot a complete system failure, only two pieces of equipment are needed: a test light, to determine that current is reaching a certain point and a current indicator (ammeter), to determine the direction of the current flow and its measurement in amps. This test works under three assumptions:

1. The battery is known to be good and fully charged.
2. The alternator belt is in good condition and adjusted to the proper tension.
3. All connections in the system are clean and tight.

➡In order for the current indicator to give a valid reading, the vehicle must be equipped with battery cables which are of the same gauge size and quality as original equipment battery cables.

Before commencing with the following tests, turn off all electrical components on the vehicle. Make sure the doors of the vehicle are closed. If the vehicle is equipped with a clock, disconnect the clock by removing the lead wire from the rear of the clock.

Battery No-Load Test

1. Ensure that the ignition switch is turned **OFF**.
2. Connect a tachometer to the engine by following the manufacturer's instructions.
3. Using a Digital Volt Ohmmeter (DVOM) measure the voltage across the positive (+) and negative
4. (–) battery terminals. Note the voltage reading for future reference.

Ensure that all electrical components on the vehicle are turned off. Be sure the doors of the vehicle are closed. If the vehicle is equipped with a clock, disconnect the clock by removing the lead wire from the rear of the clock.

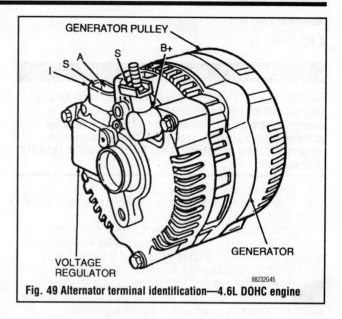

Fig. 49 Alternator terminal identification—4.6L DOHC engine

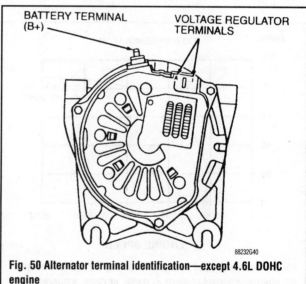

Fig. 50 Alternator terminal identification—except 4.6L DOHC engine

5. Start the engine and have an assistant run it at 1500 rpm.
6. Read the voltage across the battery terminals again. The voltage should now be 14.1–14.7 volts.

   a. If the voltage increase is less than 2.5 volts over the base voltage measured in Step 3, perform the Battery Load test.

   b. If there was no voltage increase, or the voltage increase was greater than 2.5 volts, perform the Alternator Load and No-Load tests.

Battery Load Test

1. With the engine running, turn the air conditioner ON (if equipped) or the blower motor on high speed and the headlights on high beam.
2. Have your assistant increase the engine speed to approximately 2000 rpm.
3. Read the voltage across the battery terminals again.

   a. If the voltage increase is 0.5 volts over the base voltage measured in Battery No-Load test Step 3, the charging system is working properly. If your problem continues, there may be a problem with the battery.

   b. If the voltage does not increase as indicated, perform the Alternator Load and No-Load tests.

Alternator Load Test

▶ See Figure 51

☀ WARNING

Do NOT use a normal Digital Volt Ohmmeter (DVOM) for this test; your DVOM will be destroyed by the large amounts of amperage from the car's battery. Use a tester designed for charging system analysis, such as the Rotunda Alternator, Regulator, Battery and Starter Motor Tester 010-00725 (ARBST) or equivalent

1. Switch the tester to the ammeter setting.
2. Attach the positive (+) and negative (−) leads of the tester to the battery terminals.
3. Connect the current probe to the **B+** terminal on the alternator.
4. Start the engine and have an assistant run the engine at 2000 rpm. Adjust the tester load bank to determine the output of the alternator. Alternator output should be greater than the accompanying graph; if so, continue with the Alternator No-Load test. If the output is not greater than indicated by the chart, there is a problem in the charging system. Have the system further tested by a Ford qualified automotive technician.

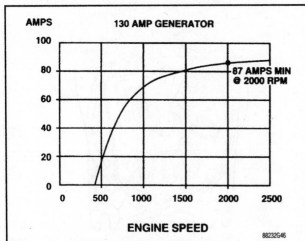

Fig. 51 Alternator Load Test graph—during the test procedure, the alternator should produce as much, or more, amperage as indicated on the graph

Alternator No-Load Test

1. Using the same tester as in the Alternator Load Test, switch the tester to the voltmeter function.
2. Connect the voltmeter positive (+) lead to the alternator **B+** terminal and the negative (−) lead to a good engine ground.
3. Turn all of the electrical accessories off and shut the doors.
4. While an assistant operates the engine at 2000 rpm, check the alternator output voltage. The voltage should be 13.0–15.0 volts. If the alternator does not produce voltage within this range, there is a problem in the charging system. Have the system further tested by a Ford qualified automotive technician.

REMOVAL & INSTALLATION

▶ See Figures 52 thru 61 (p. 26–29)

1. Disconnect the negative battery cable.
2. Remove the accessory drive belt.

3. Label and disengage all of the wiring connectors from the alternator. To disconnect push-on type terminals, depress the lock tab and pull straight off.
4. On 4.6L engines, remove the alternator bracket mounting bolts and the bracket from the engine.
5. Remove the alternator bolts, then remove the alternator from the engine.

To install:

6. Position the alternator on the engine.
7. Install the alternator mounting bolts. On 3.8L and 5.0L engines, tighten the upper bolt to 16–21 ft. lbs. (21–29 Nm) and the lower bolt to 30–40 ft. lbs. (40–55 Nm). On 4.6L engines, tighten both bolts to 15–22 ft. lbs. (20–30 Nm).

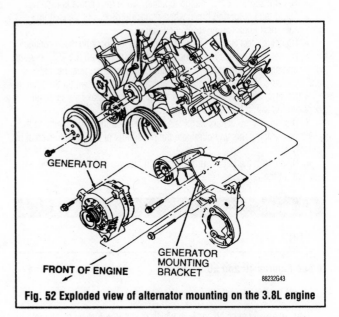

Fig. 52 Exploded view of alternator mounting on the 3.8L engine

1.	Alternator mounting bracket bolt	3.	Alternator mounting bolt
2.	Alternator mounting bracket	4.	Alternator
		5.	Engine block

Fig. 53 Exploded view of alternator mounting on the 4.6L SOHC engine

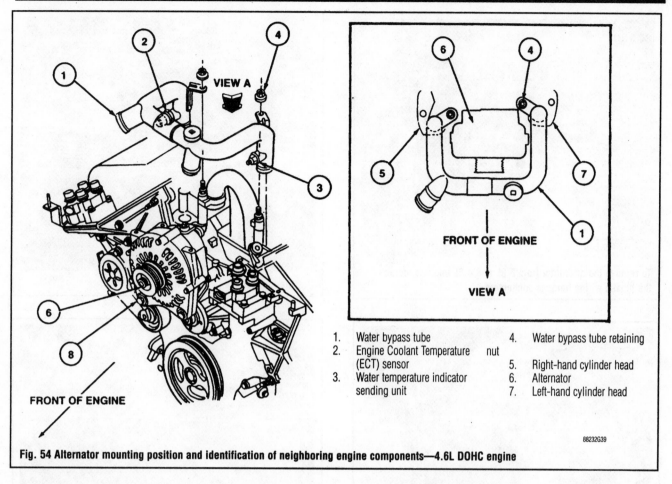

1. Water bypass tube
2. Engine Coolant Temperature (ECT) sensor
3. Water temperature indicator sending unit
4. Water bypass tube retaining nut
5. Right-hand cylinder head
6. Alternator
7. Left-hand cylinder head

88232G39

Fig. 54 Alternator mounting position and identification of neighboring engine components—4.6L DOHC engine

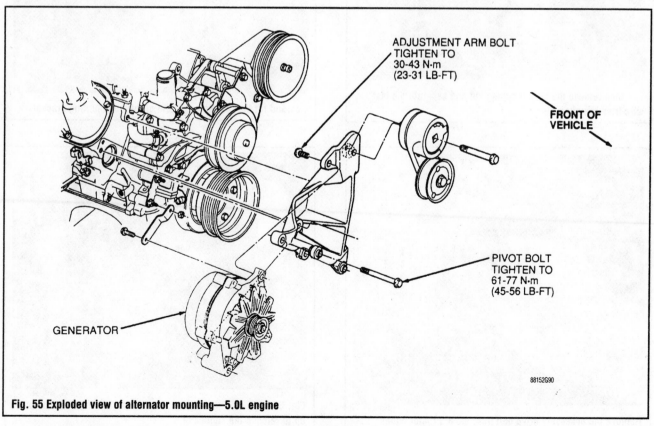

ADJUSTMENT ARM BOLT TIGHTEN TO 30-43 N·m (23-31 LB-FT)

FRONT OF VEHICLE

PIVOT BOLT TIGHTEN TO 61-77 N·m (45-56 LB-FT)

GENERATOR

88152G90

Fig. 55 Exploded view of alternator mounting—5.0L engine

To remove the alternator from 3.8L and 4.6L engines, detach the plastic wiring harness connectors . . .

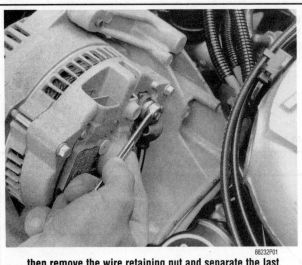

. . . then remove the wire retaining nut and separate the last wire from the alternator

Remove the accessory drive belt from the alternator pulley . . .

. . . then loosen the two mounting bolts . . .

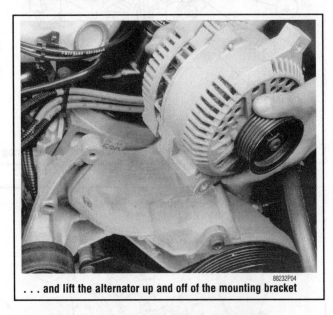

. . . and lift the alternator up and off of the mounting bracket

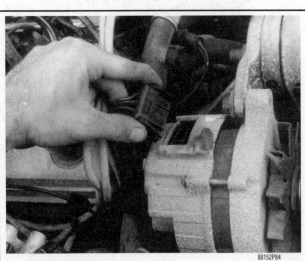

Fig. 56 For 5.0L engines, squeeze the catches together and pull up to release the connector

Fig. 57 Use a pick to release the catches on the side of the connectors if you can't access them

Fig. 60 Rotate the alternator up to access the regulator wiring if it isn't already disconnected

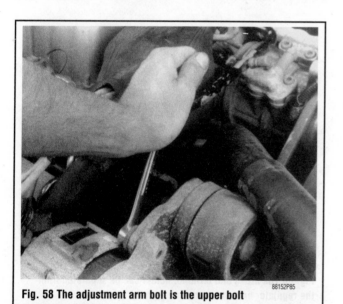

Fig. 58 The adjustment arm bolt is the upper bolt

Fig. 61 The regulator has a separate connector

8. On 4.6L engines, install the alternator mounting bracket and bolts. Tighten the bolts to 71–106 inch lbs. (8–12 Nm).

9. Install the accessory drive belt. Ensure that the drive belt is properly installed on the pulleys before starting the engine.

10. Attach all engine wiring harness connectors to the alternator.

11. Connect the negative battery cable.

Voltage Regulator

REMOVAL & INSTALLATION

Except 4.6L DOHC Engine

▶ See Figures 62 thru 68 (p. 30–31)

1. Disconnect the negative battery cable.

2. Remove 4 Torx® head screws holding the voltage regulator to the alternator rear housing. Remove the regulator, with the brush and terminal holder attached.

3. Hold the regulator in one hand and pry off the cap covering the **A** terminal screw head with a small prybar.

Fig. 59 The pivot arm bolt is the lower of the two bolts and is longer

Fig. 62 The regulator and brush/terminal holder are mounted on the backside of the alternator

Fig. 65 Slide the regulator out—the brushes will move out of the holder

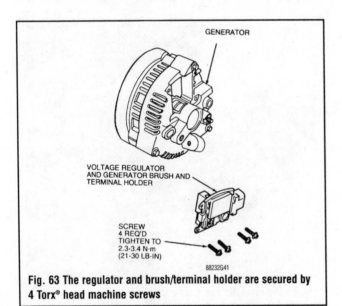

Fig. 63 The regulator and brush/terminal holder are secured by 4 Torx® head machine screws

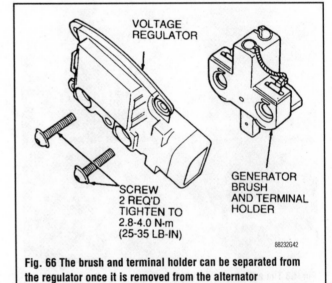

Fig. 66 The brush and terminal holder can be separated from the regulator once it is removed from the alternator

Fig. 64 Hold the regulator while removing the screws to prevent the regulator from dropping out and damaging the brushes

Fig. 67 When installing the regulator, press the brushes back into the housing

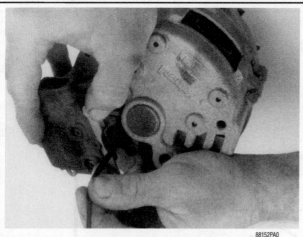

Fig. 68 Use a thin piece of soft material, like this plastic wire tie, to hold the brushes in position while replacing the regulator, or use a paper clip inserted in the hole

4. Remove 2 Torx® head screws retaining the regulator to the brush holder. Separate the regulator from the brush holder.

To install:

5. Install the brush holder on the regulator with 2 retaining screws. Tighten the screws to 25–35 inch lbs. (2.8–4.0 Nm).

6. Install the cap on the head of the **A** terminal screw.

7. Depress the brushes into the holder and hold the brushes in position by inserting a standard size paper clip, or equivalent tool, through both the location hole in the regulator and through the holes in the brushes.

8. Install the regulator/brush holder assembly and remove the paper clip. Install the attaching screws and tighten to 20–30 inch lbs. (2.3–3.4 Nm).

9. Connect the negative battery cable.

4.6L DOHC Engine

The internal voltage regulator in alternators used with 4.6L DOHC engines is not removable or serviceable in any way. If the voltage regulator is found to be defective, a new alternator must be installed.

STARTING SYSTEM

General Information

The starting system is designed to rotate the engine at a speed fast enough for the engine to start. The starting system is comprised of the following components:

- Permanent magnet gear-reduction starter motor with a solenoid-actuated drive
- Battery
- Remote control starter switch (part of the ignition switch)
- Park/Neutral Position (PNP) or Manual Lever Position (MLP) switch (on 1994 automatic transmission models) or Transmission Range (TR) sensor (on 1995–98 automatic transmission models)
- Clutch Pedal Position (CPP) switch (on manual transmission models)
- Starter relay
- Heavy circuit wiring

Heavy cables, connectors and switches are utilized by the starting system because of the large amount of amperage this system is required to handle while cranking the engine. For premium starter motor function, the resistance in the starting system must be kept to an absolute minimum.

A discharged or faulty battery, loose or corroded connections, or partially broken cables will result in slower-than-normal cranking speeds. The amount of damage evident may even prevent the starter motor from rotating the engine at all.

Vehicles equipped with a manual transmission are equipped with a Clutch Pedal Position (CPP) switch in the starter circuit, which is designed to prevent the starter motor from operating unless the clutch pedal is depressed. Vehicles equipped with automatic transmissions are equipped with either a Park/Neutral Position (PNP) switch, a Manual Lever Position (MLP) switch or a Transmission Range (TR) sensor in the starter circuit. These switches prevent the starter motor from functioning unless the transmission range selector lever is in Neutral (**N**) or Park (**P**).

The starter motor is a 12 volt assembly, which has the starter solenoid mounted on the drive end-housing. The starter solenoid energizes when the relay contacts are closed. When the solenoid energizes, the starter drive engages with the flywheel ring gear, rotating the crankshaft and starting the engine. An overrunning clutch in the starter drive assembly protects the starter motor from excessive speed when the engine starts.

Starter

TESTING

▶ **See Figures 69, 70, 71 and 72 (p. 32–34)**

Use the charts to help locate and diagnose starting system problems. Remember that the starter uses large amounts of current during operation, so use all appropriate precautions during testing.

REMOVAL & INSTALLATION

▶ **See Figures 73, 74 and 75 (p. 35–36)**

1. Disconnect the negative battery cable.
2. Raise the front of the vehicle and install jackstands beneath the frame. Firmly apply the parking brake and place blocks in back of the rear wheels.
3. Tag and disconnect the wiring at the starter.

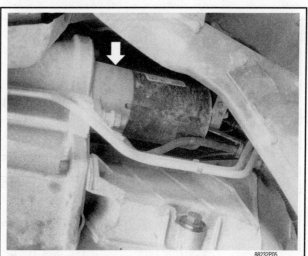

The starter motor (arrow) is mounted under the vehicle, next to the transmission

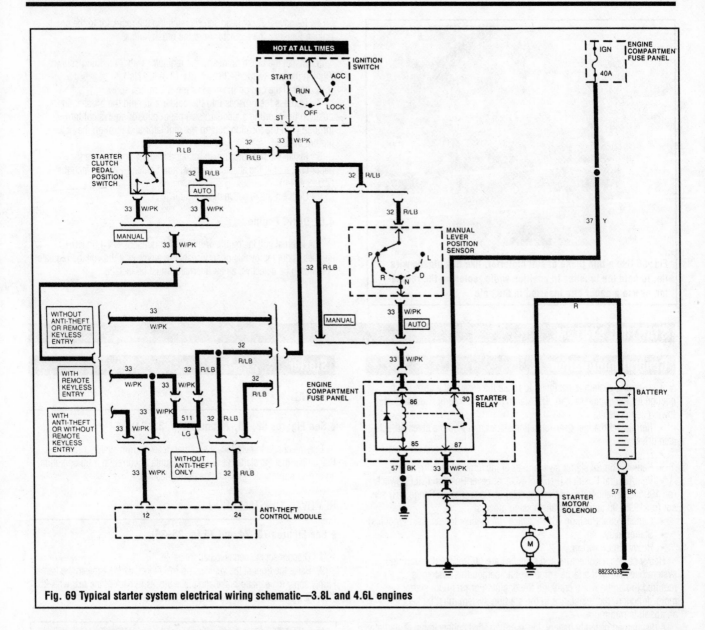

Fig. 69 Typical starter system electrical wiring schematic—3.8L and 4.6L engines

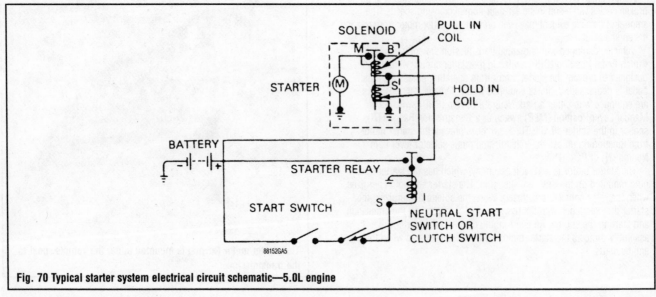

Fig. 70 Typical starter system electrical circuit schematic—5.0L engine

System Inspection

CAUTION: When disconnecting the plastic hardshell connector at the solenoid "S" terminal, grasp the plastic connector and pull lead off. DO NOT pull separately on lead wire.

WARNING: WHEN SERVICING STARTER OR PERFORMING OTHER UNDERHOOD WORK IN THE VICINITY OF THE STARTER, BE AWARE THAT THE HEAVY GAUGE BATTERY INPUT LEAD AT THE STARTER SOLENOID IS "ELECTRICALLY HOT" AT ALL TIMES.

A protective cap or boot is provided over this terminal on all carlines and must be replaced after servicing. Be sure to disconnect battery negative cable before servicing starter.

1. Inspect starting system for loose connections.

2. If system does not operate properly, note condition and continue diagnosis using the symptom chart.

WARNING: WHEN WORKING IN AREA OF THE STARTER, BE CAREFUL TO AVOID TOUCHING HOT EXHAUST COMPONENTS.

CONDITION	POSSIBLE SOURCE	ACTION
Starter solenoid does not pull-in and starter does not crank (Audible click may or may not be heard).	• Open fuse. • Low battery. • Inoperative fender apron relay. • Open circuit or high resistance in external feed circuit to starter solenoid. • Inoperative starter.	• Check fuse continuity. • Refer to appropriate battery section in this manual. • Go to Evaluation Procedure 2. • Go to Test A. • Replace starter. See removal and installation procedure.
Unusual starter noise during starter overrun.	• Starter not mounted flush (cocked). • Noise from other components. • Ring gear tooth damage or excessive ring gear runout. • Defective starter.	• Realign starter on transmission bell housing. • Investigate other powertrain accessory noise contributors. • Refer to appropriate engine section in this manual. • Replace starter. See removal and installation procedure.
Starter cranks but engine does not start.	• Problem in fuel system. • Problem in ignition system. • Engine related concern.	• Refer to appropriate fuel system section in this manual. • Refer to appropriate ignition system section in this manual. • Refer to appropriate engine section in this manual.
Starter cranks slowly.	• Low battery. • High resistance or loose connections in starter solenoid battery feed or ground circuit. • Ring gear runout excessive. • Inoperative starter.	• Refer to appropriate battery section in this manual. • Check that all connections are secure. • Refer to appropriate engine section in this manual. • Replace Starter. See removal and installation procedure.
Starter remains engaged and runs with engine.	• Shorted ignition switch. • Battery cable touching solenoid 'S' terminal (inoperative or mispositioned cable). • Inoperative starter.	• Refer to appropriate ignition system section in this manual. • Replace or relocate cable and replace starter. • Replace starter. See removal and installation procedure.

88152GA6

Fig. 71 System inspection chart

Evaluation Procedure 1

NOTE: Hoist vehicle (if necessary) to access starter solenoid terminals.

CAUTION: Remove plastic safety cap on starter solenoid and disconnect hardshell connector at solenoid 'S' terminal

CHECK STARTER MOTOR — TEST A

	TEST STEP	RESULT ▶	ACTION TO TAKE
A1	CHECK FOR VOLTAGE TO STARTER		
	• Key OFF. Transmission in Park or Neutral. • Check for voltage between starter B+ terminal and starter drive housing. • Is voltage OK? (12-12.45V)	Yes ▶ No ▶	GO to **A2**. CHECK wire connections between battery and starter solenoid and the ground circuit for open or short.
A2	CHECK STARTER MOTOR		
	• Key OFF. Transmission in Park or Neutral. • Connect one end of a jumper wire to the starter B+ terminal and momentarily touch the other end to solenoid 'S' terminal. • Does starter crank?	Yes ▶ No ▶	CHECK connections from output of fender apron relay to 'S' terminal for open or short. Defective starter. REPLACE starter.

Evaluation Procedure 2

CHECK FENDER APRON RELAY — TEST B

	TEST STEP	RESULT ▶	ACTION TO TAKE
B1	CHECK FENDER APRON RELAY		
	• Key in START. Transmission in Park or Neutral. • Is case ground OK?	Yes ▶ No ▶	GO to **B2**. SERVICE ground. GO to **B2**.
B2	CHECK VOLTAGE AT FENDER APRON RELAY START TERMINAL		
	• Key in START. Transmission in Park or Neutral. • Check for voltage between fender apron relay start terminal and case ground. • Is voltage OK? (12-12.45 V)	Yes ▶ No ▶	GO to **B3**. Open circuit or high resistance exists in external circuit wiring or components. Check the following: ● All circuit connections including plastic hardshell connector at solenoid 'S' terminal to make sure it is not broken or distorted. ● Ignition switch. ● Neutral switch or manual lever position sensor. ● Anti-theft contact.
B3	CHECK OUTPUT TERMINAL VOLTAGE		
	• Key in START. Transmission in Park or Neutral. • Check for voltage at output terminal of fender relay. • Is voltage OK?	Yes ▶ No ▶	REFER to Starter System Diagnosis in this section. Defective fender apron relay. REMOVE and REPLACE relay.

88152GA7

Fig. 72 Evaluation procedure charts

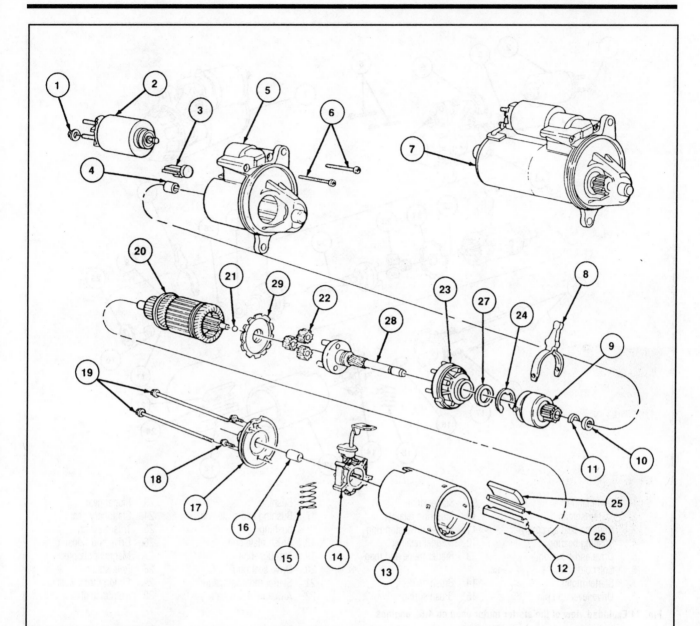

1. Terminal Nut
2. Starter Solenoid
3. Housing Seal Assy
4. Bushing Bearing
5. Drive End Housing
6. Solenoid Screw (2 Req'd)
7. Starter Motor Assy
8. Drive Lever
9. Drive Assy
10. Stop Ring Retainer
11. Stop Ring
12. Magnet Retainer (6 Req'd)
13. Starter Frame
14. Brush Assy
15. Spring
16. Bushing Bearing
17. Brush End Plate
18. Brush Plate Screw (2 Req'd)
19. Through-Bolt (2 Req'd)
20. Armature Assy
21. Armature Thrust Ball
22. Planet Gear
23. Stationary Gear Assy
24. Truarc E-Ring
25. Magnet Pole Piece (6 Req'd)
26. Pole Shunt (6 Req'd)
27. Armature
28. Shaft Assy
29. Gear Retainer

88152GA4

Fig. 73 Exploded view of the starter motor used on 3.8L and 5.0L engines

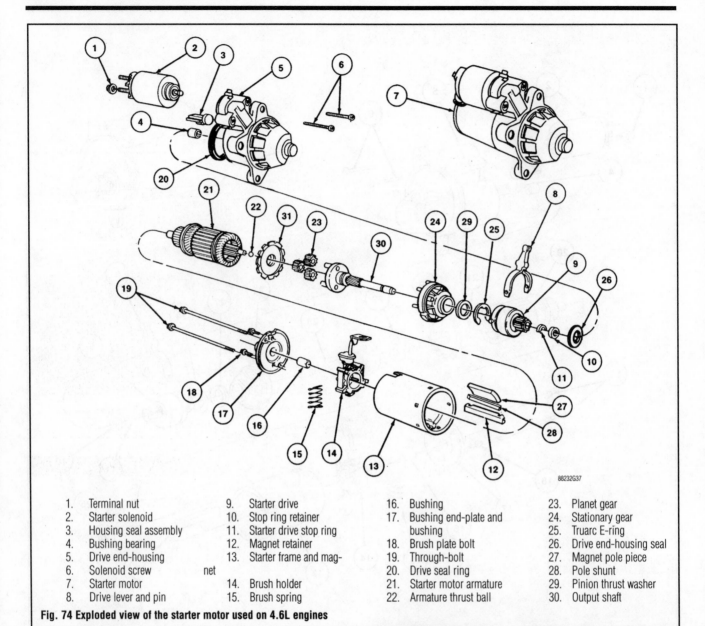

1.	Terminal nut	9.	Starter drive	16. Bushing
2.	Starter solenoid	10.	Stop ring retainer	17. Bushing end-plate and
3.	Housing seal assembly	11.	Starter drive stop ring	bushing
4.	Bushing bearing	12.	Magnet retainer	18. Brush plate bolt
5.	Drive end-housing	13.	Starter frame and mag-	19. Through-bolt
6.	Solenoid screw		net	20. Drive seal ring
7.	Starter motor	14.	Brush holder	21. Starter motor armature
8.	Drive lever and pin	15.	Brush spring	22. Armature thrust ball

23.	Planet gear
24.	Stationary gear
25.	Truarc E-ring
26.	Drive end-housing seal
27.	Magnet pole piece
28.	Pole shunt
29.	Pinion thrust washer
30.	Output shaft

Fig. 74 Exploded view of the starter motor used on 4.6L engines

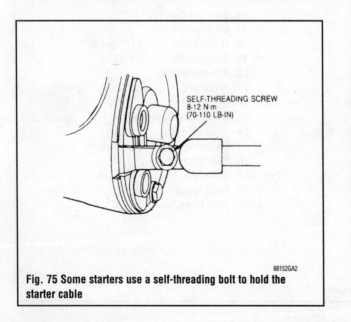

Fig. 75 Some starters use a self-threading bolt to hold the starter cable

Detach the wiring, unfasten the mounting bolts and remove the starter motor from the vehicle

4. Unfasten the starter mounting bolts and remove the starter.

To install:

5. Position the starter motor against the engine and install the mounting bolts. Tighten the mounting bolts to 15–19 ft. lbs. (21–27 Nm).

6. Install the starter solenoid connector by pushing it straight on. Ensure that the connector locks in position with a notable click.

Install the starter cable nut to the starter solenoid B-terminal. Tighten the nut to 80–123 inch lbs. (9–14 Nm).

7. Connect any remaining wiring to the starter motor.
8. Lower the front of the vehicle and remove the wheel blocks.
9. Connect the negative battery cable.

RELAY REPLACEMENT

▶ **See Figure 76**

1. Disconnect the negative battery cable from the battery.
2. If equipped, remove the power distribution box cover.
3. Disconnect the positive battery cable from the battery.
4. Remove the nut securing the positive battery cable to the relay.
5. Remove the positive cable and any other wiring under that cable.
6. Label and remove the push-on wires from the front of the relay.
7. Remove the nut and disconnect the cable from the starter side of the relay.

8. Remove the relay mounting bolts and remove the relay.

To install:

9. Install the relay and mounting bolts. Tighten the mounting bolts until snug.
10. Attach all wiring to the relay.
11. If equipped, install the power distribution box cover.
12. Connect the positive (+) cable to the battery.
13. Connect the negative (–) cable to the battery.

Fig. 76 Make sure the negative battery cable is disconnected before removing any of the relay wiring

SENDING UNITS

The following sending units are used solely to provide information to the instrument panel gauges or warning lights. Sensors which provide information to the engine and emission control system can be found in Section 4 of this manual.

Coolant Temperature Sender

The coolant temperature sender is located in the following positions:
- 3.8L engine—center front of the engine, below the cooling system air purge port
- 4.6L SOHC engine—top front of the engine, on the left-hand side
- 4.6L DOHC engine—top front of the engine, on the left-hand lower side of the water bypass tube
- 5.0L engine—top front of the engine, on the left-hand side of the distributor

TESTING

▶ **See Figures 77 and 78**

Before going to the trouble of removing the sender from the engine block and testing it, perform the tests presented in the accompanying chart to ensure that it is the sender malfunctioning, and not another part of the circuit.

1. Unscrew the coolant temperature sender from the engine block.
2. Attach an ohmmeter to the sender unit as follows:
   a. Attach one lead to the metal body of the sender unit (near the sender unit's threads).
   b. Attach the other lead to the sender unit's wiring harness connector terminal.
3. With the leads still attached, place the sender unit in a pot of cold water so that neither of the leads is immersed in the water. The portion of the sender unit which normally makes contact with the engine coolant should be submerged.

4. Measure and note the resistance.
5. Slowly heat up the pot on a stove to 190–210° F (88–99° C) and observe the resistance of the sender unit. The resistance should evenly and steadily decrease as the water temperature increases. The resistance should not jump drastically or decrease erratically.
6. If the sender unit did not function as described, replace the sender unit with a new one.

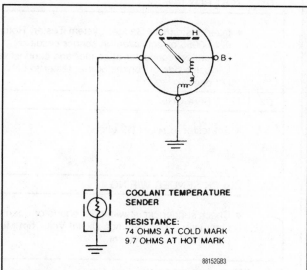

COOLANT TEMPERATURE SENDER

RESISTANCE:
74 OHMS AT COLD MARK
9.7 OHMS AT HOT MARK

Fig. 77 Common coolant temperature sender electrical circuit schematic

Temperature Gauge System

CAUTION: Do not apply 12-volts or ground directly to the temperature sender terminal. This voltage will damage the sender.

1. Verify that the engine-to-body ground strap is secure. A poor ground can cause high temperature gauge indication.

2. Idle the engine, with all accessories off, until the thermostat opens and the engine coolant temperature stabilizes. The temperature gauge pointer should indicate in the lower half of the normal band. If the coolant temperature does not stabilize, check the cooling system for proper function.

GAUGE INOPERATIVE — POINTER DOES NOT MOVE
PINPOINT TEST C

TEST STEP		RESULT ▶	ACTION TO TAKE
C1	VERIFY CONDITION		
	• Verify condition.	Gauge pointer does not move ▶	GO to **C2**.
		Gauge pointer moves ▶	GO to **D1**.
C2	CHECK OTHER GAUGES		
	• Check power to cluster. With ignition on, observe other gauges and warning lamps for proper operation. If necessary, use Rotunda Digital/Volt Ohm Meter 014-00407 or equivalent or test lamp to verify voltage at B+ terminal of cluster connector.	Other gauges and warning lamps operate correctly; voltage present at cluster ▶	GO to **D1**.
		Other gauges and warning lamps do not operate correctly; no voltage present at cluster ▶	SERVICE power to cluster.

GAUGE INACCURATE
PINPOINT TEST D

TEST STEP		RESULT ▶	ACTION TO TAKE
D1	TEST BOX CHECK		
	• Insert Instrument Gauge, System Tester, Rotunda 021-00055 or equivalent in sender circuit. Disconnect connector at sender and connect tester to cluster side of connector. Set tester to LOW (73 ohms).	Gauge reads C ▶	GO to **D2**.
		Pointer does not move ▶	GO to **D3**.
D2	TEST BOX CHECK		
	• Set tester to HIGH (10 ohms).	Gauge reads H ▶	REPLACE sender.
		Gauge does not read H ▶	GO to **D3**.
D3	CHECK SENDER WIRING		
	• Check sender circuit wiring for shorts or open with ohmmeter, using Rotunda Digital Volt/Ohm Meter 014-00407, or equivalent.	(OK) ▶	REPLACE gauge.
		(OK̸) ▶	SERVICE wiring.

88152GB4

Fig. 78 Temperature gauge diagnostic chart

REMOVAL & INSTALLATION

▶ **See Figures 79 and 80**

⁂ CAUTION

Ensure that the engine is cold prior to opening the cooling system or removing the sender from the engine. The cooling system on a hot engine is under high pressure, and released hot coolant or steam can cause severe burns.

1. Disconnect the negative battery cable.
2. Remove the radiator cap (except 4.6L engines) or the degas bottle cap (4.6L engines) to relieve any system pressure.
3. Disconnect the wiring at the sender.
4. Unscrew and remove the coolant temperature sender from the engine.

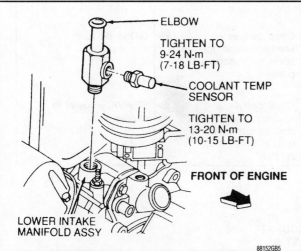

Fig. 79 Temperature gauge sender mounted in an elbow—5.0L engine

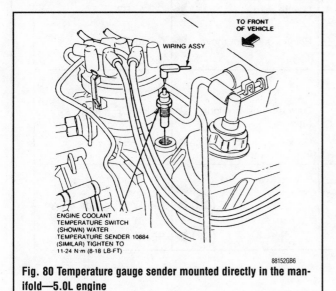

Fig. 80 Temperature gauge sender mounted directly in the manifold—5.0L engine

To install:

5. Coat the threads on the sender with Teflon® tape or electrically conductive sealer, then install the sender. Tighten the sender to 107–143 inch lbs. (12–16 Nm).
6. Attach the wiring to the sender and connect the negative battery cable.
7. If necessary, add antifreeze to replace any lost coolant, then install the radiator cap.

Oil Pressure Sender and Switch

➡**An oil pressure sender is used with an oil pressure gauge, whereas an oil pressure switch is used with a low oil warning lamp.**

The oil pressure sender/switch is located as follows:
• 3.8L engine—lower left-hand side of the engine, above the oil filter
• 4.6L and 5.0L engines—left-hand front of the engine, below the rocker arm cover

TESTING

Oil Pressure Sender

▶ **See Figures 81 and 82**

Use the accompanying diagnostic chart to help pinpoint oil pressure sender and oil pressure gauge malfunctioning.

Oil Pressure Switch

1. To test the oil pressure switch, open the hood and locate the switch.
2. Disconnect the wire from the switch. Attach one end of a jumper wire to the terminal on the end of the wire, then touch the other end of the jumper wire to a good engine ground (any bare metal engine surface). Have an assistant observe the instrument gauge cluster while you do this and tell you if the low oil warning lamp illuminates or not; the low oil warning lamp should illuminate.
   a. If the lamp does not illuminate, skip to Step 3.
   b. If the lamp does illuminate, replace the switch with a new one.

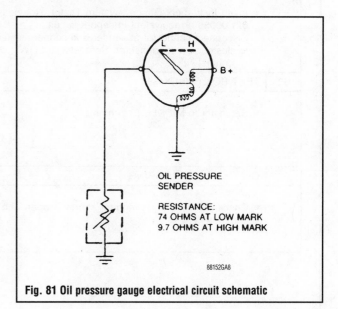

Fig. 81 Oil pressure gauge electrical circuit schematic

OIL GAUGE INOPERATIVE — POINTER DOES NOT MOVE
PINPOINT TEST A

TEST STEP	RESULT ▶	ACTION TO TAKE
A1 VERIFY CONDITION • Verify Condition.	Gauge pointer does not ▶ move	GO to **A2**.
	Gauge pointer moves ▶	GO to **B1**.
A2 CHECK OTHER GAUGES • Check power to cluster. With ignition on, observe other gauges and warning lamps for proper operation. If necessary, use voltmeter or test lamp to verify voltage at B+ terminal of cluster connector.	Other gauges and ▶ warning lamps operate correctly; voltage present at cluster	GO to **B1**.
	Other gauges and ▶ warning lamps do not operate correctly; no voltage present at cluster	SERVICE power to cluster.

OIL GAUGE INACCURATE
PINPOINT TEST B

TEST STEP	RESULT ▶	ACTION TO TAKE
B1 TEST BOX CHECK • Insert Instrument Gauge, System Tester, Rotunda 021-00055 or equivalent in sender circuit. Disconnect connector at sender and connect tester to cluster side of connector. Set tester to LOW (73 ohms).	Gauge reads L ▶	GO to **B2**.
	Pointer does not move ▶	GO to **B3**.
B2 TEST BOX CHECK • Set tester to MIDDLE (22 ohms).	Gauge reads in middle ▶ (approx.)	REPLACE sender.
	Gauge does not read ▶ in middle (approx.)	GO to **B3**.
B3 CHECK SENDER WIRING • Check sender circuit wiring for shorts or open with ohmmeter.	(OK) ▶	REPLACE gauge.
	(OK̸) ▶	SERVICE wiring.

88152GA9

Fig. 82 Oil pressure gauge diagnostic chart

3. Before jumping to any conclusions, try a different area for grounding the jumper wire on the engine. If the lamp still does not illuminate, touch the jumper wire end to the negative (–) battery post.

    a. If the lamp illuminates, the problem lies with the engine not being properly grounded.

    b. If the lamp does not illuminate, skip to Step 4.

4. Connect the original wire to the oil pressure switch. While sitting in the vehicle, turn the ignition switch to the **ON** position without actually starting the engine. Observe the other lights on the instrument cluster.

    a. If all of the other lights illuminate when turning the ignition switch **ON**, the oil pressure switch is defective and must be replaced.

    b. If none of the other lights illuminate, there is a problem with power supply to the instrument cluster and gauges.

REMOVAL & INSTALLATION

▶ **See Figure 83**

1. Disconnect the negative battery cable.
2. Disconnect the wiring at the sender/switch.
3. Unscrew and remove the oil pressure sender/switch from the engine.

To install:

4. Coat the threads with electrically conductive sealer and thread the unit into place. Tighten the sender/switch to 10–18 ft. lbs. (13–24 Nm).

5. Attach the wiring to the sender/switch and connect the negative battery cable.

Electric Fan Switch

These vehicles do not use a separate cooling fan switch; the function of the cooling fan switch is integral with the Powertrain Control Module (PCM). The PCM receives a signal from the Engine Coolant Temperature (ECT) sensor, which it uses to decide when to turn the electric cooling fan on. To turn the cooling fan on, the PCM sends a signal to the Constant Control Relay Module (CCRM), which houses the cooling fan relay and relay control unit. The cooling fan relay and relay control unit operate the cooling fan until the PCM decides the fan should be turned off.

TESTING

If the fan does not turn on at all, ensure that the fan fuse has not blown. If the fuse is blown, replace it with a new one.

Because the cooling fan is controlled by the Powertrain Control Module (PCM), it is difficult to test only the fan switch. The system should be inspected by a qualified automotive technician if the fan is malfunctioning. However, since the PCM utilizes the signal from the ECT, the ECT can be tested before the vehicle is taken to a professional. Testing for the ECT is located in Section 4 of this manual. If the ECT is found to be functioning correctly, have the rest of the system inspected by a professional.

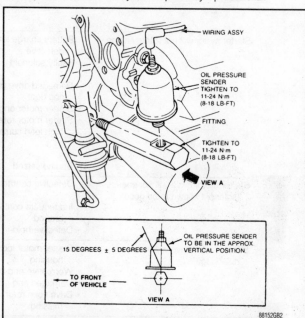

Fig. 83 When installing the oil pressure sender on 5.0L engines, ensure that it is positioned vertically (as indicated)

Troubleshooting Basic Starting System Problems

Problem	Cause	Solution
Starter motor rotates engine slowly	• Battery charge low or battery defective	• Charge or replace battery
	• Defective circuit between battery and starter motor	• Clean and tighten, or replace cables
	• Low load current	• Bench-test starter motor. Inspect for worn brushes and weak brush springs.
	• High load current	• Bench-test starter motor. Check engine for friction, drag or coolant in cylinders. Check ring gear-to-pinion gear clearance.
Starter motor will not rotate engine	• Battery charge low or battery defective	• Charge or replace battery
	• Faulty solenoid	• Check solenoid ground. Repair or replace as necessary.
	• Damaged drive pinion gear or ring gear	• Replace damaged gear(s)
	• Starter motor engagement weak	• Bench-test starter motor
	• Starter motor rotates slowly with high load current	• Inspect drive yoke pull-down and point gap, check for worn end bushings, check ring gear clearance
	• Engine seized	• Repair engine
Starter motor drive will not engage (solenoid known to be good)	• Defective contact point assembly	• Repair or replace contact point assembly
	• Inadequate contact point assembly ground	• Repair connection at ground screw
	• Defective hold-in coil	• Replace field winding assembly
Starter motor drive will not disengage	• Starter motor loose on flywheel housing	• Tighten mounting bolts
	• Worn drive end busing	• Replace bushing
	• Damaged ring gear teeth	• Replace ring gear or driveplate
	• Drive yoke return spring broken or missing	• Replace spring
Starter motor drive disengages prematurely	• Weak drive assembly thrust spring	• Replace drive mechanism
	• Hold-in coil defective	• Replace field winding assembly
Low load current	• Worn brushes	• Replace brushes
	• Weak brush springs	• Replace springs

TCCS2C01

Troubleshooting Basic Charging System Problems

Problem	Cause	Solution
Noisy alternator	• Loose mountings	• Tighten mounting bolts
	• Loose drive pulley	• Tighten pulley
	• Worn bearings	• Replace alternator
	• Brush noise	• Replace alternator
	• Internal circuits shorted (High pitched whine)	• Replace alternator
Squeal when starting engine or accelerating	• Glazed or loose belt	• Replace or adjust belt
Indicator light remains on or ammeter indicates discharge (engine running)	• Broken belt	• Install belt
	• Broken or disconnected wires	• Repair or connect wiring
	• Internal alternator problems	• Replace alternator
	• Defective voltage regulator	• Replace voltage regulator/alternator
Car light bulbs continually burn out— battery needs water continually	• Alternator/regulator overcharging	• Replace voltage regulator/alternator
Car lights flare on acceleration	• Battery low	• Charge or replace battery
	• Internal alternator/regulator problems	• Replace alternator/regulator
Low voltage output (alternator light flickers continually or ammeter needle wanders)	• Loose or worn belt	• Replace or adjust belt
	• Dirty or corroded connections	• Clean or replace connections
	• Internal alternator/regulator problems	• Replace alternator/regulator

TCCS2C02

3

ENGINE AND ENGINE OVERHAUL

GENERAL ENGINE SPECIFICATIONS

Year	Engine ID/VIN	Engine Displacement Liters (cc)	Fuel System Type	Net Horsepower @ rpm	Net Torque @ rpm (ft. lbs.)	Bore x Stroke (in.)	Compression Ratio	Oil Pressure (lbs. @ rpm)
1994	4	3.8 (3802)	SFI	140@3800	215@2400	3.81x3.39	8.2:1	40-60@2500
	D ①	5.0 (4949)	SFI	225@4200	315@2600	4.00x3.00	9.0:1	40-60@2000
	T	5.0 (4949)	SFI	200@4000	275@3000	4.00x3.00	9.0:1	40-60@2000
1995	4	3.8 (3802)	SFI	140@3800	215@2400	3.81x3.39	8.2:1	40-60@2500
	D ①	5.0 (4949)	SFI	225@4200	315@2600	4.00x3.00	9.0:1	40-60@2000
	T	5.0 (4949)	SFI	200@4000	275@3000	4.00x3.00	9.0:1	40-60@2000
1996	4	3.8 (3802)	SFI	145@4000	215@2750	3.81x3.39	9.0:1	40-60@2500
	V ①	4.6 (4593)	SFI	305@5800	300@4800	3.55x3.54	9.5:1	20-45@1500
	W	4.6 (4593)	SFI	215@4400	285@3500	3.55x3.54	9.5:1	20-45@1500
1997	4	3.8 (3802)	SFI	145@4000	215@2750	3.81x3.39	9.0:1	40-60@2500
	V ①	4.6 (4593)	SFI	305@5800	300@4800	3.55x3.54	9.5:1	20-45@1500
	W	4.6 (4593)	SFI	215@4400	285@3500	3.55x3.54	9.5:1	20-45@1500
1998	4	3.8 (3802)	SFI	150@4000	215@2750	3.81x3.39	9.0:1	40-60@2500
	V ①	4.6 (4593)	SFI	305@5800	300@4800	3.55x3.54	9.5:1	20-45@1500
	W	4.6 (4593)	SFI	225@4400	290@3500	3.55x3.54	9.0:1	20-45@1500

① Mustang Cobra model only.

88233C00

VALVE SPECIFICATIONS

Year	Engine ID/VIN	Engine Displacement Liters (cc)	Seat Angle (deg.)	Face Angle (deg.)	Spring Test Pressure (lbs. @ in.)	Approx. Free Length (in.)	Stem-to-Guide Clearance (in.) Intake	Exhaust	Stem Diameter (in.) Intake	Exhaust
1994	4	3.8 (3802)	44.47	45.80	220 @ 1.18	NA	0.0010-0.0028	0.0015-0.0033	0.3415-0.3423	0.3410-0.3418
	D	5.0 (4949)	45.00	44.00	①	②	0.0010-0.0027	0.0015-0.0032	0.3416-0.3423	0.3411-0.3418
	T	5.0 (4949)	45.00	44.00	③	④	0.0010-0.0027	0.0015-0.0032	0.3416-0.3423	0.3411-0.3418
1995	4	3.8 (3802)	44.47	45.80	220 @ 1.18	NA	0.0010-0.0028	0.0015-0.0033	0.3415-0.3423	0.3410-0.3418
	D	5.0 (4949)	45.00	44.00	①	②	0.0010-0.0027	0.0015-0.0032	0.3416-0.3423	0.3411-0.3418
	T	5.0 (4949)	45.00	44.00	③	④	0.0010-0.0027	0.0015-0.0032	0.3416-0.3423	0.3411-0.3418
1996	4	3.8 (3802)	44.47	45.80	220 @ 1.18	NA	0.0010-0.0028	0.0015-0.0033	0.3415-0.3423	0.3410-0.3418
	V	4.6 (4593)	45.00	45.50	160 @ 1.03	1.659	0.00079-0.00272	0.00181-0.00374	0.2746-0.2754	0.2736-0.2744
	W	4.6 (4593)	45.00	45.50	132 @ 1.10	1.950	0.00079-0.00272	0.00181-0.00374	0.2746-0.2754	0.2736-0.2744
1997	4	3.8 (3802)	44.47	45.80	220 @ 1.18	NA	0.0010-0.0028	0.0015-0.0033	0.3415-0.3423	0.3410-0.3418
	V	4.6 (4593)	45.00	45.50	160 @ 1.03	1.659	0.00079-0.00272	0.00181-0.00374	0.2746-0.2754	0.2736-0.2744
	W	4.6 (4593)	45.00	45.50	132 @ 1.10	1.950	0.00079-0.00272	0.00181-0.00374	0.2746-0.2754	0.2736-0.2744
1998	4	3.8 (3802)	44.47	45.80	220 @ 1.18	NA	0.0010-0.0028	0.0015-0.0033	0.3415-0.3423	0.3410-0.3418
	V	4.6 (4593)	45.00	45.50	160 @ 1.03	1.659	0.00079-0.00272	0.00181-0.00374	0.2746-0.2754	0.2736-0.2744
	W	4.6 (4593)	45.00	45.50	132 @ 1.10	1.950	0.00079-0.00272	0.00181-0.00374	0.2746-0.2754	0.2736-0.2744

NA - Not Available

① Intake valve spring: 280 lbs. @ 1.30 in.
   Exhaust valve spring: 264 lbs. @ 1.12 in.
② Intake valve spring: 2.017 in.
   Exhaust valve spring: 1.389 in.
③ Intake valve spring: 211-230 lbs. @ 1.33 in.
   Exhaust valve spring: 200-226 lbs. @ 1.15 in.
④ Intake valve spring: 2.02 in.
   Exhaust valve spring: 1.79 in.

88233C01

CAMSHAFT SPECIFICATIONS
All measurements given in inches.

Year	Engine ID/VIN	Displacement Liters (cc)	Journal Diameter					Elevation		Bearing Clearance	Camshaft End-Play
			1	2	3	4	5	Intake	Exhaust		
1994	4	3.8 (3802)	2.0505-2.0515	2.0505-2.0515	2.0505-2.0515	2.0505-2.0515	—	0.245	0.259	0.001-0.003	0.001-0.006
	D	5.0 (4949)	2.0805-2.0815	2.0655-2.0665	2.0505-2.0515	2.0355-2.0365	2.0205-2.0215	0.282	0.282	0.006	0.009
	T	5.0 (4949)	2.0805-2.0815	2.0655-2.0665	2.0505-2.0515	2.0355-2.0365	2.0205-2.0215	0.278	0.278	0.006	0.009
1995	4	3.8 (3802)	2.0505-2.0515	2.0505-2.0515	2.0505-2.0515	2.0505-2.0515	—	0.245	0.259	0.001-0.003	0.001-0.006
	D	5.0 (4949)	2.0805-2.0815	2.0655-2.0665	2.0505-2.0515	2.0355-2.0365	2.0205-2.0215	0.282	0.282	0.006	0.009
	T	5.0 (4949)	2.0805-2.0815	2.0655-2.0665	2.0505-2.0515	2.0355-2.0365	2.0205-2.0215	0.278	0.278	0.006	0.009
1996	4	3.8 (3802)	2.0505-2.0515	2.0505-2.0515	2.0505-2.0515	2.0505-2.0515	—	0.245	0.259	0.001-0.003	0.001-0.006
	V	4.6 (4593)	1.0605-1.0615	1.0605-1.0615	1.0605-1.0615	1.0605-1.0615	1.0605-1.0615	①	0.219	0.001-0.003	0.001-0.006
	W	4.6 (4593)	1.0605-1.0615	1.0605-1.0615	1.0605-1.0615	1.0605-1.0615	1.0605-1.0615	0.259	0.259	0.001-0.003	0.001-0.006
1997	4	3.8 (3802)	2.0505-2.0515	2.0505-2.0515	2.0505-2.0515	2.0505-2.0515	—	0.245	0.259	0.001-0.003	0.001-0.006
	V	4.6 (4593)	1.0605-1.0615	1.0605-1.0615	1.0605-1.0615	1.0605-1.0615	1.0605-1.0615	①	0.219	0.001-0.003	0.001-0.006
	W	4.6 (4593)	1.0605-1.0615	1.0605-1.0615	1.0605-1.0615	1.0605-1.0615	1.0605-1.0615	0.259	0.259	0.001-0.003	0.001-0.006
1998	4	3.8 (3802)	2.0505-2.0515	2.0505-2.0515	2.0505-2.0515	2.0505-2.0515	—	0.245	0.259	0.001-0.003	0.001-0.006
	V	4.6 (4593)	1.0605-1.0615	1.0605-1.0615	1.0605-1.0615	1.0605-1.0615	1.0605-1.0615	①	0.219	0.001-0.003	0.001-0.006
	W	4.6 (4593)	1.0605-1.0615	1.0605-1.0615	1.0605-1.0615	1.0605-1.0615	1.0605-1.0615	0.259	0.259	0.001-0.003	0.001-0.006

① Primary intake lobe: 0.2195 in.
  Secondary intake lobe: 0.2188 in.

88233C02

CRANKSHAFT AND CONNECTING ROD SPECIFICATIONS

All measurements are given in inches.

Year	Engine ID/VIN	Engine Displacement Liters (cc)	Crankshaft				Connecting Rod		
			Main Brg. Journal Dia.	Main Brg. Oil Clearance	Shaft End-play	Thrust on No.	Journal Diameter	Oil Clearance	Side Clearance
1994	4	3.8 (3802)	2.5190-2.5198	0.0010-0.0014	0.0040-0.0080	3	2.3103-2.3111	0.0009-0.0027	0.0047-0.0114
	D	5.0 (4949)	2.2482-2.2490	0.0004-0.0015	0.0040-0.0080	3	2.1228-2.1236	0.0008-0.0015	0.0100-0.0200
	T	5.0 (4949)	2.2482-2.2490	0.0004-0.0015	0.0040-0.0080	3	2.1228-2.1236	0.0008-0.0015	0.0100-0.0200
1995	4	3.8 (3802)	2.5190-2.5198	0.0010-0.0014	0.0040-0.0080	3	2.3103-2.3111	0.0009-0.0027	0.0047-0.0114
	D	5.0 (4949)	2.2482-2.2490	0.0004-0.0015	0.0040-0.0080	3	2.1228-2.1236	0.0008-0.0015	0.0100-0.0200
	T	5.0 (4949)	2.2482-2.2490	0.0004-0.0015	0.0040-0.0080	3	2.1228-2.1236	0.0008-0.0015	0.0100-0.0200
1996	4	3.8 (3802)	2.5190-2.5198	0.0010-0.0014	0.0040-0.0080	3	2.3103-2.3111	0.0009-0.0027	0.0047-0.0114
	V	4.6 (4593)	2.6567-2.6576	0.0010-0.0020	0.0051-0.0118	5	2.0859-2.0867	0.0010-0.0027	0.1500-0.4500
	W	4.6 (4593)	2.6567-2.6576	0.0010-0.0026	0.0051-0.0118	5	2.0859-2.0867	0.0010-0.0027	0.1500-0.4500
1997	4	3.8 (3802)	2.5190-2.5198	0.0010-0.0014	0.0040-0.0080	3	2.3103-2.3111	0.0009-0.0027	0.0047-0.0114
	V	4.6 (4593)	2.6567-2.6576	0.0010-0.0020	0.0051-0.0118	5	2.0859-2.0867	0.0010-0.0027	0.1500-0.4500
	W	4.6 (4593)	2.6567-2.6576	0.0010-0.0026	0.0051-0.0118	5	2.0859-2.0867	0.0010-0.0027	0.1500-0.4500
1998	4	3.8 (3802)	2.5190-2.5198	0.0010-0.0014	0.0040-0.0080	3	2.3103-2.3111	0.0009-0.0027	0.0047-0.0114
	V	4.6 (4593)	2.6567-2.6576	0.0010-0.0020	0.0051-0.0118	5	2.0859-2.0867	0.0010-0.0027	0.1500-0.4500
	W	4.6 (4593)	2.6567-2.6576	0.0010-0.0026	0.0051-0.0118	5	2.0859-2.0867	0.0010-0.0027	0.1500-0.4500

88233C03

PISTON AND RING SPECIFICATIONS

All measurements are given in inches.

Year	Engine ID/VIN	Engine Displacement Liters (cc)	Piston Clearance	Ring Gap			Ring Side Clearance		
				Top Compression	Bottom Compression	Oil Control	Top Compression	Bottom Compression	Oil Control
1994	4	3.8 (3802)	0.0014-0.0032	0.011-0.012	0.009-0.020	0.015-0.058	0.0016-0.0034	0.0016-0.0034	SNUG
	D	5.0 (4949)	0.0012-0.0020	0.010-0.020	0.018-0.028	0.010-0.040	0.002-0.004	0.002-0.004	SNUG
	T	5.0 (4949)	0.0012-0.0020	0.010-0.020	0.018-0.028	0.010-0.040	0.002-0.004	0.002-0.004	SNUG
1995	4	3.8 (3802)	0.0014-0.0032	0.011-0.012	0.009-0.020	0.015-0.058	0.0016-0.0034	0.0016-0.0034	SNUG
	D	5.0 (4949)	0.0012-0.0020	0.010-0.020	0.018-0.028	0.010-0.040	0.002-0.004	0.002-0.004	SNUG
	T	5.0 (4949)	0.0012-0.0020	0.010-0.020	0.018-0.028	0.010-0.040	0.002-0.004	0.002-0.004	SNUG
1996	4	3.8 (3802)	0.0014-0.0032	0.011-0.012	0.009-0.020	0.015-0.058	0.0016-0.0034	0.0016-0.0034	SNUG
	V	4.6 (4593)	0.0007-0.0018	0.010-0.020	0.009-0.019	0.006-0.026	0.0004-0.0009	0.0012-0.0031	SNUG
	W	4.6 (4593)	0.0005-0.0010	0.009-0.019	0.009-0.019	0.006-0.026	0.0016-0.0035	0.0012-0.0031	SNUG
1997	4	3.8 (3802)	0.0014-0.0032	0.011-0.012	0.009-0.020	0.015-0.058	0.0016-0.0034	0.0016-0.0034	SNUG
	V	4.6 (4593)	0.0007-0.0018	0.010-0.020	0.009-0.019	0.006-0.026	0.0004-0.0009	0.0012-0.0031	SNUG
	W	4.6 (4593)	0.0005-0.0010	0.009-0.019	0.009-0.019	0.006-0.026	0.0016-0.0035	0.0012-0.0031	SNUG
1998	4	3.8 (3802)	0.0014-0.0032	0.011-0.012	0.009-0.020	0.015-0.058	0.0016-0.0034	0.0016-0.0034	SNUG
	V	4.6 (4593)	0.0007-0.0018	0.010-0.020	0.009-0.019	0.006-0.026	0.0004-0.0009	0.0012-0.0031	SNUG
	W	4.6 (4593)	0.0005-0.0010	0.009-0.019	0.009-0.019	0.006-0.026	0.0016-0.0035	0.0012-0.0031	SNUG

88233C04

TORQUE SPECIFICATIONS
All readings in ft. lbs.

Year	Engine ID/VIN	Engine Displacement Liters (cc)	Cylinder Head Bolts	Main Bearing Bolts	Rod Bearing Bolts	Crankshaft Damper Bolts	Flywheel Bolts	Manifold Intake	Manifold Exhaust	Spark Plugs	Lug Nut
1994	4	3.8 (3802)	①	65-81	31-36	103-132	54-64	②	15-22	7-15	95
	D	5.0 (4949)	③	60-70	19-24	110-130	75-85	④	26-32	10-15	95
	T	5.0 (4949)	③	60-70	19-24	110-130	75-85	④	26-32	10-15	95
1995	4	3.8 (3802)	①	65-81	31-36	103-132	54-64	②	15-22	7-15	95
	D	5.0 (4949)	③	60-70	19-24	110-130	75-85	④	26-32	10-15	95
	T	5.0 (4949)	③	60-70	19-24	110-130	75-85	④	26-32	10-15	95
1996	4	3.8 (3802)	①	65-81	31-36	103-132	54-64	②	15-22	7-15	95
	V	4.6 (4593)	⑤	⑥	⑦	114-121	54-64	⑧	13-16	7-15	95
	W	4.6 (4593)	⑤	⑨	⑩	114-121	54-64	15-22	15-22	7-15	95
1997	4	3.8 (3802)	①	65-81	31-36	103-132	54-64	②	15-22	7-15	95
	V	4.6 (4593)	⑤	⑥	⑦	114-121	54-64	⑧	13-16	7-15	95
	W	4.6 (4593)	⑤	⑨	⑩	114-121	54-64	15-22	15-22	7-15	95
1998	4	3.8 (3802)	①	65-81	31-36	103-132	54-64	②	15-22	7-15	95
	V	4.6 (4593)	⑤	⑥	⑦	114-121	54-64	⑧	13-16	7-15	95
	W	4.6 (4593)	⑤	⑨	⑩	114-121	54-64	15-22	15-22	7-15	95

① Do not reuse cylinder head bolts!
Step 1: 15 ft. lbs.
Step 2: 29 ft. lbs.
Step 3: 37 ft. lbs.
Step 4: Loosen all bolts one at a time and retighten as follows:
Long bolts: 11-18 ft. lbs.
Short bolts: 7-15 ft. lbs.

② Step 5: Tighten an additional 85-95 degrees.
Upper intake manifold bolts
Step 1: 8 ft. lbs.
Step 2: 15 ft. lbs.
Step 3: 24 ft. lbs.
Lower intake manifold
Step 1: 13 ft. lbs.

③ Step 2: 16 ft. lbs.
Do not reuse cylinder head bolts!
Step 1: 22-35 ft. lbs.
Step 2: 44-55 ft. lbs.

④ Step 3: Tighten an additional 85-95 degrees.
Step 1: 8 ft. lbs.
Step 2: 16 ft. lbs.
Step 3: 23-25 ft. lbs.

⑤ Do not reuse cylinder head bolts!
Step 1: 27-32 ft. lbs.
Step 2: Tighten an additional 85-95 degrees.
Step 3: Repeat Step 2.

⑥ Step 1: Main bearing cap bolts – 6-9 ft. lbs.
Step 2: Outer main bearing cap bolts – 16-21 ft. lbs.
Step 3: Inner main bearing cap bolts – 27-32 ft. lbs.
Step 4: Tighten main bearing cap bolts an additional 85-95 degrees.
Step 5: Main cap adjusting screws – 4 ft. lbs., then 7.5 ft. lbs.

⑦ Step 6: Main cap side bolts – 7 ft. lbs., then 14-17 ft. lbs.
Step 1: 5 ft. lbs.
Step 2: 10 ft. lbs.
Step 3: 18-25 ft. lbs.

⑧ Step 4: Tighten an additional 85-95 degrees.
Step 1: Four inside short bolts – 9-11 ft. lbs.
Step 2: All other bolts – 13-16 ft. lbs.
Step 3: Tighten all bolts an additional 85-95 degrees.

⑨ Do not reuse main bearing cap bolts!
Step 1: Main bearing cap bolts – 22-25 ft. lbs.
Step 2: Tighten an additional 85-95 degrees.
Step 3: Main bearing cap adjusting screws – 4 ft. lbs., then 6-8 ft. lbs.
Step 4: Main bearing cap side bolts – 7 ft. lbs., then 14-17 ft. lbs.

⑩ Do not reuse connecting rod bolts!
Step 1: 12 ft. lbs.
Step 2: Tighten an additional 85-95 degrees.

88233C05

ENGINE MECHANICAL

REMOVAL & INSTALLATION

> **✳✳ CAUTION**
>
> When draining the coolant, keep in mind that cats and dogs are attracted by ethylene glycol antifreeze, and are quite likely to drink any that is left in an uncovered container or in puddles on the ground. This will prove fatal in sufficient quantity. Always drain the coolant into a sealable container. Coolant should be reused unless it is contaminated or too old.

3.8L Engine

➡On vehicles equipped with air conditioning, it is vital to refer to Section 1 prior to performing this procedure.

1. On models equipped with air conditioning, have the system discharged and evacuated by an MVAC-trained, EPA-certified automotive technician. Have the A/C compressor removed from the engine.
2. Disconnect the negative battery cable.
3. Remove the cooling fan, radiator and all cooling system hoses.
4. Label and detach all engine wiring and vacuum hoses which will interfere with engine removal.
5. Remove the hood.
6. Remove the accessory drive belt and the air intake tube.
7. Remove the Mass Air Flow (MAF) sensor.
8. Remove the power steering pump and hoses.
9. Detach the accelerator and transmission control cables from the throttle body, and the control cables' mounting bracket from the engine.
10. Release fuel system pressure, then disconnect the fuel supply and return lines from the engine.
11. Remove the A/C compressor mounting bracket and drive belt tensioner.
12. Raise the vehicle and safely support it on jackstands.

> **✳✳ CAUTION**
>
> The EPA warns that prolonged contact with used engine oil may cause a number of skin disorders, including cancer! You should make every effort to minimize your exposure to used engine oil. Protective gloves should be worn when changing the oil. Wash your hands and any other exposed skin areas as soon as possible after exposure to used engine oil. Soap and water, or waterless hand cleaner should be used.

13. Drain the engine oil and remove the oil filter.
14. Detach the exhaust system from the exhaust manifolds.
15. Label and detach any undervehicle engine wiring which will interfere with engine removal.
16. On vehicles equipped with an automatic transmission, remove the torque converter-to-flywheel bolts.
17. Remove all of the engine-to-transmission bolts.
18. If equipped, remove the transmission oil cooler line retainers from the right-hand, front engine support insulator.
19. Remove the front engine support insulator-to-crossmember retaining fasteners.
20. Remove the starter motor and starter motor wiring from the engine.
21. Partially lower the vehicle and support it with jackstands in the new position.
22. Support the transmission with a floor jack.
23. Using an engine crane or hoist, lift the engine out of the vehicle. Be sure to lift the engine slowly and check often that nothing (such as wires, hoses, etc.) will cause the engine to hang up on the vehicle.
24. At this point, the engine can be installed on an engine stand.

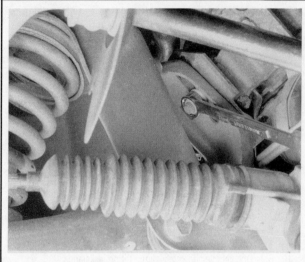

88233P00

The support insulator through-bolts can be removed with a wrench from beneath the vehicle

To install:

➡Lightly oil all bolts and stud threads, except those specifying special sealant, prior to installation.

25. Using the hoist or engine crane, slowly and carefully position the engine in the vehicle.
26. Install two engine-to-transmission bolts.

➡Seat the left-hand, front engine support insulator locating pin prior to the right-hand, front engine support insulator.

27. Lower the engine onto the front engine support insulators.
28. Detach the engine crane or hoist from the engine.
29. Remove the floor jack from beneath the transmission fluid pan.
30. Tighten the two installed engine-to-transmission bolts, then raise and securely support the vehicle on jackstands.
31. Install and tighten the remaining engine-to-transmission bolts to the following values:
   - Automatic transmission: 40–50 ft. lbs. (55–68 Nm)
   - Manual transmission: 28–38 ft. lbs. (38–51 Nm)
32. The remainder of installation is the reverse of the removal procedure. Be sure to tighten the fasteners to the values presented in the torque specification chart.

> **✳✳ WARNING**
>
> Do NOT start the engine without first filling it with the proper type and amount of clean engine oil, and installing a new oil filter. Otherwise, severe engine damage will result.

33. Fill the crankcase with the proper type and quantity of engine oil.
34. Install the air intake duct assembly.
35. Connect the negative battery cable, then fill and bleed the cooling system.
36. Bring the engine to normal operating temperature, then check for leaks.
37. Stop the engine and check all fluid levels.
38. Install the hood, aligning the marks that were made during removal.
39. If equipped, have the A/C system properly leak-tested, evacuated and charged by an MVAC-trained, EPA-certified automotive technician.

4.6L Engines

➧ See Figures 1, 2 and 3

➡On vehicles equipped with air conditioning, it is vital to refer to Section 1 prior to performing this procedure.

1. On models equipped with air conditioning, have the system discharged and evacuated by an MVAC-trained, EPA-certified automotive technician. Have the A/C compressor removed from the engine.
2. Disconnect the battery cables.
3. Remove the cooling fan, radiator and all cooling system hoses.
4. Label and detach all engine wiring and vacuum hoses which will interfere with engine removal.
5. Remove the hood.
6. Remove the engine compartment brace from the front fender apron and dash panel.
7. Detach the accelerator and transmission control cables from the throttle body, and the control cables' mounting bracket from the engine.
8. Release fuel system pressure, then disconnect the fuel supply and return lines from the engine.
9. Remove the A/C compressor mounting bracket and drive belt tensioner.
10. Raise the vehicle and safely support it on jackstands.
11. Remove the power steering pump and hoses.

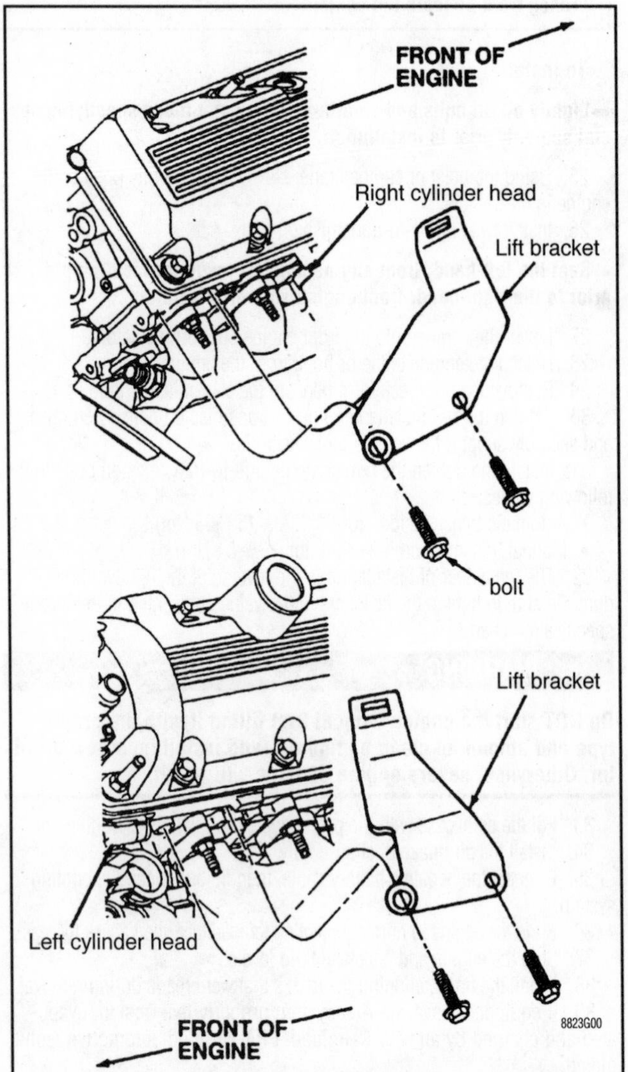

Fig. 1 Lifting Eye bracket installation positioning on the 4.6L SOHC engine

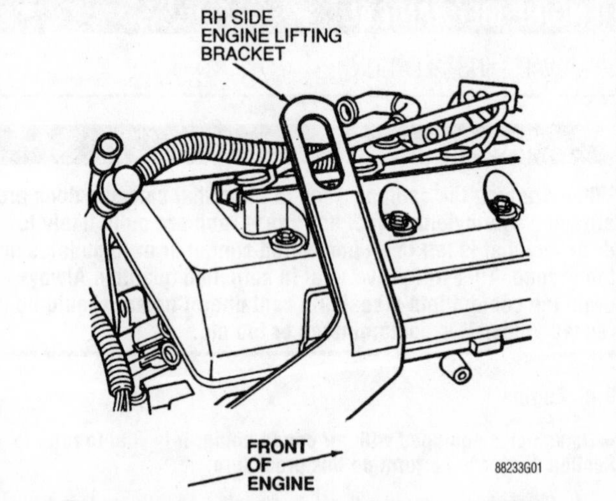

Fig. 2 Install the lifting bracket on the right-hand cylinder head in the position shown—4.6L DOHC engine

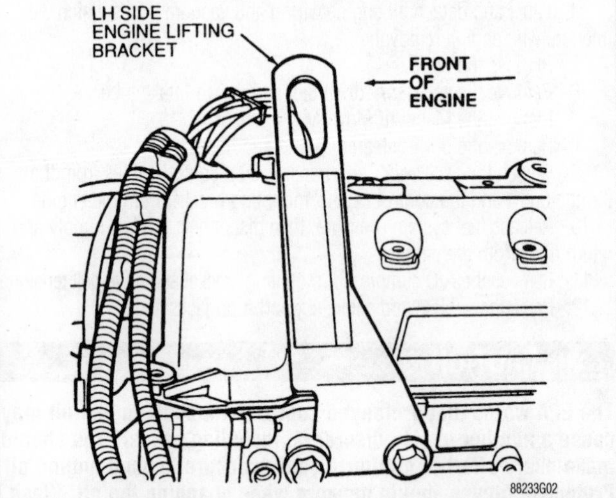

Fig. 3 The lifting bracket should be positioned on the left-hand cylinder head as shown for proper load distribution during engine removal—4.6L DOHC engine

✱✱ CAUTION

The EPA warns that prolonged contact with used engine oil may cause a number of skin disorders, including cancer! You should make every effort to minimize your exposure to used engine oil. Protective gloves should be worn when changing the oil. Wash your hands and any other exposed skin areas as soon as possible after exposure to used engine oil. Soap and water, or waterless hand cleaner should be used.

12. Drain the engine oil and remove the oil filter.
13. Detach the exhaust system from the exhaust manifolds.
14. Label and detach any undervehicle engine wiring which will interfere with engine removal.
15. Remove the transmission.
16. If equipped, remove the transmission oil cooler line retainers from the right-hand, front engine support insulator.
17. Remove the front engine support insulator-to-crossmember fasteners.
18. Remove the starter motor and starter motor wiring from the engine.
19. Partially lower the vehicle and support it with jackstands in this new position.

20. On the 4.6L SOHC engine, install the Engine Lifting Brackets D91P-6001-A, or their equivalents, onto the cylinder heads with M-12 x 1.75 x 20mm bolts.

21. On the 4.6L DOHC engine, install the lifting eyes from the Rotunda Engine Lift Bracket Set 014-00340, or their equivalents, onto the cylinder heads. Tighten the attaching bolts to 30–36 ft. lbs. (40–50 Nm).

22. Using an engine crane or hoist, lift the engine out of the vehicle. Be sure to lift the engine slowly and check often that nothing (such as wires, hoses, etc.) will cause the engine to hang up on the vehicle.

23. At this point, the engine can be installed on an engine stand.

To install:

➡ **Lightly oil all bolts and stud threads, except those specifying special sealant, prior to installation.**

24. Using the hoist or engine crane, slowly and carefully position the engine in the vehicle; lower the engine onto the front engine support insulators. Install the support through-bolts and tighten them to 15–22 ft. lbs. (20–30 Nm).

25. Detach the engine crane or hoist from the engine, and remove the lifting brackets from the cylinder heads.

26. Install the transmission.

27. The remainder of installation is the reverse of the removal procedure. Be sure to tighten the fasteners to the values presented in the torque specification chart.

❊❊ WARNING

Do NOT start the engine without first filling it with the proper type and amount of clean engine oil, and installing a new oil filter. Otherwise, severe engine damage will result.

28. Fill the crankcase with the proper type and quantity of engine oil. Adjust the transmission throttle linkage.

29. Install the air intake duct assembly.

30. Connect the negative battery cable, then fill and bleed the cooling system.

31. Bring the engine to normal operating temperature, then check for leaks.

32. Stop the engine and check all fluid levels.

33. Install the hood, aligning the marks that were made during removal.

34. If equipped, have the A/C system properly leak-tested, evacuated and charged by an MVAC-trained, EPA-certified automotive technician.

5.0L Engine

▶ **See Figures 4, 5 and 6**

➡ **On vehicles equipped with air conditioning, it is vital to refer to Section 1 prior to performing this procedure.**

1. On models equipped with air conditioning, have the system discharged and evacuated by an MVAC-trained, EPA-certified automotive technician. Have the A/C compressor removed from the engine.

2. Disconnect the negative battery cable, followed by the positive.

3. Drain the crankcase and the cooling system.

4. Properly relieve the fuel system pressure.

5. Mark the position of the hood on the hinges and remove the hood. Disconnect the battery ground cable from the cylinder block.

6. Remove the air intake duct and the air cleaner, if engine mounted.

7. Disconnect the upper radiator hose from the thermostat housing and the lower hose from the water pump. If equipped with an automatic transmission, disconnect the oil cooler lines from the radiator.

8. Remove the bolts attaching the radiator fan shroud to the radiator. Remove the radiator. Remove the fan, belt pulley and shroud.

9. Remove the alternator bolts and position the alternator out of the way.

10. Disconnect the oil pressure sending unit wire from the sending unit. Disconnect the flexible fuel line at the fuel tank line. Plug the fuel tank line.

11. Disconnect the accelerator cable from the throttle body. Disconnect the Throttle Valve (TV) rod, if equipped with an automatic transmission. Disconnect the cruise control cable, if equipped.

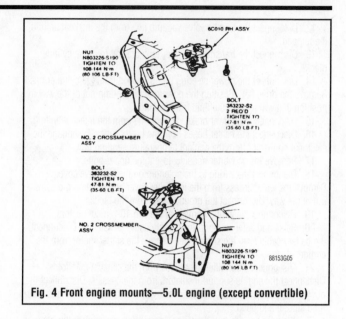

Fig. 4 Front engine mounts—5.0L engine (except convertible)

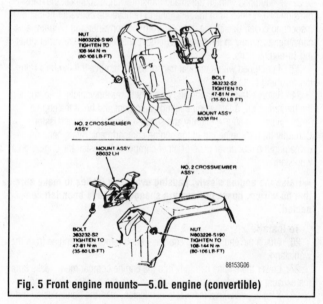

Fig. 5 Front engine mounts—5.0L engine (convertible)

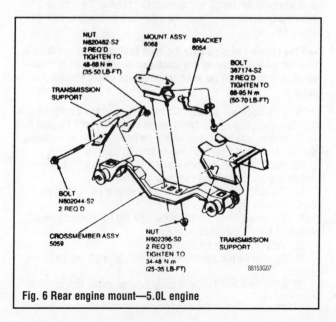

Fig. 6 Rear engine mount—5.0L engine

12. Disconnect the throttle valve vacuum line from the intake manifold, if equipped.

13. Disconnect the transmission filler tube bracket from the cylinder block.

14. Disconnect the power steering pump bracket from the cylinder head. Remove the drive belt. Position the power steering pump out of the way in a position that will prevent the fluid from leaking.

15. Disconnect the power brake vacuum line from the intake manifold.

16. Disconnect the heater hoses from the heater tubes. Disengage the electrical connector from the coolant temperature sending unit.

17. Remove the converter housing-to-engine upper bolts.

18. Disconnect the wiring to the solenoid on the left valve cover. Remove the wire harness from the left valve cover and position the wires out of the way. Disconnect the ground strap from the block.

19. Disconnect the wiring harness at the two 10-pin connectors.

20. Raise and safely support the vehicle using jackstands. Disconnect the battery cable from the starter, then remove the starter motor from the engine.

21. Disconnect the muffler inlet pipes from the exhaust manifolds. Disconnect the engine support insulators from the chassis. Disconnect the downstream thermactor tubing and check valve from the right exhaust manifold stud, if equipped.

22. If equipped with an automatic transmission, disconnect the transmission cooler lines from the retainer and remove the converter housing inspection cover. Detach the flywheel from the converter and secure the converter assembly in the housing. Remove the remaining converter housing-to-engine bolts.

23. If equipped with a manual transmission, remove the flywheel housing retaining bolts.

24. Remove the jackstands and carefully lower the vehicle, then support the transmission. Attach engine lifting equipment and hoist the engine.

25. Raise the engine slightly and separate it from the transmission. Carefully lift the engine out of the engine compartment. Avoid bending or damaging the rear cover plate or other components. Install the engine on a workstand.

➥**Raise the engine slowly, pausing every few inches to make sure that no wiring, hoses or lines are snagged or have been left connected.**

To install:

26. Attach the engine lifting equipment and remove the engine from the workstand.

27. Lower the engine carefully into the engine compartment. Make sure the exhaust manifolds are properly aligned with the muffler inlet pipes.

28. If equipped with a manual transmission, start the transmission input shaft into the clutch disc. It may be necessary to adjust the position of the transmission in relation to the engine if the input shaft will not enter the clutch disc.

➥**If the engine hangs up after the input shaft enters the clutch disc, turn the crankshaft slowly in a clockwise direction, with the transmission in gear, until the shaft splines mesh with the clutch disc splines.**

29. If equipped with an automatic transmission, start the converter pilot into the crankshaft. Align the paint mark on the flywheel with the paint mark on the torque converter. Install the converter housing upper bolts, making sure the dowels in the cylinder block engage the converter housing.

30. Install the engine support insulator-to-chassis attaching fasteners and remove the engine lifting equipment.

31. The remainder of installation is the reverse of the removal procedure.

32. Fill the crankcase with the proper type and quantity of engine oil. Adjust the transmission throttle linkage.

33. Install the air intake duct assembly.

34. Connect the negative battery cable, then fill and bleed the cooling system.

35. Bring the engine to normal operating temperature, then check for leaks.

36. Stop the engine and check all fluid levels.

37. Install the hood, aligning the marks that were made during removal.

38. If equipped, have the A/C system properly leak-tested, evacuated and charged by an MVAC-trained, EPA-certified automotive technician.

Rocker Arm (Valve) Cover

REMOVAL & INSTALLATION

3.8L Engine

▶ **See Figure 7**

1. Label and detach the spark plug wires from the plugs.

2. Remove the spark plug wire retaining clips from the valve cover mounting bolts.

3. For the left-hand valve cover, remove the oil filler cap and detach the crankcase breather hose.

4. For the right-hand valve cover, remove the air inlet tube and the PCV valve.

5. Remove the valve cover mounting bolts, then lift the cover and old gasket up and off of the engine.

To install:

➥**Lightly oil the bolt threads prior to installation.**

6. Using solvent, clean the valve cover and cylinder head gasket surfaces of all old gasket material.

7. Place the new gasket on the cylinder head, then install the valve cover.

8. Install the cover mounting bolts, and tighten them to 71–106 inch lbs. (8–12 Nm).

9. If applicable, install the oil filler cap and the crankcase breather hose, or the PCV valve and air inlet tube.

10. Install the spark plug wire retaining clips, and attach the wires to their respective plugs.

11. Start the engine and check for oil leaks.

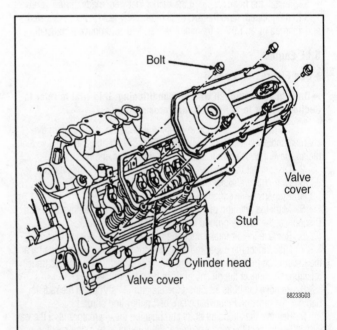

Fig. 7 Exploded view of the left-hand cylinder head and valve cover assembly (right side is similar)—3.8L engine

After removing all necessary components, remove the valve cover mounting bolts . . .

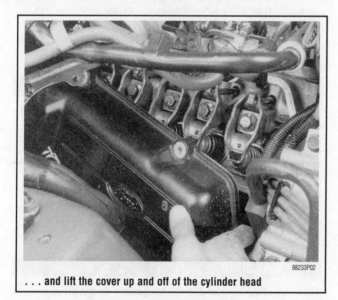

. . . and lift the cover up and off of the cylinder head

Be sure to remove and discard the old gasket, and to install a new gasket prior to reassembly

4.6L SOHC Engine

♦ See Figure 8

1. Disconnect the negative battery cable.

2. Remove the air inlet tube from the throttle body and air cleaner housing.

3. For the right-hand cover, perform the following:

   a. Detach the engine wiring from the Mass Air Flow (MAF) and Intake Air Temperature (IAT) sensors.

   b. Remove the nut that holds the A/C line to the right-hand, front fender apron, then gently lift the A/C line and feed the MAF and IAT wiring connectors under it. Position the connector out of the way.

   c. Relieve fuel system pressure, then detach the fuel lines from the engine.

   d. Remove the PCV valve from the rocker arm grommet, and position it out of the way.

4. For the left-hand cover, perform the following steps:

   a. Detach the speed control actuator cable from the throttle body and position it aside.

   b. Disengage the engine control sensor extension wire connector from the electronic variable orifice sensor and oil pressure sender. Position the wiring out of the way.

✷✷ WARNING

When separating the spark plug wires from the plugs, only pull on the plug wire boot. Otherwise, the ignition wire may separate from the connector inside the boot, which would require a replacement wire.

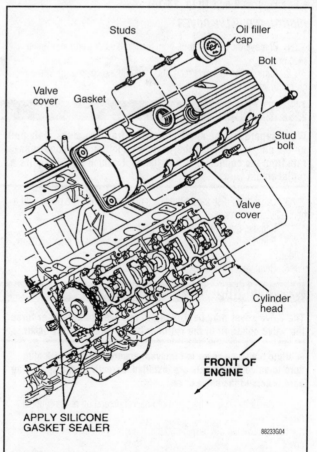

Fig. 8 Exploded view of a typical valve cover used on 4.6L SOHC engines

5. Label and disconnect the spark plug wires from the plugs.

6. Remove the spark plug wires and wire retaining clips from the valve cover studs, then set them aside.

7. Remove the valve cover mounting bolts, then lift the cover and old gasket up and off of the cylinder head.

8. Remove the old gasket from the valve cover.

To install:

9. Clean the cylinder head and valve cover gasket surfaces of all old gasket material, then cement the new gasket into the groove on the cover. Use Ford Gasket and Trim Adhesive F3AZ-19B508-B, or equivalent.

10. Apply Silicone Gasket and Sealant F6AZ-19562-A, or equivalent, in both places where the engine front cover meets the cylinder head.

➡**Install the valve cover and gasket no more than 4 minutes after applying the sealant.**

11. Install the valve cover with the new gasket onto the cylinder head. Install the mounting bolts and tighten them to 71–106 inch lbs. (8–12 Nm).

12. Attach the spark plug wire retaining clips and the plug wires.

13. For the right-hand cover, install the PCV valve, connect the fuel lines to the engine, install the air inlet tube, and reattach the wiring to the MAF and IAT sensors. Refasten the A/C line to the fender apron with the retaining nut; tighten the nut until snug.

14. For the left-hand cover, attach the wiring to the electronic variable orifice sensor and oil pressure sender. Reconnect the speed control actuator cable.

15. Connect the negative battery cable, then start the engine and check for leaks.

4.6L DOHC Engine

◆ **See Figures 9 and 10 (p. 13-14)**

RIGHT-HAND VALVE COVER

1. Remove the air inlet tube from the throttle body and air cleaner assembly.

2. Remove the four retaining nuts, then lift the spark plug wire cover off of the valve cover.

✳✳ **WARNING**

When separating the spark plug wires from the plugs, only pull on the plug wire boot. Otherwise, the ignition wire may separate from the connector inside the boot, which would require a replacement wire.

3. Label, then disconnect the spark plug wires from the plugs with a gentle twist/pull motion.

4. Remove the spark plugs from the cylinder head.

5. Remove the spark plug wires from the valve cover, then set them aside.

6. Remove the valve cover mounting bolts.

✳✳ **WARNING**

The valve cover may be difficult to remove; do not pry or force the valve cover off of the cylinder head. Damage may occur.

➡**While the valve cover is removed, ensure that the spark plug bore-to-valve cover seals are installed correctly on the spark plug bore towers of the valve cover.**

7. Carefully lift the cover and old gasket up and off of the cylinder head.

8. Remove the old gasket and the spark plug bore seals from the valve cover.

To install:

9. Clean the cylinder head and valve cover gasket surfaces of all old gasket material, then allow the valve cover and cylinder head to dry completely.

10. Install new spark plug bore-to-valve cover seals; use of sealant on these components is not necessary.

11. Cement the new gasket into the groove on the cover. Use Ford Gasket and Trim Adhesive F3AZ-19B508-B, or equivalent.

12. Apply Silicone Gasket and Sealant F6AZ-19562-A, or equivalent, in both places where the engine front cover meets the cylinder head.

➡**Install the valve cover and gasket no more than 4 minutes after applying the sealant.**

13. Install the valve cover with the new gasket onto the cylinder head. Install the mounting bolts and tighten them in the sequence shown in the accompanying illustration to 71–106 inch lbs. (8–12 Nm).

14. Install the spark plugs and plug wires.

15. Install the spark plug wire cover and retaining nuts onto the valve cover studs. Tighten them to 45–60 inch lbs. (5–7 Nm).

16. Install the air inlet tube.

17. Start the engine and check for leaks.

LEFT-HAND VALVE COVER

◆ **See Figure 11 (p. 14)**

1. Remove the windshield wiper module unit.

2. Detach the PCV valve from the grommet in the valve cover, then position it aside.

3. Remove the oil level dipstick tube retaining nut from the valve cover.

4. Remove the four retaining nuts, then lift the spark plug wire cover off of the valve cover.

✳✳ **WARNING**

When separating the spark plug wires from the plugs, only pull on the plug wire boot. Otherwise, the ignition wire may separate from the connector inside the boot, which would require a replacement wire.

5. Label, then disconnect the spark plug wires from the plugs with a gentle twist/pull motion.

6. Remove the spark plugs from the cylinder head.

7. Remove the spark plug wires from the valve cover, then set them aside.

8. Remove the valve cover mounting bolts.

✳✳ **WARNING**

The valve cover may be difficult to remove; do not pry or force the valve cover off of the cylinder head. Damage may occur.

9. Carefully lift the cover and old gasket up and off of the cylinder head.

10. Remove the old gasket and the spark plug bore seals from the valve cover.

To install:

11. Clean the cylinder head and valve cover gasket surfaces of all old gasket material, then allow the valve cover and cylinder head to dry completely.

12. Install new spark plug bore-to-valve cover seals; use of sealant on these components is not necessary.

13. Cement the new gasket into the groove on the cover. Use Ford Gasket and Trim Adhesive F3AZ-19B508-B, or equivalent.

14. Apply Silicone Gasket and Sealant F6AZ-19562-A, or equivalent, in both places where the engine front cover meets the cylinder head.

➡**Install the valve cover and gasket no more than 4 minutes after applying the sealant.**

15. Install the valve cover with the new gasket onto the cylinder head. Install the mounting bolts and tighten them in the sequence shown in the accompanying illustration to 71–106 inch lbs. (8–12 Nm).

16. Install the spark plugs and plug wires.

17. Install the spark plug wire cover and retaining nuts onto the valve cover studs. Tighten them to 45–60 inch lbs. (5–7 Nm).

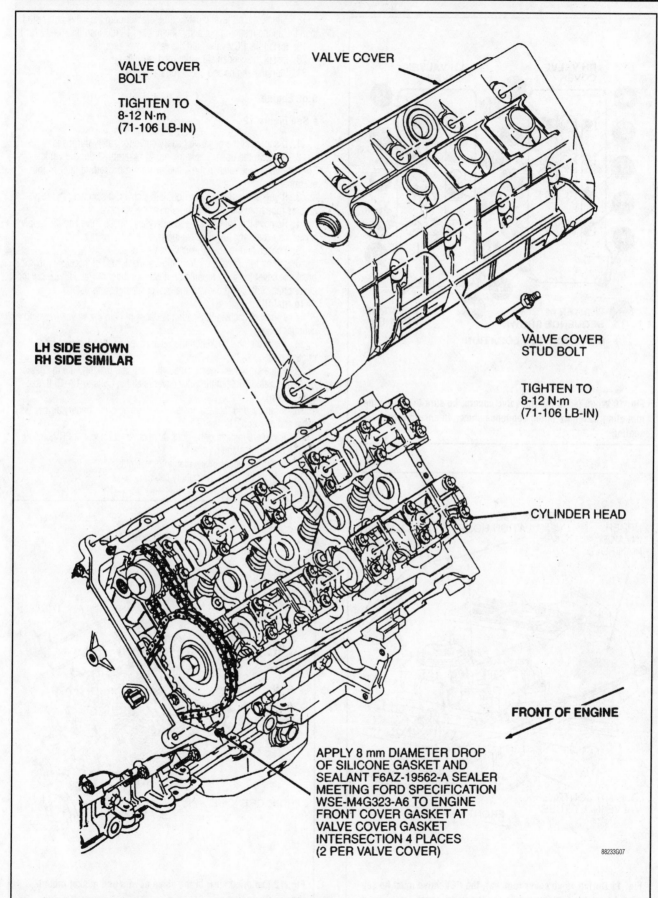

VALVE COVER
BOLT

TIGHTEN TO
8-12 N·m
(71-106 LB-IN)

VALVE COVER

LH SIDE SHOWN
RH SIDE SIMILAR

VALVE COVER
STUD BOLT

TIGHTEN TO
8-12 N·m
(71-106 LB-IN)

CYLINDER HEAD

FRONT OF ENGINE

APPLY 8 mm DIAMETER DROP
OF SILICONE GASKET AND
SEALANT F6AZ-19562-A SEALER
MEETING FORD SPECIFICATION
WSE-M4G323-A6 TO ENGINE
FRONT COVER GASKET AT
VALVE COVER GASKET
INTERSECTION 4 PLACES
(2 PER VALVE COVER)

88233G07

Fig. 9 Exploded view of a typical valve cover used on 4.6L DOHC engines

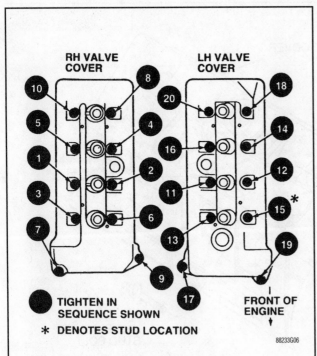

Fig. 10 When installing the valve covers, be sure to tighten the mounting fasteners in the sequence shown to ensure proper sealing

18. Situate the oil level dipstick tube bracket onto the valve cover stud, then install the retaining nut and tighten it to 71–106 inch lbs. (8–12 Nm).

19. Install the PCV valve into the valve cover grommet.

20. Install the windshield wiper module unit.

21. Start the engine and check for leaks.

5.0L Engine

▶ See Figure 12

1. Disconnect the negative battery cable for safety purposes.

2. Remove the upper intake manifold assembly from the vehicle. For details, please refer to the intake manifold procedure later in this section.

3. If you are removing the right valve cover, disconnect the PCV closure tube from the oil fill stand pipe at the valve cover.

4. Remove the Thermactor/secondary air bypass valve and air supply hoses, as necessary, to gain clearance.

5. Loosen and remove the valve cover bolts.

6. Lift off the valve cover from the engine. It may be necessary to break the cover loose by rapping on it with a rubber mallet. NEVER pry the cover off, as you could damage the gasket sealing surfaces!

To install:

7. Thoroughly clean the mating surfaces of both the valve cover and cylinder head.

8. Place the new gasket on the valve cover with the locating tabs engaging the slots.

9. Place the valve cover on the cylinder head, making sure the gasket is evenly seated. Tighten the valve cover retaining bolts to 12–15 ft. lbs. (16–20 Nm).

10. If removed for access, install the Thermactor/secondary air bypass valve and air supply hoses.

11. If you are installing the right valve cover, connect the PCV closure tube to the oil fill stand pipe.

12. Install the upper intake manifold assembly.

13. Connect the negative battery cable.

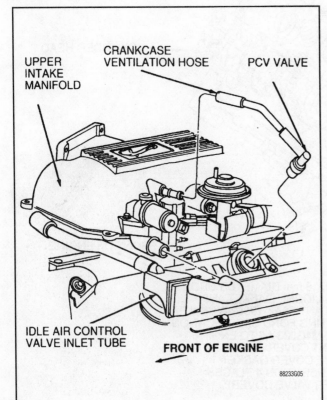

Fig. 11 During valve cover removal, the PCV valve must be separated from the rubber grommet in the valve cover

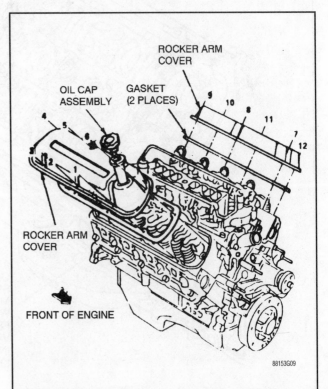

Fig. 12 Exploded view of the valve covers and gasket mounting—5.0L engine

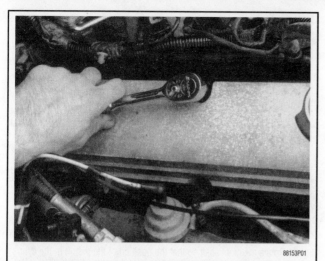

Once access to the valve covers is clear, loosen and remove the retaining bolts

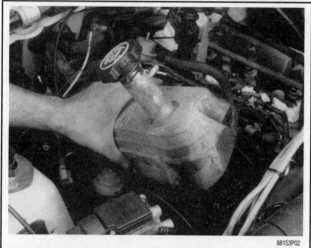

Carefully break the gasket seal and remove the valve cover from the engine

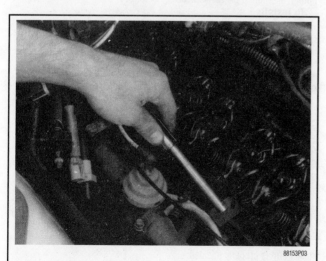

Clean the gasket mating surfaces, taking care to keep debris out of the engine

Rocker Arms

REMOVAL & INSTALLATION

3.8L Engine

➥During this procedure, always keep the parts in order so that they may be reinstalled in their original positions.

1. Remove the valve cover(s) from the engine.
2. Loosen the rocker arm fulcrum (seat) mounting bolts from the cylinder head, then lift the rocker arms, fulcrums and bolts off of the head.
3. If necessary, the pushrods may be removed from the engine at this time. If removing more than one pushrod at a time, be sure to label them so that they can be installed in their original positions..

To install:

4. If applicable, install the pushrods in their original positions, after lubricating their tips with engine assembly lube (such as Ford D9AZ-19579-D).
5. Lubricate the rocker arms and fulcrums with engine assembly lube prior to installation.
6. Install each rocker arm, one at a time, as follows:

a. Rotate the crankshaft so that the valve lifter (tappet), which corresponds to the rocker arm being installed, rests on the base circle of the camshaft (the camshaft lobe points away from the valve lifter). This position can be found by depressing the pushrod while having an assistant rotate the crankshaft with a socket and ratchet wrench on the crankshaft pulley/damper center bolt; when the pushrod is at its lowest point, the lobe is pointing away from the lifter.

b. Position the rocker arm over the pushrods and mounting bolt holes.

c. Install the rocker arm fulcrum and mounting bolt. Tighten the mounting bolt to a maximum of 44 inch lbs. (5 Nm).

7. Perform Step 4 for each of the rocker arms requiring installation.

➥For the final-tightening of the rocker arm mounting bolts, the camshaft can be in any position.

8. Final-tighten the rocker arm fulcrum bolts to 19–25 ft. lbs. (25–35 Nm) for 1994–95 models, and to 23–29 ft. lbs. (30–40 Nm) for 1996–98 models.
9. Install the valve cover(s).

After removing the valve cover, loosen the rocker arm mounting bolt . . .

... then lift the rocker arm, mounting bolt and fulcrum off of the cylinder head

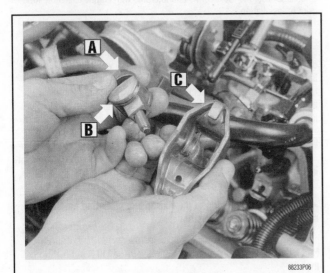

The mounting bolt (A), fulcrum (B) and rocker arm (C) can be separated once removed from the head

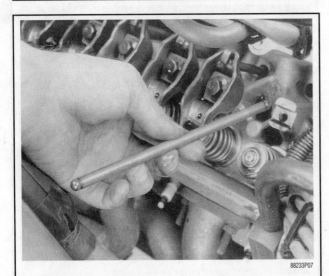

If necessary, the pushrod may be removed at this point

4.6L Engines

▶ See Figures 13, 14 and 15

On this engine, the cam followers (rocker arms) are part of the hydraulic valve lash adjustment assembly. The hydraulic lash adjusters are placed at the fulcrum point of the rocker arms and act in a manner similar to hydraulic lifters in pushrod engines.

➡Be sure to keep the rocker arms and valve tappets in order so that they can be installed in their original positions.

1. Remove the valve covers.

➡The only difference between the SOHC and DOHC engines for this procedure is simply that the DOHC ellngine has twice as many valves, rocker arms and valve tappets. The removal and installation technique is the same, regardless of which valve is being serviced, or which engine is being serviced.

2. Rotate the crankshaft so that the position of the piston in the cylinder being serviced is at the bottom of its stroke, and the base circle of the camshaft is resting against the rocker arm.

> ※※ **WARNING**

A valve spring spacer, such as Ford Tool T91P-6565-AH, must be used in order to prevent the valve spring retainer from contacting the valve stem seal, which can result in damage to the seal.

3. Install the valve spring spacer between the valve spring coils.
4. Install a valve spring compressor, such as Ford Tool T91P-6565-A, under the camshaft and on top of the valve spring retainer.
5. Slowly push down on the compressor tool until the spring is depressed far enough to allow the rocker arm to be removed, then pull the rocker arm out from underneath the camshaft.
6. Remove the valve spring compressor and spacer tools.
7. Repeat Steps 2 through 6 for all of the rocker arms needing removal.
8. If necessary, pull the hydraulic valve tappets out of the cylinder head(s).
9. Thoroughly clean the valve tappets and rocker arms with clean solvent, then wipe them with a lint-free cloth. Do not immerse the valve tappet in solvent.
10. Inspect the valve tappet, and discard it if any part shows signs of pitting, scoring, or excessive wear.

To install:

11. Apply clean engine oil to the valve stems and tips, the rocker arm roller surfaces, the valve tappets, and the valve tappet bores in the cylinder head(s).

➡The valve tappets must not have more than 0.059 in. (1.5mm) of plunger travel prior to installation.

12. If removed earlier, insert the tappets in their original bores in the cylinder head(s).
13. Rotate the crankshaft so that the position of the piston in the cylinder being serviced is at the bottom of its stroke, and the base circle of the camshaft is facing where the rocker arm will be installed.
14. Install the valve spring spacer and compressor tools as before.
15. Carefully depress the valve spring with the compressor tool until the rocker arm can be positioned between the valve stem and valve tappet, and the camshaft.
16. Slowly allow the valve spring to decompress, and ensure that the rocker arm is properly retained.
17. Remove the valve spring compressor and spacer tools.
18. Repeat Steps 13 through 17 for all of the rocker arms.
19. Install the valve covers.
20. Start the engine and check for oil leaks from the valve cover gaskets.

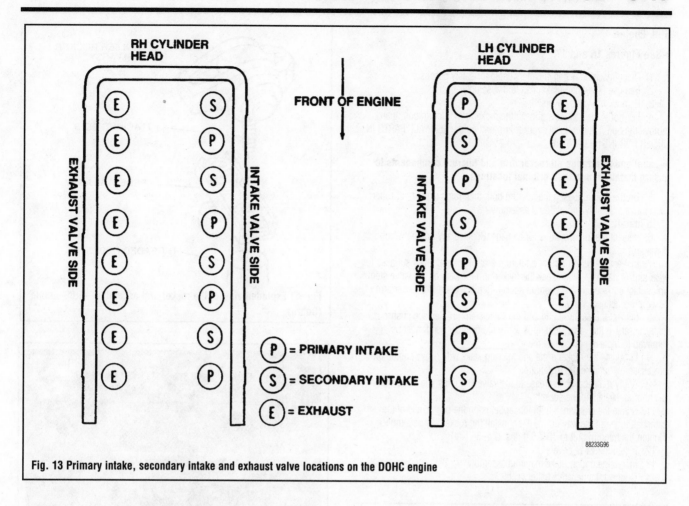

Fig. 13 Primary intake, secondary intake and exhaust valve locations on the DOHC engine

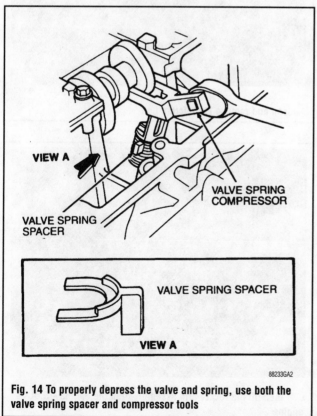

Fig. 14 To properly depress the valve and spring, use both the valve spring spacer and compressor tools

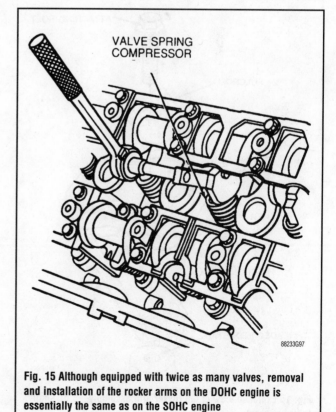

Fig. 15 Although equipped with twice as many valves, removal and installation of the rocker arms on the DOHC engine is essentially the same as on the SOHC engine

5.0L Engine

▶ See Figures 16 and 17

1. Disconnect the negative battery cable for safety purposes.
2. Remove the upper intake manifold assembly.
3. Remove the valve covers.
4. For non-Cobra models, loosen the rocker arm fulcrum bolt, then remove the bolt, fulcrum (seat), rocker arm and guide. KEEP ALL PARTS IN ORDER FOR INSTALLATION!

➡ **Label and/or arrange all rocker arm and fulcrum components to assure installation in their original locations.**

5. On the Cobra, loosen the fulcrum bolt, then remove the bolt, roller rocker arm assembly and pedestal assembly.

To install:

6. Inspect the fulcrum bolts for damage. Replace any bolt on which damage is found.
7. Inspect the rocker arm and fulcrum seat or roller contact surfaces for wear and/or damage. Also check the rocker arm for wear on the valve stem tip contact surface and the pushrod socket. Replace complete rocker arm assemblies, as necessary.
8. Inspect the pushrod end and the valve stem tip. Replace pushrods, as necessary. If the valve stem tip is worn, the cylinder head must be removed to replace or machine the valve.
9. Lubricate the rocker arms and fulcrum seats with heavy engine oil or pre-assembly lube before installation.
10. Apply multi-purpose grease to the valve stem tips, the underside of the fulcrum seats and the sockets.
11. Rotate the crankshaft until the tappet is on the base circle of the camshaft lobe (all the way down), then install the rocker arm assembly. Tighten the fulcrum bolt to 18–25 ft. lbs. (24–34 Nm).
12. Install the valve covers.
13. Install the upper intake manifold assembly.
14. Connect the negative battery cable.

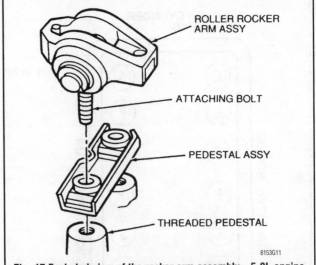

Fig. 17 Exploded view of the rocker arm assembly—5.0L engine (Cobra)

Loosen and remove the fulcrum bolt . . .

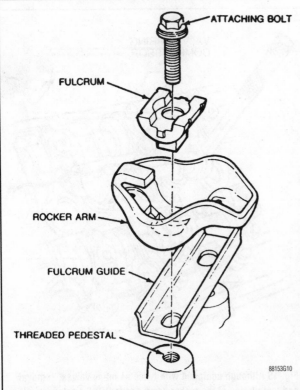

Fig. 16 Exploded view of the rocker arm assembly—5.0L engine (except Cobra)

. . . then lift the rocker arm assembly from the engine—5.0L engine

ROCKER ARM-TO-VALVE STEM CLEARANCE

◆ See Figures 18, 19, 20 and 21

➡This procedure is applicable only to pushrod engines (3.8L and 5.0L engines); the OHC engines (4.6L engines) utilize automatic hydraulic lash adjusters.

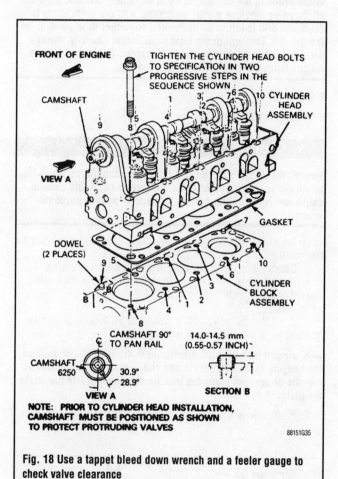

Fig. 18 Use a tappet bleed down wrench and a feeler gauge to check valve clearance

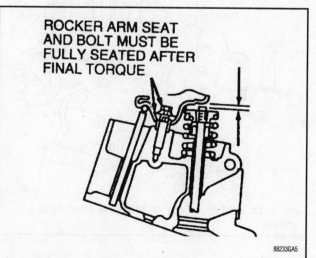

Fig. 19 Measure the clearance between the tip of the rocker arm and valve stem tip as shown

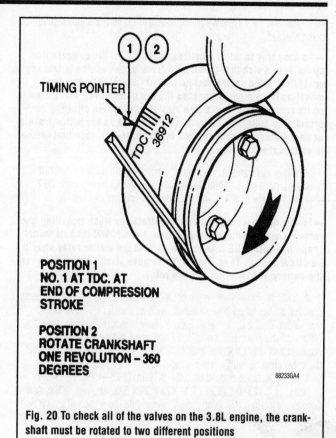

Fig. 20 To check all of the valves on the 3.8L engine, the crankshaft must be rotated to two different positions

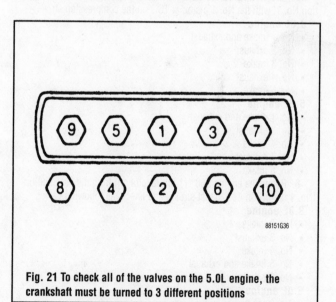

Fig. 21 To check all of the valves on the 5.0L engine, the crankshaft must be turned to 3 different positions

No periodic valve lash adjustments are necessary or possible on these engines. Even though the 3.8L and 5.0L engines utilize hydraulic valve trains to automatically maintain proper valve lash, if one of these engines is determined to have a valve tap, the following inspection procedures can help determine whether the valve tappet is to blame.

The valve lash is not adjustable. If the collapsed lifter clearance is incorrect, different length replacement pushrods are available to compensate. However, the reason for the incorrect clearance should be investigated first. The clearance could be wrong for a number of reasons, such as: worn camshaft lobe, bent pushrod, bent rocker arm, worn valve stem tip, etc.

1. Remove the valve cover(s) for access to the valves whose lash is being checked.

➡An easy way to tell if a cylinder is at TDC of the compression stroke is to watch that cylinder's valves as the engine is cranked or rotated. If the valves remain closed (the rocker arms don't move) as the piston approaches the top of its travel, that piston is on its compression stroke (the closed valves were allowing compression to build). If, instead, a valve opens as the piston travels upward (releasing compression in that cylinder), then that piston is on its exhaust stroke.

2. Either have an assistant help by cranking the engine or install a remote starter switch. Crank the engine with the ignition switch **OFF** until No.1 piston is at TDC on the compression stroke.

➡Follow the tool manufacturer's instructions when installing the remote starter switch. In most cases, the BROWN lead (terminal I) and the RED/BLUE lead (terminal S) at the starter relay should be disconnected. Then, install the remove starter switch between the battery and terminal S of the relay.

3. With the crankshaft in the positions designated in the steps below, position a lifter bleed-down wrench, such as Tool T71P-6513-B or equivalent, on the rocker arm. Slowly apply pressure to bleed down the lifter until the plunger is completely bottomed. Hold the lifter in this position and check the available clearance between the rocker arm and the valve stem tip with a feeler gauge.

4. The clearance should be 0.09–0.19 in. (2.25–4.79mm) for 3.8L engines, or 0.123–0.146 in. (3.1–3.7mm) for 5.0L engines. If the clearance is less or more than specified, investigate the reason. If everything checks out OK, install a shorter (too little clearance) or longer (too much clearance) pushrod to compensate.

5. The following valves can be checked with the crankshaft at position No. 1, with the No. 1 piston at TDC on the compression stroke:

3.8L engine
- No. 1 intake and exhaust
- No. 2 exhaust
- No. 3 intake
- No. 4 exhaust
- No. 6 intake

5.0L engine
- No. 1 intake and exhaust
- No. 3 exhaust
- No. 4 intake
- No. 7 exhaust
- No. 8 intake

6. Rotate the engine 360° (1 full revolution) from the 1st position (No. 1 is now on its exhaust stroke) and check the following valves:

3.8L engine
- No. 2 intake
- No. 3 exhaust
- No. 4 intake
- No. 5 intake and exhaust
- No. 6 exhaust

5.0L engine
- No. 2 exhaust
- No. 3 intake
- No. 6 exhaust
- No. 7 intake

7. For the 5.0L engine, rotate the engine 90° (¼ revolution) from the 2nd position and check the following valves:
- No. 2 intake and No. 4 exhaust
- No. 5 intake and No. 5 exhaust
- No. 6 intake and No. 8 exhaust

Thermostat

REMOVAL & INSTALLATION

✳✳ CAUTION

When draining the coolant, keep in mind that cats and dogs are attracted by ethylene glycol antifreeze, and are quite likely to drink any that is left in an uncovered container or in puddles on the ground. This will prove fatal in sufficient quantity. Always drain the coolant into a sealable container. Coolant should be reused unless it is contaminated or too old.

3.8L Engine

◆ See Figures 22 thru 28

✳✳ CAUTION

Never remove the radiator cap under any conditions while the engine is running, or while hot. Failure to heed this caution could result in cooling system damage or severe personal injury.

1. Drain the engine cooling system until the coolant level is below the thermostat.
2. Detach the upper radiator hose from the thermostat housing.
3. Remove the two mounting bolts, then lift the thermostat housing and old gasket off of the intake manifold.

To install:
4. Clean the gasket mating surfaces of the housing and intake manifold for all old gasket material or corrosion.

➡To prevent installing the thermostat in the incorrect orientation, the housing contains a positioning slot. Install the thermostat so that the bridge part protrudes into the housing, not into the intake manifold.

5. Position the new gasket, thermostat and housing on the intake manifold.

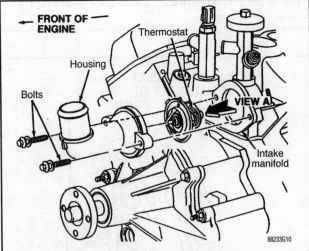

Fig. 22 Exploded view of thermostat housing mounting on 3.8L engines

Fig. 23 Depress the radiator hose clamp tangs, then detach the hose from the thermostat housing

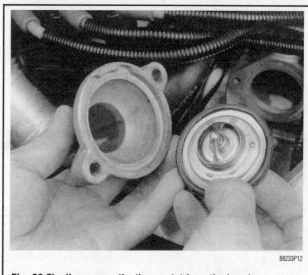

Fig. 26 Finally, remove the thermostat from the housing

Fig. 24 Loosen the two thermostat housing mounting bolts . . .

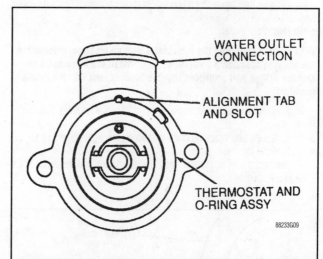

WATER OUTLET CONNECTION

ALIGNMENT TAB AND SLOT

THERMOSTAT AND O-RING ASSY

Fig. 27 Install the thermostat in the housing so that the alignment tab is inserted in the slot

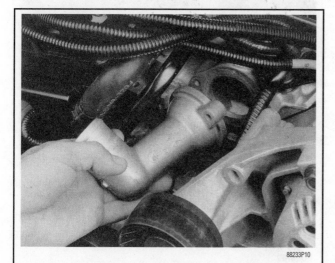

Fig. 25 . . . then separate the housing from the intake manifold

Fig. 28 The thermostat should be positioned so that the spring (arrow) protrudes away from the housing

6. Install the two mounting bolts to 71–97 inch lbs. (8–11 Nm).

7. Connect the upper radiator hose to the housing and ensure that the clamp is between the alignment marks on the hose.

8. Fill the cooling system, then start the engine and check for leaks.

9. If necessary, top off the cooling system overflow reservoir.

4.6L Engines

▶ **See Figure 29**

✳✳ CAUTION

Never remove the radiator cap under any conditions while the engine is running, or while hot. Failure to heed this caution could result in cooling system damage or severe personal injury.

1. Drain the engine cooling system until the coolant level is below the thermostat.

2. Detach the lower radiator hose, the return hose and the degas bottle hose from the thermostat housing.

3. Remove the two mounting bolts, then remove the thermostat housing.

4. Remove the O-ring and thermostat from the housing. Discard the O-ring.

To install:

➡**To prevent installing the thermostat with an incorrect orientation, the housing contains a positioning slot. Install the thermostat so that the bridge part protrudes into the housing, not into the intake manifold.**

5. Position the thermostat and a new O-ring on the housing, then install the housing.

6. Install the two mounting bolts, and alternately tighten them to 15–22 ft. lbs. (20–30 Nm).

7. Connect the lower radiator hose, the return hose and the degas bottle hose to the housing.

8. Fill the cooling system, then start the engine and check for leaks.

9. If necessary, top off the cooling system overflow reservoir.

5.0L Engine

▶ **See Figures 30 and 31**

1. Disconnect the negative battery cable for safety purposes.

2. Open the radiator drain and allow the coolant to drain out so that the coolant level is below the coolant outlet elbow which houses the thermostat.

3. Disconnect the bypass hose from the lower side of the thermostat housing.

➡**If access is difficult, it may be possible to separate the housing from the engine with this hose still attached, or it can be removed later when there is better access.**

4. Disconnect the upper radiator hose at the thermostat housing.

5. If necessary for better access, remove the distributor cap and rotor.

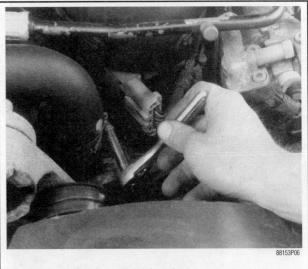

Loosen the radiator hose retaining clamp . . .

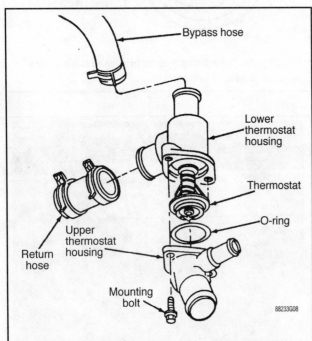

Fig. 29 Exploded view of the thermostat and housing—4.6L engines

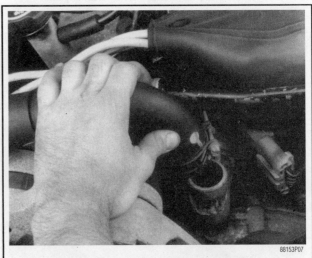

. . . then remove the upper radiator hose from the thermostat housing

Loosen and remove the housing retaining bolts (an open-end or box wrench is handy for this)

Separate the housing from the engine, then remove the thermostat

Be sure to thoroughly clean the gasket mating surfaces

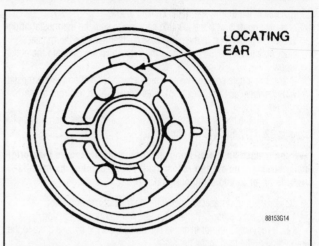

Fig. 30 Most of the engines covered by this manual utilize a thermostat equipped with locking ears to prevent improper installation

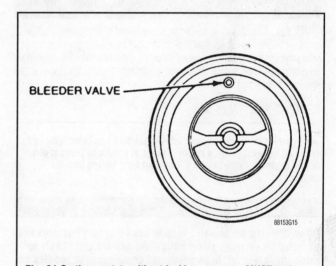

Fig. 31 On thermostats without locking ears, you MUST make sure to position the bleeder valve at 12 o'clock

6. Loosen and remove the thermostat housing retaining bolts, then carefully separate the housing from the engine.

✳✳ WARNING

On some engines, the thermostat is held into the housing by retaining flanges (locating ears) and must be removed by turning to align the flanges with the removal slots. DO NOT attempt to pry the thermostat free, as this will result in thermostat or housing damage.

7. Turn the thermostat counterclockwise in the housing until the thermostat is free, then remove it from the housing.
8. Remove the gasket.
To install:
9. Check the mating surfaces of the outlet elbow and the engine for traces of sealant, corrosion or damage. Clean the surfaces to assure a proper seal.

➡On some engines, the water outlet casting contains a lockng recess into which the thermostat is turned and locked. This is done to prevent the possibility of incorrect thermostat installation. On engines without the flanges and locating ears, care must be taken to position the bleeder valve correctly.

10. Install the thermostat in the coolant elbow.

a. On models with the locating ears, make sure the thermostat bridge section is positioned in the outlet casting, then turn the thermostat clockwise to lock it in position on the flats which are cast into the outlet elbow.

b. On models equipped with a bleeder valve, position the thermostat with the valve at 12 o'clock (top), when viewed from the front of the engine.

11. Install the thermostat housing assembly and gasket, then tighten the bolts to 12–17 ft. lbs. (16–24 Nm).

➡**If the bypass hose was removed later in the procedure than originally directed, be sure to reconnect it at that point of the installation, in order to avoid difficulty later.**

12. If removed for access, install the distributor cap and rotor.

13. Connect the upper radiator hose to the thermostat housing.

14. If removed and not installed earlier, connect the bypass hose to the lower side of the thermostat housing.

15. Connect the negative battery cable.

16. Refill the radiator. Run the engine at operating temperature and check for leaks. Recheck the coolant level.

Intake Manifolds

The 3.8L, 4.6L DOHC and 5.0L engines covered by this manual utilize an upper and lower intake manifold assembly. If necessary, only the upper intake manifold may be removed by following the intake manifold procedure up to that point. Obviously, installation would also begin at the upper intake steps.

REMOVAL & INSTALLATION

➡**Any time the upper or lower intake manifold has been removed, cover all openings with a rag or a sheet of plastic to prevent dirt, debris or, more importantly, a loose nut from falling into the engine.**

❄ CAUTION

When draining the coolant, keep in mind that cats and dogs are attracted by ethylene glycol antifreeze, and are quite likely to drink any that is left in an uncovered container or in puddles on the ground. This will prove fatal in sufficient quantity. Always drain the coolant into a sealable container. Coolant should be reused unless it is contaminated or too old.

➡**If your vehicle is equipped with air conditioning, refer to Section 1 for information regarding the implications of servicing your A/C system yourself. Only an MVAC-trained, EPA-certified automotive technician should service the A/C system or its components.**

3.8L Engine

▸ **See Figures 32 thru 47 (p. 24–27)**

1. Remove the air inlet tube from the throttle body.

2. Detach the accelerator cable from the throttle body, then remove the cable bracket bolts and position the cable and bracket aside.

3. If equipped, remove the speed control actuator.

4. Detach and label any necessary engine harness wiring connectors and vacuum lines.

5. If necessary, remove the throttle body at this time.

6. Remove the EGR valve from the Upper Intake Manifold (UIM).

7. Remove the engine support and wiring retainer bracket (located on the front, left-hand side of the engine).

➡**Note the original locations of the UIM mounting bolts/studs for reinstallation.**

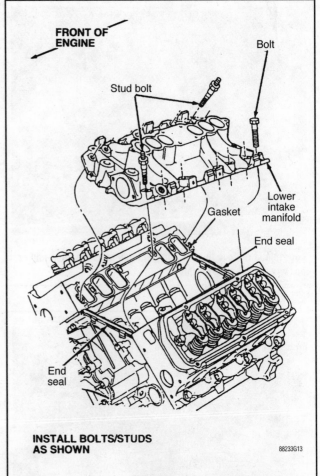

INSTALL BOLTS/STUDS AS SHOWN

88233G13

Fig. 32 Exploded view of the lower intake manifold mounting on the engine

8. Remove the UIM mounting bolts/studs.

9. Lift the UIM off of the Lower Intake Manifold (LIM). Remove the old UIM-to-LIM gasket.

➡**If only the UIM is to be serviced, stop at this point (and resume installation at Step 23).**

10. Remove the fuel injectors and fuel supply manifold.

11. Remove the heater water outlet hose from the LIM.

➡**Note the original locations of the LIM mounting bolts/studs for reinstallation.**

12. Remove the LIM mounting bolts/studs.

❄ WARNING

The LIM may be sealed at the front and rear with silicone sealant. It may be necessary to use a prytool to loosen the intake manifold. If it is necessary to use a prytool, use care to avoid damaging the manifold, cylinder head and engine block machined surfaces.

13. Lift the LIM up and off of the engine. Remove and discard the old gaskets and end seals.

14. If a new manifold is to be installed, transfer the following components to the new manifold:
- Water hose connection and thermostat
- Engine Coolant Temperature (ECT) sensor
- Coolant outlet elbow
- All vacuum and electrical fittings

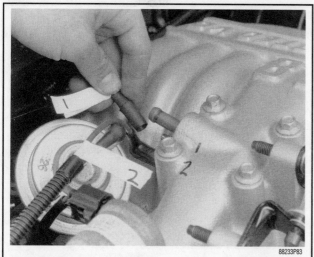

Fig. 33 To remove the upper intake manifold, label and detach all vacuum lines . . .

Fig. 36 . . . and detach the accelerator cable, then remove the cable mounting bracket and set it aside

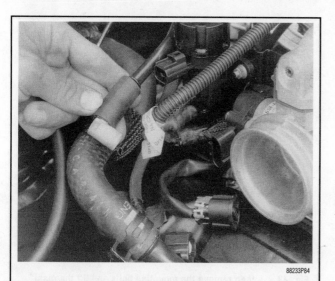

Fig. 34 . . . including the PCV valve hose

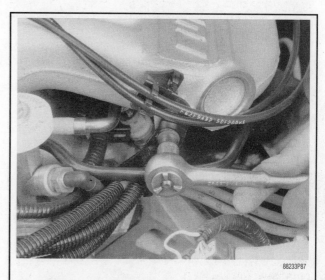

Fig. 37 Remove the intake manifold support bracket . . .

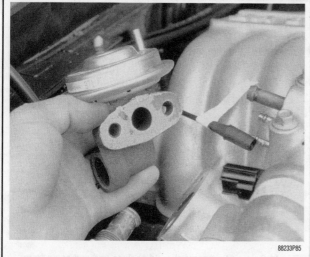

Fig. 35 Remove the EGR valve . . .

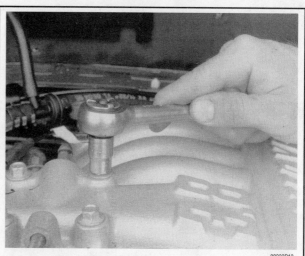

Fig. 38 . . . then loosen the upper-to-lower intake manifold attaching bolts

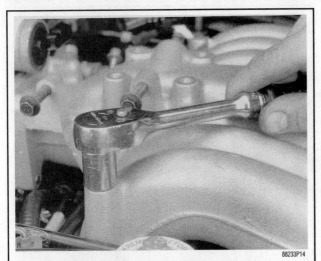

Fig. 39 Be sure to loosen all of the attaching bolts before attempting to separate the two manifolds

Fig. 40 Lift the upper manifold up and off of the lower manifold . . .

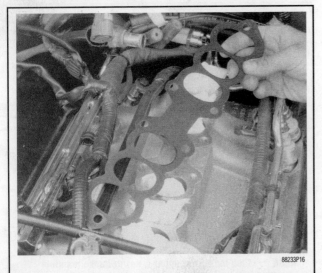

Fig. 41 . . . and be sure to remove and discard the old gasket

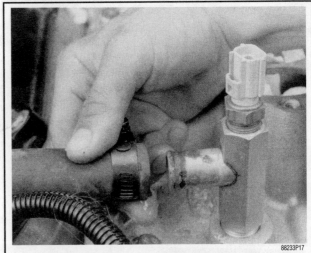

Fig. 42 To remove the lower manifold, detach all hoses and wiring from it . . .

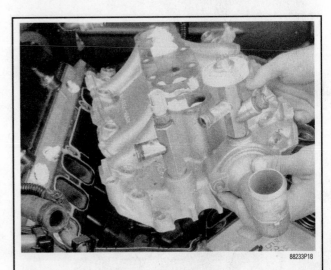

Fig. 43 . . . then remove the mounting bolts and lift the manifold up and off of the engine

Fig. 44 Be sure to remove the old gaskets and end seals from the engine block and cylinder heads

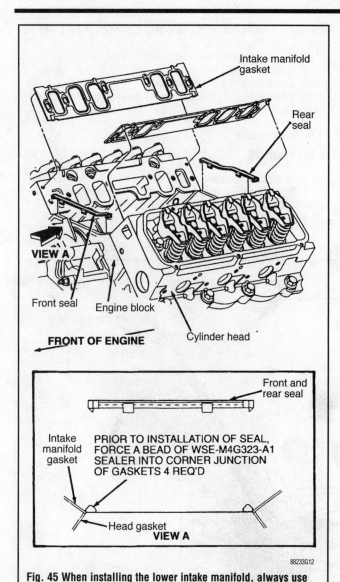

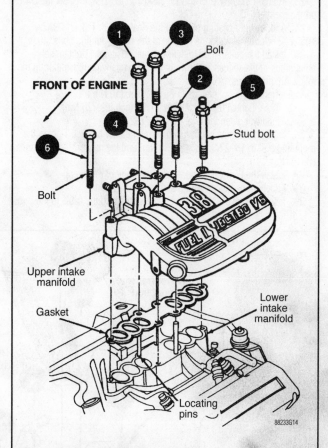

Fig. 47 When installing the upper intake manifold, tighten the upper-to-lower manifold attaching bolts in the sequence shown

Fig. 45 When installing the lower intake manifold, always use new gaskets and end seals

To install:

➡**Lightly oil all mounting bolt/stud threads before installation.**

15. Clean the UIM and LIM, cylinder head and engine block gasket surfaces of all old gasket material or dirt. Use Ford Metal Surface Cleaner F4AZ-19A536-RGH or equivalent to clean the gasket surfaces of all residue which may interfere with the new sealant's adherence.

16. Apply a dab of Ford Gasket and Trim Adhesive D7AZ-19B508-B or equivalent to each cylinder head mating surface, then press the new LIM gasket into place.

➡**When using silicone sealant, assembly must occur within 15 minutes after the sealant is applied, otherwise the sealing ability may be jeopardized.**

17. Apply a 1/8 in. (3–4mm) bead of Ford Silicone Rubber D6AZ-19562-BA or equivalent to each corner where the cylinder head meets the engine block.

18. Install the new front and rear LIM end seals.

19. Carefully lower the LIM onto the cylinder heads and engine block.

20. Install the LIM mounting bolts/studs in their original positions. Tighten the bolts/studs in the sequence shown in the accompanying illustration in the following two steps:

    a. Tighten the bolts/studs to 160 inch lbs. (18 Nm) for 1994–95 models, or to 45 inch lbs. (5 Nm) for 1996–98 models.

    b. Then, tighten the bolts/studs to 195 inch lbs. (22 Nm) for 1994–95 models, or to 71–106 inch lbs. (8–12 Nm) for 1996–98 models.

21. Install the front crankcase ventilation tube so that the retaining bracket is positioned over the LIM stud. Then, install the retaining nut and tighten it to 15–22 ft. lbs. (20–30 Nm).

22. Install the fuel injectors and fuel supply manifold.

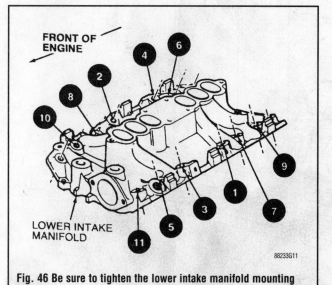

Fig. 46 Be sure to tighten the lower intake manifold mounting bolts in the sequence shown

23. Position the new UIM-to-LIM gasket on the LIM, then set the UIM on the gasket.

24. Apply a light coating of Ford Pipe Sealant with Teflon® D8AZ-19554-A, or equivalent, to the threads of the UIM mounting bolts/studs.

25. Install the bolts/studs in their original positions. Tighten the bolts/studs in the sequence shown in the accompanying illustration in the following three steps:

    a. Tighten the bolts/studs to 88 inch lbs. (10 Nm).

    b. Then, tighten the bolts/studs to 177 inch lbs. (20 Nm).

    c. Finally, tighten them to 24 ft. lbs. (32 Nm).

26. Install the engine support and wiring retainer bracket. Tighten the mounting bolt to 15–22 ft. lbs. (20–30 Nm) and the nut to 71–97 inch lbs. (8–11 Nm).

27. Install the EGR valve and the throttle body (if removed).

28. Attach all necessary wiring and vacuum lines.

29. Install the accelerator cable bracket and attach the cable to the throt-tle body. Tighten the bracket mounting bolts to 124–177 inch lbs. (14–20 Nm).

30. If applicable, attach the speed control actuator.

31. Install the air inlet tube.

32. Start the engine and check for leaks.

33. Check and adjust (if necessary) the following: accelerator cable, engine idle airflow, speed control actuator.

4.6L SOHC Engine

▶ See Figure 48

1. Disconnect the negative battery cable.

2. Drain the engine cooling system and relieve fuel system pressure. Detach the fuel lines from the fuel supply manifold.

3. Remove the air inlet tube.

4. Remove the accessory drive belt.

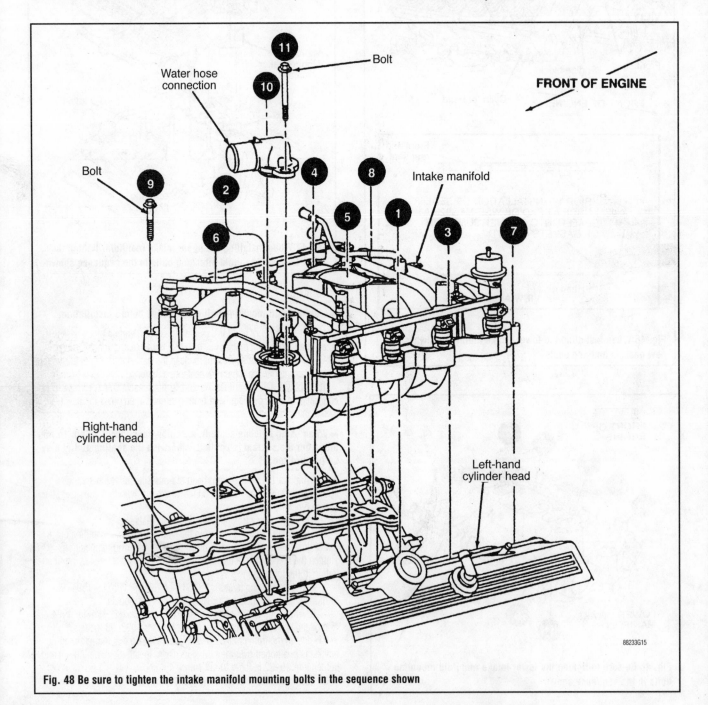

Fig. 48 Be sure to tighten the intake manifold mounting bolts in the sequence shown

When removing the spark plug wires, only pull on the spark plug wire boot. Otherwise, the wire may separate from the connector in the boot, necessitating plug wire replacement.

5. Label and remove all spark plug wires and wire separators.

6. Remove the ignition coils, the alternator and their mounting brackets from the engine.

7. Apply the parking brake and block the rear wheels, then raise and safely support the front of the vehicle on jackstands.

8. Disconnect all necessary wiring.

9. Disconnect the EGR valve-to-exhaust manifold tube from the right-hand exhaust manifold.

10. Lower the vehicle.

11. Label and disconnect all applicable wiring, vacuum lines, cooling system hoses and throttle body cables from the intake manifold or engine which will interfere with manifold removal.

➡Two water outlet connection retaining bolts also retain the intake manifold.

12. Remove the two bolts retaining the water hose connection to the manifold, then position the upper radiator hose and connection out of the way.

13. Remove the remaining bolts, then lift the manifold up and off of the engine.

14. Remove and discard the old gaskets.

➡If a replacement intake manifold is being installed, transfer all necessary components to it from the old manifold.

To install:

15. Thoroughly clean the cylinder head, engine block and intake manifold gasket surfaces.

16. Position the new intake manifold gaskets on the cylinder heads, then place the intake manifold on the heads.

➡After positioning the intake manifold, be sure that the alignment tabs on the intake manifold gasket are aligned with the holes in the cylinder heads.

17. Install and tighten intake manifold mounting bolts Nos. 1 through 9 one at a time to 15–22 ft. lbs. (20–30 Nm), in the sequence shown in the accompanying illustration.

18. Install a new O-ring on the water hose connection, then position the connection on the intake manifold and install the two mounting bolts to 15–22 ft. lbs. (20–30 Nm).

19. Attach all applicable wiring, vacuum lines, cooling system hoses and throttle body cables which were removed earlier.

20. Apply the parking brake and block the rear wheels, then raise and safely support the front of the vehicle on jackstands.

21. Connect the EGR valve-to-exhaust manifold tube to the right-hand exhaust manifold; tighten the nut to 26–33 ft. lbs. (35–45 Nm).

22. Reconnect all applicable wiring, which was disconnected earlier.

23. Lower the vehicle and remove the blocks from the wheels.

24. Install the alternator, the ignition coils and their mounting brackets.

25. Install the spark plug wires, being sure to connect them to their applicable plugs and coil terminal towers.

26. Install the accessory drive belt and the air inlet tube.

27. Attach the fuel supply and return lines to the fuel supply manifold.

28. Connect the negative battery cable.

29. Fill and bleed the engine cooling system. Refer to Section 1.

30. Start the engine and check for leaks.

4.6L DOHC Engine

▸ **See Figures 49 thru 54 (p. 29–31)**

1. Remove the engine compartment brace.
2. Disconnect the negative battery cable.

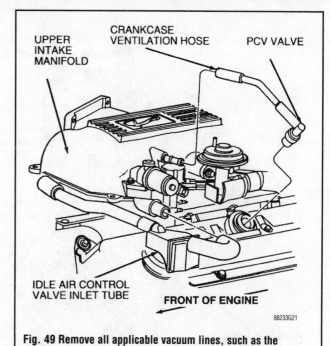

Fig. 49 Remove all applicable vacuum lines, such as the crankcase ventilation hose, in orfder to remove the intake manifold

3. Remove the air inlet tube.

4. Remove the windshield wiper module.

5. Label and disconnect all applicable wiring, vacuum lines, cooling system hoses and throttle body cables from the intake manifold or engine which will interfere with manifold removal.

6. Remove the EGR valve and gasket from the Upper Intake Manifold (UIM).

7. For Lower Intake Manifold (LIM) removal, relieve fuel system pressure. Detach the fuel lines from the fuel supply manifold.

8. Drain the engine cooling system.

9. Remove the accessory drive belt.

10. Remove the ignition wire covers from the valve covers.

When removing the spark plug wires, only pull on the spark plug wire boot. Otherwise, the wire may separate from the connector in the boot, necessitating plug wire replacement.

11. Label and remove all spark plug wires and all wire separators.

12. Remove the alternator and its mounting bracket from the engine.

13. If not already performed, detach the cooling system hoses from the water bypass tube.

14. Remove the two nuts retaining the water bypass tube to the manifold, then lift the bypass tube off of the UIM.

15. If necessary, remove the throttle body and the Idle Air Control (IAC) valve from the UIM.

16. Remove the mounting bolts, then lift the UIM up and off of the engine.

17. Remove and discard the old gaskets.

➡If only the UIM is to be serviced, stop at this point (and resume installation at Step 37).

18. Disconnect the four engine wiring harness retaining clips from the LIM studs.

19. Label and disengage all of the fuel injector wiring connectors, then position the wiring aside.

20. Loosen and remove the LIM mounting bolts and stud bolts in the sequence shown in the accompanying illustration.

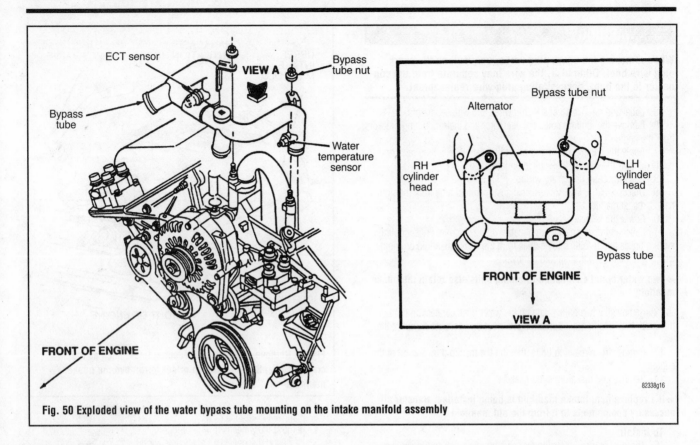

Fig. 50 Exploded view of the water bypass tube mounting on the intake manifold assembly

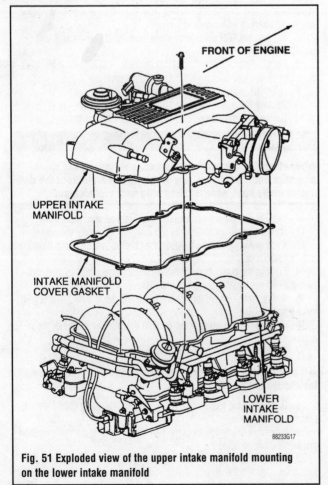

Fig. 51 Exploded view of the upper intake manifold mounting on the lower intake manifold

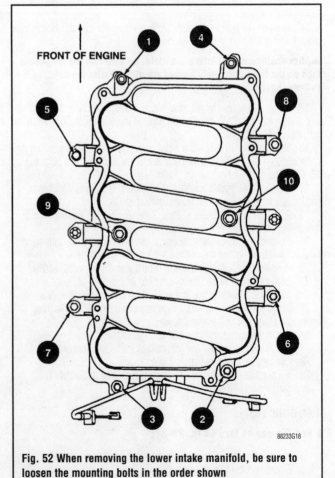

Fig. 52 When removing the lower intake manifold, be sure to loosen the mounting bolts in the order shown

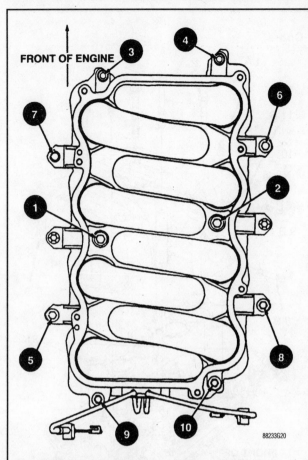

Fig. 53 When installing the lower intake manifold, tighten the mounting bolts only in the order shown

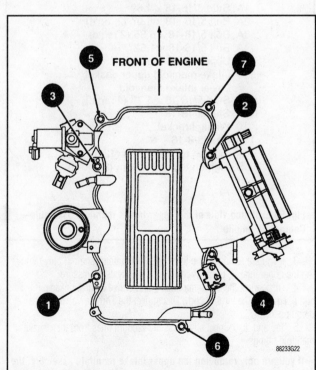

Fig. 54 Tighten the upper-to-lower intake manifold mounting bolts in the sequence shown

21. Lift the LIM and the Intake Manifold Runner Control (IMRC) manifolds as one unit. Detach the fuel charging wiring from the IMRC actuator.

22. Disconnect the IMRC actuator cables from the IMRC levers and retaining brackets.

23. Remove the fuel injection supply manifold from the LIM.

24. If necessary, separate the IMRC manifolds from the LIM by removing the attaching bolts. Retain the load limiting spacers from the IMRC manifolds for reassembly.

➡ **If a new or replacement lower or IMRC manifold is being installed, transfer all applicable components to the new manifold.**

To install:

25. Thoroughly clean all gasket surfaces. The sealing surfaces of the LIM and the IMRC manifolds should be cleaned with a suitable solvent to remove any residual adhesive film, which could adversely affect the sealing ability.

26. Inspect the LIM and IMRC manifold mating surfaces to ensure that no load limiting spacers (washers) are stuck to the surfaces.

➡ **Usually, new load limiting spacers are included with the new LIM-to-IMRC manifold gaskets.**

27. Remove the protective paper from the adhesive backing on the IMRC upper gasket, then install it onto the top of the right-hand IMRC manifold using, if necessary, tapered pins at both end bolt hole locations for proper gasket alignment. Repeat this for the left-hand IMRC manifold as well.

28. Assemble the IMRC manifolds to the LIM, and install the four attaching bolts finger-tight.

29. Install the fuel injection supply manifold and fuel injectors. Install the four retaining bolts to 71–106 inch lbs. (8–12 Nm).

30. Position new LIM gaskets on the cylinder heads using the integral locating pins to properly align the gaskets.

31. Attach the fuel charging wiring to the IMRC actuator.

32. Set the LIM/IMRC manifold assembly on the engine. Install the bolts and stud bolts in locations Nos. 7, 8, 9 and 10 (refer to the accompanying torque sequence illustration). Do NOT tighten them yet. Then, install the bolts and stud bolts in positions Nos. 1, 2, 3, 4, 5 and 6. Now hand-tighten all bolts and stud bolts.

33. Following the sequence shown in the accompanying illustration, tighten fasteners 1 through 10 to 15–22 ft. lbs. (20–30 Nm).

34. Tighten the four IMRC-to-LIM attaching bolts to 71–106 inch lbs. (8–12 Nm).

35. Connect the IMRC actuator cables to the retaining brackets and IMRC levers.

36. Reattach all fuel injection wiring to the injectors.

37. Clean the LIM-to-UIM gasket surfaces of all old gasket material and dirt, then install a new UIM-to-LIM gasket on the LIM.

38. Install and tighten the UIM mounting bolts in the sequence shown in the accompanying illustration to 71–106 inch lbs. (8–12 Nm).

39. Install the EGR valve.

40. If necessary, position the accelerator cable bracket on the UIM and install the attaching bolts to 71–106 inch lbs. (8–12 Nm).

41. If applicable, install the throttle body.

42. Install new O-rings on the water bypass tube, then install the bypass tube on the intake manifold as follows:

✳✳ WARNING

While installing the water bypass tube, be careful not to accidentally damage the new O-ring. Otherwise, coolant leakage may result.

a. Clean the O-ring sealing surface on the cylinder heads and coat the water bypass tube O-rings with a rubber lubricant (such as Ford ESE-M99B 176-A).

b. Position the bypass tube support braces over the UIM inner studs and press the bypass tube into position.

c. Install the two bypass tube retaining nuts to 71–106 inch lbs. (8–12 Nm).

43. Install the alternator and bracket on the engine. Tighten the alternator fasteners to 15–22 ft. lbs. (20–30 Nm) and the alternator bracket fasteners to 71–106 inch lbs. (8–12 Nm).

44. Reattach all necessary wiring (including spark plug wires), vacuum lines, cooling system hoses and throttle body cables, which were detached during intake manifold removal.

45. Install the accessory drive belt.

46. Attach the fuel lines to the fuel supply manifold.

47. Install the air inlet tube.

48. Install the windshield wiper module.

49. Connect the negative battery cable.

50. Fill and bleed the engine cooling system. Refer to Section 1.

51. Start the engine and check for leaks.

5.0L Engine

▶ See Figures 55 thru 81 (p. 32–37)

1. Disconnect the negative battery cable for safety purposes.

2. Drain the engine cooling system to a level below the manifold assembly.

> ※※ **CAUTION**
>
> **Fuel lines on fuel injected vehicles will remain pressurized after the engine is shut off. Fuel pressure must be relieved before servicing the fuel system.**

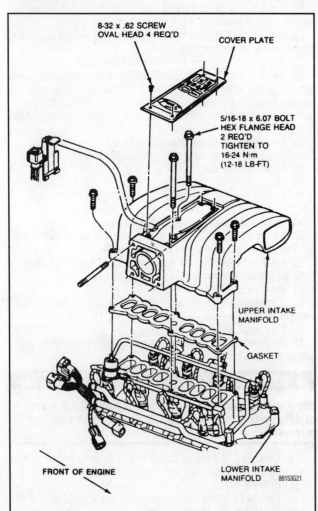

Fig. 55 Exploded view of the upper intake manifold assembly—Mustang 5.0L engine (except Cobra)

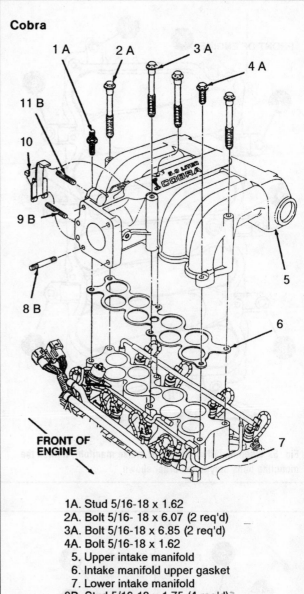

1A. Stud 5/16-18 x 1.62
2A. Bolt 5/16- 18 x 6.07 (2 req'd)
3A. Bolt 5/16-18 x 6.85 (2 req'd)
4A. Bolt 5/16-18 x 1.62
5. Upper intake manifold
6. Intake manifold upper gasket
7. Lower intake manifold
8B. Stud 5/16-18 x 1.75 (4 req'd)
9B. Stud 5/16-18
10. Wiring bracket
11B. Stud 3/8-16
A. Tighten to 16-24 N.m (12-18 lb-ft)
B. Tighten to 2.7-5.4 N.m (2-4 lb-ft)

Fig. 56 Exploded view of the upper intake manifold assembly—Cobra 5.0L engine

3. If you are removing the lower intake manifold (and not only removing the upper intake), properly relieve the fuel system pressure.

4. Disconnect the accelerator cable and cruise control linkage, if equipped, from the throttle body. Disconnect the Throttle Valve (TV) cable, if equipped.

5. Tag and disconnect all accessible vacuum lines from their intake manifold fittings.

➡**If you are only removing the upper intake manifold assembly, the distributor and spark plug wires can usually be left undisturbed. Just be careful not to hit or damage the cap, or to stress and break the wires.**

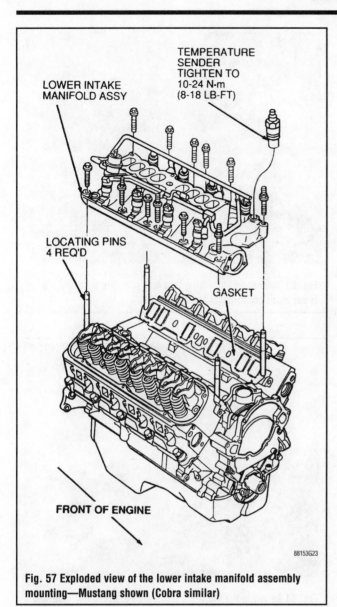

Fig. 57 Exploded view of the lower intake manifold assembly mounting—Mustang shown (Cobra similar)

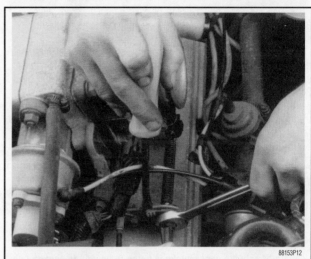

Fig. 59 Either free the cable from the bracket (as shown) or remove the bracket from the manifold

Fig. 60 Tag and disconnect the vacuum hoses from the throttle body . . .

Fig. 58 Disconnect the accelerator cable linkage from the throttle body

Fig. 61 . . . and from the rest of the upper manifold assembly

6. Tag and disconnect the spark plug wires from the spark plugs. Remove the wires and bracket assembly from the valve cover attaching stud. Remove the distributor cap and wires assembly.

7. If the lower intake is being removed, disconnect the fuel lines, then disengage the distributor wiring connector. Mark the position of the rotor on the distributor housing and the distributor housing on the engine block. Remove the hold-down bolt and remove the distributor.

8. Disconnect the upper radiator hose at the thermostat housing and the water temperature sending unit wire at the sending unit. Disconnect the heater hose from the intake manifold and disconnect the two throttle body cooler hoses.

➡Not all of these cooling system hoses must be disconnected when you are removing only the upper intake manifold. Disconnect only the hoses which are attached to the upper manifold or interfere with its removal.

9. Disconnect the water pump bypass hose from the thermostat housing.

➡Again, if only the upper intake is being removed, disengage only the wiring which is attached to or which interferes with upper intake manifold removal.

10. Tag and disengage the wiring from the manifold components including the connectors from the:
- Engine Coolant Temperature (ECT) sensor
- Intake Air Temperature (IAT) sensor
- Throttle Position (TP) sensor
- Idle Air Control (IAC) sensor
- EGR sensors
- Injector wire connections
- Fuel charging assembly wiring

11. Remove the PCV valve from the grommet at the rear of the lower intake manifold.

12. Disconnect the fuel evaporative purge hose from the plastic connector at the front of the upper intake manifold.

13. Remove the upper intake manifold cover plate and upper intake bolts. Remove the upper intake manifold.

➡Stop here if you are only removing the upper intake manifold assembly. Be sure to remove all old gasket material and to inspect the gasket mating surfaces before installation.

14. If equipped, remove the heater tube assembly from the lower intake manifold studs.

15. Remove the lower intake manifold retaining bolts and remove the lower intake manifold.

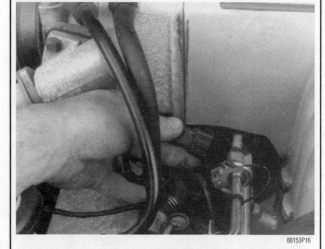

Fig. 63 Disengage any wiring that may interfere with upper or lower manifold removal (as applicable)

Fig. 64 Separate the multi-pin harnesses at the upper manifold assembly

Fig. 62 Don't forget the hoses on the "vacuum tree"

Fig. 65 Loosen and remove the upper intake manifold retaining bolts

Fig. 66 Don't forget the bolts under the upper manifold cover— loosen the cover screws . . .

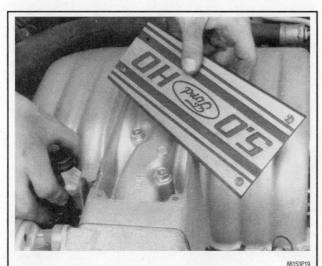

Fig. 67 . . . then remove the cover for access to the hidden manifold bolts

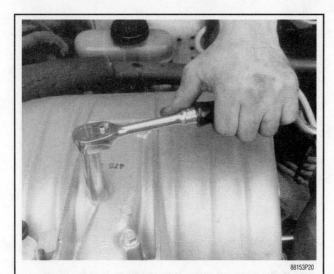

Fig. 68 Loosen and remove the remaining upper manifold bolts

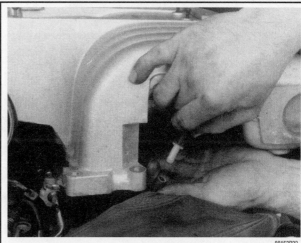

Fig. 69 Lift upward on the upper manifold for access, then disconnect the fuel evaporative purge hose

➡️If it is necessary to pry the lower intake manifold away from the cylinder heads, be careful to avoid damaging the gasket sealing surfaces.

To install:

16. Clean all gasket mating surfaces. Apply a ⅛ in. (3mm) bead of silicone sealer to the points where the cylinder block rails meet the cylinder heads.

17. Position new seals on the cylinder block and new gaskets on the cylinder heads with the gaskets interlocked with the seal tabs. Make sure the holes in the gaskets are aligned with the holes in the cylinder heads.

18. Apply a ³/₁₆ in. (5mm) bead of sealer to the outer end of each intake manifold seal for the full width of the seal. Make sure the silicone sealer will not fall into the engine and possibly block oil passages.

19. Using guide pins to ease installation, carefully lower the intake manifold into position on the cylinder block and cylinder heads.

➡️After the intake manifold is in place, run a finger around the seal area to make sure the seals are in place. If the seals are not in place, remove the intake manifold and position the seals.

20. Make sure the holes in the manifold gaskets and the manifold are in alignment. Remove the guide pins.

21. Install the intake manifold attaching bolts and tighten them, in the indicated sequence, using 3 passes:
    a. First, tighten the bolts to 8 ft. lbs. (11 Nm).
    b. Next, tighten the bolts to 16 ft. lbs. (22 Nm).
    c. Finally, tighten the bolts to 23–25 ft. lbs. (31–34 Nm).

22. Install the heater tube assembly to the lower intake manifold studs.

23. Install the water pump bypass hose on the thermostat housing. Install the hoses to the heater tubes. Connect the upper radiator hose.

24. Connect the fuel lines, then temporarily connect the negative battery cable. Cycle the ignition to pressurize the fuel system and check for leaks. Turn the ignition key back and forth (from **ON** to **OFF**) at least 6 times, leaving the key **ON** for 5 seconds each time. If no leaks are found, disconnect the negative battery cable and continue the installation.

25. If removed, install the distributor, aligning the housing and rotor with the marks that were made during removal. Install the distributor cap. Position the spark plug wires in the harness brackets on the valve cover attaching stud, and connect the wires to the spark plugs.

➡️If the engine was moved with the distributor out, rotate the crankshaft until the No. 1 piston is at TDC of the compression stroke. Align the correct initial timing mark with the pointer, then position the distributor in the block with the rotor at the No. 1 firing position and install the hold-down clamp. For more information on distributor removal and installation, and for helpful hints on figuring out when the engine is at TDC, please refer to the distributor and timing procedures in Section 1 of this manual.

Fig. 70 Carefully lift and remove the upper manifold from the engine

Fig. 71 If the lower manifold is not being removed, clean the gasket mating surfaces at this time . . .

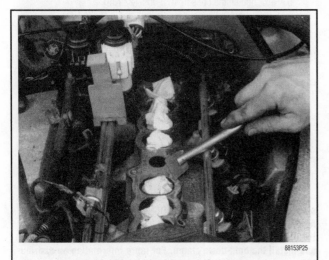

Fig. 72 . . . but be sure to cover the openings in the lower manifold to keep debris out of the engine

Fig. 73 If the lower intake manifold is also being removed, unplug the injector wiring harness connectors . . .

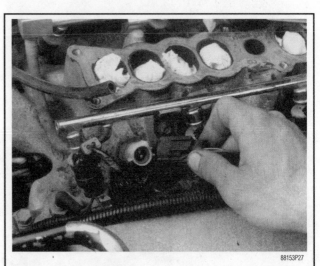

Fig. 74 . . . along with any lower manifold wiring connectors which were not unplugged earlier

Fig. 75 Make sure all wiring is disconnected from the lower manifold and nearby components

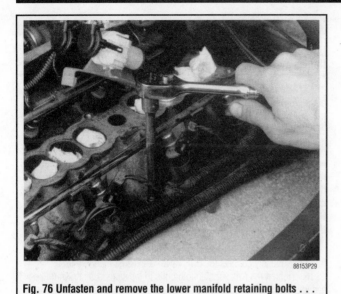

Fig. 76 Unfasten and remove the lower manifold retaining bolts . . .

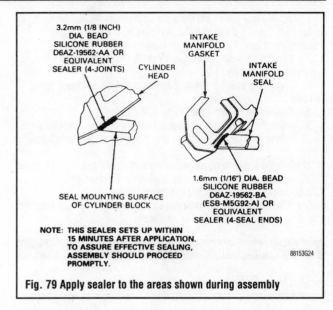

Fig. 79 Apply sealer to the areas shown during assembly

Fig. 77 . . . then break the gasket seal by lifting the manifold from the engine

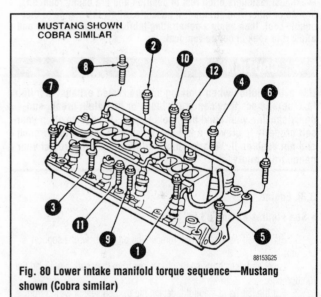

Fig. 80 Lower intake manifold torque sequence—Mustang shown (Cobra similar)

Fig. 78 Again, keep debris from falling into the engine and remove the old gaskets

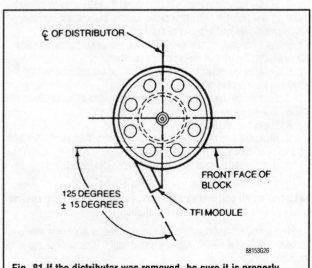

Fig. 81 If the distributor was removed, be sure it is properly aligned during installation

26. Install a new gasket and the upper intake manifold. Tighten the bolts to 12–18 ft. lbs. (16–24 Nm). Install the cover plate and connect the crankcase vent tube.

27. Connect the accelerator cable, TV cable and cruise control cable, as equipped, to the throttle body.

28. Engage the wiring connectors and vacuum lines as tagged during removal.

29. Connect the coolant hoses to the EGR spacer.

30. Install the air intake duct assembly and the crankcase vent hose.

31. Connect the negative battery cable, then fill and bleed the cooling system.

32. Run the engine to normal operating temperature and check for leaks.

33. Operate the engine at fast idle. When engine temperatures have stabilized, check the intake manifold bolt torque values.

34. If the lower intake was removed and/or the distributor was disturbed, check the ignition timing. Adjust as necessary.

Exhaust Manifold

REMOVAL & INSTALLATION

➡**Exhaust fasteners often rust in position and are easily rounded, broken or otherwise stripped. If possible, allow the engine to thoroughly cool, then apply a penetrating lubricant to the retainers and allow it to soak in before removal.**

✳✳ CAUTION

Use extra caution when working around rusted exhaust manifold fasteners, since they can break loose or just plain break, suddenly causing your hand and tools to jerk. Always position yourself properly to prevent a fall and be sure to pull on the wrench and not push on it. Wearing heavy gloves can help protect your hands from injury.

3.8L Engine

♦ **See Figures 82 and 83 (p. 39–40)**

1. For the left-hand manifold, remove the oil dipstick tube support bracket.

2. Label and detach the spark plug wires from the spark plugs and the ignition coil.

3. For the left-hand manifold, detach the oxygen sensor wiring from the engine wiring harness.

4. For the right-hand manifold, disconnect the EGR valve-to-exhaust manifold tube from the exhaust manifold. Loosen the retaining nut, then remove the heater inlet tube and heater water hose.

5. Apply the parking brake and block the rear wheels, then raise and safely support the front of the vehicle on jackstands.

6. Separate the exhaust system pipe from the exhaust manifold by removing the retaining nuts.

7. For the right-hand manifold, remove the heated oxygen sensor from the exhaust manifold.

8. Lower the vehicle.

9. Remove the exhaust manifold mounting bolts, then lift the manifold up and off of the engine.

10. Remove and discard the old exhaust manifold gasket.

To install:

➡**Lightly oil all bolt and stud threads, except any requiring special sealant, with clean oil prior to installation.**

11. If a new exhaust manifold is being installed, or if a new manifold-to-exhaust pipe stud is needed, install the stud until it is securely seated in the manifold.

12. Clean the gasket surfaces of the exhaust manifold, cylinder head and exhaust pipe.

✳✳ WARNING

Do not allow anti-seize compound to enter the oxygen sensor flutes, otherwise possible damage to the sensor may occur.

13. For the left-hand manifold, apply high-temperature anti-seize compound to the oxygen sensor threads, then install the oxygen sensor in the manifold. Tighten the sensor to 28–33 ft. lbs. (37–45 Nm).

14. Install the exhaust manifold, along with a new gasket, on the cylinder head. Install two new retaining bolts loosely to hold them in place.

➡**According to the manufacturer, if slight warpage of the exhaust manifold causes a slight misalignment between the bolt holes in the cylinder head and exhaust manifold, the holes in the exhaust manifold should be elongated to provide proper alignment. However, do NOT elongate the pilot hole (lower rear bolt hole on the No. 2 cylinder).**

15. Start the remaining mounting bolts, then (for the right-hand manifold only) loosely connect the EGR valve-to-exhaust manifold tube.

16. Tighten the exhaust manifold bolts in the sequence shown in the accompanying illustration to 22–26 ft. lbs. (30–36 Nm).

17. Apply the parking brake and block the rear wheels, then raise and safely support the front of the vehicle on jackstands.

18. Connect the exhaust pipe to the manifold, then tighten the retaining nuts to 16–23 ft. lbs. (21–32 Nm).

✳✳ WARNING

Do not allow anti-seize compound to enter the oxygen sensor flutes, otherwise possible damage to the sensor may occur.

19. For the right-hand exhaust manifold, apply high-temperature anti-seize compound to the oxygen sensor threads, then install the oxygen sensor in the manifold. Tighten the sensor to 28–33 ft. lbs. (37–45 Nm).

20. Lower the vehicle and remove the wheel blocks.

21. For the right-hand exhaust manifold, install the heater inlet tube and the heater water hose. Tighten the retaining nut to 15–22 ft. lbs. (20–30 Nm). Then, tighten the EGR valve-to-exhaust manifold tube nuts to 25–34 ft. lbs. (34–47 Nm).

22. Install the spark plug wires, then start the engine and check for exhaust leaks.

4.6L SOHC Engine

♦ **See Figures 84, 85, and 86 (p. 40)**

1. Disconnect the negative battery cable.

2. For the left-hand manifold, remove the oil dipstick tube support bracket retaining bolt.

3. Apply the parking brake and block the rear wheels, then raise and safely support the front of the vehicle on jackstands.

4. Separate the exhaust system pipe from the exhaust manifold by removing the retaining nuts. Support the exhaust system pipe from a crossmember with a piece of strong string or wire.

5. Disconnect the engine wiring from the heated oxygen sensor, installed in the exhaust manifold.

6. For the left-hand exhaust manifold, detach the steering column shaft and position it out of the way.

7. Lower the vehicle.

8. Remove the exhaust manifold retaining nuts, then lift the manifold up and off of the engine.

9. Remove and discard the old exhaust manifold gaskets.

To install:

➡**Lightly oil all bolt and stud threads, except any requiring special sealant, with clean oil prior to installation.**

10. If a new exhaust manifold is being installed, transfer the EGR valve tube to the new manifold connector. Tighten the tube fastener to 33–47 ft. lbs. (45–65 Nm).

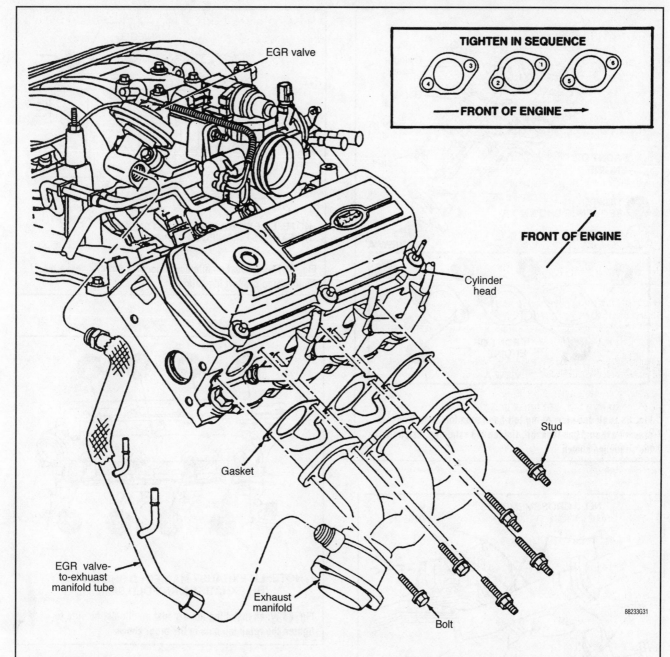

TIGHTEN IN SEQUENCE

← FRONT OF ENGINE →

EGR valve

FRONT OF ENGINE

Cylinder head

Stud

Gasket

EGR valve-to-exhuast manifold tube

Exhaust manifold

Bolt

88233G31

Fig. 82 Exploded view of the right-hand manifold mounting—be sure to tighten the mounting bolts in the sequence shown (upper right-hand corner)

11. Clean the gasket surfaces of the exhaust manifold, cylinder head and exhaust pipe.

12. Install the exhaust manifold, along with a new gasket, on the cylinder head. Install the retaining nuts and tighten them, in sequence, to 159–195 inch lbs. (18–22 Nm).

13. If applicable, reattach the steering column shaft.

➡**Loosen the line nut on the EGR valve before installing it onto the manifold.**

14. Attach the EGR valve-to-exhaust manifold tube to the left-hand exhaust manifold; tighten the tube nut to 26–33 ft. lbs. (35–45 Nm).

15. Apply the parking brake and block the rear wheels, then raise and safely support the front of the vehicle on jackstands.

➡**Ensure that the exhaust system is clear of the No. 3 crossmember; adjust it, as necessary.**

16. Connect the exhaust pipe to the manifold, then tighten the retaining nuts to 20–30 ft. lbs. (27–41 Nm).

17. Attach the engine wiring to the oxygen sensor(s), as necessary.

18. Lower the vehicle and remove the wheel blocks.

19. Connect the negative battery cable, then start the engine and check for exhaust leaks.

4.6L DOHC Engine

RIGHT-HAND MANIFOLD

▶ **See Figures 87 and 88 (p. 41)**

1. Disconnect the negative battery cable.

2. Remove the air inlet tube from the air cleaner housing and the throttle body.

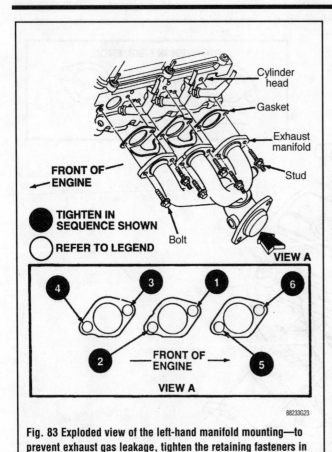

Fig. 83 Exploded view of the left-hand manifold mounting—to prevent exhaust gas leakage, tighten the retaining fasteners in the sequence shown

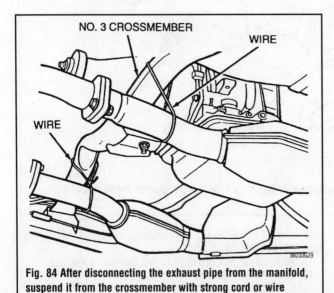

Fig. 84 After disconnecting the exhaust pipe from the manifold, suspend it from the crossmember with strong cord or wire

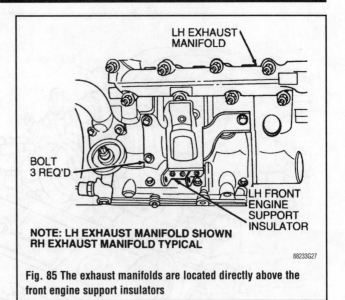

Fig. 85 The exhaust manifolds are located directly above the front engine support insulators

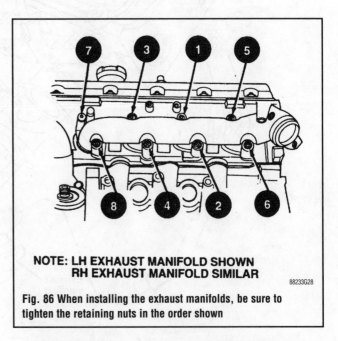

NOTE: LH EXHAUST MANIFOLD SHOWN RH EXHAUST MANIFOLD SIMILAR

Fig. 86 When installing the exhaust manifolds, be sure to tighten the retaining nuts in the order shown

6. Separate the exhaust system pipe from the exhaust manifold by removing the retaining nuts. Support the exhaust system pipe from a crossmember with a piece of strong string or wire.

7. Remove the four retaining nuts from the lower side of the manifold, then remove the manifold from the engine.

8. Remove and discard the old exhaust manifold gasket.

To install:

➡**Lightly oil all bolt and stud threads, except any requiring special sealant, with clean oil prior to installation.**

9. Clean the gasket surfaces of the exhaust manifold, cylinder head and exhaust pipe.

10. Install the exhaust manifold, along with a new gasket, on the cylinder head. Install the eight retaining nuts and tighten them, in the sequence shown in the accompanying illustration, to 159–195 inch lbs. (18–22 Nm).

3. Detach the secondary air injection manifold tube from the exhaust manifold.

4. Remove the four retaining nuts from the upper side of the exhaust manifold.

5. Apply the parking brake and block the rear wheels, then raise and safely support the front of the vehicle on jackstands.

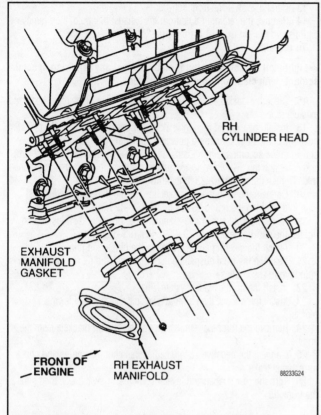

Fig. 87 Exploded view of the right-hand exhaust manifold mounting

11. Connect the exhaust pipe to the manifold, then tighten the retaining nuts to 20–30 ft. lbs. (27–41 Nm).

12. Lower the vehicle and remove the wheel blocks.

13. Reattach the secondary air injection manifold tube to the manifold. Tighten the retaining nut to 28–31 ft. lbs. (38–42 Nm).

14. Install the air inlet tube.

15. Connect the negative battery cable, then start the engine and check for exhaust leaks.

LEFT-HAND MANIFOLD

▶ **See Figures 89 and 90**

➡A Ford Three-Bar Engine Support D88L-6000-A and Engine Lifting Bracket Set 014-00340, or equivalent tools, are necessary for this procedure.

1. Open the trunk and turn the rear suspension leveler compressor switch OFF.

2. Disconnect the negative battery cable.

3. Install the engine lifting brackets on the engine, then position the three-bar engine support on the engine and attach it to the lifting brackets.

4. Loosen the front wheel lug nuts slightly, then apply the parking brake and block the rear wheels. Raise and safely support the front of the vehicle on jackstands.

5. Remove the front wheels.

6. Detach the secondary air injection manifold tube and the EGR valve-to-exhaust manifold tube from the exhaust manifold.

7. Remove the front exhaust system pipe.

8. Detach both front suspension lower control arms and outer tie rod ends from the front wheel hub/spindle assemblies.

9. Detach the steering column shaft at the pinch bolt joint and position it out of the way.

10. Support the front sub-frame assembly with a floor jack.

11. Remove the front engine support insulator through-bolts.

12. Remove the front sub-frame bolts.

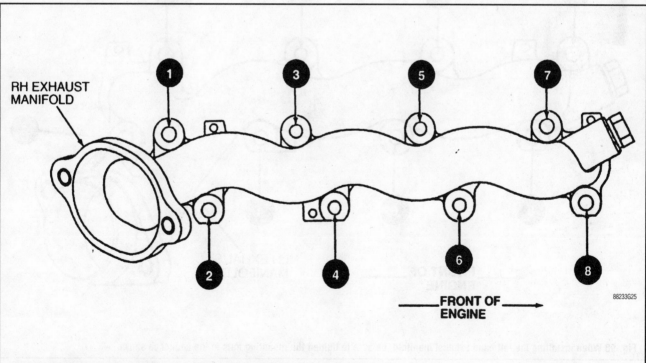

Fig. 88 Tighten the right-hand exhaust manifold retaining nuts in the order shown

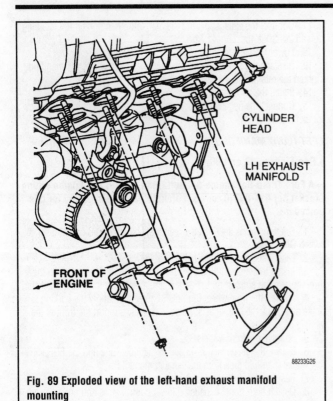

Fig. 89 Exploded view of the left-hand exhaust manifold mounting

13. Carefully lower the front sub-frame.

14. Remove the retaining nuts from the exhaust manifold, then remove and discard the old exhaust manifold gasket.

To install:

➡**Lightly oil all bolt and stud threads, except any requiring special sealant, with clean oil prior to installation.**

15. Clean the gasket surfaces of the exhaust manifold, cylinder head and exhaust pipe.

16. Install the exhaust manifold, along with new gaskets, on the cylinder head. Install the eight retaining nuts and tighten them, in the sequence shown in the accompanying illustration, to 159–195 inch lbs. (18–22 Nm).

17. Attach the EGR valve-to-exhaust manifold tube to the exhaust manifold. Tighten the nut to 30–33 ft. lbs. (40–45 Nm).

18. Connect the secondary air injection manifold tube to the exhaust manifold. Tighten the nut to 28–31 ft. lbs. (38–42 Nm).

19. Raise the front sub-frame assembly into position, then install and tighten the sub-frame bolts to 70–96 ft. lbs. (95–131 Nm).

20. Attach the steering column shaft to the pinch bolt joint.

21. Reattach the front suspension control arms and tie rod ends to the spindle/hub assemblies.

22. Install the front exhaust system pipe.

23. Install the wheels, then lower the vehicle and remove the wheel blocks.

24. Remove the three-bar engine support and lifting brackets from the engine.

25. Connect the negative battery cable, then start the engine and check for exhaust leaks.

26. Turn the rear suspension leveler compressor switch ON, then shut the trunk lid.

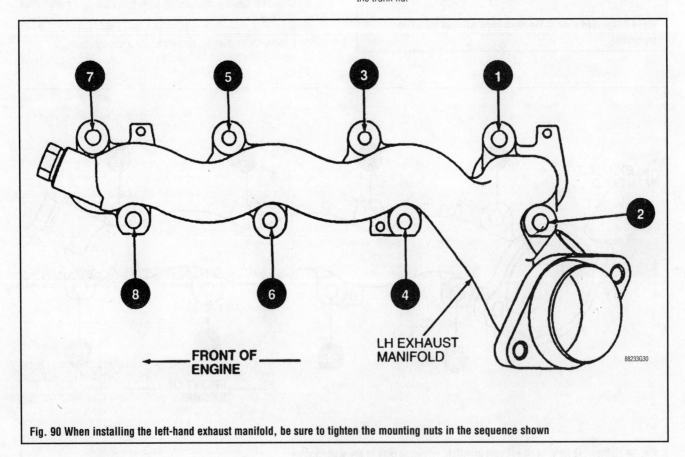

Fig. 90 When installing the left-hand exhaust manifold, be sure to tighten the mounting nuts in the sequence shown

5.0L Engine

▶ See Figures 91, 92 and 93

1. Disconnect the negative battery cable for safety purposes.
2. Remove the Thermactor/secondary air injection hardware from the right exhaust manifold.
3. If necessary, remove the air cleaner and inlet duct.
4. Tag and disconnect the spark plug wires, then remove the spark plugs from the cylinder heads.
5. If necessary, disconnect the engine oil dipstick tube from the exhaust manifold stud.

➡If the vehicle is supported at a level that allows access to both the top and bottom of the engine, you will not have to keep raising and lowering the vehicle for this procedure.

6. Raise and support the vehicle safely using jackstands.
7. Disconnect the exhaust pipe(s) from the exhaust manifold(s).
8. If necessary, remove the engine oil dipstick tube by carefully tapping upward on the tube.

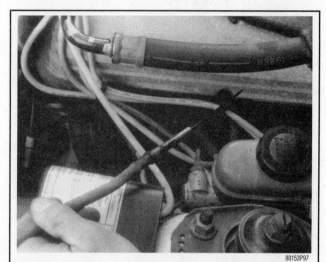

Fig. 91 On some models, it is necessary to remove the engine dipstick before the exhaust manifold

Fig. 92 From underneath the vehicle, loosen the exhaust pipe-to-manifold retainers

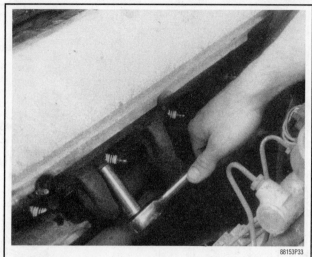

Fig. 93 Use a socket or box wrench on the bolts—avoid open-end wrenches, as these bolts are easily stripped

9. If necessary, disengage the oxygen sensor connector. If the manifold or sensor is being replaced, remove the sensor.
10. Unless upper engine access is possible in the current position, remove the jackstands and carefully lower the vehicle.
11. Remove the attaching bolts and washers, then remove the exhaust manifold(s).

To install:

12. Clean and inspect all gasket mating surfaces.
13. Position the exhaust manifold to the cylinder head using a new gasket. Retain the manifold to the engine by threading and finger-tightening the mounting bolts.
14. Working from the center to the ends, tighten the exhaust manifold attaching bolts to 26–32 ft. lbs. (35–44 Nm).
15. If lowered for access, raise and support the vehicle safely using jackstands.
16. As applicable, install the engine oil dipstick tube, then install the oxygen sensor and engage the connector.
17. Position the exhaust pipe(s) to the manifold(s). Alternately tighten the exhaust pipe flange nuts to 20–30 ft. lbs. (27–41 Nm).
18. Remove the jackstands and carefully lower the vehicle.
19. Install the spark plugs and connect the spark plug wires.
20. If removed, install the Thermactor/air injection hardware to the right exhaust manifold.
21. If removed, install the air cleaner and inlet duct.
22. Connect the negative battery cable, then start the engine and check for exhaust leaks.

Radiator

REMOVAL & INSTALLATION

▶ See Figures 94 and 95

✳ CAUTION

When draining the coolant, keep in mind that cats and dogs are attracted by ethylene glycol antifreeze, and are quite likely to drink any that is left in an uncovered container or in puddles on the ground. This will prove fatal in sufficient quantity. Always drain the coolant into a sealable container. Coolant should be reused unless it is contaminated or too old.

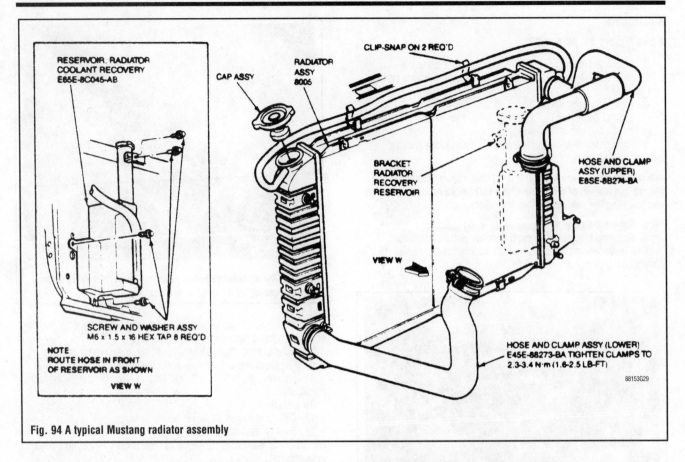

Fig. 94 A typical Mustang radiator assembly

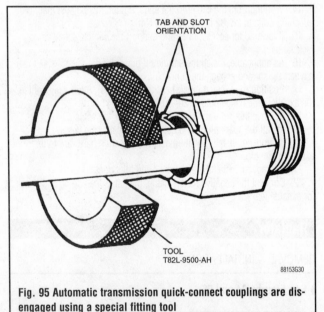

Fig. 95 Automatic transmission quick-connect couplings are disengaged using a special fitting tool

1. Disconnect the negative battery cable for safety purposes. (On vehicles with an electric cooling fan, the fan could come on at any time; disconnecting the battery cable will eliminate this risk.)

➡Before draining the cooling system is a good time to decide if it is time to replace your coolant. If not, the drain pan must be clean and free of oil or other contaminants so that the coolant can be reused. For more information, please refer to the Fluids and Lubricants information in Section 1 of this manual.

2. Make sure the engine is cool, then remove the radiator cap and drain the coolant into a suitable container.

3. Disconnect the upper, lower and coolant reservoir hoses at the radiator.

4. If equipped with an automatic transmission, disconnect the fluid cooler lines at the radiator. Depending on the year and model, your vehicle may use threaded fittings (on which a backup wrench should be used to prevent damage to the radiator) or quick-connect coupling fittings, which require a special release tool.

➡On vehicles equipped with an automatic transmission and quick-connect couplings, disconnect the fluid cooler lines at the radiator using oil cooler line quick-connect coupling tool T82L-9500-AH or equivalent.

5. On the 5.0L engine, remove the two upper fan shroud retaining bolts at the radiator support, lift the fan shroud sufficiently to disengage the lower retaining clips and lay the shroud back over the fan.

6. On some models, the coolant overflow bottle is bolted to the radiator. If so, you can ease radiator removal by unbolting and removing the overflow bottle.

7. Remove the radiator upper support retaining bolts and remove the supports. Lift the radiator from the vehicle.

To install:

8. If a new radiator is to be installed, transfer the draincock from the old radiator to the new one. If equipped with an automatic transmission and quick-connect couplings, transfer the fluid cooler line fittings from the old radiator. Use a pipe sealant with Teflon® or equivalent oil resistant sealer.

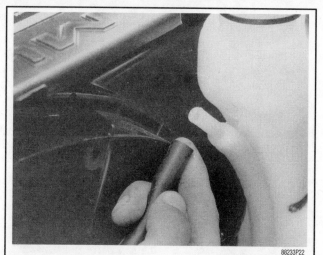

To remove a typical radiator, first detach the overflow reservoir hose . . .

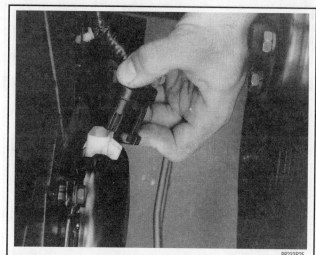

If so equipped, disengage the electrical wiring connector from the cooling fan . . .

. . . then remove the overflow reservoir mounting fasteners . . .

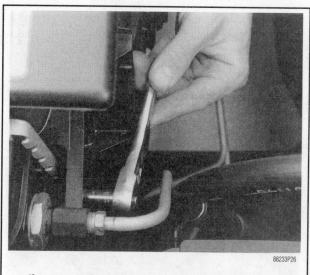

. . . then remove the cooling fan retaining fasteners . . .

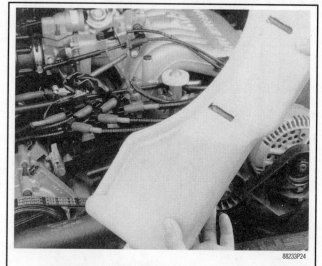

. . . and lift the reservoir up and out of the engine compartment

. . . and lift the electric cooling fan up and out of the engine compartment

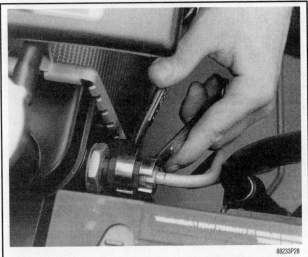

If so equipped, use two wrenches to detach the automatic transmission lines from the radiator

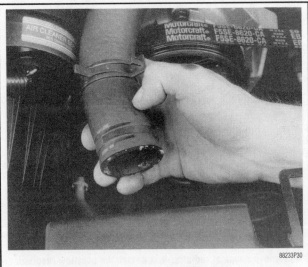

. . . and pulling the hose off of the radiator fitting

Detach the radiator hoses by depressing the clamp tangs, sliding the clamp down the hose . . .

Loosen the screws which secure the radiator cover's plastic hold-down fasteners . . .

. . . then pull the fasteners out of their mounting holes

Lift the plastic cover up and off of the radiator

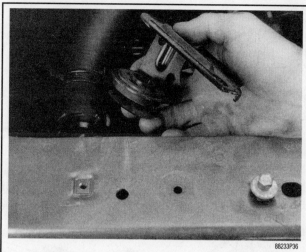

. . . then remove the retaining bracket from the support and radiator

Remove the overflow reservoir mounting bracket

Lift the radiator up and out of the engine compartment

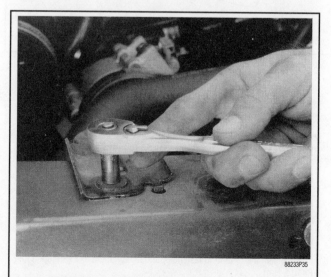

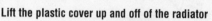

Loosen the radiator retaining bracket bolts . . .

9. Position the radiator assembly into the vehicle. Install the upper supports and the retaining bolts. If equipped with an automatic transmission, connect the fluid cooler lines.

10. If removed, install the coolant overflow bottle.

11. On the 5.0L engine, place the fan shroud into the clips on the lower radiator support and install the two upper shroud retaining bolts. Position the shroud to maintain a minimum of 0.38 in. (10mm) clearance between the fan blades and the shroud.

12. Connect the radiator hoses. Close the radiator draincock.

13. Connect the negative battery cable, then fill and bleed the cooling system.

14. Run the engine to normal operating temperature. Check for coolant and transmission fluid leaks.

15. Shut the engine **OFF**, then check the coolant and transmission fluid levels.

Engine Fan

All engines covered by this manual are equipped with a radiator mounted electric cooling fan.

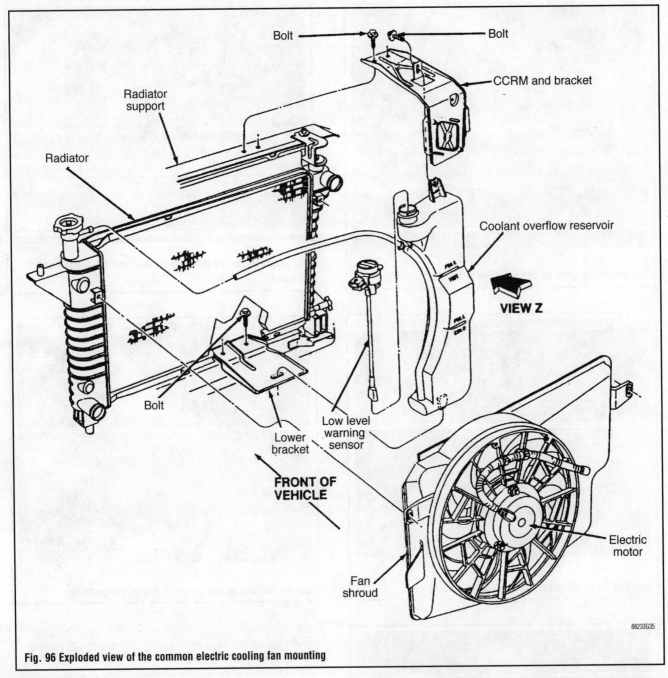

Fig. 96 Exploded view of the common electric cooling fan mounting

REMOVAL & INSTALLATION

▶ **See Figure 96**

> ❄❄ **CAUTION**
>
> **The cooling fan is automatic and may start anytime without warning. To avoid possible injury, always disconnect the negative battery cable when working near the electric cooling fan.**

1. Disconnect the negative battery cable.
2. Disengage the wiring harness connector from the electric cooling fan.
3. If necessary for added clearance or access to the fan mounting bolts, remove the coolant overflow reservoir.
4. Remove the cooling fan mounting fasteners, then lift the fan up and out of the engine compartment.

5. If necessary, the fan and motor can be separated to replace either component, as follows:
   a. Remove the retaining clip from the end of the motor shaft and remove the fan.

➡ **A metal burr may be present on the motor after the retaining clip is removed. Deburring of the shaft may be required to remove the fan.**

   b. Remove the nuts attaching the fan motor to the mounting bracket.
   To install:
6. If separated for replacement, assemble the fan and motor, as follows:
   a. Position the motor on the shroud bracket and install the retaining nuts. Tighten the nuts to 49–62 inch lbs. (5.5–7.0 Nm).
   b. Install the fan on the motor shaft using the retaining clip.
7. Install the cooling fan in its original position, against the radiator.
8. Install the mounting fasteners, and tighten them to 71–92 inch lbs. (8–10.5 Nm).
9. If applicable, install the coolant overflow reservoir.

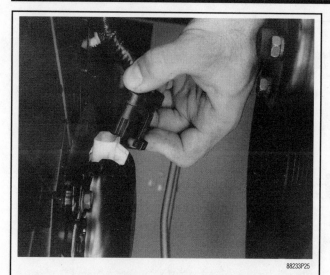

Disengage the electrical wiring connector from the cooling fan . . .

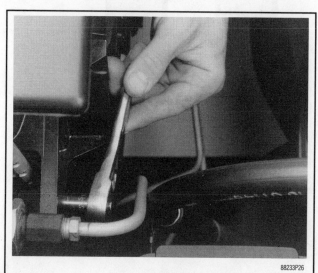

. . . then remove the cooling fan retaining fasteners . . .

. . . and lift the electric cooling fan up and out of the engine compartment

10. Fasten the motor wiring connector to the harness. Make sure the lock finger on the connector snaps firmly into place.
11. Connect the negative battery cable.
12. Run the engine and check for proper fan operation.

TESTING

▶ **See Figures 97, 98 and 99 (p. 50–51)**

The single speed electric cooling fan is attached to the fan shroud behind the radiator. The system is wired to operate only with the ignition switch in the **RUN** position. The cooling fan is controlled by a solid state Constant Control Relay Module (CCRM) and the engine control computer.

The CCRM will energize the fan with power from the fuse link when it, and the engine control module receive input from the temperature switch, indicating that the engine coolant temperature has reached at least 221°F (105°C). The fan is designed to stop once the temperature drops below 200°F (90°C). The CCRM and engine control module will also activate the cooling fan if the A/C is on and the vehicle speed does not provide a sufficient airflow (they energize the fan below 43 mph (69 km/h) and stop the fan at or above 48 mph (77 km/h).

A quick check of the fan itself can be made by circumventing the control circuit and providing battery voltage directly to the motor. If the fan works with the control circuit bypassed, the control circuit is at fault. If the fan still does not work, then the motor should be checked for binding or damage, and repaired or replaced.

Test the cooling fan as follows:
1. Disengage the electrical connector at the cooling fan motor.
2. Connect a jumper wire between the negative motor lead and a good ground.
3. Connect another jumper wire between the positive motor lead and the positive terminal of the battery.
4. If the cooling fan motor does not operate, it should be replaced. If the motor works, the control circuit is the problem and must be repaired.

Water Pump

REMOVAL & INSTALLATION

✳✳ CAUTION

When draining the coolant, keep in mind that cats and dogs are attracted by ethylene glycol antifreeze, and are quite likely to drink any that is left in an uncovered container or in puddles on the ground. This will prove fatal in sufficient quantity. Always drain the coolant into a sealable container. Coolant should be reused unless it is contaminated or too old.

3.8L Engine

▶ **See Figures 100 and 101 (p. 52–54)**

1. Drain the engine cooling system.
2. Remove the electric cooling fan from the radiator.
3. Slightly loosen the water pump pulley bolts.
4. Remove the accessory drive belt.
5. Remove the water pump pulley retaining bolts, then separate the pulley from the water pump flange.
6. Remove the ignition coil bracket mounting nuts and bolts, then position the ignition coil (with all wires still attached) aside.
7. Remove the power steering pump pulley, then remove the water pump-to-power steering pump brace.
8. Remove the heater water outlet tube retaining bolts, then separate the outlet tube from the water pump.
9. Detach the lower radiator hose from the water pump.

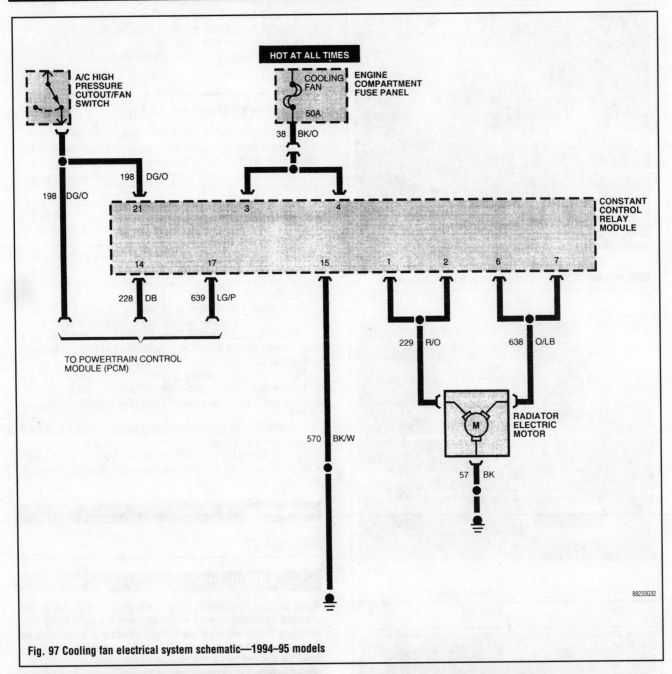

Fig. 97 Cooling fan electrical system schematic—1994–95 models

If it is necessary to utilize a prytool to separate the water pump from the engine, use caution not to damage the water pump and engine mating surfaces.

10. Loosen the water pump bolts, then pull the water pump off of the engine. Remove and discard the old water pump gasket.

To install:

➡Lightly oil all bolt and stud threads prior to assembly, except those specifying sealant, with clean engine oil.

11. Clean the gasket mating surfaces of the water pump and engine of all old gasket material and dirt.

12. Apply adhesive, such as Ford Gasket and Trim Adhesive F3AZ-19B508-B or equivalent, to the water pump gasket, then position the water pump and the new gasket on the engine.

➡The threads of the No. 1 water pump retaining bolt must be coated with a Teflon® sealant, such as Ford Pipe Sealant with Teflon® D8AZ-19554-A or equivalent, prior to installation.

13. Install the water pump retaining bolts, studs and nuts, then tighten, in the sequence shown in the accompanying illustration, the retaining bolts and studs to 15–22 ft. lbs. (20–30 Nm) and the nuts to 71–106 inch lbs. (8–12 Nm).

14. Inspect the O-ring seal on the heater water outlet tube for damage, and replace it if necessary. Then, install the outlet tube to the water pump. Tighten the retaining bolts to 71–106 inch lbs. (8–12 Nm).

15. Attach the lower radiator hose to the water pump. Ensure that the radiator hose clamps are tightened properly.

16. Install the water pump-to-power steering pump brace, then install the power steering pump pulley.

17. Install the water pump pulley and retaining bolts. Tighten the bolts to 15–21 ft. lbs. (21–29 Nm).

18. Install the accessory drive belt.

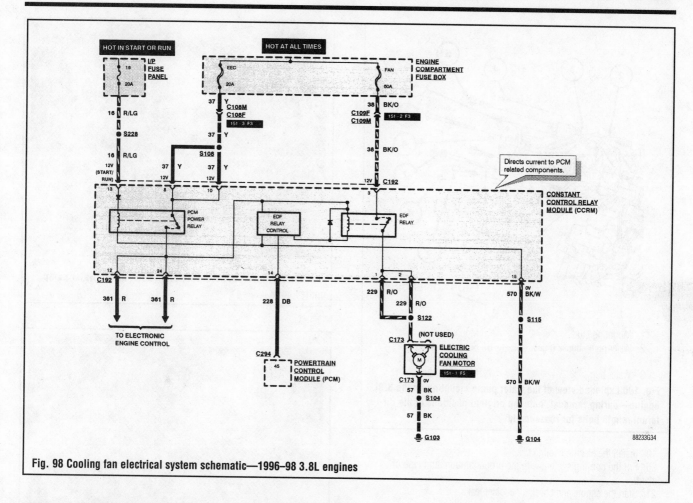

Fig. 98 Cooling fan electrical system schematic—1996–98 3.8L engines

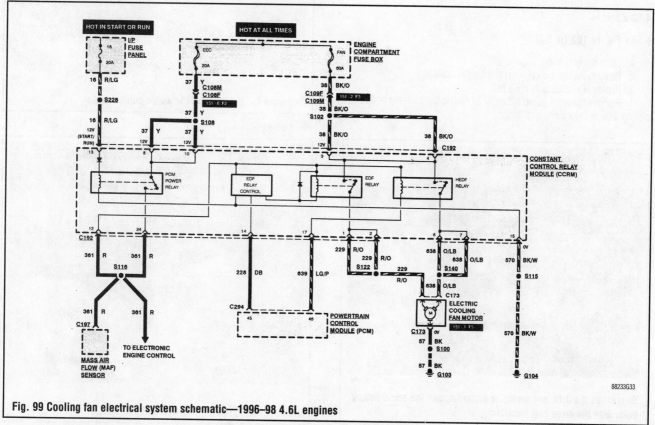

Fig. 99 Cooling fan electrical system schematic—1996–98 4.6L engines

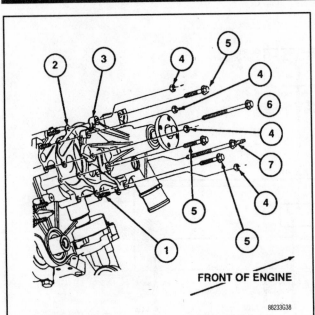

1. Mounting stud
2. Water pump housing gasket
3. Water pump
4. Mounting nuts
5. Short mounting bolts
6. Long mounting bolt
7. Mounting stud bolt

Fig. 100 Exploded view of the water pump mounting on the 3.8L engine—during removal, note the original positions of the different length bolts for reassembly

19. Install the electric cooling fan.
20. Fill the cooling system with the proper amount and type of coolant.
21. Start the engine and check for coolant leaks.

4.6L Engines

♦ See Figure 102 (p. 55)

1. Drain the engine cooling system.
2. Remove the electric cooling fan from the radiator.
3. Remove the accessory drive belt.
4. Remove the water pump pulley by loosening the retaining bolts and pulling it off of the water pump flange.

To remove the 3.8L engine water pump, loosen the pump pulley bolts with the drive belt installed . . .

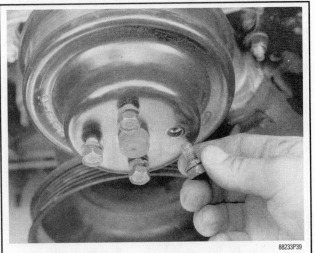

. . . then remove the accessory drive belt and the water pump pulley bolts

Separate the pulley from the water pump flange

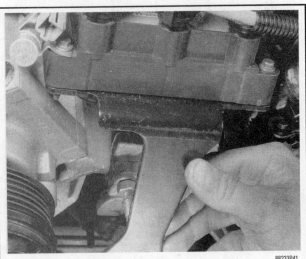

Remove the ignition coil brace and set it aside

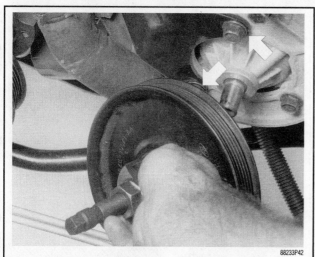

Remove the pulley from the Power Steering (PS) pump to gain access to the two PS brace bolts (arrows) . . .

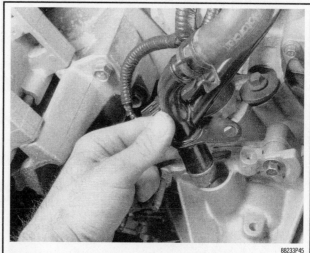

Remove the hold-down bolt, then pull the heater water outlet hose out of the water pump

. . . then remove the power steering brace bolts

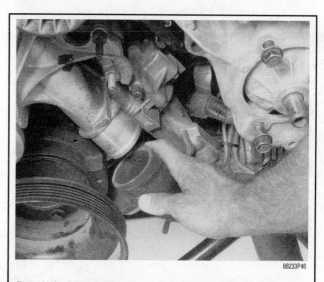

Detach the lower radiator hose from the water pump . . .

Remove the two-water pump-to-brace nuts, then remove the brace from the engine

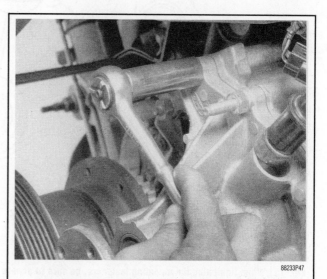

. . . then remove all of the water pump mounting fasteners

Carefully separate the water pump from the front engine cover

Be sure to remove and discard the old water pump gasket and clean the mating surfaces prior to assembly

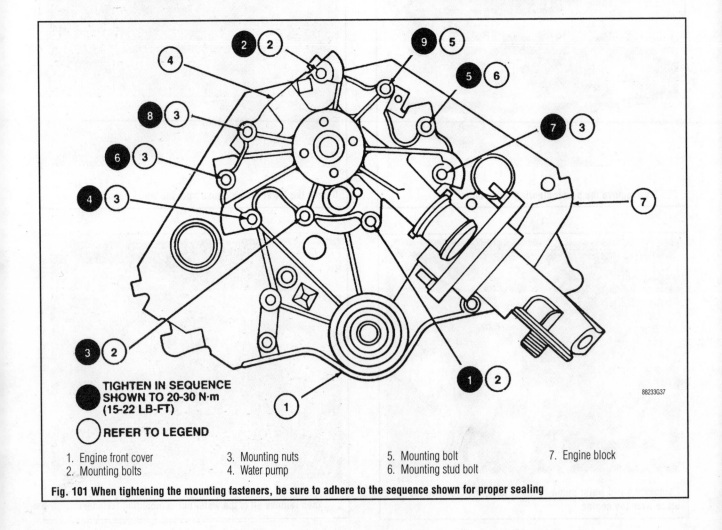

TIGHTEN IN SEQUENCE
SHOWN TO 20-30 N·m
(15-22 LB-FT)

REFER TO LEGEND

1. Engine front cover
2. Mounting bolts
3. Mounting nuts
4. Water pump
5. Mounting bolt
6. Mounting stud bolt
7. Engine block

Fig. 101 When tightening the mounting fasteners, be sure to adhere to the sequence shown for proper sealing

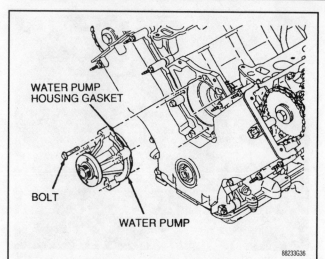

Fig. 102 Exploded view of the water pump mounting on all 4.6L engines

✳✳ WARNING

If it is necessary to utilize a prytool to separate the water pump from the engine, use caution not to damage the water pump and engine mating surfaces.

5. Loosen the water pump bolts, then separate the water pump from the engine. Remove and discard the old water pump O-ring.

To install:

➡Lightly oil all bolt and stud threads prior to assembly, except those specifying sealant, with clean engine oil.

6. Clean the mating surfaces of the water pump and engine of all corrosion and dirt.

7. Install a new O-ring in the groove on the water pump, then lubricate the O-ring with coolant, such as Ford Premium Cooling System Fluid E2Fz-19549-AA or equivalent.

8. Position the water pump, along with the new O-ring, on the engine.

9. Install the water pump retaining bolts, then tighten them 15–22 ft. lbs. (20–30 Nm) in a crisscross pattern.

10. Install the water pump pulley and retaining bolts. Tighten the bolts to 15–21 ft. lbs. (21–29 Nm).

11. Install the accessory drive belt.

12. Install the electric cooling fan.

✳✳ WARNING

Use care to prevent engine coolant from spilling on the accessory drive belt, otherwise drive belt squeal and early fatigue will result. If necessary, remove the drive belt and rinse it with clean water to clean off any antifreeze.

13. Fill the cooling system with the proper amount and type of coolant.

14. Start the engine and check for coolant leaks.

5.0L Engine

1. Disconnect the negative battery cable for safety purposes.

2. Drain the cooling system.

3. Remove the air inlet tube.

4. Remove the fan shroud attaching bolts and position the shroud over the fan.

5. Remove the fan and clutch assembly from the water pump shaft, then remove the clutch, fan and shroud from the vehicle.

6. Remove the accessory drive belt, then remove the water pump pulley.

To remove the water pump on a 5.0L engine, remove the fan assembly, the shroud, and the pump pulley . . .

. . . then loosen and remove any accessory bracket retainers which attach to the water pump

This A/C compressor bracket must also be unbolted from the A/C compressor . . .

. . . and completely removed from the engine for access to the water pump

Loosen the clamps and disconnect the hoses from the water pump assembly

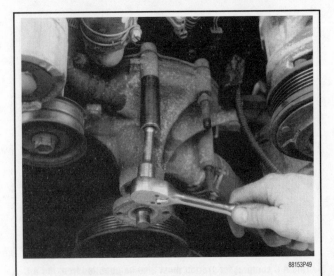

Loosen and remove the water pump retaining bolts

With the bolts removed, grasp the water pump and pull it from the engine to break the gasket seal

To assure a proper seal, remove all traces of the old gasket (being careful not to damage the surfaces)

7. Remove all accessory brackets that attach to the water pump.

8. Disconnect the lower radiator hose, heater hose and water pump bypass hose from the water pump.

9. Remove the water pump attaching bolts, then remove the water pump and discard the gasket.

To install:

10. Clean all old gasket material from the timing cover and water pump.

11. Apply a suitable waterproof sealing compound to both sides of a new gasket, then position the gasket on the timing cover.

12. Position the water pump carefully over the gasket (making sure not to dislodge it). Install and tighten the pump mounting bolts to 12–18 ft. lbs. (16–24 Nm).

13. Connect the hoses and accessory brackets to the water pump.

14. Install the pulley on the water pump shaft.

15. Install the shroud along with the clutch and fan assembly.

16. Route and install the accessory drive belt.

17. Connect the negative battery cable and refill the cooling system.

18. Run the engine and check for leaks.

Cylinder Head

REMOVAL & INSTALLATION

❈ CAUTION

When draining the coolant, keep in mind that cats and dogs are attracted by ethylene glycol antifreeze, and are quite likely to drink any that is left in an uncovered container or in puddles on the ground. This will prove fatal in sufficient quantity. Always drain the coolant into a sealable container. Coolant should be reused unless it is contaminated or too old.

3.8L Engine

▶ **See Figures 103 and 104**

1. Disconnect the negative battery cable.
2. Remove the upper and lower intake manifolds.
3. Remove the valve cover(s) and rocker arms.

➡**Be sure to label or separate all of the cylinder head components (such as pushrods, rocker arms, etc.) so that they can be installed in their original positions on the cylinder heads.**

4. Remove the exhaust manifolds.
5. If not already done, perform the following for left-hand cylinder head removal:

   a. Remove the Power Steering (PS) pump front mounting brace retaining nuts from the water pump.

   b. Remove the alternator.

   c. Remove the idler pulley.

   d. Remove the PS pump/alternator bracket mounting fasteners, then (leaving all PS hoses attached) position the PS pump and bracket aside in a position so that PS fluid does not leak out.

6. If not already done, perform the following for right-hand cylinder head removal:

   a. If equipped with A/C, remove the compressor mounting bracket bolts, then (leaving all A/C lines attached) position the compressor aside.

   b. If not equipped with A/C, remove the idler pulley.

7. Remove and discard the cylinder head mounting bolts.
8. Lift the cylinder head(s) up and off of the engine block.
9. Remove and discard the old cylinder head gasket(s).

. . . then lift the head up and off of the engine block

Be sure to remove the old cylinder head gasket and to clean all of the head and manifold mating surfaces

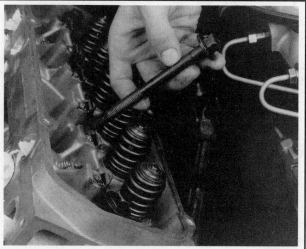

To remove the cylinder heads, remove all of the mounting bolts . . .

When tightening the cylinder head mounting bolts, be sure to use a torque wrench

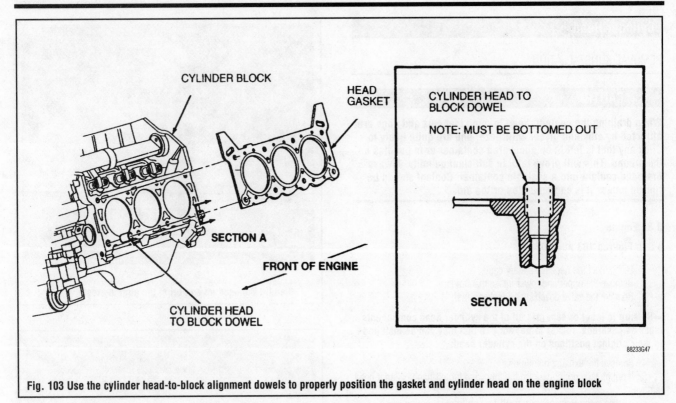

Fig. 103 Use the cylinder head-to-block alignment dowels to properly position the gasket and cylinder head on the engine block

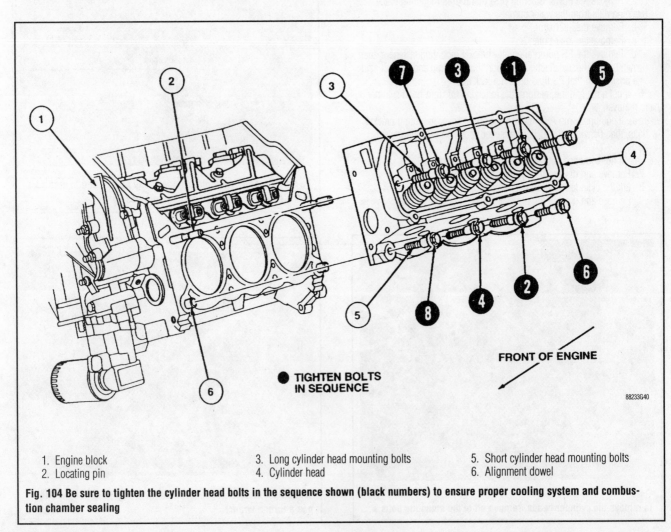

1. Engine block
2. Locating pin
3. Long cylinder head mounting bolts
4. Cylinder head
5. Short cylinder head mounting bolts
6. Alignment dowel

Fig. 104 Be sure to tighten the cylinder head bolts in the sequence shown (black numbers) to ensure proper cooling system and combustion chamber sealing

To install:

➡Lightly oil all bolt and stud threads prior to assembly, except those specifying sealant, with clean engine oil.

10. Clean the cylinder head, intake manifold and valve cover gasket mating surfaces thoroughly.

11. If a cylinder head was removed for head gasket replacement, inspect the cylinder head for warpage.

➡If a cylinder head is warped, have it ground by a competent machine shop before installing.

12. Position the new cylinder head gasket(s) on the engine block, then install the cylinder head(s).

❋❋ WARNING

Always use new cylinder head bolts to ensure a leak-tight seal. Torque values with used cylinder head bolts can vary, which may cause coolant or compression leakage.

13. Tighten the cylinder head bolts in the sequence shown in the accompanying illustration, and in the following steps to the proper values:
   a. Tighten the bolts to 15 ft. lbs. (20 Nm).
   b. Next, tighten the bolts to 29 ft. lbs. (40 Nm).
   c. Then, tighten the bolts to 37 ft. lbs. (50 Nm).

❋❋ WARNING

Do not loosen all of the bolts at the same time in the following step; only work on one bolt at a time, then move on the next bolt in the sequence.

   d. Loosen the bolts, one at a time, two or three revolutions, then retighten them as follows:

1994–95 Models
- Tighten the bolt to 133–221 inch lbs. (15–25 Nm) for a long bolt, or to 88–177 inch lbs. (10–20 Nm).
- Rotate the bolt an additional 85–95 degrees.
- Proceed to the next bolt in the sequence.

1996–98 Models
- Tighten the bolt to 29–37 ft. lbs. (40–50 Nm) for a long bolt, or to 133–221 inch lbs. (15–25 Nm) for a short bolt.
- Rotate the bolt an additional 180 degrees.
- Proceed to the next bolt in the sequence.

14. Dip each end of the pushrods in engine assembly lubricant, such as Ford D9AZ-19579-D or equivalent, then install the pushrods in their original positions.

15. Apply engine assembly lube to the rocker arms prior to installation, then install the rocker arms.

16. Install the exhaust manifolds.

17. Install the lower and upper intake manifolds.

18. Install the valve cover(s).

19. Install the spark plugs, if removed. Then, connect the spark plug wires to the plugs.

20. If necessary, install the PS pump and bracket on the engine, then install the alternator.

21. If necessary, install the A/C compressor and bracket on the engine.

22. If not already performed, install the accessory drive belt pulleys and the drive belt.

23. Connect the negative battery cable.

24. Fill the engine with the proper type and amount of coolant.

25. Start the engine and check for coolant leaks.

4.6L SOHC Engine

♦ See Figures 105, 106 and 107

1. Disconnect the negative battery cable, drain the cooling system and relieve fuel system pressure.

2. Remove the valve cover(s).

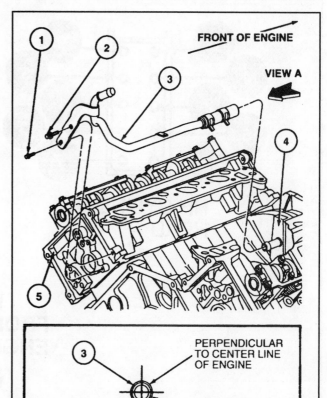

1. Mounting bolt
2. Mounting bolt
3. Heater water hose
4. Engine block
5. Left-hand cylinder head

Fig. 105 Exploded view of the heater water hose mounting on the left-hand cylinder head

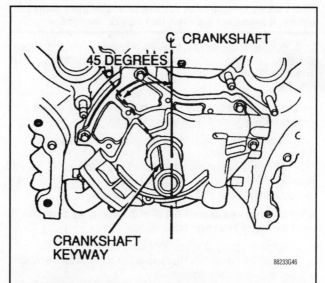

Fig. 106 Prior to installing the cylinder heads, rotate the crankshaft 45 degrees counterclockwise

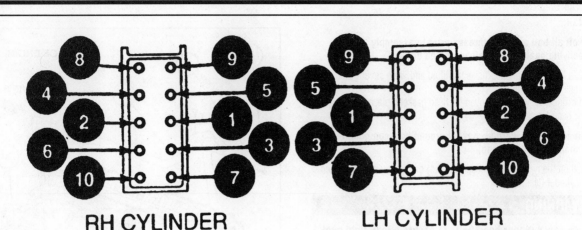

Fig. 107 When tightening the cylinder head mounting bolts, be sure to follow the order shown

3. Remove the throttle body.
4. Remove the intake manifold.
5. Disconnect the exhaust system from the exhaust manifolds.
6. Remove the engine front cover.
7. Remove the timing chains. Be sure to note the positions of the flats on the ends of the two camshafts before removing the cylinder heads.
8. Remove or detach any remaining wires, hoses or cables which will interfere with cylinder head removal.

✳✳ WARNING

Do not set the cylinder head down on its engine block mating surface; if any valves are open, they may be damaged.

9. Remove the cylinder head mounting bolts and lift the cylinder heads off of the engine block. If necessary, at this time the heater water hose can be removed from the left-hand cylinder head.

To install:

→ **Lightly oil all bolt and stud threads prior to assembly, except those specifying sealant, with clean engine oil.**

10. Clean the cylinder head, intake manifold and valve cover gasket mating surfaces thoroughly.
11. If a cylinder head was removed for head gasket replacement, inspect the cylinder head for warpage. If a cylinder head is warped, have it ground by a competent machine shop before installing.

→ **The following step ensures that all of the pistons are below the top of the engine block deck face.**

12. Rotate the crankshaft counterclockwise 45 degrees.
13. Inspect the cylinder head face surface for scratches near the coolant passages and combustion chambers.
14. Rotate the camshaft to a stable position where the valves do not extend below the cylinder head face.

15. Position the new cylinder head gasket(s) on the engine block, then install the cylinder head(s).

✳✳ WARNING

Cylinder head mounting bolts must be replaced with new bolts; do NOT reuse original cylinder head mounting bolts. They are torque-to-yield bolts and cannot be reused; otherwise, engine damage may occur.

16. Apply clean engine oil to the cylinder head mounting bolts' spot faces. Then, install the mounting bolts hand-tight.
17. Tighten the cylinder head bolts (starting with the left-hand cylinder head first) in the sequence shown in the accompanying illustration and following these steps:
   a. Tighten the bolts to 27–31 ft. lbs. (37–43 Nm).
   b. Tighten the bolts an additional 85–95 degrees.
   c. Loosen the bolts a minimum of one full revolution (360 degrees).
   d. Retighten the bolts to 27–31 ft. lbs. (37–43 Nm).
   e. Tighten the bolts an additional 85–95 degrees.
   f. Finally, tighten the bolts an additional 85–95 degrees.
18. Install the heater water hose on the left-hand cylinder head, then tighten the lower mounting bolt to 71–106 inch lbs. (8–12 Nm) and the upper mounting bolt to 15–22 ft. lbs. (20–30 Nm).
19. Using the flats matched at the center of the camshafts, rotate the camshafts until both are in time (the position they were in when the timing chains were removed).
20. Install Ford Cam Positioning Tool Adapters T92P-6256-A and Cam Positioning Tool T91P-6256-A (or their equivalents) on the flats of the camshafts to prevent them from rotating.

✳✳ WARNING

The crankshaft must only be rotated in the clockwise direction and only as far as Top Dead Center (TDC).

21. Rotate the crankshaft clockwise 45 degrees.
22. Install the timing chains.
23. Install the engine front cover.
24. Connect the exhaust system to the exhaust manifolds.
25. Install the intake manifold.
26. Install the throttle body.
27. Install the valve cover(s).
28. Install or attach any remaining wires, hoses or cables which were removed earlier.
29. Connect the negative battery cable and fill the cooling system.
30. Start the engine and check for leaks.

4.6L DOHC Engine

♦ **See Figures 108 thru 113**

➡**According to the manufacturer, the cylinder heads are not removable with the engine in the vehicle; therefore, this procedure is written with the assumption that the engine is removed from the vehicle.**

1. Remove the engine from the vehicle, as described earlier in this section.
2. Remove the valve covers.
3. Remove the engine front cover.
4. Remove the intake manifolds.
5. Remove the crankshaft position sensor pulse wheel.
6. Remove the rocker arms.
7. Remove the exhaust manifolds.
8. If not already done, drain the coolant from the engine block.
9. Rotate the engine to Top Dead Center (TDC) as follows:
   a. Remove the spark plugs from the cylinder heads.
   b. Install the crankshaft damper center bolt in the crankshaft.
   c. Position your thumb over the No. 1 cylinder's spark plug hole, so that it seals the hole completely.

➡**Only rotate the crankshaft in the clockwise direction (when looking at the front of the engine).**

   d. Have an assistant rotate the crankshaft using a breaker bar and socket on the crankshaft center bolt until you start to feel air escaping past your thumb (you will not have the strength to keep the cylinder sealed—air will escape).

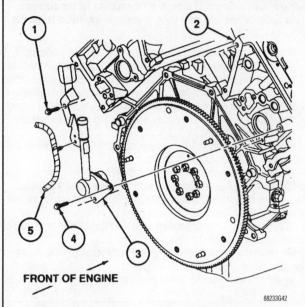

FRONT OF ENGINE

1. Mounting bolt
2. Right-hand cylinder head
3. Inlet heater water hose
4. Mounting bolts
5. Engine wiring harness

Fig. 109 Exploded view of the inlet heater water hose mounting on the right-hand cylinder head

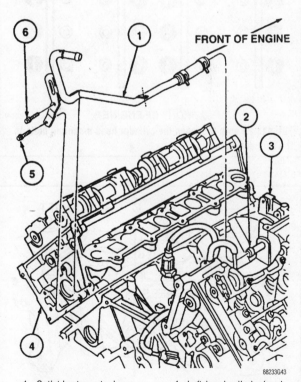

FRONT OF ENGINE

1. Outlet heater water hose
2. Connector
3. Engine block
4. Left-hand cylinder head
5. Mounting bolts
6. Mounting bolt

Fig. 110 Exploded view of the outlet heater water hose mounting on the left-hand cylinder head

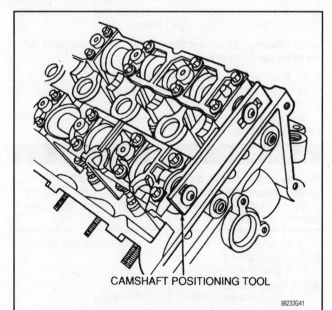

CAMSHAFT POSITIONING TOOL

Fig. 108 Use a camshaft positioning tool to hold the camshafts from rotating once the timing chains are removed

➡It may take a couple of tries to get the feeling for the air down. Have patience and take your time, it is vitally important to get the engine at TDC.

e. From that point, rotate the crankshaft until the TDC marks are aligned. The timing chain and crankshaft gears' timing marks should be aligned at this point. Also, all four valves should be closed (that is, their camshaft lobes should be pointing away from the valves and springs). If the timing chain gear marks are not aligned and all of the valves are not closed, but the TDC ignition timing marks are aligned, rotate the crankshaft one full revolution (360 degrees).

10. Install Ford Camshaft Positioning Tool T93P-6256-A, or the equivalent, in the rear D-slots of the camshafts.

11. Remove the timing chains and tensioners.

12. Disengage the engine harness wiring from the heater water hose, then remove the three bolts retaining the inlet heater water hose to the rear of the right-hand cylinder head.

13. Remove the outlet heater water hose mounting bolts from the rear of the left-hand cylinder head.

14. Using the removal sequence, shown in the accompanying illustration, remove the cylinder head mounting bolts.

15. Discard all of the old cylinder head mounting bolts.

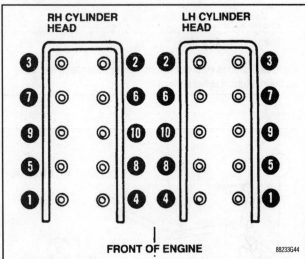

Fig. 111 Be sure to loosen the cylinder head mounting bolts in the sequence shown

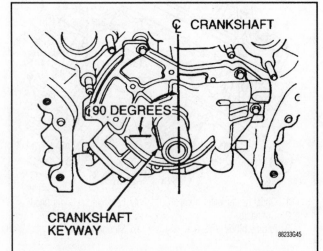

Fig. 112 Before installing the cylinder heads, rotate the crankshaft 90 degrees counterclockwise

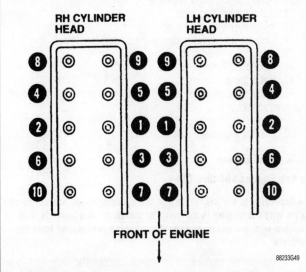

Fig. 113 Tighten the new cylinder head mounting bolts ONLY in the order shown—this will ensure proper cooling system and combustion chamber sealing

✳✳ WARNING

Do NOT set the cylinder heads down on their engine block mating surface; otherwise, damage may occur to the valve heads, which may protrude beyond the cylinder head surface.

16. Lift the cylinder heads up and off of the engine block.

17. Remove and discard the old cylinder head gaskets.

To install:

➡Lightly oil all bolt and stud threads prior to assembly, except those specifying sealant, with clean engine oil.

18. Clean the cylinder head, intake manifold, valve cover gasket mating surfaces thoroughly. Ensure that all bolt holes are clean and dry. Remove all engine coolant residue prior to reassembly.

19. If a cylinder head was removed for head gasket replacement, inspect the cylinder head for warpage. If a cylinder head is warped, have it ground by a competent machine shop before installing.

➡The following step ensures that all of the pistons are below the top of the engine block deck face.

20. Rotate the crankshaft counterclockwise 90 degrees.

21. Inspect the cylinder head face surface for scratches near the coolant passages and combustion chambers.

22. Position the new cylinder head gasket(s) on the engine block, then install the cylinder head(s).

✳✳ WARNING

Cylinder head mounting bolts must be replaced with new bolts; do NOT reuse original cylinder head mounting bolts. They are torque-to-yield bolts and cannot be reused; otherwise, engine damage may occur.

23. Apply clean engine oil to both sides of the cylinder head mounting bolts' washer faces.

24. Tighten the left cylinder head bolts in the sequence presented in the accompanying illustration, as follows:

a. Tighten the bolts to 27–32 ft. lbs. (37–43 Nm).

b. Then, tighten the bolts an additional 85–95 degrees.

c. Finally, tighten the bolts an additional 85–95 degrees again.

25. Perform Step 23 for the right-hand cylinder head as well.

26. Install the outlet heater water hose on the left-hand cylinder head.

Tighten the upper mounting bolt to 15–22 ft. lbs. (20–30 Nm) and the lower bolt to 71–106 inch lbs. (8–12 Nm).

27. Install the inlet heater water hose on the right-hand cylinder head. Tighten the upper mounting bolt to 15–22 ft. lbs. (20–30 Nm) and the two lower bolts to 71–106 inch lbs. (8–12 Nm).

28. Install the primary timing chains and set valve timing.

29. Install the rocker arms.

30. Install the crankshaft position sensor pulse wheel.

31. Install the intake manifolds.

➡**When cleaning the sealing surfaces of the engine front cover and the oil pan-to-engine block joints, be careful to avoid damaging the oil pan gasket rubber bead. If a leak develops after reassembly, the oil pan must be removed and the oil pan gasket replaced.**

32. Install the engine front cover.

33. Install the exhaust manifolds.

34. Install the engine in the vehicle.

☀ WARNING

It is very important to fill the engine with oil prior to starting it. Excessive engine damage will result if the engine is run without oil.

35. If necessary, fill the engine with the proper type and amount of clean engine oil.

36. Fill the engine cooling system.

37. Connect the positive, then the negative battery cables.

38. Start the engine and check for exhaust, coolant, fuel and oil leaks.

39. Shut the engine **OFF** and check the engine oil level; add oil, if necessary.

5.0L Engine

♦ See Figure 114

➡**If the left cylinder head is being removed and your vehicle is equipped with air conditioning, refer to Section 1 for information regarding the implications of servicing your A/C system yourself. Only an MVAC-trained, EPA-certified, automotive technician should service the A/C system or its components.**

1. For left-hand cylinder head removal, have the A/C compressor removed.

☀ WARNING

Ensure that the technician immediately caps or plugs all openings to the air conditioning system in order to prevent system contamination and damage.

2. Disconnect the negative battery cable for safety purposes.

3. Drain the cooling system and properly relieve the fuel system pressure.

4. Remove the upper and lower intake manifold assemblies, along with the throttle body.

5. If you are removing the left cylinder head, perform the following:

    a. If not done earlier, remove the drive belt from the power steering pump pulley, then disconnect the power steering pump bracket from the cylinder head. Position the pump out of the way in a position that will prevent the oil from draining out.

    b. Disconnect the oil level indicator tube bracket from the exhaust manifold stud, if necessary.

6. Remove the Thermactor/secondary air injection crossover tube from the rear of the cylinder heads.

7. If you are removing the right cylinder head, perform the following steps:

    a. Disconnect the alternator or alternator and air pump mounting bracket from the cylinder head, as equipped.

    b. Remove the fuel line from the clip at the front of the cylinder head.

88153P52

Label the pushrods to assure installation in the proper positions

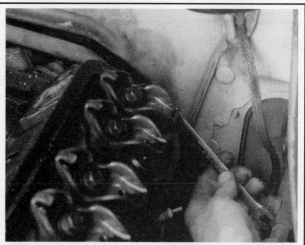

88153P53

For 5.0L engines, remove the Thermactor/secondary air injection tube from the cylinder heads . . .

88153P54

. . . then loosen the cylinder head bolts using a breaker bar and socket

Lift the cylinder head from the block, breaking the gasket seal . . .

. . . and remove the old gasket from the block

If you use a gasket scraper, be careful not to damage the surface and be sure to keep debris out of the cylinders

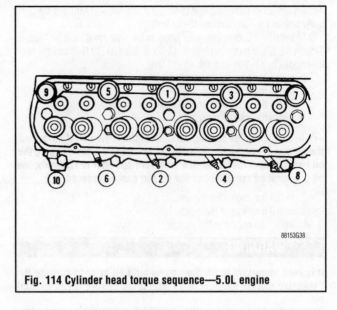

Fig. 114 Cylinder head torque sequence—5.0L engine

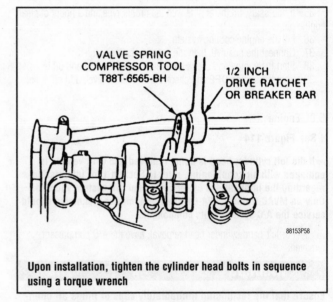

VALVE SPRING COMPRESSOR TOOL T88T-6565-BH

1/2 INCH DRIVE RATCHET OR BREAKER BAR

Upon installation, tighten the cylinder head bolts in sequence using a torque wrench

8. Apply the parking brake and block the rear wheels, then raise and safely support the front of the vehicle on jackstands.

9. Disconnect the exhaust manifolds from the muffler inlet pipes, then remove the jackstands and carefully lower the vehicle.

10. Loosen the rocker arm fulcrum bolts so the rocker arms can be rotated to the side. Remove the pushrods and tag or arrange them in sequence so they may be installed in their original positions.

➡A piece of wood or cardboard may be drilled and labelled to help sort the pushrods and make sure they are only installed to the rocker arms and lifters from which they were removed.

11. Remove the cylinder head attaching bolts and the cylinder head(s). Remove and discard the head gasket(s).

➡It may be necessary to remove the exhaust manifolds for access to the lower head bolts. If so, be sure to thoroughly clean the gasket mating surfaces and to use new exhaust manifold gaskets upon installation.

12. Clean all gasket mating surfaces. Check the flatness of the cylinder head using a straightedge and a feeler gauge. The cylinder head must not be warped any more than 0.003 in. (0.076mm) in any 6 in. (152mm) span;

0.006 in. (0.152mm) overall. Machine if necessary. For details, please refer to the Engine Reconditioning procedures later in this section.

To install:

13. Position the new cylinder head gasket(s) over the dowels on the block. Position the cylinder head(s) on the block and install the head bolts.

※※ WARNING

Cylinder head mounting bolts must be replaced with new bolts; do NOT reuse original cylinder head mounting bolts. They are torque-to-yield bolts and cannot be reused; otherwise, engine damage may occur.

14. The cylinder head bolts should be tightened in three steps of the proper sequence, as follows:

    a. Tighten the bolts to 25–35 ft. lbs. (34–47 Nm).

    b. Next, tighten the bolts to 45–55 ft. lbs. (61–75 Nm).

    c. Finally, tighten all bolts an additional ¼ turn (85–95° if a torque angle meter is available).

15. If removed, install the exhaust manifolds using new gaskets.

16. Clean the pushrods, making sure the oil passages are clean. If you have access to compressed air, blow out the passages to be sure they are clear. Check the ends of the pushrods for wear. Visually check the pushrods for straightness or check for run-out using a dial indicator. Replace pushrods, as necessary.

17. Apply a suitable multi-purpose grease to the ends of the pushrods and install them in their original positions. Position the rocker arms over the pushrods and the valves.

➡If all the original valve train parts are reinstalled and no cylinder head milling was performed, a valve clearance check is not necessary. If any valve train components are replaced, a valve clearance check must be performed.

18. Raise and support the vehicle safely using jackstands. Connect the exhaust manifolds to the muffler inlet pipes, then remove the jackstands and carefully lower the vehicle.

19. If the right cylinder head was removed, reposition and install the alternator, or alternator and air pump bracket. Install the alternator assembly.

20. Install the valve cover(s) using new gasket(s).

21. If the left cylinder head was removed, reposition and install the A/C compressor and/or the power steering pump, as equipped.

22. Install the drive belt, making sure that the belt tensioner is maintaining the proper tension and that the belt is properly aligned on all of the pulleys.

23. Install the Thermactor/secondary air injection crossover tube at the rear of the cylinder heads.

24. Install the upper and lower intake manifold assemblies.

25. Connect the negative battery cable, then fill and bleed the cooling system.

26. Bring the vehicle to normal operating temperature. Check for leaks and check all fluid levels.

27. If the A/C system was discharged, take the vehicle to a reputable service facility and have the refrigerant system leak-tested, evacuated and charged according to the proper procedures.

Oil Pan

REMOVAL & INSTALLATION

3.8L Engine

◗ See Figures 115 and 116

➡It is a good idea to place the vehicle's ignition keys in the box with the new oil containers so that you do not accidentally start the vehicle without first filling the engine with oil.

1. Disconnect the negative battery cable.

2. Remove the air inlet tube from the throttle body and air cleaner housing.

3. Remove the upper radiator plastic cover and the hood weather seal.

4. Remove the windshield wiper arms.

5. Remove the left-hand cowl vent screen and the windshield wiper module.

6. Install an engine support tool, such as the Ford Three Bar Engine Support D88L-6000-A. Do not support the weight of the engine yet.

7. Apply the parking brake and block the rear wheels, then raise and safely support the front of the vehicle on jackstands.

8. Remove the front engine mount through-bolts.

9. Using the engine support tool, raise the engine slightly.

10. Remove the starter motor.

11. If equipped, remove the automatic transmission cooler lines.

12. Drain the engine oil and remove the engine oil filter.

13. Remove the oil pan-to-bell housing bolts and the bolts at the crankshaft position sensor lower shield.

14. Remove the remaining oil pan mounting bolts.

15. Separate the steering column shaft at the pinch bolt joint.

16. Position a transmission jack under the front sub-frame, then support the front sub-frame with the jack.

17. Matchmark the sub-frame position in relation to the vehicle chassis for reinstallation purposes.

18. Remove the six rear and the two front mounting bolts from the front sub-frame.

19. Remove the lower shock absorber-to-lower control arm bolts and nuts on both sides of the vehicle.

20. Cautiously lower the front sub-frame.

21. Remove the oil pan. Pour any residual oil out of the oil pan.

22. If necessary, remove the oil pump screen and tube retainer bolts, and support bracket nut. Remove the oil pump screen cover and tube. Discard the old oil pump inlet tube gasket.

To install:

23. Install the oil pump screen cover and tube, along with a new gasket. Tighten the retaining bolts to 15–22 ft. lbs. (20–30 Nm) and the bracket nut to 30–40 ft. lbs. (40–55 Nm).

24. Trial fit the oil pan on the engine block to ensure that there is adequate clearance to prevent the new sealer from being scraped off of the engine block by the oil pan.

25. Clean the mating surfaces of the oil pan and engine block of all old sealant and oil residue with Ford Metal Surface Cleaner F4AZ-19A536-RA or equivalent.

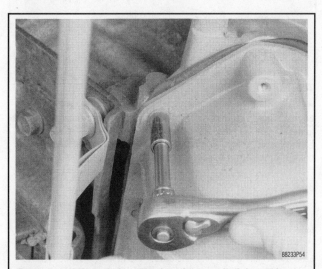

88233P54

Remove the oil pan bolts, then drop the pan off of the engine block

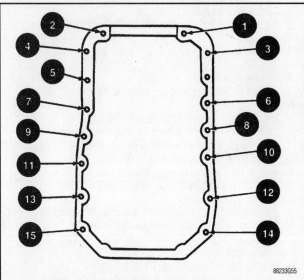

Fig. 115 Be sure to tighten the oil pan mounting bolts in the sequence shown to ensure proper sealing

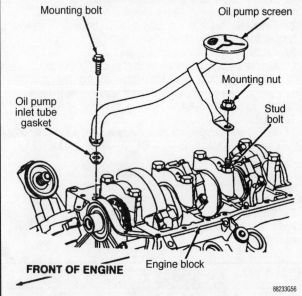

Fig. 116 Exploded view of the oil pump screen cover and tube mounting on the 3.8L engine

➡It is imperative to use the proper solvent when cleaning the engine block-to-oil pan surfaces, otherwise the new sealer may not adhere properly. Also, when using silicone sealer, assembly must be performed within 15 minutes of applying the sealer, otherwise the sealer will start to set-up and lose its sealing effectiveness.

26. Apply a bead of silicone sealer, such as Ford Silicone Gasket and Sealant F6AZ-19652-AA, to the oil pan.

27. Install the oil pan, then install all of the oil pan mounting bolts. Tighten the bolts, in the sequence shown in the accompanying illustration, to 80–106 inch lbs. (9–12 Nm).

28. Raise the front sub-frame into position, then install the lower shock absorber mounting bolts and nuts to 103–143 ft. lbs. (140–195 Nm).

29. Install the two front and six rear sub-frame bolts loosely.

30. Adjust the position of the front sub-frame assembly until the match-marks are correctly aligned. Then, tighten the large sub-frame bolts to

83–113 ft. lbs. (113–153 Nm) and the small bolts to 72–97 ft. lbs. (98–132 Nm).

➡It is important that the front sub-frame be realigned as when removed to ensure proper chassis geometry.

31. Connect the steering column shaft at the pinch bolt joint. Tighten the pinch bolt to 30–42 ft. lbs. (41–57 Nm).

32. Install the starter motor and the automatic transmission cooler lines, when applicable.

33. Install the engine oil drain plug and a new oil filter.

➡When seating the engine on the mounts, set it on the left-hand side mount first.

34. Slowly lower the engine until it is resting on the front engine mounts, then install the mount through-bolts. Tighten them to 35–50 ft. lbs. (47–68 Nm).

35. Lower the vehicle and remove the rear wheel blocks.

36. Remove the engine support tool.

37. Install the wiper module and left-hand cowl vent screen.

38. Install the windshield wiper arms and the hood weather seal.

39. Install the radiator upper plastic cover and the air inlet tube.

✳✳ WARNING

It is vitally important to fill the engine with oil prior to starting it, otherwise severe engine damage will occur.

40. Fill the engine with the proper type and amount of clean engine oil.

41. Connect the negative battery cable, then start the engine and check for oil leaks.

42. After 3–5 minutes, stop the engine and check the oil level; add more oil if necessary.

4.6L SOHC Engine

◆ See Figure 117, 118, 119 and 120 (p. 67–68)

➡If your vehicle is equipped with air conditioning, refer to Section 1 for information regarding the implications of servicing your A/C system yourself. Only a MVAC-trained, EPA-certified, automotive technician should service the A/C system or its components.

1. Have your A/C system discharged and evacuated and the A/C compressor outlet hose disconnected and sealed by a qualified automotive technician.

➡It is a good idea to place the vehicle's ignition keys in the box with the new oil containers so that you do not accidentally start the vehicle without first filling the engine with oil.

2. Disconnect the negative battery cable.

3. Remove the air inlet tube from the throttle body and air cleaner housing.

4. Drain the engine cooling system.

5. Remove the cooling fan assembly.

6. Relieve fuel system pressure, then detach the fuel lines from the engine.

7. Remove the upper radiator hose.

8. Remove the windshield wiper governor and support bracket.

9. Remove the A/C hose-to-right-hand ignition coil bracket retaining bolt.

10. Label and disengage the engine wiring harness 42-pin and 8-pin connectors.

11. Remove the EGR backpressure transducer, and disconnect the heater water hose.

12. Detach the heater water hose from the left-hand cylinder head, then position it aside.

13. Remove the heater blower switch resistor.

14. Remove the right-hand front engine mount-to-front sub-frame bolt.

15. Disconnect the vacuum hose from the EGR valve.

16. Detach the EGR backpressure transducer hoses from the EGR valve-to-exhaust manifold tube.

17. Remove the EGR valve from the throttle body.

18. Apply the parking brake and block the rear wheels, then raise and safely support the front of the vehicle on jackstands.

19. Drain the engine oil.

20. Remove both front engine mount through-bolts.

21. Remove the EGR valve-to-manifold tube nut from the left-hand exhaust manifold, then remove the tube.

22. Detach the exhaust system pipes from the exhaust manifolds. Suspend the exhaust pipes with strong cord or wire from the crossmember.

23. Position a floor jack and a block of wood beneath the oil pan, just rearward of the oil drain plug, then raise the engine approximately 4 in. (10cm). Insert two wood blocks (approximately 2.5–2.75 in./60–70mm thick) under each front engine mount. Carefully lower the engine onto the wood blocks and, once the engine is securely settled, remove the floor jack from beneath the oil pan.

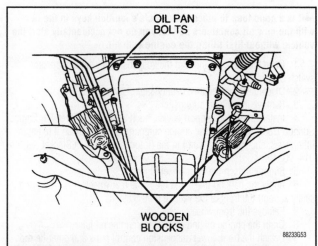

Fig. 117 Support the engine assembly with two wood blocks, positioned as shown, for adequate clearance to the oil pan mounting bolts

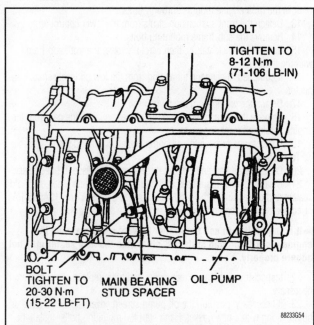

Fig. 118 When installing the oil pump screen cover and tube, tighten the fasteners to the values indicated

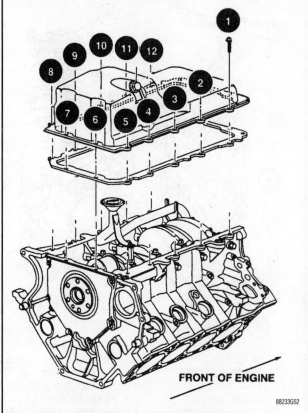

Fig. 119 Be sure to tighten the oil pan mounting bolts in the order shown for proper sealing

➥It may be necessary to loosen, not remove, the two transmission mount nuts.

24. Using a floor jack (a bottle jack may be necessary because of the lack of clearance), raise the transmission extension housing slightly.

25. Remove the oil pan mounting bolts, then lower the oil pan out of the vehicle.

26. If necessary, the oil pump screen cover and tube may be removed. Remove the old cover and tube gasket.

To install:

27. Clean the oil pan and inspect it for damage; replace it if necessary.

28. Clean the mating surfaces of the oil pan and engine block of all old sealant and oil residue with Ford Metal Surface Cleaner F4AZ-19A536-RA or equivalent.

➥It is imperative to use the proper solvent when cleaning the engine block-to-oil pan surfaces, otherwise the new sealer may not adhere properly.

29. Inspect the oil pump screen cover, tube and O-ring; replace any of them if necessary.

30. If necessary, position the oil pump screen cover and tube on the oil pump. Hand start the mounting bolts. Install the oil pump screen cover and tube-to-main bearing stud spacer retaining bolt hand-tight.

31. Tighten the oil pump screen cover and tube-to-oil pump bolts to 71–106 inch lbs. (8–12 Nm) and the oil pump screen cover and tube-to-main bearing stud spacer bolt to 15–22 ft. lbs. (20–30 Nm).

32. Install a new oil pan gasket on the oil pan.

➥When using silicone sealer, assembly must be performed within four minutes of applying the sealer, otherwise the sealer will start to set-up and lose its sealing effectiveness.

33. Apply a bead of silicone sealer, such as Ford Silicone Gasket and Sealant F6AZ-19652-AA, where the engine front cover, and the crankshaft rear oil seal retainer, meet the engine block.

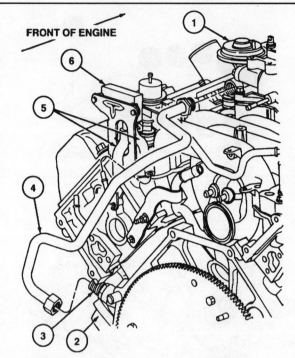

FRONT OF ENGINE

1. EGR valve
2. Left exhaust manifold
3. EGR valve tube-to-manifold connector
4. EGR valve-to-exhaust
5. EGR backpressure transducer hoses
6. EGR backpressure transduce

manifold tube

88233G51

Fig. 120 Exploded view of the EGR valve-to-exhaust manifold tube mounting on the 4.6L SOHC engine

34. Within four minutes of applying the silicone sealer, install the oil pan and retaining bolts. Tighten the bolts, in the sequence shown in the accompanying illustration, to 177 inch lbs. (20 Nm), then tighten all of the bolts an additional 60 degrees.

35. Position the floor jack under the oil pan and raise the engine to remove the wood blocks.

36. Lower the engine onto the front engine mounts, then remove the floor jack.

37. Install the front engine mounts' through-bolts and tighten them to 15–22 ft. lbs. (20–30 Nm).

➡**Prior to installation, loosen the nut at the EGR valve. This will allow adequate movement to align the EGR valve bolts.**

38. Install the EGR valve-to-exhaust manifold tube. Tighten the line nut to 26–33 ft. lbs. (35–45 Nm).

39. Attach the exhaust system pipes to the exhaust manifolds.

40. Install a new engine oil filter, and install the oil pan drain plug.

41. Lower the vehicle and remove the rear wheel blocks.

42. Install the right-hand front engine mount-to-front sub-frame retaining bolt and tighten it to 15–22 ft. lbs. (20–30 Nm).

43. Install the EGR valve along with a new gasket.

44. Install the heater blower motor switch resistor.

45. Install the EGR backpressure transducer bracket and heater water hose. Tighten the upper bolts t o 15–22 ft. lbs. (20–30 Nm) and the lower bolts to 71–106 inch lbs. (8–12 Nm).

46. Connect the heater water hose.

47. Engage the 42-pin and 8-pin engine wiring harness connectors.

48. Install the upper radiator hose.

49. Connect the fuel lines.

50. Install the windshield wiper governor and retaining bracket.

51. Install the engine cooling fan.

52. Install the air inlet tube.

✳✳ WARNING

It is vitally important to fill the engine with oil prior to starting it, otherwise severe engine damage will occur.

53. Fill the engine with the proper type and amount of clean engine oil.

54. Connect the negative battery cable, then start the engine and check for oil leaks.

55. After 3–5 minutes, stop the engine and check the oil level; add more oil if necessary.

56. Have the A/C compressor line reattached and the system evacuated and recharged by a qualified MVAC technician.

4.6L DOHC Engine

◆ See Figure 121

➡**It is a good idea to place the vehicle's ignition keys in the box with the new oil containers so that you do not accidentally start the vehicle without first filling the engine with oil.**

1. Open the trunk lid and turn the suspension leveler compressor switch OFF.

2. Disconnect the negative battery cable.

3. Remove the engine oil dipstick.

4. Install an engine support device, such as the Ford Three Bar Engine Support D88L-6000-A, in the engine compartment, and attach it to engine lifting eyes, such as those found in the Rotunda Engine Lift Bracket Set 014–00340.

5. Slightly loosen the front wheel lug nuts.

6. Apply the parking brake and block the rear wheels, then raise and safely support the front of the vehicle on jackstands.

7. Remove the front wheels.

8. Drain the engine oil and remove the engine oil filter.

9. Detach the front, lower suspension control arms and outer tie rod ends from the front wheel hubs and spindles.

10. Disconnect the steering column shaft at the pinch bolt connection.

11. Matchmark the relationship between the front sub-frame and the vehicle's chassis for reinstallation purposes.

12. Support the front sub-frame with a floor jack and jack stands, then remove the front engine mounts' through-bolts.

13. Detach the front suspension struts from the lower control arms.

14. Remove the sub-frame mounting bolts.

15. Remove the jack stands, then carefully lower the front sub-frame with the floor jack.

16. If equipped, disengage the wiring from the low oil level sensor connector.

17. Detach the wiring from the oil pan rail.

18. Remove the oil pan mounting bolts, then separate the pan from the engine block and front engine cover.

19. If necessary, remove the oil pump screen cover and tube.

To install:

20. Clean the oil pan and inspect it for damage; replace it if necessary.

21. Clean the mating surfaces of the oil pan and engine block of all old sealant and oil residue with Ford Metal Surface Cleaner F4AZ-19A536-RA or equivalent. If scraping is required, only use a plastic tool.

➡**It is imperative to use the proper solvent when cleaning the engine block-to-oil pan surfaces, otherwise the new sealer may not adhere properly.**

22. Inspect the oil pump screen cover and tube; replace either of them if necessary.

23. If necessary, position the oil pump screen cover and tube on the oil pump, along with a new gasket. Hand start the mounting bolts. Install the oil pump screen cover and tube-to-main bearing stud spacer retaining bolt hand-tight.

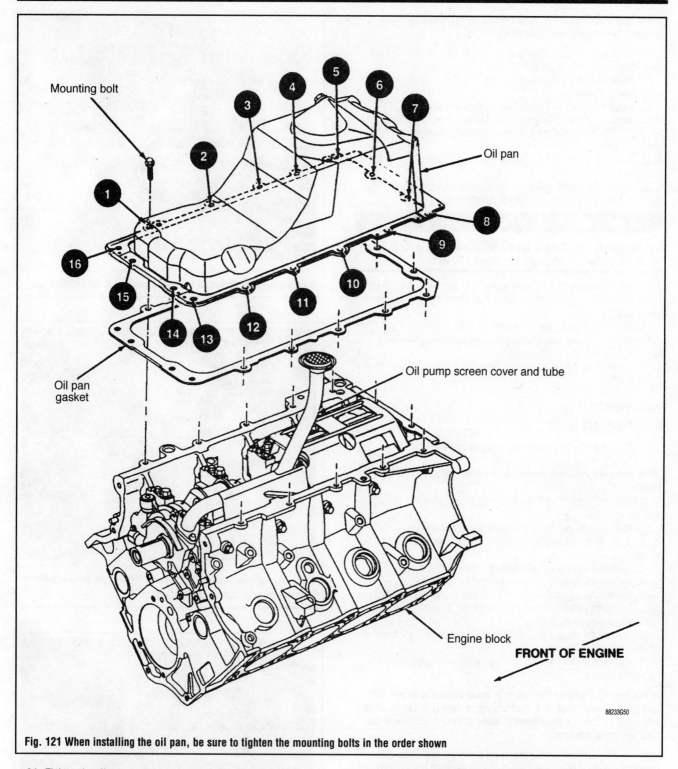

Mounting bolt

Oil pan

Oil pan gasket

Oil pump screen cover and tube

Engine block

FRONT OF ENGINE

88233G50

Fig. 121 When installing the oil pan, be sure to tighten the mounting bolts in the order shown

24. Tighten the oil pump screen cover and tube-to-oil pump bolts to 71–106 inch lbs. (8–12 Nm) and the oil pump screen cover and tube-to-main bearing stud spacer bolt to 15–22 ft. lbs. (20–30 Nm).

25. Install a new oil pan gasket on the oil pan.

→When using silicone sealer, assembly must be performed within four minutes of applying the sealer, otherwise the sealer will start to set-up and lose its sealing effectiveness.

26. Apply a bead of silicone sealer, such as Ford Silicone Gasket and Sealant F6AZ-19652-AA, where the engine front cover, and the crankshaft rear oil seal retainer, meet the engine block.

27. Within four minutes of applying the silicone sealer, install the oil pan and retaining bolts. Tighten the bolts, in the sequence shown in the accompanying illustration, to 15–22 ft. lbs. (20–30 Nm).

28. If equipped, attach the wiring to the low oil level sensor connector, and attach the wiring harness to the oil pan rail.

29. Raise the sub-frame into position, install the front engine mount through-bolts, then install the front sub-frame mounting bolts.

30. Adjust the position of the front sub-frame assembly until the match-marks are correctly aligned. Then, tighten the large sub-frame bolts to 83–113 ft. lbs. (113–153 Nm) and the small bolts to 72–97 ft. lbs. (98–132 Nm).

➡️It is important that the front sub-frame be realigned as when removed to ensure proper chassis geometry.

31. Connect the steering column shaft at the pinch bolt joint. Tighten the pinch bolt to 30–42 ft. lbs. (41–57 Nm).

32. Reconnect the lower control arms and outer tie rod ends to the front wheel hubs and spindles.

33. Install the wheels and tighten the lug nuts until snug.

34. Install the oil pan drain plug to 97–142 inch lbs. (11–16 Nm) and a new engine oil filter hand-tight (follow the oil filter manufacturer's instructions).

35. Lower the vehicle and remove the rear wheel blocks. Fully tighten the lug nuts.

36. Remove the engine support device from the engine and engine compartment. Remove the lifting eye brackets from the engine.

✳✳ WARNING

It is extremely important to fill the engine with oil prior to starting it, otherwise severe engine damage will occur.

37. Fill the engine with the proper amount and type of clean engine oil.

38. Connect the negative battery cable, then start the engine and check for oil leaks.

39. After 3–5 minutes, stop the engine.

40. Wait 10 minutes, then check the oil level with the dipstick. Add more oil, if necessary.

41. Turn the rear suspension leveler compressor switch ON, then shut the trunk lid.

5.0L Engine

▶ **See Figure 122 (p. 73)**

1. Disconnect the negative battery cable for safety.
2. Remove the air cleaner tube.
3. Remove the oil level indicator from the left side of the cylinder block.
4. Remove the fan shroud retaining bolts, then position the shroud over the fan.
5. Raise and support the vehicle safely using jackstands.
6. Drain the crankcase and remove the oil level sensor wiring from the oil pan.
7. Remove the starter motor assembly.
8. Remove the catalytic converter and muffler inlet pipes.
9. Remove the engine mount-to-No. 2 crossmember attaching bolts or nuts. Support the transmission and remove the No. 3 crossmember and rear insulator support assemblies.
10. Remove the steering gear attaching bolts and position the steering gear forward, out of the way.
11. Raise and support the engine to a position which allows clearance for oil pan removal.

➡️The best way to raise the engine is using an engine support fixture or an engine hoist. But, if necessary, a floor jack can be used under the oil pan if a large block of wood is used to distribute the load and protect the pan.

12. With the engine raised, install wood blocks between the engine mounts and frame. Then, lower the engine onto the wood blocks. If you are using an engine hoist or support fixture, leave it in place for additional safety.
13. Remove the oil pan attaching bolts and lower the pan to the No. 2 crossmember.
14. Loosen the retaining bolts, then lower the oil pump and pick-up tube assembly into the pan.
15. Remove the pan, along with the oil pump assembly, from the vehicle.

To install:
16. Clean the oil pan and the gasket mating surfaces.

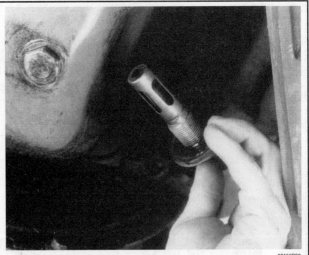

88153P98

If necessary, the threaded oil level indicator is easily removed

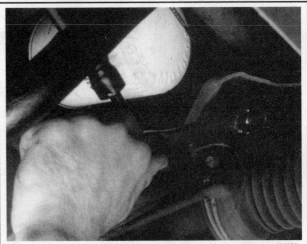

88153P65

For 5.0L engines, loosen and remove the engine mount-to-No. 2 crossmember attaching bolts or nuts . . .

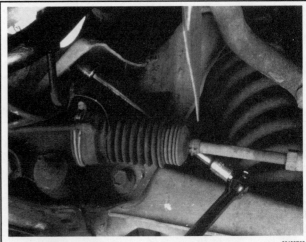

88153P66

. . . the tool you use (wrench, socket, extensions, etc.) depends on the available access

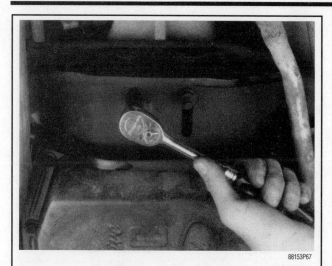

Support the transmission then remove the No. 3 insulator and rear support assemblies

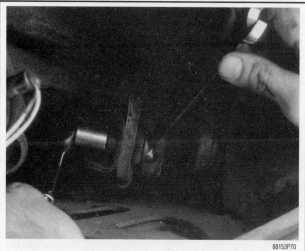

Because you are moving the steering gear, you will likely have to unbolt the input shaft from it

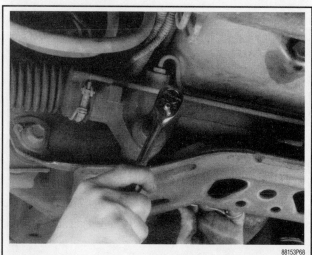

Using a backup wrench behind the crossmember, loosen the steering gear retaining bolts

Again the tools you use will depend on the access you have to the fasteners

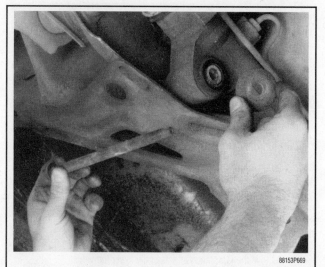

Remove the steering gear retaining through-bolts and washers

Once it is unbolted, reposition the steering gear out of the way

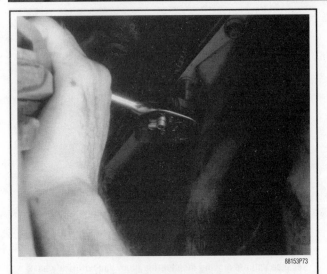

Loosen and remove the oil pan retaining bolts . . .

. . . and in this case, lower the pan reinforcements

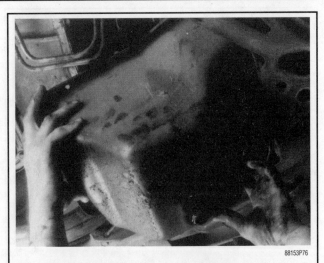

Carefully angle the pan (with the pump in it) over the cross-member and from the vehicle

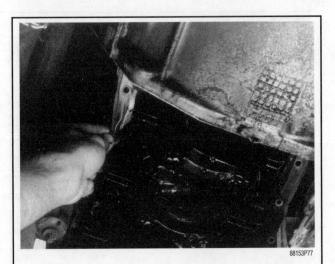

Once the oil pan is removed, check to see if the old gasket is still in place

17. Refer to the instructions included with the new oil pan gasket to determine if sealer is necessary for that type of gasket. Position the new gasket on the pan or block, as applicable.

18. With the oil pump and pick-up tube assembly positioned in the oil pan, raise the pan onto the crossmember. Install the oil pump assembly.

19. With the pump properly secured, raise the oil pan into position and install the retaining bolts. Tighten the oil pan bolts to 71–106 inch lbs. (8–12 Nm) for 1989–92 vehicles or to 80–120 inch lbs. (9–14 Nm) for ¼ in. pan bolts and 12–18 ft. lbs. (16–24 Nm) for ⅝ in. pan bolts on 1993 vehicles.

20. Carefully raise the engine and remove the wood blocks, then lower the engine and remove the lifting device.

21. Install the engine mount-to-No. 2 crossmember attaching nuts or bolts. Tighten the retainers to 80–106 ft. lbs. (108–144 Nm).

22. Position the steering gear and install the retaining bolts.

23. Install the starter motor assembly.

24. Connect the oil level sensor wire to the oil pan.

25. Install the rear insulator and the No. 3 crossmember. Tighten the retainers to 80–106 ft. lbs. (108–144 Nm).

26. Install the catalytic converter and muffler inlet pipes.

27. Remove the jackstands and carefully lower the vehicle.

28. IMMEDIATELY refill the engine crankcase to prevent an accidental attempt to start the engine without oil in it. Install the oil level indicator.

Lower the pan for access, then unbolt the oil pump and pick-up tube assembly (lay it in pan)

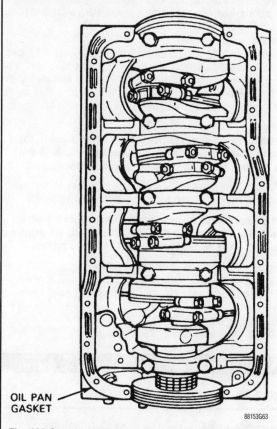

OIL PAN GASKET

88153G63

Fig. 122 On many of the engines covered by this manual, the gasket attaches to the block

29. Install the fan shroud.
30. Install the air cleaner tube.
31. Connect the negative battery cable, then start the engine and allow it to run for a few minutes. If there is no indication of oil pressure after the engine runs for a few seconds, shut it **OFF** and investigate the problem.
32. Check for leaks.

Oil Pump

REMOVAL & INSTALLATION

3.8L Engine

1. If necessary, remove the engine oil filter.
2. Remove the oil pump and filter body-to-engine front cover retaining bolts, then separate the oil pump from the front cover.
3. Inspect the oil pump sealing O-ring for damage or distortion.

To install:

4. Position the oil pump on the engine front cover, then install the mounting bolts.
5. Tighten the four large bolts to 17–23 ft. lbs. (23–32 Nm) and the two small bolts to 71–97 inch lbs. (8–11 Nm).
6. If necessary, install a new engine oil filter. Make sure to coat the new oil filter's gasket with a film of clean engine oil. Tighten the oil filter according to the manufacturer's instructions.

4.6L Engines

> **See Figure 123**

1. For the SOHC engine, remove the valve covers.
2. Remove the engine front cover.
3. Remove the oil pan, and oil pump screen cover and pick-up tube.

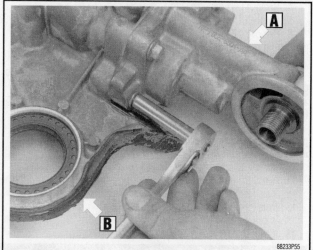

A

B

88233P55

The oil pump (A) mounts to the front engine cover (B), which is shown removed from the engine for clarity

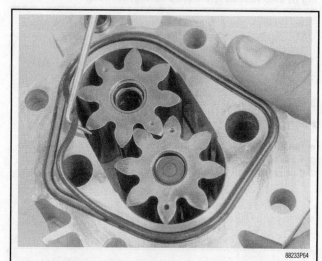

88233P64

Inspect the oil pump O-ring for damage, such as cuts, nicks, or distortion—replace it if necessary

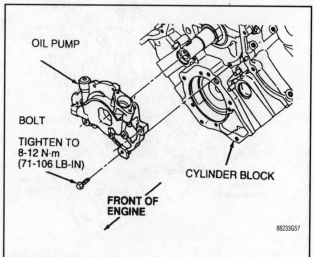

OIL PUMP

BOLT

TIGHTEN TO
8-12 N·m
(71-106 LB-IN)

CYLINDER BLOCK

FRONT OF ENGINE

88233G57

Fig. 123 Exploded view of the oil pump mounting on the 4.6L SOHC and DOHC engines

4. Remove the timing chain(s).

5. For the DOHC engine, remove the crankshaft sprockets.

6. Remove the four oil pump mounting bolts, then separate the oil pump from the engine block.

To install:

7. Rotate the inner rotor of the oil pump to align it with the flats on the crankshaft, then install the oil pump on the engine block.

8. Install the four mounting bolts and tighten them to 71–106 inch lbs. (8–12 Nm).

9. Install a new engine oil filter. Make sure to coat the new oil filter's gasket with a film of clean engine oil. Tighten the oil filter according to the manufacturer's instructions.

10. If applicable, install the crankshaft sprockets.

11. Install the timing chain.

12. Install the oil pump screen cover and pick-up tube.

13. Install the oil pan.

14. Install the engine front cover.

15. If applicable, install the valve covers.

❊❊ WARNING

It is extremely important to fill the engine with oil prior to starting it, otherwise severe engine damage will occur.

16. Fill the engine with the proper amount and type of clean engine oil.

17. Start the engine and check for oil leaks.

18. After 3–5 minutes, stop the engine.

19. Wait 10 minutes, then check the oil level with the dipstick. Add more oil, if necessary.

5.0L Engine

▶ See Figure 124

➡The oil pump and pick-up tube assembly must be unbolted and positioned in the oil pan, in order to remove the pan while the engine is installed in the vehicle.

1. Disconnect the negative battery cable for safety.

2. Remove the oil pan, along with the oil pump and pick-up tube assembly on all but early model 2.3L engines.

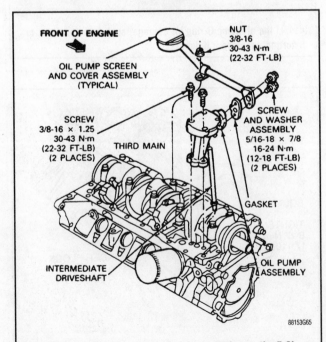

FRONT OF ENGINE

NUT
3/8-16
30-43 N·m
(22-32 FT-LB)

OIL PUMP SCREEN
AND COVER ASSEMBLY
(TYPICAL)

SCREW
3/8-16 × 1.25
30-43 N·m
(22-32 FT-LB)
(2 PLACES)

THIRD MAIN

SCREW
AND WASHER
ASSEMBLY
5/16-18 × 7/8
16-24 N·m
(12-18 FT-LB)
(2 PLACES)

GASKET

INTERMEDIATE
DRIVESHAFT

OIL PUMP
ASSEMBLY

88153G65

Fig. 124 Exploded view of the oil pump mounting on the 5.0L engine

3. If not done for pan removal, loosen the retainers, then remove the oil pump pick-up (inlet) tube and screen assembly, along with the oil pump assembly.

To install:

4. Prime the oil pump by filling either the inlet or outlet ports with engine oil and rotating the pump shaft to distribute the oil within the pump body.

5. Position the intermediate driveshaft into the distributor socket. With the shaft firmly seated in the distributor socket, the stop on the shaft should touch the roof of the crankcase. Remove the shaft and position the stop, as necessary.

➡**Remember, that on most vehicles covered by this manual, you will have to position the oil pan over the crossmember (with the pump in the pan), then raise the pump into position and install.**

6. Position a new gasket on the pump body, insert the intermediate shaft into the oil pump and install the pump and shaft as an assembly.

➡**Do not attempt to force the pump or shaft into position if it will not seat readily. The driveshaft hex may be misaligned with the distributor shaft. To align, rotate the intermediate shaft into a new position.**

7. Tighten the oil pump attaching screws to 14–21 ft. lbs. (19–29 Nm) on the 2.3L engine and 22–32 ft. lbs. (30–43 Nm) on the 5.0L engine.

8. If separated, clean and install the oil pump inlet tube and screen assembly.

9. Install the oil pan.

10. Connect the negative battery cable.

Crankshaft Damper and Front Oil Seal

REMOVAL & INSTALLATION

This procedure provides oil seal replacement for the event that the engine front cover is not going to be removed from the engine. If the front engine cover is going to be removed, use the seal replacement steps in the engine front cover removal procedure.

➡**As long as the original vibration damper is going to be reinstalled, the damper can be removed without replacing the front oil seal. However, if the damper is removed, it is good preventative maintenance to replace the oil seal (this helps avoid having to replace the oil seal at a later, less advantageous time).**

3.8L Engine

▶ See Figure 125

1. Remove the engine electric cooling fan.

2. Remove the accessory drive belt.

3. Apply the parking brake and block the rear wheels, then raise and safely support the front of the vehicle on jackstands.

4. Matchmark the crankshaft pulley to the vibration damper for reassembly.

➡**If the vibration damper is being replaced with a new one, check the original damper to ascertain whether balance pins are installed. If so, new balance pins must be installed on the new damper in the same positions as the original damper.**

5. Remove the crankshaft pulley-to-vibration damper attaching bolts, then separate the pulley from the damper.

6. Using crankshaft damper puller tools, such as the Ford Crankshaft Damper Remover T58P-6316-D and the Vibration Damper Remover Adapter T82L-6316-B, remove the vibration damper from the end of the crankshaft.

❊❊ WARNING

When removing the front oil seal, take care not to damage the oil seal bore in the front cover or the crankshaft end, otherwise future oil leakage may occur.

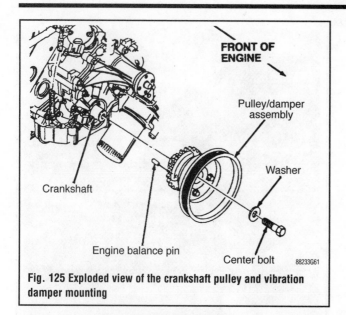

Fig. 125 Exploded view of the crankshaft pulley and vibration damper mounting

Separate the pulley from the damper . . .

To remove the damper on 3.8L engines, matchmark the pulley to the vibration damper . . .

. . . then loosen the center damper mounting bolt

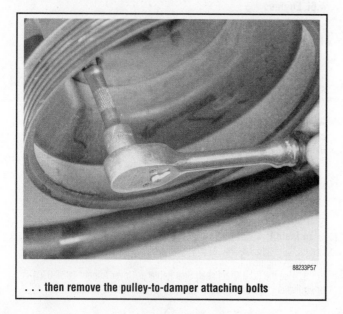

. . . then remove the pulley-to-damper attaching bolts

Withdraw the center mounting bolt and washer from the vibration damper

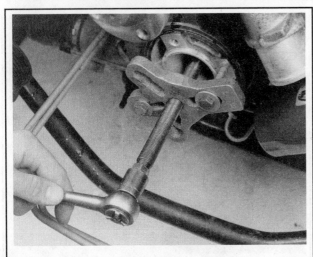

Using a damper puller, slowly draw the vibration
damper off of the end of the crankshaft . . .

88233P61

. . . then remove the damper and puller tool together from the
engine

88233P62

Carefully use a punch and hammer to remove the old oil seal
from the engine front cover

88233P63

7. If necessary, remove the crankshaft front oil seal from its bore with a
hammer and punch. Gently tap on one side (pick either the left, right, top or
bottom side) of the oil seal until it pivots in the engine front cover bore,
then pull it out of the cover with a pair of pliers. DO NOT tap the seal on
opposing sides (do not tap on both the right and left sides, or the top and
bottom sides, for example), because this will simply drive the seal further
into the front cover.

To install:

8. Inspect the engine front cover, crankshaft pulley and vibration
damper for damage, such as: nicks, burrs, roughness which may cause oil
leakage. Service or replace the components if damage is evident.

9. Lubricate the oil seal lip with clean engine oil, then install the oil
seal in the front engine cover using driver tools, such as Ford
Damper/Front Cover Seal Replacer T82L-6316-A and Front Cover Seal
Replacer T70P-6B070-A.

10. Lubricate the crankshaft front seal surface on the crankshaft vibration damper with clean engine oil. Install the damper using Ford
Damper/Front Cover Seal Replacer T82L-6316-A or equivalent. Often, a soft
block of wood and a mallet can be used to gently drive the damper onto the
crankshaft until the center damper bolt can be installed. Ensure that the
damper, if installed in this fashion, is not driven too far onto the crankshaft.

Use the center damper bolt to draw the damper into position as it is tightened to its torque specification, which is 103–132 ft. lbs. (140–180 Nm).

11. Position the pulley against the vibration damper so that the matchmarks align, then install the pulley-to-damper attaching bolts.

12. Lower the vehicle and remove the rear wheel blocks.

13. Install the engine electric cooling fan.

14. Start the engine and inspect it for oil leaks.

4.6L Engines

♦ **See Figures 126, 127, 128 and 129**

1. Disconnect the negative battery cable for safety.

2. Remove the accessory drive belt.

3. Apply the parking brake and block the rear wheels, then raise and
safely support the front of the vehicle on jackstands.

4. Remove the crankshaft pulley center bolt and washer.

➡**Often, the crankshaft pulley/damper assembly slides off of the
crankshaft without any problem, however it may be necessary to
use a pulley/damper puller tool.**

5. Install a pulley/damper removal tool, such as Ford Crankshaft
Damper Remover T58P-6316-D, on the crankshaft pulley, then draw the
pulley off of the crankshaft.

6. Using a seal removal tool, such as Ford Front Cover Seal Remover
T74P-6700-A, remove the crankshaft oil seal.

To install:

7. Lubricate the seal bore in the front engine cover and the oil seal lip
with clean engine oil.

8. Use the Ford Crankshaft Seal Replacer/Cover Aligner T88T-6701-A
or equivalent, to install the front crankshaft oil seal.

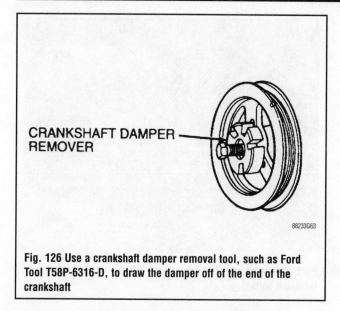

Fig. 126 Use a crankshaft damper removal tool, such as Ford Tool T58P-6316-D, to draw the damper off of the end of the crankshaft

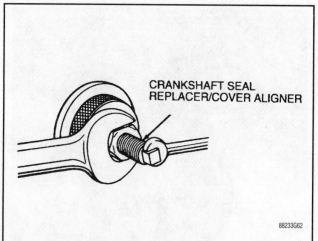

Fig. 127 Use the appropriate tool, for example Ford Tool T88T-6701-A, to properly press the front oil seal into position in the engine front cover

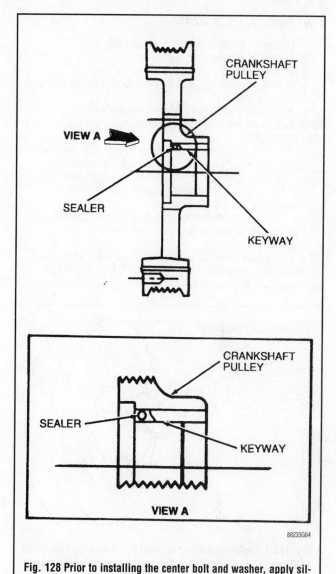

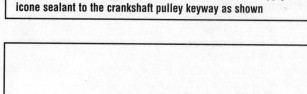

Fig. 128 Prior to installing the center bolt and washer, apply silicone sealant to the crankshaft pulley keyway as shown

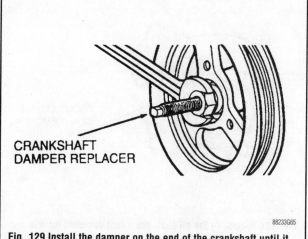

Fig. 129 Install the damper on the end of the crankshaft until it is seated properly in the engine front cover

9. Install the crankshaft pulley/damper assembly. If the pulley/damper does not simply slide onto the end of the crankshaft (as is often the case), install the crankshaft using the proper tool (such as Ford Crankshaft Damper Replacer T74P-6316-B).

10. Clean the sealing surfaces of the crankshaft pulley keyway of all oil residue with Ford Metal Surface Cleaner F4AZ-19A536-RA or equivalent.

➡ It is imperative to use the proper solvent when cleaning the keyway surfaces, otherwise the new sealer may not adhere properly.

11. Apply silicone sealer, such as Ford Silicone Gasket and Sealant F6AZ-19562-A, to the end of the crankshaft pulley keyway as shown in the accompanying illustration.

➡ Be sure that the keyway in the pulley/damper assembly is aligned with the keyway in the crankshaft.

12. Install the crankshaft pulley center bolt and washer, and tighten the center bolt to 114–121 ft. lbs. (155–165 Nm) no more than four minutes after applying the silicone sealer.

13. Lower the vehicle and remove the rear wheel blocks.

14. Install the accessory drive belt.

15. Connect the negative battery cable.

16. Start the engine and check for oil leaks.

5.0L Engine

♦ **See Figures 130, 131 and 132**

1. Disconnect the negative battery cable for safety.
2. Remove the engine electric cooling fan.
3. Remove the accessory drive belt.
4. Remove the crankshaft pulley from the vibration damper by removing the attaching bolts.
5. Remove the damper center mounting bolt and washer.
6. Install a damper puller tool on the vibration damper and draw it off of the crankshaft.
7. If the front oil seal needs to be replaced, perform the following:
   a. Position a seal removal tool, such as Ford Front Cover Seal Remover T70P-6B070-B, on the front cover, over the front oil seal.
   b. Tighten the two through-bolts until the puller is positioned between the oil seal and the front cover.
   c. Alternately tighten the four puller bolts one-half turn at a time to slowly draw the oil seal out of front engine cover.

To install:

8. Coat the new crankshaft front seal with Lubriplate®, or equivalent, and place it in the Ford Front Cover Seal Replacer T70P-6B070-A, or equivalent. Place the sleeve and front oil seal on the end of the crankshaft,

For 5.0L engines, loosen and remove the crankshaft pulley retaining bolts . . .

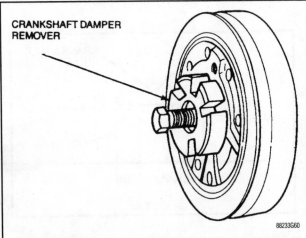

Fig. 130 A crankshaft damper removal tool draws the damper off of the end of the crankshaft without damaging the rubber layer of the damper

. . . then separate the pulley from the damper

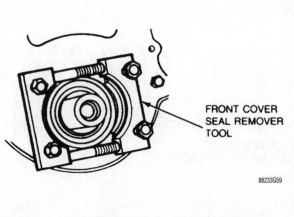

Fig. 131 To remove the oil seal, use a tool designed for this purpose, such as Ford Tool T70P-6B070-B, to prevent damaging the engine front cover or crankshaft oil seal surfaces

Loosen the crankshaft damper retaining bolt (a holding tool for the flywheel can be helpful here)

Once loosened, unthread and remove the bolt and washer from the damper

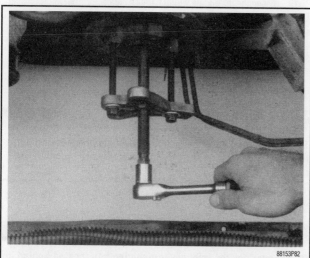

Install a suitable threaded puller (NOT a jawed puller) to the crankshaft damper . . .

. . . then thread the puller until the damper is free of the crankshaft

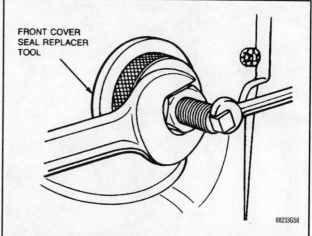

FRONT COVER SEAL REPLACER TOOL

Fig. 132 The use of a tool designed expressly for the purpose of installing the new front oil seal, will help avoid incorrect seal installation or damage

then push the front oil seal toward the engine until the oil seal starts into the engine front cover.

9. Place the installation screw, washer and nut on the end of the crankshaft. Thread the screw into the crankshaft, then tighten the nut against the washer and installation sleeve to press the front oil seal into the engine front cover.

10. Remove the installation tool from the crankshaft.

11. Apply Lubriplate®, or equivalent, to the crankshaft front oil seal rubbing surface of the vibration damper inner hub to prevent damage to the front oil seal. Apply silicone sealer, such as Ford Silicone Gasket and Sealant F1AZ-19562-A, to the keyway groove in damper prior to installing it on the crankshaft.

12. Align the crankshaft damper keyway with the crankshaft key on the crankshaft, then slide the damper on the crankshaft. Install mounting bolt and washer to 110–130 ft. lbs. (149–176 Nm).

13. Install the crankshaft pulley.

14. Install the accessory drive belt.

15. Install the engine electric cooling fan.

16. Connect the negative battery cable.

Timing Chain Cover and Seal

REMOVAL & INSTALLATION

All engines covered by this manual use timing chains and, because the timing chain is run wet (as opposed to belts which are run dry), the front crankshaft seal is found in the outer timing cover.

3.8L Engine

♦ See Figure 133 (p. 83)

1. Drain the engine cooling system.
2. Disconenct the negative battery cable.
3. Remove the air cleaner housing and air inlet tube.
4. Remove the engine electric cooling fan.
5. Remove the accessory drive belt and water pump pulley.
6. Remove the power steering pump bracket attaching bolts, then, leaving the power steering hoses attached, position the pump aside. Be sure to position the pump so that the power steering fluid will not drain out.
7. If applicable, remove the A/C compressor front brace, but leave the A/C compressor in place.
8. Remove the heater water outlet tube and O-ring from the water pump.
9. Detach the upper radiator hose from the water hose connection.

To remove the front cover on 3.8L engines, detach the radiator hoses . . .

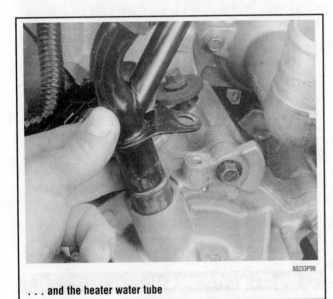

. . . and the heater water tube

Position the power steering pump and bracket aside

Then remove the ignition coil and bracket, and set it aside

10. Disengage the engine wiring harness connector from the Camshaft Position (CMP) sensor.

11. Remove the CMP sensor from the engine.

12. Apply the parking brake and block the rear wheels, then raise and safely support the front of the vehicle on jackstands.

13. Remove the crankshaft pulley and vibration damper.

14. Remove the engine oil filter.

15. Detach the lower radiator hose from the water pump.

❋❋ WARNING

The engine front cover cannot be removed without the oil pan first being lowered, otherwise possible damage to the engine may occur.

16. Remove the oil pan.

17. Lower the vehicle.

❋❋ WARNING

Do not overlook the front cover mounting bolt located behind the oil pump and filter body. The front cover will break if it is pried upon and all of the mounting bolts are not removed.

Remove the valve cover hold-down fasteners . . .

. . . then remove the valve covers from the engine

Thoroughly clean the gasket mating surfaces of all old gasket material, dirt and oil residue

18. Remove the front cover mounting bolts.
19. Remove the front cover and water pump together.
20. Remove and discard the front cover gasket and the front crankshaft oil seal.
21. If replacing the cover with a new one, remove the crankshaft position sensor, the oil pump and the water pump.

To install:

➡ **Lightly oil all bolt and stud threads prior to assembly, except those specifying sealant, with clean engine oil.**

22. Clean all of the gasket mating surfaces on the engine block, the front engine cover and other components, as necessary.
23. Install a new crankshaft oil seal in the front cover until it is flush and fully seated in its bore. You can use a tool specifically designed for this, or, if you are very careful, you can use a flat block of wood and a hammer to gently tap the seal in place; it is only important to ensure that the seal is installed flat and sits fully in its bore.
24. If a new engine front cover is being installed, be sure to transfer the oil pump and filter body, then crankshaft position sensor and the water pump to the new cover.
25. Lubricate the front crankshaft oil seal with clean engine oil.
26. Apply gasket and trim adhesive, such as Ford F3AZ-19B508-B, to

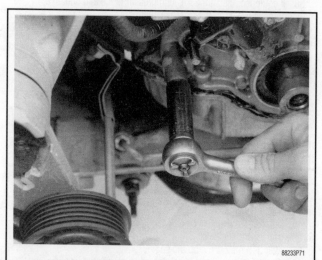

Lower the oil pan, then remove the engine front cover-to-engine block mounting bolts . . .

. . . and separate the front cover from the engine block

If necessary, install the cover components on the new cover, such as the CKP sensor—remove the nuts . . .

. . . then lift the CKP sensor cover up and off of the sensor

Remove the CKP sensor mounting nuts . . .

. . . and separate the sensor from the engine front cover—transfer all such components to the other cover

the engine front cover gasket, then position the gasket on the engine block. The adhesive should hold the gasket on the engine block for assembly.

27. Apply the gasket and trim adhesive to the engine front cover gasket surface, then install the cover on the engine block. Using dowels for alignment can help position the gasket and cover on the engine block for easier installation and less hassle.

28. Install the cover mounting bolts and tighten them, in the sequence shown in the accompanying illustration, to 15–22 ft. lbs. (20–30 Nm).

29. Raise and safely support the front of the vehicle on jackstands.

30. Install the oil pan.

31. Install the lower radiator hose.

32. Install a new engine oil filter. Be sure to coat the new filter gasket with a film of clean engine oil. Tighten the filter according to the manufacturer's instructions.

33. Install the crankshaft pulley and vibration damper.

34. Lower the vehicle and remove the blocks from the rear wheels.

35. Inspect the heater water hose O-ring for damage; replace it with a new one, if necessary. Install the heater water hose, along with the O-ring, in the water pump. Tighten the mounting fasteners to 71–106 inch lbs. (8–12 Nm).

36. Install the CMP sensor.

37. Connect the upper radiator hose to the water connection.

38. If equipped, install the A/C compressor brace and tighten the mounting bolts to 30–45 ft. lbs. (41–61 Nm).

39. Install the power steering pump and bracket, then tighten the mounting fasteners to 30–45 ft. lbs. (41–61 Nm).

40. Install the water pump pulley and tighten the mounting bolts until snug, then install the accessory drive belt. Now, tighten the water pump pulley bolts to 16–21 ft. lbs. (21–29 Nm).

41. Install the electric cooling fan.

✳✳ WARNING

It is extremely important to fill the engine with oil prior to starting it, otherwise severe engine damage will occur.

42. Fill the engine with the proper amount and type of clean engine oil.

43. Fill the cooling system.

44. Install the air cleaner housing and air inlet tube.

45. Connect the negative battery cable, then start the engine and check for oil, coolant and fuel leaks.

46. After 3–5 minutes, stop the engine.

47. Wait 10 minutes, then check the oil level with the dipstick. Add more oil, if necessary.

4.6L SOHC Engine

▶ See Figure 134 (p. 84)

1. Disconnect the negative battery cable.

2. Drain the cooling system.

3. Remove the engine electric cooling fan.

4. Loosen the water pump pulley mounting bolts.

5. Remove the accessory drive belt.

6. Remove the water pump pulley.

7. Apply the parking brake and block the rear wheels, then raise and safely support the front of the vehicle on jackstands.

8. Remove the power steering pump-to-engine block and front cover retaining bolts.

➡The front lower bolt on the power steering pump will not come all the way out.

9. Position the power steering pump out of the way.

10. Remove the oil pan and gasket.

11. Remove the crankshaft pulley and damper.

12. Lower the vehicle.

13. Remove the power steering fluid reservoir from the left-hand coil bracket and position it out of the way.

14. Remove both valve covers.

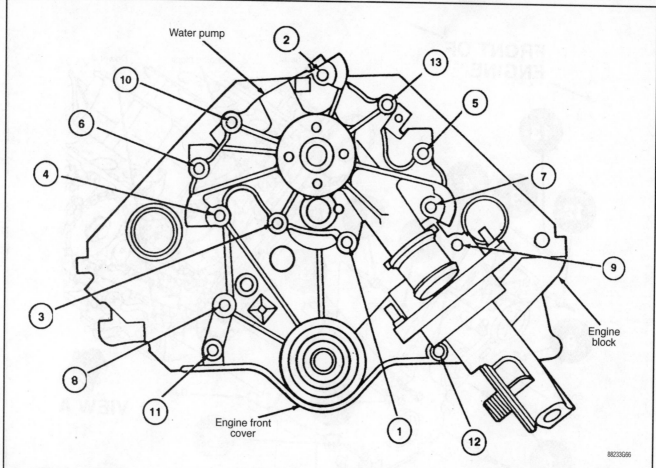

Fig. 133 When installing the engine front cover, be sure to tighten the mounting bolts in the sequence shown to ensure proper cover sealing

15. Disengage the engine wiring harness connectors from the ignition coils and the Camshaft Position (CMP) sensor.

16. Remove the right- and left-hand ignition coils and their brackets. Lay them on the engine with the spark plug wires still attached.

17. Remove the idler pulley.

18. Disengage the engine wiring harness connectors from the Crankshaft Position (CKP) sensor.

19. Remove the seven stud bolts and the four bolts retaining the engine front cover to the engine block.

20. Separate the cover from the engine.

To install:

➡**Lightly oil all bolt and stud threads prior to assembly, except those specifying sealant, with clean engine oil.**

21. Clean all of the gasket mating surfaces on the engine block, the front engine cover and other components, as necessary. Clean the surfaces with Ford Metal Surface Cleaner F4AZ-19A536-RA or equivalent.

➡**It is imperative to use the proper solvent when cleaning the keyway surfaces, otherwise the new sealer may not adhere properly.**

22. Install a new crankshaft oil seal in the front cover until it is flush and fully seated in its bore. You can use a tool specifically designed for this, or, if you are very careful, you can use a flat block of wood and a hammer to gently tap the seal in place; it is only important to ensure that the seal is installed flat and sits fully in its bore.

23. Install new engine front cover gaskets (there are three).

24. Apply an 0.32–0.47 in. (8–12mm) diameter bead of silicone sealant, such as Ford Silicone Gasket and Sealant F6AZ-19562-A, in the locations shown in the accompanying illustration.

25. Install the engine front cover on the engine block no more than four minutes after applying the sealant.

26. Install all of the engine cover fasteners, in the positions shown in the accompanying illustration, in no more than four minutes after applying the silicone sealant. Tighten the fasteners to 15–22 ft. lbs. (20–30 Nm).

27. Engage the engine wiring harness to the CKP sensor.

28. Install both ignition coils and their brackets.

29. Install the power steering reservoir.

30. Engage the engine wiring harness to the ignition coils (if not already done) and the CMP sensor.

31. Install the valve covers.

32. Raise and safely support the front of the vehicle on jackstands.

33. Install the crankshaft pulley and vibration damper.

34. Install the oil pan, along with a new gasket.

35. Install the power steering pump. Tighten the fasteners 15–22 ft. lbs. (20–30 Nm).

36. Lower the engine and remove the rear wheel blocks.

37. Install the water pump pulley and tighten the mounting bolts until snug.

38. Install the accessory drive belt, then tighten the water pump pulley mounting bolts 15–22 ft. lbs. (20–30 Nm).

39. Install the engine electric cooling fan.

✳✳ **WARNING**

It is extremely important to fill the engine with oil prior to starting it, otherwise severe engine damage will occur.

40. Fill the engine with the proper amount and type of clean engine oil.

41. Fill the cooling system.

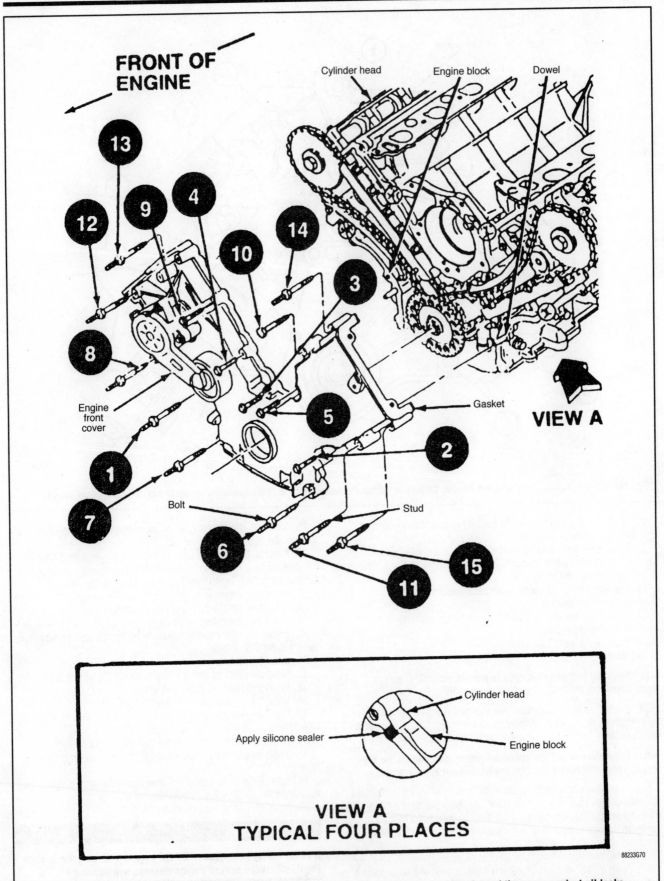

FRONT OF ENGINE

Cylinder head

Engine block

Dowel

Engine front cover

Gasket

VIEW A

Bolt

Stud

Cylinder head

Apply silicone sealer

Engine block

**VIEW A
TYPICAL FOUR PLACES**

88233G70

Fig. 134 It is important to tighten the engine front cover mounting bolts in the order shown to properly seal the cover against oil leaks

42. Connect the negative battery cable, then start the engine and check for oil, coolant and fuel leaks.

43. After 3–5 minutes, stop the engine.

44. Wait 10 minutes, then check the oil level with the dipstick. Add more oil, if necessary.

4.6L DOHC Engine

▶ See Figures 135, 136, 137 and 138

1. Disconnect the negative battery cable.
2. Remove the windshield wiper module assembly.
3. Remove the air inlet tube from the throttle body and the air cleaner housing.

4. Drain the cooling system, then remove the bypass tube-to-thermostat housing hose and the upper radiator hose from the bypass tube.

5. Remove the engine electric cooling fan.

6. Remove the engine wiring harness bracket from the front engine cover.

7. Loosen the water pump pulley mounting bolts.

8. Remove the accessory drive belt.

9. Remove the water pump pulley, then remove the lower water pump-to-engine block mounting bolt (this is necessary for engine front cover removal).

10. Remove the power steering fluid reservoir from the left-hand coil bracket and position it out of the way.

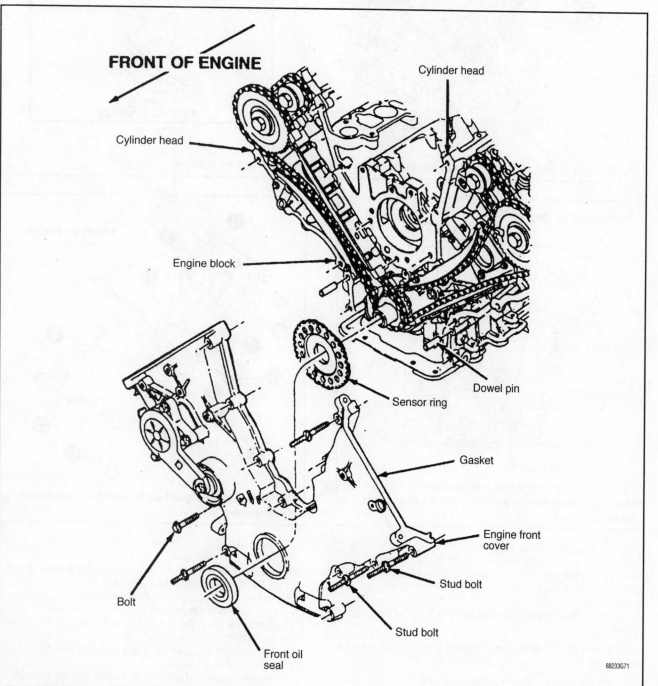

FRONT OF ENGINE

Fig. 135 Exploded view of the engine front cover mounting

88233G71

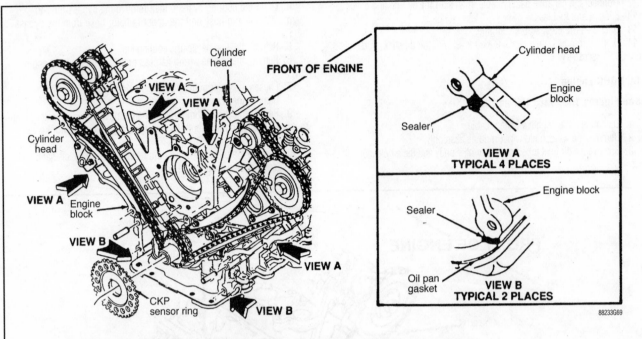

Fig. 136 Apply silicone sealant to the six locations—the view A or view B arrows indicate the locations

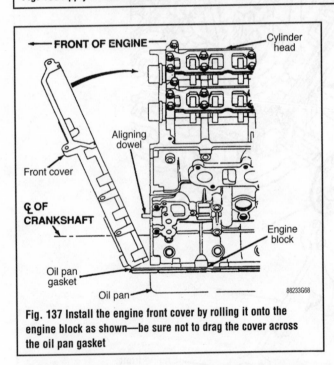

Fig. 137 Install the engine front cover by rolling it onto the engine block as shown—be sure not to drag the cover across the oil pan gasket

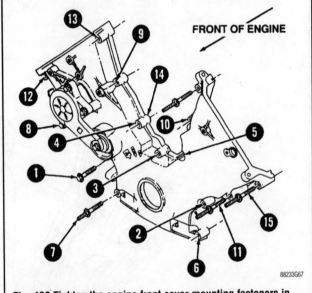

Fig. 138 Tighten the engine front cover mounting fasteners in the order shown

11. Apply the parking brake and block the rear wheels, then raise and safely support the front of the vehicle on jackstands.

12. Remove the power steering pump pulley, then remove the bolt retaining the power steering pressure hose to the power steering pump bracket.

13. Remove the power steering pump-to-engine block and front cover retaining bolts.

➡**The front lower bolt on the power steering pump will not come all the way out.**

14. Position the power steering pump out of the way.

15. Remove the four bolts retaining the front cover to the oil pan.

16. Remove the crankshaft pulley and damper.

17. Lower the vehicle.

18. Remove both valve covers.

19. Disengage the engine wiring harness connectors from the ignition coils and the Camshaft Position (CMP) sensor.

20. Remove the right- and left-hand ignition coils and their brackets. Lay them on the engine with the spark plug wires still attached.

21. Remove the idler pulley and the automatic accessory drive belt tensioner unit from the engine front cover.

22. Disengage the engine wiring harness connectors from the Crankshaft Position (CKP) sensor.

23. Remove the nine stud bolts and the six bolts retaining the engine front cover to the engine block.

24. Separate the cover from the engine.

To install:

➤**Lightly oil all bolt and stud threads prior to assembly, except those specifying sealant, with clean engine oil.**

25. Clean all of the gasket mating surfaces on the engine block, the front engine cover and other components, as necessary. Clean the surfaces with Ford Metal Surface Cleaner F4AZ-19A536-RA or equivalent.

➤**When cleaning the sealing surfaces of the engine front cover and the oil pan-to-engien block joints, use extreme care not to damage the rubber bead of the oil pan gasket. If a leak develops, the oil pan must be removed and a new gasket installed. Also, it is imperative to use the proper solvent when cleaning the keyway surfaces, otherwise the new sealer may not adhere properly.**

26. Install a new crankshaft oil seal in the front cover until it is flush and fully seated in its bore. You can use a tool specifically designed for this, or, if you are very careful, you can use a flat block of wood and a hammer to gently tap the seal in place; it is only important to ensure that the seal is installed flat and sits fully in its bore.

27. Install new engine front cover gaskets (there are three).

28. Apply silicone sealant, such as Ford Silicone Gasket and Sealant F6AZ-19562-A, in the six locations shown in the accompanying illustration.

➤**The engine front cover must be rolled into place. DO NOT slide it on the oil pan gasket.**

29. Install the engine front cover on the engine block no more than four minutes after applying the sealant.

30. Install all of the engine cover fasteners, in the positions shown in the accompanying illustration, in no more than four minutes after applying the silicone sealant. Tighten the fasteners to 15–22 ft. lbs. (20–30 Nm).

31. Install the accessory drive belt tensioner unit and the idler pulley, and tighten the mounting bolts to 15–22 ft. lbs. (20–30 Nm).

32. Engage the engine wiring harness to the CKP sensor.

33. Install both ignition coils and their brackets.

34. Install the power steering reservoir.

35. Engage the engine wiring harness to the ignition coils (if not already done) and the CMP sensor.

36. Install the valve covers.

37. Raise and safely support the front of the vehicle on jackstands.

38. Install the crankshaft pulley and vibration damper.

39. Install the four engine front cover-to-oil pan bolts and tighten them to 15–22 ft. lbs. (20–30 Nm).

40. Install the power steering pump. Tighten the fasteners 15–22 ft. lbs. (20–30 Nm).

41. Install the power steering pump pressure hose and the engine wiring harness retaining brackets.

42. Install the power steering pump pulley.

43. Lower the engine and remove the rear wheel blocks.

44. Install the water pump-to-engine block bolt to 15–22 ft. lbs. (20–30 Nm).

45. Install the water pump pulley and tighten the mounting bolts until snug.

46. Install the accessory drive belt, then tighten the water pump pulley mounting bolts 15–22 ft. lbs. (20–30 Nm).

47. Install the engine electric cooling fan.

✳✳ WARNING

It is extremely important to fill the engine with oil prior to starting it, otherwise severe engine damage will occur.

48. Fill the engine with the proper amount and type of clean engine oil.

49. Fill the cooling system.

50. Install the air inlet tube.

51. Install the windshield wiper module assembly.

52. Connect the negative battery cable, then start the engine and check for oil, coolant and fuel leaks.

53. After 3–5 minutes, stop the engine.

54. Wait 10 minutes, then check the oil level with the dipstick. Add more oil, if necessary.

5.0L Engine

◆ **See Figure 139 (p. 89)**

1. Disconnect the negative battery cable for safety.

2. Drain the cooling system and the engine crankcase oil.

3. Remove the air inlet tube.

4. Remove the fan shroud attaching bolts and position the shroud over the fan.

5. Remove the fan and clutch assembly from the water pump shaft, then remove the clutch, fan and shroud from the vehicle.

6. Remove the accessory drive belt, then remove the water pump pulley.

7. Remove all accessory brackets that attach to the water pump.

8. Disconnect the lower radiator hose, heater hose and water pump bypass hose from the water pump.

9. Remove the crankshaft pulley from the crankshaft vibration damper. Remove the damper attaching bolt and washer, then remove the damper using a suitable threaded (NOT JAWED) puller.

10. Remove the oil pan-to-front cover attaching bolts. Use a thin-bladed knife to cut the oil pan gasket flush with the cylinder block face prior to separating the cover from the cylinder block.

➤**Before removing the cover, verify that no other brackets or wires are attached.**

11. Remove the cylinder front cover and water pump as an assembly.

➤**Cover the front oil pan opening while the cover assembly is off to prevent foreign material from entering the pan.**

To install:

12. If a new front cover is to be installed, remove the water pump from the old front cover and install it on the new front cover.

➤**Ford recommends the installation of a new front cover seal whenever the cover has been removed. This is likely a precautionary measure to prevent you from having to disassemble the engine sufficiently to get at the seal, should it become worn or damaged. You will have to decide for yourself if the condition of your seal requires replacement.**

13. Clean all gasket mating surfaces. If necessary, pry the old oil seal from the front cover and install a new one, using a seal installer.

14. Coat the gasket surface of the oil pan with sealer, cut and position the required sections of a new gasket on the oil pan and apply silicone sealer at the corners. Apply sealer to a new front cover gasket, then install it on the block.

15. Position the front cover on the cylinder block. Use care to avoid seal damage or gasket dislocation. It may be necessary to force the cover downward to compress the pan gasket slightly. Use front cover aligner tool T61P-6019-B, or equivalent, to assist the operation.

16. Coat the threads of the front cover attaching screws with an oil resistant Teflon® pipe sealant and install. While pushing in on the alignment tool, tighten the oil pan-to-cover attaching screws to 12–18 ft. lbs. (16–24 Nm).

17. Tighten the front cover-to-cylinder block attaching bolts to 12–18 ft. lbs. (16–24 Nm). Remove the alignment tool.

18. Apply multi-purpose grease to the sealing surface of the vibration damper. Then apply a small amount of silicone sealant to the keyway. Align the crankshaft damper keyway with the crankshaft key, then install the damper to the crankshaft. Do NOT hammer the damper on, carefully push the damper into position and, if difficulty is encountered, use the retaining bolt and washer to draw the damper into the fully seated position.

19. Tighten the damper retaining bolt to 70–90 ft. lbs. (95–122 Nm).

20. Install the crankshaft pulley.

21. Before you go any further, REFILL THE ENGINE CRANKCASE with fresh, clean engine oil. DO IT NOW, DO NOT risk forgetting it later.

For 5.0L engine front cover removal, detach any brackets from the water pump or front cover

In this case, a bracket had to be removed in order to reach another bracket

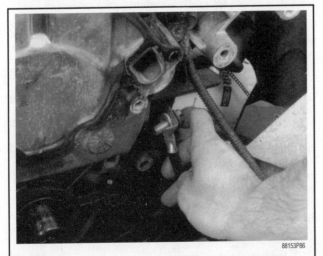

Disconnect any wiring that would interfere with front cover removal

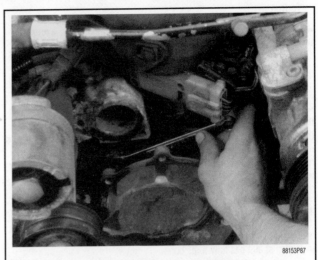

Once ALL cover bolts (including at the oil pan) are removed, gently pry to break the gasket seal

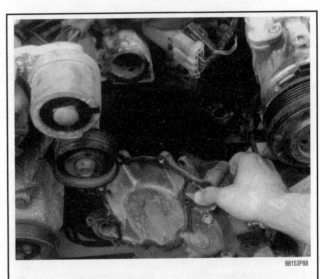

Remove the cover being careful to keep debris out of the oil pan

Clean the gasket mating surfaces (again keeping debris OUT OF the oil pan)

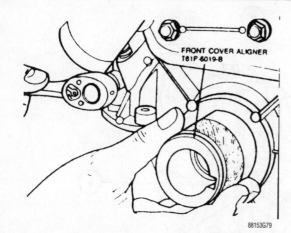

Fig. 139 A front cover alignment tool helps to align the bolt holes without having to move the cover so much that the gasket and sealant become dislodged

22. Connect the hoses and accessory brackets to the water pump.
23. Install the pulley on the water pump shaft.
24. Install the shroud along with the clutch and fan assembly.
25. Route and install the accessory drive belt.
26. Connect the negative battery cable and refill the cooling system.
27. Run the engine and check for leaks.

Timing Chain and Gears

REMOVAL & INSTALLATION

✳ CAUTION

When draining the coolant, keep in mind that cats and dogs are attracted by ethylene glycol antifreeze, and are quite likely to drink any that is left in an uncovered container or in puddles on the ground. This will prove fatal in sufficient quantity. Always drain the coolant into a sealable container. Coolant should be reused unless it is contaminated or too old.

3.8L Engine

◆ See Figures 140, 141, and 142 (p. 90–92)

1. Disconnect the negative battery cable for safety.
2. Remove the timing chain cover.
3. Remove the camshaft sprocket retaining bolt and washer, then remove the distributor drive gear from the end of the camshaft.

➡If the crankshaft gear is difficult to remove by hand, remove the camshaft gear and timing chain, then use two large prybars positioned on either side of the gear to carefully slide the gear off of the crankshaft.

4. Slide the camshaft and crankshaft gears, along with the timing chain, off of shafts at the same time.
5. Remove the timing chain tensioner (vibration damper) from the front of the engine block, then pull back on the ratcheting mechanism and insert a pin through the bracket hole to relieve the tension.

To install:

6. With the timing chain tensioner in the compressed position, install the tensioner and retaining bolts on the engine block. Tighten the bolts to 71–123 inch lbs. (8–14 Nm).
7. Rotate the crankshaft, as necessary, to position No. 1 piston at Top Dead Center (TDC) and the crankshaft keyway at the 12 o'clock position.

Familiarize yourself with the components related to the timing chain prior to disassembly

Temporarily install the camshaft gear, then rotate the camshaft so that the keyway on the camshaft is in the 6 o'clock position.

8. Lubricate the timing chain with clean engine oil, then install the camshaft gear, crankshaft gear and timing chain at the same time.

➡The timing marks should be aligned with each other; if not, remove the gears and chain and reinstall them so that they do.

9. Slide the distributor gear onto the end of the camshaft.
10. Install the camshaft sprocket retaining bolt and washer. Tighten the bolt to 30–36 ft. lbs. (40–50 Nm).
11. Pull the pin out of the timing chain tensioner to properly tension the chain.
12. Install the engine front cover.
13. Connect the negative battery cable, then start the engine and check for oil, coolant and fuel leaks.

4.6L SOHC Engine

◆ See Figures 143 thru 151 (p. 93–95)

✳ WARNING

When the timing chains are removed and the cylinder heads are installed, the crankshaft and camshafts must NEVER be rotated, otherwise valve and/or piston damage will result.

➡A camshaft gear should only be separated from the camshaft when one of them needs to be replaced.

1. Disconnect the negative battery cable.
2. Remove the valve covers, oil pan and engine front cover.
3. Remove the Crankshaft Position (CKP) sensor pulse wheel from the crankshaft.
4. Rotate the crankshaft until the No. 1 piston reaches Top Dead Center (TDC) and the timing marks on the camshaft and crankshaft gears are positioned as shown in the accompanying illustration.

➡Camshaft holding fixtures, such as Ford Cam Positioning Tool Adapters T92P-6256-A and Cam Positioning Tool T91P-6256-A, MUST be installed on the camshafts to prevent them from turning.

5. Install the camshaft holding fixtures on the flats of the camshafts.
6. Remove the right-hand timing chain tensioner from the cylinder head.
7. Remove the right-hand timing chain tensioner arm.
8. Remove the right-hand timing chain guide.
9. Remove the right-hand timing chain from the camshaft and crankshaft gears.

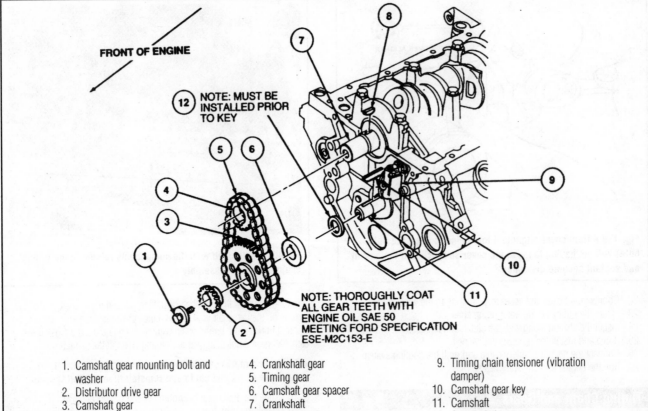

FRONT OF ENGINE

(12) NOTE: MUST BE INSTALLED PRIOR TO KEY

NOTE: THOROUGHLY COAT ALL GEAR TEETH WITH ENGINE OIL SAE 50 MEETING FORD SPECIFICATION ESE-M2C153-E

1. Camshaft gear mounting bolt and washer
2. Distributor drive gear
3. Camshaft gear
4. Crankshaft gear
5. Timing gear
6. Camshaft gear spacer
7. Crankshaft
8. Crankshaft key
9. Timing chain tensioner (vibration damper)
10. Camshaft gear key
11. Camshaft
12. Camshaft thrust spacer

88233G91

Fig. 140 Exploded view of the timing chain and gear mounting on the 3.8L engine

10. Perform Steps 5 through 9 for the left-hand timing chain.
11. Remove the crankshaft gears from the crankshaft.
12. Remove the camshaft gear mounting bolts, washers, gears and spacers from the camshafts.

✳✳ WARNING

Do not rotate the crankshaft or camshafts; possible damage to the engine may result.

13. Inspect the gears for wear or damage; replace them if any damage or wear is evident.
14. Inspect the plastic running face on the timing chain tensioner arms and chain guides. If any damage or wear is evident, install new ones, then remove and clean the oil pan and oil pump screen cover and tube.

To install:
15. Install the chain guides on both sides, then tighten the mounting bolts to 71–106 inch lbs. (8–12 Nm).
16. If removed, install the left-hand camshaft gear spacer and gear, then install the gear mounting bolt and washer hand-tight.
17. If removed, install the right-hand camshaft gear spacer and gear, then install the gear mounting bolt and washer hand-tight.

➡The two crankshaft gears are identical and must only be installed in one configuration. Refer to the accompanying illustration for correct crankshaft gear mounting. Also, ensure that the tapered part of the crankshaft gear faces away from the engine block.

18. Install the left-hand timing chain as follows:
   a. Install the inner crankshaft gear (for the left timing chain).

➡If the copper links in the timing chain are no longer visible, split both timing chains in half and mark the two opposing links as shown in the accompanying illustration.

88233P97

Remove the engine front cover for access to the timing chain and related components

Turn the crankshaft until the timing marks (arrows) on the timing chain gears are aligned

Note that the keyway (arrow) is in the 12 o'clock position when the crankshaft is properly positioned

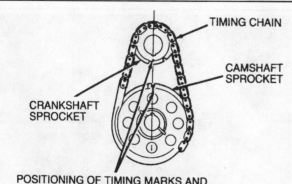

TIMING CHAIN

CAMSHAFT SPROCKET

CRANKSHAFT SPROCKET

POSITIONING OF TIMING MARKS AND KEYWAYS IN CAMSHAFT AND CRANKSHAFT SPROCKETS MUST BE IN LINE AS SHOWN WITH NO. 1 PISTON AT TOP DEAD CENTER

88233G90

Fig. 141 It is important to ensure that the timing marks on the gears are properly aligned prior to disassembly so that the timing chain can be correctly assembled later on—note that the engine is inverted in this illustration

Loosen the camshaft gear mounting bolt . . .

. . . then withdraw the bolt and washer from the end of the camshaft

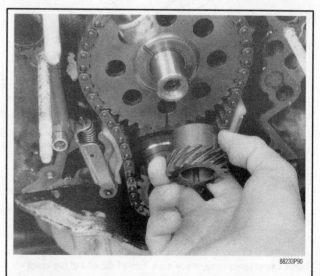

Slide the distributor drive gear off of the end of the camshaft . . .

. . . then remove the camshaft gear, crankshaft gear and timing chain together as an assembly

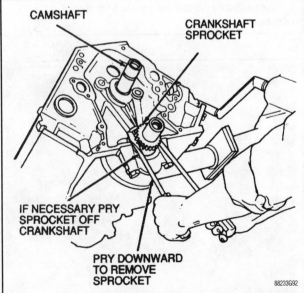

CAMSHAFT

CRANKSHAFT SPROCKET

IF NECESSARY PRY SPROCKET OFF CRANKSHAFT

PRY DOWNWARD TO REMOVE SPROCKET

Fig. 142 If the crankshaft gear is too difficult to remove by hand, use two prybars to carefully work it off of the end of the crankshaft as shown

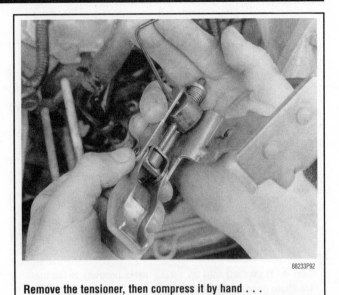

Remove the tensioner, then compress it by hand . . .

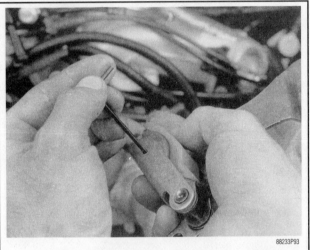

. . . and insert a sturdy pin or properly-sized Allen wrench (as shown) to hold it in this position

After installing the timing chain, remove the pin to allow the tensioner to apply pressure to the chain

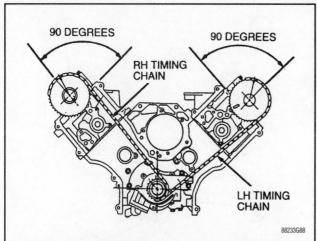

Fig. 143 Rotate the crankshaft so that the timing marks on the crankshaft gear and camshaft gears are positioned as shown when the No. 1 piston is at TDC

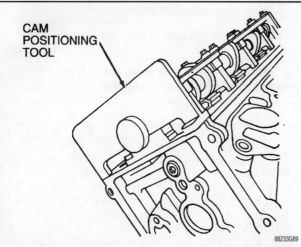

Fig. 144 Install a camshaft positioning tool on the cylinder head prior to removing the timing chain

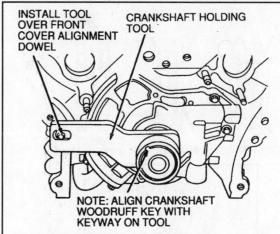

NOTE: ALIGN CRANKSHAFT WOODRUFF KEY WITH KEYWAY ON TOOL

1. Right cylinder head
2. Left cylinder head
3. Dowel
4. Left timing chain tensioner arm
5. Left timing chain tensioner
6. Bolt
7. Lock pin
8. Right timing chain tensioner
9. Right timing chain tensioner arm

Fig. 145 Exploded view of the timing chain tensioner mounting on the engine block and cylinder heads

b. Install the left timing chain on the camshaft gear. Ensure that the copper, or self-marked, link is aligned with the timing mark on the camshaft gear.

c. Install the left chain on the crankshaft sprocket so that the copper, or self-marked, link is aligned with the crankshaft gear timing mark.

19. Install the right-hand timing chain as follows:

a. Install the outer crankshaft gear (for the right timing chain).

➡If the copper links in the timing chain are no longer visible, split both timing chains in half and mark the two opposing links as shown in the accompanying illustration.

b. Install the right timing chain on the camshaft gear. Ensure that the copper, or self-marked, link is aligned with the timing mark on the camshaft gear.

c. Install the right chain on the crankshaft sprocket so that the copper, or self-marked, link is aligned with the crankshaft gear timing mark.

20. Install both timing chain tensioners. Tighten their mounting fasteners to 15–22 ft. lbs. (20–30 Nm).

21. Install a crankshaft holding fixture, such as Ford Crankshaft Holding Tool T93P06303-A, over the crankshaft end and the engine front cover alignment dowel. This is designed to properly position the crankshaft.

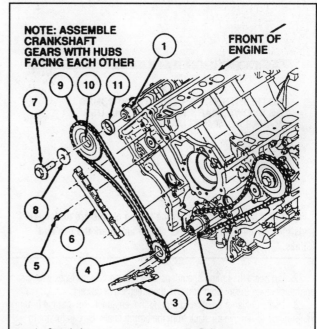

1. Camshaft
2. Crankshaft
3. Left-hand timing chain guide
4. Crankshaft gear
5. Bolt
6. Right-hand timing chain guide
7. Bolt
8. Washer
9. Right-hand timing chain
10. Camshaft gear
11. Camshaft gear spacer

Fig. 146 Exploded view of the timing chain mounting for 4.6L SOHC engines

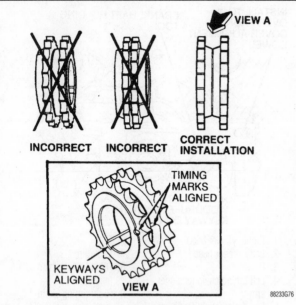

Fig. 147 Be sure to install the crankshaft gears in the correct configuration, otherwise timing chain or engine damage will result

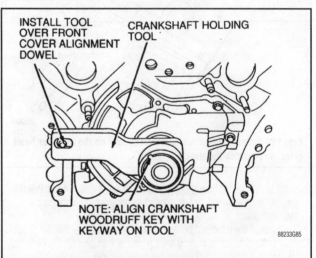

NOTE: WITH EITHER CHAIN POSITIONED AS SHOWN, MARK EACH END AND USE MARKS AS TIMING MARKS

88233G75

Fig. 148 If the copper links on the timing chains are no longer visible, lay each chain out like shown and mark the two end links

22. Lubricate the timing chain tensioner arm contact surfaces with clean engine oil, then install both arms on their respective dowels.

23. Use a C-clamp positioned around the tensioner arm and the timing chain guide to remove all slack from the timing chain. Be careful not to bend the chain guide.

24. Remove the lock pins from the tensioners and ensure that all of the timing marks are aligned.

25. Install the camshaft holding fixtures, such as Ford Cam Positioning Tool Adapters T92P-6256-A and Cam Positioning Tool T91P-6256-A, to align the camshafts, then tighten the camshaft gear center bolts to 81–95 ft. Lbs. (110–130 Nm).

26. Install a dial indicator, such as Rotunda Dial Indicator with Bracketry 014–00282, in the No. 1 cylinder spark plug hole. Ensure that the camshaft is at maximum lift for the intake valve at 114 degrees after TDC. If it is not, repeat Steps 20 through 23.

27. Remove the crankshaft and camshaft holding fixtures.

28. Install the engine front cover, the oil pan and the valve covers.

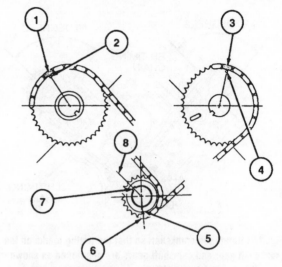

1. Right camshaft timing chain mark
2. Right camshaft gear mark
3. Left camshaft timing chain mark
4. Right camshaft gear mark
5. Crankshaft gear mark
6. Crankshaft timing chain mark
7. Crankshaft
8. Crankshaft keyway center line

88233G74

Fig. 149 After installing the two timing chains, ensure that all of the timing marks are positioned as indicated

INSTALL TOOL OVER FRONT COVER ALIGNMENT DOWEL

CRANKSHAFT HOLDING TOOL

NOTE: ALIGN CRANKSHAFT WOODRUFF KEY WITH KEYWAY ON TOOL

88233G85

Fig. 150 Install a crankshaft holding fixture to prevent it from rotating while tensioning the timing chains

❄❄ WARNING

It is extremely important to fill the engine with oil prior to starting it, otherwise severe engine damage will occur.

29. Fill the engine with the proper amount and type of clean engine oil.

30. Connect the negative battery cable, then start the engine and check for oil, coolant and fuel leaks.

31. After 3–5 minutes, stop the engine.

32. Wait 10 minutes, then check the oil level with the dipstick. Add more oil, if necessary.

NOTE: USE C-CLAMP TO REMOVE SLACK FROM CAMSHAFT TIMING CHAIN

88233G84

Fig. 151 Use a large C-clamp to tension the timing chains as shown

4.6L DOHC Engine

♦ See Figures 152 thru 161 (p. 95–99)

When the timing chains are removed and the cylinder heads are installed, the crankshaft and camshafts must NEVER be rotated, otherwise valve and/or piston damage will result.

➡A camshaft gear should only be separated from the camshaft when one of them needs to be replaced.

1. Disconnect the negative battery cable.
2. Remove the valve covers, oil pan and engine front cover.
3. Remove the rocker arms.
4. Remove the Crankshaft Position (CKP) sensor pulse wheel from the crankshaft.
5. Rotate the crankshaft until the No. 1 piston reaches Top Dead Center (TDC) and the timing marks on the camshaft and crankshaft gears are positioned as shown in the accompanying illustration.

➡Camshaft holding fixtures, such as Ford Cam Positioning Tool T93P-6256-A and Cam Holding Tool T93P-6256-AH, MUST be installed on the camshafts to prevent them from turning.

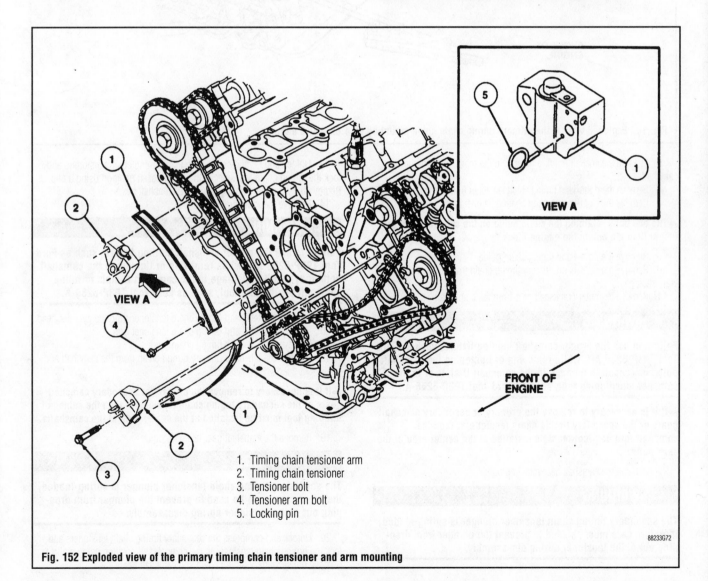

1. Timing chain tensioner arm
2. Timing chain tensioner
3. Tensioner bolt
4. Tensioner arm bolt
5. Locking pin

VIEW A

FRONT OF ENGINE

88233G72

Fig. 152 Exploded view of the primary timing chain tensioner and arm mounting

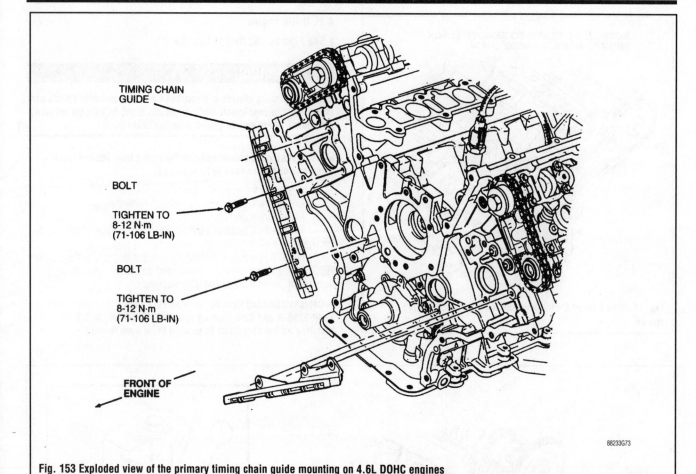

Fig. 153 Exploded view of the primary timing chain guide mounting on 4.6L DOHC engines

6. Install the camshaft holding fixtures in the rear D-slots of the camshafts.

7. Remove the right-hand timing chain tensioner from the cylinder head.

8. Remove the right-hand timing chain tensioner arm.

➡**The two bolts retaining the chain guide on the cylinder head are longer than the one in the engine block.**

9. Remove the right-hand timing chain guide.

10. Remove the right-hand primary timing chain from the camshaft and crankshaft gears.

11. Remove the outer crankshaft gear from the crankshaft.

❋❋ **WARNING**

Failure to use the proper camshaft holding fixture, such as Ford Tool T93P-6256-AH, while removing or tightening the camshaft bolts may result in damage to the camshaft D-slots or to the camshaft positioning tool, such as Ford Tool T93P-6256-A.

➡**If it is necessary to remove the primary or secondary camshaft gears or the secondary timing chain tensioners, then the camshaft torquing tool must be installed at the center area of the camshafts.**

12. Remove the camshaft gear retaining bolts.

❋❋ **WARNING**

The secondary timing chain tensioner plunger is spring-loaded, therefore care must be used to prevent the plunger from dropping out of the tensioner during disassembly.

13. Unlock and compress the secondary timing chain tensioners and lock the timing chain tensioner in the compressed position using a clip. Remove the secondary timing chain and camshaft gears.

14. Remove the inner crankshaft gear.

❋❋ **WARNING**

Failure to use the proper camshaft holding fixture, such as Ford Tool T93P-6256-AH, while removing or tightening the camshaft bolts may result in damage to the camshaft D-slots or to the camshaft positioning tool, such as Ford Tool T93P-6256-A.

15. Remove the left-hand timing chain tensioner from the cylinder head.

16. Remove the left-hand timing chain tensioner arm.

17. Remove the left-hand timing chain guide.

18. Remove the left-hand primary timing chain from the camshaft and crankshaft gears.

➡**If it is necessary to remove the primary or secondary camshaft gears or the secondary timing chain tensioners, then the camshaft torquing tool must be installed at the center area of the camshafts.**

19. Remove the camshaft gear retaining bolts.

❋❋ **WARNING**

The secondary timing chain tensioner plunger is spring-loaded, therefore care must be used to prevent the plunger from dropping out of the tensioner during disassembly.

20. Unlock and compress the secondary timing chain tensioners and lock the timing chain tensioner in the compressed position using a clip. Remove the secondary timing chain and camshaft gears.

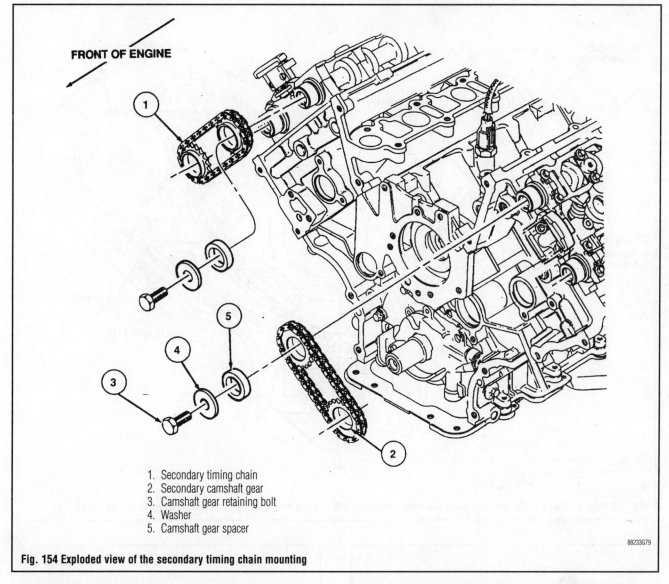

FRONT OF ENGINE

1. Secondary timing chain
2. Secondary camshaft gear
3. Camshaft gear retaining bolt
4. Washer
5. Camshaft gear spacer

88233G79

Fig. 154 Exploded view of the secondary timing chain mounting

21. Inspect the friction material on the chain tensioner arms and chain guides. If any damage or wear is evident, install new ones, then remove and clean the oil pan and oil pump screen cover and tube.

To install:

➡**Prior to installation, ensure that the tensioners are locked in the compressed positions with clips.**

22. If the cylinder head was removed from the engine block, position the crankshaft keyway at 270 degrees (9 o'clock position).

➡**The rocker arms must not be installed at this time.**

23. If removed, install the camshaft positioning fixtures (Ford Cam Positioning Tool T93P-6256-A or equivalent) in the rear D-slots of the camshafts so that the keyways of both the intake and exhaust camshafts point down toward the crankshaft.

➡**Do not remove the camshaft positioning or holding fixtures until all components are installed.**

24. Install the camshaft holding tools (Ford Tool T93P-6256-AH or equivalent) on the center of the camshafts on both cylinder heads.

25. If removed, install the left-hand secondary timing chain tensioner. Tighten the mounting bolts to 15–22 ft. lbs. (20–30 Nm).

26. If removed, install the left-hand secondary camshaft gears and tim-ing chain as an assembly. Install the gears so that the hubs of the gears face in the direction shown in the accompanying illustration.

27. Install the left-hand primary camshaft gear and spacer on the camshaft.

➡**The secondary camshaft gears must turn freely.**

28. Install the camshaft gear washers and retaining bolts; only finger-tighten them at this point.

29. Install an appropriate tensioning tool (Ford Tool T93P-6256-BH or equivalent) on the left-hand secondary timing chain tensioner.

☀☀ WARNING

Failure to use the proper camshaft holding fixture, such as Ford Tool T93P-6256-AH, while removing or tightening the camshaft bolts may result in damage to the camshaft D-slots or to the camshaft positioning tool, such as Ford Tool T93P-6256-A.

30. Tighten the camshaft gear bolts to 81–95 ft. lbs. (110–130 Nm).
31. Repeat Steps 22 through 30 for the right-hand cylinder head.

➡**The two crankshaft gears are identical and must only be installed in one configuration. Refer to the accompanying illustration for cor-rect crankshaft gear mounting. Also, ensure that the tapered part of the crankshaft gear faces away from the engine block.**

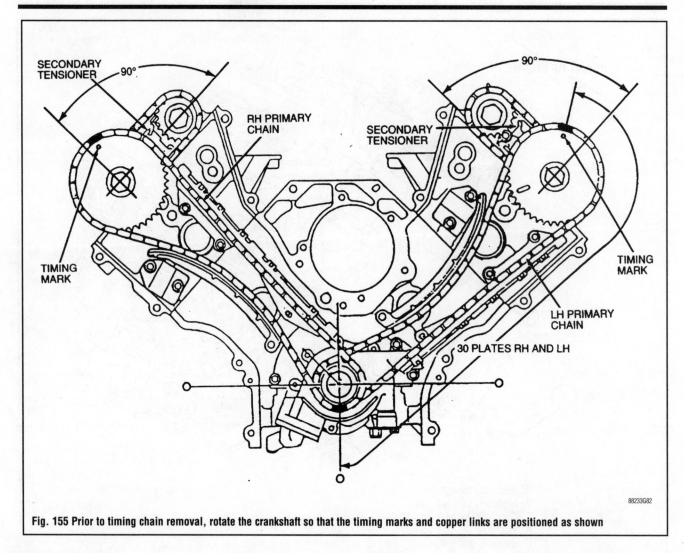

Fig. 155 Prior to timing chain removal, rotate the crankshaft so that the timing marks and copper links are positioned as shown

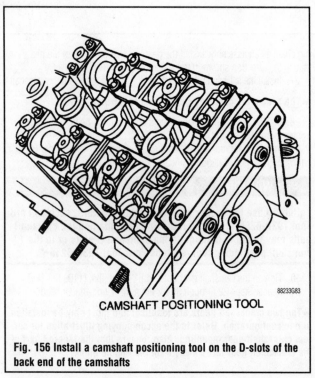

Fig. 156 Install a camshaft positioning tool on the D-slots of the back end of the camshafts

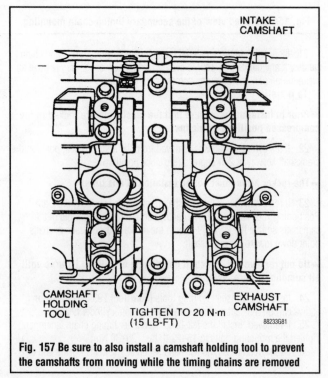

Fig. 157 Be sure to also install a camshaft holding tool to prevent the camshafts from moving while the timing chains are removed

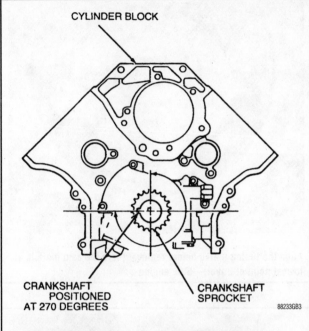

Fig. 158 If the cylinder heads were removed from the engine block, rotate the crankshaft until the keyway is positioned as shown

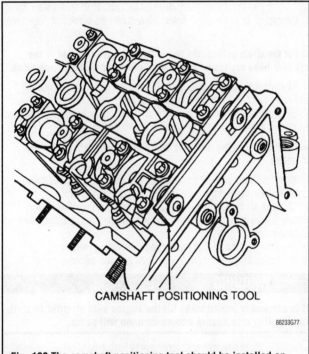

Fig. 160 The camshaft positioning tool should be installed on the back ends of the camshafts

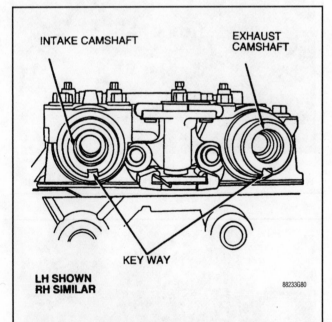

Fig. 159 Install the camshaft positioning tool so that the camshafts are held with their keyways facing the crankshaft, as shown

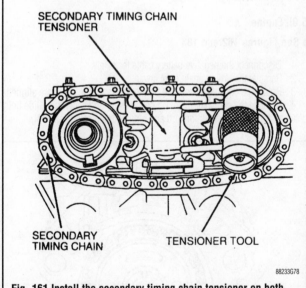

Fig. 161 Install the secondary timing chain tensioner on both cylinder heads

32. Install the left-hand primary timing chain as follows:
    a. Install the inner crankshaft gear (for the left primary timing chain).

➡️If the copper links in the timing chain are no longer visible, split both timing chains in half and mark the two opposing links as shown in the accompanying illustration.

    b. Install the left primary timing chain on the camshaft gear. Ensure that the copper, or self-marked, link is aligned with the timing mark on the camshaft gear.

    c. Install the left primary chain on the crankshaft sprocket so that the copper, or self-marked, link is aligned with the crankshaft gear timing mark.

33. Install the right-hand primary timing chain as follows:
    a. Install the outer crankshaft gear (for the right timing chain).

➡️If the copper links in the primary timing chain are no longer visible, split both timing chains in half and mark the two opposing links as shown in the accompanying illustration.

    b. Install the right primary timing chain on the camshaft gear. Ensure that the copper, or self-marked, link is aligned with the timing mark on the camshaft gear.

c. Install the right primary chain on the crankshaft sprocket so that the copper, or self-marked, link is aligned with the crankshaft gear timing mark.

➡**For the chain guides, the two bolts which are inserted in the cylinder head are longer than the bolt inserted in the engine block.**

34. Install the chain guides for both primary chains, and tighten the mounting bolts to 71–106 inch lbs. (8–12 Nm).

35. Lubricate the timing chain tensioner arm contact surfaces with clean engine oil, then install both arms using one bolt each.

➡**Do not remove the lock pins until the timing chain guides are installed.**

36. Install both primary chain tensioners, and secure them with two bolts on each. Tighten the bolts to 15–22 ft. lbs. (20–30 Nm).

37. Remove the lock pins from both primary chain tensioners, and ensure that all of the timing marks on the crankshaft and camshaft gears are aligned properly.

38. Remove the camshaft positioning and holding fixtures.

39. Install the engine front cover, the oil pan and the valve covers.

✷✷ WARNING

It is extremely important to fill the engine with oil prior to starting it, otherwise severe engine damage will occur.

40. Fill the engine with the proper amount and type of clean engine oil.

41. Connect the negative battery cable, then start the engine and check for oil, coolant and fuel leaks.

42. After 3–5 minutes, stop the engine.

43. Wait 10 minutes, then check the oil level with the dipstick. Add more oil, if necessary.

5.0L Engine

♦ See Figures 162 and 163

1. Disconnect the negative battery cable for safety.

2. Remove the timing chain front cover.

3. Rotate the crankshaft until the timing marks on the gears are aligned.

4. Remove the camshaft retaining bolt, washer and eccentric. Slide both gears and the timing chain forward and remove them as an assembly.

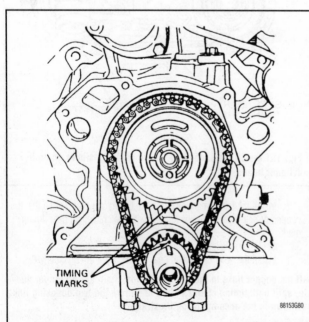

Fig. 162 The engine is properly timed when the timing marks are aligned at their closest point

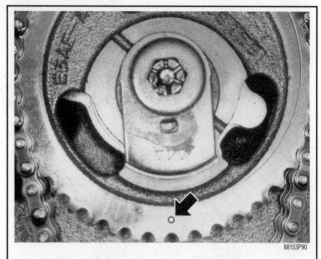

Align the timing marks before removal (here the cam mark is at lowest point of travel)—5.0L engine

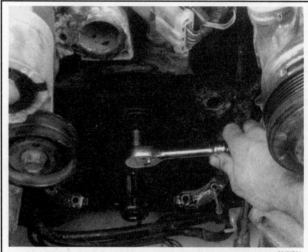

With the marks aligned, loosen the camshaft gear retaining bolt

Remove the gear retaining bolt and washer

Then, remove the timing chain and gears as an assembly

This photo shows the crankshaft gear as the timing mark was oriented prior to removal

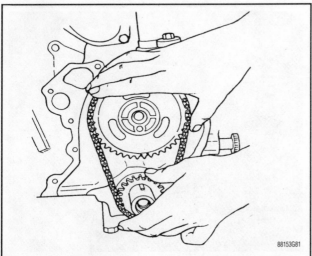

Fig. 163 The chain is most easily removed or installed together with both of the gears

To install:

5. Position the gears and timing chain on the camshaft and crankshaft simultaneously. Make sure the timing marks on the gears are aligned.

6. Install the washer, eccentric (if equipped) and camshaft gear retaining bolt. Tighten the bolt to 40–45 ft. lbs. (54–61 Nm).

7. Install the timing chain front cover.

8. Connect the negative battery cable.

Camshaft and Lifters

REMOVAL & INSTALLATION

❈❈ CAUTION

When draining the coolant, keep in mind that cats and dogs are attracted by ethylene glycol antifreeze, and are quite likely to drink any that is left in an uncovered container or in puddles on the ground. This will prove fatal in sufficient quantity. Always drain the coolant into a sealable container. Coolant should be reused unless it is contaminated or too old.

3.8L Engine

VALVE TAPPETS

➡Before replacing a valve lifter because of noisy operation, ensure that the noise is not caused by improper valve-to-rocker arm clearance, or by worn rocker arms or pushrods.

1. Remove the valve covers.
2. Remove the upper and lower intake manifolds.

➡Make sure to label or arrange the rocker arms, pushrods and valve tappets so that they can be reinstalled in their original locations.

3. Remove the rocker arms and pushrods.
4. Remove the bolts holding the two tappet retainers in place (the bolts are held captive in retainers). Remove the six valve tappet guide plates from adjacent tappets.
5. Using a magnet, remove the tappets from their bores. If the valve tappets are stuck in their bores due to excessive varnish or gum build-up, use a claw-type tappet removal tool or equivalent. When using such a tool, rotate the tappets back and forth to loosen the build-up.

Remove the valve covers and intake manifolds . . .

. . . then loosen the rocker arm hold-down bolts . . .

Remove the valve tappet retainer mounting bolts . . .

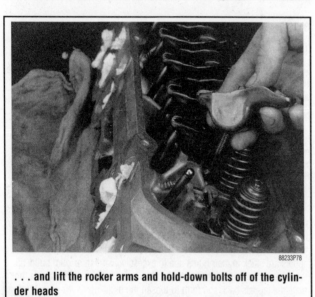

. . . and lift the rocker arms and hold-down bolts off of the cylinder heads

. . . then remove the retainers from the tappet valley . . .

Remove the pushrods and be sure to keep them in their proper order for reassembly

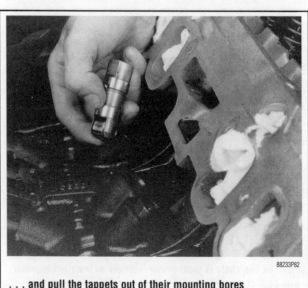

. . . and pull the tappets out of their mounting bores

To install:

➡**Lightly oil all bolt and stud threads prior to assembly, except those specifying sealant, with clean engine oil.**

6. Clean the cylinder head and valve cover sealing surfaces of all old gasket material, dirt and oil residue.

7. Lubricate each valve tappet and bore with engine assembly lubricant.

8. Insert each valve tappet into its original bore. If new tappets are being installed, check for a free fit in the bore into which they are to be installed.

9. Align the flats on the sides of the valve tappets, then install the six guide plates between adjacent tappets, making sure that the word **UP** is showing.

10. Install the valve tappet retainers and tighten the mounting bolts to 88–124 inch lbs. (10–14 Nm).

11. Install the pushrods and rocker arms.

12. Install the lower and upper intake manifolds.

13. Install the valve covers.

14. Start the engine and check for leaks.

CAMSHAFT

▶ **See Figure 164**

➡**If your vehicle is equipped with air conditioning, refer to Section 1 for information regarding the implications of servicing your A/C system yourself. Only a MVAC-trained, EPA-certified, automotive technician should service the A/C system or its components.**

1. If your vehicle is equipped with A/C, have the condenser core removed.

2. Remove the radiator and radiator grille.

3. Remove the Camshaft Position (CMP) sensor and housing.

4. Remove the valve tappets.

5. Remove the engine front cover, timing chain and camshaft sprocket spacer.

6. Remove the oil pan.

7. Remove the mounting bolts, then remove the camshaft thrust plate.

8. Carefully slide the camshaft out of the front of the engine block, making sure not to damage the camshaft bearing surfaces and lobes.

To install:

➡**Lightly oil all bolt and stud threads prior to assembly, except those specifying sealant, with clean engine oil.**

9. Lubricate the camshaft lobes and bearing journals with engine assembly lubricant.

10. Carefully slide the camshaft into the engine block, making sure not to damage the bearing or lobe surfaces.

11. Install the camshaft thrust plate, and tighten the mounting bolts to 71–124 inch lbs. (8–14 Nm).

12. Install the camshaft gear spacer, timing chain and engine front cover.

13. Install the oil pan.

14. Install the valve tappets and related components.

15. Install the upper and lower intake manifolds.

16. Install the valve covers.

17. Install the CMP sensor and housing.

18. Install the radiator grille and radiator.

❋❋❋ WARNING

It is extremely important to fill the engine with oil prior to starting it, otherwise severe engine damage will occur.

19. Fill the engine with the proper amount and type of clean engine oil.

20. Fill the cooling system.

21. Connect the negative battery cable, then start the engine and check for oil, coolant and fuel leaks.

22. After 3–5 minutes, stop the engine.

23. Wait 10 minutes, then check the oil level with the dipstick. Add more oil, if necessary.

24. If necessary, have the A/C condenser core installed and the system recharged.

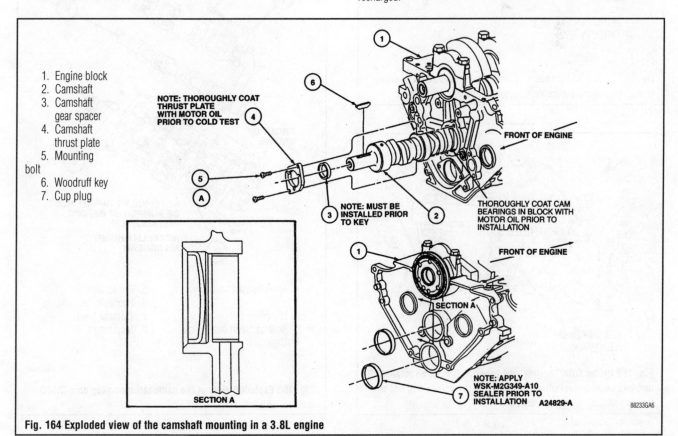

1. Engine block
2. Camshaft
3. Camshaft gear spacer
4. Camshaft thrust plate
5. Mounting bolt
6. Woodruff key
7. Cup plug

NOTE: THOROUGHLY COAT THRUST PLATE WITH MOTOR OIL PRIOR TO COLD TEST

NOTE: MUST BE INSTALLED PRIOR TO KEY

FRONT OF ENGINE

THOROUGHLY COAT CAM BEARINGS IN BLOCK WITH MOTOR OIL PRIOR TO INSTALLATION

FRONT OF ENGINE

SECTION A

NOTE: APPLY WSK-M2G349-A10 SEALER PRIOR TO INSTALLATION

A24829-A

SECTION A

88233GA6

Fig. 164 Exploded view of the camshaft mounting in a 3.8L engine

4.6L Engines

♦ **See Figures 165 thru 171 (p. 104–106)**

➡The 4.6L engines do not possess removable camshaft bearings. If the bearing surfaces are damaged, the cylinder head must either be service by a qualified machine shop, or a replacement cylinder head must be procured.

1. Remove the valve covers.
2. Remove the engine front cover.
3. Remove the timing chains.

> ❊❊ **WARNING**
>
> The crankshaft must be positioned so that the keyway is 45 degrees (SOHC engines) or 90 degrees (DOHC engines) counterclockwise from the 12 o'clock position in order to avoid damaging the valves when the camshafts are rotated.

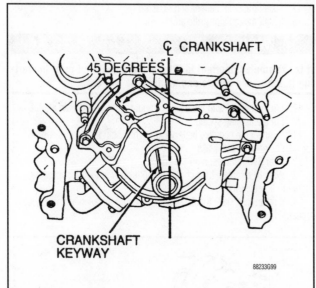

Fig. 165 On the SOHC engine, rotate the crankshaft 45 degrees counterclockwise before depressing the valve and springs

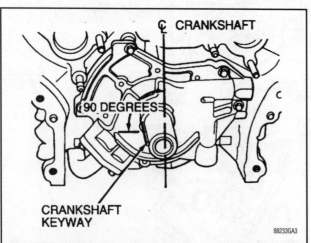

Fig. 166 On the DOHC engine, the crankshaft must be rotated 90 degrees counterclockwise to ensure that the valves will not contact the pistons when depressed

4. Rotate the crankshaft 45 degrees (SOHC engines) or 90 degrees (DOHC engines) counterclockwise.
5. Rotate the camshaft so that the base circle of the camshaft is positioned against the rocker arm being serviced.

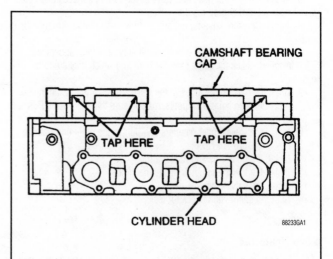

Fig. 167 To remove the camshaft bearing caps, tap the caps with a rubber or leather mallet where shown

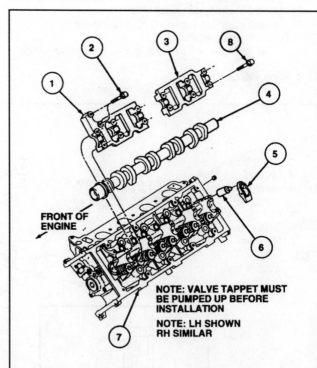

NOTE: VALVE TAPPET MUST BE PUMPED UP BEFORE INSTALLATION

NOTE: LH SHOWN RH SIMILAR

1. Front camshaft bearing cap
2. Mounting bolt
3. Rear camshaft bearing cap
4. Camshaft
5. Rocker arm
6. Hydraulic lash adjuster
7. Cylinder head
8. Mounting bolt

Fig. 168 Exploded view of the camshaft mounting on a SOHC engine

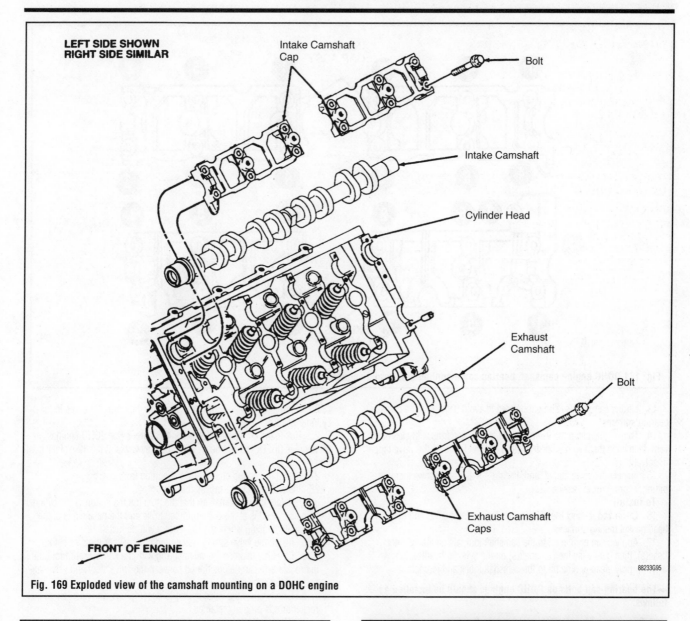

Fig. 169 Exploded view of the camshaft mounting on a DOHC engine

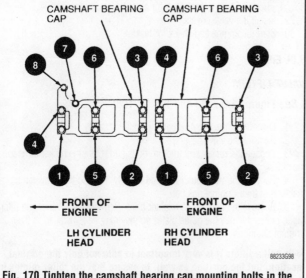

Fig. 170 Tighten the camshaft bearing cap mounting bolts in the sequence indicated—SOHC engine

✳✳ WARNING

A valve spring spacer, such as Ford Tool T91P-6565-AH, must be used in order to prevent the valve spring retainer from contacting the valve stem seal, which can result in damage to the seal.

6. Install the valve spring spacer between the valve spring coils.

7. Install a valve spring compressor, such as Ford Tool T91P-6565-A, under the camshaft and on top of the valve spring retainer.

8. Slowly push down on the compressor tool until the spring is depressed far enough to allow the rocker arm to be removed, then pull the rocker arm out from underneath the camshaft.

9. Remove the valve spring compressor and spacer tools.

10. Repeat Steps 5 through 9 until all of the rocker arms are removed from the cylinder head(s).

11. If necessary, pull the hydraulic valve tappets out of the cylinder head(s).

➡ On the DOHC engine, note the positions of the bearing cap bolts because they are various lengths.

12. Remove the camshaft bearing cap bolts from the cylinder head(s), then tap upward on the bearing caps at the positions shown in the accompanying illustration. Gradually lift the bearing caps off of the cylinder head(s).

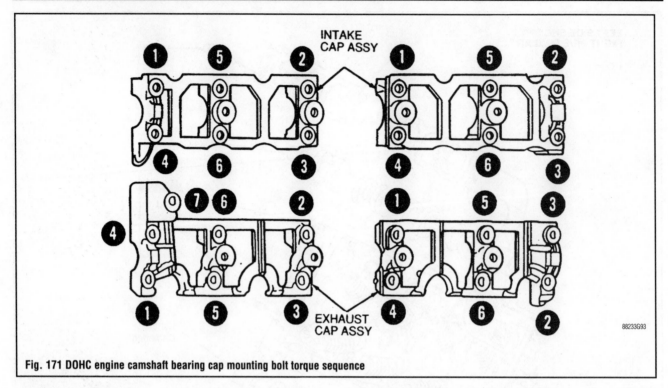

Fig. 171 DOHC engine camshaft bearing cap mounting bolt torque sequence

13. Lift the camshaft(s) straight upward to avoid damaging the camshaft bearing surfaces.

14. Thoroughly clean the valve tappets and rocker arms with clean solvent, then wipe them with a lint-free cloth. Do not immerse the valve tappet in solvent.

15. Inspect the valve tappet, and discard it if any part shows signs of pitting, scoring, or excessive wear.

To install:

16. Clean and inspect the valve cover, engine front cover and cylinder head gasket mating surfaces.

17. Apply clean engine oil to the camshaft journals on the cylinder head(s), then gently lay the camshaft(s) on the cylinder head(s).

18. Apply clean engine oil to the camshaft lobes and journals.

➡**The bearing cap bolts on DOHC engines should be installed as follows:**

• 2 in. (52mm) long bolts—intake camshaft bearing caps and inboard side of the exhaust camshaft bearing caps

• 1.6 in. (42mm) long bolts—outboard side of the exhaust camshaft bearing caps

19. Install and seat the camshaft bearing caps. Install and hand-tighten the bearing cap retaining bolts.

➡**Each camshaft bearing cap is tightened individually.**

20. Tighten the bearing cap bolts, in the sequence shown in the accompanying illustration, to 71–106 inch lbs. (8–12 Nm).

21. Loosen the bearing cap bolts approximately 2 revolutions, or until the head of the bolt turns freely.

➡**The camshaft should spin freely with a slight drag.**

22. Retighten the bearing cap bolts, in sequence, to 71–106 inch lbs. (8–12 Nm).

23. Check camshaft end-play.

24. Apply clean engine oil to the valve stems and tips, the rocker arm roller surfaces, the valve tappets, and the valve tappet bores in the cylinder head(s).

➡**The valve tappets must not have more than 0.059 in. (1.5mm) of plunger travel prior to installation.**

25. If removed earlier, insert the tappets in their original bores in the cylinder head(s).

26. Rotate the crankshaft clockwise 45 degrees (for SOHC engines) or 90 degrees (for DOHC engines)—until the keyway is at the 12 o'clock position.

27. Install the timing chains and the engine front cover.

28. Install the rocker arms, as follows:

a. Rotate the crankshaft so that the position the piston of the cylinder being serviced is at the bottom of its stroke and the base circle of the camshaft is facing where the rocker arm will be installed.

b. Install the valve spring spacer and compressor tools as before.

c. Carefully depress the valve spring with the compressor tool until the rocker arm can be positioned between the valve stem and valve tappet, and the camshaft.

d. Slowly allow the valve spring to decompress, and ensure that the rocker arm is properly retained.

e. Remove the valve spring compressor and spacer tools.

f. Repeat Steps **a** through **e** for all of the rocker arms.

29. Install the valve covers.

30. Start the engine and check for leaks.

5.0L Engine

VALVE LIFTERS

◆ **See Figures 172, 173 and 174 (p. 108)**

1. Disconnect the negative battery cable for safety.

2. Remove the valve covers.

3. Loosen the rocker arm fulcrum bolts and rotate the rocker arms to the side.

4. Remove the valve pushrods and identify them so that they can be installed in their original position.

5. Remove the lifter guide retainer bolts. Remove the retainer and lifter guide plates. Identify the guide plates so they may be reinstalled in their original positions.

➡**On roller lifters it is very important to note not only the original location, but the position as well, to assure that the roller rotates in the same direction.**

For 5.0L engines, remove the pushrod for access to the lifter . . .

. . . then remove the retainer from the center of the block's lifter valley

. . . if more than one rod is being removed, tag each to assure proper installation

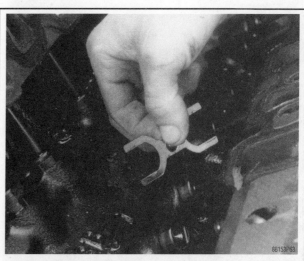

With the retainer removed, you can access the lifter guides— but be sure again, tag or arrange them

Loosen and remove the bolts securing the lifter guide retainer . . .

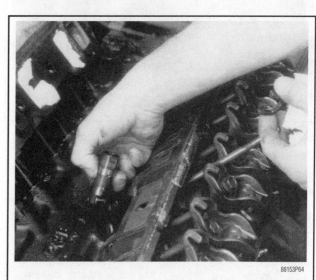

Finally, the lifter can be removed from its bore

Fig. 172 A magnet can be useful when removing lifters from their bores

Fig. 173 Stuck lifters can be freed using a slide hammer type lifter removal tool

6. Using a magnet, remove the lifters and place them in a rack so that they can be installed in their original bores.

➡If the lifters are stuck in the bores due to excessive varnish or gum deposits, it may be necessary to use a claw-type tool to aid removal. When using a remover tool, rotate the lifter back and forth to loosen it from gum or varnish that may have formed on the lifter.

To install:

7. Lubricate the lifters and install them in their original bores. If new lifters are being installed, check them for free fit in their respective bores.

8. Install the lifter guide plates in their original positions, then install the guide plate retainer.

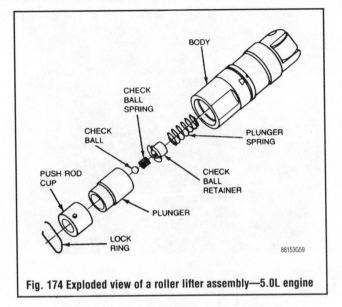

Fig. 174 Exploded view of a roller lifter assembly—5.0L engine

9. Install the pushrods in their original positions. Apply grease to the ends prior to installation.

10. Lubricate the rocker arms and fulcrum seats with heavy engine oil, then install the rocker arms and check for proper valve clearance.

11. Install the valve covers.

12. Connect the negative battery cable, then start the engine and check for leaks.

CAMSHAFT

▶ See Figure 175

➡If your vehicle is equipped with A/C, you will have to take the car to a service station to have the refrigerant discharged and recovered (using a proper recycling/recovery station) before beginning this procedure.

1. Properly discharge and recover the A/C refrigerant using a recovery station.

2. Disconnect the negative battery cable for safety.

3. Drain the cooling system and relieve the fuel system pressure.

4. Remove the radiator. If equipped with air conditioning, remove the condenser.

5. Remove the grille.

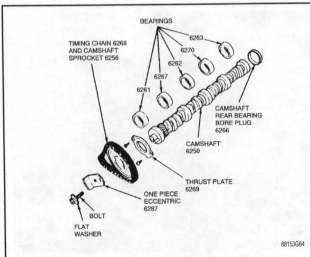

Fig. 175 Exploded view of the camshaft, bearings and related components—5.0L engine

6. Remove the upper and lower intake manifold assembly.
7. Remove the valve covers.
8. Remove the pushrods and lifters.

➡**Keep track of all valve train components. Any components which are to be reused, such as pushrods or lifters, must be reinstalled in their original locations. If necessary sort or label them during removal to assure installation in their correct positions.**

9. Remove the timing chain front cover.
10. Remove the timing chain and gears.
11. Remove the thrust plate. Remove the camshaft, being careful not to damage the bearing surfaces.

To install:

12. Lubricate the camshaft lobes and journals with heavy engine oil or a suitable engine assembly lube. An engine assembly lube is preferable if some time may pass before the job is completed and the engine is started. Install the camshaft, being careful not to damage the bearing surfaces while sliding it into position.
13. Install the camshaft thrust plate with the groove toward the cylinder block. Tighten the bolts to 9–12 ft. lbs. (12–16 Nm).
14. Check the camshaft play to determine whether or not the thrust plate must be replaced.
15. Install the lifters and pushrods.

➡**When reinstalling a camshaft, make sure the lifters and pushrods are installed in their original locations. If a new camshaft is being installed, new lifters and pushrods should be used.**

16. Install the timing chain and gears.
17. Install the engine front cover.
18. Install the valve covers.
19. Install the upper and lower intake manifolds.
20. Install the grille. If equipped with air conditioning, install the condenser.
21. Install the radiator.
22. Connect the negative battery cable, then fill and bleed the engine cooling system.
23. Run the engine and check for leaks.

INSPECTION

Camshaft Lobe Lift

Camshaft lobe lift is the amount (measured in inches or millimeters) that the camshaft is capable of LIFTING the valve train components in order to open the valves. The lobe lift is a measure of how much taller the "egg shaped" portion of the camshaft lobe is above the base or circular portion of the shaft lobe. Lift is directly proportional to how far the valves can open and a worn camshaft (with poor lobe lift) cannot fully open the valves. The lobe lift therefore can be directly responsible for proper or poor engine performance.

Lobe lift can be measured in 2 ways, depending on what tools are available and whether or not the camshaft has been removed from the engine. A dial gauge can be used to measure the lift with the camshaft installed, while a micrometer is normally only used once the shaft has been removed from the engine.

DIAL GAUGE METHOD

▶ **See Figure 176**

Lobe lift may be checked with the camshaft installed. In all cases, a dial gauge is positioned somewhere on the valve train (pushrod, lifter, or camshaft itself) and the camshaft is then turned to measure the lift.

Check the lift of each lobe in consecutive order and make a note of the reading.

1. Remove the valve cover for access to the camshaft (4.6L engines) or pushrods (3.8L and 5.0L engines).
2. On the pushrod engines, either remove the rocker arms (remember to tag or arrange them for proper installation), or loosen their mounting and

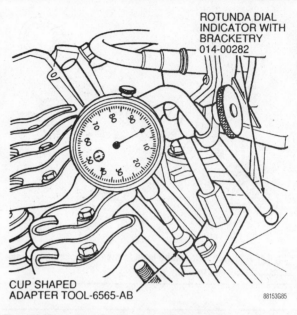

Fig. 176 Measuring lobe lift using a dial gauge on a pushrod motor such as the 5.0L engine

reposition them for access to the pushrods. Make sure the pushrod is in the valve tappet socket.
3. Install a dial indicator, such as Ford Tool D78P-4201-B, so that the actuating point of the indicator is in the pushrod socket (or the indicator ball socket adaptor tool 6565-AB is on the end of the pushrod) and in the same plane as the pushrod movement. On the OHC engines, the dial indicator may be directly placed on the camshaft.

➡**A remote starter can be used to turn the engine over during the next steps. If a remote starter is not available, remove the spark plugs in order to relieve engine compression, and turn the engine over using a large wrench or socket on the crankshaft damper bolt. BE SURE to only turn the engine in the normal direction of rotation.**

4. Turn the crankshaft over until the tappet is on the base circle of the camshaft lobe. At this position on the pushrod engines, the pushrod will be at its lowest point of travel.
5. Zero the dial indicator. Continue to rotate the crankshaft slowly until the pushrod (or camshaft lobe) is in the fully raised position.
6. Compare the total lift recorded on the dial indicator with the elevation specification shown in the Camshaft Specification chart.

To check the accuracy of the original indicator reading, continue to rotate the crankshaft until the indicator reads zero. If the lift on any lobe is below specified wear limits listed, the camshaft and the valve tappets must be replaced.

7. On 3.8L and 5.0L engines, when you are finished install the rocker arms and check the valve clearance.
8. Install the valve cover(s).

MICROMETER

▶ **See Figures 177 and 178**

A micrometer may used to measure camshaft lobe lift, but this is usually only after it has been removed from the engine. Once the valve cover is removed from the OHC engines, access may be possible (though a little awkward) to measure the camshaft lobes using a micrometer.

In any case, two measurements are necessary for each lobe. Measurement **Y** or the total LOBE HEIGHT and measurement **X** or the total LOBE WIDTH. To find the lobe lift, you simply subtract **X** from **Y** (subtract the width from the height).

Note each measurement, then make your calculation to determine the lift. Note the final results and repeat the process on the remaining camshaft

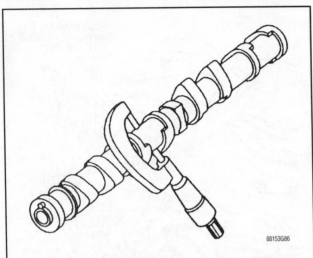

Fig. 177 A micrometer can be used to measure lobe lift with the camshaft removed from the engine

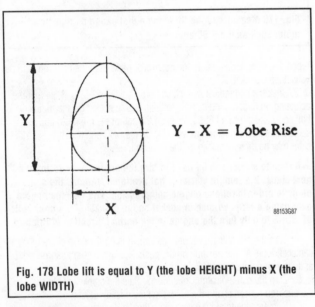

$$Y - X = \text{Lobe Rise}$$

Fig. 178 Lobe lift is equal to Y (the lobe HEIGHT) minus X (the lobe WIDTH)

lobes. Finally, you should compare your results to the specifications charts and decide if a new camshaft is in your future.

Camshaft End-Play

✳✳ WARNING

On all gasoline V6 and V8 engines, prying against the aluminum-nylon camshaft sprocket, with the valve train load on the camshaft, can break or damage the sprocket. Therefore, the rocker arms must be loosened sufficiently to free the camshaft. After checking the camshaft end-play, check the valve clearance.

1. Push the camshaft toward the rear of the engine. Install a dial indicator, such as Ford Tool D78P-D201-F and -G) so that the indicator point is on the camshaft sprocket attaching screw.
2. Zero the dial indicator. Position a prybar between the camshaft gear and the engine block or cylinder head. Pull the camshaft forward and release it. Compare the dial indicator reading with the specifications.

3. If end-play is excessive, check the spacer for correct installation before it is removed. If the spacer is correctly installed, replace the thrust plate (if equipped).
4. Remove the dial indicator.

Rear Main Oil Seal

REMOVAL & INSTALLATION

3.8L and 5.0L Engines

▶ **See Figure 179**

1. Disconnect the negative battery cable for safety.
2. Remove the flywheel or flexplate for access to the rear main seal.

✳✳ WARNING

Use extreme caution not to scratch the crankshaft oil seal surface.

3. Carefully punch 2 holes in the crankshaft rear oil seal on opposite sides of the crankshaft, just above the bearing cap-to-cylinder block split line. Install a sheet metal screw in each of the holes or use a small slide hammer to pry the crankshaft rear main oil seal from the block.

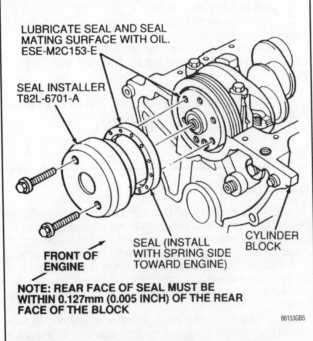

LUBRICATE SEAL AND SEAL MATING SURFACE WITH OIL. ESE-M2C153-E

SEAL INSTALLER T82L-6701-A

FRONT OF ENGINE

SEAL (INSTALL WITH SPRING SIDE TOWARD ENGINE)

CYLINDER BLOCK

NOTE: REAR FACE OF SEAL MUST BE WITHIN 0.127mm (0.005 INCH) OF THE REAR FACE OF THE BLOCK

Fig. 179 The one piece rear main seal on these engines is installed with a special installation tool—the specifications shown are for the 5.0L engine

To install:
4. Clean the oil seal recess in the cylinder block and main bearing cap.
5. Coat the seal and the seal mounting surfaces with oil.
6. Position the seal on rear main seal installer T82L-6701-A, or equivalent, then position the tool and seal to the rear of the engine.
7. Alternate tightening the seal installer tool bolts until the seal is properly seated. The rear face of the seal must be within 0.005 in. (0.127mm) of the rear face of the block for 5.0L engines, or within 0.020 in. (0.508mm) for 3.8L engines.
8. Install the flywheel or flexplate, as applicable.
9. Connect the negative battery cable.

4.6L Engines

▶ **See Figures 180, 181 and 182**

1. Disconnect the negative battery cable for safety.
2. Remove the flywheel or flexplate for access to the rear main seal.
3. Remove the crankshaft rear main oil seal retainer.

✳✳ WARNING

Use care to avoid damaging the retainer when removing the oil seal; a damaged retainer may allow oil to leak.

4. Securely support the oil seal retainer, then remove the oil seal from the retainer using a punch and a hammer.
   To install:
5. Clean the crankshaft rear oil seal retainer and retainer-to-engine block mating surfaces of all dirt, grime and oil residue. The oil residue should be cleaned from the surfaces with an appropriate metal cleaner, such as Ford Metal Surface Cleaner F4AZ-19A536-RA. Also inspect for any damage.

➡**Failure to clean the surfaces with the appropriate cleaning solvent can retard the new sealant's ability to adhere to the surfaces.**

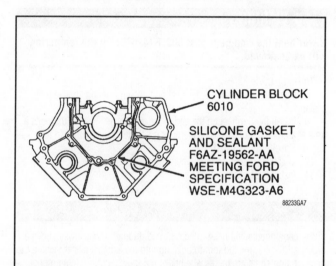

Fig. 180 Apply silicone gasket sealant to the engine block (as shown) for to prevent oil leakage from the oil seal retainer

CYLINDER BLOCK
6010

SILICONE GASKET
AND SEALANT
F6AZ-19562-AA
MEETING FORD
SPECIFICATION
WSE-M4G323-A6

88233GA7

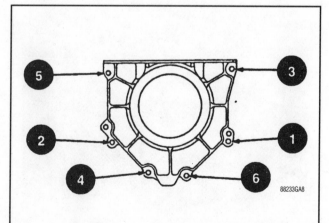

Fig. 181 Position the oil seal retainer against the engine block, then install and tighten the mounting bolts in the sequence shown

88233GA8

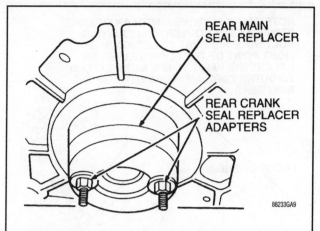

REAR MAIN
SEAL REPLACER

REAR CRANK
SEAL REPLACER
ADAPTERS

88233GA9

Fig. 182 Use a tool specifically designed for installing the rear main oil seal, otherwise the seal may not be sit correctly, leading to possible oil leakage

6. Apply a continuous 0.06 in. (1.5mm) diameter bead of silicone gasket sealant, such as Ford Sealant F6AZ-19562-A, to the engine block as shown in the accompanying illustration.
7. Install the rear oil seal retainer on the engine block, then tighten the mounting fasteners to 71–106 inch lbs. (8–12 Nm) in the sequence shown.
8. Coat the seal and the seal mounting surfaces with oil.
9. Position the seal on rear main seal installer tool (Ford T82L-6701-A or equivalent) and the adapters (Ford T91P-6701-A or equivalent), then position the tool and seal on the rear of the engine.
10. Alternate tightening the seal installer tool bolts until the seal is properly seated.
11. Install the flywheel or flexplate, as applicable.
12. Connect the negative battery cable.

Flywheel/Flexplate

➡**Flexplate is the term for a flywheel mated with an automatic transmission.**

REMOVAL & INSTALLATION

▶ **See Figures 183 and 184**

➡**The ring gear is replaceable only on engines mated with a manual transmission. Engines with automatic transmissions have ring gears which are welded to the flexplate.**

1. Remove the transmission.
2. On manual transmission vehicles, remove the clutch.
3. On automatic transmission vehicles, remove the torque converter from the flywheel.

➡**The flywheel bolts should be loosened a little at a time in a crisscross pattern to avoid warping the flywheel. Also, some vehicles will have an ORANGE bolt hole on the torque converter, which should be matched with the ORANGE line on the flexplate for proper balance. If the flywheel is not equipped with the orange markings, matchmark the flywheel to the engine block so that it can be reinstalled in the original position (of course for this to work the crankshaft cannot be rotated after the flywheel is removed).**

4. Loosen the flywheel bolts (gradually, using several passes of a crisscross pattern) and remove the flywheel from the engine.

➡**On vehicles with manual transmissions, replace the pilot bearing in the end of the crankshaft, if removing the flywheel.**

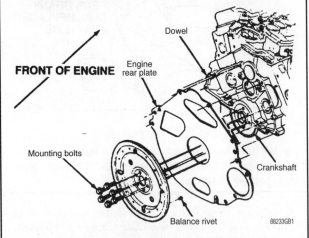

NOTE: MARK FLYWHEEL WITH AN ORANGE STRIPE AT THE CONVERTER MOUNTING BOLT HOLE NEAREST TO LOCATION OF LIGHT POINT OF THE FLYWHEEL AFTER BALANCING. PAINT STRIPE MUST EXTEND TO OUTER EDGE AND PERIPHERY OF THE RING GEAR.

FRONT OF ENGINE

Dowel

Engine rear plate

Mounting bolts

Crankshaft

Balance rivet

88233GB1

Fig. 183 Exploded view of the flywheel mounting on the 3.8L engine

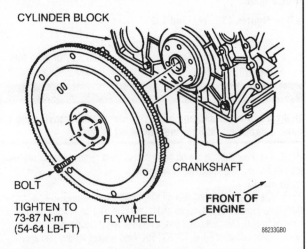

CYLINDER BLOCK

CRANKSHAFT

BOLT

TIGHTEN TO
73-87 N·m
(54-64 LB-FT)

FLYWHEEL

FRONT OF ENGINE

88233GB0

Fig. 184 Exploded view of the flywheel mounting on 4.6L engines

5. The flywheel should be checked for cracks and glazing. It can be resurfaced by a machine shop.

6. If the ring gear is to be replaced, drill a hole in the gear between two teeth, being careful not to contact the flywheel surface. Using a cold chisel at this point, crack the ring gear and remove it.

7. Polish the inner surface of the new ring gear and heat it in an oven to about 600°F (316°C). Quickly place the ring gear on the flywheel and tap it into place, making sure that it is fully seated.

✳✳ WARNING

Never heat the ring gear past 800°F (426°C), or the tempering will be destroyed.

To install:

8. Coat the threads of the flywheel bolts using a Teflon® based pipe sealant.

9. Install the flywheel on the end of the crankshaft. Tighten the bolts a little at a time, in a crisscross pattern, to the torque value shown in the Torque Specifications Chart.

10. Install the clutch or torque converter.

11. Install the transmission.

EXHAUST SYSTEM

Inspection

➡️**Safety glasses should be worn at all times when working on or near the exhaust system. Older exhaust systems will almost always be covered with loose rust particles which will shower you when disturbed. These particles are more than a nuisance and could injure your eye.**

✳✳ CAUTION

Do NOT perform exhaust repairs or inspection with the engine or exhaust hot. Allow the system to cool completely before attempting any work. Exhaust systems are noted for sharp edges, flaking metal and rusted bolts. Gloves and eye protection are required. A healthy supply of penetrating oil and rags is highly recommended.

Your vehicle must be raised and supported safely to inspect the exhaust system properly. By placing 4 safety stands under the vehicle for support should provide enough room for you to slide under the vehicle and inspect the system completely. Start the inspection at the exhaust manifold or turbocharger pipe where the header pipe is attached and work your way to the back of the vehicle. On dual exhaust systems, remember to inspect both sides of the vehicle. Check the complete exhaust system for open seams, holes loose connections, or other deterioration which could permit exhaust fumes to seep into the passenger compartment. Inspect all mounting brackets and hangers for deterioration, some models may have rubber O-rings that can be overstretched and non-supportive.

These components will need to be replaced if found. It has always been a practice to use a pointed tool to poke up into the exhaust system where the deterioration spots are to see whether or not they crumble. Some models may have heat shield covering certain parts of the exhaust system, it will be necessary to remove these shields to have the exhaust visible for inspection also.

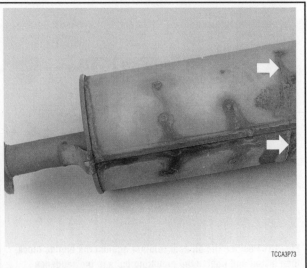

TCCA3P73

Cracks in the muffler are a guaranteed leak

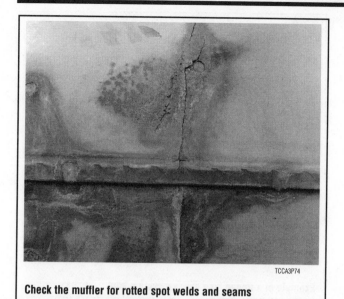

Check the muffler for rotted spot welds and seams

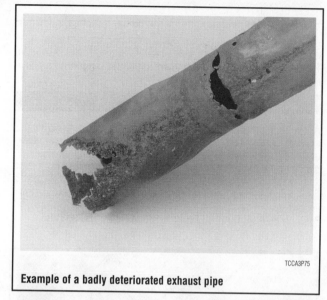

Example of a badly deteriorated exhaust pipe

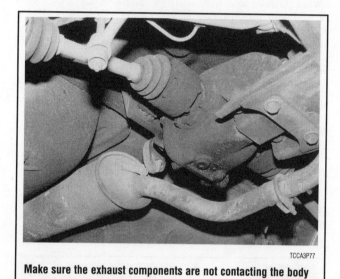

Make sure the exhaust components are not contacting the body or suspension

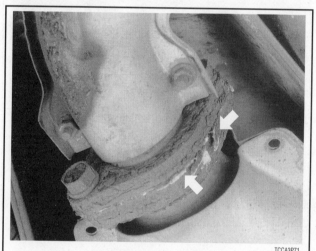

Inspect flanges for gaskets that have deteriorated and need replacement

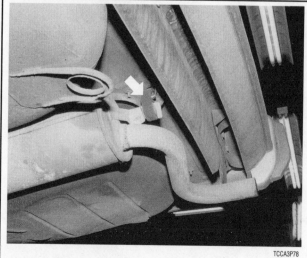

Check for overstretched or torn exhaust hangers

Some systems, like this one, use large O-rings (donuts) in between the flanges

REPLACEMENT

There are basically two types of exhaust systems. One is the flange type where the component ends are attached with bolts and a gasket in-between. The other exhaust system is the slip joint type. These components slip into one another using clamps to retain them together.

❄❄ CAUTION

Allow the exhaust system to cool sufficiently before spraying a solvent exhaust fasteners. Some solvents are highly flammable and could ignite when sprayed on hot exhaust components.

Before removing any component of the exhaust system, ALWAYS squirt a liquid rust dissolving agent onto the fasteners for ease of removal. A lot of knuckle skin will be saved by following this rule. It may even be wise to spray the fasteners and allow them to sit overnight.

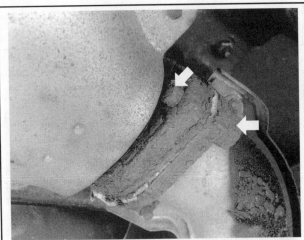

TCCA3P70

Nuts and bolts will be extremely difficult to remove when deteriorated with rust

Flange Type

❄❄ CAUTION

Do NOT perform exhaust repairs or inspection with the engine or exhaust hot. Allow the system to cool completely before attempting any work. Exhaust systems are noted for sharp edges, flaking metal and rusted bolts. Gloves and eye protection are required. A healthy supply of penetrating oil and rags is highly recommended. Never spray liquid rust dissolving agent onto a hot exhaust component.

Before removing any component on a flange type system, ALWAYS squirt a liquid rust dissolving agent onto the fasteners for ease of removal. Start by unbolting the exhaust piece at both ends (if required). When unbolting the headpipe from the manifold, make sure that the bolts are free before trying to remove them. if you snap a stud in the exhaust manifold, the stud will have to be removed with a bolt extractor, which often means removal of the manifold itself. Next, disconnect the component from the mounting; slight twisting and turning may be required to remove the component completely from the vehicle. You may need to tap on the component with a rubber mallet to loosen the component. If all else fails, use a hack-

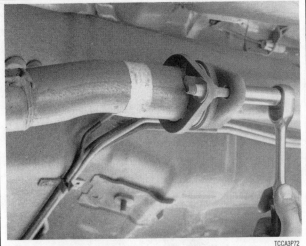

TCCA3P72

Example of a flange type exhaust system joint

saw to separate the parts. An oxy-acetylene cutting torch may be faster but the sparks are DANGEROUS near the fuel tank, and at the very least, accidents could happen, resulting in damage to the under-car parts, not to mention yourself.

Slip Joint Type

Before removing any component on the slip joint type exhaust system, ALWAYS squirt a liquid rust dissolving agent onto the fasteners for ease of removal. Start by unbolting the exhaust piece at both ends (if required). When unbolting the headpipe from the manifold, make sure that the bolts are free before trying to remove them. if you snap a stud in the exhaust manifold, the stud will have to be removed with a bolt extractor, which often means removal of the manifold itself. Next, remove the mounting U-bolts from around the exhaust pipe you are extracting from the vehicle. Don't be surprised if the U-bolts break while removing the nuts. Loosen the exhaust pipe from any mounting brackets retaining it to the floor pan and separate the components.

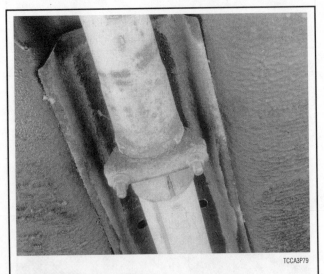

TCCA3P79

Example of a common slip joint type system

ENGINE RECONDITIONING

Determining Engine Condition

Anything that generates heat and/or friction will eventually burn or wear out (i.e., a light bulb generates heat, therefore its life span is limited). With this in mind, a running engine generates tremendous amounts of both; friction is encountered by the moving and rotating parts inside the engine and heat is created by friction and combustion of the fuel. However, the engine has systems designed to help reduce the effects of heat and friction and provide added longevity. The oiling system reduces the amount of friction encountered by the moving parts inside the engine, while the cooling system reduces heat created by friction and combustion. If either system is not maintained, a break-down will be inevitable. Therefore, you can see how regular maintenance can affect the service life of your vehicle. If you do not drain, flush and refill your cooling system at the proper intervals, deposits will begin to accumulate in the radiator, thereby reducing the amount of heat it can extract from the coolant. The same applies to your oil and filter; if it is not changed often enough it becomes laden with contaminates and is unable to properly lubricate the engine. This increases friction and wear.

There are a number of methods for evaluating the condition of your engine. A compression test can reveal the condition of your pistons, piston rings, cylinder bores, head gasket(s), valves and valve seats. An oil pressure test can warn you of possible engine bearing, or oil pump failures. Excessive oil consumption, evidence of oil in the engine air intake area and/or bluish smoke from the tail pipe may indicate worn piston rings, worn valve guides and/or valve seals. As a general rule, an engine that uses no more than one quart of oil every 1,000 miles is in good condition. Engines that use one quart of oil or more in less than 1,000 miles should first be checked for oil leaks. If any oil leaks are present, have them fixed before determining how much oil is consumed by the engine, especially if blue smoke is not visible at the tail pipe.

COMPRESSION TEST

A noticeable lack of engine power, excessive oil consumption and/or poor fuel mileage measured over an extended period are all indicators of internal engine wear. Worn piston rings, scored or worn cylinder bores, blown head gaskets, sticking or burnt valves, and worn valve seats are all possible culprits. A check of each cylinder's compression will help locate the problem.

➡A screw-in type compression gauge is more accurate than the type you simply hold against the spark plug hole. Although it takes slightly longer to use, it's worth the effort to obtain a more accurate reading.

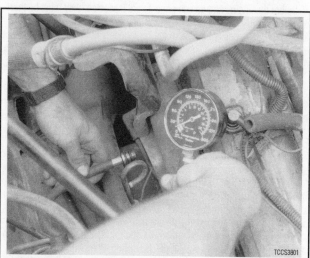

TCCS3801

A screw-in type compression gauge is more accurate and easier to use without an assistant

1. Make sure that the proper amount and viscosity of engine oil is in the crankcase, then ensure the battery is fully charged.
2. Warm-up the engine to normal operating temperature, then shut the engine **OFF**.
3. Disable the ignition system.
4. Label and disconnect all of the spark plug wires from the plugs.
5. Thoroughly clean the cylinder head area around the spark plug ports, then remove the spark plugs.
6. Set the throttle plate to the fully open (wide-open throttle) position. You can block the accelerator linkage open for this, or you can have an assistant fully depress the accelerator pedal.
7. Install a screw-in type compression gauge into the No. 1 spark plug hole until the fitting is snug.

✳✳ WARNING

Be careful not to crossthread the spark plug hole.

8. According to the tool manufacturer's instructions, connect a remote starting switch to the starting circuit.
9. With the ignition switch in the **OFF** position, use the remote starting switch to crank the engine through at least five compression strokes (approximately 5 seconds of cranking) and record the highest reading on the gauge.
10. Repeat the test on each cylinder, cranking the engine approximately the same number of compression strokes and/or time as the first.
11. Compare the highest readings from each cylinder to that of the others. The indicated compression pressures are considered within specifications if the lowest reading cylinder is within 75 percent of the pressure recorded for the highest reading cylinder. For example, if your highest reading cylinder pressure was 150 psi (1,034 kPa), then 75 percent of that would be 113 psi (779 kPa). So the lowest reading cylinder should be no less than 113 psi (779 kPa).
12. If a cylinder exhibits an unusually low compression reading, pour a tablespoon of clean engine oil into the cylinder through the spark plug hole and repeat the compression test. If the compression rises after adding oil, it means that the cylinder's piston rings and/or cylinder bore are damaged or worn. If the pressure remains low, the valves may not be seating properly (a valve job is needed), or the head gasket may be blown near that cylinder. If compression in any two adjacent cylinders is low, and if the addition of oil doesn't help raise compression, there is leakage past the head gasket. Oil and coolant in the combustion chamber, combined with blue or constant white smoke from the tail pipe, are symptoms of this problem. However, don't be alarmed by the normal white smoke emitted from the tail pipe during engine warm-up or from cold weather driving. There may be evidence of water droplets on the engine dipstick and/or oil droplets in the cooling system if a head gasket is blown.

OIL PRESSURE TEST

Check for proper oil pressure at the sending unit passage with an externally mounted mechanical oil pressure gauge (as opposed to relying on a factory installed dash-mounted gauge). A tachometer may also be needed, as some specifications may require running the engine at a specific rpm.
1. With the engine cold, locate and remove the oil pressure sending unit.
2. Following the manufacturer's instructions, connect a mechanical oil pressure gauge and, if necessary, a tachometer to the engine.
3. Start the engine and allow it to idle.
4. Check the oil pressure reading when cold and record the number. You may need to run the engine at a specified rpm, so check the specifications chart located earlier in this section.
5. Run the engine until normal operating temperature is reached (upper radiator hose will feel warm).
6. Check the oil pressure reading again with the engine hot and record the number. Turn the engine **OFF**.

7. Compare your hot oil pressure reading to that given in the chart. If the reading is low, check the cold pressure reading against the chart. If the cold pressure is well above the specification, and the hot reading was lower than the specification, you may have the wrong viscosity oil in the engine. Change the oil, making sure to use the proper grade and quantity, then repeat the test.

Low oil pressure readings could be attributed to internal component wear, pump related problems, a low oil level, or oil viscosity that is too low. High oil pressure readings could be caused by an overfilled crankcase, too high of an oil viscosity or a faulty pressure relief valve.

Buy or Rebuild?

Now that you have determined that your engine is worn out, you must make some decisions. The question of whether or not an engine is worth rebuilding is largely a subjective matter and one of personal worth. Is the engine a popular one, or is it an obsolete model? Are parts available? Will it get acceptable gas mileage once it is rebuilt? Is the car it's being put into worth keeping? Would it be less expensive to buy a new engine, have your engine rebuilt by a pro, rebuild it yourself or buy a used engine from a salvage yard? Or would it be simpler and less expensive to buy another car? If you have considered all these matters and more, and have still decided to rebuild the engine, then it is time to decide how you will rebuild it.

➡The editors at Chilton feel that most engine machining should be performed by a professional machine shop. Don't think of it as wasting money, rather, as an assurance that the job has been done right the first time. There are many expensive and specialized tools required to perform such tasks as boring and honing an engine block or having a valve job done on a cylinder head. Even inspecting the parts requires expensive micrometers and gauges to properly measure wear and clearances. Also, a machine shop can deliver to you clean, and ready to assemble parts, saving you time and aggravation. Your maximum savings will come from performing the removal, disassembly, assembly and installation of the engine and purchasing or renting only the tools required to perform the above tasks. Depending on the particular circumstances, you may save 40 to 60 percent of the cost doing these yourself.

A complete rebuild or overhaul of an engine involves replacing all of the moving parts (pistons, rods, crankshaft, camshaft, etc.) with new ones and machining the non-moving wearing surfaces of the block and heads. Unfortunately, this may not be cost effective. For instance, your crankshaft may have been damaged or worn, but it can be machined undersize for a minimal fee.

So, as you can see, you can replace everything inside the engine, but, it is wiser to replace only those parts which are really needed, and, if possible, repair the more expensive ones. Later in this section, we will break the engine down into its two main components: the cylinder head and the engine block. We will discuss each component, and the recommended parts to replace during a rebuild on each.

Engine Overhaul Tips

Most engine overhaul procedures are fairly standard. In addition to specific parts replacement procedures and specifications for your individual engine, this section is also a guide to acceptable rebuilding procedures. Examples of standard rebuilding practice are given and should be used along with specific details concerning your particular engine.

Competent and accurate machine shop services will ensure maximum performance, reliability and engine life. In most instances it is more profitable for the do-it-yourself mechanic to remove, clean and inspect the component, buy the necessary parts and deliver these to a shop for actual machine work.

Much of the assembly work (crankshaft, bearings, piston rods, and other components) is well within the scope of the do-it-yourself mechanic's tools and abilities. You will have to decide for yourself the depth of involvement you desire in an engine repair or rebuild.

TOOLS

The tools required for an engine overhaul or parts replacement will depend on the depth of your involvement. With a few exceptions, they will be the tools found in a mechanic's tool kit (see Section 1 of this manual). More in-depth work will require some or all of the following:
- A dial indicator (reading in thousandths) mounted on a universal base
- Micrometers and telescope gauges
- Jaw and screw-type pullers
- Scraper
- Valve spring compressor
- Ring groove cleaner
- Piston ring expander and compressor
- Ridge reamer
- Cylinder hone or glaze breaker
- Plastigage®
- Engine stand

The use of most of these tools is illustrated in this section. Many can be rented for a one-time use from a local parts jobber or tool supply house specializing in automotive work.

Occasionally, the use of special tools is called for. See the information on Special Tools and the Safety Notice in the front of this book before substituting another tool.

OVERHAUL TIPS

Aluminum has become extremely popular for use in engines, due to its low weight. Observe the following precautions when handling aluminum parts:
- Never hot tank aluminum parts (the caustic hot tank solution will eat the aluminum.
- Remove all aluminum parts (identification tag, etc.) from engine parts prior to the tanking.
- Always coat threads lightly with engine oil or anti-seize compounds before installation, to prevent seizure.
- Never overtighten bolts or spark plugs especially in aluminum threads.

When assembling the engine, any parts that will be exposed to frictional contact must be prelubed to provide lubrication at initial start-up. Any product specifically formulated for this purpose can be used, but engine oil is not recommended as a prelube in most cases.

When semi-permanent (locked, but removable) installation of bolts or nuts is desired, threads should be cleaned and coated with Loctite® or another similar, commercial non-hardening sealant.

CLEANING

Before the engine and its components are inspected, they must be thoroughly cleaned. You will need to remove any engine varnish, oil sludge and/or carbon deposits from all of the components to insure an accurate inspection. A crack in the engine block or cylinder head can easily become overlooked if hidden by a layer of sludge or carbon.

Most of the cleaning process can be carried out with common hand tools and readily available solvents or solutions. Carbon deposits can be chipped away using a hammer and a hard wooden chisel. Old gasket material and varnish or sludge can usually be removed using a scraper and/or cleaning solvent. Extremely stubborn deposits may require the use of a power drill with a wire brush. If using a wire brush, use extreme care around any critical machined surfaces (such as the gasket surfaces, bearing saddles, cylinder bores, etc.). USE OF A WIRE BRUSH IS NOT RECOMMENDED ON ANY ALUMINUM COMPONENTS. Always follow any safety recommendations given by the manufacturer of the tool and/or solvent. You should always wear eye protection during any cleaning process involving scraping, chipping or spraying of solvents.

An alternative to the mess and hassle of cleaning the parts yourself is to drop them off at a local garage or machine shop. They will, more than likely, have the necessary equipment to properly clean all of the parts for a nominal fee.

Use a gasket scraper to remove the old gasket material from the mating surfaces

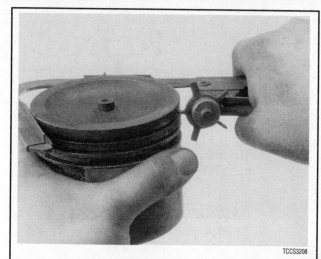
Clean the piston ring grooves using a ring groove cleaner tool, or . . .

Use a ring expander tool to remove the piston rings

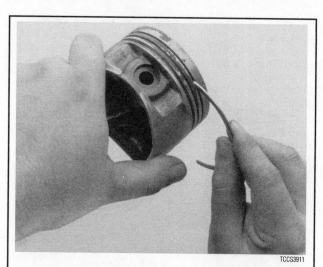
. . . use a piece of an old ring to clean the grooves. Be careful, the ring can be quite sharp

✳✳ CAUTION

Always wear eye protection during any cleaning process involving scraping, shipping or spraying of solvents.

Remove any oil galley plugs, freeze plugs and/or pressed-in bearings and carefully wash and degrease all of the engine components including the fasteners and bolts. Small parts such as the valves, springs, etc., should be placed in a metal basket and allowed to soak. Use pipe cleaner type brushes, and clean all passageways in the components. Use a ring expander and remove the rings from the pistons. Clean the piston ring grooves with a special tool or a piece of broken ring. Scrape the carbon off of the top of the piston. You should never use a wire brush on the pistons. After preparing all of the piston assemblies in this manner, wash and degrease them again.

✳✳ WARNING

Use extreme care when cleaning around the cylinder head valve seats. A mistake or slip may cost you a new seat.

When cleaning the cylinder head, remove carbon from the combustion chamber with the valves installed. This will avoid damaging the valve seats.

REPAIRING DAMAGED THREADS

▶ See Figures 185, 186, 187, 188 and 189

Several methods of repairing damaged threads are available. Heli-Coil® (shown here), Keenserts® and Microdot® are among the most widely used. All involve basically the same principle—drilling out stripped threads, tapping the hole and installing a prewound insert—making welding, plugging and oversize fasteners unnecessary.

Two types of thread repair inserts are usually supplied: a standard type for most inch coarse, inch fine, metric course and metric fine thread sizes and a spark lug type to fit most spark plug port sizes. Consult the individual tool manufacturer's catalog to determine exact applications. Typical thread repair kits will contain a selection of prewound threaded inserts, a tap (corresponding to the outside diameter threads of the insert) and an installation tool. Spark plug inserts usually differ because they require a tap equipped with pilot threads and a combined reamer/tap section. Most manufacturers also supply blister-packed thread repair inserts separately in addition to a master kit containing a variety of taps and inserts plus installation tools.

Before attempting to repair a threaded hole, remove any snapped, broken or damaged bolts or studs. Penetrating oil can be used to free frozen threads. The offending item can usually be removed with locking pliers or

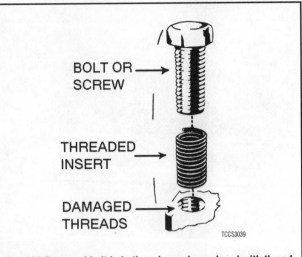

Fig. 185 Damaged bolt hole threads can be replaced with thread repair inserts

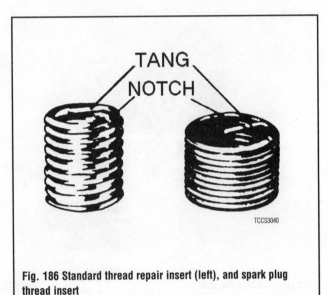

Fig. 186 Standard thread repair insert (left), and spark plug thread insert

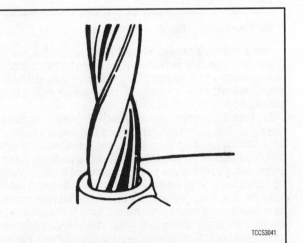

Fig. 187 Drill out the damaged threads with the specified size bit. Be sure to drill completely through the hole or to the bottom of a blind hole

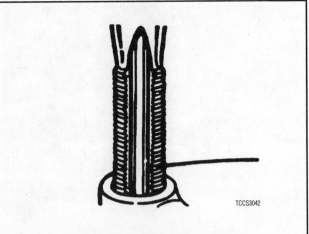

Fig. 188 Using the kit, tap the hole in order to receive the thread insert. Keep the tap well oiled and back it out frequently to avoid clogging the threads

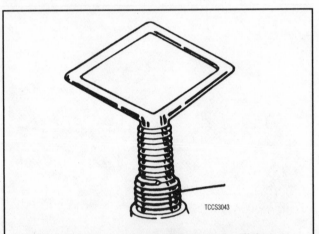

Fig. 189 Screw the insert onto the installer tool until the tang engages the slot. Thread the insert into the hole until it is ¼ –½ turn below the top surface, then remove the tool and break off the tang using a punch

using a screw/stud extractor. After the hole is clear, the thread can be repaired, as shown in the series of accompanying illustrations and in the kit manufacturer's instructions.

Engine Preparation

To properly rebuild an engine, you must first remove it from the vehicle, then disassemble and diagnose it. Ideally you should place your engine on an engine stand. This affords you the best access to the engine components. Follow the manufacturer's directions for using the stand with your particular engine. Remove the flywheel or flexplate before installing the engine to the stand.

Now that you have the engine on a stand, and assuming that you have drained the oil and coolant from the engine, it's time to strip it of all but the necessary components. Before you start disassembling the engine, you may want to take a moment to draw some pictures, or fabricate some labels or containers to mark the locations of various components and the bolts and/or studs which fasten them. Modern day engines use a lot of little brackets and clips which hold wiring harnesses and such, and these holders are often mounted on studs and/or bolts that can be easily mixed up. The manufacturer spent a lot of time and money designing your vehicle, and they wouldn't have wasted any of it by haphazardly placing brackets, clips or fasteners on the vehicle. If it's present when you disassemble it, put it back when you assemble, you will regret not remembering that little bracket which holds a wire harness out of the path of a rotating part.

You should begin by unbolting any accessories still attached to the engine, such as the water pump, power steering pump, alternator, etc. Then, unfasten any manifolds (intake or exhaust) which were not removed during the engine removal procedure. Finally, remove any covers remaining on the engine such as the rocker arm, front or timing cover and oil pan. Some front covers may require the vibration damper and/or crank pulley to be removed beforehand. The idea is to reduce the engine to the bare necessities (cylinder head(s), valve train, engine block, crankshaft, pistons and connecting rods), plus any other 'in block' components such as oil pumps, balance shafts and auxiliary shafts.

Finally, remove the cylinder head(s) from the engine block and carefully place on a bench. Disassembly instructions for each component follow later in this section.

Cylinder Head

There are two basic types of cylinder heads used on today's automobiles: the Overhead Valve (OHV) and the Overhead Camshaft (OHC). The latter can also be broken down into two subgroups: the Single Overhead Camshaft (SOHC) and the Dual Overhead Camshaft (DOHC). Generally, if there is only a single camshaft on a head, it is just referred to as an OHC head. Also, an engine with a OHV cylinder head is also known as a pushrod engine.

Most cylinder heads these days are made of an aluminum alloy due to its light weight, durability and heat transfer qualities. However, cast iron was the material of choice in the past, and is still used on many vehicles today. Whether made from aluminum or iron, all cylinder heads have valves and seats. Some use two valves per cylinder, while the more hi-tech engines will utilize a multi-valve configuration using 3, 4 and even 5 valves per cylinder. When the valve contacts the seat, it does so on precision machined surfaces, which seals the combustion chamber. All cylinder heads have a valve guide for each valve. The guide centers the valve to the seat and allows it to move up and down within it. The clearance between the valve and guide can be critical. Too much clearance and the engine may consume oil, lose vacuum and/or damage the seat. Too little, and the valve can stick in the guide causing the engine to run poorly if at all, and possibly causing severe damage. The last component all cylinder heads have are valve springs. The spring holds the valve against its seat. It also returns the valve to this position when the valve has been opened by the valve train or camshaft. The spring is fastened to the valve by a retainer and valve locks (sometimes called keepers). Aluminum heads will also have a valve spring shim to keep the spring from wearing away the aluminum.

An ideal method of rebuilding the cylinder head would involve replacing all of the valves, guides, seats, springs, etc. with new ones. However, depending on how the engine was maintained, often this is not necessary. A major cause of valve, guide and seat wear is an improperly tuned engine. An engine that is running too rich, will often wash the lubricating oil out of the guide with gasoline, causing it to wear rapidly. Conversely, an engine which is running too lean will place higher combustion temperatures on the valves and seats allowing them to wear or even burn. Springs fall victim to the driving habits of the individual. A driver who often runs the engine rpm to the redline will wear out or break the springs faster then one that stays well below it. Unfortunately, mileage takes it toll on all of the parts. Generally, the valves, guides, springs and seats in a cylinder head can be machined and re-used, saving you money. However, if a valve is burnt, it may be wise to replace all of the valves, since they were all operating in the same environment. The same goes for any other component on the cylinder head. Think of it as an insurance policy against future problems related to that component.

Unfortunately, the only way to find out which components need replacing, is to disassemble and carefully check each piece. After the cylinder head(s) are disassembled, thoroughly clean all of the components.

DISASSEMBLY

OHV Heads

Before disassembling the cylinder head, you may want to fabricate some containers to hold the various parts, as some of them can be quite small (such as keepers) and easily lost. Also keeping yourself and the components organized will aid in assembly and reduce confusion. Where possible, try to maintain a components original location; this is especially important if there is not going to be any machine work performed on the components.

1. If you haven't already removed the rocker arms and/or shafts, do so now.
2. Position the head so that the springs are easily accessed.
3. Use a valve spring compressor tool, and relieve spring tension from the retainer.

➡**Due to engine varnish, the retainer may stick to the valve locks. A gentle tap with a hammer may help to break it loose.**

4. Remove the valve locks from the valve tip and/or retainer. A small magnet may help in removing the locks.
5. Lift the valve spring, tool and all, off of the valve stem.
6. If equipped, remove the valve seal. If the seal is difficult to remove

TCCS3137

When removing an OHV valve spring, use a compressor tool to relieve the tension from the retainer

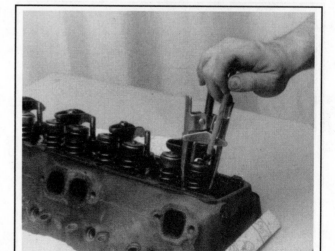

TCCS3138

A small magnet will help in removal of the valve locks

Remove the valve seal from the valve stem—O-ring type seal shown

Removing an umbrella/positive type seal

Invert the cylinder head and withdraw the valve from the valve guide bore

with the valve in place, try removing the valve first, then the seal. Follow the steps below for valve removal.

7. Position the head to allow access for withdrawing the valve.

➡Cylinder heads that have seen a lot of miles and/or abuse may have mushroomed the valve lock grove and/or tip, causing difficulty in removal of the valve. If this has happened, use a metal file to carefully remove the high spots around the lock grooves and/or tip. Only file it enough to allow removal.

8. Remove the valve from the cylinder head.

9. If equipped, remove the valve spring shim. A small magnetic tool or screwdriver will aid in removal.

10. Repeat Steps 3 though 9 until all of the valves have been removed.

OHC Heads

Whether it is a single or dual overhead camshaft cylinder head, the disassembly procedure is relatively unchanged. One aspect to pay attention to is careful labeling of the parts on the dual camshaft cylinder head. There will be an intake camshaft and followers as well as an exhaust camshaft and followers and they must be labeled as such. In some cases, the compo-

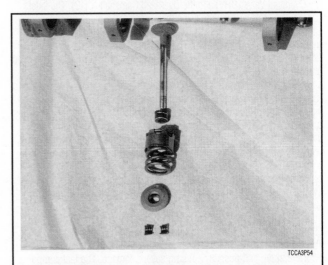

Exploded view of a valve, seal, spring, retainer and locks from an OHC cylinder head

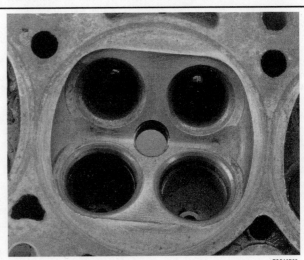

Example of a multivalve cylinder head. Note how it has 2 intake and 2 exhaust valve ports

nents are identical and could easily be installed incorrectly. DO NOT MIX THEM UP! Determining which is which is very simple; the intake camshaft and components are on the same side of the head as was the intake manifold. Conversely, the exhaust camshaft and components are on the same side of the head as was the exhaust manifold.

CUP-TYPE CAMSHAFT FOLLOWERS

Most cylinder heads with cup type camshaft followers will have the valve spring, retainer and locks recessed within the follower's bore. You will need a C-clamp style valve spring compressor tool, an OHC spring removal tool (or equivalent) and a small magnet to disassemble the head.

1. If not already removed, remove the camshaft(s) and/or followers. Mark their positions for assembly.

2. Position the cylinder head to allow use of a C-clamp style valve spring compressor tool.

➡️**It is preferred to position the cylinder head gasket surface facing you with the valve springs facing the opposite direction and the head laying horizontal.**

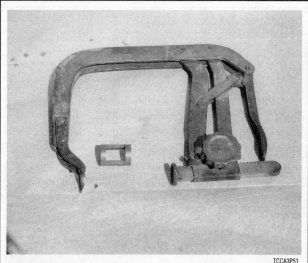

C-clamp type spring compressor and an OHC spring removal tool (center) for cup type followers

Most cup type follower cylinder heads retain the camshaft using bolt-on bearing caps

Position the OHC spring tool in the follower bore, then compress the spring with a C-clamp type tool

3. With the OHC spring removal adapter tool positioned inside of the follower bore, compress the valve spring using the C-clamp style valve spring compressor.

4. Remove the valve locks. A small magnetic tool or screwdriver will aid in removal.

5. Release the compressor tool and remove the spring assembly.

6. Withdraw the valve from the cylinder head.

7. If equipped, remove the valve seal.

➡️**Special valve seal removal tools are available. Regular or needle nose type pliers, if used with care, will work just as well. If using ordinary pliers, be sure not to damage the follower bore. The follower and its bore are machined to close tolerances and any damage to the bore will affect this relationship.**

8. If equipped, remove the valve spring shim. A small magnetic tool or screwdriver will aid in removal.

9. Repeat Steps 3 through 8 until all of the valves have been removed.

ROCKER ARM TYPE CAMSHAFT FOLLOWERS

Most cylinder heads with rocker arm-type camshaft followers are easily disassembled using a standard valve spring compressor. However, certain models may not have enough open space around the spring for the standard tool and may require you to use a C-clamp style compressor tool instead.

1. If not already removed, remove the rocker arms and/or shafts and the camshaft. If applicable, also remove the hydraulic lash adjusters. Mark their positions for assembly.

2. Position the cylinder head to allow access to the valve spring.

3. Use a valve spring compressor tool to relieve the spring tension from the retainer.

➡️**Due to engine varnish, the retainer may stick to the valve locks. A gentle tap with a hammer may help to break it loose.**

4. Remove the valve locks from the valve tip and/or retainer. A small magnet may help in removing the small locks.

5. Lift the valve spring, tool and all, off of the valve stem.

6. If equipped, remove the valve seal. If the seal is difficult to remove with the valve in place, try removing the valve first, then the seal. Follow the steps below for valve removal.

7. Position the head to allow access for withdrawing the valve.

Example of the shaft mounted rocker arms on some OHC heads

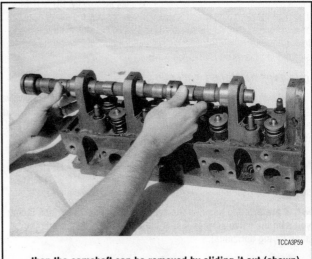

. . . then the camshaft can be removed by sliding it out (shown), or unbolting a bearing cap (not shown)

Another example of the rocker arm type OHC head. This model uses a follower under the camshaft

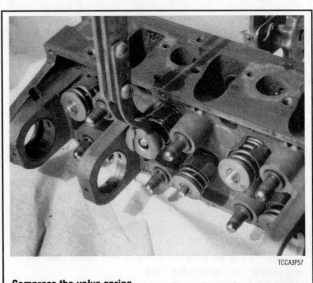

Compress the valve spring . . .

Before the camshaft can be removed, all of the followers must first be removed . . .

. . . then remove the valve locks from the valve stem and spring retainer

Remove the valve spring and retainer from the cylinder head

Remove the valve seal from the guide. Some gentle prying or pliers may help to remove stubborn ones

All aluminum and some cast iron heads will have these valve spring shims. Remove all of them as well

➡Cylinder heads that have seen a lot of miles and/or abuse may have mushroomed the valve lock grove and/or tip, causing difficulty in removal of the valve. If this has happened, use a metal file to carefully remove the high spots around the lock grooves and/or tip. Only file it enough to allow removal.

8. Remove the valve from the cylinder head.
9. If equipped, remove the valve spring shim. A small magnetic tool or screwdriver will aid in removal.
10. Repeat Steps 3 though 9 until all of the valves have been removed.

INSPECTION

Now that all of the cylinder head components are clean, it's time to inspect them for wear and/or damage. To accurately inspect them, you will need some specialized tools:

- A 0–1 inch micrometer for the valves
- A dial indicator or inside diameter gauge for the valve guides
- A spring pressure test gauge

If you do not have access to the proper tools, you may want to bring the components to a shop that does.

Valves

The first thing to inspect are the valve heads. Look closely at the head, margin and face for any cracks, excessive wear or burning. The margin is the best place to look for burning. It should have a squared edge with an even width all around the diameter. When a valve burns, the margin will look melted and the edges rounded. Also inspect the valve head for any signs of tulipping. This will show as a lifting of the edges or dishing in the center of the head and will usually not occur to all of the valves. All of the heads should look the same, any that seem dished more than others are probably bad. Next, inspect the valve lock grooves and valve tips. Check for any burrs around the lock grooves, especially if you had to file them to remove the valve. Valve tips should appear flat, although slight rounding with high mileage engines is normal. Slightly worn valve tips will need to be machined flat. Last, measure the valve stem diameter with the micrometer. Measure the area that rides within the guide, especially towards the tip where most of the wear occurs. Take several measurements along its length and compare them to each other. Wear should be even along the length with little to no taper. If no minimum diameter is given in the specifications, then the stem should not read more than 0.001 in. (0.025mm) below the specification. Any valves that fail these inspections should be replaced.

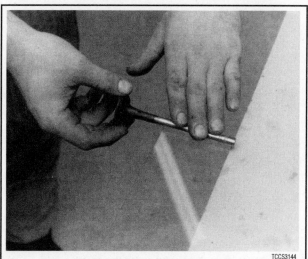

Valve stems may be rolled on a flat surface to check for bends

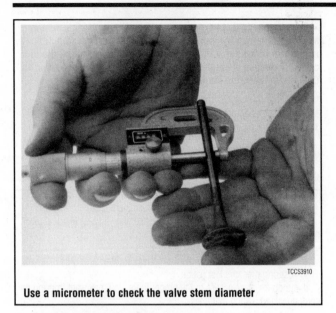

Use a micrometer to check the valve stem diameter

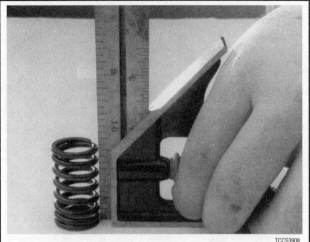

Check the valve spring for squareness on a flat surface; a carpenter's square can be used

Springs, Retainers and Valve Locks

The first thing to check is the most obvious, broken springs. Next check the free length and squareness of each spring. If applicable, insure to distinguish between intake and exhaust springs. Use a ruler and/or carpenters square to measure the length. A carpenters square should be used to check the springs for squareness. If a spring pressure test gauge is available, check each springs rating and compare to the specifications chart. Check the readings against the specifications given. Any springs that fail these inspections should be replaced.

The spring retainers rarely need replacing, however they should still be checked as a precaution. Inspect the spring mating surface and the valve lock retention area for any signs of excessive wear. Also check for any signs of cracking. Replace any retainers that are questionable.

Valve locks should be inspected for excessive wear on the outside contact area as well as on the inner notched surface. Any locks which appear worn or broken and its respective valve should be replaced.

Cylinder Head

There are several things to check on the cylinder head: valve guides, seats, cylinder head surface flatness, cracks and physical damage.

VALVE GUIDES

Now that you know the valves are good, you can use them to check the guides, although a new valve, if available, is preferred. Before you measure anything, look at the guides carefully and inspect them for any cracks, chips or breakage. Also if the guide is a removable style (as in most aluminum heads), check them for any looseness or evidence of movement. All of the guides should appear to be at the same height from the spring seat. If any seem lower (or higher) from another, the guide has moved. Mount a dial indicator onto the spring side of the cylinder head. Lightly oil the valve stem and insert it into the cylinder head. Position the dial indicator against the valve stem near the tip and zero the gauge. Grasp the valve stem and wiggle towards and away from the dial indicator and observe the readings. Mount the dial indicator 90 degrees from the initial point and zero the gauge and again take a reading. Compare the two readings for a out of round condition. Check the readings against the specifications given. An Inside Diameter (I.D.) gauge designed for valve guides will give you an accurate valve guide bore measurement. If the I.D. gauge is used, compare the readings with the specifications given. Any guides that fail these inspections should be replaced or machined.

Use a caliper to check the valve spring free-length

A dial gauge may be used to check valve stem-to-guide clearance; read the gauge while moving the valve stem

VALVE SEATS

A visual inspection of the valve seats should show a slightly worn and pitted surface where the valve face contacts the seat. Inspect the seat carefully for severe pitting or cracks. Also, a seat that is badly worn will be recessed into the cylinder head. A severely worn or recessed seat may need to be replaced. All cracked seats must be replaced. A seat concentricity gauge, if available, should be used to check the seat run-out. If run-out exceeds specifications the seat must be machined (if no specification is given use 0.002 in. or 0.051mm).

CYLINDER HEAD SURFACE FLATNESS

After you have cleaned the gasket surface of the cylinder head of any old gasket material, check the head for flatness.

Place a straightedge across the gasket surface. Using feeler gauges, determine the clearance at the center of the straightedge and across the cylinder head at several points. Check along the centerline and diagonally on the head surface. If the warpage exceeds 0.003 in. (0.076mm) within a 6.0 in. (15.2cm) span, or 0.006 in. (0.152mm) over the total length of the head, the cylinder head must be resurfaced. After resurfacing the heads of a V-type engine, the intake manifold flange surface should be checked, and if necessary, milled proportionally to allow for the change in its mounting position.

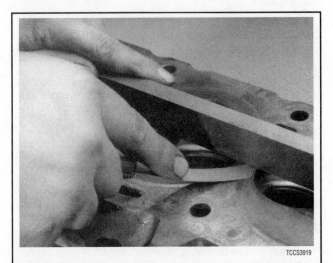

TCCS3919

Check the head for flatness across the center of the head surface using a straightedge and feeler gauge

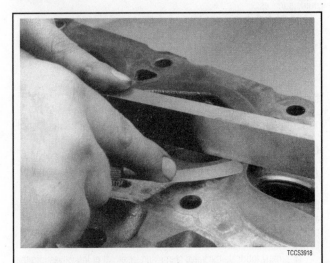

TCCS3918

Checks should also be made along both diagonals of the head surface

CRACKS AND PHYSICAL DAMAGE

Generally, cracks are limited to the combustion chamber, however, it is not uncommon for the head to crack in a spark plug hole, port, outside of the head or in the valve spring/rocker arm area. The first area to inspect is always the hottest: the exhaust seat/port area.

A visual inspection should be performed, but just because you don't see a crack does not mean it is not there. Some more reliable methods for inspecting for cracks include Magnaflux®, a magnetic process or Zyglo®, a dye penetrant. Magnaflux® is used only on ferrous metal (cast iron) heads. Zyglo® uses a spray on fluorescent mixture along with a black light to reveal the cracks. It is strongly recommended to have your cylinder head checked professionally for cracks, especially if the engine was known to have overheated and/or leaked or consumed coolant. Contact a local shop for availability and pricing of these services.

Physical damage is usually very evident. For example, a broken mounting ear from dropping the head or a bent or broken stud and/or bolt. All of these defects should be fixed or, if unrepairable, the head should be replaced.

Camshaft and Followers

Inspect the camshaft(s) and followers on OHC engines as described earlier in this section.

REFINISHING & REPAIRING

Many of the procedures given for refinishing and repairing the cylinder head components must be performed by a machine shop. Certain steps, if the inspected part is not worn, can be performed yourself inexpensively. However, you spent a lot of time and effort so far, why risk trying to save a couple bucks if you might have to do it all over again?

Valves

Any valves that were not replaced should be refaced and the tips ground flat. Unless you have access to a valve grinding machine, this should be done by a machine shop. If the valves are in extremely good condition, as well as the valve seats and guides, they may be lapped in without performing machine work.

It is a recommended practice to lap the valves even after machine work has been performed and/or new valves have been purchased. This insures a positive seal between the valve and seat.

LAPPING THE VALVES

➡**Before lapping the valves to the seats, read the rest of the cylinder head section to insure that any related parts are in acceptable enough condition to continue.**

➡**Before any valve seat machining and/or lapping can be performed, the guides must be within factory recommended specifications.**

1. Invert the cylinder head.
2. Lightly lubricate the valve stems and insert them into the cylinder head in their numbered order.
3. Raise the valve from the seat and apply a small amount of fine lapping compound to the seat.
4. Moisten the suction head of a hand-lapping tool and attach it to the head of the valve.
5. Rotate the tool between the palms of both hands, changing the position of the valve on the valve seat and lifting the tool often to prevent grooving.
6. Lap the valve until a smooth, polished circle is evident on the valve and seat.
7. Remove the tool and the valve. Wipe away all traces of the grinding compound and store the valve to maintain its lapped location.

❊❊ WARNING

Do not get the valves out of order after they have been lapped. They must be put back with the same valve seat they were lapped with.

Springs, Retainers and Valve Locks

There is no repair or refinishing possible with the springs, retainers and valve locks. If they are found to be worn or defective, they must be replaced with new (or known good) parts.

Cylinder Head

Most refinishing procedures dealing with the cylinder head must be performed by a machine shop. Read the sections below and review your inspection data to determine whether or not machining is necessary.

VALVE GUIDE

➡**If any machining or replacements are made to the valve guides, the seats must be machined.**

Unless the valve guides need machining or replacing, the only service to perform is to thoroughly clean them of any dirt or oil residue.

There are only two types of valve guides used on automobile engines: the replaceable-type (all aluminum heads) and the cast-in integral-type (most cast iron heads). There are four recommended methods for repairing worn guides.

- Knurling
- Inserts
- Reaming oversize
- Replacing

Knurling is a process in which metal is displaced and raised, thereby reducing clearance, giving a true center, and providing oil control. It is the least expensive way of repairing the valve guides. However, it is not necessarily the best, and in some cases, a knurled valve guide will not stand up for more than a short time. It requires a special knurlizer and precision reaming tools to obtain proper clearances. It would not be cost effective to purchase these tools, unless you plan on rebuilding several of the same cylinder head.

Installing a guide insert involves machining the guide to accept a bronze insert. One style is the coil-type which is installed into a threaded guide. Another is the thin-walled insert where the guide is reamed oversize to accept a split-sleeve insert. After the insert is installed, a special tool is then run through the guide to expand the insert, locking it to the guide. The insert is then reamed to the standard size for proper valve clearance.

Reaming for oversize valves restores normal clearances and provides a true valve seat. Most cast-in type guides can be reamed to accept an valve with an oversize stem. The cost factor for this can become quite high as you will need to purchase the reamer and new, oversize stem valves for all guides which were reamed. Oversizes are generally 0.003 to 0.030 in. (0.076 to 0.762mm), with 0.015 in. (0.381mm) being the most common.

To replace cast-in type valve guides, they must be drilled out, then reamed to accept replacement guides. This must be done on a fixture which will allow centering and leveling off of the original valve seat or guide, otherwise a serious guide-to-seat misalignment may occur making it impossible to properly machine the seat.

Replaceable-type guides are pressed into the cylinder head. A hammer and a stepped drift or punch may be used to install and remove the guides. Before removing the guides, measure the protrusion on the spring side of the head and record it for installation. Use the stepped drift to hammer out the old guide from the combustion chamber side of the head. When installing, determine whether or not the guide also seals a water jacket in the head, and if it does, use the recommended sealing agent. If there is no water jacket, grease the valve guide and its bore. Use the stepped drift, and hammer the new guide into the cylinder head from the spring side of the cylinder head. A stack of washers the same thickness as the measured protrusion may help the installation process.

VALVE SEATS

➡**Before any valve seat machining can be performed, the guides must be within factory recommended specifications.**

➡**If any machining or replacements were made to the valve guides, the seats must be machined.**

If the seats are in good condition, the valves can be lapped to the seats, and the cylinder head assembled. See the valves section for instructions on lapping.

If the valve seats are worn, cracked or damaged, they must be serviced by a machine shop. The valve seat must be perfectly centered to the valve guide, which requires very accurate machining.

CYLINDER HEAD SURFACE

If the cylinder head is warped, it must be machined flat. If the warpage is extremely severe, the head may need to be replaced. In some instances, it may be possible to straighten a warped head enough to allow machining. In either case, contact a professional machine shop for service.

➡**Any OHC cylinder head that shows excessive warpage should have the camshaft bearing journals align bored after the cylinder head has been resurfaced.**

✳✳ WARNING

Failure to align bore the camshaft bearing journals could result in severe engine damage including but not limited to: valve and piston damage, connecting rod damage, camshaft and/or crankshaft breakage.

CRACKS AND PHYSICAL DAMAGE

Certain cracks can be repaired in both cast iron and aluminum heads. For cast iron, a tapered threaded insert is installed along the length of the crack. Aluminum can also use the tapered inserts, however welding is the preferred method. Some physical damage can be repaired through brazing or welding. Contact a machine shop to get expert advice for your particular dilemma.

ASSEMBLY

The first step for any assembly job is to have a clean area in which to work. Next, thoroughly clean all of the parts and components that are to be assembled. Finally, place all of the components onto a suitable work space and, if necessary, arrange the parts to their respective positions.

OHV Engines

1. Lightly lubricate the valve stems and insert all of the valves into the cylinder head. If possible, maintain their original locations.
2. If equipped, install any valve spring shims which were removed.
3. If equipped, install the new valve seals, keeping the following in mind:
- If the valve seal presses over the guide, lightly lubricate the outer guide surfaces.
- If the seal is an O-ring type, it is installed just after compressing the spring but before the valve locks.
4. Place the valve spring and retainer over the stem.
5. Position the spring compressor tool and compress the spring.
6. Assemble the valve locks to the stem.
7. Relieve the spring pressure slowly and insure that neither valve lock becomes dislodged by the retainer.
8. Remove the spring compressor tool.
9. Repeat Steps 2 through 8 until all of the springs have been installed.

OHC Engines

CUP-TYPE CAMSHAFT FOLLOWERS

To install the springs, retainers and valve locks on heads which have these components recessed into the camshaft follower's bore, you will need a small screwdriver-type tool, some clean white grease and a lot of patience. You will also need the C-clamp style spring compressor and the OHC tool used to disassemble the head.

1. Lightly lubricate the valve stems and insert all of the valves into the cylinder head. If possible, maintain their original locations.
2. If equipped, install any valve spring shims which were removed.

TCCA3P64

Once assembled, check the valve clearance and correct as needed

3. If equipped, install the new valve seals, keeping the following in mind:
   • If the valve seal presses over the guide, lightly lubricate the outer guide surfaces.
   • If the seal is an O-ring type, it is installed just after compressing the spring but before the valve locks.

4. Place the valve spring and retainer over the stem.

5. Position the spring compressor and the OHC tool, then compress the spring.

6. Using a small screwdriver as a spatula, fill the valve stem side of the lock with white grease. Use the excess grease on the screwdriver to fasten the lock to the driver.

7. Carefully install the valve lock, which is stuck to the end of the screwdriver, to the valve stem then press on it with the screwdriver until the grease squeezes out. The valve lock should now be stuck to the stem.

8. Repeat Steps 6 and 7 for the remaining valve lock.

9. Relieve the spring pressure slowly and insure that neither valve lock becomes dislodged by the retainer.

10. Remove the spring compressor tool.

11. Repeat Steps 2 through 10 until all of the springs have been installed.

12. Install the followers, camshaft(s) and any other components that were removed for disassembly.

ROCKER ARM TYPE CAMSHAFT FOLLOWERS

1. Lightly lubricate the valve stems and insert all of the valves into the cylinder head. If possible, maintain their original locations.

2. If equipped, install any valve spring shims which were removed.

3. If equipped, install the new valve seals, keeping the following in mind:
   • If the valve seal presses over the guide, lightly lubricate the outer guide surfaces.
   • If the seal is an O-ring type, it is installed just after compressing the spring but before the valve locks.

4. Place the valve spring and retainer over the stem.

5. Position the spring compressor tool and compress the spring.

6. Assemble the valve locks to the stem.

7. Relieve the spring pressure slowly and insure that neither valve lock becomes dislodged by the retainer.

8. Remove the spring compressor tool.

9. Repeat Steps 2 through 8 until all of the springs have been installed.

10. Install the camshaft(s), rockers, shafts and any other components that were removed for disassembly.

Engine Block

GENERAL INFORMATION

A thorough overhaul or rebuild of an engine block would include replacing the pistons, rings, bearings, timing belt/chain assembly and oil pump. For OHV engines also include a new camshaft and lifters. The block would then have the cylinders bored and honed oversize (or if using removable cylinder sleeves, new sleeves installed) and the crankshaft would be cut undersize to provide new wearing surfaces and perfect clearances. However, your particular engine may not have everything worn out. What if only the piston rings have worn out and the clearances on everything else are still within factory specifications? Well, you could just replace the rings and put it back together, but this would be a very rare example. Chances are, if one component in your engine is worn, other components are sure to follow, and soon. At the very least, you should always replace the rings, bearings and oil pump. This is what is commonly called a "freshen up".

Cylinder Ridge Removal

Because the top piston ring does not travel to the very top of the cylinder, a ridge is built up between the end of the travel and the top of the cylinder bore.

Pushing the piston and connecting rod assembly past the ridge can be difficult, and damage to the piston ring lands could occur. If the ridge is not removed before installing a new piston or not removed at all, piston ring breakage and piston damage may occur.

➡**It is always recommended that you remove any cylinder ridges before removing the piston and connecting rod assemblies. If you know that new pistons are going to be installed and the engine block will be bored oversize, you may be able to forego this step. However, some ridges may actually prevent the assemblies from being removed, necessitating its removal.**

There are several different types of ridge reamers on the market, none of which are inexpensive. Unless a great deal of engine rebuilding is anticipated, borrow or rent a reamer.

1. Turn the crankshaft until the piston is at the bottom of its travel.

2. Cover the head of the piston with a rag.

3. Follow the tool manufacturers instructions and cut away the ridge, exercising extreme care to avoid cutting too deeply.

4. Remove the ridge reamer, the rag and as many of the cuttings as possible. Continue until all of the cylinder ridges have been removed.

DISASSEMBLY

The engine disassembly instructions following assume that you have the engine mounted on an engine stand. If not, it is easiest to disassemble the engine on a bench or the floor with it resting on the bellhousing or transmission mounting surface. You must be able to access the connecting rod fasteners and turn the crankshaft during disassembly. Also, all engine covers (timing, front, side, oil pan, whatever) should have already been removed. Engines which are seized or locked up may not be able to be completely disassembled, and a core (salvage yard) engine should be purchased.

Pushrod Engines

If not done during the cylinder head removal, remove the pushrods and lifters, keeping them in order for assembly. Remove the timing gears and/or timing chain assembly, then remove the oil pump drive assembly and withdraw the camshaft from the engine block. Remove the oil pick-up and pump assembly. If equipped, remove any balance or auxiliary shafts. If necessary, remove the cylinder ridge from the top of the bore. See the cylinder ridge removal procedure earlier in this section.

OHC Engines

If not done during the cylinder head removal, remove the timing chain/belt and/or gear/sprocket assembly. Remove the oil pick-up and pump assembly and, if necessary, the pump drive. If equipped, remove any balance or auxiliary shafts. If necessary, remove the cylinder ridge from the top of the bore. See the cylinder ridge removal procedure earlier in this section.

All Engines

Rotate the engine over so that the crankshaft is exposed. Use a number punch or scribe and mark each connecting rod with its respective cylinder number. The cylinder closest to the front of the engine is always number 1. However, depending on the engine placement, the front of the engine could either be the flywheel or damper/pulley end. Generally the front of the engine faces the front of the vehicle. Use a number punch or scribe and also mark the main bearing caps from front to rear with the front most cap being number 1 (if there are five caps, mark them 1 through 5, front to rear).

> ### ✳✳ WARNING
>
> **Take special care when pushing the connecting rod up from the crankshaft because the sharp threads of the rod bolts/studs will score the crankshaft journal. Insure that special plastic caps are installed over them, or cut two pieces of rubber hose to do the same.**

Again, rotate the engine, this time to position the number one cylinder bore (head surface) up. Turn the crankshaft until the number one piston is at the bottom of its travel, this should allow the maximum access to its connecting rod. Remove the number one connecting rods fasteners and cap and place two lengths of rubber hose over the rod bolts/studs to protect the crankshaft from damage. Using a sturdy wooden dowel and a hammer, push the connecting rod up about 1 in. (25mm) from the crankshaft and remove the upper bearing insert. Continue pushing or tapping the connecting rod up until the piston rings are out of the cylinder bore. Remove the piston and rod by hand, put the upper half of the bearing insert back into the rod, install the cap with its bearing insert installed, and hand-tighten the cap fasteners. If the parts are kept in order in this manner, they will not get lost and you will be able to tell which bearings came form what cylinder if any problems are discovered and diagnosis is necessary. Remove all the other piston assemblies in the same manner. On V-style engines, remove all of the pistons from one bank, then reposition the engine with the other cylinder bank head surface up, and remove that banks piston assemblies.

The only remaining component in the engine block should now be the crankshaft. Loosen the main bearing caps evenly until the fasteners can be

Place rubber hose over the connecting rod studs to protect the crankshaft and cylinder bores from damage

Carefully tap the piston out of the bore using a wooden dowel

turned by hand, then remove them and the caps. Remove the crankshaft from the engine block. Thoroughly clean all of the components.

INSPECTION

Now that the engine block and all of its components are clean, it's time to inspect them for wear and/or damage. To accurately inspect them, you will need some specialized tools:

- Two or three separate micrometers to measure the pistons and crankshaft journals
- A dial indicator
- Telescoping gauges for the cylinder bores
- A rod alignment fixture to check for bent connecting rods

If you do not have access to the proper tools, you may want to bring the components to a shop that does.

Generally, you shouldn't expect cracks in the engine block or its components unless it was known to leak, consume or mix engine fluids, it was severely overheated, or there was evidence of bad bearings and/or crankshaft damage. A visual inspection should be performed on all of the components, but just because you don't see a crack does not mean it is not there. Some more reliable methods for inspecting for cracks include Magnaflux®, a magnetic process or Zyglo®, a dye penetrant. Magnaflux® is used only on ferrous metal (cast iron). Zyglo® uses a spray on fluorescent mixture along with a black light to reveal the cracks. It is strongly recommended to have your engine block checked professionally for cracks, especially if the engine was known to have overheated and/or leaked or consumed coolant. Contact a local shop for availability and pricing of these services.

Engine Block

ENGINE BLOCK BEARING ALIGNMENT

Remove the main bearing caps and, if still installed, the main bearing inserts. Inspect all of the main bearing saddles and caps for damage, burrs or high spots. If damage is found, and it is caused from a spun main bearing, the block will need to be align-bored or, if severe enough, replacement. Any burrs or high spots should be carefully removed with a metal file.

Place a straightedge on the bearing saddles, in the engine block, along the centerline of the crankshaft. If any clearance exists between the straightedge and the saddles, the block must be align-bored.

Align-boring consists of machining the main bearing saddles and caps by means of a flycutter that runs through the bearing saddles.

DECK FLATNESS

The top of the engine block where the cylinder head mounts is called the deck. Insure that the deck surface is clean of dirt, carbon deposits and old gasket material. Place a straightedge across the surface of the deck along its centerline and, using feeler gauges, check the clearance along several points. Repeat the checking procedure with the straightedge placed along both diagonals of the deck surface. If the reading exceeds 0.003 in. (0.076mm) within a 6.0 in. (15.2cm) span, or 0.006 in. (0.152mm) over the total length of the deck, it must be machined.

CYLINDER BORES

The cylinder bores house the pistons and are slightly larger than the pistons themselves. A common piston-to-bore clearance is 0.0015–0.0025 in. (0.0381mm–0.0635mm). Inspect and measure the cylinder bores. The bore should be checked for out-of-roundness, taper and size. The results of this inspection will determine whether the cylinder can be used in its existing size and condition, or a rebore to the next oversize is required (or in the case of removable sleeves, have replacements installed).

The amount of cylinder wall wear is always greater at the top of the cylinder than at the bottom. This wear is known as taper. Any cylinder that has a taper of 0.0012 in. (0.305mm) or more, must be rebored. Measurements are taken at a number of positions in each cylinder: at the top, middle and bottom and at two points at each position; that is, at a point 90 degrees from the crankshaft centerline, as well as a point parallel to the crankshaft centerline. The measurements are made with either a special dial indicator or a telescopic gauge and micrometer. If the necessary precision tools to check the bore are not available, take the block to a machine shop and have them mike it. Also if you don't have the tools to check the cylinder bores, chances are you will not have the necessary devices to check the pistons, connecting rods and crankshaft. Take these components with you and save yourself an extra trip.

For our procedures, we will use a telescopic gauge and a micrometer. You will need one of each, with a measuring range which covers your cylinder bore size.

1. Position the telescopic gauge in the cylinder bore, loosen the gauges lock and allow it to expand.

➡ **Your first two readings will be at the top of the cylinder bore, then proceed to the middle and finally the bottom, making a total of six measurements.**

2. Hold the gauge square in the bore, 90 degrees from the crankshaft centerline, and gently tighten the lock. Tilt the gauge back to remove it from the bore.

3. Measure the gauge with the micrometer and record the reading.

4. Again, hold the gauge square in the bore, this time parallel to the crankshaft centerline, and gently tighten the lock. Again, you will tilt the gauge back to remove it from the bore.

5. Measure the gauge with the micrometer and record this reading. The difference between these two readings is the out-of-round measurement of the cylinder.

6. Repeat Steps 1 through 5, each time going to the next lower position, until you reach the bottom of the cylinder. Then go to the next cylinder, and continue until all of the cylinders have been measured.

The difference between these measurements will tell you all about the wear in your cylinders. The measurements which were taken 90 degrees from the crankshaft centerline will always reflect the most wear. That is because at this position is where the engine power presses the piston against the cylinder bore the hardest. This is known as thrust wear. Take your top, 90 degree measurement and compare it to your bottom, 90 degree measurement. The difference between them is the taper. When you measure your pistons, you will compare these readings to your piston sizes and determine piston-to-wall clearance.

Crankshaft

Inspect the crankshaft for visible signs of wear or damage. All of the journals should be perfectly round and smooth. Slight scores are normal for a used crankshaft, but you should hardly feel them with your fingernail. When measuring the crankshaft with a micrometer, you will take readings at the front and rear of each journal, then turn the micrometer 90 degrees and take two more readings, front and rear. The difference between the front-to-rear readings is the journal taper and the first-to-90 degree reading is the out-of-round measurement. Generally, there should be no taper or out-of-roundness found, however, up to 0.0005 in. (0.0127mm) for either can be overlooked. Also, the readings should fall within the factory specifications for journal diameters.

If the crankshaft journals fall within specifications, it is recommended that it be polished before being returned to service. Polishing the crankshaft insures that any minor burrs or high spots are smoothed, thereby reducing the chance of scoring the new bearings.

Pistons and Connecting Rods

PISTONS

The piston should be visually inspected for any signs of cracking or burning (caused by hot spots or detonation), and scuffing or excessive wear on the skirts. The wristpin attaches the piston to the connecting rod. The piston should move freely on the wrist pin, both sliding and pivoting. Grasp the connecting rod securely, or mount it in a vise, and try to rock the piston back and forth along the centerline of the wristpin. There should not be any excessive play evident between the piston and the pin. If there are C-clips retaining the pin in the piston then you have wrist pin bushings in the rods. There should not be any excessive play between the wrist pin and the rod bushing. Normal clearance for the wrist pin is approx. 0.001–0.002 in. (0.025mm–0.051mm).

Use a telescoping gauge to measure the cylinder bore diameter—take several readings within the same bore

Measure the piston's outer diameter, perpendicular to the wrist pin, with a micrometer

Use a micrometer and measure the diameter of the piston, perpendicular to the wrist pin, on the skirt. Compare the reading to its original cylinder measurement obtained earlier. The difference between the two readings is the piston-to-wall clearance. If the clearance is within specifications, the piston may be used as is. If the piston is out of specification, but the bore is not, you will need a new piston. If both are out of specification, you will need the cylinder rebored and oversize pistons installed. Generally if two or more pistons/bores are out of specification, it is best to rebore the entire block and purchase a complete set of oversize pistons.

CONNECTING ROD

You should have the connecting rod checked for straightness at a machine shop. If the connecting rod is bent, it will unevenly wear the bearing and piston, as well as place greater stress on these components. Any bent or twisted connecting rods must be replaced. If the rods are straight and the wrist pin clearance is within specifications, then only the bearing end of the rod need be checked. Place the connecting rod into a vice, with the bearing inserts in place, install the cap to the rod and torque the fasteners to specifications. Use a telescoping gauge and carefully measure the inside diameter of the bearings. Compare this reading to the rods original crankshaft journal diameter measurement. The difference is the oil clearance. If the oil clearance is not within specifications, install new bearings in the rod and take another measurement. If the clearance is still out of specifications, and the crankshaft is not, the rod will need to be reconditioned by a machine shop.

➡You can also use Plastigage® to check the bearing clearances. The assembling section has complete instructions on its use.

Camshaft

Inspect the camshaft and lifters/followers as described earlier in this section.

Bearings

All of the engine bearings should be visually inspected for wear and/or damage. The bearing should look evenly worn all around with no deep scores or pits. If the bearing is severely worn, scored, pitted or heat blued, then the bearing, and the components that use it, should be brought to a machine shop for inspection. Full-circle bearings (used on most camshafts, auxiliary shafts, balance shafts, etc.) require specialized tools for removal and installation, and should be brought to a machine shop for service.

Oil Pump

➡The oil pump is responsible for providing constant lubrication to the whole engine and so it is recommended that a new oil pump be installed when rebuilding the engine.

Completely disassemble the oil pump and thoroughly clean all of the components. Inspect the oil pump gears and housing for wear and/or damage. Insure that the pressure relief valve operates properly and there is no binding or sticking due to varnish or debris. If all of the parts are in proper working condition, lubricate the gears and relief valve, and assemble the pump.

REFINISHING

Almost all engine block refinishing must be performed by a machine shop. If the cylinders are not to be rebored, then the cylinder glaze can be removed with a ball hone. When removing cylinder glaze with a ball hone, use a light or penetrating type oil to lubricate the hone. Do not allow the hone to run dry as this may cause excessive scoring of the cylinder bores and wear on the hone. If new pistons are required, they will need to be installed to the connecting rods. This should be performed by a machine shop as the pistons must be installed in the correct relationship to the rod or engine damage can occur.

Pistons and Connecting Rods

Only pistons with the wrist pin retained by C-clips are serviceable by the home-mechanic. Press fit pistons require special presses and/or heaters to

TCCS3913

Use a ball type cylinder hone to remove any glaze and provide a new surface for seating the piston rings

remove/install the connecting rod and should only be performed by a machine shop.

All pistons will have a mark indicating the direction to the front of the engine and the must be installed into the engine in that manner. Usually it is a notch or arrow on the top of the piston, or it may be the letter F cast or stamped into the piston.

C-CLIP TYPE PISTONS

1. Note the location of the forward mark on the piston and mark the connecting rod in relation.
2. Remove the C-clips from the piston and withdraw the wrist pin.

➡Varnish build-up or C-clip groove burrs may increase the difficulty of removing the wrist pin. If necessary, use a punch or drift to carefully tap the wrist pin out.

3. Insure that the wrist pin bushing in the connecting rod is usable, and lubricate it with assembly lube.
4. Remove the wrist pin from the new piston and lubricate the pin bores on the piston.
5. Align the forward marks on the piston and the connecting rod and install the wrist pin.

TCCS3814

Most pistons are marked to indicate positioning in the engine (usually a mark means the side facing the front)

6. The new C-clips will have a flat and a rounded side to them. Install both C-clips with the flat side facing out.

7. Repeat all of the steps for each piston being replaced.

ASSEMBLY

Before you begin assembling the engine, first give yourself a clean, dirt free work area. Next, clean every engine component again. The key to a good assembly is cleanliness.

Mount the engine block into the engine stand and wash it one last time using water and detergent (dishwashing detergent works well). While washing it, scrub the cylinder bores with a soft bristle brush and thoroughly clean all of the oil passages. Completely dry the engine and spray the entire assembly down with an anti-rust solution such as WD-40® or similar product. Take a clean lint-free rag and wipe up any excess anti-rust solution from the bores, bearing saddles, etc. Repeat the final cleaning process on the crankshaft. Replace any freeze or oil galley plugs which were removed during disassembly.

Crankshaft

1. Remove the main bearing inserts from the block and bearing caps.
2. If the crankshaft main bearing journals have been refinished to a definite undersize, install the correct undersize bearing. Be sure that the bearing inserts and bearing bores are clean. Foreign material under inserts will distort bearing and cause failure.
3. Place the upper main bearing inserts in bores with tang in slot.

➡ **The oil holes in the bearing inserts must be aligned with the oil holes in the cylinder block.**

4. Install the lower main bearing inserts in bearing caps.
5. Clean the mating surfaces of block and rear main bearing cap.
6. Carefully lower the crankshaft into place. Be careful not to damage bearing surfaces.
7. Check the clearance of each main bearing by using the following procedure:

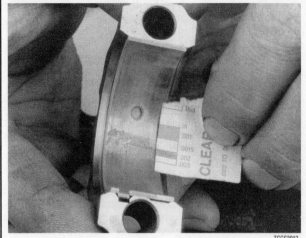

After the cap is removed again, use the scale supplied with the gauging material to check the clearance

A dial gauge may be used to check crankshaft end-play

Apply a strip of gauging material to the bearing journal, then install and torque the cap

Carefully pry the crankshaft back and forth while reading the dial gauge for end-play

a. Place a piece of Plastigage® or its equivalent, on bearing surface across full width of bearing cap and about ¼ in. off center.

b. Install cap and tighten bolts to specifications. Do not turn crankshaft while Plastigage® is in place.

c. Remove the cap. Using the supplied Plastigage® scale, check width of Plastigage® at widest point to get maximum clearance. Difference between readings is taper of journal.

d. If clearance exceeds specified limits, try a 0.001 in. or 0.002 in. undersize bearing in combination with the standard bearing. Bearing clearance must be within specified limits. If standard and 0.002 in. undersize bearing does not bring clearance within desired limits, refinish crankshaft journal, then install undersize bearings.

8. Install the rear main seal.

9. After the bearings have been fitted, apply a light coat of engine oil to the journals and bearings. Install the rear main bearing cap. Install all bearing caps except the thrust bearing cap. Be sure that main bearing caps are installed in original locations. Tighten the bearing cap bolts to specifications.

10. Install the thrust bearing cap with bolts finger-tight.

11. Pry the crankshaft forward against the thrust surface of upper half of bearing.

12. Hold the crankshaft forward and pry the thrust bearing cap to the rear. This aligns the thrust surfaces of both halves of the bearing.

13. Retain the forward pressure on the crankshaft. Tighten the cap bolts to specifications.

14. Measure the crankshaft end-play as follows:

a. Mount a dial gauge to the engine block and position the tip of the gauge to read from the crankshaft end.

b. Carefully pry the crankshaft toward the rear of the engine and hold it there while you zero the gauge.

c. Carefully pry the crankshaft toward the front of the engine and read the gauge.

d. Confirm that the reading is within specifications. If not, install a new thrust bearing and repeat the procedure. If the reading is still out of specifications with a new bearing, have a machine shop inspect the thrust surfaces of the crankshaft, and if possible, repair it.

15. Rotate the crankshaft so as to position the first rod journal to the bottom of its stroke.

Pistons and Connecting Rods

1. Before installing the piston/connecting rod assembly, oil the pistons, piston rings and the cylinder walls with light engine oil. Install connecting rod bolt protectors or rubber hose onto the connecting rod bolts/studs. Also perform the following:

a. Select the proper ring set for the size cylinder bore.

b. Position the ring in the bore in which it is going to be used.

c. Push the ring down into the bore area where normal ring wear is not encountered.

d. Use the head of the piston to position the ring in the bore so that the ring is square with the cylinder wall. Use caution to avoid damage to the ring or cylinder bore.

e. Measure the gap between the ends of the ring with a feeler gauge. Ring gap in a worn cylinder is normally greater than specification. If the ring gap is greater than the specified limits, try an oversize ring set.

f. Check the ring side clearance of the compression rings with a feeler gauge inserted between the ring and its lower land according to specification. The gauge should slide freely around the entire ring circumference without binding. Any wear that occurs will form a step at the inner portion of the lower land. If the lower lands have high steps, the piston should be replaced.

2. Unless new pistons are installed, be sure to install the pistons in the cylinders from which they were removed. The numbers on the connecting rod and bearing cap must be on the same side when installed in the cylinder bore. If a connecting rod is ever transposed from one engine or cylinder to another, new bearings should be fitted and the connecting rod should be numbered to correspond with the new cylinder number. The notch on the piston head goes toward the front of the engine.

3. Install all of the rod bearing inserts into the rods and caps.

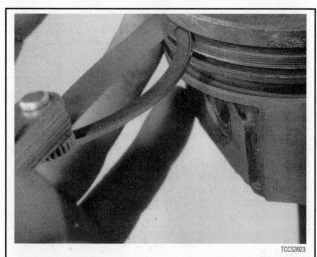

TCCS3923

Checking the piston ring-to-ring groove side clearance using the ring and a feeler gauge

TCCS3917

The notch on the side of the bearing cap matches the tang on the bearing insert

4. Install the rings to the pistons. Install the oil control ring first, then the second compression ring and finally the top compression ring. Use a piston ring expander tool to aid in installation and to help reduce the chance of breakage.

5. Make sure the ring gaps are properly spaced around the circumference of the piston. Fit a piston ring compressor around the piston and slide the piston and connecting rod assembly down into the cylinder bore, pushing it in with the wooden hammer handle. Push the piston down until it is only slightly below the top of the cylinder bore. Guide the connecting rod onto the crankshaft bearing journal carefully, to avoid damaging the crankshaft.

6. Check the bearing clearance of all the rod bearings, fitting them to the crankshaft bearing journals. Follow the procedure in the crankshaft installation above.

7. After the bearings have been fitted, apply a light coating of assembly oil to the journals and bearings.

8. Turn the crankshaft until the appropriate bearing journal is at the bottom of its stroke, then push the piston assembly all the way down until the connecting rod bearing seats on the crankshaft journal. Be careful not to allow the bearing cap screws to strike the crankshaft bearing journals and damage them.

9. After the piston and connecting rod assemblies have been installed, check the connecting rod side clearance on each crankshaft journal.

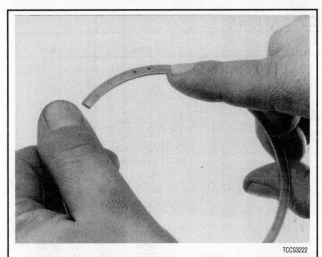

Most rings are marked to show which side of the ring should face up when installed to the piston

Install the piston and rod assembly into the block using a ring compressor and the handle of a hammer

10. Prime and install the oil pump and the oil pump intake tube.
11. Install the auxiliary/balance shaft(s)/assembly(ies).

OHV Engines

CAMSHAFT, LIFTERS AND TIMING ASSEMBLY

1. Install the camshaft.
2. Install the lifters/followers into their bores.
3. Install the timing gears/chain assembly.

CYLINDER HEAD(S)

1. Install the cylinder head(s) using new gaskets.
2. Assemble the rest of the valve train (pushrods and rocker arms and/or shafts).

OHC Engines

CYLINDER HEAD(S)

1. Install the cylinder head(s) using new gaskets.
2. Install the timing sprockets/gears and the belt/chain assemblies.

Engine Covers and Components

Install the timing cover(s) and oil pan. Refer to your notes and drawings made prior to disassembly and install all of the components that were removed. Install the engine into the vehicle.

Engine Start-up and Break-in

STARTING THE ENGINE

Now that the engine is installed and every wire and hose is properly connected, go back and double check that all coolant and vacuum hoses are connected. Check that you oil drain plug is installed and properly tightened. If not already done, install a new oil filter onto the engine. Fill the crankcase with the proper amount and grade of engine oil. Fill the cooling system with a 50/50 mixture of coolant/water.

1. Connect the vehicle battery.
2. Start the engine. Keep your eye on your oil pressure indicator; if it does not indicate oil pressure within 10 seconds of starting, turn the vehicle off.

✳✳ WARNING

Damage to the engine can result if it is allowed to run with no oil pressure. Check the engine oil level to make sure that it is full. Check for any leaks and if found, repair the leaks before continuing. If there is still no indication of oil pressure, you may need to prime the system.

3. Confirm that there are no fluid leaks (oil or other).
4. Allow the engine to reach normal operating temperature (the upper radiator hose will be hot to the touch).
5. If necessary, set the ignition timing.
6. Install any remaining components such as the air cleaner (if removed for ignition timing) or body panels which were removed.

BREAKING IT IN

Make the first miles on the new engine, easy ones. Vary the speed but do not accelerate hard. Most importantly, do not lug the engine, and avoid sustained high speeds until at least 100 miles. Check the engine oil and coolant levels frequently. Expect the engine to use a little oil until the rings seat. Change the oil and filter at 500 miles, 1500 miles, then every 3000 miles past that.

KEEP IT MAINTAINED

Now that you have just gone through all of that hard work, keep yourself from doing it all over again by thoroughly maintaining it. Not that you may not have maintained it before, heck you could have had one to two hundred thousand miles on it before doing this. However, you may have bought the vehicle used, and the previous owner did not keep up on maintenance. Which is why you just went through all of that hard work. See?

TORQUE SPECIFICATIONS

Engine	Component	Ft. Lbs.	Nm
3.8L (3802)	A/C compressor retaining bolts	30-45	41-61
	Accelerator cable bracket retainers	124-177 inch lbs.	14-20
	Automatic transmission-to-engine block bolts	40-50	55-68
	Camshaft gear-to-camshaft bolt	30-36	40-50
	Camshaft Position (CMP) sensor—1994-95 models	22-31 inch lbs.	2.5-3.5
	Camshaft Position (CMP) sensor—1996-98 models	40-61 inch lbs.	4.5-7.0
	Camshaft thrust plate bolts	71-123 inch lbs.	8-14
	Coolant temperature sender	88-177 inch lbs.	10-20
	Crankcase ventilation tube mounting bracket nut	15-22	20-30
	Crankshaft Position (CKP) sensor shield nuts	18-35	2-4
	Crankshaft Position (CKP) sensor stud bolt	71-106 inch lbs.	8-12
	Crankshaft pulley-to-damper bolt	20-28	26-38
	ECT sensor	70-115 inch lbs.	8-13
	EGR valve-to-exhaust manifold tube nuts	25-35	34-47
	EGR valve-to-intake manifold stud	15-22	20-30
	Engine front cover-to-engine block bolts	15-22	20-30
	Exhaust pipe-to-manifold nuts	16-23	21-32
	Flywheel pressure plate bolts	20-29	27-39
	Front engine mount-to-front sub-frame nut	72-98	97-133
	Front engine mount through-bolt	35-50	47-68
	Front engine mount-to-engine block bolt and stud bolt	44-59	59-81
	Fuel injection supply manifold	70-97 inch lbs.	8-11
	Fuel pressure regulator bracket bolt	15-22	20-30
	Heater elbow	75-119 inch lbs.	8.5-13.5
	Heater water outlet tube-to-water pump bolt	71-106 inch lbs.	8-12
	HO2S sensor	28-33	37-45
	IAT sensor	71-115 inch lbs.	8-13
	Oil inlet tube-to-engine block bolts	15-22	20-30
	Oil inlet tube-to-main bearing cap nuts	30-40	40-55
	Oil level dipstick tube support bracket retainer	15-22	20-30
	Oil pan drain plug	15-22	20-30
	Oil pan-to-engine block bolts	80-106 inch lbs.	9-12
	Oil pressure sender	142-212 inch lbs.	16-24
	Oil pump and filter body-to-front cover M6 bolts	70-97 inch lbs.	8-11
	Oil pump and filter body-to-front cover M8 bolts	18-22	25-30
	Power steering brace bolt	30-45	40-62
	Power steering front bracket bolt	30-45	40-62
	Retaining strap left-hand mounting bolt	34-44	45-61
	Rocker arm fulcrum-to-cylinder head bolts ①	—	—
	Shock absorber-to-control arm bolt	103-143	140-195
	Steering column shaft pinch bolt	30-42	41-57
	Tappet guide plate bolts	88-124 inch lbs.	10-14
	Thermostat housing-to-intake manifold bolts	15-22	20-30
	Throttle body retainers	15-22	20-30
	Timing chain vibration damper-to-engine block bolt	70-123 inch lbs.	8-14
	Torque converter-to-flywheel bolts	20-33	27-46
	Upper intake manifold support bolt	15-22	20-30
	Vacuum fitting-to-intake manifold	150-221 inch lbs.	17-25
	Valve cover-to-cylinder head bolts or studs	71-106 inch lbs.	8-12
	Water pump pulley bolts	15-21	20-29
	Water pump-to-front cover bolts and studs	15-22	20-30
	Water pump-to-front cover nuts—1994-95 models	53-71 inch lbs.	6-8
	Water pump-to-front cover nuts—1996-98 models	71-106	8-12

88233C06

TORQUE SPECIFICATIONS

Engine	Component	Ft. Lbs.	Nm
4.6L (4593) SOHC	A/C compressor retaining bolts	15-22	20-30
	Alternator rear mounting bracket-to-intake manifold retaining bolts	71-106 inch lbs.	8-12
	Alternator-to-engine block	15-22	20-30
	Cable bracket retaining bolt	71-106 inch lbs.	8-12
	Camshaft bearing cap-to-cylinder head bolts	71-106 inch lbs.	8-12
	Camshaft gear bolt	81-95	110-130
	CKP and CID sensor retaining bolts	71-106 inch lbs.	8-12
	Crankshaft Position (CKP) sensor bolts	71-106 inch lbs.	8-12
	Crankshaft rear oil seal retainer bolts	71-106	8-12
	EGR backpressure transducer bracket bolt	15-22	20-30
	EGR tube connector	33-47	45-65
	EGR valve-to-exhaust manifold tube connector	26-33	35-45
	EGR valve-to-throttle body adapter	15-22	20-30
	Engine front cover bolt	15-22	20-30
	Engine Coolant Temperature (ECT) sensor	142-212 inch lbs.	16-24
	Engine lifting eye bolts	30-36	40-50
	Engine-to-transmission bracket bolts	18-31	25-43
	Exhaust pipe-to-exhaust manifold nuts	20-30	27-41
	Front engine mount through-bolts	15-22	20-30
	Front engine mount-to-frame bolts	15-22	20-30
	Front sub-frame-to-body bolts (front)	83-112	113-153
	Front sub-frame-to-body bolts (rear)	70-95	95-130
	Fuel injection supply manifold retaining bolts	71-106 inch lbs.	8-12
	Heated oxygen sensor	27-33	37-45
	Idle Air Control (IAC) valve bolts	71-106 inch lbs.	8-12
	Ignition coil bracket retaining nuts	15-22	20-30
	Lower heater hose retaining bolt	71-106 inch lbs.	8-12
	Oil dipstick tube nut	71-106 inch lbs.	8-12
	Oil filter adapter bolt	15-22	20-30
	Oil inlet tube-to-oil pump bolt	71-106	8-12
	Oil inlet-to-main bearing cap nuts	15-22	20-30
	Oil pan drain plug	97-142 inch lbs.	11-16
	Oil pan-to-engine block bolts ②	—	—
	Oil pressure sensor	142-212 inch lbs.	16-24
	Oil pump-to-engine block bolts	71-106 inch lbs.	8-12
	Power steering pump-to-engine block bolts	15-22	20-30
	Rear engine mount-to-support	15-22	20-30
	Rear engine mount-to-transmission retaining bolt	30-44	40-60
	Throttle body and adapter bolts	71-106 inch lbs.	8-12
	Timing chain guide retaining bolts	71-106 inch lbs.	8-12
	Timing chain tensioner bolts	15-22	20-30
	Torque converter-to-flexplate nuts	22-25	30-35
	Transmission line bracket bolts	15-22	20-30
	Upper heater water hose retaining bolt	15-22	20-30
	Valve cover bolts	71-106 inch lbs.	8-12
	Water outlet connection bolt	15-22	20-30
	Water pump-to-engine block bolts	15-22	20-30
	Water pump-to-pulley bolt	15-22	20-30
	Water temperature indicator sending unit	142-212 inch lbs.	16-24
4.6L (4593) DOHC	A/C compressor retaining bolts	15-22	20-30
	Accelerator cable bracket	71-106 inch lbs.	8-12
	Alternator rear mounting bracket-to-intake manifold retaining bolts	71-106 inch lbs.	8-12
	Alternator-to-engine block	15-22	20-30
	Cable bracket retaining bolt	71-106 inch lbs.	8-12
	Camshaft bearing cap-to-cylinder head bolts	71-106 inch lbs.	8-12

88233C07

TORQUE SPECIFICATIONS

Engine	Component	Ft. Lbs.	Nm
4.6L (4593) DOHC continued	Camshaft gear bolt	81-95	110-130
	CKP and CID sensor retaining bolts	71-106 inch lbs.	8-12
	Crankshaft Position (CKP) sensor bolts	71-106 inch lbs.	8-12
	Crankshaft rear oil seal retainer bolts	71-106	8-12
	Drive belt idler pulley bolt	15-22	20-30
	Drive belt tensioner bolts	15-22	20-30
	EGR backpressure transducer bracket bolt	15-22	20-30
	EGR tube connector	33-47	45-65
	EGR vacuum regulator bolts	45-60 inch lbs.	5-7
	EGR valve-to-exhaust manifold tube nuts	30-33	40-45
	EGR valve-to-throttle body adapter	15-22	20-30
	EGR valve-to-upper intake manifold	15-22	20-30
	Engine front cover bolt	15-22	20-30
	Engine Coolant Temperature (ECT) sensor	142-212 inch lbs.	16-24
	Engine lifting eye bolts	30-36	40-50
	Engine oil cooler-to-oil filter adapter	59-74	80-100
	Engine-to-transmission bolts	30-44	40-60
	Exhaust pipe-to-exhaust manifold nuts	20-30	27-41
	Front engine mount through-bolts	15-22	20-30
	Front engine mount-to-frame bolts	15-22	20-30
	Front sub-frame-to-body bolts (front)	83-112	113-153
	Front sub-frame-to-body bolts (rear)	70-95	95-130
	Fuel injection supply manifold retaining bolts	71-106 inch lbs.	8-12
	Heated oxygen sensor	27-33	37-45
	Idle Air Control (IAC) valve bolts	71-106 inch lbs.	8-12
	Ignition coil bracket retaining nuts	15-22	20-30
	Inlet heater water hose-to-right cylinder head lower bolts	71-106 inch lbs.	8-12
	Inlet heater water hose-to-right cylinder head upper bolt	15-22	20-30
	Low oil level sensor	20-30	27-41
	Lower heater hose retaining bolt	71-106 inch lbs.	8-12
	Oil dipstick tube nut	71-106 inch lbs.	8-12
	Oil filter adapter bolt	15-22	20-30
	Oil inlet tube-to-oil pump bolt	71-106	8-12
	Oil inlet-to-main bearing cap nuts	15-22	20-30
	Oil pan drain plug	97-142 inch lbs.	11-16
	Oil pan-to-engine block bolts	15-22	20-30
	Oil pan-to-engine front cover bolts	15-22	20-30
	Oil pressure sensor	106-142 inch lbs.	12-16
	Oil pump-to-engine block bolts	71-106 inch lbs.	8-12
	Outlet heater water hose-to-left cylinder head lower bolt	71-106 inch lbs.	8-12
	Outlet heater water hose-to-left cylinder head upper bolt	15-22	20-30
	Power steering pump reservoir retaining bolts	71-106 inch lbs.	8-12
	Power steering pump-to-engine block bolts	15-22	20-30
	Rear engine mount-to-support	15-22	20-30
	Rear engine mount-to-transmission retaining bolt	30-44	40-60
	Secondary air injection manifold tube-to-exhaust manifold nuts	28-31	38-42
	Throttle body and adapter bolts	71-106 inch lbs.	8-12
	Timing chain guide retaining bolts	71-106 inch lbs.	8-12
	Timing chain tensioner arm bolts	88-133 inch lbs.	10-15
	Timing chain tensioner bolts	15-22	20-30
	Torque converter-to-flexplate nuts	22-25	30-35
	Transmission line bracket bolts	15-22	20-30
	Upper heater water hose retaining bolt	15-22	20-30
	Valve cover bolts	71-106 inch lbs.	8-12
	Water bypass tube nuts	71-106 inch lbs.	8-12

88233C08

TORQUE SPECIFICATIONS

Engine	Component	Ft. Lbs.	Nm
4.6L (4593) DOHC continued	Water outlet connection bolt	15-22	20-30
	Water pump-to-engine block bolts	15-22	20-30
	Water pump-to-pulley bolt	15-22	20-30
	Water temperature indicator sending unit	142-212 inch lbs.	16-24
5.0L (4949)	Alternator and secondary air injection 3/8 in. bolt	22-30	30-40
	Camshaft gear-to-camshaft bolt	40-45	54-61
	Camshaft thrust plate-to-engine block bolts	80-106 inch lbs.	9-12
	Crankshaft pulley-to-damper bolts	35-50	47-68
	Engine front cover bolt	142-212 inch lbs.	16-24
	Front engine mount nuts	72-98	97-133
	Hold-down clamp bolt	17-25	23-34
	Low oil level sensor	15-25	20-33
	Oil cooler	22-41	40-55
	Oil dipstick tube support nut	150-203 inch lbs.	17-23
	Oil filter insert-to-engine block	20-30	27-41
	Oil pan drain plug	15-25	20-34
	Oil pan-to-engine block bolt	106-142 inch lbs.	12-16
	Oil pressure sender	142-212 inch lbs.	16-24
	Oil pump screen cover and tube-to-main bearing cap nut	22-32	30-43
	Oil pump screen cover and tube-to-oil pump bolt	142-212 inch lbs.	16-24
	Oil pump-to-engine block bolt	22-32	30-43
	Pump bracket-to-cylinder head 3/8 in. bolt	22-30	30-40
	Pump bracket-to-cylinder head 7/16 in. bolt	44-60	60-81
	Rocker arm seat-to-cylinder head bolt	18-25	24-34
	Secondary air injection pump arm-to-bracket bolt	22-30	30-40
	Secondary air injection pump arm-to-water pump stud nut	142-212 inch lbs.	16-24
	Secondary air injection pump pivot bolt	22-30	30-40
	Secondary air injection pump pulley-to-pump hub bolt	79-106 inch lbs.	9-12
	Temperature indicator sending unit	88-212 inch lbs.	10-24
	Throttle body attaching stud	24-48 inch lbs.	2.7-5.4
	Throttle body mounting nuts	142-212 inch lbs.	16-24
	Vacuum fitting/plug-to-intake manifold	124-177 inch lbs.	14-20
	Valve cover bolts	142-212 inch lbs.	16-24
	Valve tappet guide plate retainer bolts	71-106 inch lbs.	8-12
	Water outlet connection bolt	142-212 inch lbs.	16-24
	Water pump pulley-to-hub bolt	15-22	20-30
	Water pump-to-engine front cover bolts	15-21	20-28

① Tighten in two steps:
  Step 1: 44 inch lbs. (5 Nm) maximum.
  Step 2: 19-25 ft. lbs. (25-35 Nm).

② Tighten in two steps:
  Step 1: 15 ft. lbs. (20 Nm).
  Step 2: Tighten an additional 60 degrees.

88233C09

USING A VACUUM GAUGE

White needle = steady needle   Dark needle = drifting needle

The vacuum gauge is one of the most useful and easy-to-use diagnostic tools. It is inexpensive, easy to hook up, and provides valuable information about the condition of your engine.

Indication: Normal engine in good condition

Gauge reading: Steady, from 17–22 in./Hg.

Indication: Sticking valve or ignition miss

Gauge reading: Needle fluctuates from 15–20 in./Hg. at idle

Indication: Late ignition or valve timing, low compression, stuck throttle valve, leaking carburetor or manifold gasket.

Gauge reading: Low (15–20 in./Hg.) but steady

Indication: Improper carburetor adjustment, or minor intake leak at carburetor or manifold

NOTE: Bad fuel injector O-rings may also cause this reading.

Gauge reading: Drifting needle

Indication: Weak valve springs, worn valve stem guides, or leaky cylinder head gasket (vibrating excessively at all speeds).

NOTE: A plugged catalytic converter may also cause this reading.

Gauge reading: Needle fluctuates as engine speed increases

Indication: Burnt valve or improper valve clearance. The needle will drop when the defective valve operates.

Gauge reading: Steady needle, but drops regularly

Indication: Choked muffler or obstruction in system. Speed up the engine. Choked muffler will exhibit a slow drop of vacuum to zero.

Gauge reading: Gradual drop in reading at idle

Indication: Worn valve guides

Gauge reading: Needle vibrates excessively at idle, but steadies as engine speed increases

TCCS3C01

Troubleshooting Engine Mechanical Problems

Problem	Cause	Solution
External oil leaks	• Cylinder head cover RTV sealant broken or improperly seated	• Replace sealant; inspect cylinder head cover sealant flange and cylinder head sealant surface for distortion and cracks
	• Oil filler cap leaking or missing	• Replace cap
	• Oil filter gasket broken or improperly seated	• Replace oil filter
	• Oil pan side gasket broken, improperly seated or opening in RTV sealant	• Replace gasket or repair opening in sealant; inspect oil pan gasket flange for distortion
	• Oil pan front oil seal broken or improperly seated	• Replace seal; inspect timing case cover and oil pan seal flange for distortion
	• Oil pan rear oil seal broken or improperly seated	• Replace seal; inspect oil pan rear oil seal flange; inspect rear main bearing cap for cracks, plugged oil return channels, or distortion in seal groove
	• Timing case cover oil seal broken or improperly seated	• Replace seal
	• Excess oil pressure because of restricted PCV valve	• Replace PCV valve
	• Oil pan drain plug loose or has stripped threads	• Repair as necessary and tighten
	• Rear oil gallery plug loose	• Use appropriate sealant on gallery plug and tighten
	• Rear camshaft plug loose or improperly seated	• Seat camshaft plug or replace and seal, as necessary
Excessive oil consumption	• Oil level too high	• Drain oil to specified level
	• Oil with wrong viscosity being used	• Replace with specified oil
	• PCV valve stuck closed	• Replace PCV valve
	• Valve stem oil deflectors (or seals) are damaged, missing, or incorrect type	• Replace valve stem oil deflectors
	• Valve stems or valve guides worn	• Measure stem-to-guide clearance and repair as necessary
	• Poorly fitted or missing valve cover baffles	• Replace valve cover
	• Piston rings broken or missing	• Replace broken or missing rings
	• Scuffed piston	• Replace piston
	• Incorrect piston ring gap	• Measure ring gap, repair as necessary
	• Piston rings sticking or excessively loose in grooves	• Measure ring side clearance, repair as necessary
	• Compression rings installed upside down	• Repair as necessary
	• Cylinder walls worn, scored, or glazed	• Repair as necessary

TCCS3C02

Troubleshooting Engine Mechanical Problems

Problem	Cause	Solution
Excessive oil consumption (cont.)	• Piston ring gaps not properly staggered • Excessive main or connecting rod bearing clearance	• Repair as necessary • Measure bearing clearance, repair as necessary
No oil pressure	• Low oil level • Oil pressure gauge, warning lamp or sending unit inaccurate • Oil pump malfunction • Oil pressure relief valve sticking • Oil passages on pressure side of pump obstructed • Oil pickup screen or tube obstructed • Loose oil inlet tube	• Add oil to correct level • Replace oil pressure gauge or warning lamp • Replace oil pump • Remove and inspect oil pressure relief valve assembly • Inspect oil passages for obstruction • Inspect oil pickup for obstruction • Tighten or seal inlet tube
Low oil pressure	• Low oil level • Inaccurate gauge, warning lamp or sending unit • Oil excessively thin because of dilution, poor quality, or improper grade • Excessive oil temperature • Oil pressure relief spring weak or sticking • Oil inlet tube and screen assembly has restriction or air leak • Excessive oil pump clearance • Excessive main, rod, or camshaft bearing clearance	• Add oil to correct level • Replace oil pressure gauge or warning lamp • Drain and refill crankcase with recommended oil • Correct cause of overheating engine • Remove and inspect oil pressure relief valve assembly • Remove and inspect oil inlet tube and screen assembly. (Fill inlet tube with lacquer thinner to locate leaks.) • Measure clearances • Measure bearing clearances, repair as necessary
High oil pressure	• Improper oil viscosity • Oil pressure gauge or sending unit inaccurate • Oil pressure relief valve sticking closed	• Drain and refill crankcase with correct viscosity oil • Replace oil pressure gauge • Remove and inspect oil pressure relief valve assembly
Main bearing noise	• Insufficient oil supply • Main bearing clearance excessive • Bearing insert missing • Crankshaft end-play excessive • Improperly tightened main bearing cap bolts • Loose flywheel or drive plate • Loose or damaged vibration damper	• Inspect for low oil level and low oil pressure • Measure main bearing clearance, repair as necessary • Replace missing insert • Measure end-play, repair as necessary • Tighten bolts with specified torque • Tighten flywheel or drive plate attaching bolts • Repair as necessary

TCCS3C03

Troubleshooting Engine Mechanical Problems

Problem	Cause	Solution
Connecting rod bearing noise	• Insufficient oil supply	• Inspect for low oil level and low oil pressure
	• Carbon build-up on piston	• Remove carbon from piston crown
	• Bearing clearance excessive or bearing missing	• Measure clearance, repair as necessary
	• Crankshaft connecting rod journal out-of-round	• Measure journal dimensions, repair or replace as necessary
	• Misaligned connecting rod or cap	• Repair as necessary
	• Connecting rod bolts tightened improperly	• Tighten bolts with specified torque
Piston noise	• Piston-to-cylinder wall clearance excessive (scuffed piston)	• Measure clearance and examine piston
	• Cylinder walls excessively tapered or out-of-round	• Measure cylinder wall dimensions, rebore cylinder
	• Piston ring broken	• Replace all rings on piston
	• Loose or seized piston pin	• Measure piston-to-pin clearance, repair as necessary
	• Connecting rods misaligned	• Measure rod alignment, straighten or replace
	• Piston ring side clearance excessively loose or tight	• Measure ring side clearance, repair as necessary
	• Carbon build-up on piston is excessive	• Remove carbon from piston
Valve actuating component noise	• Insufficient oil supply	• Check for: (a) Low oil level (b) Low oil pressure (c) Wrong hydraulic tappets (d) Restricted oil gallery (e) Excessive tappet to bore clearance
	• Rocker arms or pivots worn	• Replace worn rocker arms or pivots
	• Foreign objects or chips in hydraulic tappets	• Clean tappets
	• Excessive tappet leak-down	• Replace valve tappet
	• Tappet face worn	• Replace tappet; inspect corresponding cam lobe for wear
	• Broken or cocked valve springs	• Properly seat cocked springs; replace broken springs
	• Stem-to-guide clearance excessive	• Measure stem-to-guide clearance, repair as required
	• Valve bent	• Replace valve
	• Loose rocker arms	• Check and repair as necessary
	• Valve seat runout excessive	• Regrind valve seat/valves
	• Missing valve lock	• Install valve lock
	• Excessive engine oil	• Correct oil level

TCCS3C04

Troubleshooting Engine Performance

Problem	Cause	Solution
Hard starting (engine cranks normally)	• Faulty engine control system component	• Repair or replace as necessary
	• Faulty fuel pump	• Replace fuel pump
	• Faulty fuel system component	• Repair or replace as necessary
	• Faulty ignition coil	• Test and replace as necessary
	• Improper spark plug gap	• Adjust gap
	• Incorrect ignition timing	• Adjust timing
	• Incorrect valve timing	• Check valve timing; repair as necessary
Rough idle or stalling	• Incorrect curb or fast idle speed	• Adjust curb or fast idle speed (If possible)
	• Incorrect ignition timing	• Adjust timing to specification
	• Improper feedback system operation	• Refer to Chapter 4
	• Faulty EGR valve operation	• Test EGR system and replace as necessary
	• Faulty PCV valve air flow	• Test PCV valve and replace as necessary
	• Faulty TAC vacuum motor or valve	• Repair as necessary
	• Air leak into manifold vacuum	• Inspect manifold vacuum connections and repair as necessary
	• Faulty distributor rotor or cap	• Replace rotor or cap (Distributor systems only)
	• Improperly seated valves	• Test cylinder compression, repair as necessary
	• Incorrect ignition wiring	• Inspect wiring and correct as necessary
	• Faulty ignition coil	• Test coil and replace as necessary
	• Restricted air vent or idle passages	• Clean passages
	• Restricted air cleaner	• Clean or replace air cleaner filter element
Faulty low-speed operation	• Restricted idle air vents and passages	• Clean air vents and passages
	• Restricted air cleaner	• Clean or replace air cleaner filter element
	• Faulty spark plugs	• Clean or replace spark plugs
	• Dirty, corroded, or loose ignition secondary circuit wire connections	• Clean or tighten secondary circuit wire connections
	• Improper feedback system operation	• Refer to Chapter 4
	• Faulty ignition coil high voltage wire	• Replace ignition coil high voltage wire (Distributor systems only)
	• Faulty distributor cap	• Replace cap (Distributor systems only)
Faulty acceleration	• Incorrect ignition timing	• Adjust timing
	• Faulty fuel system component	• Repair or replace as necessary
	• Faulty spark plug(s)	• Clean or replace spark plug(s)
	• Improperly seated valves	• Test cylinder compression, repair as necessary
	• Faulty ignition coil	• Test coil and replace as necessary

TCCS3C05

Troubleshooting Engine Performance

Problem	Cause	Solution
Faulty acceleration (cont.)	• Improper feedback system operation	• Refer to Chapter 4
Faulty high speed operation	• Incorrect ignition timing • Faulty advance mechanism	• Adjust timing (if possible) • Check advance mechanism and repair as necessary (Distributor systems only)
	• Low fuel pump volume • Wrong spark plug air gap or wrong plug	• Replace fuel pump • Adjust air gap or install correct plug
	• Partially restricted exhaust manifold, exhaust pipe, catalytic converter, muffler, or tailpipe	• Eliminate restriction
	• Restricted vacuum passages • Restricted air cleaner	• Clean passages • Cleaner or replace filter element as necessary
	• Faulty distributor rotor or cap	• Replace rotor or cap (Distributor systems only)
	• Faulty ignition coil • Improperly seated valve(s)	• Test coil and replace as necessary • Test cylinder compression, repair as necessary
	• Faulty valve spring(s)	• Inspect and test valve spring tension, replace as necessary
	• Incorrect valve timing	• Check valve timing and repair as necessary
	• Intake manifold restricted	• Remove restriction or replace manifold
	• Worn distributor shaft	• Replace shaft (Distributor systems only)
	• Improper feedback system operation	• Refer to Chapter 4
Misfire at all speeds	• Faulty spark plug(s) • Faulty spark plug wire(s) • Faulty distributor cap or rotor	• Clean or relace spark plug(s) • Replace as necessary • Replace cap or rotor (Distributor systems only)
	• Faulty ignition coil • Primary ignition circuit shorted or open intermittently • Improperly seated valve(s)	• Test coil and replace as necessary • Troubleshoot primary circuit and repair as necessary • Test cylinder compression, repair as necessary
	• Faulty hydraulic tappet(s) • Improper feedback system operation • Faulty valve spring(s)	• Clean or replace tappet(s) • Refer to Chapter 4 • Inspect and test valve spring tension, repair as necessary
	• Worn camshaft lobes • Air leak into manifold	• Replace camshaft • Check manifold vacuum and repair as necessary
	• Fuel pump volume or pressure low • Blown cylinder head gasket • Intake or exhaust manifold passage(s) restricted	• Replace fuel pump • Replace gasket • Pass chain through passage(s) and repair as necessary
Power not up to normal	• Incorrect ignition timing • Faulty distributor rotor	• Adjust timing • Replace rotor (Distributor systems only)

TCCS3C06

Troubleshooting Engine Performance

Problem	Cause	Solution
Power not up to normal (cont.)	• Incorrect spark plug gap	• Adjust gap
	• Faulty fuel pump	• Replace fuel pump
	• Faulty fuel pump	• Replace fuel pump
	• Incorrect valve timing	• Check valve timing and repair as necessary
	• Faulty ignition coil	• Test coil and replace as necessary
	• Faulty ignition wires	• Test wires and replace as necessary
	• Improperly seated valves	• Test cylinder compression and repair as necessary
	• Blown cylinder head gasket	• Replace gasket
	• Leaking piston rings	• Test compression and repair as necessary
	• Improper feedback system operation	• Refer to Chapter 4
Intake backfire	• Improper ignition timing	• Adjust timing
	• Defective EGR component	• Repair as necessary
	• Defective TAC vacuum motor or valve	• Repair as necessary
Exhaust backfire	• Air leak into manifold vacuum	• Check manifold vacuum and repair as necessary
	• Faulty air injection diverter valve	• Test diverter valve and replace as necessary
	• Exhaust leak	• Locate and eliminate leak
Ping or spark knock	• Incorrect ignition timing	• Adjust timing
	• Distributor advance malfunction	• Inspect advance mechanism and repair as necessary (Distributor systems only)
	• Excessive combustion chamber deposits	• Remove with combustion chamber cleaner
	• Air leak into manifold vacuum	• Check manifold vacuum and repair as necessary
	• Excessively high compression	• Test compression and repair as necessary
	• Fuel octane rating excessively low	• Try alternate fuel source
	• Sharp edges in combustion chamber	• Grind smooth
	• EGR valve not functioning properly	• Test EGR system and replace as necessary
Surging (at cruising to top speeds)	• Low fuel pump pressure or volume	• Replace fuel pump
	• Improper PCV valve air flow	• Test PCV valve and replace as necessary
	• Air leak into manifold vacuum	• Check manifold vacuum and repair as necessary
	• Incorrect spark advance	• Test and replace as necessary
	• Restricted fuel filter	• Replace fuel filter
	• Restricted air cleaner	• Clean or replace air cleaner filter element
	• EGR valve not functioning properly	• Test EGR system and replace as necessary
	• Improper feedback system operation	• Refer to Chapter 4

TCCS3C07

Troubleshooting the Serpentine Drive Belt

Problem	Cause	Solution
Tension sheeting fabric failure (woven fabric on outside circumference of belt has cracked or separated from body of belt)	• Grooved or backside idler pulley diameters are less than minimum recommended • Tension sheeting contacting (rubbing) stationary object • Excessive heat causing woven fabric to age • Tension sheeting splice has fractured	• Replace pulley(s) not conforming to specification • Correct rubbing condition • Replace belt • Replace belt
Noise (objectional squeal, squeak, or rumble is heard or felt while drive belt is in operation)	• Belt slippage • Bearing noise • Belt misalignment • Belt-to-pulley mismatch • Driven component inducing vibration • System resonant frequency inducing vibration	• Adjust belt • Locate and repair • Align belt/pulley(s) • Install correct belt • Locate defective driven component and repair • Vary belt tension within specifications. Replace belt.
Rib chunking (one or more ribs has separated from belt body)	• Foreign objects imbedded in pulley grooves • Installation damage • Drive loads in excess of design specifications • Insufficient internal belt adhesion	• Remove foreign objects from pulley grooves • Replace belt • Adjust belt tension • Replace belt
Rib or belt wear (belt ribs contact bottom of pulley grooves)	• Pulley(s) misaligned • Mismatch of belt and pulley groove widths • Abrasive environment • Rusted pulley(s) • Sharp or jagged pulley groove tips • Rubber deteriorated	• Align pulley(s) • Replace belt • Replace belt • Clean rust from pulley(s) • Replace pulley • Replace belt
Longitudinal belt cracking (cracks between two ribs)	• Belt has mistracked from pulley groove • Pulley groove tip has worn away rubber-to-tensile member	• Replace belt • Replace belt
Belt slips	• Belt slipping because of insufficient tension • Belt or pulley subjected to substance (belt dressing, oil, ethylene glycol) that has reduced friction • Driven component bearing failure • Belt glazed and hardened from heat and excessive slippage	• Adjust tension • Replace belt and clean pulleys • Replace faulty component bearing • Replace belt
"Groove jumping" (belt does not maintain correct position on pulley, or turns over and/or runs off pulleys)	• Insufficient belt tension • Pulley(s) not within design tolerance • Foreign object(s) in grooves	• Adjust belt tension • Replace pulley(s) • Remove foreign objects from grooves

TCCS3C09

Troubleshooting the Serpentine Drive Belt

Problem	Cause	Solution
"Groove jumping" (belt does not maintain correct position on pulley, or turns over and/or runs off pulleys)	• Excessive belt speed • Pulley misalignment • Belt-to-pulley profile mismatched • Belt cordline is distorted	• Avoid excessive engine acceleration • Align pulley(s) • Install correct belt • Replace belt
Belt broken (Note: identify and correct problem before replacement belt is installed)	• Excessive tension • Tensile members damaged during belt installation • Belt turnover • Severe pulley misalignment • Bracket, pulley, or bearing failure	• Replace belt and adjust tension to specification • Replace belt • Replace belt • Align pulley(s) • Replace defective component and belt
Cord edge failure (tensile member exposed at edges of belt or separated from belt body)	• Excessive tension • Drive pulley misalignment • Belt contacting stationary object • Pulley irregularities • Improper pulley construction • Insufficient adhesion between tensile member and rubber matrix	• Adjust belt tension • Align pulley • Correct as necessary • Replace pulley • Replace pulley • Replace belt and adjust tension to specifications
Sporadic rib cracking (multiple cracks in belt ribs at random intervals)	• Ribbed pulley(s) diameter less than minimum specification • Backside bend flat pulley(s) diameter less than minimum • Excessive heat condition causing rubber to harden • Excessive belt thickness • Belt overcured • Excessive tension	• Replace pulley(s) • Replace pulley(s) • Correct heat condition as necessary • Replace belt • Replace belt • Adjust belt tension

TCCS3C10

Troubleshooting the Cooling System

Problem	Cause	Solution
High temperature gauge indication— overheating	• Coolant level low • Improper fan operation • Radiator hose(s) collapsed • Radiator airflow blocked • Faulty pressure cap • Ignition timing incorrect • Air trapped in cooling system • Heavy traffic driving • Incorrect cooling system component(s) installed • Faulty thermostat • Water pump shaft broken or impeller loose • Radiator tubes clogged • Cooling system clogged • Casting flash in cooling passages • Brakes dragging • Excessive engine friction • Antifreeze concentration over 68% • Missing air seals • Faulty gauge or sending unit • Loss of coolant flow caused by leakage or foaming • Viscous fan drive failed	• Replenish coolant • Repair or replace as necessary • Replace hose(s) • Remove restriction (bug screen, fog lamps, etc.) • Replace pressure cap • Adjust ignition timing • Purge air • Operate at fast idle in neutral intermittently to cool engine • Install proper component(s) • Replace thermostat • Replace water pump • Flush radiator • Flush system • Repair or replace as necessary. Flash may be visible by removing cooling system components or removing core plugs. • Repair brakes • Repair engine • Lower antifreeze concentration percentage • Replace air seals • Repair or replace faulty component • Repair or replace leaking component, replace coolant • Replace unit
Low temperature indication— undercooling	• Thermostat stuck open • Faulty gauge or sending unit	• Replace thermostat • Repair or replace faulty component
Coolant loss—boilover	• Overfilled cooling system • Quick shutdown after hard (hot) run • Air in system resulting in occasional "burping" of coolant • Insufficient antifreeze allowing coolant boiling point to be too low • Antifreeze deteriorated because of age or contamination • Leaks due to loose hose clamps, loose nuts, bolts, drain plugs, faulty hoses, or defective radiator	• Reduce coolant level to proper specification • Allow engine to run at fast idle prior to shutdown • Purge system • Add antifreeze to raise boiling point • Replace coolant • Pressure test system to locate source of leak(s) then repair as necessary

TCCS3C11

Troubleshooting the Cooling System

Problem	Cause	Solution
Coolant loss—boilover	· Faulty head gasket · Cracked head, manifold, or block · Faulty radiator cap	· Replace head gasket · Replace as necessary · Replace cap
Coolant entry into crankcase or cylinder(s)	· Faulty head gasket · Crack in head, manifold or block	· Replace head gasket · Replace as necessary
Coolant recovery system inoperative	· Coolant level low · Leak in system · Pressure cap not tight or seal missing, or leaking · Pressure cap defective · Overflow tube clogged or leaking · Recovery bottle vent restricted	· Replenish coolant to FULL mark · Pressure test to isolate leak and repair as necessary · Repair as necessary · Replace cap · Repair as necessary · Remove restriction
Noise	· Fan contacting shroud · Loose water pump impeller · Glazed fan belt · Loose fan belt · Rough surface on drive pulley · Water pump bearing worn · Belt alignment	· Reposition shroud and inspect engine mounts (on electric fans inspect assembly) · Replace pump · Apply silicone or replace belt · Adjust fan belt tension · Replace pulley · Remove belt to isolate. Replace pump. · Check pulley alignment. Repair as necessary.
No coolant flow through heater core	· Restricted return inlet in water pump · Heater hose collapsed or restricted · Restricted heater core · Restricted outlet in thermostat housing · Intake manifold bypass hole in cylinder head restricted · Faulty heater control valve · Intake manifold coolant passage restricted	· Remove restriction · Remove restriction or replace hose · Remove restriction or replace core · Remove flash or restriction · Remove restriction · Replace valve · Remove restriction or replace intake manifold

NOTE: *Immediately after shutdown, the engine enters a condition known as heat soak. This is caused by the cooling system being inoperative while engine temperature is still high. If coolant temperature rises above boiling point, expansion and pressure may push some coolant out of the radiator overflow tube. If this does not occur frequently it is considered normal.*

TCCS3C12

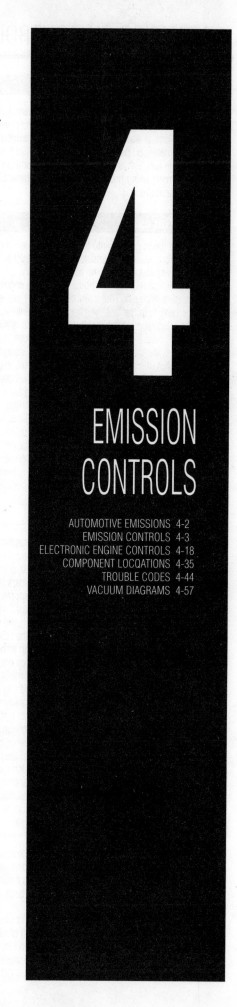

4
EMISSION CONTROLS

AUTOMOTIVE EMISSIONS

Before emission controls were mandated on internal combustion engines, other sources of engine pollutants were discovered along with the exhaust emissions. It was determined that engine combustion exhaust produced approximately 60 percent of the total emission pollutants, fuel evaporation from the fuel tank and carburetor vents produced 20 percent, with the final 20 percent being produced through the crankcase as a by-product of the combustion process.

Exhaust Gases

The exhaust gases emitted into the atmosphere are a combination of burned and unburned fuel. To understand the exhaust emission and its composition, we must review some basic chemistry.

When the air/fuel mixture is introduced into the engine, we are mixing air, composed of nitrogen (78 percent), oxygen (21 percent) and other gases (1 percent) with the fuel, which is 100 percent hydrocarbons (HC), in a semi-controlled ratio. As the combustion process is accomplished, power is produced to move the vehicle while the heat of combustion is transferred to the cooling system. The exhaust gases are then composed of nitrogen, a diatomic gas (N_2), the same as was introduced in the engine, carbon dioxide (CO_2), the same gas that is used in beverage carbonation, and water vapor (H_2O). The nitrogen (N_2), for the most part, passes through the engine unchanged, while the oxygen (O_2) reacts (burns) with the hydrocarbons (HC) and produces the carbon dioxide (CO_2) and the water vapors (H_2O). If this chemical process would be the only process to take place, the exhaust emissions would be harmless. However, during the combustion process, other compounds are formed which are considered dangerous. These pollutants are hydrocarbons (HC), carbon monoxide (CO), oxides of nitrogen (NOx) oxides of sulfur (SOx) and engine particulates.

HYDROCARBONS

Hydrocarbons (HC) are essentially fuel which was not burned during the combustion process or which has escaped into the atmosphere through fuel evaporation. The main sources of incomplete combustion are rich air/fuel mixtures, low engine temperatures and improper spark timing. The main sources of hydrocarbon emission through fuel evaporation on most vehicles used to be the vehicle's fuel tank and carburetor float bowl.

To reduce combustion hydrocarbon emission, engine modifications were made to minimize dead space and surface area in the combustion chamber. In addition, the air/fuel mixture was made more lean through the improved control which feedback carburetion and fuel injection offers and by the addition of external controls to aid in further combustion of the hydrocarbons outside the engine. Two such methods were the addition of air injection systems, to inject fresh air into the exhaust manifolds and the installation of catalytic converters, units that are able to burn traces of hydrocarbons without affecting the internal combustion process or fuel economy.

To control hydrocarbon emissions through fuel evaporation, modifications were made to the fuel tank to allow storage of the fuel vapors during periods of engine shutdown. Modifications were also made to the air intake system so that at specific times during engine operation, these vapors may be purged and burned by blending them with the air/fuel mixture.

CARBON MONOXIDE

Carbon monoxide is formed when not enough oxygen is present during the combustion process to convert carbon (C) to carbon dioxide (CO_2). An increase in the carbon monoxide (CO) emission is normally accompanied by an increase in the hydrocarbon (HC) emission because of the lack of oxygen to completely burn all of the fuel mixture.

Carbon monoxide (CO) also increases the rate at which the photochemical smog is formed by speeding up the conversion of nitric oxide (NO) to nitrogen dioxide (NO_2). To accomplish this, carbon monoxide (CO) combines with oxygen (O_2) and nitric oxide (NO) to produce carbon dioxide (CO_2) and nitrogen dioxide (NO_2). ($CO + O_2 + NO = CO_2 + NO_2$).

The dangers of carbon monoxide, which is an odorless and colorless toxic gas are many. When carbon monoxide is inhaled into the lungs and passed into the blood stream, oxygen is replaced by the carbon monoxide in the red blood cells, causing a reduction in the amount of oxygen supplied to the many parts of the body. This lack of oxygen causes headaches, lack of coordination, reduced mental alertness and, should the carbon monoxide concentration be high enough, death could result.

NITROGEN

Normally, nitrogen is an inert gas. When heated to approximately 2500°F (1371°C) through the combustion process, this gas becomes active and causes an increase in the nitric oxide (NO) emission.

Oxides of nitrogen (NOx) are composed of approximately 97–98 percent nitric oxide (NO). Nitric oxide is a colorless gas, but when it is passed into the atmosphere it combines with oxygen and forms nitrogen dioxide (NO_2). The nitrogen dioxide then combines with chemically active hydrocarbons (HC) and, when in the presence of sunlight, causes the formation of photochemical smog.

Ozone

To further complicate matters, some of the nitrogen dioxide (NO_2) is broken apart by the sunlight to form nitric oxide and oxygen. (NO_2 + sunlight = NO + O). This single atom of oxygen then combines with diatomic (meaning 2 atoms) oxygen (O_2) to form ozone (O_3). Ozone is one of the smells associated with smog. It has a pungent and offensive odor, irritates the eyes and lung tissues, affects the growth of plant life and causes rapid deterioration of rubber products. Ozone can be formed by sunlight as well as electrical discharge into the air.

The most common discharge area on the automobile engine is the secondary ignition electrical system, especially when inferior quality spark plug cables are used. As the surge of high voltage is routed through the secondary cable, the circuit builds up an electrical field around the wire, which acts upon the oxygen in the surrounding air to form the ozone. The faint glow along the cable with the engine running that may be visible on a dark night, is called the "corona discharge." It is the result of the electrical field passing from a high along the cable, to a low in the surrounding air, which forms the ozone gas. The combination of corona and ozone has been a major cause of cable deterioration. Recently, different and better quality insulating materials have lengthened the life of the electrical cables.

Although ozone at ground level can be harmful, ozone is beneficial to the earth's inhabitants. By having a concentrated ozone layer called the "ozonosphere," between 10 and 20 miles (16–32 km) up in the atmosphere, much of the ultraviolet radiation from the sun's rays are absorbed and screened. If this ozone layer were not present, much of the earth's surface would be burned, dried and unfit for human life.

OXIDES OF SULFUR

Oxides of sulfur (SOx) were initially ignored in the exhaust system emissions, since the sulfur content of gasoline as a fuel is less than $\frac{1}{10}$ of 1 percent. Because of this small amount, it was felt that it contributed very little to the overall pollution problem. However, because of the difficulty in eradicating the sulfur emissions in industrial pollution, along with the introduction of catalytic converters to automobile exhaust systems, a change was mandated. The automobile exhaust system, when equipped with a catalytic converter, changes the sulfur dioxide (SO_2) into sulfur trioxide (SO_3).

When this combines with water vapor (H_2O), a sulfuric acid mist (H_2SO_4) is formed. This is a very difficult pollutant to handle since it is extremely corrosive. This sulfuric acid mist that is formed is the same mist that rises from the vents of an automobile battery when an active chemical reaction takes place within the battery cells.

When a large concentration of vehicles equipped with catalytic converters are operating in an area, this acid mist may rise and be distributed over a large ground area causing land, plant, crop, paint and building damage.

PARTICULATE MATTER

A certain amount of particulate matter is present in the burning of any fuel, with carbon constituting the largest percentage of the particulates. In gasoline, the remaining particulates are the burned remains of the various other compounds used in its manufacture. When a gasoline engine is in good internal condition, the particulate emissions are low, but as the engine wears internally, the particulate emissions increase. By visually inspecting the tailpipe emissions, a determination can be made as to where an engine defect may exist. An engine with light gray or blue smoke emitting from the tailpipe normally indicates an increase in the oil consumption through burning due to internal engine wear. Black smoke would indicate a defective fuel delivery system, causing the engine to operate in a rich mode. Regardless of the color of the smoke, the internal part of the engine or the fuel delivery system should be repaired to prevent excess particulate emissions.

Diesel and turbine engines emit a darkened plume of smoke from the exhaust system because of the type of fuel used. Emission control regulations are mandated for this type of emission and more stringent measures are being used to prevent excess emission of the particulate matter. Electronic components have been introduced to control the injection of the fuel at precisely the proper time of piston travel, to achieve the optimum in fuel ignition and fuel usage. Other particulate afterburning components are being tested to achieve a cleaner emission.

Good grades of engine lubricating oils, which meet the manufacturers' specifications, should be used. Cut-rate oils can contribute to the particulate emission problem because of their low flash or ignition temperature point. Such oils burn prematurely during the combustion process, causing emission of particulate matter.

The cooling system is an important factor in the reduction of particulate matter. The optimum combustion will occur with the cooling system operating at a temperature specified by the manufacturer. The cooling system must be maintained in the same manner as the engine oiling system, as each system is required to perform properly in order for the engine to operate efficiently for a long time.

Crankcase Emissions

Crankcase emissions are made up of water, acids, unburned fuel, oil fumes and particulates. These emissions are classified as hydrocarbons (HC) and are formed by the small amount of unburned, compressed air/fuel mixture entering the crankcase from the combustion area (between the cylinder walls and piston rings) during the compression and power strokes. The heat of the compression and combustion help to form the remaining crankcase emissions.

Since the first engines, crankcase emissions were allowed into the atmosphere through a road draft tube, mounted on the lower side of the engine block. Fresh air came in through an open oil filler cap or breather. The air passed through the crankcase mixing with blow-by gases. The motion of the vehicle and the air blowing past the open end of the road draft tube caused a low pressure area (vacuum) at the end of the tube. Crankcase emissions were simply drawn out of the road draft tube and into the air.

EMISSION CONTROLS

Positive Crankcase Ventilation (PCV) System

OPERATION

▶ **See Figure 1**

The PCV system vents crankcase gases into the engine air intake where they are burned with the fuel and air mixture. The PCV system keeps pollutants from being released into the atmosphere, and also helps to keep the engine oil clean, by ridding the crankcase of moisture and corrosive fumes. The PCV system consists of the PCV valve, its mounting grommet, the nipple in the air intake and the connecting hoses. On some engine applications, the PCV system is connected with the evaporative emission system.

To control crankcase emissions, the road draft tube was deleted. A hose and/or tubing was routed from the crankcase to the intake manifold so the blow-by emission could be burned with the air/fuel mixture. However, it was found that intake manifold vacuum, used to draw the crankcase emissions into the manifold, would vary in strength at the wrong time and not allow the proper emission flow. A regulating valve was needed to control the flow of air through the crankcase.

Testing showed that removal of blow-by gases from the crankcase as quickly as possible was most important to the longevity of the engine. Should large accumulations of blow-by gases remain and condense, dilution of the engine oil would occur to form water, soots, resins, acids and lead salts, resulting in the formation of sludge and varnishes. This condensation of the blow-by gases occurs more frequently on vehicles used in numerous starting and stopping conditions, excessive idling and when the engine is not allowed to attain normal operating temperature through short runs.

Evaporative Emissions

Gasoline fuel is a major source of pollution, before and after it is burned in the automobile engine. From the time the fuel is refined, stored, pumped and transported, and again stored until it is pumped into the fuel tank of the vehicle, gasoline gives off unburned hydrocarbons (HC) into the atmosphere. Through the redesign of storage areas and venting systems, the pollution factor was diminished, but not eliminated, from the refinery standpoint. However, the automobile still remained the primary source of vaporized, unburned hydrocarbon (HC) emissions.

Fuel pumped from an underground storage tank is cool, but when exposed to a warmer ambient temperature, will expand. Before controls were mandated, an owner might fill the fuel tank with fuel from an underground storage tank and park the vehicle for some time in a warm area, such as a parking lot. As the fuel would warm, it would expand and, should no provisions or area be provided for the expansion, the fuel would spill out of the filler neck and onto the ground, causing hydrocarbon (HC) pollution and creating a severe fire hazard. To correct this condition, the vehicle manufacturers added overflow plumbing and/or gasoline tanks with built-in expansion areas or domes.

However, this did not control the fuel vapor emission from the fuel tank. It was determined that most of the fuel evaporation occurred when the vehicle was stationary and the engine not operating. Most vehicles carry 5–25 gallons (19–95 liters) of gasoline. Should a large concentration of vehicles be parked in one area, such as a large parking lot, excessive fuel vapor emissions would take place, increasing as the temperature increases.

To prevent the vapor emission from escaping into the atmosphere, the fuel systems were designed to trap the vapors while the vehicle is stationary, by sealing the system from the atmosphere. A storage system is used to collect and hold the fuel vapors from the carburetor (if equipped) and the fuel tank when the engine is not operating. When the engine is started, the storage system is then purged of the fuel vapors, which are drawn into the engine and burned with the air/fuel mixture.

The PCV valve controls the amount of vapors pulled into the intake manifold from the crankcase and acts as a check valve by preventing air flow from entering the crankcase in the opposite direction. The PCV valve also prevents combustion backfire from entering the crankcase, in order to prevent detonation of the accumulated crankcase gases.

TESTING

1. Remove the PCV valve from the valve cover or engine block mounting grommet. The PCV valve for the 3.8L and 4.6L SOHC engines is mounted in the right-hand valve cover, in a rubber grommet. The PCV valve for the 4.6L DOHC engine is also mounted in a rubber grommet, which is installed in the left-hand valve cover. On the 5.0L engine, the PCV valve is located on top of the block by the firewall.

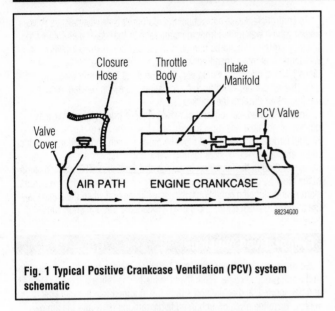

Fig. 1 Typical Positive Crankcase Ventilation (PCV) system schematic

2. Shake the PCV valve. If the valve rattles when shaken, reinstall it and proceed to Step 3. If the valve does not rattle, it is sticking and must be replaced.

3. Start the engine and bring it to normal operating temperature.

4. Disconnect the closure (fresh air) hose from the air inlet tube (connects the air cleaner housing to the throttle body).

5. Place a stiff piece of paper over the hose end and wait 1 minute.

    a. If vacuum holds the paper in place, the system is OK; reconnect the hose.

    b. If the paper is not held in place, check for loose hose connections, vacuum leaks or blockage. Correct as necessary.

REMOVAL & INSTALLATION

PCV Valve

▶ **See Figures 2, 3, 4 and 5**

1. Disconnect the vacuum hose from the PCV valve.
2. Remove the PCV valve from its mounting grommet.

To install:

3. Attach the PCV vacuum hose to the PCV valve, then insert the valve into its mounting grommet.

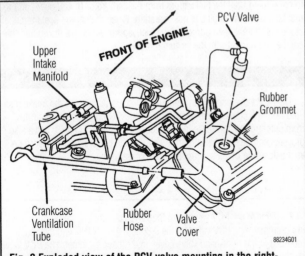

Fig. 2 Exploded view of the PCV valve mounting in the right-hand valve cover on the 3.8L engine

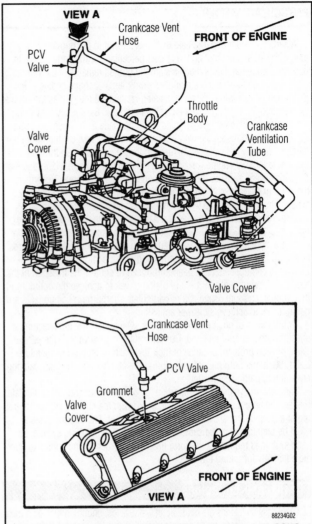

Fig. 3 Exploded view of the PCV system used on the 4.6L SOHC engine

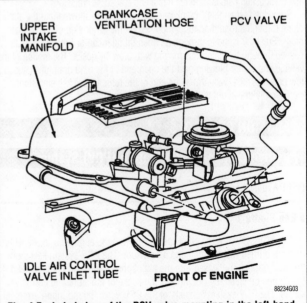

Fig. 4 Exploded view of the PCV valve mounting in the left-hand valve cover on the 4.6L DOHC engine

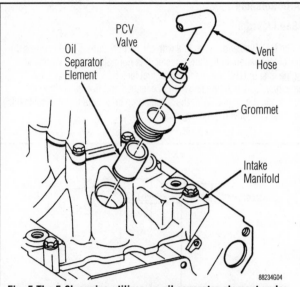

Fig. 5 The 5.0L engine utilizes an oil separator element under the PCV valve to help prevent oil from being introduced into the air intake charge

Evaporative Emission Control System

OPERATION

▶ See Figure 6

Fuel vapors trapped in the sealed fuel tank are vented through the orifice vapor valve assembly in the top of the tank. The vapors leave the valve assembly through a single vapor line and continue to the carbon canister for storage until they are purged to the engine for burning.

Purging the carbon canister removes the fuel vapor stored in the canister. The fuel vapor is purged via a Canister Purge (CANP) solenoid or vacuum controlled purge valve. Purging occurs when the engine is at normal operating temperature and off idle.

The evaporative emission control system consists of the following components: fuel vapor (charcoal) canister, orificed vapor valve, fuel vapor Canister Purge (CANP) solenoid, pressure/vacuum relief fuel tank filler cap, as well as the fuel tank and fuel tank filler pipe, vapor tube and fuel vapor hoses.

Fuel Vapor (Charcoal) Canister

▶ See Figure 7

→The fuel vapor canister is referred to as the evaporative emissions canister on 1995–98 models.

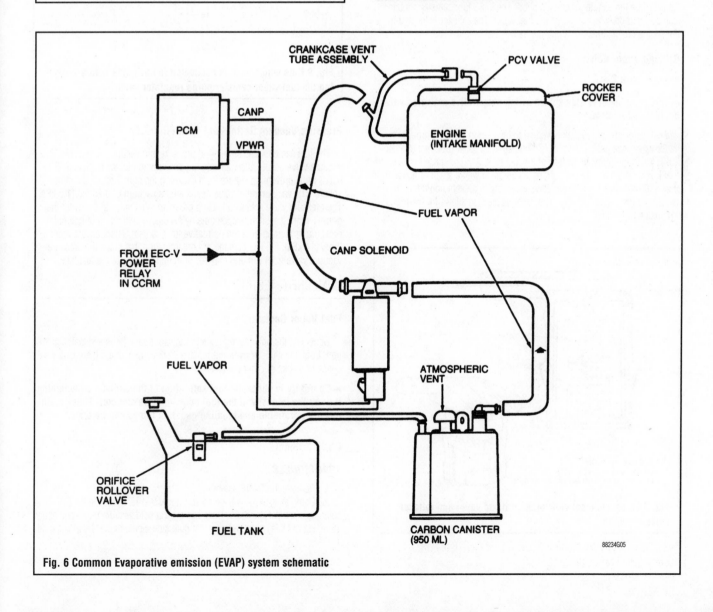

Fig. 6 Common Evaporative emission (EVAP) system schematic

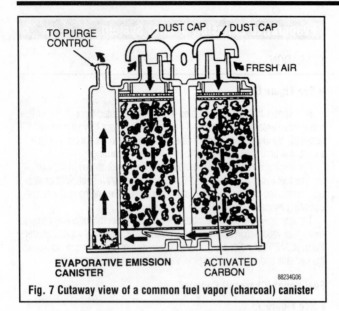

Fig. 7 Cutaway view of a common fuel vapor (charcoal) canister

The fuel vapors from the fuel tank are stored in the fuel vapor canister until the vehicle is operated, at which time the vapors will purge from the canister into the engine for consumption. The fuel vapor canister contains activated carbon, which absorbs the fuel vapor. The canister is located in the engine compartment or along the frame rail.

Orificed Vapor Valve

♦ See Figure 8

➡This component is also known as the evaporative emission valve on 1995–98 models.

Fuel vapor in the fuel tank is vented to the carbon canister through the vapor valve assembly. The valve is mounted in a rubber grommet at a central location in the upper surface of the fuel tank. A vapor space between the fuel level and the tank upper surface is combined with a small orifice and float shut-off valve in the vapor valve assembly to prevent liquid fuel from passing to the carbon canister. The vapor space also allows for thermal expansion of the fuel.

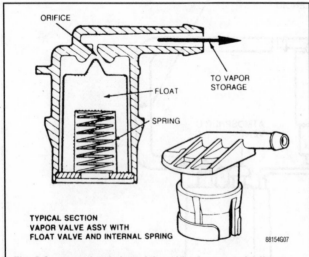

Fig. 8 Cross-sectional view of the orificed vapor and rollover valve assembly

CANP Solenoid

♦ See Figure 9

The CANP solenoid is in line with the carbon canister and controls the flow of fuel vapors out of the canister. It is normally closed. When the engine is shut **OFF**, vapors from the fuel tank flow into the canister. After the engine is started, the solenoid is engaged and opens, purging the vapors into the engine. With the solenoid open, vapors from the fuel tank are routed directly into the engine.

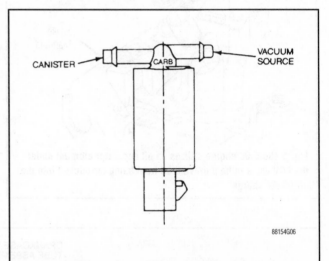

Fig. 9 Note which hose is connected to each side before removing the fuel vapor canister purge regulator valve

Pressure/Vacuum Relief Fuel Tank Filler Cap

The fuel cap contains an integral pressure and vacuum relief valve. The vacuum valve acts to allow air into the fuel tank to replace the fuel as it is used, while preventing vapors from escaping the tank through the atmosphere. The vacuum relief valve opens after a vacuum of 0.25 psi (1.7 kPa). The pressure valve acts as a backup pressure relief valve in the event the normal venting system is overcome by excessive generation of internal pressure or restriction of the normal venting system. The pressure relief is 2 psi (14 kPa). Fill cap damage or contamination that stops the pressure vacuum valve from working may result in deformation of the fuel tank.

COMPONENT TESTING

Fuel Vapor Canister

Generally, the only testing done to the vapor canister is a visual inspection. Look the canister over and replace it with a new one if there is any evidence of cracks or other damage.

➡Do not try to check the fuel saturation of the canister by weighing it or by the intensity of the fuel odor from the canister. These methods are unreliable and inhaling gasoline fumes can be toxic.

CANP Solenoid

1994 MODELS

1. Remove the CANP solenoid.
2. Using an external voltage source, apply 9–14 DC volts to the CANP solenoid electrical terminals. Then, use a hand-held vacuum pump and apply 16 in. Hg (53 kPa) vacuum to the manifold side nipple of the CANP solenoid.

a. If the solenoid opens and allows air to freely pass through it, the solenoid is working properly.

b. If the solenoid does not allow air to pass freely while energized, replace the solenoid with a new one.

1995–98 MODELS

1. Remove the CANP solenoid.
2. Measure the resistance between the two CANP terminals.
   a. If the resistance is 30–90 ohms, proceed to the Step 3.
   b. If the resistance is not 30–90 ohms, replace the CANP solenoid.
3. Attach a hand-held vacuum pump to the intake manifold vacuum side of the CANP solenoid, then apply 16 in. Hg (53 kPa) of vacuum to the solenoid.
   a. If the solenoid will not hold vacuum for at least 20 seconds, replace it with a new one.

b. If the solenoid holds vacuum, proceed to Step 4. Keep the vacuum applied to the solenoid.

4. Using an external voltage source, apply 9–14 DC volts to the CANP solenoid electrical terminals.
   a. If the solenoid opens and the vacuum drops, the solenoid is working properly.
   b. If the solenoid does not open and the vacuum remains, replace the solenoid with a new one.

EVAP System

♦ See Figures 10 and 11

To perform a general evaporation emission system inspection, follow the two diagnostic charts presented here.

Fuel Tank Evaporative Emission System

The following is a diagnostic guide for checking and / or servicing concerns of internal fuel tank pressure build-up. A typical concern may be a hissing sound as the fuel cap is removed for refueling.

The basic fuel tank venting system is typical for all vehicles.

The fuel evaporative emission system allows for controlled release of fuel tank pressure through a carbon vapor storage canister. Under normal operating conditions, this system will allow sufficient venting to prevent a build-up of internal fuel tank pressure.

Some operating conditions may cause temporary build-up of internal fuel tank pressure. Some of these conditions are:

- On warm or hot days, parking the vehicle after filling the fuel tank, the fuel is cool from underground storage and vaporizes rapidly when warmed.
- Parking after driving over rough roads, washboard, etc., after filling the fuel tank. Agitation of fuel increases vaporization.
- Parking after driving long distances in high temperature conditions.
- Climbing long grades, especially while towing a trailer, or while fully loaded.

A normally functioning evaporative emission system will relieve the pressure buildup.

No service is required if these conditions caused the customer concern. A blocked fuel evaporative emission system can cause abnormal fuel tank pressure and must be serviced. Refer to the chart for diagnosis and flow test.

PINPOINT TEST A: EVAPORATIVE EMISSIONS DIAGNOSIS

	TEST STEP	RESULT	▶	ACTION TO TAKE
A1	FUNCTIONAL TEST			
	• Test canister hose and inlet nipple for blockage. • **Are hoses or inlet blocked?**	Yes	▶	REMOVE blockage.
		No	▶	GO to **B1**.
A2	FUNCTIONAL TEST			
	• Test fuel evaporative emission system for blockage. • **Are all system passages open?**	Yes	▶	REMOVE blockage or REPLACE component.
		No	▶	GO to **B2**.
A3	VISUAL INSPECTION			
	• Inspect vapor tube and hoses for kinks or pinched areas. • **Are tube or hoses kinked or pinched?**	Yes	▶	SERVICE or REPLACE tube or hoses. VERIFY service.
		No	▶	GO to **A4**.
A4	VISUAL INSPECTION			
	• Inspect vapor hose routing between fuel tank and body for pinch. • **Is vapor hose pinched?**	Yes	▶	LOOSEN fuel tank and reroute hose. VERIFY service.
		No	▶	GO to **A5**.
A5	VISUAL INSPECTION			
	• Remove fuel tank. • Remove vapor separator valve. • Inspect valve for open air passage through orifice. • **Is air passage open?**	Yes	▶	INSTALL valve in tank. INSTALL tank system test complete.
		No	▶	REPLACE valve. VERIFY service.

Fig. 10 Evaporative emissions (EVAP) system diagnostic chart

88154G08

PINPOINT TEST B: FLOW TEST—FUEL EVAPORATIVE SYSTEM

TEST STEP		RESULT ►	ACTION TO TAKE
B1	**FLOW TEST**	Pressure drop:	
	CAUTION: Do not use other high pressure air supplies. Will result in damage to canister.	Drops to zero immediately ►	System flow OK, no servicing required.
	• Install hand pump and pressure gauge Rotunda 021-00014 Vacuum and Pressure Tester or equivalent in vapor hose at test point B1. • Hand pump to a maximum of 17.2 kPa (2.5 psi).	Holds pressure or leaks down slowly ►	PERFORM Pinpoint Test Step A3.
B2	**FLOW TEST**	Pressure drop:	
	CAUTION: Failure to remove fuel cap may result in damage to fuel tank.	Drops to zero immediately ►	System OK, no servicing required.
	• Remove fuel cap from fuel filler pipe. **CAUTION: Do not use other high pressure air supplies. May result in damage to fuel tank.** • Install hand pump and pressure gauge onto tee or canister nipple at test point B2. • Hand pump to a maximum of 17.2 kPa (2.5 psi).	Holds pressure or leaks down slowly ►	PERFORM Pinpoint Test Step A4.

TEST POINT B2 WITH TEE
TEST POINT B1 WITH TEE
TEST POINT B2 WITHOUT TEE
VAPOR HOSE
VAPOR TUBE
TO FUEL TANK
CLOSE OFF LINE
TEST POINT B1 WITHOUT TEE
CARBON CANISTER

88154G09

Fig. 11 Evaporative emissions (EVAP) system diagnostic chart (continued)

REMOVAL & INSTALLATION

Fuel Vapor Canister

▶ **See Figures 12 and 13**

➡The fuel vapor canister is referred to as the evaporative emissions canister on 1995–98 models.

1. Disconnect the vapor hoses from the canister.
2. Remove the mounting screws, then remove the canister.
To install:
3. Position the canister in place, then install the mounting screws.
4. Attach the vapor hoses to the canister.

Fuel Vapor Valve

➡This component is also known as the evaporative emission valve on 1995–98 models.

1. Disconnect the negative battery cable.
2. Relieve the fuel system pressure.
3. Remove the fuel tank, as described in Section 5 of this manual.
4. Remove the fuel vapor valve from the fuel tank.
To install:
5. Install the fuel vapor valve into the fuel tank.

6. Install the fuel tank in the vehicle.
7. Connect the negative battery cable.

CANP Solenoid

1. Disconnect the vapor hoses from the CANP solenoid.
2. Unplug the electrical connector from the CANP solenoid.
3. Remove the purge solenoid valve from the vehicle.
To install:
4. Install the CANP solenoid, then attach the engine wiring harness connector to the solenoid.
5. Connect the vapor hoses to the solenoid.

Pressure/Vacuum Relief Fuel Tank Filler Cap

1. Unscrew the fuel filler cap.

➡The cap has a pre-vent feature that allows the tank to vent for the first ¾ turn before unthreading.

2. Remove the screw retaining the fuel cap tether and remove the fuel cap.
To install:
3. Position the end of the tether against its mounting boss, then install and tighten the tether screw.
4. Thread the filler cap into the fuel tank filler tube, making sure to turn it clockwise until the ratchet mechanism gives off 3 or more loud clicks.

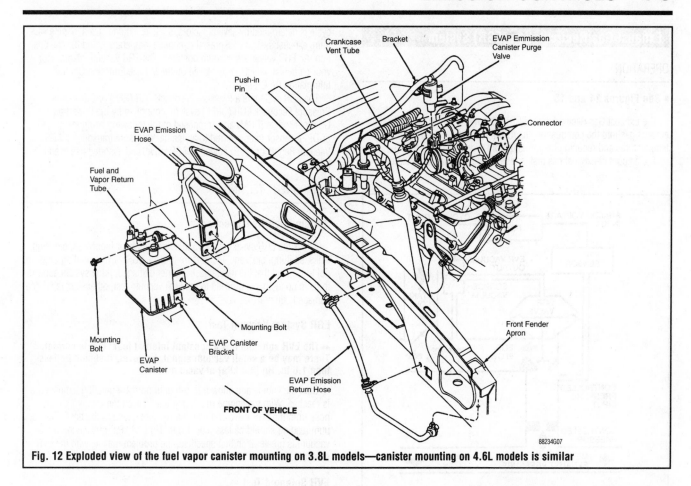

Fig. 12 Exploded view of the fuel vapor canister mounting on 3.8L models—canister mounting on 4.6L models is similar

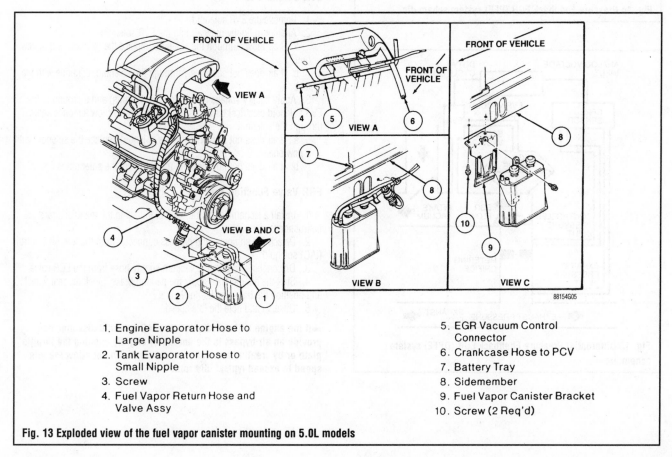

1. Engine Evaporator Hose to Large Nipple
2. Tank Evaporator Hose to Small Nipple
3. Screw
4. Fuel Vapor Return Hose and Valve Assy

5. EGR Vacuum Control Connector
6. Crankcase Hose to PCV
7. Battery Tray
8. Sidemember
9. Fuel Vapor Canister Bracket
10. Screw (2 Req'd)

Fig. 13 Exploded view of the fuel vapor canister mounting on 5.0L models

Exhaust Gas Recirculation (EGR) System

OPERATION

▶ **See Figures 14 and 15**

The Exhaust Gas Recirculation (EGR) system is designed to reintroduce exhaust gas into the combustion chambers, thereby lowering combustion temperatures and reducing the formation of Oxides of Nitrogen (NO_x).

The amount of exhaust gas that is reintroduced into the combustion cycle is determined by several factors, such as: engine speed, engine vacuum, exhaust system backpressure, coolant temperature, and throttle position. All EGR valves are vacuum operated. The EGR vacuum diagram for your particular vehicle is displayed on the Vehicle Emission Control Information (VECI) label.

The EGR system is a Pressure Feedback EGR (PFE) or Differential Pressure Feedback EGR (DPFE) system, controlled by the Powertrain Control Module (PCM) and composed of the following components: PFE or DPFE sensor (also referred to as the backpressure transducer), EGR Vacuum Regulator (EVR) solenoid, EGR valve, and assorted hoses and tubing.

COMPONENT TESTING

System Integrity Inspection

Check the EGR system hoses and connections for looseness, pinching, leaks, splitting, blockage, etc. Ensure that the EGR valve mounting bolts are not loose, and that the flange gasket is not damaged. If the system appears to be in good shape, proceed to the EGR vacuum test; otherwise, repair the damaged components.

EGR System Vacuum Test

➡ **The EVR solenoid has a constant internal leak; this is normal. There may be a small vacuum signal, however, it should be less than 1.0 in. Hg (3.4 kPa) of vacuum.**

Start the engine and allow it to run until normal operating temperature is reached. With the engine running at idle, detach the vacuum supply hose from the EGR valve and install a vacuum gauge to the hose. The vacuum reading should be less than 1.0 in. Hg (3.4 kPa) of vacuum. If the vacuum is greater than that specified, the problem may lie with the EVR solenoid.

EVR Solenoid Test

1. Remove the EVR solenoid.
2. Attempt to lightly blow air into the EVR solenoid.
   a. If air blows through the solenoid, replace the solenoid with a new one.
   b. If air does not pass freely through the solenoid, continue with the test.
3. Apply battery voltage (approximately 12 volts) and a ground to the EVR solenoid electrical terminals. Attempt to lightly blow air, once again, through the solenoid.
   a. If air does not pass through the solenoid, replace the solenoid with a new one.
   b. If air does not flow through the solenoid, the solenoid is OK.

EGR Valve Function Test

1. Install a tachometer on the engine, following the manufacturer's instructions.
2. Detach the engine wiring harness connector from the Idle Air Control (IAC) solenoid.
3. Disconnect and plug the vacuum supply hose from the EGR valve.
4. Start the engine, then apply the parking brake, block the rear wheels and position the transmission in Neutral.
5. Observe and note the idle speed.

➡ **If the engine will not idle with the IAC solenoid disconnected, provide an air bypass to the engine by slightly opening the throttle plate or by creating an intake vacuum leak. Do not allow the idle speed to exceed typical idle rpm.**

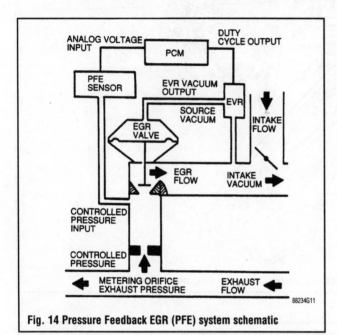

Fig. 14 Pressure Feedback EGR (PFE) system schematic

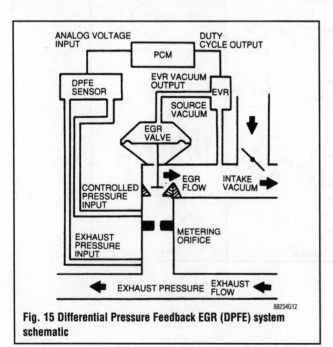

Fig. 15 Differential Pressure Feedback EGR (DPFE) system schematic

6. Using a hand-held vacuum pump, slowly apply 5–10 in. Hg (17–34 kPa) of vacuum to the EGR valve nipple.

a. If the idle speed drops more than 100 rpm with the vacuum applied and returns to normal after the vacuum is removed, the EGR valve is OK.

b. If the idle speed does not drop more than 100 rpm with the vacuum applied and return to normal after the vacuum is removed, inspect the EGR valve for a blockage; clean it if a blockage is found. Replace the EGR valve if no blockage is found, or if cleaning the valve does not remedy the malfunction.

REMOVAL & INSTALLATION

PFE/DPFE Sensor

♦ See Figures 16 and 17

➡This component is only found on 3.8L and 4.6L engines, and is also referred to as the backpressure transducer.

1. Disconnect the negative battery cable.
2. Detach and label the wiring harness connector from the PFE/DPFE sensor.
3. Disconnect all of the hoses from the sensor.
4. Remove the mounting nuts, then separate the sensor from the mounting bracket.
5. On 4.6L DOHC engines, remove the EGR tube heat shield.
6. If necessary, remove the EVR solenoid (3.8L engines only) and the PFE/DPFE mounting bracket from the upper intake manifold.

To install:

7. If removed, install the EVR solenoid and mounting bracket onto the upper intake manifold.
8. If applicable, install the EGR tube heat shield.
9. Position the PFE/DPFE sensor on the mounting bracket, then install and tighten the mounting nuts until snug.
10. Attach all necessary hoses and wiring to the sensor.
11. Connect the negative battery cable.

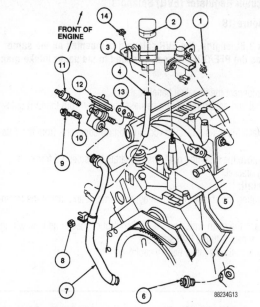

1. Mounting nut
2. PFE/DPFE sensor
3. PFE/DPFE and EVR solenoid bracket
4. PFE/DPFE sensor vacuum hose
5. Upper intake manifold
6. EGR valve-to-exhaust manifold tube connector
7. EGR valve-to-exhaust manifold tube
8. Mounting nut
9. Mounting bolt
10. EGR pressure sensor hose connector plug
11. Mounting stud/bolt
12. EGR valve
13. EGR valve gasket
14. Mounting nut

Fig. 16 Exploded view of the PFE system used by the 3.8L engine—the DPFE system is the same except that the DPFE sensor is attached to two vacuum hoses, rather than one

On 3.8L engines, the PFE/DPFE sensor (A) is mounted on the same bracket as the EVR solenoid (B)

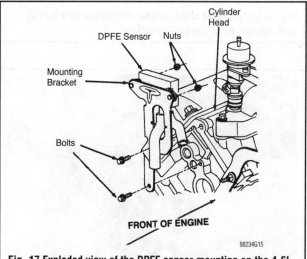

Fig. 17 Exploded view of the DPFE sensor mounting on the 4.6L SOHC engine

EGR Vacuum Regulator (EVR) Solenoid

▶ **See Figure 18**

➡On the 3.8L engine, the EVR solenoid is mounted on the same bracket as the PFE/DPFE sensor, attached to the upper intake manifold.

1. Disconnect the negative battery cable.
2. Label and detach the wiring harness connector from the EVR solenoid.
3. Detach the main emission vacuum control connector from the solenoid.
4. Remove the retaining nuts, then separate the solenoid from the mounting bracket.

To install:

5. Position the solenoid on its mounting bracket and install the retaining nuts.
6. Attach the main emission vacuum control connector and the wiring harness connector to the EVR solenoid.
7. Connect the negative battery cable.

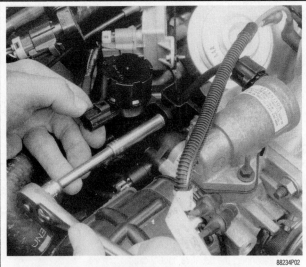

. . . then remove the mounting fasteners . . .

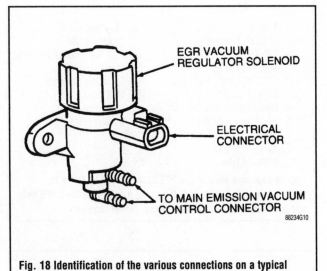

Fig. 18 Identification of the various connections on a typical EGR Vacuum Regulator (EVR) solenoid

. . . and separate the sensor from the mounting bracket

EGR Valve

3.8L AND 5.0L ENGINES

▶ **See Figure 19**

1. Disconnect the negative battery cable.
2. Remove the air inlet tube from the throttle body and air cleaner housing.
3. Label and detach all vacuum hoses from the EGR valve.
4. Label and detach any electrical wiring harness connectors from the EGR valve.
5. Disconnect the EGR valve-to-exhaust manifold tube from the EGR valve.
6. Remove the EGR valve mounting fasteners, then separate the valve from the upper intake manifold.
7. Remove and discard the old EGR valve gasket, and clean the gasket mating surfaces on the valve and the intake manifold.

To install:

8. Position the EGR valve, along with a new gasket, on the upper intake manifold, then install and tighten the mounting bolts to 15–22 ft. lbs. (20–30 Nm) on 3.8L engines, or to 106–159 inch lbs. (12–18 Nm) on 5.0L engines.

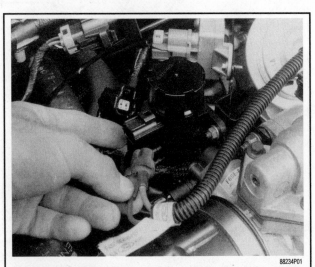

To remove the EVR solenoid on 3.8L engines, detach the engine wiring harness connector from it . . .

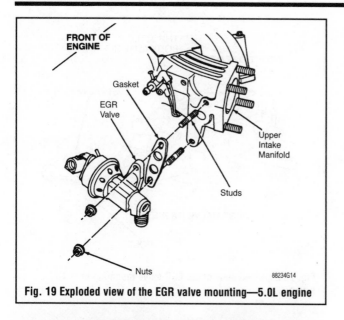

Fig. 19 Exploded view of the EGR valve mounting—5.0L engine

. . . and move the sensors and bracket aside

To remove the EGR valve on 3.8L engines, detach the engine wiring harness connectors . . .

Detach the vacuum hoses from the EGR valve . . .

. . . then remove the PFE/DPFE and EVR sensors' bracket mounting nuts . . .

. . . and disconnect the EGR valve-to-exhaust manifold tube from the valve

Remove the EGR valve mounting bolts . . .

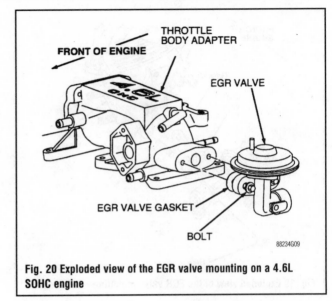

Fig. 20 Exploded view of the EGR valve mounting on a 4.6L SOHC engine

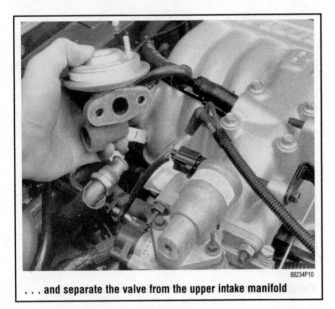

. . . and separate the valve from the upper intake manifold

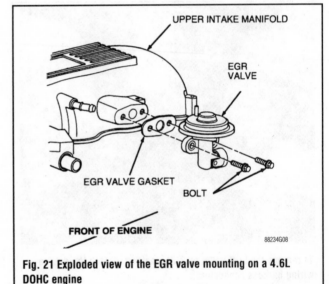

Fig. 21 Exploded view of the EGR valve mounting on a 4.6L DOHC engine

9. Connect the EGR valve-to-exhaust manifold tube to the valve, then tighten the tube nut to 30 ft. lbs. (41 Nm).

10. Connect all wiring or hoses to the EGR valve.

11. Install the air inlet tube.

12. Connect the negative battery cable.

4.6L ENGINES

◆ See Figures 20 and 21

1. On 4.6L DOHC engines, remove the EGR valve-to-exhaust manifold tube heat shield.

2. Disconnect the EGR valve-to-exhaust manifold tube from the valve.

3. Detach the vacuum hose from the EGR valve.

4. Remove the two mounting bolts, then separate the valve from the engine. Remove and discard the old EGR valve gasket.

To install:

5. Clean the EGR valve gasket surfaces with a plastic scraper to remove all traces of the old gasket.

➡**Do not tighten the EGR valve-to-exhaust manifold tube nut yet.**

6. Attach the EGR valve-to-exhaust manifold tube to the EGR valve, and loosely tighten the tube nut.

7. Install the EGR valve, along with a new gasket, on the engine.

8. Install the two mounting bolts and tighten them to 15–22 ft. lbs. (20–30 Nm).

9. Tighten the EGR valve-to-exhaust manifold tube nut until secure.

10. Attach the vacuum hose to the EGR valve.

11. On 4.6L DOHC engines, install the EGR valve-to-exhaust manifold tube heat shield.

Secondary Air Injection System

OPERATION

◆ See Figures 22 and 23

The secondary air injection system is designed to help reduce exhaust emissions during the first 20 to 120 seconds of engine operation. An Electric Air Pump (EAP) provides pressurized air to the exhaust system via tubes and hoses, and is controlled by the Powertrain Control Module (PCM).

The system is controlled by the PCM, which constantly receives information from assorted sensors telling it what is happening in the engine at

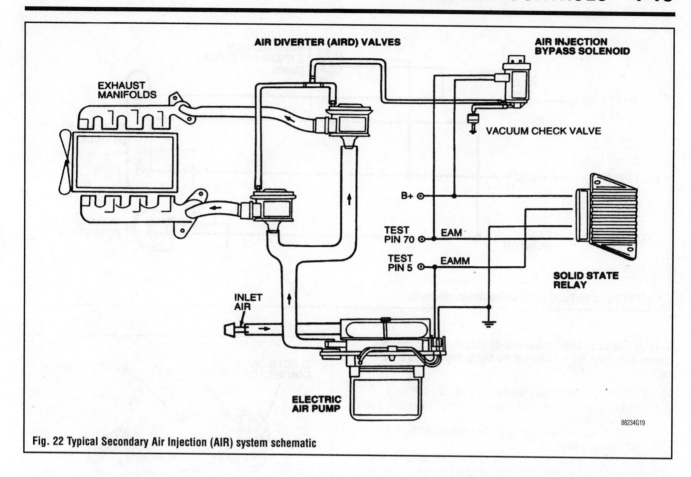

Fig. 22 Typical Secondary Air Injection (AIR) system schematic

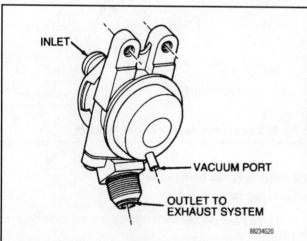

Fig. 23 The AIR Diverter (AIRD) valve, based upon incoming vacuum signals from the AIR Bypass (AIRB) valve, is what switches the pressurized air on and off to the exhaust manifolds

any given moment. The PCM energizes or de-energizes a vacuum solenoid (also known as the AIR injection Bypass or AIRB valve), which, in turn, switches a vacuum control signal going to the AIR injection Diverter (AIRD) valve on or off. When vacuum is allowed to reach the AIRD valve via the AIRB valve, the AIRD valve opens and routes pressurized air into the exhaust manifolds. The pressurized air helps complete combustion of

unburned fuel (lowering unburned hydrocarbons), and provides oxygen for the chemical reactions which take place in the catalytic converters. When vacuum is not allowed to reach the AIRD valve, the pressurized air escapes through vents into the atmosphere.

COMPONENT TESTING

Electric Air Pump (EAP)

♦ See Figure 24

> **✳ CAUTION**
>
> Use caution during this test procedure whenever working around a running engine. Personal injury can be caused by moving or hot components. Be sure to tie up long hair and to tuck in loose clothing so that they will not become caught in any moving components.

1. Disengage the wiring harness connector from the EAP.
2. Using a Digital Volt-Ohmmeter (DVOM), measure the resistance between the wiring terminals on the EAP.
   a. If the resistance measured is not 0.5–5.0 ohms, replace the EAP with a new one.
   b. If the resistance is within the range of 0.5–5.0 ohms, continue with the test.
3. Attach the DVOM to the EAIR monitor circuit terminal (on the wiring harness connector) and a good chassis ground. Start the engine and allow it to idle, then measure the voltage in the EAIR monitor circuit.

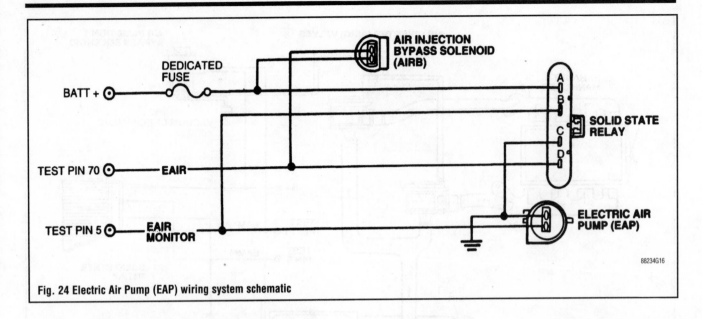

Fig. 24 Electric Air Pump (EAP) wiring system schematic

➡There may be an initial pause of 5–10 seconds after starting the engine before voltage is evident at the EAP wiring harness connector.

　a. If the voltage measured is less than 10.5 volts, the EAP is not receiving the proper amount of voltage and the wiring circuits should be inspected for problems.

　b. If the voltage is greater than 10.5 volts, continue with the test.

4. Turn the engine **OFF**.

5. Detach either hose from one of the air control valves (either the AIRD or AIRB valve). Place your hand over the detached end of the hose and have an assistant start the engine. After a 5 second delay, air flow should be felt exiting from the hose.

　a. If the air flow is felt, the EAP is functioning properly.

　b. If no air flow is felt, check the air hoses for blockages. If no blockages are evident, replace the EAP with a known good one and perform the test again.

Remaining Components

Because of the complexity and interrelationship between the secondary air injection system components, it is best to have the entire system diagnosed by a qualified automotive technician if the EAP is found to function properly, but the whole system does not.

REMOVAL & INSTALLATION

Electric Air Pump (EAP)

▶ See Figure 25

1. Disconnect the negative battery cable.

2. Label and detach all air hoses and wiring harness connectors from the EAP.

3. Remove the fasteners, then separate the EAP from the vehicle.

To install:

4. Position the EAP, then install and tighten the mounting fasteners until secure.

5. Attach all applicable hoses and wiring connectors.

6. Connect the negative battery cable.

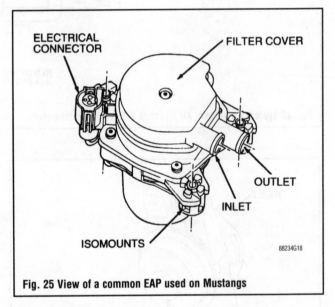

Fig. 25 View of a common EAP used on Mustangs

AIR Injection Bypass (AIRB) Valve

▶ See Figure 26

1. Remove the air inlet tube from the throttle body and the air cleaner housing.

2. Disconnect the manifold vacuum control tube from the solenoid.

3. Loosen the hose clamps from the intake and exhaust ports on the solenoid.

4. Detach the secondary air injection control valve hose and the secondary air injection pump outlet hose from the solenoid.

5. Remove the solenoid from the vehicle.

To install:

6. Attach the secondary air injection control valve hose and the secondary air injection pump outlet hose to the vacuum solenoid.

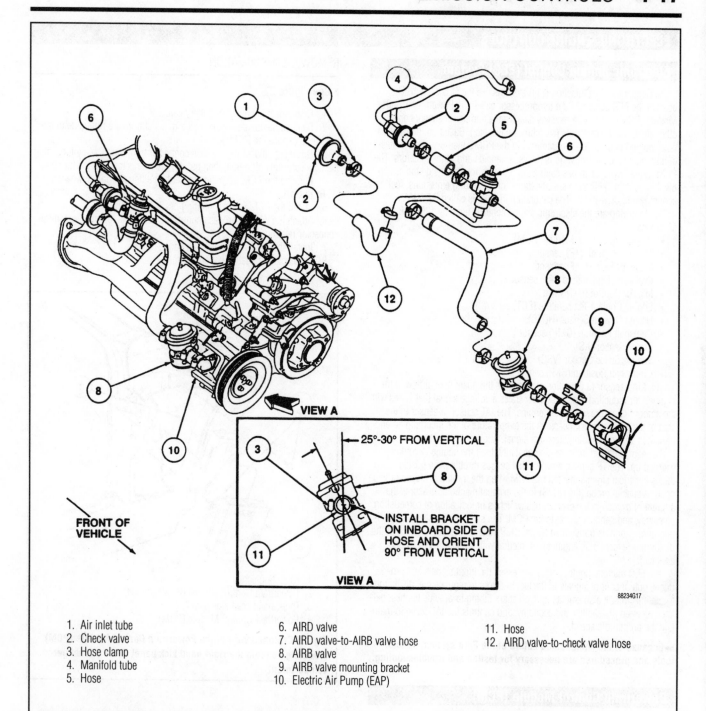

1. Air inlet tube
2. Check valve
3. Hose clamp
4. Manifold tube
5. Hose
6. AIRD valve
7. AIRD valve-to-AIRB valve hose
8. AIRB valve
9. AIRB valve mounting bracket
10. Electric Air Pump (EAP)
11. Hose
12. AIRD valve-to-check valve hose

Fig. 26 Exploded view of the AIR system used on 5.0L engines—be sure to position the AIRB valve as shown during installation

7. Tighten the intake and exhaust hose clamps until secure.
8. Attach the manifold vacuum control tube to the solenoid.
9. Install the air inlet hose.

AIR Injection Diverter (AIRD) Valve

1. Disconnect the manifold vacuum control tube from the AIRD valve.

2. Loosen the hose clamps from the intake and exhaust ports on the valve, and remove the hoses.
3. Remove the AIRD valve from the vehicle.
To install:
4. Attach the hoses to the AIRD valve.
5. Tighten the hose clamps until secure.
6. Attach the manifold vacuum control tube to the solenoid.

ELECTRONIC ENGINE CONTROLS

Electronic Engine Control (EEC) System

All Sequential Fuel Injection (SFI) systems use the EEC system. The heart of the EEC system is a microprocessor called the Powertrain Control Module (PCM). The PCM receives data from a number of sensors and other electronic components (switches, relays, etc.). Based on information received and information programmed in the PCM's memory, it generates output signals to control various relays, solenoids and other actuators. The PCM in the EEC system has calibration modules located inside the assembly that contain calibration specifications for optimizing emissions, fuel economy and driveability. The calibration module is called a PROM.

The following are the electronic engine controls used by 1994–98 Mustangs:

- Powertrain Control Module (PCM)
- Throttle Position (TP) sensor
- Mass Air Flow (MAF) sensor
- Intake Air Temperature (IAT) sensor
- Idle Air Control (IAC) valve
- Engine Coolant Temperature (ECT) sensor
- Heated Oxygen Sensor (HO2S)
- Camshaft Position (CMP) sensor
- Knock Sensor (KS)
- Vehicle Speed Sensor (VSS)
- Crankshaft Position (CKP) sensor

The MAF sensor (a potentiometer) senses the quantity of airflow in the engine's air induction system and generates a voltage signal that varies with the amount of air drawn into the engine. The IAT sensor (a sensor in the area of the MAF sensor) measures the temperature of the incoming air and transmits a corresponding electrical signal. Another temperature sensor (the ECT sensor) inserted in the engine coolant tells if the engine is cold or warmed up. The TP sensor, a switch that senses throttle plate position, produces electrical signals that tell the PCM when the throttle is closed or wide open. A special probe (the HO2S) in the exhaust manifold measures the amount of oxygen in the exhaust gas, which is in indication of combustion efficiency, and sends a signal to the PCM. The sixth signal, camshaft position information, is transmitted by the CMP sensor, installed in place of the distributor (except 5.0L engines), or integral with the distributor (5.0L engines).

The EEC microcomputer circuit processes the input signals and produces output control signals to the fuel injectors to regulate fuel discharged to the injectors. It also adjusts ignition spark timing to provide the best balance between driveability and economy, and controls the IAC valve to maintain the proper idle speed.

➡Because of the complicated nature of the Ford system, special tools and procedures are necessary for testing and troubleshooting.

Powertrain Control Module (PCM)

OPERATION

The Powertrain Control Module (PCM) performs many functions on your car. The module accepts information from various engine sensors and computes the required fuel flow rate necessary to maintain the correct amount of air/fuel ratio throughout the entire engine operational range.

Based on the information that is received and programmed into the PCM's memory, the PCM generates output signals to control relays, actuators and solenoids. The PCM also sends out a command to the fuel injectors that meters the appropriate quantity of fuel. The module automatically senses and compensates for any changes in altitude when driving your vehicle.

REMOVAL & INSTALLATION

♦ **See Figure 27**

1. Disconnect the negative battery cable.
2. Remove the inside, lower cowl trim panel from the right side of the vehicle to expose the PCM.
3. Disengage the wiring harness connector from the PCM by loosening the connector retaining bolt, then pulling the connector from the module.
4. Remove the PCM from the bracket by pulling the unit downward.
To install:
5. Install the PCM in the mounting bracket.
6. Attach the wiring harness connector to the module, then tighten the connector retaining bolt.
7. Install the right-hand cowl trim panel.
8. Connect the negative battery cable.

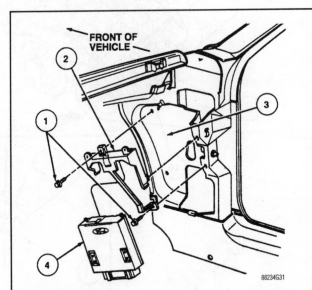

1. Mounting screw
2. Powertrain Control Module (PCM) bracket
3. Right-hand cowl side panel
4. Powertrain Control Module (PCM)

Fig. 27 Exploded view of the Powertrain Control Module (PCM) mounting beneath the right-hand kick panel in the passenger compartment

Heated Oxygen Sensors (HO2S)

OPERATION

♦ **See Figure 28**

The oxygen sensors supply the computer with a signal that indicates a rich or lean condition during engine operation. This input information assists the computer in determining the proper air/fuel ratio. A low voltage signal from one or more sensors indicates too much oxygen in the exhaust (lean condition) and, conversely, a high voltage signal indicates too little oxygen in the exhaust (rich condition).

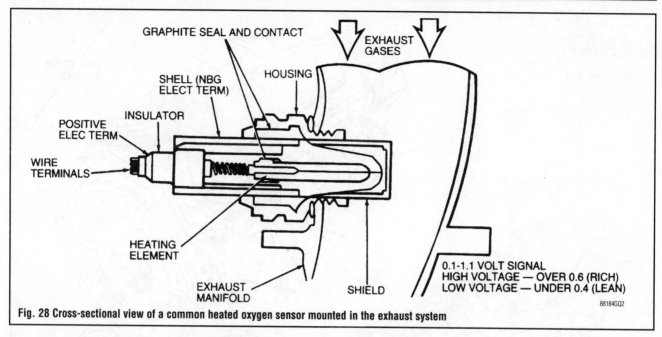

Fig. 28 Cross-sectional view of a common heated oxygen sensor mounted in the exhaust system

The oxygen sensors are threaded into the exhaust manifold and/or exhaust pipes on all vehicles. Heated oxygen sensors are used on all models to allow the engine to reach the closed loop faster.

TESTING

▶ See Figure 29

✳✳ WARNING

Do not pierce the wires when testing heated oxygen sensors, as this can lead to wiring harness damage. Backprobe the connector to properly read the voltage of HO2S.

1. Disconnect the HO2S.
2. Measure the resistance between PWR and GND terminals of the sensor. If the reading is approximately 6 ohms at 68°F (20°C), the sensor's heater element is in good condition.
3. With the HO2S connected and engine running, measure the voltage with a Digital Volt-Ohmmeter (DVOM) between terminals **HO2S** and **SIG RTN** (GND) of the oxygen sensor connector. If the voltage readings are approximately equal to those in the table, the sensor is okay.

REMOVAL & INSTALLATION

▶ See Figure 30

➡4.6L and 1996–98 3.8L engines use four heated oxygen sensors for the engine control system. The heated sensors are located before and after the dual converters in the exhaust pipes. On 5.0L and 1994–95 3.8L engines, there are two sensors; one is located in the left exhaust manifold and the other in the dual converter Y-pipe.

1. Disconnect the negative battery cable.
2. Raise and safely support the vehicle on jackstands.
3. Disconnect the HO2S from the engine control sensor wiring.

➡If excessive force is needed to remove the sensors, lubricate them with penetrating oil prior to removal.

4. Remove the sensors with a sensor removal tool, such as Ford Tool T94P-9472-A.
   To install:
5. Install the sensor in the mounting boss, then tighten it to 27–33 ft. lbs. (37–45 Nm).
6. Reattach the sensor electrical wiring connector to the engine wiring harness.
7. Lower the vehicle.
8. Connect the negative battery cable.

Condition	Voltage—Between Terminals HO2S and SIG RTN
Ignition **ON**, engine **OFF**	0V
Idle (cold)	0V
Idle (warm)	0–1.0V
Acceleration	0.5–1.0V
Deceleration	0–0.5V

88184GZA

Fig. 29 When testing the oxygen sensor voltage signal, it should correspond to the values shown in this chart

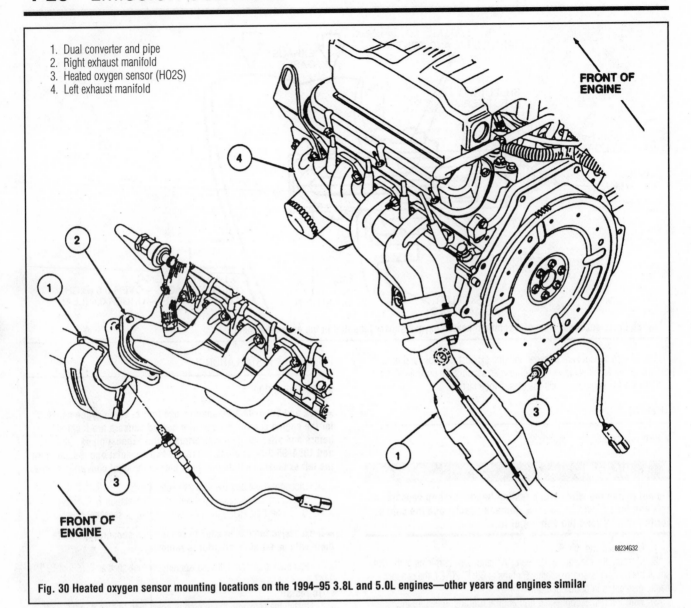

1. Dual converter and pipe
2. Right exhaust manifold
3. Heated oxygen sensor (HO2S)
4. Left exhaust manifold

FRONT OF ENGINE

FRONT OF ENGINE

88234G32

Fig. 30 Heated oxygen sensor mounting locations on the 1994–95 3.8L and 5.0L engines—other years and engines similar

88234P29

To remove an HO2S, detach the vehicle wiring harness connector from the sensor wiring harness . . .

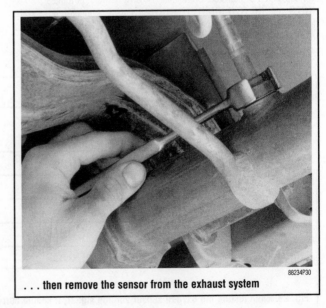

88234P30

. . . then remove the sensor from the exhaust system

Idle Air Control (IAC) Valve

OPERATION

The Idle Air Control (IAC) valve controls the engine idle speed and dashpot functions. The valve is located on the side of the throttle body. This valve allows the necessary amount of air, as determined by the Powertrain Control Module (PCM) and controlled by a duty cycle signal, to bypass the throttle plate in order to maintain the proper idle speed.

TESTING

1. Turn the ignition switch to the **OFF** position.
2. Disengage the wiring harness connector from the IAC valve .
3. Using an ohmmeter, measure the resistance between the terminals of the valve.

➡**Due to the diode in the solenoid, place the ohmmeter positive lead on the VPWR terminal and the negative lead on the ISC terminal.**

4. If the resistance is not 7–13 ohms, replace the IAC valve.

REMOVAL & INSTALLATION

▶ **See Figures 31, 32 and 33**

1. Disconnect the negative battery cable.
2. Disengage the wiring harness connector from the IAC valve.
3. Remove the two retaining screws, then remove the IAC valve and discard the old gasket.
   To install:
4. Clean the IAC valve mounting surface on the throttle body of old gasket material.
5. Using a new gasket, position the IAC valve on the throttle body. Install and tighten the retaining screws to 71–106 inch lbs. (8–12 Nm).
6. Attach the wiring harness connector to the IAC valve.
7. Connect the negative battery cable.

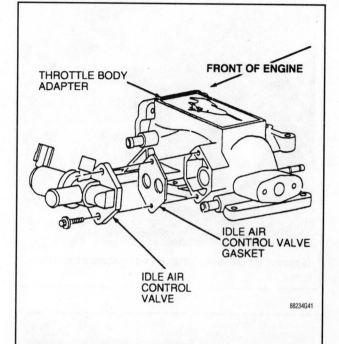

Fig. 32 On the 4.6L SOHC engine, the IAC valve is mounted on the side of the throttle body adapter

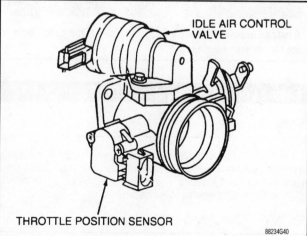

Fig. 31 The Idle Air Control (IAC) valve and the Throttle Position (TP) sensor are mounted on the throttle body on 3.8L and 5.0L engines

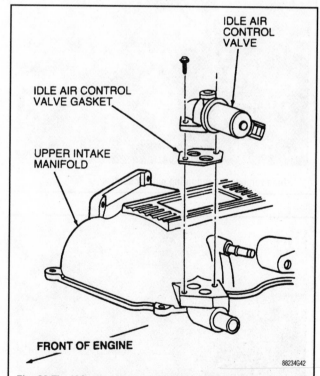

Fig. 33 The IAC valve for the 4.6L DOHC engine is the only one not mounted on the throttle body—it is mounted on a boss on the side of the upper intake manifold

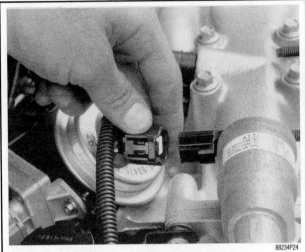

To remove the IAC valve, detach the wiring harness connector from it . . .

. . . then remove the mounting nuts or screws

Lift the IAC valve off of the throttle body or intake manifold, depending on the vehicle's engine . . .

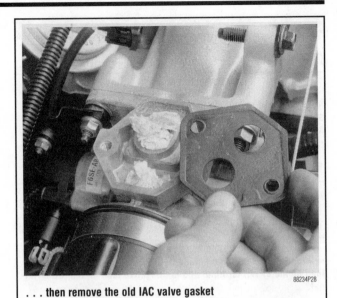

. . . then remove the old IAC valve gasket

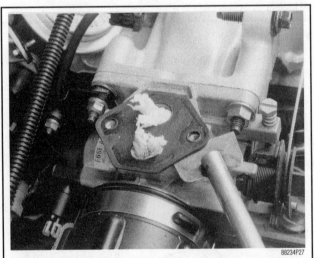

It may be necessary to use a scraper to remove the gasket from the IAC mounting surface

Engine Coolant Temperature (ECT) Sensor

OPERATION

The engine coolant temperature sensor resistance changes in response to engine coolant temperature. The sensor resistance decreases as the surrounding temperature increases. This provides a reference signal to the PCM, which indicates engine coolant temperature.

TESTING

▶ **See Figures 34, 35 and 36**

1. Disengage the engine wiring harness connector from the ECT sensor.
2. Connect an ohmmeter between the ECT sensor terminals, and set the ohmmeter scale on 200,000 ohms.
3. With the engine cold and the ignition switch in the **OFF** position, measure and note the ECT sensor resistance. Attach the engine wiring harness connector to the sensor.
4. Start the engine and allow it to warm up to normal operating temperature.
5. Once the engine has reached normal operating temperature, turn it **OFF**.

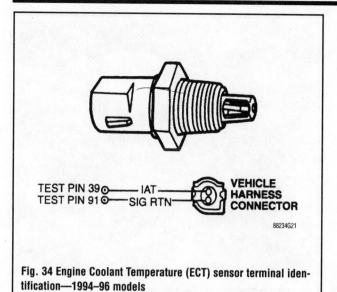

Fig. 34 Engine Coolant Temperature (ECT) sensor terminal identification—1994–96 models

Temperature		Engine Coolant/Air Charge Temperature Sensor Values	
°F	°C	Voltage (volts)	Resistance (K ohms)
248	120	.27	1.18
230	110	.35	1.55
212	100	.46	2.07
194	90	.60	2.80
176	80	.78	3.84
158	70	1.02	5.37
140	60	1.33	7.70
122	50	1.70	10.97
104	40	2.13	16.15
86	30	2.60	24.27
68	20	3.07	37.30
50	10	3.51	58.75

Fig. 36 A properly functioning Engine Coolant Temperature (ECT) sensor should exhibit the resistance values indicated in this chart

Fig. 35 The ECT and IAT sensor connectors changed shape in 1996, but the terminal identifying numbers remained the same—1997–98 models

6. Once again, detach the engine wiring harness connector from the ECT sensor.

7. Measure and note the ECT sensor resistance, then compare the cold and hot ECT sensor resistance measurements with the accompanying chart.

8. Replace the ECT sensor if the readings do not approximate those in the chart; otherwise, reattach the engine wiring harness connector to the sensor.

REMOVAL & INSTALLATION

▶ **See Figures 37 and 38**

1. Partially drain the engine cooling system until the coolant level is below the ECT sensor mounting hole.

2. Disconnect the negative battery cable.

3. Detach the wiring harness connector from the ECT sensor.

4. Using an open-end wrench, remove the coolant temperature sensor from the intake manifold.

To install:

5. Thread the sensor into the intake manifold by hand, then tighten it to the following values:
- 3.8L engine—124–168 inch lbs. (14–19 Nm)
- 4.6L SOHC engine—142–212 inch lbs. (16–24 Nm)

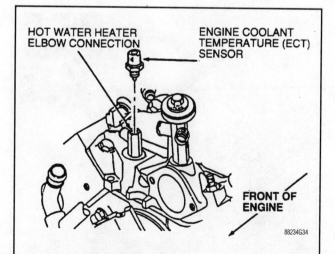

Fig. 37 Engine Coolant Temperature (ECT) sensor location on the 3.8L engine

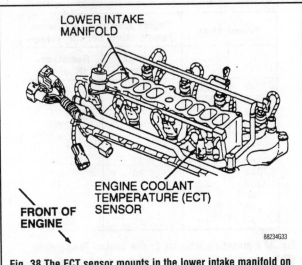

Fig. 38 The ECT sensor mounts in the lower intake manifold on 5.0L engines

To remove the ECT sensor, locate it and detach the wiring harness connector from it

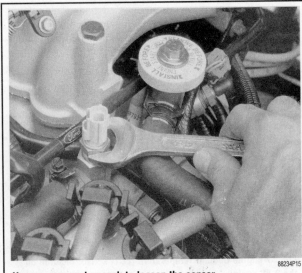

Use an open end wrench to loosen the sensor . . .

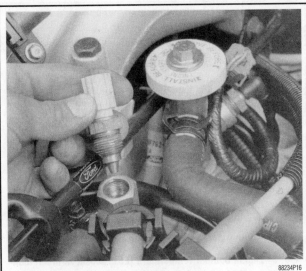

. . . then remove it from the engine

- 4.6L DOHC engine—71–106 inch lbs. (8–12 Nm)
- 5.0L engine—124–168 inch lbs. (14–19 Nm)
6. Reattach the wiring harness connector to the ECT sensor.
7. Connect the negative battery cable.
8. Refill the engine cooling system.
9. Start the engine, check for coolant leaks and top off the cooling system.

Intake Air Temperature (IAT) Sensor

OPERATION

The Intake Air Temperature (IAT) sensor resistance changes in response to the intake air temperature. The sensor resistance decreases as the surrounding air temperature increases. This provides a signal to the PCM, indicating the temperature of the incoming air charge.

TESTING

▶ See Figures 39 and 40

Turn the ignition switch **OFF** before testing the sensor.
1. Disengage the wiring harness connector from the IAT sensor.

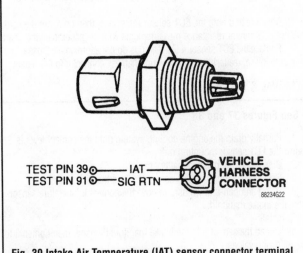

Fig. 39 Intake Air Temperature (IAT) sensor connector terminal identification—1994–96 models

Temperature		Engine Coolant/Air Charge Temperature Sensor Values	
°F	°C	Voltage (volts)	Resistance (K ohms)
248	120	.27	1.18
230	110	.35	1.55
212	100	.46	2.07
194	90	.60	2.80
176	80	.78	3.84
158	70	1.02	5.37
140	60	1.33	7.70
122	50	1.70	10.97
104	40	2.13	16.15
86	30	2.60	24.27
68	20	3.07	37.30
50	10	3.51	58.75

88184GZP

Fig. 40 A properly functioning Intake Air Temperature (IAT) sensor should exhibit the resistance values indicated in this chart

2. Using a Digital Volt-Ohmmeter (DVOM), measure the resistance between the two sensor terminals.

3. Compare the resistance reading with the accompanying chart. If the reading for a given temperature is approximately that shown in the table, the IAT sensor is okay.

4. Attach the wiring harness connector to the sensor.

REMOVAL & INSTALLATION

1. Disconnect the negative battery cable.
2. Disengage the wiring harness connector from the IAT sensor.
3. Remove the sensor from the air cleaner outlet tube.

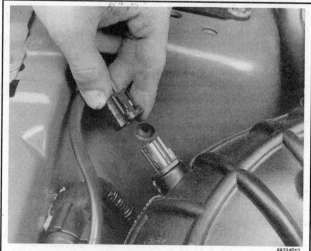

88234P12

To remove the IAT sensor, detach the wiring harness connector from it . . .

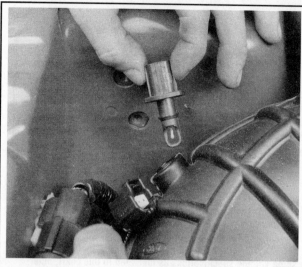

88234P13

. . . then pull it out of the air cleaner outlet tube

To install:

4. Wipe down the air cleaner outlet tube and IAT sensor mounting boss to clean the sensor area of all dirt and grime.

5. Install the sensor into the air cleaner outlet tube securely.

6. Attach the wiring harness connector to the IAT sensor.

7. Connect the negative battery cable.

Mass Air Flow (MAF) Sensor

OPERATION

The Mass Air Flow (MAF) sensor directly measures the amount of air flowing into the engine. The sensor is mounted between the air cleaner assembly and the air cleaner outlet tube.

The sensor utilizes a hot wire sensing element to measure the amount of air entering the engine. The sensor does this by sending a signal, which is generated by the sensor when the incoming air cools the hot wire, to the PCM. The signal is used by the PCM to calculate the injector pulse width, which controls the air/fuel ratio in the engine. The sensor and plastic housing are integral and must be replaced if found to be defective.

The sensing element (hot wire) is a thin platinum wire wound on a ceramic bobbin and coated with glass. This hot wire is maintained at 392°F (200°C) above the ambient temperature as measured by a constant "cold wire".

TESTING

▶ See Figures 41, 42 and 43

1. With the engine running at idle, use a DVOM to verify that there are at least 10.5 volts between terminals **A** and **B** of the MAF sensor connector. Such a reading indicates that the power input to the sensor is correct. Then, measure the voltage between MAF sensor connector terminals **C** and **D**. If the reading is approximately 0.34–1.96 volts, the sensor is functioning properly.

Engine Condition	Signal Voltage—Sensor Terminals C and D
Idle	0.60V
20 mph	1.10V
40 mph	1.70V
60 mph	2.10V

88184GZK

Fig. 41 The Mass Air Flow (MAF) sensor should exhibit the same voltage specifications as indicated in this chart; otherwise, replace the MAF sensor

REMOVAL & INSTALLATION

※ WARNING

The mass air flow sensor hot wire sensing element and housing are calibrated as a unit and must be serviced as a complete assembly. Do not damage the sensing element, or possible failure of the sensor may occur.

1. Disconnect the negative battery cable.
2. Disengage the wiring harness connectors from the IAT and MAF sensors.
3. Loosen the engine air cleaner outlet tube clamps, then remove the tube from the engine.
4. Remove the MAF sensor from the air cleaner assembly by disengaging the retaining clips.

To install:

5. Install the MAF sensor to the air cleaner assembly and ensure that the retaining clips are fully engaged.
6. Install the air cleaner outlet tube, then tighten the outlet tube clamps until snug.
7. Attach the engine wiring harness connectors to the IAT and MAF sensors.
8. Connect the negative battery cable.

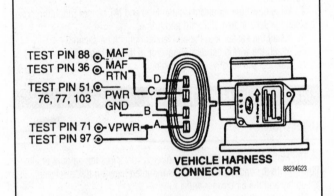

Fig. 42 MAF sensor wiring harness connector terminal identification—1994–96 models

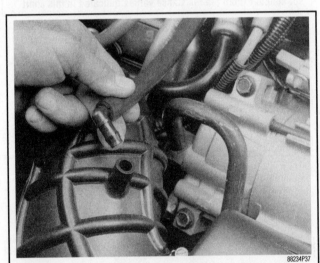

To remove the MAF sensor, disconnect the PCV system hose from the air cleaner outlet tube . . .

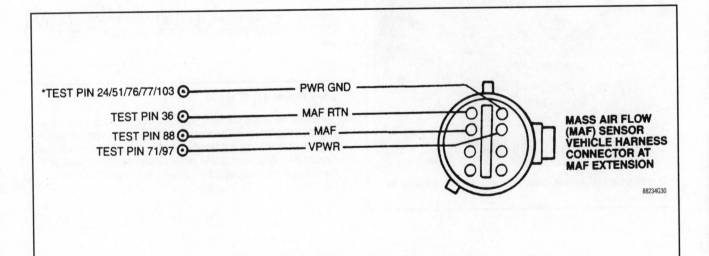

Fig. 43 MAF sensor wiring harness connector terminal identification—1997–98 models

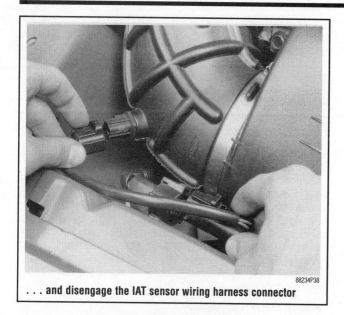

. . . and disengage the IAT sensor wiring harness connector

Loosen the outlet tube clamps . . .

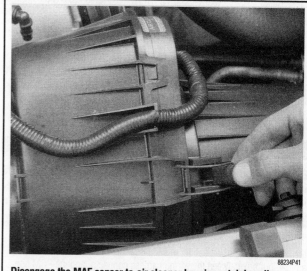

Disengage the MAF sensor-to-air cleaner housing retaining clips . . .

. . . tnen remove the MAP sensor from the vehicle

Throttle Position (TP) Sensor

OPERATION

The Throttle Position (TP) sensor is a potentiometer which provides a signal to the PCM that is directly proportional to the throttle plate position. The TP sensor is mounted on the side of the throttle body and is connected to the throttle plate shaft. The TP sensor monitors throttle plate movement and position, and transmits an appropriate electrical signal to the PCM. These signals are used by the PCM to adjust the air/fuel mixture, spark timing and EGR operation according to engine load at idle, part throttle, or full throttle. The TPS is not adjustable.

TESTING

▶ **See Figures 44 and 45**

1. Disconnect the negative battery cable.
2. Disengage the wiring harness connector from the TP sensor.

3. Using a Digital Volt-Ohmmeter (DVOM) set on ohmmeter function, probe the terminals which correspond to the brown/white and gray/white connector wires on the TP sensor. Do not measure the wiring harness connector terminals, but rather the terminals on the sensor itself.

4. Slowly rotate the throttle shaft and monitor the ohmmeter for a continuous, steady change in resistance. Any sudden jumps or irregularities in resistance (such as jumping back and forth) indicates a malfunctioning sensor.

5. Reconnect the negative battery cable.

6. Turn the DVOM to the voltmeter setting.

☀ WARNING

Ensuring that the DVOM is set to the voltmeter function is vitally important, because if you measure circuit resistance (ohmmeter function) with the battery cable connected, your DVOM will be destroyed.

7. Detach the wiring harness connector from the PCM (located behind the lower right-hand kick panel in the passenger compartment), then install a break-out box between the wiring harness connector and the PCM connector.

8. Turn the ignition switch **ON** and using the DVOM set to its voltmeter function, measure the voltage between terminals 89 and 90 of the breakout box. The specification is 0.9 volts.

9. If the voltage is outside the standard value or if it does not change smoothly, inspect the circuit wiring and/or replace the TP sensor.

REMOVAL & INSTALLATION

◆ See Figures 46 and 47

1. Disconnect the negative battery cable.
2. Disengage the wiring harness connector from the TP sensor.
3. Remove the two TP sensor mounting screws, then pull the TP sensor out of the throttle body housing.

To install:

4. Position the TP sensor against the throttle body housing, ensuring that the mounting screw holes are aligned. When positioning the TP sensor against the throttle body, slide the sensor straight onto the housing.

5. Install and tighten the sensor mounting screws until snug.

6. Attach the wiring harness connector to the sensor, then connect the negative battery cable.

➡**The TP sensor is not adjustable.**

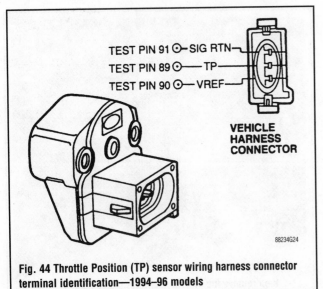

Fig. 44 Throttle Position (TP) sensor wiring harness connector terminal identification—1994–96 models

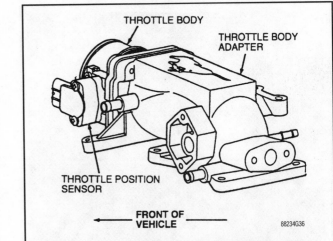

Fig. 46 The Throttle Position (TP) sensor is mounted on the side of the throttle body with two machine screws—4.6L SOHC engine

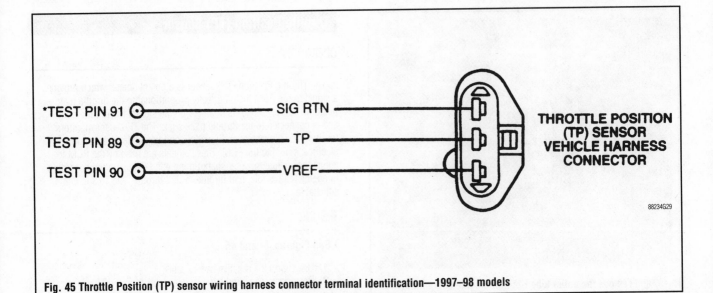

Fig. 45 Throttle Position (TP) sensor wiring harness connector terminal identification—1997–98 models

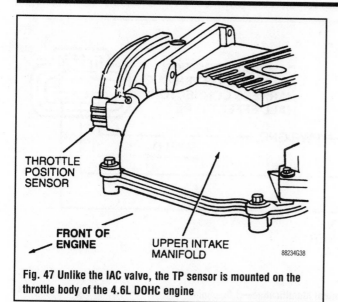

Fig. 47 Unlike the IAC valve, the TP sensor is mounted on the throttle body of the 4.6L DOHC engine

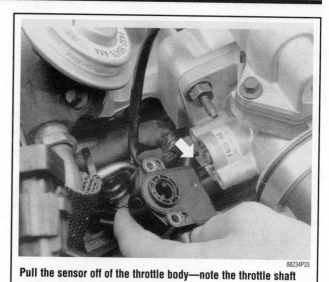

Pull the sensor off of the throttle body—note the throttle shaft tab (arrow) that actuates the sensor

To remove a TP sensor, first detach the wiring harness connector . . .

. . . then remove its mounting screws

Camshaft Position (CMP) Sensor

OPERATION

The CMP sensor provides the camshaft position information, called the CMP signal, which is used by the Powertrain Control Module (PCM) for fuel synchronization.

On the 3.8L engine, the distributor stator or Camshaft Position (CMP) sensor is a single Hall effect magnetic switch. This is activated by a single vane, and is driven by the camshaft.

On both 4.6L engines, the Camshaft Position (CMP) sensor is a variable reluctance sensor, which is triggered by the high-point mark on one of the camshaft sprockets.

The 5.0L engine does not use a separate CMP sensor. It utilizes a conventional distributor, equipped with a Hall effect device, for this function.

TESTING

Three-Wire Sensors

▶ See Figure 48

1. With the ignition **OFF**, disconnect the CMP sensor. With the ignition **ON** and the engine **OFF**, measure the voltage between sensor harness connector **VPWR** and **PWR GND** terminals (refer to the accompanying illustration). If the reading is greater than 10.5 volts, the power circuit to the sensor is okay.

2. With the ignition **OFF**, install a break-out box between the CMP sensor and the PCM. Using a Digital Volt-Ohmmeter (DVOM) set to the voltage function (scale set to monitor less than 5 volts), measure the voltage between break-out box terminals **24** and **40** with the engine running at varying RPM. If the voltage reading varies more than 0.1 volt, the sensor is okay.

Two-Wire Sensors

▶ See Figure 49

1. With the ignition **OFF**, install a break-out box between the CMP sensor and PCM.

2. Using a Digital Volt-Ohmmeter (DVOM) set to the voltage function (scale set to monitor less than 5 volts), measure the voltage between break-out box terminals **24** and **46** with the engine running at varying RPM. If the voltage reading varies more than 0.1 volt AC, the sensor is okay.

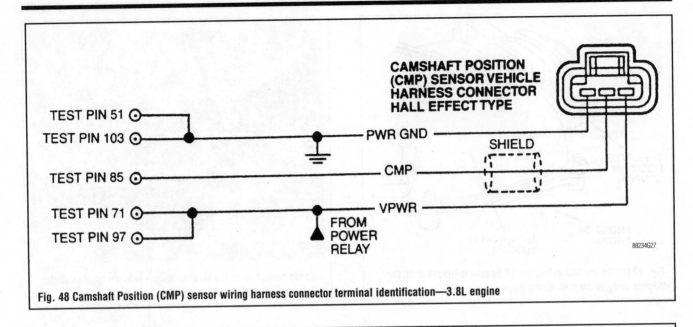

Fig. 48 Camshaft Position (CMP) sensor wiring harness connector terminal identification—3.8L engine

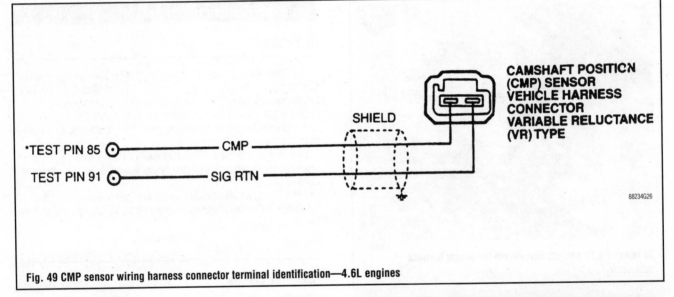

Fig. 49 CMP sensor wiring harness connector terminal identification—4.6L engines

REMOVAL & INSTALLATION

3.8L Engine

▶ See Figure 50 (p. 32)

➡If the camshaft position sensor housing does not contain a plastic locator cover tool, a special service tool such as T89P-12200-A, or equivalent, must be obtained prior to installation. Failure to follow this procedure may result in improper stator alignment. This will result in the fuel system being out of time with the engine, possibly causing engine damage.

1. Disconnect the negative battery cable.
2. Remove the ignition coil, radio capacitor and ignition coil bracket.
3. Disengage the wiring harness connector from the CMP sensor.

➡Prior to removing the camshaft position sensor, set the No. 1 cylinder to 10° After Top Dead Center (ATDC) of the compression stroke. Note the position of the sensor's electrical connection. When installing the sensor, the connection must be in the exact same position.

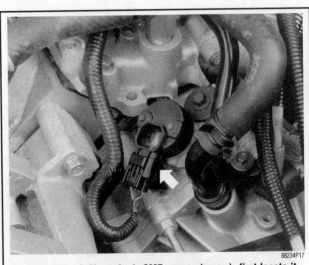

To remove the 3.8L engine's CMP sensor (arrow), first locate it at the front of the engine block . . .

. . . then detach the wiring harness connector from the sensor

88234P18

Remove the hold-down bolt and washer . . .

88234P19

4. Position the No. 1 cylinder at 10° ATDC, then matchmark the CMP sensor terminal connector position with the engine assembly.

5. Remove the camshaft position sensor retaining screws and sensor.

6. Remove the retaining bolt and hold-down clamp.

➡The oil pump intermediate shaft should be removed with the camshaft sensor housing.

7. Remove the CMP sensor housing from the front engine cover.
To install:

8. If the plastic locator cover is not attached to the replacement camshaft position sensor, attach a synchro positioning tool, such as Ford Tool T89P-12200-A or equivalent. To do so, perform the following:

   a. Engage the sensor housing vane into the radial slot of the tool.

   b. Rotate the tool on the camshaft sensor housing until the tool boss engages the notch in the sensor housing.

➡The cover tool should be square and in contact with the entire top surface of the camshaft position sensor housing.

9. Transfer the oil pump intermediate shaft from the old camshaft position sensor housing to the replacement sensor housing.

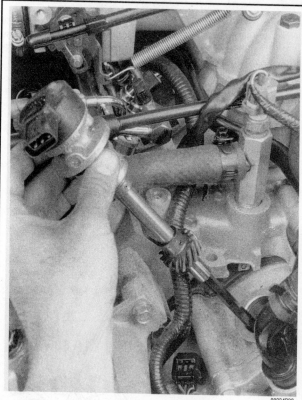

. . . then pull the sensor and housing out of the engine front cover

88234P20

10. Install the camshaft sensor housing so that the drive gear engagement occurs when the arrow on the locator tool is pointed approximately 30° counterclockwise from the face of the cylinder block. (The sensor terminal connector should be aligned with its matchmarks.)

11. Install the hold-down clamp and bolt, then tighten the bolt to 15–22 ft. lbs. (20–30 Nm).

12. Remove the synchro positioning tool.

⁂ WARNING

If the sensor connector is positioned correctly, DO NOT reposition the connector by rotating the sensor housing. This will result in the fuel system being out of time with the engine. This could possibly cause engine damage. Remove the sensor housing and repeat the installation procedure beginning with Step 1.

13. Install the sensor and retaining screws, and tighten the screws to 22–31 inch lbs. (2–4 Nm).

14. Attach the engine control sensor wiring connector to the sensor.

15. Install the ignition coil bracket, radio ignition capacitor and ignition coil.

16. Connect the negative battery cable.

4.6L Engine

♦ **See Figure 51**

1. Disconnect the negative battery cable.

2. Disconnect the engine control sensor wiring from the camshaft position sensor.

3. Remove the sensor retaining screw and the sensor from the front of the engine front cover.

1. Synchro positioning tool
2. Engine front cover
3. Hold-down clamp
4. Oil pump intermediate shaft
5. CMP sensor housing
6. Camshaft Position (CMP) sensor
7. Mounting screw

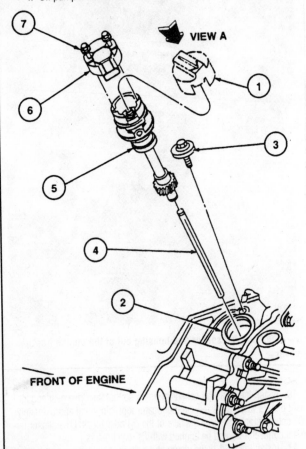

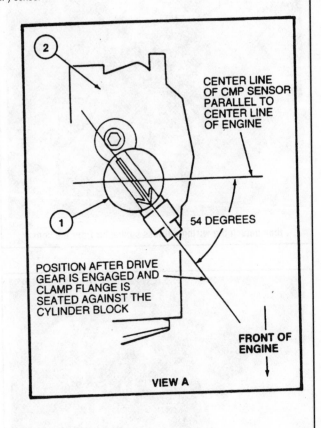

CENTER LINE OF CMP SENSOR PARALLEL TO CENTER LINE OF ENGINE

54 DEGREES

POSITION AFTER DRIVE GEAR IS ENGAGED AND CLAMP FLANGE IS SEATED AGAINST THE CYLINDER BLOCK

FRONT OF ENGINE

VIEW A

FRONT OF ENGINE

88234G35

Fig. 50 When installing the CMP sensor and housing, ensure that the sensor terminal connector is situated 30–36° from the face of the block (or 54–60° from the engine block centerline)

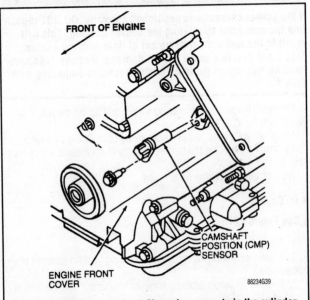

FRONT OF ENGINE

CAMSHAFT POSITION (CMP) SENSOR

ENGINE FRONT COVER

88234G39

Fig. 51 The CMP sensor for 4.6L engines mounts in the cylinder head since these engines utilize overhead camshafts

To install:

4. Make sure the camshaft position sensor mounting surface is clean and the O-ring is positioned correctly.

5. Position the sensor, then install the retaining screw and tighten it to 71–106 inch lbs. (8–12 Nm).

✳✳ WARNING

Do not overtighten the screw; you may damage the sensor if the retaining screw is overtightened.

6. Engage the wiring harness connector to the CMP sensor.
7. Connect the negative battery cable.

5.0L Engine

Refer to Section 2 in this manual for distributor removal and installation.

Crankshaft Position (CKP) Sensor

OPERATION

◆ See Figure 52

The Crankshaft Position (CKP) sensor, located on the front cover (near the crankshaft pulley) is used to determine crankshaft position and crank-

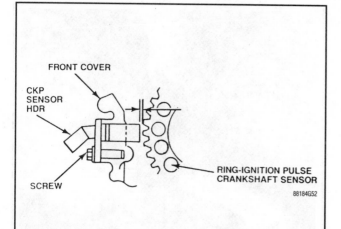

Fig. 52 The Crankshaft Position (CKP) sensor is mounted on the engine front cover, and senses the teeth on the sensor ring as they pass through its magnetic field

The CKP sensor responds to the sensor ring's teeth (arrow) as they pass through its magnetic field

shaft rpm. The CKP sensor is a reluctance sensor which senses the passing of teeth on the sensor ring because the teeth disrupt the magnetic field of the sensor. This disruption creates a voltage fluctuation, which is monitored by the PCM.

TESTING

Using a DVOM set to the AC scale to monitor less than 5 volts, measure the voltage between the sensor Cylinder Identification (CID) terminal and ground by backprobing the sensor connector. If the connector cannot be backprobed, fabricate or purchase a test harness. The sensor is okay if the voltage reading varies more than 0.1 volt with the engine running at varying RPM.

REMOVAL & INSTALLATION

1. Disconnect the negative battery cable.
2. Disengage the wiring harness connector from the CKP sensor.
3. Remove the CKP sensor cover retaining nuts, then lift the cover off of the CKP sensor stud/bolts.

Remove the crankshaft damper (A) and the four sensor ring mounting bolts (B) to replace the sensor ring

The CKP sensor (arrow) is mounted on the front of the engine, near the crankshaft pulley

4. Loosen the CKP sensor mounting stud/bolts, then separate the sensor form the engine front cover.
To install:
5. Position the sensor against the engine front cover, then install the mounting stud/bolts. Tighten them until snug.
6. Install the CKP sensor cover and retaining nuts; tighten the nuts until snug.
7. Reattach the wiring harness connector to the CKP sensor.
8. Connect the negative battery cable.

Vehicle Speed Sensor (VSS)

OPERATION

The Vehicle Speed Sensor (VSS) is a magnetic pick-up that sends a signal to the Powertrain Control Module (PCM). The sensor measures the rotation of the transmission and the PCM determines the corresponding vehicle speed.

TESTING

▶ **See Figures 53 and 54**

1. Turn the ignition switch to the **OFF** position.
2. Disengage the wiring harness connector from the VSS.
3. Using a Digital Volt-Ohmmeter (DVOM), measure the resistance (ohmmeter function) between the sensor terminals. If the resistance is 190–250 ohms, the sensor is okay.

REMOVAL & INSTALLATION

The VSS is located half-way down the right-hand side of the transmission assembly.

1. Apply the parking brake, block the rear wheels, then raise and safely support the front of the vehicle on jackstands.
2. From under the right-hand side of the vehicle, disengage the wiring harness connector from the VSS.
3. Loosen the VSS hold-down bolt, then pull the VSS out of the transmission housing.

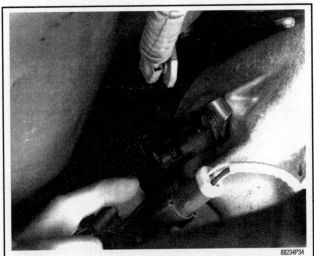

To remove the VSS, detach the wiring harness connector from it . . .

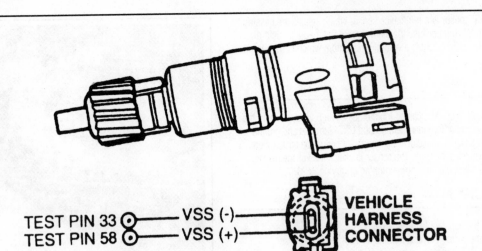

Fig. 53 Vehicle Speed Sensor (VSS) wiring harness connector terminal identification—1994–96 models

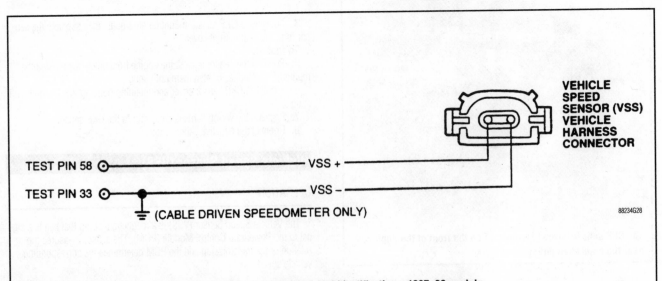

Fig. 54 Vehicle Speed Sensor (VSS) wiring harness connector terminal identification—1997–98 models

To install:

4. If a new sensor is being installed, transfer the driven gear retainer and gear to the new sensor.

5. Ensure that the O-ring is properly seated in the VSS housing.

6. For ease of assembly, engage the wiring harness connector to the VSS, then insert the VSS into the transmission assembly.

7. Install and tighten the VSS hold-down bolt to 62–88 inch lbs. (7–10 Nm).

8. Lower the vehicle and remove the wheel blocks.

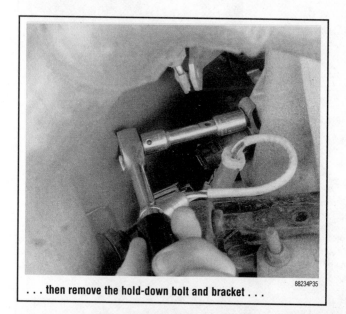

. . . then remove the hold-down bolt and bracket . . .

88234P35

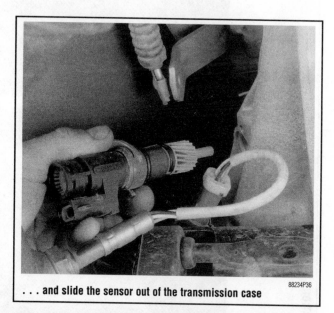

. . . and slide the sensor out of the transmission case

88234P36

COMPONENT LOCATIONS

▶ See Figures 55 thru 67 (p. 35–43)

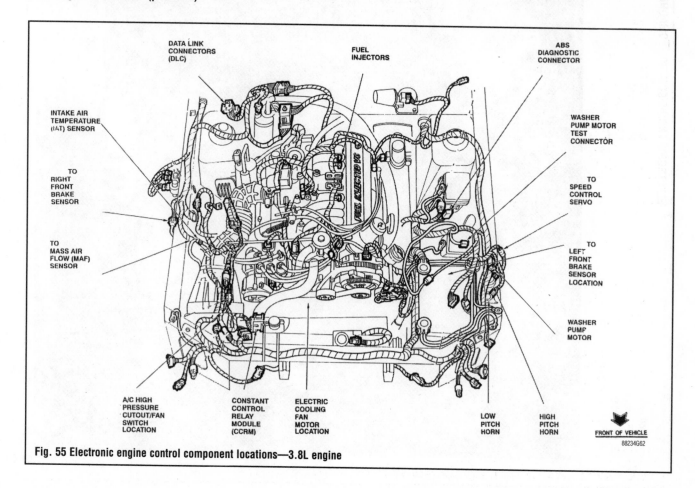

Fig. 55 Electronic engine control component locations—3.8L engine

88234G62

ELECTRONIC ENGINE CONTROL COMPONENT LOCATIONS—3.8L ENGINE

1. MAF sensor
2. IAT sensor
3. IAC valve
4. TP sensor (behind IAC valve)
5. PFE/DPFE sensor
6. EVR solenoid
7. EGR valve
8. CMP sensor
9. ECT sensor
10. Power distribution box
11. ABS diagnostic connector

88234P54

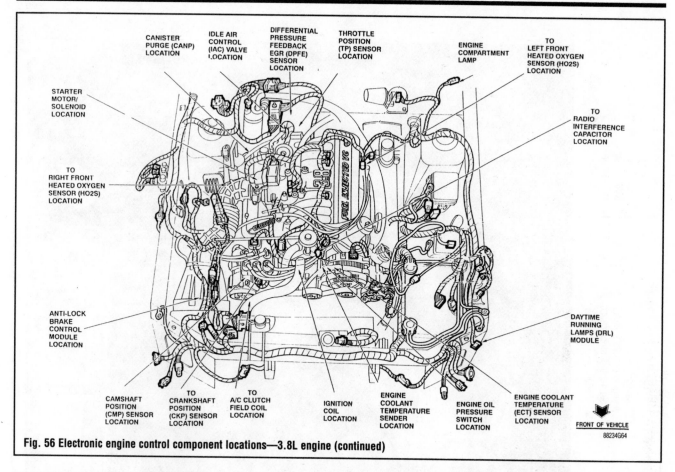

Fig. 56 Electronic engine control component locations—3.8L engine (continued)

88234G64

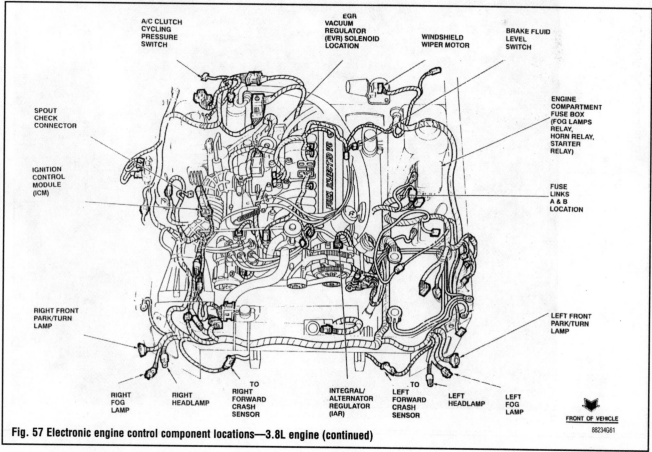

Fig. 57 Electronic engine control component locations—3.8L engine (continued)

88234G61

ELECTRONIC ENGINE CONTROL COMPONENT LOCATIONS—4.6L SOHC ENGINE

1. EVAP canister purge valve
2. EVAP purge flow sensor (beneath the air outlet tube)
3. TP sensor
4. IAC valve
5. EGR valve
6. DPFE sensor
7. Power distribution box
8. ECT sensor
9. Low engine coolant switch
10. Left radio interference capacitor
11. ECT sensor
12. Right radio interference capacitor
13. MAF sensor
14. IAT sensor
15. Constant control relay module

88234P53

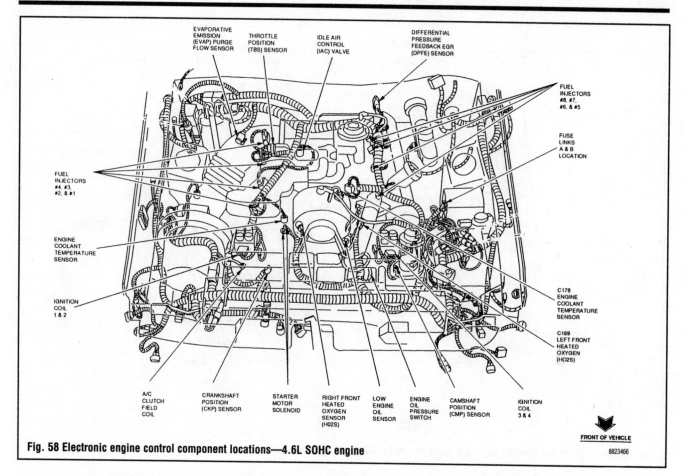

EVAPORATIVE
EMISSION
(EVAP) PURGE
FLOW SENSOR

THROTTLE
POSITION
(TBS) SENSOR

IDLE AIR
CONTROL
(IAC) VALVE

DIFFERENTIAL
PRESSURE
FEEDBACK EGR
(DPFE) SENSOR

FUEL
INJECTORS
#8, #7,
#6, & #5

FUSE
LINKS
A & B
LOCATION

FUEL
INJECTORS
#4, #3,
#2, & #1

ENGINE
COOLANT
TEMPERATURE
SENSOR

IGNITION
COIL
1 & 2

C178
ENGINE
COOLANT
TEMPERATURE
SENSOR

C169
LEFT FRONT
HEATED
OXYGEN
(HO2S)

A/C
CLUTCH
FIELD
COIL

CRANKSHAFT
POSITION
(CKP) SENSOR

STARTER
MOTOR
SOLENOID

RIGHT FRONT
HEATED
OXYGEN
SENSOR
(HO2S)

LOW
ENGINE
OIL
SENSOR

ENGINE
OIL
PRESSURE
SWITCH

CAMSHAFT
POSITION
(CMP) SENSOR

IGNITION
COIL
3 & 4

FRONT OF VEHICLE

Fig. 58 Electronic engine control component locations—4.6L SOHC engine

8823466

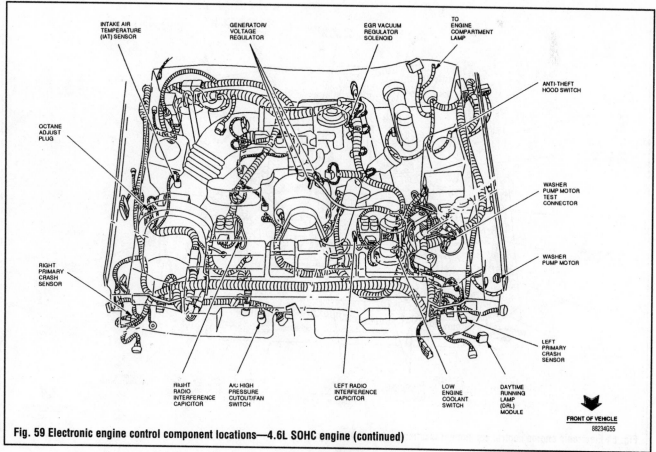

INTAKE AIR
TEMPERATURE
(IAT) SENSOR

GENERATOR/
VOLTAGE
REGULATOR

EGR VACUUM
REGULATOR
SOLENOID

TO
ENGINE
COMPARTMENT
LAMP

ANTI-THEFT
HOOD SWITCH

OCTANE
ADJUST
PLUG

WASHER
PUMP MOTOR
TEST
CONNECTOR

WASHER
PUMP MOTOR

RIGHT
PRIMARY
CRASH
SENSOR

LEFT
PRIMARY
CRASH
SENSOR

RIGHT
RADIO
INTERFERENCE
CAPICITOR

A/C HIGH
PRESSURE
CUTOUT/FAN
SWITCH

LEFT RADIO
INTERFERENCE
CAPICITOR

LOW
ENGINE
COOLANT
SWITCH

DAYTIME
RUNNING
LAMP
(DRL)
MODULE

FRONT OF VEHICLE

Fig. 59 Electronic engine control component locations—4.6L SOHC engine (continued)

88234G55

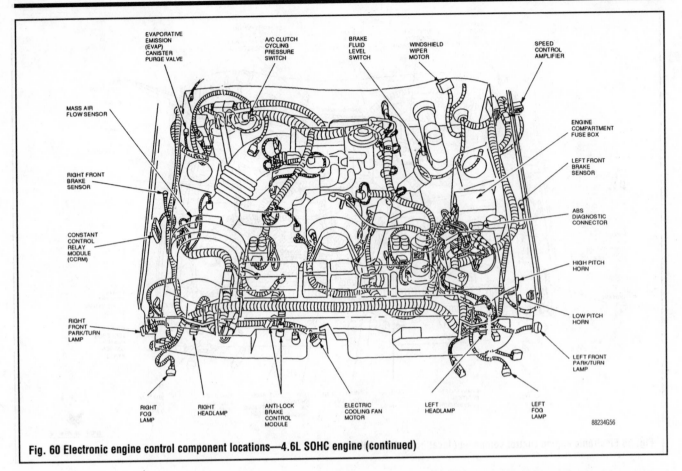

Fig. 60 Electronic engine control component locations—4.6L SOHC engine (continued)

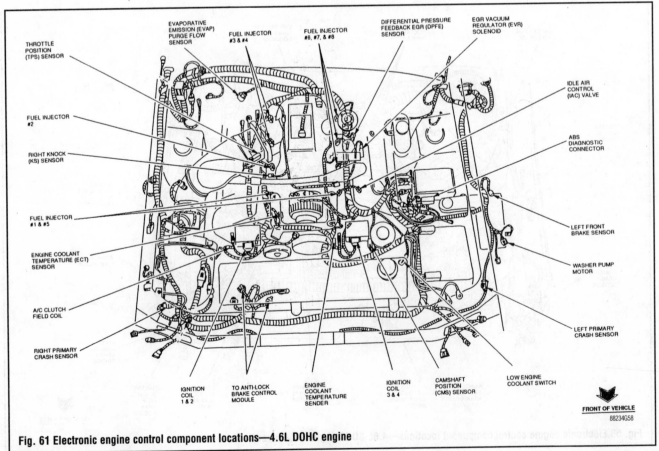

Fig. 61 Electronic engine control component locations—4.6L DOHC engine

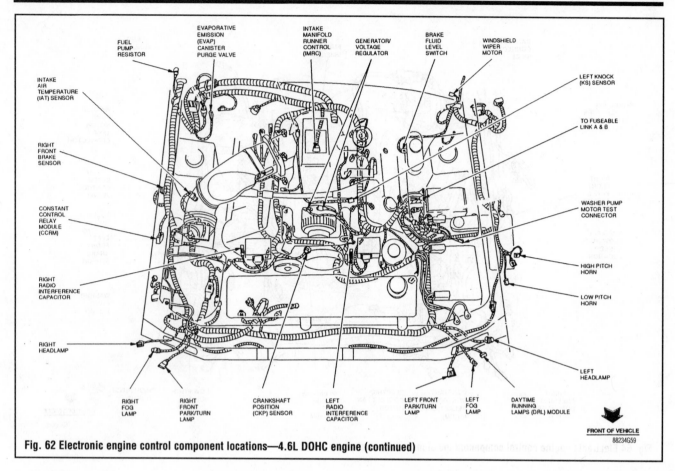

Fig. 62 Electronic engine control component locations—4.6L DOHC engine (continued)

FRONT OF VEHICLE

88234G59

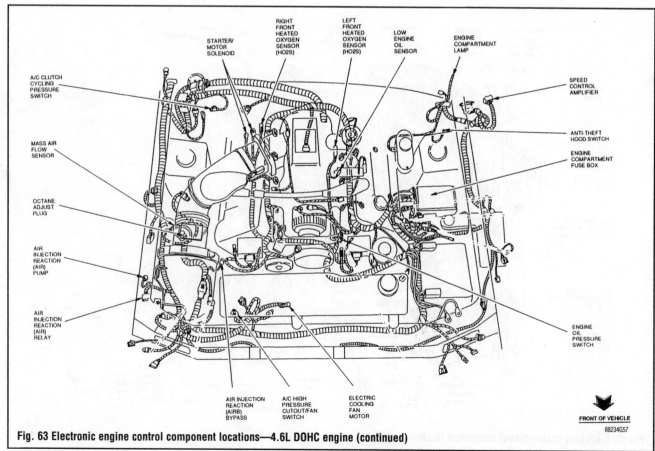

Fig. 63 Electronic engine control component locations—4.6L DOHC engine (continued)

FRONT OF VEHICLE

88234G57

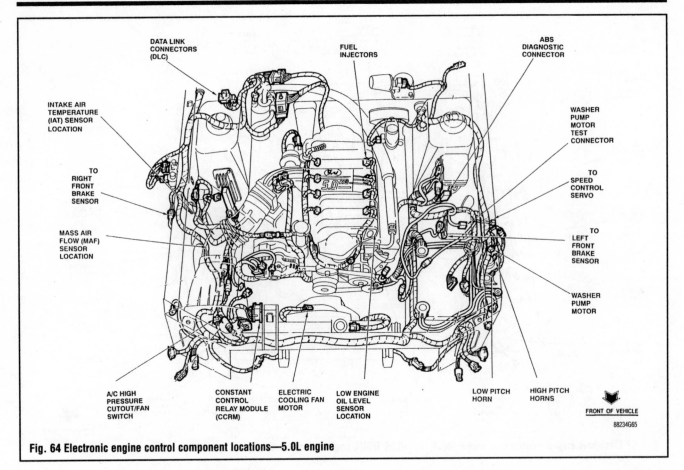

Fig. 64 Electronic engine control component locations—5.0L engine

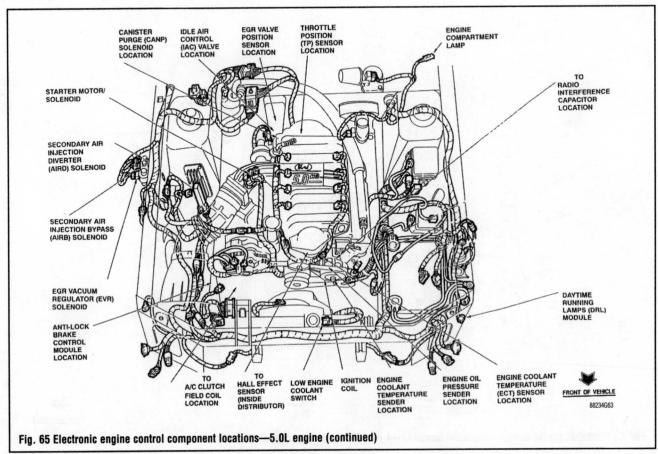

Fig. 65 Electronic engine control component locations—5.0L engine (continued)

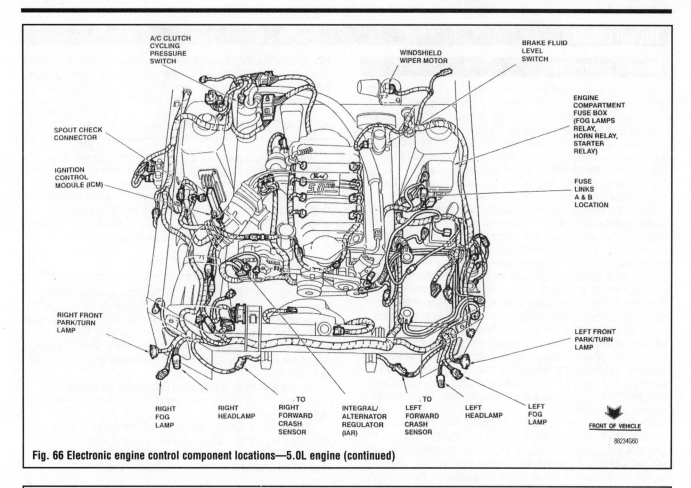

Fig. 66 Electronic engine control component locations—5.0L engine (continued)

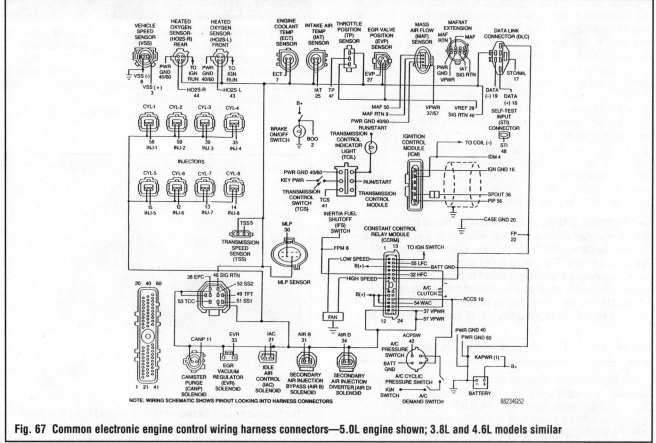

Fig. 67 Common electronic engine control wiring harness connectors—5.0L engine shown; 3.8L and 4.6L models similar

TROUBLE CODES

General Information

Ford Mustang vehicles employ the Electronic Engine Control (EEC) system to manage fuel, ignition and emissions on vehicle engines.

The Powertrain Control Module (PCM) is responsible for the operation of the emission control devices, cooling fans, ignition/advance and, in some cases, automatic transmission functions. Because the EEC oversees both the ignition timing and the fuel injector operation, a precise air/fuel ratio will be maintained under all operating conditions. The PCM is a microprocessor or small computer which receives electrical inputs from several sensors, switches and relays on and around the engine.

Based on combinations of these inputs, the PCM controls outputs to various devices concerned with engine operation and emissions. The engine control assembly relies on the signals to form a correct picture of current vehicle operation. If any of the input signals is incorrect, the PCM reacts to whatever picture is painted for it. For example, if the coolant temperature sensor is inaccurate and reads too low, the PCM may see a picture of the engine never warming up. Consequently, the engine settings will be maintained as if the engine were cold. Because so many inputs can affect one output, correct diagnostic procedures are essential on these systems.

One part of the PCM is devoted to monitoring both input and output functions within the system. This ability forms the core of the self-diagnostic system. If a problem is detected within a circuit, the controller will recognize the fault, assign it an identification code, and store the code in a memory section. Depending on the year and model, the fault code(s) may be represented by two or three-digit numbers. The stored code(s) may be retrieved during diagnosis.

While the EEC system is capable of recognizing many internal faults, certain faults will not be recognized. Because the computer system sees only electrical signals, it cannot sense or react to mechanical or vacuum faults affecting engine operation. Some of these faults may affect another component which will set a code. For example, the PCM monitors the output signal to the fuel injectors, but cannot detect a partially clogged injector. As long as the output driver responds correctly, the computer will read the system as functioning correctly. However, the improper flow of fuel may result in a lean mixture. This would, in turn, be detected by the oxygen sensor and noticed as a constantly lean signal by the PCM. Once the signal falls outside the pre-programmed limits, the engine control assembly would notice the fault and set an identification code.

Additionally, the EEC system employs adaptive fuel logic. This process is used to compensate for normal wear and variability within the fuel system. Once the engine enters steady-state operation, the engine control assembly watches the oxygen sensor signal for a bias or tendency to run slightly rich or lean. If such a bias is detected, the adaptive logic corrects the fuel delivery to bring the air/fuel mixture towards a centered or 14.7:1 ratio. This compensating shift is stored in a non-volatile memory which is retained by battery power even with the ignition switched **OFF**. The correction factor is then available the next time the vehicle is operated.

➡**If the battery cable(s) is disconnected for longer than 5 minutes, the adaptive fuel factor will be lost. After repair it will be necessary to drive the car at least 10 miles to allow the processor to relearn the correct factors. The driving period should include steady-throttle open road driving if possible. During the drive, the vehicle may exhibit driveability symptoms not noticed before. These symptoms should clear as the PCM computes the correction factor. The PCM will also store Code 19 indicating loss of power to the controller.**

FAILURE MODE EFFECTS MANAGEMENT (FMEM)

The engine controller assembly contains back-up programs which allow the engine to operate if a sensor signal is lost. If a sensor input is seen to be out of range—either high or low—the FMEM program is used. The processor substitutes a fixed value for the missing sensor signal. The engine will continue to operate, although performance and driveability may be noticeably reduced. This function of the controller is sometimes referred to as the limp-in or fail-safe mode. If the missing sensor signal is restored, the FMEM system immediately returns the system to normal operation. The dashboard warning lamp will be lit when FMEM is in effect.

HARDWARE LIMITED OPERATION STRATEGY (HLOS)

This mode is only used if the fault is too extreme for the FMEM circuit to handle. In this mode, the processor has ceased all computation and control; the entire system is run on fixed values. The vehicle may be operated but performance and driveability will be greatly reduced. The fixed and default settings provide minimal calibration, allowing the vehicle to be carefully driven in for service. The dashboard warning lamp will be lit when HLOS is engaged. Codes cannot be read while the system is operating in this mode.

MALFUNCTION INDICATOR LAMP (MIL)

The CHECK ENGINE or SERVICE ENGINE SOON dashboard warning lamp is referred to as the Malfunction Indicator Lamp (MIL). The lamp is connected to the engine control assembly and will alert the driver to certain malfunctions within the EEC system. When the lamp is lit, the PCM has detected a fault and stored an identity code in memory. The engine control system will usually enter either FMEM or HLOS mode and driveability will be impaired.

The light will stay on as long as the fault causing it is present. Should the fault self-correct, the MIL will extinguish but the stored code will remain in memory.

Under normal operating conditions, the MIL should light briefly when the ignition key is turned **ON**. As soon as the PCM receives a signal that the engine is cranking, the lamp will be extinguished. The dash warning lamp should remain out during the entire operating cycle.

Diagnostic Connector

To read Diagnostic Trouble Codes (DTC's), the test connector for the EEC system must be used. This connector, which is known as the Assembly Line Diagnostic Link (ALDL) connector on vehicles with 5.0L engines, or the Data Link Connector (DLC) on all other models, is located in the passenger compartment. It is attached to the underside of the instrument panel and is accessible from the driver's side of the vehicle.

The connector is trapezoidal in shape and can accommodate up to 16 terminals.

88234P11

The Diagnostic Link Connector or DLC (arrow) is located under the driver's side of the instrument panel

Reading Codes

3.8L AND 4.6L ENGINES

♦ See Figure 68

The 3.8L and 4.6L engines utilize On Board Diagnostic II (OBD-II) Diagnostic Trouble Codes (DTC's), which are alpha-numeric (they use letters and numbers). The letters in the OBD-II DTC's make it highly difficult to convey the codes through the use of anything but a scan tool. Therefore, in order to read the OBD-II DTC's on these vehicles, it is necessary to utilize an OBD-II compatible scan tool.

1. Ensure that the ignition switch is in the **OFF** position.
2. Apply the parking brake.
3. Ensure that the transmission gearshift is in either Park (automatic transmissions) or Neutral (manual transmissions).
4. Block the rear wheels.
5. Turn off all electrical loads, such as the heater blower motor, radio, rear defroster, etc.
6. Connect the scan tool to the Data Link Connector. Make certain that the test button on the scan tool is unlatched or up.
7. Turn the ignition switch to the **ON** position without starting the engine (KOEO).
8. Using the scan tool, retrieve and record any continuous memory DTC's.
9. Turn the ignition switch to the **OFF** position.
10. Start the engine and run it until normal operating temperature is reached.
11. Turn the engine **OFF** and wait 10 seconds.
12. Turn the ignition switch **ON**, but do not start the engine.
13. Activate the KOEO self-test. Retrieve and record any KOEO DTC's after the KOEO test is complete.

➡Ignore DTC 1000.

14. If any DTC's were present, refer to the accompanying OBD-II charts to locate the problem(s).

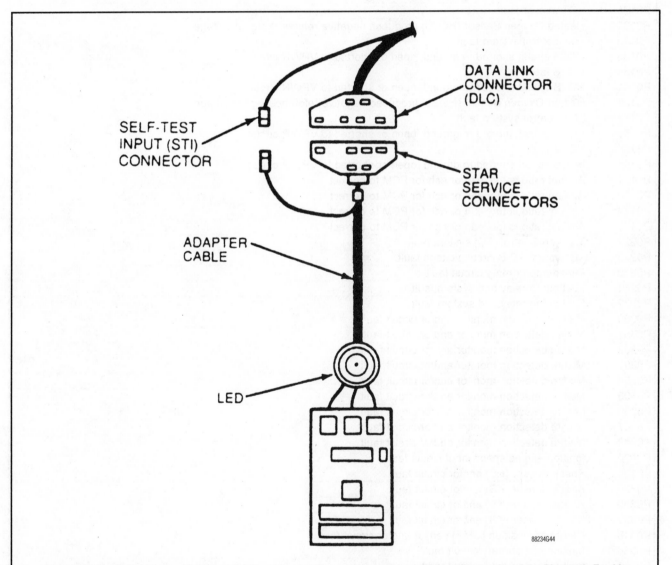

Fig. 68 For OBD-II vehicles (those with 3.8L and 4.6L engines) only a scan tool can be used to retrieve and read the Diagnostic Trouble Codes (DTC's)

OBD-II DIAGNOSTIC TROUBLE CODE (DTC) APPLICATIONS

DTC	Applicable System or Component
Constant Memory Trouble Codes	
P0102	MAF sensor reference signal voltage too low
P0103	MAF sensor reference signal too high
P0112	IAT or ECT intermittent fault
P0113	IAT or ECT intermittent fault
P0117	IAT or ECT intermittent fault
P0118	IAT or ECT intermittent fault
P0121	TP sensor fault
P0122	TP sensor reference signal voltage too low
P0123	TP sensor reference signal voltage too high
P0125	ECT sensor fault
P0131	Heated Oxygen Sensor (HO2S) produced negative reference signal voltage
P0133	Fuel control system fault
P0135	HO2S circuit shorted to ground, open or shorted to VPWR circuit
P0136	HO2S fault
P0141	HO2S circuit shorted to ground, open or shorted to VPWR circuit
P0151	Heated Oxygen Sensor (HO2S) produced negative reference signal voltage
P0153	Fuel control system fault
P0155	HO2S circuit shorted to ground, open or shorted to VPWR circuit
P0156	HO2S fault
P0161	HO2S circuit shorted to ground, open or shorted to VPWR circuit
P0171	Air/fuel ratio is too lean or rich for PCM to correct
P0172	Air/fuel ratio is too lean or rich for PCM to correct
P0174	Air/fuel ratio is too lean or rich for PCM to correct
P0175	Air/fuel ratio is too lean or rich for PCM to correct
P0222	Traction Control (TC) system fault
P0223	TC system TP-B circuit voltage fault
P0230	Fuel pump primary circuit fault
P0231	Fuel pump relay and system fault
P0232	Fuel pump relay and system fault
P0300	Misfire detection monitor and/or circuit fault
P0301	Misfire detection monitor and/or circuit fault
P0302	Misfire detection monitor and/or circuit fault
P0303	Misfire detection monitor and/or circuit fault
P0304	Misfire detection monitor and/or circuit fault
P0305	Misfire detection monitor and/or circuit fault
P0306	Misfire detection monitor and/or circuit fault
P0307	Misfire detection monitor and/or circuit fault
P0308	Misfire detection monitor and/or circuit fault
P0320	Ignition engine speed input circuit fault
P0325	Knock Sensor (KS) and/or circuit fault
P0326	Knock Sensor (KS) and/or circuit fault
P0330	Knock Sensor (KS) and/or circuit fault
P0331	Knock Sensor (KS) and/or circuit fault
P0340	Camshaft Position (CMP) sensor and/or circuit fault
P0350	Ignition coil primary circuit fault
P0351	Ignition coil primary circuit fault
P0352	Ignition coil primary circuit fault
P0353	Ignition coil primary circuit fault

OBD-II DIAGNOSTIC TROUBLE CODE (DTC) APPLICATIONS

DTC	Applicable System or Component
Constant Memory Trouble Codes (continued)	
P0354	Ignition coil primary circuit fault
P0401	Insufficient EGR flow detected
P0402	EGR flow at idle fault
P0411	Electric air pump hose fault
P0412	Secondary Air Injection (AIR) system fault
P0413	AIR injection VPWR circuit voltage fault
P0414	AIR injection VPWR circuit voltage fault
P0416	AIR injection VPWR circuit voltage fault
P0417	AIR injection VPWR circuit voltage fault
P0420	Catalyst efficiency monitor and/or exhaust system fault
P0430	Catalyst efficiency monitor and/or exhaust system fault
P0442	Evaporative Emission (EVAP) system leak detected
P0443	Intermittent EVAP canister purge valve fault
P0446	EVAP system Fuel Tank Pressure (FTP) sensor fault
P0452	FTP sensor circuit input signal too low
P0453	FTP sensor circuit input signal too high
P0455	Evaporative Emission (EVAP) system leak detected
P0460	Fuel level input circuit fault
P0500	Vehicle Speed Sensor (VSS) and/or circuit fault
P0501	Vehicle Speed Sensor (VSS) and/or circuit fault
P0503	Intermittent VSS and/or circuit fault
P0552	Power Steering Pressure (PSP) sensor and/or circuit fault
P0553	Power Steering Pressure (PSP) sensor and/or circuit fault
P0703	BOO switch input signal fault
P0704	CPP or PNP switch fault, or CPP or PNP switch voltage is too high or open when it should be low or closed
P0707	Manual transmission fault
P0708	Manual transmission fault
P0712	Manual transmission fault
P0713	Manual transmission fault
P0715	Manual transmission fault
P0720	Manual transmission fault
P0721	Manual transmission fault
P0731	Manual transmission fault
P0732	Manual transmission fault
P0733	Manual transmission fault
P0734	Manual transmission fault
P0735	Manual transmission fault
P0736	Manual transmission fault
P0741	Manual transmission fault
P0743	Manual transmission fault
P0746	Manual transmission fault
P0750	Manual transmission fault
P0751	Manual transmission fault
P0755	Manual transmission fault
P0756	Manual transmission fault
P0760	Manual transmission fault
P0761	Manual transmission fault
P0765	Manual transmission fault

88234G84

OBD-II DIAGNOSTIC TROUBLE CODE (DTC) APPLICATIONS

DTC	Applicable System or Component
Constant Memory Trouble Codes (continued)	
P0781	Manual transmission fault
P0782	Manual transmission fault
P0783	Manual transmission fault
P0784	Manual transmission fault
P1000	All OBD-II monitors not yet successfully tested
P1100	MAF sensor reference signal voltage out of specifications
P1112	IAT or ECT intermittent fault
P1117	IAT or ECT intermittent fault
P1120	TP sensor reference voltage out of specifications
P1121	TP sensor reference signal inconsistent with MAF sensor reference signal
P1125	TP sensor reference voltage out of specifications
P1130	HO2S fault
P1131	HO2S fault
P1132	HO2S fault
P1150	HO2S fault
P1151	HO2S fault
P1152	HO2S fault
P1220	TC system series throttle system fault
P1224	Series throttle assembly fault
P1232	Low speed fuel pump primary circuit fault
P1233	Fuel pump driver module and/or system circuit fault
P1234	Fuel pump driver module and/or system circuit fault
P1235	Fuel pump circuit, fuel pump driver module or PCM fault
P1236	Fuel pump circuit, fuel pump driver module or PCM fault
P1237	Fuel pump driver module circuit fault
P1238	Fuel pump driver module circuit fault
P1260	Anti-theft system detected a break-in
P1270	Engine and/or vehicle speed exceeded calibrated limits during vehicle operation
P1285	Engine overheat condition was sensed by PCM
P1289	Intermittent CHT sensor and/or circuit fault
P1290	Intermittent CHT sensor and/or circuit fault
P1299	Engine overheat condition was sensed by PCM
P1309	CMP sensor output signal fault
P1400	Exhaust Gas Recirculation (EGR) system fault
P1401	PFE/DPFE sensor signal voltage fault
P1405	Upstream pressure hose connection fault
P1406	Downstream pressure hose connection fault
P1409	EGR vacuum regulator solenoid fault
P1411	AIR injection is not being diverted when requested
P1413	AIR injection solid state relay voltage fault
P1414	AIR injection EAIR monitor circuit fault
P1442	Evaporative Emission (EVAP) system leak detected
P1443	Idle Air Control (IAC) valve speed fault
P1444	PF circuit input signal too low
P1445	PF circuit input signal too high
P1450	EVAP system unable to bleed fuel tank vacuum fault
P1451	EVAP system Canister Vent (CV) solenoid fault
P1452	EVAP system unable to bleed fuel tank vacuum fault

OBD-II DIAGNOSTIC TROUBLE CODE (DTC) APPLICATIONS

DTC	Applicable System or Component
Constant Memory Trouble Codes (continued)	
P1455	EVAP system fault
P1460	Wide Open Throttle A/C (WAC) circuit fault occurred during vehicle operation
P1461	Air Conditioning Pressure (ACP) sensor and/or circuit fault
P1462	ACP sensor reference signal too low
P1463	ACP sensor did not detect a pressure change in A/C system when activated
P1469	Frequent A/C compressor clutch cycling detected
P1474	Fan control circuit failure detected during vehicle operation
P1479	Fan control circuit failure detected during vehicle operation
P1483	Power-to-cooling fan circuit exceeded normal current draw when fan was activated
P1484	Variable load control module (VLCM) and/or circuit fault
P1500	Intermittent VSS reference signal fault
P1504	Idle Air Control (IAC) valve and/or circuit fault
P1505	IAC valve and/or circuit fault
P1506	IAC valve overspeed fault
P1507	Idle Air Control (IAC) valve and/or circuit fault
P1512	Intake Manifold Runner Control (IMRC) fault
P1513	Intake Manifold Runner Control (IMRC) fault
P1516	Intake Manifold Runner Control (IMRC) fault
P1517	Intake Manifold Runner Control (IMRC) fault
P1518	Intake Manifold Runner Control (IMRC) fault
P1519	Intake Manifold Runner Control (IMRC) fault
P1520	Intake Manifold Runner Control (IMRC) fault
P1530	Power-to-A/C clutch circuit open or short to power
P1537	Intake Manifold Runner Control (IMRC) fault
P1538	Intake Manifold Runner Control (IMRC) fault
P1539	Power-to-A/C clutch circuit exceeded normal current draw when A/C was activated
P1549	IMT valve and/or circuit fault
P1550	Power Steering Pressure (PSP) sensor and/or circuit fault
P1625	Open battery supply voltage to VLCM fan or A/C circuit detected
P1626	Open battery supply voltage to VLCM fan or A/C circuit detected
P1651	Power Steering Pressure (PSP) switch and/or circuit fault
P1701	Manual transmission fault
P1714	Manual transmission fault
P1715	Manual transmission fault
P1716	Manual transmission fault
P1717	Manual transmission fault
P1719	Manual transmission fault
P1728	Manual transmission fault
P1741	Manual transmission fault
P1742	Manual transmission fault
P1743	Manual transmission fault
P1744	Manual transmission fault
P1746	Manual transmission fault
P1747	Manual transmission fault
P1749	Manual transmission fault
P1751	Manual transmission fault
P1754	Manual transmission fault
P1756	Manual transmission fault

88234G86

OBD-II DIAGNOSTIC TROUBLE CODE (DTC) APPLICATIONS

DTC	Applicable System or Component
Constant Memory Trouble Codes (continued)	
P1760	Manual transmission fault
P1761	Manual transmission fault
P1762	Manual transmission fault
P1767	Manual transmission fault
P1783	Manual transmission fault
P1784	Manual transmission fault
P1785	Manual transmission fault
P1786	Manual transmission fault
P1787	Manual transmission fault
P1788	Manual transmission fault
P1789	Manual transmission fault
U1020	Manual transmission fault
U1021	PCM-to-VLCM two-way communication fault
U1039	Manual transmission fault
U1051	Manual transmission fault
U1073	PCM-to-VLCM two-way communication fault
U1135	Manual transmission fault
U1256	PCM-to-VLCM two-way communication fault
U1451	Manual transmission fault
Key On, Engine Off (KOEO) Trouble Codes	
135P0	HO2S circuit shorted to ground, open or shorted to VPWR circuit
P0103	MAF sensor reference signal too high
P0112	IAT or ECT sensor reference signal voltage too low
P0113	IAT or ECT sensor reference signal voltage too high
P0117	Cylinder Head Temperature (CHT) sensor and/or circuit fault
P0118	IAT or ECT sensor reference signal voltage too high
P0122	TP sensor reference signal voltage too low
P0123	TP sensor reference signal voltage too high
P0141	HO2S circuit shorted to ground, open or shorted to VPWR circuit
P0155	HO2S circuit shorted to ground, open or shorted to VPWR circuit
P0161	HO2S circuit shorted to ground, open or shorted to VPWR circuit
P0222	Traction Control (TC) system fault
P0223	TC system TP-B circuit voltage fault
P0230	Fuel pump relay fault
P0231	Fuel pump secondary circuit fault
P0232	Fuel pump FPM circuit voltage too high
P0411	Electric air pump hose fault
P0412	Secondary Air Injection (AIR) system fault
P0413	AIR injection VPWR circuit voltage fault
P0414	AIR injection VPWR circuit voltage fault
P0416	AIR injection VPWR circuit voltage fault
P0417	AIR injection VPWR circuit voltage fault
P0443	Evaporative Emission (EVAP) system fault
P0452	FTP sensor circuit input signal too low
P0453	FTP sensor circuit input signal too high
P0460	Fuel level input circuit fault
P0603	Keep Alive Power (KAPWR) circuit and/or PCM fault
P0605	Defective PCM; replace the PCM

OBD-II DIAGNOSTIC TROUBLE CODE (DTC) APPLICATIONS

DTC	Applicable System or Component
Key On, Engine Off (KOEO) Trouble Codes (continued)	
P0704	CPP or PNP switch fault, or CPP or PNP switch voltage is too high or open when it should be low or closed
P0705	Manual transmission fault
P0712	Manual transmission fault
P0713	Manual transmission fault
P0743	Manual transmission fault
P0750	Manual transmission fault
P0755	Manual transmission fault
P0760	Manual transmission fault
P1000	DTC 1000 should be ignored; continue with other codes
P1101	Manifold Air Flow (MAF) sensor output voltage fault
P1116	Intake Air Temperature (IAT) or Engine Coolant Temperature (ECT) sensor fault
P1120	TP sensor reference voltage out of specifications
P1124	Throttle Position (TP) reference voltage out of specifications
P1151	HO2S fault
P1220	TC system series throttle system fault
P1224	Series throttle assembly fault
P1232	Low speed fuel pump primary circuit fault
P1233	Fuel pump driver module and/or system circuit fault
P1234	Fuel pump driver module and/or system circuit fault
P1235	Fuel pump circuit, fuel pump driver module or PCM fault
P1236	Fuel pump circuit, fuel pump driver module or PCM fault
P1237	Fuel pump driver module circuit fault
P1238	Fuel pump driver module circuit fault
P1288	Cylinder Head Temperature (CHT) sensor fault
P1289	CHT sensor reference signal too high
P1290	CHT sensor reference signal too low
P1390	Octane Adjust (OCT ADJ) system fault
P1400	Exhaust Gas Recirculation (EGR) system fault
P1401	PFE/DPFE sensor signal voltage fault
P1409	EGR vacuum regulator solenoid fault
P1411	AIR injection is not being diverted when requested
P1413	AIR injection solid state relay voltage fault
P1414	AIR injection EAIR monitor circuit fault
P1451	EVAP system Canister Vent (CV) solenoid fault
P1460	Wide Open Throttle A/C (WAC) circuit fault
P1461	Air Conditioning Pressure (ACP) sensor and/or circuit fault
P1462	ACP sensor reference signal too low
P1464	ACCS input signal too high
P1473	Power-to-cooling fan circuit open or short to power
P1474	Fan control relay and/or circuit fault
P1479	Fan control relay and/or circuit fault
P1483	Power-to-cooling fan circuit exceeded normal current draw when fan was activated
P1484	Variable load control module (VLCM) and/or circuit fault
P1504	Idle Air Control (IAC) valve and/or circuit fault
P1505	IAC valve and/or circuit fault
P1516	Intake Manifold Runner Control (IMRC) fault
P1517	Intake Manifold Runner Control (IMRC) fault
P1518	Intake Manifold Runner Control (IMRC) fault

88234G88

OBD-II DIAGNOSTIC TROUBLE CODE (DTC) APPLICATIONS

DTC	Applicable System or Component
Key On, Engine Off (KOEO) Trouble Codes (continued)	
P1519	Intake Manifold Runner Control (IMRC) fault
P1520	Intake Manifold Runner Control (IMRC) fault
P1530	Power-to-A/C clutch circuit open or short to power
P1537	Intake Manifold Runner Control (IMRC) fault
P1538	Intake Manifold Runner Control (IMRC) fault
P1539	Power-to-A/C clutch circuit exceeded normal current draw when A/C was activated
P1549	IMT valve and/or circuit fault
P1625	Battery voltage to VLCM fan or A/C circuit not detected
P1626	Battery voltage to VLCM fan or A/C circuit not detected
P1650	Power Steering Pressure (PSP) switch and/or circuit fault
P1703	Signal from Brake On/Off (BOO) switch detected when brake pedal is not applied
P1705	Manual transmission fault
P1709	Park/Neutral Position (PNP)/Clutch Pedal Position (CPP) switches and/or circuit fault
P1711	Manual transmission fault
P1746	Manual transmission fault
P1747	Manual transmission fault
P1754	Manual transmission fault
P1760	Manual transmission fault
P1767	Manual transmission fault
P1788	Manual transmission fault
P1789	Manual transmission fault
U1021	PCM-to-VLCM two-way communication fault
U1073	PCM-to-VLCM two-way communication fault
U1256	PCM-to-VLCM two-way communication fault

88234G89

5.0L ENGINE

The 5.0L engines use an older diagnostic system to monitor and report engine related malfunctions. This older system is known as On Board Diagnostics (OBD-I). The Diagnostic Trouble Codes (DTC's) are two or three-digit numbers, and can be read through the use of a scan tool, an analog voltmeter, or with the Malfunction Indicator Lamp (MIL) located on the instrument cluster. Use the accompanying OBD-I DTC charts to decipher the DTC's for the identification of the malfunctioning component or circuit.

Scan Tool Method

♦ See Figures 69 and 70

1. Connect the scan tool to the self-test connectors. Make certain the test button is unlatched or up.
2. Start the engine and run it until normal operating temperature is reached.
3. Turn the engine **OFF** and wait 10 seconds.
4. Activate the test button on the STAR tester.
5. Turn the ignition switch **ON**, but do not start the engine.
6. The codes will be transmitted. Six to nine seconds after the last code, a single separator pulse will be transmitted. Six to nine seconds after this pulse, the codes from the Continuous Memory will be transmitted.
7. Record all service codes displayed. Do not depress the throttle during the test.
8. After the test, compare the DTC's retrieved with the accompanying OBD-I code identification charts.

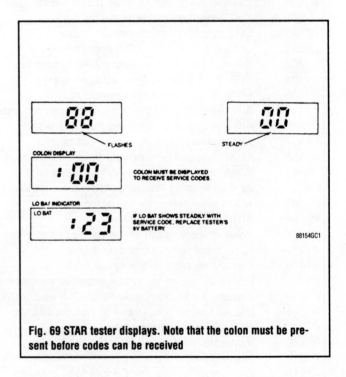

Fig. 69 STAR tester displays. Note that the colon must be present before codes can be received

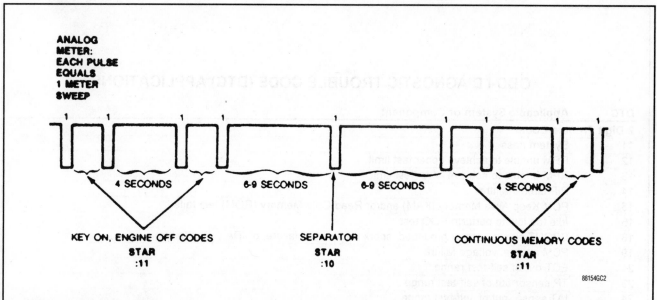

Fig. 70 Code transmission using a scan tool—note that the continuous memory codes are transmitted after a brief pause and separator pause

Analog Voltmeter Method

♦ See Figures 71 and 72

In the absence of a scan tool, an analog voltmeter may be used to retrieve stored fault codes. Set the meter range to read 0–15 volts DC. Connect the positive lead of the meter to the battery positive terminal and connect the negative lead of the meter to the Self-Test Output (STO) pin of the diagnostic connector.

Follow the directions given previously for performing the scan tool procedure. To activate the procedure, use a jumper wire to connect the signal return pin on the diagnostic connector to the self-test input connector. The self-test input line is the separate wire and connector with or near the diagnostic connector.

The codes will be transmitted as groups of needle sweeps. This method may be used to read either 2 or 3-digit codes. The Continuous Memory codes are separated from the other codes by 6 seconds, a single sweep and another 6 second delay.

1. After the test, compare the DTC's retrieved with the accompanying OBD-I code identification charts.

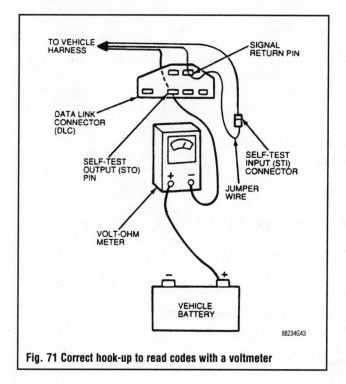

Fig. 71 Correct hook-up to read codes with a voltmeter

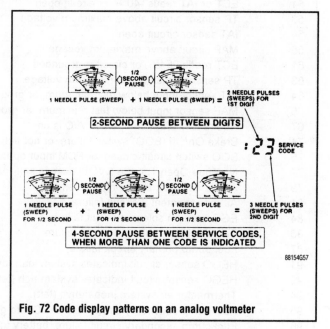

Fig. 72 Code display patterns on an analog voltmeter

OBD-I DIAGNOSTIC TROUBLE CODE (DTC) APPLICATIONS

DTC	Applicable System or Component
2-Digit Trouble Codes	
11	System pass
12	RPM unable to achieve upper test limit
13	RPM unable to achieve lower test limit
14	PIP circuit failure
15	PCM Keep Alive Memory (KAM) and/or Read Only Memory (ROM) test failed
16	Idle too low to perform EGO test
18	SPOUT circuit open or grounded, spark angle word failure, or IDA circuit failure
19	PCM internal voltage failure
21	ECT out of self-test range
23	TP sensor out of self-test range
24	IAT sensor out of self-test range
25	Knock not sensed during dynamic test
26	MAF out of self-test range
29	Insufficient input from VSS
31	PFE, EVP or EVR circuit below minimum voltage
32	EVP voltage below closed limit
33	EGR valve opening not detected
34	EVP voltage above closed limit
35	PFE or EVP circuit above maximum voltage
41	HEGO sensor circuit indicates system lean, or no HEGO switching detected (right)
42	HEGO sensor circuit indicates system rich (right)
44	Thermactor air system inoperative (right)
45	Thermactor air upstream during self-test
46	Thermactor air not bypassed during self-test
51	ECT or IAT reads -40°F, or circuit open
53	TP sensor circuit above maximum voltage
54	IAT sensor circuit open
56	MAF circuit above maximum voltage
61	ECT reads 254°F, or circuit is grounded
63	TP sensor circuit below minimum voltage
64	IAT sensor input below test minimum, or grounded
66	MAF sensor input below test minimum, or grounded
67	Neutral/Drive switch open, or A/C is on
74	Brake On/Off (BOO) switch failure, or not actuated
75	BOO switch circuit closed, or PCM input open
77	No Wide Open Throttle (WOT) seen in self-test, or operator error
79	A/C or defroster on during the self-test
81	Air management 2 circuit failure
84	EGR vacuum solenoid circuit failure
85	Canister purge solenoid circuit failure
87	Fuel pump primary circuit failure
91	HEGO sensor circuit indicates system lean, or no HEGO switching detected (left)
92	HEGO sensor circuit indicates system rich (left)
94	Thermactor air system inoperative (left)
95	Fuel pump secondary circuit failure, PCM to ground
96	Fuel pump secondary circuit failure, battery to PCM
98	Hard fault present

OBD-I DIAGNOSTIC TROUBLE CODE (DTC) APPLICATIONS

DTC	Applicable System or Component
3-Digit Trouble Codes	
111	System pass
112	IAT sensor circuit grounded or reads 254°F
113	IAT sensor circuit open, or reads -40°F
114	IAT outside test limits during KOEO test
116	ECT outside limits during KOEO test
117	ECT sensor circuit grounded
118	ECT sensor circuit above maximum voltage, or reads -40°F
121	Closed throttle voltage higher or lower than expected
122	TP sensor circuit below minimum voltage
123	TP sensor circuit above maximum voltage
124	TP sensor voltage higher than expected, but with specified range
125	TP sensor voltage lower than expected, but with specified range
129	Insufficient MAF sensor change during Dynamic Response test
136	HEGO shows system always lean (left)
137	HEGO shows system always rich (left)
139	No HEGO switching (left)
144	No HEGO switching (right)
157	MAF sensor circuit below minimum voltage
158	MAF sensor circuit above maximum voltage
159	MAF sensor higher or lower than expected during KOEO test
167	Insufficient TP sensor change during Dynamic Response test
172	No HEGO switching detected, indicates lean (right)
173	HEGO shows system always rich (rear) or no HEGO switching detected, indicates rich
174	HEGO switching time is slow (right)
175	No HEGO switching, system at adaptive limit (left)
177	HEGO shows system always lean (left)
178	HEGO switching time is slow (left)
179	System at lean adaptive limit at part throttle, system rich (right)
181	System at rich adaptive limit at part throttle, system rich (right)
182	System at lean adaptive limit at idle, system rich (right)
183	System at rich adaptive limit at idle, system rich (right)
184	MAF higher than expected
185	MAF lower than expected
186	Injector pulse width higher than expected
187	Injector pulse width lower than expected
188	System at lean adaptive limit at part throttle, system rich (left)
189	System at rich adaptive limit at part throttle, system rich (left)
191	System at lean adaptive limit at idle, system rich (left)
192	System at rich adaptive limit at idle, system rich (left)
211	PIP circuit fault
212	Loss of IDM input to PCM or SPOUT circuit grounded
213	SPOUT circuit open
311	Thermactor air system inoperative (right)
313	Thermactor air not bypassed during self-test
314	Thermactor air system inoperative (left)
327	EVP or DPFE circuit below minimum voltage
328	EGR closed voltage lower than expected

OBD-I DIAGNOSTIC TROUBLE CODE (DTC) APPLICATIONS

DTC	Applicable System or Component
3-Digit Trouble Codes (continued)	
332	Insufficient EGR flow detected
334	EGR closed voltage higher than expected
337	EVP or DPFE circuit above maximum voltage
452	Insufficient input from VSS
511	EEC processor ROM test failed
512	Keep Alive Memory test failed
513	Failure in EEC processor internal voltage
522	Vehicle not in Park or Neutral during KOEO test
539	A/C or defroster on during KOEO test
542	Fuel pump secondary circuit failure, PCM to ground
543	Fuel pump secondary circuit failure, battery to PCM
552	Air management 1 circuit failed
556	Fuel pump primary circuit failure
558	EGR vacuum regulator circuit failure
565	Canister purge circuit failure
998	Hard fault present

88234G82

Malfunction Indicator Lamp (MIL) Method

◗ **See Figures 73 and 74**

The Malfunction Indicator Lamp (MIL) on the dashboard may also be used to retrieve the stored codes. This method displays only the stored codes and does not allow any system investigation. It should only be used in field conditions where a quick check of stored codes is needed.

Follow the directions given previously for performing the scan tool procedure. To activate the tests, use a jumper wire to connect the signal return pin on the diagnostic connector to the Self-Test Input (STI) connector. The self-test input line is the separate wire and connector with or near the diagnostic connector.

Codes are transmitted by place value with a pause between the digits; for example, code 32 would be sent as 3 flashes, a pause and 2 flashes. A slightly longer pause divides codes from each other. Be ready to count and record codes; the only way to repeat a code is to recycle the system. This

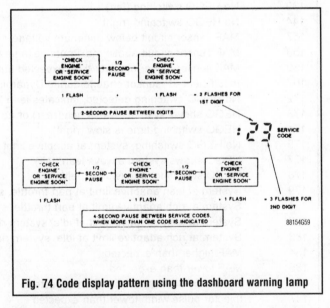

Fig. 74 Code display pattern using the dashboard warning lamp

method may be used to read either 2 or 3-digit codes. The Continuous Memory codes are separated from the other codes by 6 seconds, a single flash and another 6 second delay.

Clearing Codes

CONTINUOUS MEMORY CODES

These codes are retained in memory for 40 warm-up cycles. To clear the codes for purposes of testing or confirming repair, perform the code reading procedure. When the fault codes begin to be displayed, de-activate the test either by disconnecting the jumper wire (if using a meter, MIL or message center) or by releasing the test button on the hand scanner. Stopping the test during code transmission will erase the Continuous Memory. Do not disconnect the negative battery cable to clear these codes; the Keep Alive memory will be cleared and a new code, 19, will be stored for loss of PCM power.

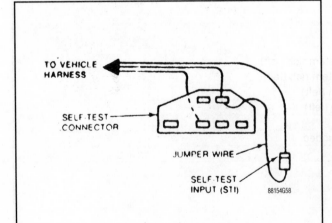

Fig. 73 Only one jumper wire is needed to read codes through the MIL or the message center

KEEP ALIVE MEMORY

The Keep Alive Memory (KAM) contains the adaptive factors used by the processor to compensate for component tolerances and wear. It should not be routinely cleared during diagnosis. If an emissions related part is replaced during repair, the KAM must be cleared. Failure to clear the KAM may cause severe driveability problems, since the correction factor for the old component will be applied to the new component.

To clear the Keep Alive Memory, disconnect the negative battery cable for at least 5 minutes. After the memory is cleared and the battery reconnected, the vehicle must be driven at least 10 miles so that the processor may relearn the needed correction factors. The distance to be driven depends on the engine and vehicle, but all drives should include steady-throttle cruising on open roads. Certain driveability problems may be noted during the drive because the adaptive factors are not yet functioning.

VACUUM DIAGRAMS

Following are vacuum diagrams for most of the engine and emissions package combinations covered by this manual. Because vacuum circuits will vary based on various engine and vehicle options, always refer first to the Vehicle Emission Control Information (VECI) label, if present. Should the label be missing, or should the vehicle be equipped with a different engine than the vehicle's original equipment, refer to the following diagrams for the same or similar configuration.

If you wish to obtain a replacement emissions label, most manufacturers make the labels available for purchase. The labels can usually be ordered from a local dealer.

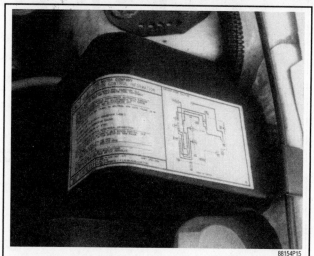

The vacuum diagram and emissions information is on a sticker under the hood of the car

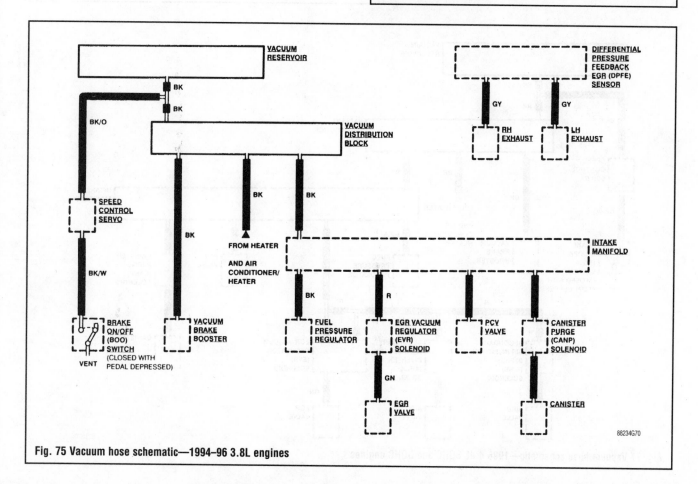

Fig. 75 Vacuum hose schematic—1994–96 3.8L engines

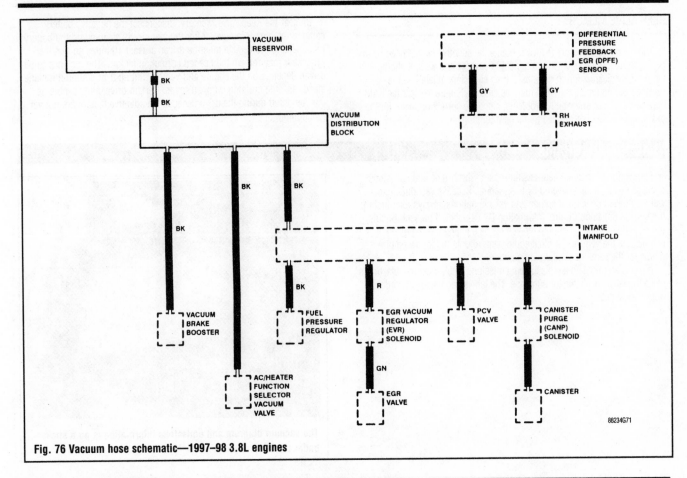

Fig. 76 Vacuum hose schematic—1997–98 3.8L engines

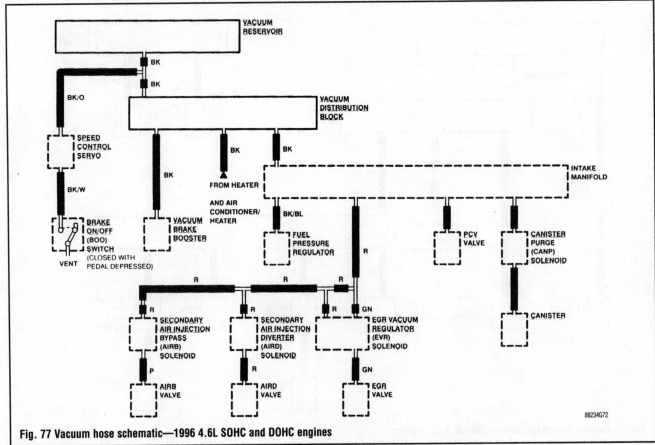

Fig. 77 Vacuum hose schematic—1996 4.6L SOHC and DOHC engines

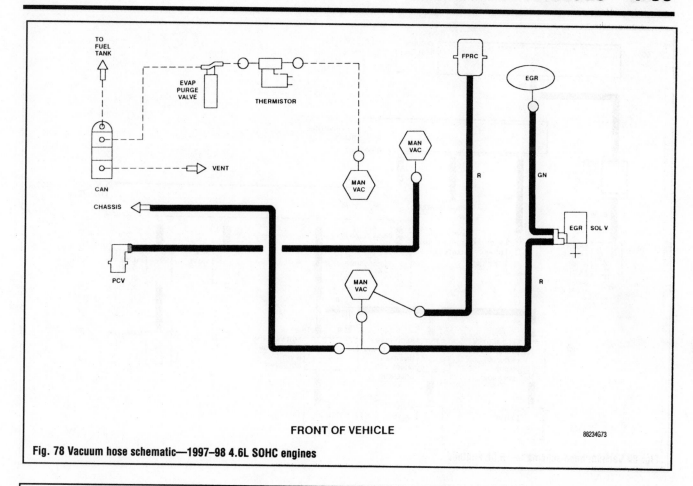

Fig. 78 Vacuum hose schematic—1997–98 4.6L SOHC engines

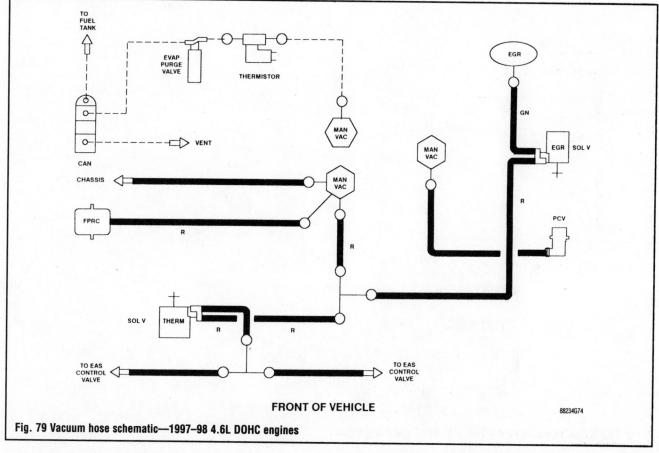

Fig. 79 Vacuum hose schematic—1997–98 4.6L DOHC engines

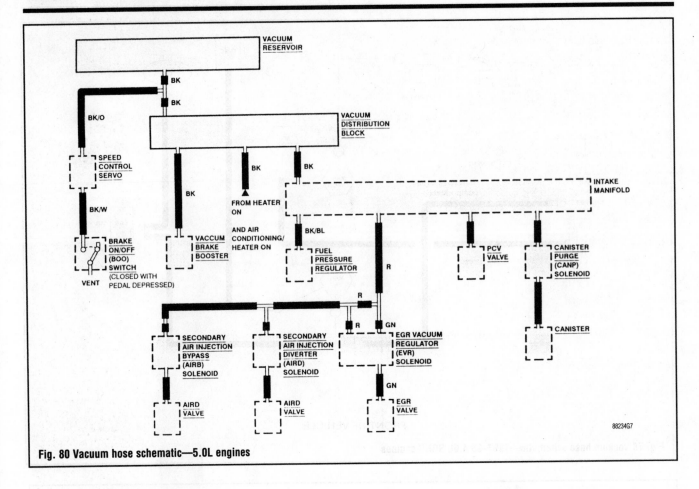

Fig. 80 Vacuum hose schematic—5.0L engines

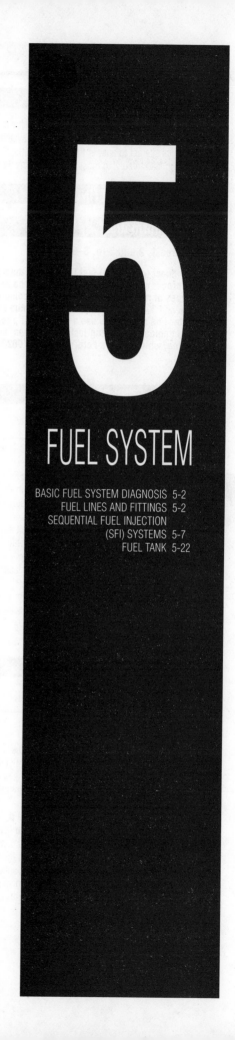

5

FUEL SYSTEM

BASIC FUEL SYSTEM DIAGNOSIS

When there is a problem starting or driving a vehicle, two of the most important checks involve the ignition and the fuel systems. The questions most mechanics attempt to answer first, "is there spark?" and "is there fuel?" will often lead to solving most basic problems. For ignition system diagnosis and testing, please refer to the information on engine electrical components and ignition systems found earlier in this manual. If the ignition system checks out (there is spark), then you must determine if the fuel system is operating properly (is there fuel?).

FUEL LINES AND FITTINGS

General Information

◆ See Figures 1, 2 and 3 (p. 3–5)

➡Quick-connect (push-type) fuel line fittings must be disconnected using the proper procedure or the fitting may be damaged. There are two types of retainers used on the quick-connect fittings. Line sizes of ⅜ and ⁵⁄₁₆ in. diameter use a hairpin clip retainer. The ¼ in. diameter line connectors use a duck-bill clip retainer. In addition, some engines use spring-lock connections, secured by a garter spring, which require Ford Tool T81P-19623-G (or equivalent) for removal.

Hairpin Clip Fitting

REMOVAL & INSTALLATION

◆ See Figure 4 (p. 6)

1. Clean all dirt and grease from the fitting. Spread the two clip legs about ⅛ in. (3mm) each to disengage from the fitting and pull the clip outward from the fitting. Use finger pressure only; do not use any tools.
2. Grasp the fitting and hose assembly and pull away from the steel line. Twist the fitting and hose assembly slightly while pulling, if the assembly sticks.
3. Inspect the hairpin clip for damage, and replace the clip if necessary. Reinstall the clip in position on the fitting.
4. Inspect the fitting and inside of the connector to ensure freedom from dirt or obstruction. Install the fitting into the connector and push together. A click will be heard when the hairpin snaps into the proper connection. Pull on the line to ensure full engagement.

Duckbill Clip Fitting

REMOVAL & INSTALLATION

◆ See Figure 5 (p. 6)

1. A special tool is available from Ford and other manufacturers for removing the retaining clips. Use Ford Tool T82L-9500-AH or equivalent. If the tool is not on hand, go on to step 2. Align the slot on the push-type connector removal tool with either tab on the retaining clip. Pull the line from the connector.
2. If the special clip tool is not available, use a pair of narrow 6-inch slip-jaw pliers with a jaw width of 0.2 in. (5mm) or less. Align the jaws of the pliers with the openings of the fitting case and compress the part of the retaining clip that engages the case. Compressing the retaining clip will release the fitting, which may be pulled from the connector. Both sides of the clip must be compressed at the same time to disengage.
3. Inspect the retaining clip, fitting end and connector. Replace the clip if any damage is apparent.
4. Push the line into the steel connector until a click is heard, indicating the clip is in place. Pull on the line to check engagement.

Spring Lock Coupling

REMOVAL & INSTALLATION

◆ See Figures 6 and 7 (p. 6–7)

The spring lock coupling is held together by a garter spring inside a circular cage. When the coupling is connected together, the flared end of the

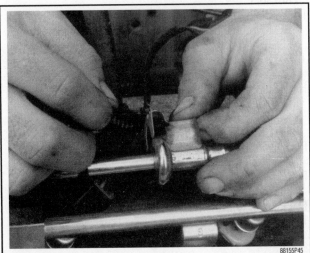

To disengage a spring lock coupling, pull the clip back off the coupling after cleaning the area . . .

88155P45

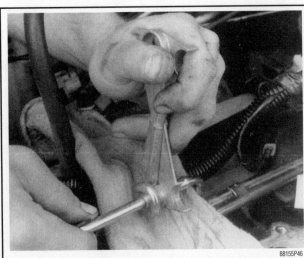

. . . then insert a removal tool into the coupling to release the spring

88155P46

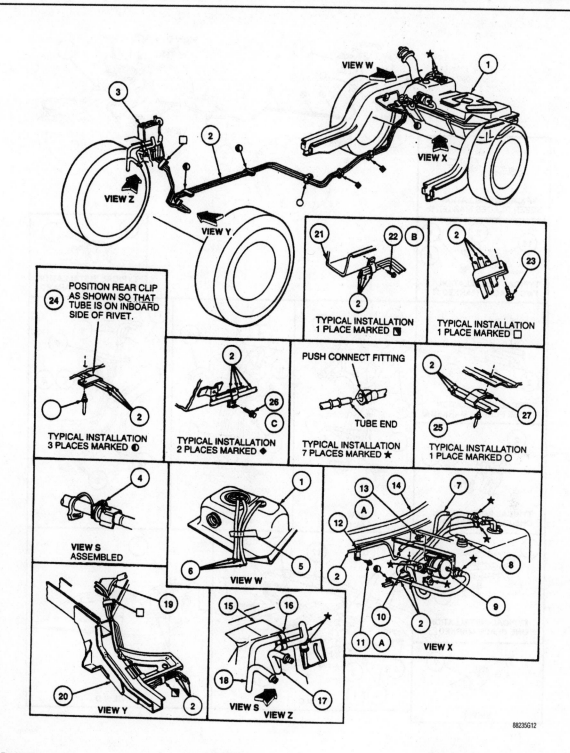

Fig. 1 Fuel line/hose routing and fitting locations on Mustang models equipped with the 3.8L engine

1. Fuel tank
2. Fuel and vapor return tube
3. Fuel vapor canister
4. Retainer
5. 2 in. wide tape
6. Fuel pump-to-injector hose
7. Fuel hose
8. Fuel vapor valve
9. Fuel filter and base
10. Tie strap
11. Bolt
12. Clamp
13. Bolt
14. Side member
15. Shock tower
16. Fuel tube retainer
17. Fuel tube hose
18. Fuel return hose
19. Vapor line
20. Front side rear member
21. Front side member dash mounting gusset
22. Bolt
23. Bolt
24. Clamp
25. Rivet
26. Bolt
27. Clamp

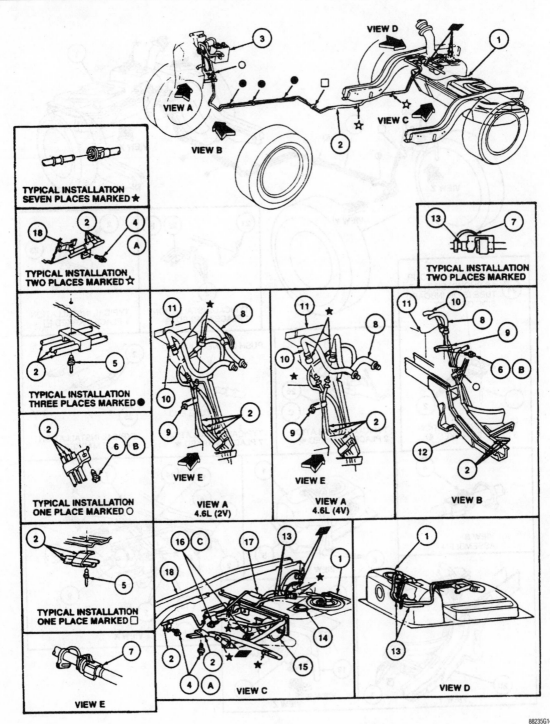

TYPICAL INSTALLATION SEVEN PLACES MARKED ★

TYPICAL INSTALLATION TWO PLACES MARKED ☆

TYPICAL INSTALLATION THREE PLACES MARKED ●

TYPICAL INSTALLATION ONE PLACE MARKED ○

TYPICAL INSTALLATION ONE PLACE MARKED □

TYPICAL INSTALLATION TWO PLACES MARKED

VIEW A

VIEW B

VIEW C

VIEW D

VIEW E

VIEW A 4.6L (2V)

VIEW A 4.6L (4V)

VIEW B

VIEW C

VIEW D

VIEW E

88235G14

1. Fuel tank
2. Fuel and vapor return tube
3. Evaporative emissions canister
4. Mounting bolt
5. Rivet
6. Mounting bolt
7. Retainer
8. Fuel supply hose
9. Fuel tube clip
10. Fuel return hose
11. Front fender apron
12. Front side member dash mounting gusset
13. Fuel pump-to-injector hose
14. Evaporative emission valve
15. Fuel filter and base
16. Mounting bolt
17. Rubber hose
18. Rear floor side member

Fig. 2 Fuel line/hose routing and fitting locations on Mustang models equipped with either 4.6L engine

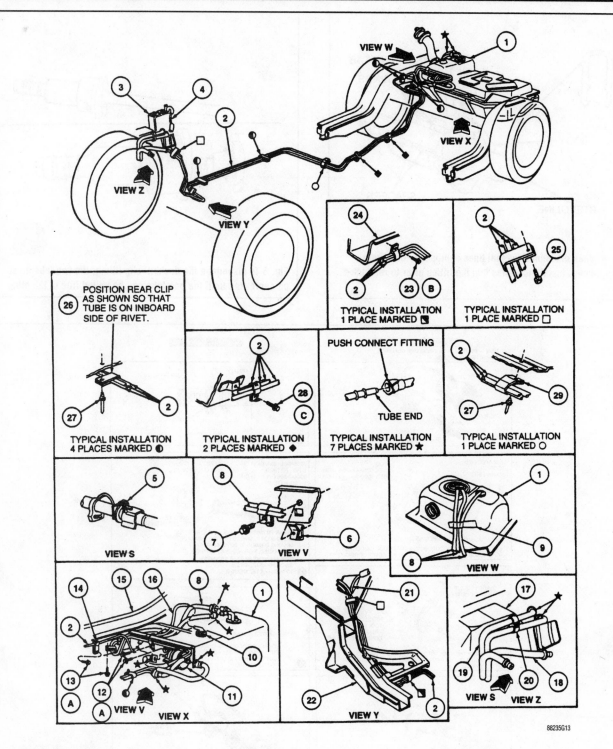

1. Fuel tank
2. Fuel and vapor return tube
3. Fuel vapor canister
4. Fuel tank vent tube
5. Retainer
6. Clip
7. Bolt
8. Fuel pump-to-injector hose
9. 2 in. wide tape
10. Fuel vapor valve
11. Fuel filter and base
12. Bolt
13. Bolt
14. Clamp
15. Rear floor side member
16. Fuel hose
17. Front suspension housing
18. Fuel tube hose
19. Fuel return hose
20. Fuel tube retainer
21. Vapor line
22. Front side rear member
23. Bolt
24. Front side member dash mounting gusset
25. Bolt
26. Clamp
27. Rivet
28. Bolt
29. Clamp

Fig. 3 Fuel line/hose routing and fitting locations on Mustang models equipped with the 5.0L engine

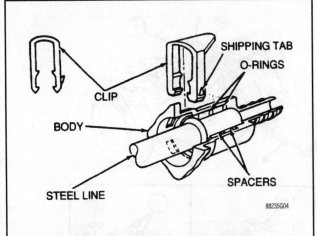

Fig. 4 When disconnecting fuel lines equipped with hairpin clips, always install new clips into the fitting prior to reattachment

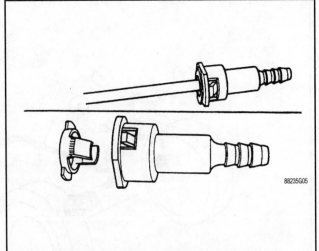

Fig. 5 To disengage the duckbill clip fitting, the two tabs must be depressed until the one tube can be pulled free of the other

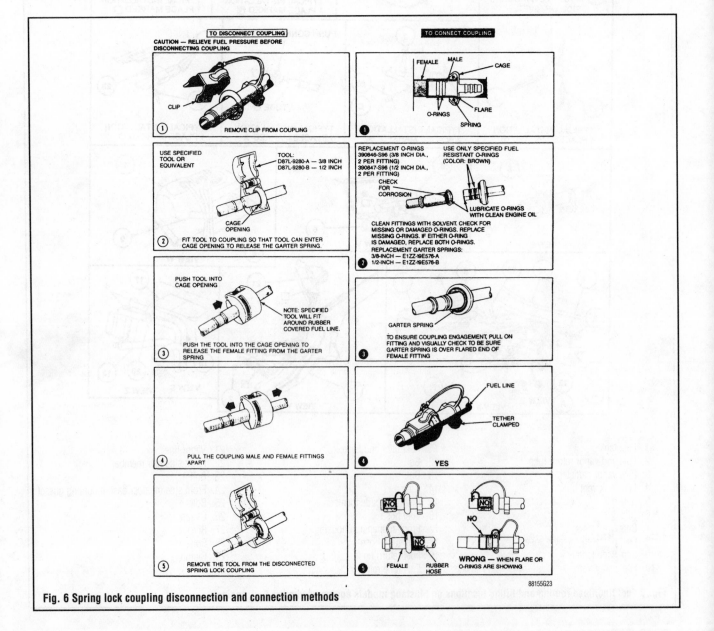

Fig. 6 Spring lock coupling disconnection and connection methods

female fitting slips behind the garter spring inside the cage of the male fitting. The garter spring and cage then prevent the flared end of the female fitting from pulling out of the cage. As an additional locking feature, most

vehicles have a horseshoe-shaped retaining clip that improves the retaining reliability of the spring lock coupling.

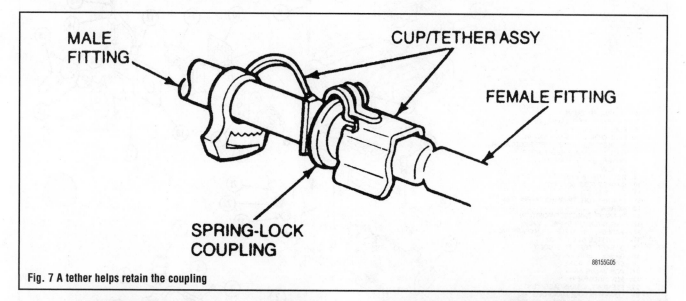

Fig. 7 A tether helps retain the coupling

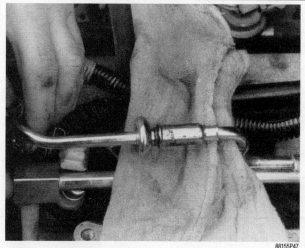

Use a rag to catch any spilled fuel while pulling the coupling apart . . .

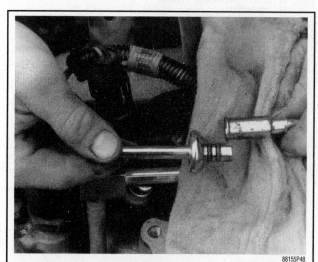

. . . and be sure to check the O-rings for damage; replace them if necessary

SEQUENTIAL FUEL INJECTION (SFI) SYSTEM

General Information

▶ **See Figures 8 and 9**

The Sequential Fuel Injection (SFI) system includes a high pressure, inline electric fuel pump mounted in the fuel tank, a fuel supply manifold, a throttle body (which meters the incoming air charge for the correct mixture with the fuel), a pressure regulator, fuel filters and both solid and flexible fuel lines. The fuel supply manifold includes 6 or 8 electronically-controlled fuel injectors, each mounted directly above an intake port in the lower intake manifold. Each injector fires once every other crankshaft revolution, in sequence with the engine firing order.

The fuel pressure regulator maintains a constant pressure drop across the injector nozzles. The regulator is referenced to intake manifold vacuum and is connected in parallel to the fuel injectors; it is positioned on the far end of the fuel rail. Any excess fuel supplied by the fuel pump passes through the regulator and is returned to the fuel tank via a return line.

➡**The pressure regulator reduces fuel pressure to 39–40 psi under normal operating conditions. At idle or high manifold vacuum condition, fuel pressure is further reduced to approximately 30 psi.**

The fuel pressure regulator is a diaphragm-operated relief valve, in which the inside of the diaphragm senses fuel pressure and the other side senses manifold vacuum. Normal fuel pressure is established by a spring preload applied to the diaphragm. Control of the fuel system is maintained through the Powertrain Control Module (PCM), although electrical power is routed through the fuel pump relay and an inertia switch. The fuel pump relay is normally located on a bracket somewhere above the Electronic Control Assembly (ECA) and the inertia switch is located in the trunk. The inline fuel pump is usually mounted on a bracket at the fuel tank, or on a frame rail. Tank-mounted pumps can be either high or low pressure, depending on the model.

The inertia switch opens the power circuit to the fuel pump in the event of a collision. Once tripped, the switch must be reset manually by pushing the reset button on the assembly.

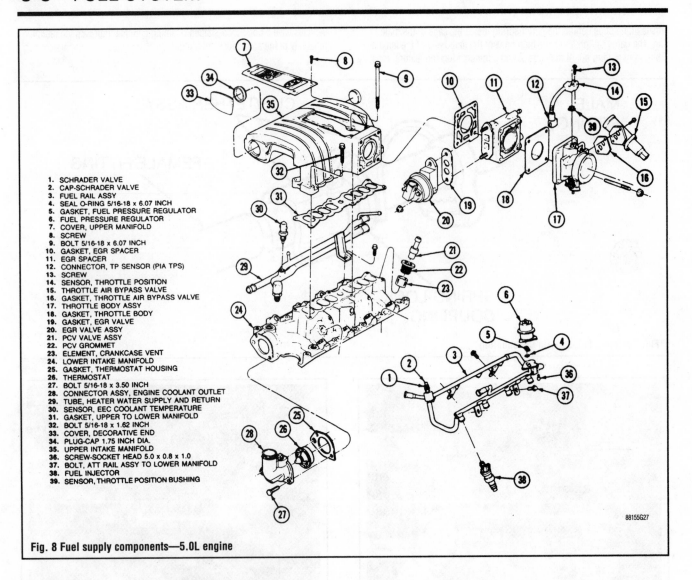

1. SCHRADER VALVE
2. CAP-SCHRADER VALVE
3. FUEL RAIL ASSY
4. SEAL O-RING 5/16-18 x 6.07 INCH
5. GASKET, FUEL PRESSURE REGULATOR
6. FUEL PRESSURE REGULATOR
7. COVER, UPPER MANIFOLD
8. SCREW
9. BOLT 5/16-18 x 6.07 INCH
10. GASKET, EGR SPACER
11. EGR SPACER
12. CONNECTOR, TP SENSOR (PIA TPS)
13. SCREW
14. SENSOR, THROTTLE POSITION
15. THROTTLE AIR BYPASS VALVE
16. GASKET, THROTTLE AIR BYPASS VALVE
17. THROTTLE BODY ASSY
18. GASKET, THROTTLE BODY
19. GASKET, EGR VALVE
20. EGR VALVE ASSY
21. PCV VALVE ASSY
22. PCV GROMMET
23. ELEMENT, CRANKCASE VENT
24. LOWER INTAKE MANIFOLD
25. GASKET, THERMOSTAT HOUSING
26. THERMOSTAT
27. BOLT 5/16-18 x 3.50 INCH
28. CONNECTOR ASSY, ENGINE COOLANT OUTLET
29. TUBE, HEATER WATER SUPPLY AND RETURN
30. SENSOR, EEC COOLANT TEMPERATURE
31. GASKET, UPPER TO LOWER MANIFOLD
32. BOLT 5/16-18 x 1.62 INCH
33. COVER, DECORATIVE END
34. PLUG-CAP 1.75 INCH DIA.
35. UPPER INTAKE MANIFOLD
36. SCREW-SOCKET HEAD 5.0 x 0.8 x 1.0
37. BOLT, ATT RAIL ASSY TO LOWER MANIFOLD
38. FUEL INJECTOR
39. SENSOR, THROTTLE POSITION BUSHING

88155G27

Fig. 8 Fuel supply components—5.0L engine

The inertia switch, behind the rear panel in the trunk, is reset by pushing the button mounted on top

88155P56

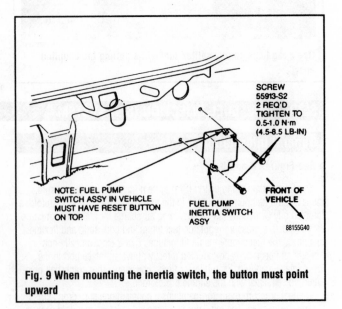

SCREW
55913-S2
2 REQ'D
TIGHTEN TO
0.5-1.0 N·m
(4.5-8.5 LB-IN)

NOTE: FUEL PUMP
SWITCH ASSY IN VEHICLE
MUST HAVE RESET BUTTON
ON TOP.

FUEL PUMP
INERTIA SWITCH
ASSY

FRONT OF
VEHICLE

88155G40

Fig. 9 When mounting the inertia switch, the button must point upward

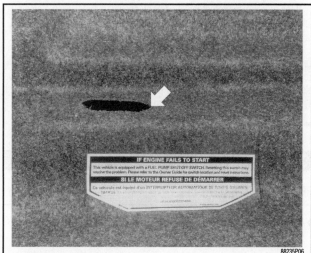

The inertia or fuel pump shut-off switch has an access hole (arrow) in the trunk . . .

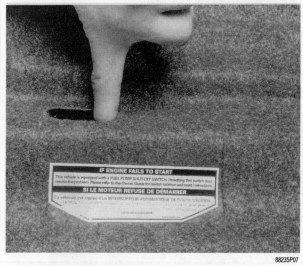

. . . so that you can reset it by hand, if necessary

➡️Check that the inertia switch is reset before diagnosing power supply problems to the fuel pump.

The fuel injectors used with SFI system are electro-mechanical (solenoid) type, designed to meter and atomize fuel delivered to the intake ports of the engine. The injectors are mounted in the lower intake manifold and positioned so that their spray nozzles direct the fuel charge in front of the intake valves. The injector body consists of a solenoid-actuated pintle and needle valve assembly. The control unit sends an electrical impulse that activates the solenoid, causing the pintle to move inward off the seat and allow the fuel to flow. The amount of fuel delivered is controlled by the length of time the injector is energized (pulse width), since the fuel flow orifice is fixed and the fuel pressure drop across the injector tip is constant. Correct atomization is achieved by contouring the pintle at the point where the fuel enters the pintle chamber.

➡️Exercise care when handling fuel injectors during service. Be careful not to lose the pintle cap and always replace O-rings to assure a tight seal. Never apply direct battery voltage to test a fuel injector.

The injectors receive high pressure fuel from the fuel supply manifold (fuel rail) assembly. The complete assembly includes a single, pre-formed tube with six or eight connectors, the mounting flange for the pressure regulator, mounting attachments to locate the manifold and provide the fuel injector retainers and a Schrader® quick-disconnect fitting used to perform fuel pressure tests.

The fuel manifold is normally removed with the fuel injectors and pressure regulator attached. Fuel injector electrical connectors are plastic and have locking tabs that must be released when disconnecting the wiring harness.

FUEL SYSTEM SERVICE PRECAUTIONS

Safety is the most important factor when performing not only fuel system maintenance, but any type of maintenance. Failure to conduct maintenance and repairs in a safe manner may result in serious personal injury or death. Work on a vehicle's fuel system components can be accomplished safely and effectively by adhering to the following rules and guidelines.

• To avoid the possibility of fire and personal injury, always disconnect the negative battery cable unless the repair or test procedure requires that battery voltage be applied.

• Always relieve the fuel system pressure prior to disconnecting any fuel system component (injector, fuel rail, pressure regulator, etc.) fitting or fuel line connection. Exercise extreme caution whenever relieving fuel system pressure to avoid exposing skin, face and eyes to fuel spray. Please be advised that fuel under pressure may penetrate the skin or any part of the body that it contacts.

• Always place a shop towel or cloth around the fitting or connection prior to loosening to absorb any excess fuel due to spillage. Ensure that all fuel spillage is quickly removed from engine surfaces. Ensure that all fuel-soaked cloths or towels are deposited into a flame-proof waste container with a lid.

• Always keep a dry chemical (Class B) fire extinguisher near the work area.

• Do not allow fuel spray or fuel vapors to come into contact with a spark or open flame.

• Always use a second wrench when loosening or tightening fuel line connection fittings. This will prevent unnecessary stress and torsion on fuel piping. Always follow the proper torque specifications.

• Always replace worn fuel fitting O-rings with new ones. Do not substitute fuel hose where rigid pipe is installed.

Relieving Fuel System Pressure

All SFI engines are equipped with a pressure relief valve located on the fuel supply manifold. Remove the fuel tank cap and attach fuel pressure gauge T80L-9974-B, or equivalent, to the valve to release the fuel pressure. Be sure to drain the fuel into a suitable container and to avoid gasoline spillage. If a pressure gauge is not available, disconnect the vacuum hose from the fuel pressure regulator and attach a hand-held vacuum pump. Apply about 25 in. Hg (84 kPa) of vacuum to the regulator to vent the fuel system pressure into the fuel tank through the fuel return hose.

➡️This procedure will remove the fuel pressure from the lines, but not the fuel. Take precautions to avoid the risk of fire and use clean rags to soak up any spilled fuel when the lines are disconnected.

Fuel Pump

REMOVAL & INSTALLATION

◗ See Figure 10

➡️To gain access to the fuel pump, it is necessary to remove the fuel tank.

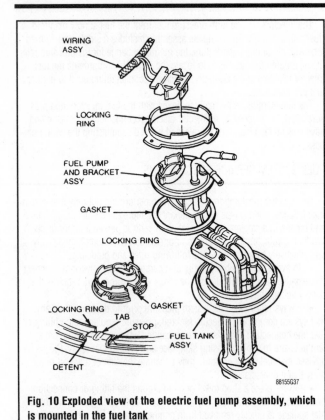

Fig. 10 Exploded view of the electric fuel pump assembly, which is mounted in the fuel tank

1. Depressurize the fuel system, then drain and remove the fuel tank from the vehicle.

2. Remove any dirt that has accumulated around the fuel pump attaching flange, to prevent it from entering the tank during service.

3. Turn the fuel pump locking ring counterclockwise using a locking ring removal tool, then remove the ring.

4. Remove the fuel pump and bracket assembly.

5. Remove the seal gasket and discard it.

To install:

6. Put a light coating of heavy grease on a new seal ring to hold it in place during assembly. Install it in the fuel tank ring groove.

7. Insert the fuel pump assembly into the fuel tank, then secure it in place with the locking ring. Tighten the ring until secure.

8. Install the fuel tank in the vehicle.

9. Add a minimum of 10 gallons of fuel and check for leaks.

10. Install a pressure gauge on the throttle body valve and turn the ignition **ON** for 3 seconds. Turn the key **OFF**, then repeat the key cycle five to ten times until the pressure gauge shows at least 30 psi. Reinspect for leaks at the fittings.

11. Remove the pressure gauge. Start the engine and check for fuel leaks.

TESTING

◆ **See Figures 11 thru 16 (p. 11–16)**

✳✳ CAUTION

Fuel pressure must be relieved before attempting to disconnect any fuel lines.

The diagnostic pressure valve (Schrader valve) is located on the fuel supply manifold (rail). This valve provides a convenient point for service personnel to monitor fuel pressure, relieve the system pressure prior to maintenance, and to bleed out air which may become trapped in the system during pressure replacement. A pressure gauge with an adapter is required to perform pressure tests.

If the pressure tap is not installed or an adapter is not available, use a T-fitting to install the pressure gauge between the fuel filter line and the throttle body fuel inlet or fuel rail.

To test the fuel pump, follow the accompanying diagnostic charts. Testing fuel pressure requires the use of a special pressure gauge (Ford Tool T80L-9974-B, Rotunda Fuel Pressure Testing Kit 014-00447, or equivalent) that attaches to the diagnostic pressure tap fitting. To perform the fuel system test, a scan tool is necessary to access the different test modes.

➡**Depressurize the fuel system before disconnecting any lines.**

Throttle Body Assembly

REMOVAL & INSTALLATION

◆ **See Figures 17, 18 and 19 (p. 17)**

1. Loosen the air inlet tube clamps, then separate the tube from the throttle body and air cleaner housing. Remove the tube from the vehicle.

2. Detach the accelerator cable and, if equipped, speed control cable from the throttle body lever.

To remove the throttle body, first detach the air inlet hose from it . . .

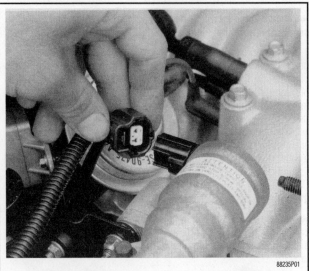

. . . then disengage all engine wiring harness connectors

TEST STEP	RESULT	▶	ACTION TO TAKE
HC1 CHECK SYSTEM INTEGRITY			
• Key off. • Visually inspect the complete fuel delivery system, including fuel lines, connections, pump, pressure regulator and injector areas for leaks, looseness, cracks, kinks, pinching, or abrasion caused by an accident, collision, mishandling, etc. • Visually inspect electrical harness and connectors for loose pins, corrosion, abrasion, or other damage from accident, mishandling, etc. • Verify vehicle has followed maintenance schedule. • Verify Inertia Fuel Shutoff (IFS) switch set. • Verify vehicle battery is fully charged. • Verify electrical / fuse integrity. • Verify sufficient fuel in the tank. • **Has any problem been found?**	Yes No	▶ ▶	SERVICE as necessary. RERUN Quick Test. GO to HC2.
HC2 CHECK FUEL PRESSURE			
WARNING: BEFORE SERVICING OR REPLACING ANY COMPONENTS IN THE FUEL SYSTEM, REDUCE THE POSSIBILITY OF INJURY OR FIRE BY FOLLOWING DIRECTIONS IN FUEL SYSTEM "CAUTION, HANDLING AND WARNING" AT THE BEGINNING OF THIS PINPOINT TEST. • Key off. • Release the fuel pressure. • Install fuel pressure tester. • Scan Tool connected. • Key on, engine off. • Enter Output Test Mode (refer to Section 2) and run the fuel pump to obtain maximum fuel pressure. • **Is fuel pressure between 35 and 40 psi (240-280 kPa)?**	Yes No	▶ ▶	GO to HC3. GO to HC9.
HC3 CHECK FUEL PRESSURE LEAKDOWN			
• Fuel pressure tester installed. • Scan Tool connected. • Key on, engine off. • Enter Output Test Mode and run fuel pump to obtain maximum fuel pressure. • Exit Output Test Mode, key off. • Verify fuel pressure remains within 5 psi of the maximum pressure for 1 minute after turning pump off. • **Does fuel pressure remain within 5 psi?**	Yes No	▶ ▶	GO to HC5. GO to HC4.

88235G00

Fig. 11 General fuel system diagnosis for 3.8L and 4.6L engines—this test inspects the fuel pump, pressure regulator, fuel filter, vacuum supply and injectors

	TEST STEP	RESULT	▶	ACTION TO TAKE
HC4	**CHECK PRESSURE REGULATOR DIAPHRAGM**			
	• Key off. • Fuel pressure tester installed. • Start and run engine for 10 seconds. • Key off, wait 10 seconds. • Start and run engine for 10 seconds. • Key off, remove vacuum hose from fuel pressure regulator. • Inspect for fuel in the vacuum hose or regulator port. • **Is vacuum hose and regulator port free of fuel?**	Yes No	▶ ▶	GO to HC11. REPLACE fuel pressure regulator. RERUN Quick Test.
HC5	**CHECK FUEL PRESSURE, ENGINE RUNNING**			
	• Key off. • Fuel pressure tester installed. • Disconnect vacuum hose at the fuel pressure regulator and plug it. • Drive vehicle with heavy accelerations while observing fuel pressure gauge reading. • **Does fuel pressure reading hold steady within 3 psi during test?**	Yes No	▶ ▶	UNPLUG vacuum hose and RECONNECT to the regulator. GO to HC6. GO to HC8.
HC6	**CHECK FUEL PRESSURE REGULATOR RESPONSE TO VACUUM**			
	• Key off. • Fuel pressure tester installed. • Install vacuum gauge to intake manifold. • Start engine and observe both gauges. • Accelerate and decelerate engine speed to vary the vacuum gauge reading. • **Does fuel pressure gauge reading increase as vacuum gauge reading decreases, or does fuel pressure gauge reading decrease as vacuum gauge reading increases?**	Yes No	▶ ▶	REMOVE vacuum gauge and fuel pressure tester. Problem is elsewhere. RETURN to Section 4, Symptom Flow Charts, for further direction. GO to HC7.
HC7	**CHECK VACUUM SUPPLY**			
	• Key off. • Fuel pressure tester installed. • Vacuum hose disconnected and plugged at the regulator. • Install hand held vacuum pump to the fuel pressure regulator. • Start engine, run at idle. • Observe fuel pressure while applying vacuum. • **Does the fuel pressure change as the vacuum changes?**	Yes No	▶ ▶	SERVICE vacuum system. UNPLUG vacuum hose and RECONNECT to the pressure regulator. RERUN Quick Test. REPLACE fuel pressure regulator. RERUN Quick Test.

88235G01

Fig. 12 General fuel system diagnosis for 3.8L and 4.6L engines (continued)

	TEST STEP	RESULT	▶	ACTION TO TAKE
HC8	**CHECK FUEL FILTER**			
	• Key off. • Scan Tool connected. • Replace in-line fuel filter, if not replaced recently (check maintenance log). • Key on, engine off. • Enter Output Test Mode (OTM) to run the fuel pump. • Check fuel pressure. • **Is fuel pressure within specification?**	Yes No	▶ ▶	GO to **HC3**. GO to **HC12**.
HC9	**CHECK REGULATOR FOR HIGH PRESSURE CAUSE**			
	• Key off. • Scan Tool connected. • Remove fuel return line at the fuel rail and connect a short hose from rail to a measured container of at least one quart capacity. • Key on, engine off. • Enter Output Test Mode (OTM) and run the fuel pump. • Record fuel pressure and note whether fuel is being returned to the measured container. • Exit OTM to shut off the fuel pump, key off. • **Is fuel pressure between 35 and 40 psi (240-280 kPa) and is fuel returning to the container?**	Yes No	▶ ▶	GO to **HC10**. REPLACE fuel pressure regulator. RERUN Quick Test.
HC10	**CHECK FUEL RETURN SYSTEM**			
	• Key off. • Fuel line disconnected at the fuel pressure regulator. • Check the fuel return system for restriction due to blockage, kinking, or pinching. • Disconnect the fuel return line near the fuel tank. • Apply 3-5 psi regulated shop air to the return line at the pressure regulator side. • **Does air flow freely through the line?**	Yes No	▶ ▶	REPLACE the fuel pump assembly. RERUN Quick Test. SERVICE the fuel return line. RERUN Quick Test.

88235G02

Fig. 13 General fuel system diagnosis for 3.8L and 4.6L engines (continued)

TEST STEP	RESULT	▶	ACTION TO TAKE
HC11 CHECK FUEL INJECTOR LEAKAGE AND FLOW ● Key off. ● Check injectors for leakage and flow rate, using Rotunda Injector Tester 113-00001 and Rotunda Fuel Pump Check Valve-Pressure Regulator and Injector Leakage Tool 113-00010, SBDS Injector Tester or equivalent. ● **Is the flow rate for each injector within specification?**	Yes No	▶ ▶	VERIFY no other leaks. If none are found, REPLACE fuel pump assembly. RERUN Quick Test. REPLACE the defective injector. RECONNECT all components. RERUN Quick Test.
HC12 CHECK FUEL PUMP VOLTAGE ● Key off. ● Scan tool connected. ● Disconnect the electrical fuel pump vehicle harness connector. Inspect for damaged or pushed out pins, corrosion, loose wires, etc. Service as necessary. ● Key on, engine off. ● Enter Output Test Mode and turn on the fuel pump circuit. ● Use DVOM to check voltage to the fuel pump, at the fuel pump connector, fuel pump relay, VCRM or CCRM. (Refer to the EVTM for the specified vehicle.) ● **Is the voltage greater than 10.5 volts?**	Yes No	▶ ▶	CHECK for fuel pump ground connection, REPAIR as required. If OK, REPLACE fuel pump. RECONNECT all components. GO to HC2 for verification. LOCATE cause of low voltage in fuel pump circuit. REPAIR as required. GO to HC2 for verification.

88235G03

Fig. 14 General fuel system diagnosis for 3.8L and 4.6L engines (continued)

FUEL PUMP DIAGNOSIS

TEST STEP	RESULT	▶	ACTION TO TAKE
A1 CHECK STATIC FUEL PRESSURE			
• Check for adequate fuel supply, fill as required.	Yes	▶	GO to **A3**.
• Key OFF, install EFI and CFI fuel pressure gauge T80L-9974-B or equivalent on Shrader valve or engine fuel rails. Install test lead to FP lead of VIP test connector.	No	▶	GO to **A2**.
VIP SELF TEST CONNECTOR SIGNAL RETURN SELF TEST OUT FP (FUEL PUMP) LEAD (SHORT END OF CONNECTOR)			
• Turn key to ON position. Ground test lead to run fuel pump.			
• Refer to Fuel Pressure Specifications Chart in this Section. Is pressure within acceptable limits?			
A2 HYDRAULIC AND ELECTRICAL CIRCUIT CHECK			
• Plugged fuel line filter (replace filter and check again for proper pressure)?	Yes	▶	If service was required and made. Pressure must be checked again REPEAT STEP **A1**.
• Check for system leaks.			
• Check for kinked/restricted fuel lines.	No	▶	If no service was required, REPLACE fuel pump. REPEAT STEP **A1**.
• Low voltage to fuel pump (should be within 0.5 volts of battery voltage at pump connection)?			
• Disconnect return fuel line and note if fuel is returning. If fuel is being returned, adjust or replace pressure regulator and check again for proper pressure.			
• Inertia switch open? (Reset switch as required.)			
• Wiring at fuel pump/tank connector loose or open?			
• Fuel pump ground connection at chassis loose or damaged?			
• Improper fuel pump relay operation (should operate when FP (test) lead is grounded with ignition switch in RUN position).			
• EEC relay not operating if fuel pump relay is not operating.			
A3 CHECK VALVE TEST			
• Remove ground from test lead and note pressure on gauge.	Yes	▶	GO to **A5**.
• Does pressure remain within .14 kPa (2 psi) for 3 minutes after lead is ungrounded.	No	▶	GO to **A4**.

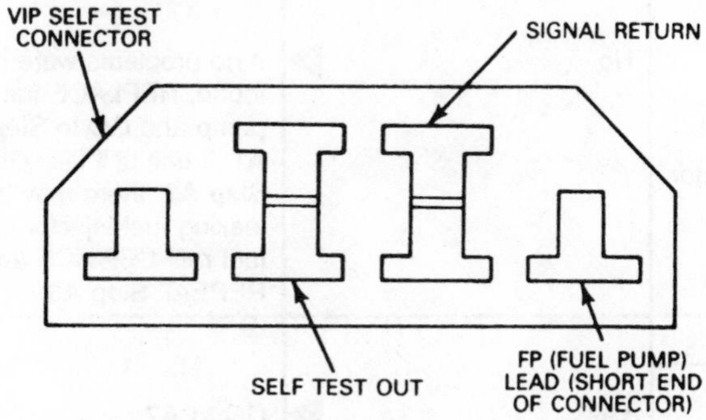

88155G38

Fig. 15 Fuel pump diagnosis for the 5.0L engine

FUEL PUMP DIAGNOSIS — Continued

	TEST STEP	RESULT	▶	ACTION TO TAKE
A4	**CIRCUIT LEAK CHECK**			
	• Fuel lines or connectors leaking?	Yes	▶	If service was made, GO to Step **A1**.
	• Disconnect fuel return line and plug engine side.			
	• Momentarily activate fuel pump by grounding test lead.	No	▶	If no problems were found, REPLACE fuel pump and GO to Step **A1**. If unit still fails GO to Step **A3**, there may be a leaking fuel injector or fuel rail. SERVICE and REPEAT Step **A3**.
	• Raise pressure to approximate operating pressure.			
	• Repeat Step **A3**. If pressure holds, replace regulator and repeat Step **A3**.			
A5	**ENGINE ON TEST**			
	• If engine is equipped with fuel rail injectors, disconnect injectors and plug the vacuum line connected to the pressure regulator.	Yes	▶	GO to **A7**.
	• Start engine and run at idle. Fuel pressure should be as indicated in chart for Ignition On, Engine Off.	No	▶	GO to **A6**.
A6	**IDLE ENGINE SERVICE**			
	• Fuel filter restricted?	Yes	▶	If damage has been found and serviced GO to **A1**.
	• Improper fuel pressure regulator adjustment?			
	• Fuel line restricted?			
	• Improper voltage to fuel pump (battery voltage at pump connections)?	No	▶	REPLACE fuel pump and GO to **A1**.
A7	**HIGH SPEED TEST**			
	• With engine running at idle and vacuum line disconnected from pressure regulator if required from Step A5, note the fuel rail pressure.	Yes	▶	Fuel pump is OK. DISCONNECT test connections and connect vacuum and fuel lines as required.
	• Rapidly accelerate engine and watch fuel pressure. Does pressure remain within .35 kPa (5 psi) of starting pressure?			
	NOTE: Road test vehicle while monitoring pressure may give a better test under load conditions.	No	▶	GO to **A6**.

88155G39

Fig. 16 Fuel pump diagnosis for the 5.0L engine (continued)

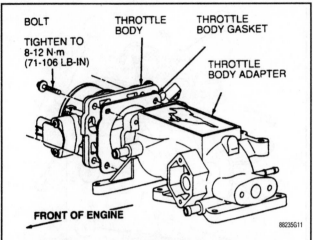

Fig. 17 The throttle bodies on all engines covered by this manual are attached to the intake manifold with four fasteners—4.6L engine shown

Disconnect the accelerator cable (A) from the throttle body lever (B) . . .

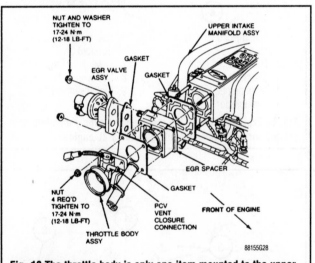

Fig. 18 The throttle body is only one item mounted to the upper manifold; all are held by the same four studs—5.0L engine

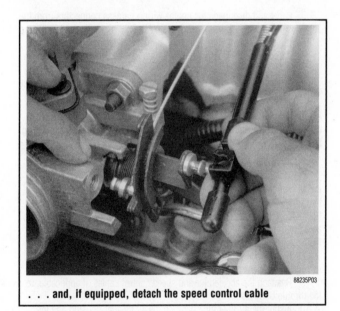

. . . and, if equipped, detach the speed control cable

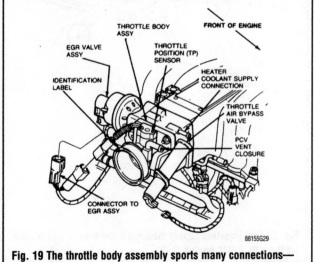

Fig. 19 The throttle body assembly sports many connections—5.0L engine

Support the throttle body with your hand and remove the four throttle body mounting nuts . . .

. . . then separate the throttle body from the upper intake manifold

3. Label and disengage the engine wiring harness connectors from the Throttle Position (TP) sensor and the Idle Air Control (IAC) valve (3.8L and 5.0L engines only); both are mounted on the throttle body.

4. Remove the four mounting nuts, then carefully separate the throttle body from the upper intake manifold.

5. Remove and discard the old throttle body-to-intake manifold gasket.

To install:

➡**If scraping is necessary to clean the remaining gasket material off of the mating surfaces, take care to avoid scratching or gouging the soft aluminum.**

6. Clean the gasket mating surfaces of any residual gasket material.

7. Install the throttle body, along with a new gasket, onto the upper intake manifold. Install and tighten the mounting nuts in a crisscross pattern to 15–22 ft. lbs. (20–30 Nm) for the 3.8L engine, to 71–106 inch lbs. (8–12 Nm) for the 4.6L SOHC engine, to 71–89 inch lbs. (8–10 Nm) plus an additional 85–95 degrees for the 4.6L DOHC engine, or to 141–212 inch lbs. (16–24 Nm) for the 5.0L engine.

8. Engage the TP sensor and IAC valve (3.8L and 5.0L engines only) wiring connectors and remove the temporary labels.

9. Reattach the accelerator and speed control cables, if applicable, to the throttle body lever.

10. Install the air inlet tube between the air cleaner housing and the throttle body. Tighten the tube clamps until snug.

Fuel Supply Manifold and Injectors

REMOVAL & INSTALLATION

▶ **See Figures 20, 21 and 22**

1. Remove the upper intake manifold (except 4.6L SOHC engine). Be sure to depressurize the fuel system before disconnecting any fuel lines.

2. Disconnect the fuel supply and return line retaining clips.

3. Detach the vacuum line from the fuel pressure regulator.

4. Disconnect the fuel chassis inlet and outlet fuel hoses from the fuel supply manifold.

5. Remove the four fuel supply manifold retaining bolts.

6. Carefully disengage the fuel rail assembly from the fuel injectors by lifting and gently rocking the rail.

7. Remove the fuel injectors from the intake manifold by lifting while gently rocking them from side to side

8. Place all removed components on a clean surface to prevent contamination by dirt or grease.

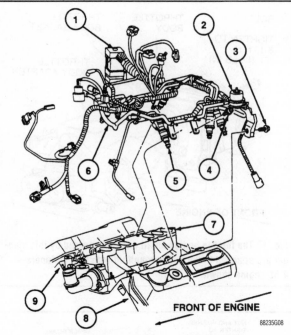

1. Fuel injection wiring harness
2. Fuel pressure regulator
3. Mounting bolt
4. Mounting bolt
5. Fuel injector
6. Fuel injection supply manifold
7. Lower intake manifold
8. Left cylinder head
9. Right cylinder head

Fig. 20 Exploded view of the fuel injection supply manifold and related wiring harness mounting on the 3.8L engine

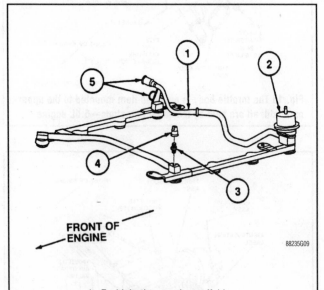

1. Fuel injection supply manifold
2. Fuel pressure regulator
3. Fuel pressure relief valve
4. Fuel pressure relief valve cap
5. Fuel line fittings

Fig. 21 Fuel injection supply manifold component identification for the 4.6L SOHC engine

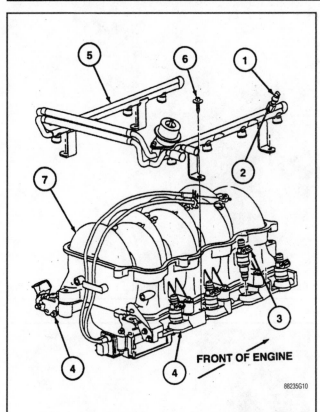

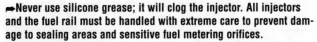

FRONT OF ENGINE

88235G10

1. Fuel pressure relief valve cap
2. Fuel pressure relief valve
3. Fuel injector
4. Intake Manifold Runner Control (IMRC) assemblies
5. Fuel injection supply manifold
6. Mounting bolt
7. Lower intake manifold

Fig. 22 Fuel injection supply manifold component identification and exploded view on the 4.6L DOHC engine

→**Never use silicone grease; it will clog the injector. All injectors and the fuel rail must be handled with extreme care to prevent damage to sealing areas and sensitive fuel metering orifices.**

9. Examine the injector O-rings for deterioration or damage; replace them as needed.

10. Make sure the injector caps are clean and free from contamination or damage.

To install:

11. Lubricate all O-rings with clean engine oil, then install the injectors into the fuel rail using a light twisting/pushing motion.

12. Carefully install the fuel rail assembly and injectors into the lower intake manifold. Make certain to correctly position the insulators. Push down on the fuel rail to make sure the O-rings are seated.

13. Hold the fuel rail assembly in place and install the retaining bolts finger-tight. Then, tighten the bolts to 15–22 ft. lbs. (20–30 Nm) for the 3.8L and 5.0L engines, or to 71–106 inch lbs. (8–12 Nm) for the 4.6L SOHC and DOHC engines.

14. Connect the fuel supply and return lines.

15. Attach the vacuum hose to the fuel pressure regulator.

16. Connect the fuel injector wiring harness at the injectors.

17. Connect the vacuum line to the fuel pressure regulator, if removed.

18. Install the air intake and throttle body assembly.

19. Run the engine and check for fuel leaks.

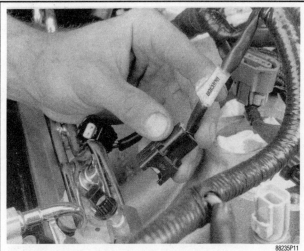

To remove the fuel injectors and supply manifold, label and detach all wiring harness connectors . . .

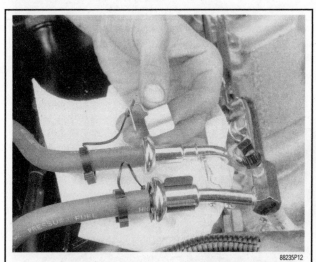

. . . and disconnect the fuel lines by first removing the retaining clip

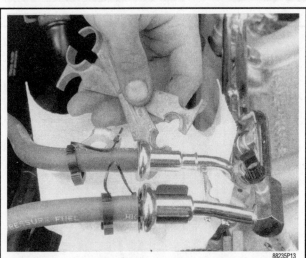

A disconnection tool is necessary to separate the fuel line fittings

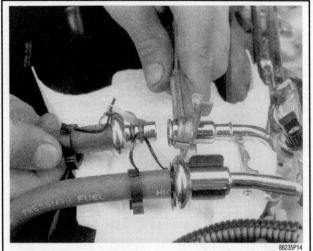

Slide the proper end of the disconnection tool into the fitting, then pull the fittings apart

Remove the mounting bolts, then lift the fuel supply manifold up and off of the intake manifold

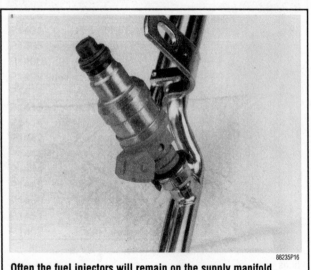

Often the fuel injectors will remain on the supply manifold, rather than staying on the engine

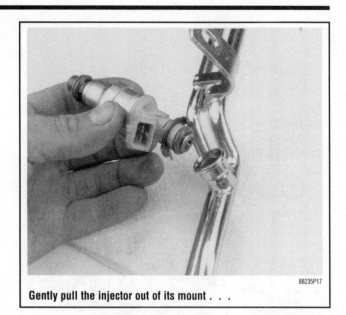

Gently pull the injector out of its mount . . .

. . . then inspect the O-ring for damage and replace it if necessary

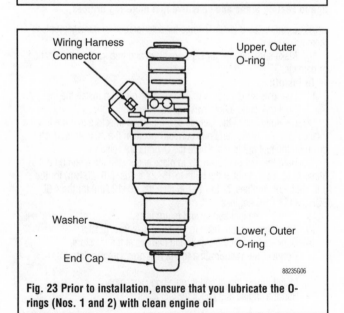

Fig. 23 Prior to installation, ensure that you lubricate the O-rings (Nos. 1 and 2) with clean engine oil

Wiring Harness Connector

Upper, Outer O-ring

Washer

Lower, Outer O-ring

End Cap

FUEL INJECTOR TESTING

If you want to test the fuel injectors because of a fuel system problem, it is a good idea to test the entire system; refer to the fuel system test charts earlier in this section.

The fuel injectors can be tested, however, with a Digital Volt-Ohmmeter (DVOM). To test an injector, detach the engine wiring harness connector from it. This may require removing the upper intake manifold or other engine components.

Once access to the injector is gained and the wiring is disconnected from it, set the DVOM to measure resistance (ohms). Measure the resistance of the injector by probing one terminal with the positive DVOM lead and the other injector terminal with the negative lead. The resistance measured should be 11–18 ohms. If the resistance is not within this range, the fuel injector is faulty and must be replaced with a new one.

Fuel Pressure Regulator

REMOVAL & INSTALLATION

▶ See Figures 24, 25 and 26

1. Depressurize the fuel system; remove shielding as needed.
2. Remove the vacuum line at the pressure regulator.
3. Remove the Allen® head retaining screws from the regulator housing.
4. Remove the pressure regulator assembly, gasket and O-ring. Discard the gasket and check the O-ring for signs of cracks or deterioration.

To install:

5. Clean the gasket mating surfaces. If scraping is necessary, be careful not to damage the fuel pressure regulator or supply line gasket mating surfaces.
6. Lubricate the pressure regulator O-ring with light engine oil. Do not use silicone grease; it will clog the injectors.
7. Install the O-ring and a new gasket on the pressure regulator.
8. Install the pressure regulator on the fuel manifold and tighten the retaining screws to 27–40 inch lbs. (3–4 Nm).
9. Install the vacuum line at the pressure regulator.
10. Build fuel pressure in the system by turning the ignition **ON** and **OFF** (without starting the engine) at least five times. Leave the ignition **ON** at least 5 seconds each time. Check for fuel leaks.

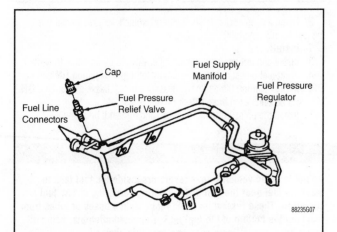

Fig. 24 The fuel pressure regulator and the fuel pressure relief valve are both mounted on the fuel injection supply manifold—3.8L engine shown; other engines are similar

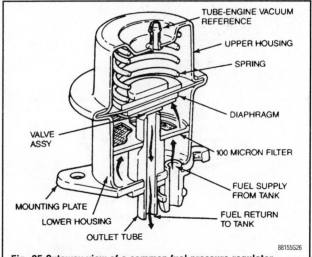

Fig. 25 Cutaway view of a common fuel pressure regulator, showing the interior working components

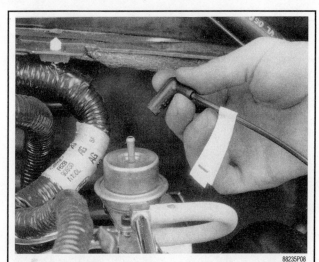

To remove the pressure regulator, label and detach the vacuum hose from it . . .

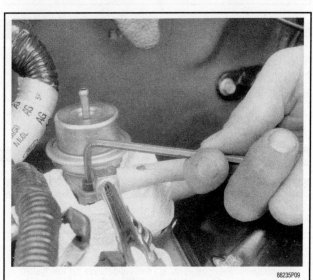

. . . then loosen the Allen® head screws

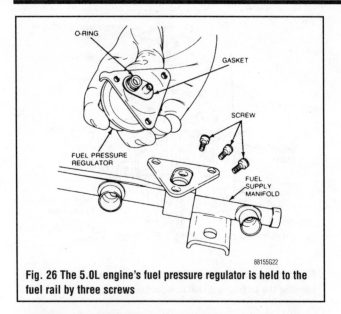

Fig. 26 The 5.0L engine's fuel pressure regulator is held to the fuel rail by three screws

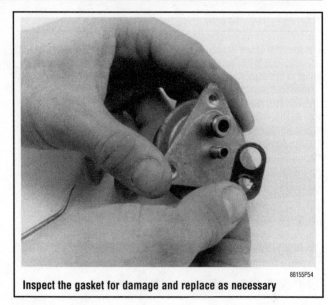

Inspect the gasket for damage and replace as necessary

Separate the regulator from the fuel supply manifold

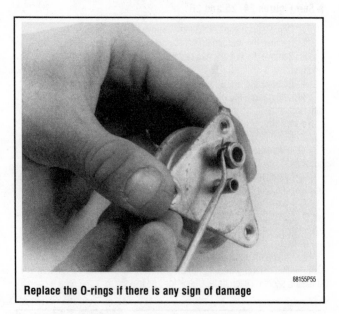

Replace the O-rings if there is any sign of damage

Pressure Relief Valve

REMOVAL & INSTALLATION

➡The fuel pressure relief valve cap on the valve must be removed.

1. If the fuel supply manifold is installed on the engine, remove the fuel tank filler cap and relieve fuel system pressure.

2. Using a deep socket or an open-end wrench, remove the valve from the fuel supply manifold.

To install:

3. Install and tighten the pressure relief valve to 69 inch lbs. (8 Nm).

4. Build fuel pressure in the system by turning the ignition **ON** and **OFF** (without starting the engine) at least five times. Leave the ignition **ON** at least 5 seconds each time. Check for fuel leaks.

5. Install the pressure relief valve cap and tighten it until snug.

FUEL TANK

Tank Assembly

REMOVAL & INSTALLATION

♦ See Figures 27, 28, 29 and 30 (p. 23–26)

1. Disconnect the negative battery cable and relieve the fuel system pressure.

2. Siphon or pump as much fuel as possible out through the fuel filler pipe.

➡Fuel injected vehicles have reservoirs inside the fuel tank to maintain fuel near the fuel pick-up during cornering or low-fuel operation. These reservoirs could block siphon hoses or tubes from reaching the bottom of the fuel tank. Repeated attempts, using different hose orientations, can overcome this obstacle.

3. Raise and safely support the vehicle.

4. Disconnect the fuel fill and vent hoses connecting the filler pipe to the tank. Disconnect one end of the vapor crossover hose at the rear, over the driveshaft.

5. On vehicles equipped with a metal retainer fastening the filler pipe to the fuel tank, remove the screw holding the retainer to the fuel tank flange.

6. Disengage the fuel lines and the electrical connections to the fuel tank sending unit/fuel pump assembly. On some vehicles, these are inaccessible on top of the tank. In this case, they must be disconnected when the tank is partially lowered.

7. Place a safety support (such as a floor jack) beneath the fuel tank and remove the bolts from the fuel tank straps. Allow the straps to swing out of the way. Be careful not to deform the fuel tank.

8. Lower the tank a few inches, then detach the fuel lines and electrical connection from the sending unit/fuel pump assembly, if required.

9. Remove the tank from the vehicle.

To install:

10. Before installation, it would be wise to perform the following:

   a. Double-check the tightness of the sending unit/fuel pump locking ring. If it is already loose, now would be a good time to remove it and check the condition of the gasket underneath.

   b. Ensure that all metal shields are reinstalled in their original positions and that the fasteners are secure.

   c. Be sure that the fuel vapor valve is completely installed on top of the fuel tank.

   d. Make all necessary fuel line or wiring connections which will be inaccessible after the fuel tank is installed.

11. Raise the fuel tank into position in the vehicle. If necessary, attach the fuel lines and sending unit electrical connector before the tank is in its final position.

12. Lubricate the fuel filler pipe with a water-based lubricant. Install the tank onto the filler pipe, then bring the tank into final position. Be careful not to deform the tank.

13. Position the tank straps around the tank and start the retaining nut or bolt. Align the tank with the straps. If equipped, be sure the fuel tank shields are installed with the straps and are positioned correctly.

14. Check the hoses and wiring on top of the tank. Make sure they are correctly routed and will not be pinched between the tank and body.

15. Tighten the fuel tank strap retaining nuts or bolts to 20–30 ft. lbs. (28–41 Nm).

16. If not already attached, connect the fuel hoses and lines. Make sure the fuel supply, fuel return (if present) and vapor vent attachments are made properly. If not already attached, connect the sending unit.

17. Lower the vehicle.

18. Fill the tank with fuel and check all connections for leaks.

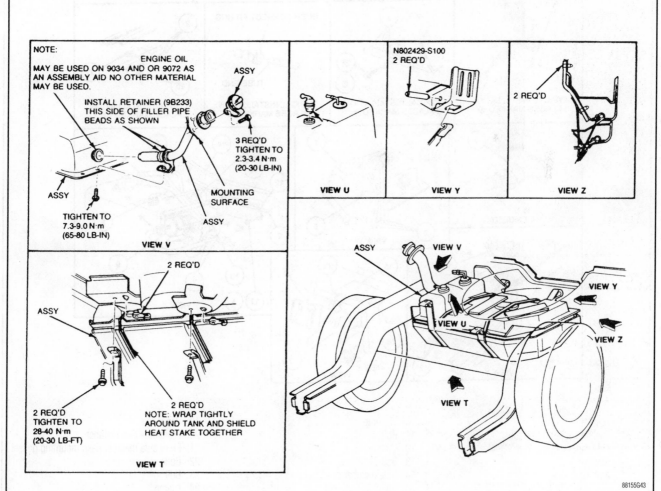

Fig. 27 The fuel tanks on all Mustang models are mounted beneath the car, between the frame rails at the rear of the vehicle

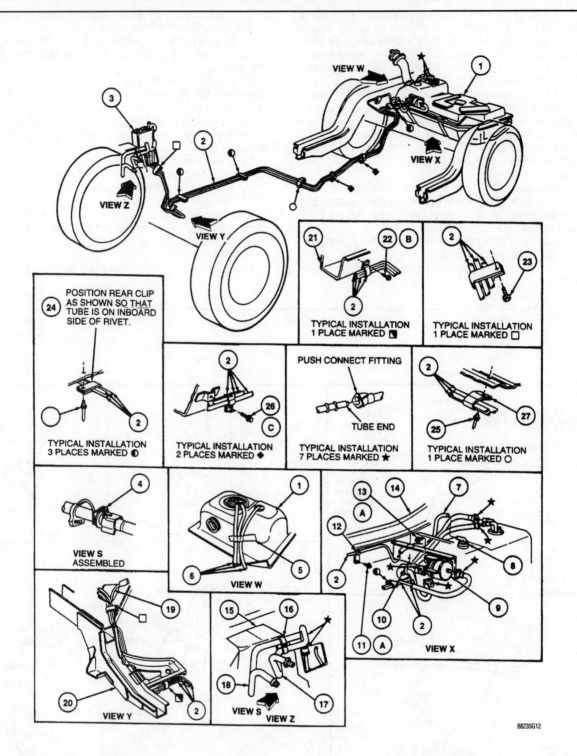

1. Fuel tank
2. Fuel and vapor return tube
3. Fuel vapor canister
4. Retainer
5. 2 in. wide tape
6. Fuel pump-to-injector hose
7. Fuel hose
8. Fuel vapor valve
9. Fuel filter and base
10. Tie strap
11. Bolt
12. Clamp
13. Bolt
14. Side member
15. Shock tower
16. Fuel tube retainer
17. Fuel tube hose
18. Fuel return hose
19. Vapor line
20. Front side rear member
21. Front side member dash mounting gusset
22. Bolt
23. Bolt
24. Clamp
25. Rivet
26. Bolt
27. Clamp

Fig. 28 Fuel tank placement and fuel line routing for Mustangs equipped with the 3.8L engine

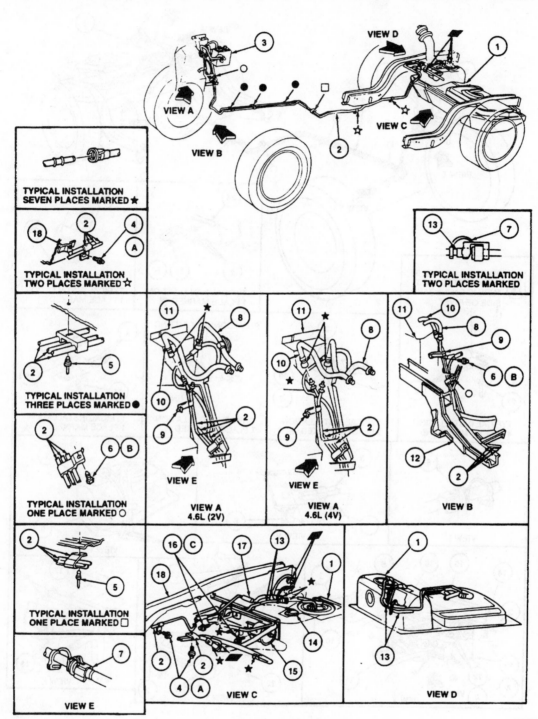

1. Fuel tank
2. Fuel and vapor return tube
3. Evaporative emissions canister
4. Mounting bolt
5. Rivet
6. Mounting bolt
7. Retainer
8. Fuel supply hose
9. Fuel tube clip
10. Fuel return hose
11. Front fender apron
12. Front side member dash mounting gusset
13. Fuel pump-to-injector hose
14. Evaporative emission valve
15. Fuel filter and base
16. Mounting bolt
17. Rubber hose
18. Rear floor side member

Fig. 29 Fuel tank placement and fuel line routing for Mustangs equipped with either 4.6L engine

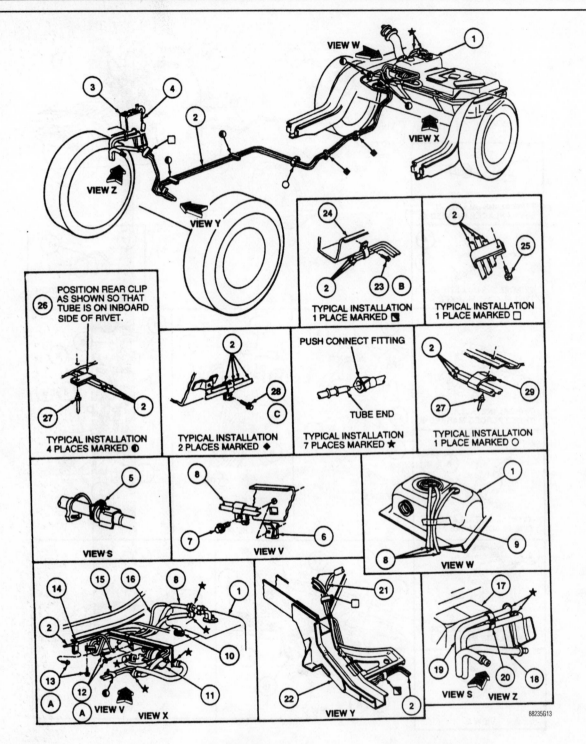

1. Fuel tank
2. Fuel and vapor return tube
3. Fuel vapor canister
4. Fuel tank vent tube
5. Retainer
6. Clip
7. Bolt
8. Fuel pump-to-injector hose
9. 2 in. wide tape
10. Fuel vapor valve
11. Fuel filter and base
12. Bolt
13. Bolt
14. Clamp
15. Rear floor side member
16. Fuel hose
17. Front suspension housing
18. Fuel tube hose
19. Fuel return hose
20. Fuel tube retainer
21. Vapor line
22. Front side rear member
23. Bolt
24. Front side member dash mounting gusset
25. Bolt
26. Clamp
27. Rivet
28. Bolt
29. Clamp

Fig. 30 Fuel tank placement and fuel line routing for Mustangs equipped with the 5.0L engine

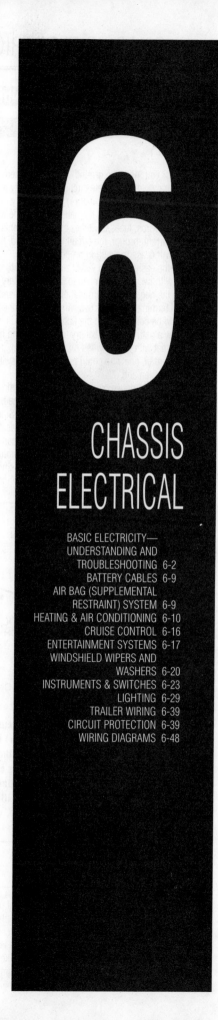

6

CHASSIS
ELECTRICAL

BASIC ELECTRICITY—UNDERSTANDING AND TROUBLESHOOTING

Basic Electrical Theory

▶ See Figure 1

For any 12 volt, negative ground, electrical system to operate, the electricity must travel in a complete circuit. This simply means that current (power) from the positive terminal (+) of the battery must eventually return to the negative terminal (–) of the battery. Along the way, this current will travel through wires, fuses, switches and components. If, for any reason, the flow of current through the circuit is interrupted, the component fed by that circuit will cease to function properly.

Perhaps the easiest way to visualize a circuit is to think of connecting a light bulb (with two wires attached to it) to the battery (em dash) one wire attached to the negative (–) terminal of the battery and the other wire to the positive (+) terminal. With the two wires touching the battery terminals, the circuit would be complete and the light bulb would illuminate. Electricity would follow a path from the battery to the bulb and back to the battery. It's easy to see that with longer wires on our light bulb, it could be mounted anywhere. Further, one wire could be fitted with a switch so that the light could be turned on and off.

The normal automotive circuit differs from this simple example in two ways. First, instead of having a return wire from the bulb to the battery, the current travels through the chassis of the vehicle. Since the negative (–) battery cable is attached to the chassis and the chassis is made of electrically conductive metal, the chassis of the vehicle can serve as a ground wire to complete the circuit. Secondly, most automotive circuits contain multiple components which receive power from a single circuit. This lessens the amount of wire needed to power components on the vehicle.

TCCS2004

Fig. 1 This example illustrates a simple circuit. When the switch is closed, power from the positive (+) battery terminal flows through the fuse and the switch, and then to the light bulb. The light illuminates and the circuit is completed through the ground wire back to the negative (-) battery terminal. In reality, the two ground points shown in the illustration are attached to the metal chassis of the vehicle, which completes the circuit back to the battery.

THE WATER ANALOGY

Electricity is the flow of electrons—hypothetical particles thought to constitute the basic "stuff" of electricity. Many people have been taught electrical theory using an analogy with water. In a comparison with water flowing through a pipe, the electrons would be the water.

The flow of electricity can be measured much like the flow of water through a pipe. The unit of measurement used is amperes, frequently abbreviated as amps (a). When connected to a circuit, an ammeter will measure the actual amount of current flowing through the circuit. When relatively few electrons flow through a circuit, the amperage is low. When many electrons flow, the amperage is high.

Just as water pressure is measured in units such as pounds per square inch (psi), electrical pressure is measured in units called volts (v). When a voltmeter is connected to a circuit, it is measuring the electrical pressure. The higher the voltage, the more current will flow through the circuit. The lower the voltage, the less current will flow.

While increasing the voltage in a circuit will increase the flow of current, the actual flow depends not only on voltage, but also on the resistance of the circuit. Resistance is the amount of force necessary to push the current through the circuit. The standard unit for measuring resistance is an ohm (Ω or omega). Resistance in a circuit varies depending on the amount and type of components used in the circuit. The main factors which determine resistance are:

• Material—some materials have more resistance than others. Those with high resistance are said to be insulators. Rubber is one of the best insulators available, as it allows little current to pass. Low resistance materials are said to be conductors. Copper wire is among the best conductors. Most vehicle wiring is made of copper.

• Size—the larger the wire size being used, the less resistance the wire will have. This is why components which use large amounts of electricity usually have large wires supplying current to them.

• Length—for a given thickness of wire, the longer the wire, the greater the resistance. The shorter the wire, the less the resistance. When determining the proper wire for a circuit, both size and length must be considered to design a circuit that can handle the current needs of the component.

• Temperature—with many materials, the higher the temperature, the greater the resistance. This principle is used in many of the sensors on the engine.

OHM'S LAW

The preceding definitions may lead the reader into believing that there is no relationship between current, voltage and resistance. Nothing can be further from the truth. The relationship between current, voltage and resistance can be summed up by a statement known as Ohm's law.

Voltage (E) is equal to amperage (I) times resistance (R): $E = I \times R$

Other forms of the formula are $R = E/I$ and $I = E/R$

In each of these formulas, E is the voltage in volts, I is the current in amps and R is the resistance in ohms. The basic point to remember is that as the resistance of a circuit goes up, the amount of current that flows in the circuit will go down, if voltage remains the same.

Electrical Components

POWER SOURCE

The power source for 12 volt automotive electrical systems is the battery. In most modern vehicles, the battery is a lead/acid electrochemical device consisting of six 2 volt subsections (cells) connected in series, so that the unit is capable of producing approximately 12 volts of electrical pressure. Each subsection consists of a series of positive and negative plates held a short distance apart in a solution of sulfuric acid and water.

The two types of plates are of dissimilar metals. This sets up a chemical reaction, and it is this reaction which produces current flow from the battery when its positive and negative terminals are connected to an electrical load. The power removed from the battery is replaced by the alternator, which forces electrons back through the battery, reversing the normal flow, and restoring the battery to its original chemical state.

GROUND

Two types of grounds are used in automotive electric circuits. Direct ground components are grounded through their mounting points. All other components use some sort of ground wire which is attached to the body or chassis of the vehicle. The electrical current runs through the chassis of the vehicle and returns to the battery through the ground (–) cable; if you look, you'll see that the battery ground cable connects between the battery and the body or chassis of the vehicle.

➡️**It should be noted that a good percentage of electrical problems can be traced to bad grounds.**

PROTECTIVE DEVICES

It is possible for large surges of current to pass through the electrical system of your vehicle. If this surge of current were to reach the load in the circuit, it could burn it out or severely damage it. To prevent this, fuses, circuit breakers and/or fusible links are connected into the supply wires of the electrical system. These items are nothing more than a built-in weak spot in the system. When an abnormal amount of current flows through the system, these protective devices work as follows to protect the circuit:

• Fuse—when an excessive electrical current passes through a fuse, the fuse "blows" (the conductor melts) and opens the circuit, preventing the passage of current.

• Circuit Breaker—a circuit breaker is basically a self-repairing fuse. It will open the circuit in the same fashion as a fuse, but when the surge subsides, the circuit breaker can be reset and does not need replacement.

• Fusible Link—a fusible link (fuse link or main link) is a short length of special, Hypalon high temperature insulated wire that acts as a fuse. When an excessive electrical current passes through a fusible link, the thin gauge wire inside the link melts, creating an intentional open to protect the circuit. To repair the circuit, the link must be replaced. Some newer type fusible links are housed in plug-in modules, which are simply replaced like a fuse, while older type fusible links must be cut and spliced if they melt. Since this link is very early in the electrical path, it's the first place to look if nothing on the vehicle works, but the battery seems to be charged and is properly connected.

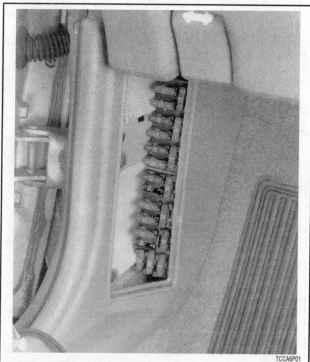

TCCA6P01

Most vehicles use one or more fuse panels. This one is located in the driver's side kick panel

Always replace fuses, circuit breakers and fusible links with identically rated components. Under no circumstances should a component of higher or lower amperage rating be substituted.

SWITCHES AND RELAYS

♦ **See Figure 2**

Switches are used in electrical circuits to control the passage of current. The most common use is to open and close circuits between the battery and the various electric devices in the system. Switches are rated according to the amount of amperage they can handle. If a sufficient amperage rated switch is not used in a circuit, the switch could overload and cause damage.

Some electrical components which require a large amount of current to operate use a special switch called a relay. Since these circuits carry a large amount of current, the thickness of the wire in the circuit is also greater. If this large wire were connected from the load to the control switch on the dashboard, the switch would have to carry the high amperage load and the dash would be twice as large to accommodate the increased size of the wiring harness. To prevent these problems, a relay is used.

Relays are composed of a coil and a switch. These two components are linked together so that when one operates, the other operates at the same time. The large wires in the circuit are connected from the battery to one side of the relay switch and from the opposite side of the relay switch to the load. Most relays are normally open, preventing current from passing through the circuit. Additional, smaller wires are connected from the relay coil to the control switch for the circuit and from the opposite side of the relay coil to ground. When the control switch is turned on, it grounds the smaller wire to the relay coil, causing the coil to operate. The coil pulls the relay switch closed, sending power to the component without routing it through the inside of the vehicle. Some common circuits which may use relays are the horn, headlights, starter, electric fuel pump and rear window defogger systems.

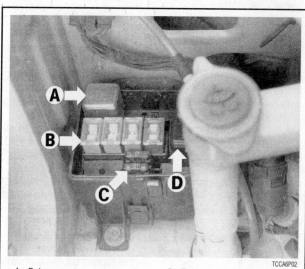

TCCA6P02

A. Relay   C. Fuse
B. Fusible link   D. Flasher

The underhood fuse and relay panel usually contains fuses, relays, flashers and fusible links

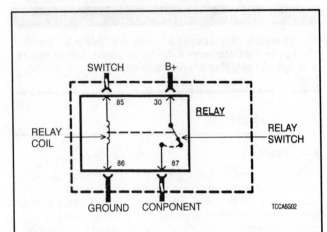

Fig. 2 Relays are composed of a coil and a switch. These two components are linked together so that when one operates, the other operates at the same time. The large wires in the circuit are connected from the battery to one side of the relay switch (B+) and from the opposite side of the relay switch to the load (component). Smaller wires are connected from the relay coil to the control switch for the circuit and from the opposite side of the relay coil to ground.

LOAD

Every complete circuit must include a "load" (something to use the electricity coming from the source). Without this load, the battery would attempt to deliver its entire power supply from one pole to another. The electricity would take a short cut to ground and cause a great amount of damage to other components in the circuit by developing a tremendous amount of heat. This condition could develop sufficient heat to melt the insulation on all the surrounding wires and reduce a multiple wire cable to a lump of plastic and copper.

WIRING AND HARNESSES

The average automobile contains about 1/2 mile of wiring, with hundreds of individual connections. To protect the many wires from damage and to keep them from becoming a confusing tangle, they are organized into bundles, enclosed in plastic or taped together and called wiring harnesses. Different harnesses serve different parts of the vehicle. Individual wires are color coded to help trace them through a harness where sections are hidden from view.

Automotive wiring or circuit conductors can be either single strand wire, multi-strand wire or printed circuitry. Single strand wire has a solid metal core and is usually used inside such components as alternators, motors, relays and other devices. Multi-strand wire has a core made of many small strands of wire twisted together into a single conductor. Most of the wiring in an automotive electrical system is made up of multi-strand wire, either as a single conductor or grouped together in a harness. All wiring is color coded on the insulator, either as a solid color or as a colored wire with an identification stripe. A printed circuit is a thin film of copper or other conductor that is printed on an insulator backing. Occasionally, a printed circuit is sandwiched between two sheets of plastic for more protection and flexibility. A complete printed circuit, consisting of conductors, insulating material and connectors for lamps or other components is called a printed circuit board. Printed circuitry is used in place of individual wires or harnesses in places where space is limited, such as behind instrument panels.

Since automotive electrical systems are very sensitive to changes in resistance, the selection of properly sized wires is critical when systems are

repaired. A loose or corroded connection or a replacement wire that is too small for the circuit will add extra resistance and an additional voltage drop to the circuit.

The wire gauge number is an expression of the cross-section area of the conductor. The most common system for expressing wire size is the American Wire Gauge (AWG) system. As gauge number increases, area decreases and the wire becomes smaller. An 18 gauge wire is smaller than a 4 gauge wire. A wire with a higher gauge number will carry less current than a wire with a lower gauge number. Gauge wire size refers to the size of the strands of the conductor, not the size of the complete wire. It is possible, therefore, to have two wires of the same gauge with different diameters because one may have thicker insulation than the other.

12 volt automotive electrical systems generally use 10, 12, 14, 16 and 18 gauge wire. Main power distribution circuits and larger accessories usually use 10 and 12 gauge wire. Battery cables are usually 4 or 6 gauge, although 1 and 2 gauge wires are occasionally used.

It is essential to understand how a circuit works before trying to figure out why it doesn't. An electrical schematic shows the electrical current paths when a circuit is operating properly. Schematics break the entire electrical system down into individual circuits. In a schematic, no attempt is made to represent wiring and components as they physically appear on the vehicle; switches and other components are shown as simply as possible. Face views of harness connectors show the cavity or terminal locations in all multi-pin connectors to help locate test points.

CONNECTORS

Three types of connectors are commonly used in automotive applications—weatherproof, molded and hard shell.

• Weatherproof—these connectors are most commonly used in the engine compartment or where the connector is exposed to the elements. Terminals are protected against moisture and dirt by sealing rings which provide a weathertight seal. All repairs require the use of a special terminal and the tool required to service it. Unlike standard blade type terminals, these weatherproof terminals cannot be straightened once they are bent. Make certain that the connectors are properly seated and all of the sealing rings are in place when connecting leads.

• Molded—these connectors require complete replacement of the connector if found to be defective. This means splicing a new connector assembly into the harness. All splices should be soldered to insure proper contact. Use care when probing the connections or replacing terminals in them, as it is possible to create a short circuit between opposite terminals. If this happens to the wrong terminal pair, it is possible to damage certain components. Always use jumper wires between connectors for circuit checking and NEVER probe through weatherproof seals.

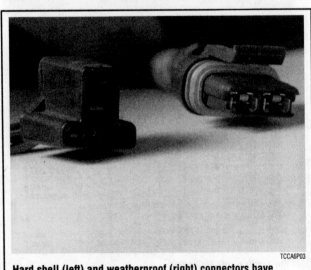

Hard shell (left) and weatherproof (right) connectors have replaceable terminals

Weatherproof connectors are most commonly used in the engine compartment or where the connector is exposed to the elements

- Hard Shell—unlike molded connectors, the terminal contacts in hard-shell connectors can be replaced. Replacement usually involves the use of a special terminal removal tool that depresses the locking tangs (barbs) on the connector terminal and allows the connector to be removed from the rear of the shell. The connector shell should be replaced if it shows any evidence of burning, melting, cracks, or breaks. Replace individual terminals that are burnt, corroded, distorted or loose.

Test Equipment

Pinpointing the exact cause of trouble in an electrical circuit is most times accomplished by the use of special test equipment. The following describes different types of commonly used test equipment and briefly explains how to use them in diagnosis. In addition to the information covered below, the tool manufacturer's instructions booklet (provided with the tester) should be read and clearly understood before attempting any test procedures.

JUMPER WIRES

⁂ CAUTION

Never use jumper wires made from a thinner gauge wire than the circuit being tested. If the jumper wire is of too small a gauge, it may overheat and possibly melt. Never use jumpers to bypass high resistance loads in a circuit. Bypassing resistances, in effect, creates a short circuit. This may, in turn, cause damage and fire. Jumper wires should only be used to bypass lengths of wire.

Jumper wires are simple, yet extremely valuable, pieces of test equipment. They are basically test wires which are used to bypass sections of a circuit. Although jumper wires can be purchased, they are usually fabricated from lengths of standard automotive wire and whatever type of connector (alligator clip, spade connector or pin connector) that is required for the particular application being tested. In cramped, hard-to-reach areas, it is advisable to have insulated boots over the jumper wire terminals in order to prevent accidental grounding. It is also advisable to include a standard automotive fuse in any jumper wire. This is commonly referred to as a

"fused jumper". By inserting an in-line fuse holder between a set of test leads, a fused jumper wire can be used for bypassing open circuits. Use a 5 amp fuse to provide protection against voltage spikes.

Jumper wires are used primarily to locate open electrical circuits, on either the ground (-) side of the circuit or on the power (+) side. If an electrical component fails to operate, connect the jumper wire between the component and a good ground. If the component operates only with the jumper installed, the ground circuit is open. If the ground circuit is good, but the component does not operate, the circuit between the power feed and component may be open. By moving the jumper wire successively back from the component toward the power source, you can isolate the area of the circuit where the open is located. When the component stops functioning, or the power is cut off, the open is in the segment of wire between the jumper and the point previously tested.

You can sometimes connect the jumper wire directly from the battery to the "hot" terminal of the component, but first make sure the component uses 12 volts in operation. Some electrical components, such as fuel injectors, are designed to operate on about 4 volts, and running 12 volts directly to these components will cause damage.

TEST LIGHTS

The test light is used to check circuits and components while electrical current is flowing through them. It is used for voltage and ground tests. To use a 12 volt test light, connect the ground clip to a good ground and probe wherever necessary with the pick. The test light will illuminate when voltage is detected. This does not necessarily mean that 12 volts (or any particular amount of voltage) is present; it only means that some voltage is present. It is advisable before using the test light to touch its ground clip and probe across the battery posts or terminals to make sure the light is operating properly.

⁂ WARNING

Do not use a test light to probe electronic ignition spark plug or coil wires. Never use a pick-type test light to probe wiring on computer controlled systems unless specifically instructed to do so. Any wire insulation that is pierced by the test light probe should be taped and sealed with silicone after testing.

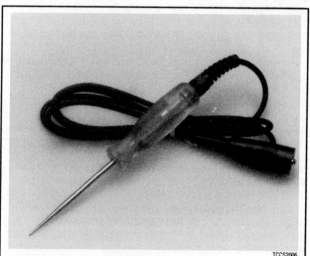

A 12 volt test light is used to detect the presence of voltage in a circuit

Like the jumper wire, the 12 volt test light is used to isolate opens in circuits. But, whereas the jumper wire is used to bypass the open to operate the load, the 12 volt test light is used to locate the presence of voltage in a circuit. If the test light illuminates, there is power up to that point in the circuit; if the test light does not illuminate, there is an open circuit (no power). Move the test light in successive steps back toward the power source until the light in the handle illuminates. The open is between the probe and a point which was previously probed.

The self-powered test light is similar in design to the 12 volt test light, but contains a 1.5 volt penlight battery in the handle. It is most often used in place of a multimeter to check for open or short circuits when power is isolated from the circuit (continuity test).

The battery in a self-powered test light does not provide much current. A weak battery may not provide enough power to illuminate the test light even when a complete circuit is made (especially if there is high resistance in the circuit). Always make sure that the test battery is strong. To check the battery, briefly touch the ground clip to the probe; if the light glows brightly, the battery is strong enough for testing.

➡**A self-powered test light should not be used on any computer controlled system or component. The small amount of electricity transmitted by the test light is enough to damage many electronic automotive components.**

MULTIMETERS

Multimeters are an extremely useful tool for troubleshooting electrical problems. They can be purchased in either analog or digital form and have a price range to suit any budget. A multimeter is a voltmeter, ammeter and ohmmeter (along with other features) combined into one instrument. It is often used when testing solid state circuits because of its high input impedance (usually 10 megaohms or more). A brief description of the multimeter main test functions follows:

• Voltmeter —the voltmeter is used to measure voltage at any point in a circuit, or to measure the voltage drop across any part of a circuit. Voltmeters usually have various scales and a selector switch to allow the reading of different voltage ranges. The voltmeter has a positive and a negative lead. To avoid damage to the meter, always connect the negative lead to the negative (-) side of the circuit (to ground or nearest the ground side of the circuit) and connect the positive lead to the positive (+) side of the circuit (to the power source or the nearest power source). Note that the negative voltmeter lead will always be black and that the positive voltmeter will always be some color other than black (usually red).

• Ohmmeter —the ohmmeter is designed to read resistance (measured in ohms) in a circuit or component. All ohmmeters will have a selector switch which permits the measurement of different ranges of resistance (usually the selector switch allows the multiplication of the meter reading by 10, 100, 1,000 and 10,000). Since the meters are powered by an internal battery, the ohmmeter can be used as a self-powered test light. When the ohmmeter is connected, current from the ohmmeter flows through the circuit or component being tested. Since the ohmmeter's internal resistance and voltage are known values, the amount of current flow through the meter depends on the resistance of the circuit or component being tested.

The ohmmeter can also be used to perform a continuity test for suspected open circuits. In using the meter for making continuity checks, do not be concerned with the actual resistance readings. Zero resistance, or any ohm reading, indicates continuity in the circuit. Infinite resistance indicates an opening in the circuit. A high resistance reading where there should be none indicates a problem in the circuit. Checks for short circuits are made in the same manner as checks for open circuits, except that the circuit must be isolated from both power and normal ground. Infinite resistance indicates no continuity to ground, while zero resistance indicates a dead short to ground.

✳✳ WARNING

Never use an ohmmeter to check the resistance of a component or wire while there is voltage applied to the circuit.

• Ammeter—an ammeter measures the amount of current flowing through a circuit in units called amperes or amps. At normal operating voltage, most circuits have a characteristic amount of amperes, called "current draw" which can be measured using an ammeter. By referring to a specified current draw rating, then measuring the amperes and comparing the two values, one can determine what is happening within the circuit to aid in diagnosis. An open circuit, for example, will not allow any current to flow, so the ammeter reading will be zero. A damaged component or circuit will have an increased current draw, so the reading will be high.

The ammeter is always connected in series with the circuit being tested. All of the current that normally flows through the circuit must also flow through the ammeter; if there is any other path for the current to follow, the ammeter reading will not be accurate. The ammeter itself has very little resistance to current flow and, therefore, will not affect the circuit, but it will measure current draw only when the circuit is closed and electricity is flowing. Excessive current draw can blow fuses and drain the battery, while a reduced current draw can cause motors to run slowly, lights to dim and other components to not operate properly.

Troubleshooting

When diagnosing a specific problem, organized troubleshooting is a must. The complexity of a modern automotive vehicle demands that you approach any problem in a logical, organized manner. There are certain troubleshooting techniques which are standard:

• Establish when the problem occurs. Does the problem appear only under certain conditions? Were there any noises, odors or other unusual symptoms?

• Isolate the problem area. To do this, make some simple tests and observations, then eliminate the systems that are working properly. Check for obvious problems, such as broken wires and loose or dirty connections. Always check the obvious before assuming something complicated is the cause.

• Test for problems systematically to determine the cause once the problem area is isolated. Are all the components functioning properly? Is there power going to electrical switches and motors. Performing careful, systematic checks will often turn up most causes on the first inspection, without wasting time checking components that have little or no relationship to the problem.

• Test all repairs after the work is done to make sure that the problem is fixed. Some causes can be traced to more than one component, so a careful verification of repair work is important in order to pick up additional malfunctions that may cause a problem to reappear or a different problem to arise. A blown fuse, for example, is a simple problem that may require more than another fuse to repair. If you don't look for a problem that caused a fuse to blow, a shorted wire (for example) may go undetected.

Experience has shown that most problems tend to be the result of a fairly simple and obvious cause, such as loose or corroded connectors, bad grounds or damaged wire insulation which causes a short. This makes careful visual inspection of components during testing essential to quick and accurate troubleshooting.

Testing

OPEN CIRCUITS

1. Isolate the circuit from power and ground.
2. Connect the self-powered test light or ohmmeter ground clip to a good ground and probe sections of the circuit sequentially.
3. If the light is out or there is infinite resistance, the open is between the probe and the circuit ground.
4. If the light is on or the meter shows continuity, the open is between the probe and end of the circuit toward the power source.

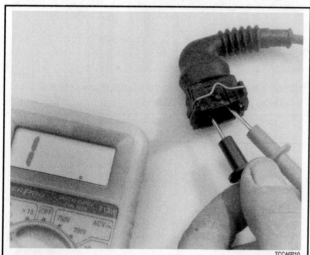

The infinite reading on this multimeter (1   .) indicates that the circuit is open

SHORT CIRCUITS

➥**Never use a self-powered test light to perform checks for opens or shorts when power is applied to the electrical system under test. The 12 volt vehicle power will quickly burn out the light bulb in the test light.**

1. Isolate the circuit from power and ground.
2. Connect the self-powered test light or ohmmeter ground clip to a good ground and probe any easy-to-reach test point in the circuit.
3. If the light comes on or there is continuity, there is a short somewhere in the circuit.
4. To isolate the short, probe a test point at either end of the isolated circuit (the light should be on or the meter should indicate continuity).
5. Leave the test light probe engaged and sequentially open connectors or switches, remove parts, etc. until the light goes out or continuity is broken.
6. When the light goes out, the short is between the last two circuit components which were opened.

VOLTAGE

This test determines voltage available from the battery and should be the first step in any electrical troubleshooting procedure. Many electrical problems, especially on computer controlled systems, can be caused by a low

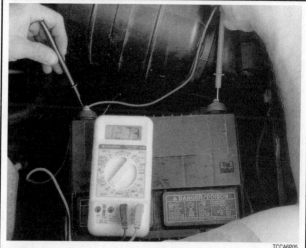

Using a multimeter to check battery voltage. This battery is fully charged

Testing voltage output between the alternator's BAT terminal and ground. This voltage reading is normal

state of charge in the battery. Excessive corrosion at the battery cable terminals can cause poor contact that will prevent proper charging and full battery current flow.

1. Set the voltmeter selector switch to the 20V position.
2. Connect the multimeter negative lead to the battery's negative (−) post or terminal and the positive lead to the battery's positive (+) post or terminal.
3. Turn the ignition switch **ON** to provide a load.
4. A well charged battery should register over 12 volts. If the meter reads below 11.5 volts, the battery power may be insufficient to operate the electrical system properly.

VOLTAGE DROP

When current flows through a load, the voltage beyond the load drops. This voltage drop is due to the resistance created by the load and also by

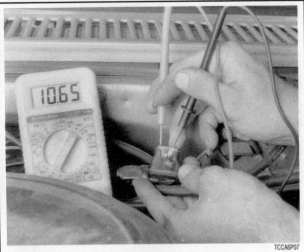

This voltage drop test revealed high resistance (low voltage) in the circuit

Checking the resistance of a coolant temperature sensor with an ohmmeter. Reading is 1.04 kilohms

small resistances created by corrosion at the connectors and damaged insulation on the wires. The maximum allowable voltage drop under load is critical, especially if there is more than one load in the circuit, since all voltage drops are cumulative.

1. Set the voltmeter selector switch to the 20 volt position.
2. Connect the multimeter negative lead to a good ground.
3. Operate the circuit and check the voltage prior to the first component (load).
4. There should be little or no voltage drop in the circuit prior to the first component. If a voltage drop exists, the wire or connectors in the circuit are suspect.
5. While operating the first component in the circuit, probe the ground side of the component with the positive meter lead and observe the voltage readings. A small voltage drop should be noticed. This voltage drop is caused by the resistance of the component.
6. Repeat the test for each component (load) down the circuit.
7. If a large voltage drop is noticed, the preceding component, wire or connector is suspect.

RESISTANCE

✳✳ WARNING

Never use an ohmmeter with power applied to the circuit. The ohmmeter is designed to operate on its own power supply. The normal 12 volt automotive electrical system current could damage the meter!

1. Isolate the circuit from the vehicle's power source.
2. Ensure that the ignition key is **OFF** when disconnecting any components or the battery.
3. Where necessary, also isolate at least one side of the circuit to be checked, in order to avoid reading parallel resistances. Parallel circuit resistances will always give a lower reading than the actual resistance of either of the branches.
4. Connect the meter leads to both sides of the circuit (wire or component) and read the actual measured ohms on the meter scale. Make sure the selector switch is set to the proper ohm scale for the circuit being tested, to avoid misreading the ohmmeter test value.

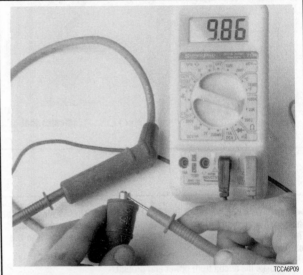

Spark plug wires can be checked for excessive resistance using an ohmmeter

Wire and Connector Repair

Almost anyone can replace damaged wires, as long as the proper tools and parts are available. Automotive wire and terminals are available to fit almost any need. Even the specialized weatherproof, molded and hard shell connectors are now available from aftermarket suppliers.

Be sure the ends of all the wires are fitted with the proper terminal hardware and connectors. Wrapping a wire around a stud is never a permanent solution and will only cause trouble later. Replace wires one at a time to avoid confusion. Always route wires exactly the same as the factory.

➡**If connector repair is necessary, only attempt it if you have the proper tools. Weatherproof and hard shell connectors require special tools to release the pins inside the connector. Attempting to repair these connectors with conventional hand tools will damage them.**

BATTERY CABLES

Disconnecting the Cables

When working on any electrical component on the vehicle, it is always a good idea to disconnect the negative (—) battery cable. This will prevent potential damage to many sensitive electrical components such as the Engine Control Module (ECM), radio, alternator, etc.

➡Any time you disengage the battery cables, it is recommended that you disconnect the negative (—) battery cable first. This will prevent your accidentally grounding the positive (+) terminal to the body of the vehicle when disconnecting it, thereby preventing damage to the above mentioned components.

. . . then loosen the clamp bolt and lift the cable terminal off of the battery post

To disconnect the battery cables, first remove the access cover . . .

Before you disconnect the cable(s), first turn the ignition to the **OFF** position. This will prevent a draw on the battery which could cause arcing (electricity trying to ground itself to the body of a vehicle, just like a spark plug jumping the gap) and, of course, damaging some components such as the alternator diodes.

When the battery cable(s) are reconnected (negative cable last), be sure to check that your lights, windshield wipers and other electrically operated safety components are all working correctly. If your vehicle contains an Electronically Tuned Radio (ETR), don't forget to also reset your radio stations. Ditto for the clock.

AIR BAG (SUPPLEMENTAL RESTRAINT) SYSTEM

General Information

The 1994–98 Mustang vehicles are available with an air bag Supplemental Restraint System (SRS). The SRS is designed to work in conjunction with the standard three-point safety belts to reduce injury in a head-on collision.

✳✳ WARNING

The SRS can actually cause physical injury or death if the safety belts are not used, or if the manufacturer's warnings are not followed. The manufacturer's warnings can be found in your owner's manual, or, in some cases, on your sun visors.

The SRS is comprised of the following components:
• Driver's side air bag module
• Passenger's side air bag module
• Right-hand and left-hand primary crash front air bag sensors
• Air bag diagnostic monitor computer
• Electrical wiring

The SRS primary crash front air bag sensors are hard-wired to the air bag modules and determine when the air bags are deployed. During a frontal collision, the sensors quickly inflate the two air bags to reduce injury by cushioning the driver and front passenger from striking the dashboard, windshield, steering wheel and any other hard surfaces. The air bag inflates so quickly (in a fraction of a second) that in most cases it is fully inflated before you actually start to move during an automotive collision.

Since the SRS is a complicated and essentially important system, its components are constantly being tested by a diagnostic monitor computer, which illuminates the air bag indicator light on the instrument cluster for approximately 6 seconds when the ignition switch is turned to the **RUN** position when the SRS is functioning properly. After being illuminated for the 6 seconds, the indicator light should then turn off.

If the air bag light does not illuminate at all, stays on continuously, or flashes at any time, a problem has been detected by the diagnostic monitor computer.

✳✳ WARNING

If at any time the air bag light indicates that the computer has noted a problem, have your vehicle's SRS serviced immediately by a qualified automotive technician. A faulty SRS can cause severe physical injury or death.

SERVICE PRECAUTIONS

Whenever working around, or on, the air bag supplemental restraint system, ALWAYS adhere to the following warnings and cautions.

• Always wear safety glasses when servicing an air bag vehicle and when handling an air bag module.

• Carry a live air bag module with the bag and trim cover facing away from your body, so that an accidental deployment of the air bag will have a small chance of personal injury.

• Place an air bag module on a table or other flat surface with the bag and trim cover pointing up.

• Wear gloves, a dust mask and safety glasses whenever handling a deployed air bag module. The air bag surface may contain traces of sodium hydroxide, a by-product of the gas that inflates the air bag and which can cause skin irritation.

• Ensure to wash your hands with mild soap and water after handling a deployed air bag.

• All air bag modules with discolored or damaged cover trim must be replaced, not repainted.

• All component replacement and wiring service must be made with the negative and positive battery cables disconnected from the battery for a minimum of one minute prior to attempting service or replacement.

• NEVER probe the air bag electrical terminals. Doing so could result in air bag deployment, which can cause serious physical injury.

• If the vehicle is involved in a fender-bender which results in a damaged front bumper or grille, have the air bag sensors inspected by a qualified automotive technician to ensure that they were not damaged.

• If at any time, the air bag light indicates that the computer has noted a problem, have your vehicle's SRS serviced immediately by a qualified automotive technician. A faulty SRS can cause severe physical injury or death.

DISARMING THE SYSTEM

1. Disconnect the negative battery cable from the battery.
2. Disconnect the positive battery cable from the battery.
3. Wait one minute. This time is required for the back-up power supply in the air bag diagnostic monitor to completely drain. The system is now disarmed.

If you are disarming the system with the intent of testing the system, do not! The SRS is a sensitive, complex system and should only be tested or serviced by a qualified automotive technician. Also, specific tools are needed for SRS testing.

ARMING THE SYSTEM

1. Connect the positive battery cable.
2. Connect the negative battery cable.
3. Stand outside the vehicle and carefully turn the ignition to the **RUN** position. Be sure that no part of your body is in front of the air bag module on the steering wheel, to prevent injury in case of an accidental air bag deployment.
4. Ensure the air bag indicator light turns off after approximately 6 seconds. If the light does not illuminate at all, does not turn off, or starts to flash, have the system tested by a qualified automotive technician. If the light does turn off after 6 seconds and does not flash, the SRS is working properly.

HEATING & AIR CONDITIONING

Blower Motor

REMOVAL & INSTALLATION

▶ **See Figures 3 and 4**

➡**The heater/air conditioning blower motor is mounted in the heater case assembly, under the instrument panel on the passenger's side of the vehicle.**

1. Disconnect the negative battery cable.
2. From under the instrument panel on the passenger's side of the vehicle, remove the three blower motor mounting screws, then remove the blower motor cover and stiffener (if equipped).

3. Disconnect electrical wiring harness from the blower motor.
4. Pull the blower motor and wheel out of the heater case. Discard the old gasket.
5. If the blower wheel must be replaced or transferred to a new motor, remove the wheel retaining nut. Slide the wheel off of the blower motor shaft.

To install:
6. If necessary, slide the blower wheel onto the motor shaft and install the retaining nut until secure.
7. Install a new gasket onto the blower motor, then insert the motor and wheel in the blower motor cover.
8. Position the blower motor, stiffener (if equipped) and cover in the heater case. Install and tighten the retaining screws until secure.
9. Reattach the wiring harness connector to the blower motor terminals.
10. Attach the negative battery cable.

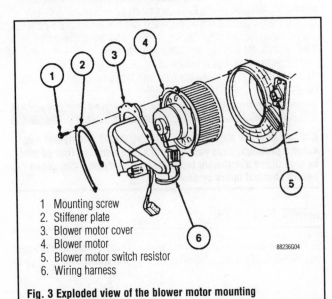

1 Mounting screw
2. Stiffener plate
3. Blower motor cover
4. Blower motor
5. Blower motor switch resistor
6. Wiring harness

88236G04

Fig. 3 Exploded view of the blower motor mounting

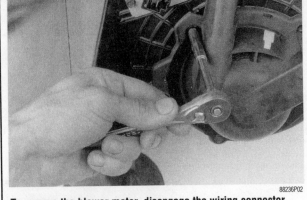

88236P02

To remove the blower motor, disengage the wiring connector and remove the mounting screws . . .

. . . then remove the stiffener plate, if equipped

88236P03

Pull the blower motor out of the heater case assembly

88236P04

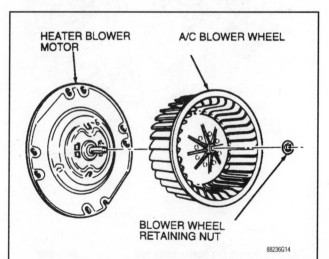

HEATER BLOWER MOTOR

A/C BLOWER WHEEL

BLOWER WHEEL RETAINING NUT

88236G14

Fig. 4 The blower wheel is secured to the blower motor shaft with a retaining nut—be sure that this nut is tight during installation

Heater Core

✳✳ CAUTION

All models covered by this manual are equipped with a Supplemental Restraint System (SRS), which uses an air bag. Whenever working near any of the SRS components, such as the impact sensors, the air bag module, steering column and instrument panel, disconnect the negative, then the positive battery cables and wait one minute. Disconnecting the battery cables and waiting for one minute will allow any residual power in the system to drain. Failure to properly disconnect both battery cables may result in accidental air bag deployment, which could easily result in severe personal injury or death. Also, never attempt any electrical diagnosis or service to the SRS components and wiring; this work should only be performed by a qualified automotive technician.

REMOVAL & INSTALLATION

⬥ **See Figures 5, 6, 7, 8 and 9**

1. Disconnect the negative battery cable.
2. Remove the instrument panel.
3. Remove the heater case assembly as follows:
   a. Position a drain pan under the heater water hose connections at the cowl panel.

✳✳ CAUTION

When draining engine coolant, keep in mind that cats and dogs are attracted to ethylene glycol antifreeze and could drink any that is left in an uncovered container or in puddles on the ground. This will prove fatal in sufficient quantity. Always drain coolant into a sealable container. Coolant should be reused unless it is contaminated or is several years old.

   b. Detach the coolant hoses from the heater core tubes, then plug the smaller coolant hose with a ⅝ in. plug and the larger hose with a ¾ in. plug.
   c. Cap the heater core tubes to prevent coolant spillage during heater case removal.
   d. Detach and label the heater case vacuum hose from the engine vacuum connector.
   e. Remove the heater case-to-cowl panel mounting nut (in the engine compartment) and screw (located at the bottom of the heater case in the passenger compartment).
   f. Remove the nut and screw retaining the heater case mounting bracket to the cowl top panel.
   g. Disengage the wiring harness connector from the blower motor.
   h. Carefully pull the heater case away from the cowl panel, then remove the case from the vehicle as an assembly.
4. Position the heater case on a clean, stable workbench.
5. Remove the heater core cover retaining screws, then remove the heater core cover from the heater case.
6. Remove the heater dash panel seal from the heater core tubes, then separate the heater core from the case.
To install:
7. Install a new heater core case seal, then position the heater core in the case.
8. Slide the new heater dash panel seal onto the heater core tubes, then position the cover over the heater core. Install the cover mounting screws and tighten them until snug.
9. Install the heater case assembly as follows:
   a. Position the heater case on the cowl panel of the vehicle, making sure that all hoses and tubes are properly routed through the cowl panel into the engine compartment, then install the case-to-top mounting bracket nut. Tighten the nut to 90–122 inch lbs. (10–14 Nm).

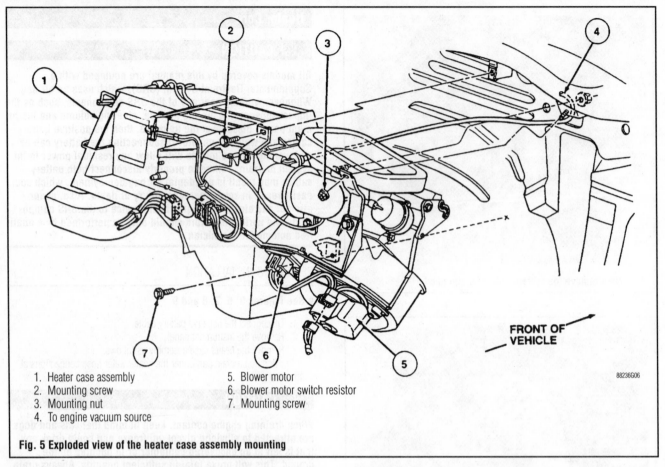

FRONT OF VEHICLE

88236G06

1. Heater case assembly
2. Mounting screw
3. Mounting nut
4. To engine vacuum source
5. Blower motor
6. Blower motor switch resistor
7. Mounting screw

Fig. 5 Exploded view of the heater case assembly mounting

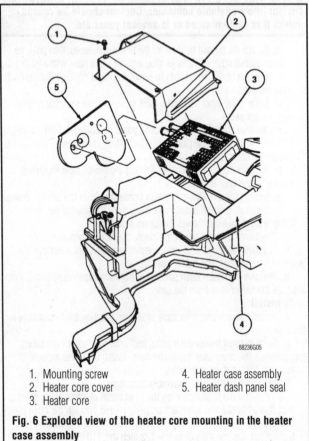

88236G05

1. Mounting screw
2. Heater core cover
3. Heater core
4. Heater case assembly
5. Heater dash panel seal

Fig. 6 Exploded view of the heater core mounting in the heater case assembly

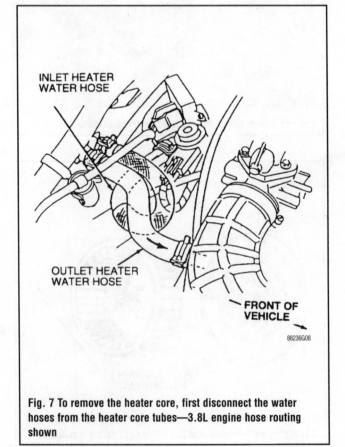

INLET HEATER WATER HOSE

OUTLET HEATER WATER HOSE

FRONT OF VEHICLE

88236G08

Fig. 7 To remove the heater core, first disconnect the water hoses from the heater core tubes—3.8L engine hose routing shown

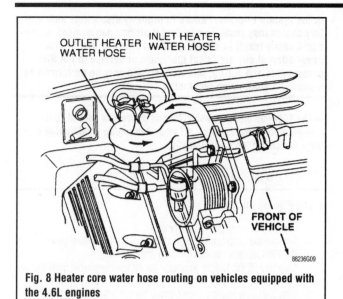

Fig. 8 Heater core water hose routing on vehicles equipped with the 4.6L engines

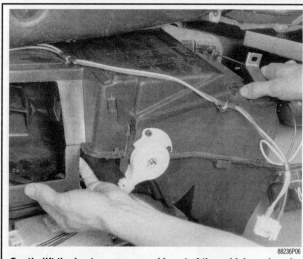

Gently lift the heater case assembly out of the vehicle and position it on a sturdy, clean work surface . . .

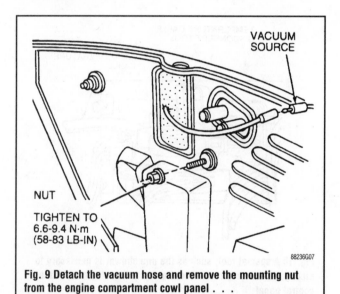

Fig. 9 Detach the vacuum hose and remove the mounting nut from the engine compartment cowl panel . . .

. . . then remove the heater core cover retaining screws

. . . then remove the mounting fasteners from inside the passenger's compartment

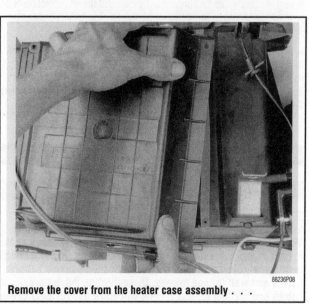

Remove the cover from the heater case assembly . . .

. . . then pull the heater core out of the case

b. Install the case-to-top mounting bracket screw, and tighten it to 90–122 inch lbs. (10–14 Nm).

c. Install the lower case-to-cowl panel retaining screw, and tighten it until snug.

d. From inside the engine compartment, install the case-to-cowl panel retaining nut, and tighten it until snug.

e. Reattach the vacuum supply hose in the engine compartment.

f. Attach the two coolant hoses to the heater core tubes.

10. Install the instrument panel.

11. Connect the negative battery cable.

12. Fill the engine cooling system as required.

Air Conditioning Components

REMOVAL & INSTALLATION

Repair or service of air conditioning components is not covered by this manual, because of the risk of personal injury or death, and because of the legal ramifications of servicing these components without the proper EPA certification and experience. Cost, personal injury or death, environmental damage, and legal considerations (such as the fact that it is a federal crime to vent refrigerant into the atmosphere), dictate that the A/C components on your vehicle should be serviced only by a Motor Vehicle Air Conditioning (MVAC) trained, and EPA certified automotive technician.

➡If your vehicle's A/C system uses R-12 refrigerant and is in need of recharging, the A/C system can be converted over to R-134a refrigerant (less environmentally harmful and expensive). Refer to Section 1 for additional information on R-12 to R-134a conversions, and for additional considerations dealing with your vehicle's A/C system.

Control Cable

✳✳ CAUTION

All models covered by this manual are equipped with a Supplemental Restraint System (SRS), which uses an air bag. Whenever working near any of the SRS components, such as the impact sensors, the air bag module, steering column and instrument panel, disconnect the negative, then the positive battery cables and wait for one minute. Disconnecting the battery cables and waiting for one minute will allow any residual power

in the system to drain. Failure to properly disconnect both battery cables may result in accidental air bag deployment, which could easily result in severe personal injury or death. Also, never attempt any electrical diagnosis or service to the SRS components and wiring; this work should only be performed by a qualified automotive technician.

➡The 1994–98 Mustang vehicles only utilize one control cable (temperature control cable), all other heating/air conditioning settings are controlled electronically.

REMOVAL & INSTALLATION

▶ **See Figures 10 and 11**

1. Disconnect the negative battery cable.
2. Remove the control panel assembly from the instrument panel.
3. On 1994 models, remove the instrument panel.
4. Carefully lift the locktab to detach the temperature cable from the control door shaft.
5. Note the cable routing, then remove the cable from the vehicle.

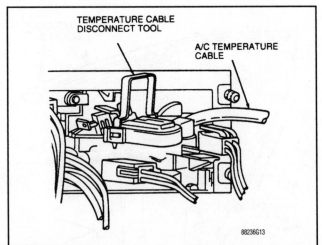

Fig. 10 A special tool, such as the one shown, is necessary to disengage the temperature control cable from the back of the control panel

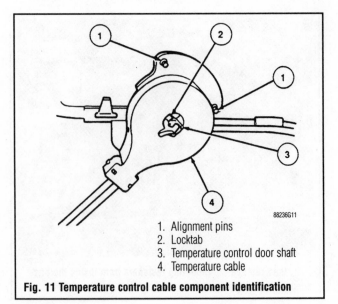

1. Alignment pins
2. Locktab
3. Temperature control door shaft
4. Temperature cable

Fig. 11 Temperature control cable component identification

To install:

6. Route the cable behind the instrument panel, then engage the alignment pins and attach the temperature cable to the control door shaft until the locktab snaps into the groove on the shaft.

7. If necessary, install the instrument panel.

8. Engage the cable end with the cable actuator on the control assembly. Install the control assembly in the instrument panel.

9. Connect the negative battery cable and check the system for proper operation.

Control Panel

REMOVAL & INSTALLATION

▶ **See Figures 12 and 13**

1. Disconnect the negative battery cable.

2. Remove the snap-in trim moulding in the center console to expose the four control assembly attaching screws. Remove the four screws attaching the control assembly to the instrument panel.

3. Roll the control panel out of the opening in the console.

4. Detach the temperature control cable from the control panel by using Ford Temperature Cable Disconnect tool T94P-18532-A, or equivalent, to release the side locking tube, and a small flat-bladed prytool to release the top locking tab. Pull the temperature cable away from the heater control.

5. Remove the two mounting nuts, then separate the vacuum hose and wiring harness connectors from the back of the damper door switch.

6. Detach the wiring harness connectors from the back of the blower motor switch and the light bulbs.

7. Remove the control panel from the center console.

To install:

8. Position the temperature cable at the midpoint of its travel, directly between the H and C markings. Position the temperature control knob at

the midpoint of its range, then connect the temperature cable to the geared arm on the blower motor wheel. Rotate the temperature control knob from maximum cold to maximum warm to verify proper range of motion.

9. Install the electrical connector at the following locations: blower switch, control assembly illumination bulbs and damper door switch.

10. Install the vacuum harness connector for the function selector knob and tighten the mounting nuts until snug.

11. Roll the control assembly into position against the instrument panel and install the four attaching screws until snug.

12. Snap the console trim moulding into position, connect the negative battery cable and check the system for proper operation.

To remove the control panel, first remove the trim cover and remove the panel mounting screws . . .

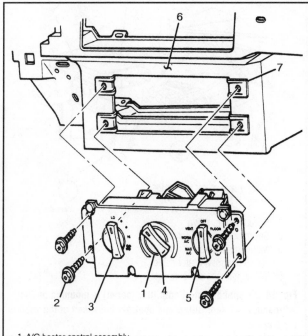

1. A/C-heater control assembly
2. Screw - (Control assy. to instrument panel) (4 req'd)
3. Blower motor speed selector knob
4. Temperature selector knob
5. Function selector knob
6. Instrument panel
7. Nut - (purchased as part of instrument panel assy.)

81556G04

Fig. 12 Exploded view of the heater control panel mounting

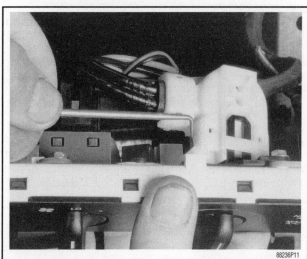

. . . then disengage the locking tabs on the temperature control cable . . .

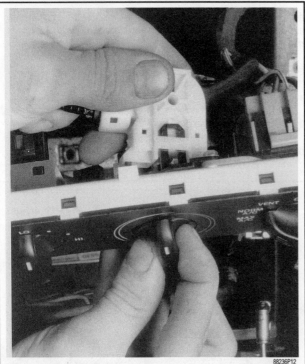

. . . and detach the control cable. Detach all wiring harness connectors and remove the panel

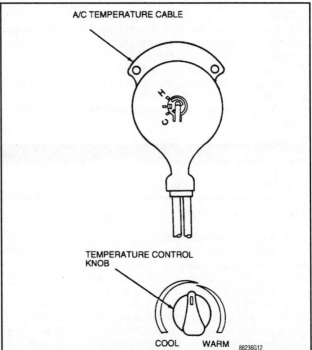

Fig. 13 Prior to installing the temperature control cable, turn the control knob and the cable indicator to the mid-points of their ranges

CRUISE CONTROL

▶ **See Figure 14**

1994–98 Mustang vehicles were available with a speed control system. This system automatically controls the speed of the vehicle when cruising at a stable highway speed. The speed control system consists of the following:

- Speed control amplifier
- Speed control cable
- Vehicle Speed Sensor (VSS)
- Horn relay and bracket
- Speed control actuator switch
- Stop light switch
- Deactivator switch
- Clutch pedal position switch (manual transmissions only)

The speed control system operates independently of engine vacuum and, therefore, does not utilize any vacuum lines.

The speed control amplifier, mounted on the left-hand door hinge pillar, integrates the system electronics, thereby eliminating any other electronic control modules in the vehicle. The amplifier controls the vehicle's speed via a cable attached to the throttle body lever.

The speed control actuator switch assembly is mounted on the steering wheel and allows the driver to control the system's operation. The switch assembly contains five control buttons for system functioning, namely: ON, OFF, RESUME, SET ACCEL, COAST.

The system will continue to control the vehicle's speed until the OFF button is used, or the brake pedal or clutch pedal (manual transmissions only) is depressed.

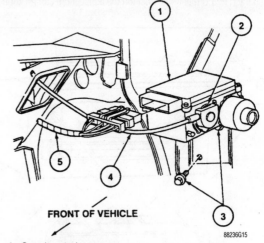

FRONT OF VEHICLE

1. Speed control servo
2. Speed control actuator cap
3. Mounting screws
4. Speed control actuator cable
5. Wiring harness and connector

Fig. 14 The speed control amplifier (servo) is mounted on the left-hand, front door pillar, and controls the speed of the vehicle via a cable

CRUISE CONTROL TROUBLESHOOTING

Problem	Possible Cause
Will not hold proper speed	Incorrect cable adjustment
	Binding throttle linkage
	Leaking vacuum servo diaphragm
	Leaking vacuum tank
	Faulty vacuum or vent valve
	Faulty stepper motor
	Faulty transducer
	Faulty speed sensor
	Faulty cruise control module
Cruise intermittently cuts out	Clutch or brake switch adjustment too tight
	Short or open in the cruise control circuit
	Faulty transducer
	Faulty cruise control module
Vehicle surges	Kinked speedometer cable or casing
	Binding throttle linkage
	Faulty speed sensor
	Faulty cruise control module
Cruise control inoperative	Blown fuse
	Short or open in the cruise control circuit
	Faulty brake or clutch switch
	Leaking vacuum circuit
	Faulty cruise control switch
	Faulty stepper motor
	Faulty transducer
	Faulty speed sensor
	Faulty cruise control module

Note: Use this chart as a guide. Not all systems will use the components listed.

TCCA6C01

ENTERTAINMENT SYSTEMS

Precautions

Electronic modules, such as instrument clusters, powertrain controls and sound systems are sensitive to static electricity and can be damaged by static discharges which are below the levels that you can hear snap or detect on your skin. A detectable snap or shock of static electricity is in the 3,000 volt range. Some of these modules can be damaged by a charge of as little as 100 volts.

The following are some basic safeguards to avoid static electrical damage:
• Leave the replacement module in its original packing until you are ready to install it.
• Avoid touching the module connector pins.
• Avoid placing the module on a non-conductive surface.
• Use a commercially available static protection kit. These kits contain such things as grounding cords and conductive mats.

Radio Receiver/Tape Player/CD Player

REMOVAL & INSTALLATION

♦ See Figure 15

➡These vehicles have DIN-standard radios; Ford Tool T87P-19061-A, or equivalent, is required to release the clips and remove the radio from the vehicle.

1. Disconnect the negative battery cable.
2. Insert the two radio removing tools (T87P-19061-A or equivalents) into the radio face plate. Push the tools in approximately 1 in. (25mm) to release the retaining clips.

➡DO NOT use excessive force when inserting the radio removal tools, as this will damage the retaining clips.

3. Apply a light spreading force on the tools and pull the radio out of the center console.
4. Disengage the wiring and antenna connectors from the rear of the radio.

To install:
5. Engage the wiring and antenna connectors to the rear of the radio.
6. Slide the radio into the instrument panel, ensuring that the rear radio bracket is engaged on the upper support rail.
7. Connect the negative battery cable. Check the radio for proper operation.

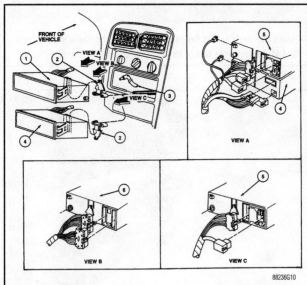

1. Radio/cassette player
2. Radio support bracket
3. Antenna lead-in cable
4. Compact Disc (CD) player
5. Radio/electronic search cassette or premium analog cassette player
6. Electronic search radio

88236G10

Fig. 15 Exploded view of the radio/tape player and optional CD player mounting

To remove the radio, two of these special tools are needed

88236P13

Insert the tools in the holes on the side of the radio's front face and slide the radio out of its recess . . .

88236P14

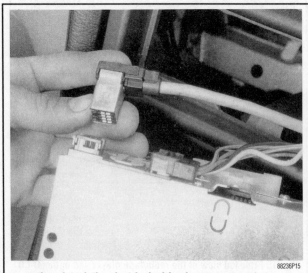

. . . then detach the electrical wiring harness connector . . .

88236P15

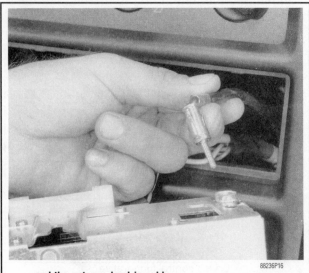

. . . and the antenna lead-in cable

88236P16

Speakers

REMOVAL & INSTALLATION

Door Trim Panel Speakers

▶ See Figure 16

1. Disconnect the negative battery cable.
2. Remove the door trim panel.
3. If equipped, remove the speaker access cover.
4. Remove the speaker retaining screws.
5. Separate the speaker from the door and disengage the speaker wiring harness connector.

To install:

6. Reattach the speaker wiring harness connector to the speaker, then position the speaker in the door. Install the retaining screws until snug.
7. If equipped, install the speaker access cover.
8. Install the door trim panel and connect the negative battery cable.
9. Turn the radio on to ensure that the speaker functions properly.

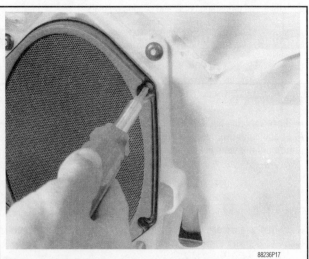

After removing any trim pieces for access, remove the speaker mounting screws . . .

88236P17

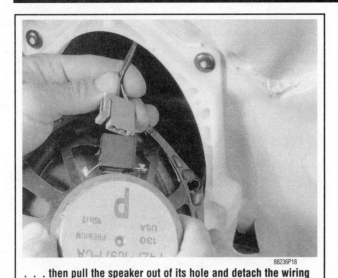

. . . then pull the speaker out of its hole and detach the wiring harness connector

Rear Quarter Trim Panel Speakers

♦ See Figures 17 and 18

1. Disconnect the negative battery cable.
2. Remove the rear seat from the vehicle.

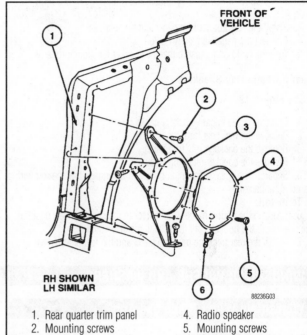

RH SHOWN
LH SIMILAR

88236G03

1. Rear quarter trim panel
2. Mounting screws
3. Radio speaker mounting plate
4. Radio speaker
5. Mounting screws
6. Chassis main wiring harness connector

Fig. 17 Exploded view of the woofer speaker mounting in the rear quarter trim panel

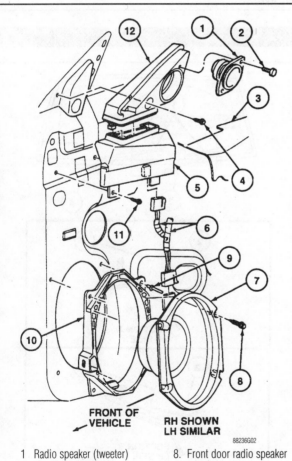

FRONT OF VEHICLE

RH SHOWN
LH SIMILAR

88236G02

1. Radio speaker (tweeter)
2. Mounting screws
3. Front door trim panel
4. Mounting screw
5. Radio speaker base assembly
6. Radio speaker wiring
7. Radio speaker (woofer)
8. Front door radio speaker retaining screw
9. Rivet
10. Radio speaker mounting spacer
11. Mounting screws
12. Radio speaker housing

Fig. 16 Exploded view of the speaker mounting in the front door

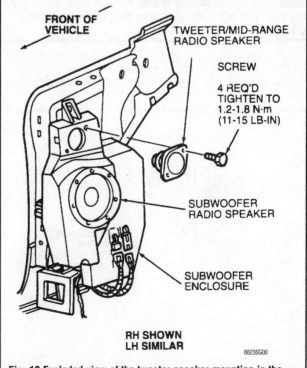

FRONT OF VEHICLE

TWEETER/MID-RANGE RADIO SPEAKER

SCREW

4 REQ'D TIGHTEN TO 1.2-1.8 N·m (11-15 LB-IN)

SUBWOOFER RADIO SPEAKER

SUBWOOFER ENCLOSURE

RH SHOWN
LH SIMILAR

88236G00

Fig. 18 Exploded view of the tweeter speaker mounting in the subwoofer enclosure

3. Remove the rear quarter trim panel.

4. Remove the speaker retaining screws.

5. Separate the speaker from the body and disengage the speaker wiring harness connector.

To install:

6. Reattach the wiring harness connector to the speaker, then position the speaker in the body. Install the retaining screws until snug.

7. Install the rear quarter trim panel and the rear seat.

8. Connect the negative battery cable.

9. Turn the radio on to ensure that the speaker functions properly.

Rear Package Tray Speakers

♦ **See Figure 19**

1. Disconnect the negative battery cable.

2. Remove the rear seat from the vehicle.

3. Remove the package tray trim panel.

4. Remove the speaker retaining screws.

5. Separate the speaker from the body and disengage the speaker wiring harness connector.

To install:

6. Reattach the wiring harness connector to the speaker, then position the speaker in the body. Install the retaining screws until snug.

7. Install the rear package tray trim panel and the rear seat.

8. Connect the negative battery cable.

9. Turn the radio on to ensure that the speaker functions properly.

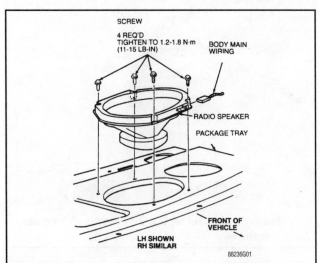

Fig. 19 Exploded view of the speaker mounting in the rear package tray

---

WINDSHIELD WIPERS AND WASHERS

Windshield Wiper Blade and Arm

REMOVAL & INSTALLATION

♦ **See Figures 20, 21 and 22**

> ⁕⁕ **WARNING**
>
> **When removing the wiper arm from the pivot shaft, do not pry the wiper arm with a metal or sharp tool. Otherwise, paint or glass damage may be the result.**

1. From inside the vehicle, turn the windshield wiper switch to the **LOW** position and allow the wipers to operate through three or four cycles, then turn the switch **OFF**. This will ensure that the wipers are in the Park position.

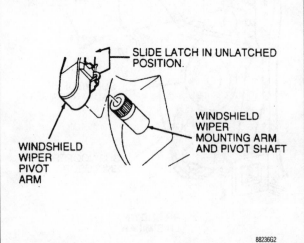

Fig. 20 Pull the slide latch out and lift the wiper arm up and off of the pivot shaft

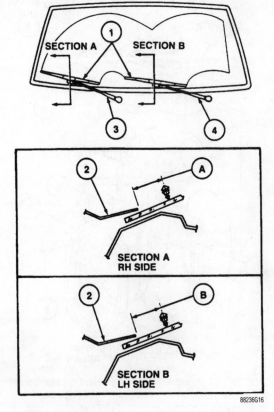

1. Windshield wiper blade
2. Cowl vent screen
3. Right-hand pivot arm
4. Left-hand pivot arm
A. 2.16-3.18 in. (55-81mm)
B. 2.20-3.14 in. (56-80mm)

Fig. 21 Be sure to install the wiper arms and blades so that they are positioned as indicated—this will ensure the proper sweep range of the wiper blades on the windshield

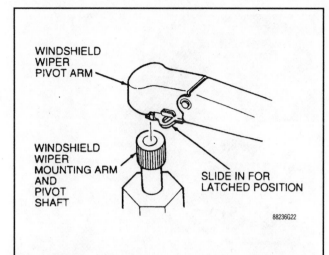

Fig. 22 After installing the wiper arms on the pivot shafts, push the slide latch in to secure the arms in place

2. While holding the wiper arm, push down slightly on the wiper arm head, then swing the outer end of the arm up and away from the windshield glass to its highest position.

3. With the wiper arm pointing upward, use your fingers to grasp the slide latch tab and pull the latch out from underneath the wiper arm head.

4. Remove the wiper arm from the pivot shaft by lifting it straight up and off of the shaft.

To install:

➡️**Prior to installation, ensure that the wiper motor is in the Park position.**

5. Position the windshield wiper so that the arm is parallel with the top edge of the cowl vent screen, then, with the slide latch tab in the unlatched position, slide the arm head over the pivot shaft and depress it until it is fully seated on the shaft.

6. While depressing the wiper arm head, lift the outer end of the arm until the slide latch tab can be fully locked under the arm and pivot shaft.

7. Gently lower the outer end of the wiper arm until it rests against the glass. Ensure that the wiper arm and blade is positioned as indicated in the accompanying illustration. If it is not, remove the wiper arm and reposition it.

8. Turn the wiper switch **ON** to check the wiper system operation. The wiper arms or blades should not contact any of the metal windshield trim or body work.

Windshield Wiper Motor

REMOVAL & INSTALLATION

▸ **See Figures 23 and 24**

❋ WARNING

The magnets used inside the windshield wiper motor are constructed of a ceramic material. Care must be taken when handling the motor to avoid dropping it or hitting it against a hard surface or object, to prevent breaking the magnets.

1. Disconnect the negative battery cable.
2. Remove the windshield wiper arms and blades.
3. Loosen the cowl vent screen retaining screws, then carefully pry up on the rear edge of the cowl vent screen to remove it from the cowl panel.
4. Remove the cowl top extension from the vehicle.
5. Detach the wiper motor link from the motor pivot shaft by disengaging the retaining clip.

6. Detach the linkage drive arm from the wiper motor.
7. Disengage the electrical wiring harness connector from the wiper motor.
8. Remove the mounting bolts, then lift the wiper motor up and through the cowl panel opening.

To install:

➡️**When installing the drive arm to a new wiper motor, follow the instructions provided with the new wiper motor.**

9. Position the wiper motor through the cowl panel opening and against the cowl panel, aligning the mounting bolt holes. Install and tighten the bolts to 115–150 inch lbs. (13–17 Nm).

10. Engage the electrical wiring harness connector in the wiper motor until the connector retaining tabs are fully seated.

11. Connect the negative battery cable.

12. Turn the wiper motor to the **LO** position and allow it to cycle for approximately 10–15 seconds, then turn it **OFF**. This will ensure that the motor is in the Park position.

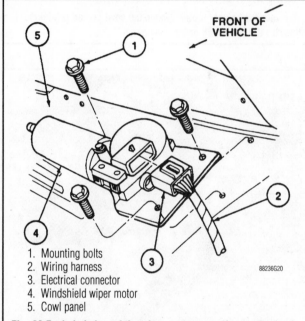

1. Mounting bolts
2. Wiring harness
3. Electrical connector
4. Windshield wiper motor
5. Cowl panel

Fig. 23 Exploded view of the wiper motor mounting on the cowl panel

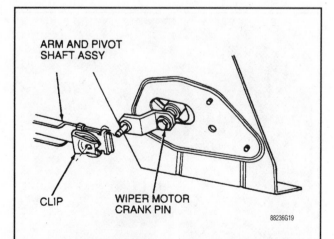

Fig. 24 The wiper linkage uses retaining clips to secure the various arms to their connections, as shown here with the pivot shaft and motor crank arm

To remove the wiper motor, loosen the cowl screen retainers, then lift the screen off of the cowl panel

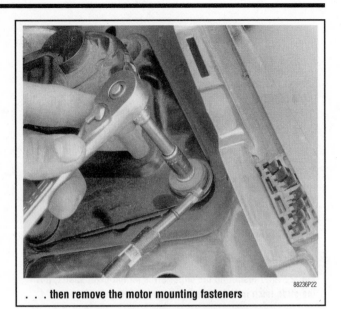

. . . then remove the motor mounting fasteners

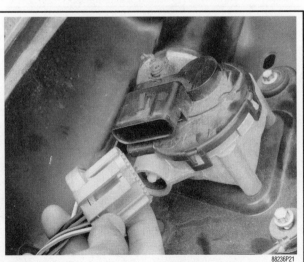

Loosen the fasteners, then remove the cowl extension

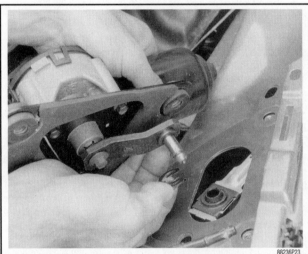

Lift the motor up slightly, then detach it from the linkage arm by removing the retaining clip

13. Install the linkage drive arm onto the wiper motor.

14. Attach the wiper motor link on the motor pivot shaft, and secure it in place with a retaining clip.

15. Install the cowl top extension, then install the cowl vent screen by aligning the retainer holes, installing the retainer screws, then tightening the retainer screws until the vent screen is securely held onto the cowl panel.

16. Install the wiper blades, making sure that they are positioned as shown in the accompanying illustration.

17. Turn the wiper switch to the **LO** and **HI** positions to ensure that the wipers are working properly.

Windshield Washer Motor

REMOVAL & INSTALLATION

◆ See Figures 25 and 26

1. Disconnect the wiring at the pump motor. Use a small prytool to unlock the connector tabs.

2. Detach the washer hose from the washer pump motor.

Disengage the wiring harness connector from the wiper motor . . .

3. Remove the left-hand front, inner fender splash shield.
4. Remove the reservoir attaching screws or nuts and lift the assembly from the vehicle.
5. Using a small prytool, pry out the motor retaining ring.
6. Using a pliers, grip one edge of the electrical connector ring and pull the motor, seal and impeller from the reservoir.

➡️**If the seal and impeller come apart from the motor, it can all be reassembled.**

To install:
7. Take the time to clean out the reservoir before installing the motor.

8. Coat the seal with a dry lubricant, such as powdered graphite or spray Teflon®. This will aid assembly.
9. Align the small projection on the motor end cap with the slot in the reservoir and install the motor so that the seal seats against the bottom of the motor cavity.
10. Press the retaining ring into position. A 1 in. (25mm), 12-point socket or length of 1 in. (25mm) tubing, will do nicely as an installation tool.
11. Install the reservoir and connect the wiring.

➡️**It's not a good idea to run a new motor without filling the reservoir first. Dry-running may damage a new motor.**

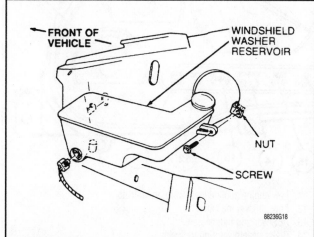

Fig. 25 To replace the washer pump motor, first remove the washer fluid reservoir from the inner fender apron in the engine compartment

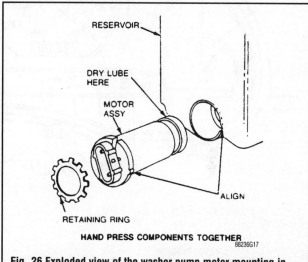

Fig. 26 Exploded view of the washer pump motor mounting in the bottom of the washer fluid reservoir

INSTRUMENTS AND SWITCHES

Precautions

Electronic modules, such as instrument clusters, powertrain controls and sound systems are sensitive to static electricity and can be damaged by static discharges which are below the levels that you can hear snap or detect on your skin. A detectable snap or shock of static electricity is in the 3,000 volt range. Some of these modules can be damaged by a charge of as little as 100 volts.

The following are some basic safeguards to avoid static electrical damage:
• Leave the replacement module in its original packing until you are ready to install it.
• Avoid touching the module connector pins.
• Avoid placing the module on a non-conductive surface.
• Use a commercially available static protection kit. These kits contain such things as grounding cords and conductive mats.

Instrument Cluster

✳️✳️ CAUTION

All models covered by this manual are equipped with a Supplemental Restraint System (SRS), which uses an air bag. Whenever working near any of the SRS components, such as the impact sensors, air bag module, steering column and instrument panel, disconnect the negative, then the positive battery cables and wait one minute. Disconnecting the battery cables and waiting one minute will allow any residual power in the system to drain. Failure to properly disconnect both battery cables may result in accidental air bag deployment, which could easily result in severe personal injury or death. Also, never attempt any electrical diagnosis or service to the SRS components and wiring; this work should only be performed by a qualified automotive technician.

REMOVAL & INSTALLATION

▶ **See Figures 27, 28 and 29 (p. 24–25)**

1. Disconnect the negative battery cable for safety purposes.
2. Pull the headlight switch knob to the **HEAD** position, then, reaching through the instrument panel opening, depress the headlight switch knob shaft release button and withdraw the knob and shaft from the headlight switch.
3. Remove the two upper retaining screws from the instrument cluster trim panel, then remove the trim panel.
4. Remove the four mounting screws from the instrument cluster, then pull the cluster out of its recess.
5. Detach the two wiring harness connectors from the receptacles in the cluster backplate.
6. Remove the instrument cluster from the instrument panel.

✳️✳️ WARNING

If the cluster is being removed with the intent of replacing one or more of the gauges, DO NOT remove the gauge pointers; the magnetic gauges cannot be recalibrated and would, therefore, need to be replaced.

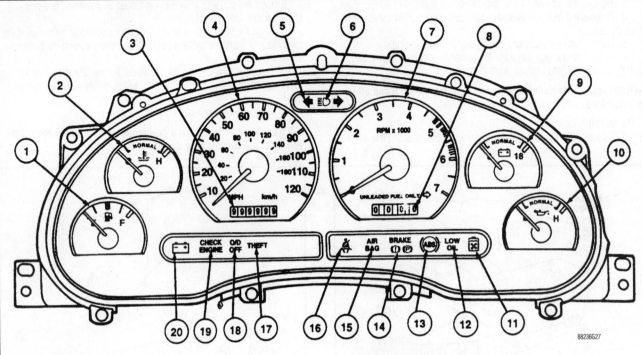

1. Fuel gauge
2. Engine coolant temperature gauge
3. Odometer
4. Speedometer
5. Turn signal/hazard indicator
6. High beam indicator
7. Tachometer
8. Trip odometer
9. Voltmeter
10. Oil pressure gauge
11. Low engine coolant level warning indicator
12. Low oil level indicator
13. ABS warning indicator
14. Brake system warning indicator
15. Air bag warning indicator
16. Safety belt warning indicator
17. Anti-theft indicator
18. Overdrive indicator (automatic transmissions)
19. Malfunction Indicator Lamp (MIL)
20. Charging system warning indicator

Fig. 27 Instrument gauge cluster component identification

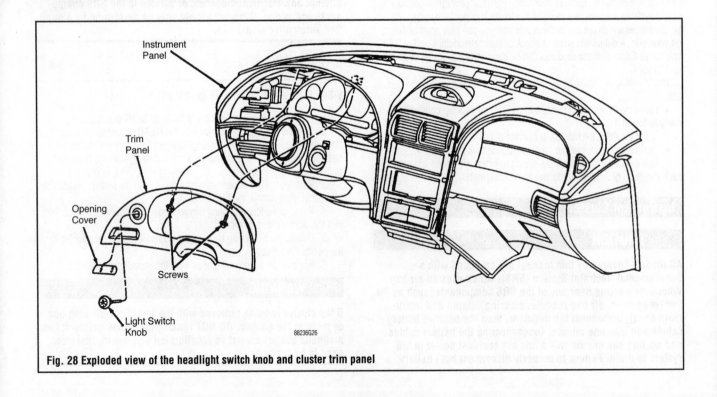

Fig. 28 Exploded view of the headlight switch knob and cluster trim panel

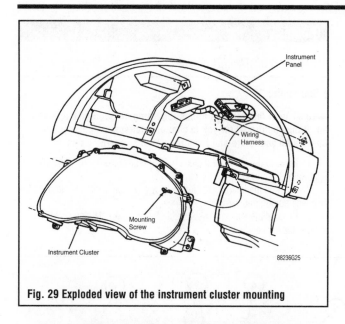

Fig. 29 Exploded view of the instrument cluster mounting

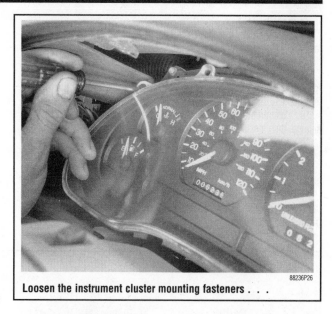

Loosen the instrument cluster mounting fasteners . . .

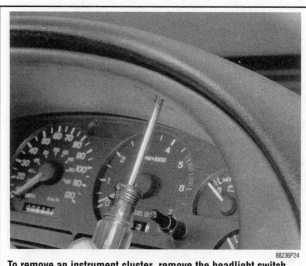

To remove an instrument cluster, remove the headlight switch knob and the trim panel retaining screws . . .

. . . and roll the cluster out of the instrument panel opening

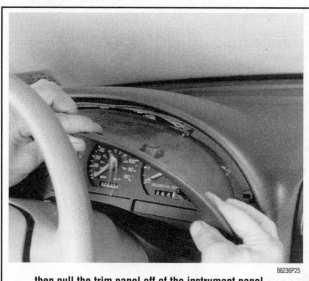

. . . then pull the trim panel off of the instrument panel

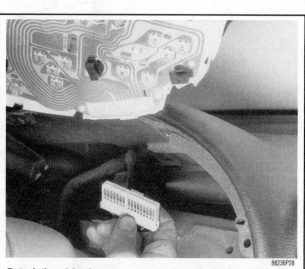

Detach the wiring harness connector from the back of the instrument cluster

To install:

7. Position the cluster in front of the instrument panel hole and reattach the two wiring harness connectors. Be sure that they are fully seated in their receptacles and that the retaining tabs are engaged.

8. Push the wiring harness up toward the top of the instrument cluster to avoid interference between it and the warning light bulbs or the tripmeter/odometer stepper motor.

9. Position the instrument cluster so that the mounting holes are aligned, then install the mounting screws and tighten them until snug.

10. Position the trim panel over the instrument cluster and install the two retaining screws.

11. Install the light switch knob, then connect the negative battery cable.

12. Turn the ignition to the **RUN** position to verify that all of the warning lights work properly. Then, road test the vehicle to ensure that all of the gauges are functioning

Gauges

REMOVAL & INSTALLATION

▶ **See Figure 30**

➡ **Because of federal regulations regarding mileage on the odometer, it may be illegal for you to change your speedometer yourself. Check with your state and local regulations regarding this.**

1. Remove the instrument cluster, then remove the instrument cluster light bulbs from the back of the cluster.

2. Position the instrument cluster on a workbench with the clear plastic face lens pointing upward.

3. Remove the lens and instrument cluster mask retaining screws, then remove the lens and mask from the cluster assembly.

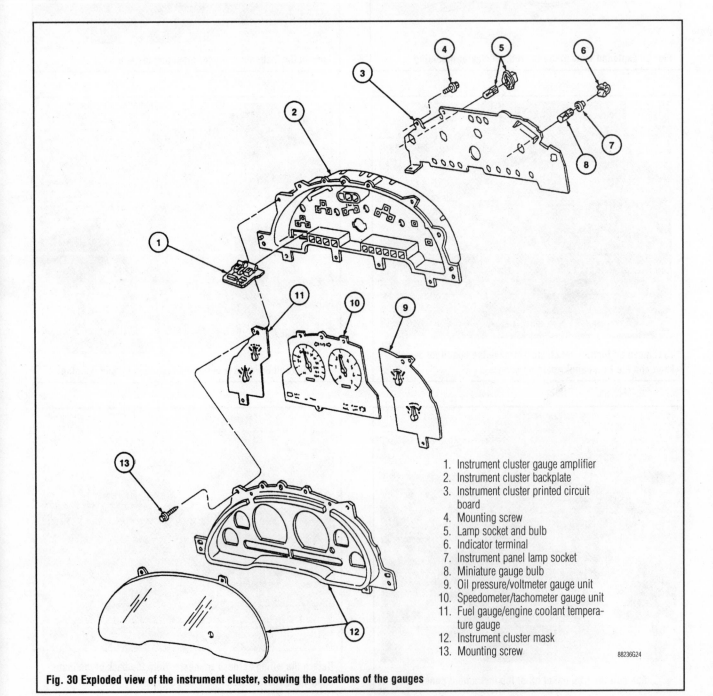

1. Instrument cluster gauge amplifier
2. Instrument cluster backplate
3. Instrument cluster printed circuit board
4. Mounting screw
5. Lamp socket and bulb
6. Indicator terminal
7. Instrument panel lamp socket
8. Miniature gauge bulb
9. Oil pressure/voltmeter gauge unit
10. Speedometer/tachometer gauge unit
11. Fuel gauge/engine coolant temperature gauge
12. Instrument cluster mask
13. Mounting screw

88236G24

Fig. 30 Exploded view of the instrument cluster, showing the locations of the gauges

Once the cluster is removed, the illumination gauge bulbs can be replaced with good ones, if necessary

➡**The fuel gauge/engine coolant temperature gauge and the instrument gauge amplifier are calibrated together and MUST be replaced as a single unit.**

4. Remove the fuel/engine coolant temperature gauge, the oil pressure gauge, the voltmeter, and the speedometer/tachometer from the cluster assembly housing.

5. Remove and discard all push-in connector cups and illumination bulbs from the back of the cluster assembly housing.

6. If replacing the fuel gauge/engine coolant temperature gauge, depress the connector tab, then slide the instrument gauge cluster amplifier/low coolant control module out.

7. If necessary, remove the printed circuit board from the instrument cluster.

To install:

8. Position the printed circuit board on the housing, ensuring that the alignment pins are properly inserted in the holes in the circuit board.

9. Insert the gauge amplifier/low coolant control module in the guides, align the terminals over the center of the circuit board connection, then press the amplifier/module into position until it clicks in place.

10. Install the instrument panel light bulbs and new snap-in connector clips.

11. Install the gauges into the assembly housing, then position the mask and instrument cluster lens on the housing. Install the retaining screws and tighten until snug.

12. Install the instrument cluster in the instrument panel.

Windshield Wiper Switch

REMOVAL & INSTALLATION

The windshield wiper switch is an integral part of the turn signal combination switch. Please refer to the Turn Signal (Combination) Switch procedure in Section 8 of this manual.

Headlight Switch

REMOVAL & INSTALLATION

➡**There are two possible ways to remove the headlight switch: the Ford recommended way and an alternative method.**

Recommended Method

◆ **See Figures 31 and 32**

1. Disconnect the negative battery cable for safety purposes.

2. Just below the headlight switch knob is a small access trim panel. Remove this panel to access the switch knob shaft release button.

3. Pull the headlight switch to the **HEAD** position, then, reaching through the instrument panel opening, depress the headlight switch knob shaft release button and withdraw the knob and shaft from the headlight switch.

4. Remove the two upper retaining screws from the instrument cluster trim panel, then the trim panel.

5. Remove the headlight retaining nut and pull the switch through the opening in the instrument panel bracket.

6. Disengage the wiring harness connector from the switch.

To install:

7. Attach the wiring harness connector to the headlight switch, then position the switch through the instrument panel opening.

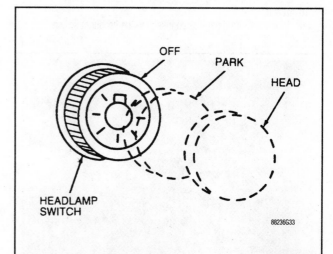

Fig. 31 Before removing the headlight switch knob, pull it out to the HEAD position

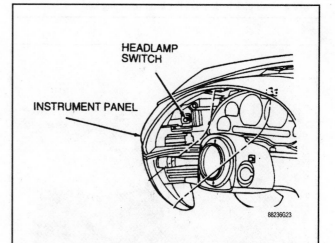

Fig. 32 The headlight switch is located to the left of the instrument cluster

8. Position the headlight switch so that the threaded portion projects through the mounting bracket, then install and tighten the retaining nut until it is snug.

9. Position the trim panel over the instrument cluster and install the two retaining screws.

10. Insert the light switch knob and shaft into the switch until it clicks in place, then connect the negative battery cable. Install the small trim panel just below the headlight switch knob.

11. Start the engine and check the function of the headlight switch.

Alternative Method

1. Disconnect the negative battery cable for safety purposes.
2. Use a small pick to disengage the knob from the switch shaft.
3. Remove the two upper retaining screws from the instrument cluster trim panel, then remove the trim panel.
4. Remove the two bracket fasteners and remove the switch from the opening.
5. Disengage the wiring harness connector from the switch.

To install:
6. Attach the wiring harness connector to the headlight switch.

Remove the instrument cluster trim panel retaining screws . . .

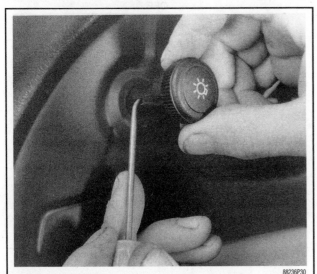
Use a small pick to depress the knob retaining tabs . . .

. . . then pull the trim panel off of the instrument panel

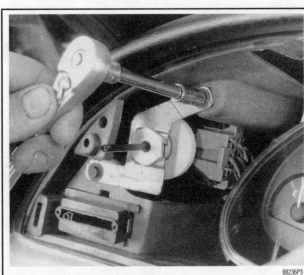
. . . then pull the knob off of the switch shaft

Remove the two headlight switch bracket retaining screws . . .

. . . then pull the switch out and disengage the wiring harness connector retaining tabs

Pull the wiring harness connector out of the headlight switch—alternative method shown

7. Position the switch and bracket to align the mounting holes, and install the mounting fasteners.

8. Position the trim panel over the instrument cluster and install the two retaining screws.

9. Push the switch knob onto the shaft until fully seated, then connect the negative battery cable.

10. Start the engine and check the function of the headlight switch.

LIGHTING

Headlights

REMOVAL & INSTALLATION

♦ See Figure 33

❋❋ WARNING

Don't remove the old bulb until you are ready to immediately replace it! Leaving the headlamp assembly open, without a bulb, will allow foreign matter such as water, dirt, leaves, oil, etc. to enter the housing. This type of contamination will cut down on the amount and direction of light emitted, and eventually cause premature blow-out of the bulb.

➡**A properly aimed headlamp should not need re-aiming after removing and installing the headlight bulb.**

1. Make sure that the headlight switch is **OFF**.

2. Raise the hood, then remove the cover from the rear of the headlamp assembly as follows:

a. Loosen and remove the hold-down plastic finger screws from the cover.

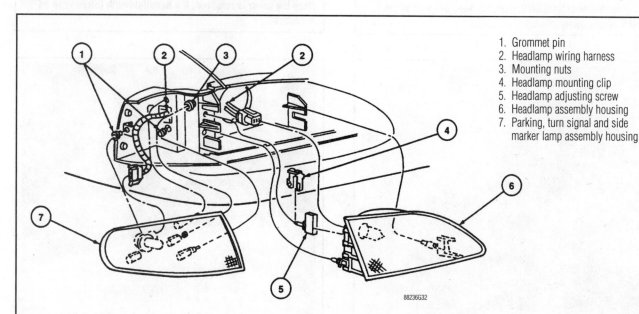

1. Grommet pin
2. Headlamp wiring harness
3. Mounting nuts
4. Headlamp mounting clip
5. Headlamp adjusting screw
6. Headlamp assembly housing
7. Parking, turn signal and side marker lamp assembly housing

Fig. 33 Exploded view of the front headlamp and side marker/parking/turn signal lamp assemblies

b. Lift the cover off of the headlamp assembly.

3. Remove the bulb and socket from the headlamp assembly by loosening the plastic retaining sleeve and pulling the socket out of the back of the headlamp housing.

4. Disconnect the wiring by disengaging the retaining tab(s), grasping the connector and pulling it firmly out of the socket.

✳✳ WARNING

The headlamp bulb contains high pressure halogen gas. The bulb may shatter if scratched or dropped! Hold the bulb by its plastic base only. If you touch the glass portion with your fingers, or if any dirt or oily deposits are found on the glass, it must be wiped clean with an alcohol soaked paper towel. Even the oil from your skin will cause the bulb to burn out prematurely due to hot-spotting.

5. Rotate the bulb retaining ring counterclockwise (rear view) about ⅛ turn and slide it off the bulb base. Don't lose it; it's re-usable.

To install:

6. Install the plastic retaining ring on the new headlight bulb, then engage the wiring harness connector to the headlight bulb socket.

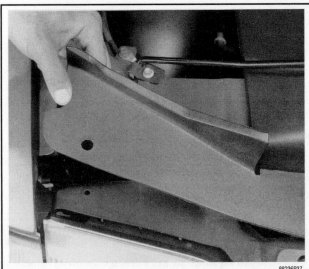

Remove the headlight bulb cover   88236P37

To remove the headlight bulb, open the hood and loosen the cover's plastic finger screws . . .   88236P35

Once the cover is removed, the headlight bulb (arrow) can be accessed   88236P38

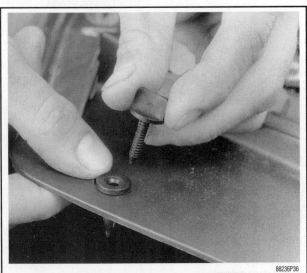

. . . then remove the screws and lift up the cover   88236P36

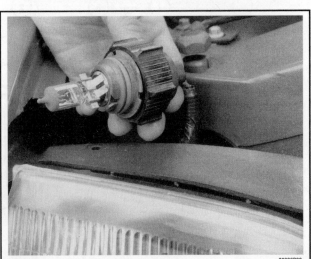

Remove the bulb and socket assembly from the headlamp housing . . .   88236P39

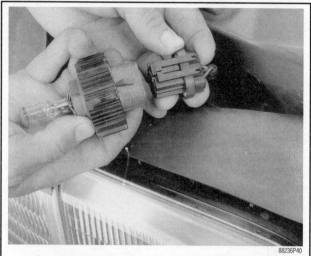

. . . then disengage the wiring harness connector from the bulb's socket

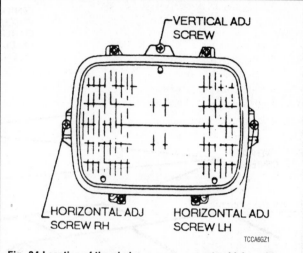

Fig. 34 Location of the aiming screws on most vehicles with sealed beam headlights

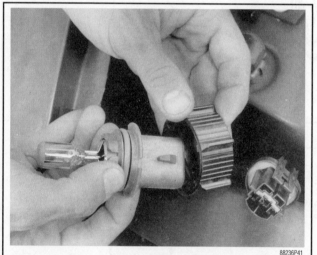

Remove the plastic retaining ring from the old bulb—it is reusable

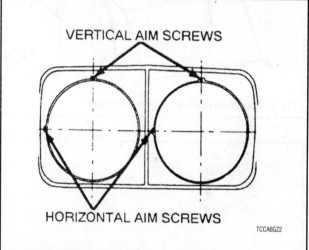

Fig. 35 Dual headlight adjustment screw locations—one side shown here (other side should be mirror image)

7. Insert the headlight bulb into the headlamp housing with the flat side of the bulb base facing upward. You may have to turn the bulb slightly to align the locating tabs. Once aligned, push the bulb firmly into place until the bulb base contacts the mounting flange in the socket.

8. Push the retaining ring against the mounting flange and rotate it clockwise to lock it. It should lock against a definite stop when fully engaged.

9. Turn the headlights **ON** to check that the new bulb functions properly. If it does not, determine the source of the problem (defective bulb, dirty socket, faulty wiring, blown fuse, etc.) and correct the situation.

10. Position the headlamp cover in place and install the hold-down retainers until snug.

11. Close the hood.

AIMING

▶ **See Figures 34, 35, 36, 37 and 38**

The headlights must be properly aimed to provide the best, safest road illumination. The lights should be checked for proper aim and adjusted as necessary. Certain state and local authorities have requirements for headlight aiming; these should be checked before adjustment is made.

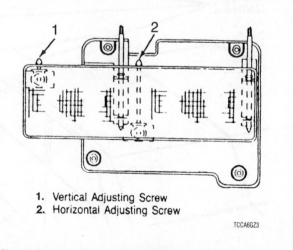

1. Vertical Adjusting Screw
2. Horizontal Adjusting Screw

Fig. 36 Example of headlight adjustment screw location for composite headlamps

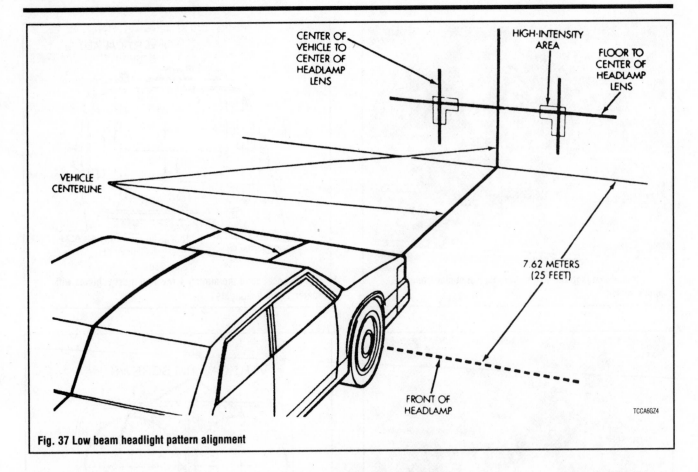

Fig. 37 Low beam headlight pattern alignment

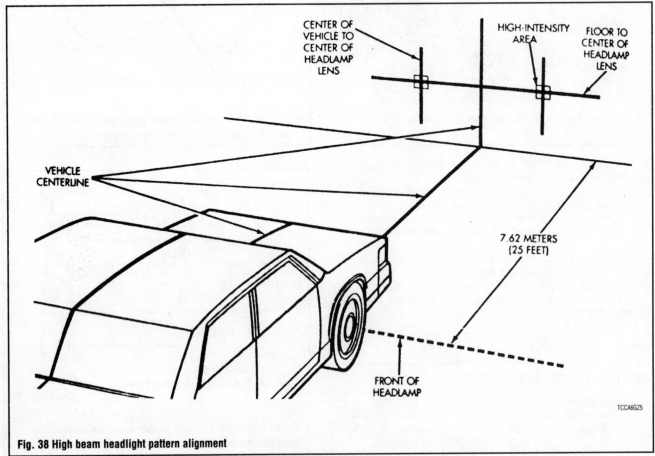

Fig. 38 High beam headlight pattern alignment

About once a year, when the headlights are replaced or any time front end work is performed on your vehicle, the headlights should be accurately aimed by a reputable repair shop using the proper equipment. Headlights not properly aimed can make it virtually impossible to see and may blind other drivers on the road, possibly causing an accident. Note that the following procedure is a temporary fix, until you can take your vehicle to a repair shop for a proper adjustment.

Headlight adjustment may be temporarily made using a wall, as described below, or on the rear of another vehicle. When adjusted, the lights should not glare in oncoming car or truck windshields, nor should they illuminate the passenger compartment of vehicles driving in front of you. These adjustments are rough and should always be fine-tuned by a repair shop which is equipped with headlight aiming tools. Improper adjustments may be both dangerous and illegal.

For most of the vehicles covered by this manual, horizontal and vertical aiming of each sealed beam unit is provided by two adjusting screws which move the retaining ring and adjusting plate against the tension of a coil spring. There is no adjustment for focus; this is done during headlight manufacturing.

➡**Because the composite headlight assembly is bolted into position, no adjustment should be necessary or possible. Some applications, however, may be bolted to an adjuster plate or may be retained by adjusting screws. If so, follow this procedure when adjusting the lights, BUT always have the adjustment checked by a reputable shop.**

Before removing the headlight bulb or disturbing the headlamp in any way, note the current settings in order to ease headlight adjustment upon reassembly. If the high or low beam setting of the old lamp still works, this can be done using the wall of a garage or a building:

1. Park the vehicle on a level surface, with the fuel tank about ½ full and with the vehicle empty of all extra cargo (unless normally carried). The vehicle should be facing a wall which is no less than 6 feet (1.8m) high and 12 feet (3.7m) wide. The front of the vehicle should be about 25 feet (7.6m) from the wall.

2. If aiming is to be performed outdoors, it is advisable to wait until dusk in order to properly see the headlight beams on the wall. If done in a garage, darken the area around the wall as much as possible by closing shades or hanging cloth over the windows.

3. Turn the headlights **ON** and mark the wall at the center of each light's low beam, then switch on the brights and mark the center of each light's high beam. A short length of masking tape which is visible from the front of the vehicle may be used. Although marking all four positions is advisable, marking one position from each light should be sufficient.

4. If neither beam on one side is working, and if another like-sized vehicle is available, park the second one in the exact spot where the vehicle was and mark the beams using the same-side light. Then switch the vehicles so the one to be aimed is back in the original spot. It must be parked no closer to or farther away from the wall than the second vehicle.

5. Perform any necessary repairs, but make sure the vehicle is not moved, or is returned to the exact spot from which the lights were marked. Turn the headlights **ON** and adjust the beams to match the marks on the wall.

6. Have the headlight adjustment checked as soon as possible by a reputable repair shop.

Signal and Marker Lights

REMOVAL & INSTALLATION

Front Turn Signal, Parking and Side Marker Lights

Don't remove the old bulb until you are ready to immediately replace it! Leaving the lamp assembly open, without a bulb,

will allow foreign matter such as water, dirt, leaves, oil, etc. to enter the housing. This type of contamination will cut down on the amount and direction of light emitted, and eventually cause premature blow-out of the bulb.

1. Make sure that the headlight switch is **OFF**.
2. Raise the hood, then remove the cover from the rear of the headlamp assembly as follows:
   a. Loosen and remove the hold-down plastic finger screws from the cover.
   b. Lift the cover off of the headlamp assembly.
3. Remove the turn signal housing retaining nuts, then carefully pull the housing away from the body.
4. If extra clearance is needed, disengage the wiring harness connectors from the backside of the turn signal housing.
5. Grasp the light bulb socket and turn it ⅛ to ¼ turn counterclockwise to disengage the locking tabs from the turn signal housing, then withdrawal the bulb and socket together from the housing.
6. Gently pull the bulb out of the bulb socket.

To install:
7. Prior to installation, ensure that the light bulb contacts in the socket are clean and free of corrosion.

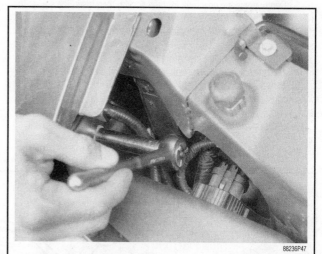

To remove the front turn signal light, remove the plastic cover and loosen the retaining nuts . . .

88236P47

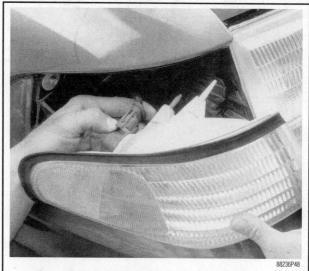

. . . then pull the lamp assembly out from the body

88236P48

Remove the socket from the lamp assembly, then pull the bulb out of the socket

8. Gently press the new bulb into the socket, then insert the socket in the housing and lock it in place by turning it ⅛ to ¼ turn clockwise. Be sure that the socket terminal connector faces the same direction as it did before removal.

9. If disengaged, insert the wiring harness connector into the bulb socket and press it in until the retaining tabs are fully engaged.

10. Turn the lights on to check that the new bulb functions properly. If it does not, determine the source of the problem (defective bulb, dirty socket, faulty wiring, blown fuse, etc.) and correct the situation.

11. Position the lamp housing against the body and install the retaining nuts until secure.

12. Position the headlamp cover in place and install the hold-down retainers until snug.

13. Close the hood.

Rear Turn Signal, Brake and Parking Lights

♦ See Figure 39

1. Open the trunk and remove the luggage compartment rear trim panel to gain access to the rear lamp housing retaining nuts.

2. Remove the rear lamp housing retaining nuts, then carefully pull the housing away from the body.

3. If extra clearance is necessary for bulb removal, disengage the wiring harness connectors from the backside of the turn signal housing.

4. Grasp the light bulb socket and turn it ⅛ to ¼ turn counterclockwise to disengage the locking tabs from the turn signal housing, then withdraw the bulb and socket together from the housing.

5. Gently pull the bulb out of the bulb socket.

To install:

6. Prior to installation, ensure that the light bulb contacts in the socket are clean and free of corrosion.

7. Gently press the new bulb into the socket, then insert the socket in the housing and lock it in place by turning it ⅛ to ¼ turn clockwise. Be sure that the socket terminal connector faces the same direction as it did before removal.

8. If disengaged, insert the wiring harness connector into the bulb socket and press it in until the retaining tabs are fully engaged.

9. Turn the lights on to check that the new bulb functions properly. If it does not, determine the source of the problem (defective bulb, dirty socket, faulty wiring, blown fuse, etc.) and correct the situation.

10. Position the lamp housing against the body and install the retaining nuts until secure.

11. Install the luggage compartment rear trim panel in place.

12. Close the trunk.

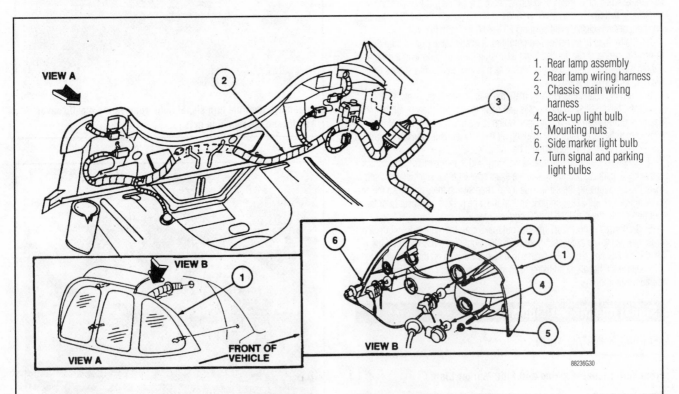

1. Rear lamp assembly
2. Rear lamp wiring harness
3. Chassis main wiring harness
4. Back-up light bulb
5. Mounting nuts
6. Side marker light bulb
7. Turn signal and parking light bulbs

Fig. 39 Exploded view of the rear brake/turn signal/parking/side marker lamp assembly

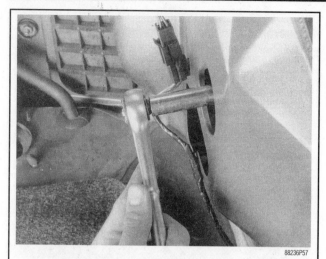

To remove the rear lights, remove the trunk trim panel, then remove the lamp housing retaining nuts

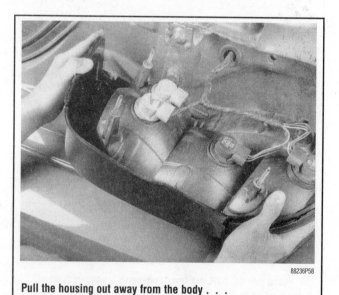

Pull the housing out away from the body . . .

Remove the bulb and socket from the lamp housing by rotating it ⅛ to ¼ turn counterclockwise . . .

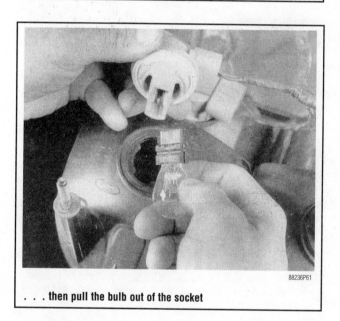

. . . then pull the bulb out of the socket

High-Mounted Brake Light

◆ **See Figure 40**

1. Open the trunk lid.
2. Disengage the wiring harness connector from the high-mounted brake lamp housing.
3. Remove the lamp housing retaining fasteners, then remove the housing from the trunk lid.
4. Remove the light bulb(s) from the housing.
To install:
5. Install the light bulb(s) in the lamp housing.
6. Turn the lights on to check that the new bulb functions properly. If it does not, determine the source of the problem (defective bulb, dirty socket, faulty wiring, blown fuse, etc.) and correct the situation.
7. Position the lamp assembly against the inside of the trunk lid, then install the retaining screws. Tighten the retaining screws until secure.
8. Engage the wiring harness connector to the lamp housing.
9. Close the trunk lid.

. . . and you can rest it on the bumper while removing the bulb(s)

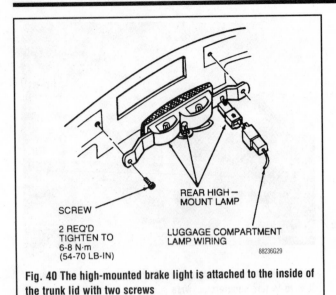

Fig. 40 The high-mounted brake light is attached to the inside of the trunk lid with two screws

Dome/Map Lights

♦ See Figure 41

1. Using a thin-bladed prytool, remove the lens from the dome/map lamp housing.

2. To remove the dome light bulb, pull the bulb out from between the two terminals.

3. To remove the map lights, perform the following:

   a. Remove the three housing retaining screws, then lower the housing.

   b. Detach the wiring harness connector from the housing.

   c. Remove the small metal reflector, then pull the bulb out from between the terminals.

To install:

➡ Prior to installation, ensure that the electrical terminals are clean and free of corrosion.

4. Install the map light bulb(s) as follows:

   a. Gently press the bulb(s) in the housing so that the metal ends are between the terminals. Turn the lights on to check that the new bulb functions properly. If it does not, determine the source of the problem (defective bulb, dirty socket, faulty wiring, blown fuse, etc.) and correct the situation.

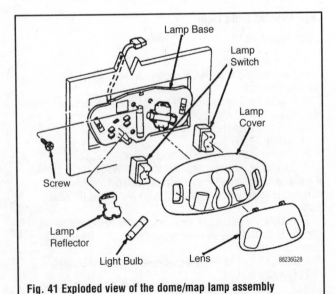

Fig. 41 Exploded view of the dome/map lamp assembly

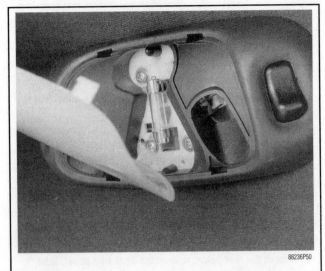

To remove the dome light bulb, first remove the lens cover . . .

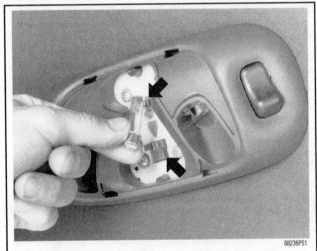

. . . then pull the bulb out from between the electrical terminals (arrows)

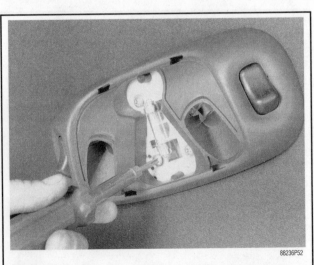

To access the map light bulbs, remove the lens cover and the retaining screws . . .

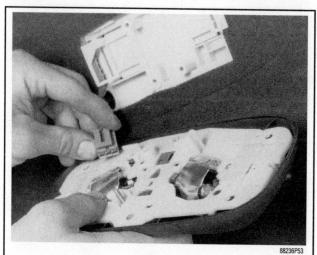

. . . then lower the lamp housing and detach the wiring harness connector

The small metal reflector (arrow) must be removed to access the bulb

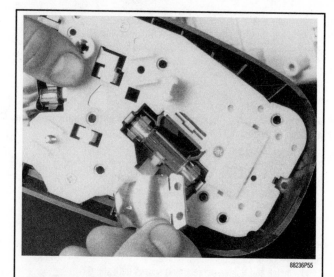

Unclip the reflector from above the bulb and remove it . . .

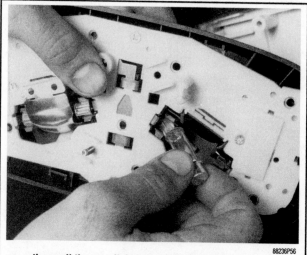

. . . then pull the map light bulb out from between the terminals

b. Install the metal reflector(s).

c. Position the lamp housing against the trim panel, then install the three retaining screws and tighten them until snug.

5. Install the dome light bulb by gently pressing the bulb in the housing so that the light bulb's metal ends are between the terminals. Turn the lights on to check that the new bulb functions properly. If it does not, determine the source of the problem (defective bulb, dirty socket, faulty wiring, blown fuse, etc.) and correct the situation.

6. Install the lens cover onto the housing until all retaining tabs are properly engaged.

License Plate Lights

▶ See Figure 42

1. For better access, open the trunk lid.

2. Remove the license plate lamp housing retaining screws. It may be easier to completely remove them if you can apply pressure to the plastic screw anchors.

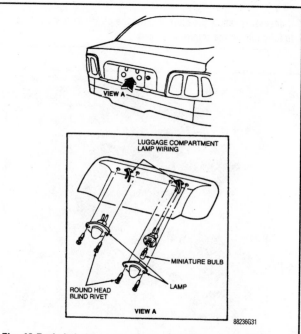

Fig. 42 Exploded view of the license plate lamp assemblies

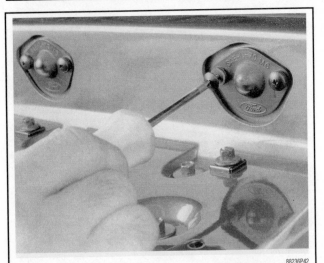

To remove the license plate bulbs, loosen the retaining screws

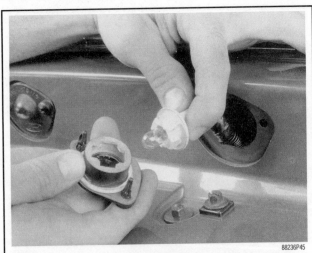

. . . then remove the light bulb and socket assembly by twisting it ⅛ turn counterclockwise

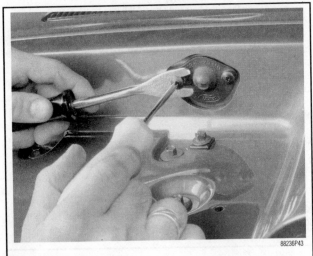

If necessary, apply pressure against the plastic screw anchors to fully loosen the retaining screws

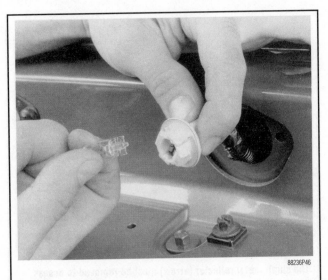

Carefully pull the bulb out of the socket

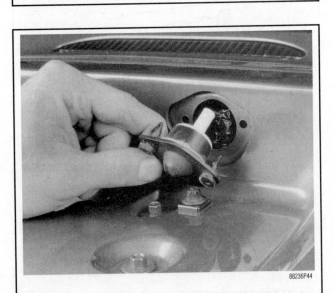

Pull the license plate lamp assembly free of the trunk lid . . .

3. Pull the lamp assembly off of the trunk lid.

4. Grasp the bulb socket and twist it ⅛ turn counterclockwise to disengage the retaining tabs, the pull it free of the lamp housing.

5. Gently pull the light bulb out of the socket.

6. If necessary, remove the other license plate light in the same manner.

To install:

➡ Prior to installation, ensure that the electrical terminals are clean and free of corrosion.

7. Insert the bulb into the socket until it is fully seated.

8. Install the bulb and socket assembly into the lamp housing, then lock it in place by twisting the socket ⅛ turn clockwise.

9. Turn the lights on to check that the new bulb functions properly. If it does not, determine the source of the problem (defective bulb, dirty socket, faulty wiring, blown fuse, etc.) and correct the situation.

10. Position the lamp housing against the trunk lid, making sure that the plastic screw anchors are properly inserted through the two small holes on either side of the larger housing hole.

11. Install and tighten the retaining screws until snug.

12. Close the trunk lid.

Fog/Driving Lights

REMOVAL & INSTALLATION

Except Cobra Models

> ※※ **WARNING**
>
> **DO NOT touch the new bulb with bare hands. The stains will cause contamination of the quartz which may result in early failure of the light. Do not remove the protective plastic sleeve until the light is inserted into the socket. Ensure that the circuit is not energized. If the quartz was inadvertently handled, it should be cleaned with a clean cloth moistened with alcohol before installation.**

1. Lift up on the lens assembly retaining tab securing the lens assembly to the light housing. Use caution to avoid dropping the lens.
2. Remove the lens assembly from the light housing and turn it to gain access to the rear of the light body.
3. Unplug the bulb wire lead from the pigtail connector.
4. Release the bulb socket retainer from the locking tab.
5. Remove the bulb and socket assembly from the light body and pull the bulb directly out of the socket.

To install:

6. Insert the new bulb into the lens assembly and secure it with the retainer. Connect the wire lead to the pigtail connector.
7. Turn the lights on to check that the new bulb functions properly. If it does not, determine the source of the problem (defective bulb, dirty socket, faulty wiring, blown fuse, etc.) and correct the situation.
8. Position the lens assembly right side up (as indicated on the lens) into the light housing.

➡ **There is a vertical tab on the bottom of the housing.**

9. Secure the lens assembly to the light housing with the retaining tab.

Cobra Models

1. Disengage the electrical wiring harness connector from the backside of the lamp assembly.
2. Remove the light bulb from the fog light housing by twisting it counterclockwise until it is disengaged, then pull it out of the housing.

To install:

3. Insert the new bulb into the light housing and twist it clockwise to lock it in place.
4. Attach the wiring harness connector to the backside of the housing.
5. Test the lights for proper operation. If the bulb does not function properly, determine the source of the problem (defective bulb, dirty socket, faulty steering, blown fuse, etc.) and correct the situation.

TRAILER WIRING

Wiring the vehicle for towing is fairly easy. There are a number of good wiring kits available and these should be used, rather than trying to design your own.

All trailers will need brake lights and turn signals, as well as tail lights and side marker lights. Most areas require extra marker lights for overwide trailers. Also, most areas have recently required back-up lights for trailers, and most trailer manufacturers have been building trailers with back-up lights for several years.

Additionally, some Class I, most Class II and just about all Class III trailers will have electric brakes. Add to this number an accessories wire, to operate trailer internal equipment or to charge the trailer's battery, and you can have as many as seven wires in the harness.

Determine the equipment on your trailer and buy the wiring kit necessary. The kit will contain all the wires needed, plus a plug adapter set which includes the female plug, mounted on the bumper or hitch, and the male plug, wired into, or plugged into the trailer harness.

When installing the kit, follow the manufacturer's instructions. The color coding of the wires is usually standard throughout the industry. One point to note: some domestic vehicles, and most imported vehicles, have separate turn signals. On most domestic vehicles, however, the brake lights and rear turn signals operate with the same bulb. For those vehicles without separate turn signals, you can purchase and install an isolation unit, so that the brake lights won't blink whenever the turn signals are operated. The isolation units are simple and quick to install.

One final point—the best kits are those with a spring loaded cover on the vehicle mounted socket. This cover prevents dirt and moisture from corroding the terminals. Never let the vehicle socket hang loosely; always mount it securely to the bumper or hitch.

CIRCUIT PROTECTION

Fuses

REPLACEMENT

♦ **See Figure 43**

The 1994–98 Mustang vehicles are equipped with two fuse boxes, or locations: the fuse junction panel and the power distribution box.

The fuse junction panel is located under the left-hand side of the instrument panel and is an integral part of the chassis wiring harness. The fuse junction panel contains only some of the fuses and circuit breakers for the vehicle.

The other location for fuses and relays is the power distribution box, which is located in the engine compartment on the left-hand, front fender apron. This box contains the high power fuses and was designed to take the place of most of the fusible links.

To replace a blown fuse, perform the following:

> ※※ **WARNING**
>
> **Always disconnect the negative battery cable before removing or servicing the fuses, relays or fusible links. Otherwise, component damage may result.**

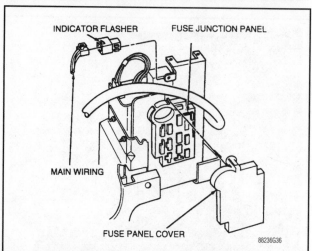

88236G36

Fig. 43 The indicator flasher and fuse junction panel are located under the left-hand side of the instrument panel, to the left of the steering column

1. Disconnect the negative battery cable.

➡ **The fuse junction panel cover is equipped with extra fuses and a fuse removal tool.**

2. Remove the cover from the appropriate fuse box (junction panel or power distribution box).

3. Using your fingers or a fuse removal tool, pull the bad fuse out of its electrical terminals.

To install:

❊❊ WARNING

Always be sure of the fuse rating of the fuse you are replacing. Component damage or, perhaps, a car fire may result from installing an improper fuse. Refer to your owner's manual for the proper fuse ratings, or look at the fuse you are removing.

4. Insert a new fuse into the fuse block. Ensure that it is fully seated between the electrical terminals.

5. Install the fuse box cover.

6. Connect the negative battery cable. If the fuse blows again, there is a problem somewhere in your vehicle's wiring. Have the wiring harness inspected or inspect it yourself for problems.

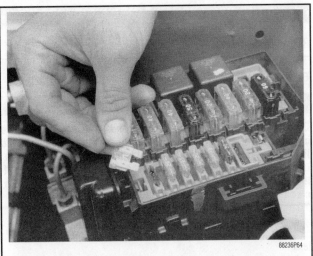

To remove a fuse, you can use a fuse puller, or simply pull it out of the distribution box with your fingers

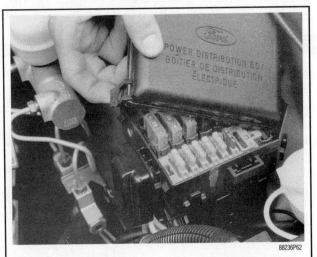

To access the fuses in the power distribution box, remove the panel cover

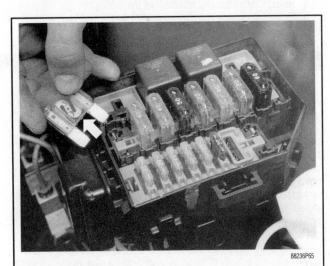

Note that when the metal strip (arrow) in the fuse is not broken or burned, the fuse is okay

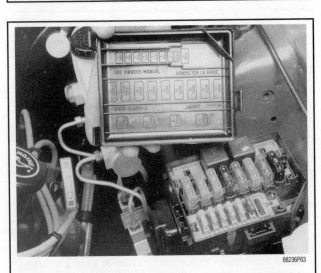

Note that the identification of the fuses and relays is embossed into the power distribution box cover

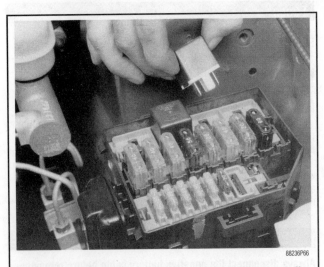

The relays can be removed by pulling them out of the power distribution box as well

To access fuses in the junction panel, remove the lower trim panels and the junction panel cover

The fuse junction panel cover is equipped with a few spare fuses and a fuse removal tool (arrow)

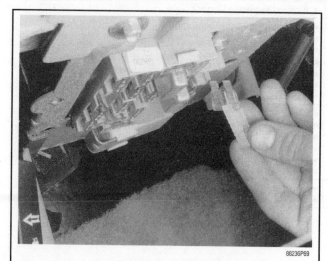

Use the fuse removal tool like a pair of tweezers to grasp the fuse and pull it out of the junction panel

Fusible Links

The fusible link is a short length of special, Hypalon (high temperature) insulated wire, integral with the engine compartment wiring harness, and should not be confused with standard wire. It is several wire gauges smaller than the circuit which it protects. Under no circumstances should a fusible link replacement repair be made using a length of standard wire cut from bulk stock or from another wiring harness.

The 1994–95 models utilize fusible links to protect three circuits: the heated back window circuit, the load circuit, and the engine compartment lamp circuit. The heated back window fusible link is located in the engine compartment, whereas the other two are located in their respective circuits.

In 1996–98 models, there are generally two fusible links between the power distribution box and the alternator/voltage regulator. They are both 16 gauge and are designed to burn through in the event that a short to ground occurs in the wiring harness, or if a booster battery is incorrectly connected to your vehicle.

➡**Do not mistake a resistor wire for a fusible link. The resistor wire is generally longer and has print stating, "Resistor: don't cut or splice."**

Circuit Breakers

RESETTING

The 1994–95 models utilize circuit breakers to protect three circuits: the headlamps and high beam indicator circuit (20 amps); the power windows, power seat, and power door lock circuit (20 amps); and the convertible top (if equipped) circuit (25 amps). The headlamp and high beam indicator circuit breaker is an integral part of the headlight switch; if it becomes faulty, the entire switch must be replaced. The power window/seat/lock circuit breaker is located near the starter motor relay. The convertible top circuit breaker is located in the fuse junction panel, under the left-hand side of the instrument panel.

The 1996–98 models only utilize the headlamp and high beam indicator circuit breaker, which is still an integral part of the headlight switch.

All of these circuit breakers are self-resetting and do not need to be manually reset. If the breakers do not reset themselves, they must be replaced with new ones.

Flashers

REPLACEMENT

The 1994–98 models only use one flasher, which is an electronic solid-state indicator flasher for the turn signals and hazard lights. The electronic solid-state construction eliminates electronic interference and heat associated with the thermo-electric flashers used on earlier models.

The flasher is located in the fuse junction panel, under the left-hand side of the instrument panel.

To replace the flasher unit, perform the following:
1. Disconnect the negative battery cable.
2. Remove the fuse junction panel cover.
3. Pull the indicator flasher straight out from the fuse junction panel.

To install:
4. Align the indicator flasher with the fuse junction panel and press it into place until it is fully seated.
5. Install the fuse junction panel cover.
6. Connect the negative battery cable.

Fuse Function Panel Fuse Identification—1994 Models

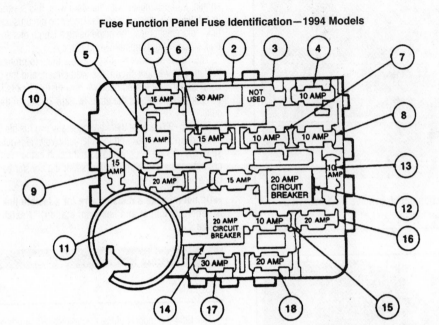

Cavity Number	Fuse Rating	Color	Circuit Protected
1	15 Amp	Light Blue	• Turn Signal Lamps • Turn Signal Cluster Indicator Lamp • Back Up Lamps • Air Bag Diagnostic Monitor • DRL Module, IGN Power • Illuminated Entry Actuator Shut Off Power • Heated Back Window Control Relay Coil in Switch • Convertible Top Relay Coil • Heated Back Window Defrost Relay Coil in Switch • Transmission Control Switch • Brakeshift Interlock Signal Feed
2	30 Amp	Light Green	• Windshield Wiper—High • Washer Pump
3	—	—	Not Used
4	10 Amp	Red	• Air Bag Diagnostic Monitor
5	15 Amp	Light Blue	• Warning Chime (Headlamp On) • Clock • Front Park Lamps • Rear Tail Lamps • License Plate Lamps • Rear Side Marker Lamps • Fuse 13
6	15 Amp	Light Blue	• Clock—Display • Speed Control Amplifier • Warning Chime Module • A/C Clutch Coil • Door Lock Control Processor • Anti-Theft Alarm Control
7	10 Amp	Red	• Anti-Lock Brake Control Module • Low Oil Relay

88236G38

Fuse Function Panel Fuse Identification (continued)—1994 Models

Cavity Number	Fuse Rating	Color	Circuit Protected
8	10 Amp	Red	• Power Mirror Motor • Radio Memory • Courtesy Lamp Switch (Door Open Signal) • Clock Operation • Door Lock Control Processor Battery Save/Power • Dome Lamp • Map Lamp • Luggage Compartment Door Lamp • Visor Vanity Lamps • Engine Compartment Lamp • Glove Compartment Lamp • Warning Chime (Key-In/Headlamp On)
9	15 Amp	Light Blue	• Hazard Lamps-Front • Hazard Lamps-Rear • Hazard Cluster Indicator Lamps • Stop Lamps • High Mount Rear Lamp • Brakeshift Interlock Solenoid
10	20 Amp	Yellow	HO2S Sensors (5.0L)
11	15 Amp	Light Blue	Radio
12	20 Amp C.B.	—	• Luggage Compartment Door Remote Control • Door Lock Control Processor • Power Door Locks
13	10 Amp	Red	• Clock Illumination • Radio Illumination • Heated Back Window Switch—Illumination • Instrument Cluster Illumination • A/C Heater Control Illumination • Transmission Range Indicator Lamp Illumination • Ash Receptacle Lamp Illumination • Fog Lamp Switch—Illumination
14	20 Amp C.B.	—	Power Windows
15	10 Amp	Red	• Air Bag Indicator Lamp • Air Bag Diagnostic Monitor • Low Oil Relay • Fuel Gauge • Temperature Gauge • Instrument Gauge Amplifier Module • Transmission Control Indicator Lamp • Malfunction Indicator (Check Engine) Lamp • Speedometer • Anti-Theft Lamp • Gauge • Oil Gauge • Low Oil Level Lamp (5.0L) • Tachometer • Anti-Lock Brake Indicator Lamp • Parking Brake Lamp • Low Coolant Lamp (5.0L) • Low Coolant Switch (5.0L) • Seatbelt Warning Lamp/Chime
16	20 Amp	Yellow	• Headlamp Flash-to-Pass • Anti-Theft Alarm Control Module
17	30 Amp	Light Green	AC—Heater Blower Motor

88236G39

Fuse Function Panel Fuse Identification (continued)—1994 Models

Cavity Number	Fuse Rating	Color	Circuit Protected
18	20 Amp	Yellow	3.8L • CCRM Power • Ignition Coil • Charging System Warning Lamp • Regulator Signal 5.0L • CCRM Power • Ignition Coil • Charging System Warning Lamp • Transmission Control Switch Module (5.0L) • Ignition Control Module (5.0L) • Regulator Signal

88236G40

Fuse Junction Panel Fuse Identification—1995 Models

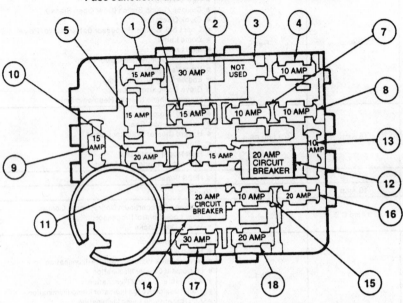

Cavity Number	Fuse Rating	Circuit Protected
1	15 Amp	Turn Signal Lamps, Turn Signal Cluster Indicator Lamp, Back Up Lamps, Air Bag Diagnostic Monitor, DRL Module, IGN Power, Illuminated Entry Actuator Shut Off Power, Heated Back Window Control Relay Coil in Switch, Convertible Top Relay Coil, Heated Back Window Defrost Relay Coil in Switch, Transmission Control Switch, Brakeshift Interlock Signal Feed.
2	30 Amp	Windshield Wiper—High, Washer Pump.
3	—	Not Used
4	10 Amp	Air Bag Diagnostic Monitor
5	15 Amp	Warning Chime (Headlamp On), Clock, Front Park Lamps, Rear Tail Lamps, License Plate Lamps, Rear Side Marker Lamps, Fuse 13.
6	15 Amp	Clock—Display, Speed Control Amplifier, Warning Chime Module, A/C Clutch Coil, Door Lock Control Processor, Anti-Theft Alarm Control.
7	10 Amp	Anti-Lock Brake Control Module, Low Oil Relay.
8	10 Amp	Power Mirror Motor, Radio Memory, Courtesy Lamp Switch (Door Open Signal), Clock Operation, Door Lock Control Processor Battery Save/Power, Dome Lamp, Map Lamp, Luggage Compartment Door Lamp, Visor Vanity Lamps, Engine Compartment Lamp, Glove Compartment Lamp, Warning Chime (Key-In/Headlamp On).
9	15 Amp	Hazard Lamps-Front, Hazard Lamps-Rear, Hazard Cluster Indicator Lamps, Stop Lights, High Mount Rear Lamp, Brakeshift Interlock Solenoid.
10	20 Amp	HO2S Sensors (5.0L)
11	15 Amp	Radio
12	20 Amp C.B.	Luggage Compartment Door Remote Control, Door Lock Control Processor, Power Door Locks.
13	10 Amp	Clock Illumination, Radio Illumination, Heated Back Window Switch—Illumination, Instrument Cluster Illumination, A/C Heater Control Illumination, Transmission Range Indicator Lamp Illumination, Ash Receptacle Lamp Illumination, Fog Lamp Switch—Illumination.
14	20 Amp C.B.	Power Windows

88236G42

Fuse Junction Panel Fuse Identification (continued)—1995 Models

Cavity Number	Fuse Rating	Circuit Protected
15	10 Amp	Air Bag Indicator Lamp, Air Bag Diagnostic Monitor, Low Oil Relay, Fuel Gauge, Temperature Gauge, Instrument Gauge Amplifier Module, Transmission Control Indicator Lamp, Maifunction Indicator (Check Engine) Lamp, Speedometer, Anti-Theft Lamp, Gauge, Oil Gauge, Low Oil Level Lamp (5.0L), Tachometer, Anti-Lock Brake Indicator Lamp, Parking Brake Lamp, Low Coolant Lamp (5.0L), Low Coolant Switch (5.0L), Safety Belt Warning Lamp / Chime.
16	20 Amp	Headlamp Flash-to-Pass, Anti-Theft Alarm Control Module.
17	30 Amp	AC—Heater Blower Motor
18	20 Amp	3.8L CCRM Power, Ignition Coil, Charging System Warning Lamp, Regulator Signal. 5.0L CCRM Power, Ignition Coil, Charging System Warning Lamp, Transmission Control Switch Module (5.0L), Ignition Control Module (5.0L), Regulator Signal.

88236G43

Fuse Function Panel Fuse Identification—1996–98 Models

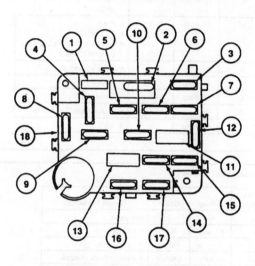

Cavity No.	Fuse Rating	Circuit Protected
8	10A	Power Mirror Motor, Radio Memory, Courtesy Lamp Switch (Door Open Signal), Clock Operation, Door Lock Control Processor Battery Save / Power, Dome Lamp, Map Lamp, Luggage Compartment Door Lamp, Visor Vanity Lamps, Engine Compartment Lamp, Glove Compartment Lamp, Warning Chime (Key-In / Headlamp On)
9	10A	Hazard Lamps-Front, Hazard Lamps-Rear, Hazard Cluster Indicator Lamps, Stop Lights, High Mount Rear Lamp, Brakeshift Interlock Solenoid
10	15A	Intake Manifold Runner (4.6L 4V)
11	15A	Radio
12	20A C.B.	Luggage Compartment Door Remote Control, Door Lock Control Processor, Power Door Locks
13	10A	Clock Illumination, Radio Illumination, Heated Back Window Switch—Illumination, Instrument Cluster Illumination, A / C Heater Control Illumination, Transmission Range Indicator Lamp Illumination, Ash Receptacle Lamp Illumination, Fog Lamp Switch—Illumination
14	20A C.B.	Power Windows
15	10A	Air Bag Indicator Lamp, Air Bag Diagnostic Monitor, Low Oil Relay, Fuel Gauge, Temperature Gauge, Instrument Gauge Amplifier Module, Transmission Control Indicator Lamp, Malfunction Indicator (Check Engine) Lamp, Speedometer, Anti-Theft Lamp, Voltmeter, Oil Gauge, Low Oil Level Lamp, Tachometer, Anti-Lock Brake Indicator Lamp, Parking Brake Lamp, Low Coolant Lamp, Low Coolant Switch, Safety Belt Warning Lamp / Chime
16	20A	Headlamp Flash-to-Pass, Anti-Theft Alarm Control Module
17	30A	AC—Heater Blower Motor
18	20A	CCRM Power, Ignition Coil, Charging System Warning Lamp

Cavity No.	Fuse Rating	Circuit Protected
1	15A	Turn Signal Lamps, Turn Signal Cluster Indicator Lamp, Back Up Lamps, Air Bag Diagnostic Monitor, DRL Module, IGN Power, Illuminated Entry Actuator Shut Off Power, Heated Back Window Control Relay Coil in Switch, Convertible Top Relay Coil, Transmission Control Switch, Brakeshift Interlock Signal Feed
2	30A	Windshield Wiper—High, Washer Pump
3	—	Not Used
4	10A	Air Bag Diagnostic Monitor
5	15A	Warning Chime (Headlamp On), Clock, Front Park Lamps, Rear Tail Lamps, License Plate Lamps, Rear Side Marker Lamps, Fuse 13
6	15A	Clock—Display, Speed Control Amplifier, Warning Chime Module, A / C Clutch Coil, Door Lock Control Processor, Anti-Theft Alarm Control
7	10A	Anti-Lock Brake Control Module

88236G34

Power Distribution Box Fuse Identification—1994 Models

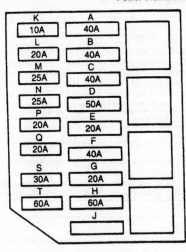

Cavity Number	Fuse Rating	Color	Circuit Protected
E	20 Amp	Light Green	• PCM • Fuel Pump • HO2S (3.8L) • Canister Purge Solenoid • EVR Solenoid • Ignition Control Module (3.8L) • IAC Solenoid • Fuel Injector • Automatic Transmission • Camshaft Position Sensor (3.8L) • MAF Sensor
F	40 Amp	Orange	• Heated Back Window
G	20 Amp	Yellow	• Fuel Pump
H	60 Amp	Blue	• Fan Control
J	—	—	Not Used
K	10 Amp	Blue	• Anti-Lock Brake Control Module
L	20 Amp	Red	• Fan Control Monitor (PCM)
M	25 Amp	Yellow	• Horn • Foglamps • Daytime Running Lights Control Module
N	25 Amp	Clear	• Fuses 5 and 9
P	20 Amp	Clear	• Radio Amplifier
Q	20 Amp	Yellow	• Generator
S	30 Amp	Yellow	• Convertible Top Motor
T	60 Amp	—	• ABS

Cavity Number	Fuse Rating	Color	Circuit Protected
A	40 Amp	Orange	• Ignition Switch
B	40 Amp	Orange	• Ignition Switch
C	40 Amp	Orange	• Ignition Switch
D	50 Amp	Red	• Headlamp Switch • Instrument Panel Fuses 4, 8 and 16 • Instrument Panel Circuit Breaker 12

88236G46

Power Distribution Box Fuse Identification—1995 Models

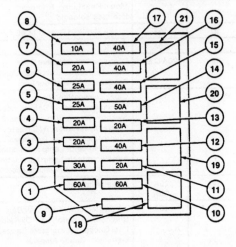

Cavity Number	Rating	Color	Circuit Protected
9	—	—	Not Used
10	60 Amp	Blue	• Fan Control
11	20 Amp	Yellow	• Fuel Pump
12	40 Amp	Orange	• Heated Back Window
13	20 Amp	Yellow	• PCM • Fuel Pump • HO2S (3.8L) • Canister Purge Solenoid • EVR Solenoid • Ignition Control Module (3.8L) • IAC Solenoid • Fuel Injector • Automatic Transmission • Camshaft Position Sensor (3.8L) • MAF Sensor
14	50 Amp	Red	• Headlamp Switch • Instrument Panel Fuses 4, 8 and 16 • Instrument Panel Circuit Breaker 12
15	40 Amp	Orange	• Ignition Switch
16	40 Amp	Orange	• Ignition Switch
17	40 Amp	Orange	• Ignition Switch
18	Relay	—	Fog Lamp
19	Relay	—	Starter Relay
20	Relay	—	Horn Relay
21	Relay	—	Spare (Open)

Cavity Number	Rating	Color	Circuit Protected
1	60 Amp	Blue	• ABS
2	30 Amp	Green	• Convertible Top Motor
3	30 Amp	Green	• Power Seats / Cigar Lighter
4	20 Amp	Yellow	• Generator
5	25 Amp	Clear	• Radio Amplifier
6	25 Amp	Clear	• Fuses 5 and 9
7	20 Amp	Yellow	• Horn • Fog Lamps • Daytime Running Lights Control Module
8	10 Amp	Red	• Fan Control Monitor (PCM)

88236G45

Power Distribution Box Fuse Identification—1996–98 Models

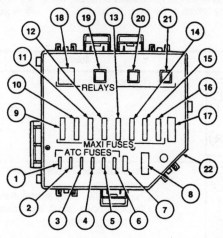

Cavity Number	Rating	Color	Circuit Protected
7	30A	Circuit Breaker	Convertible Top Motor
8	60A	Lt. Blue	Anti-Lock Brake System (ABS)
9	40A	Amber	Ignition Switch
10	40A	Amber	Ignition Switch
11	40A	Amber	Ignition Switch
12	50A	Red	Headlamps
13	20A	Yellow	Electronic Engine Control
14	40A	Amber	Heated Back Window
15	20A	Yellow	Fuel Pump
16	60A	Lt. Blue	Engine Cooling Fan
17	30A	Lt. Green	Thermactor Air Pump (4.6L 4V Only)
18	—	—	Not Used
19	Relay	—	Horn
20	Relay	—	Starter
21	Relay	—	Fog Lamps
22	—	—	Power Distribution Box

Cavity Number	Rating	Color	Circuit Protected
1	25A	Natural	Power Seats
2	20A	Yellow	Horn Fog Lamps Daytime Running Lamps Control Module
3	25A	Natural	Interior Lamps
4	25A	Natural	Audio
5	20A	Yellow	Alternator
6	30A	Lt. Green	Cigar Lighter

88236G35

Circuit Breaker and Fusible Link Applications—1994 Models

Circuit	Circuit Protection and Rating	Location
Headlamps and High Beam Indicator	20 Amp. CB	Integral with Lighting Switch
Heated Back Window	16 GA Fuse Link	Engine Compartment
Power Windows, Power Seat, Power Door Locks	20 Amp. CB	Starter Motor Relay
Load Circuit	Fuse Link	In Harness
Engine Compartment Lamp	Fuse Link	In Harness
Convertible Top	25 Amp. CB	Lower Instrument Panel-Reinforcement

88236G41

Circuit Breaker and Fusible Link Applications—1995 Models

Circuit	Circuit Protection and Rating	Location
Headlamps and High Beam Indicator	20 Amp CB	Integral with Lighting Switch
Heated Back Window	16 GA Fuse Link	Engine Compartment
Power Windows, Power Seat, Power Door Locks	20 Amp CB	Starter Motor Relay
Load Circuit	Fuse Link	In Harness
Engine Compartment Lamp	Fuse Link	In Harness
Convertible Top	25 Amp CB	Lower Instrument Panel-Reinforcement

88236G44

Circuit Breaker and Fusible Link Applications—1996–98 Models

Circuit	Circuit Protection and Rating	Location
Headlamps and High Beam Indicator	20 Amp CB	Integral with Lighting Switch
Generator	16 GA Fuse Link	Engine Compartment

88236G37

Most problems in the turn signals or flasher system can be reduced to defective flashers or bulbs, which are easily replaced. Occasionally, problems in the turn signals are traced to the switch in the steering column, which will require professional service.

F = Front   R = Rear   ● = Lights off   o = Lights on

Problem		Solution
Turn signals light, but do not flash		• Replace the flasher
No turn signals light on either side		• Check the fuse. Replace if defective. • Check the flasher by substitution • Check for open circuit, short circuit or poor ground
Both turn signals on one side don't work		• Check for bad bulbs • Check for bad ground in both housings
One turn signal light on one side doesn't work		• Check and/or replace bulb • Check for corrosion in socket. Clean contacts. • Check for poor ground at socket
Turn signal flashes too fast or too slow		• Check any bulb on the side flashing too fast. A heavy-duty bulb is probably installed in place of a regular bulb. • Check the bulb flashing too slow. A standard bulb was probably installed in place of a heavy-duty bulb. • Check for loose connections or corrosion at the bulb socket
Indicator lights don't work in either direction		• Check if the turn signals are working • Check the dash indicator lights • Check the flasher by substitution

One indicator light doesn't light		• On systems with 1 dash indicator: See if the lights work on the same side. Often the filaments have been reversed in systems combining stoplights with taillights and turn signals.
		    Check the flasher by substitution
		• On systems with 2 indicators: Check the bulbs on the same side
		    Check the indicator light bulb
		    Check the flasher by substitution

TCC8823

WIRING DIAGRAMS

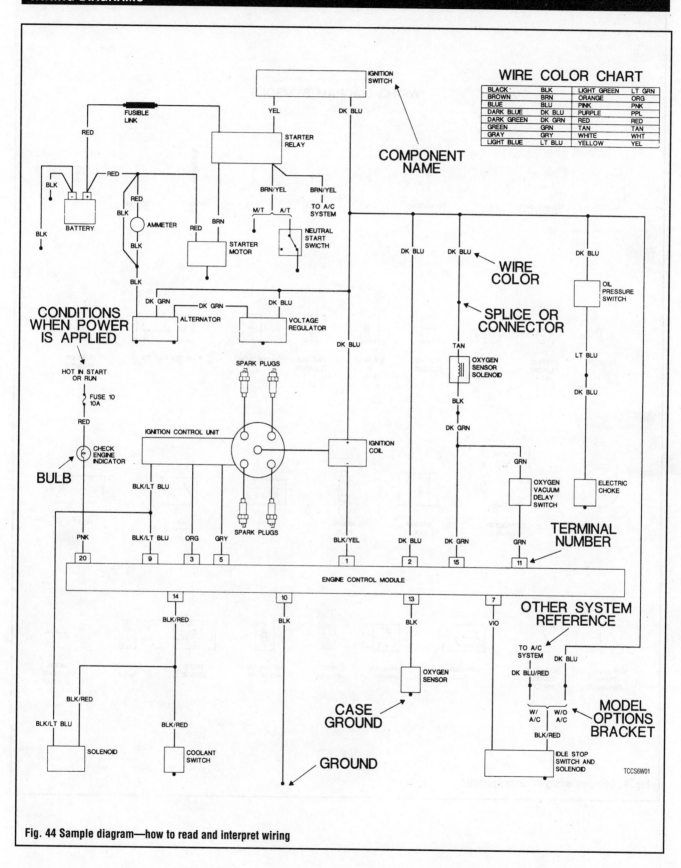

WIRE COLOR CHART

BLACK	BLK	LIGHT GREEN	LT GRN
BROWN	BRN	ORANGE	ORG
BLUE	BLU	PINK	PNK
DARK BLUE	DK BLU	PURPLE	PPL
DARK GREEN	DK GRN	RED	RED
GREEN	GRN	TAN	TAN
GRAY	GRY	WHITE	WHT
LIGHT BLUE	LT BLU	YELLOW	YEL

COMPONENT NAME

WIRE COLOR

SPLICE OR CONNECTOR

CONDITIONS WHEN POWER IS APPLIED

BULB

TERMINAL NUMBER

OTHER SYSTEM REFERENCE

CASE GROUND

GROUND

MODEL OPTIONS BRACKET

Fig. 44 Sample diagram—how to read and interpret wiring

TCCS6W01

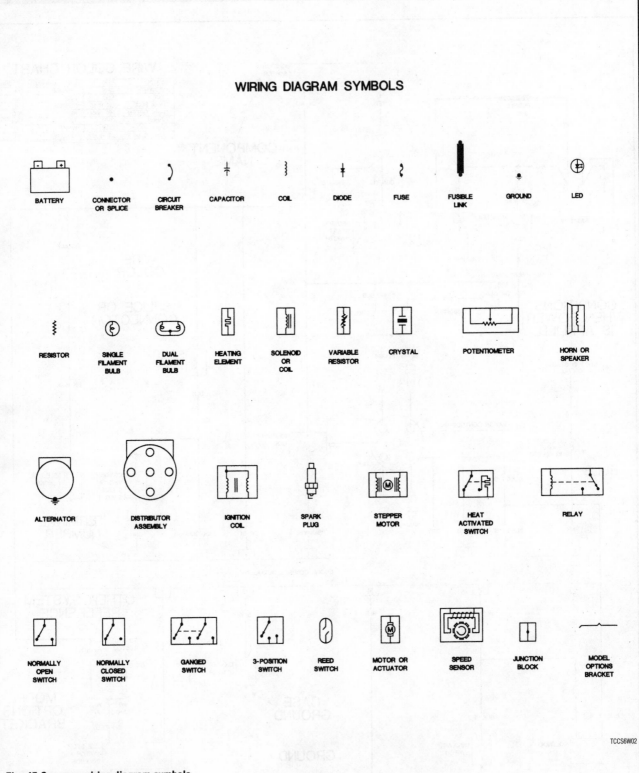

Fig. 45 Common wiring diagram symbols

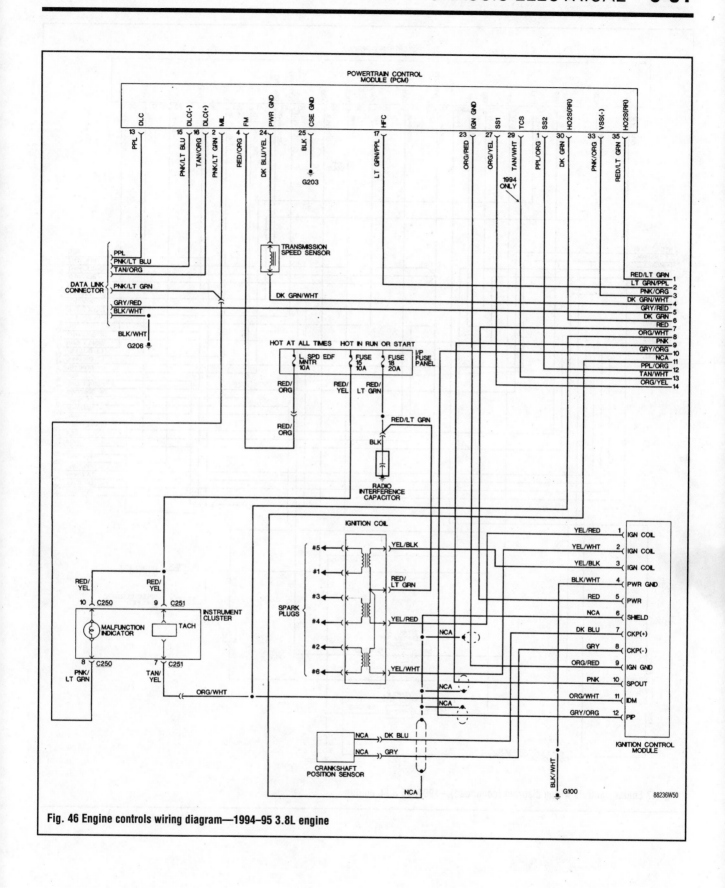

Fig. 46 Engine controls wiring diagram—1994–95 3.8L engine

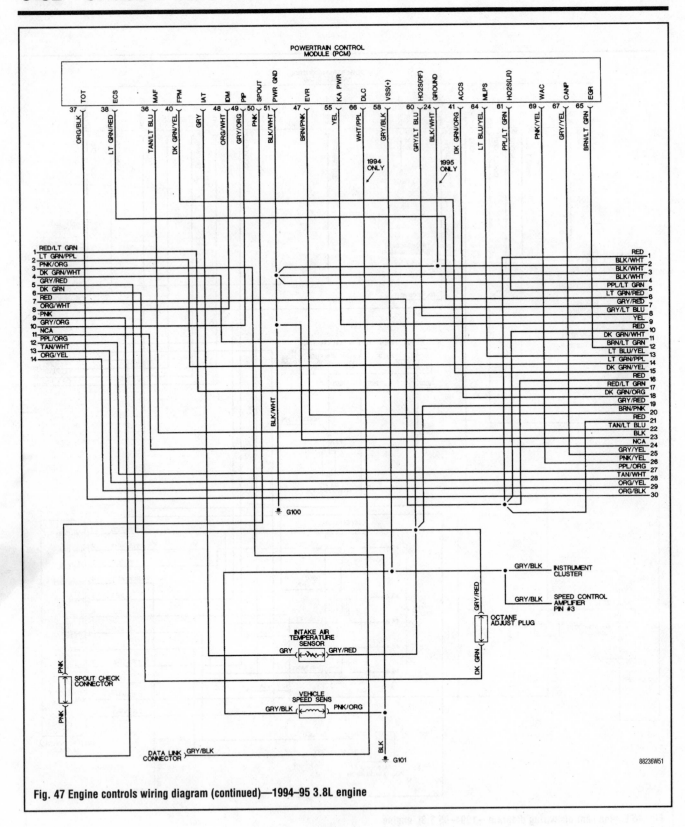

Fig. 47 Engine controls wiring diagram (continued)—1994-95 3.8L engine

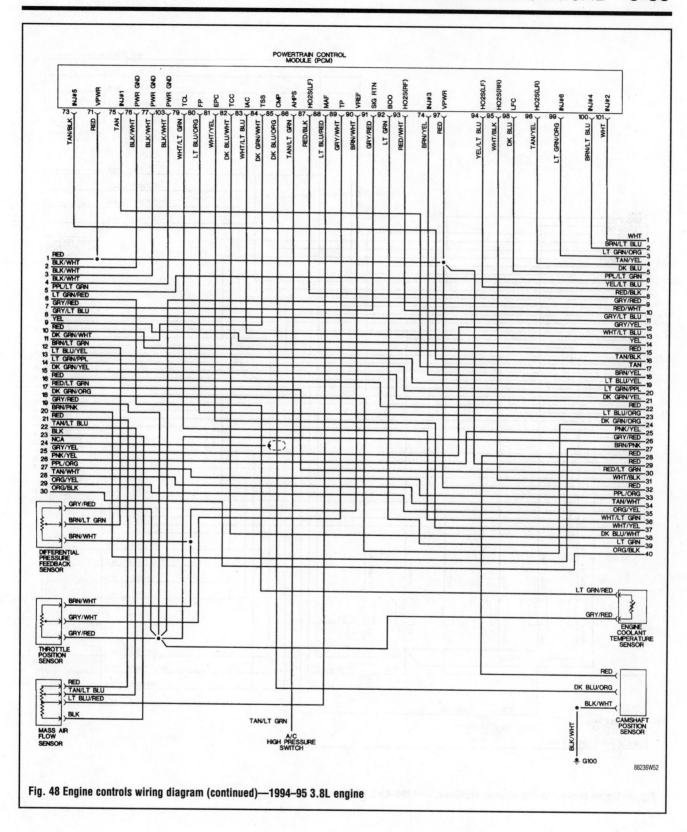

Fig. 48 Engine controls wiring diagram (continued)—1994–95 3.8L engine

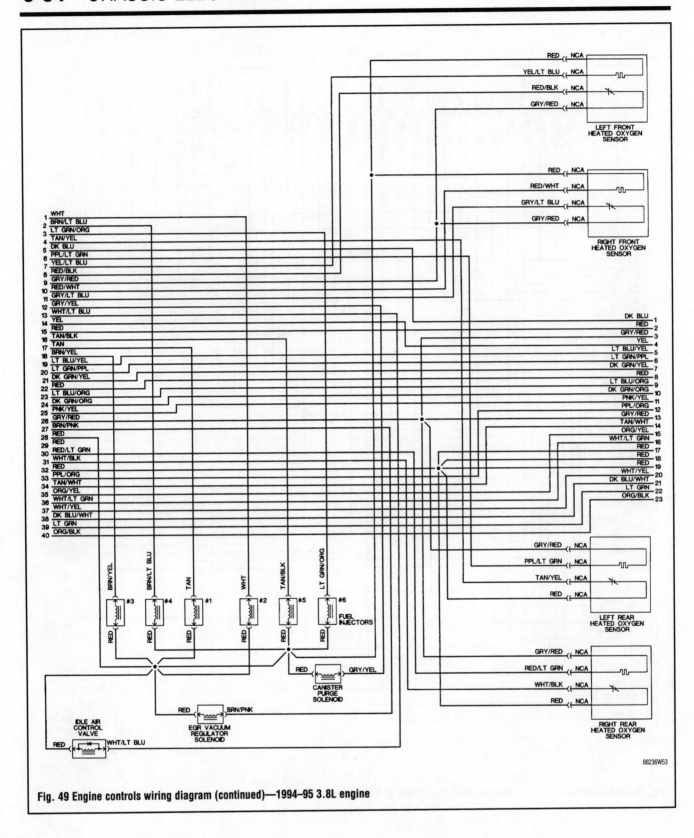

Fig. 49 Engine controls wiring diagram (continued)—1994–95 3.8L engine

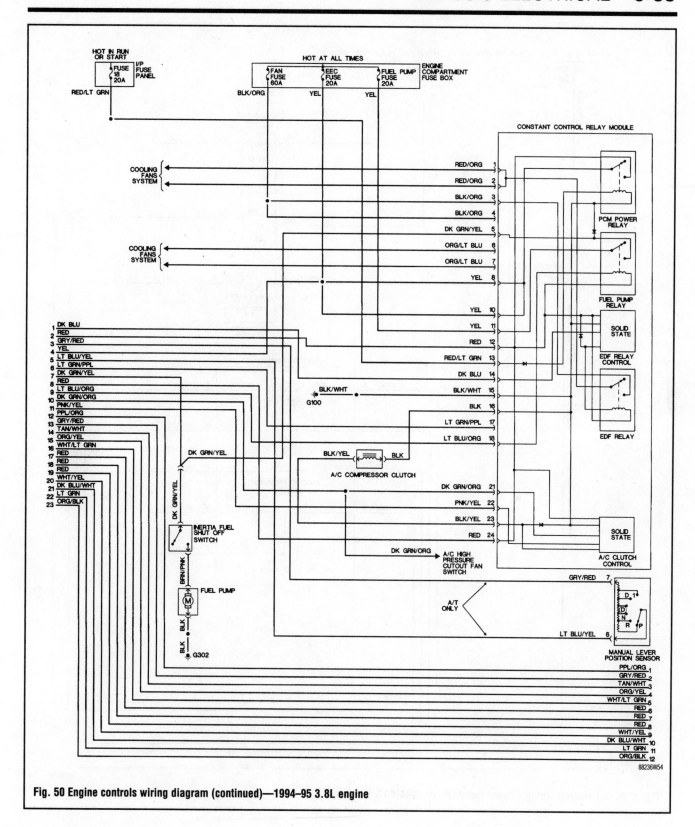

Fig. 50 Engine controls wiring diagram (continued)—1994–95 3.8L engine

88236W54

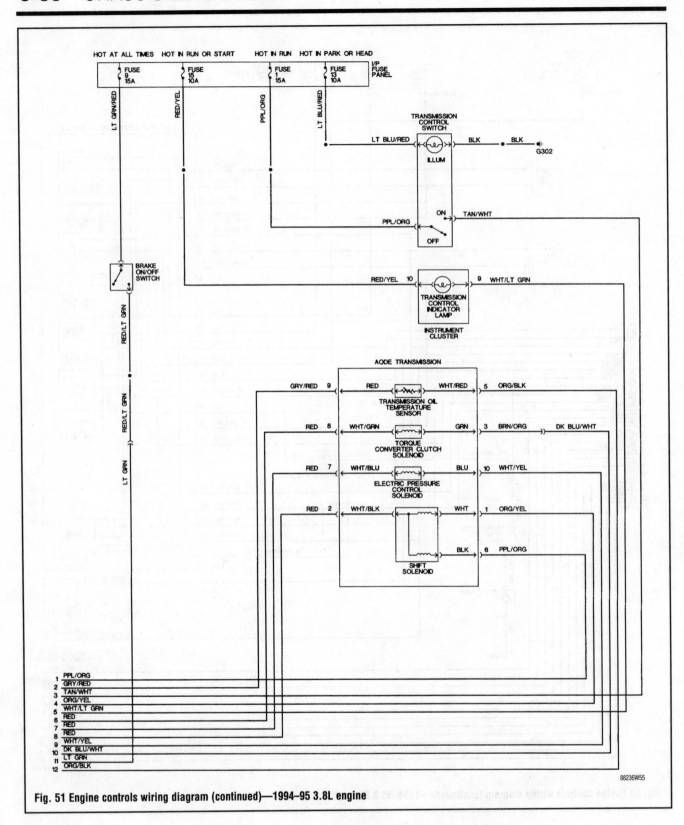

Fig. 51 Engine controls wiring diagram (continued)—1994–95 3.8L engine

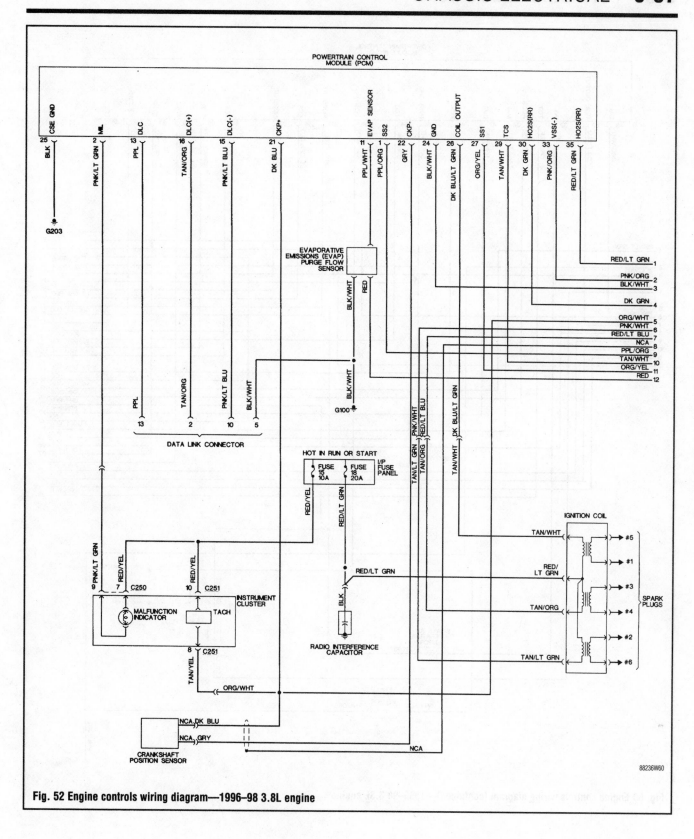

Fig. 52 Engine controls wiring diagram—1996–98 3.8L engine

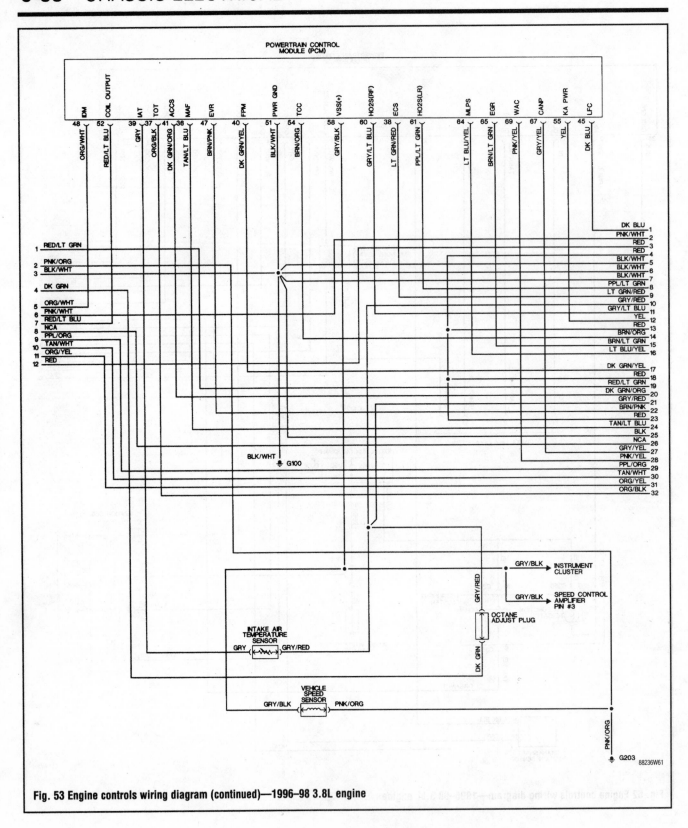

Fig. 53 Engine controls wiring diagram (continued)—1996–98 3.8L engine

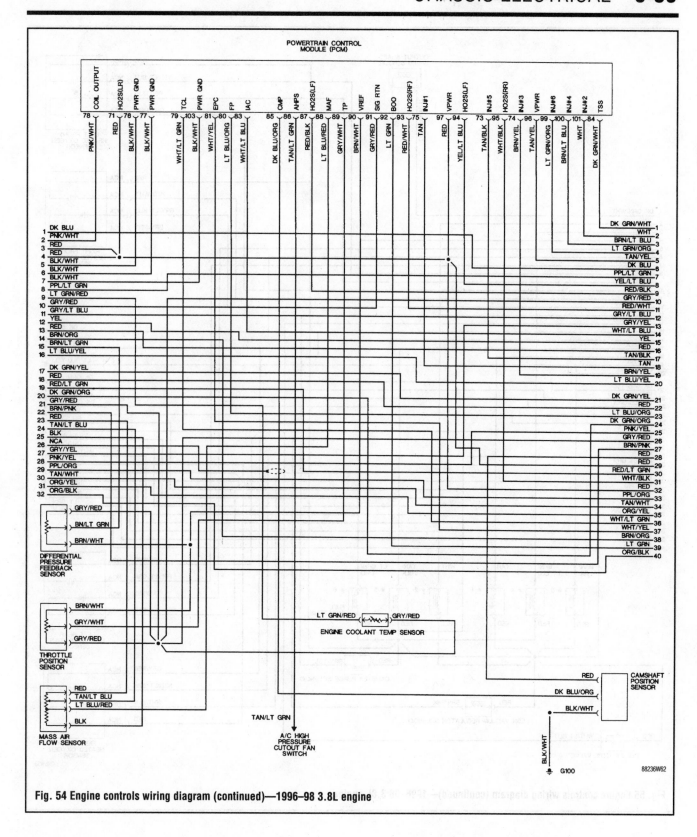

Fig. 54 Engine controls wiring diagram (continued)—1996–98 3.8L engine

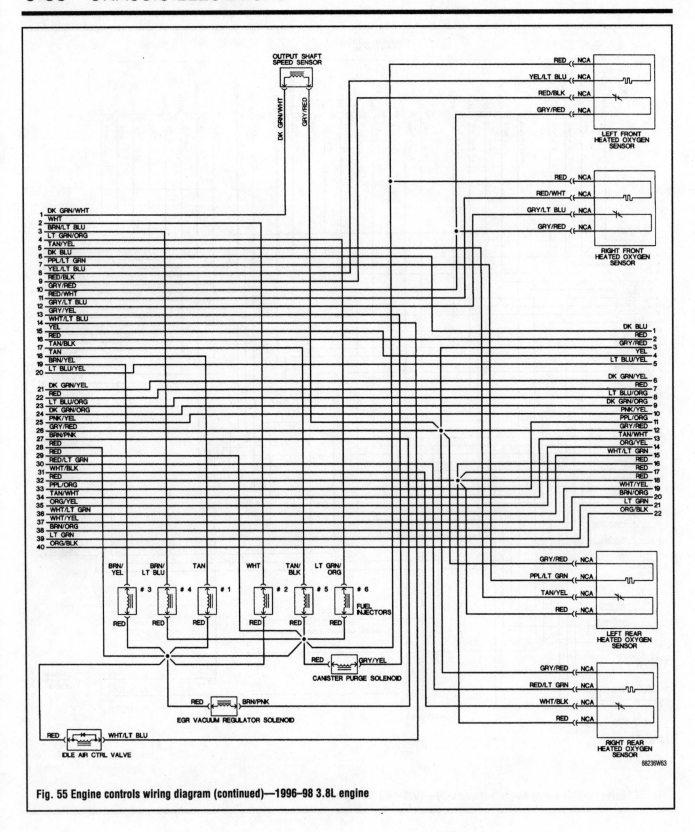

Fig. 55 Engine controls wiring diagram (continued)—1996–98 3.8L engine

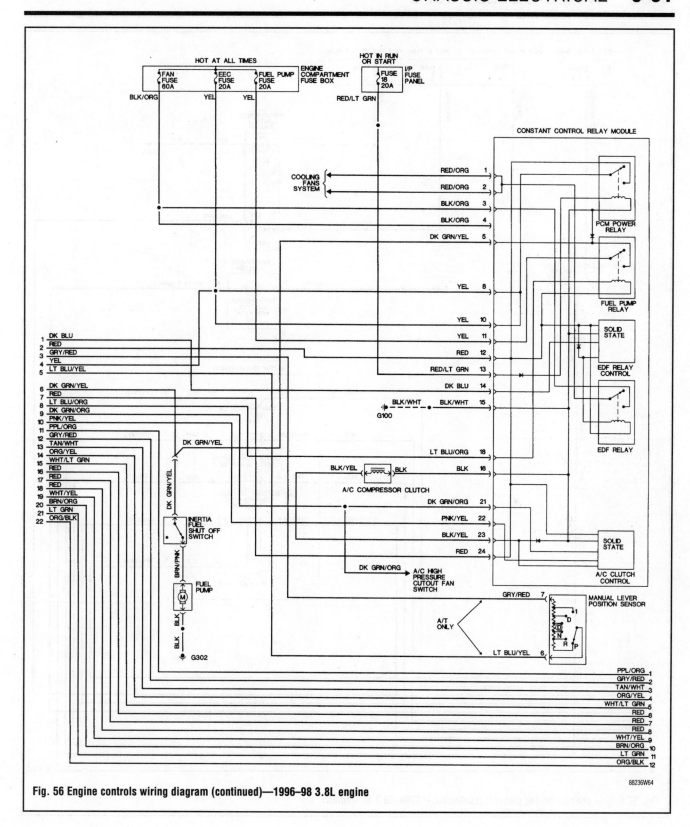

Fig. 56 Engine controls wiring diagram (continued)—1996–98 3.8L engine

88236W64

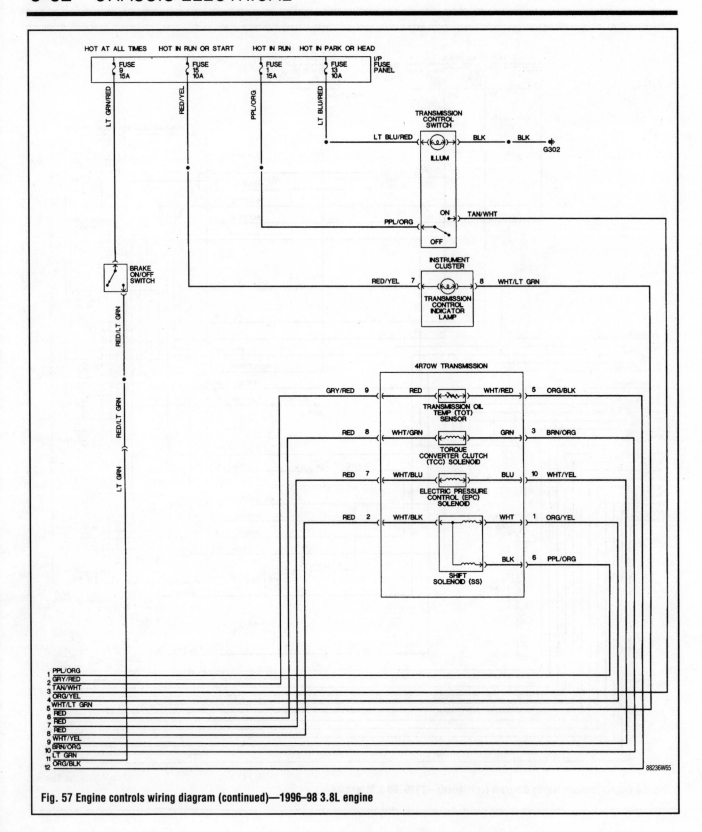

Fig. 57 Engine controls wiring diagram (continued)—1996–98 3.8L engine

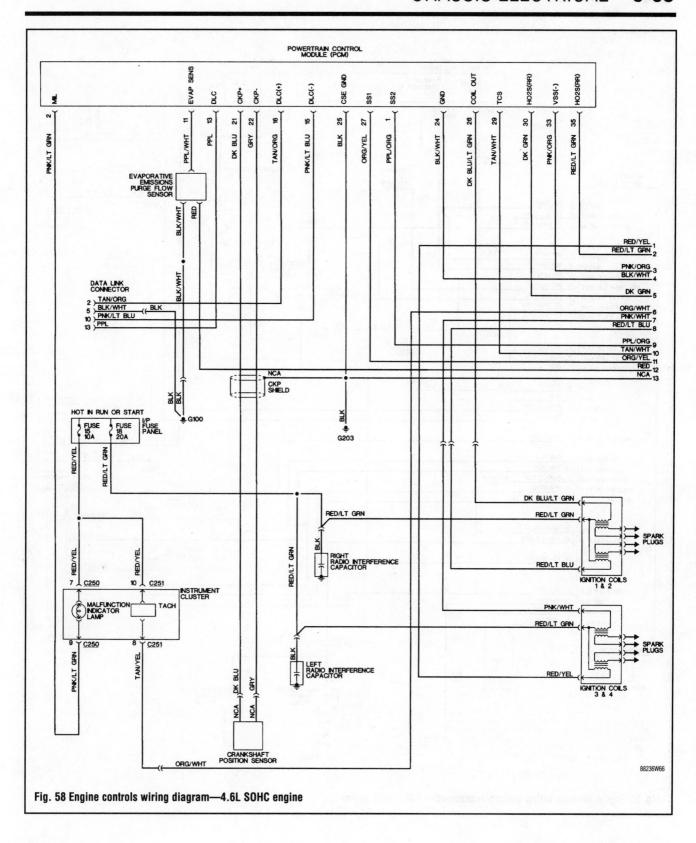

Fig. 58 Engine controls wiring diagram—4.6L SOHC engine

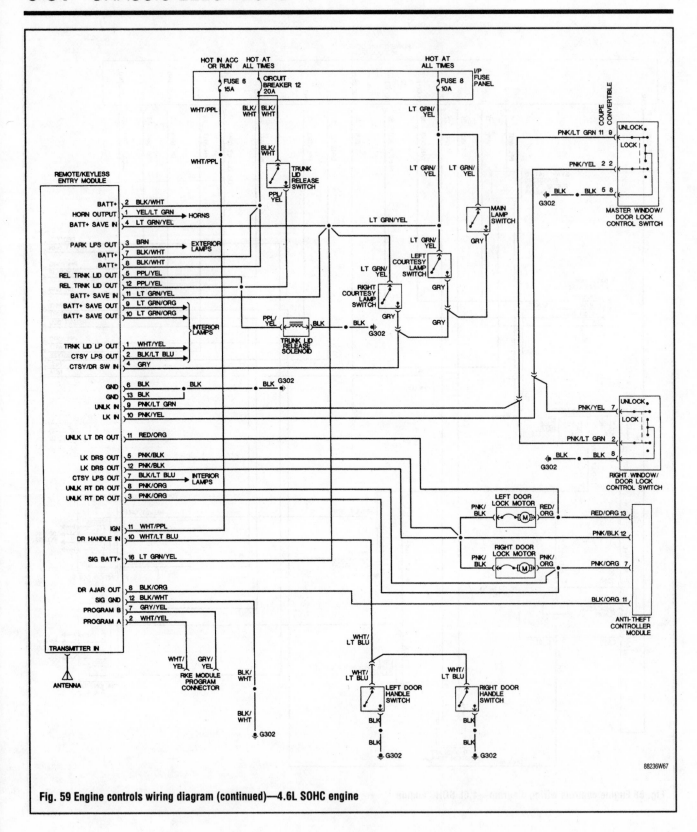

Fig. 59 Engine controls wiring diagram (continued)—4.6L SOHC engine

88236W67

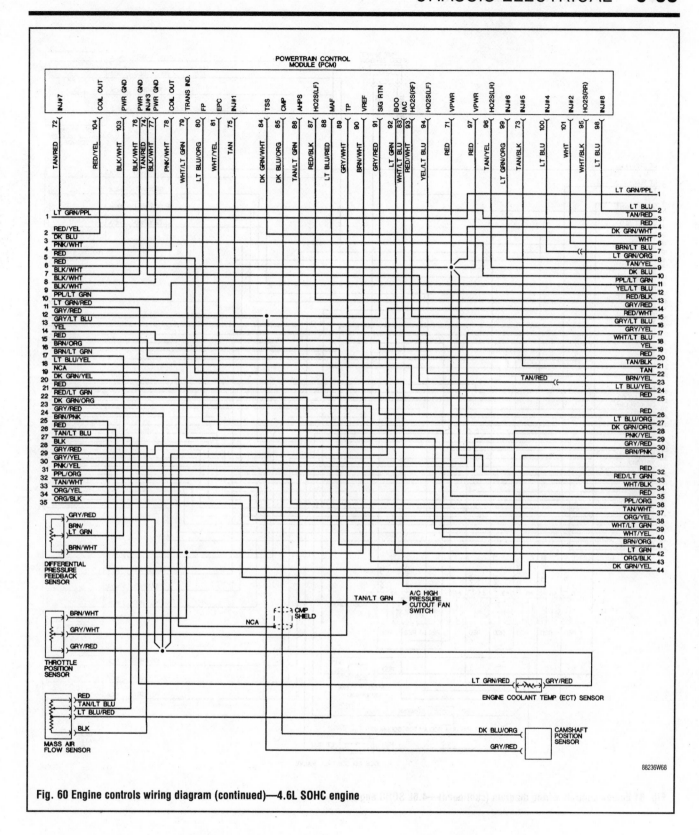

Fig. 60 Engine controls wiring diagram (continued)—4.6L SOHC engine

88236W68

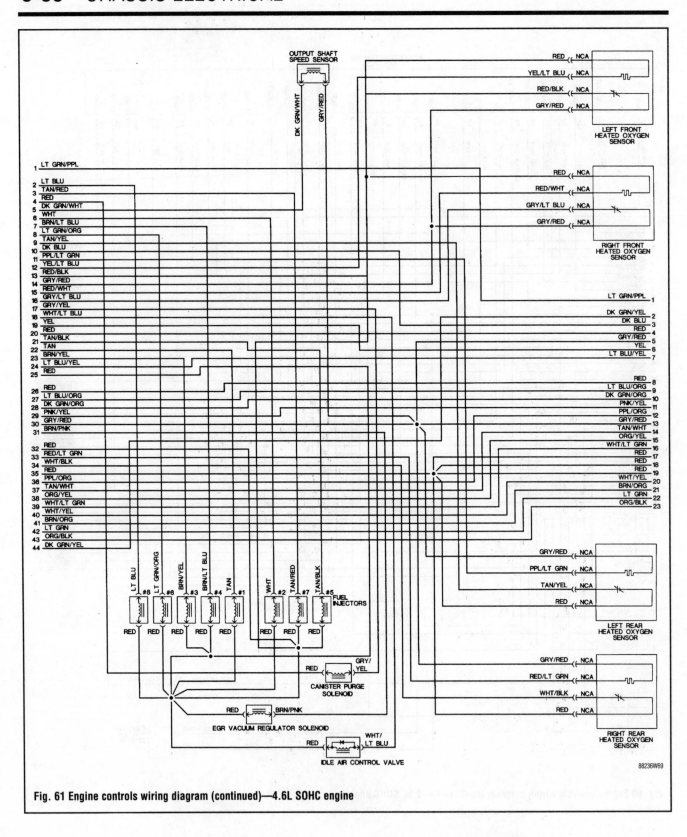

Fig. 61 Engine controls wiring diagram (continued)—4.6L SOHC engine

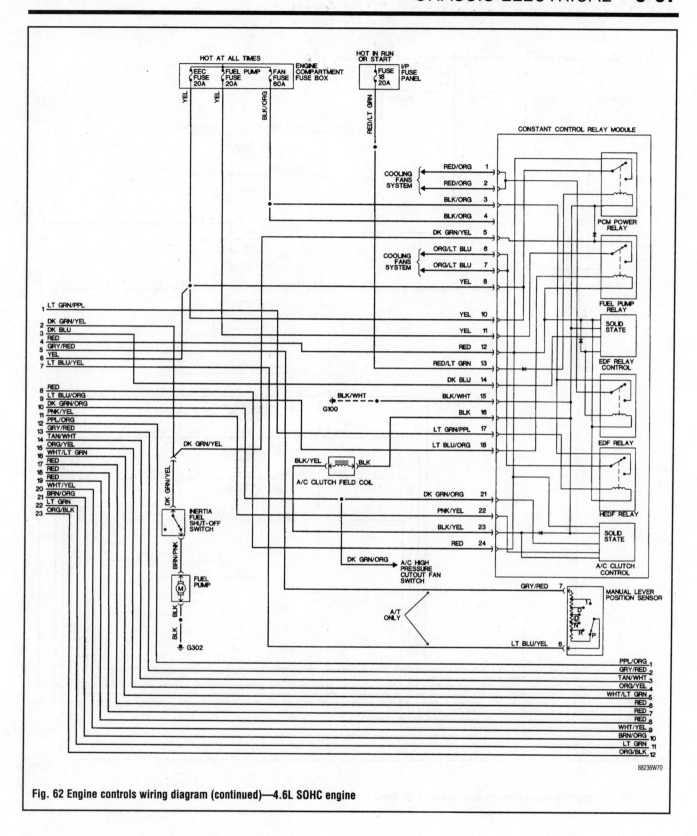

Fig. 62 Engine controls wiring diagram (continued)—4.6L SOHC engine

88236W70

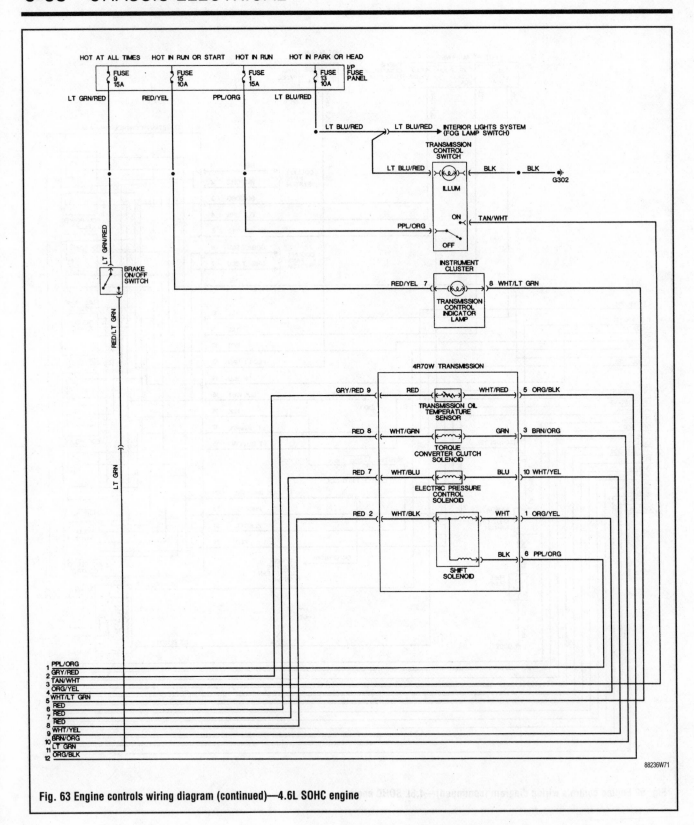

Fig. 63 Engine controls wiring diagram (continued)—4.6L SOHC engine

88236W71

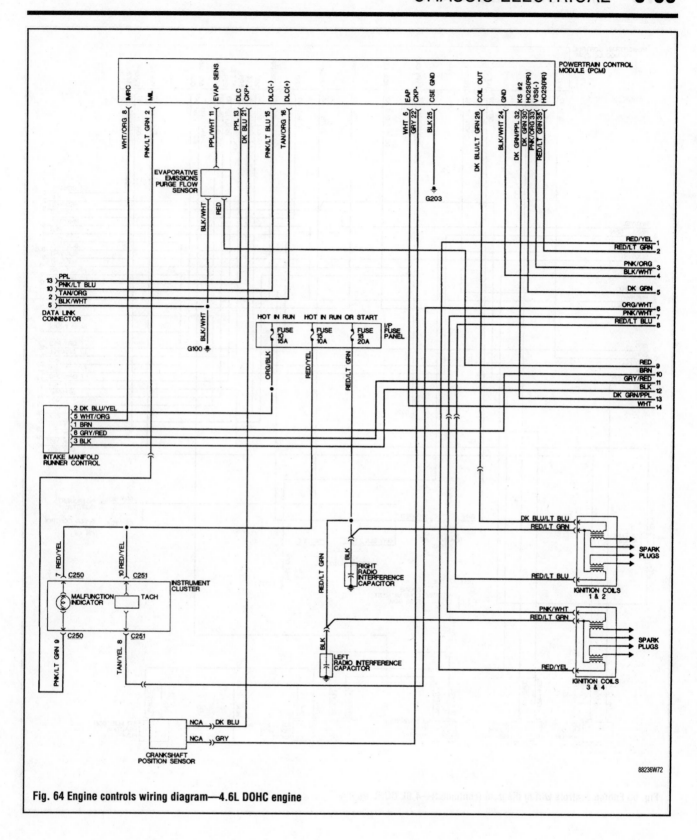

Fig. 64 Engine controls wiring diagram—4.6L DOHC engine

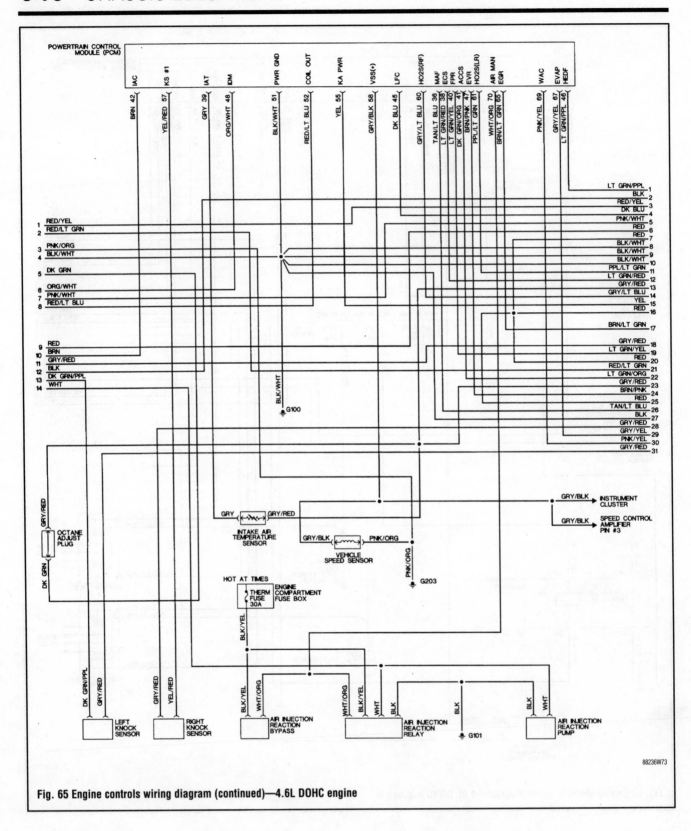

Fig. 65 Engine controls wiring diagram (continued)—4.6L DOHC engine

88236W73

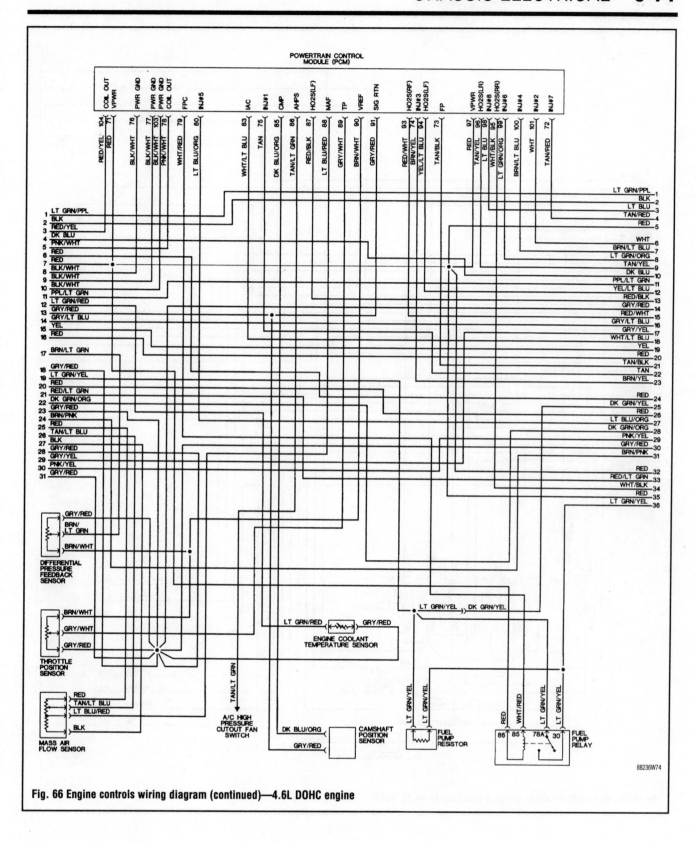

Fig. 66 Engine controls wiring diagram (continued)—4.6L DOHC engine

88236W74

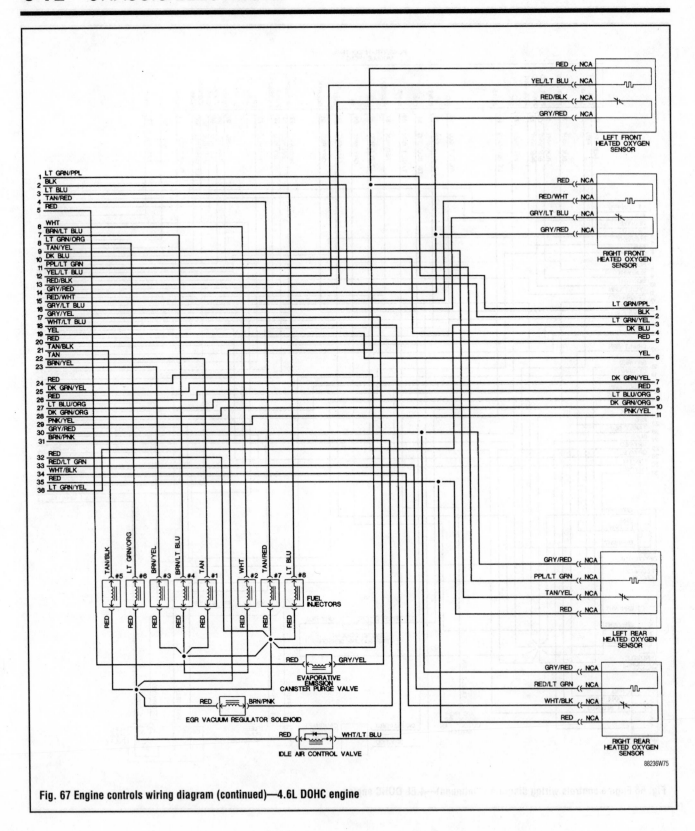

Fig. 67 Engine controls wiring diagram (continued)—4.6L DOHC engine

88236W75

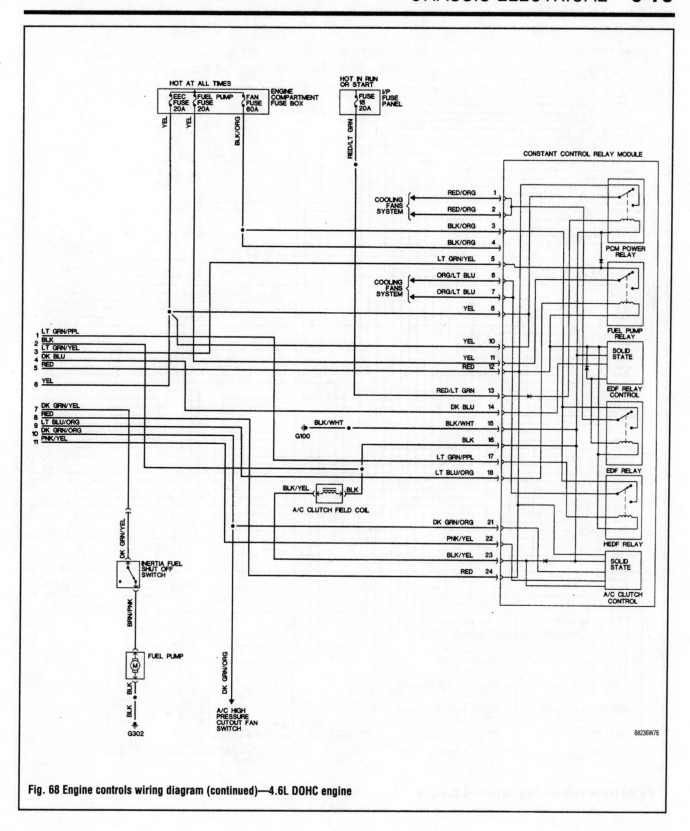

Fig. 68 Engine controls wiring diagram (continued)—4.6L DOHC engine

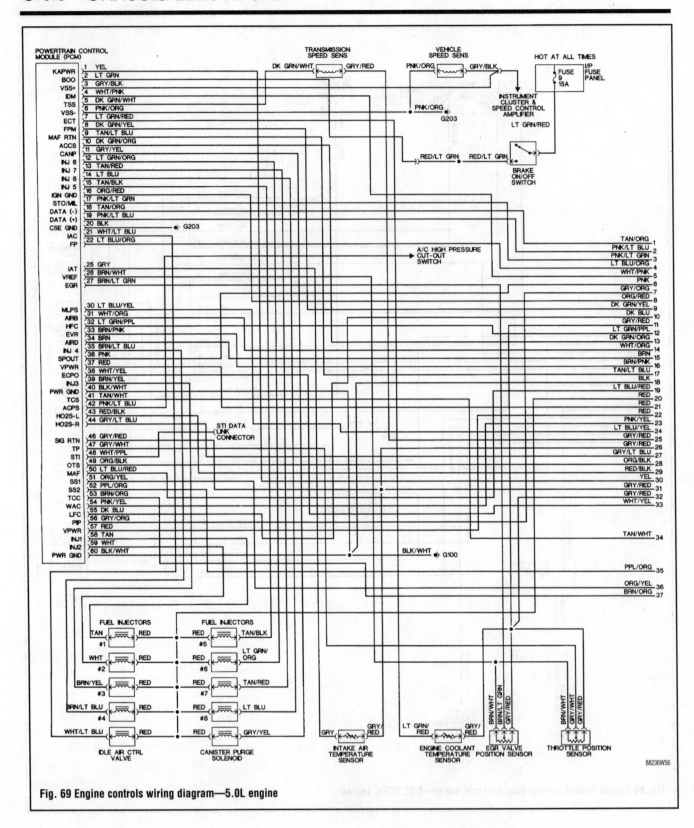

Fig. 69 Engine controls wiring diagram—5.0L engine

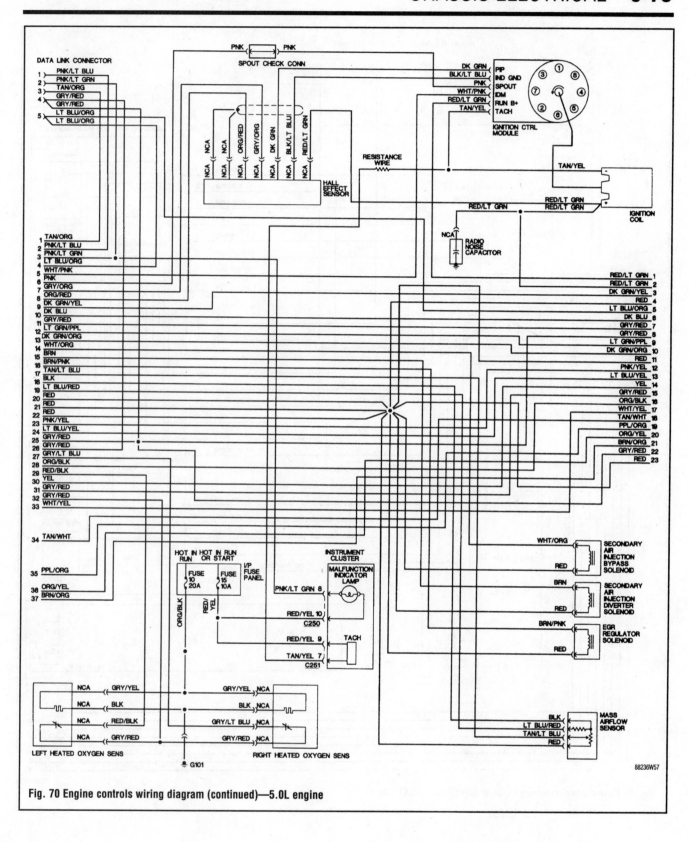

Fig. 70 Engine controls wiring diagram (continued)—5.0L engine

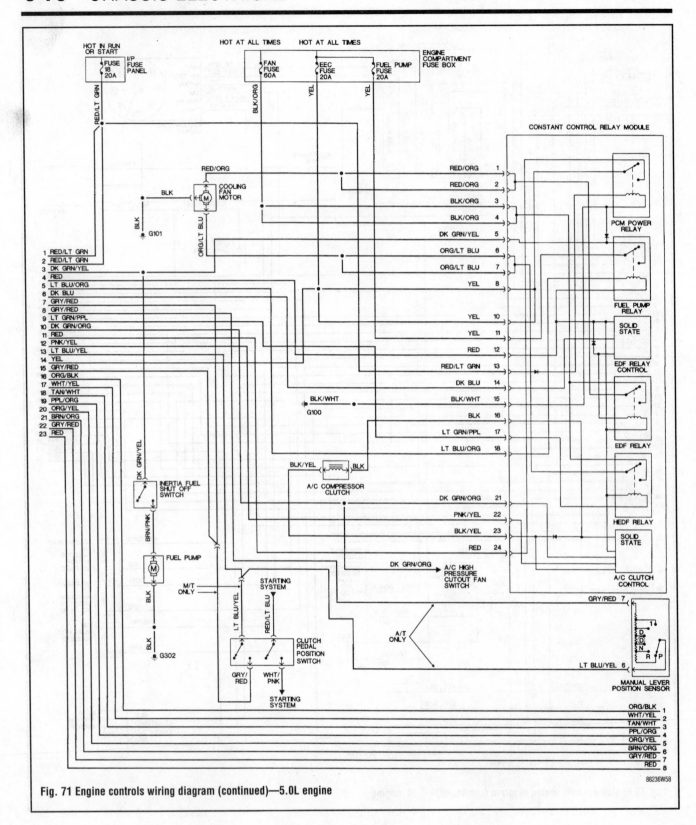

Fig. 71 Engine controls wiring diagram (continued)—5.0L engine

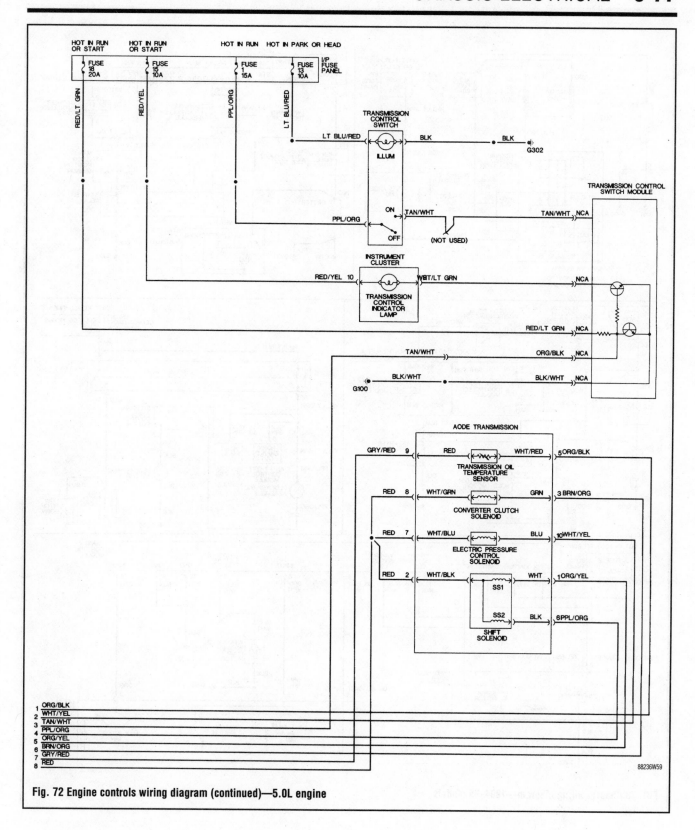

Fig. 72 Engine controls wiring diagram (continued)—5.0L engine

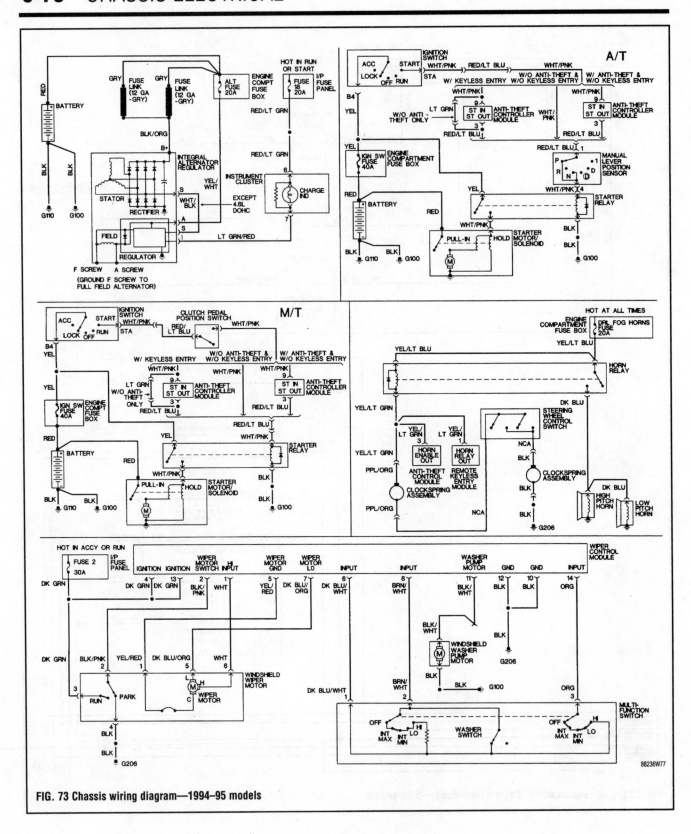

FIG. 73 Chassis wiring diagram—1994–95 models

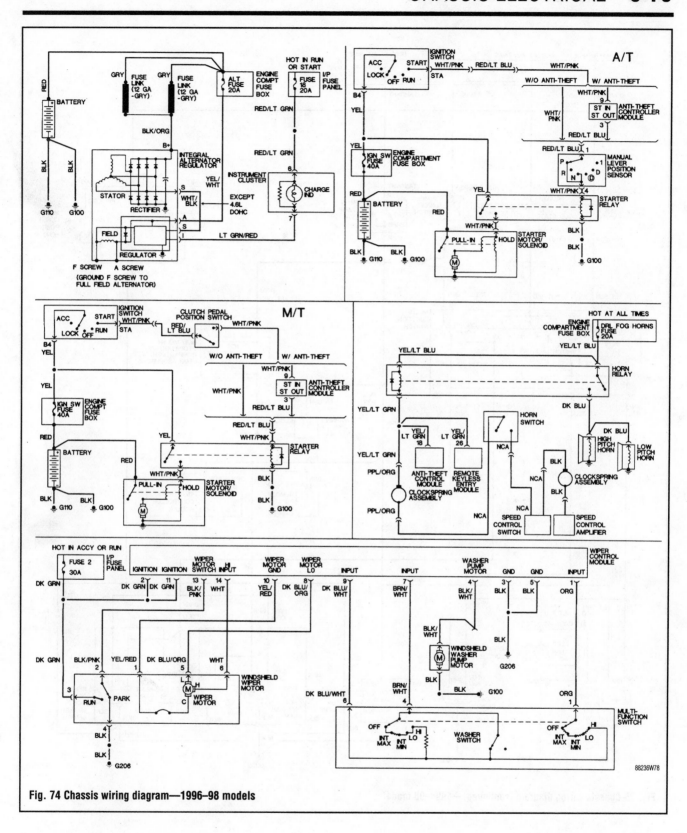

Fig. 74 Chassis wiring diagram—1996–98 models

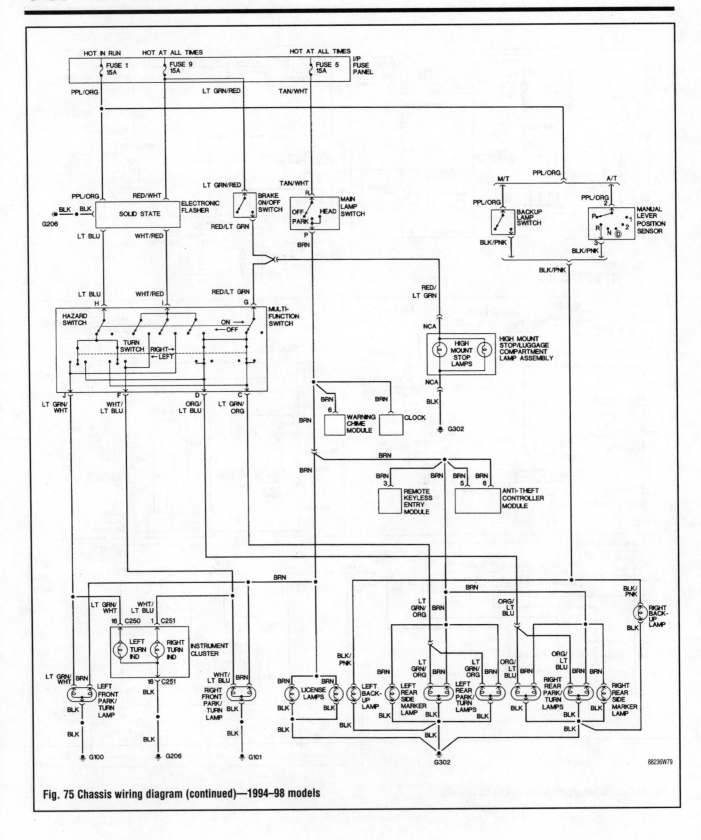

Fig. 75 Chassis wiring diagram (continued)—1994–98 models

88236W79

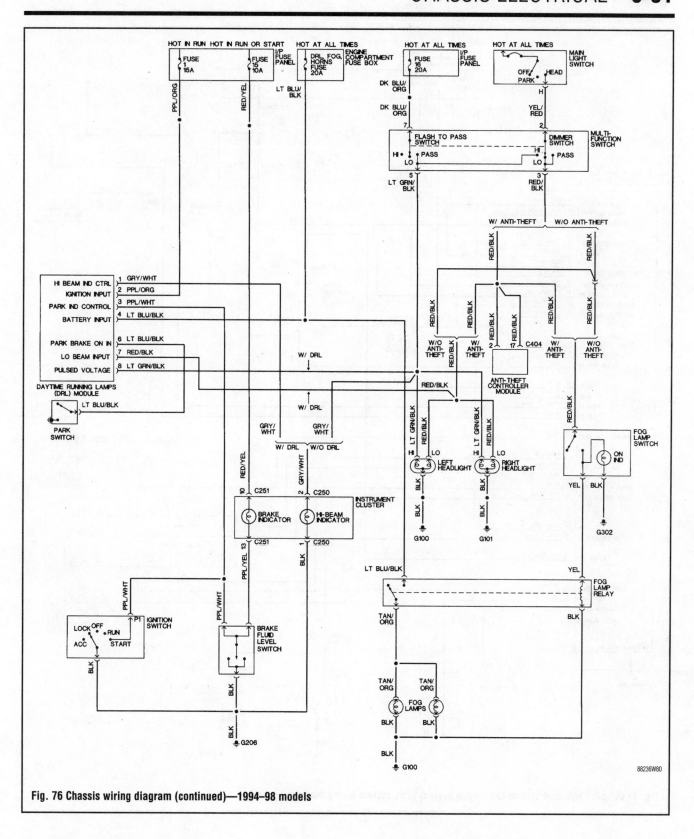

Fig. 76 Chassis wiring diagram (continued)—1994–98 models

88236W80

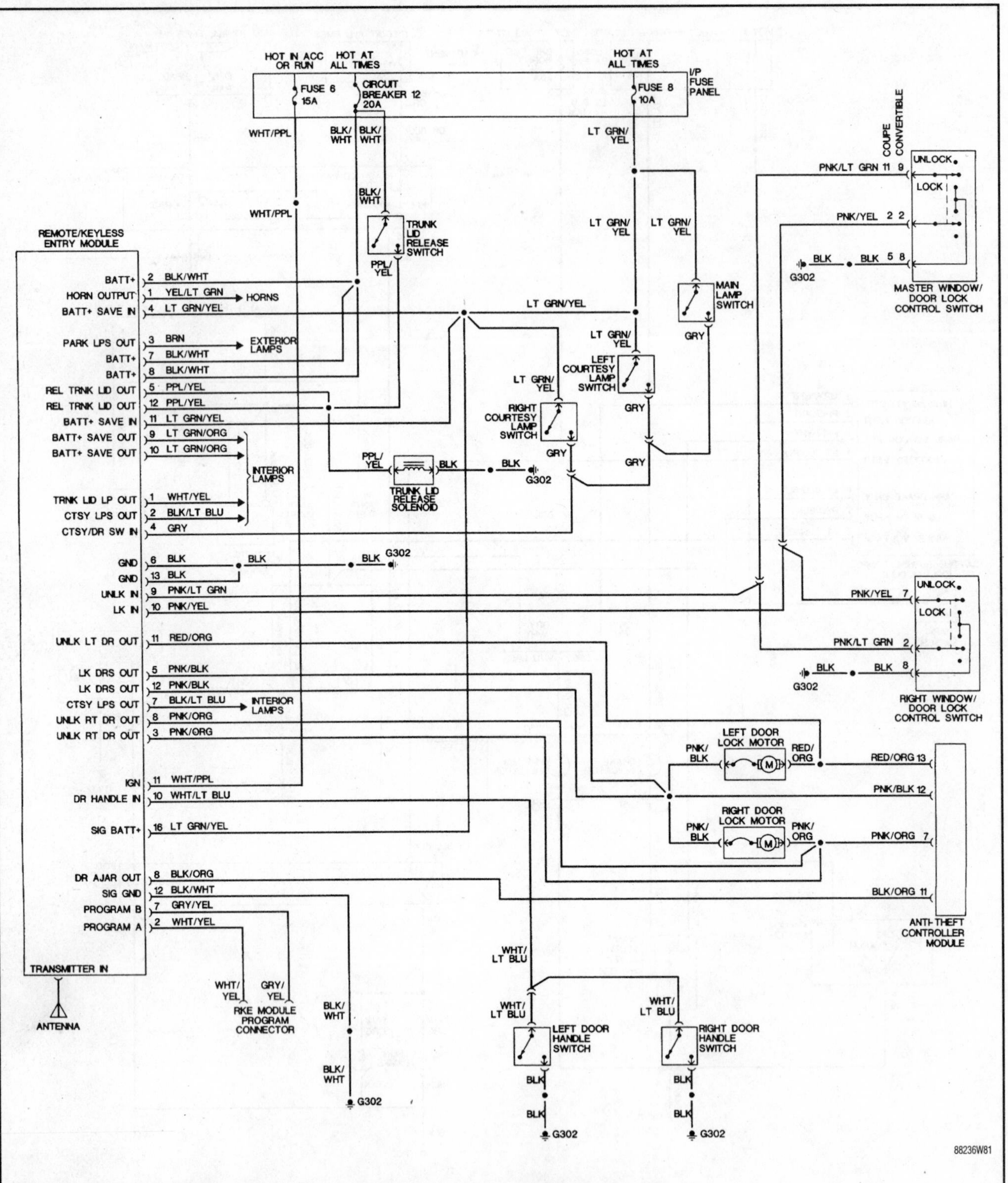

Fig. 77 Optional anti-theft system and remote keyless entry system wiring diagram—all models

88236W81

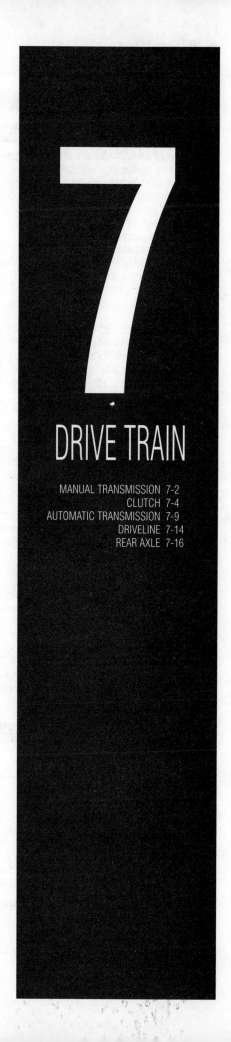

7

DRIVE TRAIN

MANUAL TRANSMISSION

Understanding the Manual Transmission

Because of the way an internal combustion engine breathes, it can produce torque (or twisting force) only within a narrow speed range. Most overhead valve pushrod engines must turn at about 2500 rpm to produce their peak torque. Often by 4500 rpm, they are producing so little torque that continued increases in engine speed produce no power increases.

The torque peak on overhead camshaft engines is, generally, much higher, but much narrower.

The manual transmission and clutch are employed to vary the relationship between engine RPM and the speed of the wheels so that adequate power can be produced under all circumstances. The clutch allows engine torque to be applied to the transmission input shaft gradually, due to mechanical slippage. The vehicle can, consequently, be started smoothly from a full stop.

The transmission changes the ratio between the rotating speeds of the engine and the wheels by the use of gears. 4-speed or 5-speed transmissions are most common. The lower gears allow full engine power to be applied to the rear wheels during acceleration at low speeds.

The clutch driveplate is a thin disc, the center of which is splined to the transmission input shaft. Both sides of the disc are covered with a layer of material which is similar to brake lining and which is capable of allowing slippage without roughness or excessive noise.

The clutch cover is bolted to the engine flywheel and incorporates a diaphragm spring which provides the pressure to engage the clutch. The cover also houses the pressure plate. When the clutch pedal is released, the driven disc is sandwiched between the pressure plate and the smooth surface of the flywheel, thus forcing the disc to turn at the same speed as the engine crankshaft.

The transmission contains a mainshaft which passes all the way through the transmission, from the clutch to the driveshaft. This shaft is separated at one point, so that front and rear portions can turn at different speeds.

Power is transmitted by a countershaft in the lower gears and reverse. The gears of the countershaft mesh with gears on the mainshaft, allowing power to be carried from one to the other. Countershaft gears are often integral with that shaft, while several of the mainshaft gears can either rotate independently of the shaft or be locked to it. Shifting from one gear to the next causes one of the gears to be freed from rotating with the shaft and locks another to it. Gears are locked and unlocked by internal dog clutches which slide between the center of the gear and the shaft. The forward gears usually employ synchronizers, friction members which smoothly bring gear and shaft to the same speed before the toothed dog clutches are engaged.

Shift Handle

REMOVAL & INSTALLATION

♦ See Figure 1

1. Remove the shift knob by rotating it counterclockwise.
2. Remove the console trim and lift the boot over the shift lever.
3. Remove the two bolts retaining the shift lever to the transmission.
To install:
4. Position the shift lever to the transmission, then install the two retaining bolts and tighten to 23–32 ft. lbs. (31–43 Nm).

➡**Shift lever bolts must only be installed in one direction, from the left side of the shift lever.**

5. Install the console trim and the shift boot.
6. Install the shift knob by screwing it into place. When tension is felt, rotate it an additional 180 degrees to align the graphics on the knob.

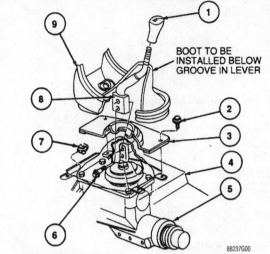

1. Gearshift handle knob
2. Mounting bolts
3. Rubber secondary gearshift boot
4. Front floor pan
5. Transmission
6. Gearshift handle-to-transmission bolts
7. J-nuts
8. Gearshift handle
9. Console gearshift trim panel and leather primary boot

Fig. 1 Exploded view of the transmission shift handle mounting

Back-up Light Switch

REMOVAL & INSTALLATION

♦ See Figures 2 and 3

1. Raise and support the vehicle safely using jackstands.

➡**Be sure to block the wheels remaining on the ground. If the front end is being raised, firmly set the parking brake.**

2. Disengage the wiring harness connector from the back-up light switch, located on the left-hand side of the transmission case.

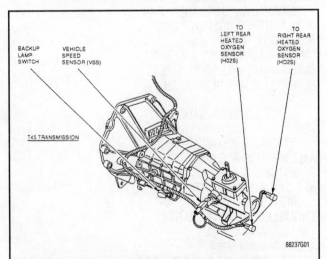

Fig. 2 The back-up light switch on the T45 transmission is located on the left-hand side of the case—4.6L engines

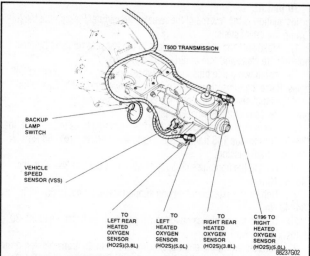

Fig. 3 On the T50D transmission, the back-up switch is also located on the left-hand side—3.8L and 5.0L engines

3. Unthread the switch from the transmission case.

To install:

4. Thread the new switch into position and tighten it to 20–35 ft. lbs. (27–47 Nm).

5. Attach the wiring harness connector to the switch.

6. Remove the jackstands and carefully lower the vehicle.

7. Start the vehicle, depress the clutch and the brake pedals and position the shift handle in Reverse. Have an assistant, standing off to one side of the rear of the vehicle, check your back-up lights to verify proper operation of the switch; the back-up lights should only illuminate when the shift handle is in Reverse.

Extension Housing Seal

REMOVAL & INSTALLATION

▶ **See Figures 4 and 5**

1. Raise and safely support the vehicle on jackstands.
2. Remove the driveshaft from the vehicle.

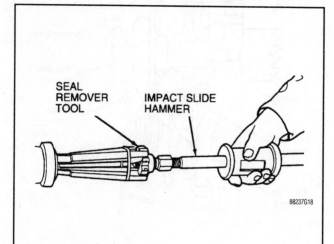

Fig. 4 Use an impact slide hammer and an oil seal remover tool/adapter to pull the seal out of the extension housing

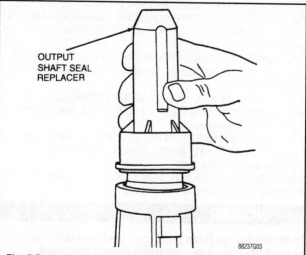

Fig. 5 Press the new oil seal into the extension housing with a properly-sized driver

❋❋ WARNING

Avoid damaging (scratching, gouging, etc.) the oil seal bore in the extension housing; otherwise, oil leaks may occur after the new seal is installed.

3. Using an impact slide hammer (such as Ford Tool T50T-100-A) and a seal remover adapter (such as Ford Tool 1175-AC), pull the old seal out of the extension housing. It may also be possible to use a prytool oil seal removal tool; however, this method is not recommended by the manufacturer.

To install:

4. Use Ford Output Shaft Seal Replacer T96P-7127-A (for the T45 transmission), Ford Extension Housing Seal Replacer T94P-7657-A (for the T50D transmission), or an equivalent properly-sized seal driver, to seat the new oil seal in the extension housing. Ensure that the seal is installed so that it is not cocked in the housing and that it is fully seated.

5. Install the driveshaft.

6. Lower the vehicle.

Manual Transmission Assembly

REMOVAL & INSTALLATION

1. Disconnect the negative battery cable for safety purposes.
2. Remove the gearshift handle.
3. Firmly set the parking brake and block the drive wheels, then raise and support the front of the vehicle safely using jackstands.
4. Drain the transmission fluid.
5. Matchmark the driveshaft for reassembly. Disconnect the driveshaft from the rear U-joint flange. Slide the driveshaft off the transmission output shaft, then install an extension housing seal installation tool into the extension housing to prevent residual lubricant from leaking.

➡**If a seal tool is not available, place a plastic bag over the extension housing and secure it with one or more rubber bands. This will help prevent a mess of transmission fluid.**

6. Remove the mounting fasteners, then remove the dual catalytic converter Y-pipe from the vehicle.

7. Remove the retaining bolt and the clutch release lever dust shield, then disconnect the clutch cable.

8. Remove the two nuts attaching the rear transmission support to the crossmember, then remove the retaining bolts.

9. Use a floor jack to support the engine and transmission assembly. Always use a block of wood between the engine/transmission and the floor jack to spread the load, and to prevent damage to the engine and drive train components.

10. Remove the two nuts from the crossmember bolts. Remove the bolts, then use the jack to raise the transmission slightly and remove the crossmember.

11. Disengage the wiring harness connectors from the back-up lamp switch and the Vehicle Speed Sensor (VSS). On the 5.0L engine, disconnect the Neutral sensing switch.

12. If equipped, remove the bolt from the speedometer cable retainer, then remove the speedometer driven gear from the transmission.

13. Remove the starter motor.

14. Position a jackstand under the back of the engine to support it while the transmission is removed from the vehicle.

✷✷ WARNING

Do not depress the clutch pedal while the transmission is removed from the engine, otherwise damage may result.

15. Remove the transmission-to-flywheel housing retaining bolts.

16. Remove the transmission and jack rearward until the transmission input shaft clears the flywheel housing. If necessary, lower it enough to obtain clearance for removing the transmission.

✷✷ WARNING

Do NOT depress the clutch while the transmission is removed. To prevent this, it is usually wise to either block the pedal in the upward position or to tie it up to the steering column.

CLUTCH

✷✷ CAUTION

The clutch driven disc may contain asbestos, which has been determined to be a cancer-causing agent. Never clean clutch surfaces with compressed air. Avoid inhaling any dust from any clutch surface. When cleaning clutch surfaces, use a commercially-available brake cleaning fluid.

Understanding the Clutch

▶ See Figure 6

The purpose of the clutch is to disconnect and connect engine power at the transmission. A vehicle at rest requires a lot of engine torque to get all that weight moving. An internal combustion engine does not develop a high starting torque (unlike steam engines) so it must be allowed to operate without any load until it builds up enough torque to move the vehicle. To a point, torque increases with engine rpm. The clutch allows the engine to build up torque by physically disconnecting the engine from the transmission, relieving the engine of any load or resistance.

The transfer of engine power to the transmission (the load) must be smooth and gradual; if it weren't, driveline components would wear out or break quickly. This gradual power transfer is made possible by gradually releasing the clutch pedal. The clutch disc and pressure plate are the connecting link between the engine and transmission. When the clutch pedal is released, the disc and plate contact each other (the clutch is engaged), physically joining the engine and transmission. When the pedal is pushed down, the disc and plate separate (the clutch is disengaged), disconnecting the engine from the transmission.

Most clutch assemblies consists of the flywheel, the clutch disc, the clutch pressure plate, the throwout bearing and fork, the actuating linkage and the pedal. The flywheel and clutch pressure plate (driving members) are connected to the engine crankshaft and rotate with it. The clutch disc is

To install:

Installation is the reverse of the removal procedure. Please note the following important steps:

17. Make sure the mounting surface of the transmission and flywheel housing are clean and free of dirt, paint and burrs.

18. Install two guide pins in the flywheel housing lower mounting bolt holes. Raise the transmission, then move it forward onto the guide pins until the input shaft splines enter the clutch hub splines and the case is positioned against the flywheel housing.

19. Tighten the transmission-to-flywheel retaining bolts to 28–38 ft. lbs. (38–52 Nm) for the T45 transmission, or to 45–64 ft. lbs. (61–88 Nm) for the T50D transmission.

20. Tighten the transmission support attaching bolts to 36–50 ft. lbs. (48–68 Nm).

21. Tighten the extension housing support retaining nut to 25–35 ft. lbs. (34–48 Nm).

22. Tighten the catalytic converter Y-pipe attaching fasteners to 20–30 ft. lbs. (27–41 Nm).

23. Before starting the engine, be sure to install the transmission drain plug, fill the transmission with 5.6 pts. (for the T50D), or with 6.4–6.7 pts. (for the T45) of Mercon® multi-purpose automatic transmission fluid, and to install the transmission fluid fill plug. Use a pipe sealant with Teflon® on the drain and fill plugs, and tighten them to 13–21 ft. lbs. (17–29 Nm).

24. After installing the shift handle, check the shift and crossover motion for full shift engagement and smooth crossover operation.

➡**Remember to remove the wheel blocks before attempting to move the vehicle.**

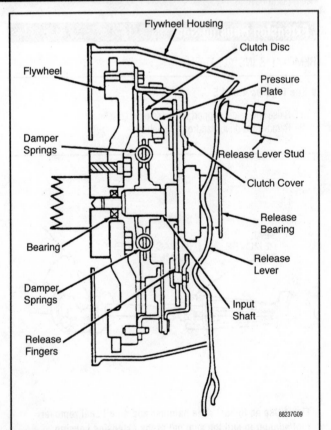

Fig. 6 Cutaway view of the typical clutch system used on 1994–98 Mustang vehicles

located between the flywheel and pressure plate, and is splined to the transmission shaft. A driving member is one that is attached to the engine and transfers engine power to a driven member (clutch disc) on the transmission shaft. A driving member (pressure plate) rotates (drives) a driven member (clutch disc) on contact and, in so doing, turns the transmission shaft.

There is a circular diaphragm spring within the pressure plate cover (transmission side). In a relaxed state (when the clutch pedal is fully released) this spring is convex; that is, it is dished outward toward the transmission. Pushing in the clutch pedal actuates the attached linkage. Connected to the other end of this is the throwout fork, which holds the throwout bearing. When the clutch pedal is depressed, the clutch linkage pushes the fork and bearing forward to contact the diaphragm spring of the pressure plate. The outer edges of the spring are secured to the pressure plate and are pivoted on rings so that when the center of the spring is compressed by the throwout bearing, the outer edges bow outward and, by so doing, pull the pressure plate in the same direction, away from the clutch disc. This action separates the disc from the plate, disengaging the clutch and allowing the transmission to be shifted into another gear.

A coil type clutch return spring attached to the clutch pedal arm permits full release of the pedal. Releasing the pedal pulls the throwout bearing away from the diaphragm spring, resulting in a reversal of spring position. As bearing pressure is gradually released from the spring center, the outer edges of the spring bow outward, pushing the pressure plate into closer contact with the clutch disc. As the disc and plate move closer together, friction between the two increases and slippage is reduced until, when full spring pressure is applied (by fully releasing the pedal), the speed of the disc and plate are the same. This stops all slipping, creating a direct connection between the plate and disc, which results in the transfer of power from the engine to the transmission. The clutch disc is now rotating with the pressure plate at engine speed and, because it is splined to the transmission shaft, the shaft now turns at the same engine speed.

The clutch is operating properly if:

1. It will stall the engine when released with the vehicle held stationary.

2. The shift lever can be moved freely between 1st and reverse gears when the vehicle is stationary and the clutch disengaged.

Driven Disc and Pressure Plate

REMOVAL & INSTALLATION

▶ See Figures 7 and 8 (p. 6–7)

1. Disconnect the negative battery cable for safety purposes.

✳✳ WARNING

The clutch release lever cable should never be removed from the clutch and brake pedal pivot shaft with a prying instrument such as a prybar.

2. Lift the clutch pedal to its upwardmost position to disengage the pawl and quadrant. Push the quadrant forward, unhook the cable from the quadrant and allow it to slowly swing rearward.

3. Raise and support the vehicle safely using jackstands. Remove the clutch release lever dust shield.

4. Disconnect the cable from the release lever. Remove the retaining clip and remove the clutch cable from the flywheel housing.

5. Remove the starter motor and the bolts holding the engine rear plate to the lower part of the flywheel housing.

6. Remove the transmission from the vehicle. Remove the bolts attaching the flywheel housing to the engine block, then remove the flywheel housing from the vehicle.

7. Remove the clutch release lever from the housing by pulling it through the window in the housing until the retainer spring is disengaged from the pivot. Remove the release bearing from the release lever.

8. Loosen the pressure plate cover attaching bolts evenly, to release spring tension gradually and avoid distorting the cover. If the same pressure plate and cover are to be reinstalled, matchmark the cover and flywheel so that the pressure plate can be installed in its original position. Remove the pressure plate and clutch disc from the engine.

9. Inspect the flywheel for scoring, cracks or other damage. Machine or replace as necessary. Inspect the pilot bearing for damage and free movement. Replace as necessary.

To install:

10. If removed, install the flywheel. Make sure the mating surfaces of the flywheel and the crankshaft flange are clean prior to installation. Tighten the flywheel bolts to 54–64 ft. lbs. (73–87 Nm) for 3.8L and 4.6L engines, or to 75–85 ft. lbs. (102–115 Nm) for the 5.0L engine.

11. Position the clutch disc and pressure plate assembly on the flywheel. The three dowel pins on the flywheel must be properly aligned with the pressure plate. Bent, damaged or missing dowels must be replaced. Start the pressure plate bolts, but do not tighten them.

12. Align the clutch disc using a disc alignment tool inserted into the pilot bearing. Alternately tighten the bolts a few turns at a time, until they are all tight. Then, tighten all the bolts to 12–24 ft. lbs. (17–32 Nm) for 1994–95 models, to 20–28 ft. lbs. (27–39 Nm) for 1996–98 3.8L engines, or to 19–24 ft. lbs. (25–33 Nm) for 4.6L engines, then remove the alignment tool.

Loosen the pressure plate bolts evenly to gradually release the spring tension . . .

. . . then remove the pressure plate and clutch disc from the flywheel

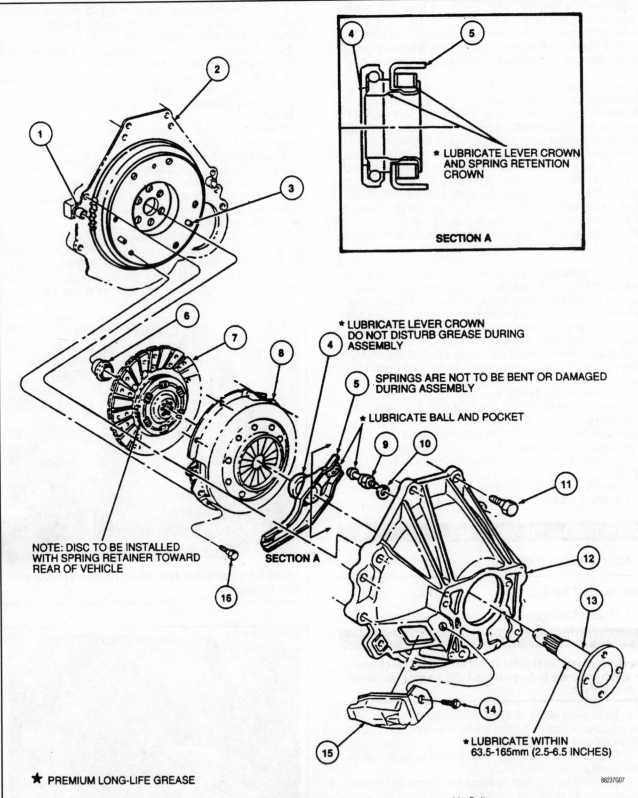

★ LUBRICATE LEVER CROWN
AND SPRING RETENTION
CROWN

SECTION A

★ LUBRICATE LEVER CROWN
DO NOT DISTURB GREASE DURING
ASSEMBLY

SPRINGS ARE NOT TO BE BENT OR DAMAGED
DURING ASSEMBLY

★ LUBRICATE BALL AND POCKET

NOTE: DISC TO BE INSTALLED
WITH SPRING RETAINER TOWARD
REAR OF VEHICLE

SECTION A

★ LUBRICATE WITHIN
63.5–165mm (2.5–6.5 INCHES)

88237G07

★ PREMIUM LONG-LIFE GREASE

1. Flywheel housing-to-engine block
   dowel
2. Rear face of engine block and flywheel
3. Flywheel-to-clutch cover alignment
   dowel
4. Release bearing

5. Clutch release lever
6. Pilot bearing
7. Clutch disc
8. Clutch pressure plate
9. Clutch release lever stud
10. Washer

11. Bolt
12. Flywheel housing
13. Main drive gear bearing retainer
14. Bolt
15. Clutch release lever dust shield
16. Screw and washer

Fig. 7 Exploded view of the clutch system used on all 1994–95 Mustang models

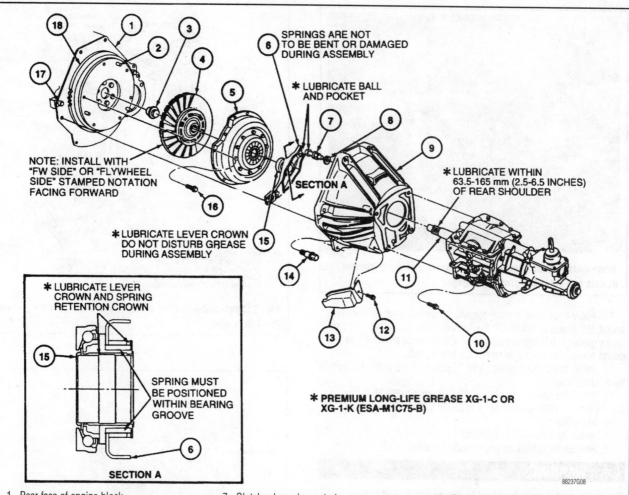

SPRINGS ARE NOT
TO BE BENT OR DAMAGED
DURING ASSEMBLY

* LUBRICATE BALL
AND POCKET

SECTION A

* LUBRICATE WITHIN
63.5-165 mm (2.5-6.5 INCHES)
OF REAR SHOULDER

NOTE: INSTALL WITH
"FW SIDE" OR "FLYWHEEL
SIDE" STAMPED NOTATION
FACING FORWARD

* LUBRICATE LEVER CROWN
DO NOT DISTURB GREASE
DURING ASSEMBLY

* LUBRICATE LEVER
CROWN AND SPRING
RETENTION CROWN

SPRING MUST
BE POSITIONED
WITHIN BEARING
GROOVE

SECTION A

* PREMIUM LONG-LIFE GREASE XG-1-C OR
XG-1-K (ESA-M1C75-B)

88237G08

1. Rear face of engine block
2. Flywheel-to-clutch cover alignment dowel
3. Pilot bearing
4. Clutch disc
5. Clutch pleasure plate
6. Clutch release lever
7. Clutch release lever stud
8. Lockwasher
9. Flywheel housing
10. Bolt
11. Input shaft
12. Bolt
13. Clutch release lever dust shield
14. Bolt
15. Clutch release bearing
16. Bolt
17. Flywheel housing-to-engine block dowel

Fig. 8 Exploded view of the clutch system components used on all 1996–98 Mustang models

TCCS7142

Use an alignment tool of the same size and spline pattern as the transmission input shaft for assembly

TCCS7128

Insert the alignment arbor to properly position the clutch disc and pressure plate during installation

When installing the pressure plate, ensure that the alignment dowels and holes are properly engaged

13. Apply a light coat of multi-purpose grease to the release lever pivot pocket, the release lever fork and the flywheel housing pivot ball. Fill the grease groove of the release bearing hub with the same grease. Clean all excess grease from the inside bore of the bearing hub.

14. Install the release bearing on the release lever and install the lever in the flywheel housing.

15. Install the flywheel housing. Tighten the bolts to 38–55 ft. lbs. (52–74 Nm) on 1994–95 models, or to 28–38 ft. lbs. (38–52 Nm) on 1996–98 models.

16. Install the remaining components.

17. Remove the jackstands and carefully lower the vehicle.

✳✳ WARNING

The clutch pedal must be lifted to disengage the adjusting mechanism during clutch release lever cable installation. If this is not done, damage to the self-adjuster mechanism will occur.

18. Install the clutch release lever cable by lifting the clutch pedal to disengage the clutch and brake pedal pivot shaft, then push the pivot shaft forward and hook the end of the clutch release cable over the rear of the pivot shaft.

19. Depress and lift the clutch several times to allow the self-adjusting mechanism to properly set the free-play.

20. Connect the negative battery cable, then check for proper clutch operation.

ADJUSTMENTS

Free-Play

◆ See Figures 9, 10 and 11

The clutch free-play is adjusted automatically by a built-in clutch control mechanism. This device allows the clutch controls to self-adjust during normal operation.

The system consists of a spring-loaded gear quadrant, a spring-loaded pawl and a clutch cable which is spring-loaded to preload the release lever bearing. This compensates for movement of the release lever, as the clutch disc wears. The pawl, located at the top of the clutch pedal, engages the gear quadrant when the clutch pedal is depressed and pulls the cable through its continuously adjusted stroke. Clutch cable adjustments are not required because of this feature.

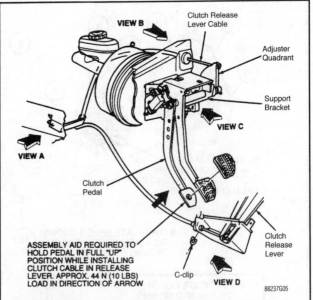

Fig. 9 Clutch self-adjusting system component identification for the 3.8L engine

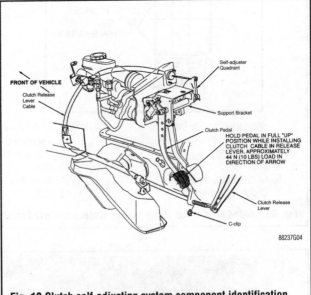

Fig. 10 Clutch self-adjusting system component identification for the 4.6L engines

CHECKING ADJUSTMENT

The self-adjusting feature should be checked every 5,000 miles (8,000 km). This is accomplished by ensuring that the clutch pedal travels to the top of its upward position. Grasp the clutch pedal with your hand or put your foot under the clutch pedal, and pull up on the pedal until it stops. Very little effort is required (about 10 lbs./4.5 kg). Finally, depress the clutch pedal and listen for an audible "click." If you hear a sound, the clutch was in need of adjustment, and it has just adjusted itself.

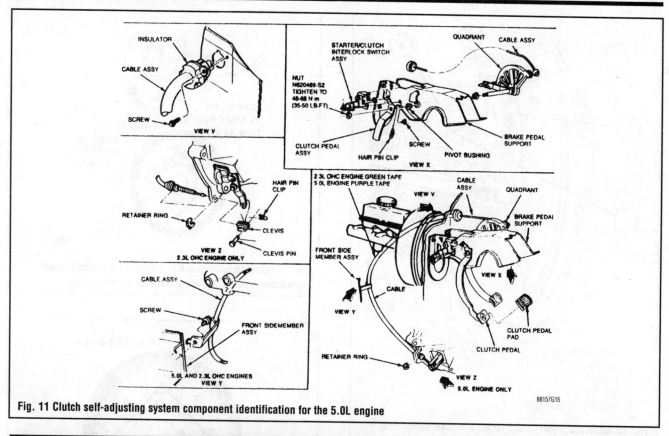

Fig. 11 Clutch self-adjusting system component identification for the 5.0L engine

AUTOMATIC TRANSMISSION

Understanding Automatic Transmissions

The automatic transmission allows engine torque and power to be transmitted to the rear wheels within a narrow range of engine operating speeds. It will allow the engine to turn fast enough to produce plenty of power and torque at very low speeds, while keeping it at a sensible rpm at high vehicle speeds (and it does this job without driver assistance). The transmission uses a light fluid as the medium for the transmission of power. This fluid also works in the operation of various hydraulic control circuits and as a lubricant. Because the transmission fluid performs all of these functions, trouble within the unit can easily travel from one part to another. For this reason, and because of the complexity and unusual operating principles of the transmission, a very sound understanding of the basic principles of operation will simplify troubleshooting.

TORQUE CONVERTER

♦ See Figures 12 and 13

The torque converter replaces the conventional clutch. It has three functions:

• It allows the engine to idle with the vehicle at a standstill, even with the transmission in gear.

• It allows the transmission to shift from range-to-range smoothly, without requiring the driver to close the throttle during the shift.

• It multiplies engine torque to an increasing extent as vehicle speed drops and throttle opening is increased. This has the effect of making the transmission more responsive and reduces the amount of shifting required.

The torque converter is a metal case which is shaped like a sphere that has been flattened on opposite sides. It is bolted to the rear end of the engine's crankshaft. Generally, the entire metal case rotates at engine speed and serves as the engine's flywheel.

The case contains three sets of blades. One set is attached directly to the case. This set forms the torus or pump. Another set is directly connected to

the output shaft, and forms the turbine. The third set is mounted on a hub which, in turn, is mounted on a stationary shaft through a one-way clutch. This third set is known as the stator.

A pump, which is driven by the converter hub at engine speed, keeps the torque converter full of transmission fluid at all times. Fluid flows continuously through the unit to provide cooling.

Under low speed acceleration, the torque converter functions as follows:

The torus is turning faster than the turbine. It picks up fluid at the center of the converter and, through centrifugal force, slings it outward. Since the outer edge of the converter moves faster than the portions at the center, the fluid picks up speed.

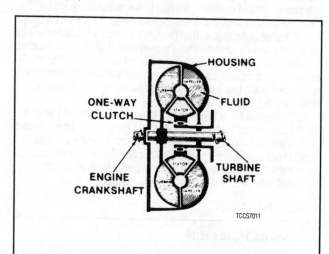

Fig. 12 The torque converter housing is rotated by the engine's crankshaft, and turns the impeller. The impeller then spins the turbine, which gives motion to the turbine shaft, driving the gears

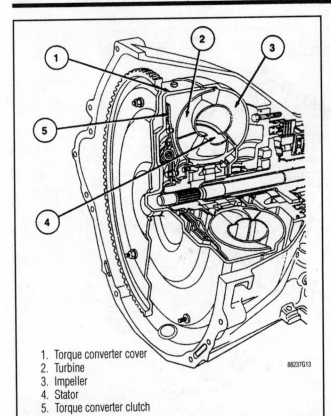

1. Torque converter cover
2. Turbine
3. Impeller
4. Stator
5. Torque converter clutch

Fig. 13 Automatic transmission torque converter component identification

The fluid then enters the outer edge of the turbine blades. It then travels back toward the center of the converter case along the turbine blades. In impinging upon the turbine blades, the fluid loses the energy picked up in the torus.

If the fluid was now returned directly into the torus, both halves of the converter would have to turn at approximately the same speed at all times, and torque input and output would both be the same.

In flowing through the torus and turbine, the fluid picks up two types of flow, or flow in two separate directions. It flows through the turbine blades, and it spins with the engine. The stator, whose blades are stationary when the vehicle is being accelerated at low speeds, converts one type of flow into another. Instead of allowing the fluid to flow straight back into the torus, the stator's curved blades turn the fluid almost 90° toward the direction of rotation of the engine. Thus the fluid does not flow as fast toward the torus, but is already spinning when the torus picks it up. This has the effect of allowing the torus to turn much faster than the turbine. This difference in speed may be compared to the difference in speed between the smaller and larger gears in any gear train. The result is that engine power output is higher, and engine torque is multiplied.

As the speed of the turbine increases, the fluid spins faster and faster in the direction of engine rotation. As a result, the ability of the stator to redirect the fluid flow is reduced. Under cruising conditions, the stator is eventually forced to rotate on its one-way clutch in the direction of engine rotation. Under these conditions, the torque converter begins to behave almost like a solid shaft, with the torus and turbine speeds being almost equal.

PLANETARY GEARBOX

♦ **See Figures 14, 15 and 16**

The ability of the torque converter to multiply engine torque is limited. Also, the unit tends to be more efficient when the turbine is rotating at relatively high speeds. Therefore, a planetary gearbox is used to carry the power output of the turbine to the driveshaft.

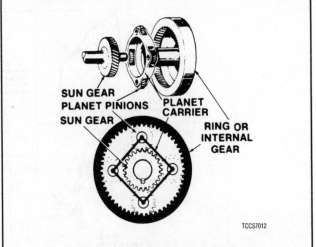

Fig. 14 Planetary gears work in a similar fashion to manual transmission gears, but are composed of three parts

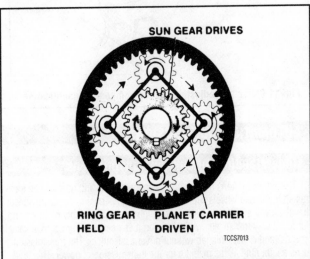

Fig. 15 Planetary gears in the maximum reduction (low) range. The ring gear is held and a lower gear ratio is obtained

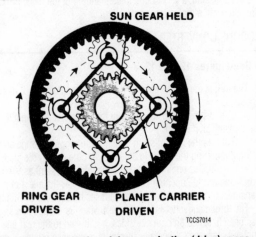

Fig. 16 Planetary gears in the minimum reduction (drive) range. The ring gear is allowed to revolve, providing a higher gear ratio

Planetary gears function very similarly to conventional transmission gears. However, their construction is different in that three elements make up one gear system, and in that all three elements are different from one another. The three elements are: an outer gear that is shaped like a hoop, with teeth cut into the inner surface; a sun gear, mounted on a shaft and located at the very center of the outer gear; and a set of three planet gears, held by pins in a ring-like planet carrier, meshing with both the sun gear and the outer gear. Either the outer gear or the sun gear may be held stationary, providing more than one possible torque multiplication factor for each set of gears. Also, if all three gears are forced to rotate at the same speed, the gearset forms, in effect, a solid shaft.

Most automatic transmissions use the planetary gears to provide various reductions ratios. Bands and clutches are used to hold various portions of the gearsets to the transmission case or to the shaft on which they are mounted. Shifting is accomplished, then, by changing the portion of each planetary gearset which is held to the transmission case or to the shaft.

SERVOS & ACCUMULATORS

♦ See Figure 17

The servos are hydraulic pistons and cylinders. They resemble the hydraulic actuators used on many other machines, such as bulldozers. Hydraulic fluid enters the cylinder, under pressure, and forces the piston to move to engage the band or clutches.

The accumulators are used to cushion the engagement of the servos. Transmission fluid must pass through the accumulator on the way to the servo. The accumulator housing contains a thin piston which is sprung away from the discharge passage of the accumulator. When fluid passes through the accumulator on the way to the servo, it must move the piston against spring pressure, and this action smooths out the action of the servo.

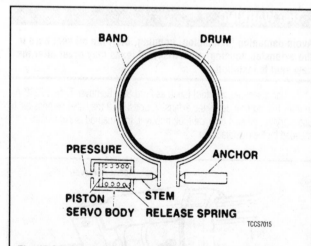

TCCS7015

Fig. 17 Servos, operated by pressure, are used to apply or release the bands, to either hold the ring gear or allow it to rotate

HYDRAULIC CONTROL SYSTEM

The hydraulic pressure used to operate the servos comes from the main transmission oil pump. This fluid is channeled to the various servos through the shift valves. There is generally a manual shift valve which is operated by the transmission selector lever and an automatic shift valve for each automatic upshift the transmission provides.

➡**Many new transmissions are electronically controlled. On these models, electrical solenoids are used to better control the hydraulic fluid. Usually, the solenoids are regulated by an electronic control module.**

There are two pressures which effect the operation of these valves. One is the governor pressure which is effected by vehicle speed. The other is the modulator pressure which is effected by intake manifold vacuum or throttle position. Governor pressure rises with an increase in vehicle speed, and modulator pressure rises as the throttle is opened wider. By responding to these two pressures, the shift valves cause the upshift points to be delayed with increased throttle opening to make the best use of the engine's power output.

Most transmissions also make use of an auxiliary circuit for downshifting. This circuit may be actuated by the throttle linkage which actuates the modulator, by a cable or by a solenoid. It applies pressure to a special downshift surface on the shift valve or valves.

The transmission modulator also governs the line pressure, used to actuate the servos. In this way, the clutches and bands will be actuated with a force matching the torque output of the engine.

Fluid Pan

REMOVAL, FILTER CHANGE & INSTALLATION

This procedure is covered under Fluids and Lubricants in Section 1 of this manual.

Neutral Safety and Back-up Light Switches

REMOVAL & INSTALLATION

♦ See Figure 18

➡**For this procedure, the Ford MLP/TR Sensor Alignment Tool T93P-70010-A, or equivalent, is required.**

The neutral safety and back-up light switches on these models are incorporated into the Manual Lever Position (MLP) sensor, also known as the

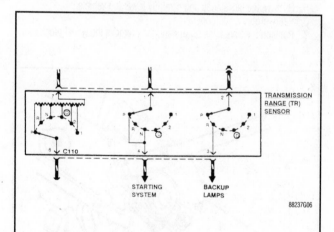

88237G06

Fig. 18 The Manual Lever Position (MLP) sensor, also known as the Transmission Range (TR) sensor, incorporates the neutral safety and back-up light switches into one component

Transmission Range (TR) sensor on newer models. The MLP sensor houses the starting circuits for the ignition system, to allow the vehicle to be started in Park (P) or Neutral (N), and the back-up light circuits, which are closed in Reverse (R). This sensor is used by the transmission control module to determine the transmission gear selection.

1. Apply the parking brake, block the rear wheels and position the transmission gearshift in Neutral.

2. Disconnect the negative battery cable.

3. Raise and support the front of the car safely using jackstands.

4. Disconnect the wiring harness from the sensor by disengaging the retaining tab and pulling the connector out of the sensor.

5. Remove the two sensor mounting bolts, then remove the sensor from the side of the transmission.

To install:

6. Ensure that the manual control lever on the transmission is in the Neutral position, then install the MLP sensor on the transmission case. Loosely install the mounting bolts.

7. Align the MLP sensor slots using the alignment tool (T93P-70010-A or equivalent). Tighten the retaining bolts to 62–88 inch lbs. (7–10 Nm), then remove the alignment tool.

8. Attach the wiring harness connector to the sensor until the retaining tab is fully engaged.

9. Remove the jackstands and carefully lower the vehicle.

10. Connect the negative battery cable.

11. Verify proper switch operation.

12. Position the transmission in Park, then remove the wheel blocks.

ADJUSTMENT

▶ See Figures 19 and 20

➡For this procedure, the Ford MLP/TR Sensor Alignment Tool T93P-70010-A, or equivalent, is required.

1. Apply the parking brake, block the rear wheels and position the transmission gearshift in Neutral.

2. Raise and support the front of the car safely using jackstands.

3. From under the vehicle, loosen the two sensor mounting bolts.

4. Install the alignment tool (T93P-70010-A or equivalent) onto the MLP sensor to align it, tighten the retaining bolts to 62–88 inch lbs. (7–10 Nm), then remove the alignment tool.

5. Remove the jackstands and carefully lower the vehicle.

6. Verify proper switch operation.

7. Position the transmission in Park, then remove the wheel blocks.

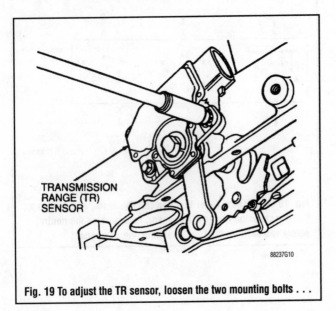

Fig. 19 To adjust the TR sensor, loosen the two mounting bolts . . .

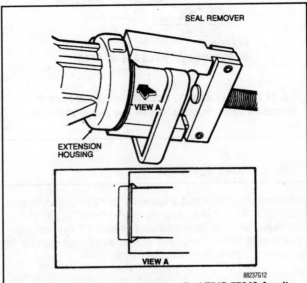

Fig. 20 . . . and install the alignment tool to properly position the sensor, then retighten the mounting bolts

Extension Housing Seal

REMOVAL & INSTALLATION

▶ See Figures 21 and 22

1. Raise and safely support the vehicle on jackstands.

2. Remove the driveshaft from the vehicle, as described later in this section.

✳✳ WARNING

Avoid damaging (scratching, gouging, etc.) the oil seal bore in the extension housing; otherwise, oil leaks may occur after the new seal is installed.

3. Use a seal removal tool (such as Ford Seal Remover T74P-77248-A) to draw the old seal out of the extension housing. It may also be possible to use a prytool oil seal removal tool; however, this method is not recommended by the manufacturer.

Fig. 21 Use either Ford Seal Remover Tool T74P-77248-A or its equivalent to draw the old oil seal out of the extension housing

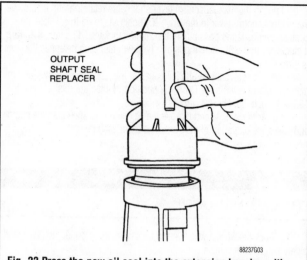

Fig. 22 Press the new oil seal into the extension housing with a properly-sized driver

To install:

4. Use an extension housing seal installation tool (such as Ford Tool T61L-7657-B) to seat the new oil seal in the extension housing. Ensure that the seal is installed so that it is not cocked in the housing and that it is fully seated.

5. Install the driveshaft.

6. Lower the vehicle.

7. Warm the engine to normal operating temperature and check the transmission fluid level; add fluid if necessary.

Transmission

REMOVAL & INSTALLATION

1. Disconnect the negative battery cable for safety purposes.

2. Raise and support the vehicle safely using jackstands.

3. Place a drain pan under the transmission fluid pan. Starting at the rear of the pan and working toward the front, loosen the attaching bolts and allow the fluid to drain. Finally, remove all of the pan attaching bolts except two at the front, to allow the fluid to further drain. With the fluid drained, install two bolts on the rear side of the pan to temporarily hold it in place.

4. Remove the front exhaust pipes, as necessary, for transmission removal.

5. Remove the torque converter cover from the lower end of the converter housing and the adapter plate bolts from the engine oil pan.

➡**Never rotate the crankshaft counterclockwise (looking at the engine from the front of the car).**

6. Remove the converter-to-flywheel attaching nuts. Place a wrench on the crankshaft pulley attaching bolt to turn the crankshaft and, therefore, the torque converter to gain access to the nuts.

7. If equipped with a torque converter drain plug, place a drain pan under the converter to catch the fluid. With the wrench on the crankshaft pulley attaching bolts, turn the converter to gain access to the converter drain plug and remove the plug. After the fluid has been drained, reinstall the plug.

8. Disconnect the driveshaft from the rear axle and slide the shaft rearward from the transmission. Position a seal installation tool in the extension housing to prevent fluid leakage.

➡**If a seal installation tool is not available, slip a plastic bag over the extension housing and secure it using rubber bands. This will help to keep the fluid from leaking and causing a mess during the procedure.**

9. Remove the Vehicle Speed Sensor (VSS) from the transmission case.

10. Carefully detach the shift cable from the transmission control lever at the transmission by removing the adjusting nut.

11. Disengage all transmission wiring harness and starter motor connectors and position the wiring harness aside. Remove the starter motor.

12. Position a transmission floor jack under the transmission and raise it slightly.

13. Remove the engine rear support-to-crossmember bolts.

14. Remove the crossmember-to-frame side support retaining bolts, then remove the engine and transmission support mount. Remove the engine and transmission support and engine damper mounting body bracket.

15. Lower the transmission jack and allow the transmission to hang.

16. Using a floor jack beneath the front of the engine, raise the engine to gain access to the two upper converter housing-to-engine block attaching bolts.

17. Detach the automatic transmission fluid cooler lines from the transmission, and plug the lines to prevent contamination.

18. Remove the lower transmission-to-engine bolts, then remove the transmission fluid fill tube.

19. Secure the transmission to the jack with a chain.

➡**If the transmission is to be removed from the vehicle for an extended period of time, support the back end of the engine with a jackstand and wooden block.**

20. Remove the two upper transmission-to-engine bolts, then carefully move the transmission and converter assembly away from the engine and, at the same time, lower the jack to clear the underside of the vehicle.

21. Remove the converter and mount the transmission in a holding fixture.

To install:

22. Position the converter on the transmission, making sure the converter drive flats are fully engaged in the pump gear by rotating the converter through what feels like two bumps or "notches".

23. With the converter properly installed, place the transmission on the jack. Secure the transmission to the jack with a safety chain.

24. Rotate the converter until the studs and drain plug are in alignment with the holes in the flywheel.

25. Lubricate the pilot bushing.

26. Align the yellow balancing marks on the converter and flexplate on models with the 5.0L engine.

✳✳ WARNING

While moving the transmission into position, avoid allowing it to tip into a nose-down position, because this can allow the converter to move forward and disengage from the pump gear. The converter housing is guided into position by the dowels in the rear of the engine block.

27. Move the converter and transmission assembly forward into position, taking care not to damage the flywheel and converter pilot. The torque converter must rest squarely against the flywheel, which indicates that the converter pilot is not binding in the engine crankshaft.

➡**Prior to installing and tightening the engine housing-to-flywheel retaining nut, a check should be made to ensure that the torque converter is properly installed. The torque converter should move freely with respect to the flywheel. If it will not move, or moves only grudgingly, remove the transmission and torque converter and reposition the torque converter so that it is properly installed.**

28. Install and tighten the bolts between the converter housing and the engine to specifications.

29. The remainder of installation is the reverse of the removal procedure.

30. Be sure to fill the transmission with 3–4 qts. (2.8–3.8L) of clean, new Mercon® Automatic Transmission Fluid (ATF) prior to starting the engine.

31. Allow the engine to reach normal operating temperature, then check the ATF level. Add fluid until the transmission is full.

ADJUSTMENTS

Shift Linkage

➡The transmission range selector lever (gearshift handle) should be held against the rearward Drive (D) stop when the linkage is adjusted.

1. Position the transmission gearshift handle in the Drive (D) position. Be sure that the lever is tight against the rearward Drive (D) stop.
2. Apply the parking brake, block the rear wheels, then raise the front of the vehicle and safely support it on jackstands.

3. Loosen the manual control lever shift cable retaining nut, then move the manual control lever to the Drive (D) position. To do this, rotate the control lever as far as possible in the counterclockwise direction, then turn it clockwise to the 3rd detent position (you will feel each detent as the lever is turned).
4. With the gearshift handle held against the rear Drive (D) stop and the manual control lever in the Drive (D) position, tighten the retaining nut to 150–203 inch lbs. (17–23 Nm).
5. Lower the vehicle and remove the wheel blocks, then start the engine and check the operation of the transmission in each range.

DRIVELINE

Driveshaft and U-joints

◆ See Figure 23

The driveshaft is the means by which the power from the engine and transmission (which are in the front of the car) can be transferred to the differential, rear axles and finally to the rear wheels. The driveshaft assembly incorporates two universal joints, one at each end, and a slip yoke (at the front end of the assembly), which fits into the back of the transmission.

All driveshafts are balanced when installed in a car. It is, therefore, imperative that before applying undercoat to the chassis, the driveshaft and universal joint assembly be completely covered or removed to prevent the accidental application of undercoating to the surfaces and the subsequent loss of balance. For this same reason, it is also a good idea to matchmark the driveshaft to the rear axle drive pinion flange before removal.

REMOVAL & INSTALLATION

1. Block the wheels which are to remain on the ground, then raise and safely support the vehicle.

➡If the front end is raised, be sure to block the drive wheels and firmly set the parking brake before lifting the vehicle. If the rear is raised, then the front wheels MUST be blocked, but the parking brake will be of no use. Also, keep in mind that lifting the vehicle at the rear may help prevent transmission fluid from leaking out of the transmission extension housing.

2. Matchmark the relationship of the rear driveshaft yoke and the drive pinion flange of the axle. If the original yellow marks are visible, there is no need for new marks. The marks facilitate installation of the assembly in its exact original position, thereby assuring you will maintain the proper balance.

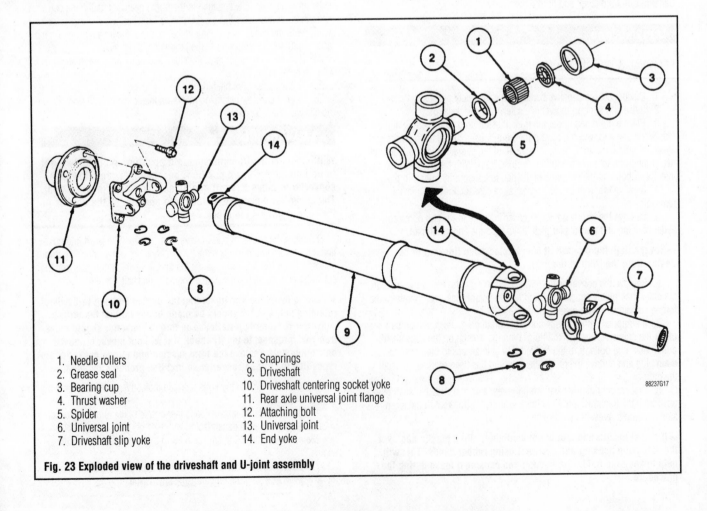

1. Needle rollers
2. Grease seal
3. Bearing cup
4. Thrust washer
5. Spider
6. Universal joint
7. Driveshaft slip yoke
8. Snaprings
9. Driveshaft
10. Driveshaft centering socket yoke
11. Rear axle universal joint flange
12. Attaching bolt
13. Universal joint
14. End yoke

Fig. 23 Exploded view of the driveshaft and U-joint assembly

88237G17

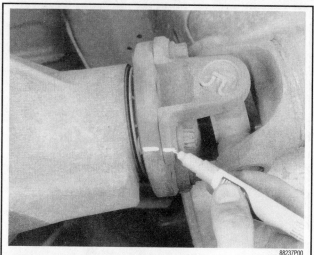

Matchmark the driveshaft and differential flanges so that they can be assembled in the same position . . .

. . . then remove the flange mounting bolts and separate the driveshaft from the differential flange

3. Remove the four bolts or U-clamps which hold the rear universal joint to the pinion flange. Wrap tape around the loose bearing caps in order to prevent them from falling off the spider.

4. Pull the driveshaft toward the rear of the vehicle until the slip yoke clears the transmission housing and the seal. Plug or cover the hole at the rear of the transmission housing (a plastic bag and a few rubber bands are helpful for this) or place a container under the opening to catch any fluid which might leak.

To install:

5. Carefully inspect the rubber seal on the output shaft and the seal in the end of the transmission extension housing. Replace them if they are damaged.

6. Examine the lugs on the axle pinion flange and replace the flange if the lugs are shaved or distorted.

7. Coat the yoke spline with special-purpose lubricant. The Ford part number for this product is B8A-19589-A.

8. If installed to prevent fluid leakage, remove the plug or cover from the rear of the transmission housing.

9. Insert the yoke into the transmission housing and onto the transmission output shaft. Make sure that the yoke assembly does not bottom on the output shaft with excessive force.

10. Locate the alignment marks made (or the original marks noted) during removal. Install the driveshaft assembly with the marks properly aligned.

11. Install the U-bolts and nuts or bolts which attach the universal joint to the pinion flange. Tighten the U-bolt nuts to 8–15 ft. lbs. (11–20 Nm) or the flange bolts to 70–95 ft. lbs. (95–130 Nm).

12. Remove the jackstands and carefully lower the vehicle.

U-JOINT REPLACEMENT

◗ See Figure 24, 25 and 26

1. Position the driveshaft assembly in a sturdy soft-jawed vise, BUT DO NOT place a significant clamp load on the shaft or you will risk deforming and ruining it.

2. Remove the snaprings which retain the bearings in the slip yoke (front only) and in the driveshaft (front and rear).

➡**A U-joint removal and installation tool (which looks like a large C-clamp) is available to significantly ease the task, but it is very possible to replace the U-joints using an arbor press or a large vise and a variety of sockets.**

3. Using a large vise or an arbor press along with a socket smaller than the bearing cap (on one side) and a socket larger than the bearing cap (on the other side), drive one of the bearings in toward the center of the universal joint, which will force the opposite bearing out.

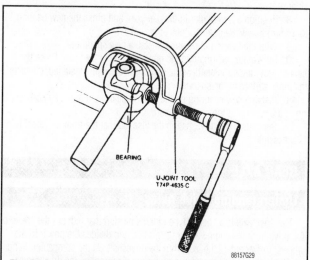

Fig. 24 A special tool (which looks like a C-clamp) is available to remove or install U-joints—removal shown here

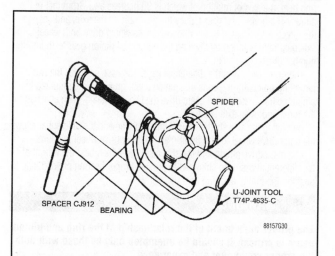

Fig. 25 The tool comes with special drivers or spacers such as the spacer shown here that is used when installing the U-joint

➡The smaller socket is used as a driver here, as it can pass through the opening of the U-joint or slip yoke flange. The larger socket is used to support the other side of the flange so that the bearing cap has room to exit the flange (into the socket).

4. As each bearing is forced far enough out of the universal joint to be accessible, grip it with a pair of pliers and pull it from the driveshaft yoke. Drive the spider in the opposite direction in order to make the opposite bearing accessible and pull it free with a pair of pliers. Use this procedure to remove all the bearings from both universal joints.

5. After removing the bearings, lift the spider from the yoke.

6. Thoroughly clean all dirt and foreign matter from the yokes on both ends of the driveshaft.

❊❊ WARNING

When installing new bearings in the yokes, it is advisable to use an arbor press or the special C-clamp tool. If this tool is not available, the bearings should be driven into position with extreme care, as a heavy jolt on the needle bearings can easily damage or misalign them. This will greatly shorten their life and hamper their efficiency.

7. Start a new bearing into the yoke at the rear of the drive-shaft.

8. Position a new spider in the rear yoke and press the new bearing ¼ in. (6mm) below the outer surface of the yoke.

9. With the bearing in position, install a new snapring.

10. Start a new bearing into the opposite side of the yoke. Press the bearing until the opposite bearing, which you have just installed, contacts the inner surface of the snapring.

11. Install a new snapring on the second bearing. It may be necessary to grind the surface of the second snapring.

12. Reposition the driveshaft in the vise, so that the front universal joint is accessible.

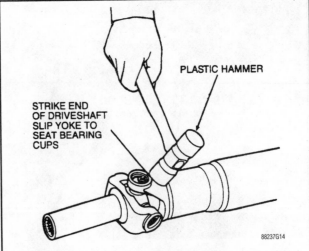

STRIKE END OF DRIVESHAFT SLIP YOKE TO SEAT BEARING CUPS

PLASTIC HAMMER

88237G14

Fig. 26 If the bearing caps do not seat properly during installation, strike the yoke, as shown, to position them

13. Install the new bearings, new spider and new snaprings in the same manner as for the previously assembled rear joint.

14. Position the slip yoke on the spider. Install new bearings, nylon thrust bearings and snaprings.

15. Check both reassembled joints for freedom of movement, If misalignment of any part is causing a bind, a sharp rap on the side of the yoke with a brass hammer should seat the needle bearings and provide the desired freedom of movement. Care should be exercised to firmly support the shaft end during this operation, as well as to prevent blows to the bearings themselves. Under no circumstance should the driveshaft be installed in a car if there is any binding in the universal joints.

REAR AXLE

Understanding Drive Axles

The drive axle is a special type of transmission that reduces the speed of the drive from the engine and transmission and divides the power to the wheels. Power enters the axle from the driveshaft via the companion flange, which is mounted on the drive pinion shaft. From there, the drive pinion shaft (which turns at engine/transmission speed) and gear carry the power into the differential. The gear on the end of the pinion shaft drives a large ring gear, the axis of rotation of which is 90 degrees away from that of the pinion. The pinion and gear reduce the gear ratio of the axle, and change the direction of rotation to turn the axle shafts which drive both wheels. The axle gear ratio is found by dividing the number of pinion gear teeth into the number of ring gear teeth.

The ring gear drives the differential case. The case provides the two mounting points for the ends of a pinion shaft, on which are mounted two pinion gears. These pinion gears drive the two side gears, each attached to the inner end of an axle shaft.

By driving the axle shafts through this arrangement, the differential allows the outer drive wheel to turn faster than the inner drive wheel in a turn.

The main drive pinion and the side bearings, which bear the weight of the differential case, are shimmed to provide proper bearing preload, and to position the pinion and ring gears properly.

❊❊ WARNING

The proper adjustment of the relationship of the ring and pinion gears is critical. It should be attempted only by those with both the proper equipment and experience.

Limited-slip differentials include clutches which tend to link each axle shaft to the differential case. Clutches may be engaged either by spring action or by pressure produced by the torque on the axles during a turn. When turning on dry pavement, the effects of the clutches are overcome and each wheel turns at the required speed. When slippage occurs at the either wheel, however, the clutches will transmit some of the power to the wheel with the greater amount of traction. Because of the clutches, limited-slip units often require a special lubricant.

Determining Axle Ratio

The drive axle is said to have a certain axle ratio (meaning the amount which the rear axle reduces the turning speed of the engine/transmission as it transmits this motion to the rear wheels. This number is actually a comparison of the number of gear teeth on the ring gear and pinion gear. For example, a 4.11 rear means that there are 4.11 teeth on the ring gear for every tooth on the pinion gear. Put another way, the driveshaft must turn 4.11 times to turn the rear wheels once. Actually, on a 4.11 rear, there might be 37 teeth on the ring gear and 9 on the pinion gear. By dividing the number of teeth on the pinion gear into the number of teeth on the ring gear, the numerical axle ratio is obtained. This also provides a good method of ascertaining the axle ratio with which your car is equipped.

Another, less accurate but quicker, method of determining gear ratio is to jack up and support the car so that BOTH rear wheels are off the ground. Make a chalk mark on the rear wheel and driveshaft, then place the transmission in Neutral and turn the rear wheel one complete turn (exactly). While turning the rear wheel, count the number of turns that the driveshaft makes (an assistant makes this a little easier). The number of turns made by the driveshaft (during one complete rotation of the rear wheel) is an approximation of the rear axle ratio. Again, if the driveshaft turned just a little bit more than 4 times, you have a 4.11 or similar gear ratio.

Rear Axle Shaft, Bearing and Seal

REMOVAL & INSTALLATION

▶ **See Figures 27, 28 and 29 (p. 17–20)**

1. Block the front wheels, then loosen the lug nuts on the rear wheel that is being removed.
2. Raise and support the vehicle safely using jackstands.
3. Remove the wheel, then remove the rear brake caliper and rotor.
4. If equipped, remove the anti-lock brake speed sensor.
5. Clean all dirt from the area of the axle housing cover. Drain the axle lubricant by removing the housing cover. For details, please refer to the Fluid and Lubricant information in Section 1 of this manual.
6. Remove the differential pinion shaft lockbolt and pinion shaft.
7. Push the flanged end of the axle shaft toward the center of the vehicle (to create the necessary play and free the C-lock), then remove the C-lock from the button end of the axle shaft.
8. Slowly withdraw the axle shaft from the housing, being careful not to damage the oil seal (unless you are replacing it anyway).
9. If the seal is being replaced (or if you damaged it on the way out)

insert a wheel bearing and seal replacement tool, such as T85L-1225-AH or equivalent, in the bore and position it behind the bearing so the tangs on the tool engage the bearing outer race. Remove the bearing and seal as a unit, using an impact slide hammer.

➡**If only the seal is being replaced, use a seal removal tool to pry ONLY THE SEAL from the axle housing.**

To install:

10. If removed, lubricate the new bearing with rear axle lubricant. Install the bearing into the housing bore with a bearing installer.
11. If removed, install a new axle seal using a seal installer. Essentially, the installation tool is a driver of the right diameter; a smooth socket or piece of pipe can also be used as a driver, just be careful not to damage the seal.

➡**Check for the presence of an axle shaft O-ring on the spline end of the shaft; install one if none is found.**

12. Carefully slide the axle shaft STRAIGHT into the axle housing, without damaging the bearing or seal assembly. Start the splines into the side gear and push firmly until the shaft splines engage. It may be necessary to rotate the axle slightly to align the splines.

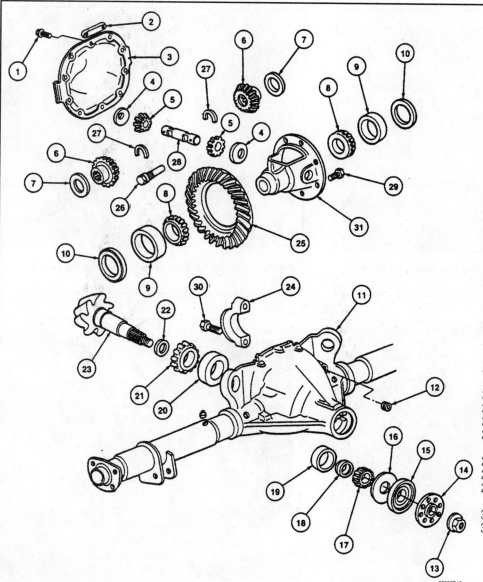

1. Mounting bolt
2. Brake line clip
3. Axle housing cover
4. Differential pinion thrust washer
5. Differential pinion gear
6. Differential side gear
7. Differential side gear thrust washer
8. Differential bearing
9. Differential bearing cup
10. Differential bearing shim
11. Axle housing
12. Filler plug
13. Pinion nut
14. Rear axle universal joint flange
15. Flange yoke seal
16. Rear axle drive pinion shaft oil slinger
17. Differential pinion bearing
18. Differential drive pinion bearing spacer
19. Differential pinion bearing cup
20. Rear axle pinion bearing cup
21. Rear axle pinion bearing cone and roller
22. Drive pinion bearing adjustment shim
23. Drive pinion
24. Bearing cap
25. Ring gear
26. Differential pinion shaft lockbolt
27. Rear axle shaft retaining C-clip
28. Differential pinion shaft
29. Rear axle differential gear case bolt
30. Mounting bolt
31. Differential case

Fig. 27 Exploded view of the rear axle assembly

99237G16

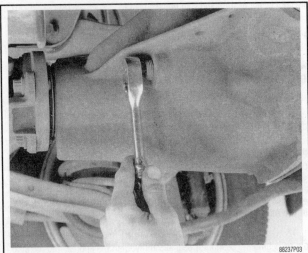

To remove an axle shaft, first remove the housing's fill plug to ensure that it is not frozen in place . . .

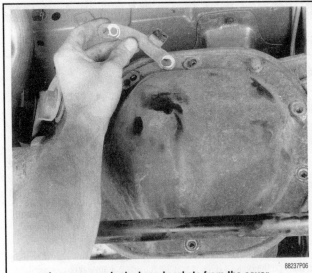

. . . and remove any brake hose brackets from the cover

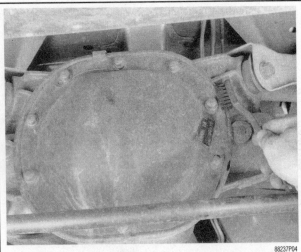

. . . then clean all dirt and debris from the cover to prevent it from entering the differential

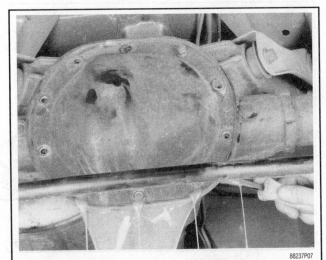

Pry the cover away from the housing and allow the fluid to drain . . .

Remove all but one or two upper mounting bolts from the axle housing cover . . .

. . . then remove the cover

Once the cover is removed, the differential unit (arrow) can be accessed

. . . and pull it out enough to clear the pinion shaft (arrow)

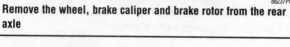

Remove the wheel, brake caliper and brake rotor from the rear axle

Pull the pinion shaft out of the differential unit . . .

Loosen the pinion shaft lockbolt . . .

. . . then push the axle shaft in and remove the C-clip retainer

Carefully pull the axle shaft out of the rear axle housing

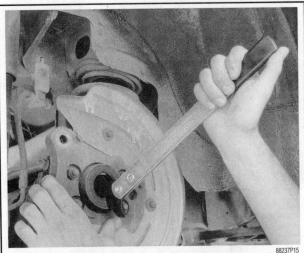

It is a good idea to replace the axle shaft oil seal at this time—be careful not to damage the seal bore

Use a properly-sized driver to install a new oil seal into the axle shaft housing

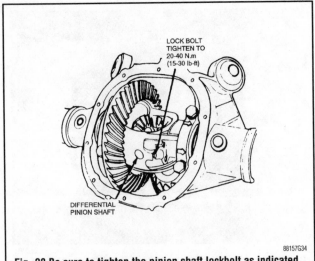

Fig. 28 Be sure to tighten the pinion shaft lockbolt as indicated to prevent it from accidentally loosening . . .

. . . then cover the differential unit with a clean rag and clean the gasket mating surface with a scraper

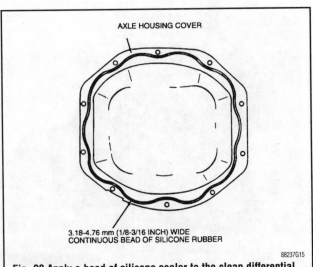

Fig. 29 Apply a bead of silicone sealer to the clean differential cover and install it on the axle housing . . .

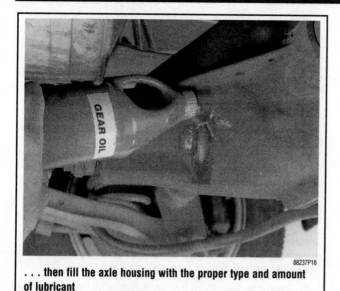

... then fill the axle housing with the proper type and amount of lubricant

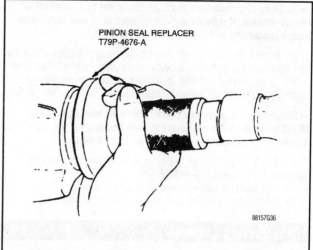

Fig. 30 A new pinion shaft seal should be installed using a suitable driver

13. Install the C-lock, then pull outward slightly on the axle shaft and make sure the C-lock seats in the counterbore of the differential side gear.

14. Insert the differential pinion shaft through the case and pinion gears, aligning the hole in the shaft with the lockbolt hole. Apply a suitable locking compound to the lockbolt and insert it through the case and pinion shaft. Tighten the lockbolt to 15–30 ft. lbs. (20–41 Nm).

15. Cover the inside of the differential case with a shop rag and clean the machined surface of the carrier and cover. Remove the shop rag.

16. Carefully clean the gasket mating surfaces of the cover and axle housing of any remaining gasket or sealer. A putty knife is a good tool to use for this. You may want to cover the differential gears using a rag or piece of plastic to prevent contaminating them with dirt or pieces of the old gasket.

17. Install the rear cover using a new gasket and sealant. Tighten the retaining bolts using a crosswise pattern.

➡**Make sure the vehicle is level before attempting to add fluid to the rear axle or an incorrect fluid level will result. You may have to lift all four corners of the vehicle and support it using 4 jackstands in order to do this.**

18. Refill the rear axle housing using the proper grade and quantity of lubricant as detailed in Section 1. Install the filler plug.

19. If removed, install the anti-lock speed sensor and tighten the retaining bolt to 40–60 inch lbs. (5–7 Nm).

20. Install the brake caliper and rotor.

21. Install the wheel, then remove the jackstands and carefully lower the vehicle.

Pinion Seal

REMOVAL & INSTALLATION

♦ **See Figures 30 and 31**

1. Raise and support the vehicle safely using jackstands.
2. Matchmark the rear driveshaft yoke and the companion flange so they may be reassembled in the same orientation to maintain balance.
3. Disconnect the driveshaft from the rear axle companion flange, then remove the driveshaft from the extension housing. Plug or cover the extension housing to prevent leakage. A plastic bag and a few rubber bands work well to cover the housing.
4. Install an inch pound torque wrench on the pinion nut and record the torque required to maintain rotation of the pinion through several revolutions.
5. While holding the companion flange with holder tool No. T78P-4851-A, or equivalent, remove the pinion nut.

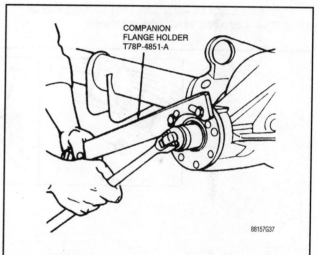

Fig. 31 A holding fixture tool is necessary when loosening or tightening the pinion shaft nut

6. Clean the area around the oil seal and place a pan under the seal.
7. Mark the companion flange in relation to the pinion shaft so the flange can be installed in the same position.
8. Remove the rear axle companion flange using tool No. T65L-4851-B, or equivalent.
9. Pry the seal out of the housing with a prytool.

To install:

10. Clean the oil seal seat surface and install the seal in the carrier using seal replacer tool T79P-4676-A, or equivalent. Apply lubricant to the lips of the seal.

11. Apply a small amount of lubricant to the companion flange splines, then align the marks on the flange and pinion shaft and install the flange.

12. Install a new nut on the pinion shaft and apply lubricant on the washer side of the nut.

13. Hold the flange with the holder tool while tightening the nut. Rotate the pinion to ensure proper seating and take frequent pinion bearing torque preload readings until the original recorded reading (before disassembly) is obtained.

14. If the original recorded preload is less than the minimum specification of 170 ft. lbs. (230 Nm) for the 7.5 in diameter ring gear axle, or 140 ft. lbs. (190 Nm) for the 8.8 in. diameter ring gear axle, tighten the nut to specification. If the preload is higher than specification, tighten to the original reading as recorded.

→Under no circumstance should the pinion nut be backed off to reduce preload. If reduced preload is required, a new collapsible pinion spacer and pinion nut should be installed.

15. Remove the plug or cover from the transmission extension housing and install the front end of the driveshaft on the transmission output shaft.

16. Connect the rear end of the driveshaft to the axle companion flange, aligning the scribed marks. Tighten the four bolts to 71–95 ft. lbs. (95–130 Nm).

→Remember that when you check fluid in the rear axle, the car MUST be level. If it is necessary to raise and support the vehicle for access, then it must be supported at all four corners.

17. Add rear axle lubricant to the carrier. Install the filler plug and tighten to 15–30 ft. lbs. (20–41 Nm).

18. Make sure the axle vent is not plugged with debris.

19. Remove the jackstands and carefully lower the vehicle.

Axle Housing Assembly

REMOVAL & INSTALLATION

◆ See Figure 32 and 33

1. Raise and support the vehicle safely using jackstands. Position additional jackstands under the rear frame crossmember.

2. Remove the axle housing cover and drain the lubricant.

3. Remove the wheel and tire assemblies.

4. Remove the brake rotors.

5. Remove the lockbolt from the pinion shaft and remove the shaft.

6. If equipped, remove the anti-lock brake sensors before removing the axle shafts.

7. Push the axle shafts inward to remove the C-locks and remove the axle shafts.

8. If necessary, remove the bolt attaching the brake line junction block to the rear cover.

9. Remove the brake lines from the clips and position them out of the way.

10. Matchmark the driveshaft yoke and companion flange. Disconnect the driveshaft at the companion flange and wire it to the underbody.

11. Support the axle housing with jackstands. Disengage the brake line from the clips that retain the line to the axle housing.

12. Disconnect the axle vent(s) from the rear axle housing.

→Some axle vents may be secured to the housing assembly through the brake line junction block. Upon assembly, a thread-lock/sealer must be applied to ensure retention.

13. Remove the lower shock absorber studs from the mounting brackets on the axle housing. If equipped, detach the quad shock from the quad shock bracket.

14. Disconnect the upper arms from the mountings on the axle housing ear brackets.

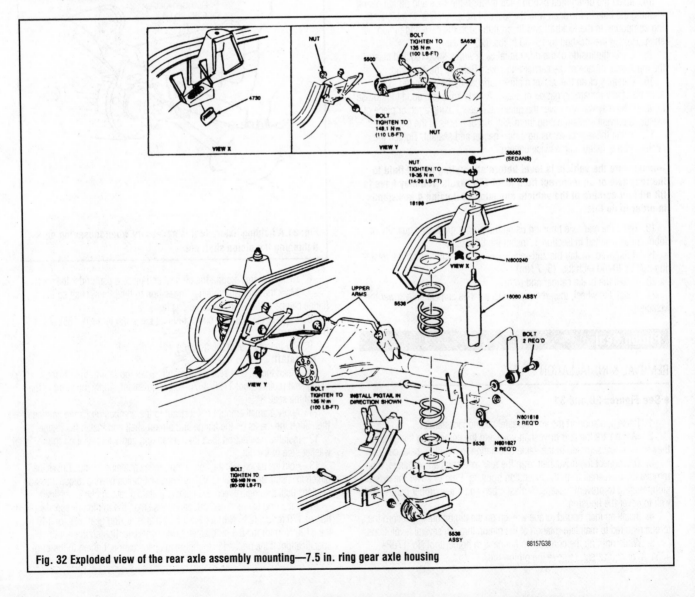

Fig. 32 Exploded view of the rear axle assembly mounting—7.5 in. ring gear axle housing

15. Lower the axle housing assembly until the coil springs are released and lift out the coil springs.

16. Disconnect the lower suspension arms at the axle housing.

17. Lower the axle housing and remove it from the vehicle.

To install:

18. Position the axle housing under the vehicle and raise the axle with a hoist or jack. Connect the lower suspension arms to their mounting brackets on the axle housing. Do not tighten the bolts and nuts at this time.

19. Reposition the rear coil springs.

20. Raise the housing into position.

21. Connect the upper arms to the mounting ears on the housing. Tighten the nuts and bolts to 70–100 ft. lbs. (95–135 Nm). Tighten the lower suspension arm bolts to 70–100 ft. lbs. (95–135 Nm).

22. Install the axle vent(s) and the brake line to the clips that retain the line to the axle housing.

23. Connect the lower shock absorber studs to the mounting bracket on the axle housing. If equipped, attach the quad shock to the quad shock bracket.

24. Connect the driveshaft to the companion flange and tighten the bolts to 70–95 ft. lbs. (95–130 Nm).

25. Slide the rear axle shafts into the housing until the splines enter the side gear. Push the axle shafts inward and install the C-lock at the end of each shaft spline. Pull the shafts outward until the C-lock enters the recess in the side gears.

26. Install the pinion shaft and the pinion shaft lockbolt. Tighten to 15–30 ft. lbs. (20–41 Nm).

27. Install the anti-lock sensor, if it was removed.

28. Install the rear brake rotors and calipers.

29. Install the axle housing cover.

30. Install the brake junction block on the cover and tighten to 10–18 ft. lbs. (14–24 Nm).

31. Properly refill the rear axle with the recommended lubricant (refer to Section 1 of this manual). Remember that the vehicle MUST be level to ensure that a proper amount of fluid is added.

32. Remove the jackstands and carefully lower the vehicle.

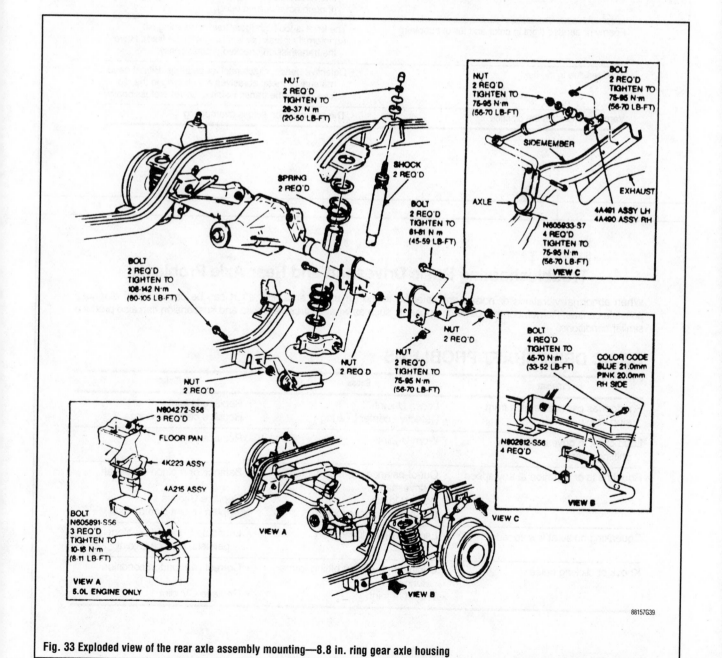

Fig. 33 Exploded view of the rear axle assembly mounting—8.8 in. ring gear axle housing

Transmission Fluid Indications

The appearance and odor of the transmission fluid can give valuable clues to the overall condition of the transmission. Always note the appearance of the fluid when you check the fluid level or change the fluid. Rub a small amount of fluid between your fingers to feel for grit and smell the fluid on the dipstick.

If the fluid appears:	It indicates:
Clear and red colored	· Normal operation
Discolored (extremely dark red or brownish) or smells burned	· Band or clutch pack failure, usually caused by an overheated transmission. Hauling very heavy loads with insufficient power or failure to change the fluid, often result in overheating. Do not confuse this appearance with newer fluids that have a darker red color and a strong odor (though not a burned odor).
Foamy or aerated (light in color and full of bubbles)	· The level is too high (gear train is churning oil) · An internal air leak (air is mixing with the fluid). Have the transmission checked professionally.
Solid residue in the fluid	· Defective bands, clutch pack or bearings. Bits of band material or metal abrasives are clinging to the dipstick. Have the transmission checked professionally.
Varnish coating on the dipstick	· The transmission fluid is overheating

88237C02

Troubleshooting Basic Driveshaft and Rear Axle Problems

When abnormal vibrations or noises are detected in the driveshaft area, this chart can be used to help diagnose possible causes. Remember that other components such as wheels, tires, rear axle and suspension can also produce similar conditions.

BASIC DRIVESHAFT PROBLEMS

Problem	Cause	Solution
Shudder as car accelerates from stop or low speed	· Loose U-joint · Defective center bearing	· Replace U-joint · Replace center bearing
Loud clunk in driveshaft when shifting gears	· Worn U-joints	· Replace U-joints
Roughness or vibration at any speed	· Out-of-balance, bent or dented driveshaft · Worn U-joints · U-joint clamp bolts loose	· Balance or replace driveshaft · Replace U-joints · Tighten U-joint clamp bolts
Squeaking noise at low speeds	· Lack of U-joint lubrication	· Lubricate U-joint; if problem persists, replace U-joint
Knock or clicking noise	· U-joint or driveshaft hitting frame tunnel · Worn CV joint	· Correct overloaded condition · Replace CV joint

88237C03

TORQUE SPECIFICATIONS

Year	Component	Ft. Lbs.	Nm
T45 Manual Transmission			
1996-98	Transmission support bolts	35-50	48-68
	Gearshift lever-to-transmission fasteners	20-25	26-35
	Back-up light switch	20-35	27-47
	Flywheel housing-to-transmission bolts	15-25	20-34
	Clutch release lever dust shield retaining bolt	150-203 inch lbs.	17-23
	Drain plug	97-212 inch lbs.	11-24
T50D Manual Transmission			
1994-98	Drain plug	12-22	17-29
	Transmission-to-flywheel housing bolts	45-65	61-88
	Speedometer cable retaining bolt	54-115 inch lbs.	6-13
	Transmission support bolts	35-50	48-68
	Shift lever-to-transmission fasteners	23-32	31-43
	Back-up light switch	20-35	27-47
	Neutral sensing switch	20-35	27-47
Clutch			
1994	Flywheel housing-to-engine block bolts—3.8L engine	28-38	38-52
	Flywheel housing-to-engine block bolts—5.0L engine	38-55	52-74
	Clutch pressure plate-to-flywheel bolt—3.8L engine	20-29	27-39
	Clutch pressure plate-to-flywheel bolt—5.0L engine	12-24	16-33
1995	Flywheel housing-to-engine block bolts—3.8L engine	28-38	38-52
	Flywheel housing-to-engine block bolts—5.0L engine	38-55	52-74
	Clutch pressure plate-to-flywheel bolt—3.8L engine	30-37	40-50
	Clutch pressure plate-to-flywheel bolt—5.0L engine	18-24	24-32
1996-98	Flywheel housing-to-engine block bolts—all engines	28-38	38-52
	Clutch pressure plate-to-flywheel bolt—3.8L engine	20-28	27-39
	Clutch pressure plate-to-flywheel bolt—4.6L engines	19-24	25-33
Automatic Transmission			
1994	Automatic Transmission Fluid (ATF) pan bolts	106-133 inch lbs.	12-15
	Crossmember-to-transmission bolts	65-81	87-110
	Converter-to-flywheel nuts	20-33	2746
	Converter housing drain plug	21-22	28-30
	Converter housing-to-engine bolts	28-38	38-51
	Cooler lines-to-transmission case	15-19	20-26
	Manual Lever Position (MLP) sensor mounting bolts	62-88 inch lbs.	7-10
	Transmission Speed Sensor (TSS) retaining bolt	62-88 inch lbs.	7-10
	Converter access plate bolts	22-32 inch lbs.	2.5-3.6
	Fluid filler tube bolt	28-38	38-51
	Transmission linkage adjustment nut	168-230 inch lbs.	19-26
1995	Automatic Transmission Fluid (ATF) pan bolts	106-133 inch lbs.	12-15
	Crossmember-to-transmission bolts	65-81	87-110
	Converter-to-flywheel nuts	20-33	2746
	Converter housing drain plug	21-22	28-30
	Converter housing-to-engine bolts	28-38	38-51
	Cooler lines-to-transmission case	15-19	20-26
	Transmission Range (TR) sensor mounting bolts	80-100 inch lbs.	9-11
	Vehicle Speed Sensor (VSS) retaining bolt	44-71 inch lbs.	5-8
	Converter access plate bolts	22-32 inch lbs.	2.5-3.6
	Fluid filler tube bolt	28-38	38-51
	Transmission linkage adjustment nut	168-230 inch lbs.	19-26
1996-98	Automatic Transmission Fluid (ATF) pan bolts	106-133 inch lbs.	12-15
	Crossmember-to-transmission bolts	65-81	87-110
	Converter-to-flywheel nuts	20-33	2746

88237C00

TORQUE SPECIFICATIONS

Year	Component	Ft. Lbs.	Nm
1996-98 continued	Converter housing drain plug	21-22	28-30
	Converter housing-to-engine bolts	41-50	55-68
	Cooler lines-to-transmission case	15-19	20-26
	Transmission Range (TR) sensor mounting bolts	62-88 inch lbs.	7-10
	Vehicle Speed Sensor (VSS) retaining bolt	62-88 inch lbs.	7-10
	Converter access plate bolts	142-195 inch lbs.	16-22
	Fluid filler tube bolt	28-38	38-51
	Transmission linkage adjustment nut	168-230 inch lbs.	19-26
Drive Train and 7.5 in. Rear Axle			
1994-98	U-joint flange bolts	71-95	95-130
	Pinion shaft lockbolt	15-30	20-41
	Axle housing cover bolts—1994 models	28-38	38-52
	Axle housing cover bolts—1995-97 models	18-28	24-38
	Oil fill plug	15-30	20-41
	Rear suspension arm and bushing-to-axle bolts	70-100	95-135
	Rear suspension arm and bushing-to-chassis bolts	110	149
	Brake line clip retaining bolt	88-124 inch lbs.	10-14
	Rear suspension lower arm-to-axle	70-100	95-135
	Rear suspension lower arm-to-chassis	77-105	104-142
	Rear shock absorber lower mounting bracket bolt	56-77	76-104
	Pinion nut	140	190
Drive Train and 8.8 in. Rear Axle			
1994-98	U-joint flange bolts	71-95	95-130
	Pinion shaft lockbolt	15-30	20-41
	Axle housing cover bolts (except ratio tag bolt)	28-38	38-52
	Axle housing cover ratio tag bolt	18-28	24-38
	Oil fill plug	15-30	20-41
	Rear suspension arm and bushing-to-axle bolts	70-100	95-135
	Rear suspension arm and bushing-to-chassis bolts	77-105	104-142
	Brake line clip retaining bolt	88-124 inch lbs.	10-14
	Rear suspension lower arm-to-axle	70-100	95-135
	Rear suspension lower arm-to-chassis	77-105	104-142
	Rear shock absorber lower mounting bracket bolt and nut	57-77	76-104
	Axle damper front bolt	57-75	76-103
	Axle damper rear nut	57-75	76-103
	Axle damper bracket bolt	57-75	76-103
	Stabilizer bar-to-lower arm bolts	33-52	45-70

88237C01

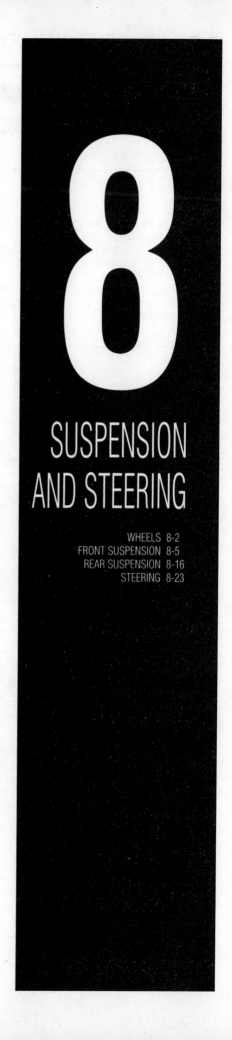

SUSPENSION
AND STEERING

WHEELS

Wheels

REMOVAL & INSTALLATION

▶ **See Figure 1**

1. Park the vehicle on a level surface.
2. Remove the jack, tire iron and, if necessary, the spare tire from their storage compartments.
3. Check the owner's manual or refer to Section 1 of this manual for the jacking points on your vehicle. Then, place the jack in the proper position.
4. If equipped with lug nut trim caps, remove them by either unscrewing or pulling them off the lug nuts, as appropriate. Consult the owner's manual, if necessary.

5. If equipped with a wheel cover or hub cap, insert the tapered end of the tire iron in the groove and pry off the cover.
6. Apply the parking brake and block the diagonally opposite wheel with a wheel chock or two.

➡**Wheel chocks may be purchased at your local auto parts store, or a block of wood cut into wedges may be used. If possible, keep one or two of the chocks in your tire storage compartment, in case any of the tires has to be removed on the side of the road.**

7. If equipped with an automatic transmission/transaxle, place the selector lever in **P** or Park; with a manual transmission/transaxle, place the shifter in Reverse.
8. With the tires still on the ground, use the tire iron/wrench to break the lug nuts loose.

Place the jack at the proper lifting point on your vehicle

With the vehicle still on the ground, break the lug nuts loose using the wrench end of the tire iron

Before jacking the vehicle, block the diagonally opposite wheel with one or, preferably, two chocks

After the lug nuts have been loosened, raise the vehicle using the jack until the tire is clear of the ground

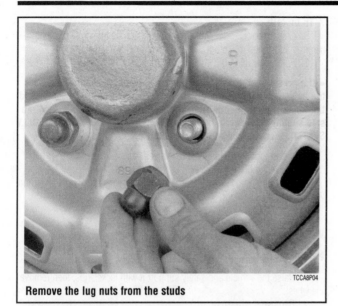

Remove the lug nuts from the studs

TCCA8P04

Remove the wheel and tire assembly from the vehicle

TCCA8P05

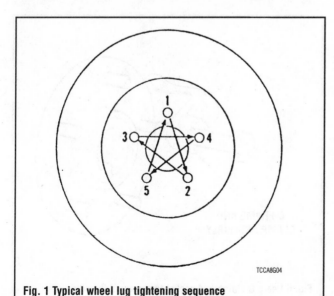

TCCA8G04

Fig. 1 Typical wheel lug tightening sequence

➡If a nut is stuck, never use heat to loosen it or damage to the wheel and bearings may occur. If the nuts are seized, one or two heavy hammer blows directly on the end of the bolt usually loosens the rust. Be careful, as continued pounding will likely damage the brake drum or rotor.

9. Using the jack, raise the vehicle until the tire is clear of the ground. Support the vehicle safely using jackstands.

10. Remove the lug nuts, then remove the tire and wheel assembly.

To install:

11. Make sure the wheel and hub mating surfaces, as well as the wheel lug studs, are clean and free of all foreign material. Always remove rust from the wheel mounting surface and the brake rotor or drum. Failure to do so may cause the lug nuts to loosen in service.

12. Install the tire and wheel assembly and hand-tighten the lug nuts.

13. Using the tire wrench, tighten all the lug nuts, in a crisscross pattern, until they are snug.

14. Raise the vehicle and withdraw the jackstand, then lower the vehicle.

15. Using a torque wrench, tighten the lug nuts in a crisscross pattern to 85–105 ft. lbs. (115–142 Nm). Check your owner's manual or refer to Section 1 of this manual for the proper tightening sequence.

✖ WARNING

Do not overtighten the lug nuts, as this may cause the wheel studs to stretch or the brake disc (rotor) to warp.

16. If so equipped, install the wheel cover or hub cap. Make sure the valve stem protrudes through the proper opening before tapping the wheel cover into position.

17. If equipped, install the lug nut trim caps by pushing them or screwing them on, as applicable.

18. Remove the jack from under the vehicle, and place the jack and tire iron/wrench in their storage compartments. Remove the wheel chock(s).

19. If you have removed a flat or damaged tire, place it in the storage compartment of the vehicle and take it to your local repair station to have it fixed or replaced as soon as possible.

INSPECTION

Inspect the tires for lacerations, puncture marks, nails and other sharp objects. Repair or replace as necessary. Also check the tires for treadwear and air pressure as outlined in Section 1 of this manual.

Check the wheel assemblies for dents, cracks, rust and metal fatigue. Repair or replace as necessary.

Wheel Lug Studs

REPLACEMENT

With Disc Brakes

♦ See Figures 2, 3 and 4

1. Raise and support the appropriate end of the vehicle safely using jackstands, then remove the wheel.

2. Remove the brake pads and caliper. Support the caliper aside using wire or a coat hanger. For details, please refer to Section 9 of this manual.

3. Remove the outer wheel bearing and lift off the rotor. For details on wheel bearing removal, installation and adjustment, please refer to Section 1 of this manual.

4. Properly support the rotor using press bars, then drive the stud out using an arbor press.

➡If a press is not available, **CAREFULLY** drive the old stud out using a blunt drift. **MAKE SURE** the rotor is properly and evenly supported or it may be damaged.

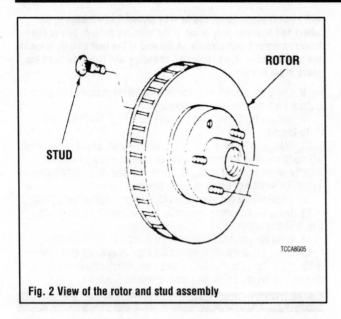

Fig. 2 View of the rotor and stud assembly

To install:

5. Clean the stud hole with a wire brush and start the new stud with a hammer and drift pin. Do not use any lubricant or thread sealer.

6. Finish installing the stud with the press.

➡**If a press is not available, start the lug stud through the bore in the hub, then position about 4 flat washers over the stud and thread the lug nut. Hold the hub/rotor while tightening the lug nut, and the stud should be drawn into position. MAKE SURE THE STUD IS FULLY SEATED, then remove the lug nut and washers.**

7. Install the rotor and adjust the wheel bearings.

8. Install the brake caliper and pads.

9. Install the wheel, then remove the jackstands and carefully lower the vehicle.

10. Tighten the lug nuts to the proper torque.

With Drum Brakes

◗ **See Figures 5, 6 and 7**

1. Raise the vehicle and safely support it with jackstands, then remove the wheel.

2. Remove the brake drum.

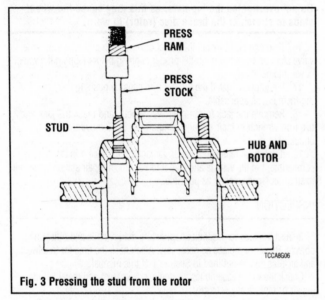

Fig. 3 Pressing the stud from the rotor

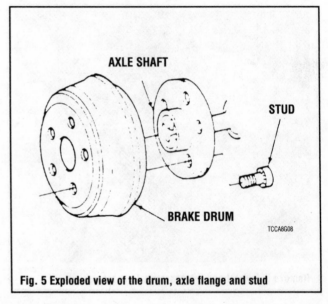

Fig. 5 Exploded view of the drum, axle flange and stud

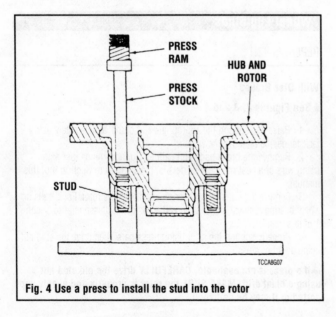

Fig. 4 Use a press to install the stud into the rotor

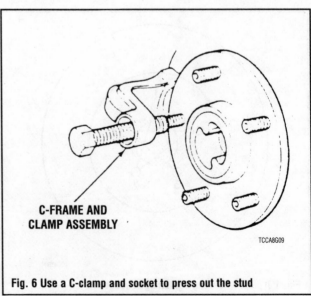

Fig. 6 Use a C-clamp and socket to press out the stud

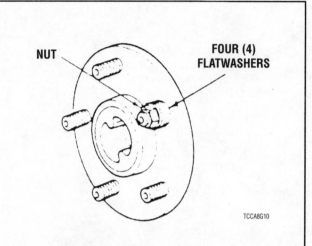

Fig. 7 Force the stud onto the axle flange using washers and a lug nut

3. If necessary to provide clearance, remove the brake shoes, as outlined in Section 9 of this manual.

4. Using a large C-clamp and socket, press the stud from the axle flange.

5. Coat the serrated part of the stud with liquid soap and place it into the hole.

To install:

6. Position about 4 flat washers over the stud and thread the lug nut. Hold the flange while tightening the lug nut, and the stud should be drawn into position. MAKE SURE THE STUD IS FULLY SEATED, then remove the lug nut and washers.

7. If applicable, install the brake shoes.

8. Install the brake drum.

9. Install the wheel, then remove the jackstands and carefully lower the vehicle.

10. Tighten the lug nuts to the proper torque.

FRONT SUSPENSION

Coil Springs

✳✳ CAUTION

Always use extreme caution when working with coil springs. Always use the proper spring compression tools, since the springs are VERY strong and, if pressure is released suddenly (and without control), serious personal injury could result. Also, ALWAYS be sure the vehicle is very well supported when working around springs.

REMOVAL & INSTALLATION

◆ See Figures 8, 9, 10, 11 and 12 (p. 7–8)

➡This procedure REQUIRES the use of a coil spring compression tool. This tool can usually be rented for a one-time use; otherwise, it can be purchased from your local parts store.

1. Loosen the front wheel lug nuts only slightly.

2. Raise and support the vehicle safely using jackstands, but allow the control arms to hang free.

3. Remove the wheel and tire assembly.

4. Remove the brake caliper. Suspend the caliper with a length of wire; DO NOT let the caliper hang by the brake hose.

5. Disconnect the tie rod end from the steering spindle and disconnect the stabilizer link from the lower arm.

6. If necessary, remove the steering gear (rack and pinion) bolts and reposition the gear so the suspension arm-to-No. 2 crossmember mounting bolts can be removed.

7. On models equipped with the 3.8L engine, use a coil spring compressor, such as Ford Coil Spring Compressor T82P-5310-A, and install the upper plate in the spring pocket cavity on the crossmember. The hooks on the plate should be facing toward the center of the vehicle.

8. On Mustangs with the 4.6L or 5.0L engines, use spring compressor tool D78P-5310-A or equivalent, to install a plate between the coils near the toe of the spring. Mark the location of the upper plate on the coils for installation.

9. Install the compression rod into the lower arm spring pocket hole, through the coil spring and into the upper plate.

10. Install the lower plate, lower ball nut, thrust washer and bearing, and forcing nut onto the compression rod. Tighten the forcing nut until a drag on the nut is felt.

11. Remove the suspension arm-to-crossmember nuts and bolts. The compressor tool forcing nut may have to be tightened or loosened for easy bolt removal.

12. Pull the lower control arm down and remove the spring from the suspension.

13. Loosen the compression rod forcing nut until spring tension is relieved and remove the forcing nut. Remove the compression rod and coil spring.

To install:

14. Place the insulator on top of the spring. Position the spring into the lower arm pocket. Make sure the spring pigtail is positioned between the two holes in the lower arm spring pocket.

15. Position the spring into the upper spring seat in the crossmember.

16. On Mustangs with the 3.8L engine, insert the compression rod through the control arm and spring, then hook it to the upper plate. The upper plate is installed with the hooks facing the center of the vehicle.

17. On Mustangs with either the 4.6L or 5.0L engines, install the upper plate between the coils in the location marked during removal.

18. Install the lower plate, ball nut, thrust washer and bearing, and forcing nut onto the compression rod.

19. Tighten the forcing nut, position the lower arm into the crossmember and install new lower arm-to-crossmember bolts and nuts. Do not tighten at this time.

20. Remove the spring compressor tool from the vehicle. Raise the suspension arm to a normal attitude position with a jack. With the suspension in the normal ride-height position, tighten the lower arm-to-crossmember attaching nuts to specifications. Carefully lower the suspension again and remove the jack.

21. If repositioning, install the steering gear (rack and pinion)-to-crossmember bolts and nuts. Hold the bolts and tighten the nuts to specifications.

22. Connect the stabilizer bar link to the lower suspension arm. Tighten the attaching nut to specifications.

FRONT SUSPENSION AND STEERING COMPONENTS

1. Sway bar
2. Power steering gear fluid lines
3. Coil springs
4. Struts
5. Outer tie rod ends
6. Knuckle/spindle assemblies
7. Ball joints
8. Coil spring mounting cups
9. Lower control arms
10. Sway bar end links
11. Control arm rear mounting bolts
12. Control arm front mounting bolts
13. Power steering gear mounting nuts
14. No. 2 crossmember
15. Power steering rack and pinion

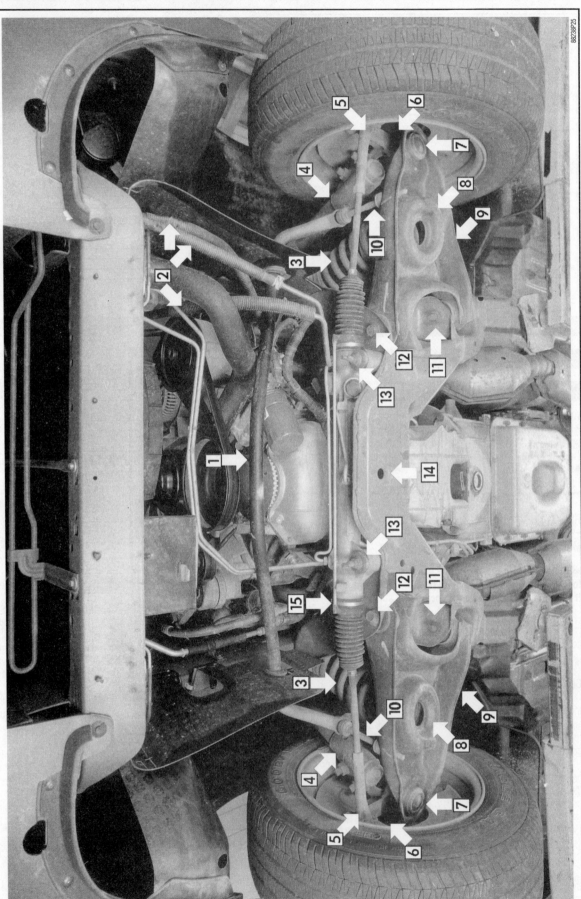

8238P25

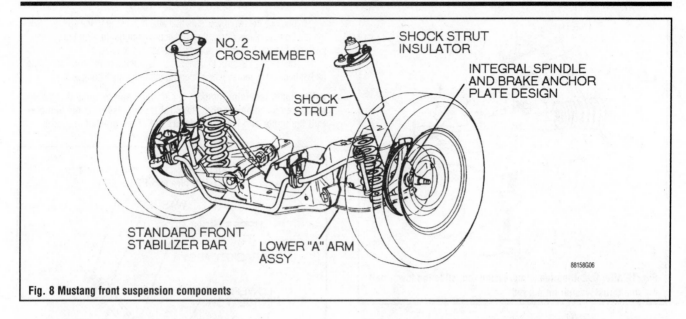

Fig. 8 Mustang front suspension components

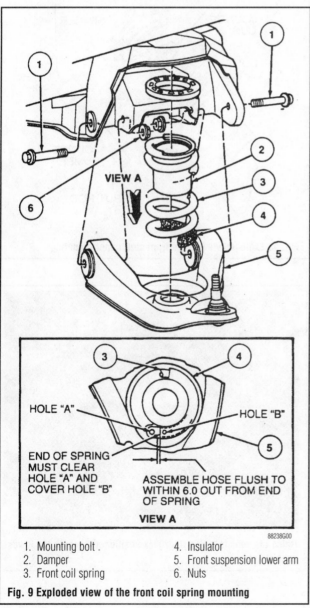

Fig. 9 Exploded view of the front coil spring mounting

1. Mounting bolt
2. Damper
3. Front coil spring
4. Insulator
5. Front suspension lower arm
6. Nuts

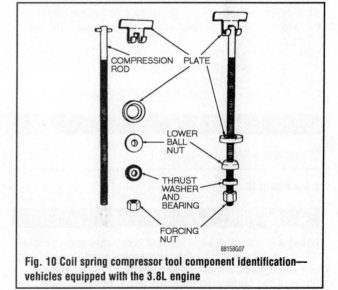

Fig. 10 Coil spring compressor tool component identification—vehicles equipped with the 3.8L engine

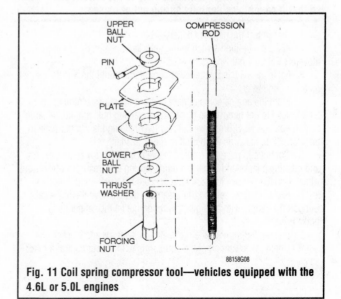

Fig. 11 Coil spring compressor tool—vehicles equipped with the 4.6L or 5.0L engines

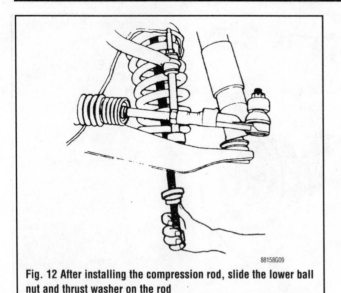

Fig. 12 After installing the compression rod, slide the lower ball nut and thrust washer on the rod

23. Position the tie rod into the steering spindle and install the retaining nut. Tighten the nut to the specified torque value and continue tightening the nut to align the next castellation with the hole in the stud. Install a new cotter pin.
24. Install the brake caliper.
25. Install the wheel and tire assembly, then remove the jackstands and carefully lower the vehicle.
26. Tighten the wheel lug nuts to the specified torque value.

Struts

REMOVAL & INSTALLATION

▶ See Figure 13

✳✳ CAUTION

During this procedure when the strut is detached from the spindle, if the floor jack under the lower control arm is lowered, the coil spring, under a great amount of tension, can be abruptly released and cause severe physical injury. As a precaution, chain the bottom end of the coil spring to the lower control arm so that it cannot accidentally spring out of its seat.

1. Disconnect the negative battery cable.
2. Place the ignition switch in the unlocked position to permit free movement of the front wheels.
3. Raise the vehicle by the lower control arms until the wheels are just off the ground.
4. From the engine compartment, remove the strut's central upper mount nut. Do not remove the three small retaining nuts around the larger central nut, and NEVER remove the pop rivet holding the camber plate in position. Slide the large washer off of the strut shaft.
5. Continue to raise the front of the vehicle by the lower control arm and position a jackstand under the frame jacking pad, rearward of the front wheel. Do NOT remove the jack from beneath the lower control arm!
6. Remove the wheel and tire assembly, then remove the brake caliper. Support the caliper with a length of wire; do not let the caliper hang by the brake hose.
7. If equipped, remove the brake anti-lock sensor and bracket.
8. Chain the lower end of the coil spring to the lower control arm for safety.

9. Remove the two lower nuts that attach the strut to the spindle, leaving the bolts in place. Carefully remove both spindle-to-strut bolts, then push the bracket free of the spindle and remove the strut.
10. Compress the strut to clear the upper mount of the body mounting pad. If necessary, remove the upper mount and jounce bumper.

➡**The upper insulator mounts, if damaged and in need of replacement, can be removed after the strut is removed from the vehicle. Pull the upper and lower insulators out of the bracket assembly.**

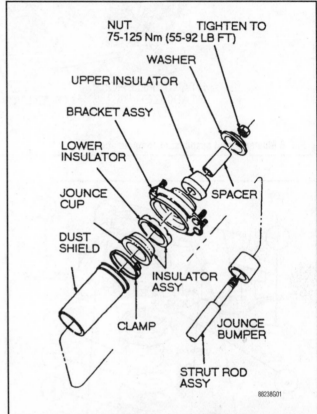

Fig. 13 Exploded view of the front strut upper mounting

Raise the vehicle with a floor jack positioned beneath the lower control arm . . .

. . . then loosen the central mounting nut (A) while holding the strut shaft (B) from rotating

Remove the central mounting nut and washer from the strut shaft

Remove the strut lower mounting bolts and nuts . . .

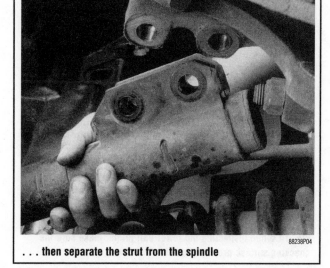

. . . then separate the strut from the spindle

To install:

11. If removed, install the upper insulators in the bracket assembly.

12. Position the upper strut shaft through the insulator mounts and camber plate, then start the central mounting nut.

13. Compress the strut and position the lower end in the spindle. Install two new lower retaining bolts and hand-start the nuts. Remove the suspension load from the control arm by slowly lowering the floor jack until the arm hangs without any support from the jack. Tighten the lower retaining nuts to the figures given in the torque specifications chart.

14. Raise the suspension control arm (to position the suspension at normal ride height) and tighten the upper mount retaining nut to 55–92 ft. lbs. (75–125 Nm).

15. Remove the safety chain from the lower control arm and coil spring.

16. Install the brake anti-lock sensor bracket, along with the anti-lock sensor, caliper and front wheel.

17. Remove the jackstands and carefully lower the vehicle to the ground.

18. Tighten the wheel lug nuts in a crisscross pattern to specifications.

19. Have the front end alignment checked and adjusted, if necessary, by a professional automotive technician.

Lower Ball Joints

INSPECTION

▶ **See Figure 14**

1. Raise and support the vehicle on jackstands so that the suspension control arms hang and the wheels are off of the ground.

2. Use a floor jack to support the lower control arm, then attempt to wobble the wheel in a vertical motion by holding the top of the tire with one hand and the bottom of the tire with the other. If any movement is felt, have an assistant wobble the wheel and look for movement between the lower control arm and the spindle; the spindle and arm should not move independently of each other. If there is movement, replace the lower ball joint.

3. If the ball joint appears fine, check the front wheel bearing, then repeat this test to ensure that the ball joint is in good condition.

The ball joints on 1994 models can also be inspected as follows:

4. Support the vehicle in a normal driving position with the ball joints loaded.

5. Wipe the wear indicator and ball joint cover surface clean.

6. The ball joint wear indicator should project at least ³⁄₆₄ in. (1.2mm) from the cover surface. If the indicator does not project at least ³⁄₆₄ in. from the cover surface, replace the lower ball joint.

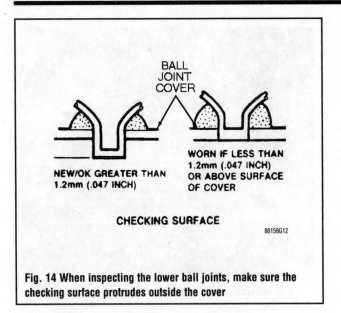

Fig. 14 When inspecting the lower ball joints, make sure the checking surface protrudes outside the cover

REMOVAL & INSTALLATION

◆ See Figures 15 and 16

1. Either remove the front suspension lower control arm from the vehicle, or remove the front strut and spindle from the vehicle.
2. If the lower control arm was removed from the vehicle, position the lower control arm in a vise so that the ball joint is easy to service.
3. Using a large C-clamp and adapters, such as Ford Tools T74P-4635-C, D89P-3010-A and D84P-3395-A4, carefully press the old ball joint out of the lower control arm.

   To install:

➡ **When installing a new front ball joint, leave the protective cover in place to protect the ball joint seal. It may be necessary to cut off the end of the cover to allow it to pass through the receiving cup adapter tool.**

4. Press the new ball joint into the lower control arm with Ford's Ball Joint Replacer D89P-3010-B, Cup D84P-3395-A4 and C-Frame T74P-4635C, or their equivalents, until it is fully seated in the control arm.

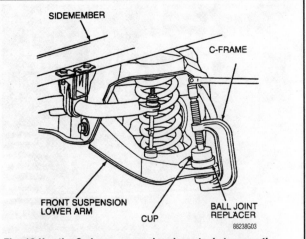

Fig. 16 Use the C-clamp, cup and replacer tools to press the new ball joint into the lower control arm until it is fully seated in its bore

5. Discard the ball joint protective cover and inspect the ball joint to ensure that it is fully seated in its bore and that it is free of cuts or tears.
6. Install the lower control arm in the vehicle or install the front strut and spindle, whichever is applicable.

Sway Bar

REMOVAL & INSTALLATION

◆ See Figure 17

1. Apply the parking brake, block the rear wheels, then raise and safely support the front of the vehicle on jackstands beneath each lower control arm.
2. Remove all end link retaining nuts, bushings and washers. Remove the end link studs from the lower control arms and the sway bar.
3. Remove the two bolts from both sway bar mounting brackets, then remove the sway bar from the vehicle.
4. Remove the mounting brackets and bushings from the sway bar.

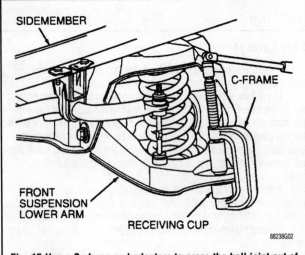

Fig. 15 Use a C-clamp and adapters to press the ball joint out of the lower control arm

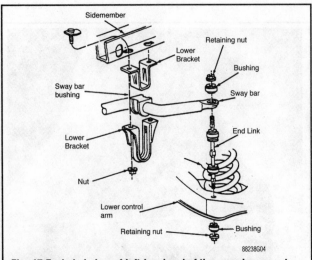

Fig. 17 Exploded view of left-hand end of the sway bar mounting—right-hand end is the same

To install:

5. Coat the rubber components used on the sway bar with rubber lubricant (such as Ford Rubber Suspension Insulator Lube E25Y-19553-A) prior to installation.

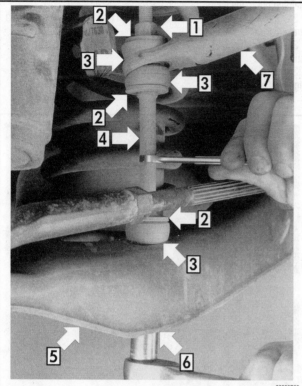

1. Retaining nut	4. End link	6. Retaining nut (not
2. Washers	5. Lower control	visible in photo)
3. Bushings	arm	7. Sway bar

To remove the sway bar, detach the end links by removing the retaining nuts, bushings and washers . . .

. . . then remove the sway bar mounting bracket nuts

6. Install the mounting bushings and brackets on the sway bar, then position the sway bar in the vehicle with the ends of the bar over the lower control arms. Install the mounting bracket bolts and tighten them to specifications.

7. Install the end links in the lower control arms and sway bar. Install the washers, bushings and retaining nuts. Tighten the retaining nuts to specifications.

8. Lower the vehicle.

Lower Control Arm

REMOVAL & INSTALLATION

✷✷ CAUTION

Always use extreme caution when working with coil springs. Always use the proper spring compression tools, since the springs are VERY strong and, if pressure is released suddenly (and without control), serious personal injury could result. Also, ALWAYS be sure the vehicle is very well supported when working around springs.

1. Loosen the front wheel lug nuts slightly (no more than ½ turn).

2. Apply the parking brake, block the rear wheels, then raise and safely support the front of the vehicle on jackstands, ensuring that the control arms hang free.

3. Remove the wheel and tire assembly.

4. If necessary, remove the brake caliper and suspend it with a length of wire; do NOT let the caliper hang by the brake hose. Remove the brake rotor and dust shield.

5. Disconnect the tie rod end from the steering spindle. Disconnect the stabilizer bar link from the lower control arm.

6. If necessary for suspension arm mounting bolt removal, remove the steering gear (rack and pinion) bolts and lower the gear out of the way to provide access.

7. Remove the cotter pin and loosen the lower ball joint stud nut 1–2 turns. **Do not completely remove the nut at this time.** Tap the spindle boss sharply with a brass mallet to relieve the stud pressure; the lower control arm and ball joint should "pop" loose from the spindle (leaving the nut on the ball joint prevents the arm from completely disengaging from the spindle, which would allow the coil spring to jump out of the lower arm cup, possibly causing severe personal injury).

8. Install a suitable spring compressor and compress the coil spring until it can be moved freely in the lower control arm seat.

➡**For more information on coil spring compression or removal, refer to the coil spring procedure earlier in this section.**

9. Remove and discard the ball joint nut, then raise the entire strut and spindle assembly up and off of the ball joint stud. Wire the strut/spindle out of the way to obtain working room.

10. Remove and discard the suspension arm-to-crossmember nuts and bolts. Remove the lower control arm and coil spring from the vehicle.

To install:

11. Position the compressed coil spring into the lower arm pocket. Make sure the spring pigtail is positioned between the two holes in the pocket.

12. Position the lower arm ends in the crossmember brackets and install new arm-to-crossmember bolts and nuts. Do not tighten at this time.

13. Remove the retaining wire from the strut/spindle assembly, then position the spindle over the ball joint stud.

14. Raise the control arm with a jack to the normal vehicle resting position, ensuring the ball joint stud is inserted into the spindle hole. Install the ball joint nut loosely.

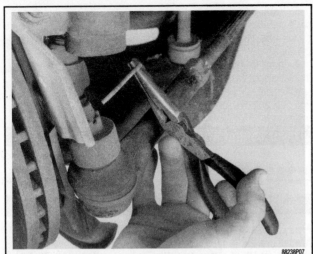

88238P07

To detach the tie rod end from the spindle, remove the cotter pin . . .

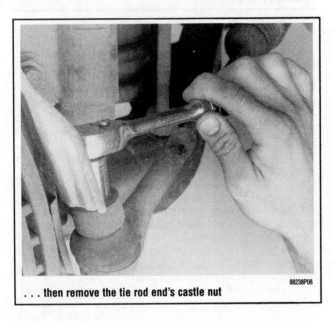

88238P08

. . . then remove the tie rod end's castle nut

15. With the jack in place, tighten the lower arm-to-crossmember attaching nuts to the figures given in the torque specifications chart.

➡ When tightening the ball joint nut, do not loosen the nut to install the cotter pin. Tighten the nut until the next set of grooves are aligned with the stud hole, then install the new cotter pin.

16. Tighten the ball joint stud nut to the figures given in the torque specifications chart and install a new cotter pin; bend the cotter pin ends over. Remove the floor jack.

17. If removed, install the dust shield, rotor and brake caliper.

18. If removed, install the steering gear (rack and pinion)-to-crossmember bolts and nuts. Hold the bolts and tighten the nuts to the figures given in the torque specifications chart.

➡ When tightening the tie rod end nut, do not loosen the nut to install the cotter pin. Tighten the nut until the next set of grooves are aligned with the stud hole, then install the new cotter pin.

19. Position the tie rod into the steering spindle and install the retaining nut. Tighten the nut to the figures given in the torque specifications chart and continue tightening the nut to align the next castellation with the hole in the stud. Install a new cotter pin and bend its ends over.

20. Connect the stabilizer bar link to the lower control arm. Tighten the retaining nut to the figures given in the torque specifications chart.

21. Install the wheel and tire assembly, then remove the jackstands and carefully lower the vehicle.

22. Tighten the wheel lug nuts to the figures given in the torque specifications chart.

23. Have the front end alignment checked by a qualified automotive alignment technician.

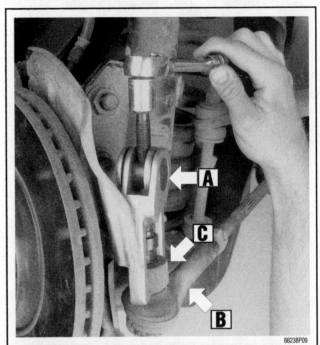

88238P09

Press the tie rod end (B) from the spindle (C) using a tool designed specifically for this (A) . . .

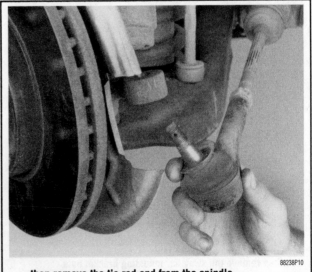

88238P10

. . . then remove the tie rod end from the spindle

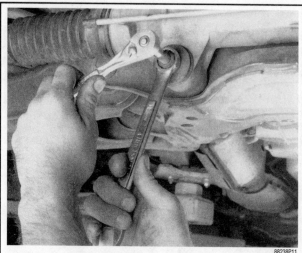

If access to the arm mounting nuts is tight, remove the nuts and lower the steering gear until access is gained

88238P11

Knuckle and Spindle

REMOVAL & INSTALLATION

1. Break the wheel lug nuts free (do not loosen them more than ½ turn).
2. Apply the parking brake, block the rear wheels, then raise and safely support the front of the vehicle on jackstands placed beneath the frame rails.
3. Remove the wheel and tire assembly.
4. If equipped, remove the anti-lock brake sensor from the wheel spindle.
5. Remove the caliper and suspend it out of the way.
6. Remove the hub and rotor assembly.
7. Remove the rotor dust shield.
8. Unbolt the stabilizer link from the control arm.
9. Using a tool specifically designed for this purpose (tie rod end separator), disconnect the tie rod end from the spindle.
10. Remove the cotter pin and loosen the lower ball joint stud nut 1–2 turns. **Do not completely remove the nut at this time.** Tap the spindle boss sharply with a brass mallet to relieve the stud pressure; the lower control arm and ball joint should "pop" loose from the spindle (leaving the nut on the ball joint prevents the arm from completely disengaging from the spindle, which would allow the coil spring to jump out of the lower arm cup, possibly causing severe personal injury).
11. Support the lower control arm with a floor jack.
12. Using a coil spring compressor, remove the spring tension from the lower arm. For more information on coil spring compressor tools, refer to the coil spring removal procedure.
13. Remove the ball joint stud nut.
14. Remove the two bolts and nuts attaching the spindle to the strut. Compress the strut until working clearance is obtained.
15. Remove the spindle from the vehicle.

To install:
16. Place the spindle on the lower control arm ball joint stud, and install the stud nut finger-tight.
17. Install the lower end of the strut between the spindle brackets so that the attaching holes are aligned. Install two new bolts and nuts.
18. Tighten the ball stud nut to the figures given in the torque specifications chart, and install the cotter pin.

19. Tighten the strut-to-spindle attaching nuts to the figures given in the torque specifications chart.
20. Ensure that the coil spring is properly positioned in the control arm cup, then remove the compressor tool.
21. Install the stabilizer links. Tighten the nuts to the specified value.
22. Lower the floor jack.
23. Position the tie rod into the steering spindle and install the retaining nut. Tighten the nut to the figures given in the torque specifications chart and continue tightening the nut to align the next castellation with the hole in the stud. Install a new cotter pin and bend its ends over.
24. Install the rotor dust shield.
25. Install the hub and rotor assembly.
26. Reposition and secure the brake caliper.
27. Install the wheel and snug the lug nuts.
28. Remove the jackstands and carefully lower the vehicle.
29. Tighten the wheel lug nuts in a crisscross pattern to the figures given in the torque specifications chart.

Front Hub and Bearing

INSPECTION

➡**Be sure not to confuse the lower ball joint looseness with wheel bearing looseness.**

Wheel bearings that need replacing may be indicated by a noise that occurs only during turning. Diagnose the wheel bearings as follows:
1. Road test the vehicle on a smooth road. Make sharp turns to the right and left.
   a. If the vehicle makes noises on right turns, the left wheel bearing may need to be replaced.
   b. If the vehicle makes noises on left turns, the right wheel bearing may need to be replaced.
2. Apply the parking brake and block the rear wheels, then raise and safely support the front of the vehicle on jackstands.
3. Using one hand on top of the tire and one hand on the bottom, rock the wheel assembly to check for wheel bearing looseness.
4. Spin the tire quickly by hand and be sure that the tire rotates smoothly and without noise from the wheel bearings.
5. Remove the wheel and disc brake caliper.
6. Position a dial indicator, such as Ford Position Dial Indicator with Bracketry TOOL-4201-C, against the wheel bearing hub. Push and pull on the hub and read the hub movement range on the dial indicator. The maximum allowable hub play is 0.002 in. (0.05mm). If end-play exceeds the specified value, replace the wheel hubs.

REMOVAL & INSTALLATION

♦ See Figures 18 and 19 (p. 14–15)

➡**The front wheel bearings, hub and anti-lock sensor ring (where applicable) are one unit and cannot be separately serviced or replaced. Therefore, when the wheel bearings are faulty, the entire assembly must be replaced.**

1. Loosen the front wheel lug nuts ½ turn only.
2. Apply the parking brake, block the rear wheels, then raise and safely support the front of the vehicle on jackstands.
3. Using a prytool, remove the plastic hub grease cap and discard it.
4. Remove the brake caliper and suspend it with strong cord or wire from the chassis.

To remove the front wheel bearings, use a prytool to loosen the grease cap (arrow) . . .

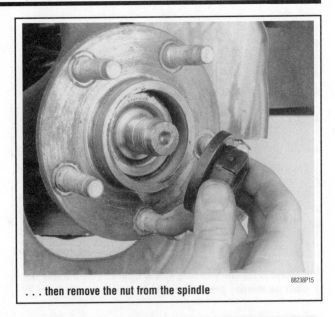

. . . then remove the nut from the spindle

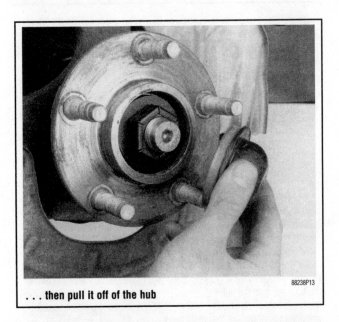

. . . then pull it off of the hub

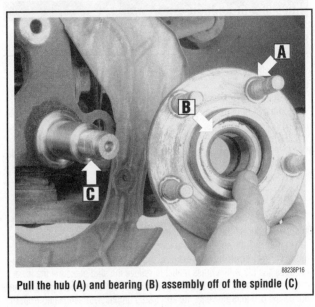

Pull the hub (A) and bearing (B) assembly off of the spindle (C)

Use a breaker bar to loosen the hub retaining nut . . .

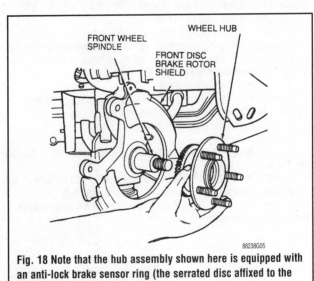

Fig. 18 Note that the hub assembly shown here is equipped with an anti-lock brake sensor ring (the serrated disc affixed to the inboard side of the hub assembly)

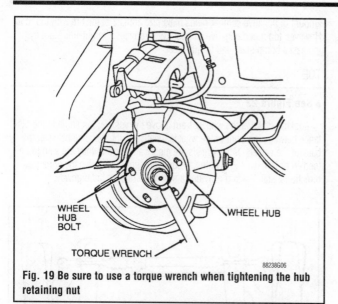

Fig. 19 Be sure to use a torque wrench when tightening the hub retaining nut

WHEEL HUB BOLT

WHEEL HUB

TORQUE WRENCH

88238G06

✳✳ WARNING

Do not allow the brake caliper to hang from its brake hose.

5. Remove the front disc brake rotor.
6. Remove the front axle wheel hub retainer and discard it.
7. Pull the wheel hub and bearing assembly off of the spindle. If the assembly cannot be removed by hand, use Ford Front Hub Remover/Replacer T81P-1104-C or equivalent.

To install:

8. Install the hub/bearing assembly on the wheel spindle.
9. Install a new front axle wheel hub retainer and tighten it to the figures given in the torque specifications chart.
10. Install the front disc brake rotor and new push-on nuts.
11. Install a new front hub grease cap, being cautious to avoid damaging or distorting the grease cap.
12. Install the brake caliper.
13. Install the wheel and tire assembly, and snug the wheel lug nuts.
14. Lower the vehicle and remove the rear wheel blocks.
15. Tighten the wheel lug nuts in a crisscross pattern to the figures given in the torque specifications chart.

Wheel Alignment

If the tires are worn unevenly, if the vehicle is not stable on the highway or if the handling seems uneven in spirited driving, the wheel alignment should be checked. If an alignment problem is suspected, first check for improper tire inflation and other possible causes. These can be worn suspension or steering components, accident damage or even unmatched tires. If any worn or damaged components are found, they must be replaced before the wheels can be properly aligned. Wheel alignment requires very expensive equipment and involves minute adjustments which must be accurate; it should only be performed by a trained technician. Take your vehicle to a properly equipped shop.

Following is a description of the alignment angles which are adjustable on most vehicles and how they affect vehicle handling. Although these angles can apply to both the front and rear wheels, usually only the front suspension is adjustable.

CASTER

♦ **See Figure 20**

Looking at a vehicle from the side, caster angle describes the steering axis rather than a wheel angle. The steering knuckle is attached to a control arm or strut at the top and a control arm at the bottom. The wheel pivots around the line between these points to steer the vehicle. When the upper point is tilted back, this is described as positive caster. Having a positive caster tends to make the wheels self-centering, increasing directional stability. Excessive positive caster makes the wheels hard to steer, while an uneven caster will cause a pull to one side. Overloading the vehicle or sagging rear springs will affect caster, as will raising the rear of the vehicle. If the rear of the vehicle is lower than normal, the caster becomes more positive.

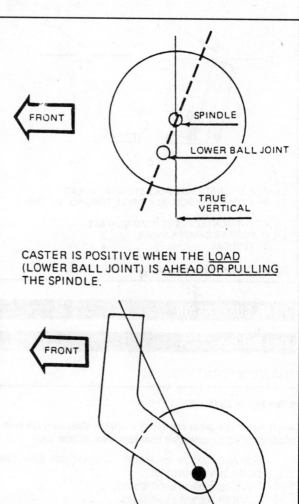

FRONT

SPINDLE

LOWER BALL JOINT

TRUE VERTICAL

CASTER IS POSITIVE WHEN THE LOAD (LOWER BALL JOINT) IS AHEAD OR PULLING THE SPINDLE.

FRONT

LOAD IS PULLING THE WHEEL.

TCCA8G01

Fig. 20 Caster affects straight-line stability. Caster wheels used on shopping carts, for example, employ positive caster

CAMBER

♦ **See Figure 21**

Looking from the front of the vehicle, camber is the inward or outward tilt of the top of wheels. When the tops of the wheels are tilted in, this is negative camber; if they are tilted out, it is positive. In a turn, a slight amount of negative camber helps maximize contact of the tire with the road. However, too much negative camber compromises straight-line stability, increases bump steer and torque steer.

TOE

♦ **See Figure 22**

Looking down at the wheels from above the vehicle, toe angle is the distance between the front of the wheels, relative to the distance between the back of the wheels. If the wheels are closer at the front, they are said to be toed-in or to have negative toe. A small amount of negative toe enhances directional stability and provides a smoother ride on the highway.

A A CYLINDER WILL ROLL STRAIGHT AHEAD
B A CONE WILL ROLL IN A CIRCLE TOWARD THE SMALL END
C TIRE CONTACTS THE ROAD SURFACE
D POSITIVE CAMBER ANGLE
E VERTICAL

TCCA8G02

Fig. 21 Camber influences tire contact with the road

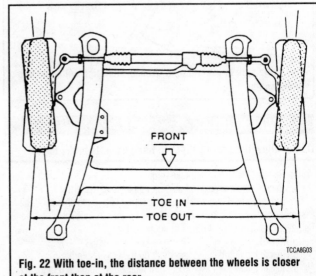

TCCA8G03

Fig. 22 With toe-in, the distance between the wheels is closer at the front than at the rear

REAR SUSPENSION

Coil Springs

REMOVAL & INSTALLATION

♦ **See Figure 23 (p. 18)**

➡**It is easier to replace one spring at a time; otherwise, the axle housing will be disconnected from both lower control arms.**

1. Raise and support the vehicle safely using jackstands. Support the body at the rear body crossmember.
2. If equipped, remove the stabilizer bar.
3. Support the axle with a suitable jack.
4. Place another jack under the lower arm axle pivot bolt. Remove and discard the bolt and nut. Lower the jack slowly until the coil spring load is relieved.
5. Remove the coil spring and insulator from the vehicle.
   To install:
6. Place the upper spring insulator on top of the spring. Place the lower spring insulator on the lower arm.
7. Position the coil spring on the lower arm spring seat, so the pigtail on the lower arm is at the rear of the vehicle and pointing toward the left side of the vehicle.
8. Slowly raise the jack until the arm is in position. Insert a new rear pivot bolt and nut, with the nut facing outward. Do not tighten them at this time.

9. Raise the axle to curb height. Tighten the lower arm-to-axle pivot bolt to the figures given in the torque specifications chart.
10. If equipped, install the stabilizer bar.
11. Remove the crossmember supports and carefully lower the vehicle.

Shock Absorbers

REMOVAL & INSTALLATION

♦ **See Figure 24 (p. 19)**

➡**Some Ford Mustangs use Torx® head bolts to retain the shocks at the lower mounts. Check to make sure you have the proper drivers before beginning this procedure.**

1. Open the luggage compartment (trunk) lid.
2. Remove the trim panels, as necessary, to gain access to the upper shock absorber mount.
3. Remove the shock absorber retaining nut washer and insulator.
4. Raise the vehicle and support it safely using jackstands under the rear axle housing.
5. From under the vehicle, remove the shock absorber bolt, washer and nut at the lower arm and remove the shock absorber.

➡**These vehicles are equipped with gas pressurized shock absorbers which will extend unassisted.**

REAR SUSPENSION COMPONENTS

1. Sway bar
2. Upper control arms
3. Coil springs
4. Shock absorbers
5. Shock absorber lower mounts
6. Lower control arm-to-axle assembly mounts
7. Lower control arms

88238P26

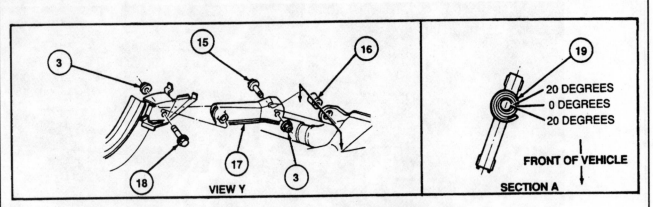

1. Upper shock mount
2. Mounting bolt
3. Mounting nut
4. Lower shock mount bracket
5. Axle assembly
6. Mounting nut
7. Lower control arm
8. Lower spring insulator
9. Mounting bolt
10. Mounting bolt
11. Coil spring damper
12. Coil spring
13. Upper spring insulator
14. Shock absorber
15. Mounting bolt

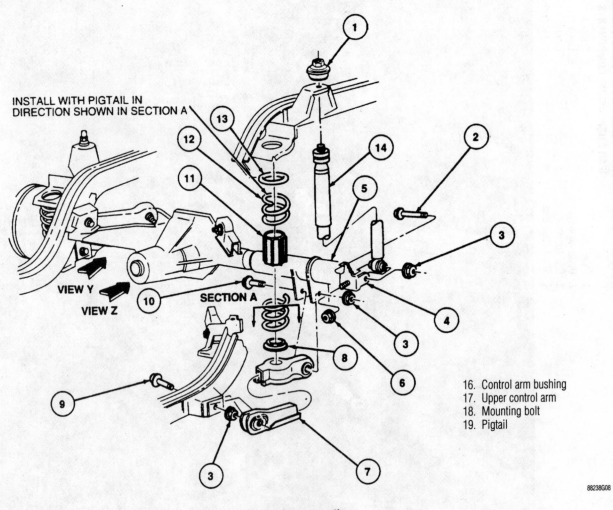

INSTALL WITH PIGTAIL IN
DIRECTION SHOWN IN SECTION A

16. Control arm bushing
17. Upper control arm
18. Mounting bolt
19. Pigtail

88238G08

Fig. 23 Exploded view of the rear suspension coil spring and control arm mounting

To install:

6. Prime the new shock absorber as follows:

   a. With the shock absorber right side up, extend it fully.

   b. Turn the shock absorber upside down and fully compress it.

   c. Repeat the previous two steps at least three times to make sure any trapped air has been expelled.

7. From under the vehicle, place the inner washer and insulator on the upper retaining stud and position the stud through the shock tower mounting hole.

8. Attach the lower end of the shock absorber with the retaining bolt and nut. Tighten the bolt to the figures given in the torque specifications chart.

9. Remove the jackstands and carefully lower the vehicle.

10. Install the upper insulator, washer and retaining nut, then tighten the nut to the figures given in the torque specifications chart.

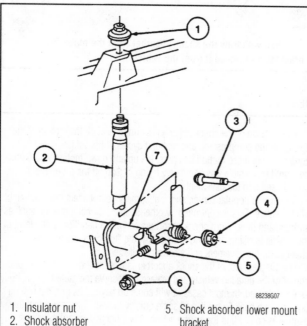

1. Insulator nut
2. Shock absorber
3. Mounting bolt
4. Mounting nut
5. Shock absorber lower mount bracket
6. Mounting nut
7. Rear axle housing

88238G07

Fig. 24 Exploded view of the rear shock absorber mounting

88238P18

. . . then remove the cover from the trunk

88238P19

Unfasten all of the trunk's rear carpet retainers and remove the carpet trim panel . . .

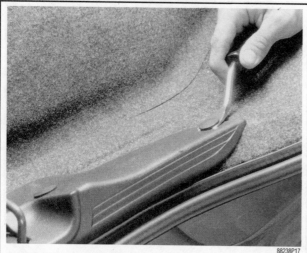

88238P17

To gain access to the upper shock absorber mount, remove the trunk latch cover retainers . . .

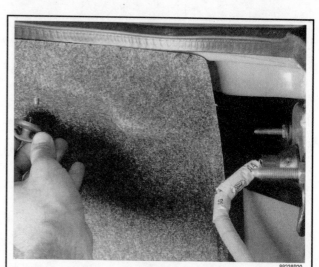

88238P20

. . . then unfasten the retainers and remove the side carpet trim as well

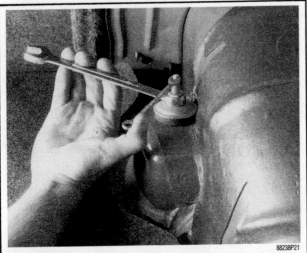

Use a back-up wrench to hold the shock absorber shaft while loosening the retaining nut

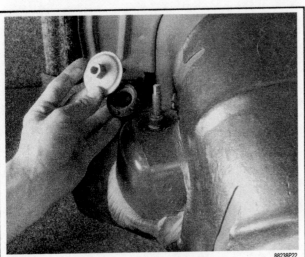

Remove the nut/washer and rubber insulator from the shock absorber shaft

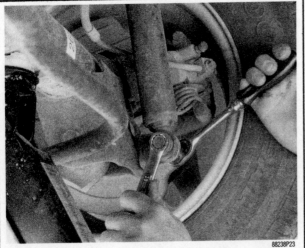

From under the vehicle, remove the shock absorber mounting bolt and nut . . .

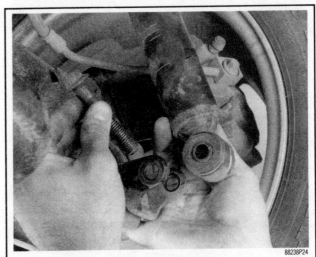

. . . then withdraw the shock absorber from the mounting bracket and remove it from the vehicle

TESTING

The purpose of the shock absorber is simply to limit the motion of the spring during compression and rebound cycles. If the vehicle is not equipped with these motion dampers, the up and down motion would multiply until the vehicle was alternately trying to leap off the ground and pound itself into the pavement.

Contrary to popular rumor, shock absorbers do not affect the ride height of the vehicle. This is controlled by other suspension components, such as springs, and tires. Worn shock absorbers can affect handling; if the front of the vehicle is rising or falling excessively, the "footprint" of the tires changes on the pavement and steering is affected.

The simplest test of the shock absorber is to simply push down on one corner of the unladen vehicle and release it. Observe the motion of the body as it is released. In most cases, it will come up beyond its original resting position, dip back below it, and settle quickly to rest. This shows that the damper is controlling the spring action. Any tendency toward excessive pitch (up-and-down) motion or failure to return to rest within 2-3 cycles is a sign of poor function within the shock absorber. Oil-filled shock absorbers may have a light film of oil around the seal, resulting from normal breathing and air exchange. This should NOT be taken as a sign of fail-

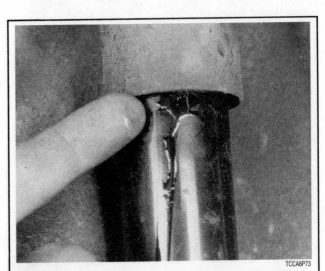

When fluid is seeping out of the shock absorber, it's time to replace it

ure, but any sign of thick or running oil definitely indicates failure. Gas filled shock absorbers may also show some film at the shaft; if the gas has leaked out, the shock will have almost no resistance to motion.

While each shock absorber can be replaced individually, it is recommended that they be changed as a pair (both front or both rear) to maintain equal response on both sides of the vehicle. Chances are quite good that if one has failed, its mate is also weak.

Axle Damper

REMOVAL & INSTALLATION

▶ **See Figure 25**

Models equipped with the handling suspension package are equipped with an axle damper (a horizontal shock absorber for the rear axle).

1. Loosen the lug nuts on the wheel which is being removed (on the same side as the axle damper).
2. Raise and support the rear of the vehicle safely.
3. Remove the tire and wheel assembly.
4. Loosen and remove the front retaining pivot bolt (damper-to-rear axle). A back-up wrench should be used to keep the fasteners from spinning.
5. Loosen and remove the rear axle damper retaining nut (damper-to-frame rail).
6. Remove the damper from the vehicle.

To install:

7. Position the damper to the vehicle and loosely install the fasteners.
8. Tighten the rear retaining nut and then the front retaining bolt to the figures given in the torque specifications chart.
9. Install the tire and wheel assembly.
10. Remove the jackstands and carefully lower the vehicle.

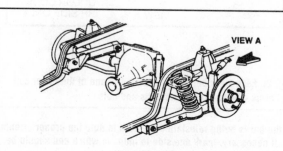

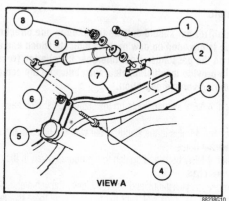

1. Mounting bolt
2. Bracket
3. Exhaust pipe
4. Mounting bolt
5. Axle assembly
6. Axle Damper
7. Sidemember
8. Mounting nut
9. Washer

Fig. 25 Exploded view of the rear axle damper mounting

Remove the tire and wheel assembly for access to the axle damper (arrow)

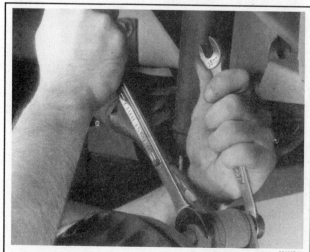

Use a back-up wrench when loosening the front retaining pivot bolt from the axle

A wrench or socket and driver can be used to loosen the rear damper retaining nut

Control Arms

REMOVAL & INSTALLATION

Upper Arm

➡For safety, even if only one arm needs to be replaced, the other arm should be replaced as well.

1. Raise and support the vehicle safely using jackstands at the rear crossmember.
2. Position a floor jack beneath the differential unit to support the axle assembly.
3. Remove and discard the upper arm pivot bolts and nuts, then remove the control arm.

To install:

4. Position the upper arm in the body side rail bracket. Install a new pivot bolt and nut finger-tight with the nut facing outward. Do not tighten them at this time.
5. Using the floor jack, raise the suspension until the upper arm-to-axle pivot hole is in position with the hole in the axle bushing. Install a new pivot bolt and nut with the nut facing inward.
6. Raise the suspension to normal curb height. Tighten the front upper arm and the rear upper arm bolts to the figures given in the torque specifications chart.
7. Remove the jackstands and carefully lower the vehicle.

Lower Arm

➡For safety, even if only one arm needs to be replaced, the other arm should be replaced as well.

1. Raise and support the vehicle safely using jackstands at the rear crossmember.
2. If equipped, remove the stabilizer bar.
3. Place a jack under the lower arm-to-axle pivot bolt. Remove and discard the bolt and nut. Lower the jack slowly until the coil spring can be removed.
4. Remove and discard the lower arm-to-frame pivot bolt and nut. Remove the lower arm.

To install:

5. Position the lower arm assembly into the front arm bracket. Install a new pivot bolt and nut finger-tight with the nut facing outward. Do not tighten at this time.
6. Position the coil spring on the lower arm spring seat, so the pigtail on the lower arm is at the rear of the vehicle and pointing toward the left side of the vehicle.
7. Slowly raise the jack until the arm is in position. Insert a new rear pivot bolt and nut finger-tight with the nut facing outward. Do not tighten at this time.
8. Raise the axle to normal curb height. Tighten the lower arm front and rear bolts to the figures given in the torque specifications chart.
9. If equipped, install the stabilizer bar.
10. Remove the jackstands from the crossmember and carefully lower the vehicle.

Sway Bar

REMOVAL & INSTALLATION

♦ **See Figure 26**

1. Raise and support the vehicle safely using jackstands.
2. Remove and discard the 4 bolts and stamped nuts attaching the sway (stabilizer) bar to the brackets in the lower control arms.
3. Remove the stabilizer bar from the vehicle.

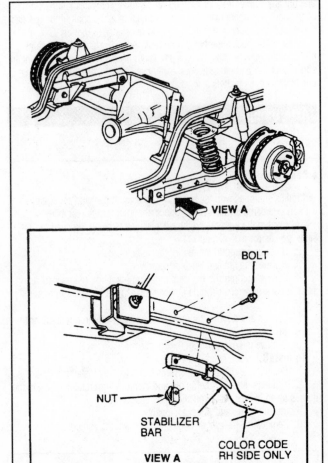

Fig. 26 Each sway bar end is attached to one of the lower control arms with two mounting bolts and nuts

➡If the bar is being reinstalled, be sure to note the proper orientation. If necessary, mark one side to indicate which end should be installed on the passenger side of the vehicle.

To install:

➡The stabilizer bar should only be installed in one direction. A color code is provided on new parts to indicate which end should be installed on the passenger side. Improper installation (reversing sides) will provide insufficient clearance between the control arm and bar during vehicle operation.

4. Install 4 NEW stamped nuts on the stabilizer bar over each retaining hole.
5. Align the 4 holes in the stabilizer bar with the holes in the lower control arm bracket holes.
6. Install 4 NEW bolts and tighten to the figures given in the torque specifications chart.
7. Remove the jackstands and carefully lower the vehicle.
8. Visually inspect the stabilizer bar to make sure there is adequate clearance between the bar and lower arm.

STEERING

FRONT SUSPENSION AND STEERING COMPONENTS

1. Sway bar
2. Power steering gear fluid lines
3. Coil springs
4. Struts
5. Outer tie rod ends
6. Knuckle/spindle assemblies
7. Ball joints
8. Coil spring mounting cups
9. Lower control arms
10. Sway bar end links
11. Control arm rear mounting bolts
12. Control arm front mounting bolts
13. Power steering gear mounting nuts
14. No. 2 crossmember
15. Power steering rack and pinion

Steering Wheel

✳✳ CAUTION

All models covered by this manual are equipped with a Supplemental Restraint System (SRS), which uses an air bag. Whenever working near any of the SRS components, such as the impact sensors, air bag module, steering column or instrument panel, disconnect the negative, then the positive battery cables and wait at least one minute. Disconnecting the battery cables and waiting one minute will allow any residual power in the system to drain. Failure to properly disconnect both battery cables may result in accidental air bag deployment, which could easily result in severe personal injury or death. Also, never attempt any electrical diagnosis or service to the SRS components and wiring; this work should only be performed by a qualified automotive technician.

REMOVAL & INSTALLATION

♦ See Figure 27

➡Prior to servicing the steering wheel, please read the Supplemental Restraint System (SRS) precautions in Section 6 of this manual.

1. Center the front wheels to the straight-ahead position and lock the steering column in this position with the ignition switch.
2. Disconnect the negative battery cable, then the positive battery cable. Wait at least one minute for the residual power in the air bag assembly to drain.
3. Using a small plastic or wooden prytool, remove the access plugs from both sides of the steering wheel. Using a socket with an extension and a ratchet, remove the two bolts through the access holes.
4. Lift the driver's side air bag carefully off of the steering wheel.
5. Disengage the air bag wiring harness connector from the air bag module, then remove the module from the vehicle. Place the air bag module on a clean work bench with the outside face of the module facing up.
6. Detach the horn and speed control connector from the steering wheel.
7. Remove and discard the steering wheel retaining bolt.

Before servicing the air bag module, disconnect both battery cables and wait at least one minute

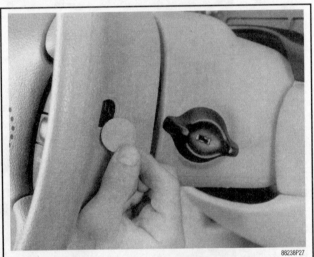

Remove the small access covers from both sides of the steering wheel . . .

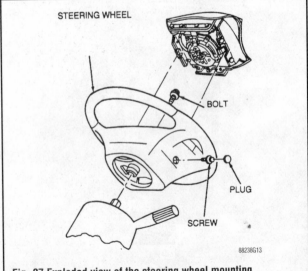

Fig. 27 Exploded view of the steering wheel mounting

STEERING WHEEL

BOLT

PLUG

SCREW

88238G13

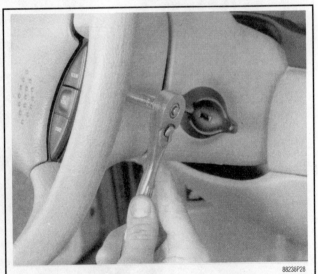

. . . then remove the air bag module retaining bolts

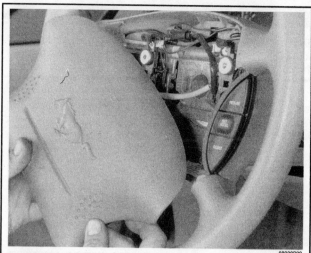

Lift the driver's side air bag module up and off of the steering wheel . . .

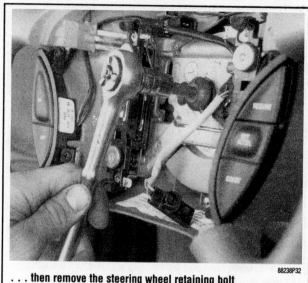

. . . then remove the steering wheel retaining bolt

. . . then detach the wiring harness connector from the module

Matchmark the steering column shaft (A) with the steering wheel (B)

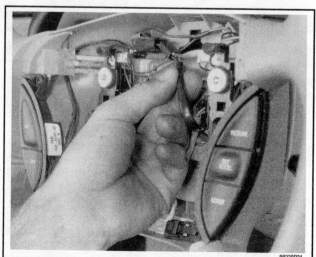

Disengage the horn and speed control connector from the steering wheel . . .

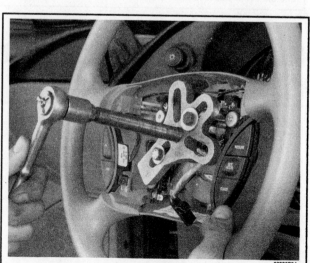

Use a steering wheel puller to draw the wheel off of the steering column shaft . . .

... and, while removing the steering wheel, route the wiring harness through the wheel

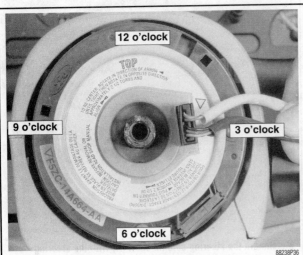

Before installing the wheel, be sure the wires are not pinched and the connector is in the 3 o'clock position

✳✳ WARNING

When removing the steering wheel from the column, take care to avoid catching the wiring harness on the wheel.

8. Matchmark the steering column shaft and the steering wheel for added insurance against incorrect positioning during reassembly. Using a steering wheel puller, such as Ford Tool T67L-3600-A, remove the wheel from the steering column. Route the wiring harness through the steering wheel as it is lifted off of the steering column shaft.

To install:
9. Ensure that the front wheels are pointing straight ahead.

✳✳ WARNING

Be sure that the air bag sliding contact wire is not pinched or kinked; otherwise, the air bag monitor will detect a system fault.

10. Position the steering wheel on the tip of the steering column shaft and route the wiring harness through the wheel at the 3 o'clock position. Slide the wheel completely onto the steering shaft. The matchmarks should be aligned.
11. Install a new steering wheel retainer bolt and tighten it to the value presented in the torque specifications chart.
12. Attach the horn and speed control wiring harness connector to the steering wheel and engage the wiring harness in the steering wheel clip, if equipped.
13. Position the air bag module near the steering wheel, and connect the wiring harness to it. Ensure that the connectors are fully seated.

✳✳ WARNING

Be sure that the wiring is not pinched or kinked between the steering wheel and the air bag module, otherwise the air bag monitor will detect a system fault.

14. Position the air bag module on the steering wheel and install the retaining bolts through the two access holes on the sides. Tighten them to specifications.
15. Connect the positive, then the negative battery cables.
16. Verify that the air bag warning indicator lamp indicates a satisfactory air bag system condition.

The air bag indicator light on the instrument cluster will illuminate for approximately 6 seconds when the ignition switch is turned to the **RUN** position if the SRS is functioning properly. After being illuminated for the 6 seconds, the indicator light should then turn off. If the air bag light does not illuminate at all, stays on continuously, or flashes at any time, a problem has been detected by the diagnostic monitor computer.

✳✳ WARNING

If at any time the air bag light indicates that the computer has noted a problem, have your vehicle's SRS serviced immediately by a qualified automotive technician. A faulty SRS can cause severe physical injury or death.

Combination Switch

✳✳ CAUTION

All models covered by this manual are equipped with a Supplemental Restraint System (SRS), which uses an air bag. Whenever working near any of the SRS components, such as the impact sensors, air bag module, steering column or instrument panel, disconnect the negative, then the positive battery cables and wait at least one minute. Disconnecting the battery cables and waiting one minute will allow any residual power in the system to drain. Failure to properly disconnect both battery cables may result in accidental air bag deployment, which could easily result in severe personal injury or death. Also, never attempt any electrical diagnosis or service to the SRS components and wiring; this work should only be performed by a qualified automotive technician.

The combination switch incorporates the turn signal, dimmer, hazard lights and wiper switch functions on the Mustang.

REMOVAL & INSTALLATION

◆ See Figure 28

1. To prevent accidental air bag deployment, disconnect the negative battery cable, then the positive battery cable to allow residual energy in the air bag system to drain.
2. Remove the steering column shroud retaining screws, then remove the upper and lower shrouds.
3. Remove the switch retaining screws and lift the switch assembly off of the column.
4. With the wiring exposed, carefully lift the wiring harness connector retainer tabs and disengage the connectors.

To install:
5. Engage the wiring harness connectors for the combination switch, then position the switch against the steering column. Install the self-tapping retaining screws and tighten them to 18–26 inch lbs. (2–3 Nm).
6. Position the steering column shrouds on the column and secure them in place with the mounting screws. Tighten the screws until snug.
7. Connect the positive, then the negative battery cables to the battery.
8. Start the engine and check the combination switch for proper function.

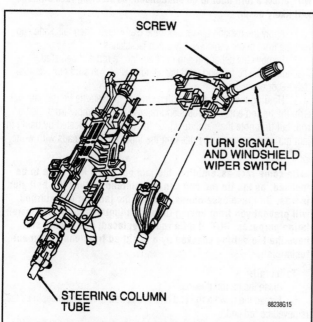

SCREW

TURN SIGNAL AND WINDSHIELD WIPER SWITCH

STEERING COLUMN TUBE

88238G15

Fig. 28 Exploded view of the combination switch mounting on the steering column

Ignition Switch

❋❋ CAUTION

All models covered by this manual are equipped with a Supplemental Restraint System (SRS), which uses an air bag.

Whenever working near any of the SRS components, such as the impact sensors, air bag module, steering column or instrument panel, disconnect the negative, then the positive battery cables and wait at least one minute. Disconnecting the battery cables and waiting one minute will allow any residual power in the system to drain. Failure to properly disconnect both battery cables may result in accidental air bag deployment, which could easily result in severe personal injury or death. Also, never attempt any electrical diagnosis or service to the SRS components and wiring; this work should only be performed by a qualified automotive technician.

REMOVAL & INSTALLATION

1. To prevent accidental air bag deployment, disconnect the negative battery cable, then the positive battery cable to allow residual energy in the air bag system to drain.
2. Remove the steering column shroud(s).
3. Disengage the wiring harness connector from the ignition switch.
4. Insert the key into the ignition switch, then rotate the ignition key lock cylinder to the **RUN** position.
5. Remove the two screws attaching the ignition switch.
6. Disengage the ignition switch from the actuator pin and remove the switch.

To install:
➡A new ignition switch purchased from Ford will already be set in the RUN position.

7. Adjust the new ignition switch by sliding the carrier to the **RUN** position.
8. Check to ensure that the ignition key lock cylinder is in the **RUN** position. The **RUN** position is achieved by rotating the key lock cylinder approximately 90 degrees from the **LOCK** position.
9. Install the ignition switch onto the actuator pin.
10. Align the switch mounting holes and install the attaching screws. Tighten the screws to 50–69 inch lbs. (6–8 Nm).
11. Attach the electrical connector to the ignition switch.
12. Connect the positive, then the negative battery cables. Check the ignition switch for proper function in **START** and **ACC** positions. Make sure the column is locked in the **LOCK** position.
13. Install the steering column shroud(s).

Ignition Lock Cylinder

❋❋ CAUTION

All models covered by this manual are equipped with a Supplemental Restraint System (SRS), which uses an air bag. Whenever working near any of the SRS components, such as the impact sensors, air bag module, steering column or instrument panel, disconnect the negative, then the positive battery cables and wait at least one minute. Disconnecting the battery cables and waiting one minute will allow any residual power in the system to drain. Failure to properly disconnect both battery cables may result in accidental air bag deployment, which could easily result in severe personal injury or death. Also, never attempt any electrical diagnosis or service to the SRS components and wiring; this work should only be performed by a qualified automotive technician.

REMOVAL & INSTALLATION

◆ **See Figures 29 and 30**

1. To prevent accidental air bag deployment, disconnect the negative battery cable, then the positive battery cable to allow residual energy in the air bag system to drain.

2. Remove the steering column shroud(s).

3. Insert the key into the ignition switch, then rotate the ignition key lock cylinder to the **RUN** position.

4. Place a ⅛ in. (3mm) diameter wire pin or small drift punch in the hole in the casting surrounding the lock cylinder, and depress the retaining pin while pulling out on the lock cylinder to remove it from the column housing.

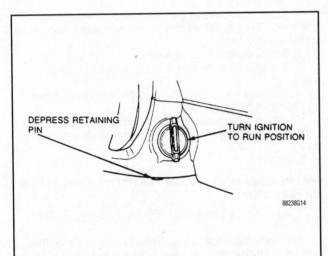

Fig. 29 To remove the ignition lock cylinder, turn the lock cylinder to the RUN position . . .

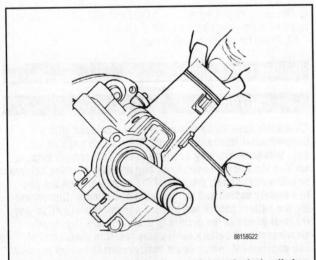

Fig. 30 . . . depress the retaining pin and draw the lock cylinder out of the housing

To install:

5. Turn the lock cylinder to the **RUN** position and depress the retaining pin. Insert the lock cylinder into its housing in the lock cylinder casting.

6. Make sure that the cylinder is fully seated and aligned in the interlocking washer before turning the key to the **OFF** position. This action will permit the cylinder retaining pin to extend into the hole in the lock cylinder housing.

7. Using the ignition key, rotate the cylinder to ensure correct mechanical operation in all positions.

8. Connect the positive, then the negative battery cables and check for proper operation in **P** or **N**. Also make sure that the start circuit cannot be actuated in **D** or **R** positions and that the column is locked in the **LOCK** position.

9. Install the trim shrouds.

Steering Linkage

REMOVAL & INSTALLATION

Tie Rod Ends

◆ **See Figure 31**

➡**If a steering boot or inner rod is damaged on the rack and pinion assembly, they are easily replaced after tie rod end removal. DO NOT allow a torn boot to go unattended, as steering rack damage will likely occur.**

1. Apply the parking brake, block the rear wheels, then raise and support the front of the vehicle safely using jackstands.

2. Remove the cotter pin and nut from the tie rod end ball stud. Disconnect the tie rod end from the spindle using ball stud remover tool 3290-D or equivalent.

3. Holding the tie rod end with a wrench, loosen the tie rod jam nut. Grip the tie rod end with pliers and remove the assembly from the tie rod, but first note the depth to which the tie rod was located by using the jam nut as a marker, or by marking the inner tie rod threads with white paint.

➡**On some rack assemblies, the jam nut DOES NOT have to be touched, as the tie rod end can be unthreaded once the ball stud is free. On these assemblies, leaving the jam nut undisturbed will prevent you from having to make alignment marks for installation purposes. BUT, if a tie rod is replaced, you should still have the toe setting checked by a qualified front end alignment technician.**

To install:

4. Clean the tie rod threads.

5. Thread the new tie rod end onto the tie rod to the same depth as the removed tie rod end.

6. Place the tie rod end ball stud into the spindle and install the nut. Make sure the front wheels are in the straight-ahead position.

7. Tighten the nut to the specified value, and continue tightening the nut to align the next castellation of the nut with the cotter pin hole in the stud. Install a new cotter pin.

8. Tighten the jam nut to the figures given in the torque specifications chart.

9. Have the front end alignment checked by a qualified automotive technician.

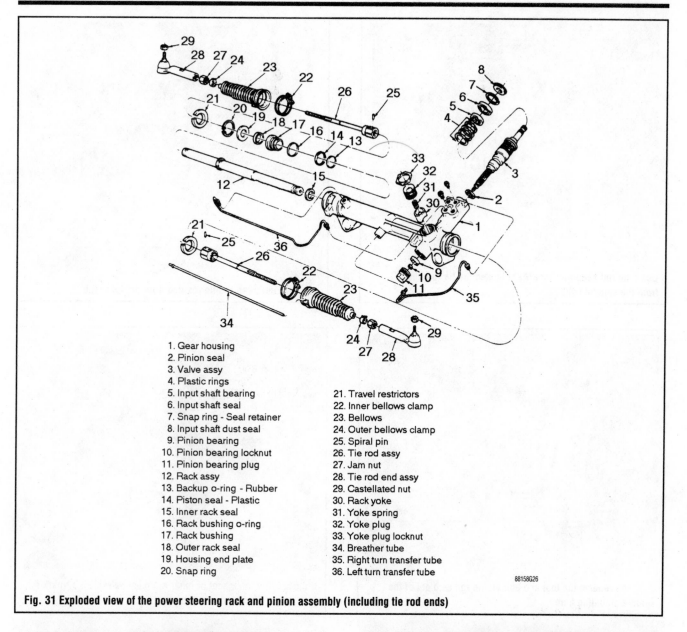

1. Gear housing
2. Pinion seal
3. Valve assy
4. Plastic rings
5. Input shaft bearing
6. Input shaft seal
7. Snap ring - Seal retainer
8. Input shaft dust seal
9. Pinion bearing
10. Pinion bearing locknut
11. Pinion bearing plug
12. Rack assy
13. Backup o-ring - Rubber
14. Piston seal - Plastic
15. Inner rack seal
16. Rack bushing o-ring
17. Rack bushing
18. Outer rack seal
19. Housing end plate
20. Snap ring

21. Travel restrictors
22. Inner bellows clamp
23. Bellows
24. Outer bellows clamp
25. Spiral pin
26. Tie rod assy
27. Jam nut
28. Tie rod end assy
29. Castellated nut
30. Rack yoke
31. Yoke spring
32. Yoke plug
33. Yoke plug locknut
34. Breather tube
35. Right turn transfer tube
36. Left turn transfer tube

88158G26

Fig. 31 Exploded view of the power steering rack and pinion assembly (including tie rod ends)

To remove the outer tie rod end, first remove the cotter pin . . .

88238P07

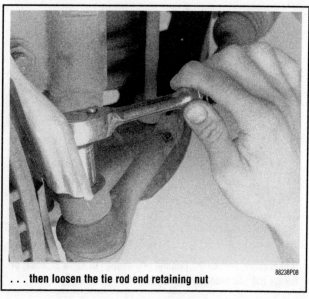

. . . then loosen the tie rod end retaining nut

88238P08

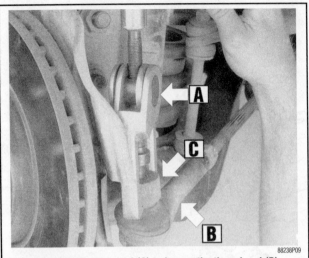

Use a tie rod separator tool (A) to loosen the tie rod end (B) from the spindle (C) . . .

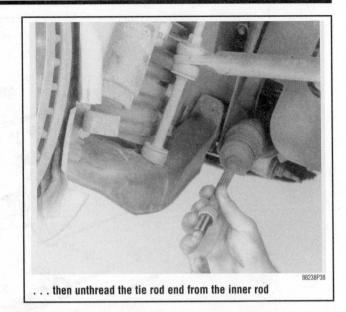

. . . then unthread the tie rod end from the inner rod

. . . then remove the tool and pull the tie rod stud out of the spindle mounting bore

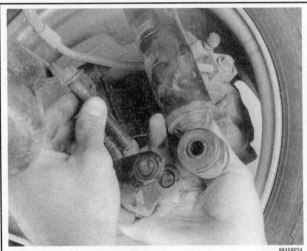

If the steering rack boot or inner rod must be replaced, mark the jam nut positioning on the inner rod . . .

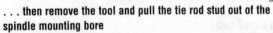

If necessary, loosen the jam nut just enough to allow removal of the tie rod end (about ½ turn) . . .

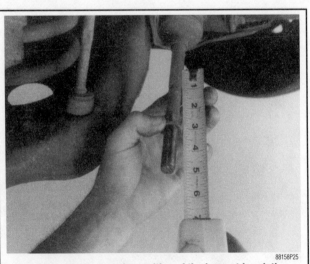

. . . or you can measure the position of the jam nut in relation to the inner rod threads

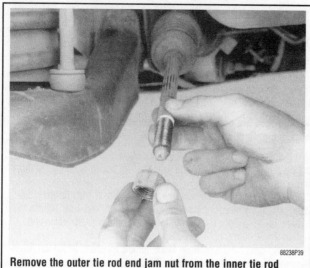

Remove the outer tie rod end jam nut from the inner tie rod shaft

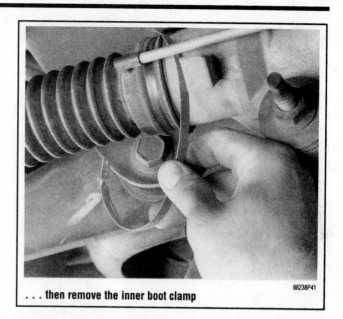

. . . then remove the inner boot clamp

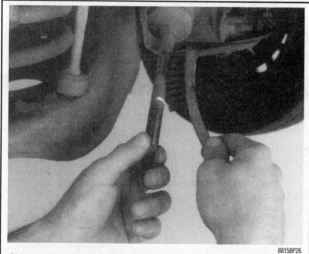

Clean the inner rod threads thoroughly to prevent damage (and to make installation easier)

Slide the damaged boot off of the inner rod

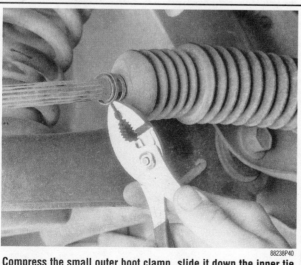

Compress the small outer boot clamp, slide it down the inner tie rod . . .

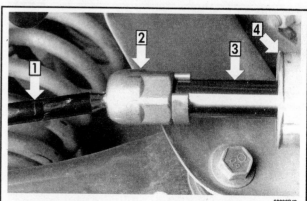

1. Inner tie rod end
2. Fitting
3. Power steering rack and pinion shaft
4. Power steering rack and pinion

The inner rod attaches to the power steering rack and pinion at this fitting; unthread it to separate the two

Power Steering Rack and Pinion

REMOVAL & INSTALLATION

▶ **See Figure 32**

1. Disconnect the negative battery cable. Turn the ignition switch to the **RUN** position so that the front wheels can be turned while working on the power rack and pinion.
2. Loosen all of the wheel lug nuts ½ turn to break them free.
3. Raise and support the vehicle safely using jackstands. Position a drain pan to catch the fluid from the power steering lines.
4. Remove the one bolt retaining the steering column shaft flexible coupling to the input shaft.
5. Remove the front wheel and tire assemblies. Remove the cotter pins and nuts from the tie rod ends, then separate the tie rod studs from the spindles.
6. Remove the two nuts, insulator washers and bolts retaining the steering rack to the crossmember. Remove the front rubber insulators.

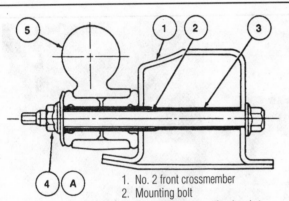

1. No. 2 front crossmember
2. Mounting bolt
3. Steering gear mounting bracket
4. Retaining nut
5. Power steering rack and pinion

88238G12

Fig. 32 Power steering rack and pinion mounting on the No. 2 crossmember

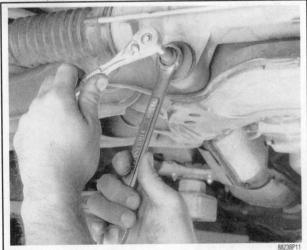

88238P11

When loosening the retaining nut, hold the mounting stud with a second wrench

7. Position the rack to allow access to the hydraulic lines and disconnect the lines.
8. Remove the steering rack from the vehicle.

To install:

9. Install new plastic seals on the hydraulic line fittings.
10. Install the rack on the mounting studs, and connect the hydraulic lines to the rack and pinion. Tighten the fittings to the figures given in the torque specifications chart.

➡**The hoses are designed to swivel when properly tightened. Do not attempt to eliminate looseness by overtightening the fittings.**

11. Install the front rubber insulators. Make sure all rubber insulators are pushed completely inside the gear housing before installing the mounting bolts.
12. Insert the input shaft into the steering column shaft flexible coupling. Install the mounting bolts, insulator washers and nuts. Tighten the nuts to the figures given in the torque specifications chart. Install and tighten the flexible coupling bolt to the specified values.
13. Connect the tie rod ends to the spindle arms and install the retaining nuts. Tighten the nut to the specified value, and continue tightening the nut to align the next castellation of the nut with the cotter pin hole in the stud. Install a new cotter pin.
14. Remove the jackstands and carefully lower the vehicle.
15. Turn the ignition switch **OFF** and connect the negative battery cable.
16. Fill the power steering system with the proper type and quantity of fluid.
17. If the tie rod ends were loosened, have the front end alignment checked by a qualified automotive suspension technician.

Power Steering Pump

REMOVAL & INSTALLATION

▶ **See Figure 33**

1. Disconnect the negative battery cable.
2. Disconnect the fluid return hose at the reservoir and drain the fluid into a container.
3. Remove the pressure hose from the pump and, if necessary, drain the fluid into a container. Do not remove the fitting from the pump.
4. Remove the serpentine accessory drive belt.
5. Using a pulley removal tool, such as Ford Tool T69L-10300-B, draw the pulley off of the pump shaft.
6. Remove the steering pump mounting bolts, then remove it from the

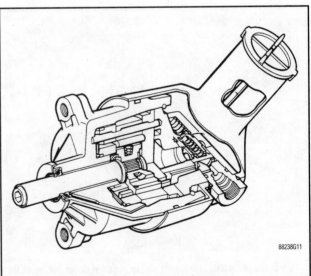

88238G11

Fig. 33 Cutaway view of the power steering pump

vehicle.

To install:

7. Position the pump on the mounting bracket and install the bolts at the front of the pump. Tighten them to the figure given in the torque specifications chart.

8. Install the power steering pump pulley using an installation tool specifically designed for this purpose, such as Ford Tool T65P-3A733-C.

9. Install the serpentine accessory drive belt.

10. Install the pressure hose to the pump fitting. Tighten the tube nut with a flare nut wrench, rather than with an open-end wrench. Tighten the fitting to the figure given in the torque specifications chart.

➡**Do not overtighten this fitting. Swivel and/or end-play of the fitting is normal and does not indicate a loose fitting. Overtightening the tube nut can collapse the tube nut wall, resulting in a leak and requiring replacement of the entire pressure hose assembly. Use of an open-end wrench to tighten the nut can deform the tube nut hex, which may result in improper torque and may make further servicing of the system difficult.**

11. Connect the return hose to the pump and tighten the clamp. Fill the reservoir with the proper type and quantity of fluid.

12. Connect the negative battery cable and properly bleed the power steering system.

BLEEDING

1. Disconnect the ignition coil and raise the front wheels off the floor.
2. Fill the power steering fluid reservoir.
3. Crank the engine with the starter and add fluid until the level remains constant.

4. While cranking the engine, rotate the steering wheel from lock-to-lock.

➡**The front wheels must be off the floor during lock-to-lock rotation of the steering wheel.**

5. Check the fluid level and add fluid, if necessary.

6. Connect the ignition coil wire. Start the engine and allow it to run for several minutes.

7. Rotate the steering wheel from lock-to-lock.

8. Shut off the engine and check the fluid level. Add fluid, if necessary.

9. If air is still present in the system, purge the system of air using power steering pump air evacuator tool 021-00014 or equivalent, as follows:

a. Make sure the power steering pump reservoir is full to the FULL COLD mark on the dipstick.

b. Tightly insert the rubber stopper of the air evacuator assembly into the pump reservoir fill neck.

c. Apply 20–25 in. Hg (68–85 kPa) maximum vacuum on the pump reservoir for a minimum of three minutes with the engine idling. As air purges from the system, vacuum will fall off. Maintain adequate vacuum with the vacuum source.

d. Release the vacuum and remove the vacuum source. Fill the reservoir to the FULL WARM or center reservoir mark.

e. With the engine idling, apply 15 in. Hg vacuum to the pump reservoir. Slowly cycle the steering wheel from lock-to-lock every 30 seconds for approximately five minutes. Do not hold the steering wheel at its stops while cycling. Maintain adequate vacuum with the vacuum source as the air purges.

f. Release the vacuum and remove the vacuum source.

10. Lower the front end of the vehicle, and fill the reservoir until full.

11. Start the engine and cycle the steering wheel. Check for oil leaks at

TORQUE SPECIFICATIONS

System	Component	Ft. Lbs.	Nm
Front Suspension			
	Ball joint-to-spindle nut	109-149	148-202
	Lower control arm-to-crossmember nuts and bolts	141-191	191-259
	Lug nuts	85-105	115-142
	Spindle-to-strut nuts and bolts—1994-95 models	141-199	190-271
	Spindle-to-strut nuts and bolts—1996-98 models	141-191	190-259
	Sway bar end link nuts	11-16	16-22
	Sway bar mounting bracket bolts	44-59	60-80
	Upper strut mounting central nut	56-92	75-125
	Wheel hub/bearing assembly retaining nut—1994 models	221-295	300-400
	Wheel hub/bearing assembly retaining nut—1995 models	189-254	255-345
	Wheel hub/bearing assembly retaining nut—1996-98 models	221-295	300-400
Rear Suspension			
	Axle damper front bolt	57-75	76-103
	Axle damper rear nut	57-75	76-103
	Clevis bracket-to-axle nut—1994 models	57-75	76-103
	Clevis bracket-to-axle nut—1995 models	67-80	90-108
	Clevis bracket-to-axle nut—1996-98 models	57-75	76-103
	Lower control arm-to-axle bolts	71-97	97-132
	Lower control arm-to-frame bracket bolts	71-97	97-132
	Lower shock absorber mounting nut and bolt	57-75	76-103
	Lug nuts	85-105	115-142
	Shock absorber-to-clevis bracket bolt	56-76	77-104
	Sway bar-to-lower control arm bolts	29-37	40-54
	Upper control arm-to-axle bolts—1994-95 models	70-100	95-135
	Upper control arm-to-axle bolts—1996-98 models	71-97	98-132
	Upper control arm-to-frame bracket bolts	77-105	104-142
	Upper shock absorber retaining nut—1994 models	20-25	26-35
	Upper shock absorber retaining nut—1995 models	25-34	34-46
Steering			
	Lower power steering bolt—1994-95 models	30-40	41-54
	Outer tie rod end jam nut	35-50	48-68
	Outer tie rod end-to-spindle nut	35-47	47-64
	Power steeirng pump-to-support bracket bolts—1994-95 models	30-45	40-62
	Power steering bracket bolt—1994-95 models	58-70	79-95
	Power steering pump bracket-to-rear support—models with A/C	18-24	24-32
	Power steering pump bracket-to-rear support—models without A/C	30-45	40-62
	Power steering pump pivot bolt—1994-95 models	30-45	40-62
	Power steering pump pressure hose fitting—1994 models	10-15	14-20
	Power steering pump pressure hose fitting—1995-98 models	26-33	34-46
	Power steering pump-to-bracket bolts	30-45	40-62
	Rack and pinion line fittings	20-25	27-34
	Rack and pinion-to-crossmember retaining nuts	30-40	41-54
	Rear support-to-cylinder head—1994-95 models	30-45	40-62
	Steering column flex joint nut	20-30	28-40
	Steering wheel retaining nut	22-33	31-45
	Support bracket-to-water pump bolts	30-45	40-62

88238C0

all connections.

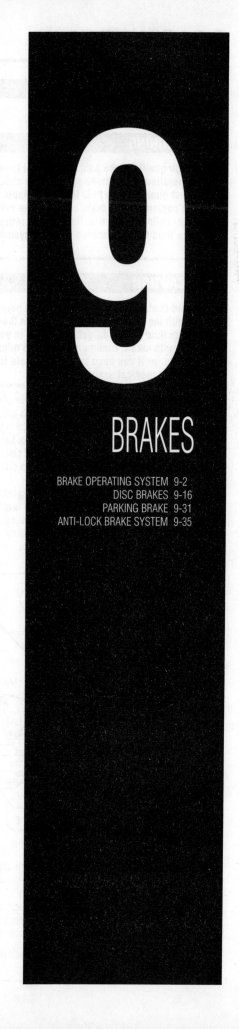

9

BRAKES

BRAKE OPERATING SYSTEM

▶ See Figure 1

Hydraulic systems are used to actuate the brakes of all modern automobiles. The system transports the power required to force the frictional surfaces of the braking system together from the pedal to the individual brake units at each wheel. A hydraulic system is used for two reasons.

First, fluid under pressure can be carried to all parts of an automobile by small pipes and flexible hoses without taking up a significant amount of room or posing routing problems.

Second, a great mechanical advantage can be given to the brake pedal end of the system, and the foot pressure required to actuate the brakes can be reduced by making the surface area of the master cylinder pistons smaller than that of any of the pistons in the wheel cylinders or calipers.

The master cylinder consists of a fluid reservoir, along with a double

cylinder and piston assembly. Double type master cylinders are designed to separate the front and rear braking systems hydraulically in case of a leak. The master cylinder coverts mechanical motion from the pedal into hydraulic pressure within the lines. This pressure is translated back into mechanical motion at the wheels by the caliper.

Steel lines carry the brake fluid to a point on the vehicle's frame near each of the vehicle's wheels. The fluid is then carried to the calipers by flexible tubes, in order to allow for suspension and steering movements.

In drum brake systems, each wheel cylinder contains two pistons, one at either end, which push outward in opposite directions and force the brake shoes into contact with the drum.

In disc brake systems, the cylinders are part of the calipers. At least one cylinder in each caliper is used to force the brake pads against the disc.

All pistons employ some type of seal, usually made of rubber, to minimize fluid leakage. A rubber dust boot seals the outer end of the cylinder against dust and dirt. The boot fits around the outer end of the caliper piston.

The hydraulic system operates as follows: When at rest, the entire system, from the piston(s) in the master cylinder to those in the calipers, is full of brake fluid. Upon application of the brake pedal, fluid trapped in front of the master cylinder piston(s) is forced through the lines to the calipers. Here, it forces the pistons inward toward the disc. The motion of the pistons is opposed by spring seals.

Upon release of the brake pedal, a spring located inside the master cylinder immediately returns the master cylinder pistons to the normal position. The pistons contain check valves and the master cylinder has compensating ports drilled in it. These are uncovered as the pistons reach their normal position. The piston check valves allow fluid to flow toward the calipers as the pistons withdraw. Then, as the return springs force the brake pads or shoes into the released position, the excess fluid returns to the reservoir through the compensating ports. It is during the time the pedal is in the released position that any fluid that has leaked out of the system will be replaced through the compensating ports.

Dual circuit master cylinders employ two pistons, located one behind the other, in the same cylinder. The primary piston is actuated directly by mechanical linkage from the brake pedal through the power booster. The secondary piston is actuated by fluid trapped between the two pistons. If a leak develops in front of the secondary piston, it moves forward until it bottoms against the front of the master cylinder, and the fluid trapped between the pistons will operate the rear brakes. If the rear brakes develop a leak, the primary piston will move forward until direct contact with the secondary piston takes place, and it will force the secondary piston to actuate the front brakes. In either case, the brake pedal moves farther when the brakes are applied, and less braking power is available.

All dual circuit systems use a switch to warn the driver when only half of the brake system is operational. This switch is usually located in a valve body which is mounted on the firewall or the frame below the master cylinder. A hydraulic piston receives pressure from both circuits, each circuit's pressure being applied to one end of the piston. When the pressures are in balance, the piston remains stationary. When one circuit has a leak, however, the greater pressure in that circuit during application of the brakes will push the piston to one side, closing the switch and activating the brake warning light.

This valve body also contains a metering valve and, in some cases, a proportioning valve. The metering valve keeps pressure from traveling to the disc brakes on the front wheels until the brake pads on the rear wheels have contacted the discs, ensuring that the front brakes will never be used alone. The proportioning valve controls the pressure to the rear brakes to lessen the chance of rear wheel lock-up during very hard braking.

Warning lights may be tested by depressing the brake pedal and holding it while opening one of the wheel cylinder bleeder screws. If this does not cause the light to turn on, substitute a new lamp, make continuity checks and, finally, replace the switch as necessary.

The hydraulic system may be checked for leaks by applying pressure to the pedal gradually and steadily. If the pedal sinks very slowly to the floor,

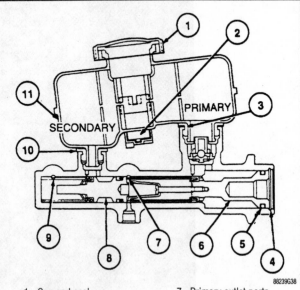

1. Cap and seal
2. Fluid level indicator
3. Primary seal
4. Snapring
5. O-ring
6. Primary piston assembly
7. Primary outlet ports
8. Secondary piston assembly
9. Secondary outlet port
10. Secondary seal
11. Brake master cylinder

88239G38

Fig. 1 Cross-sectional view of the dual circuit master cylinder used in all 1994–98 Mustangs

the system has a leak. This is not to be confused with a springy or spongy feel due to the compression of air within the lines. If the system leaks, there will be a gradual change in the position of the pedal with a constant pressure.

Check for leaks along all lines and at wheel cylinders. If no external leaks are apparent, the problem is inside the master cylinder.

DISC BRAKES

Instead of the traditional expanding brakes that press outward against a circular drum, disc brake systems utilize a disc (rotor) with brake pads positioned on either side of it. An easily-seen analogy is the hand brake arrangement on a bicycle. The pads squeeze onto the rim of the bike wheel, slowing its motion. Automobile disc brakes use the identical principle, but apply the braking effort to a separate disc instead of the wheel.

The disc (rotor) is a casting, usually equipped with cooling fins between the two braking surfaces. This enables air to circulate between the braking surfaces, making them less sensitive to heat buildup and more resistant to fade. Dirt and water do not drastically affect braking action, since contaminants are thrown off by the centrifugal action of the rotor or scraped off the rotor by the pads. Also, the equal clamping action of the two brake pads tends to ensure uniform, straight line stops. Disc brakes are inherently self-adjusting. There are three general types of disc brake:

- Fixed caliper
- Floating caliper
- Sliding caliper

The fixed caliper design uses two pistons mounted on either side of the rotor (in each side of the caliper). The caliper is mounted rigidly and does not move.

The sliding and floating designs are quite similar. In fact, these two types are often lumped together. In both designs, the pad on the inside of the rotor is moved into contact with the rotor by hydraulic force. The caliper, which is not held in a fixed position, moves slightly, bringing the outside pad into contact with the rotor. There are various methods of attaching floating calipers. Some pivot at the bottom or top, and some slide on mounting bolts. In any event, the end result is the same.

POWER BOOSTERS

3.8L and 5.0L Engines

◆ See Figure 2

Virtually all modern vehicles use a vacuum assisted power brake system to multiply the braking force and reduce pedal effort. Since vacuum is always available when the engine is operating, the system is simple and efficient. A vacuum diaphragm is located on the front of the master cylinder and assists the driver in applying the brakes, reducing both the effort and travel he must put into moving the brake pedal.

The vacuum diaphragm housing is normally connected to the intake manifold by a vacuum hose. A check valve is placed at the point where the hose enters the diaphragm housing, so that during periods of low manifold vacuum, braking assist will not be lost.

Depressing the brake pedal closes off the vacuum source and allows atmospheric pressure to enter on one side of the diaphragm. This causes the master cylinder pistons to move and apply the brakes. When the brake pedal is released, vacuum is applied to both sides of the diaphragm and springs return the diaphragm and master cylinder pistons to the released position.

If the vacuum supply fails, the brake pedal rod will contact the end of the master cylinder actuator rod and the system will apply the brakes without any power assistance. The driver will notice that much greater pedal effort is needed to stop the car and that the pedal feels harder than usual.

VACUUM LEAK TEST

1. Operate the engine at idle without touching the brake pedal for at least one minute.
2. Turn off the engine and wait one minute.
3. Test for the presence of assist vacuum by depressing the brake pedal and releasing it several times. If vacuum is present in the system, light application will produce less and less pedal travel. If there is no vacuum, air is leaking into the system.

SYSTEM OPERATION TEST

1. With the engine **OFF**, pump the brake pedal until the supply vacuum is entirely gone.
2. Put light, steady pressure on the brake pedal.
3. Start the engine and let it idle. If the system is operating correctly, the brake pedal should fall toward the floor when constant pressure is maintained.
4. Power brake systems may be tested for hydraulic leaks just as ordinary systems are tested.

4.6L Engines

◆ See Figure 3

The 4.6L engines utilize a different type of power booster than the conventional vacuum-type. The power booster is called a Hydro-Boost booster and is manufactured by Bendix.

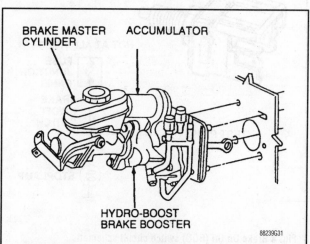

88239G32

Fig. 2 The vacuum booster used by Mustang models equipped with either the 3.8L or the 5.0L engine is a large metal cylinder

BRAKE MASTER CYLINDER   ACCUMULATOR

HYDRO-BOOST BRAKE BOOSTER

88239G31

Fig. 3 Vehicles equipped with 4.6L engines utilize a Hydro-Boost booster because the engine does not produce sufficient vacuum to activate a vacuum booster

The Hydro-Boost booster is powered by power steering fluid. Brake fluid and power steering fluid are not compatible and, if mixed, will result in damage to the brake system.

The Hydro-Boost booster uses pressurized power steering fluid, provided by the power steering pump, to multiply the effectiveness of brake pedal movement. In the event of disrupted flow of power steering fluid from the pump, the booster has a reserve system (accumulator) which can store enough pressurized power steering fluid to provide at least two power-assisted brake applications. After the reserve fluid pressure has been used, the brake system functions as a conventional manual system. The Hydro-Boost booster is mounted in the same place (between the master cylinder and engine firewall) as the conventional vacuum power booster.

Brake Light Switch

OPERATION

▶ **See Figures 4 and 5**

The stop light switch, referred to as the stoplight or Brake On/Off (BOO) switch by the manufacturer, turns power on and off to the rear brake lamps when the brake pedal is depressed. The BOO switch also provides reference signals to the Anti-lock Brake System Control Module (ABS-CM), the Powertrain Control Module (PCM), the shift lock actuator, and the speed control servo (if equipped).

REMOVAL & INSTALLATION

❊❊❊ **WARNING**

Do not pull on the connector or on the harness with excessive force to disengage the switch wiring. Connector and/or wiring harness damage will result.

1. Detach the wiring harness connector from the BOO switch by using a small pick or prytool to lift the connector retaining tab up, then pulling the connector from the switch.

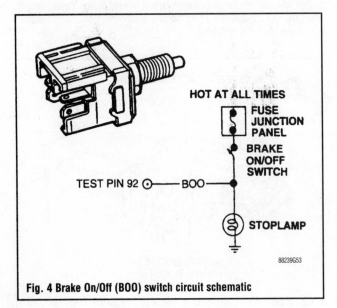
88239G53

Fig. 4 Brake On/Off (BOO) switch circuit schematic

➡Since the side plate of the BOO switch nearest the brake pedal is slotted, it is not necessary to remove the brake master cylinder pushrod and one spacer from the brake pedal pin.

2. Disengage the hairpin retainer, then slide the BOO switch, pushrod, nylon washers and bushing away from the brake pedal. Detach the BOO switch from the bracket by sliding it up or down.
   To install:

❊❊❊ **WARNING**

Only use hairpin retainers specifically designed for the BOO switch.

3. Position the BOO switch so that the U-shaped side is nearest the brake pedal and directly over the pin. Slide the switch down until it has trapped the master cylinder pushrod and blade bushing between its side-plates.
4. Press the BOO switch and pushrod firmly toward the brake pedal arm, then assemble the outside white nylon washer to the pin.
5. Install the hairpin retainer to securely hold the entire assembly.

➡The BOO switch wiring harness must have sufficient slack to allow brake pedal movement. After attaching the connector to the switch, ensure that there is enough play in the harness.

6. Insert the wiring harness connector into the BOO switch connector until the retaining tab is fully engaged.
7. Have an assistant sit in the vehicle and apply the brake pedal while you watch the brake lamps for proper function. The brake lights should illuminate even with the ignition switch in the **OFF** position. If they do not illuminate when the pedal is depressed, there is a problem within the switch or circuit.

Master Cylinder

▶ **See Figure 6**

❊❊❊ **WARNING**

Clean, high quality brake fluid is essential to the safe and proper operation of the brake system. You should always buy the highest quality brake fluid that is available. If the brake fluid becomes contaminated, drain and flush the system, then refill the master cylinder with new fluid. Never reuse any brake fluid. Any brake fluid that is removed from the system should be discarded.

❊❊❊ **CAUTION**

Brake fluid contains polyglycol ethers and polyglycols. Avoid contact with the eyes and wash your hands thoroughly after handling brake fluid. If you do get brake fluid in your eyes, flush your eyes with clean, running water for 15 minutes. If eye irritation persists, or if you have taken brake fluid internally, IMMEDIATELY seek medical assistance.

➡On models equipped with an Anti-lock Brake System (ABS), if, during brake system service or because of a fluid leak, the level of fluid in the system ever falls below that of the Hydraulic Control Unit (HCU), refer to the bleeding procedure in the ABS portion of this section. To properly bleed the HCU, an expensive scan tool is necessary; take this into consideration when contemplating brake system service. However, if only the brake pads, calipers, master cylinder, and other non-ABS components are being removed and installed, bleeding the HCU is not necessary and, therefore, the scan tool is not necessary.

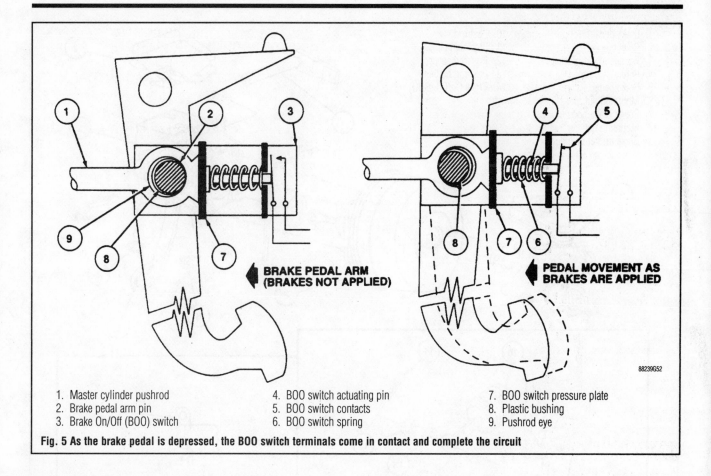

1. Master cylinder pushrod
2. Brake pedal arm pin
3. Brake On/Off (BOO) switch
4. BOO switch actuating pin
5. BOO switch contacts
6. BOO switch spring
7. BOO switch pressure plate
8. Plastic bushing
9. Pushrod eye

88239G52

Fig. 5 As the brake pedal is depressed, the BOO switch terminals come in contact and complete the circuit

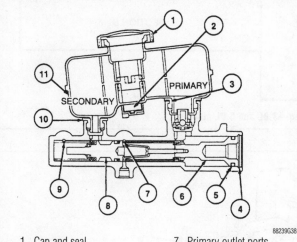

1. Cap and seal
2. Fluid level indicator
3. Primary seal
4. Snapring
5. O-ring
6. Primary piston assembly
7. Primary outlet ports
8. Secondary piston assembly
9. Secondary outlet port
10. Secondary seal
11. Brake master cylinder

88239G38

Fig. 6 The same master cylinder is used with vacuum-activated and Hydro-Boost power brake boosters

REMOVAL & INSTALLATION

◆ See Figures 7 and 8

1. Help avoid brake fluid spills by siphoning as much brake fluid out of the reservoir as possible. A clean turkey baster makes an ideal brake fluid siphon.

2. Tag and remove the brake lines from the primary and secondary outlet ports of the master cylinder.

3. On models equipped with a manual transmission, remove the clutch cable retaining bolt.

4. Disengage the brake fluid level indicator connector.

5. Remove the nuts attaching the master cylinder to the brake booster assembly.

6. Slide the master cylinder forward and upward from the vehicle.

To install:

7. Position the master cylinder over the booster pushrod and onto the two mounting studs, then install and tighten the retaining nuts to 16–22 ft. lbs. (21–29 Nm).

8. Attach the brake fluid lines to the master cylinder.

9. If applicable, install the clutch cable bracket bolt.

10. Attach the brake fluid level indicator connector.

11. Fill the brake master cylinder with clean, new DOT 3 brake fluid to the MAX line on the reservoir.

12. Bleed the master cylinder, then the entire brake system. Operate the brakes several times, then check for external hydraulic leaks.

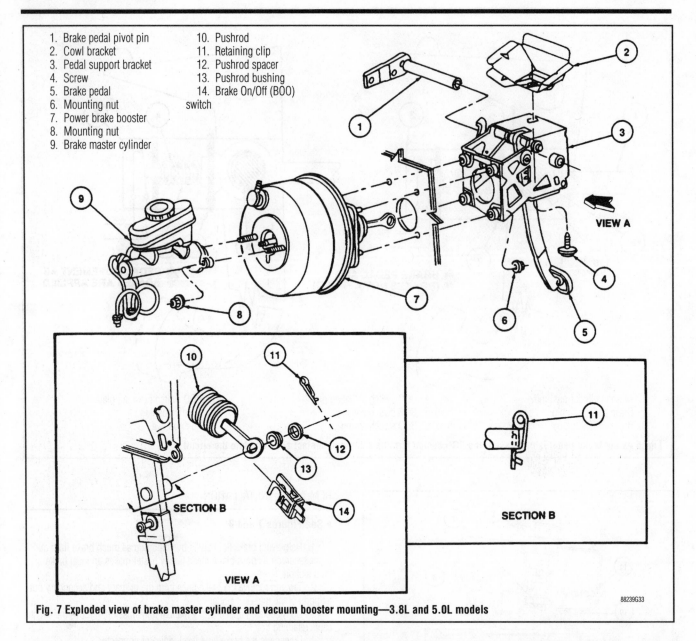

1. Brake pedal pivot pin
2. Cowl bracket
3. Pedal support bracket
4. Screw
5. Brake pedal
6. Mounting nut
7. Power brake booster
8. Mounting nut
9. Brake master cylinder
10. Pushrod
11. Retaining clip
12. Pushrod spacer
13. Pushrod bushing
14. Brake On/Off (BOO) switch

Fig. 7 Exploded view of brake master cylinder and vacuum booster mounting—3.8L and 5.0L models

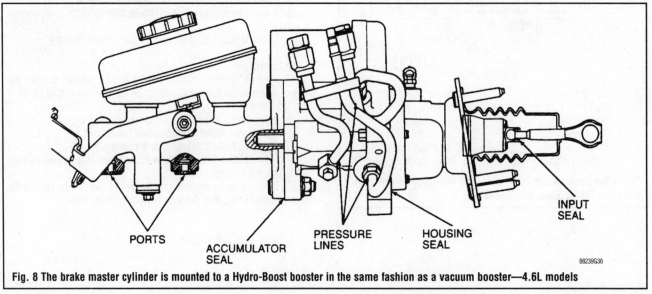

PORTS

ACCUMULATOR SEAL

PRESSURE LINES

HOUSING SEAL

INPUT SEAL

Fig. 8 The brake master cylinder is mounted to a Hydro-Boost booster in the same fashion as a vacuum booster—4.6L models

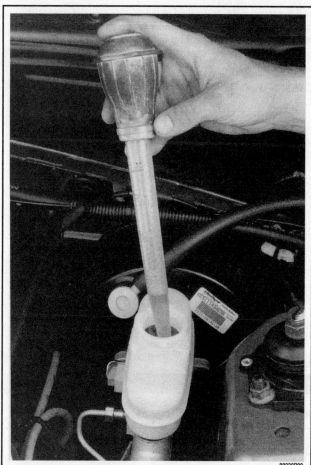

To remove the master cylinder, siphon as much brake fluid from the reservoir as possible . . .

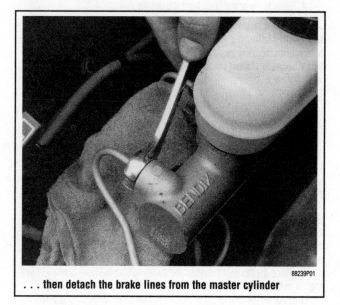

. . . then detach the brake lines from the master cylinder

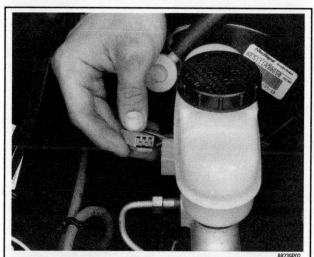

Disengage the wiring harness connector from the low fluid level indicator switch . . .

. . . then remove the master cylinder retaining nuts . . .

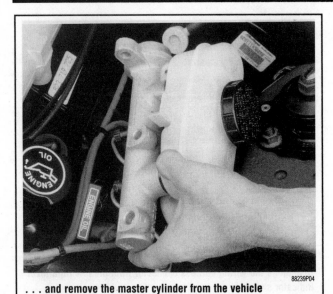

88239P04

. . . and remove the master cylinder from the vehicle

BLEEDING THE MASTER CYLINDER

Master Cylinders With Bleeder Valves

➡**During this procedure, do not allow the master cylinder to empty of brake fluid; otherwise, the entire procedure must be performed again.**

1. Install the master cylinder in the vehicle and attach the brake fluid lines to it, if not already done.
2. Fill the brake master cylinder with clean, new DOT 3 brake fluid.

➡**For 4.6L engine-equipped vehicles, only use the bleeder valves on the engine side of the master cylinder, rather than the Hydro-Boost bleed screw located near the firewall on the booster unit.**

3. Locate the two bleeder valves on the engine side of the master cylinder.
4. Attach a clear plastic drain tube to the bleeder valve nipple closest to the firewall. Submerge the other end of the tube in a container partially filled with clean, new DOT 3 brake fluid.
5. Loosen the bleeder valve about ¾ turn.
6. Have a helper depress the brake pedal all the way to the floor and hold it there. Close the bleeder valve, THEN have your helper release the brake pedal.
7. Fill the master cylinder to the Full level, if necessary.
8. Wait three seconds, then repeat Steps 5 through 7 until no air bubbles appear in the plastic drain tube when the brake pedal is depressed.
9. Perform Steps 4 through 8 for the other master cylinder bleeder valve, then repeat the procedure for the first bleeder valve.

Master Cylinders Without Bleeder Valves

1. Install the master cylinder in the vehicle, if not already done. If the master cylinder is already installed, detach the two brake lines from it.

➡**For the next step, bleeder kits are commercially available. These kits include flexible plastic hoses and fittings designed for your master cylinder brake line fittings.**

2. Either install a commercially available bleeder kit on the master cylinder, or install short brake lines on the master cylinder; ensure that the fittings are tightened. Bend the short brake lines so that they curve up and into the master cylinder reservoir. The ends of the brake lines should be positioned so that when the reservoir is full, the ends of the lines will be submerged approximately ½–¾ in. (13–19mm) beneath the surface of the fluid.

➡**If the level of the brake fluid in the master cylinder ever falls below the ends of the brake bleeder tubes, the entire procedure must be repeated from the beginning.**

3. If necessary, fill the master cylinder fluid reservoir until full.
Cover the brake master cylinder reservoir with a clean shop rag; this will prevent any brake fluid from shooting out of the reservoir while allowing air to breathe into and out of the master cylinder.
4. Have an assistant depress the brake pedal slowly and steadily all the way to the floor, then let it up slowly. Have your helper repeat this until no air bubbles are present in the brake fluid expelled from the brake bleeder tubes or in the master cylinder reservoir.
5. Remove the bleeder tubes and reinstall the vehicle brake lines to the master cylinder to 123–212 inch lbs. (14–24 Nm), then bleed each brake line at the master cylinder as follows:
    a. Have an assistant sitting in the driver's seat depress and release the brake pedal ten times, then hold it depressed.
    b. Loosen the brake line fitting closest to the firewall with a flare nut wrench until brake fluid seeps from the junction. Tighten the fitting after the brake pedal travels to the floor, THEN have your assistant release the brake pedal.
    c. Repeat sub-steps 6a and 6b until the brake fluid coming from the brake line-to-master cylinder junction is free of all air bubbles.
    d. Tighten the brake line fitting to 123–212 inch lbs. (14–24 Nm).
    e. Proceed to the brake line fitting farthest away from the firewall and repeat sub-steps 6a through 6d for this brake line.
6. Bleed the rest of the brake system.

Power Brake Booster

REMOVAL & INSTALLATION

3.8L and 5.0L Engines

1. Disconnect the negative battery cable.
2. Label and detach the vacuum hose from the power booster check valve.
3. Depress the brake pedal several times to deplete the vacuum in the booster.
4. Detach the brake lines from the master cylinder.

➡**Although it is possible to remove the master cylinder with the brake lines attached (to avoid bleeding the system) to remove the brake booster, this can result in brake line damage. If the brake lines become kinked or cracked, the brake line MUST be replaced with a new one.**

5. Remove the brake master cylinder-to-power booster retaining nuts, then remove the master cylinder from the vehicle.
6. If the vehicle is equipped with a manual transmission, disconnect the clutch cable routing bracket from the frame side rail, then move the clutch cable toward the engine to provide added maneuvering room for the power brake booster.
7. Detach the accelerator cable at the dash panel and at the accelerator pedal and shaft. Move it aside for added working clearance.
8. From inside the vehicle, under the instrument panel, detach the Brake On/Off (BOO) switch wiring harness connector, then loosen the four booster retaining nuts and the bolt securing the pedal support bracket to the firewall.
9. Remove the BOO switch.
10. Slide the booster pushrod and brake master cylinder pushrod bushing off of the brake pedal pin.
11. Loosen the four booster stud nuts that hold the pedal support bracket onto the booster and firewall.
12. From inside the engine compartment, pull the booster forward until the mounting studs clear the firewall. Turn the front of the booster toward the engine and remove it by lifting it upward until clear of all obstructions.

To install:

13. Position the booster against the firewall so that all four studs protrude into the passengers' compartment. It is easiest to position the booster against the firewall so that the stud which corresponds to the smallest firewall hole is inserted first, followed by the stud with the slotted hole, and finally by the two studs with large round holes.

14. From inside the vehicle, under the instrument panel, pull the booster studs through the firewall and pedal support bracket.

15. Install the booster pushrod and bushings onto the brake pedal pin.

16. Install the booster-to-firewall mounting nuts, then install the BOO switch. Tighten the four retaining nuts to 16–21 ft. lbs. (21–29 Nm), then tighten the brake pedal support bracket mounting bolt to 168–230 inch lbs. (19–26 Nm).

17. Reattach the BOO switch electrical wiring harness connector.

18. Detach the speed control deactivation switch from the adapter on the brake pedal arm, and push the adjuster mechanism toward the switch pivot. Depress the brake pedal, then reattach the speed control deactivation switch to the adapter on the brake pedal arm. Pull up on the brake pedal to complete the adjustment.

19. Attach the manifold vacuum hose to the power booster check valve.

20. Install the master brake cylinder and attach the brake fluid lines to it. Tighten the brake line fittings to 123–212 inch lbs. (14–24 Nm).

21. Bleed the brake system.

22. Attach the accelerator cable to the pedal and shaft and to the pedal support bracket. On vehicles equipped with manual transmissions, reattach the clutch cable routing bracket to the frame side rail.

23. Connect the negative battery cable.

24. Start the engine and check the power brake function.

BOOSTER PUSHROD ADJUSTMENT

According to Ford, some brake boosters are equipped with an adjustable output pushrod, which is used to compensate for dimensional differences in an assembled brake booster. After booster assembly, the pushrod length is adjusted at the factory to compensate for these differences. Therefore, a properly adjusted brake booster pushrod, which remains assembled to the power brake booster with which it was matched at the factory, should NEVER require readjustment.

4.6L Engines

◢ See Figure 9

➡The master brake cylinder is removed from the vehicle along with the Hydro-Boost unit.

❊❊ CAUTION

The power brake booster should never be carried by, or dropped on, the accumulator. Also, if you must dispose of the accumulator or brake booster for some reason, take it to your local Ford dealer for proper disposal. The accumulator contains pressurized nitrogen gas, which can be hazardous if mishandled.

❊❊ WARNING

Never depress the brake pedal, or otherwise actuate, the power brake booster when the master cylinder is removed from the vehicle.

1. Disconnect the negative battery cable.

2. Depress the brake pedal numerous times to dispel any residual brake booster pressure.

❊❊ WARNING

Clean, high quality brake fluid is essential to the safe and proper operation of the brake system. You should always buy the highest quality brake fluid that is available. If the brake fluid

becomes contaminated, drain and flush the system, then refill the master cylinder with new fluid. Never reuse any brake fluid. Any brake fluid that is removed from the system should be discarded. Do not allow brake fluid to come in contact with painted surfaces.

❊❊ CAUTION

Brake fluid contains polyglycol ethers and polyglycols. Avoid contact with the eyes and wash your hands thoroughly after handling brake fluid. If you do get brake fluid in your eyes, flush your eyes with clean, running water for 15 minutes. If eye irritation persists, or if you have taken brake fluid internally, IMMEDIATELY seek medical assistance.

3. Detach the brake fluid lines from the proportioning valve, then disengage the brake fluid level indicator connector from the master cylinder.

4. On models equipped with automatic transmissions, detach the shifter interlock cable.

5. On models equipped with manual transmissions, disconnect the clutch cable from the routing bracket on the master cylinder.

6. Remove the hose routing bracket from the master cylinder.

7. Position a drain pan under the power steering pressure lines, then disconnect the hoses from the Hydro-Boost tubes. Drain any residual fluid out of the tubes into the drain pan, then position the tubes aside.

8. From inside the vehicle, under the instrument panel, detach the Brake On/Off (BOO) switch wiring harness connector, then loosen the four booster retaining nuts and the bolt securing the pedal support bracket to the firewall.

9. Remove the brake switch.

10. Slide the booster pushrod bushing off of the brake pedal pin.

11. Loosen the four booster stud nuts that hold the pedal support bracket onto the booster and firewall.

➡Avoid damaging the brake tubes during removal and installation of the Hydro-Boost unit.

12. From inside the engine compartment, pull the booster forward until the mounting studs clear the firewall, then lift it upward until clear of the engine compartment.

13. If necessary, the brake master cylinder can be separated from the booster at this time.

To install:

14. If removed, install the master cylinder on the Hydro-Boost unit.

15. Position the booster against the firewall so that all four studs protrude into the passengers' compartment.

16. From inside the vehicle, under the instrument panel, install the booster-to-firewall retaining nuts loosely.

17. Install the booster pushrod and bushings onto the brake pedal pin, then install the BOO switch. Tighten the four retaining nuts to 16–21 ft. lbs. (21–29 Nm) and the brake pedal support bracket mounting bolt to 168–230 inch lbs. (19–26 Nm).

18. Reattach the BOO switch electrical wiring harness connector.

19. If equipped, detach the speed control deactivation switch from the adapter on the brake pedal arm, and push the adjuster mechanism toward the switch pivot. Depress the brake pedal, then reattach the speed control deactivation switch to the adapter on the brake pedal arm. Pull up on the brake pedal to complete the adjustment.

20. Attach the brake fluid lines to the proportioning valve and tighten the fittings to 123–212 inch lbs. (14–24 Nm).

21. Reattach the master cylinder fluid level indicator connector.

➡If installing a new Hydro-Boost booster, but not new hoses, one of the two tube nuts that come with a new booster can be used for the third tube.

22. Connect the power steering pressure hoses and power steering return line hose to the Hydro-Boost tubes. Tighten them to 124–177 inch lbs. (14–20 Nm).

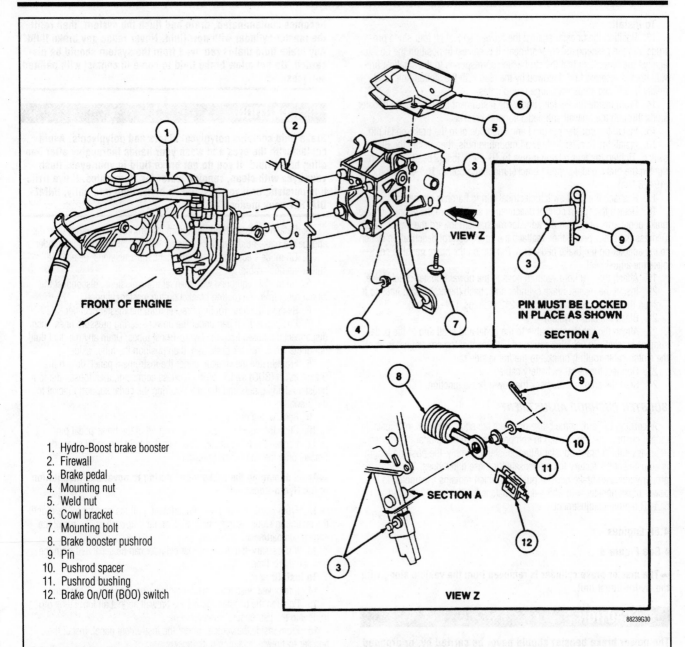

1. Hydro-Boost brake booster
2. Firewall
3. Brake pedal
4. Mounting nut
5. Weld nut
6. Cowl bracket
7. Mounting bolt
8. Brake booster pushrod
9. Pin
10. Pushrod spacer
11. Pushrod bushing
12. Brake On/Off (BOO) switch

FRONT OF ENGINE

VIEW Z

**PIN MUST BE LOCKED
IN PLACE AS SHOWN**

SECTION A

SECTION A

VIEW Z

88239G30

Fig. 9 Exploded view of the Hydro-Boost booster mounting on models equipped with one of the 4.6L engines—notice that the brake master cylinder is removed attached to the booster

23. Bleed the brake system, including the two bleeder screws located on the master cylinder.

24. On automatic transmission models, connect the shifter interlock cable to the master cylinder.

25. On models equipped with manual transmissions, secure the clutch cable on the routing bracket to the master cylinder.

26. Mount the power steering tubes and hoses to the bracket on the master cylinder.

27. Connect the negative battery cable.

28. Satrt the engine and check the power brake function.

29. Bleed the Hydro-Boost power brake booster of air trapped in the power steering fluid.

HYDRO-BOOST BLEEDING

➡The power steering fluid level in the reservoir will rise and fall as the accumulator is discharged and charged. Fill the reservoir to the MAX line when the accumulator is discharged. To discharge the accumulator, depress the brake pedal 10 times with the engine OFF.

1. Release fluid from the booster by depressing the brake pedal ten times with the engine OFF.

2. Using Ford Vacuum Pump D83L-7059-A, or its equivalent, extract air from the power steering fluid by applying 24–29 in. Hg (81–98 kPa) vacuum to the power steering reservoir for three minutes.

3. Loosen the bleeder screw located on top of the booster housing between the firewall and the accumulator.

4. Using the vacuum pump, extract air from the booster cavity, then tighten the bleeder screw and disconnect the vacuum pump.

5. Add Mercon® Automatic Transmission Fluid (ATF) to the power steering fluid reservoir until the fluid level reaches the FULL mark.

➡For the following step, the front of the vehicle may be raised and safely supported on jackstands to reduce the effort required to turn the steering wheel.

6. With the engine **OFF**, disconnect the vacuum hose and turn the steering wheel lock-to-lock twice, then return the wheel to the center position.

7. Once again using the vacuum pump, remove any air from the fluid by applying 24–29 in. Hg (81–98 kPa) vacuum to the power steering fluid reservoir.

8. Start the engine and turn the steering wheel lock-to-lock.

9. Turn the engine **OFF**, then depress the brake pedal at least 10 times to empty the booster of fluid.

10. Loosen the bleeder screw located on top of the booster housing between the firewall and the accumulator.

11. Using the vacuum pump, extract air from the booster cavity, then tighten the bleeder screw and disconnect the vacuum pump.

12. Start the engine and turn the steering wheel. Check the power steering fluid level and add Mercon® ATF if necessary.

Brake Pressure Control Valve

▶ See Figure 10

✳✳ WARNING

Clean, high quality brake fluid is essential to the safe and proper operation of the brake system. You should always buy the highest quality brake fluid that is available. If the brake fluid becomes contaminated, drain and flush the system, then refill the master cylinder with new fluid. Never reuse any brake fluid. Any brake fluid that is removed from the system should be discarded. Also, do not allow any brake fluid to come in contact with a painted surface; it will damage the paint.

✳✳ CAUTION

Brake fluid contains polyglycol ethers and polyglycols. Avoid contact with the eyes and wash your hands thoroughly after handling brake fluid. If you do get brake fluid in your eyes, flush your eyes with clean, running water for 15 minutes. If eye irritation persists, or if you have taken brake fluid internally, IMMEDIATELY seek medical assistance.

➡On models equipped with an Anti-lock Brake System (ABS), if during brake system service, or because of a fluid leak, the level of fluid in the system ever falls below that of the Hydraulic Control Unit (HCU), refer to the bleeding procedure in the ABS portion of this section. To properly bleed the HCU, an expensive scan tool is necessary; take this into consideration when contemplating brake system service. However, if only the brake pads, calipers, master cylinder, and other non-ABS components are being removed and installed, bleeding the HCU is not necessary and, therefore, the scan tool is not necessary.

REMOVAL & INSTALLATION

1. Detach the brake fluid lines from the valve.

2. Remove the valve mounting nuts, then pull the valve off of the frame member.

To install:

3. Position the valve on the mounting studs, then install the mounting nuts. Tighten the nuts to 97–142 inch lbs. (11–16 Nm).

4. Connect the brake fluid lines to the valve and tighten the line fittings to 124–212 inch lbs. (14–24 Nm).

5. Bleed the hydraulic brake system.

Brake Hoses and Pipes

▶ See Figures 11 and 12 (p. 12–13)

Metal lines and rubber brake hoses should be checked frequently for leaks and external damage. Metal lines are particularly prone to crushing and kinking under the vehicle. Any such deformation can restrict the proper flow of fluid and, therefore, impair braking at the wheels. Rubber hoses should be checked for cracking or scraping; such damage can create a weak spot in the hose and it could fail under pressure.

Any time the lines are removed or disconnected, extreme cleanliness must be observed. Clean all joints and connections before disassembly (use a stiff bristle brush and clean brake fluid); be sure to plug the lines and ports as soon as they are opened. New lines and hoses should be flushed clean with brake fluid before installation to remove any contamination.

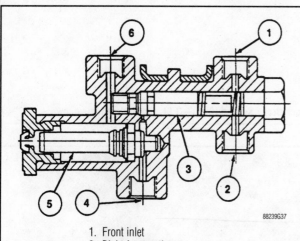

88239G37

1. Front inlet
2. Right front outlet
3. Shuttle valve
4. Rear outlet
5. Proportioning valve
6. Rear inlet

Fig. 10 Cross-sectional view of the internal components of the brake pressure control valve

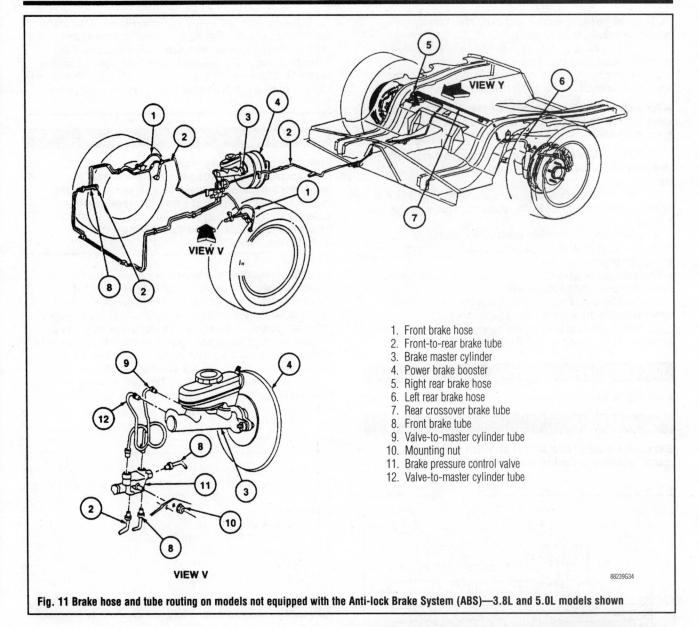

1. Front brake hose
2. Front-to-rear brake tube
3. Brake master cylinder
4. Power brake booster
5. Right rear brake hose
6. Left rear brake hose
7. Rear crossover brake tube
8. Front brake tube
9. Valve-to-master cylinder tube
10. Mounting nut
11. Brake pressure control valve
12. Valve-to-master cylinder tube

VIEW V

88239G34

Fig. 11 Brake hose and tube routing on models not equipped with the Anti-lock Brake System (ABS)—3.8L and 5.0L models shown

REMOVAL & INSTALLATION

1. Disconnect the negative battery cable.
2. Raise and safely support the vehicle on jackstands.
3. Remove any wheel and tire assemblies necessary for access to the particular line you are removing.
4. Thoroughly clean the surrounding area at the joints to be disconnected.
5. Place a suitable catch pan under the joint to be disconnected.
6. Using two wrenches (one to hold the joint and one to turn the fitting), disconnect the hose or line to be replaced.
7. Disconnect the other end of the line or hose, moving the drain pan if necessary. Always use a back-up wrench to avoid damaging the fitting.
8. Disconnect any retaining clips or brackets holding the line and remove the line from the vehicle.

➟**If the brake system is to remain open for more time than it takes to swap lines, tape or plug each remaining clip and port to keep contaminants out and fluid in.**

To install:

9. Install the new line or hose, starting with the end farthest from the master cylinder. Connect the other end, then confirm that both fittings are

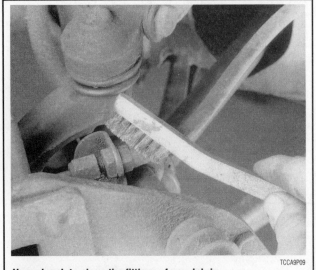

TCCA9P09

Use a brush to clean the fittings of any debris

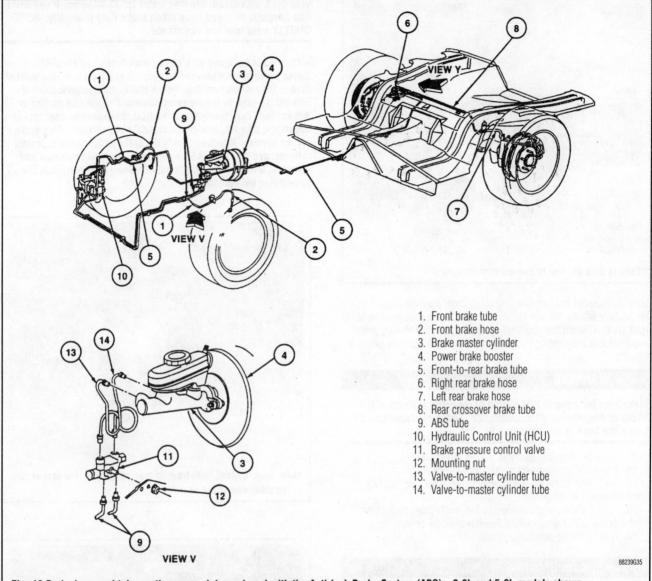

1. Front brake tube
2. Front brake hose
3. Brake master cylinder
4. Power brake booster
5. Front-to-rear brake tube
6. Right rear brake hose
7. Left rear brake hose
8. Rear crossover brake tube
9. ABS tube
10. Hydraulic Control Unit (HCU)
11. Brake pressure control valve
12. Mounting nut
13. Valve-to-master cylinder tube
14. Valve-to-master cylinder tube

Fig. 12 Brake hose and tube routing on models equipped with the Anti-lock Brake System (ABS)—3.8L and 5.0L models shown

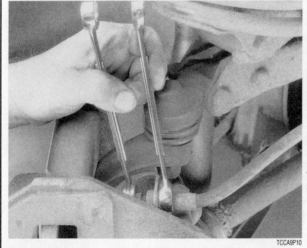

Use two wrenches to loosen the fitting. If available, use flare nut type wrenches

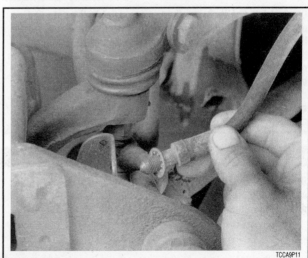

Any gaskets/crush washers should be replaced with new ones during installation

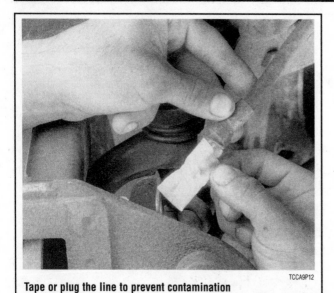

Tape or plug the line to prevent contamination

TCCA9P12

correctly threaded and turn smoothly using finger pressure. Make sure the new line will not rub against any other part. Brake lines must be at least 1/2 in. (13mm) from the steering column and other moving parts. Any protective shielding or insulators must be reinstalled in the original location.

❊ WARNING

Make sure the hose is NOT kinked or touching any part of the frame or suspension after installation. These conditions may cause the hose to fail prematurely.

10. Using two wrenches as before, tighten each fitting.
11. Install any retaining clips or brackets on the lines.
12. If removed, install the wheel and tire assemblies, then carefully lower the vehicle to the ground.
13. Refill the brake master cylinder reservoir with clean, fresh brake fluid, meeting DOT 3 specifications. Properly bleed the brake system.
14. Connect the negative battery cable.

Brake System Bleeding

❊ WARNING

Clean, high quality brake fluid is essential to the safe and proper operation of the brake system. You should always buy the highest quality brake fluid that is available. If the brake fluid becomes contaminated, drain and flush the system, then refill the master cylinder with new fluid. Never reuse any brake fluid. Any brake fluid that is removed from the system should be discarded. Also, do not allow any brake fluid to come in contact with a painted surface; it will damage the paint.

❊ CAUTION

Brake fluid contains polyglycol ethers and polyglycols. Avoid contact with the eyes and wash your hands thoroughly after handling brake fluid. If you do get brake fluid in your eyes, flush your eyes with clean, running water for 15 minutes. If eye irritation persists, or if you have taken brake fluid internally, IMMEDIATELY seek medical assistance.

➡On models equipped with an Anti-lock Brake System (ABS), if during brake system service, or because of a fluid leak, the level of fluid in the system ever falls below that of the Hydraulic Control Unit (HCU), refer to the bleeding procedure in the ABS portion of this section. To properly bleed the HCU, an expensive scan tool is necessary; take this into consideration when contemplating brake system service. However, if only the brake pads, calipers, master cylinder, and other non-ABS components are being removed and installed, bleeding the HCU is not necessary and, therefore, the scan tool is not necessary.

Make sure to bleed both front or rear calipers before proceeding to the other end of the vehicle

88239P05

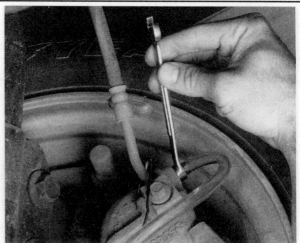

Use a clear plastic tube when bleeding the brakes so that you can see the air bubbles in the fluid

88239P06

The front and rear brake hydraulic circuits are individual and must be bled separately. Therefore, either the front or rear brakes can be bled first, so long as both of the front or rear wheels are bled before moving to the other circuit. This procedure starts with the rear circuit first.

1. Bleed the master cylinder if not already done.
2. Fill the master cylinder with clean, new DOT 3 brake fluid. Leave the clean shop rag on the master cylinder while bleeding it.
3. Block the front wheels, then raise and support the rear of the vehicle on jackstands.
4. Position a box-end wrench on the right-rear caliper bleeder valve, then install a clear plastic tube on the bleeder valve nipple. Submerge the other end of the tube in a container partially filled with new, clean brake fluid.
5. Open the bleeder valve approximately ¾ turn.
6. Have an assistant sit in the driver's seat and depress the brake pedal all the way to the floor and hold it there.
7. Close the bleeder valve, THEN have the helper release the brake pedal.
8. Check the brake master cylinder level and fill it if necessary; the master cylinder should never be allowed to empty of brake fluid. If it does, the master cylinder and brake system must be rebled.
9. Repeat Steps 5–8 until no air bubbles appear in the brake fluid emitted from the bleeder tube.
10. Position a box-end wrench on the left-rear caliper bleeder valve, then install a clear plastic tube on the bleeder valve nipple. Submerge the other end of the tube in a container partially filled with new, clean brake fluid.
11. Open the bleeder valve approximately ¾ turn.
12. Have an assistant sit in the driver's seat and depress the brake pedal all the way to the floor and hold it there.
13. Close the bleeder valve, THEN have the helper release the brake pedal.
14. Check the brake master cylinder level and fill it if necessary; the master cylinder should never be allowed to empty of brake fluid. If it does, the master cylinder and brake system must be rebled.
15. Repeat Steps 11–14 until no air bubbles appear in the brake fluid emitted from the bleeder tube.
16. Lower the rear of the vehicle.
17. Apply the parking brakes, block the rear wheels, then raise and support the front of the vehicle on jackstands.
18. Position a box-end wrench on the right-front caliper bleeder valve, then install a clear plastic tube on the bleeder valve nipple. Submerge the other end of the tube in a container partially filled with new, clean brake fluid.
19. Open the bleeder valve approximately ¾ turn.
20. Have an assistant sit in the driver's seat and depress the brake pedal all the way to the floor and hold it there.
21. Close the bleeder valve, THEN have the helper release the brake pedal.
22. Check the brake master cylinder level and fill it if necessary; the master cylinder should never be allowed to empty of brake fluid. If it does, the master cylinder and brake system must be rebled.
23. Repeat Steps 20–23 until no air bubbles appear in the brake fluid emitted from the bleeder tube.

24. Position a box-end wrench on the left-front caliper bleeder valve, then install a clear plastic tube on the bleeder valve nipple. Submerge the other end of the tube in a container partially filled with new, clean brake fluid.
25. Open the bleeder valve approximately ¾ turn.
26. Have an assistant sit in the driver's seat and depress the brake pedal all the way to the floor and hold it there.
27. Close the bleeder valve, THEN have the helper release the brake pedal.
28. Check the brake master cylinder level and fill it if necessary; the master cylinder should never be allowed to empty of brake fluid. If it does, the master cylinder and brake system must be rebled.
29. Repeat Steps 26–29 until no air bubbles appear in the brake fluid emitted from the bleeder tube.
30. Lower the front end of the vehicle.
31. On models equipped with master cylinders containing bleeder valves, perform the following:
    a. If necessary, refill the brake master cylinder with clean, new DOT 3 brake fluid.
    b. Locate the two bleeder valves on the engine side of the master cylinder.
    c. Attach a clear plastic drain tube to the bleeder valve nipple closest to the firewall. Submerge the other end of the tube in a container partially filled with clean, new DOT 3 brake fluid.
    d. Loosen the bleeder valve about ¾ turn.
    e. Have a helper depress the brake pedal, from the passengers' compartment, all the way to the floor and hold it there. Close the bleeder valve, THEN have your helper release the brake pedal.
    f. Fill the master cylinder to the full level, if necessary.
    g. Wait three seconds, then repeat sub-steps 32d through 32g until no air bubbles appear in the plastic drain tube when the brake pedal is depressed.
    h. Perform Steps 32a through 32g for the other master cylinder bleeder valve, then repeat the procedure for the first bleeder valve again.
32. On models equipped with master cylinders without bleeder valves, perform the following:
    a. Have an assistant sit in the driver's seat and depress and release the brake pedal ten times, then hold it depressed.
    b. Loosen the brake line fitting closest to the firewall with a flare nut wrench until brake fluid seeps from the junction. Tighten the fitting after the brake pedal travels to the floor, THEN have your assistant release the brake pedal.
    c. Repeat sub-steps 33a and 33b until the brake fluid emitted from the brake line-to-master cylinder junction is free of all air bubbles.
    d. Tighten the brake line fitting to 123–212 inch lbs. (14–24 Nm).
    e. Move onto the brake line fitting farthest away from the firewall and repeat sub-steps 33a through 33d for this brake line.

The brake system is now completely bled. If the brake pedal feels spongy and your Mustang is equipped with ABS, refer to the ABS bleeding procedure later in this section; air may have become trapped in the Hydraulic Control Unit (HCU). If your Mustang does not have ABS, or the HCU has already been bled, a qualified automotive technician can pressure bleed your brake system to remove any residual trapped air.

DISC BRAKES

♦ See Figure 13

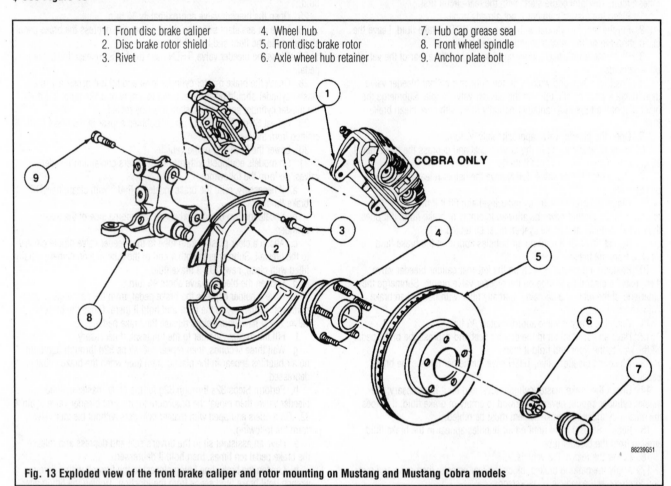

1. Front disc brake caliper
2. Disc brake rotor shield
3. Rivet
4. Wheel hub
5. Front disc brake rotor
6. Axle wheel hub retainer
7. Hub cap grease seal
8. Front wheel spindle
9. Anchor plate bolt

COBRA ONLY

88239G51

Fig. 13 Exploded view of the front brake caliper and rotor mounting on Mustang and Mustang Cobra models

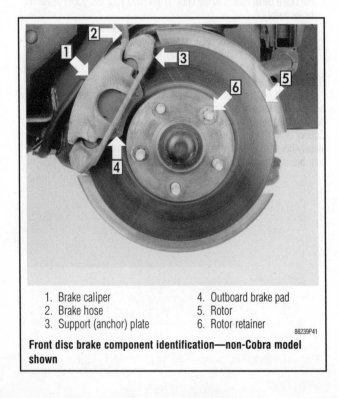

1. Brake caliper
2. Brake hose
3. Support (anchor) plate
4. Outboard brake pad
5. Rotor
6. Rotor retainer

88239P41

Front disc brake component identification—non-Cobra model shown

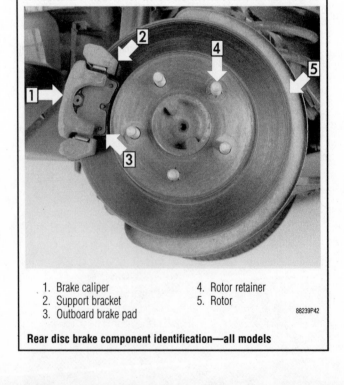

1. Brake caliper
2. Support bracket
3. Outboard brake pad
4. Rotor retainer
5. Rotor

88239P42

Rear disc brake component identification—all models

Brake Pads

REMOVAL & INSTALLATION

✳✳ CAUTION

Older brake pads may contain asbestos, which has been determined to be a cancer-causing agent. Never clean brake surfaces with compressed air. Avoid inhaling any dust from any brake surface. When cleaning brake surfaces, use a commercially available brake cleaning fluid. Also, always replace the brake pads on both front wheels at the same time.

Front

➡The Mustang Cobra model utilizes dual piston front calipers, whereas all other models covered by this manual utilize single piston front brake calipers.

EXCEPT COBRA MODEL

▶ **See Figure 14**

1. Remove and discard half of the brake fluid in the master cylinder reservoir.
2. Raise and safely support the vehicle. Remove the front wheel(s).

➡To replace the brake pads, it is not necessary to disconnect the brake fluid hose from the caliper. If the hose is detached from the caliper, the brake system will need to be bled.

3. Remove the brake caliper anchor plate mounting bolts, then, using a pivoting motion, lift the caliper and anchor plate away from the disc brake rotor.

✳✳ WARNING

Do not let the caliper hang by the brake hose; otherwise, damage to the hose may occur, necessitating brake hose replacement.

4. Suspend the caliper inside the fender housing with a length of wire or strong cord.
5. Remove the outer brake pad from the anchor plate by sliding the brake pad away from the outer leg.

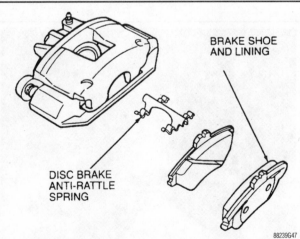

Fig. 14 Always replace all four front brake caliper pads at the same time—do not replace the brake pads on one wheel only, as this practice can lead to uneven and dangerous braking conditions

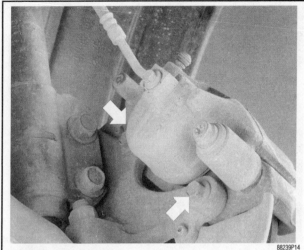

To replace the front disc pads, locate the caliper and anchor plate bolts (arrows) . . .

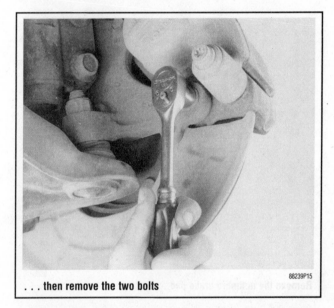

. . . then remove the two bolts

Slide the caliper and anchor plate off of the rotor . . .

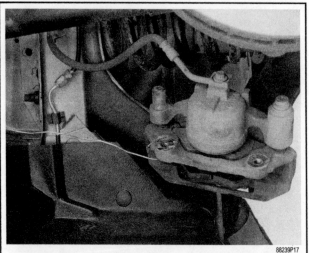

. . . then suspend the caliper with strong cord or wire to prevent damaging the brake hose

Use a small prytool to pop one edge of the anti-rattle spring up . . .

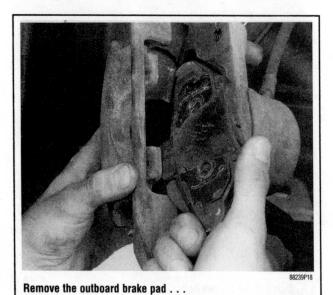

Remove the outboard brake pad . . .

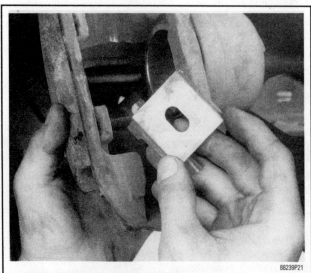

. . . then pull the spring off of the caliper

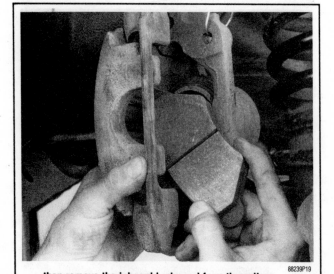

. . . then remove the inboard brake pad from the caliper

Use a 4 in. C-clamp and a small block of wood to seat the caliper's piston prior to NEW pad installation

6. Remove the inboard pad by separating the pad from the caliper piston and anchor plate, then remove the anti-rattle spring from the caliper. A small prytool may be necessary to remove the anti-rattle spring.

To install:

7. Inspect the brake rotor for scoring and wear; minor scoring or disc pad lining build-up does not require disc machining or replacement. If heavy scoring, cracks or other damage is evident, replace or have the rotor machined, as necessary.

8. Glaze on the rotor can be removed by hand-sanding it with medium grit garnet paper or aluminum oxide sandpaper.

9. While the brake pads are removed, it is a good time to inspect the caliper piston boot and caliper pin boots for damage, such as tearing. Replace the boots if any damage is evident.

10. Use a 4 in. (10cm) C-clamp and a small block of wood to press the caliper piston back into its bore until it is fully seated. This must be done to provide adequate assembly clearance, since the new brake pads will be thicker than the old ones that were removed.

➡**The brake caliper is designed to have the anti-rattle spring installed in one orientation only. The right-hand and left-hand springs are identical, but installed in opposite directions. The spring should be installed from the disc brake pad side.**

11. Thoroughly clean all dirt and other residue from the disc caliper, especially from the brake pad lining abutments. Install the anti-rattle clip and the hold-down spring.

12. Peel the protective paper from the backside of the disc brake pad. Do not allow the sticky backside of the brake pad to become contaminated with dirt.

13. Install the inboard and outboard brake pads into the brake caliper and anchor plate. Be sure that the brake pad anti-rattle springs are fully engaged in the caliper assembly.

14. Install the caliper onto the disc brake rotor, then install the anchor mounting bolts to 95 ft. lbs. (130 Nm).

✳✳ WARNING

Failure to tighten the lug nuts in a star pattern may result in high rotor run-out, which speeds up the onset of rotor roughness, shudder and vibration.

15. Install the wheel and lug nuts. Have an assistant depress the brake pedal, while you tighten the lug nuts in a star pattern to 85–105 ft. lbs. (115–142 Nm).

16. Lower the vehicle.

17. Pump the brake pedal prior to moving the vehicle to seat the brake pads. Refill the master cylinder.

COBRA MODEL

1. Remove and discard half of the brake fluid in the master cylinder reservoir.

2. Raise and safely support the vehicle. Remove the front wheel(s).

➡**To replace the brake pads, it is not necessary to disconnect the brake fluid hose from the caliper. If the hose is detached from the caliper, the brake system will need to be bled.**

3. Remove the retaining clip, washer and caliper mounting pin, then separate the caliper from the anchor plate and disc brake rotor.

✳✳ WARNING

Do not let the caliper hang by the brake hose; otherwise, damage to the hose may occur, necessitating brake hose replacement.

4. Suspend the caliper inside the fender housing with a length of wire or strong cord.

➡**Mark the removed brake pads as right or left to aid in identifying replacement parts.**

5. Remove both brake pads from the caliper.

To install:

6. Thoroughly clean all dirt and other residue from the disc brake caliper and anchor plate, especially from the brake pad lining abutments.

7. Inspect the brake rotor for scoring and wear; minor scoring or disc pad lining build-up does not require disc machining or replacement. If heavy scoring, cracks or other damage is evident, replace or have the rotor machined, as necessary.

8. Glaze on the rotor can be removed by hand-sanding it with medium grit garnet paper or aluminum oxide sandpaper.

9. While the brake pads are removed, it is a good time to inspect the caliper piston boot and caliper pin boots for damage, such as tearing. Replace the boots if any damage is evident.

➡**There are four different brake pads included with the new brake pad kit. The outboard brake pads, equipped with the insulating backing, are installed in the caliper housing, whereas the two inboard pads are installed in the caliper's pistons. Differently positioned retaining springs prevent the inboard pads from being installed in the outboard positions and vice versa. Use the removed brake pads for reference when installing the new pads.**

10. Peel the protective paper from the backside of the disc brake pad. Do not allow the sticky backside of the brake pad to become contaminated with dirt.

11. Install the inboard and outboard brake pads. Press the outboard pads against the caliper housing, and the inboard pads against the caliper pistons, until they are fully seated.

12. Install the caliper onto the disc brake rotor and anchor plate, ensuring that the guiding surfaces of the brake pad and anchor plate are seating correctly.

13. Install the disc brake caliper locating pin by depressing the front disc brake caliper, to compress the bias spring, and sliding the locating pin into position. Secure the locating pin with the washer and retaining clip.

✳✳ WARNING

Failure to tighten the lug nuts in a star pattern may result in high rotor run-out, which speeds up the onset of rotor roughness, shudder and vibration.

14. Install the wheel and lug nuts. Have an assistant depress the brake pedal, while you tighten the lug nuts in a star pattern to 85–105 ft. lbs. (115–142 Nm).

15. Lower the vehicle.

16. Pump the brake pedal prior to moving the vehicle to seat the brake pads. Refill the master cylinder, if necessary.

Rear

◗ See Figures 15 and 16 (p. 20–21)

➡**To seat the piston in the caliper for brake pad installation, a specific tool (Ford Tool T87P-2588-A or equivalent) is necessary.**

1. Remove and discard half of the brake fluid in the master cylinder reservoir.

2. Loosen the rear wheel lug nuts ½ turn to break them loose.

3. Block the front wheels, then raise and safely support the rear of the vehicle on jackstands.

4. Remove the wheel.

5. Separate the brake hose mounting bracket from the shock absorber bracket by removing the retaining screw.

6. Detach the parking brake cable and conduit from the rear brake calipers, as follows:

   a. Use a pair of needlenose pliers to pull the retaining E-clip off of the end of the parking brake cable conduit.

   b. Using a large pair of pliers, or an equivalent tool, compress the parking brake cable lever, then, using a second pair of pliers, pull the cable out as far as possible. With the cable extended as far as possible, disengage the cable from the lever.

   c. Once the cable is free of the lever, release it. Then, withdraw the cable and conduit from the caliper mounting boss.

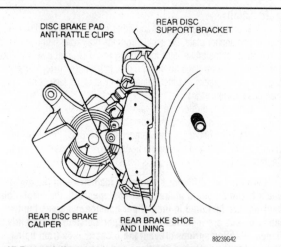

DISC BRAKE PAD
ANTI-RATTLE CLIPS

REAR DISC
SUPPORT BRACKET

REAR DISC BRAKE
CALIPER

REAR BRAKE SHOE
AND LINING

88239G42

Fig. 15 Do not fully remove the rear brake caliper for pad replacement—simply remove the top locating pin and pivot the caliper out and away from the rotor

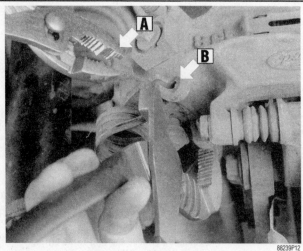

Manipulate the cable end (A) to disengage it from the brake lever (B)

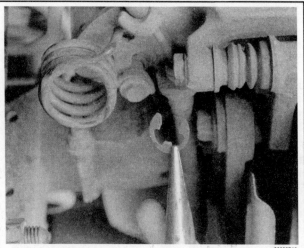

To detach the cable from the rear caliper, first remove the conduit retaining E-clip . . .

. . . then withdraw the cable and conduit from the brake cable mounting boss (arrow)

. . . then compress the cable lever and grasp the cable end using pliers

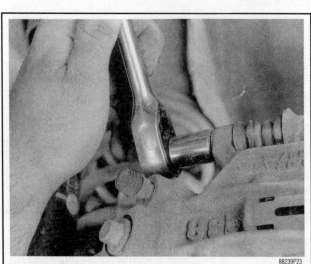

Remove the top locating pin, then pivot the caliper down and out from the rotor

If so desired, the entire caliper can be removed from the rotor for pad replacement

Suspend the caliper with wire or strong cord (arrow) while removing and installing the brake pads

Remove the outboard brake pad . . .

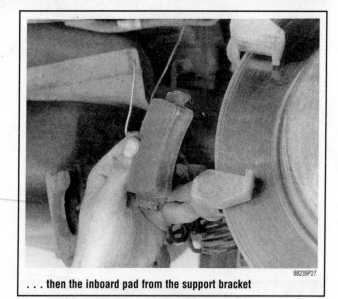

. . . then the inboard pad from the support bracket

7. Hold the caliper locating pin hex head with an open-end wrench, then remove the upper pin retainer.

8. Pivot the caliper down and away from the rotor.

9. Remove the inner and outer brake pads and anti-rattle clips from the support bracket.

To install:

➡Ensure that one of the two indentations on the caliper piston face is situated so that it will engage the nib on the brake pad when installed.

10. Use a caliper piston adjuster tool (Ford Tool T87P-2588-A or equivalent) to turn the piston clockwise until it is fully seated.

※※ WARNING

NEVER attempt to seat the rear brake caliper piston by using a C-clamp, as with the front calipers—the rear calipers are not designed to be seated in this manner and you WILL ruin the caliper. Also, do not try to use needlenose pliers (or another incorrect tool) to turn the piston and seat it; the piston surface, indentations, and dust boots can be easily damaged.

Fig. 16 A brake caliper adjuster tool must be used to seat the rear caliper piston—never substitute another tool, such as a C-clamp or needlenose pliers, to seat the piston

11. Install the anti-rattle clips and brake pads on the caliper.

12. Pivot the caliper up and onto the rotor. Ensure that the brake pads and anti-rattle clips are properly positioned once the caliper is installed.

13. Apply a threadlocking compound, such as Ford Threadlock and Sealer E0AZ-19554-AA, to the upper locating pin threads. Install the locating pin retainer and tighten it to 23–26 ft. lbs. (31–35 Nm) while holding the locating pins with an open-end wrench.

14. Connect the parking brake cable and conduit to the rear brake caliper as follows:

    a. Insert the cable and conduit through the rear caliper mounting boss until the stop on the conduit contacts the mounting boss.

    b. Using a pair of needlenose pliers, install a new E-clip onto the cable conduit, ensuring that the clip is properly seated in the conduit retaining groove.

    c. Use the large pair of pliers to compress the parking brake cable lever, then grasp the end of the cable with a second pair of pliers.

    d. Manipulate the cable so that it is engaged by the cable lever, then release the cable.

    e. Slowly release the brake cable lever until it rests against the parking brake cable end stop.

❈❈ WARNING

Failure to tighten the lug nuts in a star pattern may result in high rotor run-out, which speeds up the onset of rotor roughness, shudder and vibration.

15. Install the wheel and lug nuts. Have an assistant depress the brake pedal, while you tighten the lug nuts in a star pattern to 85–105 ft. lbs. (115–142 Nm).

16. Lower the vehicle.

17. Pump the brake pedal prior to moving the vehicle to seat the brake pads. Refill the master cylinder, if necessary.

INSPECTION

Front and Rear

Remove the brake pads and measure the thickness of the lining. If the lining at any point on any of the front pads is less than 0.125 in. (3mm), replace all four front disc brake pads. Also replace all of the front pads if any of them shows any cracking, separation, or contamination from oil, grease or brake fluid.

Brake Caliper

REMOVAL & INSTALLATION

❈❈ WARNING

Clean, high quality brake fluid is essential to the safe and proper operation of the brake system. You should always buy the highest quality brake fluid that is available. If the brake fluid becomes contaminated, drain and flush the system, then refill the master cylinder with new fluid. Never reuse any brake fluid. Any brake fluid that is removed from the system should be discarded. Also, do not allow any brake fluid to come in contact with a painted surface; it will damage the paint.

❈❈ CAUTION

Brake fluid contains polyglycol ethers and polyglycols. Avoid contact with the eyes and wash your hands thoroughly after handling brake fluid. If you do get brake fluid in your eyes, flush your eyes with clean, running water for 15 minutes. If eye irritation persists, or if you have taken brake fluid internally, IMMEDIATELY seek medical assistance.

➡ If your vehicle is equipped with ABS, and during the brake caliper removal procedure the brake fluid level drops below that of the hydraulic control unit (a very large amount of brake fluid would need to leak out for this to occur), a specific scan tool will be necessary for hydraulic control unit bleeding. Be sure to plug the brake fluid hoses when they are detached from the caliper. If in doubt, refer to the bleeding procedure earlier in this section, and to the ABS procedures later in this section.

Front

❈❈ CAUTION

Older brake pads may contain asbestos, which has been determined to be a cancer-causing agent. Never clean brake surfaces with compressed air. Avoid inhaling any dust from any brake surface. When cleaning brake surfaces, use a commercially available brake cleaning fluid. Also, always replace the brake pads on both front wheels at the same time

➡ The Mustang Cobra model utilizes dual piston front calipers, whereas all other models covered by this manual utilize single piston front brake calipers.

EXCEPT COBRA MODEL

▶ See Figure 17

1. Loosen all front wheel lug nuts ½ turn to break them free.

2. Raise and safely support the vehicle. Remove the front wheel(s).

3. If both front brake calipers are being removed and reinstalled, mark them to avoid confusion, since they must be reinstalled on their original sides.

4. Disconnect the front brake hose from the caliper by removing the hollow retaining bolt that connects the brake hose to the caliper. Plug the hose to prevent contamination and leakage of the brake fluid, then position the hose out of the way.

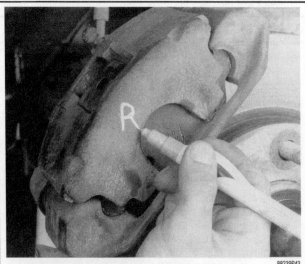

88239P43

Mark the brake calipers before removal for reassembly

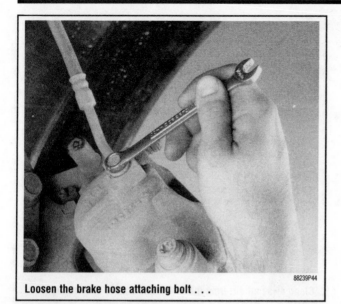

Loosen the brake hose attaching bolt . . .

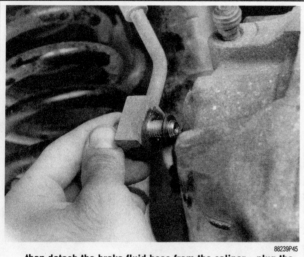

. . . then detach the brake fluid hose from the caliper—plug the hose to avoid fluid contamination

Remove the lower caliper-to-support bracket location mounting pin . . .

. . . then pivot the caliper up and away from the rotor, and remove it from the support bracket

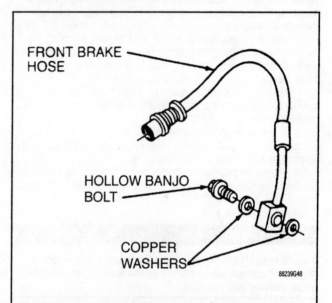

Fig. 17 Always utilize two new copper washers when attaching the brake hose to the caliper

5. Remove the lower brake caliper mounting pin, pivot the bottom edge of the caliper up and out approximately 90 degrees, then pull the caliper away from the anchor plate until it is fully disengaged from the upper mounting pin.

6. Remove the caliper from the vehicle.

To install:

7. Install the caliper onto the rotor and anchor plate by engaging the upper caliper end under the upper mounting pin, then pivoting the caliper down and onto the rotor.

➡**Using a new mounting pin is recommended by the manufacturer, due to the threadlocking compound on the pin.**

8. Install the lower caliper mounting pin, and tighten it to 64 ft. lbs. (88 Nm).

9. Remove the plug from the front brake hose, then, using a new copper washer on each side of the hose fitting, connect the hose to the caliper. Tighten the hose fitting bolt to 29 ft. lbs. (40 Nm).

10. Bleed the brake system.

Failure to tighten the lug nuts in a star pattern may result in high rotor run-out, which speeds up the onset of rotor roughness, shudder and vibration.

11. Install the wheel and lug nuts. Have an assistant depress the brake pedal, while you tighten the lug nuts in a star pattern to 85–105 ft. lbs. (115–142 Nm).

12. Lower the vehicle.

13. Pump the brake pedal prior to moving the vehicle to seat the brake pads. Refill the master cylinder with new clean DOT 3 brake fluid, if necessary.

COBRA MODEL

1. Loosen all front wheel lug nuts ½ turn to break them free.

2. Raise and safely support the vehicle. Remove the front wheel(s).

3. If both front brake calipers are being removed and reinstalled, mark them to avoid confusion, since they must be reinstalled on their original sides.

4. Disconnect the front brake hose from the caliper by removing the hollow retaining bolt that connects the brake hose to the caliper. Plug the hose to prevent contamination and leakage of the brake fluid, then position the hose out of the way.

5. Remove the retaining clip, washer and brake caliper locating pin, then remove the caliper from the anchor plate and rotor.

6. Clean the anchor plate of any dirt, grime or other residue.

To install:

7. Install the caliper onto the rotor and anchor plate. Ensure that the guiding surfaces on the brake shoe and disc brake caliper anchor plate are positioned correctly.

8. Install the caliper locating pin by depressing the caliper, to compress the bias spring, and sliding the locating pin into position. Secure the locating pin with the washer and retaining clip.

9. Remove the plug from the front brake hose, then, using a new copper washer on each side of the hose fitting, connect the hose to the caliper. Tighten the hose fitting bolt to 29 ft. lbs. (40 Nm).

10. Bleed the brake system.

Failure to tighten the lug nuts in a star pattern may result in high rotor run-out, which speeds up the onset of rotor roughness, shudder and vibration.

11. Install the wheel and lug nuts. Have an assistant depress the brake pedal, while you tighten the lug nuts in a star pattern to 85–105 ft. lbs. (115–142 Nm).

12. Lower the vehicle.

13. Pump the brake pedal prior to moving the vehicle to seat the brake pads. Refill the master cylinder with new clean DOT 3 brake fluid, if necessary.

Rear

▶ See Figures 18 and 19

➡To seat the piston in the caliper for brake pad installation, a specific tool (Ford Tool T87P-2588-A or equivalent) is necessary.

1. Loosen the rear wheel lug nuts ½ turn to break them loose.

2. Block the front wheels, then raise and safely support the rear of the vehicle on jackstands.

3. Remove the wheel.

4. Separate the brake hose from the rear brake caliper by removing the hollow banjo bolt from the hose fitting. Immediately plug the hose to prevent brake fluid contamination and leakage.

5. Detach the parking brake cable and conduit from the calipers, as follows:

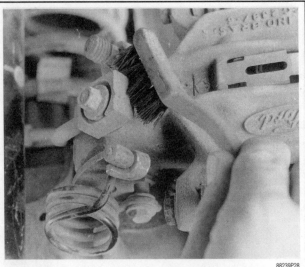

Clean away all dirt from the rear brake caliper hose fitting . . .

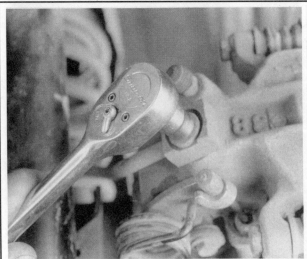

. . . then loosen the brake hose fitting banjo bolt

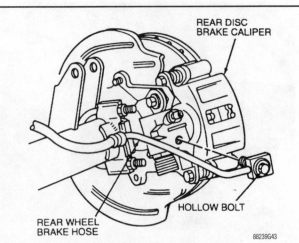

Fig. 18 The hollow banjo bolt is designed to hold the brake hose to the caliper, while allowing fluid to flow through it for brake operation

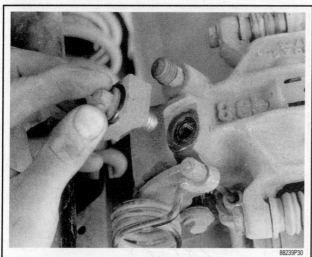

Separate the brake hose fitting from the caliper—plug the hose immediately to avoid contamination

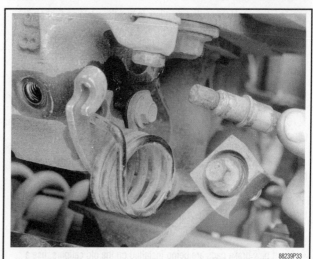

. . . then withdraw the cable and conduit from the brake cable mounting boss

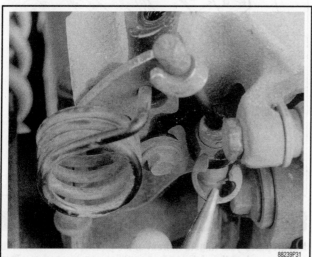

To detach the cable from the rear caliper, first remove the conduit retaining E-clip . . .

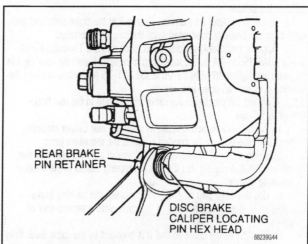

REAR BRAKE PIN RETAINER

DISC BRAKE CALIPER LOCATING PIN HEX HEAD

Fig. 19 Use two wrenches to remove the brake pin retainers—one to hold the locating pins steady and one to loosen the retainers . . .

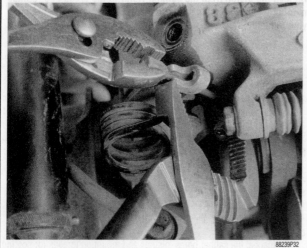

. . . then compress the cable lever and grasp the cable end with pliers. Disengage the cable from the lever . . .

. . . then pull the caliper off of the brake pads and support bracket

a. Use a pair of needlenose pliers to pull the retaining E-clip off the end of the parking brake cable conduit.

b. Using a large pair of pliers, or an equivalent tool, compress the parking brake cable lever, then, using a second pair of pliers, pull the cable out as far as possible. With the cable extended as far as possible, disengage the cable from the lever.

c. Once the cable is free of the lever, release it. Then, withdraw the cable and conduit from the caliper mounting boss.

6. Hold the caliper locating pin hex head with an open-end wrench and remove the pin retainer. Repeat for the other pin retainer.

7. Slide the caliper off of the rotor.

8. Remove the brake caliper locating pins and boots from the support bracket.

To install:

9. Apply silicone dielectric grease, such as Ford D7AZ-19A331-A, to the inside of the locating pin boots and to the locating pins.

10. Position the brake caliper locating pins and boots in the support bracket.

11. If new brake pads are being installed on the old calipers, use a caliper piston adjuster tool (Ford Tool T87P-2588-A or equivalent) to turn the piston clockwise until it is fully seated. Ensure that one of the two indentations on the caliper piston face is situated so that it will engage the nib on the brake pad when installed. Install the anti-rattle clips and brake pads on the caliper.

12. Install the caliper on the rotor. Ensure that the brake pads and anti-rattle clips are properly positioned once the caliper is installed.

13. Apply a threadlocking compound, such as Ford Threadlock and Sealer E0AZ-19554-AA, to the locating pin threads. Install the locating pin retainers and tighten them to 23–26 ft. lbs. (31–35 Nm) while holding the locating pins with an open-end wrench.

14. Connect the parking brake cable and conduit to the rear brake caliper as follows:

a. Insert the cable and conduit through the rear caliper mounting boss until the stop on the conduit contacts the mounting boss.

b. Using a pair of needlenose pliers, install a new E-clip onto the cable conduit, ensuring that the clip is properly seated in the conduit retaining groove.

c. Use the large pair of pliers to compress the parking brake cable lever, then grasp the end of the cable with a second pair of pliers.

d. Manipulate the cable so that it is engaged by the cable lever, then release the cable.

e. Slowly release the brake cable lever until it rests against the parking brake cable end stop.

⁕⁕⁕ WARNING

Failure to tighten the lug nuts in a star pattern may result in high rotor run-out, which speeds up the onset of rotor roughness, shudder and vibration.

15. Install the wheel and lug nuts. Have an assistant depress the brake pedal, while you tighten the lug nuts in a star pattern to 85–105 ft. lbs. (115–142 Nm).

16. Lower the vehicle.

17. Pump the brake pedal prior to moving the vehicle to seat the brake pads. Refill the master cylinder, if necessary.

OVERHAUL

◗ **See Figures 20 thru 30 (p. 26–29)**

➡**Some vehicles may be equipped with dual piston calipers. The procedure to overhaul those calipers is essentially the same, with the exception of multiple pistons, O-rings and dust boots.**

1. Remove the caliper from the vehicle and place on a clean workbench.

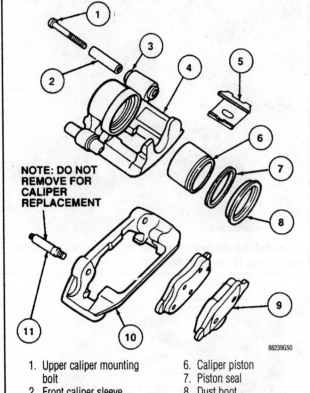

NOTE: DO NOT REMOVE FOR CALIPER REPLACEMENT

88239G50

1. Upper caliper mounting bolt
2. Front caliper sleeve
3. Insulator
4. Caliper housing
5. Anti-rattle clip
6. Caliper piston
7. Piston seal
8. Dust boot
9. Brake pad
10. Brake caliper anchor plate
11. Locating pin

Fig. 20 Exploded view of the front brake caliper—non-Cobra model

⁕⁕⁕ CAUTION

NEVER place your fingers in front of the pistons in an attempt to catch or protect the pistons when applying compressed air. This could result in personal injury!

➡**Depending upon the vehicle, there are two different ways to remove the piston from the caliper. Refer to the brake pad replacement procedure to make sure you have the correct procedure for your vehicle.**

2. The first method is as follows:

a. Stuff a shop towel or a block of wood into the caliper to catch the piston.

b. Remove the caliper piston using compressed air applied into the caliper inlet hole. Inspect the piston for scoring, nicks, corrosion and/or worn or damaged chrome plating. The piston must be replaced if any of these conditions is found.

3. For the second method, you must rotate the piston to retract it from the caliper.

4. If equipped, remove the anti-rattle clip.

5. Use a prytool to remove the caliper boot, being careful not to scratch the housing bore.

6. Remove the piston seals from the groove in the caliper bore.

7. Carefully loosen the brake bleeder valve cap and valve from the caliper housing.

8. Inspect the caliper bores, pistons and mounting threads for scoring or excessive wear.

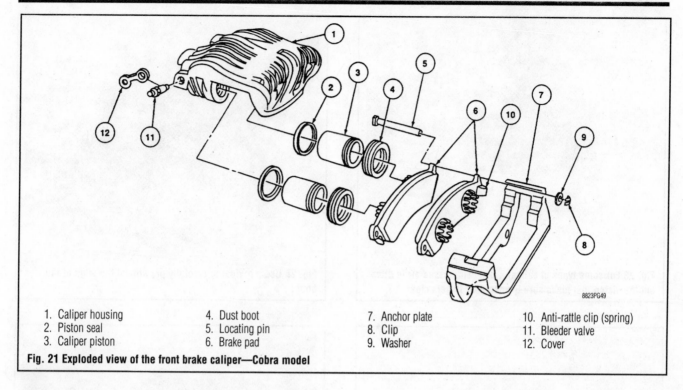

1. Caliper housing
2. Piston seal
3. Caliper piston
4. Dust boot
5. Locating pin
6. Brake pad
7. Anchor plate
8. Clip
9. Washer
10. Anti-rattle clip (spring)
11. Bleeder valve
12. Cover

8823PG49

Fig. 21 Exploded view of the front brake caliper—Cobra model

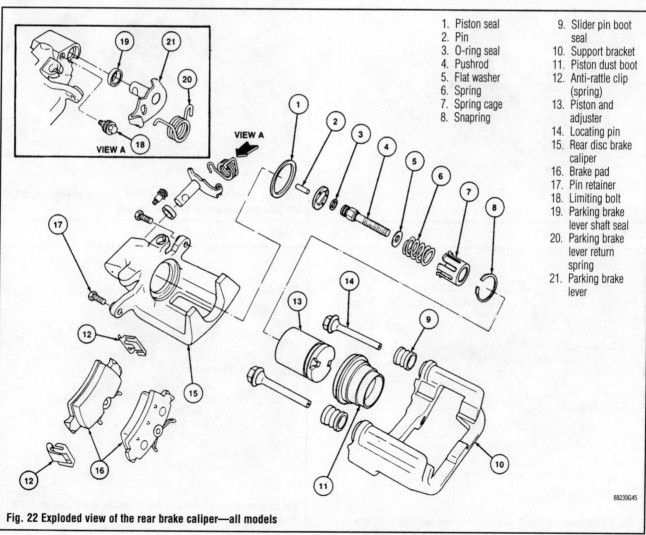

1. Piston seal
2. Pin
3. O-ring seal
4. Pushrod
5. Flat washer
6. Spring
7. Spring cage
8. Snapring
9. Slider pin boot seal
10. Support bracket
11. Piston dust boot
12. Anti-rattle clip (spring)
13. Piston and adjuster
14. Locating pin
15. Rear disc brake caliper
16. Brake pad
17. Pin retainer
18. Limiting bolt
19. Parking brake lever shaft seal
20. Parking brake lever return spring
21. Parking brake lever

VIEW A

88239G45

Fig. 22 Exploded view of the rear brake caliper—all models

Fig. 23 For some types of calipers, use compressed air to drive out the piston, but make sure to keep your fingers clear

Fig. 24 Withdraw the piston from the caliper bore

Fig. 25 On some vehicles, you must remove the anti-rattle clip

Fig. 26 Use a prytool to carefully pry around the edge of the boot . . .

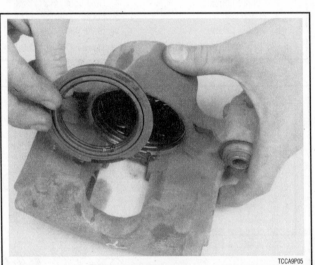

Fig. 27 . . . then remove the boot from the caliper housing, taking care not to score or damage the bore

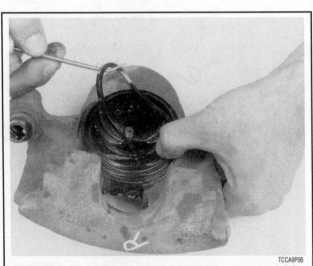

Fig 28 Use extreme caution when removing the piston seal; DO NOT scratch the caliper bore

9. Use crocus cloth to polish out light corrosion from the piston and bore.

10. Clean all parts with denatured alcohol and dry with compressed air.

To assemble:

11. Lubricate and install the bleeder valve and cap.

12. Install the new seals into the caliper bore grooves, making sure they are not twisted.

13. Lubricate the piston bore.

14. Install the pistons and boots into the bores of the calipers and push to the bottom of the bores.

15. Use a suitable driving tool to seat the boots in the housing.

16. Install the caliper in the vehicle.

17. Install the wheel and tire assembly, then carefully lower the vehicle.

18. Properly bleed the brake system.

Fig. 30 There are tools, such as this Mighty-Vac, available to assist in proper brake system bleeding

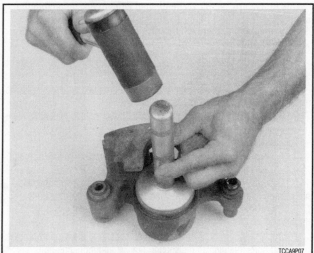

Fig. 29 Use the proper size driving tool and a mallet to properly seat the boots in the caliper housing

Brake Disc (Rotor)

REMOVAL & INSTALLATION

Front

▶ **See Figure 31**

1. Raise and safely support the vehicle. Remove the front wheel(s).
2. Remove the caliper, as follows:
   a. Remove and discard half of the brake fluid in the master cylinder reservoir.

➡ **To remove the disc brake rotor, it is not necessary to disconnect the brake fluid hose from the caliper. If the hose is detached from the caliper, the brake system will need to be bled.**

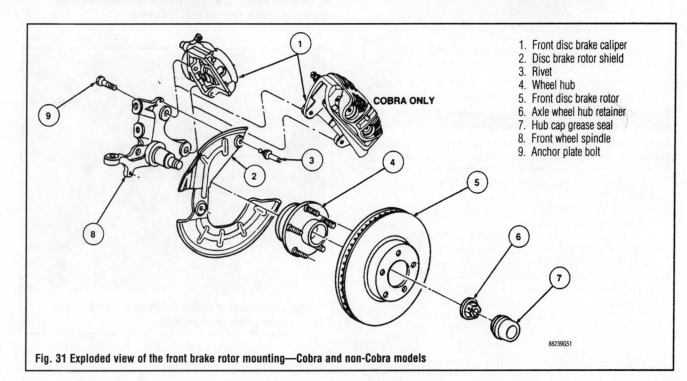

COBRA ONLY

1. Front disc brake caliper
2. Disc brake rotor shield
3. Rivet
4. Wheel hub
5. Front disc brake rotor
6. Axle wheel hub retainer
7. Hub cap grease seal
8. Front wheel spindle
9. Anchor plate bolt

Fig. 31 Exploded view of the front brake rotor mounting—Cobra and non-Cobra models

Remove the brake caliper, then remove the brake rotor retaining nuts from the lug studs . . .

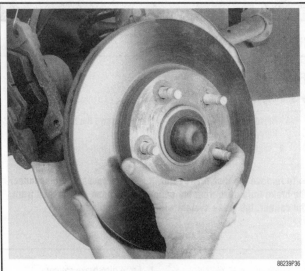

. . . and pull the rotor off of the wheel bearing/hub assembly

   b. Remove the brake caliper anchor plate mounting bolts, then, using a pivoting motion, lift the caliper and anchor plate away from the rotor.

❊❊ WARNING

Do not let the caliper hang by the brake hose; otherwise, damage to the hose may occur, necessitating brake hose replacement.

   c. Suspend the caliper inside the fender housing with a length of wire or strong cord.
   3. If equipped, remove any rotor retaining clips with a pair of needlenose pliers or similar tool.
   4. Slide the rotor off of the wheel bearing/hub assembly. If the rotor is difficult to remove, spray a rust penetrating lubricant on the rotor and wheel bearing/hub mating surfaces, then strike the rotor between the wheel lug studs with a plastic mallet. If this does not loosen the rotor sufficiently to allow removal, use a 3-jawed puller and a slide hammer to remove the rotor.
   To install:
   5. If a new rotor is being installed, remove the protective film from the rotor with a metal brake parts cleaner.

   6. Slide the rotor onto the wheel lug studs and push it onto the wheel bearing/hub assembly until completely seated.
   7. Install the caliper onto the rotor, then install the anchor mounting bolts to 95 ft. lbs. (130 Nm).

❊❊ WARNING

Failure to tighten the lug nuts in a star pattern may result in high rotor run-out, which speeds up the onset of rotor roughness, shudder and vibration.

   8. Install the wheel and lug nuts. Tighten the lug nuts in a star pattern to 85–105 ft. lbs. (115–142 Nm).
   9. Lower the vehicle.
   10. Pump the brake pedal prior to moving the vehicle to seat the brake pads. Refill the master cylinder.

Rear

➡**This procedure can be accomplished without disconnecting the brake hose from the caliper. If, during the caliper removal procedure, you detach the brake fluid hose from the caliper, the brake system will require bleeding.**

   1. Remove the rear caliper without disconnecting the hydraulic brake hose.
   2. Remove the caliper support bracket mounting bolts, then remove the bracket.
   3. Remove the nuts retaining the rotor to the axle shaft, then slide the rotor off of the lug studs and axle flange.
   To install:
   4. If a new rotor is being installed, remove the protective film from the rotor with a metal brake parts cleaner.
   5. Slide the rotor onto the wheel lug studs and push it onto the axle flange until completely seated, then install the retaining nuts securely.
   6. Clean the rear disc brake support bracket and retaining bolt threads.
   7. Apply one drop of a threadlocking compound to the support bracket mounting bolts, then install the support bracket and mounting bolts. Tighten the bolts to 64–88 ft. lbs. (87–119 Nm).
   8. Install the rear disc brake caliper.

➡**If the brake fluid hose was not disconnected from the brake caliper, the system does not need to be bled.**

The caliper and support caliper can be removed together by removing the anchor mounting bolts . . .

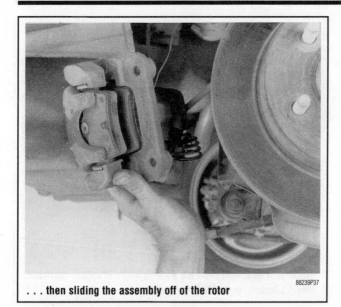

. . . then sliding the assembly off of the rotor

88239P37

Remove the brake rotor retaining nuts from the lug studs . . .

88239P39

Suspend the brake caliper by strong cord or wire while removing the rotor

88239P38

. . . then pull the rotor off of the rear axle flange

88239P40

INSPECTION

Front and Rear

Inspect the brake rotor for scoring and wear; minor scoring or disc pad lining buildup does not require rotor machining or replacement. If heavy scoring, cracks or other damage is evident, replace or have the rotor machined, as necessary.

Glaze on the rotor can be removed by hand-sanding it with medium grit garnet paper or aluminum oxide sandpaper.

The minimum thickness of each brake rotor is indicated on the rotor itself. Do not utilize a rotor which is worn below the minimum allowable thickness. If rotor damage cannot be corrected by grinding to these minimums, the rotor must be replaced.

Rotor lateral run-out must not be more than 0.001 in. (0.035mm).

PARKING BRAKE

Rear Cables

REMOVAL & INSTALLATION

◗ See Figure 32

➡If any of the parking brake components needs servicing, or if the rear axle assembly must be removed, parking brake cable tension must be relieved.

1. Place the parking brake control in the released position. Release the cable tension as follows:
   a. Remove the top panel of the floor console.

✳✳ CAUTION

Make sure the vehicle is securely supported, because you must sit in the raised vehicle while your assistant is under the vehicle. If the vehicle is not properly supported, the vehicle may fall and cause severe injury or death.

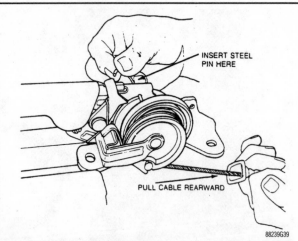

Fig. 32 While your assistant pulls rearward on the parking brake equalizer, insert a steel lockpin through the handle bracket and adjuster reel to release cable tension

While your assistant pulls the parking brake equalizer rearward, insert a lockpin in this hole (arrow)

Remove the floor console to gain access to the parking brake lever assembly

To detach the cable from the rear caliper, first remove the conduit retaining E-clip . . .

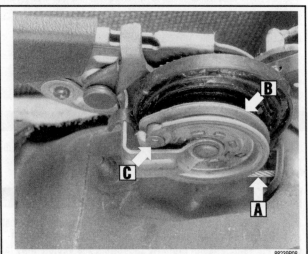

The front brake cable (A) attaches to the adjuster reel (B) by using a cylindrical fitting (C)

. . . then compress the cable lever and grasp the cable end using pliers

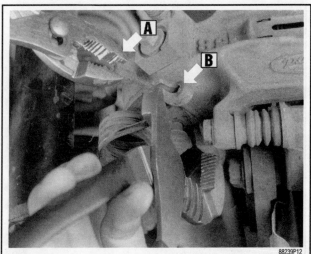

Manipulate the cable end (A) to disengage it from the brake lever (B)

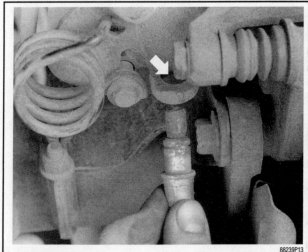

. . . then withdraw the cable and conduit from the brake cable mounting boss (arrow)

b. Raise and safely support the vehicle on jackstands.

c. From beneath the vehicle, have an assistant pull the parking brake cable and equalizer rearward approximately 1–2½ in. (26–63mm) to rotate the self-adjuster reel backward.

d. Insert a steel lockpin (an appropriately-sized Allen wrench works well) through the holes in the lever and control assembly. This locks the ratchet wheel in the cable-release position.

➡**Do not remove the lockpin until the cables are connected to the equalizer. Pin removal releases the tension in the ratchet wheel, causing the spring to unwind and release its tension. If the pin is removed without the cables attached, the entire assembly must be removed to reset the spring tension.**

2. Detach the parking brake cable and conduit from the rear brake calipers, as follows:

a. Use a pair of needlenose pliers to pull the retaining E-clip off the end of the parking brake cable conduit.

b. Using a large pair of pliers, or an equivalent tool, compress the parking brake cable lever, then, using a second pair of pliers, pull the cable out as far as possible. With the cable extended as far as possible, disengage the cable from the lever.

c. Once the cable is free of the lever, release it. Then, withdraw the cable and conduit from the caliper mounting boss.

3. Remove the cable snap fitting from the body. Remove the retaining clip that attaches the cable to the underbody.

4. Detach the rear cable from the parking brake cable and equalizer, then remove the cable from the vehicle.

To install:

➡**Do not remove the lockpin until the cables are connected to the equalizer. Pin removal releases the tension in the ratchet wheel, causing the spring to unwind and release its tension. If the pin is removed without the cables attached, the entire assembly must be removed to reset the spring tension.**

5. Route the parking brake cable in the vehicle as before removal.

6. Engage the cable and conduit in all of the body retaining clips.

7. Attach the cable to the equalizer.

8. Connect the parking brake cable and conduit to the rear brake caliper as follows:

a. Insert the cable and conduit through the rear caliper mounting boss until the stop on the conduit contacts the mounting boss.

b. Using a pair of needlenose pliers, install a new E-clip onto the cable conduit, ensuring that the clip is properly seated in the conduit retaining groove.

c. Use the large pair of pliers to compress the parking brake cable lever, then grasp the end of the cable with a second pair of pliers.

d. Manipulate the cable so that it is engaged by the cable lever, then release the cable.

e. Slowly release the brake cable lever until it rests against the parking brake cable end stop.

9. From beneath the vehicle, have an assistant pull the parking brake cable and equalizer rearward to remove the parking brake adjuster tension from the steel lockpin. While your assistant is pulling on the cable, remove the lockpin from the parking brake lever. Have your assistant slowly release the parking brake equalizer until the self-adjuster reel takes up all cable slack.

10. Lower the vehicle and install the top panel on the floor console.

11. Apply the parking brake several times. Make certain that the brakes apply and that the BRAKE warning lamp on the instrument panel illuminates when the lever is engaged.

ADJUSTMENT

The parking brake system utilizes a self-adjuster mechanism, which is an integral component of the parking brake lever assembly. Manual adjustment of the parking brake cable is not necessary.

Parking Brake Lever and Front Cable

REMOVAL & INSTALLATION

♦ **See Figure 33**

➡**If any of the parking brake components needs servicing, or if the rear axle assembly must be removed, parking brake cable tension must be relieved.**

1. Place the parking brake control in the released position. Release the cable tension as follows:

a. Remove the top panel of the floor console.

❊❊ CAUTION

Make sure the vehicle is securely supported, because you must sit in the raised vehicle while your assistant is under the vehicle. If the vehicle is not properly supported, the vehicle may fall and cause severe injury or death.

b. Raise and safely support the vehicle on jackstands.

c. From beneath the vehicle, have an assistant pull the parking brake cable and equalizer rearward approximately 1–2½ in. (26–63mm) to rotate the self-adjuster reel backward.

d. Insert a steel lockpin (an appropriately-sized Allen wrench works well) through the holes in the lever and control assembly. This locks the ratchet wheel in the cable-release position.

➡**Do not remove the lockpin until the cables are connected to the equalizer. Pin removal releases the tension in the ratchet wheel, causing the spring to unwind and release its tension. If the pin is removed without the cables attached, the entire assembly must be removed to reset the spring tension.**

2. Disconnect the equalizer from the control.
3. Remove the bolts attaching the parking brake lever to the floorpan.

To install:

➡**Do not remove the lockpin until the cables are connected to the equalizer. Pin removal releases the tension in the ratchet wheel, causing the spring to unwind and release its tension. If the pin is removed without the cables attached, the entire assembly must be removed to reset the spring tension.**

4. Route the cable and equalizer around the control assembly pulley. Install the cable anchor pin in the pivot hole in the ratchet.
5. Connect the rear cable to the equalizer.
6. With the cable attached, position the control assembly on the floorpan. Install and tighten the bolts to 10–16 ft. lbs. (12–21 Nm).
7. From beneath the vehicle, have an assistant pull the parking brake cable and equalizer rearward to remove the parking brake adjuster tension from the steel lockpin. While your assistant is pulling on the cable, remove the lockpin from the parking brake lever. Have your assistant slowly release the parking brake cable and equalizer until the self-adjuster reel takes up all cable slack.
8. Lower the vehicle and install the top panel on the floor console.
9. Apply the parking brake several times. Make certain that the brakes apply and that the BRAKE warning lamp on the instrument panel illuminates when the lever is engaged.

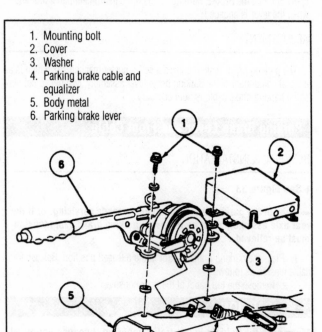

1. Mounting bolt
2. Cover
3. Washer
4. Parking brake cable and equalizer
5. Body metal
6. Parking brake lever

88239G40

Fig. 33 Exploded view of the parking brake lever mounting

88239P07

To release cable tension, remove the floor console to gain access to the parking brake lever assembly

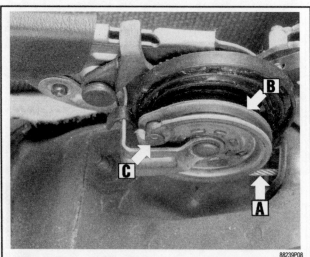

88239P08

The front brake cable (A) attaches to the adjuster reel (B) by using a cylindrical fitting (C)

88239P09

While your assistant pulls the parking brake equalizer rearward, insert a lockpin in this hole (arrow)

ANTI-LOCK BRAKE SYSTEM

General Information

♦ See Figures 34 and 35

➥Whenever service is performed on the Hydraulic Control Unit (HCU), a specific procedure must be performed to bleed the system to ensure that no air is trapped in the HCU. To perform this procedure, the New Generation Start (NGS) Tester, or an equivalent brake tool, is necessary.

The 1994–98 Mustang models were available with a Bosch 2U four-wheel Anti-lock Brake System (ABS) as an option. The ABS is designed to prevent wheel lock-up under heavy braking on almost any road surface by controlling the amount of brake system pressure applied to each wheel. By preventing the wheels from locking up, enhanced steering and braking integrity is maintained. During ABS operation, the driver of the vehicle will feel a pulsation in the brake pedal. Under normal conditions, the ABS allows the brake system to function in the same fashion as any conventional vacuum-boost brake system.

The Bosch 2U system is composed of the following components:
• Hydraulic Control Unit (HCU)
• ABS Control Module (ABS-CM)
• Front and rear wheel ABS sensors

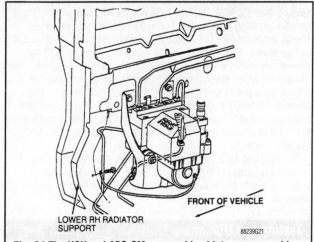

Fig. 34 The HCU and ABS-CM are combined into one assembly, which is mounted to the lower, right-hand radiator support in the engine compartment

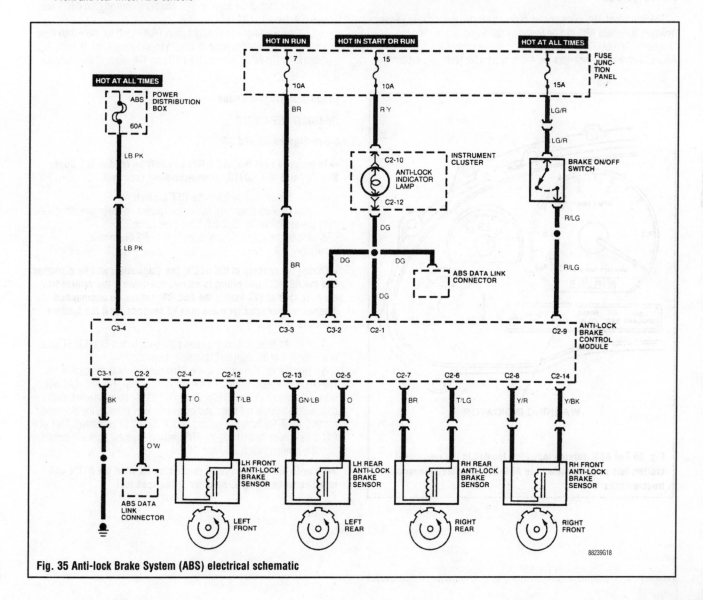

Fig. 35 Anti-lock Brake System (ABS) electrical schematic

The ABS works as follows:

ABS sensors mounted at each wheel on the vehicle electrically sense each tooth of the ABS sensor indicator ring as it passes through the ABS sensor's magnetic field. This data is sent to the ABS-CM, which translates the incoming signals, based upon their frequencies, into wheel speeds. Since the ABS-CM constantly monitors the rotational speeds of all four wheels, it can use this incoming data to activate the ABS only when an impending wheel lock-up is evident. In such an event, the ABS-CM decides which wheel(s) need(s) to be controlled, and sends the appropriate signal to the HCU. The HCU, in turn, manipulates (rapidly opens and closes) the appropriate internal solenoid valves to regulate brake pressure at the designated wheel(s). This manipulation of the internal solenoid valves is what results in the brake pedal pulsations felt by the vehicle operator.

The HCU and ABS-CM are contained within one assembly. This assembly is located in the right-hand, lower front corner of the engine compartment, next to the bottom of the white radiator coolant reservoir.

Testing and Diagnosis

SYSTEM TESTS

♦ See Figure 36

The individual ABS components cannot be tested individually per se; however, the entire ABS can be tested by retrieving and reading the Diagnostic Trouble Codes (DTC's) stored in the control module. The ABS-CM constantly monitors the entire system for faults or problems.

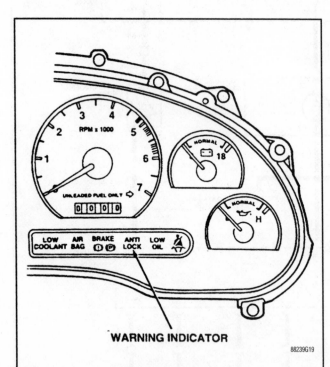

WARNING INDICATOR

88239G19

Fig. 36 The ABS warning indicator, located in the instrument cluster, lets you know when the ABS-CM has stored diagnostic trouble codes

When the ABS is operating normally, the ABS warning indicator light (on the instrument panel) will illuminate for approximately three seconds when the ignition key is turned **ON** or when the engine is started. If the warning indicator light stays illuminated for more than three seconds, or illuminates while driving, then a malfunction has been detected by the ABS-CM. If a problem is found by the ABS-CM, it will store a DTC corresponding to the component which exhibited the problem. Up to three DTC's can be stored by the ABS-CM at one time. The DTC does not only refer to the component in question, but also to the component's wiring harness circuit. If a code is detected, check the component's wiring for a short-to-ground or an open circuit before replacing the component; doing so may save you a lot of money, if the problem lies within the wiring.

➡**It is important to perform the quick test prior to retrieving the ABS diagnostic trouble codes; it may save you some time and effort.**

Quick Test

1. Turn the ignition switch to the **ON** position.
2. Note the activity of the ABS warning indicator light on the instrument cluster:
    a. The ABS warning indicator light should illuminate for approximately three seconds when the ignition key is turned **ON** or when the engine is started. If the warning light functions normally, no DTC's are stored in the ABS-CM.
    b. If the warning indicator light stays illuminated for more than three seconds, or illuminates while driving, then a malfunction has been detected by the ABS-CM; read the DTC's for the cause of the malfunction.

Diagnostic Trouble Codes

READING THE CODES

♦ See Figures 37 and 38

➡**To properly read the ABS DTC's can only be read with a Super Star Tester II 007–0041B, or an equivalent scan tool.**

1. Turn the ignition switch to the **OFF** position.
2. Find the ABS diagnostic connector, located on the engine compartment power distribution box (left-hand inner fender).
3. Attach the scan tool connector to the ABS diagnostic connector.

➡**During the reading of the DTC's, the diagnostics will be disrupted and the ABS-CM will return to normal operation if the vehicle travels over 15 mph (24 km/h), the ABS-CM senses an ungrounded diagnostic connector for more than 15 seconds, or if the ignition switch is turned OFF.**

4. Turn the scan tool on, then move the latch button to the TEST position. Ensure that the scan tool is in slow mode.
5. Turn the ignition switch to the **RUN** position (with the engine off). The DTC's will begin to flash on the scan tool screen. The ABS-CM will store a maximum of three DTC's. If any DTC's have been detected, each code will be flashed out once, and only once, after entering the diagnostic mode. If no DTC's have been stored, a DTC 12 will be presented. After all DTC's have been flashed out, the ABS warning indicator light will remain on until the ignition switch is turned **OFF**.

➡**Refer to the accompanying illustration for what the DTC's will look like when being flashed out by the scan tool.**

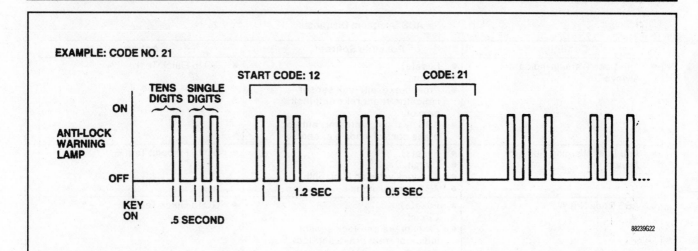

Fig. 37 Before the individual trouble codes are displayed by the scan tool, code 12 will be flashed three times to signal the beginning of code flash out

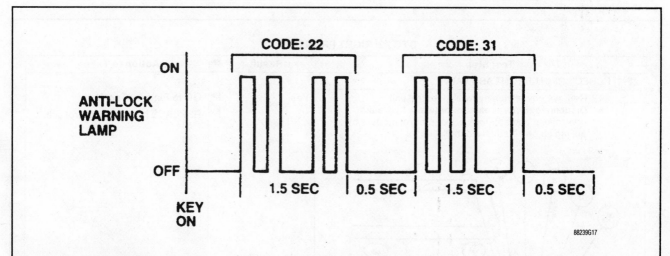

Fig. 38 The difference between code 22 and code 31 is shown here—the first set of flashes for each code group represent the tens and the second set of flashes represent the ones

CODE IDENTIFICATION

The diagnostic trouble codes are as follows:
- Code 12—system OK
- Code 19—ABS-CM
- Code 22—right, front internal solenoid valve
- Code 24—left, front internal solenoid valve
- Code 26—rear internal solenoid valve
- Code 31—right, front ABS sensor continuity
- Code 32—right, rear ABS sensor continuity
- Code 33—left, front ABS sensor continuity
- Code 34—left, rear ABS sensor continuity
- Code 41—right, front ABS sensor
- Code 42—right, rear ABS sensor
- Code 43—left, front ABS sensor
- Code 44—left, rear ABS sensor
- Code 61—pump motor/pump motor relay fault
- Code 63—voltage supply interruption
- Code 69—vehicle battery voltage less than 10 volts
- Code 78—ABS sensor frequency fault

DIAGNOSTIC PINPOINT TESTS

Depending on the DTC's read from your system, refer to the accompanying diagnostic charts. The corresponding tests for each DTC are as follows:
- Codes 12, 19, 61, 63, and 69—use pinpoint test E
- Code 22—use DTC 22 pinpoint test
- Code 24—use DTC 24 pinpoint test
- Code 26—use DTC 26 pinpoint test
- Codes 31 and 41—use pinpoint test A
- Codes 32 and 42—use pinpoint test B
- Codes 33 and 43—use pinpoint test C
- Codes 34 and 44—use pinpoint test D
- Code 78—inspect the ABS sensors and ABS sensor indicator rings for physical damage, then refer to pinpoint test D

ABS Symptom Diagnosis

Condition	Possible Source	Action
• Anti-Lock Warning Indicator Always On	• Fuse(s). • Circuit. • Front brake anti-lock sensor indicator / rear brake anti-lock sensor. • ABS hydraulic actuator / anti-lock brake control module assembly.	• GO to Quick Test.
• Anti-Lock Warning Indicator Always Off	• Fuse(s). • Circuit. • Anti-lock warning lamp bulb. • ABS control module.	• GO to Pinpoint Test F.
• ABS Does Not Work	• Fuse(s). • Circuit. • Front brake anti-lock sensor indicator / rear brake anti-lock sensor. • ABS hydraulic actuator / anti-lock brake control module assembly.	• GO to Quick Test.

88239G16

DTC 22: RIGHT FRONT VALVE

Test Step	Result	▶	Action to Take
22-1 CHECK RIGHT FRONT ABS VALVE			
• Remove cover from hydraulic control unit. • Disconnect 6-pin connector between hydraulic control unit and anti-lock brake control module by pulling up on plastic hardshell.	Yes No	▶ ▶	GO to Pinpoint Test D. REPLACE hydraulic control unit.

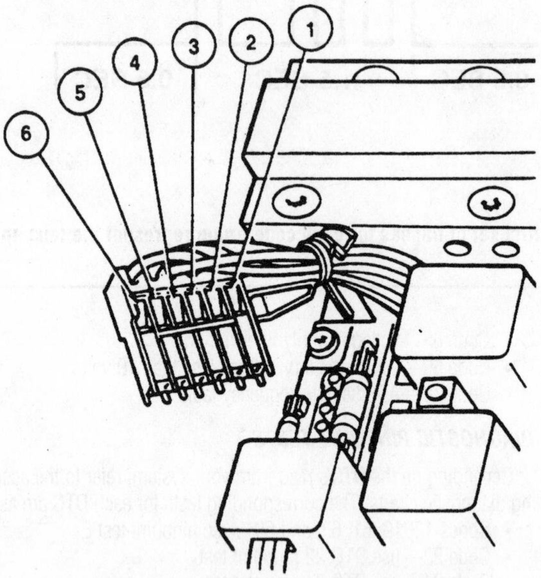

• Measure resistance of right front ABS valve at Pins 3 and 4 of valve connector hardshell. • **Is resistance between 1.0 and 1.5 ohms?**			

88239G15

DTC 24: LEFT FRONT VALVE

Test Step	Result	▶	Action to Take
24-1 CHECK LEFT FRONT ABS VALVE			
• Remove cover from hydraulic control unit. • Disconnect 6-pin connector between hydraulic control unit and anti-lock brake control module by pulling up on plastic hardshell.	Yes No	▶ ▶	GO to Pinpoint Test D. REPLACE hydraulic control unit.

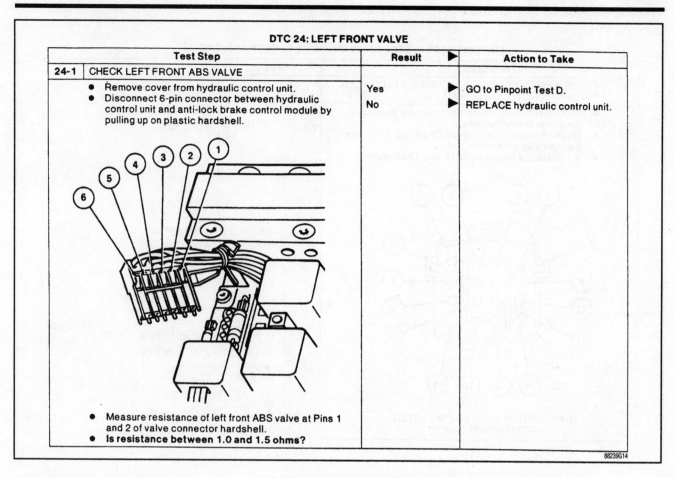

• Measure resistance of left front ABS valve at Pins 1 and 2 of valve connector hardshell.
• **Is resistance between 1.0 and 1.5 ohms?**

88239G14

DTC 26: REAR ABS VALVE

Test Step	Result	▶	Action to Take
26-1 CHECK REAR AXLE ABS VALVE			
• Remove cover from hydraulic control unit. • Disconnect 6-pin connector between hydraulic control unit and anti-lock brake control module by pulling up on plastic hardshell. • Measure resistance of rear ABS valve at Pins 5 and 6 of valve connector hardshell. • **Is resistance between 1.0 and 1.5 ohms?**	Yes No	▶ ▶	GO to Pinpoint Test D. REPLACE hydraulic control unit.

88239G13

PINPOINT TEST A: DTCs 31, 41 RH FRONT SENSOR AND CIRCUIT

	Test Step	Result	▶	Action to Take
A1	CHECK RESISTANCE PIN C1-2, CIRCUIT 514 (Y/R) TO PIN C1-13, CIRCUIT 516 (Y/BK)			
	• Disconnect 16-pin connector on jumper from ABS assembly to wire harness. • Measure resistance between Pins 2 and 13 on wire harness side connector. • **Is resistance between 1015 and 1245 ohms?**	Yes No	▶ ▶	GO to **A3**. GO to **A2**.

1. Left, rear brake sensor terminal
2. Right, front brake sensor terminal
3. Left, front sensor ground terminal
4. Not used
5. Right, rear brake sensor ground terminal
6. Left, rear brake sensor ground terminal
7. Left, front brake sensor terminal
8. Not used
9. Right, rear brake sensor terminal
10. ABS data link connector terminal
11. Not used
12. Not used
13. Right, front brake sensor ground terminal
14. Not used
15. Brake light switch input terminal
16. Anti-lock indicator output terminal

16-PIN ANTI-LOCK BRAKE CONNECTOR BODY HARNESS SIDE C1

88239G12

PINPOINT TEST A: DTCs 31, 41 RH FRONT SENSOR AND CIRCUIT (Continued)

	Test Step	Result	▶	Action to Take
A2	CHECK RIGHT FRONT BRAKE ANTI-LOCK SENSOR RESISTANCE			
	• Disconnect right front sensor from wire harness. • Measure resistance between Pins 1 and 2 on sensor connector. • **Is resistance between 1015 and 1245 ohms?**	Yes No	▶ ▶	SERVICE or REPLACE cable harness Circuit 514 or 516. REPLACE right front brake anti-lock sensor.

RH FRONT BRAKE ANTI-LOCK SENSOR

	Test Step	Result	▶	Action to Take
A3	CHECK CIRCUITS 514 (Y/R) AND 516 (Y/BK) AT JUMPER HARNESS			
	• Remove cover from hydraulic control unit. • Disconnect jumper harness from anti-lock brake control module. • Check for broken or damaged wire in jumper between Pin 2 (16-pin side) and Pin 8 (15-pin side) or between Pin 13 (16-pin side) and Pin 14 (15-pin side). • **Are both wires OK?**	Yes No	▶ ▶	GO to **A4**. SERVICE or REPLACE broken or damaged wire in jumper.

88239G11

PINPOINT TEST A: DTCs 31, 41 RH FRONT SENSOR AND CIRCUIT (Continued)

Test Step	Result	▶	Action to Take
A4 CHECK RIGHT FRONT BRAKE ANTI-LOCK SENSOR			
• Remove cover from hydraulic control unit. • Disconnect jumper harness from anti-lock brake control module. • Check for a short between Pin 8 or Pin 14 of the 15-pin connector to ground. • Check for short between Pin 14 of the 15-pin connector to ground. • **Does a short to ground exist and are both wires OK?**	Yes No	▶ ▶	SERVICE or REPLACE jumper, Circuit 514 or 516, or right front brake anti-lock sensor. GO to **A5**.

ANTI-LOCK BRAKE CONTROL MODULE CONNECTOR C2

88239G10

1. Anti-lock indicator output terminal
2. ABS data link connector terminal
3. Not used
4. Left, front brake sensor terminal
5. Left, rear brake sensor ground terminal
6. Right, rear brake sensor ground terminal
7. Right, rear brake sensor terminal
8. Right, front brake sensor terminal
9. Brake light switch input terminal
10. Not used
11. Not used
12. Left, front brake sensor ground terminal
13. Left, rear brake sensor terminal
14. Right, front brake sensor ground terminal

PINPOINT TEST A: DTCs 31, 41 RH FRONT SENSOR AND CIRCUIT (Continued)

	Test Step	Result	▶	Action to Take
A5	CHECK RIGHT FRONT BRAKE ANTI-LOCK SENSOR AIR GAP • Remove the right front wheel and tire. • Check for damage to the front brake anti-lock sensor or front brake anti-lock sensor indicator. • Check for objects sticking to the front brake anti-lock sensor or front brake anti-lock sensor indicator. • Check the air gap between the front brake anti-lock sensor indicator and front brake anti-lock sensor (0.5 mm-0.95 mm specification). • Check for excessive wheel bearing end play. • **Are the conditions OK?**	Yes No	▶ ▶	If light is coming on all the time, REPLACE anti-lock brake control module. SERVICE condition as required.

PINPOINT TEST B: DTCs 32, 42 RH REAR SENSOR AND CIRCUIT

	Test Step	Result	▶	Action to Take
B1	CHECK RIGHT REAR BRAKE ANTI-LOCK SENSOR RESISTANCE PIN C1-5, CIRCUIT 494 (T/LG) TO PIN C1-9, CIRCUIT 492 (BR) • Disconnect 16-pin connector on jumper from ABS assembly to wire harness. • Measure resistance between Pins 9 and 5 on wire harness side connector. • **Is resistance between 2187 and 2673 ohms?**	Yes No	▶ ▶	GO to B3. GO to B2.
B2	CHECK RESISTANCE AT SENSOR • Disconnect right rear brake anti-lock sensor from wire harness. • Measure resistance between Pins 1 and 2 on sensor connector. • **Is resistance between 2187 and 2673 ohms?** RH REAR BRAKE ANTI-LOCK SENSOR	Yes No	▶ ▶	SERVICE or REPLACE cable harness Circuit 492 or 494. REPLACE right rear brake anti-lock sensor.
B3	CHECK CIRCUIT 492 (BR) AND 494 (T/LG) AT JUMPER HARNESS • Remove cover from hydraulic control unit. • Disconnect jumper harness from anti-lock brake control module. • Check for broken or damaged wire in jumper between Pin 9 (16-pin side) and Pin 7 (15-pin side) or between Pin 5 (16-pin side) and Pin 6 (15-pin side). • **Are both wires OK?**	Yes No	▶ ▶	GO to B4. SERVICE or REPLACE broken or damaged wire in jumper.
B4	CHECK RIGHT REAR BRAKE ANTI-LOCK SENSOR CIRCUIT FOR SHORT TO GROUND • Remove cover from hydraulic control unit. • Disconnect jumper harness from anti-lock brake control module. • Check for a short between Pin 6 of the 15-pin connector to ground. • Check for short between Pin 7 of the 15-pin connector and ground. • **Does a short to ground exist at either of the two pins?**	Yes No	▶ ▶	SERVICE or REPLACE jumper, Circuit 494 or 492, or right rear brake anti-lock sensor. GO to B5.

88239G09

PINPOINT TEST B: DTCs 32, 42 RH REAR SENSOR AND CIRCUIT (Continued)

	Test Step	Result	▶	Action to Take
B5	CHECK RIGHT REAR BRAKE ANTI-LOCK SENSOR AIR GAP			
	• Remove the right rear wheel and tire. • Check for damage to the rear brake anti-lock sensor or rear brake anti-lock sensor indicator. • Check for objects sticking to the rear brake anti-lock sensor or rear brake anti-lock sensor indicator. • Check the air gap between the rear brake anti-lock sensor indicator and rear brake anti-lock sensor (0.6 mm-1.6 mm specification). • Check for excessive axle bearing end play. • **Are the conditions OK?**	Yes No	▶ ▶	If light is coming on all the time, REPLACE anti-lock brake control module. SERVICE condition as required.

PINPOINT TEST C: DTCs 33, 43 LH FRONT SENSOR AND CIRCUIT

	Test Step	Result	▶	Action to Take
C1	CHECK RESISTANCE PIN C1-3, CIRCUIT 527 (T/BK) TO PIN C1-7, CIRCUIT 521 (T/O)			
	• Disconnect 16-pin connector on jumper from ABS assembly to wire harness. • Measure resistance between Pins 3 and 7 on wire harness side connector. • **Is resistance between 1015 and 1245 ohms?**	Yes No	▶ ▶	GO to C3. GO to C2.
C2	CHECK SENSOR RESISTANCE			
	• Disconnect left front brake anti-lock sensor from wire harness. • Measure resistance between Pins 1 and 2 on sensor connector. • **Is resistance between 1015 and 1245 ohms?**	Yes No	▶ ▶	SERVICE or REPLACE cable harness Circuit 521 or 522. REPLACE left front brake anti-lock sensor.

LH FRONT BRAKE ANTI-LOCK SENSOR

	Test Step	Result	▶	Action to Take
C3	CHECK CIRCUIT 521 (T/O) AND 522 (T/BK) AT JUMPER HARNESS			
	• Disconnect jumper harness from anti-lock brake control module. • Check for broken or damaged wire in jumper between Pin 7 (16-pin side) and Pin 4 (15-pin side) or between Pin 3 (16-pin side) and Pin 12 (15-pin side). • **Are both wires OK?**	Yes No	▶ ▶	GO to C4. SERVICE or REPLACE broken or damaged wire in jumper.
C4	CHECK LEFT FRONT BRAKE ANTI-LOCK SENSOR CIRCUITS FOR SHORT TO GROUND			
	• Remove cover from hydraulic control unit. • Disconnect jumper harness from anti-lock brake control module. • Check for a short between Pin 4 of the 15-pin connector to ground. • Check for a short between Pin 12 of the 15-pin connector to ground. • **Does a short to ground exist at either of the two pins?**	Yes No	▶ ▶	SERVICE or REPLACE jumper, Circuit 521 or 522, or left front brake anti-lock sensor. GO to C5.

88239G08

PINPOINT TEST C: DTCs 33, 43 LH FRONT SENSOR AND CIRCUIT (Continued)

	Test Step	Result	▶	Action to Take
C5	CHECK LEFT FRONT SENSOR AIR GAP			
	• Remove the left front wheel and tire. • Check for damage to the front brake anti-lock sensor or front brake anti-lock sensor indicator. • Check for objects sticking to the sensor or ring. • Check the air gap between the ring and sensor (0.5 mm-0.95 mm specification). • Check for excessive wheel bearing end play. • **Are the conditions OK?**	Yes No	▶ ▶	If light is coming on all the time, REPLACE anti-lock brake control module. SERVICE condition as required.

PINPOINT TEST D: DTCs 34, 44 LH REAR SENSOR AND CIRCUIT

	Test Step	Result	▶	Action to Take
D1	CHECK RESISTANCE PIN C1-1, CIRCUIT 499 (GY / BK) TO PIN C1-6, CIRCUIT 496 (O)			
	• Disconnect 16-pin connector on jumper from ABS assembly to wire harness. • Measure resistance between Pins 1 and 6 on wire harness side connector. • **Is resistance between 2187 and 2673 ohms?**	Yes No	▶ ▶	GO to **D3**. GO to **D2**.
D2	CHECK LEFT REAR BRAKE ANTI-LOCK SENSOR RESISTANCE			
	• Disconnect left rear rear brake anti-lock sensor from wire harness. • Measure resistance between Pins 1 and 2 on sensor connector. • **Is resistance between 2187 and 2673 ohms?** **LH REAR BRAKE ANTI-LOCK SENSOR**	Yes No	▶ ▶	SERVICE or REPLACE cable harness Circuit 496 or 499. REPLACE left rear brake anti-lock sensor.
D3	CHECK CIRCUITS 499 (GY / BK) AND 496 (O) AT JUMPER HARNESS			
	• Disconnect jumper harness from anti-lock brake control module. • Check for broken or damaged wire in jumper between Pin 1 (16-pin side) and Pin 13 (15-pin side) or between Pin 6 (16-pin side) and Pin 5 (15-pin side). • **Are both wires OK?**	Yes No	▶ ▶	GO to **D4**. SERVICE or REPLACE broken or damaged wire in jumper.
D4	CHECK LEFT REAR BRAKE ANTI-LOCK SENSOR CIRCUITS FOR SHORT TO GROUND			
	• Disconnect jumper harness from anti-lock brake control module. • Check for short between Pin 5 of the 15-pin connector to ground. • Check for short between Pin 13 of the 15-pin connector to ground. • **Does a short to ground exist at either of the two pins?**	Yes No	▶ ▶	SERVICE or REPLACE jumper, Circuit 499 or 496, or left rear brake anti-lock sensor. GO to **D5**.

88239G07

PINPOINT TEST D: DTCs 34, 44 LH REAR SENSOR AND CIRCUIT (Continued)

	Test Step	Result	▶	Action to Take
D5	CHECK LEFT REAR SENSOR AIR GAP			
	• Remove the left rear wheel and tire. • Check for damage to the rear brake anti-lock sensor or rear brake anti-lock sensor indicator. • Check for objects sticking to the rear brake anti-lock sensor or rear brake anti-lock sensor indicator. • Check the air gap between the rear brake anti-lock sensor indicator and rear brake anti-lock sensor (0.6 mm-1.6 mm specification). • Check for excessive axle bearing end play. • **Are the conditions OK?**	Yes No	▶ ▶	If light is coming on all the time, REPLACE anti-lock brake control module. SERVICE condition as required.

PINPOINT TEST E: HYDRAULIC PUMP MOTOR AND RELAY

	Test Step	Result	▶	Action to Take
E1	CHECK 60A ABS FUSE			
	• Check the 60A ABS fuse located in the LH engine compartment power distribution panel. • **Is the fuse OK?**	Yes No	▶ ▶	GO to **E4**. GO to **E2**.
E2	CHECK HYDRAULIC MOTOR SYSTEM			
	• Ignition switch OFF. • Replace the 60A ABS fuse. • Inspect the fuse. • **Does the fuse fail again?**	Yes No	▶ ▶	GO to **E3**. GO to **E4**.
E3	CHECK FOR SHORT TO GROUND IN HYDRAULIC MOTOR POWER CIRCUIT			
	• Ignition switch OFF. • Remove the 60A ABS fuse. • Remove cover from hydraulic control unit. • Disconnect the 16-pin connector located at the hydraulic control unit. NOTE: Circuit 601 changes color from LB/PK to R as it passes through the harness connector. • Measure the resistance of Circuit 601 (R) between the 60A ABS fuse terminal and ground. • **Is the resistance greater than 10,000 ohms?**	Yes No	▶ ▶	GO to **E4**. SERVICE Circuit 601 (R) between the engine compartment fuse panel and the hydraulic control unit.
E4	CHECK POWER SUPPLY TO HYDRAULIC CONTROL UNIT			
	• Ignition switch OFF. • Disconnect the hydraulic control unit connector. NOTE: Circuit 601 changes color from LB/PK to R as it passes through the harness connector. • Ignition switch ON. • Measure the voltage on Circuit 601 (R) at the hydraulic actuator assembly connector. • **Is the voltage greater than 10 volts?**	Yes No	▶ ▶	GO to **E5**. SERVICE Circuit 601 (R) between the engine compartment fuse panel and the hydraulic control unit.
E5	CHECK HYDRAULIC ACTUATOR ASSEMBLY GROUND			
	• Ignition switch OFF. • Measure the resistance of the BK wire between the screw terminal on the right side of the hydraulic control assembly and ground. • **Is the resistance less than 5 ohms?**	Yes No	▶ ▶	REPLACE ABS unit. SERVICE the BK wire.

PINPOINT TEST F: NO ANTI-LOCK BRAKE INDICATOR ON WHEN IGNITION SWITCH ON

	Test Step	Result	▶	Action to Take
F1	CHECK CLUSTER FUSE			
	• Check 10A instrument cluster fuse in power distribution box. • **Is the fuse OK?**	Yes No	▶ ▶	GO to **F4**. GO to **F2**.

88239G06

PINPOINT TEST F: NO ANTI-LOCK BRAKE INDICATOR ON WHEN IGNITION SWITCH ON (Continued)

Test Step	Result	▶	Action to Take
F2 CHECK FOR SHORT			
• Ignition switch OFF. • Replace instrument cluster fuse (10A). • Ignition switch ON. • **Does fuse fail again?**	Yes No	▶ ▶	GO to **F3**. GO to **F4**.
F3 CHECK FOR SHORT CIRCUIT 640			
• Ignition switch OFF. • Remove instrument cluster fuse (10A). • Remove instrument cluster. Refer to Section 13-01. • Measure resistance of Circuit 640 (R/Y) wire between the fuse terminal and ground. • **Is the resistance greater than 10,000 ohms?**	Yes No	▶ ▶	SERVICE short in instrument cluster. SERVICE Circuit 640 (R/Y) wire between the interior fuse and instrument cluster.

1. Ground terminal
2. Ground terminal
3. Oil pressure gauge feed terminal
4. 12 volt input terminal
5. Illumination lamps feed terminal
6. Low coolant indicator feed terminal
7. Ground terminal
8. Tachometer feed terminal
9. Ground terminal
10. 12 volt input terminal
11. Low oil indicator terminal
12. Anti-lock indicator feed terminal
13. Brake indicator feed terminal
14. Air Bag indicator feed terminal
15. Fasten Belts indicator terminal
16. Right turn indicator terminal

**INSTRUMENT CLUSTER
CONNECTOR C2**

88239G05

PINPOINT TEST F: NO ANTI-LOCK BRAKE INDICATOR ON WHEN IGNITION SWITCH ON (Continued)

Test Step	Result	▶	Action to Take
F4 CHECK FOR OPEN CIRCUIT			
• Ignition switch OFF. • Disconnect 4-pin and 15-pin connectors at ABS unit. • Jump Pin 1 Circuit 603 (DG) of 15-pin connector to ground. • Ignition switch ON. • **Does ABS indicator illuminate?**	Yes No	▶ ▶	GO to **F9**. GO to **F5**.

1. Anti-lock indicator output terminal
2. ABS data link connector terminal
3. Not used
4. Left, front brake sensor terminal
5. Left, rear brake sensor ground terminal
6. Right, rear brake sensor ground terminal
7. Right, rear brake sensor terminal
8. Right, front brake sensor terminal
9. Brake light switch input terminal
10. Not used
11. Not used
12. Left, front brake sensor ground terminal
13. Left, rear brake sensor terminal
14. Right, front brake sensor ground terminal

**ANTI-LOCK BRAKE
CONTROL MODULE CONNECTOR C2**

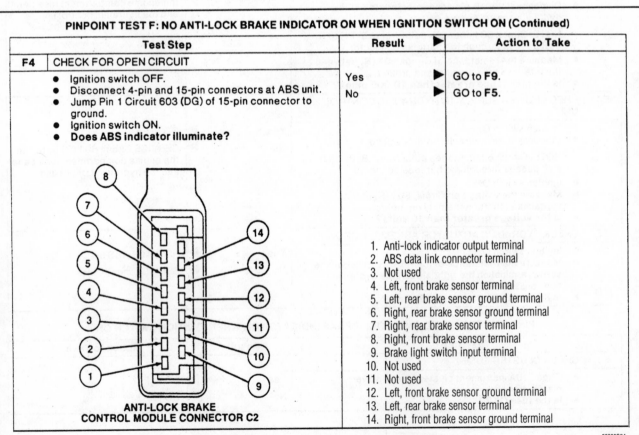

88239G04

PINPOINT TEST F: NO ANTI-LOCK BRAKE INDICATOR ON WHEN IGNITION SWITCH ON (Continued)

	Test Step	Result	▶	Action to Take
F6	CHECK ANTI-LOCK WARNING INDICATOR BULB			
	• Ignition switch OFF. • Remove anti-lock lamp bulb. • Measure the resistance between the two bulb terminals. • **Is resistance approximately 15 ohms?**	Yes No	▶ ▶	GO to **F7**. SERVICE Circuit 640 (R / Y) wire between instrument cluster and power distribution box.
F7	CHECK CIRCUIT 603 (Y) BETWEEN INSTRUMENT CLUSTER AND ABS CONTROL MODULE JUMPER CONNECTOR			
	• Ignition switch OFF. Disconnect 4-pin and 15-pin connectors at the ABS unit. • Measure resistance between Pin 2 (Y) of the 4-pin connector and Pin 1 (DG) of the 15-pin connector. • **Is resistance less than 5 ohms?**	Yes No	▶ ▶	GO to **F8**. SERVICE Circuit 603 (Y) for open. NOTE: Circuit 603 changes color from DG to Y as it passes through the harness connector.
F8	CHECK CIRCUIT 603 (Y) BETWEEN INSTRUMENT CLUSTER AND ABS CONTROL MODULE			
	• Ignition switch OFF. NOTE: Circuit 603 changes color from DG to Y as it passes through the harness connector. • Measure resistance between Pin 2 (Y) of the 4-pin connector and Pin 5 (DG) of the instrument cluster connector. • **Is resistance less than 5 ohms?**	Yes No	▶ ▶	GO to **F9**. SERVICE Circuit 603 (Y) for open.
F9	CHECK ABS CONTROL MODULE GROUND			
	• Ignition switch OFF. • Measure resistance between Pin 1 (BK) of the 4-pin connector and ground. • **Is the resistance less than 5 ohms?**	Yes No	▶ ▶	SERVICE Circuit 57 (BK) for open. REPLACE anti-lock brake control module

**ANTI-LOCK BRAKE CONTROL MODULE
CONNECTOR POWER JUMPER HARNESS C3**

1. Ground terminal
2. Anti-lock indicator output terminal
3. Ignition switch RUN power terminal
4. Battery power terminal
5. Connector guide pin

88239G03

PINPOINT TEST G: ANTI-LOCK BRAKE WARNING INDICATOR ON AFTER ENGINE STARTS (WITH ANTI-LOCK BRAKE WARNING INDICATOR OFF)

	Test Step	Result	▶	Action to Take
G1	CHECK ABS INDICATOR LAMP • Ignition switch OFF. • Disconnect 4-pin and 15-pin connectors at anti-lock brake control module. • Ignition switch ON. • **Does ABS indicator illuminate?**	Yes No	▶ ▶	GO to **G2**. REPLACE anti-lock brake control module.
G2	CHECK CIRCUIT BETWEEN INSTRUMENT CLUSTER AND ABS UNIT • Ignition switch OFF. • Disconnect 4-pin and 15-pin connectors at ABS unit. • Remove instrument cluster. • Disconnect 16-pin instrument cluster. • Measure resistance between Pin 5 of the 16-pin connector and ground. • **Is resistance less than 5 ohms?**	Yes No	▶ ▶	SERVICE short in Circuit 603 (DG) wire to ground. REPLACE anti-lock brake control module.

88239G02

Anti-lock Brake System Control Module (ABS-CM)

➡ Whenever service is performed on the Hydraulic Control Unit (HCU), a specific procedure must be performed to bleed the system to ensure that no air is trapped in the HCU. To perform this procedure, the New Generation Start (NGS) Tester, or an equivalent brake tool, is necessary.

REMOVAL & INSTALLATION

▶ **See Figure 39**

➡ The ABS-CM and HCU are one assembly.

1. Remove the HCU from the vehicle.
2. Remove the Torx® head screws from the black plastic cover on the HCU.
3. Disengage the 15-pin and 4-pin connectors.
4. Loosen the Torx® head retaining screws, then separate the ABS-CM from the HCU.

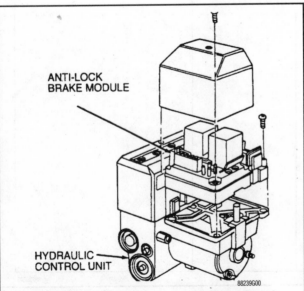

ANTI-LOCK BRAKE MODULE

HYDRAULIC CONTROL UNIT

88239G00

Fig. 39 Exploded view of the Anti-lock Brake System Control Module (ABS-CM) mounting

To install:
5. Carefully slide the ABS-CM down onto the HCU, over the ground post.
6. Install the retaining screws and tighten them until snug.
7. Install the 15-pin and 4-pin connectors, then position the plastic cover over the ABS-CM.
8. Install the cover retaining screw.
9. Install the HCU in the engine compartment.

Hydraulic Control Unit (HCU)

➡ Whenever service is performed on the Hydraulic Control Unit (HCU), a specific procedure must be performed to bleed the system to ensure that no air is trapped in the HCU. To perform this procedure, the New Generation Start (NGS) Tester, or an equivalent brake tool, is necessary.

REMOVAL & INSTALLATION

▶ **See Figure 40**

✳✳ CAUTION

Brake fluid contains polyglycol ethers and polyglycols. Avoid contact with the eyes and wash your hands thoroughly after handling brake fluid. If you do get brake fluid in your eyes, flush your eyes with clean, running water for 15 minutes. If eye irritation persists, or if you have taken brake fluid internally, IMMEDIATELY seek medical assistance.

1. Disconnect the negative battery cable.
2. Remove any components necessary for access to the HCU, located at the bottom of the right-hand side of the radiator in the engine compartment.
3. Disengage the two wiring harness connectors from the HCU.
4. Detach the five brake tubes from the HCU.
5. Detach the HCU ground wire.
6. Loosen the four mounting bolts, then remove the HCU from the vehicle.
7. If necessary, separate the mounting bracket from the HCU by removing the three attaching nuts.

To install:
8. If applicable, position the mounting bracket on the HCU and install the retaining nuts. Tighten the nuts to 88–176 inch lbs. (10–20 Nm).

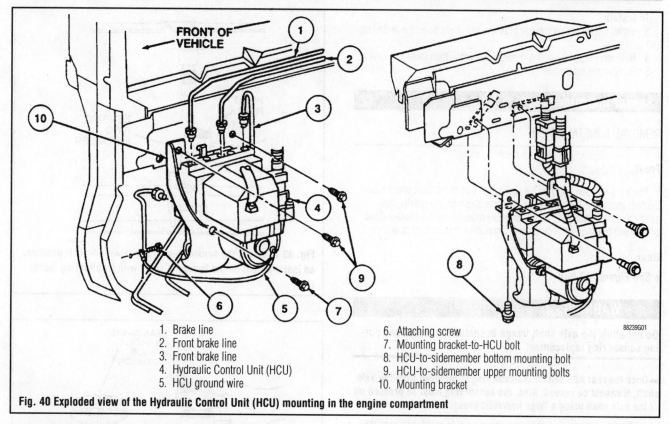

1. Brake line
2. Front brake line
3. Front brake line
4. Hydraulic Control Unit (HCU)
5. HCU ground wire

6. Attaching screw
7. Mounting bracket-to-HCU bolt
8. HCU-to-sidemember bottom mounting bolt
9. HCU-to-sidemember upper mounting bolts
10. Mounting bracket

88239G01

Fig. 40 Exploded view of the Hydraulic Control Unit (HCU) mounting in the engine compartment

9. Position the HCU in the engine compartment and install the mounting bolts. Tighten the bottom bolts to 88–124 inch lbs. (10–14 Nm). Tighten the remaining bolts to 160–230 inch lbs. (18–26 Nm).
10. Attach the HCU ground wire and attaching screw. Tighten the screw until snug.
11. Reattach the five brake lines to the unit, then connect the negative battery cable.
12. Bleed the brake system, as described later in this section.

Speed Sensors

REMOVAL & INSTALLATION

➡This procedure applies to the sensors, not the toothed sensor indicator rings.

Front

1. Loosen all of the front wheel lug nuts ½ turn to break them free.
2. Apply the parking brake, block the rear wheels, then raise and safely support the front of the vehicle on jackstands.
3. Remove the front wheel(s).
4. Remove the ABS sensor mounting bolt, and pull the sensor away from the wheel spindle.
5. Remove the ABS sensor cable bracket bolts and brackets, then remove the cable bracket-to-inner wheel well screws.
6. Push the cable grommet through the wheel well opening.
7. Disengage the ABS sensor wiring harness connector in the engine compartment, then remove the harness retainer.
8. Remove the front ABS sensor from the vehicle.
To install:
9. Position the sensor in the vehicle, then reattach the wiring harness retainer to it.
10. Engage the electrical wiring harness connector to the sensor.
11. Install the wheel well grommet, position the cable on the inner wheel well and install the retaining screws until snug.

12. Position the sensor brackets on the strut, then install the mounting bolts.
13. Position the sensor on the wheel spindle and install the retaining bolt. Tighten the bolt to 124–133 inch lbs. (11–15 Nm).
14. Install the front wheel(s) and lower the vehicle.

Rear

▶ See Figure 41

1. Block the front wheels securely, then raise and safely support the rear of the vehicle on jackstands.
2. Remove the ABS sensor mounting bolt, then disengage the sensor wiring harness connector and separate the sensor from the rear brake caliper.

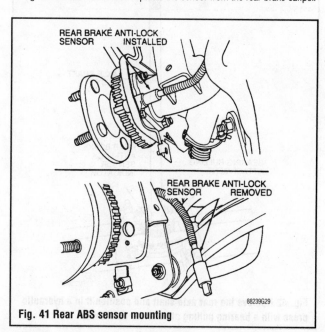

REAR BRAKE ANTI-LOCK SENSOR INSTALLED

REAR BRAKE ANTI-LOCK SENSOR REMOVED

88239G29

Fig. 41 Rear ABS sensor mounting

To install:

3. Install the sensor on the rear brake caliper, and tighten the mounting bolt until snug.

4. Reattach the sensor wiring harness connector, then lower the vehicle.

5. Remove the front wheel blocks.

Sensor Indicator Ring

REMOVAL & INSTALLATION

Front

The front ABS sensor rings are an integral part of the front wheel bearing/hub assembly. The ring cannot be separated from the bearing/hub assembly and, if faulty, the entire assembly must be replaced with a good one. Wheel bearing/hub removal and installation is presented in Section 8.

Rear

♦ **See Figures 42 thru 47**

☼ WARNING

Do not allow the axle shaft flange to contact the press bed during sensor ring replacement.

➡ Once the rear ABS sensor indicator ring is removed from the axle shaft, it cannot be reused. Also, the sensor ring must be pressed off of the axle shaft using a large hydraulic press.

1. Remove the rear axle shaft from the same side of the vehicle as the sensor ring needing to be removed.

2. Position the axle shaft in a hydraulic press, as indicated in the accompanying illustration, then press the sensor ring off of the shaft.

3. Discard the sensor ring.

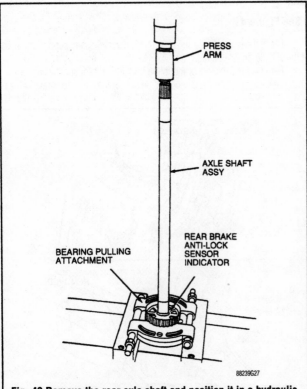

Fig. 42 Remove the rear axle shaft and position it in a hydraulic press with a bearing pulling attachment as shown

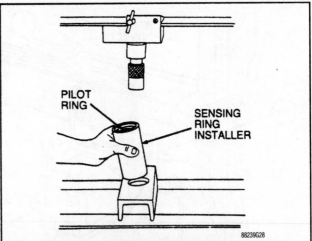

Fig. 43 To install the sensor ring on the axle shaft, first position an installer tool on the hydraulic press with its pilot ring facing up

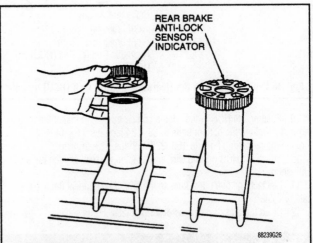

Fig. 44 Place the sensor ring on the installer tool in the orientation shown—the side of the sensor ring with a lip should face down

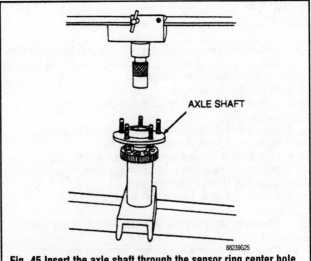

Fig. 45 Insert the axle shaft through the sensor ring center hole until it rests on the sensor ring . . .

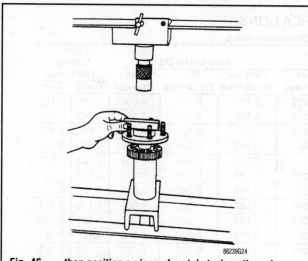

Fig. 46 . . . then position a piece of metal stock on the axle shaft flange as shown

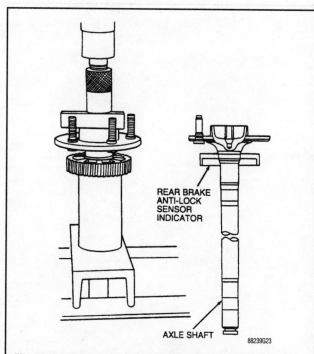

Fig. 47 Use the hydraulic press to drive the axle shaft into the sensor ring to the proper depth (1.25–1.35 in./3.18–3.43cm)

To install:

4. Position Ford Sensing Ring Installer T89P-20202-A, or equivalent, on the press with the pilot ring facing up.

5. Position the new sensor ring on the installer tool, as indicated in the accompanying illustration. Ensure that it is oriented correctly.

6. Insert the inner end of the axle shaft through the sensor ring until it rests on the ring.

7. Position a flat piece of steel on the axle shaft flange, as shown in the illustration.

8. Press the axle shaft into the sensor ring until the outer face of the sensor ring is 1.25–1.35 in. (3.18–3.43cm) from the outer face of the axle shaft flange.

9. Install the axle shaft.

Bleeding the ABS System

Whenever service is performed to the Hydraulic Control Unit, a specific procedure must be performed to bleed the system to ensure that no air is trapped in the HCU.

➡**To perform this procedure, the New Generation Start (NGS) Tester, or an equivalent brake tool, is necessary.**

1. Bleed the entire hydraulic system using the same procedure used for a non-ABS system. (Refer to the brake bleeding procedure, earlier in this section.)

2. Attach the NGS tester to the underdash serial link connector, as though retrieving engine trouble codes.

3. Turn the ignition switch to the **RUN** position.

4. Follow the instructions on the NGS screen. Choose the correct vehicle and model year, then go to the "Diagnostic Data Link" menu item. Choose the ABS module, then "Function Tests" and "Service Bleed."

5. The NGS will instruct you to depress the brake pedal. Ensure that you push hard on the pedal. The pedal must be held down for approximately 5 seconds while the NGS opens the outlet valves in the HCU. When the outlet valves open, the brake pedal should immediately drop; make sure to depress the brake pedal all the way to the floor. This is VERY important to do!

6. The NGS will then prompt you to release the pedal. After the pedal is released, the NGS will run the ABS hydraulic pump motor for approximately 15 seconds.

7. Repeat Step 5 to ensure that all air has been flushed from the HCU. Upon completion, the NGS will show the "Service Bleed Procedure Completed" message.

8. Once again, bleed the rest of the hydraulic system as for a non-ABS model.

BRAKE SPECIFICATIONS
All measurements in inches unless noted

Year	Model	Master Cylinder Bore	Front Brake Disc			Rear Brake Disc			Min. Lining Thickness	
			Original Thickness	Min. Thickness	Max. Run-out	Original Thickness	Min. Thickness	Max. Run-out	Front	Rear
1994	Mustang	1.060	1.030	0.970	0.002	0.550	0.500	0.002	0.040	0.123
	Mustang Cobra	1.000	1.100	1.040	0.002	0.550	0.500	0.002	0.040	0.123
1995	Mustang	1.060	1.030	0.970	0.002	0.550	0.500	0.002	0.040	0.123
	Mustang Cobra	1.000	1.100	1.040	0.002	0.550	0.500	0.002	0.040	0.123
1996	Mustang ①	1.060	1.030	0.970	0.001	0.550	0.500	0.002	0.125	0.123
	Mustang ②	1.000	1.030	0.970	0.002	0.550	0.500	0.002	0.125	0.123
	Mustang Cobra	1.000	1.100	1.040	0.001	0.710	0.660	0.002	0.125	0.123
1997	Mustang ①	1.060	1.030	0.970	0.001	0.550	0.500	0.002	0.125	0.123
	Mustang ②	1.000	1.030	0.970	0.002	0.550	0.500	0.002	0.125	0.123
	Mustang Cobra	1.000	1.100	1.040	0.001	0.710	0.660	0.002	0.125	0.123
1998	Mustang ①	1.060	1.030	0.970	0.001	0.550	0.500	0.002	0.125	0.123
	Mustang ②	1.000	1.030	0.970	0.002	0.550	0.500	0.002	0.125	0.123
	Mustang Cobra	1.000	1.100	1.040	0.001	0.710	0.660	0.002	0.125	0.123

① 3.8L engine
② 4.6L SOHC engine

88239C01

10

BODY AND TRIM

EXTERIOR

Doors

REMOVAL & INSTALLATION

▶ See Figure 1

➡An assistant is necessary to safely remove the door from the vehicle.

1. Open the door.
2. Using a floor jack with a soft-faced pad or folded towel on the jack support pad, slightly support the door.
3. Disengage any applicable vehicle wiring harness connectors from the door harness connectors.
4. If the original door is going to be reinstalled, matchmark the hinges to the door.
5. Remove the hinge-to-door retaining bolts, then carefully lift the door away from the vehicle.
6. If the front door is going to be replaced with another door, transfer the following components to the new door:
   - Front door trim panel and watershield
   - Door lock and door latch
   - Window regulator, equalizer arm bracket and door glass
   - Front door weatherstripping
   - Door wiring harness

To install:

7. Using your assistant's help, support the door on the padded floor jack and maneuver it close to the vehicle. Position the door so that the hinges can be placed on the door.
8. Install the door hinge retaining bolts finger-tight.
9. Align the door in the door opening as described later in this section.
10. Tighten the retaining bolts to 18–26 ft. lbs. (25–35 Nm).
11. Reattach all applicable wiring harness connectors.
12. Carefully close and open the door to ensure that it is properly aligned to the body.

ADJUSTMENT

▶ See Figure 2

The door hinges allow sufficient movement to correct most door misalignment conditions. The hinge mounting holes are elongated to provide such movement for door alignment.

➡Never attempt to remedy door misalignment by repositioning the latch striker.

1. Determine which hinge bolts are to be loosened and back them out just enough to allow movement.
2. Move the door safely by using a padded prybar to correct the misalignment condition. When the door is in the proper position, tighten the bolts to 18–26 ft. lbs. (25–35 Nm), then check door operation. There should be no binding or other interference when the door is either closed or opened.
3. Repeat Steps 1 and 2 until the door is properly aligned in the door opening. The gap between the edge of the door and the body should be uniform all around the door's perimeter.
4. Door closing adjustment can also be affected by the position of the lock striker plate. Loosen the striker plate bolts and move the striker plate just enough to permit proper closing and latching/locking of the door.

➡On convertible models, the quarter glass may need adjusting to be properly aligned with the roof rail and vertical weatherstripping. Refer to the door glass removal and installation procedure later in this section.

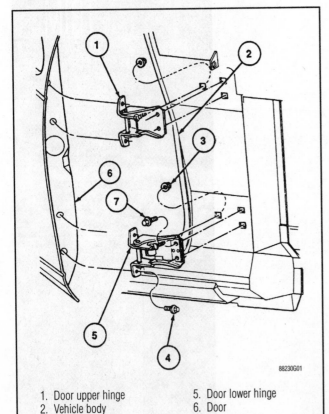

1. Door upper hinge
2. Vehicle body
3. Nut and washer
4. Bolt and washer
5. Door lower hinge
6. Door
7. Mounting bolt

88230G01

Fig. 1 Unfasten the door-to-hinge bolts, then remove the hinges by unfastening the hinge-to-body bolts

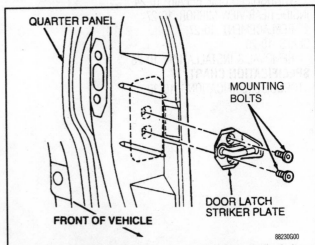

QUARTER PANEL

MOUNTING BOLTS

DOOR LATCH STRIKER PLATE

FRONT OF VEHICLE

88230G00

Fig. 2 To adjust the latch striker, loosen the two mounting bolts until the striker plate can be moved to the proper position, then tighten the bolts to 16–22 ft. lbs. (21–29 Nm)

Hood

REMOVAL & INSTALLATION

◗ **See Figure 3**

1. Open and support the hood.

➡ **If the vehicle does not contain a built-in support rod, you can use an old broom handle or other long piece of wood to prop open the hood, but first wrap clean rags or padding around the wood's ends to protect the vehicle from scratches or chips.**

2. Position fenders covers or old blankets over both fenders to protect the paint, in case the hood accidentally strikes the painted surface of the fenders.

3. It may be necessary to remove the underhood insulation pad to access the underhood lamp wiring harness. To remove this pad, pry the plastic retainers out of the hood, then pull the pad off of the underside of the hood. The old plastic retainers can be reused if they are not damaged during removal; otherwise, new ones can be purchased at many automotive parts retailers, or from your local Ford dealership parts department.

4. Detach the hood ground strap by removing the retaining bolt.

5. Disengage the underhood lamp wiring harness connector.

6. Matchmark the hood-to-hinge positions to make aligning the hood easier during installation.

7. Have an assistant support the hood while you remove the hinge-to-hood nuts.

✳✳ WARNING

An assistant is needed to keep the hood from sliding back and damaging the windshield once the nuts are removed. Positioning a folded-up old blanket on the bottom 10–12 in. (25–30cm) of the windshield may help protect it in the event that the hood slips and hits it.

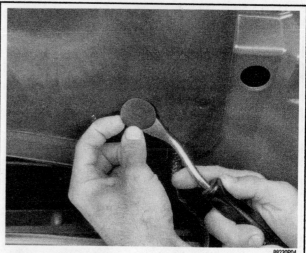

To remove the hood, first remove all plastic retainers and the underhood insulator pad . . .

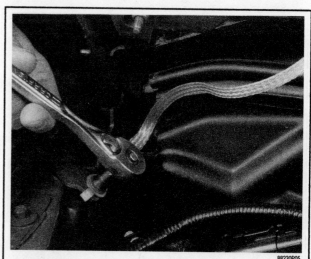

. . . then disconnect the hood ground strap by removing the attaching bolt

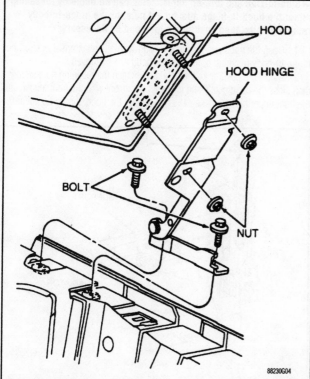

Fig. 3 Exploded view of the hinge-to-hood and hinge-to-body mounting

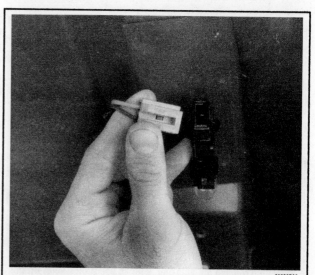

Disengage the underhood lamp wiring harness connector . . .

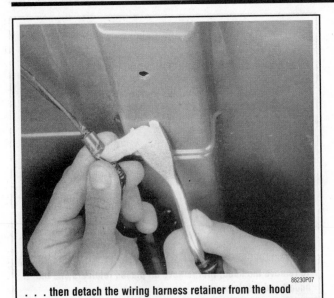

. . . then detach the wiring harness retainer from the hood

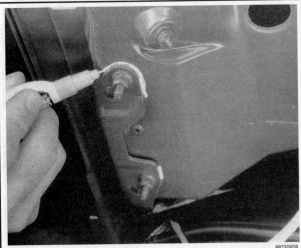

Before loosening the hood-to-hinge retaining nuts, matchmark the hinge positions on the hood . . .

. . . then remove the nuts and, with an assistant's help, lift the hood off of the vehicle

8. Once the nuts are removed, carefully lift the hood (with the help of your assistant) and position it aside. You may wish to place the hood on a soft, protective surface such as carpet remnants or some clean rags.

To install:

9. With the aid of your helper, position the hood on the vehicle so that the hinge-to-hood mounting studs align with the holes in the hinges.

10. Have your helper hold the hood steady while you install the retaining nuts finger-tight.

11. If the original hood is being installed, position the hood so that the hinge matchmarks are aligned. If a replacement hood is being installed, align it with the front fenders and the upper, front bumper assembly. The gap around the hood should be uniform in width.

➡**If, after the original hood is installed and the matchmarks are aligned, the gap around the hood is not uniform, adjust the hood until it is.**

12. Once the hood is properly aligned, tighten the hood-to-hinge retaining nuts to 88–124 inch lbs. (10–14 Nm).

13. Close and open the hood several times slowly and carefully to ensure that there is not binding or interference between the hood, the fenders and the upper bumper panel. If there is interference or binding, realign the hood until these conditions no longer exist.

14. Open the hood and support it with the hood support rod or a fabricated, padded prop rod. Reattach the hood ground strap and the underhood lamp wiring harness.

15. With the help of an assistant, position the insulator pad on the underside of the hood so that the mounting holes are aligned. Insert the plastic retainers through the pad and into the hood sheet metal until fully engaged. If any of the old retainers are damaged so that they will not hold the pad securely against the hood, purchase and install new retainers.

16. If necessary, adjust the hood latch by loosening the attaching bolts and moving it accordingly.

ALIGNMENT

▶ **See Figure 4**

➡**Side-to-side and fore-aft adjustments can be made by loosening either the hood-to-hinge attachment nuts, or the hinge-to-body retaining bolts, then positioning the hood as necessary.**

1. Open the hood and loosen the hood-to-hinge attachment nuts or the hinge-to-body retaining bolts until the hood can be moved.

2. Adjust the position of the hood and tighten the retaining nuts snugly, then close the hood gently and check its alignment with the front fenders and the front upper bumper panel. The gap around the hood should be uniform.

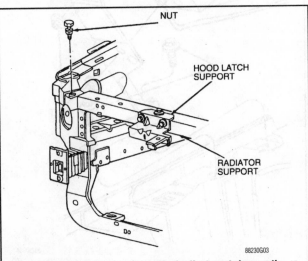

Fig. 4 To fine-tune the hood's vertical adjustment, loosen the jam nuts and loosen or tighten the rubber hood bumpers

3. Repeat Steps 1 and 2 until the hood is properly positioned, then tighten either the hood-to-hinge nuts to 88–124 inch lbs. (10–14 Nm), or the hinge-to-body bolts to 142–239 inch lbs. (16–27 Nm).

➡**The hood's vertical fit can be adjusted by raising or lowering the front hood bumpers.**

4. Inspect the level of the front of the hood in relation to the fender level. If the hood is not flush with the fenders, open the hood. Adjust the front bumpers as follows:

    a. Loosen the lower jam nut on each of the two front bumpers.

    b. Loosen the two front hood bumpers to raise the front of the hood, or tighten them to lower the front of the hood.

    c. Close the hood and inspect it for a flush fit with the fenders.

    d. If further aligning is necessary, open the hood and repeat Steps 4b and 4c until the hood is properly adjusted.

    e. Tighten the bumper lower jam nuts until secure.

5. Close the hood once again to ensure that it is properly adjusted side-to-side, fore-and-aft, and up-and-down. Realign the hood, if necessary.

Trunk Lid

REMOVAL & INSTALLATION

◆ **See Figure 5**

➡**The aid of an assistant is necessary to safely lift the trunk lid off of the vehicle.**

1. Open and support the trunk lid. You can use part of an old broom handle or other 3–4 ft. (1m) long piece of wood.

2. Position fender covers or old blankets over both rear fenders to protect the paint in case the trunk lid accidentally strikes the painted surface of the fenders.

3. If equipped, label and disengage the inside trunk lid lamp wiring harness connector.

4. Matchmark the trunk lid-to-hinge positions to make aligning the trunk lid easier during installation.

5. Remove both trunk lid support cylinders as follows:

    a. At the lower end of the support cylinder, use a small pick or prytool to disengage the retaining clip by pulling it out from the cylinder attachment joint housing.

    b. Detach the lower end of the cylinder by pulling the cylinder end away from the mounting ball until it disengages.

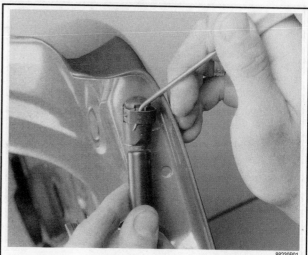

To remove the support cylinders, use a pick or prytool to disengage the cylinder's retaining clips . . .

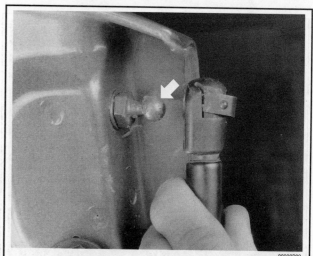

. . . and pull the cylinder away from the upper and lower mounting ball studs (arrow) . . .

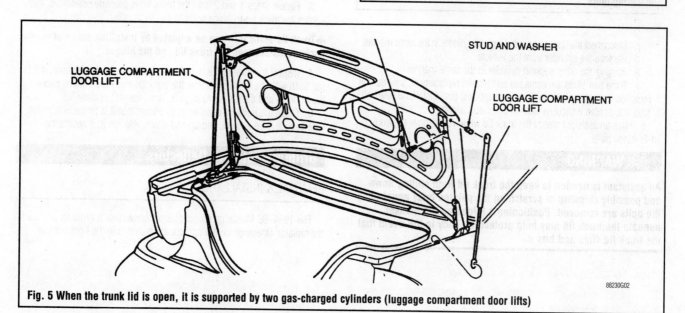

Fig. 5 When the trunk lid is open, it is supported by two gas-charged cylinders (luggage compartment door lifts)

LUGGAGE COMPARTMENT DOOR LIFT

STUD AND WASHER

LUGGAGE COMPARTMENT DOOR LIFT

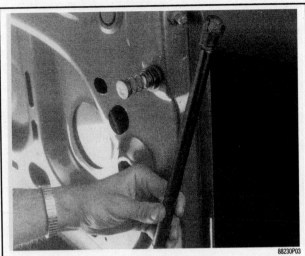

... then remove the cylinder from the vehicle—remove the other cylinder in the same manner

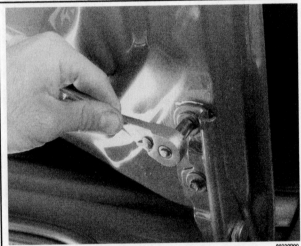

After matchmarking the hinges to the trunk lid, remove the mounting bolts

c. Disconnect the upper end of the support cylinder in the same manner.

d. Remove the cylinder from the vehicle.

e. Remove the other support cylinder in the same manner.

f. If the ball studs are damaged and require replacement, they can be removed by loosening them like a conventional bolt. Install the new ball stud and tighten it securely with an open-end wrench.

6. Have an assistant steady the trunk lid while you remove the trunk lid-to-hinge bolts.

✳✳ WARNING

An assistant is needed to keep the trunk lid from sliding down and possibly chipping or scratching the painted body panel once the bolts are removed. Positioning a folded-up old blanket beneath the trunk lid may help protect the body in the event that the trunk lid slips and hits it.

7. Once the bolts are removed, carefully lift the trunk lid (with the help or your assistant) and position it aside. You may wish to place it on a soft, protective surface such as carpet remnants or clean rags.

To install:

8. With the aid of your helper, position the trunk lid on the vehicle so that the hinge-to-hood mounting holes are aligned.

9. Ask your helper to hold the trunk lid steady while you install the retaining bolts finger-tight.

10. If the original trunk lid is being installed, position it so that the hinge matchmarks are aligned. If a replacement trunk lid is being installed, align it with the rear fenders and the upper, rear bumper assembly. The gap around the trunk lid should be uniform in width.

➡️**If, after the original trunk lid is installed and the matchmarks are aligned, the perimeter gap is not uniform, adjust the trunk lid until it is.**

11. Once the trunk lid is properly aligned, tighten the trunk lid-to-hinge nuts to 44–75 inch lbs. (5–8 Nm).

12. Close and open the trunk lid several times slowly and carefully to ensure that there is not binding or interference between the trunk lid, the fenders and the upper bumper panel. If there is interference or binding, realign the trunk lid until these conditions no longer exist.

13. Open the trunk lid and support it with the piece of wood used earlier. Reattach the trunk lid support cylinders as follows:

a. Position the upper end of the support cylinder over the mounting ball stud on the side of the trunk lid, then press it toward the trunk lid until it snaps in place. Push the retaining clip in until it is fully seated.

b. Position the lower end of the support cylinder over the mounting ball stud on the side of the trunk opening, then depress it until it snaps in place. Push the retaining clip in until it is fully seated.

c. Install the other support cylinder in the same manner.

14. If applicable, reconnect the inside trunk lid lamp wiring harness.

ALIGNMENT

➡️**Side-to-side and fore-aft adjustments can be made by loosening the trunk lid-to-hinge attachment bolts.**

1. Open the trunk lid and loosen the hinge-to-lid mounting bolts until the trunk lid can be moved.

2. Adjust the position of the trunk lid and tighten the mounting bolts snugly, then close the trunk lid gently and check its alignment with the fenders and the upper bumper panel. The gap around the perimeter of the trunk lid should be uniform.

3. Repeat Steps 1 and 2 until the trunk lid is properly positioned, then tighten the trunk lid-to-hinge bolts to 44–75 inch lbs. (5–8 Nm).

➡️**Trunk lid vertical fit can be adjusted by installing shims of varying thicknesses between the trunk lid and the hinges.**

4. Inspect the level of the trunk lid in relation to the fender level. If it is not flush with the fenders, remove the trunk lid and install shims between the trunk lid and the hinges to align it. Then, install the trunk lid.

5. Close the trunk lid once again to ensure that it is properly adjusted side-to-side, fore-and-aft, and up-and-down. Realign it, if necessary.

Grille/Radiator Air Deflectors

REMOVAL & INSTALLATION

The 1994–98 Mustangs do not utilize a conventional grille for air flow to the radiator. Openings for the radiator are provided in the front bumper cover above and below the front bumper. Air deflectors surrounding the radiator channel air through the radiator. Deflector removal and installation is covered here.

Side and Upper Deflectors

1. Open the hood and secure it with the support rod.
2. Remove the upper radiator sight shield by loosening the plastic screws, then lifting the shield up and off of the radiator upper support.
3. Disengage the deflector shield push-pins from the radiator support, then remove the air deflectors.

To install:

4. Position the deflectors in the vehicle and secure them in place by engaging all of the push-pin retainers.
5. Install the upper radiator sight shield, making sure that the plastic anchors are properly inserted in their mounting holes. Tighten the plastic screws until snug; do not overtighten these screws, since they are only plastic and will break easily if given the chance.
6. Close the hood.

Lower and Front Deflectors

1. Apply the parking brake, block the rear wheels, then raise and safely support the front of the vehicle on jackstands.
2. Disengage the four plastic rivets holding the lower radiator air deflectors onto the support, then remove the deflectors from the vehicle.

➡**Some of the rivets can be removed by prying the retaining pin out of the center, then removing the pin and anchor. The other type of rivets must be broken to remove them, so new rivets will have to be installed.**

3. Remove the front deflector by detaching it from the lip on the front edge of the radiator.

To install:

4. Position the front deflector in the vehicle, then secure it by engaging it onto the radiator lip.
5. Hold the lower deflectors against the support and press new plastic rivets through the mounting holes until properly engaged.
6. Lower the vehicle and remove the wheel blocks.

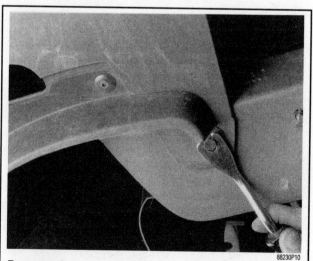

88230P10

To remove the anchor-type retainers, pry the center pin out of the anchor . . .

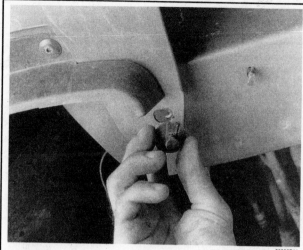

88230P11

. . . then remove the anchor and pin together from the body panels

Outside Mirror

REMOVAL & INSTALLATION

♦ See Figure 6

➡**Outside mirrors that are frozen must be thawed prior to adjustment. Do not attempt to free-up the mirror by pressing on the glass assembly.**

1. Disconnect the negative battery cable.
2. Remove the door trim panel.
3. Use a small plastic or wooden tool to pry the inside mirror cover off of the door.
4. Disengage the mirror assembly's wiring connector. Remove the necessary wiring guides/retainer clips.
5. Remove the three mirror retaining nuts, then remove the mirror while guiding the wiring and connector through the hole in the door.

To install:

6. Install the mirror assembly by routing the connector and wiring through the hole in the door, then secure the mirror on the door with the three retaining nuts. Tighten the retaining nuts to 53–71 inch lbs. (6–8 Nm).
7. Engage the mirror wiring connector and install the wiring guides.
8. Install the inside mirror cover.
9. Install the door trim panel.
10. Connect the negative battery cable.

Antenna

REMOVAL & INSTALLATION

♦ See Figure 7

1. Remove the radio and disconnect the antenna cable at the radio by pulling it straight out of the unit.
2. Remove the right-hand cowl side trim panel.

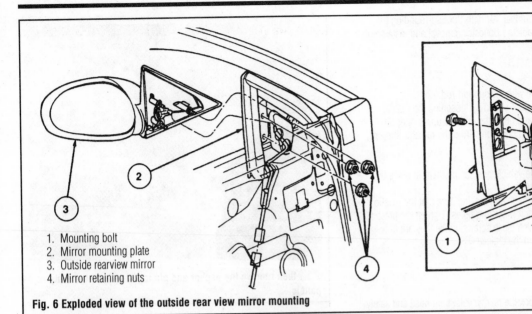

1. Mounting bolt
2. Mirror mounting plate
3. Outside rearview mirror
4. Mirror retaining nuts

Fig. 6 Exploded view of the outside rear view mirror mounting

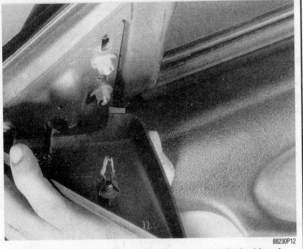

To remove the outside rear view mirror, remove the inside mirror cover . . .

. . . then loosen the retaining nuts and separate the mirror from the door

3. Remove the antenna cable clips holding the antenna cable to the heater assembly, and disconnect the two antenna cable halves near the heater assembly.

4. Remove the antenna cap and antenna base retaining screws, then pull the cable through the holes in the door hinge pillar and fender. Remove the antenna base and two cable halves.

To install:

5. With the right-hand door open, position the antenna assembly in the fender opening, put the gasket in position on the antenna and install the antenna base to the fender.

6. Pull the antenna lead through the door hinge pillar opening. Seat the grommet by pulling the cable from inside the vehicle.

7. Connect the two antenna cable halves, and route the cable behind the heater assembly. Attach the locating clips.

8. Connect the antenna lead to the rear of the radio, then install the radio.

9. Install the right side cowl trim panel.

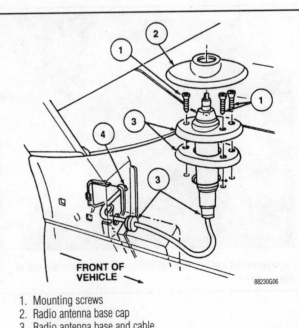

1. Mounting screws
2. Radio antenna base cap
3. Radio antenna base and cable
4. Antenna cable (to radio assembly)

Fig. 7 Exploded view of the antenna and base mounting

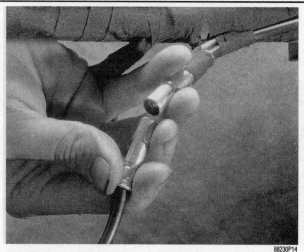

Detach the two cable halves at the junction near the heater assembly

Fenders

REMOVAL & INSTALLATION

▶ See Figures 8 and 9

1. Open the hood.
2. Remove the front bumper cover assembly, as follows:
   a. If equipped, drill out the four license plate rivets.
   b. Remove the fog lamp assemblies.
   c. Remove the two nuts and one bolt retaining the front bumper to each front fender.
   d. Remove the four screws retaining the front bumper to each front fender splash shield.
   e. Remove the push-pins attaching the front bumper cover to the radiator support.
   f. Remove the two upper blind rivets holding the bumper cover to the radiator grille opening panel reinforcement, then remove the front bumper cover.
3. Remove the headlamp and parking lamp assemblies.
4. Remove the front fender splash shield.

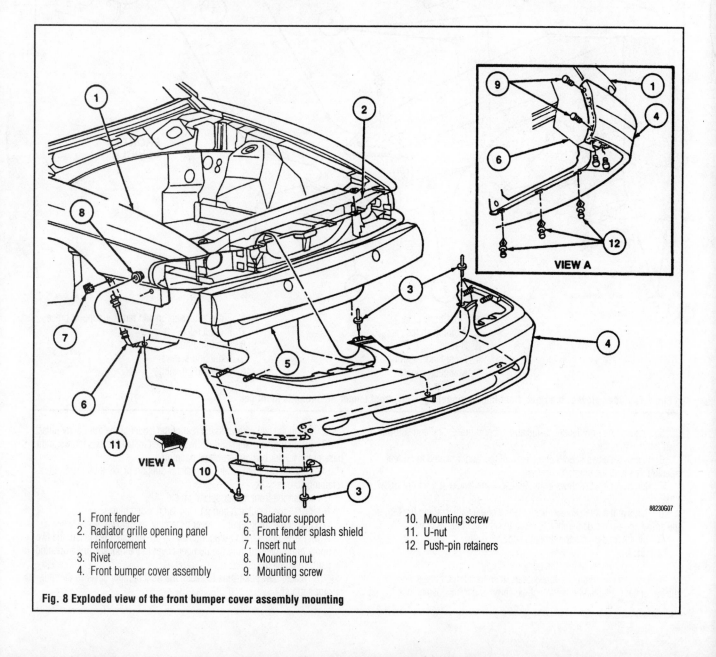

1. Front fender	5. Radiator support	10. Mounting screw
2. Radiator grille opening panel reinforcement	6. Front fender splash shield	11. U-nut
	7. Insert nut	12. Push-pin retainers
3. Rivet	8. Mounting nut	
4. Front bumper cover assembly	9. Mounting screw	

Fig. 8 Exploded view of the front bumper cover assembly mounting

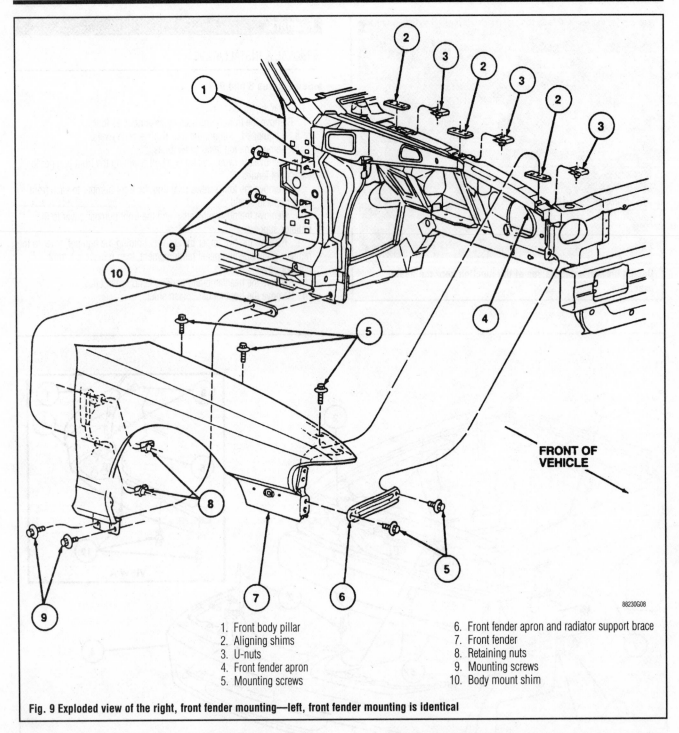

1. Front body pillar
2. Aligning shims
3. U-nuts
4. Front fender apron
5. Mounting screws
6. Front fender apron and radiator support brace
7. Front fender
8. Retaining nuts
9. Mounting screws
10. Body mount shim

Fig. 9 Exploded view of the right, front fender mounting—left, front fender mounting is identical

5. Remove the front fender-to-radiator support brace retaining screws, then remove the brace.

6. Remove the two screws at the base of the fender behind the wheel opening. Remove the shim, if necessary.

7. Remove the two screws from the rear of the fender at the front body pillar.

8. Remove the three screws from the top of the fender, along the top of the apron and front sidemember. Remove the shims, if necessary.

9. Lift the fender up and off of the body.

To install:

10. Position the fender on the body.

11. Install aligning shims, if necessary, then install the three screws in the top of the fender, along the top of the apron and front sidemember.

12. Install the two screws in the rear of the fender at the front body pillar.

13. Install aligning shims, if necessary, then install the two screws at the base of the fender behind the wheel opening.

14. Position the front fender-to-radiator support brace, then install the retaining screws.

15. Install the front fender splash shield.

16. Install the headlamp and parking lamp assemblies.

17. Install the front bumper cover assembly, as follows:

    a. Position the front bumper cover on the vehicle, then install the two upper blind rivets to hold the bumper cover to the radiator grille opening panel reinforcement.

    b. Install new push-pins to attach the front bumper cover to the radiator support.

c. Install the four screws to retain the front bumper to each front fender splash shield.

d. Install the two nuts and one bolt to retain the front bumper to each front fender.

e. Install the fog lamp assemblies.

f. If equipped, install four new license plate rivets.

18. Close the hood and check the fender alignment in relation to the hood, door and front bumper assembly. The fender can be positioned by adding or subtracting aligning shims.

Convertible Top

MOTOR REPLACEMENT

1. Open the top to the fully raised position.
2. Disconnect the negative battery cable.
3. Remove the rear seat cushion and seat back.
4. Remove the rear quarter trim panels.
5. Disengage the folding top compartment trim from the 19 tackstrip nuts.
6. Unfasten the folding top motor upper and lower hoses from the holding clips. On vehicles equipped with Super Sound audio systems, unfasten the two amplifier clips.

7. Disengage the up and down relays from the motor plate.
8. Detach the connector from the vehicle wiring harness.
9. Unseat the folding top lift motor and plate grommets from the lift motor and plate kit.
10. Remove the cylinder rod shoulder screws, then remove the hydraulic bracket retaining nuts and the control link brackets.
11. Remove the hydraulic lift motor and plate kit, and the hydraulic cylinder from the vehicle.

To install:

12. Position the hydraulic cylinder, lift motor and plate kit in the vehicle.
13. Reinstall the control link brackets and hydraulic bracket retaining nuts. Install and tighten the cylinder shoulder screws.
14. Attach the plate grommets and folding top lift motor to the lift motor and plate kit.
15. Engage the motor connector to the vehicle wiring harness.
16. Install the up and down relays on the motor plate.
17. If equipped, fasten the two amplifier clips.
18. Attach the folding top motor upper and lower hoses to the holding clips.
19. Reattach the folding top compartment trim to the 19 tackstrips nuts.
20. Install the rear quarter trim panels, and the rear seat cushion and seat back.
21. Connect the negative battery cable.

INTERIOR

Instrument Panel and Pad

REMOVAL & INSTALLATION

♦ **See Figures 10, 11 and 12**

✳✳ CAUTION

Most vehicles are equipped with air bags. Before attempting to service air bag-equipped vehicles, be sure that the system is properly disarmed and all safety precautions are taken. Serious personal injury and vehicle damage could result if this note is disregarded. Refer to the Supplemental Restraint System coverage in Section 6 for air bag precautions and procedures.

➡**Removal and installation of the instrument panel is easier to perform with an assistant.**

1. Disconnect the negative battery cable, then the positive battery cable.
2. Disengage all underhood wiring harness connectors from the main wiring harness. Remove the rubber grommet seal from the dash panel, then feed the wiring harness through the firewall into the passenger compartment.

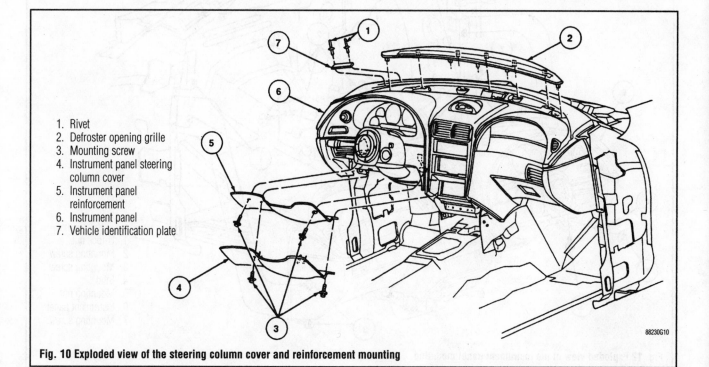

1. Rivet
2. Defroster opening grille
3. Mounting screw
4. Instrument panel steering column cover
5. Instrument panel reinforcement
6. Instrument panel
7. Vehicle identification plate

88230G10

Fig. 10 Exploded view of the steering column cover and reinforcement mounting

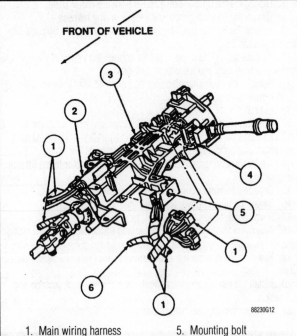

FRONT OF VEHICLE

88230G12

1. Main wiring harness
2. Shift solenoid
3. Steering column tube
4. Multi-function switch
5. Mounting bolt
6. Horn and speed control switch wiring harness

Fig. 11 Steering column component identification

3. Loosen the instrument panel steering column cover retaining screws and the instrument panel reinforcement screws, then remove the instrument panel steering column cover.

4. Remove the instrument panel reinforcement bolts, then remove the reinforcement.

5. Remove the floor console.

6. Lock the steering column to prevent it from turning.

7. Remove the steering column upper and lower shrouds, then disengage the wiring connectors from the ignition switch and shift lock actuator.

8. Remove the multi-function switch from the steering column.

9. Remove the steering column-to-instrument panel support mounting nuts, then carefully lower the steering column.

10. Remove the ignition switch and tilt column lever, if equipped.

11. Remove the right-hand and left-hand side cowl trim panels.

12. Remove the hood latch control handle and cable retaining screw, then detach the handle and cable from the instrument panel.

13. Disengage the wiring harness connectors at the lower right-hand and left-hand cowl sides.

14. Remove the instrument panel cowl side retaining bolts and nut (two bolts on the right-hand side and one bolt and one nut on the left-hand side).

15. Remove the instrument panel defroster grille, then loosen the three cowl top screw attachments.

16. Open the glove compartment fully, then detach the antenna lead cable halves and the wiring harness connector from the A/C or heater blower motor.

17. Pull the carpet up from the front floor pan to expose the diagnostic monitor. Disconnect the diagnostic monitor.

18. Remove the weatherstripping from the door opening.

19. Remove the four bolts holding the instrument panel to the floor bracket.

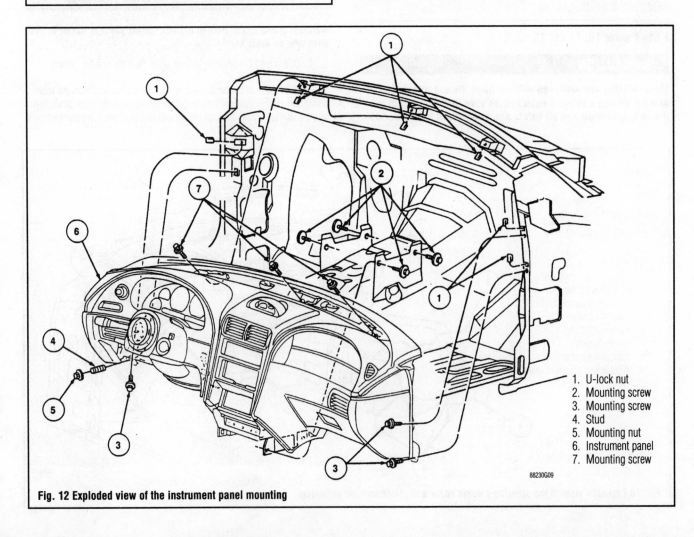

1. U-lock nut
2. Mounting screw
3. Mounting screw
4. Stud
5. Mounting nut
6. Instrument panel
7. Mounting screw

88230G09

Fig. 12 Exploded view of the instrument panel mounting

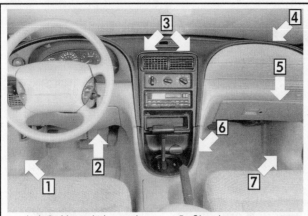

1. Left side cowl trim panel
2. Steering column cover
3. Defroster grille
4. Instrument panel
5. Glove box
6. Floor console
7. Right side cowl trim panel

88230P15

Instrument panel and related components

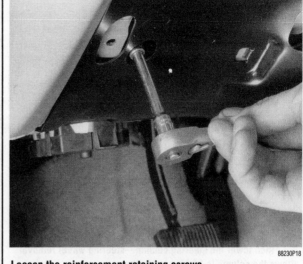

88230P18

Loosen the reinforcement retaining screws . . .

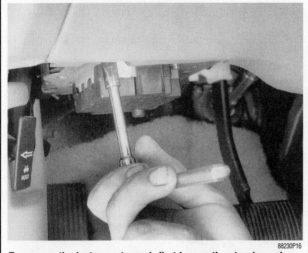

88230P16

To remove the instrument panel, first loosen the steering column cover retaining fasteners . . .

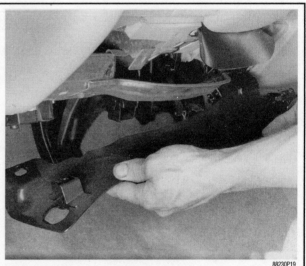

88230P19

. . . then remove the reinforcement from the instrument panel

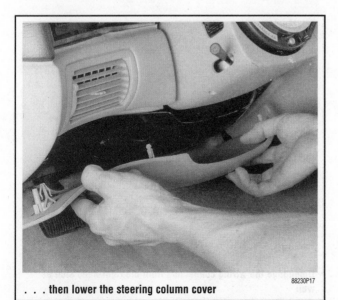

88230P17

. . . then lower the steering column cover

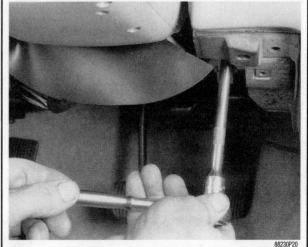

88230P20

Loosen the steering column-to-instrument panel mounting bolts . . .

. . . then lower the steering column—steering wheel removal allows the column to be lowered further

88230P21

. . . then pull the connectors out from the panel recess; loosen the connector retaining bolt

88230P24

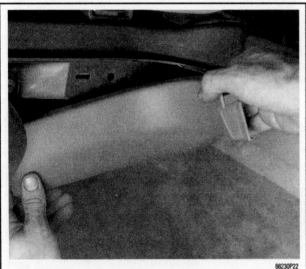

Remove the right and left side cowl trim panels

88230P22

. . . and separate the connector halves

88230P25

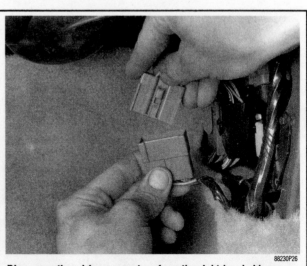

To disengage the left side wiring harness connectors, first remove the securing bolt . . .

88230P23

Disengage the wiring connectors from the right-hand side as well

88230P26

Remove the instrument panel's side mounting fasteners . . .

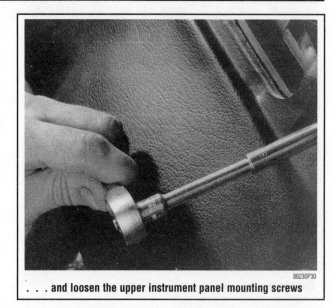

. . . and loosen the upper instrument panel mounting screws

Be sure not to miss the fastener located in the glove box opening

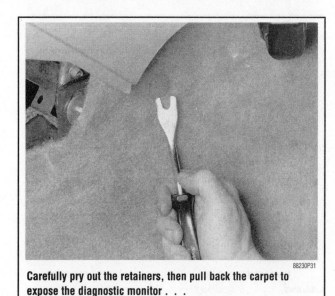

Carefully pry out the retainers, then pull back the carpet to expose the diagnostic monitor . . .

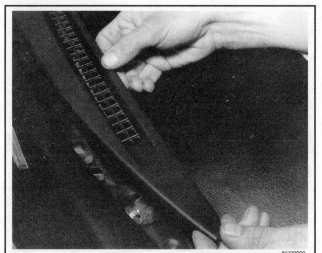

Remove the defroster grille from the top of the instrument panel . . .

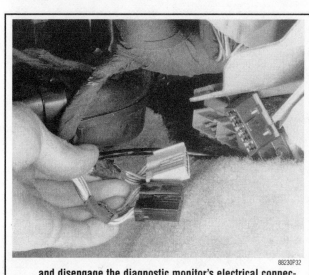

. . . and disengage the diagnostic monitor's electrical connectors

Remove the door opening weatherstripping . . .

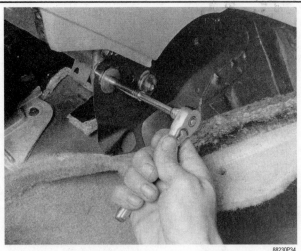

. . . then remove the four instrument panel lower mounting screws

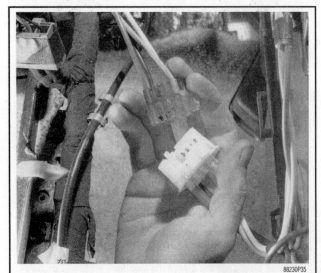

Detach the vacuum hose connector from the A/C housing hoses

With the help of an assistant, remove the instrument panel from the vehicle

20. If equipped, detach the pull cable from the A/C housing and the A/C vacuum harness connector.

21. Remove the instrument panel from the vehicle.

22. If a new instrument panel is being installed, transfer all components, wiring and hardware to the new panel.

To install:

23. Position the instrument panel in the vehicle.

24. If equipped, attach the A/C vacuum harness connector and the pull cable to the A/C housing.

25. Install and tighten the four instrument panel-to-floor bracket bolts to 68–91 inch lbs. (7–10 Nm).

26. Install the weatherstripping in the door opening.

27. Reattach the diagnostic monitor wiring, then position the carpeting back on the floor pan to hide the monitor.

28. Continue the installation in the reverse order of the removal procedure. Keep the following in mind during installation:

• Tighten the instrument panel mounting nut to 30–41 ft. lbs. (40–56 Nm).

• Tighten the instrument panel retaining screws to 68–91 inch lbs. (8–10 Nm).

• Tighten the steering column opening cover and reinforcement to 68–91 inch lbs. (8–10 Nm).

• Tighten the ignition switch connector to 15–19 inch lbs. (1.6–2.2 Nm).

29. Route the engine wiring harness through the firewall and install the opening grommet.

30. From the engine compartment, reattach all wiring harness connectors.

31. Connect the positive battery cable, and then the negative battery cable.

32. If so equipped, check for proper operation of the air bag indicator. Check for proper operation of all components.

Console

REMOVAL & INSTALLATION

▶ **See Figure 13**

1. Disconnect the negative battery cable.

2. Use a prytool to carefully remove the console finish panel.

3. Disengage the cigarette lighter wiring harness connector.

4. Remove the two rubber bumpers, two screws and storage compartment from the console.

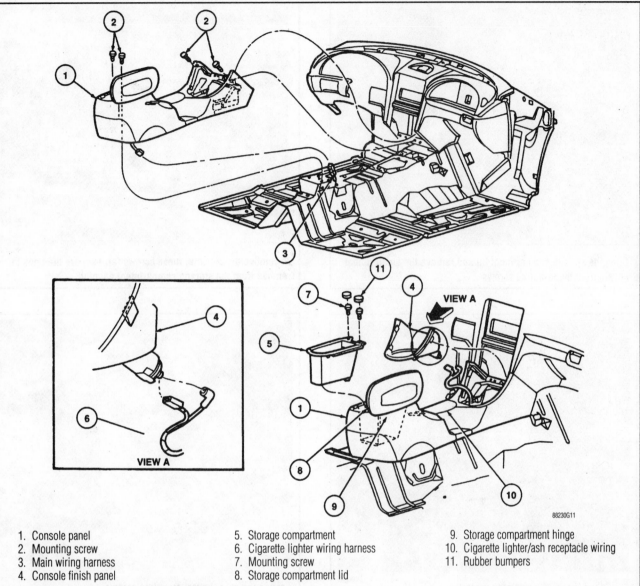

1. Console panel
2. Mounting screw
3. Main wiring harness
4. Console finish panel
5. Storage compartment
6. Cigarette lighter wiring harness
7. Mounting screw
8. Storage compartment lid
9. Storage compartment hinge
10. Cigarette lighter/ash receptacle wiring
11. Rubber bumpers

Fig. 13 Exploded view of the console mounting

To remove the console, first remove the console trim panel . . .

. . . then detach the cigarette lighter wiring harness connector

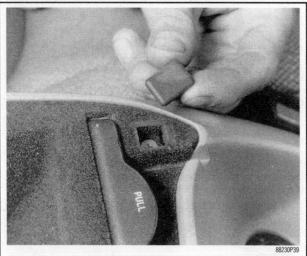

Open the storage compartment lid and remove the small rubber covers from the retaining screws . . .

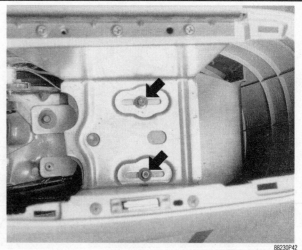

To remove the console, these screws (arrows) are the ones to remove from the storage compartment opening

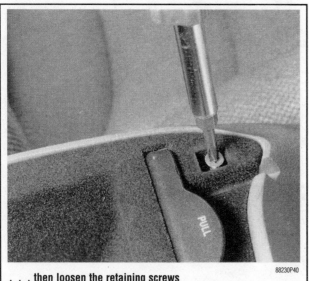

. . . then loosen the retaining screws

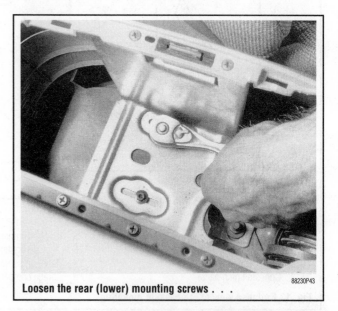

Loosen the rear (lower) mounting screws . . .

Lift the storage compartment up and out of the console

. . . then remove the two front (upper) screws

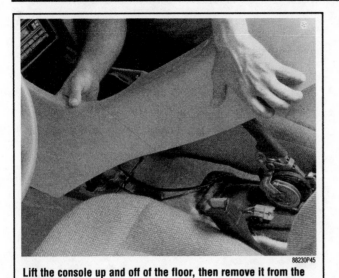

Lift the console up and off of the floor, then remove it from the vehicle

5. Remove the four mounting screws (two at the front of the console in the instrument panel and two under the console's storage compartment).

6. Move the parking brake hand lever to the upright position.

7. Remove the console by moving it up and back, then detach the console panel wiring harness connectors.

To install:

8. Install the console and reattach the wiring harness connectors.

9. Release the parking brake lever.

10. Install the four console mounting screws and tighten them until snug.

11. Install the storage compartment, the two screws and rubber bumpers in the console.

12. Reattach the cigarette lighter wiring harness connector.

13. Position the console finish panel over the opening and secure it in place by pressing until the retaining clips are fully engaged.

14. Connect the negative battery cable.

Door Panels

REMOVAL & INSTALLATION

1. If equipped with manually operated windows, remove the window regulator handle.

2. Cautiously pry the top edge of the window regulator switch plate down.

3. Raise the window regulator switch plate approximately 1 in. (25mm) to release the front of the switch plate.

➡Do NOT twist the window regulator switch plate during removal. Grasp the plate at the front and rear, then pull it straight upward with a quick, firm motion.

4. Remove the front window regulator wiring screws, then remove the wiring.

5. Remove the side rear view mirror inner cover by pulling outward on it.

6. Remove the inside door handle cup.

7. Remove the one plastic rivet and two screws from the front door trim panel.

8. Unhook the trim panel from the door at the top, as well as the locating tab slots in the inner door panel, by pulling the panel upward.

9. If necessary, remove the watershield from the inside surface of the door.

To install:

10. If removed, install the watershield onto the inside surface of the door.

To remove the door panel, first detach the window regulator switch plate from the panel . . .

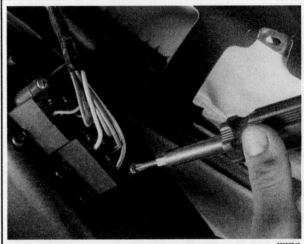

. . . then remove the regulator wiring by unfastening the retaining screws . . .

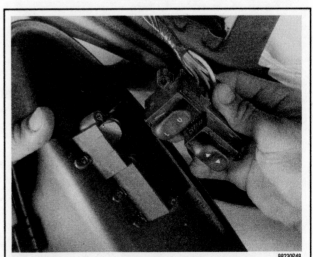

. . . and separating the regulator switch and wiring from the switch plate

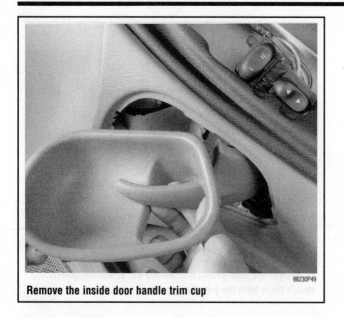

Remove the inside door handle trim cup

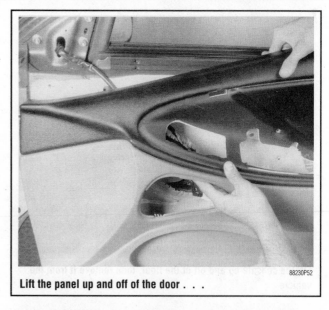

Lift the panel up and off of the door . . .

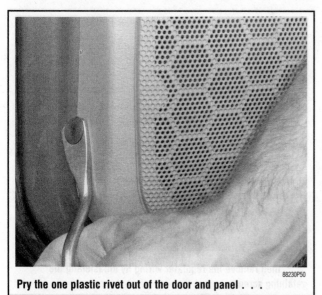

Pry the one plastic rivet out of the door and panel . . .

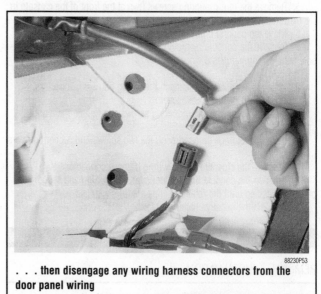

. . . then disengage any wiring harness connectors from the door panel wiring

. . . then remove the two retaining screws (arrows)

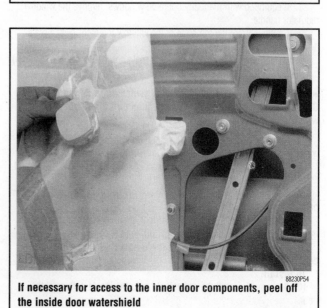

If necessary for access to the inner door components, peel off the inside door watershield

11. Position the door panel on the door and press it in place until all retaining clips are fully engaged.

12. Install the two mounting screws and a new plastic rivet to secure the door panel in place.

13. Install the inside door handle cup, then install the side rear view mirror inner cover by positioning it so that the retaining clips are aligned with the clip holes, then pressing it against the door until the clips are fully engaged.

14. Install the regulator wiring, then secure it with the regulator wiring screws.

15. Install the window regulator switch plate.

16. If equipped with manually operated windows, install the window regulator handle.

Door Lock Cylinder

REMOVAL & INSTALLATION

▶ **See Figure 14**

➡**It is a good idea to replace all lock cylinders on a vehicle whenever one of them is faulty, so that you do not have to carry an extra key which fits only one lock cylinder.**

1. Remove the door trim panel and peel the watershield away from the door until the access holes are exposed.

2. Remove the door lock retaining clip by pulling it away from the door lock cylinder.

3. Detach the door latch control rod from the door lock cylinder.

4. Pull the door lock cylinder out of the door.

5. Transfer the lock cylinder arm to the new door lock cylinder. If signs of damage or wear are present, replace the door lock retaining clip with a new one.

To install:

6. Slide the new door lock cylinder into the door until it is fully seated.

7. Attach the control rod to the door lock cylinder, then slide the retaining clip onto the cylinder to secure it in place.

8. Install the watershield and door trim panel.

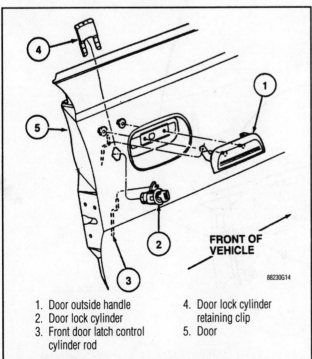

1. Door outside handle
2. Door lock cylinder
3. Front door latch control cylinder rod
4. Door lock cylinder retaining clip
5. Door

Fig. 14 Exploded view of the door lock cylinder mounting

Trunk Lid Lock Cylinder

REMOVAL & INSTALLATION

▶ **See Figure 15**

➡**It is a good idea to replace all lock cylinders on a vehicle whenever one of them is faulty, so that you do not have to carry an extra key which fits only one lock cylinder.**

1. Open the trunk lid.

2. Detach the trunk lid lock actuator from the lock cylinder plate.

3. Remove the trunk lid cylinder lock retaining rivet by using a narrow punch to hammer the center pin of the rivet, then using a drill to remove the remainder of the rivet from the trunk lid. Do not enlarge the rivet hole.

4. Pull the lock cylinder out of the trunk lid.

To install:

5. Slide the new lock cylinder into the trunk lid until it is fully seated.

6. Using a rivet gun, install a new retaining rivet to hold the lock cylinder in place.

7. Reattach the trunk lid lock actuator to the lock cylinder plate.

8. Before closing the trunk lid, test the new lock cylinder and key to ensure that they function properly.

9. Close the trunk lid.

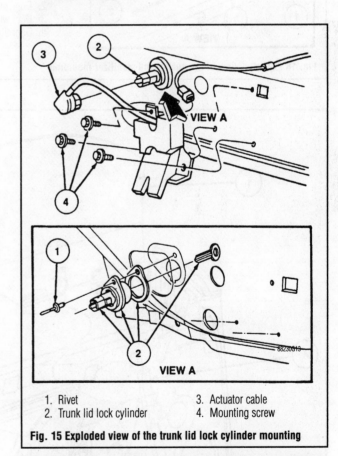

1. Rivet
2. Trunk lid lock cylinder
3. Actuator cable
4. Mounting screw

Fig. 15 Exploded view of the trunk lid lock cylinder mounting

Door Glass and Regulator

REMOVAL & INSTALLATION

▶ **See Figures 16, 17 and 18 (p. 22–23)**

1. Remove the door trim panel and watershield.
2. Remove the door belt line inside weatherstripping.

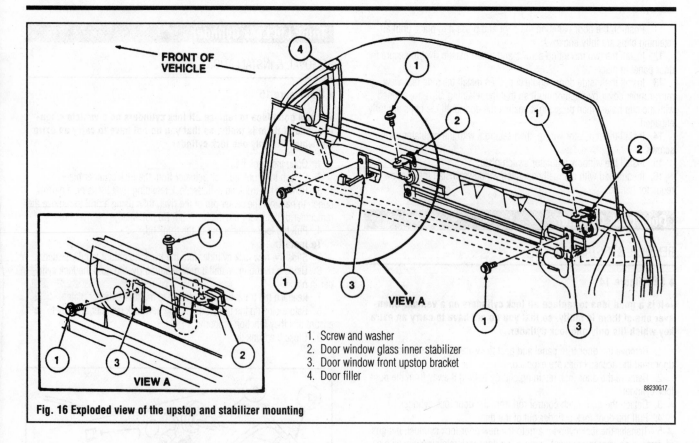

1. Screw and washer
2. Door window glass inner stabilizer
3. Door window front upstop bracket
4. Door filler

88230G17

Fig. 16 Exploded view of the upstop and stabilizer mounting

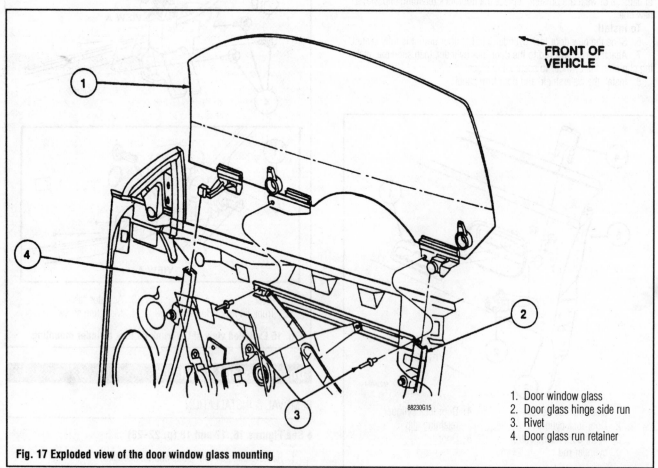

1. Door window glass
2. Door glass hinge side run
3. Rivet
4. Door glass run retainer

88230G15

Fig. 17 Exploded view of the door window glass mounting

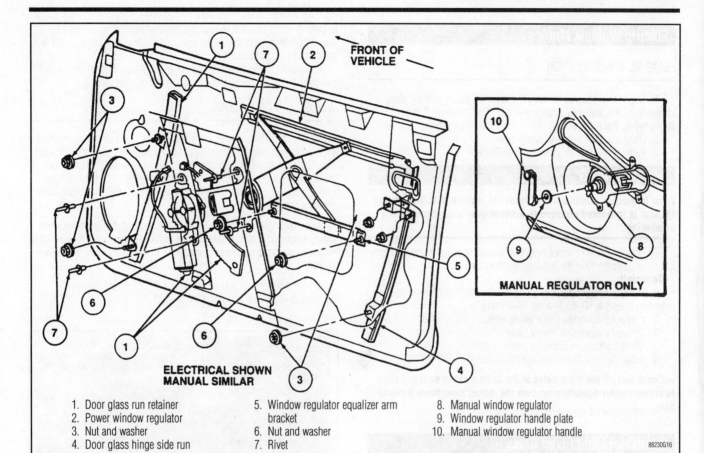

ELECTRICAL SHOWN
MANUAL SIMILAR

1. Door glass run retainer
2. Power window regulator
3. Nut and washer
4. Door glass hinge side run
5. Window regulator equalizer arm bracket
6. Nut and washer
7. Rivet
8. Manual window regulator
9. Window regulator handle plate
10. Manual window regulator handle

88230G16

Fig. 18 Door window regulator-related component identification—power and manual windows

3. Remove the attaching screws, then the door window glass inner stabilizers.

4. Remove the door window front upstop bracket attaching screws, then remove the upstop brackets from the door assembly.

5. Remove the one rivet with a drill, then remove the door belt line outside weatherstripping from the door.

6. Lower the door window so that you can access the door window channel bracket attaching rivets.

❋❋ WARNING

Be careful when drilling out the rivet so that the window channel bracket and spacer holes are not enlarged. Otherwise, the window glass channel bracket retainer will be damaged.

7. Using a narrow drift punch, hammer out the center pin of each rivet attaching the door window glass to the door window channel bracket. Then, using a ¼ inch drill bit, ream out the remainder of the rivet.

8. Tip the front of the door glass down to clear the door filler, then remove the window glass by sliding it up and out of the door assembly.

9. If equipped with power windows, disengage the window regulator wiring from the motor.

10. Remove the regulator equalizer arm bracket.

❋❋ CAUTION

If the regulator counterbalance spring must be removed or replaced for any reason, ensure that the regulator arms are in a fixed position prior to removal, to prevent possible injury during C-spring unwinding.

❋❋ WARNING

Be careful when drilling out the rivet that the window channel bracket and spacer holes are not enlarged. Otherwise, the window glass channel bracket retainer will be damaged.

11. Remove the four rivets attaching the window regulator to the inner door panel, by using a narrow drift punch to hammer out the center pin of each rivet. Then, use a ¼ inch drill bit to ream out the remainder of the rivet.

12. Remove the door regulator from the access hole.

To install:

13. Position the regulator against the inner door panel by installing it through the access hole, then install two ¼ in. blind rivets or two ¼–20 x ½ in. hex head bolts with two nuts and washers to secure the regulator to the inner door panel. If using nuts and bolts, tighten them to 90–122 inch lbs. (10–14 Nm).

14. On models equipped with power windows, reattach the regulator wiring harness connector to the motor.

15. Position the window glass to the door window regulator, then install two ¼ in. blind rivets or two ¼–20 x ½ in. hex head bolts with two nuts and washers to secure the glass to the window regulator. If using nuts and bolts, tighten them to 90–122 inch lbs. (10–14 Nm).

16. Loosely install the door window glass inner stabilizers and upstops.

17. Adjust the window glass as follows:
  a. Close the door.
  b. Loosen the door window stop bracket nuts.
  c. Raise the door window to the proper height, then tighten the window stop bracket nuts to 88–124 inch lbs. (10–14 Nm).

18. Install the belt line weatherstripping.

19. Cycle the door window glass to check for proper operation.

20. When the door window glass cycles properly, tighten the stabilizer retaining screws to 88–124 inch lbs. (10–14 Nm).

21. Install the door watershield and trim panel.

Electric Window Motor

REMOVAL & INSTALLATION

1. Raise the window to the full UP position, if possible. If the glass cannot be raised, and is in a partially or fully down position, it must be supported so that it will not fall into the door well during motor removal.
2. Disconnect the negative battery cable.
3. Remove the door trim panel and watershield.

❊❊❊ WARNING

Prior to electric window motor removal, ensure that the regulator arm is in a fixed position to prevent counterbalance spring unwinding.

4. Remove the three motor mounting screws, then disengage the motor and drive assembly from the regulator quadrant gear.

To install:

5. Install the new motor and drive assembly. Tighten the three motor mounting screws to 50–85 inch lbs. (6–10 Nm).
6. Connect the window motor wiring leads.
7. Connect the negative battery cable.
8. Check the power window for proper operation.
9. Install the door trim panel and the watershield.

➡**Check that all the drain holes at the bottom of the door are open to prevent water accumulation over the motor; clear them if necessary.**

Windshield and Fixed Glass

REMOVAL & INSTALLATION

If your windshield, or other fixed window, is cracked or chipped, you may decide to replace it with a new one yourself. However, there are two main reasons why replacement windshields and other window glass should be installed only by a professional automotive glass technician: safety and cost.

The most important reason a professional should install automotive glass is for safety. The glass in the vehicle, especially the windshield, is designed with safety in mind in case of a collision. The windshield is specially manufactured with two panes of specially-tempered glass with a thin layer of transparent plastic between them. This construction allows the glass to "give" in the event that a part of your body hits the windshield during the collision, and prevents the glass from shattering, which could cause lacerations, blinding and other harm to passengers of the vehicle. The other fixed windows are designed to be tempered so that if they break during a collision, they shatter in such a way that there are no sharp or pointed edges on the glass pieces. The professional automotive glass technician knows how to install the glass in a vehicle so that it will function optimally during a collision. Without the proper experience, knowledge or tools, installing a piece of automotive glass yourself could lead to additional harm if an accident should ever occur.

Cost is also a factor when deciding to install automotive glass yourself. Performing this could cost you much more than a professional may charge to do the same job. Since the windshield is designed to break under stress, an often life saving characteristic, windshields tend to break VERY easily when an inexperienced person attempts to install one. Do-it-yourselfers buying two, three or even four windshields from a salvage yard because they have broken them during installation are common stories. Also, since the automotive glass is designed to prevent the outside elements from entering your vehicle, improper installation can lead to water and air leaks. Annoying whining noises at highway speeds from air leaks or inside body panel rusting from water leaks can add to your stress level and subtract from your wallet. After buying two or three windshields, installing them and

ending up with a leak that produces a noise while driving and water damage during rainstorms, the cost of having a professional do it correctly the first time may be much more alluring.

We here at Chilton, therefore, advise you to have a professional automotive glass technician service any broken glass on your vehicle.

WINDSHIELD CHIP REPAIR

There is something, however, that you can do to prolong or even prevent the need for replacement of a chipped windshield. There are many companies, such as Loctite®, which offer windshield chip repair products, such as the Bullseye™ Windshield Repair Kit (Part No. 16067). These kits are not meant to correct cracks or holes in your windshield, only chips caused by gravel or stones.

➡**Check with your state and local authorities on the laws for state safety inspection. Some states or municipalities may not allow chip repair as a viable option for correcting stone damage to your windshield.**

To fix a stone chip in your windshield with the Loctite® Bullseye™ Windshield Repair Kit, perform the following:

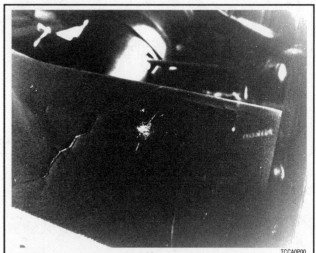

TCCA0P00

Small chips on your windshield can be fixed with an aftermarket repair kit, such as the one from Loctite®

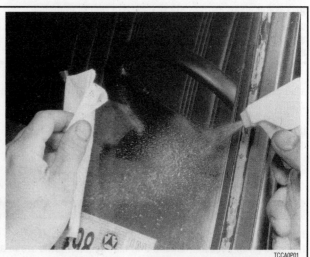

TCCA0P01

To repair a chip, clean the windshield with glass cleaner and dry it completely

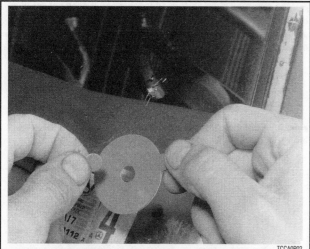

Remove the center from the adhesive disc and peel off the backing from one side of the disc . . .

. . . then press it on the windshield so that the chip is centered in the hole

Be sure that the tab points upward on the windshield

Peel the backing off the exposed side of the adhesive disc . . .

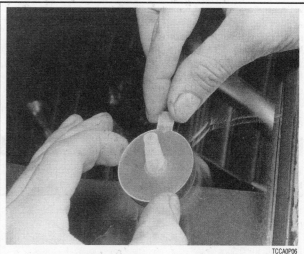

. . . then position the plastic pedestal on the adhesive disc, ensuring that the tabs are aligned

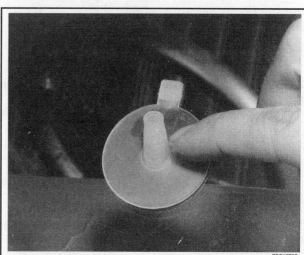

Press the pedestal firmly on the adhesive disc to create an adequate seal . . .

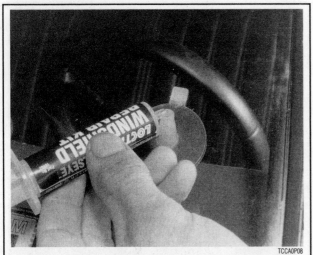

. . . then install the applicator syringe nipple in the pedestal's hole

➡Loctite Corporation recommends that their repair kits should be applied outside in the sunlight, which, evidently, helps cure the repair solution much faster. In one of our experiments with these kits, performed in a shop using fluorescent lights and without any sunlight, the solution had not cured even after 18 hours. Therefore, it is highly recommended that the solution be allowed to cure in sunlight.

1. Clean the damaged area of your windshield with glass cleaner, then dry the area completely.

✳✳ WARNING

The fluid contained in chip repair kits may damage paint; be sure to cover any exposed areas with clean shop rags.

2. Cover any painted surfaces with a clean shop rag, because the chip repair fluid may damage or remove paint.
3. Remove the adhesive disc from the kit, then remove the center hold plug from the disc.
4. Peel the backing off one side of the disc, then, with the disc tab pointing upward, line up the hole in the disc with the center of the chip on the windshield. Press the disc onto the windshield.
5. Remove the plastic pedestal from the kit. Peel the paper off of the other side of the disc, then align the pedestal with the disc, making sure that the tabs are also aligned. Press the pedestal firmly onto the disc.
6. Remove the fluid applicator (syringe) from the kit and remove the cap from its tip.
7. Thread the syringe into the pedestal tube.

➡During the next step, pull the plunger back until you feel it hit the stop on the inside of the syringe.

8. While holding the syringe with one hand, gently pull back the syringe's plunger with the other hand, hold it there for 5–10 seconds, then abruptly release the plunger. Repeat this step 10 times.
9. Allow the entire assembly to sit, undisturbed, for 30 minutes.
10. From inside the vehicle, inspect the damaged area for any residual air bubbles. A flashlight may be necessary. If any air bubbles remain, repeat Steps 8 and 9.
11. Allow the repair kit to sit undisturbed until the solution has finally hardened or set. The light level where you are performing the repair largely dictates the length of time the repair solution needs to completely set. If the repair is performed in a bright, sunny area, it should set up in approximately 1 hour. If the repair is performed inside or on a cloudy day, allow 4–5 hours for it to fully set.

➡If the repair must be performed indoors and it does not set in a few hours, an ultraviolet lamp may help expedite the curing process. However, according to the manufacturer, this should not be necessary.

12. Remove the stringe from the pedestal.
13. Using a pair of pliers or a utility knife, if necessary, remove the pedestal and adhesive disc from the windshield.
14. Clean up any excess compound with glass cleaner.

➡For other brands of windshield repair kits, follow the manufacturer's instructions enclosed with the kit.

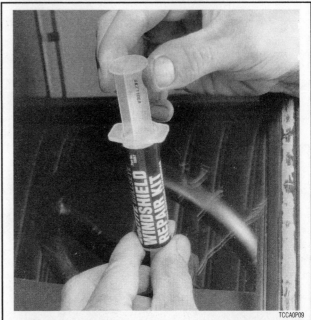

Hold the syringe in one hand while pulling the plunger back with the other hand

After applying the solution, allow the entire assembly to sit until it has set completely

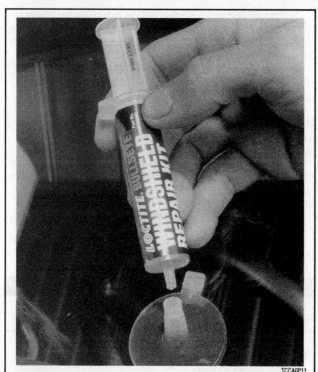

After the solution has set, remove the syringe from the pedestal . . .

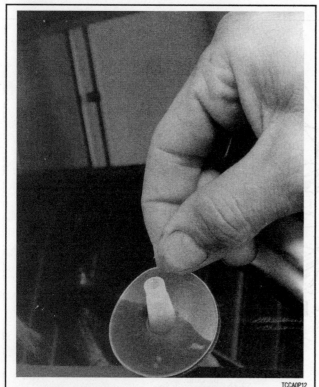

. . . then peel the pedestal off of the adhesive disc . . .

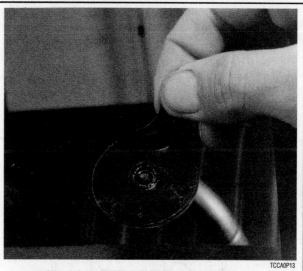

. . . and peel the adhesive disc off the windshield

The chip will still be slightly visible, but it should be filled with the hardened solution

Inside Rear View Mirror

REPLACEMENT

▶ **See Figure 19**

➡Breakaway mounts are used with the inside rear view mirrors in 1994–98 Mustangs. The breakaway mounts are designed to detach from the mirror bracket in the event of an air bag deployment during a collision. Excessive force, up-and-down, or side-to-side movement can cause the mirror to detach from the windshield glass.

1. Loosen the mirror assembly-to-mounting bracket setscrew.
2. Remove the mirror assembly by sliding it upward and away from the mounting bracket.

3. If the bracket vinyl pad remains on the windshield, apply low heat from an electric heat gun until the vinyl softens. Peel the vinyl off the windshield and discard.

To install:

4. Make sure the glass, bracket and adhesive kit (such as Ford's Rear View Mirror Repair Kit D9AZ-19554-B or equivalent) are at least at a room temperature of 65–75° F (18–24° C).

5. Locate and mark the mirror mounting bracket location on the outside surface of the windshield with a wax pencil.

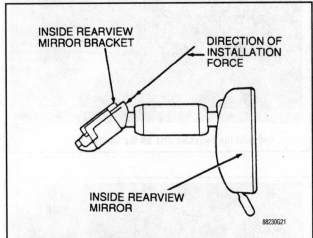

Fig. 19 When installing the mirror on the bracket, slide it down until it is fully engaged—be careful, as too much force can break the bracket off of the windshield

6. Thoroughly clean the bonding surfaces of the glass and bracket to remove the old adhesive. Use a mild abrasive cleaner on the glass and fine sandpaper on the bracket to lightly roughen the surface. Wipe it clean with the alcohol-moistened cloth.

7. Crush the accelerator vial (part of Rear View Mirror Repair Kit D9AZ-19554-B or equivalent), and apply the accelerator to the bonding surface of the bracket and windshield. Let it dry for three minutes.

8. Apply two drops of adhesive (from Rear View Mirror Repair Kit D9AZ-19554-B or equivalent) to the mounting surface of the bracket. Using a clean toothpick or wooden match, quickly spread the adhesive evenly over the mounting surface of the bracket.

9. Quickly position the mounting bracket on the windshield. The ⅜ in. (10mm) circular depression in the bracket must be toward the inside of the passenger compartment. Press the bracket firmly against the windshield for one minute.

10. Allow the bond to set for five minutes. Remove any excess bonding material from the windshield with an alcohol dampened cloth.

11. Attach the mirror to the mounting bracket and tighten the setscrew to 10–20 inch lbs. (1–2 Nm).

Seats

REMOVAL & INSTALLATION

Front

▶ See Figures 20 and 21

1. If equipped with power seats, disconnect the negative battery cable.

2. Slide the front seat belt out of the front seat strap loop shield.

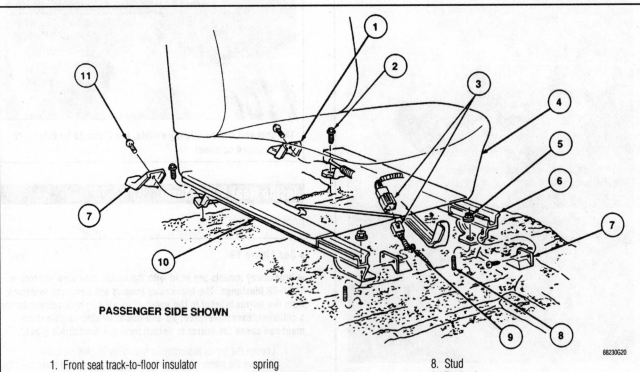

PASSENGER SIDE SHOWN

1. Front seat track-to-floor insulator
2. Screw
3. Power lumbar support connector
4. Front seat cushion frame and

    spring
5. Nut and washer
6. Left-hand front seat track
7. Front seat track-to-floor insulator

8. Stud
9. Push-pin
10. Right-hand front seat track
11. Push-pin

Fig. 20 Exploded view of the front seat mounting—manually adjustable seat

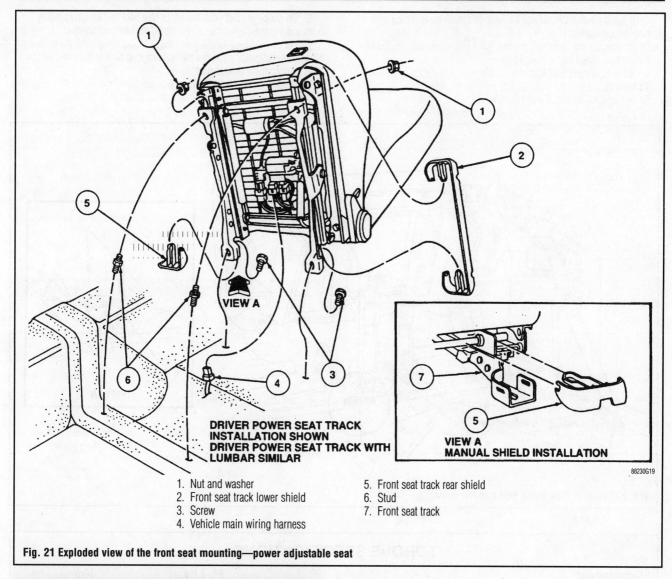

DRIVER POWER SEAT TRACK
INSTALLATION SHOWN
DRIVER POWER SEAT TRACK WITH
LUMBAR SIMILAR

VIEW A
MANUAL SHIELD INSTALLATION

88230G19

1. Nut and washer
2. Front seat track lower shield
3. Screw
4. Vehicle main wiring harness
5. Front seat track rear shield
6. Stud
7. Front seat track

Fig. 21 Exploded view of the front seat mounting—power adjustable seat

---

Use care when handling the seat and track assembly. Dropping the assembly or sitting on a seat not secured in the vehicle may result in damage to the seat or track.

3. Remove the push-pins and the front seat track-to-floor insulator nuts and bolts.

4. Remove the two bolts and nuts retaining the seat to the floor, then disengage the wiring harness connectors and remove the seat from the vehicle.

To install:

5. Position the seat in the vehicle and reattach the wiring harness connectors.

6. Install the seat-to-floor retaining bolts and nuts; tighten the fasteners to 25–34 ft. lbs. (34–46 Nm).

7. Install the front seat track-to-floor insulator nuts and push-pins.

8. Position the seat belt strap in the loop shield, then connect the negative battery, if applicable.

Rear

SEAT CUSHION

▶ See Figure 22

1. Release the anchor pins from their locks by pressing the release button under the rear seat cushion.

2. Pull the rear safety belt and buckle through the openings in the rear seat cushion pad and frame, then remove the cushion pad and frame.

To install:

3. Position the seat cushion in the vehicle, then route the safety belts and buckles through the cushion and frame openings.

4. Press down on the seat cushion until the anchor pins fully engage their retaining locks.

SEAT BACK

1. Remove the rear seat cushion.

2. For convertible models, perform the following:

a. Remove the two bolts retaining the rear seat back pad and frame to the body.

b. Lift the seat back pad and frame up to detach the retaining hooks from the crossmember.

3. On coupe models, remove the rear seat bolster, then remove the four seat back-to-package tray retaining bolts.

4. Remove the seat back from the vehicle.

To install:

5. Position the seat back in the vehicle.

6. On coupe models, install the four seat back-to-rear package tray bolts and tighten them until secure. Install the rear seat bolster.

7. For convertible models, press the seat back down until the retaining hooks are engaged, then install the two rear seat back and frame-to-body bolts; tighten them until secure.

8. Install the rear seat cushion.

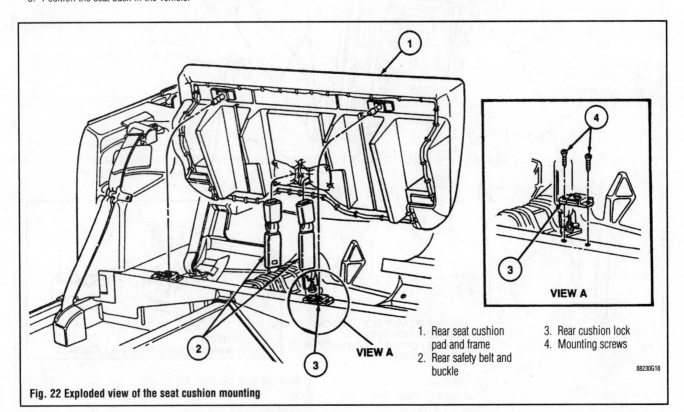

1. Rear seat cushion pad and frame
2. Rear safety belt and buckle
3. Rear cushion lock
4. Mounting screws

Fig. 22 Exploded view of the seat cushion mounting

TORQUE SPECIFICATIONS

Component	Ft. Lbs.	Nm
Door hinge-to-door bolts	18-26	25-35
Door latch striker bolts	16-22	21-19
Electric window motor mounting screws	50-85 inch lbs.	6-10
Front seat-to-floor retaining bolts and nuts	25-34	34-46
Hood hinge-to-body bolts	142-239 inch lbs.	16-27
Hood-to-hinge nuts	88-124 inch lbs.	10-14
Ignition switch connector securing bolt	15-19 inch lbs.	1.6-2.2
Inside rear view mirror-to-mounting bracket setscrew	10-20 inch lbs.	1.1-2.3
Instrument panel mounting nut	30-41	40-56
Instrument panel retaining screws	68-91 inch lbs.	7.6-10.4
Instrument panel-to-floor bracket bolts	68-91 inch lbs.	7.6-10.4
Outside rear view mirror mounting nuts	53-71 inch lbs.	5.9-8.1
Regulator-to-inner door panel nuts and bolts	90-122 inch lbs.	10.2-13.8
Steering column opening cover and reinforcement screws	68-91 inch lbs.	7.6-10.4
Trunk lid-to-hinge nuts	44-75 inch lbs.	5.0-8.5
Window stabilizer retaining screws	88-124 inch lbs.	10-14
Window stop bracket nuts	88-124 inch lbs.	10-14

88230C00

GLOSSARY

AIR/FUEL RATIO: The ratio of air-to-gasoline by weight in the fuel mixture drawn into the engine.

AIR INJECTION: One method of reducing harmful exhaust emissions by injecting air into each of the exhaust ports of an engine. The fresh air entering the hot exhaust manifold causes any remaining fuel to be burned before it can exit the tailpipe.

ALTERNATOR: A device used for converting mechanical energy into electrical energy.

AMMETER: An instrument, calibrated in amperes, used to measure the flow of an electrical current in a circuit. Ammeters are always connected in series with the circuit being tested.

AMPERE: The rate of flow of electrical current present when one volt of electrical pressure is applied against one ohm of electrical resistance.

ANALOG COMPUTER: Any microprocessor that uses similar (analogous) electrical signals to make its calculations.

ARMATURE: A laminated, soft iron core wrapped by a wire that converts electrical energy to mechanical energy as in a motor or relay. When rotated in a magnetic field, it changes mechanical energy into electrical energy as in a generator.

ATMOSPHERIC PRESSURE: The pressure on the Earth's surface caused by the weight of the air in the atmosphere. At sea level, this pressure is 14.7 psi at 32°F (101 kPa at 0°C).

ATOMIZATION: The breaking down of a liquid into a fine mist that can be suspended in air.

AXIAL PLAY: Movement parallel to a shaft or bearing bore.

BACKFIRE: The sudden combustion of gases in the intake or exhaust system that results in a loud explosion.

BACKLASH: The clearance or play between two parts, such as meshed gears.

BACKPRESSURE: Restrictions in the exhaust system that slow the exit of exhaust gases from the combustion chamber.

BAKELITE: A heat resistant, plastic insulator material commonly used in printed circuit boards and transistorized components.

BALL BEARING: A bearing made up of hardened inner and outer races between which hardened steel balls roll.

BALLAST RESISTOR: A resistor in the primary ignition circuit that lowers voltage after the engine is started to reduce wear on ignition components.

BEARING: A friction reducing, supportive device usually located between a stationary part and a moving part.

BIMETAL TEMPERATURE SENSOR: Any sensor or switch made of two dissimilar types of metal that bend when heated or cooled due to the different expansion rates of the alloys. These types of sensors usually function as an on/off switch.

BLOWBY: Combustion gases, composed of water vapor and unburned fuel, that leak past the piston rings into the crankcase during normal engine operation. These gases are removed by the PCV system to prevent the buildup of harmful acids in the crankcase.

BRAKE PAD: A brake shoe and lining assembly used with disc brakes.

BRAKE SHOE: The backing for the brake lining. The term is, however, usually applied to the assembly of the brake backing and lining.

BUSHING: A liner, usually removable, for a bearing; an anti-friction liner used in place of a bearing.

CALIPER: A hydraulically activated device in a disc brake system, which is mounted straddling the brake rotor (disc). The caliper contains at least one piston and two brake pads. Hydraulic pressure on the piston(s) forces the pads against the rotor.

CAMSHAFT: A shaft in the engine on which are the lobes (cams) which operate the valves. The camshaft is driven by the crankshaft, via a belt, chain or gears, at one half the crankshaft speed.

CAPACITOR: A device which stores an electrical charge.

CARBON MONOXIDE (CO): A colorless, odorless gas given off as a normal byproduct of combustion. It is poisonous and extremely dangerous in confined areas, building up slowly to toxic levels without warning if adequate ventilation is not available.

CARBURETOR: A device, usually mounted on the intake manifold of an engine, which mixes the air and fuel in the proper proportion to allow even combustion.

CATALYTIC CONVERTER: A device installed in the exhaust system, like a muffler, that converts harmful byproducts of combustion into carbon dioxide and water vapor by means of a heat-producing chemical reaction.

CENTRIFUGAL ADVANCE: A mechanical method of advancing the spark timing by using flyweights in the distributor that react to centrifugal force generated by the distributor shaft rotation.

CHECK VALVE: Any one-way valve installed to permit the flow of air, fuel or vacuum in one direction only.

CHOKE: A device, usually a moveable valve, placed in the intake path of a carburetor to restrict the flow of air.

CIRCUIT: Any unbroken path through which an electrical current can flow. Also used to describe fuel flow in some instances.

CIRCUIT BREAKER: A switch which protects an electrical circuit from overload by opening the circuit when the current flow exceeds a predetermined level. Some circuit breakers must be reset manually, while most reset automatically.

COIL (IGNITION): A transformer in the ignition circuit which steps up the voltage provided to the spark plugs.

COMBINATION MANIFOLD: An assembly which includes both the intake and exhaust manifolds in one casting.

COMBINATION VALVE: A device used in some fuel systems that routes fuel vapors to a charcoal storage canister instead of venting them into the atmosphere. The valve relieves fuel tank pressure and allows fresh air into the tank as the fuel level drops to prevent a vapor lock situation.

COMPRESSION RATIO: The comparison of the total volume of the cylinder and combustion chamber with the piston at BDC and the piston at TDC.

CONDENSER: 1. An electrical device which acts to store an electrical charge, preventing voltage surges. 2. A radiator-like device in the air conditioning system in which refrigerant gas condenses into a liquid, giving off heat.

CONDUCTOR: Any material through which an electrical current can be transmitted easily.

CONTINUITY: Continuous or complete circuit. Can be checked with an ohmmeter.

COUNTERSHAFT: An intermediate shaft which is rotated by a mainshaft and transmits, in turn, that rotation to a working part.

CRANKCASE: The lower part of an engine in which the crankshaft and related parts operate.

CRANKSHAFT: The main driving shaft of an engine which receives reciprocating motion from the pistons and converts it to rotary motion.

CYLINDER: In an engine, the round hole in the engine block in which the piston(s) ride.

CYLINDER BLOCK: The main structural member of an engine in which is found the cylinders, crankshaft and other principal parts.

CYLINDER HEAD: The detachable portion of the engine, usually fastened to the top of the cylinder block and containing all or most of the combustion chambers. On overhead valve engines, it contains the valves and their operating parts. On overhead cam engines, it contains the camshaft as well.

DEAD CENTER: The extreme top or bottom of the piston stroke.

DETONATION: An unwanted explosion of the air/fuel mixture in the combustion chamber caused by excess heat and compression, advanced timing, or an overly lean mixture. Also referred to as "ping".

DIAPHRAGM: A thin, flexible wall separating two cavities, such as in a vacuum advance unit.

DIESELING: A condition in which hot spots in the combustion chamber cause the engine to run on after the key is turned off.

DIFFERENTIAL: A geared assembly which allows the transmission of motion between drive axles, giving one axle the ability to turn faster than the other.

DIODE: An electrical device that will allow current to flow in one direction only.

DISC BRAKE: A hydraulic braking assembly consisting of a brake disc, or rotor, mounted on an axle, and a caliper assembly containing, usually two brake pads which are activated by hydraulic pressure. The pads are forced against the sides of the disc, creating friction which slows the vehicle.

DISTRIBUTOR: A mechanically driven device on an engine which is responsible for electrically firing the spark plug at a predetermined point of the piston stroke.

DOWEL PIN: A pin, inserted in mating holes in two different parts allowing those parts to maintain a fixed relationship.

DRUM BRAKE: A braking system which consists of two brake shoes and one or two wheel cylinders, mounted on a fixed backing plate, and a brake drum, mounted on an axle, which revolves around the assembly.

DWELL: The rate, measured in degrees of shaft rotation, at which an electrical circuit cycles on and off.

ELECTRONIC CONTROL UNIT (ECU): Ignition module, module, amplifier or igniter. See Module for definition.

ELECTRONIC IGNITION: A system in which the timing and firing of the spark plugs is controlled by an electronic control unit, usually called a module. These systems have no points or condenser.

END-PLAY: The measured amount of axial movement in a shaft.

ENGINE: A device that converts heat into mechanical energy.

EXHAUST MANIFOLD: A set of cast passages or pipes which conduct exhaust gases from the engine.

FEELER GAUGE: A blade, usually metal, or precisely predetermined thickness, used to measure the clearance between two parts.

FIRING ORDER: The order in which combustion occurs in the cylinders of an engine. Also the order in which spark is distributed to the plugs by the distributor.

FLOODING: The presence of too much fuel in the intake manifold and combustion chamber which prevents the air/fuel mixture from firing, thereby causing a no-start situation.

FLYWHEEL: A disc shaped part bolted to the rear end of the crankshaft. Around the outer perimeter is affixed the ring gear. The starter drive engages the ring gear, turning the flywheel, which rotates the crankshaft, imparting the initial starting motion to the engine.

FOOT POUND (ft. lbs. or sometimes, ft.lb.): The amount of energy or work needed to raise an item weighing one pound, a distance of one foot.

FUSE: A protective device in a circuit which prevents circuit overload by breaking the circuit when a specific amperage is present. The device is constructed around a strip or wire of a lower amperage rating than the circuit it is designed to protect. When an amperage higher than that stamped on the fuse is present in the circuit, the strip or wire melts, opening the circuit.

GEAR RATIO: The ratio between the number of teeth on meshing gears.

GENERATOR: A device which converts mechanical energy into electrical energy.

HEAT RANGE: The measure of a spark plug's ability to dissipate heat from its firing end. The higher the heat range, the hotter the plug fires.

HUB: The center part of a wheel or gear.

HYDROCARBON (HC): Any chemical compound made up of hydrogen and carbon. A major pollutant formed by the engine as a byproduct of combustion.

HYDROMETER: An instrument used to measure the specific gravity of a solution.

INCH POUND (inch lbs.; sometimes in.lb. or in. lbs.): One twelfth of a foot pound.

INDUCTION: A means of transferring electrical energy in the form of a magnetic field. Principle used in the ignition coil to increase voltage.

INJECTOR: A device which receives metered fuel under relatively low pressure and is activated to inject the fuel into the engine under relatively high pressure at a predetermined time.

INPUT SHAFT: The shaft to which torque is applied, usually carrying the driving gear or gears.

INTAKE MANIFOLD: A casting of passages or pipes used to conduct air or a fuel/air mixture to the cylinders.

JOURNAL: The bearing surface within which a shaft operates.

KEY: A small block usually fitted in a notch between a shaft and a hub to prevent slippage of the two parts.

MANIFOLD: A casting of passages or set of pipes which connect the cylinders to an inlet or outlet source.

MANIFOLD VACUUM: Low pressure in an engine intake manifold formed just below the throttle plates. Manifold vacuum is highest at idle and drops under acceleration.

MASTER CYLINDER: The primary fluid pressurizing device in a hydraulic system. In automotive use, it is found in brake and hydraulic clutch systems and is pedal activated, either directly or, in a power brake system, through the power booster.

MODULE: Electronic control unit, amplifier or igniter of solid state or integrated design which controls the current flow in the ignition primary circuit based on input from the pick-up coil. When the module opens the primary circuit, high secondary voltage is induced in the coil.

NEEDLE BEARING: A bearing which consists of a number (usually a large number) of long, thin rollers.

OHM: (Ω) The unit used to measure the resistance of conductor-to-electrical flow. One ohm is the amount of resistance that limits current flow to one ampere in a circuit with one volt of pressure.

OHMMETER: An instrument used for measuring the resistance, in ohms, in an electrical circuit.

OUTPUT SHAFT: The shaft which transmits torque from a device, such as a transmission.

OVERDRIVE: A gear assembly which produces more shaft revolutions than that transmitted to it.

OVERHEAD CAMSHAFT (OHC): An engine configuration in which the camshaft is mounted on top of the cylinder head and operates the valve either directly or by means of rocker arms.

OVERHEAD VALVE (OHV): An engine configuration in which all of the valves are located in the cylinder head and the camshaft is located in the cylinder block. The camshaft operates the valves via lifters and pushrods.

OXIDES OF NITROGEN (NOx): Chemical compounds of nitrogen produced as a byproduct of combustion. They combine with hydrocarbons to produce smog.

OXYGEN SENSOR: Use with the feedback system to sense the presence of oxygen in the exhaust gas and signal the computer which can reference the voltage signal to an air/fuel ratio.

PINION: The smaller of two meshing gears.

PISTON RING: An open-ended ring with fits into a groove on the outer diameter of the piston. Its chief function is to form a seal between the piston and cylinder wall. Most automotive pistons have three rings: two for compression sealing; one for oil sealing.

PRELOAD: A predetermined load placed on a bearing during assembly or by adjustment.

PRIMARY CIRCUIT: the low voltage side of the ignition system which consists of the ignition switch, ballast resistor or resistance wire, bypass, coil, electronic control unit and pick-up coil as well as the connecting wires and harnesses.

PRESS FIT: The mating of two parts under pressure, due to the inner diameter of one being smaller than the outer diameter of the other, or vice versa; an interference fit.

RACE: The surface on the inner or outer ring of a bearing on which the balls, needles or rollers move.

REGULATOR: A device which maintains the amperage and/or voltage levels of a circuit at predetermined values.

RELAY: A switch which automatically opens and/or closes a circuit.

RESISTANCE: The opposition to the flow of current through a circuit or electrical device, and is measured in ohms. Resistance is equal to the voltage divided by the amperage.

RESISTOR: A device, usually made of wire, which offers a preset amount of resistance in an electrical circuit.

RING GEAR: The name given to a ring-shaped gear attached to a differential case, or affixed to a flywheel or as part of a planetary gear set.

ROLLER BEARING: A bearing made up of hardened inner and outer races between which hardened steel rollers move.

ROTOR: 1. The disc-shaped part of a disc brake assembly, upon which the brake pads bear; also called, brake disc. 2. The device mounted atop the distributor shaft, which passes current to the distributor cap tower contacts.

SECONDARY CIRCUIT: The high voltage side of the ignition system, usually above 20,000 volts. The secondary includes the ignition coil, coil wire, distributor cap and rotor, spark plug wires and spark plugs.

SENDING UNIT: A mechanical, electrical, hydraulic or electro-magnetic device which transmits information to a gauge.

SENSOR: Any device designed to measure engine operating conditions or ambient pressures and temperatures. Usually electronic in nature and designed to send a voltage signal to an on-board computer, some sensors may operate as a simple on/off switch or they may provide a variable voltage signal (like a potentiometer) as conditions or measured parameters change.

SHIM: Spacers of precise, predetermined thickness used between parts to establish a proper working relationship.

SLAVE CYLINDER: In automotive use, a device in the hydraulic clutch system which is activated by hydraulic force, disengaging the clutch.

SOLENOID: A coil used to produce a magnetic field, the effect of which is to produce work.

SPARK PLUG: A device screwed into the combustion chamber of a spark ignition engine. The basic construction is a conductive core inside of a ceramic insulator, mounted in an outer conductive base. An electrical charge from the spark plug wire travels along the conductive core and jumps a preset air gap to a grounding point or points at the end of the conductive base. The resultant spark ignites the fuel/air mixture in the combustion chamber.

SPLINES: Ridges machined or cast onto the outer diameter of a shaft or inner diameter of a bore to enable parts to mate without rotation.

TACHOMETER: A device used to measure the rotary speed of an engine, shaft, gear, etc., usually in rotations per minute.

THERMOSTAT: A valve, located in the cooling system of an engine, which is closed when cold and opens gradually in response to engine heating, controlling the temperature of the coolant and rate of coolant flow.

TOP DEAD CENTER (TDC): The point at which the piston reaches the top of its travel on the compression stroke.

TORQUE: The twisting force applied to an object.

TORQUE CONVERTER: A turbine used to transmit power from a driving member to a driven member via hydraulic action, providing changes in drive ratio and torque. In automotive use, it links the driveplate at the rear of the engine to the automatic transmission.

TRANSDUCER: A device used to change a force into an electrical signal.

TRANSISTOR: A semi-conductor component which can be actuated by a small voltage to perform an electrical switching function.

TUNE-UP: A regular maintenance function, usually associated with the replacement and adjustment of parts and components in the electrical and fuel systems of a vehicle for the purpose of attaining optimum performance.

TURBOCHARGER: An exhaust driven pump which compresses intake air and forces it into the combustion chambers at higher than atmospheric pressures. The increased air pressure allows more fuel to be burned and results in increased horsepower being produced.

VACUUM ADVANCE: A device which advances the ignition timing in response to increased engine vacuum.

VACUUM GAUGE: An instrument used to measure the presence of vacuum in a chamber.

VALVE: A device which control the pressure, direction of flow or rate of flow of a liquid or gas.

VALVE CLEARANCE: The measured gap between the end of the valve stem and the rocker arm, cam lobe or follower that activates the valve.

VISCOSITY: The rating of a liquid's internal resistance to flow.

VOLTMETER: An instrument used for measuring electrical force in units called volts. Voltmeters are always connected parallel with the circuit being tested.

WHEEL CYLINDER: Found in the automotive drum brake assembly, it is a device, actuated by hydraulic pressure, which, through internal pistons, pushes the brake shoes outward against the drums.

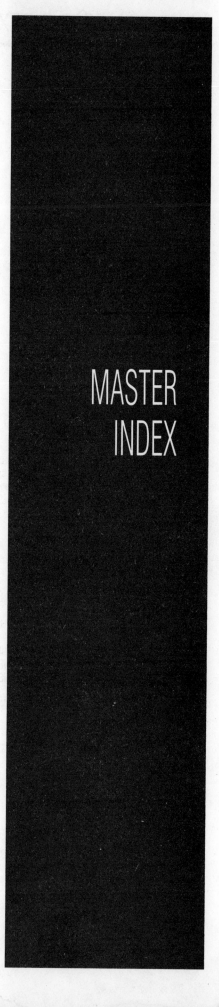

MASTER
INDEX